Indo-European Numerals

Trends in Linguistics
Studies and Monographs 57

Editor
Werner Winter

Mouton de Gruyter
Berlin · New York

Indo-European Numerals

Edited by

Jadranka Gvozdanović

Mouton de Gruyter
Berlin · New York 1992

Mouton de Gruyter (formerly Mouton, The Hague)
is a division of Walter de Gruyter & Co., Berlin.

⊗ Printed on acid-free paper which falls within the guidelines
of the ANSI to ensure permanence and durability.

Library of Congress Cataloging in Publication Data

Indo-European numerals / edited by Jadranka Gvozdanović,
p. cm. — (Trends in linguistics. Studies and monographs ; 57)
Includes bibliographical references and index.
ISBN 3-11-011322-8 (cloth: acid free paper)
1. Indo-European languages — Numerals. I. Gvozdanović, Jadranka. II. Series.
P643.I53 1991 91-36751
410—dc20 CIP

Die Deutsche Bibliothek — Cataloging in Publication Data

Indo-European numerals / ed. by Jadranka Gvozdanović. —
Berlin ; New York : Mouton de Gruyter, 1991
(Trends in linguistics : Studies and monographs ; 57)
ISBN 3-11-011322-8
NE: Gvozdanović, Jadranka [Hrsg.]; Trends in linguistics / Studies and monographs

Typesetting: Arthur Collignon GmbH, Berlin. — Printing: Gerike, Berlin. —
Binding: Lüderitz & Bauer GmbH, Berlin.
Printed in Germany.

Preface

This volume on Indo-European numerals has its origin two decennia ago, when the late A. S. C. Ross approached Hermann Berger, Robert G. G. Coleman, Bernard Comrie, Heiner Eichner, Ronald Emmerick, David Greene, G. Klingenschmitt, Kenneth R. Norman, Edgar C. Polomé, Glanville Price, H. Thesleff and Werner Winter proposing that they write chapters on numerals in the Indo-European language(s) in which they were specializing. They did so, and their original contributions date from late 1960s and early 1970s. A. S. C. Ross provided some general comments on Indo-European numerals, supplemented by an excursus on Tocharian *tumane* by H. W. Bailey and an excursus on Mesopotamian numerals by W. G. Lambert. A. S. C. Ross also wrote a chapter on Germanic, notes on analogy as mentioned in the various chapters, and compiled a list of lesser-known languages and localities mentioned in the various chapters. In the process of editing the volume, A. S. C. Ross retyped the original manuscripts using his own system of cross-referencing. Unfortunately, he passed away before he was able to accomplish the task to an extent which would have made it possible to publish the volume; this was partly due to missing bibliographical data which had been planned to be presented in an integrated bibliography of the entire volume.

After A. S. C. Ross's death, Mouton Publishers tried to proceed with the publication of this volume and W. Winter, the editor of Trends in Linguistics, devised a system of chapter organization so as to make the presented information more easily accessible. In the process of editing the volume, however, W. Winter found himself in a position when essential information was missing which seemed impossible to supply; in any case the task at hand exceeded by far the usual work of an editor, especially in view of new data on numerals which had became available since the beginning of the preparatory work on this volume.

Due to these circumstances, the Indo-European numerals volume seemed to be doomed to remain unpublished. However, the manuscripts were still being kept at the Linguistics Department of the University of Kiel when I arrived there as a Humboldt scholar in order to investigate numeral change and decay in the Tibeto-Burman languages of East Nepal, on the basis of the Linguistic Survey of Nepal questionnaires at the

University of Kiel, in addition to my own field-work in Nepal. It struck me that the manuscripts on Indo-European numerals contained too many valuable data on numeral developments, and extensive comparative evidence, to remain unpublished. On the basis of W. Winter's advice and with Mouton's consent, I took up the publication of this volume after completing my Tibeto-Burman numeral investigations.

In the process of the preparation of this volume, I wrote to the contributors to the volume (with the exception of D. Greene and A. S. C. Ross, who were no longer alive any more, and with the exception of Sir Walter Bailey and W. G. Lambert, due to a more limited new conception of the volume), asking them whether they were still in agreement with the publication of their manuscripts, and, if so, to send me their original bibliographies and any text revisions they might wish. With the exception of G. Klingenschmitt and H. Thesleff (who had contributed chapters on Albanian and Greek respectively), all the authors approached agreed to have their texts published in the volume I was proposing to edit. G. Klingenschmitt had decided to publish his manuscript on Albanian numerals elsewhere, and H. Thesleff had no time to revise his manuscript on Greek numerals, a revision of which he considered necessary. On the basis of these reactions, W. Winter and I proposed that E. Hamp should write a chapter on Albanian numerals and F. M. J. Waanders on Greek numerals. In addition to these changes as compared with the original conception of the volume, we also had to face the fact that two authors, H. Berger and Edgar C. Polomé, had published the texts originally intended for this volume elsewhere (i.e., Berger in *Münchener Studien zur Sprachwissenschaft* 47, 1986: 23 – 70, and Polomé in the *Journal on Indo-European Studies* 14: 1 – 2, 1986: 185 – 189). We finally decided to publish Berger's somewhat modified English version of his original chapter on Modern Indo-Aryan numerals, and to reprint Polomé's "A Note on Thraco-Phrygian numerals" with the consent of the editor of the *Journal on Indo-European Studies*, and with an *addendum* by Polomé in concern of recent evidence on Thraco-Phrygian. A major revision of the original chapter on Germanic numerals, needed in view of incomplete references and new evidence which had become available in the meantime, was carried out by J. Berns.

In addition to these chapters, which were already present in the original conception of this volume, there are also two newly written ones: a general chapter about Indo-European numeral reconstruction, called "Some thoughts about Indo-European numerals", and a chapter entitled "Remarks on numeral systems" which tries to formulate a link between the Indo-European tradition of numeral investigation and recent theoretical interest in numerals which has been developed independently of Indo-European studies. The present volume presents a comprehensive survey of Indo-European evidence on numerals based on our knowledge from two decennia ago and updated where the authors considered it appropriate (which applied especially in the case of Tocharian, Thraco-Phrygian, Greek, and Germanic).[1]

The basic arrangement of each chapter is the following throughout the volume:

X.0 Introduction
X.1. Cardinals
X.1.0. Introduction
X.1.1. 'One'
etc.
X.1.10. 'Ten'
X.1.11. 'Teens'
X.1.12. 'Twenty'
X.1.13. 'Thirty' – 'ninety'
X.1.14. 'Hundreds'
X.1.15. 'Thousands' (and upwards)
X.2. Ordinals
X.2.0. Introduction, etc. as above
X.3. Fractions
X.3.0. Introduction, etc., as above
X.4. Other categories as needed
X.4.0. Introduction, etc., as above

('X' refers to the number of the chapter. Finer divisions reflect the author's own subdivision of the text – if any, as no guidelines had been given to the authors before they wrote their texts.)

Major deviations from this schema are found in the chapters on Anatolian and Balto-Slavonic. In the chapter on Anatolian, the second figure denotes the numeral discussed, and the third figure denotes either a cardinal numeral, if it is "1", or an ordinal numeral, if it is "2" – e.g. "3.1.1." denotes that within the third chapter (Anatolian) the cardinal numeral "one" is being discussed. In the chapter on Balto-Slavonic, on the other hand, the second figure denotes the numeral discussed, and the last figure – if it is not preceded by "0" – denotes a cardinal numeral if it is "1", and an ordinal numeral if it is "2".

The chapters are (whenever possible) based on the original manuscripts supplied by the authors and on their original bibliographies. Where appropriate, an explanatory list of the abbreviations used in the text has been included at the end of the chapter. In several chapters, the authors have chosen to make a distinction between minor references, fully given in the text, and major references, given in the bibliography. The major references have been standardized. The minor references aim at giving sufficient information to the reader, though it has not been possible to fully standardize these.[2] Bibliographical abbreviations follow the system used in *Linguistic Bibliography*, with additions in several chapters which have been explained separately.

It wish to thank the authors for their willingness to reconsider their manuscripts, and all the people who have contributed towards this publication in the course of the years. Among them, I especially wish to thank the editor of Trends in Linguistics for his constructive contributions, and the Editor in Chief of Mouton de Gruyter for all the stimulating efforts towards this publication.

It seems more than appropriate to dedicate this volume to the memory of its initiator, Alan S. C. Ross.

Jadranka Gvozdanović

Notes

1. Among recent studies mentioning numeral etymologies, I would like to draw the reader's attention to T. V. Gamkrelidze – V. V. Ivanov (1984): *Indoevropejskij jazyk i indoevropejcy*, (Tblisi, Izdatel'stvo Tbilisskogo Universiteta) 2: 842 – 855 ("Čislitel'nye i sistema sčeta" [Numerals and the system of counting]).
2. The authors' own reconstruction and transcription preferences were followed as much as possible:
   - in the presence vs. absence of a reconstructed series of palatal velars;
   - in the transcription of the laryngeals as H_1, H_2, H_3, or H_e, H_a, H_o, or *E*, *A*, *O*, or $ə_1$, $ə_2$, $ə_3$;
   - in the glide transcription, where *y* and *w* were used whenever possible, and otherwise *i̯* and *u̯* were respected.

Contents

Chapter 1
Remarks on numeral systems

Jadranka Gvozdanović

Numerals are language signs, with forms and meanings which fit in with the language structures in which they occur. In most languages, numerals are characterized by relatively transparent form-meaning relations, which enable us to study patterning of numeral meanings (also referred to as "numbers") in a relatively straightforward way.

Cross-linguistic studies of numerals (especially Greenberg 1978) in terms of the mathematical structure of numeral meanings, the order of elements in numeral phrases, and the syntactic relation to the head noun, showed that there is a high level of generalizability and regularity in the embedding into the language structure. Subsequently, Chomsky (1980: 248 f.) suggested that the property of the human mind to develop certain forms of mathematical understanding, especially concerning the number system, abstract geometrical space, continuity, and related notions, might be enlightening as regards deep and fundamental characteristics of the human species. And in a later publication (1982: 20 ff.), Chomsky suggested that what underlies both the human language faculty and the number faculty is a kind of computational complexity that is equipped to deal with discrete infinities.

Against the background of this type of interest in numerals from the universalist and cognitive points of view, Hurford (1975, 1987) investigated numeral systems assuming that they lie in the intersection of the human language faculty and the number faculty. The relevant features of the language faculty include in his opinion the pairing of word forms with concepts and highly recursive syntax. In addition to a generative treatment of morphological and syntactic properties of numeral forms, Hurford (1987) especially concentrated on cognitive – mainly acquisitional and partly also variational – properties of the numeral meanings. Concerning the pairing of forms and meanings in numeral morphosyntax, Hurford (especially 1987) established a general tendency by which languages prefer to form numeral expressions by combining constituents whose meanings correspond with arithmetical values which are maximally far apart. This tendency corresponds in his opinion to a general output constraint in language which tends to prohibit sequences of identical morphs.[1] It forms part of the general principles of numeral syntax, for which Hurford proposed an analysis in terms of phrase structure rules and additional language-specific constraints, such as the so-called "Packing Strategy" in English. The proposed simplified version of the phrase structure rules for English numerals is given in (1).

(1) A simplified version of the phrase structure rules for English numerals (Hurford 1987: 245):

NUMBER → { DIGIT / PHRASE (NUMBER) } ('DIGIT' expands to any of the words *one, two, ..., eight, nine.*)

PHRASE → NUMBER M

M → { -ty / hundred / thousand / million / billion }

An example of a structure generated by (1) is given in (2).

(2) The phrase structure for *two thousand one hundred* in English (Hurford 1987: 246):

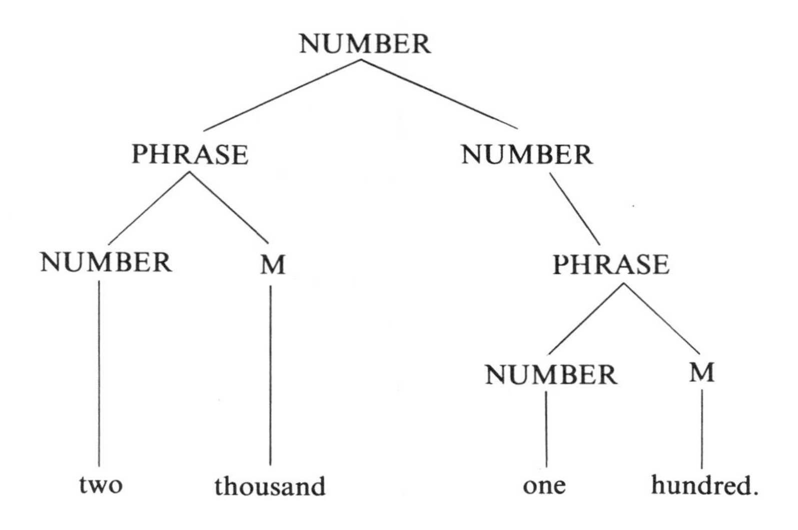

Corresponding to the pre-theoretical intuitive account of the facts, by which in additive constructions the highest-valued constituent is put first, Hurford's Packing Strategy states: "pack the highest-valued constituent as near as possible to the root (top) of the tree" (Hurford 1987: 246 f.). This can account for the fact that English *two thousand one hundred* is standard, but **one hundred two thousand* is not. Given its general formulation, the Packing Strategy captures also the pretheoretical intuitive account by which in multiplicative constructions the highest-valued constituent is put second, thus accounting for the fact that English *two hundred thousand* is standard, but **two thousand hundred* is not.

In addition to such morphological and syntactic generalizations, Hurford (1987: 305) established the following innate contributions to the organization of numeral systems:

1) the concepts of collection and individual object, and the relations between them;
2) the ability to represent arbitrary links between signified and signifier (the Saussurean Sign);
3) the disposition to make the sizeable inductive leap from a memorized sequence of words to the use of these words expressing the cardinality of collections (the Cardinality Principle);
4) the ability to acquire and control syntactic rules forming longer expressions out of the simple vocabulary, together with associated semantic interpretation rules;
5) the ability to assemble such rules into highly recursive rule sets.

"Out of these capacities", Hurford (1987: 305) wrote, "only the third, the Cardinality Principle, is special to numeral systems; the rest are very familiar in human language more generally." The Cardinality Principle, by which an inference regarding the cardinality of a set is made from an instance of the counting activity ending with a particular numeral word, is directly related to the ordering of numeral expressions, a feature which in Hurford's opinion sets apart numerals from other language elements, such as the set of noun phrases, or prepositional phrases, or other elements, which are in Hurford's opinion all unordered sets. This basic assumption, which is partly due to Hurford's generative background, was not exposed to further investigation. And it is at this point that one might speak of a missed opportunity for shedding more light onto the human cognitive capacities which underlie both the human language faculty and the number faculty.

In fact, arguments in favour of similarity between numeral ordering and ordering in the other parts of language can be found both syntagmatically and paradigmatically. These arguments can be understood if one views

a) the presence of ordering among forms as reflecting ordering among the meanings of these forms, and
b) the basis of ordering as being constituted by asymmetrical implication of the type "B implies A, but A does not imply B"; asymmetrical implication affecting elements of the same level is traditionally referred to as "markedness", and asymmetrical implication affecting elements across levels is traditionally referred to as "hierarchy".

If understood in this, more general, sense, then ordering which can be established for the number system (i. e., the system of numeral meanings, as reflected by the numeral forms) does appear to be comparable to ordering which can be established for the other parts of language.

A syntagmatic argument can be deduced i. a. from phenomena captured by the so-called Packing Strategy constraint described above, by which "the highest-valued constituent" is packed "as near as possible to the root (top) of the tree". This constraint shows that fixed ordering holds among numeral forms if their meanings are mutually hierarchically differentiated. The observed effect of meaning hierarchy on the order of the forms representing these meanings holds for numerals in a way comparable to that obtaining for the other parts of language. This principle was already implicitly recognized by Hurford (1978), who formulated the Packing Strategy constraint with reference to morphosyntactic principles which are in this type of approach applicable to the other parts of language as well. What I am doing here is in fact reformulating them in terms of form—meaning relations and ordering. In this reformulation of the principles already recognized by Hurford, the ordering which is characteristic of numeral phrases parallels the ordering which is characteristic of, e. g., Heads and Modifiers in noun phrases, and this ordering of forms follows from their meanings, such that Heads denote entities and Modifiers denote properties. Between these categories, there is asymmetrical implication in the sense that entities are characterized by properties, and if so, implied by them (a property may either characterize an entity or an event; in the latter case, it shows up as a Modifier of a verb phrase, not a noun phrase). It is on the basis of this asymmetrical implication that a hierarchy obtains by which a nominal Head is dominating and its Modifier subordinate. Languages tend to express this meaning hierarchy by means of formal phenomena such as the Modifier's copying, e. g., gender and number from its Head and/or by means of word order constraints. In the numeral system, this is paralleled by the difference between so-called building blocks (e. g., 'ten', i. e., not fully equalling Hurford's category 'M', as will be shown below) and so-called numeral elements (e. g., 'one'): if present, a numeral building block dominates numeral elements, but numeral elements need not imply a building block (for cross-linguistic variational data, e. g., from Tibeto-Burman, cf. Gvozdanović 1985). It is this asymmetrical implication holding for the different categories of numeral meanings which underlies the hierarchy that plays the relevant rôle in the morphosyntactic constraints such as the Packing Strategy discussed above.

If the meanings of the categories involved are mutually characterized by asymmetrical implication, this has consequences for their syntagmatic usage possibilities. Paradigmatic characterization and syntagmatic usage possibilities consequently fit in within one whole. It is on the basis of paradigmatic asymmetrical implication that not only the morphosyntactic phenomena discussed above can be explained, but also usage possibilities of a bare hierarchically dominating category with reference to its (potentially) subordinate ones. This is a well-known phenomenon of generic expressions in language (by which, e. g., *a monkey* or *monkeys* can be used with reference to any of the possible properties of the given set of entities). A nominal Head can be used in this way, but if a Modifier is to be used in a similar way, then languages tend to develop additional adjustment means (such as saying, e. g., *a beautiful one* in English, with *one* referring to the corresponding dominating category). In the numeral system we have the same phenomenon of usage possibilities of a dominating category with reference to its (potentially) subordinate ones in the usage possibility of any of the numeral building blocks or a multiplication of it with reference to any of its subordinate building blocks and/or any of the possible numeral elements further specifying it (such as saying in English, e. g., *this happened in the eighteen hundreds* or *this happened in the eighteen hundred twenties*, with referential applicability to any of the decads and specific years of the nineteenth century in the first example, and with reference to any of the specific years within the given decad of the nineteenth century in the second example).

In addition to these principled similarities between the numeral system and the remaining parts of language, there is a well-known difference, too. It is found in the presence of full ordering among the numeral meanings, which is not to such an extent found in the remaining parts of language. However, even though there is full ordering, there are alternatives in its patterning, demonstrated by language-specific differences in the building blocks as used in the numeral hierarchies. Depending on the language, the building blocks can be based on the meaning of 'five', 'ten', 'twenty', 'hundred', etc., and only the ways in which these building blocks participate in hierarchies with respect to each other and with respect to the numeral elements show basic cross-linguistic similarities. These similarities, all deriving from the same principle of asymmetrical implication at the level of numeral meaning, are revealed by the principles of linear ordering at the level of numeral forms, which fit in with – and are hence indicative of – the general principles of linear ordering in a given language, and which reveal the meanings of the units undergoing this ordering.

It is in respect of hierarchy that numeral systems can be assumed to fit in within one whole with fundamental characteristics of language systems. And it is in this respect that a study of numeral systems, with their relatively straightforward patterning of form and meaning in the derived forms and syntagms, can be revealing with respect to fundamental characteristics of the human mind.

What kind of independent evidence can be given for the idea presented here that the numeral system is organized hierarchically, such that there are level differences as described above? From what kind of data can the existence of levels be deduced?

The relevant sort of data would be of the sort showing that the so-called building blocks are units comparable to each other and different from the so-called basic elements. If there is such a phenomenon among numeral meanings, we can expect it to show up in similarities among the forms connected with these meanings, such that numeral building blocks are, or become, similar to each other in a way distinguishing them from the so-called basic elements 'one', 'two', etc. Whereas similarity among basic numeral elements is by nature linear, similarity among building blocks – if it is attested – is by nature nonlinear and unexplainable by any linear principle, unless it takes into account levels.

The relevant sort of data concerning nonlinearity within numeral systems can be derived from studies of analogy, such as Winter's (1969). Winter discusses analogy in language, including numerals, as similarity in form which originates from similarity in meaning: in the case of numerals, it is often – but apparently not always – based on contiguity,

i. e., linear ordering in counting, as shown by the following Sanskrit examples.

(3) Analogy in the ordinal numerals of Sanskrit (from Winter 1969: 36):

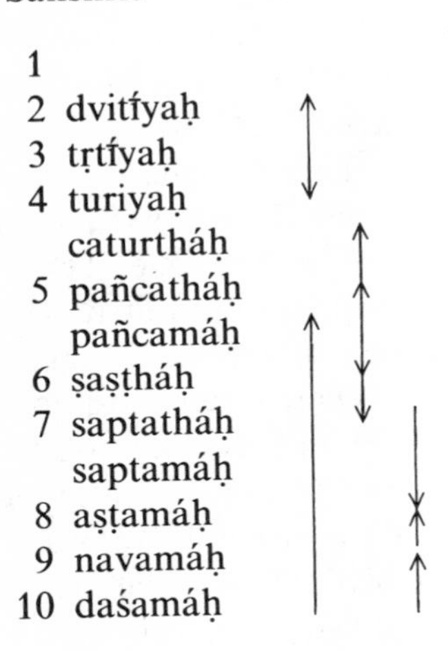

The only exception to contiguity as underlying analogical formation in the ordinal numerals of the first decad in Sanskrit is found in the influence of the *-m-* suffix of *daśamáḥ* (i. e. *daśamás*) 'tenth' on the form for 'fifth'. Winter (1969: 38) concludes that an explanation for this phenomenon can be given only in connection with an investigation of the higher numerals. This statement is correct, and now that more extensive numeral data have been collected for this volume, we can see that in another case of analogy in Old Indian (which comprises Sanskrit), *pañcát-* 'group of five' is due to influence of *daśát-* 'group of ten', which in its turn owes its accentuation to the other tens (cf. chapter 5 (5.3.5.4) of the present volume). This shows that in Old Indian, 'five' was apparently a unit on a par with 'ten' and the higher tens, i. e., it was apparently a building block and in this sense similar to 'ten' and the higher tens, and distinguished from the basic numeral elements. Such data on non-linear analogies are indicative of the existence of paradigmatic level differences among the numerals, and apparently of the type which may be claimed to be reflected by syntagmatic rules such as Hurford's Packing Strategy. As the analogies show that such paradigmatic differences can claim independent existence, we are justified in assuming that the observed syntagmatic level differences follow from the corresponding paradigmatic ones, and that numeral systems are not only linearly, but also hierarchically ordered.

The hypothesis about the relevance of numeral systems to our insight into cognitive capacities which underlie language as a human communication system can now be formulated as follows: *the relation between meaning and form in numeral systems reflects the principles of ordering within and among levels which are fully applicable and hence more transparent than those in the remaining parts of language, which are of the same type, but not always applicable to the same extent.* This hypothesis contains two subparts: one concerning principles in numeral systems, and one concerning their parallels in the remaining parts of language. The first subpart of this hypothesis can be tested and further elaborated on the basis of extensive numeral data from a set of genetically related languages, such as those contained in the present volume. Whereas derived numeral forms reveal the principles of ordering in a straightforward way, basic numeral forms and those whose derivation is not transparent any more so that they may be called "pseudo-basic" reveal the principles of ordering only through analogies in which they were involved. Given the fact that analogy is a possibility in language, never a necessity, ordering need not be fully revealed by analogy. This means that the hypothesis about ordering among basic and pseudo-basic numerals cannot be fully tested. Language speakers know that their meanings are ordered, but as their language system does not have full ordering, the language forms used for expressing the numeral meanings do not fully reflect the ordering among the numeral meanings. It is at this point that an extensive set of data from genetically related languages can give us indications about ordering in various parts of the numeral systems which, if taken together, can give a full picture of the principles involved.

The present volume contains extensive data on Indo-European numerals. Its purpose is descriptive and its organization such that it can enable the reader to draw conclusions about the principles of ordering outlined above. The reader is invited to pay special attention to data on analogy and new formations presented in the various chapters of this book. For a better understanding of these data, special attention should be paid to language-specific numeral building blocks, also called "numeral bases". They are crucial to our understanding of analogy and new formations as affected by level differences. The following types of numeral systems emerge from the data on Indo-European:

- the system based on 'five', i. e., the quinary system, in Welsh, and with sporadic evidence in Old Indian;
- the system based on 'ten', i. e., the decimal system, which is the main system in Indo-European languages;
- the system based on 'twenty', i. e., the vigesimal system, in Iranian, Indo-Aryan, Albanian, Celtic, Romance, North Germanic, and sporadically as borrowed in Slavic;
- the system based on 'hundred', in Modern Indo-Aryan (where contemporary non-derivability of the lower numerals is due to a mixed effect of sound change and analogy).

Starting form the present collection of data, an investigation of how the principles underlying the structure of numeral systems relate to the principles underlying other parts of language will hopefully belong to our immediate future tasks.

Note

1. I am obliged to state that counterexamples to this "constraint" do occur in languages, but with a meaning modification. For example, in Limbu, a Tibeto-Burman language from East Nepal, *thik* means 'one' and *thik thik*, 'one each' (cf. also Gvozdanović 1985: 162).

References

Chomsky, Noam
1980 *Rules and representations* (Oxford: Basil Blackwell).
1982 *The generative enterprise: a discussion with Riny Huybregts and Henk van Riemsdijk* (Dordrecht: Foris).
Greenberg, Joseph H.
1978 "Generalizations about numeral systems", in: J. H. Greenberg (ed.), *Universals of human language: word structure* (Stanford: Stanford University Press): 249–295.
Gvozdanović, Jadranka
1985 *Language system and its change (on theory and testability)* (Berlin/New York/Amsterdam: Mouton de Gruyter).

Hurford, James R.
1975 *The linguistic theory of numerals* (Cambridge: Cambridge University Press).
1987 *Language and number* (Oxford: Basil Blackwell).
Winter, Werner
1969 "Analogischer Sprachwandel und semantische Struktur", *Folia Linguistica* 3: 29–45.

Chapter 2
Some thoughts about Indo-European numerals*

Werner Winter

Carl Darling Buck voiced a commonly held opinion when he stated (1949: 936):

> No class of words, not even those denoting family relationship, has been so persistent as the numerals in retaining the inherited words.
>
> Except for some suffix-variation and actual substitution in the case of 'one' (13.32), the IE words for 'one' to 'ten' have persisted everywhere with only slight changes other than phonetic; likewise the IE word for 'hundred', while for 'thousand' there are several different groups.

Buck then went on to make some remarks about the '-teens', the decads, and the ordinals (multiples of 'one hundred' were left unmentioned), pointing out some disturbances in these sets of numerals, but feeling no need for even a mild qualification of his opening sentence. It would not seem unfair, though, to revise his statement so as to read: "No class of words (in Indo-European languages) has been as persistent as the set of cardinals 'two' to 'ten' in retaining the inherited words".

Even in this toned-down version, a number of facts have to be disregarded. Some years ago, when discussing the possibility of utilizing evidence from analogical change as an indication of semantic structure, I placed side by side (Winter 1969: 34–35) those forms of lower cardinals in Sanskrit, Greek, Latin, Germanic (represented by Modern Low German), Slavic (with data from Russian), Baltic (Lithuanian), Tocharian (B), and Armenian which had undergone irregular development under the influence of adjacent cardinals. With the exception of 'ten', not a single lower cardinal had remained unaffected. At the time, I interpreted these findings as support for the very natural claim that lower numerals

* An earlier version of this paper was read at the symposium honoring the memory of Sir William Jones, which was held in 1986 in Calcutta, India.

formed a closely-knit semantic field with a fairly well definable internal structure. I rejected the assumption that the analogical changes had taken place due to adjacency in actual counting because of the fact that analogical reshaping was even more common in ordinals than in cardinals and that an enumeration of ordinals in a sequence of numerals uninterrupted by non-numeral forms was too unnatural in actual language use to have triggered the introduction of, say, Skt. *dvitī́yaḥ* 'second' shaped after Skt. *tṛtī́yaḥ* 'third' (Winter 1969: 38). Whether one wants to accept this conclusion or not, the fact remains that even the low cardinals do not show the resistance to irregular change attributed to them by Buck. Still, one will not want to deny that 'two' through 'ten' reflect, though here and there with slight distortion, a set of fairly well reconstructible Proto-Indo-European forms.

However, even these forms present their problems. 'Two' is a dual based on a thematic stem **dwe/o-*; 'three', a plural form with a stem **trey-* subject to ablaut variation. 'Four' is more peculiar: it, too, is a plural form, but the stem is not a simple one, but has, in the masculine, the **-e . . o-* vowel pattern of a compound. However, this is an observation in terms of form only: it cannot be supplemented by an identification of the two elements of the compound with surviving simple stems or roots. Thus, 'four' remains, in spite of its formal complexity, an unmotivated lexeme, at least at the level of reconstruction which can be reached using the methods available to us.

Lack of motivation is not uncommon in lower numerals. Thus, it seems impossible to find a connection of **septm̥* with any other element of the Proto-Indo-European lexicon; 'seven' just means 'seven' and nothing else. This does not alter the fact that **septm̥* is a strange form; it remains tempting to identify final **m̥* with the accusative ending of consonant stems. Even if one were to take **-t-* as a consonant-stem variant of **-ti-* found elsewhere in cardinals, the remaining **sep-*, while now acceptable in terms of Proto-Indo-European root structure, would remain an isolate: if indeed **sept-* originally should have denoted a heptad rather than mere 'seven', the underlying **sep-* would still require a rendering as 'seven' and only as that.

Moreover, residual problems of considerable weight persist. We would have to assume that an accusative form was generalized; this in itself is not an impossibility, witness the spread of descendants of the Latin accusative in Old French. Somewhat less anticipated would, at first glance, seem the occurrence of a singular rather than a plural form; this objection can be neatly handled by referring to the claim that nothing but a singular form should be expected if **sept-* did indeed mean 'heptad' – witness the plural form used in Russian in the declension of *tri* 'three' as against the singular forms found for *pjat'* 'five', etc. What remains an unanswerable question, though, is why it should have been only 'seven' that was expressed by an abstract noun. Or is it that one could ascribe a special status to a numeral which could be used referring to the fourth part of a lunar month? Rather than complicate the issue by alluding to, and elaborating on, the possibility that 'seven' might have been borrowed from a Semitic language (cf. Møller 1909: 124, where, of course, a claim for Urverwandtschaft is involved), I prefer to limit myself to showing up a possible option and to leave the matter at that.

Attempts at finding motivation in other lower cadinals have been made in the past. The fact that the word for 'eight' shows the ending of a masculine dual has been taken as an indication of the use of an old quaternary system in Proto-Indo-European. Taken by itself, this is a rash conclusion. Even if Avest. *ašti-* 'width of four fingers' (cf. Henning 1948: 69) could be taken as pointing toward a related PIE **ok̓to-*, which might tentatively be rendered by *'pertaining to a group of four' (with no connection whatsoever with PIE *k^{w}etwores* 'four'), PIE **ok̓tōw* would not contain more than a hint of a system or subsystem in which multiplication could be used to express non-prime numbers.

The quaternary hypothesis would be considerably strengthened if the old assumption (cf. Walde – Hofmann 1954: 180) could be made plausible that the word for 'nine' was related to the word for 'new'. If Gk. *nearós* 'youngster', Arm. *nor* 'new' can both be considered derivations from an *-*r*-stem noun PIE **newr̥*, then it is not impossible that beside the *-*r*-stem, an *-*n*-stem should also have existed. **newn̥* could then perhaps be an endingless locative (cf., with different ablaut grade, OInd. *udán* 'in the water'); its meaning 'in the new' could have been reinforced by preposing **en* 'in', which would then be reflected in Gk. *ennéa*, Arm. *inn* 'nine'. If this interpretation were correct, the apparently optional addition of **en* might constitute a shared innovation of Greek and Armenian. If, on the other hand, Gk. *e-* and Arm. *i-* are 'prothetic vowels', they must be taken to reflect a Proto-Indo-European laryngeal, and both the common innovation and the connection with 'new' would have to be dropped from our list of potential hypotheses concerning Gk. *ennéa* and Arm. *inn*. As it is, the assumption of an addition of **en* provides a neat explanation for the (double) *-nn-* of Gk. *ennéa*; on the other hand, the Greek ordinal *énatos* / *eínatos* / *ḗnatos* / *énotos* 'ninth', which seems to have replaced an older **enwanos* (cf., *mutatis mutandis*, Sommer 1951: 25–36), appears to be unaccounted for without elaborate additional assumptions.

To sum up the points just discussed: It seems to me that the arguments in favor of a connection of 'nine' and 'new' do not carry enough weight to consider the hypothesis proved that 'nine' marked overtly the onset of a new set of numbers; even less can the assumption that Proto-Indo-European had a quaternary system at some point in its prehistory be deemed sufficiently supported. Ossetic *farast* 'nine', literally 'beyond eight', is taken by Abaev (1958: 419–420) to show that 'eight' was a round number, at least from an Ossetic point of view, but he is cautious enough to add 'just like ten', which prevents one from citing the Ossetic form in support of a quaternary hypothesis.

Szemerényi (1960: 78–79) enumerates arguments which may be adduced to posit an underlying **weḱs* for the Indo-European forms for 'six'. In footnote 55, he then suggests a connection with PIE **(H)weḱs-* 'to grow', "so that '6' would be 'the increase' after the first 'hand'"; **s-* in the widespread **sweḱs* he considers "secondary", "obviously from the following numeral **septm̥*". If these assumptions are warranted, 'six' would indeed be a clear case of motivation in a lower cardinal. While the basic thrust of the argument seems to be well-founded, certain details need further elaboration.

Before a root noun **Aweḱs* 'increment' can be posited as underlying the Indo-European forms for 'six', explanations have to be found for the vacillation found between forms with and without **-w-* and for the onsets Skt. *ṣ-*, OInd. **kṣ-* as reflected by Middle and New Indic forms with initial *ch-*, Avest. *xšv-*, Slav. *š-*, and Lith. *š-*.

OInd. **kṣ-* and Avest. *xšv-* show the reflex of PIE **s* regular in a *ruki* environment. Sanskrit *ṣ-* is regular if a *ruki* environment can be reconstructed; so is Balto-Slavic *š-* before *-e-*, given the same condition. To posit a Proto-Indo-European onset **ksw-*, with simplification of the original cluster in most daughter languages, would mean positing a monstrosity violating all we know about root structure and clustering rules in Proto-Indo-European. If then **k-* cannot be part of the root of 'six' and cannot be a proper onset of the word for 'six', what could be its origin?

There is nothing to recommend claiming the presence of a prefix **k-* since no meaning or function can be ascribed to it, nor would it be at all likely that a cluster **ksw-* would have survived without either consonant deletion or vowel insertion.

The *ruki* environment must therefore be sought outside, and that means preceding, the lexeme 'six', which can indeed be reconstructed, in almost full agreement with Szemerényi (1960: 78), as **sweḱs*.

The word which one does expect to find preceding 'six' in an ordered sequence of cardinals, no matter whether the sequence was one encountered in an actual counting enumeration or rather one in the speaker's memory as reconstructible from the evidence of analogical reshaping (as pointed out earlier), is the word for 'five'. This very observation seems to lead us into a blind alley: the combined evidence of the cardinals Skt. *páñca*, Gk. *pénte*, Arm. *hing* (if taken together with Arm. *hngetasan* 'fifteen'), Tocharian B *piś*, A *päñ*, leaves no doubt that the underlying Proto-Indo-European word must be posited as **penk*^{w}*e*; this in turn means that 'five' would not provide a *ruki* environment as *-*k*^{w}- is not immediately adjacent to *-*s*- of **sweḱs*.

Now, in spite of its easy reconstructibility, PIE **penk*^{w}*e* does not appear to be a Proto-Indo-European form of long standing. Two arguments can be raised against it: For one, **penk*^{w}*e* has two full-grade vowels, and this is in violation of old ablaut rules. The second point is just as serious: the use of the ordinal suffix *-*to*- outside 'tenth' is secondary according to, among others, Szemerényi (1960: 86–87). One has to agree with Szemerényi (1960: 85) that it is "inevitable to conclude that '5th' ... was originally **penk*^{w}*o*-, or rather **pn̥k*^{w}*o*-". Strangely enough, the comparative evidence is overwhelmingly in favor of the full-grade, rather than the zero-grade, form (cf. Gk. *pémptos*, Lat. *quīntus*, OHG *fimfto*, Lith. *peñktas*, Tocharian B *piṅkte* vs. OInd. *pakthā́ḥ* and perhaps – in spite of the vigorous objections by Szemerényi (1960: 71–74) – forms from High as well as Low German: from my own dialect of Low German, *dı föftı* 'the fifth' as against *fị̄f* 'five' may be quoted here). The preponderance of apparent full-grade forms is matched in 'sixth' even where **sw*- has been preserved, and of course in 'seventh' where zero-grade forms of **sept*- would not agree with rules of Proto-Indo-European syllable structure. The important point to be made here, however, is that the ordinals show a trace of the final *-*e* of 'five' only in some clearly secondary formations (cf., e.g., Pokorny 1959: 808). As **p(e)nk*^{w}*os* is to be segmented as **p(e)nk*^{w}*-o-s*, we are free to assume that *-*e* in **penk*^{w}*e* is a development (comparable to *-*e* of the third person singular perfect) introduced to permit the occurrence of underlying **penk*^{w}, with an inadmissible final consonant cluster *-*nk*^{w}*#*, as a free surface form. The alternative to the addition of an "empty" protecting vowel would have been the deletion of final *-*k*^{w}; it is highly doubtful whether this substance-destroying alternative was ever made use of – **pen*- in ordinals like dialectal Gk. *péntos*, Tocharian A *pänt* 'fifth' seems to be insufficient evidence for raising such a claim.

In a rapidly produced counting sequence, however, the underlying form **penk*ʷ could surface, provided the word boundary between 'five' and 'six' was eliminated so that 'six' could "protect" 'five'. As a result of such a development, phonological processes blocked by word boundary could become operative: just as in rapid-speech counting the sequence -*s* + *s*- in slow-speech Engl. *six seven* is reduced to a single -*s*- in allegro [sɪksɛvm̩], so stem-final *-*k*ʷ of **penk*ʷ 'five' could now provide the proper environment for the immediately adjacent initial **s*- of 'six' to cause application of the *ruki* rule in Indo-Iranian and Balto-Slavic. The close sequence 'five-six' thus could become Proto-Indo-Iranian **pank*⁽ʷ⁾*šwac*. (I have included the velar element of the labiovelar to be able to account for the difference between Skt. *ṣaṭ* and Avest. *xšvas*; cf. below, Proto-Balto-Slavic **penkšeš*.) Decomposition of the sequence *-*nk*⁽ʷ⁾*ṣ*- could now bring into existence forms for 'six' with rather different onsets: **š*- in Skt. *ṣaṭ*, Lith. *šešì*, OCS *šestĭ*; **kṣ* in the Old Indic form underlying Middle and Modern Indic *ch*- and in Khotan Saka *kṣai*; **kšw*- in Avest. *xšvas*. **k*ʷ thus remained with 'five' or was interpreted as shared by 'five' and 'six', so that the insertion of a protective *-*e* could lead to the re-creation of **penk*ʷ*e* even on the basis of the allegro form (however, there is no need to stress this point: allegro and lento forms should have existed side by side so that we merely have to assume that *ruki*-affected forms were introduced in the lento set, replacing there forms with a plain **s(w)*-onset).

Armenian seems to show a special reflex of the allegro configuration: If Olsen (1981: 5) is right in deriving Arm. *veç* 'six' from earlier **huwe*-, then the deviant insertion of a Sievers-Edgerton *-*u*- is easy to understand if we envisage **swe*- as occurring in position after the cluster *-*nk*ʷ of the allegro form for 'five'.

The distribution of **s*- and **sw*- is erratic: clear instances of *-*w*- are found in Avestan, Armenian, Greek, Celtic, and Baltic (forms such as OPruss. *uschts* 'sixth' seem to point to a dissimilatory reduction of **šuštas* rather than to a survival of a form without an **s*- onset, as Szemerényi 1960: 78 would want to have it). The simplest explanation for such a distribution is to assume that *-*w*- was lost by dissimilation against the labial element of the labiovelar of 'five', either by distant dissimilation in the lento set or, perhaps more likely so, by contact dissimilation in the allegro sequence. The dissimilation hypothesis requires a relatively late survival of labiovelars even in satem languages; as there is some evidence for just that in Albanian and in Armenian, the proposal made here cannot be rejected outright, but should be taken under advisement.

Szemerényi (1960: 69 with fn. 69) joins others who proposed before him that PIE **deḱm̥t* should be analyzed as **de-ḱm̥t* and rendered by 'two hands'. The difficulty remains that the evidence for a set of forms for 'two' without *-*w*- is at best shaky. While 'two hands' is a perfectly reasonable rendering of 'ten' in a quinary system, all depends on a demonstration that Proto-Indo-European had such a quinary system at least in its first decad of numerals. To prove this point, it has to be shown that **penk*^{w} can be identified as related to Indo-European words for 'hand'. A connection has indeed been suggested between **penk*^{w}*e* 'five' and OHG *fūst*, ORuss. *pjast'* 'fist' (cf. e.g., Pokorny 1959: 839, Vasmer 1953: 477 for literature). An *-*st* suffix is not uncommon in – above all paired – body parts (cf., e.g., OInd. *muṣṭiḥ*, Tocharian B *maśce* 'fist', Lith. *kùmstė* 'fist'). **penk*^{w} might then originally have referred to the hand clenched to form a fist; by way of contrast, one could imagine that **oḱto-*, reflected by Avest. *ašti-* 'width of four fingers' and PIE **oḱtōw* 'eight' might have designated four fingers outstretched, with the thumb turned in.

The time seems to have come to try and sum up our findings so far: The lower cardinals up to 'three' are unmotivated forms. 'Four', considered a compound, so far defies analysis. 'Five' is, if correctly analyzed, a motivated formation, with 'fist' as the primary meaning of **penk*^{w}. 'Six' may ultimately be an elliptic expression "increment (of 'five')". 'Seven' is unanalyzable: the possibility of its being a very old loanword from a Semitic language cannot be ruled out entirely. 'Eight' may mean 'both sets of four (outstretched) fingers'. Unless 'nine' can be connected with 'newness' (which is difficult in view of some Greek forms), it remains unanalyzable. For 'ten', an interpretation 'two hands' has been suggested; this sounds persuasive as far as the meaning is concerned; but **de-* causes difficulties, and so does the fact that 'two' would have been expressed by a numeral rather than a dual form of 'hand' being used.

All higher cardinals, beginning with 'eleven' are syntagms (in a broad sense of the term), that is, they are based on lower numerals either derivationally or through processes of composition or phrase formation, with the possibility of elliptic reduction of complex forms. This is a very natural state of affairs. Numbers are an open-ended semantic field (at least potentially so, although speakers of numerous languages stop counting at a very early point); unless the counting potential has been left undeveloped, it is in principle impossible to name the highest number of any full-fledged system. The property of nonfiniteness makes it impractical to use separate lexical items for any but a few lower numbers; the situation in Modern Indo-Aryan, with its relegation of all numbers up to 'one hundred' to the lexicon as items to be learned separately and not to be derived by palpable rules, is quite exceptional and hard, if not impossible, to explain.

What is needed to cope with the necessities of a nonfinite universe of numbers, is a set of building blocks and a set of operations to be applied to these building blocks.

In theory, it would be possible to base a nonfinite set of units (disregarding fractions, that is) on one unit, viz., 'one', and one operation, viz., addition. This solution is thoroughly impractical, as can easily be shown: Suppose I say, preferably in a monotone, 'one' + 'one' + 'one' + 'one' + 'one' + 'one' + 'one' + 'one' + 'one' + 'one', and then ask which number I had just uttered, only very few listeners would be able to give the correct answer, viz., 'ten'. If, on the other hand, I had pointed out that in Bantawa Rai, a Tibeto-Burman language of Eastern Nepal, *chuk* meant 'hand', *ʔükchuk* 'one hand; five', and that *hüwa-* was one of the variants of 'two', used in bound forms, probably few, if any listeners would have difficulties in determining that *hüwachuk* denoted 'ten'. There would have been no difficulty because we had all learned to apply an operation other than addition, too, viz., multiplication. That multiplication and not addition or subtraction was called for had been indicated by giving the information that the compound form *ʔükchuk* meant 'one hand = 1 × hand = five' and not 'one plus hand = six' or 'hand minus one = four'. The logically possible operation *ʔükchuk* 'one hand = five divided by one = 5', so that *hüwachuk* would require a reading 'five divided by two = 2.5', would probably occur to no one since the effectiveness of division (as of subtraction) is very limited in sets of natural numbers: without the use of other, conflicting operations, it would be quite impossible to cope with the task of forming increasingly high numbers.

Lexicalization and addition are the only operations which, in theory, could be applied in isolation to express a set of integers, but both are ruled out in practice for that purpose. Total lexicalization is, on the one hand, too cumbersome for memory storage and for learning to use it for anything but very short sequences of numbers (the situation in Modern Indo-Aryan presents an extreme case of lexical-set extension); on the other, it would require the creation of a new lexical item for every new number one wanted to express, which in turn would constantly increase the weight of the storage-and-learning problem; moreover, there seems to be ample evidence that creation *ex nihilo* is found very rarely in natural languages.

Addition used by itself runs into another difficulty, as we have seen a short while ago: there are rather severe limitations on the scope of human perception as far as the number of elements that can be evaluated without naturally provided breaks is concerned. Very few listeners would be able to identify properly the value of moderately high numbers if they were to be expressed as sequences of 'one'.

Multiplication cannot be applied to complete sets of integers for a simple non-linguistic reason: prime numbers cannot be expressed as products. Subtraction pure and simple could only be used if one was to deal with a finite set of numbers, the highest member of which could be taken as a starting point. However, such a set would lack the property of being expandable at will, and therefore be of fairly little use. Division, taken by itself, suffers from the shortcomings of multiplication (now taken in reverse) and subtraction combined: it can thus be only of very limited use under special circumstances.

The optimal solution then is a combination of addition and multiplication; slightly inferior, as soon as more than a few relatively low numbers have to be expressed, is a process of addition to lexicalized higher numbers reflected by numerals not derivable from smaller entities. An example, for simplicity's sake presented in English translation, could be cited again from Tibeto-Burman. As competing expressions for 'twenty' are found, one multiplicative 'four hand', one independent, viz., 'heap' (for which we may use 'score' as an English parallel), 'twenty-one' can be expressed either by saying 'four hand plus one' or by employing 'one score plus one'. The 'score' approach obviously suffers from the same weakness as was encountered in a purely lexical solution: too many entities would have to be learned and stored. Note here that even languages with an extensive use of lexicalized numerals such as the modern Indo-Aryan ones, extend this approach only to very few numbers higher than 'one hundred' – there is 'one thousand', 'a hundred thousand', 'ten million', but no separate lexical item for, say, 'five hundred' or 'twelve thousand'.

Multiplication is a very effective way of abbreviating the expression of higher numbers; addition, and, more rarely so, subtracton is the means of coping with numbers that cannot be analyzed as multiples of the multiplicand or multiplicands utilized in a particular counting system. Thus, if, as in a language of the Yuman group in California, 'six' is expressed as 'two times three' and 'nine' as 'three times three', 'eight' will have to make reference to either 'six' or 'nine' by addition or subtraction, respectively, or else a separate lexical item has to be used (unless, of course, 'four' is also employed as a multiplicand, so that 'eight' could become 'two times four'; 'seven', however could in no case be handled by multiplication).

It seems to be normal to select as high as possible a multiplicand as the basis for higher numerals, apparently with the proviso that a numeral so chosen should be unanalyzable as a complex term synchronically. More than one multiplicand may be chosen as the counting progresses to ever higher numbers. Thus, it is quite common in languages of the world to find a combination of a quinary and a vigesimal system; modern Indo-Aryan languages progress from a system with 'hundred' as a unit of multiplication to higher systems with 'one thousand' and 'one hundred thousand' as multiplicands; modern French starts out decadic, then turns vigesimal, then moves on to 'hundred', 'thousand', 'million', etc., as multiplicands; Tocharian has 'ten', 'hundred', 'thousand', 'ten thousand', and, in a context influenced by Indic tradition, 'ten million' as multiplicands.

For Proto-Indo-European, the condition that a numeral used as a multiplicand should be unanalyzable synchronically leads one to consider Late Proto-Indo-European a language characterized by 'ten' and 'hundred' as multiplicands, while at an earlier stage of the language, at which 'hundred' was still recognizably derived from 'ten', there was a purely decimal system, as far as all numbers above ten are concerned. The higher numeral 'thousand', to the extent that its various forms permit an analysis, seems to contain a reference to a basic notion 'hundred', be it explicitly, as in Goth. *þūsundi* and its Germanic congeners as well as in OPruss. *tūsimtons*, OCS *tysęšti*, be it in an elliptic form like Tocharian B *yaltse*, A *wälts*, which could be analyzed as a nominalized adjective (B *-tse*, A *-ts* can be rendered by 'provided with') derived from a root noun pre-Toch. **wel-* whose **-i*-stem counterpart can be seen in Slav. **velĭ* reflected by OCS *velĭmi* 'very' and later Slavic forms (cf. Vasmer 1953: 181 with earlier literature; for the Tocharian forms cf. van Windekens 1976: 555 with literature – no connection with B A *wälts-** '± condense' should be attempted); a slightly different interpretation of the Tocharian forms is included in chapter 4 of the present volume. Germanic and Balto-Slavic forms could be read directly as conveying the meaning 'strength hundred', the Tocharian ones as '(the hundred) with strength'. It would be highly satisfactory if Gk. *khī́lioi*/*kheílioi*/*khéllioi*/*khḗlioi*, OInd. *sahás-*

ram, Avest. *ha-zaŋrəm*, Khotan Saka *ysāra*, Lat. *mīlle* could be tacked on; however, all attempts made so far remain fraught with difficulties (cf., e.g., Frisk 1970: 1099–1100); a detailed discussion would take up too much time here.

No matter how one wants to evaluate details, the overall picture remains very much as outlined by Szemerényi (1960: 1):

> "1000" appears in forms based on an IE **gheslo-* in Aryan and Greek, probably also in Latin, and this fact would suggest that in the Southern part of the IE area, at any rate, even this number was well established. But we must also acknowledge that this number is expressed by different words in the other dialects – expecially in Germanic and Balto-Slavic – and, although it is not impossible that **gheslo-* was lost in these areas, it is perhaps safer to admit that the word for "1000" was not fully established in the last period of the IE community.

One could perhaps paraphrase what is said in the last sentence, in a way more in line with earlier formulations in the present paper, to wit: while there were ways in the Late Proto-Indo-European to express the notion 'one thousand', the results of the formation processes used were still different enough not to permit one lexicalization applicable to the whole of the Indogermania. If it should prove possible to analyze **gheslo-* as motivated in ways similar to what has been suggested here for the Tocharian forms, one could feel tempted to submit that there may have been a notion 'strength hundred' used in more subareas than those of the Germanic, Balto-Slavic, and Tocharian languages, but that the notion was cast in different forms so that the reconstruction of a form 'one thousand' would remain impossible even for Late Proto-Indo-European.

But what about numbers below 'one thousand'? Is it a fact that, as Szemerényi (1960: 1) states, "the agreement in the formation of the hundreds is so close that their development must be ascribed to Indo-European"?

When we look at actually attested numerals above 'ten', we find that it is not only minor changes, which we may ascribe to analogical distortions of an earlier state of affairs, that occur in ample numbers, but that the operations used in employing the building blocks provided by lower (or, marginally, higher) numerals to express higher numbers, are subject to drastic changes in periods open to inspection because of adequate attestation of data.

Let me just list a few instances. 'Eleven' and 'twelve' are based on 'ten' and 'one' or 'two' respectively (indirectly also in Germanic and Baltic), but the operations used vary: the digit may precede or follow 'ten', the components may be fused into a single word or a phrasal status might be preserved; the constituents may be just 'ten' plus digit, or a connective may be added; 'ten' may appear as such, or it may be modified; the same may happen to the digit; finally, changes might totally obscure the constituents and 'eleven' and 'twelve' may become lexicalized as such. To illustrate the types of representation, a few examples (for 'twelve' only) will suffice:

Juxtaposition without connective: Toch. B *śak wi*
Juxtaposition with connective: Gk. *dúo kaì déka*, Toch. A *śäk wepi*
Fusion without connective: OInd. *dvādaśa*, Lat. *duōdecim*, Gk. *duṓdeka, duódeko*
Fusion with connective: Russ. *dvenadcat'*
'Ten' modified: Arm. *erkotasan*
'Two' modified: Gk. *dṓdeka*
Lexicalization: Fr. *douze*, Hindi *bārah*

There would be a need for further sub- and cross-classification if all details were taken into full consideration, but the rough classification will suffice. Once we turn toward 'eighteen' and 'nineteen', the picture gets even more involved: while the operations used to form 'eleven' and 'twelve' outside Germanic and Baltic all involved addition to 'ten', forms like Lat. *ūndēvīgintī* 'nineteen' and *duōdēvīgintī* 'eighteen' show subtraction employed. The examples given by Schwyzer (1939: 594) prove that, while never systematized as in Latin, subtraction could be used in forming numerals with 'eight' and 'nine' in digit position by speakers of Greek as well. That an option for subtraction may well be open under special circumstances even when addition is the rule can be shown by such examples as the expressions for '6:20' and '6:40' in normal, non-timetable German: *zwanzig nach sechs,* but *zwanzig vor sieben.* In this type of German, closeness to the higher number causes addition to be overruled by subtraction. In English, the same applies to the expression of fifteen-minute periods (*quarter past six*, but *quarter to seven*) and that of minutes (*twenty past six, twenty to seven*) just as in German, but the half-hour is expressed differently: by addition in English (*half past six*), by subtraction in German (*halb sieben*). French largely follows the pattern found in

English (*six-heures-et-quart*, *six-heures-et-demie*, but *sept-heures-moins-le-quart*). Russian uses an even more complex system: full hours are referred to with cardinals, as in French (*v šest' časov* = *à six heures*); quarter past and half past express that one fourth and one half of the distance to the next full hour have been covered, this hour now expressed as an ordinal (*četvert' sed'mogo* '6:15', *pol-sed'mogo* '6:30'); for '6:45' however, a formulation 'seven (cardinal) without a fourth' (*bez četverti sem'*) is used. The last-mentioned form is purely subtractive; those for '6:15' and '6:30' in Russian are different in that the speaker both moves backward from a point in the future (in expressing the hour) and forward (in naming quarter and half-hour): we thus have subtraction and addition combined in a very strange way, as we also find in German *fünf nach halb sechs* '5:35'.

A further point should be made here: it is not uncommon that within one and the same language variation will be tolerated to an amazing degree. Thus, 'quarter to seven' has in Modern High German the regional variants *viertel vor sieben* and *dreiviertel sieben* which, as was seen in the case of Russian, differ strongly in their internal structure, although they, of course, taken as a whole, denote one and the same thing. In this respect, the German phrases then offer a good parallel to what could be observed in the case of Greek renderings of 'twelve' mentioned earlier: Gk. *dúo kaì déka* showed juxtaposition of 'two' and 'ten' with the connective 'and'; Gk. *duṓdeka* and *duódeko*, fusion without connective; Gk. *dṓdeka*, fusion with concurrent change of 'two'.

My purpose in discussing such variation is of course more than to provide some possibly entertaining, yet anecdotal, material. What I am basically interested in, is the observation that experience shows that speakers of a language frequently have more than one avenue open to them when they set out to express particular numerical notions. A generalization seems called for: as long as the constituents of a complex expression remain recognizable and as long as only known operations are employed, the speaker has a certain amount of freedom of choice.

In present-day English, one and the same speaker may say with equal ease *three thousand five hundred dollars* and *thirty-five hundred dollars*, and a moment later neither he nor the persons spoken to might actually be able to remember which form he used. In other cases, one variant will be the preferred one: I cannot conceive of my ever using *one thousand nine-hundred and twenty-three* for my year of birth, while everybody seems to be talking about the year *two thousand*. Stylistic considerations might lead one to use *four-score-and-ten years* rather than the more natural *ninety years*, but one would not dare to say that one paid *four-score-and-ten rupees* for a taxi ride. Clearly, acceptability, governed by a variety of criteria, is more of a criterion than intelligibility of a form. But the fact remains that variation within the range of intelligibility is tolerated in principle, and, while it may be the rule that after a period of fluctuation, one variant might win out and become the norm, there are enough cases of a coexistence of variants.

It is a sound tenet of linguistic reconstruction that one should let oneself be guided by observations made with living languages. If we find that variation within the range of intelligibility is tolerated in living languages and that indeed it is a necessary prerequisite for change and its explanation, it is a methodological error to assume that all variation observed in languages of a given family has to be ascribed to later developments while for the parent language a highly consistent pattern should be reconstructed at all cost. To be sure, the building blocks deserve to be viewed as basically stable so that it is very well worth our concerted efforts to try to determine the shape and, to the extent that this can be done, a possible "basic" meaning of the building blocks. But given the variation we observe in living languages in the expression of complex numbers, one has to doubt whether attempts to reconstruct such complex numers for the parent language can be meaningful at all. At best we can hope to find that several variants have a claim to being old; to single out just one of them as being the primeval form makes one the victim of one's own prejudices, the more so as the comparative evidence usually does not suffice and internal reconstruction has to take over. Internal reconstruction, however, aims at consistent patterns, and, as has been seen, consistency and variation do not exclude each other, but coexist to an astonishing degree, in living languages.

It makes sense, under the circumstances, to approach the area of complex numerals from an onomasiological point of view: Given building blocks such as 'nine', 'ten', 'twenty', and 'hundred', and given the basic arithmetic operations, how could the number 'ninety' be expressed?

Using multiplication only, 'nine times ten'/'nine decads' and 'ten times nine'/'ten enneads' could be introduced. Subtraction would lead to 'one hundred minus ten'. A combination of multiplication and addition could yield, e.g., 'four-score plus ten', multiplication and subtraction, e.g., 'five-score minus ten'. If 'decad' was simply implied, 'ninety' could be referred to as 'the decad associated with nine as a multiplicator', and this could be expressed in various ways, i.a., by referring to 'ennead'.

Multiplication is attested in the following cases:
with 'ten' as the multiplicand, e.g., in OCS *devętĭ desętŭ*;
with 'ennead' as the multiplicand, in Goth. *niuntēhund (*with PIE **t* replaced by **d* as in Gk. *ennead-*).
Subtraction is found in Russ. *devjanosto* (not all details of the form are clear).
Multiplication plus addition occurs in Fr. *quatre-vingt-dix*; multiplication plus subtraction in Dan. *halvfems*.
The use of 'ennead' is encountered in OInd. *navatíḥ*.

Without ellipsis of the reference to the decad, 'nine', is referred to by the more complex notion 'associated with nine' in Gk. *enenḗkonta* (the arguments whether we are dealing with 'nine' or 'ninth' here — a central concern of Sommer 1951 and Szemerényi 1960 — are rather pointless: 'ninth' is nothing but a special use of more general 'associated with nine, pertaining to nine'); it should be noted that a *constructio ad sensum* has moved a singular 'decad pertaining to nine' to the plural in the Greek form.

A partial, though formally irregular, reference to the decad is found in Tocharian B *ñumka*, A *nmuk* (and of course in such recent forms as Engl. *ninety* and German *neunzig*).

What all the forms mentioned have in common is the clear reference to 'nine' (even Russ. *devjanosto* introduces it in a rather "illogical" way) whenever the system remains decadic; application of a vigesimal approach, as in French and Danish, of course, of necessity has to make mention of 'four' or 'five', respectively, instead of alluding to 'nine'.

The central role of the decad as a building block is above all indicated by the ease with which it can be implied. OInd. *navatíḥ* 'ninety' has already been mentioned as a case in point. Even more striking an example is the word for 'hundred'.

I am in perfect agreement with Szemerényi (1960: 140) and his predecessors in their interpretation of PIE **k̑m̥tom* as an original genitive, denoting 'of decads'. On the other hand, I see no need to introduce a pre-form **(d)km̥̄km̥tom* in which then 'because of the frequent usage the antepenult was shortened and the resulting **km̥km̥tom*, by haplology, reduced to **km̥tom'*. Ellipsis plain and simple suffices, so it would seem.

If PIE **(d)k̑m̥tom* could be matched by a fuller form **(d)k̑m̥tom dek̑m̥t-* 'decad of decads' (by the way, a neat match of Goth. *taihuntēhund* 'one hundred'), one may well ask whether alternative expressions for the construct 'decad of decads' could be proposed. Considering the affinity, and often interchangeability, of genitive and adjective, one could well imagine that a variant **(d)ḱm̥tyo- deḱm̥t-* (with the ending of the adjective dependent on the gender of the word for 'decad') might have existed alongside **(d)ḱm̥tom deḱm̥t-*. Ellipsis of **deḱm̥t-* would lead not to **(d)ḱm̥tom*, but to **(d)ḱm̥tyo-*.

Positing an elliptic construction with an overt adjectival provides for a very simple explanation for the multiples of 'one hundred' in Greek, which are characterized by either *-kátioi* or *-kósioi* (cf. Schwyzer 1939: 593): they could be rendered by '(decad) of twenties, thirties, forties, etc.', in close agreement with '(decad) of tens' in 'one hundred'. Again, as in the case of the forms of the type of Gk. *enenḗkonta* 'ninety', discussed earlier, a *constructio ad sensum* would have replaced the old singular form of *-kátioi/-kósioi* which is to be assumed to have been in concord with the word for 'decad'.

It is obvious that a discussion of details of more than a few selected forms would far exceed the time limits set for the present paper. However, it does not seem to be too early to try to present a few general conclusions.

We have seen by inspecting a fair number of examples that there is considerable leeway for the construction of complex numerical terms provided the building blocks used remain recognizable or can be inferred with sufficient certainty and the operations used in combining the elements of a complex entity are apt to be discovered by the language user. During times for which we can be sure of historical developments, we can observe variation within these limitations, and we can observe selection from variants which for a given time and a given language may eliminate variation to a considerable extent. The fact that there are wide areas of disagreement among Indo-European languages, not excluding the oldest ones, should lead us to recognize variation in numeral formation as a characteristic of reconstructed Proto-Indo-European. It is better to describe the range of variation and to determine the kind of variation found than to try to reconstruct, without sufficient comparative evidence, a unitary set, say, of multiples of 'ten' or 'hundred', for Proto-Indo-European. While the interpretation of some of the data — and only some could be discussed here — provides strong arguments against attempts to reconstruct "the" Proto-Indo-European 'tens' and 'hundreds', it also does away with the opposite extreme: if there are conflicting data, and if these data are at variance to such an extent that all reconstruction would be highly subjective if one wanted to eliminate one set of data and retain the other so that a point could be proved, still there is no need now to claim that numerals such as 'seventy, eighty, ninety' did not exist in Proto-Indo-European. To be sure, one cannot argue as Mańczak (1985: 351) does, that because a term for 'one hundred' can be reconstructed, there also had to be established terms for 'eighty' and 'ninety'. Experience with "exotic" languages makes one reluctant to accept reasoning of such a modern type. Judging from what we have encountered in the discussion offered here, we can very well conclude that, although there is not enough solid evidence to reconstruct one Proto-Indo-European term for, say, 'ninety', the building blocks and the ways of putting them together were available, which meant that differently structured variants could be created whenever the need arose, conflicting variants, to be sure, but all with a claim to being Proto-Indo-European. After all, there were the building blocks, 'ten', 'hundred', also 'twenty', which could be combined with the available digits using methods of simple arithmetic. Thus, in an unexpected way, everything seems to have been – and to be – quite simple.

References

Abaev, Vasilij Ivanovič
1958 *Istoriko-ètimologičeskij slovar' osetinskogo jazyka* I (Moskva – Leningrad: Izdatel'stvo Akademii Nauk SSSR).

Buck, Carl Darling
1949 *A dictionary of selected synonyms in the principal Indo-European languages* (Chicago – London: University of Chicago Press.).

Frisk, Hjalmar
1970 *Griechisches etymologisches Wörterbuch* II (Heidelberg: Winter).

Henning, Walter Bruno
1948 *"Oktō(u)", Transactions of the Philological Society:* 69.

Mánczak, Witold
1985 "Indo-European numerals and the sexagesimal system", in: Jacek Fisiak (ed.), *Papers from the Sixth Conference on Historical Linguistics*, 347 – 352. (Amsterdam: Benjamins, Poznań: UAM)

Møller, Hermann
1909 *Indoeuropæiskt-semitisk sammenlignende Glossarium* (in: *Festskrift udgivet af Kjøbenhavns Universitet i Anledning af Universitets Aarsfest*) (Kjøbenhavn).

Olsen, Birgit
1981 "IE *Vwe/i = Arm. Vwe/i (Vve/i)?", in: *Arbejdspapirer, Institut for Lingvistik*, Københavns Universitet BO: 1 – 9.

Pokorny, Julius
1959 *Indogermanisches etymologisches Wörterbuch* I (Bern – München): Francke).

Schwyzer, Eduard
1939 *Griechische Grammatik* I (München: Beck).

Sommer, Ferdinand
1951 *Zum Zahlwort* (Sitzungsberichte, Bayerische Akademie der Wissenschaften, Philosophisch-historische Klasse 1950. 7) (München: Bayerische Akademie der Wissenschaften).

Szemerényi, Oswald
1960 *Studies in the Indo-European system of numerals* (Heidelberg: Winter).

Vasmer, Max
1953 *Russisches etymologisches Wörterbuch* I (Heidelberg: Winter).

Walde, Alois – Johann Baptist Hofmann
1954 *Lateinisches etymologisches Wörterbuch*[3] II (Heidelberg: Winter).

Windekens, Albert Joris van
1976 *Le tokharien confronté avec les autres langues indo-européennes I: La phonétique et le vocabulaire* (Louvain: Centre International de Dialectologie Générale).

Winter, Werner
1969 "Analogischer Sprachwandel und semantische Struktur", *Folia Linguistica* 3: 29 – 45.

Chapter 3
Anatolian

Heiner Eichner

3.0. Introduction

The syllabic transcription of Hittite cuneiform signs follows J. Friedrich (1960), *Hethitisches Keilschriftlesebuch* II (with *u̯* replaced by *w* and *i̯* by *y*) or W. von Soden – W. Röllig (1967), *Das akkadische Syllabar*; for the reading of the ideograms, H. G. Güterbock (1973) "Einige seltene oder schwierige Ideogramme in der Keilschrift von Boğazköy", *Otten Fs.* pp. 71–86, has also been taken into account. Sumerograms are given in capitals, akkadograms in italic capitals. Sumerian sequences of signs are joined by full stops on the line (e. g. GIŠ.KÍN), Akkadian and Hittite ones by hyphens. Determinatives, rendered by raised small capital or lower-case letters, are not to be read phonetically. Thus we have ^{URU} with the names of towns, ^{LÚ} with male names of occupations, ^{SAL} with female ones and female personal names, ^{m} with male personal names, ^{d} with god-names. Determinatives usually stand before the words they refer to, but the signs ^{MEŠ} and $^{\text{HI.A}}$, which serve as plural determinatives, are placed after them (e. g. ŠAH.TUR$^{\text{HI.A}}$). In the rendering of Hittite words and word-stems in non-syllabic transcription I largely follow Friedrich (1952), abbreviated as *HW*, without considering satisfactory the procedure made use of there. Restored portions of text are given in square brackets [ ]; signs which are partially damaged are placed in parentheses; severe damage is indicated by a subscript dot. Signs inadvertently missed by the scribe are given in pointed brackets ⟨ ⟩, superfluous signs in curly brackets { }. The translation of restored passages is also given in square brackets; e. g., [no single thi]ng (3.1.1.4.2.) means that the first half of the logogram translated by 'thing' and the word standing in front of it are restored. Non-literal translations departing markedly from the original text are printed in italics. An unknown or unidentifiable sign is represented by the symbol "x". Signs (and tablet-columns) that cannot be identified with certainty are indicated by one, respectively, two, superscript question marks. Attention is called to the corrected reading of obvious miswritings by an superscript exclamation mark.

The quotations from cuneiform texts are taken from the editions which have so far appeared (including *Keilschrifturkunden aus Boghazköi* (*KUB*) XLIV and *Keilschrifttexte aus Boghazköi* (*KBo*) XXII), also from the card-index of unpublished tablets of Professor Otten (Marburg). A fully identified quotation contains, in this order, indicators of the edition-series (sigla: *KUB*[1] and *KBo*); the numbering of the volume (roman numbers); the numbering of the tablet (arabic numbers) within the volume; the column-reference if it can be given (roman numbers, or, in the case of one-column tablets o. = obverse, r. = reverse); and the line-number (arabic); in the case of a lost beginning of a tablet with following apostrophe). For instance, "*KBo* III 4 II 27" means *Keilschrifttexte aus Boghazköi*, vol. 3, tablet 4, column 2, line 27. "XIX 7 line 8" means *Keilschrifturkunden aus Boghazköi*, vol. 19, tablet 7, line 8 (no column-indication). Where there is no risk of confusion, a reduced indication may appear; thus "XXIV 8 I 16', II 3' " means *Keilschrifturkunden aus Boghazköi*, vol. 24, tablet 8, column 1, line 16', and the same, vol. 24, tablet 8, column 2, line 3'. The plus sign between two references (as *KBo* I 44 + *KBo* XIII) indicates that two fragments of tablets which have been published separately actually join. Frequently only one fragment is mentioned (e.g., XXXII 14 +), especially in the case of complicated joins. Unpublished tablets are cited with sigla such as *VAT* [*Vorderasiatische Texte*], *Bo* [unpublished texts from Boğazköy], .../n, and inventory numbers; thus *Bo* 620, *VAT* 13016, 1103/u, 277/p. From these the specialist is informed as to the origin and place of keeping (Berlin, Istanbul) of the tablets; thus the reference "277/p II? 3" contains, in sequence, the inventory-number 277/p – it tells us that the tablet was found in one of the campaigns of excavation conducted by K. Bittel in Boğazköy in 1957 –, the supposed (but uncertain) column-number (II), and the line-number (3). If, instead of the edition or inventory number, a special text designation is given, e. g. "*Maštigga*", "*Targašnalli*", or, abbreviated as ("*BdU*" [*Beschwörung der Unterirdischen*]), this gives an indication of the appropriate discussion in the specialist literature; here will be found information as to further details, which cannot be mentioned in the present chapter.

The quotations from Hieroglyphic Luvian texts essentially follow Laroche (1960), abbreviated as *HH*, and his system. Raised *n* (as in *tuwi^{n}za*) indicates the anteconsonantal nasal, which is not written. "M 129", etc., refer to the sign numbers in Meriggi (1962). Hieroglyphic Luvian logograms are given in capitals and in English translation (as SPEAK); for the logograms which refer to numbers, which can be evaluated as true ideograms, arabic numbers are given.

Lycian inscriptions are quoted according to J. Friedrich, *Kleinasiatische Sprachdenkmäler* (*Kleine Texte für Vorlesungen und Übungen* LXIII; 1932).

The oblique stroke as in *nala/i-* indicates that both the interpretations *nala-* and *nali-* are possible.

Phonematic interpretations of Anatolian words are given between slanting lines (as /duia-/).

3.0.1. General comments on Anatolian numerals

Little is known of the numerals of the Anatolian branch of the Indo-European family, because, in most cases, the texts use numeral-ideograms. Thus, additional information has to be obtained by carefully observing the phonetic complementation of these numeral-ideograms, and by adducing derived words which permit conclusions as to the phonetics, morphology, and inflection of the numerals.

The present chapter represents a first attempt to discuss exhaustively an, admittedly somewhat inextensive, section of the comparative grammar of the Anatolian languages. The material derives from Hittite, Cuneiform Luvian, Hieroglyphic Luvian, and Lycian (A, B – Lycian A is for the most part not expressly indicated); the sources yield nothing for Palaean and little more for Lydian (but cf. 3.14.2.). Etruscan, as to whose membership of Indo-European Anatolian there is as yet no agreement, is excluded from the discussion. But this does not mean that anything here has been prejudged.

The vocabulary of the Anatolian languages is distinguished by a relatively small store of lexemes, which often show a great range of meanings. This phenomenon is often to be noticed, too, in the domain of the numerals, in which there exist the most favourable preconditions for strict class-formation within the lexicon. For this reason terms such as "numeral", "cardinal", "ordinal" are not used here to indicate closed word-classes, the individual members of which have become consistently specialised in respect to specific numeric concepts. Here all the words are included whose spectrum of meaning comprises, among other things, specific numeric quantifiers (such as "one", "first", "once", "a third"); the domain of general quantifiers (such as "many", "a few", "some", "often") is left out of account.

In the presentation of the phonetic complementation of numeral-signs in Hittite texts, I have been able to rely on the splendid collections of the Marburg Hittite Thesaurus. My sincere thanks are due to Professor Otten, who, with great friendliness, has made access to this material possible for me, and who has, further, given me information and advice. I am also grateful to Professors Cowgill (Yale), Neu (Bochum), and Watkins (Harvard) for important information from unpublished works.

3.1. The Anatolian numerals 'one' and their derivatives

3.1.1. The Hittite cardinal 'one'

The numeral sign "1" appears with phonetic complements.

3.1.1.1. *-a*-stem

Forms: Singular; Common	nom. 1-*aš*
	acc. 1-*an*
	gen. 1-(*e*-)*el* XXIII 103 r. 5; 1103/u r. 8
	dat. 1-*e-da-ni* (old loc 1-*e-da*, see 3.1.1.6.
	instr. 1-*e-ta-an-da* *KBo* XXII 203 I 1'? (context fragmentary)
	*1-*e-it*, see 3.1.1.7.
	abl. 1-*e-da-az*
	1-*e-az*? XIV 1 r. 25; XXX 15 o. 27 (error for 1-*e-da-az*?)
	1-*e-iz* Bo 620 r. 19' (bis); 159/w
Singular: Neuter	nom. 1-*e*??, 1-*an*??; no clear examples; *HW* p. 301 quotes 1-*an*; see 3.1.1.4. for this; 1-*e*/ *1-*i* and, above all, *1-*at* are more likely; see below.
Plural: Common	nom.? (1-*e* would be expected, see 3.1.1.1.2.)
	acc. (?) 1-*EN-aš* in the construction 1-*EN-aš*, ⟨1-⟩*EN-aš* VII 1 II 4 (= 1-*EN* 1-*EN-aš* in dupl. XLIII 52 II 12)
	gen. – (*1-*en-za-an* would be expected)
	dat. 1-*e-da-aš*
	instr. –
	abl. –

3.1.1.1.1. Notes

3.1.1.1.1.1. For 1-*at-ta* [X] *KBo* XVII 104 II 7 see 3.1.1.7.
3.1.1.1.1.2. 1-*e* *KBo* XVIII 172 o. 16', corresponding to the unknown gender and number (plurale tantum) of the word it qualifies, may be either nominative-accusative singular neuter, nominative plural common, or nominative-accusative plural neuter: 2 ^{GIŠ}*ŠU-RI-EN-NU* ŠÀ-*BA* 1 2 GIŠ.KÍN KUBABBAR 1-*e-ma* 1 GIŠ.KÍN KUBABBAR 'two š.-emblems, of which one with two GIŠ.KÍN of silver, but the other with one GIŠ.KÍN of silver (?)'. An identification as a plural form would be the most convincing from the point of view of the morphology (cf. 2-*e*, 3-*e*), but it is only possible if the qualified word in Hittite is a plurale tantum. Since these are not very common among designations of objects, the force of 1-*e* as nominative-accusative singular neuter must be seriously considered.

3.1.1.1.2. Declension

Possibly the same as the normal declension of pronouns, with *e* in most of the oblique cases < PIE **e* (cf. gen.sg. **téso* 'this') and PIE **ey*/*oy* (cf. gen.pl. **tóysōm*). The assumption of a half nominal, half pronominal mixed inflection (Friedrich (1940–46: § 130), following Sommer (1932: 164)), which would be comparable with Latin *ūnum, ūnīus, ūnī* and Vedic *ékam, ékasmin*, depends on the assessment of the nominative-accusative singular neuter form (1-*an* would agree in its ending with Latin *ūnum*, Vedic *ékam*). Today this assessment has to take place under changed conditions, because, in the meantime, an -*nt*-stem (to which 1-*an* can belong) has been found to be attested with certainty, and, on the other hand, a possible example of 1-*e* (?) has become known (cf. *ki-e* 'this'; if this form is old, it should be referred to PIE **ḱé*; the usual form *ki-i* goes back to something like **ḱi*, **gi*, **ǵhi*). We have in addition the fact that 1-*at-ta* (3.1.1.7.) presupposes a nom.-acc. sg. *1-*at*, that is, it clearly points to pronominal inflection (for the variation 1-*at*/1-*e*, cf. 2-*at*/2-*e*, 3.2.1.1.1.). For instr. 1-*etanda*, cf. instr. sg. *apēdanda* 'that', *kīdanda* 'this'. For the forms 1-*ela*, 1-*eda*, 1-*etta*, taken from the paradigmatic nexus, see 3.1.1.5–7. Acc.pl. 1-*aš* in a text, which, with the corresponding form of the personal pronoun -*a*- 'he, she', uses the variant -*uš* (not -*aš*), is surprising, but not objectionable.

3.1.1.1.3. Reading

Unknown. Goetze (1935) suggests **šanna-*, which Kronasser (1956: 152) also takes into consideration. (Friedrich 1952: 301 is against this.) Later, Goetze (1949: 288 ff.) puts in a plea for **ašma-* (to be rejected; see 3.1.4.). In my view, a reading **ā-* (< **oyo-* or **oiyo-*) is, rather, to be contemplated.

3.1.1.2. *-i*-stem

This stem can only be distinguished from the *-a*-stem in the nominative-accusative singular.

3.1.1.2.1. Forms

Nom.sg. 1-*iš*, about twenty examples, of which none are Old Hittite. For instance *KBo* V 2 III 41 (bis); X 34 I 8,9; XVIII 69 r. 11'; *KUB* XIV 1 (*Madd* [*Madduwattaš*] o. 57; XVIII 5 I 15; XXVIII 107 II 1, 6, 9, 12, 15, 18; XXXIII 5 III 10'; XLI 23 II 20', 21'. 1-*iš* LÚ*ME-ŠE-DI* 'one (single) MEŠEDI-man' XI 29 V 11 is in alternation with 1-*aš* LÚ*ME-ŠE-DI KBo* IV 9 V 4.

Acc.sg. 1-*in* 277/p II? 3 (1-*iš* 1-*in*).

3.1.1.2.2. Reading

The reading is unknown. At least in part of the examples probably only a stem-variant to 1-*aš*, corresponding to the frequent passage of *-a*-stems to *-i*-stems (cf. 1-*aš* XXVIII 107 I 9, 11, 13, 15: 1-*iš* XXVIII 107 II 1, 6, 9, 12, 15, 18). In the case of an *-a*-stem inflected pronominally one must especially consider analogy with the paradigm of the interrogative pronoun (*kuel, kuedani : kuiš, kuin ::* 1-*el*, 1-*edani :* 1-*iš*, 1-*in*).

3.1.1.3. Meaning and use of 1-*aš*, 1-*iš*

The phonetically complemented numeral-sign "1" is found mostly in non-attributive use. The boundaries between the meanings given in the following are often fluid.

1) Indication of the singular of specimens of a particular object or of a group of persons: *KBo* V 9 IV 4 1-*aš* ^{LÚ}*ME-ŠE-DI* 'one (single) MEŠEDI man'; XXVIII 107 II 1, 6, 9, 12, 15, 18 1-*iš hal-za-a-i* 'a single person calls'.

2) Stressing of isolation or uniqueness, 'single', 'alone', 'without companion': *KBo* III 4 II 77 1!-*aš* SAG.DU-*aš iš*! -*pár-za-aš-ta* '(PN) escaped as the only (or a single) one' (see also XIV o. 57 1-*iš*); *KBo* V 6 II 9 f. ^{URU}*kar-ga-miš-aš-pát* 1-*aš* URU-*aš* (10) *Ú-UL ták-šu-la-it* 'the town of K. was the only town that did not make peace'; *KBo* IV 14 II 9 ^{URU}*ni-hi-ir-ya-za-kán Ú-UL* 1-*aš ar-ha u-un-na-ah-hu-un* 'had I not all alone to hurry forth from the town of N.?' (similarly *KBo* IV 14 II 11; *KUB* XXI 1 II 69').

3) Stressing of the unity of a combination of two or several parts, 'one, united, joined into one': XXXIII 5 III 9 f. *nu-uš-ma-aš* (10) [*iš-ta-an-za-aš-mi-i*]*š ga-ra-az-ši-iš* 1-*iš ki-i-ša-ri* 'and to them their souls and the inside of their bodies become one' (similarly XLI 23 II 20 f.).

4) Use in repeated placement of 1-*a*- ... 1-*a*-, with various nuances of meaning.

4a) Successive-distributive, 'one after the other, each single one': *VAT* 13016 IV? 10 f. *ta* EN ERÍN^{MEŠ}[x] (11) 1-*an* 1-*an anda tarnieškizzi* 'he admits the military commanders one after the other'; VII 1 II 4 f. *nu-uš ha-aš-ša-az* EGIR-*pa iš-pa-an-ni-it* 1-*EN-aš* ⟨1-⟩*EN-aš da-aš-ki-iz-zi* 'he takes them [sc. the twice seven dumplings] in alternation, the one set after the other [i. e., first the first seven, then the seven others] with a spit from the fireplace [and eats them one after the other]' (differently, H. Kronasser, *Die Sprache* vii, 1961: 150). With a slightly different nuance we have XIII 4 III 5 1-*aš* 1-*aš* 'the one like the other, each single one'.

4b) Reciprocal, 'one another, mutual': *KBo* II 5 IV 18 [X 1]-*aš* 1-*an ku-wa-aš-ki-it* 'one killed the other continuously'; *KBo* V 4 r. 3 ff. *nu* 1-*aš* 1-*e-da-ni li-e i-da-la-a-u-e-eš-zi nu-kán* 1-*aš* 1-*e-da-aš-ša-an* ÌR-*iš* (4) [^{LÚ}*pít-ti-ia-a*]*n-ti-li li-e pa-iz-zi nu* 1-*aš* 1-*an ku-na-an-na li-e ša-an-ha*[-*zi*] '(of you three) one is not to think of evil against the other, and one is not to seek his refuge as a servant with the other [i. e., with one of the two others], and one is not to strive to kill the other'; XXI 1 III 76 f. *ki-i-ma A-WA-TE*^{MEŠ} *Ú-UL ku-it-ki* 1-*e-da-az* 1-*e-da-az* (77) *IŠ-TU* KUR ^{URU}*ha-at-ti-at* 'these terms of Treaty are in no way mutually [binding]; they are [binding] in respect of the Land of the Hatti'.

3.1.1.4. *-nt*-stem

3.1.1.4.1. Forms

Nom.-acc.pl.neut. Old Hittite 1-*an-ta* ... 1-*an-ta* 'the ones ... the others' *KBo* XVII 3 IV 25 (cf. duplicate *KBo* XVII 1 IV 27, both tablets in the "typically old ductus", see H. Otten – V. Souček, *Studien zu den Boğazköy-Texten* (in future abbreviated *StBoT*) viii (1969: 38), as attribute to ^{GIŠ}*harpa* 'heap' (of logs?). Acc.pl.comm. *harpuš* (H. Kümmel, *StBoT* iii, 1967: 78 n. 8) cannot be adduced as an argument against the identification of ^{GIŠ}*harpa*, and, with it, 1-*anta*, as nominative-accusative plural neuter, cf. *harpa : harpuš :: alpa : alpuš* 'cloud' :: *hašša hanzašša : haššuš hanzaššuš* 'grandchildren and great-grandchildren' (see E. Neu, *IF* lxxiv, 1969: 240).

Nom.-acc.sg.neut. 1-*an KBo* XI 49 I 15; *KUB* IX 31 III 21; 32 o. 8; XIII 4 III 50; XIV 3 III 63; XIX 9 II 21; XXIV 8 I 16', II 3'; L. King, *Hittite texts in the cuneiform character from tablets in the British Museum* (1920), 1 III 11 can likewise be assigned to the *-nt*-stem.

3.1.1.4.2. Comments

The *-nt*-stem does not point to an entirely different word, but to a derivative of the *-a-* or *-i*-stem; cf. *dapi- : dapiyant-* 'complete, whole', and probably also *hūmant-* 'whole, each'. Following from the suggestion made above (3.1.1.1.3.), the reading **ānt-* (??) is to be assumed. The meaning 'only a single one, only one' and 'something which forms a unit', clearly distinguishable in the case of the form 1-*an*, deserves notice; see Sommer (1932: 164); in the *Treaty with Targašnalli* II 9 (Friedrich 1926: I.60), Hitt. 1-*an* alternates with Akkadian 1-*NU-TUM* '(individual) unit'. As opposed to this, still other nuances of meaning appear to play a part in the case of 1-*aš* and 1-*iš*. If 1-*an* is an *-nt*-stem, this finding can be explained by means of the opposition to the antonymic nom. *dapiyan* 'whole, complete, altogether' (*-nt*-stem, cf. H. Eichner, *KZ* lxxxii, 1968: 215 n. 11).

From the point of view of the history of the language, the *-nt*-stem can be variously assessed. On the one hand, the suffix *-nt-* is to be taken into consideration; cf. the adjectives *nekumant-* 'naked' (: Av *maγnəṇta-*) : **neg^{w}mó-* (Vedic *nagná-*), *tangarant-* 'sober' : **donḱró-* (> German *zanger*), etc.; further also *hūmant-* 'all, whole, each' (**H_2áw-mo-nt-*). On the other hand a collective or abstract formation in *-and-* (Greek -αδ-, **-n̥-d-*) could be present. In Hittite, both types fell together from phonological causes (nom.sg. **-ant-s* and **-and-s* > *-anza*, dat.sg. **-ant-i* and **-and-i*

> *-anti*, then confusion in other forms too) and were probably also fused semantically. Thus Hitt. **ānt-* (??) may combine both components (**ā-nt-* and **ā-and-*).

ānt- is very probably to be established on the basis of the vocabulary *KBo* XIII 10 (Laroche, *Catalogue des textes hittites,* 1971: 309). Here there are the following consecutive lemmata:

o.?	4	[X]	x-*iš-ka-aš*
	5	[X]	*ne-ku-uz me-hur*
	6	[X]	*a-a-an-za* INIM-*aš*
	7	[X] xx	*a-a-an-za* INIM-*aš ku-e-da-ni e-eš-ta*
	8	[X IN]IM-aš	*ku-e-da-ni* NU.GÁL

Since the participle *ānt-* 'hot' can hardly be present here, and also because a reading A.A.-*an-za* (something like **muwanza*) does not seem to make sense, I should like to suggest the translations 'one (single) thing' for line 6 and 'someone who had one (single) thing' for line 7. Line 8 may be completed as 'someone who has [no (single) thi]ng'; that the text already begins in the neighbouring rubric on the left is not too surprising in view of the other irregularities of this kind in the vocabularies. And as a support for this interpretation a further vocabulary passage can be added: *KBo* I 44 o. 9 f. NU.GÁL-*kán ku-e-da-ni ku-it* 'someone/something [nominative or some other case] who does not have anything' (NU.GÁL = *natta* '(is) not'; *kuit* = *kuitki* 'something', see W. H. Held on the text, *The Hittite relative sentence* (*Language Dissertation* 55) (1957: 43), cf. *The Assyrian dictionary of the Oriental Institute of the University of Chicago* (ed. J. Gelb) Z p. 170a (H. Otten, *StBoT* vii, 1968: 9 to be rejected). The circle of the lucubrations closes if, further, we restore the reading X (1?)-*iš*(-)INIM-*aš* 'one (single) thing' in *KBo* XIII 10 o. 4.

The hyperplene writing of the vowel of the first syllable (*a-a-an-za*) finds its explanation in the fact that the initial contraction-vowel (*ā̂* < *aa* < *aya*) is over-long and is thus phonologically different from the usual initial long vowels; hyperplene writing indicates over-length, normal plene writing normal length. The two theoretically possible alternative readings *aant-* (more accurately *āant-* or *aānt-*, disyllabic, with hiatus) must be eliminated from our considerations. The first, because vowels of the same quality are contracted in Hittite (cf., for instance, 3.2.4., for the shortening of unstressed long vowels derived from contraction); the second because it is not consistent with Hittite scribal habits (A. Goetze *JCS* xvi: 32; *JAOS* lxxiv: 187, to be rejected). On the other hand it is not possible to decide the question whether the contraction-length (*ā̂*) in *ā̂nza* (*a-a-an-za*) has been regularly preserved or only been based analogically on nom.-acc.sg.neut. **ā̂n* (1-*an*-). For if initial long vowels derived from contraction are regularly shortened before two consonants, the lack of the hyperplene writing in *a-an-ki* 'once' (3.1.3.) could be phonologically justified. But, on the other hand, in *a-an-ki* an inaccurate writing instead of **a-a-an-ki* = / *ā̂nki* / could be present. The same problem is posed in the verb *ā̂*- 'to be hot' (3 pl. *a-a-an-ta* with *ā̂*), which, possibly, has been restored analogically on the basis of forms such as 3 sg. *a-a-ri* = / *ā̂ri* / or nom.-acc.sg.neut.ptc. *a-a-an* = / *ā̂n* /.

3.1.1.5. 1-*e-la*

1-*e-la* 'alone, single' *Bo* [unpublished texts from Boğazköy] 1806 line 7' and *Bo* 2701 III? 12' (dU AN-*E* 1-*e-la a-ku-wa-an-zi* 'they drink to the Weather-God of Heaven alone (as the only one)': 1-*e-la-aš* (= Akk. *e-te-nu* (*ēdēnû*) 'single' in Vocabulary *KBo* I 44 + *KBo* XIII 1 o. 34 (H. Otten – W. von Soden, *StBoT* vii, 1968: 11 line 17).

We are here concerned with the extension of the adverbial genitive 1-*el** 'as a single one'. For this use of the genitive, adverbs of the type *ašandaš* 'sitting, seated' ← 'as sitter(s)' – singular or plural – are to be compared. The postulated adverbial use of 1-*el* has a firm support in the attested 2-*el* 'both together, both' (see 3.2.1.6.–9.). The form 1-*ela* appears to be an adverbial locative (1-*el* : 1-*ela* on the pattern of *šiuat* : *šiuatta* 'by day', *lukkat* : *lukkatta* 'on the next morning'?). The secondary -*a*-stem 1-*ela*- 'single' could arise (by hypostasis) from 1-*ela* (cf. 2-*ela*-, 3.2.1.6., 3.2.1.9.). In 1-*el*, 1-*ela* (and 2-*el*), which arose correctly, the Hittites perhaps saw, because of a new, etymologically "false" analysis, an adverbial ending -*el* -*ela*, which they carried over into the personal pronouns, cf. *ukel*, *ukela*/*ukila* 'myself', *zikela*/*zikila* 'you yourself', *apašila* 'he himself, that one' (singular: *KBo* XIV 8 II 3; plural: see *HW* s. vv.; for acc.pl. *apašilus*, cf. nom.sg. 1-*elaš*), *šumašila* 'you yourself'. So we have an explanation of these hybrid formations, about which there has been much puzzlement: they start from the numeral, especially from 1-*el*, 1-*ela*. The postulated development would moreover present itself as considerably simpler still, if the suggestion made in 3.1.1.3. as to the initial of the numeral for "1" being *ā* should be correct. **ēl* **ēla* (secondarily, unstressed **ĭl* **ĭla*) would have to be considered as the reading of 1-*el* 1-*ela*, nom. **āš* : gen. **ēl*, like nom. *apāš* 'that one' : gen. *apēl*, nom. *kāš* 'this one' : gen. *kēl*. In *ukel ukela ukila* there could then be present a conflation of the phrase **uk ēl(a)* 'I as the only one, I alone' (→ 'I of my own initiative', 'I in my own person', 'I myself'), as similarly in *zikela/ zikila* and *apašila; šumašila* (cf. A. Kammenhuber, *KZ* lxxxiii, 275) is, rather, a later imitation.

3.1.1.6. 1-*e-da*

1-*eda* 'on one's own, isolated' is an original locative form taken out of the paradigmatic nexus (i. e., no longer freely formable). It is found in *KBo* IV 14 II 60, 64, 70 in the phrase 1-*eda tiyawar* 'to put oneself in isolation, stay in isolation, keep oneself out of' (?) in an enumeration of three kinds of breach of duty to assist in case of war. Before the phrase there is *allallā pāwar* 'to become unloyal', whereas, after it, there is *pidikan wahnumar* 'to turn back on the spot'; from this collocation, the meaning of 1-*eda tiyawar* is to some extent defined. A further example of 1-*eda* occurs in the phrase 1-*eda leng-* XXVI 1 III 54 'to swear for oneself alone' in an order concerning people who are absent at the general oath-taking (see Sommer – Falkenstein 1938: 143; E. von Schuler, *Hethitische Dienstanweisungen für höhere Hof- und Staatsbeamte* (*AfO* Beiheft 10) 1957: 14 'together' is not to be preferred). The difference between 1-*ela* (3.1.1.5.) and 1-*eda* does not lie in the meaning, but in the syntactic use.

3.1.1.7. 1-*etta* (1-*ašša**)

1-*e-it-ta nai-* 'to unite someone, make politically one' (XXI 37 o. 17; XXI 42 II 6 = dupl. XXVI 12 II 30) probably originally means 'to direct to one particular side, to make into one special party'. The grammatical determination of the form 1-*etta*, so far unsuccessful, depends upon one's assessment of the syntax. Among the morphologically possible alternatives, the syntactic properties of the verb *nai-* 'to step forward on someone's side, to turn to someone's party (middle reflexive)' determine the form 1-*etta* clearly as an instrumental. Cf. Goetze, *Ḫattušiliš* (1925: IV 10 f.) 'and the whole of Hattusa will concur in the matter of thy husband / will take up the party of thy husband' *IŠ-TU ŠA* [LÚ]*MU-DI-KA ne-ya-ri* (the Akkadian flexion-indicators must here denote a pendent genitive in the function of an instrumental or ablative), and, for a verb related in meaning, *Kup* § 13* C 7 f. (Friedrich 1926: I. 122; E. Neu, *StBoT*, 1968: 7) *IŠ-TU ŠA* [d]UTU-*ŠI ma*[-*ah-ha-an*] *ar-ta-ti* (8) *nu IŠ-TU ŠA* [d]UTU-*ŠI-pát* EGIR-*an ar-hu-ut* 'as thou (in the past) wast on the side of The Majesty, so mayest thou in the future be on the side of The Majesty'. Cf., further XIV 1 r. 25 (Goetze, *Madduwattaš*, 1928/68: 27) 1-*e* < *-da*? > *-az ti-ya-mi* '[against the land of Hapalla] I will make common cause [with thee]', lit. 'I will step forward on one side'.

Since the instrumental ending terminates with *-t* in postvocalic position (*-ta* only postconsonantal), 1-*etta* must be analyzed as *1-*et* + *-a* 'and, also', and thus leads to positing 1-*ašša** '(only) one single one, one and the same'. The difficulties of deriving this meaning from the two elements 1-*aš* 'one, one single one' and *-a* 'and, also' can be eliminated by starting from the negated **natta* 1-*ašša* 'and not a single one, not even one'. '(Only) a single one, just a single one' is yielded as one of the semantic possibilities of the use of this combination of words in the positive; for another semantic possibility, see 3.1.1.8. The further example 1-*e-it-ta* *KBo* III 4 III 33 (Goetze 1933: 76) is not unambiguous; the context allows the meanings 'everything in one, all together' or 'taken on its own, even alone'.

In conclusion it is to be observed that the interpretation of 1-*etta* as locative (cf. *tamatta* 'somewhere else', *kuwatta* 'whither', *apadda* 'thither'), to be found in the literature, comes to grief on the *e*-vocalism of the form; *1-*atta* would necessarily be required, or 1-*eda* with a single dental, see 3.1.1.6.

Now a form 1-*atta* is actually recorded *KBo* XVII 104 II 7, but it is to be identified as nominative-accusative singular neuter to 1-*ašša**; its meaning is 'ditto, of the same kind, the same' (lit. 'one and the same'). By means of intratextual comparison (lines 8, 9 KI.MIN) and of placing it beside the duplicate *KBo* XI 14 II 8 ff., it follows cogently in fact that 1-*at-ta* is a heterogram for KI-MIN and takes the place of a clause which is to be repeated several times ('give me the sacrificer back'), which is only once written out in full. Nevertheless I should not wish to exclude the possibility that KI.MIN (written KI.2) has still other Hittite correspondences than 1-*at-ta*; those possible are *kīpat* 'the same, exactly that one' (Friedrich 1959, abbreviated as *HG*, i § 64) in alternation with *QA-TAM-MA-pát*, *apeniššan* 'just so' (see *HW* 311 f.), and *katta* 'likewise, correspondingly' (the question mark after this meaning, *HW* 105, is to be deleted).

Bo 2933 II 5' *na-an* 1-*e-it-ta da-a-i* (*hīli pedai* in front of it) is not clear. Perhaps this example is to be placed with the cases just mentioned and is to be translated 'he puts him on (one and) the same side'. In this case 1-*e-it-ta* would be a further example for the "lateral" instrumental ('on the side of'; see *HG* i § 22 A *kēt* 'this side of') for 1-*ašša**.

3.1.1.8. 1-*ašša*

1-*aš-ša* (1-*aš* 'one' + *a-* 'and') 'each single one' occurs XLIII 23 r. 21'. H. Ehelolf (1933: 5), who interpreted the passage (*Orientalistische Literaturzeitung* xxxvi, 5), called attention to *kuišša* (*kwiš* 'who' + *a-* 'and') 'each', whose semantic history (cf. Latin *quisque*) rests however on conditions ('whoever it may be') which cannot be present in the case of 1-*ašša*. For this reason a further investigation of the evidence becomes necessary.

XLIII 23 r. 19' ff. *nu-za* 1 ŠAH *ma-a-ah-ha-an* (20') ŠAH. TUR^HI.A^ *me-ik-ku-uš ha-aš-ki-iz-zi ki-e-el-la-az ŠA* ^GIŠ^SAR. G[EŠTIN] (21') 1-*aš-ša* ^GIŠ^*ma-a-ah-la-aš* ŠAH-*aš i-wa-ar mu-u-ri-uš* (22') *me-ik-ku-uš ha-aš-ki-id-du* 'Just as one sow usually bears many piglets, so also is each single vine of this vineyard to bear many grapes just as the sow does'. (The attraction of the comparandum to the comparatum is typical of the style of Hittite comparisons.) Therefore the meaning given by Ehelolf is plausible; since the particle *-a* 'and, also' is already present with *kēl* 'of this' (genitive singular), taking 1-*ašša* to be a separate lexeme (and not just as a word-connection) should be justified (cf. *HW*, 302). The meaning of this lexeme is explained most simply if, once again, we start from negative formulations (cf. 3.1.1.7.). The material for demonstration can be extracted from the Hittite texts themselves.

XIII 4 III 51 f. *nu wa-as-túl ku-iš i-ya-zi na-aš QA-DU* NUMUN-*ŠU* (52) *har-ak-zi-pát ku-e-ša-at-kán ku-i-e-eš im-ma* ŠÀ É DINGIR-*LIM nu* 1-*aš-ša* (53) TI-*nu-ma-aš Ú-UL e-eš-zi* '... so he who trespasses must nevertheless (*-pat*) perish. And of all those who are still in the temple as well, not one single one must be left alive'. Since the expression 'not one single one' is synonymous with 'no single one', the remaining 1-*ašša* can, after taking out the negation, be taken as 'each single one, each separate one'. So the two meanings of 3.1.1.7. and 3.1.1.8. depend on the fact that, to the negative concept 'not a single one, no single one', there corresponds, on the positive side, not only 'a single one' but also 'every single one'.

3.1.1.9. 1-*li* (?)

An apparent Old Hittite 1-*li KBo* VII 14 (old ductus) o. 8 is a constituent of PN ^m^LI.KASKAL-*iš* (Laroche 1966, no. 1750) – Professor Neu has kindly called my attention to this fact; 1-*li KBo* XX 21 line 7' f. does not belong here. The abbreviation 1 *LI* for Akk. 1 *LI-IM* '1000' (cf. von

Soden (1965–81: 553)) could be present: [X 1? *L*]*I* 5 *ME* ERÍN^{MEŠ}-*aš* *ha-a-li-iš* 20-*iš* 5 ME ^{NINDA}ha[x] ('8') [X + ?] 1 *LI* NINDA $^{HI.A}$ 30-*iš* 1 *LI* NINDA? ... [X]. Unfortunately the entire tablet is broken in such a way that it is not possible to determine with certainty to what word 1-*li* / 1 *LI* refers.

3.1.2. The Hieroglyphic Luvian cardinal 'one'

The numeral-sign "1" is used with phonetic complements (cf. Meriggi, *Glossar*[2] 1962: 165).

3.1.2.1. Forms

Singular: scc. 1-*na*, 1-*ti-na*
dat.abl. 1?-*ti-na*

3.1.2.2. Comments

Further examples are obscure. The reading is unknown. With some reservations the coexistence of an unextended stem and one extended by -*nt*- (or derived by means of *-*and*-) can be postulated, as in Hittite, perhaps **a*- (??) and **anti*- (??). An argument for the establishment of a stem **a*- 'one' in Hieroglyphic Luvian could be seen in the writing Kululu 2 B *arha* '1' -*wa-há-a*?, if the meaning 'I came out' and the reading *arha awaha* (in my view, rather *awiha*; WA = wa, wí) could be assumed. It should be a rebus-like writing; for the form *awaha*, see J. D. Hawkins, *RHA* xxix (1966: 129). But this argument vanishes if, with Meriggi *Manuale* ii (1967: 46), the sign WA in this place has a "thorn", i.e., a little oblique stroke added, as actually the photograph H. T. Bossert, *Jahrbuch für kleinasiatische Forschung* (1950: Plate XXX) suggests. [Hieroglyphic Luvian *nala/i*- 'nullus' (Meriggi 1962: 86) is a wrong reading for **hantili*- 'prior, former' (J. D. Hawkins, *Anatolian Studies* 25, 1975: 148–150), therefore not to be analysed as **ne oyolo*-.]

3.1.3. Hittite *ānki*

The hitherto unrecognized hittitogram for 1-ŠU ~ 1-*an-ki* 'once' occurs in *a-an-ki KUB* IV 2 IV 36, 38 (in alternation with 1-ŠU and 1-*an-ki*). The sequence **ān* which remains after the removal of the adverbial suffix -*ki* is to be regarded as nominative-accusative singular neuter. This form can belong to an *-nt*-stem, **ānt-*, or continue directly an old nominative-accusative singular neuter with *-n* < *-m*. The unextended stem *ā-* probably contains a long vowel due to contraction, and points to **oy-o-* or **oy-yo-*, and is thus a derivative of PIE **oy*, meaning something like 'one, single' (adverb), somewhat different from the well-known stems **oy-ko-*, **oy-wo-*, **oy-no-* which are represented in the non-Anatolian branches of Indo-European (Pokorny 1959: 286). **oy* lying at the base of it is probably to be regarded as an old locative singular **o-i* 'with the one, in the one, on its own' of the pronoun *e-/o-* 'this, the, the one mentioned', from which the semantic constituent 'one, alone' is derivable from the grammatical function of the Indo-European singular.

Further reflexes could be present in Hitt. *āšma* 'firstly' (see 3.1.4.) and – quite uncertain – in the word *ayawala-* XIV 3 I 12, which is probably not true Hittite but comes from some dialect, if this is to be taken as something like 'of equal birth' (*'being of one and the same rank'; **oyo-wo-lo-* – for the formation cf. Vedic *kévala-* 'alone; whole, complete').

3.1.4. Hittite *āšma*

Hitt. *āšma* 'firstly, on the first occasion (?), for the first time (?)' is always written *a-aš-ma*.

XXXIII 120 I 31 ff. in the series *āšmatta* … *dānmatta* … 3-*annatta* 'at first/firstly … but secondly … and (finally) thirdly [have I impregnated thee]'; XXXIII 106 IV 13 *āšma-an hullanun* 'first I struck him'. Further possibly XXIV 8 II 14, where the translation is perhaps 'for the first time' (sense something like 'for the first time the Sun-god comes to visit us! Has something dreadful happened?'). x-*ma-an-da* XXXIII 120 II 78 probably does not belong here (against H. G. Güterbock, *Kumarbi* (*Istanbuler Schriften* XVI), 1946: 79).

There are two possible explanations:
(1) Connection with *ānki* 'once', **ā-* (??) 'one'. Stem **ā-*, or, more probably, loc. **ā* 'at the one' (formed like *kā* 'here, hither') was extended by a particle-like element *-š-* (something like PIE **sé*/**só*, cf. Vedic *sá yathā* 'as'; also in Hitt. *kāša, kāšma* 'look here' and *naššu* ... *našma*/*naššuma* 'either … or', something like **no-se/o-we*) and by emphatic *-ma* (cf. *aru-mma* 'excessively', *imma* 'over and above' < **id-ma* or **im-ma*). Phonologically, the form *āšma* derives either by the route **ā́še* > **ā́š* (regular loss of final postconsonantal *-e*) with later addition of *-ma*, or by the alternative route **ā́šama*/**ā́šema* > **ā́šma*, with syncope of the vowel of the middle syllable after a long first syllable. In the series 'to

one ... to another ... to a third' a semantic shift → 'in the first place ... in the second place ... thirdly' could easily occur; cf. also Goetze's reference to Akkadian (Goetze 1949: 297 n. 46). The conjectural meaning 'firstly, on the first occasion (?)' is also easily explainable.
(2) **ō-smō*, lit. 'at the one', from prep. **o* [*o-H_1] = Vedic *ā́* 'to, around', and a case-form of PIE **sem* 'one'. This interpretation is suggested by E. Neu, *StBoT* xviii (1974: 98 n. 210); it presents no difficulties and, moreover, finds support in further Hittite material.

3.1.5. Hittite *hantezzi(ya)-*

hantezziya- / *hantezzi-* 'first, anterior' is used as an ordinal. The word was apparently coined as an antonym to the perhaps inherited *appezzi̯ia-* / *appezzi-* (**ope-tyo-* 'last, posterior, later', cf. Vedic *ápatya-* 'progeny' or **opi-tyo-*, cf. Greek ὀπίσσω; whether the Hittite word had *e* or *i* in the second syllable is not determinable); cf. J. F. Lohmann, *IF* li (1933: 324). Hitt. *hantezziya-* cannot derive directly from ?H_2*anti-tyo-* (cf. Greek ἀντί Latin *ante*), as is often said in the literature, because, in this case, **hanzizziya-* would have to be expected. It is probably an innovation starting from the dative, which had already fallen in with the locative, which happened at a time when *H_2*n̥téi* had already become **hantḗ* 'in front' (see H. Eichner, *MSS* xxxi, 1973: 77), but had not yet undergone the further development of final *-*ē* (< *-*ey*) to *ī* (cf. Hittite adv. *ha-an-ti-i* 'separate', originally 'front, to be found in the first place, especially'). [Or was *H_2*ante-tyo-* due to the influence of **ope-tyo-*?]

There are some derivatives to *hantezziya-* / *hantezzi-* (verb *hantezzi-yahh-* XXXI 147 II 21; noun d. *hantezumni* 'in the front room'); of these, *hantezzili* XXX 39 II 4 (*HW*, 53 'at the first time, at first') is the only one with a numeral concept.

3.1.5.1. Cuneiform Luvian *hanteli-*

In Luvian the equivalent is *hanteli-* 'first' (Laroche 1959: 40), the corresponding ordinal. Just as in Hittite, a dative-locative form **hantē* (< *H_2*n̥téy*), to which the suffix *-li-* has been added, probably underlies it. For the method of formation, the name of the originally second Roman month is, in my view, to be compared: *aprīlis* (ls. **apere*/*oy* + *-li-*). There also occurs a (not necessarily Luvian) PN *Hanteli* / *Hantili*; see Laroche (1966: no. 275); for the motive for giving such a name, one may want to consider joy at the birth of the first son (in this case, then, with the meaning of the ordinal), but also the wish for high social position of the bearer of this name (in this case, then, with the meaning 'foremost, high in rank, of the first rank'). For Lycian, closely related to Luvian, from *χñwatawat-* 'ruler, king' (dat.loc. *-a*; for the formation cf. the Hittite suffix *-att-*, also Cuneiform Luvian *handawati-* 'ruler') we can construct a denominative verb **χñtawa-* (for the formation, cf. Hittite *-ai-* verbs, e. g., *hantai-* 'to arrange' and *appai-* 'to be finished') 'to be a leader, find oneself in front'; and further adj. **χñtewe* (or **χñtawa-*) 'foremost, first, leader', which is derived, by means of the suffix *-we-* (*-wo-*), from an adverbial *a*-locative **χñta* (this would be something like a Hitt. **handa*). Hitt. *hantezzi(i̯a)-* is to Lycian **χñtewe-* as is Hitt. *šanizzi-* 'pleasant' to Hieroglyphic Luv. *sanawa-* 'good' (see 3.1.6.). A Lycian equivalent of Luvian *hanteli-* 'first' can be assumed, as Professor Neumann (Würzburg) has pointed out to me, in gen.sg. *χñtlah*, which is probably used as a surname [Hier.-luv. **hantili*, 3.1.2.2.].

3.1.6. Hittite *šanaiš** / *šaniš**

Hitt. *šanai-*? / *šani-* 'one and the same, a single one' raises complicated problems. For the most part several possibilities call for consideration in the interpretation of the quotations; there is an additional complication by reason of the possibility of confusion with Akk. *šanû* 'second'.

Old Hittite *KBo* III 22 (E. Forrer, *Die Boghazköi-Texte im Umschrift* [*Wissenschaftliche Veröffentlichungen der Deutschen Orient-Gesellschaft* XI, XII], abbreviated as *BoTU*; 7, old ductus) o. 10 *ša-ni-ia ú-it-ti* could mean 'in the same year', 'within the space of a year', or 'in the first year'. Further, the meaning 'in the next/second year' is not to be excluded, but, then, the necessary assumption of an akkadogram *ŠANIYA* would not yield a correct syntagma (adverbial accusative singular masculine or suffixed pronoun of the first person singular in the genitive – both are little used). *KBo* III 20 o. 60 *ša-ni-ya ši-wa-at-t*[*i*] is best interpreted as 'on one and the same day'. In the Laws § 191 (II § 97) *ša-ni-ya pí-di* '(if they) (are) at one and the same place' alternates with XXIX 34 IV 16' 2-*el pí-di* '(if they) both (are) on the spot', whereby the same content is given in another formulation. The reading 2-*el* (not 1-*el*) is certain according to Otten (Friedrich, in *Pagliaro Fs.* ii, 1969: 139 n. 1). The meaning 'one and the same' for Hitt. *šani-* is made certain by the passage from the Laws (see *HG* II § 97).

Recently E. Neu, *StBoT* xviii (1974: 20 f.) has taken up a position with regard to Hitt. *šaniya*; essentially, I follow him. He puts in a plea for an akkadogram *ŠA-NI-I pí-di KBo* IV 9 I 15 (otherwise *HW*) and *ŠA-NI-E pí-di* XII 50, line 10' (with duplicate). Admittedly the context does not permit a perfectly clearcut decision. According to Neu, the form *ša-a-ni-ta* does not belong here, as not certainly attested; otherwise Goetze (1949: 291 and n. 19).

3.1.6.1. Etymology

Kronasser (1956: 152) and Neu (op. cit.) (1974: 98 n. 210) suggest a connection with PIE **sem-* 'one'. Kronasser's derivation **sm̥-ni* should have yielded **samni-* or **šanni-*, not *šani-*, but this is hardly tenable, while Neu's referral to a neuter **san-* (with *-n* from *-m*) is unobjectionable. The protoform **šan* may constitute an equation with Greek ἕν, if weak stress can be assumed to here caused Hitt. *a* instead of *e*. Whether in **šani-* there is a functionless stem-extension (transference of a consonant-stem to the *-i*-stems) or a derivative from an adverbial *šan*, cannot be decided. Also analogical shaping of a **šami-* (*-i*-stem for *-a*-stem) 'the same' (cf. Vedic *samá-* 'just, like, the same', Pokorny (1959: 904)) on the basis of nom.-acc.sg.neut. **šan* or **šen* should be considered (protoform something like **sm̥ó-*).

3.1.6.1.1. Additional remarks

The neuter **sem* is probably also reflected in adv. *kiššan* 'thus, in the following way', which can be interpreted as a conflation (univerbalisation) of an expression **kí šan* < **kí šen* (**ḱí/gí/ǵʰí sém*) 'in this one way, exactly so'. Adverbs such as *eniššan* 'thus, in the manner mentioned', *apeniššan* 'thus, in that way', *keniššan* 'thus, in this way', were then formed (always with *šš*) in addition to *kiššan* (which is best considered as a sequence of two nominative-accusative neuter forms). In the adverb of time *kuššan* 'when?' (beside *annišan* 'formerly') we must correspondingly assume a conflation of the old locative **kʷu* 'where, when?' (in Vedic *kvà* 'where?', *kúha* 'where?' = Old Church Slavonic *kŭde*) with adv. **sém* **sóm*. In its turn **sém* **sóm* is probably also a locative ('in one' = 'together'). The Hittite particle of place *-ššan*, too, goes back to adv. **sém* **sóm*.

On the other hand, in my view, the following words do not belong here: *šannapi šannapi* (āmreḍita) 'each for itself, separate, scattered' (with derivative *šannapili-* 'empty, alone; not impregnated'); *šanezzi-* / *šanizzi-* 'pleasant, first class' (correspondingly Hieroglyphic Luv. *saniwa-*), which are no doubt to be assigned to **sen-i-* 'on its own, separated' (Pokorny 1959: 907).

3.2. The Anatolian numerals 'two' and their derivatives

3.2.1. The Hittite cardinal 'two'

The numeral-sign "2" is found with phonetic complements.

3.2.1.1. Forms

The stem-class is not certain, but there are indications of an *-a*-stem (cf. 2-*at*).

Plural common	nom.	2-*e* (probably *Bo* 3542 II 10' *ku-i-e-eš* 'the two, which') (2-*uš*, see *HW*; cf. however 3.2.1.6.) 2-*at*, see 3.2.1.2. 2-*ah-hi* ??, see 3.2.1.3.
	acc.	(2-*e* ??, see 3.2.1.1.1.)
	gen.	2-(*e*)-*el* (?), see 3.2.1.5.
	dat.	2-(*e-ta-*)*aš*, see *HW*
	abl.	2-*az*, see 3.2.1.4.
neuter nom.-acc.		2-*e* e. g., *KBo* XVII 11 I 21', a tablet in typically old ductus; also in later duplicate 74 I 36', see E. Neu, *StBoT* xii (1970: 14); further *Bo* 2410 2-*e huppar* GEŠTIN 'two bowls of wine', and XXX 41 II 9'; see also 3.2.1.1.1. For 2-*at* ?, see 3.2.1.2.

3.2.1.1.1. Notes

2-*e* is taken by Friedrich as accusative plural common for a series of quotations which are listed *HW* 302 (*KBo* XVII 74 II 14, II 8'; E. Neu, *StBoT* xii, 1970: 18, 24 are to be added). If this interpretation were right, it would be possible, or indeed necessary, because of the coincidence of nominative and accusative *-e*, to consider 2-*e* the descendant of an Indo-European dual form, having in mind the Indo-European masculine dual ending *-e* (or to be put as $-H_1e$ in ablaut to $-H_1ə$ – fn. iH_1, with secondarily accreted *i*?). Admittedly this ending would have to be taken over on to the numeral "2" only secondarily, since the Indo-European form is to be put as $*d(u)wóH_1$ $*dóH_1$ (traditionally **d(u)wō *dō*), and, beside it, with a still obscure extension in *u*, $*d(u)wóH_1u$? etc. or

$*d(u)w\acute{\bar{o}}w$ (PIE final °oH_1w > IE °*ōw*?), from which, in Hittite, a descendant with final °*ă̄* or °*au* would regularly result.

The quotations for 2-*e* are in expressions of the following kind. *KBo* IV 9 III 16 f. LUGAL-*uš* GUB-*aš* 2-*e e-ku-zi* (17) ᵈ*hal-ma-aš-šu-ut-tu₄* ᵈZA.BA₄.BA₄ 'standing, the King drinks (to?) two: to the goddess of the throne and to Zababa'; from other passages it is seen that the names of the gods are in the accusative; for *eku-* + accusative 'to drink to someone / in honour of someone', see J. Puhvel, *MIO* v (1957: 32) – Engl. *to toast somebody* fits; XX 19 III 4 f. LUGAL-*ùš* KISLAH-*ni a-ri* 2-*e ir-ha-a-iz-zi* (5) ᵈ*še-pu-ru-ú*? ᵈ*te-li-pí-nu-ú* 'the King comes to the threshing-floor and completes (?) two (i. e. given operations); to the honour of Šepuru and Telipinu'; or, better, '... he memorializes two in common, Šepuru and Telipinu' – other passages show the accusative of the god-names; *irhai-* perhaps similar to *kalutiya-* 'to sacrifice in common / in one round'. In expressions of this kind, 3-*e* occurs too instead of 2-*e* (XI 30 IV 7'; *IBoT* I 2 III 10); it must originally have been formed analogically on 2-*e*.

The determination of the forms 2-*e*, 3-*e* as nominative-accusative plural neuter is more probable than Friedrich's view (*HW* 302) of these forms as accusative plural common. Then there are two possibilities of interpretation:

1) There is ellipse of a neuter substantive, of which the meaning would be something like 'drink, draught of honour'. Neu, who inaugurated this view (*StBoT* xii 1970: 19, 25, 39), thinks of 'beaker' (Hitt. *zeri-* n.), but, against this, there is the fact that, in many cases, only a single vessel seems to be used (also *KUB* I 17 I 4 f.).

2) 2-*e* (in the event, 3-*e*) refers to the gods honoured. Kammenhuber (1971: 143 ff.) emphatically proposes this solution. Admittedly its basis is surprising: in Old Hittite the difference in gender in the (lower) numerals is, she says, weakly developed (1971: 147). It is not clear what is to be understood by this. The missing gender-concord is however quite easily to be explained from a particular function of the Hittite neuter, one that may be called "complexive". The complexive neuter is usually still coupled with the (collective) singular; but, in the case of the numerals, this interpretation is really excluded because of their special meaning. It is to be remembered here that the replacement of the Old Hittite form of the anaphoric pronoun of the third person, nom.pl.common -*e*, by the original form of the nominative-accusative singular neuter, -*at* (< -*ed*), in Modern Hittite can only be explained from these syntactic conditions; that only the nominative plural common, and not the accusative plural common

too, is affected by this, must be due to a difference in the placing of the subject- and object-pronoun, which has not been sufficiently investigated.

Finally we must consider the question of stem-formation, which is decisive for the assessment of 2-*e*. Here I would like to put forward for discussion the question whether it would not be better to separate 2-*e* (and 3-*e*) from the basic stem, and assign it to the -*nt*-stem (thus 2-*e* = *2-*ante*). From the point of view of the meaning, a collective formation (-*and*-) 'two in common' would fit excellently. For the ending -*e* in the nominative-accusative plural neuter, reference may be made to the occasionally recorded *waššante* 'covered' (*KBo* XI 29 o. 7). It would thus have remained as a nominal ending in the ritual formula 2-*e ekuzi* / *irhaizzi*, whereas, otherwise, it has – as is generally the case in the nominative-accusative plural neuter – been eliminated in favour of the competing ending -*a* to such an extent, that it merely occurs as a very rare variant. The cause of this lies in the striving for differentiation of nominal (-*a*) and pronominal (-*e*) declension. That -*e* has a firm place precisely in the case of *2-*ante* in the ritual language would not come as a surprise. The regular descendant of the Indo-European dual ending of the thematic stems must appear in Hittite as -*e* (nom.-acc. neuter dual < Proto-Anatolian -*e* < PIE $\textit{-o-iH}_1$), corresponding to -*i* (< $\textit{-iH}_1$) in the stems ending in a consonant (cf. nom.-acc.pl.neut. *aniyatti IBoT* II 130 r. 5 from *aniyatt*- 'instalment, priestly dress of the Hittite king'). The confusion of the ending of thematic and consonant-stems corresponds precisely to the linguistic development of Hittite, which I cannot discuss here; a dual form *2-*ante* would be just as possible as the singular form (accusative common) which *2-*antan* actually is (with ending -*an* < -*o*-*m* instead of -*un* < -*m̥*). When, after the – possibly very late – merger of the dual and plural categories, the endings -*e*/-*i* (dual $\textit{-o-iH}_1\textit{/-iH}_1$) and -*a* (from plural $\textit{-a-H}_2\textit{/ə}_2$) became functionless variants, which were, however, in part distributionally kept apart, *2-*ante* might at first retain its dual ending. In the later process of the elimination of *2-*ante* in favour of *2-*anta* (attested in the writing 2-*ta*, see 3.2.1.5.) in historical Hittite, the ritual form then remained excluded; this stylistic peculiarity of the ritual terminology could then bring about the imitation *3-*ante ekuzi* / *irhaizzi*.

So we see how Neu's suggestion as to the dual origin of 2-*e* is indeed vindicated by the assessment of this form as *2-*ante*. While the ending -*e* quite corresponds to the norm in the pronominal declension, which the -*nt*-stems follow, it is something unusual, and its consistent use precisely in the case of *2-*ante* must have a special cause.

In support of the interpretation of 2-*e* as *2-*ante* I may adduce an example of a different kind: *KBo* XI 49 I 14' ff. 3 NINDA*par-šu-ul-li* (15') *tág-na-aš* dUTU-*i iš-ta-na-ni* ZAG-*na-az* 1-*an* GÙB-*la-az-ma* 2-*e da-a-i* 'he puts two crumble cakes on the altar of the sun-divinity of the earth, that is, one (one specimen) on the right side, and two (two specimens) on the left side'. Since in view of 1-*at-ta* (3.1.1.7.), 1-*an* should be considered as nominative-accusative singular neuter of the -*nt*-stem, 2-*e* should also be an -*nt*-stem. Therefore the example shows (with good probability) that the writing 2-*e* is actually used instead of *2-*ante*.

A further possible support for *2-*ante* is yielded from the passage *KUB* IV 1 II 10f. *ma-ši-ia-an-te-ma-aš-ma-aš a-aš-šu* (11) *nu a-pí-ni-eš-šu-wa-an a-ku-wa-an-zi* (E. H. Sturtevant, *Language* x, 1934: 272f.) 'as many [nom-acc.pl.neuter] as seem good to them, that many they drink'. This formation is of course patterned after the usual syntagma 2-*e*/3-*e akuwanzi*; it is crucial that here it is not the basic stem but the -*nt*-stem. Nom.-acc.sg.neuter *āššu* is syntactically correct, since the predicative adjective can appear in the neuter singular independently of the gender and number of the noun that goes with it; *apinieššuwan* is a "complexive" neuter singular. The emendation of *mašiyante* to **mašiyanki* put forward by A. Goetze, *Neue Bruchstücke zum großen Text des Ḫattušiliš und den Paralleltexten* (1930: 36) and Sommer–Falkenstein (1938: 165 n. 1) is unnecessary.

3.2.1.2. 2-*at*

XXX 41 II 7' *nam-ma-kán* 2 GIŠ*zu-up-pa-a*[*n* X] (8') *šu-un-na-i* 2-*at-kan wa-al-*[*hi-it*] (9') 2-*e-ma-kán ta-wa-li-it šu-un-na-an-zi* 'Further they fill two *zuppa* in pairs. They fill two with *ualhi*, the other two with *taual*'. That *zuppa*- here shows neuter gender – otherwise only common gender is recorded, see H. Otten, *StBoT* xv (1971: 5) – need not be assumed, because of the possibility of a regular gender-discord (complexive-anaphoric neuter); the point is that 2-*at* here can be regarded as *2-*ante* + -*at* (nom.pl.common 'they'), and so does not present a nom.-acc.pl.neuter *2-*at*, which, in itself, would be conceivable. But 2-*at* is recorded with certainty as nominative plural common, *KBo* XX 83 I 4' 2-*at* 2-*at* (context fragmentary), something like '(they march) in groups of two, one behind the other; two by two' (cf. 1-*an* 1-*an* 'one after the other'). Nom.pl. common 2-*at* is formed to nom.pl.common, 2-*e* on the pattern nom.pl. common -*e* 'they' (older): nom.pl.common, -*at* 'they' (later). [2-*at* also 114/d I 11'].

3.2.1.3. 2-*AH-hi*

KBo XVII 74 II 31, non liquet. E. Neu, *StBoT* xii (1970: 21, 41, 92), operates with a 3 sg. pres. 'he doubles', i. e., 'takes double, takes twofold', Hitt. **dayahhi* (?). On the other hand C. Watkins, *Akten der 5. Fachtagung der Indogermanischen Gesellschaft*, Regensburg (1974: 369), sees here the continuation of an Indo-European dual (-aH_2-iH_1), cf. Latin *duae*, Old Church Slavonic *dŭvě*. This view is decidedly favoured by the parallels to the passage adduced by Neu (1970: 41). The new example *KBo* XXI 14 o. 8' 9-*an* 9-*AH-ha iš-pí-ir-te-en* 'nine (or nine times?) ninefold have you spread out' makes the assumption of a special, non-verbal numeral-formation in *-hh-* necessary, but creates a problem in that, now, the locative to a numeral-abstract *2-*ahh-* 'duality, doubleness' is rather to be envisaged ('in duality', i. e., 'divided' or 'doubled'; for the word-formation cf. *maninkuyahhi* XXIV 9 I 18 'in the neighbourhood'). A reading 2-*ih-hi* seems to me less suitable; for the consequences of this view for the assessment of the morphology, see (3.7.2.; 3.9.1.5.).

In this connection I may further call attention to the remarkable passage VII 1 II 9 f. It reads *ma-a-an* ᴸᵁ́MAŠDÁ-*ma nu ka-ra-a-du-uš ku-wa-pí* (10) *ú-e-mi-ia-az-zi nu* 2-*ŠU* 3-*ŠU nu-uš e-iz-za-i* 'if he (i. e. the sacrificer) is however a poor man, as soon as he finds (gets) entrails, thus ... and then he eats them'. A finite verb is missing in the part of the sentence left untranslated, but the assumption of an ellipse (cf. A. Goetze, *Die Sprache* viii, 1962: 10) would be very difficult. The problem is solved if for 2-*ŠU*, 3-*ŠU* we introduce the reading **t*/*dayahhi* (or the like; in the event, **t*/*danki*), **teriyahhi* (3 sg.), for then we obtain a parallel to II 1 f. — 'he makes twice three portions out of it' — to be recommended on the basis of the text-structure *nu* 2-*ŠU* 7 *ša-la-kar* DUMU-*li i-e-iz-zi za-nu-uz-zi* 'and then, for the child, he makes twice seven *šalakar* and roasts them'. The representation of the verbal form *teriyahhi* (to the verb *teriyahh-*, see 3.3.6.) 'he divides into three portions (?)' by 3-*ŠU* (really, 'thrice') becomes intelligible if there are locatives **t*/*dayahhi* (or the like) 'in twoness, twofold, double' and **teriyahhi* 'in threeness, threefold', which are homonyms with finite verbal forms of the meaning 'he divides into two, respectively, three parts' (or the like). Kronasser's translation of this passage (*Die Sprache* vii, 1961: 151) "sobald er die Eingeweide findet, dann isst er sie zwei mal und drei mal" goes against the Hittite sentence-boundary which is marked by *nu* and is also not a possible representation semantically — the entrails can only be eaten *once*.

3.2.1.4. 2-*az*

617/p II 10' ff. *ma-a-an* 2-*az-ma* (11') [KASKAL-*az na-aš-ma*] 3-*az* 4-*az* 5-*az* 6-*az* 7*az* KASKAL-*az* (meaning not clear); perhaps the assignment of this ablative form to the cardinal is not quite certain (= abl.sg. *damedaz*, 'other').

3.2.1.5. *-nt-stem*

Nom.-acc.pl.neut. 2-*ta* ^{GIŠ}*šar-pa* 'two ^{GIŠ}*šarpa*' *KBo* XIII 172 o. 10'. Because of KUR-*e-ta-aš* 'of the lands' XXIV 8 II 15 (*-nt-stem*), 2-*e-ta-aš* could also theoretically belong to the *-nt*-stem, but the probability of this is extremely small because of the *-e-*, which would then be hard to explain. On the other hand, the examples for 2-*e* (= *2-*ante*) discussed in 3.2.1.1.1., probably do belong to the *-nt*-stem. For the mode of formation in general, see 3.1.1.4.2.

3.2.1.6. 2-*el*, 2-*ela* / 2-*ila*

This, meaning 'two together, both in common', is used in the meaning given by way of a pendent genitive; cf. 1-*el*, 1-*ela*, 3.1.1.5. Attestations allow an exposition of its use.

1) In the function of a nominative:

XIX 7 (*BoTU* 43) line 8 f. *na-at* 2-*e-la A-NA A-B*[*U-IA* X] (9) *kat-ta-an ú-e-ir* 'they came two together / both in common to my father'; *KUB* I 6 II 8 (= Goetze, *Ḫattušiliš*, 1925: II, 14) 2-*e-el iš-pár-zi-ir* 'they came away from there two together' (i. e. they were the only two); *HG* II § 97 (= § 191) j (= *KBo* VI 26) *tak-ku* 2-*el pí-di* 'if they (the girls) are on the spot two/both together' as a variant to the older (0_6 = XXXIX 34) *tak-ku ša-ni-ia pí-di* 'if they are in one and the same place'.

2) In the function of an accusative:

XIII 9 III 18 2-*i-la-pát ša-ku-wa-an-zi* 'the two of them will be looked at' (i. e. called to account, or the like).

3) Hypostasized, with flexional ending (cf. 1-*elaš*, *apašiluš* 3.1.1.5.):

VIII 50 III 18' f. (E. Laroche, *RHA* xxvi 1968: 20) *na-at-kán* 2-*e-lu-ušpát A-NA* ^{GIŠ}MÁ *ša-ra-a* [*pa-a-ir* ?] (19') ^dGIŠ.GÍM.MAŠ-*uš* ^m*ur-ša-na-bi-iš-ša* 'thereupon they (*-at*) went the two of them / both together on board the ship, Gilgameš and Uršanabi'. The complete parallelism of the use suggests that the form cited *HW*, 302, npc. 2-*uš*, as short for 2-*eluš*, should be included here too (so already Kronasser 1962: 363). XIII 4 II

50 2-*uš-pát-at ak-kán-du* and XIII 4 III 83 2-*uš-ša-at* (= 2-*uš* + -*a* + *at*) *ak-kán-d*[*u*] 'two together both of them, they (-*at*) must die'. (XIII 4 II 49 dative plural is however not relevant.) Matters are perhaps different with regard to 2-*uš* XVI 29 line 25 (bis), but the syntax of the damaged passage is not clearly recognisable.

Whether the form 2-*el* continues a genitive form contained in the paradigm of the cardinal (cf. *anzel* 'of us', *šumel* 'of you') or represents a direct imitation on *1-*el*, 1-*ela* and cannot stand attributively cannot be decided out of hand.

3.2.1.7. Declension

The declension is pronominal. For the analogically formed 2-*at*, cf. 3.2.1.2. The possibility of a direct reflection of the dual offers itself, if the grammatical determination of 2-*e* as accusative plural common and 2-*AH-hi* as plural common / nominative neuter is right. However, this is not very probable, because of better alternative possibilities. On the other hand a completely clear reflex of the dual would be present if 2-*e* were to be taken as nominative-accusative plural neuter of the -*nt*-stem, as is suggested in 3.2.1.1.1.

3.2.1.8. Reading

The reading is unknown. Etymological attempts would lead to the establishment of **da*- (< **dó*-), **duwa*- (< **dwó*-) or *d*/*tuma* (< *duwó-); they can be supported (see 3.2.2.—3.2.4.) but not rendered sure. The probability that an inherited word is present in the Hittite cardinal is however to be estimated as considerable. The view (*HW*, 302) that a phonetic realisation **dā*- from *dān* 'second' and *dāiuga*- 'two years old' is directly to be inferred, is erroneous; see 3.2.3.—3.2.3.5. It is merely that certain variations in the phonetic form of these words permit an indirect reference to an analogical influencing by the cardinal, which may be shown to have *d*- as initial.

3.2.1.9. Meaning

While 'two' is a certain meaning, it cannot be decided whether the numeral-sign "2" also stands for a continuation of the Indo-European special indicator for 'both' (Pokorny 1959: 34 f.). The attempt to attribute the meanings 'two' (2-*e*) and 'both' (2-*uš*) to different formations, which the data *HW*, 302 suggest, leads to the surprising result that 2-*uš*, at least in the quotations mentioned *HW*, may represent an abbreviation for 2-*e-lu-uš* (3.1.1.5.; 3.2.1.6.).

3.2.2. Forms of the Hieroglyphic Luvian cardinal 'two'

The accusative plural common is *tu-wa-i*; see Meriggi (1962: 138 and 1966: 128, 1967: 59). According to recent opinions, *tuwa^{n}za* or *tuwi^{n}za* (initial *t* or *d*) is to be read, for which I have received strong suggestions from Professor Neumann. The further phonetic complementations (1962: 164) 2-*i-a*, 2-*i*, 2-?-*ī*, are in agreement with this finding.

3.2.3. Hittite (*)*t*/*dā* 'second'

To be compared is adv. *t*/*dān* 'for the second time'. This almost obsolete word stem seems once to have functioned as an ordinal. In addition, etymological attempts allow a stem **duiia-* or **duia-* to be postulated, but a reflex of it seems to be confined to Luvian. The usual Hittite ordinal is *t*/*damai-*, see 3.2.4. – 3.2.4.1.

3.2.3.1. Locative *tā*

A remnant of the inflected paradigm is formed in dat.-loc. *tā*: XXXII 123 III 5 *ha-an-te-iz-zi* UD-*ti* ... *ta-a* UD-*ti* 'on the first day ... one the second day'; Old Hitt. *KBo* III 46 (*BoTU* 17, later copy) o. 14 *ta-a-ma ú-it-ti* 'but in the next year'.

For the formation of the form *tā*, cf. *kā* 'here, hither'. In the first passage there could be an error (*HW*), in the second, nasal reduction from **tānma* (E. Neu, *StBoT* xviii, 1974: 98 n. 210). But the two quotations mutually support one another and contain a correctly formed and properly used form. In *IBoT* II 97 line 7' *da-a-an* UD-*ti*, the adverbial form *dān* (with the later phonetic realisation *d-*) has spread into the correct old syntagma *tā* UD-*ti*. For this cf. further *KBo* IV 4 III 58 *da-a-an* KASKAL-*ši* 'for the second time' (Goetze 1933: 130 f.); 2-*an* (+*za*) *pidi* 3.3.3.2.1.

3.2.3.2. Adverb *tān*/*dān*

The form is an isolated nom.-acc.sg.neut. *tān, dān, HW* 209; older writing *tān*, according to H. Otten, *StBoT* xi (1969: 20) (with examples).

1) Adverbial use in the meaning 'for the second time, secondly, again'; examples for the independent use, see *HW*. Also with enclitic *-a*, f. i. *KBo*

XX 40 Col. *b* 6' *ta-a-na* 'at the second time, secondly' ... 8' *te-ri-an-na* 'and (finally) at the third time'; cf. also *KBo* V 2 II 59 2-*an-na* (later 3-*an-na*, 4-*in*, 5-*na*, 6-*na*, etc.).

2) The word group *dān pedaš*, something like 'of the second rank, second-ranking' has attracted much attention. It might be imagined that this expression could have arisen in syntagmas such as 'so-and-so is of the second rank / the second choice (*dān pedan*)' and was then used as an indication of quality either parenthetically ('it is the second choice', nominal phrase with no subject pronoun) or in the attributive or predicative genitive, in which case only the second part would be inflected, because, in the meantime, the stem *t/dā-* had become obsolete, apart from the fossilised form *t/dān*. Indeed some passages allow it to be supposed that there arose a new adjective (*)*dānpeda-* (written with a space, *dān peda-*) 'of the second rank, second class, of the second quality', as a semantic opposition to *hantezzi(ya)-* 'of the first rank, first class, of the first quality' (cf. *HW* 1 *Ergänzungen*, 1957: 20), but clearcut examples are lacking. Cf. *KBo* III 1 + 68 (*BoTU* 23A) II 36 ff. *ták-ku* DUMU.LUGAL (37) *ha-an-te-iz-zi-iš* NU.GÁL *nu ku-iš ta-a-an pí-e-da-aš* DUMU-*RU nu* LUGAL-*uš a-pa-a-aš* (38) *ki-ša-ru* 'If there is no king's son of the first rank, then shall someone who is a son of the second rank become king' (variant *da-a-an pí-e-da-an* in dupl. *KBo* XII 4 II 6'); X 13 III 4 ff. *A-NA* ^{LÚ}SANGA 1 TÚG *ha-an-te-i*[*z-zi-in*] (5) *pí-an-zi* ^{LÚ}*ta-az-zi-e*[*l-li-ya*?] (6) 1 TÚG *da-a-an pí-e-da-an pí-*[*an-zi*] (7) ^{LÚ}*ha-mi-na-a-i* 1 TÚG (8) *da-a-an pí-e-da-an pí-an-zi* 'To the *sanga*-priest they give a garment of the first quality, to the *tazzielli*-priest a garment of the second quality, to the chamberlain (??) a garment of the second quality'; *Bo* 3371 line 8 ff. (see H. Otten *AFO* xxiii, 1962: 38 n. 18) ^{LÚ}KAŠ$_4$.E (sic) *tar-ah-zi ku-iš UŠ-G*[*I-EN*] (9) *ta-a-an pi-e-da-aš-ša* ^{LÚ}KAŠ$_4$.E *ku-iš* (10) LUGAL-*i UŠ -GI-EN* 'the runner who wins (in the race) may bow, and also the runner who comes in second place (lit. he who is of the second place / rank) may bow before the king' (cf. also *IBoT* I 8 II 4–6; I 13 V 14 ff.).

The verb *tān pedaššahh-* (Goetze, *Madduwattaš*, 1928/68) does not belong here, for it does not mean 'to make someone of the second rank' (so *HW*, 168, 209), but 'to put someone again (*tān*, § 39.1) in this place / in his rank'; see already H. Otten, *StBoT* xi (1969: 20). The verb *pedaššahh-* is based on a hybrid stem **pedašša-*, which can be abstracted from the – predicatively used – genitive *pedaš-šaš* 'of his place', for *pedaššahh-* is equivalent to **pedaš-šaš iya-*, lit. 'to make someone of his place'. In other texts *pedaššahh-* (without *t/dān*) has the meaning 'to bring to the spot' (cf. H. Otten, *Hethitische Totenrituale* (DAWBIO

XXXVII) 1958: 143); this use is clearly to be brought into connection with the expression *pe/idišši* 'on the spot', lit. 'in its place'.
3) A univerbalisation with *dān* is probably present in the word UZU*dān-hašti-* (neuter), which Neumann (1964: 51) (cf. *HW* 3 *Ergänzungen*, 1966: 31) has interpreted as 'double bone'. The univerbalisation may be relatively old, for neither member appears any longer in historical Hittite with the presupposed form (nom.-acc.sg.n. *hašti* with *-i* < *-ei* or *-i* against *haštai* with *-ai* < *-ēi* or *-ōi*) or meaning (*dān* *'doubled').

3.2.3.3. *tāuga-, t/dāiuga-*

The stem *t/dā-* which is comprised in the compound *tāuga-* (thus the phonologically correct form; beside it *tāiuga-, dāiuga-*) 'two years old' has placed an important part in the determination of the numeral "2" in Hittite; see Hrozný (1917: I, 93); Friedrich *HW* (1952: 302), Kronasser (1962–66: 362). Identification of the first element *t/dā* with the expected descendant of PIE **d(w)ó-* (stem) or even nom.acc.masc.dual **d(w)óh*$_1$ is, however, not convincing; since the compound must be relatively old, the Indo-European compound-stem **dwi-* (cf. Greek δι- Latin *bi-*, Vedic *dvi-*, etc.) should appear in the first element. Kronasser's comparison with Greek δώδεκα is not apt; the latter is a dvandva not a bahuvrīhi like Hitt. *tāuga-*. For a better explanation, see 3.2.3.4.

3.2.3.4. Etymology

With regard to the etymology of *t/dā-* I follow (with an inessential modification) a suggestion made to me by Professor Cowgill (Yale). Hitt. *t/dā-* goes back to **doyó-* (his **dwoiyo-*) 'twofold, double', a phonological variant of PIE **dwoyó-*, cf. Greek δοιός and Old Church Slavonic *dŭvójĭ* (initial *dŭv-* perhaps originally from *dŭva*). Adv. *tān* < **doyóm* (Greek δοιόν) represents a correct form of the paradigm (nominative-accusative singular neuter). The slight semantic shift is simply explained; for instance, 'to make something doubled' is, in many situations, equivalent to 'to do an action twice / for the second time'; similarly 'to give something twofold' = 'to give something twice'; cf. XIII 9 + IV 7 f. (E. von Schuler, *Festschrift Johannes Friedrich zum 65. Geburtstag am 27. August 1958 gewidmet* (1959: 448, 451) *na-aš-za ku-it ku-it da-a-an har-zi* (8) *hu-u-ma-an ta-a-an pi-eš-ki-iz-zi*, where one is tempted to translate 'whatever he has taken for himself, he must replace everything twofold (not: again)', although, according to Hittite interpretation, *tān* here = 2-*ŠU* 'twice', as follows from other texts. The compound *tāuga-* must thus originally have meant 'having the yoke twofold / for the second time' or 'having the time-span *H_1iugó-* twofold', that is then 'two years old' or 'just over two years old'.

Little attention has hitherto been paid to the cause of the variation of the initial writing TA/DA. If *d-* > *t-* has come into being regularly initially before unstressed *a* (at the stage **dayá-* or **daá* > **tayá-* or **taá* with secondary contraction to *tā*), as I would assume – only this assumption will correspond to the complicated graphical data, cf. *tan-garant-* 'sober' < **donḱró-nt-* = German *zanger* – then the dominant Modern Hittite form of the initial with *d-* must be due to analogical influence of the cardinal, which may then unambiguously be determined as the descendant of PIE **d(w)ó-*. Before directly following accent, initial media (and media aspirata) stay preserved at least before *a*, cf. *dāi* 'takes' (root *deH_3*) and *dāi* 'puts down' (*d^hóH_1yei*); occasional deviant writings can easily be explained on the basis of this assumption. So Professor Cowgill's etymology permits a satisfactory explanation both of the morphology and also of the varying phonetic form of *t/dā-* and *t/dān*, is thus well based, and is to be preferred to the thoroughly unsatisfactory earlier assumptions.

3.2.4. Hittite *t/damai-*

Hitt. *t/damai* 'other, second' is an extension of the wordstem discussed in 3.2.3. – 3.2.3.4. The anachronistic form **doyomṓi-* obtained by transposing this into Indo-European terms allows the formation and phonology clearly to be recognised. Undoubtedly we have a suffix *-mo-*, which reappears in various languages in ordinals, cf. e.g., the Vedic new formation *pañcamá-* 'fifth' (5.2.5.). Whether this suffix was obtained secondarily by false division from ordinals such as **sebdmó-* 'seventh' and then carried over other ordinals, or is to be identified with the suffix in words such as **medhyo-mo-* 'middle', **upo-mo-* 'uppermost' can be left out of account. Passage to the *ai*-stems no doubt happened late by analogy with other pronouns (*dapi-* 'whole', *tagai-** or *taki-** 'other'). From **doyomṓi* there developed **taamái-* (finally **tāmái-*) via **dayamái-*; the long vowel of the first syllable, due to contraction, was not shortened in the unstressed position until after the development of intervocalic *m* to *mm* after a short syllable in the neighbourhood of the accent was completed (cf. H. Eichner, *MSS* xxxi, 1973: 100 n. 88). An occasionally appearing *mm* was no doubt originally taken over secondarily from the pronoun of the first person; cf. for instance the opposition XIII 35 II 3f. *am-me-el* 'of me': *ta-me-el* 'of another'. The occasional long vowel of the first syllable is decidedly secondary (f.i. *KBo* VI 5 III 1 *da-a-me-e-da-ni* 'to another' as a Modern Hittite variant writing for *ta-me-e-da-ni, HG* I § 28); it has been taken over from *t/dān* (3.2.3.2.). One must be clear on the point that the single *-m-* of *t/damai-*, which, because of the lack of parallel formations, can hardly have originally been introduced analogically, shows a late – Primitive Hittite – shortening of an unstressed long vowel which is due to contraction. Unstressed inherited long vowels (from Indo-European long vowels or short vowel + tautosyllabic *y, w,* $H_{1/3}$) were already shortened in Primitive Anatolian time, long before the development *-m-* > *-mm-*, which even appears in Primitive Hittite *m* originating from *w*. With this, the etymology put forward in 3.2.4. may be sufficiently proved. Initially, *ta-* is phonologically regular; for *da-* the same source as for *dān* (3.2.3.2.) is to be assumed. See now O. Carruba, *RLL* cviii (1974: 590) on Hitt. "*damai-* 'altro', che etimologizziamo, dividendola nei suoi componenti **duwa-ma-i-*, con tematizzione in *-i* di un antico **duo-mo-* 'secondo, altro' ".

3.2.4.1. Inflection

The inflection is pronominal, gen. *tamēl*, dat. *tamēdani*, etc.; in all forms the accent is situated consistently on the second syllable (paradigm with deuterostatic accent); its vowel can be written plene, which is not the case for the vowel of the next following syllables (*tamēdănĭ*, etc.). In the dative(-locative) there is an old secondary form *tamatta* (e.g. XLIII 23 o. 5 *ta-ma-at-ta-ma* KUR-*e* 'in another land however'), which is to be compared with *kuwatta* 'where, whither' and *apadda* 'there, thither', and, further, with Lycian *eptte* 'to them' (< **ăbătăs*, see H. Eichner, *MSS* xxxi, 1973: 81).

3.2.4.2. Meaning

As to the meaning of *tamai-*, the only peculiarities which I point out here are *Maštigga* III 5 (L. Rost, *MIO* i, 1953: 358) 'one again, one new one' and XXX 10 r. 15 (with dupl. 11 r. 11') *ta-ma-at-ta pí-e-di* 'at a repeated time, repeated again and again'.

3.2.4.3. Derivatives

tameuma(n)- 'belonging to other people / to the enemy, enemy (adj.)' (cf. *HW* 208 – *KBo* XVI 46 o. 11' is to be added) is a derivative of *tamai-*, further the verbs *tameumeš-* and *tameummahh-* (mid.) 'to alter (intr.)'; the additional meaning 'to be angry, become annoyed' (examples see E. Neu, *StBoT* v, 1968: 166) is a calque on Akk. *nakāru* (von Soden 1965–81: 718 ff.); cf. *KBo* I 11 r. 23 *šarru ut-ta-ka$_4$-ar* 'the king gets into a rage (?)'.

The adjective *damme/ili-* 'fresh, undisturbed, unworked' (so Güterbock with convincing arguments, see *HW* 3 *Ergänzungen*, 1966: 31) does not belong to *tamai-* (against N. van Brock, *RHA* xx, 1962: 122) but to the family of *dammeda(r)* 'plenty, abundance'; it must have been used originally of wild, proliferating plant-growth in nature. The *-mm-* of the word is justified only with this derivation, which is also semantically without objection. It must however be admitted that the expressions *dammili pedi* and *tamedani pedi* have, to a great extent, mutually approximated; cf. the examples cited by E. Neu, *StBoT* xviii (1974: 21); also, e. g. XL 17 IV 19' *gi-im-ri* ... *ta-me-e-da-ni pí-e-di* 'in the plain ... at another place'; an example such as VII 13 I 26' *ta-me-li* could be explained from this (with *t-* and *-m-*; but cf. *ta-mi-e-ta* VIII 22 III 3).

This short conspectus of the derivatives of *tamai-* makes plain how far this word is from being limited to its function as an ordinal. For the most part the meanings of Hittite words appear to us to have a very wide range. It is precisely in the case of the lower numerals that we must not expect that the concept – in some sort apt for modern languages – of the semantic categories "cardinal" and "ordinal" can materialize in Anatolian as lexeme-classes (of which the individual members have in the first place or exclusively pure numeral concepts attached to them).

3.2.5. Hittite *tagaiš*/takiš**

Dat.sg. *takiya* ... *takiya* (correlative, *HG* §§ 77, 82) too belongs to a word *tagaiš** or *takiš** 'other, second', which is to be regarded as a derivative of *tā-* (3.2.3.). At the base of it there is a formation **doyo-ghó-* (parallel to **doyo-mó-*, 3.2.4.–3.2.4.1.; less probably, **do-ghó-* directly from the cardinal), which contains a suffix which is doubtless present in Gothic *manags* 'many' (**mon-o-gho-*) and Old Church Slavonic *mŭnogŭ* (**mn̥-o-gho-*). The initial writing *tā-* and the absence of plene writings in the first syllable correspond to what is phonologically to be expected. The word became extinct early and is no longer affected by the workings of analogy which are present in the case of *tamai-*.

The nature of the use deserves attention; it departs markedly from that which we see in Latin *alter* ... *alter*. *HG* ii § 77 *ka-a-aš-ma ta-ki-ya ut-ne-e ka-a-aš-ša ta-ki-ya ut-ne-e-ya* '(if) the one is in the one land and the other in the other land'. Here *kāš* ... *kāš* functions as the normal correlative distributive; *takiya* ... *takiya* stands as an additional correlative for emphasising diversity. In English what is meant must be reproduced in the following way: 'if the one is in a land *other* than where the *other* one is'. The Hittite formulation is a consequence of the circumstance that, in this language, there is no direct possibility of expressing relations such as 'bigger than' and 'other than'. The etymological connection with *tā-* (3.2.3.) is thus correct; a connection with PIE **two-* ... *two-* (as in Vedic and Avestan) would leave unexplained the type of use which is characteristic of *takiya*.

3.2.6. Hieroglyphic Luvian *tu-wa-na*

For this form Meriggi (1962: 135, 1966: 59) proposes the meaning 'secundum' or 'duplicem', which is perfectly possible. The series of signs can be interpreted as *tuwān* (< **dwoyóm* cf. Hitt. *t/dān*, or **dweyóm*, cf. Vedic *dvayá-*) or *tuwin* (initial *t* or *d*), cf. Lycian *kbi* (3.2.7.).

3.2.7. Lycian *tbi*, *kbi*

Lycian B *tbi*, A *kbi* 'another, second' (G. Neumann 1969: 394) is an *-i-*stem from an original *-ya-*stem, as can indeed be seen from the derivative A *kbijehi-* 'foreign' (< **dwiyasi-*); for an old *-i-*stem, **kbehi-*, would be expected as the derivative (otherwise E. Laroche, *Bulletin de la Société de Linguistique de Paris* lxii, 1967: 47). The protoform **dwi(y)o-* can be analysed as **dwi-ó-* or **dwi-yo-*. Both possibilities are plausible; for *-o-*, cf. **sebdmó-* / *septm̥ó-* 'seventh'; for *-yo*, **alyo-*, **anyo-* 'other'. It is important that the stem **dwi-* functions as the basis of derivation, as in Indo-Iranian (Vedic *dvitī́ya-*, Gāthic *daibitiia*, YAv. *bitiia* 'second'). Elsewhere this stem is very rare; it has its place in composition (as front element) and in adv. **dwís* 'twice' (gen.abl.sg.), also in some derivatives (cf. 4.). But originally **dwi-* must have stood beside **dwo-*, as *k^{w}*i-* is found beside *k^{w}*o-* in the question-pronoun. The semantic difference between such stem-doublets has not been sufficiently investigated. For the retreat of the stem **dwi-*, in spite of support by **tri-* 'third', must be due to some special circumstance. It is to be supposed that this circumstance is to be seen in the fact that the special meaning of the stem **dwi-* overlaps with one of the types of use of the Indo-European dual (the "natural", "anaphoric", "elliptic" dual), and that, therefore, the stem **dwi-* was replaced by the use of the dual by itself. So precisely those cases of the survival of **dwi-* can be understood to whose assessment Lycian offers an important contribution. The possibility of explanation sketched here is intended more as a call for further investigation than as a concrete suggestion as to solution. *kbijẽti* 44c4 is a derivative of *kbi-*; a further derivative, used as a personal name, is *kbijẽtezi huzetẽi*, from a newly-discovered inscription, see G. Neumann, in: J. Borchardt et al. (eds.), *Myra* (*Istanbuler Forschungen* XXX) (1975: 152). He compares the personal name(s) *trijẽtezi* 7,2; 8,2, which is derived from **tri-* 'third' (?).

3.2.8. Hittite *duianalli-*

Hitt. ᴸᵁ́*duianalli-* 'officer of the second rank' (Güterbock, see *HW* 2 *Ergänzungen*, 1961: 25) is, in my view, a loan-word from Luvian; for justification, see 3.3.3.4.–3.3.3.5.2. Here we are concerned with a derivative by means of the suffix *-alli-* from a basis **duiana-* 'to be found in the second place' (ord. **dwiyó-* 'second', cf. 3.2.7. + *-no-* suffix indicative of position – cf. Vedic *dakṣiṇá-* 'right'), or **dwiyan* 'secondly' (adverbial nominative-accusative singular neuter). It is not necessary, with N. van Brock, *RHA* xx (1962: 111 No. 209), to postulate a word **duyana-* 'deuxième'. Having in mind the etymology, there is no need for */dwia-/* or */dwiya-/* to be read, for *w* (consonantal *u*) in such a position has perhaps become *u* (vocalic *u*) for Hittite; see H. Eichner, *MSE* xxxi (1973: 82). So the no doubt careless reading *duyanalli-*, *HW*, 227, could be right.

F. Sommer's old postulate (*IF* lix, 1948: 205 ff.) **duya-* 'quartus' < **dur(i)ya-* = Vedic *turī́ya-* rests of an understandable misinterpretation and seems, indeed, in the meantime generally to have been abandoned.

3.2.9. Lycian *tbisu*, etc.

Lycian B *tbisu* 44 c 41, 64; A *kbihu* 44 b 6, 7 (bis) – Neumann (1969: 394) – presumably means 'twice'. Probably we have here before us an endingless locative, **dwiswé* 'twice', of a *-wo*-derivative to **dwis* 'twice', with which Old High German *zwiro* 'twice' and, quite probably also Av. *bižuuat̰* 'twice' (**dwis-wn̥t* – cf. 8.3.1.6.) is to be compared. If we only consider Lycian, an adverbial nominative-accusative of a syncopated *-wa-*

stem would also seem possible (*-wan* > *-un* > Lycian *-u*), but a Hieroglyphic Luvian piece of evidence (3.3.4.1.) is in opposition to this explanation, which might at first sight be preferred to the one given first.

Lycian B *tbiplẽ* (multiplicative, distributive, or the like) could be derived from **dwiplom* (cf. Latin *duplum*) or **dwipelom* 'twofold, double'. For another possibility, see Neumann (1969: 394).

The lack of syncope in *tbisu* / *kbihu* and *tbiplẽ* causes difficulties. Probably the initial has been analogically affected by *tbi*/*kbi* 'other, second' (3.2.7.), perhaps especially by an adverbial nominative-accusative singular neuter **tbi*/**kbi* 'for the second time'. It is less probably a matter of a derivative of the stem **dwi(y)o-* right from the beginning.

For Lycian *kbisñni* and *tupm̃me*, see 3.13.1.1.

3.2.10. Miscellaneous Hittite items

These are written with the numeral sign "2" with Hittite phonetic complements, in diverse value.

3.2.10.1. 2-*an-ki*, 2-*ki*

The meaning is 'twice, to a double level' (*HW*, 302); the reading uncertain, possibly **t*/*dānki*.

3.2.10.2. 2-*an*, 2-*anna*

2-*an* and 2-*anna* occur with a meaning 'the second, secondly, the second time'. The Hittite reading is presumably *t*/*dān* and *t*/*dānna*. The complex 2-*an-na* is to be analysed as 2-*an* + *-a* 'and, but' (geminating) and should not be regarded as a special numeral formation in *-anna*, as has hitherto happened (*HW*, 302, according to Sommer 1932: 272 n. 1). Cf. 888/z IV 7' 2-*an-za pí-di* ... 3-*an-na pí-di* ... 4-*an-za pí-di* (particles *-za* and *-a* on the numerals); *KBo* V 2 II 59 ff. 2-*an-na* ... 3-*an-na* ... 4-*in* ... 5-*na* ... etc.

3.2.10.3. 2-*iš*

2-*iš* 'twice'? XXXI 143 II 1, 8, 15 f.; cf. E. Laroche, *JCS* i (1947: 205). If the meaning is correctly determined, a variant of 2-*an-ki*, 2-*ki* (3.2.10.1.) could be taken into account — thus something like **t*/*dānkiš*. Theoretically, a reading **duiš* would come under consideration as a descendant of PIE **dwís* 'twice' (Latin *bis*). The form **duiš* (instead of the phonologically regular **duš*) would have been retained or restored in analogy with the other multiplicatives in *-iš*; cf., further, analogical *kuiš* 'who, which?', beside the rarely evidenced phonologically regular *kuš* (< **kuiš* < **k^{w}is*). If we consider such a possibility, we must at all events be aware that it is not very probable.

3.2.10.4. *takšan*

2-*an* = *takšan* (reading made certain by alternative parallel passages) in the expression UTÚL $^{HI.A}$ *tak-ša-an* (or 2-*an*) *šar-ra-(at-)ta-ri* 'the things to eat are halved (?)'; see the quotations *HW* 2 *Ergänzungen* (1961: 32) and E. Neu, *StBoT* v (1968: 153) below. Probably the juxtaposition *takšan šarra* here shows a semantic shift from 'to divide into two parts, to halve' to 'to divide into (as many) parts (as you like), distribute, divide out', similar to German *entzwei* (J. L. C. and W. G. Grimm, *Deutsches Wörterbuch*, 1854–60: ii. 672). At all events this meaning seems to me to fit better in the situation of use – distribution of the portions of food to the religious "gathering" – than 'to halve' (so E. Neu, *StBoT* v 1968: 153). Nevertheless for *takšan šarra-* the meaning 'to divide into two parts, to halve' (Friedrich 1959: i § 31) is also evidenced in *takšan arha šarra-* 'to divide (youths) into two groups' (XVII 35 III 9). *takšan šarran* 'half-share, half; piece?', too, is perhaps originally nominative-accusative singular neuter of the participle (Kronasser 1962–66: 532); but an *-a*-stem *takšan šarra* (*HW* 204: *-aš* XIII 4 I 56, now rendered sure by dupl. XL 63 I 5) is attested. For its part *takšan* could equally be nominative-accusative singular neuter to *takš-* 'to join together'. Originally *takšan* was certainly used, like Greek σύμβολον, for the indication of two pieces, which, joined together, gave a complete whole. So in Anatolian territory a new formation came into being, which shows semantic properties similar to Proto-Indo-European adj. **sēmí-* 'half' (Pokorny 1959: 905 f.), originally probably 'belonging to a unity, forming a whole' (word-formation difficult; perhaps double vṛddhi-derivative, zero-grade stem **sm-* 'one', to which ***semó-* 'unit', to which **sēmí-* 'forming a unit'), cf. Gonda, *Reflections on the numerals 'one' and 'two' in the ancient Indo-European languages* (1953: 35 ff.) (with a partly differing semantic argumentation). In *takšan* we have the only directly palpable Anatolian term for a fraction.

Whether adv. *takšan* (*HW* 204) 'in common, together, two together' is also a participle, or an endingless locative of a substantive (*)*takšan-* 'connection, juncture' may be left undecided. If IX 34 III 29 *ták-ša-ni* (not clear to me) were to mean, not 'in the middle', but 'in common', there would be an argument in favour of the latter possibility. We must be clear that the homonymy of *takšan* 'half, a half' and *takšan* '(also) two together' (e. g. XXXII 135 I 9; Friedrich 1959: i § 53) has led to the first word being written with the numeral sign "2" (2-*an*). Admittedly "$\frac{1}{2}$" also occurs in the meaning 'a half' ($\frac{1}{2}$-*AM* XV 31 II 28, Goetze, *Verstreute Boghazköi-Texte*, 1930: 24 I 38 f.); $\frac{1}{2}^{\mathrm{HI.A}}$ XVII 28 IV 48, *Bo* 1078 III 7' ff.), but up to now there are lacking Hittite complementations – XX 99 II 11 contains only particles – or parallel passages with the phonetic writing *takšan*. So it is not to be precluded that there exists a further word for "a half" (not homonymous with *takšan* 'two together' and thus not written 2-*an*).

I have not investigated whether in ornithomantic texts 2-*an* really means 'half-way' (a suggestion of Sommer's, see *HW* 302). At all events easily misleading comments *HW* 302 and *HW* 2 *Ergänzungen*, 32 (as if 2-*an* 'half-way' = *takšan* were proved) are to be modified.

3.3. The Anatolian numerals 'three' and their derivatives

3.3.1. The Hittite cardinal

The number is written using the numeral sign "3", or sequence *teri*-, both with phonetic complements. No clear evidence can be adduced for an -*nt*-stem.

3.3.1.1. Forms written with the numeral sign

Plural common	nom.	3-*i-e-eš* X 55 line 12
		3-*e-eš* XV 31 I 6; *IBoT* I 36 II 35, III 13
	acc.	3-*uš* IX 31 I 11 (in the margin); *KBo* XII 85 I 48
	gen.	3-*aš*, see 3.3.1.1.1.1.
	dat.	3-*ta-aš* 1175/u r. 7′ (-*nt*-stem?)
	instr.	–
	abl.	3-*az*, see 3.3.1.1.1.
Plural neuter	nom.-acc.	(3-*e*, see 3.3.1.1.1.2.)

3.3.1.1.1. Comments

3.3.1.1.1.1. Gen. 3-*aš* and abl. 3-*az*. *IBoT* II 5 r. 4 ff. [^{NINDA}*t*]*a-pár-wa*$_a$-*šu-uš ŠA* UDU. [NITÁ] (5) [*še-i*]*r* 3-*aš* ^{UZU}ÚR-*az n*[*a-aš-ta*?] (6) *šar-ra-an-zi* 'A *taparwa*$_a$*šu*-loaf ('men's virility loaf') from rams. On top it is covered with the penises (^{UZU}ÚR 'penis') of three of them. It is divided (distributed?)'. (Not understood by A. Goetze, *Journal of Cuneiform Studies* ii, 1948: 31 and *HW*: ^{UZU}ÚR.) Cf. XX 78 III 5' ff. ^{NINDA}*ta-pár-wa-šu-uš-wa* ^{d}U-*aš* NINDA *har-ši-iš* (6') *še-ir-wa-kán* UDU.NITÁ-*az* 3-*az* (7') ^{UZU}ÚR-*az* '*t*.-bread is the normal bread of the weather-god. On top it is covered/to be covered with three ram-penises'. The ablative UDU.NITÁ-*az* (instead of the genitive) is part of a badal construction or is due to case-attraction. Whether 3-*az* belongs to ^{UZU}ÚR-*az* or to UDU.NITÁ-*az* is unimportant. For the titbits ^{UZU}ÚR cf. also IX 32 o. 20 f. (H. Kümmel *StBoT* iii, 1967: 120 below) and *KBo* IV 2 II 10. E. Laroche (1967: 170 n. 31) gives the quotations for the *taparw*$_a$*ašu*-bread; for the operation of the covering which is described *KUB* II 10 IV 16 ff. (cf. *KBo* XX 67 III 20 ff.) in all details, cf. above all XI 13 V 11 f. *še-ir-ra-aš-ša-an ŠA* UDU.NITÁ (12) 3 ^{UZU}ÚR *wa-aš-šu-u-ar*! (13) *wa-aš-šu-wa-an-zi* 'And on it three ram-penises are to be put as a covering' (figura etymologica). As a consequence of these parallels the forms 3-*aš* and 3-*az* may, despite the elliptic (or brachylogical) mode of expression, be clearly determined from the actual quotations.

3.3.1.1.1.2. Nominative-accusative plural neuter 3-*e*: IX 30 IV 7 3-*e*! *ir-ha-a-iz-zi*; *IBoT* I 2 III 10 f. LUGAL-*uš* 3-*e* (11) *ir-ha-a-u-wa-an-zi* 'The King has task of bestowing a round of three' (for the construction cf. Friedrich 1940–46: i § 274 n.); 355/t r. 8' 3-*e irha*[X]; *Bo* 2692 V 23' 3-*e e-ku-zi*; 428/s II 3'. Possibly 3-*e* belongs to the -*nt*-stem; for discussion of the problem, see 3.2.1.1.1.

3.3.1.2. Forms written with *teri-*

Plural gen. *te-ri-ia-aš* UD-*aš* XLIII 60 (*Bo* 2533) I 9' '(a distance) of three days' (Güterbock 1957), see *HW* 2 *Ergänzungen* (1961: 25).

3.3.1.3. Inflection

The pattern is nominal or mixed nominal-pronominal. Gen. *teriyaš* (3-*aš*) follows the nominal pattern, dat. 3-*ta-aš* and nominative-accusative neuter 3-*e* the pronominal, unless both forms belong to the -*nt*-stem. The pronominally inflected forms, if these exist, are nearest to the paradigm of *kuiš* 'who?' (dative pl. *kued/taš*, nominative common pl. *ku-i-e-es*, occasionally *ku-e-eš*, nominative-accusative neuter pl. *ku-e*, rarely *ku-i-e*).

3.3.1.4. Etymology

Hitt. *teri-* is clearly a descendant of the Proto-Indo-European cardinal **tri-*. The nominative masc. **tréyes* should regularly result in Hitt. **terḗš*, which was altered to **teriḗš* (written 3-*i-e-eš*; in the -*i*-stems -*iēš* in general replaces the ending -*ēš* < -*éyes*). Gen. **triyóm* (with *iy* instead of *y* by Sievers' Rule) or **tr̥yóm* should really give **tariyan* or **tariyán* > ? (probably **tariyan* rather than **tarriyan*). The old ending -*an* is, as usual, replaced by -*aš*. For the variation in the anaptyctic vowels cf. nom. *gerēz* 'flood' (K. K. Riemschneider, *Otten Fs.*, 1973: 279); gen. *karittaš* < PIE nom. **ǵróyts*, gen. **ǵritós* (J. Schindler 1972: 35) or nom. *karaiz* (equivalent to **ǵrṓits*). The other variant of genitive **tréyō̆m* should lead directly to Hitt. **teriyan, teriyaš*. The initial of the original nominative appears to have been introduced analogically into the whole paradigm. PIE **tríns* must have led to Hitt. **tariš*; as elsewhere, the ending is altered to -*iuš*. The marked feminine forms (n. **tis(o)res*), which were perhaps not obligatory in Indo-European, have been eliminated in Hittite, in accordance with the general course of development.

We must allow for the possibility that forms of a word nominative-accusative singular neuter **teriyan* < **tereyan* < **treyóm* 'group of three' merged with the paradigm of the Hittite cardinal. Anyone who, because of 3-*e* and 3-*aš*, wants to assume a pronominal type of inflection, could in such a way explain the deviant gen. *teriyaš* (3-*aš*). **treyóm* 'group of three' would be a substantivized adjective **treyó-* 'consisting of three, threefold' (Vedic *trayá-*), which is derived by means of a thematic vowel and Kuryłowicz vr̥ddhi from **tri-*. In this connection the existence of a vr̥ddhi-derivative with another position of the stem-infix *e*, **teryo-*, too, would be theoretically possible, but without support from non-Anatolian material.

Finally it may be noted that the widespread rejection of an anaptyctic vowel in words like *teri-* has never been sufficiently supported, in particular the assumption of "Pleneschreibungen für nicht gesprochene Vokale" (Kammenhuber 1968: 204) is completely unfounded. It has for long been supposed that the writing of the Aryan numeral compound *ti-e-ra-wa-ar-ta-an-na* (initially, consistent *ti-e-*, otherwise with variants) could depend upon the influence of the Hittite word for "3"; see Mayrhofer, *Indo-*

Arier (1966: 16 n. 1, 19 with n. 1). The unexpected plene-writing is perhaps to be explained by the fact that the anaptyctic vowel came secondarily under the word-accent; a cause for the use of the initial TI instead of TE is however not apparent.

3.3.2. The Hieroglyphic Luvian cardinal

The numeral-sign "3" appears with phonetic complements; see Meriggi (1962: 164). The accusative 3-*i-a* is probably to be read as **tarï*^{n}*za* (or **trï*^{n}*za*); cf. 3.2.2. 3-*i*, too, is possibly **tarï*^{n}*za/i*. It should be noted that the numeral-sign "3" (beside its variant augmented by a "thorn") can also be used as a phonetic sign. In Laroche (1960: no. 388), the values *tara/i* or *tra/i* are assigned for "3" and (no. 389) the values *tar* or *tra* for "3" + "thorn" (for which Meriggi 1962: no. 370 has only *tar*). For systematic reasons, it is, however, preferable that the values *tara/i* should be assigned to either sign; if either of the two vowels assumes zero value, *tar(a/i)* or *t(a)ra/i*, the signs represent *tar* and *tra*/**tri*. In particular the non-recognition of the value *tari* for "3" + "thorn" on the part of Meriggi and Laroche leads to bizarre readings, e. g. *tar-su-u* 'thrice' (Lycian *trisu*!), SPEAK *ta-tar-ā* (Cuneiform Luv. *tatariyaman*-!).

3.3.3. The Hittite ordinal and related material

3.3.3.1. *teriya-*

KBo XVI 49 IV 2' *nu a-pa-a-aš te-ri-aš-mi-iš* (context fragmentary) '(±) that one is the third of them'; for the surprising use of the personal pronoun (lit. 'that one is their third', cf. *KBo* III 20 I 4 [*ha-a*]*n-te-iz-zi-ya-aš-mi-iš* LUGAL-*uš* 'my earlier king' i. e. 'the king previous to me'; *KBo* XX 32 III 13 *ha-an-te-iz-zi-ya-aš-mi-iš* 'their first', i. e. 'the first of them'. *KBo* V 2 II 60 3-*an-na hu-up-ru-uš-hi-in* 'and the third tureen (he libates for Kumarbi)'. The analysis 3-*ann* + -*a* 'and' (cf. already Hrozný 1917: 95 f.) is necessary; Sommer (1932: 272 n. 1) is to be rejected. See also *teriyala*-, 3.3.3.3.

3.3.3.2. *teriyan, terin*

3.3.3.2.1. Forms

teriyan, teriyann + -*a* (3-*an*, 3-*an-na*, 3-*na*), *terin* (*3-*in*) 'thirdly; at / for the third time'.

KBo XX 40 V 4' ff. [*nu*?] 3.TA.ÀM *tar-ku-wa-an-zi* [–] // (5') ^LÚ.MEŠ^*zi-in-hu-u-ri-eš* ^SAL.MEŠ^*zi-in-t* [*u-hi-ša*?] (6') SÌR-*RU ta-a-na hu-u-ma-an-ti-iš* (7') *tar-ku-wa-an-zi* ^SAL.MEŠ^*zi-in-tu-hi-e-eš* (8') *Ú-UL* SÌR-*RU te-ri-ya-an-na* (9') *iš-hi-ma-na-an ap-pa-an-zi* (10') ^GIŠ^ ^d^INANNA^HI.A^ *ha-az-zi-ya-an-zi* (11') [^GIŠ^*a*]*r-ga-mi wa-al-ha-an-zi* '(±) 'They dance three times. // (First) the *zinhuri*-men (dance and) the *zintuhi*-women sing. At the second time they all dance, but the *zintuhi*-women do not sing. And (finally) at the third time they seize a rope, pluck the ^d^INANNA-instruments and strike the tambourine (?)'.

KBo III 18 (*BoTU* 4B) r. 4 ff. [*ha-a*]*n-te-iz-zi-ya pal-ši* ... *t* [*a-a-an*] ... [*te-ri-*]*ya-an-na*, for which dupl. 16 (*BoTU* 4A) r. 1 has [*ha-an-te-iz-*]*zi pal-ši* ... *ta-a-an* ... 3-*na* 'At the first time ... at the second time ... and (finally) at the third time'; XXXIII 120 I 33 3-*an-na-at-ta* 'and (finally) thirdly' (32: *da-an-ma-at-ta* 'at the second time ...'.

KUB II 10 IV 33' *nam-ma* 3-*an pí-di* 'at the third time again' (i. e. if the third penis is laid on the *taparwa*$_a$*šu*-loaf); in IV 24 there corresponds *nam-ma da-a-an* 'at the second time again', 888/z 3-*an-na pí-di* (between 2-*an-za pí-di* and 4-*an-za pí-di*); *KBo* XIII 145 o. 3' *te-ri-in* 4-*in* (context fragmentary); the duplicate *KBo* XI 14 II 15 ff. gives the full wording, but in a condition difficult to read: *zi-iq-qa* ^d^UTU-*uš i-*(*it*?) nu *t* (*e*!)-*ri-in* (4̣)-*in* (5̣)-*in* [–] (16) *ú-e-*(*eḷ*?)-(*lụ*?)-*i-*(*kạn*??) (*na*?)-(*ya*?) (??; or °*i* (*tụ*)-*ri-*(*yạ*)??) etc. 'But thou, sun-god, get up and drive for the third time, for the fourth time, for the fifth time, around the plain! Unharness (thereupon) the tired (draught animal) and harness a rested one'. The attempt at an interpretation, which does not yet give perfectly correct Hittite, should only allow the sentence-structure to be approximately recognised; that *terin* belongs under 3.3.3.1. is not entirely excluded.

3.3.3.2.2. Inflection

The inflection is that of *-ya*-stems. The form *terin* must show syncope (cf. H. Eichner 1968: 215 n. 11) if has been correctly identified as a nominative-accusative singular neuter.

3.3.3.2.3. Word formation

We must posit either a derivative from the cardinal **tr-i-* by means of the suffixes *-o-* (^+^*tri-ó* ⟶ **triyó-* / **tr̥yó-* or *-io-* (^+^*tri-ió-* ⟶ **triyó-*) or else a direct derivative of the "numeral root" **t(e)r* by means of the suffix *-io-* (^+^*tér-io-* ⟶ **téryo-* or ^+^*tr-ió-* ⟶ **triyó-* or **tr̥yó-*). That both alternatives really have to be admitted is shown by the comparison with Latin *tertius* and Gothic *þridja* (**trityón-*, from the cardinal) and Vedic *tṛtī́ya-* (from the "root"). In addition a vṛddhi derivative of the cardinal would seem possible ($^+$*ter-io-* → **teryo-*). Since the sound changes to be assumed have not yet been fully elucidated and analogies with the cardinal could play their part, no decision can be reached. As the most probable phonological development we might assume

**tr̥yó-*	(← $^+$*tri-ó-* / $^+$*tr-ió-*)	>	Hitt. **tariya-*
**triyó-*	(← $^+$*tri-ó-* / $^+$*tri-ió-* / $^+$*tr-ió-*)	>	Hitt. **tariya-*
**téryo-*	(← $^+$*tér-io-* / $^+$*téri-o-*)	>	Hitt. **tḗriya-*

Thus the postulates $^+$*tri-ó-* and $^+$*tr-ió-*, in their coincident realisations **triyó-* and **tr̥yó-*, would yield Hitt. *tariya-* (perhaps still preserved as a variant of a derivative, see 3.3.3.3.). Hitt. *teriya-* could not have arisen in a phonologically correct manner in this way; it must have taken its *e* from the cardinal. Reconstructed $^+$*t(e)r-io-*, with its two ablaut doublets $^+$*tér-io-* → **teryo-* and $^+$*tr-ió-* → **triyó-* / **tr̥yó-* (essentially already Benveniste 1962: 87), would yield all the Hittite phonetic forms in question (*teriya-* and *tariyala-*), but is doubtful on other grounds.

3.3.3.3. Hittite *teriyalla, tariyala*

Ehelolf recognised that the derivative *teriyalla* / *tariyala*, a drink, belongs here (see *HW*, 221). There are the following attestations: *KBo* V 1 IV 35 f. *nu ši-ip-ta-mi-ya te-ri-ya-al-la ši-pa-an-da-an-zi* 'They libate *šiptamiya* and *teriyalla*'; *Bo* 4951 [X] 3-*ya-al-la* 7-*mi-ia ši-pa-an-ta-an-zi* 'do.'; *Bo* 2375 (with dupl. *Bo* 553) III 14 1 GAL GIR$_4$ *ta-ri-ya-la* 'a vessel of fired clay (?) with / for *tariyala* (?)'.

3.3.3.3.1. Inflection

If it is not just the stem-form that is used (as is probably the case at least in *Bo* 2375), *teriyalla* is to be idenfied as nominative-accusative plural neuter of an *-a-* or an *-i-*stem.

3.3.3.3.2. Word formation

Because of parallel *šiptamiya*, a derivative from the ordinal is probably present. The basic meaning would then not be 'drink from three ingredients' (cf. English *punch*, Hobson-Jobson 737–738) but something like 'drink of one-third', whatever may be implied by that. Friedrich's reference (*HW* 194) to Akk *šikar šalultum* '"one-third" beer' supports the suggestion. Perhaps in *teriyalla* and *šiptamiya* there is an indirect attestation for Anatolian fraction-formations. The morphological analysis leads either to an *-alli*-derivative or a (typologically older) *-la*-derivative from the ordinal *teriya-* / **tariya-*; the single *l* in *tariyala* can have been influenced by other *l*-formations.

3.3.3.4. Hittite *teriyala-* 'mediator'

In the Old Hittite ritual (Laroche, *Catalogue des textes hittites*, 1971: 416), we find II 56 (= *KBo* XVII 3 II 13', old ductus) a group of signs *te*(?)*-ri-ia-la-aš-mi-iš* for which H. Otten and V. Souček venture the interpretation (*StBoT* viii, 1969: 29 n. 9) 'my/our third' and further suggest that a circumlocution for the "mediator" (intermediary) is to be seen in the term "third". This suggestion fits the context of the passage extremely well and has important support in Hieroglyphic Luv. *tariwana/i-* (3.3.4. – 3.3.4.1.). The word *teriyala-* (this reading of the initial is virtually certain because of a lack of suitable alternatives) can now be analysed in two ways:

1) As a derivative of the ordinal *teriya-* (3.3.3.1.) by means of a formant *-la-*. In this case there could be identity with the material of 3.3.3.3., as already suggested by Otten and Souček.

2) As a nomen agentis, derived by means of the formant *-ala-* (Friedrich 1940 – 46: i § 46 c) from a verb **teriya-* 'to be the third, to function as third' or also directly from the ordinal *teriya-*.

3.3.3.5. Hittite *tarriyanalli-*

This adjective, meaning 'of the third rank, to be found in the third place; of third quality', has long erroneously been regarded as an ordinal (*HW*, 214, with literature). The correct determination of the meaning goes back to H. G. Güterbock, see *HW* 2 *Ergänzungen* (1961: 24).

3.3.3.5.1. Attestation

Nominative singular common ^{LÚ}*tar-ri-ya-na-al-li-iš IBoT* I 36 I 38; dat. *-li* I 37 'man (officer) of the third rank' or 'man in the third place'; further 4 TÚG *tar-ri-y*[*a-na-liš*] *KBo* XVIII 181 r. 3'; 3 TÚG *tar-ri-ya-na-liš* r. 8; 6 TÚG *tar-ya-na-liš* (abbreviated writing because of lack of space);

186 left margin 4 'third-quality garments' according to a suggestion of H. G. Güterbock, *KBo* XVIII, p. VII. (The writing with the sign LIŠ in *KBo* XVIII is to be assessed as an "abbreviated" writing, similar to, e. g., *kiš-an* for *ki-iš-ša-an* 'as follows'; what is meant phonetically is most probably Hitt. as in *IBoT* I 36.)

3.3.3.5.2. Linguistic assessment

Just as in the case of *duianalli-* (3.2.8.) an *-alli-* derivative is probably present. As the basis we must infer **tarriyana-* 'to be found in the third place' (ord. **tarriya-* + suffix *-na-* indicating position) or perhaps also an adv. **tarriyan* 'thirdly'. If, as has hitherto been usual, it is desired to consider the word as of Hittite origin, the explanation of the *-rr-* — about which it is indeed believed that one should not worry — would cause the greatest difficulties. PIE *r* gives Hitt. *r* between unstressed vowels (cf. H. Eichner 1973: 100 n. 86), as also after stressed etymologically short or long vowel (cf. *hā́raš* 'eagle' < **H₂árō*, *pḗru* 'rock' < **pérwr̥*, *pḗran* 'in front' < **pérom* or **pérām*; in *arraš* 'arse' < **H₁órsos* the *rr* goes back to **rs*, not **r*). As a consequence, the position before directly following accent is the only possible condition for *rr* < *r* (*warri-* 'helpful' must thus tentatively be derived from **worí-*, *šarrizzi* 'transgresses' from **so-réyeti*, etc.). This is however certainly not the case if the Hittite vowel preceding the *r* has been inserted in an original group of consonants by anaptyxis (cf. *geréz, karáiz* 'flood', *parā́* 'forward < **proH₁*, *karā́uar* 'pair of horns'). The only remaining possibility is at best to posit **tr̥yó-* < **təryá-*, provided the change **r̥* > **ər* took place very early (earlier than the development of an anaptyctic vowel in **tr-*), and, further, that postvocalic **r* was doubled before *y* too: **təryó-* > **tarriya-*. For the latter hypothesis reference could indeed be made to *anturriya-* 'inland' (beside *anturiya-*). But this assumption, too, loses probability if words such as *tūriya-* 'to harness' (< **dhwr̥h-yé-*) are adduced, particularly when *rr* of *anturriya-* can have been taken over analogically from *katterra-* 'lower' (anachronistically **kmt-eró-*, a replacement of **n̥dʰero-*; beside it also *kattera-* with a different accent, or analogical *r*).

But all problems are resolved if *tarriyanalli-* is considered an originally Luvian word. Luvian *rr* is a normal correspondence of Hitt. *r*, to which, above all, B. Čop, *IF* lxxv (1970: 86 f.) has called attention. The textual evidence (clear luvisms in *IBoT* I 36!) and the word formation (suffix *-alli-* more productive in Luvian than in Hittite in the case of such words as *mawalli-*, 3.4.4.1.) are reconcilable with the hypothesis that *tarriyanalli-* is Luvian. We then obtain the correspondences Hitt. *dān pedaš*, **teriyan / *teriyaš pedaš*: Luvian *duianalli-*, *tarriyanalli-*.

Hitt. *teriya-* and Luvian **tarriya-* 'third' can be equated on the basis of (Proto-Anatolian or Common Anatolian) **ter(i)ya-*. If the *e* of this form goes back to PIE *e*, Luvian *tarriyanalli-* would be the only word in the whole of the Indo-European material which requires a form **teryo-* with *e* after C_1- and thus provides proof for Benveniste's reconstruction **teryono-* (1962: 87).

But, as far as I can see, there is no cogent ground for the assumption that Luvian *rr* next to an accent — this condition must not be overlooked — could not have arisen after an anaptyctic vowel, too (*šarra* 'on' corresponds to Hitt. *šarā́*, at first < **šrā́?*). In Luvian *atari-* : Hitt. *etriya-* 'to nourish', Luvian *hattarai-* : Hitt. *hatrāi-* 'to write', Luvian *huppara-* : Hitt. *hupra-* 'sort of girdle', Luvian *immari-* : Hitt. *gimra-* 'field, plain', Luvian *iššari* : Hitt. *keššar* 'hand' (see Laroche 1959), the *r* does not necessarily occur after an originally stressed vowel (***H_1*ed-ri-yé-* 'to nourish', ***H_2*atra*H_2*-yé-* 'to scratch', **ǵhésr̥* 'hand'). Initial stress in **gémra-* 'plain' is probably indicated by Hittite dat. *-ri* (not *-ri-i*). Luvian *pari* (Laroche 1959: 78) on its part, can no longer be directly equated to Hitt. *parā*, and, for Luvian *kuranni-* 'section (??)' (Laroche 1959: 57), original final stress, an aberrant development *kurá-* < **k*^{w}*rá-*, or borrowing from Hittite must be assumed. Even this short sketch makes it probable that Benveniste's reconstruction **teryono-* is not unavoidable.

From the data the conclusion may be drawn that the Luvian cardinal (*sic*) "3" is to be posited as **tarri-* < **trí-*; as in Hittite, it is the phonological form of the cardinal that became decisive, and probably caused a reshaping of the ordinal **tariya-* (< **triyó-*, by far the most probable protoform) to **tarriya-*. In its turn, **tarriya-* is attested by *tarriyanalli-*, indirectly to be sure, but nevertheless undoubtedly.

3.3.4. Hieroglyphic Luvian *tariwana-*

The very common Hieroglyphic Luvian epithet of the ruler, *tariwana-* (perhaps to be put phonetically as **tarriwanni-* — but this question is not significant in our connection) has been approximately identified by Meriggi (1962) and Laroche (1960: i. no. 371) (both read *tarwana-*) as 'righteous one' or 'judge'; the two meanings are best joined together as 'righteous judge'. The sphere of meaning is in any case fixed by the related abstract **tariwana-* 'righteousness' (a meaning assured by the Phoenician translation), probably originally as *ya*-derivative (*-aya-* > *-a-*) like Hitt. *pittuliya-* 'anxiety' to *pittula-* 'noose'. A word 'judge' as the title of a prince naturally does not surprise us; Laroche calls attention to the political meaning of Semitic *špṭ*; we need only think of the rôle of the "judges" in the Old Testament.

If it is assumed that the basic meaning is 'impartial person, arbitrator', the etymology is of course clear: *tariwana-* denoted the impartial "third", who – in certain circumstances on account of his power and of the regard in which he is held – has to settle the dispute of two parties in a law suit (not the criminal judge). For the historical importance of the office of arbitrator as early as the time of the Hittite Great Kingdom reference should be made to the "Arbitrament of Muršili II in respect of Barga" iii, 27 f. (H. Klengel, *Or.* N.S. xxxii, 1963: 38, 44, 53), where "the Priest" (epithet of Telipinu of Aleppo) is named as the competent court for any disputes between Muršili's Syrian vassals. Perhaps it is no coincidence that this rule concerns precisely a region which belongs to the area in which, later, the *tariwanas* officiated.

3.3.4.1. Word formation

If fundamentally there are no objections to raise against positing **tri-wo-n-* 'third' (with characteristic *-n*-suffix) or **tri-wo-no-* 'to be found in third place' (cf. Vedic *pūr-vá-* 'first', also Lycian *χñtawati* 'ruler'), it is worthy of thought that, in the Luvian domain, there should be a further formation too, **tarriwa-* or **tarriwana/i-*, beside **tarriya-* 'third' (= Hitt. *teriya-*) or **tarriyana-*. But all doubts can be eliminated by reference to a further Anatolian word, to which *tariwana-* can have been assimilated (see 3.4.6.).

For the details of the reading, see 3.3.2. Under no circumstances can the controversial state of affairs lead to doubt about the etymology. Those researchers who want to read *tarwana-* also interpret the multiplicative *tar(r)iš(š)u* as *tarsu*, see 3.3.2. and 3.3.5.1.

3.3.5. Luvo-Lycian multiplicative adverbs, etc.

3.3.5.1. Hieroglyphic Luv. *tarisu* 'three times' (?) (= **tarriššu*?), see Meriggi (1962: 165); Laroche (1960: i. no. 388). The writing is *tari-su-u*, with the first sign "3" + "thorn".

Lycian B *trisu* 44c 51, d 70 'three times' (?), A **trihu*, corresponds to Hieroglyphic Luv. *tarisu*; for possible syncope, cf. Lycian *hri* = Hieroglyphic Luv. *šarri* 'above'. To be derived from ± **tris-wé*; for an explanation see 3.2.9.

3.3.5.2. Lycian B *trpplẽ* 44 c 53 (beside *tbiplẽ*), derived from ± **triplom* or **tripelom*; after the syncope of the *i, p* was regularly doubled in the position after a consonant. For the word formation, see 3.2.9.

3.3.5.3. Lycian *trppeme* 109,5 (numeral ??): *hrppibeije : tãtu : epñte : trppeme* 'so afterwards they must be enjoined *trppeme*'. The form is thus to be identified as nominative-accusative plural neuter (admittedly dative plural would also be possible). It is hard to say whether a meaning '$3\frac{1}{2}$' or '$2\frac{1}{2}$' would be apt. All the same, because of *tupm̃ne* and *mupm̃me*, this possibility must be considered. See 3.13.1.6.. For the proper name *trijẽ-tezi-*, see 3.2.7.

3.3.6. Miscellaneous Hittite items

The writing is with the numeral sign "3" with various Hittite phonetic complements.

3.3.6.1. 3-*an-ki* 'three times' Goetze, *Verstreute Boghazköi-Texte* (1930: 111 III 22'); 482/z line 2; to be read **teriyanki* (??).

3.3.6.2. 3-*iš*, 3-*kiš* 'three times' (?); see *HW*, 303; to be read **teriyankiš* (??). For 3-*iš* the assumption of a direct continuation of PIE **trís* (> Hitt. **tariš*, analogically **teriš*) would be improbable. For 3-*kiš* there is a quotation on a tablet in typically old ductus (*KBo* XVII i I 3').

3.3.6.3. 3-*li* (?) *KBo* III 56 (*BoTu* 19) line 13' (or 3-*li*-(*x̣*)[X]).

3.3.6.4. 3-*yahh* and 4-*yahh* (verb-stems); according to *HW*, 303 'to make threefold' and 'to make fourfold'; but the meaning is not clear. The quotations for 3-*iahhahh*- and 4-*iahhahh*- (IX 4 II 35) are possibly to be regarded as dittographic (with *HW*), but, on the other hand, we can also seek a connection with verbs such as *teriyahh*- (**teriyahhahh*- would be the normal factitive to the participle **teriyahhant*-) or with the numeral formations in -*hh* (cf. 3.2.1.3.).

One could attempt to connect 3 pl.pret. *te-ri-ir* XXXIII 60 r. 14 (Laroche, *RHA* xxiii, 1968: 154) with a verb **teriya*- 'to divide into three parts, to be one of three (or the like)' because of the shortly preceding (r. 11) 3 DUMU^{MEŠ}-ŠU 'three children from him (from her?)'. However we probably have here just the third plural preterite of the verb *tar*- 'to speak', which is not recorded elsewhere.

3.4. The Anatolian numerals 'four' and their derivatives

3.4.1. The Hittite cardinal

3.4.1.1. Forms written with the numeral sign '4'

The phonetic complements indicate both root-stem and *-nt*-stem.

Plural common acc.	4-*uš* *KBo* XVII 1 II 8' (Otten – Souček, *StBoT* viii, 1969: II 22'), tablet in typically old ductus
dat.	4-*ta-aš* XXXIII 51 line 7' (*-nt*-stem?)
instr.	4-*it* 1238/v line 11'; 941/z r.? 5'
abl.	(4-*az* 617/p, see 3.2.1.4.)
Plural neuter nom.-acc.	4-*ta*, see 3.4.1.1.1.2.

3.4.1.1.1. Notes

3.4.1.1.1.1. 4-*aš* (?) *IBoT* II 97 line 4 (*HW*, 303) does not exist. Instead of this we should read [X ^{GIŠ}ZA.LAM.] GAR-*aš-ma kat-ta-an tar-na-an-zi* 'they put a tent up'; cf. line 3'. ^{GIŠ}ZA[.LAM.GAR.X].
3.5.1.1.1.2. Plural neuter nom.-acc. 4-*ta*: *KUB* V 7 o. 30 4-*ta TA-PAL* EZEN ITU.KAM *ku-it kar-ša-an e-eš-ta* 'which concerns the fact that four pairs of month-festivals have been neglected'. The form belongs to the *-nt*-stems (*4-*ant*-). The writing of the next line but one, 4 *TA-PAL* ITU.KAM, shows that, in the case of numerals too, the graphic indication of the *-nt*-stem can be entirely omitted.
3.4.1.1.1.3. On the problem 4. (KI.) GUB 'standing with four legs' (*HW*, 303, 2 *Ergänzungen*, 1961: 32) light is thrown by *Bo* 6514 IV 3' f. (H. G. Güterbock, *Oriens* x, 1957: 361) *IŠ-TU BI-IB-RI* GUD.AMAR 4-*i*[*t* GÌR^{MEŠ}-*it* ?] (4') *a-ra-an-te-it a-ku-wa-an-zi* 'they drink out of a calf's rhyton standing on (all) four feet'; cf. 1238/v line 11' 4-*it* GIR-x̣[X] and X 89 I 20 f. 4 *arantet* (O. Carruba, *Kadmos* vi, 1967: 93).
3.4.1.1.1.4. [X](x̣) 4-*at irhaizzi Bo* 7967 line 5'. A passage which poses a riddle. If correctly read, 4-*at* would have to be compared with 2-*at* : 2-*e* and 1-*at* : 1-*e* (an instrumental in *-at* is excluded). Is it a special kind of numeral? Since the accusative is required syntactically, 4-*at* must formally be the nominative-accusative singular neuter. The explanation of this form will only be possible with additional material and will have consequences for the assessment of other forms (e. g., 2-*e*).

3.4.1.2. Forms written with *mieu-*

Hitt. *mieu-, miu* denotes 'member of a group of four; four?' (according to H. G. Güterbock, see *HW* 2 *Ergänzungen* 1961: 18).

Plural common nom.		*mi-e-wa-aš- ABoT* 44 I 54
		mi-e-ia-wa-aš I 55
	acc.	*mi-e-ú-uš* I 52
	gen.	*mi-i-ú-wa* ⟨*-aš*⟩ XLIII 60 I 11.

3.4.1.2.1. Notes

ABoT 44 shows the word applied to the sun-god's four-in-hand: I 52 ff. *nu mi-e-ú-uš ku-i-uš tu-u-ri-ya-an har-ši* (53) *nu-uš-ma-aš ka-a-ša* DUMU.NAM.LÚ.ULU^{LU}*-aš hal-ki-in šu-uh-ha-aš* (54) *nu mi-e-wa-aš-ti-iš ka-ri-ip-pa-an-du nu ku-it-ma-an* (55) *mi-e-ya-wa-aš-te-eš hal-ki-in ka-ri-ip-pa-an-zi,* etc. 'Look, the mortal man has heaped up grain for the four which thou hast yoked! Now may thy four eat! And while thy four eat the grain – mayst thou live, O sun-god! – look, then will the mortal man, thy servant, address the word to thee and will listen to thy words'. Hitt. *mieu-* stands here without additional substantive for the parties concerned in a collective of four: the quadriga of the sun-god. A corresponding content may be present in the further passage, in which admittedly an assessment of *mi(e)u-* as a simple numeral is also possible: XLIII 60 I 10 f. NIM.LÀL *te-ri-ya-aš* UD-*aš* (11) *mi-i-ú-wa* ⟨*-aš*⟩ UD-*aš* KASKAL-*an pa-a-an-du* 'the bees shall put behind them a journey of three days, of four days'. Perhaps here the idea of the nature of a 'three-days' journey', 'four-days' journey' is intended, and not simply 'three journeys of a day', 'four journeys of a day'. For the time being, then, the situation does not yet permit the definitive statement that *mieu-* is the normal Hittite cardinal; it could be a case of a special collective nomenclature.

3.4.1.2.2. Inflection

The pattern is that of a *-u*-stem with traces of suffix-ablaut as found in the "proterodynamic" inflection, which, in Hittite, for the most part occurs in adjectives. But in respect to the typology of the ablaut, the substantive *he(i)u-* 'rain' is comparable, too. The form of the nominative plural common *mieyawaš* is decisive for the determination as a *-u*-stem; in the case of an *-a*-stem, *miewa- miwa-*, as we should normally posit it (cf. Laroche's *mauwa-* for Luvian – see 3.3.3.5.2.), the ablaut would come as something of a surprise. The ending *-aš* is to be assessed as an archaism or hyperarchaism merely conditioned by the text – originally *-aš* belongs to the *-a*-stems, PIE *-ōs*, cf. I 61 *ú-e-⟨ri-⟩te-ma-aš* 'the terrors'.

3.4.1.2.3. Etymology

Cf. A. Heubeck, *Die Sprache* ix (1963: 201 f.); G. Neumann, *Innsbrucker Beiträge zur Kulturwissenschaft*, Sonderheft xxiv (1967: 24 f.).

We must start out from a Proto-Indo-European adjective stem **méy-u* 'little, small'. **meyu-* became Hitt. *miu-*, **meyw-*, Hitt. **mēw-*; by mixture of these, *mīw-*, *miew-*; Proto-Indo-European forms such as nominative plural masc. **meyowes* > Hitt. **miyaw-* or **m(i)-yéwes* > Hitt. *miew-* are to be considered. Heubeck suggests convincingly that a designation of the "little" hand (without the thumb) is to be seen in **meyu-*. The word formation is most easily to be understood if a substantivized neuter adjective **méyu-* is assumed (type **pélH₁u* > Gothic *filu* 'much'), to which there would belong a thematic derivative **meiw-o-* '(plural) belonging to the little hand', i. e., 'the four long fingers', and transferred, 'the members of a group of four; the four'. In Hittite the two formations would be conflated.

The postulated adjective, **mey-u-*, is directly derived from the root *mey-* 'to be little, small' (cf. Pokorny 1959: 711). A denominative *n*-present **minéwti* 'to make less, make smaller' served as a Proto-Indo-European factitive to this adjective. (I owe the hint for this important assumption to Professor Klingenschmitt.) Parallel to it a denominative *n*-present to a substantive **m(e/o/0)y-eH₂* 'lack, diminution' was formed, **minéH₂ti* 'to cause diminution', Vedic *mināti* 'to harm, diminish, injure'; we must be clear that, in the case of **minéwti* and **minéH₂ti* with *n* as stem-infix, a very old type of formation in present, which, in contradistinction to the well-known type with *n* (or *ne/n*) as root-infix, must be primary, for root-infixation is not consonant with the structure of Indo-European morphology elsewhere, whereas for stem-infixation, reference can, after all, be made to the morpheme *-e-* of "vṛddhi-derivation" (which does not start from the root but from a stem). Starting from **minéwti* a new adjective **minu-* '(too) small, less' was formed still in Proto-Indo-European times, evidenced by the reflexes found in Greek, Latin, Celtic(?), Germanic, Slavic. (A secondary formation of the same type is Vedic *dhṛṣṇú-* 'bold' beside *dhṛṣṇóti* 'to the bold'; the old adjective is represented by Greek θρασύς.) But if, beside **méyu-*, there was the new formation **minu-*, it may be suggested that, already in Indo-European, **méyu-* could have developed its special use as a numeral, thus PIE **méyu-* '1. little; 2. (substantivized neuter) little hand': PIE **minu-* 'less, (too) small'. The Anatolian languages preserve thus something very old in Hitt. *mi(e)u-* together with its Luvian correspondences, as should have become clear after this excursus into questions of word formation; **méyu-* must be older than **minéwti* and this again older than the adjective **minu-*, and even this must be a Proto-Indo-European form. And even without a consideration of the background, it would be difficult to assume a Hittite-Luvian innovation, since there is no other trace of the relevant Indo-European root in Anatolian (Laroche 1959: 70).

3.4.2. The Cuneiform Luvian numeral 'four'

3.4.2.1. Forms written with the numeral sign '4' with phonetic complements: nominative plural common 4-*zi*?; instrumental plural 4-*ti* (= *māuwăti*), see 3.4.2.2.
3.4.2.2. Forms written with phonetic signs plus complements. The stem is *mauwa-* (or *mauwi- mau-*?). Instrumental plural *ma-a-u-wa-a-ti pa*[-*a-a*-]*r-ta-a-ti* XXXV 54 III 10 'of/with the four sides'; likewise *ma-a-u-wa-ti p*[*a* X] XXXV 21 r. 4; in alternation with 4-*ti* p. 43 II 12 III 24, 33 III 7 (restored); XXXII 14 + line 6.
3.4.2.3. Discussion. The phonological development is hard to assess: **meyaw-* > **maaw-* > *māw-*, but also **meyw-* > **mew-* > **maw-* (Heubeck) may have to be considered. It is hardly possible to argue here from the plene writings, since the attested forms are too few and occur in passages where one must certainly reckon with emphatic lengthenings (conjuration-formulae!); the emphatic lengthenings are quite obvious in XXXV 54 III 10 (see above; twice double-plene). It is not clear whether by-forms **mu(wa)-* (< **mau* < **meyu-*???) and **miu*, **miwa-* are to be assumed. And no certainty is to be attained concerning the stem-formation (stem *mawi-*?; the instrumental *-ati* would be regular for this stem too). However, in any event, because of the connection with the Hittite, we must posit a *-u-*stem as original for Luvian also – which was secondarily extended to an *-i-* or *-a-*stem – and not seek some direct connection with Old Icel. *mær mjór* 'slim, narrow' and Tocharian B **maiwe* 'young' (**moywo-*).

3.4.3. The Hieroglyphic Luvian numeral 'four'

Written with the numeral sign "4" with phonetic complements (Meriggi 1962: 165; *HH* I, No. 391).

Accusative plural common 4-*i* (two examples), 4-*i-a*, to be read 4-*za*, 4-*za-a* (see 3.2.2.) = **mawī*^{n}*za*?

3.4.3.1. Discussion

The numeral sign "4" has also the phonetic values *mi, ma*, which have been derived from the numeral according to the acrophonic principle. The value *mi* agrees with Hitt. *mieu-, miu-*; since it is already attested in the time of the Great Kingdom, it could derive from the Hittite numeral (?). With due caution, notice should be taken of a possible phonetic variant **muwa-* indicated by WOMAN – M 129 4-*tà* (= [1 +]3-*tà* according to a brilliant suggestion of Mittelberger's in Meriggi 1962: 85) 'woman's power' i. e. 'weakness'; the word is in opposition to M 129 *mu-wa-a-tà-na* '(man's) power'; for the passage, see Meriggi (1967: 67 f.); for the realia see also Goetze, *Verstreute Boghazköi-Texte* (1930: 24 I 28 f.).

3.4.4. Miscellaneous forms derived from stems studied in 3.4.1.—3.4.3.

3.4.4.1. Accusative singular common *mawalli-* XXXI 66 IV 14 (Laroche 1959: 70), in reference to a horse, perhaps 'belonging to a four-in-hand' (?). The word is obviously of Luvian origin.

3.4.4.2. Hitt. (?) *mi-u-wa-ni-ya-an-t-* and *mu-u-wa-n*[*i-ya-an-t-*] (of horses), perhaps 'harnessed in fours' (??), according to a suggestion by Kammenhuber see *HW* 2 *Ergänzungen* (1961: 18). The alternative, that there is a connection with a higher numeral derived from "four" ('forty, four hundred', something like 'accomplishing a distance of four hundred measuring units'), which comes to mind because of the Lycian type *kbisñtãta, nuñtãta* (ending *-nta*), does not seem applicable.

3.4.4.3. Luvian *ma-a-wa-ni-in-ta* (Kammenhuber 1961: 152) can be the Luvian or luvianizing correspondent of *miuwaniyant-*. The textual surroundings perhaps contain further related expressions, but the beginnings of the lines are lost: x̣ *ta-aš-ta-a-ri-in-ta* 2 *ME gipeššar* '... *taštārinta* (**ta-* "double" at the beginning of the word?), two hundred ells' and [X]x-*an-ti-in-ta* 3 DANNA 'x (containing "three" in the lost beginning?), three miles', then finally our [X 4 ?? DAN]NA *māuwaninta* '[x 4 ?? mi]les *māuwaninta*'.

3.4.4.4. Hieroglyphic Luv. 4-*su-u* 'four times' (?); see Meriggi (1962: 165); cf. 3.2.9.

3.4.4.5. Hitt. 4-*iahh-*, 4-*iahhahh-*, see 3.3.6.4.

3.4.4.6. Hitt. 4-*iš*, see *HW*, 303.

3.4.5. The Hittite ordinal and related material

The words earlier included here (*HW*, 303) must now in part be assessed differently. For LÚ*duianalli-*, see 3.2.8.; for 4-*na* (*IBoT* II 91 III 9, before it III 5, 7 3-*ŠU*, meaning ± 'a fourth time'?) and 4-*in* (*KBo* V 2 II 61; *KBo* XI 14 II 15; *KBo* XIII 145 o.? 3'), cf. 3.3.3.2.1.

3.4.6. Hittite *kutruwan-* 'witness'

This form, originally an -*n*-stem, secondarily also -*a*-stem, is, according to what has been said in 3.3.4., to be analysed as *k^w*tru-(y)ó-n-* or as *k^w*tr̥w-(y)ó-n-*(?) 'the fourth'. It is a derivative formed by means of a suffix -*o-* or -*io-* to the zero-grade stem of the cardinal *k^w*tru-* (cf. Greek τρυφάλεια, Avest. *caθru-*, Latin *quadru-*); a protoform without the metathesis of *w* and *r* but with dissimilatory loss of the *w* perhaps also calls for consideration (*k^w*-twr̥-wó-n-* > *k^w*tr̥-wón-*).

This etymology poses an interesting phonological problem. The descendants of Indo-European labiovelars (before consonant and word-boundary) are generally not written plene in Hittite; at all events in the checking of about a thousand passages for forms like *ku-na-an-zi* 'they strike', *ku-ra-an-zi* 'they cut', *e-ku-zi* 'drinks', *tak-ku* 'if', *ne-ku-ma-an-za* 'naked', I could not detect a single plene writing. All but one of the examples of *kutruwan-* — and its derivatives — conform to this rule too; nevertheless there occurs *KBo* IV 4 IV 7 (late tablet) the writing *ku-u-ut-ru-wa-a-iz-zi* 'he declares it before witnesses' (Friedrich 1959: 56f.). In my view, this isolated plene writing is on a par with *KUB* VI 46 I 39 *i-iš-ta-ma-aš-ša-du* 'they shall hear' (apart from this the prothetic vowel *i* is never written plene — in hundreds, indeed perhaps thousands, of examples). Just as, because of this isolated spelling, a derivation of *ištamaš-* from a protoform beginning, not with *st-*, but with *ist-* or *eist-* has little to recommend it, so can the writing *ku-u-ut-* not be adduced as an argument against a protoform *k^w*t-*. On the other hand, in my view, it proves the existence of a pronunciation *kut-* (instead of or beside k^w*t-*) just as well as the spelling *i-iš-ta-ma-aš-ša-du* decides the question of the phonological reality of the prothetic vowel in the positive sense (to add Friedrich 1940–46: § 24); against the assumption of plene writings of unpronounced vowels, cf. 3.3.1.4. According to a view often presented, the labiovelars are however preserved as consonants (monophonematically) in Hittite — see, above all, F. O. Lindeman, *Revue hittite et asianique* lxxvi (1965: 29–32). This view may be supported by writings such as *e-*

uk-zi 'drinks', *e-uk-ta* 'drank', *e-uk-ši* 'you drink' (*KBo* XXII 1 o. 28), which are occasionally to be encountered; from the variation *e-uk-zi* ~ *ekuzi* etc. we assume a phoneme k^w (written KU, UK). This conclusion is however not certain, for the variation of the *eukzi* ~ *ekuzi* cases may be based on the differing position of an anaptyctic vowel (*taruhzi* 'defeats' ~ *tarhudu*, see *HW*, 123; from this first, *tarukzi* ~ *tarkuzi* 'dances', from the root *terk*^{w}- 'to turn oneself'; then *eukzi* ~ *ekuzi*), cf. secondary *me-uh-ni* (VIII 21, 8, thus to be read in my view) against *me-hu-ni* from *mehur* 'time' — the assumption of spelling mistakes, confusion of the signs KU and UK, etc., would be very improbable for these cases). On the other hand the fixed points for the phonological disintegration of the labiovelars (*watkut* 'jumped' from the root *tek*^{w}-; *kuiš* < *kwiš* < *k^w*is* 'who?', 3.2.10.3.), which have been little considered in the discussion so far, are really hard to discount; in addition, the form *kūtruwāizzi* 'he declares it before witnesses' would come as a further argument. It cannot however be passed over in silence that, as an alternative, a pre-Anatolian postulate with schwa secundum (*$k^w{}_e$*tru-*) also comes into question, just as, for instance, it is unavoidable for Latin *quadru-*. The reflex of the schwa secundum as *u* is conditioned by the vicinity of the labiovelar (*$k^w{}_e$*t-* > *k^w*ut-*, in the event further to *kut-*); cf. Greek κύκλος < *$k^w{}_e k^w$*los*, etc.; for the assimilatory labialisation of secondary vowels in Hittite, cf. my suggestions put forward in *MSS* xxxi (1973: 76). And, too, whichever of the two alternatives (*k^w*t-* or *$k^w{}_e$*t-*) one decides on, the consequences for the phonology are, in each case, considerable.

For prehistoric Anatolian we thus obtain the following word-range: the two contracting parties before a court are denoted by one word, which survives in Hitt. *hannitalwan(a)-* (? word formation); the judge functions as an impartial third, **teriyan-* (altered to **teriwan-*), and, as 'fourth', the witnesses, **kutruwaneš*, are brought in. Thus it is clear how the difference in the nomenclature as against Latin *testis* came about.

C. H. Carruthers, *Language* ix (1933: 152) first proposed the etymology of Hitt. *kutruwan-* presented here; he also discussed the semantics: "If the judge is considered as a major party in the case, he will normally be the *third* person present, and the witness, when called, will obviously be the *fourth*" (in addition a very improbable semantic hypothesis, going back to Sturtevant, was given as an option). Carruthers was certainly wrong in the matter of the word formation, for he lets "Hitt. *kutrus*" derive from "*q^u*tru*"; as we know today, the stem *kutru-* (instead of *kutruwan-*) is secondary in Hittite; further, PIE *k^w*tru-* belongs to the cardinal, not the ordinal, and could also not be used as nominative in the ablaut-grade attested. Despite this misconception, the sharp rejection which Carruthers' suggestion has experienced, on the part of H. Pedersen *Archív orientální* v (1933: 178) and Benveniste (1962: 110) ("H. Pedersen a fait justice de ces fantaisies") is not justified at all.

Pedersen's connection of *kutruwan-* with Lith. *gudrùs* 'clever, cunning, wily' can now be dismissed. The Lithuanian word was perhaps secondarily altered from *gudras* to a *-u-*stem; in its turn, *gudras* may be a relatively late Baltic innovation as could be formed at any time, which then would have little relevance for comparative reconstruction (*gudrùs* must be viewed ultimately as derivative of *gùsti gundù* 'be accustomed, obtain experience' (Fraenkel, *Litauisches etymologisches Wörterbuch* 1, 1962: 141).

3.5. The Anatolian numerals 'five' and their derivatives

3.5.1. Hittite data

These data are extremely scanty. Synopsis of the material:
3.5.1.1. Cardinal. 5-*az* (?), see 3.2.1.4.; it is not clear whether there is a phonetic complement in *KBo* XX 67 III 15 f.
3.5.1.2. Ordinal and related material. (5̣?)-*in* *KBo* XI 14 II 15, see 3.3.3.2.1. (probably syncopated from *5-*yan*); 5-*an* VIII 62 IV 8' (?); 5-*an-na* XVII 1 II 7' 'and/but (-*a*) for the fifth time'; 5-*na* *KBo* V 2 III 1 'and the fifth', see 3.2.3.2.; 3.3.3.2.1.; not clear: MU.3.KAM (5̣)-*ia* ITU-*mi* *Bo* 6828 IV 9 (dative ending or -*ia* 'and'?).
3.5.1.3. 5-*an-k*[*i* X] *KBo* XXII 79 line 1'; see also *HW*, 303.
3.5.1.4. 5-*li-eš* XXXVI 89 o. 5' 'containing five units of measure' (of loaves) (?); see *HW* 1 *Ergänzungen* (1957: 30).

3.5.2. Hieroglyphic Luvian data

The forms are written with the numeral sign "5" with phonetic complements.

Acc.sg. 5-*wa-sà-pa-* (before a consonant) 'fivefold' (?); 5-*na-a* can be a shorter writing for this (see Meriggi 1962: 165, where taking a clear stand is avoided – probably intentionally. Cf. however Meriggi 1966: § 108 n. 2).

If, with Meriggi (1966: § 108), a suffix *-apa-/-api-* (or *-aspa-/-aspi-* too, possibly even *-asampa/i-*) is assumed, the initial bit 5-*w(a)-*, shows a word that, in its final, can be compared with PIE **pénk^{w}e*; **pa^{n}ku* would be expected.

3.5.3. Hittite *panku-*

A discussion of the suggestion that Hitt. *panku* 'whole, all, totality, generality, etc.' should be connected with PIE **pénk^{w}e* can be omitted here, for, according to this suggestion, Hitt. *panku-* would not be the reflex of a Proto-Indo-European numeral, but merely that of a root from which, in Proto-Indo-European, a numeral had been derived. See E. C. Polomé, *Pratidānam. Indian, Iranian and Indo-European studies presented to Franciscus Bernardus Jacobus Kuiper on his sixtieth birthday* (1968: 98 ff.), and N. van Brock, *Mélanges de linguistique et de philologie grecque offerts à Pierre Chantraine (Études et commentaires* LXXIX) (1972: 266 f.).

3.6. The Anatolian numerals 'six' and their derivatives

3.6.1. Hittite data

3.6.1.1. Cardinal. 6-*az* (?) 617/p II 11'; see 3.2.1.4.
3.6.1.2. Ordinal and related material: (6̣?)-*an* VIII 62 IV 17'; 6-*an-na-za* XVIII 1 II 9' 'and for the sixth time' (= 6-*ann* + -*a* + -*za*); 6-*na KBo* V 2 III 2 'and/but the sixth', see 3.2.3.2.; 3.3.3.2.1.

3.6.2. Cuneiform Luvian data

(6̣?)-*un* (??) *KBo* XI 145 II 11-3 (ter, Laroche 1959: 125); reading of the numeral in all three cases uncertain, emendation to (9̣)!-*un* should be considered.

3.7. The Anatolian numerals 'seven' and their derivatives

3.7.1. Hittite data

The forms are written with the numeral-sign "7" with phonetic complements.
3.7.1.1. Cardinal. 7-*an* ~ UH_4-*an* XXVII 29 I 28'; *KBo* XI 11 II 5 f. *ki-e-iz 7-an pa-ah-hur ki-e-iz-zi-ya* (6) *7-an pa-ah-hur pa-ri-ih-hi* 'one the

one side I kindle seven fires and on the other side seven fires'; 297/d V 4' f. *nu 7-an 7-an an-da iš-hi-iš-kán-z*[*i* X] (5') *nu iš-hi-ya-tar* AN.TAH.ŠUM^SAR *i-ya-an*[*-zi* X] 'they bind seven at a time onto it and make a bundle from A.-plants' (?); 7-*az* 617/p II 11'; see 3.2.1.4. The complementation 7-*an* could point to **se*/*iptan*-. Phonologically this phonetic form could not go back to PIE **septm̥* (*-*m̥* > -*un*, proved by the first person singular preterite of the athematic verbs), but possibly to **septm̥t*-. The final -*an* could also have been taken over from other numerals, for instance from "10", where a Proto-Indo-European form **dḱm̥t*- 'decad' beside **déḱm̥* '10' is well attested (Old Church Slavonic locative *desęt-e*, etc.; see Pokorny 1959: 191). It would thus present a problem similar to that of Germanic "7" (Gothic *sibun*, etc., with preserved -*n*). On the other hand 7-*an* can belong to the -*nt*-stem; because of the examples just given ('seven here' ... 'seven there', 'seven at a time'); I would give preference to this possibility.

3.7.1.2. Ordinal and related material. 7-*an-na-za-kán* XXVII 11 II 11' 'and/but for the seventh time' (7-*ann* + -*a* + -*za* + -*kán*); 7-*na KBo* V 2 III 3 'and/but the seventh'; perhaps Hitt. **šiptama*- or **šiptamiya*-.

3.7.1.3. 7-*an-ki* XXXIII 105 I 5'–8' (quater).

3.7.1.4. 7-*iš KBo* XVII 50 r (?) 5' (tablet in old ductus); perhaps = *7-*ankiš* (?).

3.7.2. Hittite *šiptamiya*-

šiptamiya KBo V 1 IV 35 in alternation with 7-*miya* (discussion of the examples, 3.3.3.3.), as the name of a drink, is a derivative of an original ordinal **šiptama*- < **sebdmó*- (or from a secondary, but perhaps still Proto-Indo-European, **sebdm̥ó*-), or, more probably, **septmó*- (**septm̥ó*-), with *pt* analogically restored from the cardinal (Hittite writing with TA, not DA). For the semantics, see 3.3.3.3. The attempt, often undertaken, to infer a cardinal **šiptam* on the basis of *šiptamiya* (e. g. Kronasser 1962–66: 365; also *HW* 303, with a question-mark) represents a gross error; a Hittite word, as is well-known, cannot end in -*m*. Every attempt to wish to see in *šiptamiya* an intra-Hittite derivative of the cardinal comes to grief because of the regularity of the sound change -*m* > -*n* (also in -*m̥* > -*un*).

If *šiptamiya* is anachronistically expressed by a Proto-Indo-European formula, **septmeyo*- (**septm̥eyo*-) or **septmiyo*- (also **septm̥yo*-?) would result. In the first case the Old Indian type *dvi-maya*- 'containing the double, consisting of something in two parts out of three' (Wackernagel,

Altindische Grammatik, 1896–1957: II/2, 770, with literature; *-maya-* in my view by "suffix-extension" from *-a-ya-* would be comparable). In the latter case *-iyo-* would be a Sievers variant of the suffix *-yo-*; the suffix traditionally postulated as *-iyo-* can be disregarded, as Hitt. *-iḫḫa-* (*-iH₂o-*) should correspond to it (perhaps attested in 9-*AḪ-ḫa* = 9-*iḫ-ḫa*?, 3.9.1.5.). Typologically perhaps the Roman name *Septimius* is comparable.

In **septmiyo-*, *i*-umlaut would probably occur (cf. **mélit* > Hitt. *milit* 'honey'), but the writing of the initial with the sign ŠI (instead of ŠE), which occurs only once, can be otherwise explained, and can hardly contribute anything to the decision of the question of the word formation.

A further indirect piece of evidence for the Hittite ordinal is probably present in the Cappadocian female PN *ša-áp-ta-ma-ni-ga* (Laroche 1966, No. 1111), which can be interpreted as 'the seventh (*šaptama-*) sister (*niga-*)'. Cf. G. Neumann in: M. Mayrhofer et al. (eds.), *Gedenkschrift H. Güntert* (1974: 279). Above all it is the vocalism of the first syllable that remains obscure (dialectal sound-change *e* > *a* or assimilation to the vowels of the following syllable ?).

3.8. The Anatolian numerals 'eight' and their derivatives

3.8.1. Hittite data

The forms are written with the numeral sign "8" with phonetic complements.

3.8.1.1. Cardinal. 8-*ta-aš* XXXI 143 II 1.8 etc. (E. Laroche, *JCS* i, 1947: 205 f.), probably, rather an *-nt*-stem than a direct reflex of PIE *H_2*oḱtó-*.

3.8.1.2. Ordinal. 8-*na KBo* V 2 III 7 'and/but the eight'.

3.8.1.3. 8-*anki KBo* XXI 90 o. 11 'eight times'.

3.8.1.4. 8-*iš* (4-*ŠU* follows) 913/z IV 6'.

3.8.2. Hieroglyphic Luvian data

The writing is with the numeral sign "8" with phonetic complements (Meriggi 1962: 165). 8-*wa-a-ī* = ± 8-*ua^{n}zi/a*. Etymological attempts lead to the reconstruction of **hak?taua^{n}zi* (??), which implies a **haktau* (derived from PIE *H_2*oḱtṓu*) carried over into the plural. Thus the dual ending *ōw*, which would be hard to explain on the basis of the laryngeal theory, is, for the first time, required by Anatolian; perhaps PIE **ōw* goes back to earlier *oH_1w* (**w* would be a deictic particle, cf. Vedic *u*).

On the other hand the Hieroglyphic Luvian form could be influenced by the numeral "9", see 3.9.1.
3.8.3. Hitt. 8-*in-zu* in the passages given *HW*, 303 is not clear.

3.9. The Anatolian numerals 'nine' and their derivatives

3.9.1. Hittite data

The forms are written with the numeral sign "9" with phonetic complements.
3.9.1.1. Cardinal. Dat.sg. 9-*an-ti happešni* 'to/on the nine limbs' *KBo* XXI 14 o. 13'; 9-*an-ti-ma* KASKAL-*ši IBoT* II 128 r. 5', see 3.9.2.3.; abl.sg./pl. 9-*za KBo* XIII 109 II 3'; gen.pl. 9-*aš* XXXVI 89 r. 4 (see V. Haas, *Der Kult von Nerik*, *Studia Pohl* IV, 1972: 150 f.); dat.pl. 9?-*an-da-aš happešnaš šer* 'on the nine limbs' *Bo* 2533 I 23; 9-*aš* (?) *KBo* XVII r. 7'; XXXVI 49 I 9', 89 r. 4 (?).
3.9.1.2. 9-*an*: – *KBo* XI 10 II 17'; 72 III 28; *KBo* XII 70 II 11', 16'; *KBo* XIII 94 line 4'; *KBo* XVII 1 I 9' (typically old ductus); 88 III (?) 9' (bis); *KBo* XX 59 line 15'; *KBo* XXI 14 o. 8'; Goetze, *Verstreute Boghazköi-Texte* (1930: 58 IV 12'). Several passages are enigmatic; in others, a form of the cardinal could be present (3.9.1.1.), e. g. *KBo* XII 70 II 11'. The meaning 'ninefold' (*HW* 303), too, would fit some passages, e. g., *KBo* XI 72 III 28; Goetze, *Verstreute Boghazköi-Texte* (1930: 58 IV 12').
3.9.1.3. Ordinal. 9-*na KBo* V 2 III 8' 'and/but the ninth'; (9̣?)-*ti*-(*mạ*?) MU-*ti* XXXIII 120 I 12 'but in the ninth year'. The second example could contain the cardinal, if, in dates, the construction 'in the year 9' should also be possible; then we should not have to postulate the coexistence of base-stem and -*nt*-stem for the ordinals, too. An analogical argument applies to *BdU* II 60 E (*IBoT* II 128 r. 5') 9-*an-ti-ma* KASKAL-*ši* 'but at the ninth time'.
3.9.1.4. 9-*al-li-uš Bo* 5149 line 7 (Sommer 1948: 206 n. 1), 9-*li* 9/y line 5', 654/z line 2'; here perhaps also 9-*iš* VII 17 line 12' (*9-alliš ?). Not clear: 9-*at* = 9-*la*! (?), see *HW* 1 *Ergänzungen* (1957: 30) (against it Kronasser 1962–66: 365).
3.9.1.5. 9-*AH-ha KBo* XXI 14 o. 8' [X] x̣ 9-*an* 9-*AH-ha iš-pí-ir-te-en* ('... ye have spread out'), for the construction cf. *KBo* XIII 94 line 4' 9-*an* 9-*an-ki še-eš-zi* ('... he sleeps (with?)'). For the assessment of a form

9-*ah-ha*, see 3.2.1.3. The reading 9-*ih-ha* too is possible (theoretically further 9-*uh-ha*), for the morphology, see 3.7.2.
3.9.1.6. 9-*an-ki* *KBo* XIII 94 line 4' 'nine times' (3.9.1.5.).
3.9.1.7. 9-*iš* VII 17 line 12' (see 3.9.1.4.).

3.9.2. Luvo-Lycian data

The Luvo-Lycian forms are (*)*nunzi/a*, (*)*nuwanzi/a*.
3.9.2.1. Cuneiform Luv 9-*un-za* (Laroche 1959: 125); see also 3.6.2. ((9̣?)-*un*?).
3.9.2.2. Hieroglyphic Luvian material (Meriggi 1962: 165; *HH* I, no. 395):

> 9-*ī* or *nu-ī*, to be read as 9-*za/i* or *nu*^{n}*za/i*.
> 9-*wa-a-ī*, to be read as 9-*wa*^{n}*za/i* or *nuwa*^{n}*za/i* A 13 d 4

(according to Laroche; non vidi).
The numeral sign "9" (nine vertical strokes) has the phonetic value *nu*.
3.9.2.3. Lycian *nuñtãta*. This numeral of unknown meaning is obviously derived from the word for "nine" ('19', '90', '190', '900'?). If, in Lycian, single nasal after *u* and before consonant vanishes without trace (**unt* > **ũt* > **ut* (denasalized]), as is to be expected on the basis of parallelism with *i* (**int* > **ĩt* > **it*, e. g. in 3 pl. *tubeiti* 'they strike' 57,8; 59,3; 88,5; 101,4), *nuñt-* must be derived from **nunant-*, just as *miñti* from **mina-nt(i)-* (-*nt*-formation to *mina-*, cf. Hieroglyphic Luv. TOWN *mina-* 'town'). The Lycian -*nt*-stem **nunant-* (possibly syncopated from **nu-wanant-*) or **nunanti-*, which is then to be assumed, can be directly equated with Hitt. 9-*ant-* (3.9.1.1.).
The material points to a Proto-Luvo-Lycian cardinal **nuwan* or **nun*, which, in Luvian, secondarily acquired plural endings.
The etymological connection with PIE **newn̥* (variant **enun* > Arm. *inn*) is evident, but the phonological derivation remains unclear. Perhaps the old ordinal **newnó-*, which would have given Proto-Anatolian **nuná-*, influenced the phonetic form of the cardinal. However, anyone who wants to maintain the direct derivation from **newn̥* can point to the variants *muwaniyant-* and **muwa-* from 3.4.4.1. and assume the development **néwn̥* > **newən* > **newun* (this state approximately Proto-Anatolian) > **naun* > **nun* (with secondary monophthongisation, cf. the suggestion **meyu-* > **mau* > **mu* from 3.4.1.2.3.).

3.10. The Anatolian numerals 'ten' and their derivatives

3.10.1. Hittite data

The writing is with the numeral sign "10" with phonetic complements.
3.10.1.1. Cardinal. Instr.sg. 10-*an-ti-it kalulupit* 'the ten fingers' *KBo* XVII 32 line 12' (relatively old ductus).
3.10.1.2. Ordinal. 10-*na* *KBo* V 2 III 9 'and/but the tenth'.
3.10.1.3. 10-*an-ki* *KBo* I 42 I 40' 'ten times'.
3.10.1.4. 10-*pa* XXXIII 87 I 36' approximately 'tenfold' (adv.), see H. G. Güterbock, *Journal of Cuneiform Studies* vi (1952: 12f.); for the formation-type 3.10.2. and 3.5.2. are perhaps to be compared (Meriggi 1966: 59).
3.10.1.5. 10-*iš*, see *HW*, 304; cf. 3.9.1.7.
3.10.1.6. 10-*li-iš* VII 29 I 12; XXXII 123 II 14'; 10.ÀM-*liš* XLI 36 II? 4; *KBo* XXI 1 I 4 2 NINDA.GIDIM 10-*iš* 2 ^{NINDA}*mar-ki-iš-sar* 10-*li* 2 NINDA.ERÍN^{MEŠ}10-*iš* perhaps points to a paradigm common nom. 10-*iš*: neuter nom.acc. 10-*li*.

3.10.2. Hieroglyphic Luvian data

For acc.sg. 10-*ha-sà-pi-na*, as well as 10-*ta*, both something like 'tenfold', see Meriggi (1962: 165). For the initial sequence 10-*h*-, 2-*AH-hi*, 3.2.1.3., and 9-*AH-ha*, 3.9.1.5., should be compared.

3.11. The Anatolian numerals 'twelve' and their derivatives

3.11.1. Hittite forms

3.11.1.1. ERÍN^{MEŠ}-*an* 12-*an* 148/r line 7'.
3.11.1.2. 12-*iš*, e. g., *KBo* XI 36 V 8 1 ^{NINDA}*pi-ia-an-ta-al-li-iš* 12-*iš*.
3.11.1.3. Higher numeral: *LI-IM-aš* KUR-*e-aš* XXXI 142 r. 4 'of a thousand countries'.

3.11.2. Cuneiform Luvian forms

Instr. 12-*ta-a-ti*, see Laroche (1959: 125); very probably an -*nt*-stem.

3.12. Derivatives of higher numerals

3.12.1. Hittite forms

3.12.1.1. 15-*anki*, 20-*anki* 'fifteen times', 'twenty times', see *HW*, 304.
3.12.1.2. 15-*iš* (e.g. *KBo* XVII 14 line 4', typically old ductus), 20-*iš* (*KBo* XVII 100 IV 3'; *KBo* XX 3 r. 9'); 25-*iš* (*KBo* XVII 29 I 7', old ductus); 30-*iš* (e.g. *KBo* V 5 r. 9'); 40-*iš* (e.g. *KBo* XVII 100 IV 2'); 50-*iš* (e.g. *KBo* XX 3 o. 14'; 21 o. 9'; *IBot* II 93 line 3'); *ŠU-ŠI-iš* (968/z, left col. K 7'); 70-*iš* (*KBo* XX 3 o. 14'; VII 17 line 15'); 80-*iš* (*IBot* II 93 line 4'); 90-*iš* (VII 17 line 14'); the formation-type probably belongs to one paradigm with 2.12.1.3., cf. 3.9.1.4.
3.12.1.3. 20-*li-eš* (XXXVI 89 o. 5); 30-*li* (e.g. *Bo* 2309 III 15); 30-*li-eš* (XXXVI 89 o. 5); 70-*la* (?) VIII 72 o. 7; the enumeration XXXVI 89 o. 5 3 NINDA.KUR$_4$.RA 5-*li-eš* 20 NINDA.KUR$_4$.RA 20-*li-eš* 20 NINDA.KUR$_4$.RA 30-*li-eš* suggests that here indications of size are given in the form of fractions; obviously smaller baked goods are produced in a greater number than big ones (cf. also the passages cited in 3.1.1.9.). As a consequence 20-*alli-* is to be interpreted as '(containing) a twentieth (of a particular unit of weight)'. The same type of word formation is present as in the case of *teriyalla*, 3.3.3.3.

3.13. Numerals of unknown meaning

3.13.1. Miscellaneous Lycian numerals

Several Lycian numerals elude an identification of their meaning (cf. Neumann 1969: 394).
3.13.1.1. *kbisñni* 26,17 and *trisñmi* 26,18; 44b, 45 (both times beside *wawã*). It has been suggested that these are multiplicatives, distributives, or the like. Also the meanings 'twenty', 'thirty' (H. L. Stoltenberg, *Die termilische Sprache Lykiens*, 1955) or 'twelve', 'thirteen', are not entirely excluded. Analysis: *kbi* ('second', 'for the second time'?) / **tri* ('third', 'for the third time')? + *-sñn* + ending. The forms might be derivatives (note the suffix *-sñ* in, e.g., *trm̃misñ*) or compounds. In the latter case a connection with PIE **dék̂m̥* (> **tesñ*, with syncope > **tsñ* > Lycian **sñ*??) should be considered.
3.13.1.2. *aitãta* 102, 3. The beginning of the word may contain "one" or "once", a meaning 'ten', 'eleven', 'one hundred ten' should perhaps

be considered. The sequence *it* can have developed phonologically from **ind* (**ind* > **indd* > **ĩt* > **it*). The form is to be analyzed either as a derivative by means of the collective suffix Proto-Anatolian *-and-* (< PIE **-n̥-d-*) to the *-nt*-stem **aiti-* (equivalent to **oye-nt-i-*), thus something like **ay(n)tay-and-a*, or a compound **ain(t)-dayant-a* (**deḱont-ə₂??*).

3.13.1.3. *kbisñtãta* 111, 3.4. Meaning: probably in the area 'twelve', 'twenty', 'one hundred twenty' or 'two hundred'. Analysis: *kbisñ* (3.13.1.1.) + **dayant-a* (< **deḱont-ə₂??*) or *kbi-* + **sñtãta*, in which case *-sñtãta* is either a compound **sñ-dãta* (**déḱm̥ *deḱont-ə* ??) or an *-and-* collective formation (plural ?) to *sñta* (5).

3.13.1.4. *nuñtãta* 131, 3. Meaning in the area 'nineteen, 'ninety' or 'one hundred ninety' (Neumann 1969: 394 'ninety'?). "9" is contained in the beginning of the word – see 3.9.1.3.; for further analysis, see 3.13.1.2.3.

3.13.1.5. *sñta* 112,6; 149,9. The meaning is something like 'ten' or 'hundred'. *sñta* could be interpreted as a descendant of PIE **ḱm̥tóm* (> **sñtñ*, then secondarily altered to *sñta* after other numerals??), or as a derivative to **sñ* (3.13.1.1.). J. E. Rasmussen, *Haeretica indogermanica* (*KDVS* XLVIII.3 1974: 56 n. 15) points out that *sñta* is "in all probability a loan-word from Persian *sada*" and therefore "not diagnostic for the assignment of the labels *satem* and *centum*".

3.13.1.6. It is not clear whether the following Lycian words belong to the designations of numbers: *tupm̃me* 57,6; *trppeme* 109,5; *mupm̃me* 149,14; 57,4 ff. serves as the point of departure for the determination of the meaning: *sei pijẽtẽ* (5) *pijatu : miñti : ẽtri : χupu : siχli : aladehχχãne : se hrzzi* (6) *tupm̃me siχla* 'And for the town authority (??) he has ordered as an order: the lower grave-chamber for one shekel (dative singular) *aladehχχãne* (infinitive) and the upper for *tupm̃me* shekels'. Since the interpretation of E. Torp (*Lykische Beiträge*, 1853–1916: ii, 25) of *tupm̃me* as 'two each' and that of W. Deecke (*Lükische Geschichten und Sagen*, 1852) as 'double' (criticised by Torp) do not quite satisfy from the realia point of view, it would be preferable to think of $2 \pm \frac{1}{2}$ and correspondingly for *trppeme* and *mupmme* as $3 \pm \frac{1}{2}$ and $4 \pm \frac{1}{2}$ respectively. The upper grave-chamber is the more valuable one (cf. Friedrich 1932: no. 36).

tusñti 44a, 12 (meaning 'twelve' because of δώδεκα c 22?) could perhaps be adduced for **tu-* 'two' (with syncope of a vowel, < **dwo* or **dwi*). The suggestion that *tusñti* is 'twelve' has recently received noteworthy support in that E. Laroche, *Fouilles de Xanthos* V (ed. P. Demargue) (1974: 146) has recovered a part of the destroyed context with the aid of a newly-found fragment. Line 44 a 12 now reads *ñte* *ma[h]ãnaha : tusñtiti*[, with which the correspondence a 12 *ma[h]ãnaha tusñti* (with a form of adj. *mahãnahi* 'divine; of the gods') to c 22 δώδεκα θεοῖς is evident. So Laroche, *Les noms des hittites* (1966: n. 41) himself offers the following thought: "N'avons-nous pas ici le nom de nombre 'douze' en lycien? On rapprochera d'une part, les δώδεκα θεοῖς de c 22, d'autre part, le nom de nombre *sñta*. D'où *tu-sñti* '2 + 10'; le thème *tu(i)*- est connu par **twi*- donnant *kbi* ..., et *kbisñtata* [sic] serait non pas '200' mais '20', proprement 'deux dizaines': *sñtata* [sic] dérivé en *-at-* [sic] de *sñta/i-* '10' ". Already W. Deecke and S. Bugge, *Lykische Studien* (1897: i, 50) had taken *tusñti* to be a form of a numeral (*tu-sñta* '200'), to which P. Meriggi (*Germanen und Indogermanen. Festschrift für Herman Hirt, IB* III.15, 1936: ii) energetically raised objections. In the meantime O. Carruba has produced a detailed account of the determination of the Lycian numerals in an article entitled "I termini per *mese, anno* e i numerali in Licio", (*RIL* cviii 1974: 575–97, especially 583–93). For the cardinals he reaches the results *sñta* 'one', **tuwa-* 'two', **tri(ja)* 'three', *teteri* 'four', *aitãta* 'eight', *nuñtãta* 'nine', *tuweri* 'twelve'; for the other numerals, inter alia, *tupm̃me* 'second' (?), *kbisñni* 'di due anni', *trisñni* 'di tre anni'. I cannot agree with his system. For instance *teteri* 'four' is falsified by the newly-found trilingual from the Letoron of Xanthos, which shows that it has the meaning 'city', see E. Laroche, *RFil* cxvii (1965: 119).

3.13.2. Cuneiform Luvian data

For the sake of completeness I would like to mention Cuneiform Luv. *ta-aš-ta-a-ri-in-ta*; see Kammenhuber, *Hippologia Hethitica* (1961: 152 f.) with Note a. "Für t., falls luvische Entsprechung zu 200 (Ellen), fehlt es an vergleichbarem Material für Hunderter aus dem Hethitischen".

3.14. On the diverse numeral categories in Anatolian

3.14.1. Cardinals

As a consequence of a Common Anatolian innovation, it seems that an *-nt*-stem existed beside the basic form throughout the cardinals. It is therefore not possible to determine whether the plain cardinals from "5" onwards were in part indeclinable as in Proto-Indo-European. The complete phonetic form of a cardinal is known only in the case of Hitt. *ãnt-*

(?) 'one', Hitt. *teri-* 'three', Hitt. *mi(e)u-* 'four', Cuneiform Luv. *mau(wa/i)-* and also Hieroglyphic Luv. *tu-wa-i* 'two' (something like (*d/tuwa*^{n}*za/i-*) and Hieroglyphic Luv. 9/*nu-ī*, 9/*nu-wa-a-ī*? 'nine' (something like *nu*^{n}*za/i, nuwa*^{n}*za/i*).

As far as can be seen, the cardinals are, in their entirety, inherited from Indo-European. An exception in the case of the word "1" is probably based on the fact that here no true cardinal existed in the parent language. In the case of "4", the counting term **méyu-* – probably already in existence in Indo-European –, possibly completely eliminated the cardinal **k*^{w}*etwóres*, in its turn originally a counting-word too. The most important indication for this lies in the phonetic value of the Hieroglyphic Luvian numeral sign "4"; the Hittite and Cuneiform Luvian examples occur under such conditions that a special collective terminology could be present.

In several instances phonetic complements of numerals written only with numeral signs fit the reconstructable descendants of Proto-Indo-European cardinals, as in the cases of "5" and "8" in Hieroglyphic Luvian, "9" in Cuneiform Luvian, and "7"(?) in Hittite.

3.14.2. Ordinals

For 'first', we find in Hitt. *hantezzi(ya)-*, Cuneiform Luv. *hanteli-* and Lycian **χñtewe-*(?), Anatolian innovations independent of the cardinal. In the case of 'second', the Anatolian languages show a split: in Hittite the descendant of PIE **doyó-* 'twofold, double' (with various derivatives) was used; cf. Hitt. *tā, t/dān, takiya, t/damai*. Luvo-Lycian employed a derivative of the stem **dwi-* (**dwi-o-* or **dwi-yo-*), Luvian (sic) *duianalli-*, Lycian B *tbi*, A *kbi*. Lydian apparently used for 'second' the descendant of PIE **alyo-*, see R. Gusmani, *Lydisches Wörterbuch* (1965: 56) (*aλa*). For 'third' there seems to have been a uniform Anatolian formation ($^{+}$*tri-o-* or $^{+}$*tri-io-* ⟶ **triyo-* > Proto-Anatolian **tariya-*), which appears in Hitt. *teriya-* (with *e* from the cardinal) and Luvian **tarriya-* (with *rr* from the cardinal); Hieroglyphic Luv. *tariwana-* 'arbitrator' (⟵ 'third') is a reshaped derivative. An old term for 'fourth' survives, I think, in Hitt. *kutruwan-* 'witness'; the normal ordinal seems however to have been a *-ya*-stem.

An inspection of the Marburg Hittite Thesaurus shows clearly that the Hittite ordinals in *-anna*, which have hitherto been assumed (Friedrich 1940–46: i § 133*b*) do not exist; see 3.2.3.2., 3.3.3.2.1., 3.5.1.2., 3.7.1.2.

3.14.3. Multiplicatives, etc.

With respect to such forms, the Anatolian languages are widely divergent. For the meaning '*n* times', Hittite uses formations with the suffix *-ki* (also in *mašiyan-ki* 'how many times, how often?'), which, together with Greek -κι can be taken back to PIE **ḱi* (taken by itself Hitt. *-ki* is also derivable from **gi/ǵhi*, even, less probably, from **ke/ḱe*). The variant, Hitt. *-kiš*, Greek -κις, is due to an assimilation to the type **dwis* 'twice, twofold'. We know the complete phonetic form of a Hittite multiplicative adverb only in the case of *ānki* 'once'. In the meaning 'for/at the *n*th time' several possible expressions were available: the unextended nominative-accusative singular neuter of the ordinal (*t/dān, teriyan*) was used adverbially; for clarification the dative sg. (!) *pedi/pidi* to *pedan* 'time, turn' could be added (this use should be listed *HW*, 168). Furthermore Hitt. *palši* could appear in the meaning 'times', e. g. *hantezzi palši* 'at the first time'. Whether in 9-*anti* KASKAL-*ši* (probably = *palši*) 'for the ninth time' a cardinal or an ordinal is used must remain an open question. *hantezzili* 'for the first time' and *āšma* 'first, at first, for the first time' are outside the fixed series of formation. For further details, see the discussion in 3.1. The group of multiplicative expressions needs still further investigation.

In Luvo-Lycian, formations with the ending *-su* (**s-wé*) are usual, note Hieroglyphic Luv. 3/*tari-su*, 4-*su*, Lycian B *tbisu, trisu,* A *kbihu.* The interpretation '*n* times' has unfortunately not hitherto been rendered certain. Hitt. 1-*ŠU*, 2-*ŠU* etc. can – contrary to Merrigi (1966: 59) – have nothing to do with this type, for the complement is Akkadian, as clearly follows from the graphic variation *ŠU/ŠÚ* (1-*ŠÚ*, e. g. *KBo* II 4 I 4).

Hitt. 9-*an*, 10-*pa* (adverb) and Hieroglyphic Luv. 5-*was(am?)pa-* and 10-*has(am?)pi-* appear to occur in the meaning '*n*-fold'. In Lycian this value is perhaps to be assigned to the class B *tbiplẽ trpplẽ.*

3.14.4. Fractions

In the meaning 'half, a half', Hittite had the innovation *takšan*. Otherwise nothing is known for certain. Some *-lli*-formations appear either to be themselves fractions or derivatives based on fractions (which are then probably to be equated with the simple ordinal); see 3.3.3.5., 3.11.1. In Hittite the connection of whole numbers with fractions could be expressed by means of addition, for which I know of only one certain example: VII 24 I 2 1 *še-kan* ½*še-kán-na* 'one-and-a-half spans'. For Lycian, I would assume compound formations, see 3.12.1.1.

3.14.5. Some other numeral formations

In the meaning 'of the first rank' we have Hitt. *hantezzi(ya)-*, 'of the second, third rank' Hitt. *dān pedaš*, and, of Luvian origin, *duianalli-* and *tarriyanalli-*. The *-nt*-derivatives of the basic numeral (3.14.3.) appear in part to have complex meanings (9-*ant-* 'a complex of nine parts'). In place of the distributives there were perhaps in Hittite iterated groups (1-*aš* 1-*aš*, 1-*an* 1-*an*, 7-*an* 7-*an*). The formations in *-hh-* are not yet quite clear, but they are obviously of the greatest importance for the historical grammar of the Anatolian languages; see 3.9.1.5.

Note

1. The siglum *KUB* is left out in the case of volume-numbers above 7; thus "XIII 4 III 5'" means *Keilschrifturkunden aus Boghazköi*, vol. 13, tablet 4, column 3, line 51.

References (major titles)

ABOT
Ankara Arkeoloji Müzesinde bulunan Boğazköy tabletleri = T. C. Milli Eğitim Bakanlıgı Eski Eserler ve Müzeler genel Müdürlüğü Yayınlarından III.3.

Benveniste, Emile
1962 *Hittite et Indo-Européen (= HIE) (p. 78–87: Formation de quelques numéraux)* (Paris: Maisonneuve).

Ehelolf, Hans
1929 "Hethitisches *tri* und *si/epta* = 'drei' und 'sieben'", *Orientalische Literaturzeitung* 32, 322–328.

Friedrich, Johannes
1926–32 *Staatsverträge des Hatti-Reiches in hethitischer Sprache,* vols. I–II *(Mitteilungen der Vorderasiatisch-Aegyptischen Gesellschaft* 31.1–34.1) (Leipzig).
1940–46 *Hethitisches Elementarbuch,* 1. Teil: *Kurzgefasste Grammatik* (§§ 129–134 *Zahlwort*) (2nd edition, 1960 = HE I²). (Heidelberg: Winter.)

1952 *Hethitisches Wörterbuch* (= *HW*), with three additional volumes (= 1., 2., 3. *Erg.*), published in 1957–1966 (Heidelberg: Winter).
1959 *Die hethitischen Gesetze (Transkription, Übersetzung, sprachliche Erläuterungen und vollständiges Wörterverzeichnis)* (Leiden/Köln: Brill).
1966 "Eine neue Art hethitischer Zahlwörter?", *Festschrift Pagliaro*, II: 139–140 (Roma).

Goetze, Albrecht
1933 *Die Annalen des Muršiliš (Mitteilungen der Vorderasiatisch-Aegyptischen Gesellschaft* 38) (Leipzig).
1935 "Hittite *šanna* – 'one' ", *Language* 11, 185–190.
1949 "Hittite *šani/a, šannapili*", *Archiv Orientální* 17/1, 288–297.

Güterbock, Hans G.
1957 "Lexicographical notes", Revue hittite et asianique 60, 1–6.

Hrozný, Bedřich
1917 *Die Sprache der Hethiter (Boghazköi-Studien* I, 92–96: *Zahlwörter)* (Leipzig).

IBoT
Istanbul Arkeoloji Müzelerinde bulunan Boğazköy tabletlerinden seçme metinler: I *T. C. Maarif Vekilligi Antikite ve Müzeler Müdürlüğü Yayınlarından III.i;* II *T. C. Milli Egitim Bakanlıgı Eski Eserler ve Müzeler Genel Müdürlüğü Yayınlarından III.ii;* III *T. C. Maarif Vekaleti Eski Eserler ve Müzeler Genel Müdürlüğü Yayınlarından III.5.*

Kammenhuber, Annelies
1971 "Heth. *haššuš 2-e ekuzi* 'Der König trinkt zwei' ", *Studi Micenei ed Egeo-anatolici* 14: 143–159.

Kronasser, Heinz
1956 *Vergleichende Laut- und Formenlehre des Hethitischen (= VLFH), Numeralia* (Heidelberg: Winter).
1962–1966 *Etymologie der hethitischen Sprache (= EHS)* (p. 361–362: *Zahladverbia;* p. 362–365: *Zahlwörter*) (Wiesbaden: Harrassowitz).

Laroche, Emmanuel
1959 *Dictionnaire de la langue louvite (= DLL)* (Paris: Maisonneuve).
1960 *Les hiéroglyphes hittites* I (= *HH* I) (especially p. 203–205) (Paris: Centre National de la Recherche Scientifique).

Meriggi, Piero
1936 "Der Indogermanismus des Lykischen", *Festschrift Hirt* II, 257–290 (especially p. 266–268) (Heidelberg: Winter).
1962 *Hieroglyphisch-hethitisches Glossar,* 2nd edition (= Glossar^{2}) (especially pp. 164–166) (Wiesbaden: Harrassowitz).
1966–1967 *Manuale di eteo geroglifico (= Manuale),* I (1966) (pp. 58–59: *Numerali*), II (1967) (Roma: Ed. dell' Ateneo).

Neu, Erich
1974 *Der Anitta-Text* (Wiesbaden: O. Harrassowitz).

Neumann, Günter
1969 *Lykisch. Handbuch der Orientalistik* I.II, 1/2, 2 (= *HdO Lykisch*) (§ 32: *Zahlwörter*) (Leiden/Köln: Brill).
Pedersen, Holger
1948 *Hethitisch und die anderen indoeuropäischen Sprachen* (pp. 51–54: heth. *damaiš* griech. δᾶμος) (København).
Pokorny, Julies
1959 *Indogermanisches etymologisches Wörterbuch*, 2 vols. (Bern/München: Francke).
Soden, W. von
1965–1981 *Akkadisches Wörterbuch*. Unter Benutzung des lexikalischen Nachlasses von Bruno Meissner (1868–1947), bearbeitet von W. von Soden, vols. 1–3 (Wiesbaden: Harrassowitz).
Sommer, Ferdinand
1932 *Die Ahhijavā-Urkunden (Abhandlungen der Bayerischen Akademie der Wissenschaften, Philosophisch-historische Abteilung, N.F.)* (München: Bayerische Akademie der Wissenschaften).
1948 "Hethitisch [LÚ]duianalli-", *Indogermanische Forschungen* 59/2; 205–207.
1951 *Zum Zahlwort (Sitzungsberichte der Bayerischen Akademie der Wissenschaften, Philosophisch-historische Klasse)* (München: Bayerische Akademie der Wissenschaften).
Sommer, Ferdinand – A. Falkenstein
1938 *Die hethitisch-akkadische Bilingue des Hattušili* I/*Labarna* II /*Abhandlungen der Bayerischen Akademie der Wissenschaften, Philosophisch-historische Abteilung)* (München: Bayerische Akademie der Wissenschaften).
Sturtevant, Edgar Howard
1951 *A comparative grammar of the Hittite language* (New Haven).
Szemerényi, O.
1960 *Studies in the Indo-European system of numerals* (s. *Index* p. 183: *Hittite*) (Heidelberg: Winter).
1970 *Einführung in die vergleichende Sprachwissenschaft* (s. pp. 204–211: *Das Zahlwort*) (Darmstadt: Wissenschaftliche Buchgesellschaft).
Watkins, Calvert
1961 "Anatolian evidence on a Germano-Slavic isogloss: Past passive participles in *-*e/ono*- and the Hittite ordinal", *International Journal of Slavic Linguistics and Poetics* 4; 7–12.

Note

Further references have been given in the text. I have not been able to consult Kellogg, *Hittite numerals*, mentioned by Sturtevant in *Language* 4 (1928: 6 fn. 2). Citation and abbreviations follow *HW* and *Linguistic Bibliography*.

Chapter 4
Tocharian

Werner Winter

4.0. Introductory remarks

In the following pages, I will try to present a fairly complete survey of the field of Tocharian numerals; gaps in our knowledge prevent the coverage from being truly exhaustive. Wherever possible and useful, reference will be made to the texts, with first preference given to published ones. In case of ample attestation, special attention will be paid to the inclusion of dialectal variants.

The principal emphasis will be on the presentation of forms and on their interpretation in a Tocharian context, with attention paid wherever possible to a discussion of the Indo-European background as I see it. In those cases where competing hypotheses exist in the literature, I will adduce interpretations other than those which I consider acceptable by way of a brief reference unless I feel that a detailed discussion is warranted by the facts. It cannot be avoided that my approach, as obviously that of others, will show a certain amount of personal bias; but as my evaluations have been made against the background of a fairly long tradition of etymological work in the field of Tocharian, it seems reasonable to hope that they may turn out to be more than just subjective. It goes without saying that my preferences will show wherever new proposals are offered.

As sources of information about previous studies, three recent books by van Windekens (1976, 1979, 1982) are of considerable value; the author's original proposals, as well as his assessment of the work of others, should, however, be used with much caution and under no circumstances be taken at face value.

Since quite a few uncertainties in matters of detail still have to be removed, I find it necessary to give preference to the interpretation of individual forms and their derivatives within Tocharian rather than try to embark upon attempts at reconstructing possible Proto-Indo-European systems or subsystems. Whatever Tocharian evidence may contribute to such a discussion, is best relegated to the general chapter of this book.

4.1. Cardinal numbers

4.1.0. The numerals 'one' through 'four' are inflected for gender (except for 'two' in Tocharian B and 'four' in Tocharian A). 'One' is also inflected for number.

Case forms are also found of some higher numerals; genitives show plural ending in B (*piśants-o* 'of five', *oktaṃts* 'of eight'), singular ending in A (*oktis*), but the latter is not surprising in view of the fact that in plurals with nominative and accusative identical, genitive singular A *-is* is quite common beside genitive plural A *-śśi*, and A *okät* 'eight' occurs both in the nominative (A 366 b 4) and the accusative (A 236 a 2).

4.1.1. 'One'

4.1.1.0. The paradigms of 'one' in Tocharian B and A are:

			Masculine	Feminine
B	Singular	nominative	*ṣe*	*sana*
		accusative	*ṣeme*	*sanai/somo*
		genitive	*ṣemepi*	
	Plural	nominative	*ṣemi*	*somona*
		accusative	*ṣemeṃ*	*somona*
		genitive	*ṣemeṃts*	*somonaṃts*
A	Singular	nominative	*sas*	*säṃ*
		accusative	*ṣom*	*ṣom*
		genitive	*ṣomāp*	
	Plural	nominative	*ṣome*	*ṣomaṃ*
		accusative	*ṣomes*	*ṣomaṃ*
		genitive	*ṣomeśśi*	

The feminine nominative singular form B *somo*, listed in Krause – Thomas (1960: 158) and discussed in considerable detail in van Windekens (1976: 415, 1979: 276, with thoroughly wrong conclusions about allegedly parallel items), is a ghost form wrongly extracted by Sieg – Siegling (1949: 48, 187) from B 29 b 1 (where *somo* does not modify the following nominative *ytārye* 'path', but is merely cited as the first part of the compound *somwaiñyai* 'ekāyana'; the following *somo* is best interpreted as an adverb – cf. B *ysomo* 'all in one').

4.1.1.1. A very detailed analysis of earlier proposals, combined with new ones of his own, is in Jörundur Hilmarsson's study of the Tocharian paradigms of 'one' (Hilmarsson 1984); the following remarks overlap to a large extent with Hilmarsson's findings.

Even a mere inspection of the sets of forms for 'one' in Tocharian B and A shows that a reconstruction of Common Tocharian forms can be achieved only by an elimination of language-specific innovations. The major discrepancies are:

a) the difference in the forms of the masculine nominative singular, B *ṣe* vs. A *sas*;
b) presence vs. absence of initial palatalization in feminine forms such as A *ṣomaṃ* : B *somona*;
c) the contrast between B *-e-* and A *-o-* in forms such as B *ṣeme* : A *ṣom*.

4.1.1.2. While B *ṣe* and A *sas* cannot be directly matched, there is a form for 'one' that agrees in every detail with B *ṣe* to be found in the bound variant of A *sas* as it occurs in A *śäk ṣapi* 'eleven'. The numerals A *śäk wepi* 'twelve' and *śäk täryāpi* 'thirteen' contain clear nonmasculine forms of 'two' and 'three'; hence it is reasonable to assume that A *ṣa-* is a reflex of the old neuter nominative-accusative PIE **sem* as represented by Gk. *hén*. B *ṣe*, in its turn, is also to be identified as derived from the neuter, and not the masculine, nominative of the Proto-Indo-European cardinal 'one'; generalization of the neuter, and not the masculine, form recurs in B *wi* 'two', but only in this language and not in A.

It is thus only A *sas* that is to be compared with Gk. *heîs* and to be derived from a Proto-Indo-European nominative singular masculine form **sem-s*.

The absence of initial palatalization in A *sas* poses no problem; it can be explained as the result of an assimilation process as found reflected in A *säksäk* 'sixty' (cf. 4.1.16.1.) or, *mutatis mutandis*, in the demonstrative nominative masculine singular A *säs* beside the nominative-accusative neuter A *täṣ* (cf. Pedersen 1941: 116).

B *-e-*, A *-a-* in B *ṣe*, A *ṣa-*, A *sas* require a special explanation in view of the fact that the normal continuation of PIE **e* is (palatalizing) B A /ə/. Attempts to posit an underlying form with a Proto-Indo-European lengthened grade have little in their favor; in particular, a lengthening in the unmarked neuter form is hardly to be expected. Instead, a special reflex of PIE **e* in old monosyllables may be assumed on the strength of B *śem* 'he came' : Skt. *ágan*.

The forms of the second stem of the masculine in B and A cannot be derived directly from the consonant stem of 'one' as found in the forms of the nominative singular. The second stem contains formations based on a thematic stem. If one were to consider B *ṣeme* a regular development from such a stem, one would have no alternative but to derive it from a hypothetical Proto-Indo-European form **sēmo-m*. It would be part of an adjectival paradigm of the type found in B *astare* 'clear', as indicated by B *ṣemi* and *ṣemeṃ*. Precisely the same comments apply to A *ṣom, ṣome, ṣomes*. A replacement of the regular correspondence pattern B *e* : A *a* by B *e* : A *o* in the position before (morphophonemically) heterosyllabic *-m-* is limited to such cases where B *e*, A *a* derive from old long vowels (cf. B *ñem*, A *ñom* 'name', B *emalle*, A *omäl* 'hot', as against B *keme*, A *kam* 'tooth', A *nam* 'reverence'); both A and B forms support the reconstruction of a Common Tocharian form with a long vowel in the first syllable.

It is desirable to be able to decide whether such a form is to be taken to be a reflex of PIE **sēmo-*, or whether it is a Common Tocharian thematicization of the athematic nominative singular stem with its lengthened vowel developed in the monosyllabic form. As there are no outside parallels to support a Proto-Indo-European **sēmo-* 'one', it seems best to give preference to the assumption of an intra-Tocharian development, hence to the second alternative just given.

The last discrepancy to be explained is that listed above under (b). Here the suggestion by Hilmarsson (1984: 145) applies, that leveling reduced earlier diversity. If the analysis given for the second stem of the masculine is correct, the forms of the feminine can be said to contain the second stem of the masculine, too, in the case of A; in B, initial **ṣ-* as found in B *ṣe, ṣeme* would then have been replaced by the onset of the feminine nominative singular *s-*. As a result, the B paradigm shows greater consistency in the feminine, but the original agreement found between masculine singular and feminine (formerly: neuter) plural has been eliminated.

4.1.1.3. The forms of the nominative singular of the feminine, B *sana*, A *säṃ* (*snā-* in A *snāki* 'alone' cf. 4.3.5.), plus the feminine accusative singular form B *sanai*, have provoked a great deal of controversy. The co-occurrence of a feminine nominative singular B *-a* and a feminine accusative singular B *-ai* is extremely common in adjectives (cf. Krause – Thomas 1960: 144 – 158) in forms which are clearly to be interpreted as containing the suffix B *-ya* < PIE **-yA*. It would thus be only natural to propose equating B *sana*, A *säṃ* directly with Gk. *mía* < PIE **sm-yA*; the proposal has indeed been made repeatedly (cf. Hilmarsson

1984: 138). One difficulty, however, remained: a replacement of a sequence **-my-* by (unpalatalized) *-n-* is somewhat surprising, and one would like to have this sound change demonstrated to have occurred not only in the form in need of explanation. A parallel, which has so far been overlooked, seems indeed to exist: The Tocharian A term for 'earth, ground' is *tkaṃ* (B has reduced *keṃ*), a form which is to be compared with Gk. *khthṓn*, etc. (cf. Pokorny 1959: 414–416); Greek and Tocharian share the loss of labiality in the stem-final consonant, a loss which must have originated in the nominative singular. Greek has, however, a number of forms in which the paradigmatically conditioned change **m > n* did not occur – cf. *khthamalós* 'lowly', *khamaí* 'on the ground', etc. In Tocharian A, a word of unknown meaning (cf. Sieg–Siegling–Schulze 1931: 111 fn. 3) is found in two nearly identical passages, which should be considered in our context. We note A *tkani* in

A 400 a 6 *tkani top trāṅk kl.||*
400 a 7 *|| top trāṅk tkani nkäṃsanträ*

It is not clear whether A *trāṅk* '?', found only in this text, can be connected with B *troṅk*, A *truṅk* 'cave' (one would have to assume membership in quite different morphological classes), but the idea is tempting in view of the fact that A *top* (B *taupe*) has the meaning 'mine'. The two nouns then would denote two different types of hole in the ground. If so, an interpretation of A *tkani* as an adjective derived from A *tkaṃ* 'ground' would be quite natural: a 6 would read 'a mine in the ground (and) a cave(?)', a 7 'a mine (and) a cave(?) in the ground, they perish'. A derivation of A *tkani* from the secondary *-n-* stem as found in attested A *tkaṃ* is most unlikely in view of a form such as A *ṣāmañi* 'monastic' : A *ṣāmaṃ* 'monk'.

The natural equation of B *sana*, A *säṃ* with Gk. *mía*, Arm. *mi* can thus be maintained, the only difference between the Tocharian form on the one side and the Greek and Armenian ones on the other being that they seem to represent two Sievers-Edgerton variants: **$s_o$myA* > B *sana*, A *säṃ* : **sm$_o$yA* > Gk. *mía*, Arm. *mi*.

4.1.1.4. The question whether B *somo* or B *sanai* is the more archaic form for the feminine accusative singular, can be answered as follows: As pointed out above, an accusative in B *-(y)ai* is extremely common alongside a nominative in B *-(y)a*; the pattern B *-ya* : *-o* recurs in one single adjective, viz., B *allek* 'other' – here the nominative singular of the feminine is B *alyāk*, the accusative, B *allok*. As a matter of general principle, one will always want to consider a recessive pattern a more likely candidate for greater antiquity than a dominant one; hence, B *sanai* should be an innovation.

The *-o-* in B *somo*, as in B *somona* and *somonaṃts*, is due to umlaut caused by the following *-o-*, itself a regular reflex of PIE *-*ā*- (cf. Hilmarsson 1984: 144).

4.1.1.5. The numeral 'one' occurs before noun forms in one of three combinations:

a) Both the numeral and the noun have the shape of free forms: there is number, gender, and case concord (the latter limited by the characteristics of "group inflection").
b) The numeral has the shape of a free form; there is gender concord (the problem of number selection will be taken up in 4.1.21.1.); the noun in second position does not have the stress marking which occurs in free forms.
c) The numeral deviates in shape from the free form which may be expected to occur preposed to a particular noun; the noun itself deviates in stress from its free form.

The combination described under (a) is that of a noun phrase with a numeral as its first element. Combinations (b) and (c) may be said to represent two degrees of composition, both with an elimination of free-form status for the second (nominal) element. To permit concise formulations in the later discussion, a combination (b) will be referred to as a "juxtapound", a combination (c), as a "compound". It goes without saying that an identification of a specific combination type will be possible only in those cases where graphic properties of a sequence of lexemes provide the necessary information.

An example of a compound in the narrow sense is B *ṣeñemnats* (FY 3 b 1) 'of those (illnesses) having one [and the same] name' (cf. Bernhard 1958: 184); for a free form of 'one' to combine with the feminine plural B *ñemana** it would have to be B *somona*. While the B form for 'one' used in this compound is that of the neuter nominative-accusative (which is identical with the nominative singular masculine also in other adjectives – cf. B *kartse* 'good', nominative masculine and nominative-accusative neuter vs. B *krent* accusative masculine), a bound form of the accusative singular masculine is found in A *ṣomapācär* 'having one [and the same] father'. The difference in the first members of the compounds may reflect an old difference between neuters and nonneuters. If so, one would have to recognize spread of the nonneuter form in A *ṣomaṣärpāṣluneyum** 'pointing [only] to one [thing]'. If A *ṣomakälyme* 'in one direction [only]; to the exclusion of everything else', a compound in the narrow sense, provides strong enough arguments for assigning its equivalent B *somo+kälymi* (B 630 a 6) to category (c) and not to (b), one would have to note gender agreement in (c) forms, too. In this case, B *somotkäññe* 'uniformly' (cf. Thomas 1952: 27) would have to be interpreted as derived from a noun in second position with feminine gender (*/tə́ke/?). B *ṣeme+yärm* 'to one [and the same] extent', B *ṣeme+ykne* 'in one [and the same] manner', B *ṣeme+pälsko* 'of one mind', however, all of which should be old neuters, would reflect a state of affairs where the singular had been reinterpreted as a masculine. In view of the difference between B *ṣe+ñem* and B *ṣeme+yärm*, it seems advisable to include the latter type in category (b); whether B *somo+kälymi* should be given the same interpretation after all, has to be left open.

In order to distinguish between the categories proposed, it seems advantageous to use different transcriptional conventions. Obviously, the free forms in (a) should be separated by a blank. For (b), the use of a hyphen seems indicated, for (c), one-word rendering. In this way, the bound-form status of the second element in B *ṣeme-pälsko* would be underlined, yet the different nature of the combination of 'one' and 'father' in A *ṣomapācär* would not be obscured.

4.1.2. 'Two'

4.1.2.0. The forms attested are:

B *wi* (*wi*), used for both masculine and feminine;
A masculine *wu*, feminine *we*.

4.1.2.1. A *wu* derives from the Proto-Indo-European masculine form **dwōw* (cf. Skt. *dváu*; note also A *oktuk* 'eighty', for which 4.1.18.1. is to be compared). An identification with the Proto-Indo-European variant **dwō*, as proposed of late by Hilmarsson (1986: 155–156), seems unlikely in view of B *-e* found in the dual marker, which can hardly have an origin other than PIE *-*ō* (cf. Winter 1962: 127), and of B *e-* : A *a-*/*o-* in such forms as B *epiṅkte* : A *opänt** 'inbetween' (cf. Winter 1983: 322).

A *we* obviously reflects a Proto-Indo-European diphthong. If A *we* and B *wi* are developments from a single Common Tocharian item, the underlying form cannot have contained PIE **a* (as assumed by Pedersen

1941: 76 and reasserted by van Windekens 1976: 585), since PIE **-ay* should have resulted in B *-ai*. Instead, the source has to be late PIE **-oy* (absence of palatalization, plus the development of A *-e*, precludes PIE **-ey*). One difficulty remains: in a monosyllabic word one would have expected the diphthong to be preserved as such in B – note the dual form B *tai* of the demonstrative. The only explanation that occurs is that B *-i* may have been reduced from **-ai* under the influence of B *antapi* 'both', that is, of a multisyllabic construct.

4.1.2.2. For A *wu* (used both as a nominative in, e. g., A 353 b 6, and as an accusative in, e. g., A 150 b 6), a second stem *wun-* is found not only in the univerbal ablative case *wunäṣ* (A 108 a 5), but also in the postpositional phrase A *wun-yo* (A 3 a 4). A *-n-* will be discussed in 4.2.2.2.

Whether the translation of Sieg–Siegling–Schulze (1931: 197) for the passage A 186 a 3, which contains the only attestations of A *weśäl* ('je zu zweien aufeinander gestützt'), is correct, remains doubtful: the word is not a well-formed comitative (cf. Sieg–Siegling–Schulze 1931: 135) – hence it might be better to disregard A *weśäl* in the present context.

4.1.2.3. In compounds of 'two', B *wästo-* (*wasto*), A *wäst* are found in lieu of B *wi* and A *wu, we* (cf. 4.3.2). In juxtapounds, B *wi-* occurs in B *wī-ykne* 'twofold' and *wi-dhatuṣṣe** 'of two dhātus' (cf. Bernhard 1958: 209); it is well-attested in forms for 'two hundred' (cf. 4.1.21.0.), 'two thousand' (cf. 4.1.23.0.), and 'twenty thousand' (cf. 4.1.25.1.). It is also to be noted in the accusative plural B *wi-pewaṃ* 'bipeds'; see also 4.1.4.3. for the comparable term B *śwer-pewä* 'quadruped'.

In A, the feminine (formerly: neuter) form *we* is incurred in A *śäk wepi* 'twelve' (cf. 4.1.11.1.), *wiki wepi-* 'twenty-two' (in the ordinal, cf. 4.1.12.4.), *taryāk wepi* 'thirty-two' (cf. 4.1.13.3.); note that in the digit *we* is used even if the noun modified is a masculine (cf. A 151 a 2, if correctly supplied by Sieg and Siegling). *we-* is also found in the juxtapounds A *we-känt* 'two hundred' (cf. 4.1.21.0.), *we-wälts* 'two thousand' (cf. 4.1.23.0.), that is in forms which are likely to derive from old neuters; hence here the use of A *we-* may be primary and not due to generalization as in A *śäk wepi*, etc.

4.1.3. 'Three'

4.1.3.0. The forms attested are:

masculine B *trai*, A *tre*;
feminine B *tarya* (*täryā-*), A *tri* (*täryā-*).

4.1.3.1. In spite of the overt similarity with forms such as Gk. _treîs_ and Skt. _tráyaḥ_, the masculine forms B _trai_, A _tre_ cannot directly reflect PIE _*treyes_ (this would have yielded Common Tocharian _*trəyə_); they are best derived from a blending of a descendant of PIE _*treyes_ and one of PIE _*troyo-_; the former would account for the consonant stem, the latter, for the vocalism of the first syllable. OCS _troji_ provides a parallel (cf. van Windekens 1976: 513); even closer is Russ. _troe_.

The feminine reflects the neuter (collective) form PIE _*tryA_ (cf. Gk. _tría_, Skt. _trī́_, etc.) in its Sievers-Edgerton variant _*t_{o}ryA_; in view of the general replacement of feminine plural forms by collective ones in Tocharian adjectival paradigms, there is no need to have recourse to Proto-Indo-European feminine forms.

4.1.3.2. B _tarya_ is found inflected, or extended by postposition, when used in phrase-final position. Examples are: genitive _taryaṃts_ (B 170 b 1), _täryānts-o_ (B 251 b 5); ablative _täryyāmeṃ_ (B 275 b 6); instrumental _tarya-sa_ (B 543 b 5).

4.1.3.3. In A, the unreduced equivalent of feminine _tri_, A _täryā-_, occurs only in the digits of higher numerals: A _śäk täryāpi_ 'thirteen', A _wiki täryāpi-_ 'twenty-three' (in an ordinal, cf. 4.2.12.3.).

Forms with an onset A _tri-_ should be classified as juxtapounds and not as compounds in the narrow sense (cf. 4.1.1.5.). It is to be noted that just like A _we-_ in the forms cited in 4.1.2.3., A _tri-_ combines with a singular of the second element in the construct: 'three times' is A _tri-lkwär_ (A 222 b 3), 'three ways' is A _tri-wkäṃ*_, 'three garments', A _tri-wsāl*_ (cf. Bernhard 1958: 210). 'Three hundred' is unattested, but 'of three thousand' occurs as A _tri-wältseṃ_. The proposal by Bernhard (1958: 209) to render A _tri-ñemi_ by 'jewel triad' is quite persuasive; an intra-Tocharian formulation, however, would have to be content with a statement that while there is number concord in nominal phrases that include a numeral, there is none in juxtapounds.

Bernhard (1958: 210) offers parallels from B to the type A _tri-wsāl_ 'triad of garments', among them the equivalent of the A term, B _tarya-wassi_. This form is identifiable as a member of category (b) by virtue of its opening with the free form B _tarya_ and not with bound B _täryā-_ and of its showing lack of number concord.

Genuine compounds, and not juxtapounds, are to be recognized in items like B _täryāyäkne_ 'threefold' and possibly – unless the unpublished Berlin text is of extreme MQ type – in B _täryakänte_ 'three hundred'.

It is tempting to speculate whether the juxtapound and compound forms without number concord reflect an old state of affairs where nonsingular marking was suppressed in position after a numeral higher than 'one' (a situation which would find its parallel in Armenian), or whether in configurations denoting inseparable groups of two, three, etc., entities, singular number of the entire construct reflected its unitary character.

4.1.3.4. One B text, of Western origin contains two rather curious forms with 'three' as their first element. In B 148 a 1 and B 148 b 1 Skt. *trisaṃndhi* is rendered by B *treyameskem*, in B 148 a 2 Skt. *trayāśraya* is translated by B *treyasaim*. *treya-* might be interpreted as a compounding form of B *trai*, with stressed /ə/ appearing as *-a-*. What remains troublesome is that B *saim* 'protection' is an old neuter, and one would expect to find B *tarya* combining with it. B *meske* is masculine, so that B *treyameskeṃ* could readily have replaced a phrase **trai meski* 'three connections'. To be sure, no plural is attested for B *saim*, but it seems only natural to view this word as the reflex of an old **-mn-* stem, hence a neuter, and one would not think that a phrase that could be taken to underlie B *treyasaim* would have contained nonneuter B *trai*. It seems hard to avoid the conclusion that at least B *treyasaim* is due to a mistake on the part of the scribe or the translator.

4.1.3.5. An adjective A **treyo** 'threefold', identified by Sieg (1952: 15) does not exist; A *tre yo* is nothing but a postpositional phrase with the masculine form of 'three', which in A 67 b 3 fully agrees with the masculine gender of A *āṅkari* 'tusks' (note als Krause—Thomas 1960: 158).

4.1.4. 'Four'

4.1.4.0. The forms found are:

B: masculine *śtwer* (*śwer*); feminine *śtwāra* (*śwāra*), in bound forms: *śtwarā-*;
A: masculine/feminine *śtwar*, in bound forms: *śtwar-*.

B forms with an onset *św-* are usually of Eastern origin.

4.1.4.1. B *śtwer* and probably also A *śtwar* can be equated with Arm. *č'ork'* and, if Brugmann's law applies, Skt. *śatvāraḥ*. B *ctwāra*, if derived by *-a-* umlaut from a Common Tocharian form with a long vowel before **-r-*, is to be compared with Goth. *fidwor*, Skt. *catvāri*. Contrary to what van Windekens (1976: 489 and elsewhere) believes, B *-a-* in this form cannot be taken to be a direct reflex of PIE **-ō-*.

No explanation can be given for the use of A *śtwar* in the role of a feminine; one would have expected to have an A **śtwār* match B *śtwāra*.

4.1.4.2. No case forms of 'four' have been preserved. B *śtwerne*, which is listed by Thomas – Krause (1964: 248), van Windekens (1976: 489) as a locative, requires a different explanation. If days of the month are numbered (as in B 435.3 and B 588 b 3), this is done by way of an elliptic construction. This is indicated by the fact that in B 433.11, 14, 15, 20, 21, etc., we find the postposition *-ne* 'in' seemingly used as a free form after a genitive; yet, postpositions occur in B (and A) only after an accusative. Hence, the formula B *wi meñantse ne* in B 433.11 is to be interpreted as a conventionalized abbreviation of B *wi meñantse* (*kom*)-*ne* 'on (day) two of the month'. This interpretation should also apply to numbers of days of the month above 'ten', where B *meñantse* 'of the month' is omitted, as, e. g., in B *śak ṣuk-ne* (B 455.2) 'on the seventeenth', *ikäṃ ṣuk-ne* (B 459.5) 'on the twenty-seventh'; note also B *śäk śtwer-ne śäk piś-ne* 'on the fourteenth and fifteenth' in B 588 b 3.

4.1.4.3. All combinations of 'four' and a second lexeme in A have to be classified as juxtapounds and not compounds as A *śtwar-* is identical with the free form A *śtwar*; note A *śtwar p*^{u}*kul* (written as two separate words!) 'quadrennium', *śtwar-pāk* 'in four parts', etc. Even where one would have expected to find a bound form on the strength of items with A *täryāpi*, the free form of 'four' prevails: 'sixty-four' is A *säksäk śtwar-pi*.

In B, both compounds and juxtapounds have survived: a bound form of 'four' is found in B *śtwarāyäkne* (*śwarāykne, śwaraikne*) 'fourfold', free forms occur in B *śtwer-meñ-tsa* 'for a period of four months', *śwer-pewä* 'quadruped' and B *śtwāra-känte* 'four hundred'.

4.1.5. 'Five'

4.1.5.0. The forms attested are B *piś* (*pīś*), A *päñ*.

4.1.5.1. Both the B and the A forms derive from PIE **penk*^{w}*e*; cf. Gk. *pénte*, Skt. *páñca*, etc. B *pi-* is the regular development of Common Tocharian **p'ə-* and so is A *pä-* (cf. B *pīle*, A *päl* 'wound'). Loss of a nasal before a spirant recurs in B *mīsa* 'meat'; the B form thus can be considered fully explained. In A, though, one would have expected to find **päñś**; a possible explanation for the loss of *-ś* may be that a simplification of the sequence **-ś ṣ-* occurred in rapid counting bringing **päñś* 'five' and *ṣäk* 'sic' into immediate adjacency. The suggestion that the A form may have been influenced by the second stem of the A ordinal, viz., A *päñc-* (van Windekens 1976: 361) suffers from the difficulty that in those cases where a cardinal was in all likelihood reshaped after the ordinal (cf. 4.1.6.1., 4.1.12.1.), it was the first stem of the ordinal that was replicated.

4.1.5.2. No case forms of A *päñ* can be found. The genitive (with plural ending as in 'three', cf. 4.1.3.2.) is attested in B in several variants: B *piśäts* in B 255 b 6; B *piśants-o* in B 5 b 6; *piśats* has been supplied for B 173 a 1 by Sieg and Siegling. For B *piś ne* (B 447.3) cf. 4.1.4.2.

4.1.5.3. Of possible combinations with 'five' as first member, only juxtapounds, and not compounds, are attested. From A, the following examples may be cited: *päñ-känt* (A 4 a 5) 'five hundred', *päñ-wälts* (A 255 a 4) 'five thousand', *päñ-tmāṃ* (A 295 b 2) 'fifty thousand', *päñ-wäknā* (A 345 b 3) 'fivefold'. Juxtapounds from B are: *piś-känte* (B 400 a 2) 'five hundred', *piś-iltse-mpa* (B 398 a 1) 'with five thousand', *piś-yäkne-sa* (B 11 b 7) 'fivefold', *piś-cmelṣeṃ* (B 220 a 1) 'those of the five births', *piś-antseṣṣai* (B 168 frg. e) 'pertaining to the five skandhas'.

4.1.6. 'Six'

4.1.6.0. The forms found in the texts are: B *ṣkas, ṣkass, ṣkass-o, ṣkäs, ṣkäss*; A *ṣäk, ṣäkk*.

4.1.6.1. The form corresponding to Lat. *sex*, etc., must have been subjected to cluster alleviation by shwa insertion in Proto-Tocharian times. In this process, PIE **seḱs*, one of the more wide-spread variants of 'six', became PToch. **s'əkəs*. This form should have lost its final consonant, with a result that is clearly reflected in A *ṣäk*. In the corresponding ordinal, CToch. **šəkəstV-* yielded, quite regularly, A *ṣkäṣt*, B *ṣkaste*. It seems likely that B *ṣkas* came into existence instead of expected B **ṣäk** by a removal of the ordinal marker B *-te* from the ordinal form. The argumentation found in van Windekens (1976: 450) can be disregarded.

4.1.6.2. Of inflected forms, a genitive (with plural ending) B *ṣkässaṃts* is found in B 173 a 3.

4.1.6.3. B *ṣkässaṃts* may be taken as an indication that in compounds B *ṣkas* should be replaced by **ṣkässa-* (or **ṣäksa-*), with *-a-* for /ə́/. Hence, the following forms have to be classified as juxtapounds: *ṣkas-känte* 'six hundred', *ṣkas-yiltse* 'six thousand', *ṣkas-tmane* (B 3 b 1) 'sixty thousand'. In B 3 b 1, *ṣkas* is separated by virāma writing from the following lexeme, hence identified as a free form; the second lexeme, however, is characterized by absence of stress-marking as a bound item. These facts serve to illustrate rather neatly the intermediate status of juxtapounds between phrases of free forms and univerbal compounds.

Outside the domain of higher numerals, a matching pair of juxtapounds is found in B *ṣkas-yäkne-sa* : A *ṣäk-wäknā* 'sixfold'.

4.1.7. 'Seven'

4.1.7.0. The A form is *ṣpät* throughout; in B, variants are found: *ṣukt, ṣūkt, ṣukt-o, ṣuk* – with the latter occurring outside of juxtapounds only in Eastern texts.

4.1.7.1. As in the case of 'six', the A form for 'seven' is a regular reflex of a Proto-Indo-European item: A *ṣpät* corresponds neatly to Gk. *heptá*, Skt. *saptá*, Lat. *septem*, all descended from PIE **septṃ*. The B forms pose problems. B *-kt*, to be sure, may be ascribed to the influence of B *okt* 'eight' (cf. van Windekens 1976: 461, with references; the additional speculations offered are of no value). As to the origin of B *-u-*, a very tentative suggestion may be made: In a fairly large number of B forms, there is graphic indication of a subphonemic "lenition" of /p/ between sonorants (cf. Krause–Thomas 1960: 69). If one supposes now that CToch. **śəpətə*, the form underlying A *ṣpät*, developed in pre-B to **śəwət*, shwa deletion in open syllable would have resulted in a later pre-B form **śwət*. Under stress, this should have been reflected by **ṣwat*, with unstressed counterparts being **ṣwät* and **ṣut*. The latter form then would have undergone the influence of 'eight', with **-t* replaced by *-kt*. The weakness in this chain of arguments is that we do not know whether "lenition"-derived B *-w-* participated in an alternation /wə/ : /u/ as found, e. g., in B *kwarsär*, plural *kwärsarwa* / *kursarwa* 'mile; vehicle'.

4.1.7.2. The alleged locative forms of B *ṣuk* in B 455 and B 459 are to be interpreted as elliptical constructions; cf. 4.1.4.2.

Plural forms of A *ṣpät* 'seven' are found in A *ṣäptantu* (A 146 a 2) and *ṣäptäntu* (A 204 b 6) 'hebdomads'; they occur in a multiplicative expression 'seven times seven days; seven weeks'.

4.1.7.3. A compound in the narrow sense is found in A *ṣäptakoñi** 'of seven days; of [one] week', attested in the accusative phrase *ṣäptakoñiṃ walunt* '[him], having been dead for a week'. *-a-* of the A form in all probability owes its existence to a transfer from compound forms of 'eight', such as A *oktapuklyi* 'of eight years'; cf. 4.1.8.3.

Juxtapounds are fairly common. For B, the passage B 522 b 3, in a manuscript from Šorčuq, provides the number '77700', *ṣuk-tmane ṣuk-*

yältse ṣu-känte (with 'seven hundred' showing a simplification of *-kk-* resulting from a reduction of the cluster *-ktk-*). An expression for 'sevenfold' is found in B *ṣuk-yäkne-sa* (LS 3 a 3). Quite common is the term B *ṣuk-kauṃ* 'seven days; week' (cf. B 16 a 2, 22 a 7, with the Eastern variant B *ṣuk-kom* occurring in B 296 b 1). Contrary to the view of Bernhard (1958: 285) I prefer, in view of the numerous cases of a combination of a numeral higher than 'one' with a noun in the singular in juxtapounds, not to take B *kauṃ* to be a reduction of the accusative plural B *kaunäṃ*; the constructions *ad sensum* listed by Bernhard do not seem to provide a strong enough argument. On the other hand, a clear case for a juxtapound A *ṣpät-koṃ* 'week' can be made only for the singular expression A *ṣpät-*(*ṣpät*)*-koṃ*, rendered by Bernhard (1958: 284) as 'immer nach sieben Tagen(?)', while A *ṣpät koṃsaṃ* 'in seven days', with its plural form of the noun, is best taken as a phrase consisting of two free forms.

On the other hand, there are, parallel to forms in B, clear instances of juxtapounds among the higher numerals: A *ṣäptuk-ṣpät-pi* (A 316 b 7) 'seventy-seven', *ṣpät-känt* (A 29 a 2) 'seven hundred', *ṣpät-wältsä* (A 316 b 7) 'seven thousand', *ṣpä-tmāṃ* (A 441 a 2) 'seventy thousand'.

4.1.8. 'Eight'

4.1.8.0. The forms incurred are B *okt, ok* (Eastern variant); A *okät.*

4.1.8.1. In spite of their overt similarity with forms from other Indo-European languages (cf., e. g., Lat. *octō*, Gk. *oktṓ*), the Tocharian terms for 'eight' pose some difficult problems; a good summary of earlier proposals, and a new suggestion, are found in Hilmarsson (1986). As I agree with Hilmarsson in finding the earlier proposals largely unconvincing, but also have to take exception to his own analysis, I will present here my own line of argumentation.

PIE **o-* should be reflected by B *e-*, A *a-* (note in particular B *ek*, A *ak* 'eye' where this development remains unaffected even before *-k* deriving from a Proto-Indo-European labiovelar); B A *o-* thus requires a special explanation. PIE **-ōw* should have resulted in a final diphthong in B and in a monophthongized diphthong in A. As far as PIE **-ō* is concerned, it should have resulted in B *-a* (reduced from **-e* in absolute final) and in pre-A **-a*, later lost like all other simple vowels in end position. The reflex A *a* has been preserved in secondary internal, and thus protected, position in A *oktapuklyi* 'of eight years' and A *oktats* 'with eight parts'; A *oktuk* 'eighty', on the other hand, has to be taken to reflect PIE *-*ōw* monophthongized in A final and carried over into internal position. In B, PIE **ōw* should have resulted in a diphthong in final and secondarily internal position; there is no trace whatsoever of a diphthongal reflex in B forms connected with 'eight'. As to Hilmarsson's assumption that PIE **ō* became B (and A) *u*, which then was lost in unprotected final, the only clear instances of such a development are limited to positions after the reflex of CToch. **w* (cf. Hilmarsson 1986: 155–159). B *okt*, etc., therefore, call for a retention of the earlier explanation that 'eight' was adapted to 'seven' and 'nine' in its final. For A *okät*, a decision between former *-*m̥* and former *-*ō* is not possible because of the loss of all final simple vowels in A, although it would seem that a slight preference is to be given to the assumption that an adaptation to 'seven', etc., did not take place in A because A *oktats* presupposes A *okta-* < PIE **oḱtō-* while B *oktatse*, with /ə́/ in the second syllable, is best derived from what could be written **oḱtm̥* in Proto-Indo-European terms.

There being no sufficient grounds for positing a Common Tocharian form ending in *-*u* which could have led to umlaut of the initial vowel, the question needs to be reconsidered whether B *o-* : A *o-* is regular under certain conditions, whether these conditions can be said to prevail, or to have prevailed, in forms for 'eight' or closely related items, and whether, if analogical reshaping should be involved, parallels can be shown to be available.

As already pointed out, B *okt* : A *okät* cannot be derived by normal rules from PIE **oḱt-*; the counterexample is B *ek*, A *ak* 'eye' (< PIE *ok^{w}-). On the other hand, B *-o-* : *-o-* is found in a context favoring labialization whenever the B *-e-* : A *-a-* one would expect to find derives from Common Tocharian long or lengthened **e*; examples for old long **ē* are to be found in B A *yok* 'body hair; color' and in the *s*-aorist based preterit forms B *yopsa*, A *yowäs* 'he entered' (: PIE *yebh-*); a case of Lachmann-type lengthening occurs in B A *yoktsi* 'to drink' (if < PIE *eg^{w}- < *Eeg^{w}- and not < *ēg^{w}h-). The oldest reconstructable from for 'eighth' is early PIE **OektOwos* > later PIE **ogdOwos*, as reflected by Gk. *ógdoos*. In Common Tocharian, a syllabified laryngeal (in Brugmannian terms: PIE *ə) was assimilated to following *-*w-* to become *-*u-*; the sequence *-*uw-* was then treated as though it were a Sievers-Edgerton variant of *-*w-* (cf. B *pärweṣṣe* 'first', A *pärwat* 'first-born'). Before the reflex of PIE *-*gd-*, Lachmann-type lengthening brought a long vowel into existence in the first syllable of 'eighth' in Common Tocharian; the reflex of **d* was lost in *-*dw-* (cf. 4.1.2.1.). The form resulting from these processes for 'eighth' was now **ōkwV-* (the precise nature of the Common Tocharian development from lengthened PIE **-o-* need not concern us here). If the forms for 'eight' and 'eighth' had been taken over as such from Common Tocharian by B and A, we would have had a rather disparate subset in B **ektV* : B **okwe* and in A **akt-* : A **okw-*. It is only natural that a leveling should have taken place. This leveling was bidirectional (the order of the steps involved cannot be determined): the cardinal was changed so as to contain the onset of the ordinal, the ordinal received the *-kt-* of the cardinal stem. As a final adjustment, this time to a numeral other than 'eighth', the B cardinal had its reflex of final PIE **-ō(w)* replaced by that of a final sonantic nasal (as found in 'seven' and 'nine'), a reflex which was eventually reduced to zero phonetically.

4.1.8.2. The genitive forms B *oktaṃts*, A *oktis* 'of eight' have been mentioned and discussed in 4.1.0.

4.1.8.3. A compound form of 'eight' occurs in A *oktapuklyi* 'of eight years' (A 293 b 2).

Examples for juxtapounds are B *ok-yiltse* 'eight thousand', *ok-tmane* (LS 8 a 4) 'eighty thousand', *ok-pokai* 'with eight arms', and A *śäkk-okät-pi* (A 227–228 a 3) 'eighteen', *oktuk-okät-pi* (A 398 b 2) 'eighty-eight', *okät-wälts* (A 255 a 6) 'eight thousand', *okät-tmāṃ* (A 227–228 a 0–1) and *ok-tmāṃ* (A 289 a 5) 'eighty thousand'.

4.1.9. 'Nine'

4.1.9.0. The forms attested are B *ñu, ñū*; A *ñu*.

4.1.9.1. For Common Tocharian, a form **ńəwə* is to be reconstructed. Final **-ə* probably derives from **-m̥* introduced for earlier **-n̥* under the influence of the word for 'ten' (cf. Krause–Thomas 1960: 159). The underlying form is late PIE **newn̥*.

4.1.9.2. No case forms seem have survived; the alleged locatives listed by Thomas–Krause (1964: 195) are to be interpreted as elliptic expressions as pointed out in 4.1.4.2.

4.1.9.3. Of possible combinations with 'nine', only juxtapounds seem to have survived.

Terms for higher numbers occur in A *ñu-känt* (A 229 a 6) 'nine hundred', A *ñu-wälts* (A 255 a 1) 'nine thousand'; for B *ñu-ltse* (B 45 b 3) 'nine thousand' see 4.1.23.0. A juxtapound used as the nucleus of a derived adjective is found in B *ñu-kalpaṣṣa* 'of nine kalpas' (B 296 b 2; an emendation to **ñu-kalpanmaṣṣa** is precluded by the fact that a four-syllable subcolon is required).

4.1.10. 'Ten'

4.1.10.0. The forms found are A *śäk, śäkk*; B *śak, śśak, śäk.*
4.1.10.1. There can be no doubt that B *śak,* A *śäk* has to be connected with Gk. *déka*, Lat. *decem*, etc., from PIE **deḱm̥*. It is, however, only with difficulty that a decision can be reached as to whether B A *śə-* is a regular development from PIE **de-* or not: there are no immediately obvious parallels to be found for B *śak*, A *śäk*. There are, though, also no certain cases to support a claim that PIE **de-* was reflected by anything other than B A *śə-*: none of the examples adduced by van Windekens (1976: 81–82) to prove a development of the palatalized descendant of PIE **d* to B A *c* carries any weight. In Winter (1962), I have presented arguments for a development of PIE **d* before vowel other than PIE **e* to B A *ts*; I consider these findings to be still valid. In A, we note that there is an alternation between *ts* and *ś* in one and the same verbal paradigm, with A *ś* the palatalized counterpart of A *ts*; witness A *śuk* '(he) drank' (A 84 b 2) vs. A *tsuko* 'drunk' (A 44 a 1). In B, examples are harder to find; the best of them is B *śūke* (: A *śuk*) 'taste', which is to be connected with the same root for 'drink'. With a handful of good examples from A and one or two from B showing the same development as that found in B *śak*, A *śäk* we may confidently consider the Tocharian forms for 'ten' regular developments from PIE **deḱm̥*.

There is only an indirect indication that labiality of the underlying nasal was preserved in (pre-)Tocharian until a fairly late date: the *-m-* found in B *ñumka*, A *nmuk* 'ninety' can be explained only by the assumption that the Common Tocharian word for 'nine' was reshaped after 'ten'; cf. 4.1.9.1.
4.1.10.2. No case forms of 'ten' are found in accessible texts; a postpositional phrase B *śak-sa* may be seen in B 247 a 1. A plural form of 'ten', B *śkanma*, used to denote 'decads' has been noted (cf. Thomas–Krause 1964: 244); the derived form B *śtwer-śkänmaṣṣ*' in B 248 b 2 is grammatically faulty. B *śkanma* is best explained as having originated at a time when the reflex of PIE **-m̥*, was still **-əm* that is, the underlying form with **-əmna* seems to go back to Common Tocharian.
4.1.10.3. Compound forms of B *śak*, A *śäk* are found in the renderings of the Sanskrit term *daśabala* 'possessing the ten powers', viz., B *śka-maiyya*, A *śkatampeyum*. The B form reflects in its first element pre-B **śəkə-*, with stress on the second shwa, as indicated clearly by the MQR form B *śkämaiyyai* (accusative singular). The second element is the second

stem (accusative) of B *maiyyo* 'power'. The A form poses no problem in the material following *śka-*: A *tampe* is 'energy, force', A *-um* a suffix commonly found in bāhuvrīhi compounds. A *śka-*, though, is not easily explained. A *-a-* cannot be identified as a precise match of B *-a-* in *śkamaiyya*; the suggestion made by Bernhard (1958: 46) that both B *-a-* and A *-a-* should be derived from a generalized thematic vowel **-o-*, is demonstrably wrong: even in Bernhard's analysis there is no question but that PIE **-o-* became B *-e-*. It seems that the simplest solution to be offered is the assumption that the string of compounds with a first member in A *-a-* beginning with A *ṣäptakoñi** 'of seven days' and A *oktapuklyi* 'of eight years' continued through unattested A **ñwa-* to A *śkatampeyum*. A *-a-* can be readily explained in A *okta-* (cf. 4.1.8.1); in the other members of the string it must be taken to be due to analogical transfer.

Juxtapounds with 'ten' as their first element are more widely attested. Of higher numerals and their derivatives, the following may be cited: B *śak-piśaṣṣe* 'of fifteen', B *śak-ṣkäs* (B 66 b 3) 'sixteen', B *śak-ṣkässaṣṣe* (B 364 a 7) 'of sixteen', A *śäk-ṣäk-piṣi* (A 217 b 1) 'of sixteen (i. e., of the sixteenth night)', A *śäk-tmāṃ* (A 308 a 1) '100,000'. From other domains, these forms may be mentioned: A *śäk-puklyi** (A 285 a 7) 'of ten years', B *śak-yāmorṣṣe** (B 574 b 1) 'of ten actions', B *śak-karmaṣṣe** 'of ten actions'.

4.1.11. 'Eleven' through 'nineteen'

4.1.11.0. Attested forms for the 'teens' are:

B:	
'eleven'	*śak-ṣe* (B 433.31)
'twelve'	*śak-wi* (B 33 b 2)
'thirteen'	*śak-trai* (Krause – Thomas 1960: 159)
	śak-tarya (Krause – Thomas 1960: 159)
'fourteen'	*śak-śtwer* (LP 5 a 5), *śak-śwer* (B 435.3),
	śäk-śtwer (B 588 b 3)
	śak-śtwāra (Krause – Thomas 1960: 159)
'fifteen'	*śak-piś* (B 192 b 3), *śäk-piś* (B 588 b 3)
'sixteen'	*śak-ṣkäs* (B 497 a 4), *śa-skas* (B 429 a 5)
'seventeen'	*śak-ṣuk* (B 455.2), *śäk-ṣukt-o* (B 127 a 2)
'eighteen'	*śak-okt* (B 45 b 5), *śak-ok* (B 492 a 4), *śäk-okt* (B 212 a 3)
'nineteen'	*śak-ñu* (LP 42 a 2)

A:

'eleven'	*śäk-ṣapi* (A 397 a 6)
'twelve'	*śäk-wepi* (A 222 b 1)
'thirteen'	*śäk-täryāpi* (A 371 a 1)
'fourteen'	(unattested)
'fifteen'	*śäk-päñpi* (A 336 a 4)
'sixteen'	*śäk-ṣäkpi* (A 300 a 5)
'seventeen'	(attested only in ordinal *śäk-ṣpätpint*)
'eighteen'	*śäk-okätpi* (A 321 a 3), *śäkk-okätpi* (A 227/228 a 3)
'nineteen'	(attested only in ordinal *śäk-ñupint*)

4.1.11.1. The only etymological issue to be raised here is the question of the origin of A *-pi*. A comparison with the clausal (politeness?) particle B *-pi* (Thomas – Krause 1964: 210) seems improbable for semantic reasons; that with A *pe* 'also' (Fraenkel 1932: 99), however, may be considered acceptable provided that A *-pi* was treated as the reflex of a Proto-Indo-European diphthong **-oy* (cf. Latv. *pìe* 'near') in a polysyllabic form, while A *pe* represents the outcome of the same sequence in a monosyllabic word (cf. A *āmpi* 'both' : A *we* 'two', and note van Windekens 1976: 126).

4.1.1.2. The B form for 'sixteen', found three times in the shape B *śak ṣkäs* in B 497 a 3, 4, a text from Šorčuq, beside a form for 'six', B *ṣkas*, marked for stress, permits a clear identification of the B expression for 'sixteen' as a juxtapound with a bound, and not a free, form as its second member; yet, the boundary between the two lexemes involved remains preserved graphically. On the other hand, two forms taken from Krause – Thomas (B *śak tarya* 'thirteen', *śak śtwāra* 'fourteen') mark both 'ten' and the following digit for stress. The conclusion seems inescapable that while 'teens were subject to juxtapounding, a phrasal status of the complex numeral could be retained (or, for that matter, re-introduced): unfortunately, items such as 'eleven', 'twelve', 'seventeen' do not permit a decision between juxtapound and phrase, as B *e, i, u* do not allow a safe identification of stressedness or absence of stress.

As far as A is concerned, the presence of a word boundary before A *-pi* is impossible to claim for 'thirteen' and rather unlikely for 'eleven' (but note 4.1.1.5.). At the same time, the expression for 'eighteen' provides clear evidence (as seen by Sieg – Siegling – Schulze 1931: 195) for the fact that the full string 'ten' + 'eight' + A *-pi* does not constitute a compound. It thus seems likely that, as in B, the 'teens of A should be classified as juxtapounds. The combination of digit and A *-pi* shows inconsistency in that the lower teens contain certain or possible bound forms, while 'eighteen' has for a digit an unambiguously free form A *okät* and not a bound variant **okta-* or **oktä-*; it seems likely that a free form replaced a bound one, a conclusion that could be extended to cover 'fifteen' and 'sixteen' as well.

4.1.12. 'Twenty'

4.1.12.0. The forms attested are B *ikäṃ* (*ikaṃ* only in B 584), *īkäṃ*; A *wiki* (*viki* in A 370), *wīki*.

4.1.12.1. B *i-* must be the overtly palatalized counterpart of A *wi-*. As the reflex of PIE *-*i*- does not cause palatalization in either B or A (cf. B *wase*, A *wäs* 'poison' : Skt. *viṣám*; B *wikṣeñca* 'avoiding'; B *wate*, A *wät* 'second' : Skt. *dvitáḥ* – see 4.2.2.2.), B *i-* for **yV-* cannot be from PIE **wi-*. However, a B *-i-* derived from PIE *-*ī*- (in Brugmannian terms) does palatalize a preceding consonant – note the athematic optative forms such as B *eñcimar, taśim, trañci, pyāśim*, etc. (cf. Krause 1952: 119–120). PIE *-*ī*- is required for 'twenty' by Av. *vīsa'ti*, Lat. *vīgintī*, Homeric Gk. *eeíkosi* (cf. Frisk 1960: 453). In laryngealist terms, PIE *-*ī*- is to be reanalyzed as *-*yE*; B *i-*, A *wi-* thus represent old dual forms whose neuter gender matches that of the higher decades. The 'prothetic vowel' in Greek leads one to posit an early Proto-Indo-European onset **Ew-yE-*; whether **E-* resulted from a dissimilation of older **d-* before original **d-* of the decad, need not concern us here.

As for A *-i*, a comparison with *-i* in A *āmpi* 'both' (cf. 4.3.4.) seems acceptable. For a possible antecedent of A *wiki*, see 4.2.12.2.

In B, one would expect to find a form **ikäñc** (cf. B *asāñc-ne-sa* 'on the buttocks' : B *asānänta* 'seats'). It is tempting to consider the possibility that B *-ṃ* in 'twenty' way a regular reflex of PIE *-*nti* (with *-*i* instead of *-*i* < *-*yE* having originated in prevocalic position) if PIE *-*nti* could be identified as the source of B *-ṃ* in the third person plural of present and optative verb forms; here, however, an alternative explanation is at our disposal, viz., that what survives in B is the "secondary" ending PIE *-*nt* (cf. Krause 1952: 201). The proposal by Pedersen (1941: 253 n. 1) that B *ikäṃ* should be interpreted as having developed from a neuter form in PIE *-*ḱm̥t* is unobjectionable as far as the form goes, but it would place 'twenty' in perfect isolation over against the other decads (which show a marking for old neuter plural). The simplest explanation is probably that offered for B *ṣkas* (cf. 4.1.6.1.): Suppose the regular form for 'twenty' was B **ikäñc**. In the corresponding ordinal, **ikäñcte**, a cluster reduction (similar to that which led to A *pänt* 'fifth', cf. 4.2.5.1.) would have caused (attested) B *ikänte* 'twentieth' to come into existence; deletion of the ordinal marker B *-te* could then result in a back-formation B *ikäṃ*.

4.1.12.2. No case forms of 'twenty' have survived.

4.1.12.3. The numerals 'twenty-one' through 'twenty-nine' are fairly well attested in references to days of the month and to regnal years. The following forms can be listed:

B:	
'twenty-one'	*ikäṃ ṣe* (LP 2 a 2); *ikäṃ ṣeme* (B 252 a 3)
'twenty-two'	*ikäṃ wi* (B 459.3)
'twenty-three'	*ikäṃ trai* (PK 36.10[1])
'twenty-four'	*ikäṃ śwer* (G-Su 7)
'twenty-five'	*ikäṃ piś* (B 454.2)
'twenty-six'	*ikäṃ ṣkas* (B 484.1)
'twenty-seven'	*ikäṃ ṣuk* (B 459.5)
'twenty-eight'	*ikäṃ okt* (B 497.9)
'twenty-nine'	*ikäṃ ñu* (B 433.4)
A:	
'twenty-one'	*wiki ṣapi-* (in ordinal); *wiki śkaṃ ṣapi* (A 229 a. 6)
'twenty-two'	*wiki wepi-* (in ordinal)
'twenty-three'	*wiki täryāpi-* (in ordinal)
'twenty-four'	(unattested)
'twenty-five'	*wiki päñpi* (A 281 a 8)
'twenty-six'	*wiki ṣäkpi-* (in ordinal)
'twenty-seven'	*wiki ṣpätpi-* (in ordinal)
'twenty-eight'	*wiki °kätpi* (A 395 b 5), *viki okätpi* (A 370.5)
'twenty-nine'	*wiki ñupi* (A 290 a 3; text faulty)

The difference in the structure of numeral combinations of B and A that was noticeable in 'eleven' through 'nineteen' recurs in 'twenty-one' through 'twenty-nine' (as well as in higher number expressions containing a combination of decad and digit): in B, an asyndetic construction is used, in A, the digit is extended by A *-pi*.

'Twenty' is found in more complex configurations just as was the case with lower numerals. Expressions for higher numbers are, e. g., A *känt wiki* '120' (A 255 b 1), A *ñu-känt wiki śkaṃ ṣapi* '921' (A 229 a 6; *śkaṃ* 'and' has been inserted to complete the first colon – which, by the way, indicates that A *ṣapi* was a sequence without an internal boundary apt to be matched with a caesura); B *kante ikäṃ* '120' (B 108 a 4), B *kant' īkäṃ okt* '128' (B 497 b 9). 'Twenty years old' is expressed by A *wiki-puklyiñi* (A 285 a 8; nominative plural masculine), 'twenty-nine years old' by A *wiki-ñupi-puklyi* (A 290 a 3; text faulty), 'less than twenty years old' by B *(me)ṅki-ikäṃ-pikwalaṃñepi* (H 149.3 a 1) (genitive singular masculine).

4.1.13. 'Thirty'

4.1.13.0. Forms attested are B *täryāka,* A *taryāk.*

4.1.13.1. The A form is due to an innovation (if *-a-* was old, *-ā-* would have been changed to **-a-**); it is simplest to assume that earlier A **täryāk(V)* was affected by analogical change under the influence of A *śtwarāk(V)* 'forty'; a transfer of *-a-* (/ə/) from B *tarya* 'three' (van Windekens 1976: 494) can be ruled out.

-ka in B *täryāka* (and the higher decads) is not a regular development from PIE **-ḱomtA* or **-ḱm̥tA*; neither is A *-k*. Numerals seem to be subject, in Tocharian and elsewhere, to irregular reshaping to a particularly high degree (note 4.1.23.0.); hence it seems warranted to consider number expressions in B *-ka*, A *-k* allegro forms. What has been replaced by these items cannot be directly identified; however, the ordinals in A (cf. 4.2.12.2.) do provide a strong argument in favor of **-ḱm̥tA*. Except for the reduction in the second lexeme and for **-A* rather than **-eA* of the ending, B *täryāka* 'thirty' could thus be a very close equivalent of Lat. *trīgintā*; both could be taken to derive from PIE **tryA-(d)ḱm̥tA*.

4.1.13.2. No case forms of 'thirty' are attested.

4.1.13.3. Just like the lower decads, 'thirty' combines with digits as well as with higher numerals. Examples are: A *taryāk wepi* 'thirty-two' (A 67 b 5), *taryāk ṣäkpi* 'thirty-six' (A 17 a 4), A *känt taryāk* '130' (A 248 b 3), A *we-känt taryāk śkaṃ koris śtwar-känt-tmāṃ* '2,304,000,000' (A 229 a 5; *śkaṃ* 'and' again has been inserted so as not to make the word *koris* straddle a caesura); B *täryāka wī* 'thirty-two' (B 76 b 5), B *täryāka ṣukt* 'thirty-seven' (B 54 b 2). A complex construction is to be found in A *taryāk-päñpi-puklyi* 'thirty-five years old' (A 255 b 1).

4.1.14. 'Forty'

4.1.14.0. Forms attested are B *śtwārka* (*śtvārka*), A *śtwarāk.*

4.1.14.1. Van Windekens (1976: 489) implies that the B form ought to have been **stwarāka*, a suggestion that can be accepted. He further thinks that the older form was changed to attested B *śtwārka* under the influence of monosyllabic B *śtwer*. The trouble with this proposal is that the feminine (formerly neuter) form B *śtwāra* is very well attested in our texts, and that B *śtwarā-* is the form used in complex configurations, above all in high numerals (cf. 4.1.4.3.); thus the alleged impact of B *śtwer* is hard to understand. Therefore, in spite of all overt similarity with other Indo-European forms for 'forty', B *śtwārka* remains opaque to some extent. For a further suggestion cf. 4.1.15.1.

The A form *śtwarāk* is irregular, too, but here an explanation for the deviation from the expected can be given. Matching the feminine form B *śtwāra* one would anticipate finding A **śtwār*, **śtwārā-* (later syncopated to **śtwāra-* and **śtwār-*); as the equivalent of reconstructed B **śtwarāka*, pre-A should have had **śtwārākə*. When the forms for 'four' were leveled in A to become *śtwar*, the onset of 'forty' was reshaped accordingly, but *-ā-* was preserved in the second syllable (or, as an alternative suggestion, it may have been reintroduced from 'fifty' – cf. 4.1.15.1.).

4.1.14.2. No case forms of 'forty' have survived.

4.1.14.3. 'Forty' is used in forming higher numerals: In A 372 b 5 *päñ śtwarāk puklā* may mean 'five (times) forty years' rather than 'five (and) forty years' as Sieg–Siegling–Schulze (1931: 196) think. For A 278 b 2 *säksäk-śtwarāk-kalpaṣi ṣtare*, an additive reading 'an effort of sixty (plus) forty kalpas' is, however, probably to be preferred. B provides avery high number in *(śt)w(ā)rka-tmane koṭänma* (B 252 b 2) '4,000,000,000,000'.

The use of 'forty' in an adjective based on a juxtapound can be illustrated by B *śtvārka-yṣiṣṣe* 'of forty nights' in H 149 add. 19 b 5 (B *yṣi-*, free form *yaṣi*, is an accusative singular).

4.1.15. 'Fifty'

4.1.15.0. Forms attested are B *piśāka, pśāka*; A *pñāk*.

4.1.15.1. A *pñāk* shows no trace of a reflex of PIE *-k^w-; its first part consists of what appears to be a variant of 'five' that arose in a certain preconsonantal position (cf. 4.1.5.1.); the form thus has no claim at all to being old. Since A *pñāk* is to A *päñ* 'five' as A *śtwarāk* 'forty' is to A *śtwar* 'four', it probably came into existence only after the developments sketched in 4.1.14.1. had taken place.

No reconstruction of a Common-Tocharian word for 'fifty' on the basis of a comparison of A *pñāk* and B *piśāka* is possible. In order to determine the status of B *piśāka*, the question has to be asked as to what would be the form to be expected for Common Tocharian (and for B) on the strength of what is known about 'fifty' in other Indo-European languages.

It has been mentioned briefly (4.1.13.1.) that there is reason to believe that Tocharian decads in B *-ka*, A *-k* are abbreviated forms replacing the regular development of PIE **-ḱm̥tA*. Suppose now that the onset of 'fifty' corresponded to that found in Gk. *pentēkonta*, Skt. *pañcāṣat-*; what would one expect to find in Common Tocharian? The answer is quite simple indeed: the unreduced form would be CToch. **p'ənśēkənta*. After the allegro form (which has to be assigned to Common Tocharian because of the agreement between B *-ka* and A *-k*) came into existence, CToch. **p'ənśēka* was affected by *-a-* umlaut (again a Common-Tocharian phenomenon). The form resulting, CToch. **p'ənśāka*, provides a perfect base for the derivation of B *piśāka* (for the loss of the nasal, cf. 4.1.5.1.).

To be sure, if the B word for 'fifty' had been derived from 'five' in the same mechanical way in which A *pñāk* was created after A *päñ*, the outcome in B would also have been B *piśāka*. However, the argument in the case of B suffers from the fact that between the alleged starting point of the spread of B *-āka,* B *täryāka* 'thirty', and B *piśāka* 'fifty', there was B *śtwārka* 'forty' without an *-a-* before *-ka*, a form that should have blocked the transfer of B *-āka* to 'fifty'. As B *piśāka* can be explained without recourse to assumptions about analogical reshaping, the claim that this word is a form descended from Common Tocharian will be maintained (against van Windekens 1976: 361).

4.1.15.2. No case forms of 'fifty' are found. A plural of B *piśāka*, B *piśakānta* 'groups of fifty', is attested in B 252 b 4. The selection of B *-nta* as a plural suffix (rather than that of B *-nma* as in B *śkanma* 'decads', B *käntenma* 'hundreds', etc.) was probably triggered by the fact that B *piśāka* had more than two (morphophonemic) syllables, while B *śak, kante*, etc., had just two (for related data see Krause – Thomas 1960: 122, 125).

4.1.15.3. No complex configurations involving 'fifty' have been found.

4.1.16. 'Sixty'

4.1.16.0. The forms attested are B *ṣkaska, ṣkäska*; A *säksäk*.

4.1.16.1. Both B and A form derive from CToch. **šəkəska*; this in turn echoes what may be projected back as PIE **seḱs-(d)ḱm̥tA* (cf. 4.1.13.1.). The form in B shows only the expected developments; in A, initial **ṣ-* was assimilated to internal *-s-* (see 4.1.1.2.; cf. Pedersen 1941: 240).

4.1.16.2. No case forms of 'sixty' have survived.
4.1.16.3. Complex constructions involving 'sixty' are A *säksäk śtwarpi* 'sixty-four' (A 323 a 3), B *ṣkaska śtwāra* 'sixty-four' (B 497.3), B *ṣkaska ṣkas* 'sixty-six' (B 624 b 3); the B forms must be viewed as having the status of phrases and not of juxtapounds because of the presence of stress on both decade and digit. The precise function of 'sixty' (probably additive rather than multiplicative) in A *säksäk-śtwārak-kalpaṣi* 'of sixty plus (or: times) forty kalpas' (A 278 b 2) remains in slight doubt; cf. 4.1.14.3.

4.1.17. 'Seventy'

4.1.17.0. Forms attested are B *ṣuktaṅka*, A *ṣäptuk*.
4.1.17.1. The B form reflects, except for the reshaping of its first element (cf. 4.1.7.1.), CToch. **šəpətənka*; the A word, more regular in its first part, shows the results of a transfer of A *-u-* from the form for 'eighty'.
4.1.17.2. No case forms of 'seventy' seem to have survived.
4.1.17.3. The A word for 'seventy' forms part of the number 16,777,216 (= 2^{24}) preserved in A 316 b 7 + 315 b 8: *wälts ṣäk-kät ṣäptuk ṣpätpi tmānäntu ṣpät-wälts we-(känt ṣä)k-ṣapi.*

4.1.18. 'Eighty'

4.1.18.0. Forms surviving are B *oktaṅka, oktaṃka, oktamka*; A *oktuk*.
4.1.18.1. The A form derives (in Brugmannian terms) from PIE **oḱtōw* plus **(d)ḱm̥tə* (< **(d)ḱm̥tA*); A *oktuk* is therefore very close to Lat. *octōgintā*.

B |-ən-| in B *oktaṅka* and B *oktaṃka* must be due to a reshaping after the more conservative of the forms for 'ninety', B *ñuṅka* (< *|ṅəwə́nka|). B *oktamka*, attested in the unpublished Berlin text 3008. 2+8 b 2 (K. T. Schmidt, personal communication), shows the influence of the more recent form B *ñumka* 'ninety'.
4.1.18.2. No case forms of 'eighty' appear to have survived.
4.1.18.3. Of complex constructions, A *oktuk okätpi* 'eighty-eight' (A 398 b 2) and B *ṣkas-känte oktaṅka ṣe* '681' can be cited.

4.1.19. 'Ninety'

4.1.19.0. Forms attested are B *ñuṅka, ñumka*; A *nmuk*.
4.1.19.1. Neither A *nmuk* nor B *ñumka* are regular. For A *nmuk*, one has to assume a transfer of *-uk* from A *oktuk* 'eighty', analogous to that

claimed for A *ṣäptuk* 'seventy' (cf. 4.1.17.1.). The suggestion by van Windekens (1976: 120, 319) that *-u-* in A *nmuk* owed its place to metathesis, is unsupported by parallels. The depalatalization of the initial consonant of A *nmuk* can merely be noted; no explanation can be given. A *-m-* must have been transferred from a pre-A form for 'ten' to a pre-A form for 'nine' before the difference in the reflexes of PIE **-m̥* and PIE **-n̥* had become obliterated; it subsequently was introduced in the form for 'ninety'.

The same kind of double transfer led to the form B *ñumka*; the variant A *ñuṅka* may be viewed as a more conservative form retaining the reflex of PIE **-n̥-* and not of PIE **-m̥-*. A comment is in order concerning the vocalism of the first syllable of the B word for 'ninety'. The material preceding B *-ka* should be reconstructed as Common Tocharian **ńəwən-* or **ńəwəm-*; as a reflex, one would expect to find B **ñwaṅka** (|ńəwə́nka|) or B **ñwamka* (|ńəwə́mka|), respectively. However, both B *ñuṅka* and B *ñumka* are forms in full agreement with a rule in Tocharian B to the effect that in a sequence *|Vwə́| accented shwa is deleted and the accent transferred to the preceding syllable. This rule will be documented and discussed elsewhere (Winter forthcoming).

4.1.19.2. No case forms of 'ninety' can be cited.

4.1.19.3. Examples for the use of 'ninety' in complex forms are B *ñumka ṣkass-o* 'ninety-six' (LS 6 b 6) and A *śtwar-känt nmuk pänpi* '495' (A 348 a 2).

4.1.20. 'One hundred'

4.1.20.0. Attested forms are B *kante, känte*; A *känt*.

4.1.20.1. The Tocharian words for 'hundred' match other Indo-European forms, such as Lat. *centum*, and derive regularly from PIE **ḱm̥tom*.

4.1.20.2. No case forms of 'one hundred' seem to have survived.

In both languages, the numeral can be pluralized; the forms are: B *käntenma* (B 618 b 3); A *käntant* (A 225 a 5), *käntantu* (A 254 b 7). No Common-Tocharian form can be reconstructed – it seems that both the B and the A words are of recent origin; for B, such an assumption is supported by the mechanically conditioned selection of the plural marker (cf. 4.1.15.2.).

4.1.20.3. The terms for '101' through '199' are formed as asyndetic phrases, with the higher numeral preceding the lower one. Examples are: A *känt wiki* '120' (A 19 a 1), B *kant' ïkäṃ ok(t)* '128' (B 497 b 9).

4.1.21. Multiples of 'one hundred'

4.1.21.0. The following forms can be cited from published texts and other materials:

B:	
'two hundred'	*wī-känte* (unpublished Berlin text), *wi-käṃnte* (Paris text)
'three hundred'	*tärya-känte* (unpublished Berlin text)
'four hundred'	*śtwārā-känte* (B 297.2 a 1), *św ā ra-känte* (B 429 a 1)
'five hundrd'	*piś-känte* (B 23 a 1), *piś-känte* (B 525 a 1)
'six hundred'	*ṣkas-känte* (PR 36.21), *ṣkas kante* (B 525 a 2)
'seven hundred'	*ṣu(k)-känte* (B 525 a 2)
'eight hundred'	(unattested)
'nine hundred'	(unattested)
A:	
'two hundred'	*we-känt* (A 229 a 5)
'three hundred'	(unattested)
'four hundred'	*śtwar-känt* (A 229 a 5)
'five hundred'	*päñ-känt* (A 4 a 5)
'six hundred'	*ṣäk-känt* (A 234 b 6), *ṣäk-kät* (A 316 b 7)
'seven hundred'	*ṣpät-känt* (A 29 a 2)
'eight hundred'	(unattested)
'nine hundred'	*ñu-känt* (A 167 b 4)

4.1.21.1. Absence of number concord would not *eo ipso* rule out free-form status for 'hundred'; note the use of the singular in German *fünf Pfund* 'five pounds' and the like. However, the almost general absence of stress indication of the form for 'hundred' in B signals a bound item. Even in the lower hundreds, no support can be found for a claim that the complex constructions were compounds in the narrow sense; in A, the crucial term for 'three hundred' has not been preserved, and without a closer inspection of the text, it cannot be decided whether B *tärya-* in *tärya-känte* should be viewed as the equivalent of standard B *tarya* or *täryā-*.

4.1.21.2. An ablative of 'three hundred' has survived in an unpublished Berlin text, viz., B *tärya-käntemeṃ*. Allegro forms of 'five hundred' occur in Paris texts (cf. Schmidt 1986: 645): B *piś-känt-sa* (PR 36.3), B *piś-käṃnt-sa* (PR 36.1), B *pis-käṃt-sa* (PR 37.53), and B *piś-käts-tsa* (PR 37.36).

4.1.21.3. Complex numerals with multiples of 'hundred' as constituents are found quite often. Examples are: A *we-känt täryāk śkaṃ koris* '2,300,000,000' (A 229 a 5), A *śtwar-känt nmuk päñpi* '495' (A 348 a 2); B *ṣkas kante ikäṃ* '620' (B 525 a 2), B *ṣkas-känte oktaṅka ṣe* '681' (PR 36.21), A *ok-yiltse wi-käṃnte pśāka* '8,250' (PR 36.24).

4.1.22. 'One thousand'

4.1.22.0. Forms attested are: A *wälts*; B *yaltse, yältse, yiltse.*

4.1.22.1. Earlier etymologies proposed for A *wälts*, B *yaltse* have been listed by van Windekens (1976: 555); he is inclined to perfer the comparison with OCS *velĭjĭ* 'great', etc., suggested by Meillet (1912: 292). The weakness of this analysis is that the internal structure of the Tocharian numerals cannot be accounted for, and that no precise parallel can be adduced from other Indo-European languages; therefore, the alleged preform **weltyom* remains most uncertain. Under the circumstances, it seems appropriate to propose a number of modifications.

In view of the explanations given for the Germanic words for 'thousand' (cf. Lehmann 1986: 368), it seems reasonable to consider Meillet's comparison of B *yaltse*, A *wälts* with Slavic items referring to greatness plausible on semantic grounds; all thus depends on the cogency of an analysis of the Tocharian forms.

There can be no doubt that the onsets B *yal-*, A *wäl-* require the recognition of underlying PIE **wel-*, that is, of a root in the full grade. B A *-ts-* is taken by van Windekens to reflect an underlying sequence PIE **-ty-*; it should be noted, though, that *-ts-* after *-l-* could very well derive from pre-Tocharian **-s-*, a fact which has hitherto not been taken into consideration. Hence, the reconstruction of an underlying form **welsom* is a possible choice. Such a form could be a thematic derivative (possibly a nominalized adjective) based on an *-s-* stem noun PIE **welos* 'greatness'; for a parallel see Skt. *vatsáḥ* 'calf, young of an animal': PIE **wetos* (cf. Mayrhofer 1976: 132–133 with references). The alternative offered in my Calcutta paper (see chapter 2 in this volume) now strikes me as less attractive.

The form reflected by B *yaltse*, A *wälts* may first have been an adjective 'pertaining to greatness' modifying the noun 'hundred'; when it became possible to express the notion 'thousand' elliptically, nominalization of the adjective would have taken place.

4.1.22.2. No case forms of 'thousand' are attested.

As with 'hundred', a plural is found in both languages: B *yältsenma*; A *wältsant, wältsantu* (cf. 4.1.20.2. and 4.1.15.2.). Postpositional phrases occur in B *yältsenma-sa* (LS 8 a 3), A *wältsant-yo* (A 340 a 6), A *wältsantu-yo* (A 340 a 8) 'by thousands'.

4.1.22.3. As to be expected, the expressions for 'thousand' occur in complex numerals (to avoid duplication, no multiples of 'one thousand' will be cited in this paragraph); examples are B *yältse trey* '1,003' (B 108 b 3), B *yältse ṣkas* '1,006' (B 497 a 3); a reason for the absence of stress indication on the first syllable of 'thousand' cannot be given.

A *(wä)lts atrat(am)p(e)s* in A 128 a 3–4 is in all likelihood not a juxtapound with A *wälts* (cf. Sieg–Siegling–Schulze 1931: 205), but a sequence of two parallel modifiers: '... thousand having the strength of heroes'; the only combinations in which B *yaltse*, A *wälts* have been found to occur are then terms denoting multiples of 'one thousand' – see 4.1.23.

4.1.23. Multiples of 'one thousand'

4.1.23.0. Forms for '2,000' through '9,000' are found in two sets in B, in one in A. The A items will be listed first, as they require no comment. The two sets in B are clearly in complementary distribution: whenever the preceding digit phonemically ends in consonant, the fuller form (B *-yältse, -yiltse, -iltse*) is used; after a final vowel of the digit, a reduction of '1,000' to B *-ltse* appears to have taken place. The starting point for this development probably was the word for '2,000' – the sequence **wíyə-* (or **wíyi-*) was contracted to *wí-*, the shorter form for 'thousand' was extracted from B *wiltse* and transferred to B *ñultse*; whether the development from B *tarya/täryā-* plus *yaltse/yältse* proceeded through an intermediate assimilated stage **təryiyəltse*, cannot be decided (Schmidt 1986: 645, to whom I owe the references to several of the items cited here, limits himself to an ordered presentation of more and more reduced form of '3,000'); in any case, a reduced stem of 'three' came into existence, to which stress was assigned. While B *wiltse* and B *ñultse* could be viewed as juxtapounds, B *tarältse*, etc., with two bound forms conjoined, must be classified as a compound proper; it seems reasonable, though not absolutely necessary, to treat '2,000' and '9,000' as perfect parallels to '3,000' and to identify them as compounds in the narrow sense, too. Once

A:	
'two thousand'	*we-wälts* (A 375 a 5)
'three thousand'	*tri-wälts-* (A 314 b 1)
'four thousand'	*śtwar-wälts* (A 255 a 3)
'five thousand'	*päñ-wälts* (A 255 a 4)
'six thousand'	*ṣäk-wälts* (A 255 a 7)
'seven thousand'	*ṣpät-wältsä* (A 316 b 7)
'eight thousand'	*okät-wälts* (A 255 a 6)
'nine thousand'	*ñu-wälts* (A 255 a 1)
B:	
'two thousand'	(I) *wiltse* (PR 37.53; Ot 13.1.2)
'three thousand'	(I) *(tä)r(y)yäl(ts)e* (B 274 b 6),
	(I) *täryältse* (PK NS 10568),
	(I) *tarältse* (B 563 a 1),
	(I) *tarltse* (PK NS 34 b 1),
	(I) *tarse* (PK 36.1), *tarsse* (HW 4.7)
'four thousand'	(I) *śtwārältse* (PK AS 17 A b 5),
	(I) *śwārse* (PR 36.22)
'five thousand'	(II) *piś-yältse* (PR 37.35),
	(II) *piś-iltse* (B 398 a 1, 399 a 1)
'six thousand'	(II) *ṣkas-yiltse* (PR 37.3; Otani text)
'seven thousand'	(II) *ṣuk-yältse* (B 522 b 3)
'eight thousand'	(II) *ok-yiltse* (B 401 b 3; PR 36.24)
'nine thousand'	(I) *ñul(tse)* (B 45 b 3)

/a/ was deleted in '3,000', analogy could lead to a comparable suppression in '4,000'.

4.1.23.1. No further etymological comments are required.

4.1.23.2. A postpositional phrase is found in B 398 a 1 (and B 399 a 1) *ṣuk-tmane piś-iltse-mpa* 'with 75,000'.

4.1.23.3. The occurrence of multiples of 'one thousand' in more complex expressions of numbers is to be expected. Examples are: A *tmāṃ śtwar-wälts* '14,000' (A 255 a 3), A *okät-tmāṃ śtwar-wälts* '84,000' (A 130 a 3); B *piś-tᵘmane ṣkas-yiltse wi-käṃnte ikäṃ ok* '56,228' (Otani text), B *tarya-tᵘmane wiltse piś-käṃnte pśāka* '32,550' (Otani text).

Bracketed constructions containing multiples of 'one thousand' are well attested in A. On the one hand, we find A *tri-wältseṃ ārkiśoṣi* (A 314 b 1) as the translation of Skt. *trisāhasralokadhātu* (cf. Sieg – Siegling – Schulze 1931: 27); on the other, there is a whole string of adjectives meaning 'of *n* years': A *tri-wälts-puklyi* (A 255 a 4), *ṣäk-wälts-puklyi* (A 255 a 2), *okät-wälts-puklyi* (A 255 a 7), *ñu-wälts-puklyi* (A 255 b 3). Finally, a fairly complex configuration may be mentioned: A *tmāṃ-ṣäk-wälts-pᵘkul* 'comprising 16,000 years' (A 255 b 5).

4.1.24. 'Ten thousand'

4.1.24.0. The forms attested are A *tmāṃ*; B *tmāne* (*-tmane*), *tumane* (*-tᵘmane*).

B *tumane* is found once in published or otherwise accessible texts (B 401 b 3). The bound form *-tᵘmane* occurs in B *tarya-tᵘmane* (Otani 3.1); *tᵘmāne** is also preserved in the plural form *tᵘmanenma* (B 110 b 9). All three texts are of known Eastern origin or of Eastern type; conversely, disyllabic *tmāne* is not attested in Eastern texts.

4.1.24.1. The observations just made are of crucial importance for any attempt at an etymology of the term for 'ten thousand': *-u-* is not present in A, and marginally – and only regionally – found in B. The accentuation pattern precludes an identification of B *tmāne* as a mediopassive present participle (this form is stressed on the vowel preceding B *-mane* – cf. Krause 1952: 60 for such examples from Central B as *miwamane* 'shaking', *smimane* 'smiling', plus several relevant parallels from Hoernle texts). A derivation from a base *tu-* (otherwise nonexistent in Tocharian B) could therefore have yielded nothing but Central B **tūmane** or **tumane** with stressed and stable *-u-*. Such a form does not occur; any etymology along the lines originally suggested by Meillet (1913: 19) and since then frequently repeated, must be rejected outright. (There is no need to point out that PIE **tewX-* or **teXw-* would not have been reflected by a zero-grade form B *tu-* anyhow.) All this almost certainly makes B *tmāne*, A *tmāṃ* loanwords (or, as an alternative, forms descended from a Common-Tocharian loanword). It is rather unlikely that Old Turkish *tümän* was the source, as the direction Tocharian-Turkish borrowing took was usually from Tocharian (and specifically from Tocharian A) into Turkish. The transfer is more likely to have occurred between an Iranian language and Tocharian; for a detailed presentation of hypotheses cf. Isebaert (1980: 102–103).

4.1.24.2. No case forms of the singular have been found in B; in A, a locative *tmānaṃ* (A 222 b 6) has survived.

A plural was formed in the way encountered with 'hundred' and 'thousand': B *tmanenma*; A *tmānantu* (*tmānäntu* with dotted fremdzeichen in A 316 b 7 is likely to be a mistake). Postpositional phrases are found (or to be supplied) in A *tmānantu-yo* (A 254 b 7), B *(tmanenma)-sa* (B 350 a 6), B *tᵘmanenma(-sa)* (B 110 b 9).

4.1.24.3. B *tmāne* and A *tmāṃ* occur in complex configurations (multiples of '10,000' will be treated in 4.1.25.).

B *tmān(e) ñul(tse)* '19,000' is found in B 45 b 3. From A, more forms can be listed: A *tmāṃ we-wälts* '12,000' (A 255 a 4), A *tmāṃ śtwar-wälts* '14,000' (A 255 a 3), A *tmāṃ ṣäk-wälts* '16,000' (A 255 a 1), A *tmāṃ ñu-wälts* '19,000' (A 255 a 1).

A bracketed form, A *tmāṃ-puklyi* 'ten thousand years old', occurs in A 255a 5.

4.1.25. Multiples of 'ten thousand'

4.1.25.0. As 'ten thousand' is used in expressing any multiple of 'ten thousand' (unless A *kor*, B *koṭ-* 'koṭi' is utilized – cf. 4.1.26.), no listing of forms found in the texts will yield more than examples from an open-ended set; hence, no tabulation will be attempted.

4.1.25.1. The following multiples of 'ten thousand' have been noted in B texts: B *wī-tmāne* '20,000' (B 45 b 3), B *(ta)rya-tmane* '30,000' (B 590 a 7–8), B *ṣkas-tmane* '60,000' (B 3 b 1; *ṣkas tmāne* in B 3 b 8), B *ok-tmane* '80,000' (B 595 b 2; *ok-tmāne* in B 213 b 4), B *śak-tman(e)* '100,000' (B 399 a 3), B *śak-ṣkäs-tm(ane)* '16,000' (B 66 b 3), B *(śt)w(ā)rka-tmane* '400,000' (B 252 b 2).

For A, the list includes: A *tri-tmāṃ* '30,000' (A 255 a 6), A *päñ-tmāṃ* '50,000' (A 295 b 2), A *ṣäk-tmāṃ* '60,000' (A 255 a 3), A *ṣpät-tmāṃ* '70,000' (A 295 b 3), A *okät-tmāṃ* '80,000' (A 314 b 2), A *śäk-tmāṃ* '100,000' (A 308 a 1), *(śä)k-wepi tmāṃ* '120,000' (A 376 b 4–5), A *śtwar-känt tmāṃ* '4,000,000' (A 229 a 5), A *ṣäk-känt tmāṃ* '6,000,000' (A 234 b 6).

4.1.25.2. No case forms of multiples of 'ten thousand' have been found.

4.1.25.3. Multiples of 'ten thousand' can be expected to occur in complex configurations. Examples are: B *tarya-tᵘmane wiltse piś-käṃnte pśāka wi* '32,552' (Otani 3.2–3), B *piś-tᵘmane ṣkas-yiltse wi-käṃnte ikäṃ ok* '56,228' (Otani 3.3–4), B *ṣuk-tmane piś-iltse-mpa* 'with 75,000' (B 398 a 1), B *ṣuk-tmane ṣuk-yältse ṣu(k)-känte* '77,700' (B 522 b 3); A *(we)-tmāṃ we-wälts* '22,000' (A 255 a 6), A *śtwar-tmāṃ päñ-wälts* '45,000' (A 255 b 3), A *okät-tmāṃ śtwar-wälts* '84,000' (A 256 a 5), A *śäk-ṣapi-tmāṃ okät-wälts* '118,000' (A 305 a 8).

Bracketed constructions are: B *ok-tmān'-āntseṃ* 'with 80,000 skandhas' (LS 5 b 4) and B *ṣkas-tmane-pikᵘla* 'of 60,000 years' (B 3 b 1).

B *(o)ktmanema(ñ)ñe*, rendering Skt. *(aśītisā)hasra* in B 538 b 1 and probably to be corrected to read B *ok-tmanenma-ññe*, is the only known case of a plural used in expressing a multiple of 'ten thousand' and embedded in a bracketed construction.

4.1.26. 'One hundred thousand'

4.1.26.0. A *lakṣ* is attested in A 47 a 5.
4.1.26.1. The source form is Skt. *lakṣá-* 'lakh; 100,000'.

4.1.27. 'Ten million'

4.1.27.0. The A form is *kor*. In B, beside *kor*, there is also a learned variant *koṭ-*.
4.1.27.1. The source of the borrowed items is Skt. *koṭiḥ* 'crore; 10,000,000'. In A, *kor* was treated as a nonneuter consonant stem; in B, the word was included in a declension class that has a number of loanwords with less than three morphophonemic syllables as members.
4.1.27.2. Oblique case forms are attested in A *koris* (A 315 b 3) and in the (nominative-)accusative B *ko(ra)nma*. Postpositional phrases are found in B *k(o)ṭanma-sa* (B 290.2), B *(ko)ränma-sa* (B 203 b 1), and A *koris-yo* (A 26 b 1) 'by crores'.
4.1.27.3. In both languages, 'crore' is used to express very high numbers. Thus one finds: A *taryāk ṣäkpi koris* '360,000,000' (A 17 a 4), A *we-känt taryāk śkaṃ koris śtwar-känt-tmāṃ* '2,304,000,000' (A 229 a 5); B *(śt)w(ā)rka-tmane ko(ra)nma* '4,000,000,000,000' (B 252 b 2).

4.2. Ordinal numbers

4.2.0. As in other Indo-European languages, 'first' stands apart from all other ordinals: it shows no formal relationship whatsoever with the corresponding cardinal 'one'.

The other Tocharian ordinals, including 'second', are derived from the same lexical nuclei as the corresponding cardinals. Ordinals differ from these by the presence of a suffix or a suffix complex. Descriptively speaking, three such configurations are to be noted: (1) B *-te*, A *-t*; (2) B *-(a)nte*, A *-(ä)nt*; (3) A *-iñci*.
4.2.0.1. B *-te* and A *-t* correspond to *-tos* in Gk. *tétartos* 'fourth', *pémptos* 'fifth', etc.

B *-(a)nte*, A *-(ä)nt* resulted from a resegmentation of forms in B *-te*, A *-t* after the final nasal of the stem of a cardinal when this final nasal had been lost at the end of a free form: when, e. g., the reflex of PIE **deḱm̥* had become CToch. **śəkə* (> B *śak*, A *śäk*), the Common Tocharian ordinal **śəkəntV* ceased to be analyzed as **śəkən-tV*, but was now interpreted as **śəkə-ntV*; the new suffix complex could then be transferred to forms without an old nasal (note in particular 4.2.11.).

A *-iñci*, in its turn, shows the reflex of a **-yo-* suffix seemingly attached to the secondary suffix complex A *-änt*; however, as will be seen later (cf. 4.2.12.1.), a different analysis seems preferable.

4.2.0.2. The paradigms that can be extracted from attested ordinals, are the following:

Type 1				
Singular	masculine	nominative:	B *-te*	A *-t*
		accusative:	B *-ce*	A *-c, -cäṃ*
		genitive:	B *-cepi*	
	feminine	nominative:	B *-ca*	A *-ci*
		accusative:	B *-cai*	A *-ccāṃ*
Plural	masculine	nominative:	B *-ci*	A *-ce*
		accusative:	B *-ceṃ*	A *-ces*
	feminine	nominative:	B *-tona**	A *-taṃ**
		accusative:	B *-tona**	A *-taṃ**
Type 2				
Singular	masculine	nominative:	B *-nte*	A *-nt*
		accusative:	B *-ñce*	A *-ñcäṃ*
		genitive:	B *-ñcepi**	
	feminine	nominative:	B *-ñca*	A *-ñci**
		accusative:	B *-ñcai**	A *-ñcāṃ*
Plural	masculine	nominative:	B *-ñci**	A *-ñce*
		accusative:	B *-ñceṃ*	A *-ñces*
	feminine	nominative:	B *-ntona**	A *-ntaṃ**
		accusative:	B *-ntona**	A *-ntaṃ**
Type 3				
Singular	masculine	nominative:		A *-ñci*
		accusative:		A *-ñciṃ*
		genitive:		A *-ñcināp**
Plural	masculine	nominative:		A *-ñciñi**
		accusative:		A *-ñcinäs*

(As no feminine form survived of type 3, no feminine paradigm will be posited here; this decision does not imply the assumption that no such paradigm existed in Tocharian A.)

4.2.0.2.1. The paradigms of B *-te*, A *-t*, and B *-nte*, A *-nt* show the usual reshaping of the adjectival inflection after the pattern of the demonstratives – a palatalized stem is introduced as the second masculine stem of an adjective agreeing in its nominative stem with forms like Gk. *tétartos* 'fourth'. The feminine nominatives B *-ca*, A *-ci*, and B *-ñca*, A *-ñci** reflect the presence of the normal gender-shifting suffix of Tocharian adjectives, viz., CToch. **-ya* < PIE **-yA*; the feminine accusative forms of the singular show the extension of the first stem to the accusative singular (as opposed to the preservation of the second stem in B *allok* 'other'; cf. 4.3.6.1.) generally found in Tocharian adjectives. The feminine plural forms have at present only a hypothetical status; there is a remote possibility that B *-tona** may have to be replaced by B *-cana**.

The development PIE **-tyA* > CToch. **-ča* (> B *-ca*, A *-ci*), natural as it may seem, poses some problems. There are several good examples to support a claim that PIE **-t-yA* resulted in B *-tsa*, A *-ts* (cf. Winter 1962: 20–22; none of the additional cases in van Windekens 1976: 81 carries much weight). Obviously, one cannot be satisfied with having to posit different developments under identical conditions. However, a possibility may be worth considering: van Windekens (1976: 80) assumes that PIE **-ti-* resulted in B A *-ci-*; those of his examples that seem immediately persuasive, involve not just PIE **-ti-*, but PIE **-tiy-* (as a Sievers-Edgerton variant of PIE **-ty-*); this sequence may have had a palatalizing influence even if **-i-* by itself did not affect a preceding CToch. **t* (cf. B *tin-* 'be soiled(?)', B *stinäsk-* 'silence(?)'). To be sure, the question why one should find A *lāñci* 'royal' but B *lāntsa*, A *lāntsa-* 'queen' remains unsettled and unsettling; it seems noteworthy that several of the probable cases of a development PIE **-tyV-* > CToch. **-tsV-* involve positions after Common Tocharian vowels so that one might feel tempted to think of B A *-ts-* as descended from the postvocalic Sievers-Edgerton variant of PIE **-tyV-*. If the reflexes of Proto-Indo-European nasales sonantes retained a vocalic status in Common Tocharian, even feminine forms of adjectives in what became *-w* in B might be accommodated; B *lāntsa*, A *lāntsa-* 'queen' and A *pontsāṃ* (accusative singular feminine) continue to present difficulties.

If the hypothesis advanced here is adequate, then a form like A *wci* 'second' (nominative singular feminine) will have to be explained, along with B *trica* 'third' (nominative singular feminine) as owing its *-c-* instead of *-ts-* to a transfer from higher cardinals such as B *starte* 'fourth', B *piṅkte* 'fifth', etc., in which *-c-* was developed regularly if the above proposal is warranted.

4.2.0.2.2. Reference to case forms attested will be made with the appropriate individual ordinals.

4.2.1. 'First'

4.2.1.0. The forms of B and A are not related: B renders 'first' by *pärweṣṣe*, A, by *maltow-inu*. The forms of B *pärweṣṣe* are those of normal (denominative) adjectives in B *-ṣṣe* 'pertaining to X'; beside the masculine singular nominative A *maltow-inu*, only the accusative A *maltow-inunt* has survived; 'first' thus seems to fall in with the adjectives or, alternatively, with the participles in A *-u* (cf. Sieg – Siegling – Schulze 1931: 161).

4.2.1.1. The noun form from which B *pärweṣṣe* 'first' was derived, is attested in the prefix-bearing adverb B *yparwe* '(at) first'. B *parwe* 'first' is attested in B *parwe kṣuṃ-tsa* 'in the first regnal year' (cf. Pinault 1987: 81). B *parwe* in B *yparwe* is to be identified as an old neuter singular, reflecting PIE **prXwom*; other developments from PIE **prXwo-* are Skt. *pū́rvaḥ*, OCS *prĭvŭ* 'first'. The sequence **-Xw-* developed to **-uw-* in Common Tocharian, which then was reinterpreted as a Sievers-Edgerton variant of **-w-* and reduced to **-w-*. That this was a Common Tocharian development is indicated by the fact that B *parwe** had its counterpart in *pärwa-* in A *pärwat* 'first-born (son)'.

The very existence of A *pärwat* confirms the status of A *maltow-inu* as an innovation. A *maltow-* remains unchanged in the accusative form A *maltow-inunt*, which means that it cannot be a modifying adjective, but must be viewed as an old neuter used adverbially (cf. A *malto* 'first' occurring in its sandhi form *maltw* in A 217 a 5). The masculine nominative A *malto** must have been derived by means of a suffix reflecting PIE **-went-*, etc., 'provided with X; possessing X' from an unattested noun A *malta-** corresponding neatly to B *melte* 'elevation'.

For A *-inu*, B *ynūca* 'walker' is to be compared. The suffix B *-ca* was usually added to past participles to form agent nouns (cf. Krause 1952: 44); a B participle **inu* would have A *inu* as its expected equivalent. The only problematic point is that A *inu* does not have preterit function, as far as can be determined; but neither have the agent nouns in B *-uca*, etc.

The alternative proposal made by Krause – Thomas (1960: 161) cannot be accepted: PIE **eynowent-s* would have yielded not A *inu*, but **ino**.

4.2.2. 'Second'

4.2.2.0. The attested nominative singular masculine forms are B *wate, wäte*; A *wät*.

4.2.2.1. The underlying Common-Tocharian form is **wətV-*. The projection backwards yields PIE **dwito-* (cf. Penney 1976–1977: 90 n. 67), which allows us to recognize Skt. *Dvitáḥ* (cf. also Skt. *dvitā́* 'doubly so') and Khotanese Saka *śäta-* 'second' (cf. Bailey 1951: 41) as exact parallels, though not as forms offering sufficient support for a **dwito-* as part of the Proto-Indo-European lexicon. For Tocharian forms that can be used to back up the reconstruction favored here cf. 4.1.12.1. A derivation from otherwise nonexistent **dweto-* (van Windekens 1976: 566) fails to account for the absence of palatalization in B *wate*.

As an association of the ordinal 'second' with the cardinal 'two' in all probability does not go back to Common Indo-European times, and as a borrowing of the form underlying Khotanese Saka *śäta-*, viz., **dwita-*, does not seem very likely, an independent development has to be assumed for a period not later than Common Tocharian. Apparently a spread of the ordinal suffix *-*tV-*, which had earlier affected 'third' (cf. 4.2.3.2.), extended to 'second', where the compound form of 'two' (PIE **dwi-*) was selected as the basis for the new ordinal. (Toch. B /wə-/ < **dwi-* may have been reshaped to *wi-* under the influence of the cardinal 'two' in B *wipew-* 'biped'; cf. 4.1.2.3.) This selection has a parallel in Indo-Iranian, cf. Skt. *dvitī́yah*, OPers. *duvitīyam*, etc.

4.2.2.2. In B, one finds inflectional forms of the masculine and feminine that agree with the normal adjectival paradigm, and forms of the neuter that follow the pattern of nouns. Examples are:

Singular	masculine	nominative:	*wate* (B 8 b 3), *wäte* (H 149.291 b 5)
		accusative:	*wace* (B 27 b 5), *wce* (B 29 a 5)
		genitive:	*wcepi* (B 474.4, cf. B 467.1)
		dative:	*wace-śc-o* (Berlin text)
	feminine	nominative:	*waca**
		accusative:	*wacai**

Plural	masculine	nominative:	*waci**
		accusative:	*wacemṃ* (B 603 a 1)
	feminine	nominative/ accusative:	*wtona**
Singular	neuter	nominative/ accusative:	*wate* (B 25 b 3)
		genitive:	*wtentse* (B 3 a 4), *wteṃtse* (B 22 a 5)
		instrumental:	*wate-sa* (B 108 a 3)
		dative:	*wteś* (B 318 a 3)

(The genitive appears to have been reinterpreted as a neuter in B 512 a 1, so that a hybrid instrumental B *wtentse-sa* could come into existence; an interpretation as an elliptic construction does not seem likely.)

In A, the situation is essentially comparable to that in B, but it is complicated by the fact that two types of masculine singular forms occur:

Singular	masculine	nominative:	*wät* (A 3 a 5)
		accusative:	(1) *wäc* (A 394 b 1), *-wäc* (A 155 a 4)
			(2) *wcaṃ* (A 150 b 6)
		genitive:	(2) *wcanis* (A 150 b 6)
		instrumental:	(1) *-wcā* (A 331 b 5)
			(2) *-wcanā* (A 186 a 3)
		comitative:	(1) *-wcaśśäl* (A 277 b 4)
		dative:	(1) *-wcac* (A 15 a 1)
			(2) *-wcanac* (A 336 a 3)
		ablative:	(1) *-wcäṣ* (A 347 a 3)
			(2) *-wcanäṣ* (A 212 a 2)
		locative:	(2) *-wcanaṃ* (A 262 b 7), *wcanan-äkk* (A 18 a 6)
	feminine	nominative:	*wci* (A 291 a 2)
		accusative:	*wäccāṃ* (A 145 a 4)
Plural	masculine	nominative:	*wce**
		accusative:	*wces* (A 305 a 4)

Items with preposed hyphen occur only in A *ālamwäc* 'each other' and its case forms; for A *ālamwäc* and its counterpart B *alyewce, alyauce*, cf. 4.3.7.

The A paradigm (1) agrees with the paradigm of the masculine oblique forms of B. It seems possible to assume that A **wəca-* was transferred to the adjectival declension prior to the loss of a final vowel; the result was that the short forms (A *wäc, wcā*, etc.) continued to reflect the pronominal declension also found in B, the longer ones (A *wcan-*, etc.), the adjectival declension. What then needs an explanation is why A *-a-* was once lost, once retained. One may think of different tactic conditions – **wəca* in the interior of a noun phrase may have been protected from vowel loss, while **wəca* without a following noun or adjective may have undergone vowel reduction. The *-n-* marking forms of pattern (2) seem to have been transferred also to A *wu* 'two' (cf. 4.1.2.2.); note that A *wcan-* and A *wun-* are masculine forms.

The neuter accusative of A *wät* appears to be present in the rendering of 'dvitināma' in A 384 b 2 *wät-ñom*. The instrumental is found in A *wtā* (A 94 a 4), *wtā-k* (A 67 a 1) 'again'; the ablative, in A *wtaṣ* 'a second time' (A 432 a 3).

4.2.2.3. Reference has already been made to the compound forms B *ālyewce, ālyauce*, A *ālamwäc* 'each other' (cf. 4.3.7.). B *wace* is also found in a juxtapound bracketed to form an adjective, viz., B *wace-dhyanaṣṣana* 'pertaining to the second dhyāna' (PK AS 19.4 a 3).

The neuter stem forms the basis for another B *-ṣṣe* adjective, B *wteṣṣe* 'of the second degree(?)'.

4.2.3. 'Third'

4.2.3.0. The lead forms attested are B *trīte* (*trite*), A *trit*.

4.2.3.1. Common Tocharian **tritV-* cannot be compared directly with Gk. *trítos* 'third' – PIE **-i-* should have become CToch. **-ə-* as in B *wase*, A *wäs* 'poison'; B *wate*, A *wät* 'second' (cf. 4.2.2.1.); B *wasto*, A *wäṣt* 'twofold' (cf. 4.3.3.); B *k^{u}se*, A *kus* 'who?' (cf. Penney 1976–1977: 90 n. 67). If Szemerényi is justified in believing that Proto-Indo-European ordinals were basically thematizations of the cardinals, then the expected form of the ordinal was PIE **triyos* (cf. Szemerényi 1960: 82). Now, if a Common Tocharian form **trəyV-* (or even its Proto-Tocharian antecedent **triyV-*) was subjected to an analogical reshaping under the influence of 'fourth', the outcome would have to be CToch. **tritV-*.

4.2.3.2. The inflectional forms and postpositional phrases cover roughly the same range as those for 'second'.

In B, one finds: Singular masculine nominative B *trīte* (B 8 b 3), *trite* (B 199 a 2), accusative B *trīce* (B 184.2), *trice* (B 591 a 1), genitive B *tricepi* (B 297.1 a 2), ablative B *tricemeṃ* (B 3 a 8); plural masculine accusative B *trīceṃ* (B 603 a 2). The neuter is attested in the instrumental B *trite-sa* 'for the third time' (B 25 b 3).

In A, the forms are: Singular masculine nominative A *trit* (A 307 a 4), accusative A *tricäṃ* (A 394 b 1), locative A *tricnaṃ* (A 397 a 4). Of the neuter, the ablative is attested in A *tritaṣ* 'for the third time' (A 432 a 3). The transfer of the accusative singular form of the masculine to the adjectival declension must have taken place later for 'third' (and 'fourth', 'fifth', etc.) than for 'second' because A *tric-* and not **trica-** is expanded by *-ṃ*; cf. 4.2.2.2.

4.2.3.3. A *tricäṃ-dhyāṃ-ṣiṃ* 'pertaining to the third dhyāna' is to be compared with B *wace-dhyanaṣṣana* mentioned in 4.2.2.3.

A B *-ṣṣe* adjective derived from the neuter B *trīte* is found in B *(tri)teṣṣa* 'of the third degree(?)' (B 327 B 3–4).

4.2.4. 'Fourth'

4.2.4.0. The lead forms attested are B *śtarte* (*śtartte*), A *śtärt*.

4.2.4.1. Common Tocharian **śətərtV-* has a perfect parallel in Gk. *tétartos, tétratos*; cf. Van Windekens (1976: 489).

4.2.4.2. Surviving case forms and postpositional phrases are:

B: Singular masculine nominative B *śtarte* (B 484.4), *śtartte* (B 177 b 7), accusative B *śtarce* (B 333 b 6), *śtarcce* (B 462.1), genitive B *śtärcepi* (B 510 a 1), instrumental B *śtarce-sa* (H 150.50 a 4); feminine nominative B *śtarca* (B 11 a 1); plural masculine accusative B *śtarceṃ* (B 603 a 3).

A: Singular masculine nominative A *śtärt* (A 307 b 4), accusative A *śtärc* (type 1; A 299 b 1), *śtärcäṃ* (type 2; A 394 b 1); plural masculine accusative A *śtärces* (A 305 a 5).

4.2.4.3. An adjective derived by bracketing is again found in A *śtärcäṃ-dhyāṃ-ṣiṃ* 'pertaining to the fourth dhyāna' (A 397 b 3); cf. 4.2.2.3. and 4.2.3.3.

4.2.5. 'Fifth'

4.2.5.0. The lead forms attested are B *piṅkte*, A *pänt*.

4.2.5.1. Common Tocharian **p'ənktV-*, the source of both B *piṅkte* and – with cluster reduction – A *pänt*, is the exact equivalent of Gk. *pémptos*, Lith. *peñktas*, etc.

4.2.5.2. Forms attested in B are: Singular masculine nominative B *piṅkte* (B 461.4), accusative B *piṅkce* (B 37 a 1), *piṅce* (LP 104 a 2), genitive B *piṅce(pi)* (B 510 a 3), *piṃce(pi)* (B 510 a 5), instrumental B *piñce-sa* (H 150.50 a 4); feminine nominative B *p(i)ṅkca* (B 131 frg. 2.2); plural masculine accusative B *(pi)ṅk(c)eṃ* (B 603 a 4). For forms of the neuter, cf. 4.2.5.3.

In A, one finds: singular masculine nominative A *pänt* (A 3 a 1), accusative A *päñcäṃ* (type 2; A 280 a 4); feminine accusative A *päñcāṃ* (A 145 a 6); plural masculine accusative A *päñces* (A 305 a 6).

4.2.5.3. A neuter form is the second element of B *epiṅkte* (*epiṅte*) 'between', more literally 'in the fifth (place)', that is, in a position added to those given by the four cardinal points (cf. Winter 1983: 321–322). It is treated as a noun in the locative phrase B *teṃ-epiṅkte-ne* 'in between' (B 107 a 3) and in the compound B *snai-epiṅkte* 'immediately' (B 107 a 8). Forms with cluster reduction are fairly common, cf. B *epiṅte* in B 22 a 6, *epiṅte-ne* in B 358 a 3.

An ablative is formed from the equivalent of B *epiṅkte* in A: the line A 383 a 2 contains A *opäntäṣ*.

4.2.6. 'Sixth'

4.2.6.0. The lead forms are B *ṣkaste*, A *ṣkäṣt*.

4.2.6.1. Common Tocharian **šəkəstV-* is the regular equivalent of forms such as Lat. *sextus*, Goth. *saihsta*; the underlying form is PIE **sek̑sto-* without *-*w*- and with *-*s*-.

4.2.6.2. Attested forms in B include: Singular masculine nominative B *ṣkaste* (B 199 a 3), *ṣkäste* (B 342 a 2), accusative B *ṣkaśce* (LP 114 a 1), *ṣkasce* (G-Qa 1.1), *ṣkacce* (B 198 a 4; G-Su 36.1), genitive B *ṣkace(pi)* (B 510 b 3); plural masculine accusative B *ṣka*(*cceṃ*?) (B 603 b 1). A nominative feminine singular may be found in B *ṣkäśca* (B 131 frg. 3.1; cf. fragment 4). The expected development outside the masculine nominative singular is B -*śc*-, with dialectally conditioned variants -*śś*- and -*ṣc*-; no explanation can be given for attested -*sc*-, -*cc*-, and -*c*-.

In A, one finds singular masculine nominative A *ṣkäṣt* (A 156 a 4), accusative A *ṣkäśśäṃ* (type 2; A 218 a 3).

4.2.7. 'Seventh'

4.2.7.0. Lead forms are B *ṣuktante* (*ṣuktänte*), A *ṣäptänt*.

4.2.7.1. B *ṣukt*- has been discussed in 4.1.7.1. A *ṣäptänt* has the appearance of being an exact match of Lith. *septiñtas*, but since this form is of more recent attestation than Lith. *sẽkmas* (cf. Fraenkel 1965: 772), the agreement must be due to independent parallel development. A *ṣäptänt* reflects Proto-Tocharian **s'əpətəntV-* (or **-mtV-*), a form in which the ordinal suffix **-tV-* had been added to the cardinal. When **-əN* was reduced to **-ə* in Common Tocharian, the ordinal suffix could be reinterpreted as **-ntV-* (just as in 'tenth'); cf. 4.2.0.1.

4.2.7.2. From published texts, the following forms can be cited for B: Singular masculine nominative B *ṣuktante* (B 183 a 4), *ṣuktänte* (B 135 b 3), accusative B *ṣuktañce* (B 461.5), *ṣuktaṃñce* (LP 6 a 1), *ṣuktäñce* (B 132 b 5).

Forms from A are: Singular masculine nominative A *ṣäptänt* (A 303 b 3), accusative A *ṣäptäñcäṃ* (A 78 b 4); feminine accusative A *ṣäptä(ñcāṃ)* (A 145 b 1).

4.2.8. 'Eighth'

4.2.8.0. The lead forms are B *oktante*, A *oktänt**.

4.2.8.1. A reconstruction of an earlier form for 'eighth' has been undertaken in 4.1.8.1. The replacement of this earlier form by an analogically reshaped one must be ascribed to Common Tocharian. CToch. **-tV-* of the ordinal probably had its origin in 'tenth' and was transferred from there to 'ninth', 'eighth', and 'seventh' (for 'seventh', a continuation of the old **-tV-* sequence 'fourth', 'fifth', 'sixth' is of course also possible, should one prefer to consider the reshaping of 'eighth' relatively late). CToch. **-əntV-* in 'eighth' seems likely to be due to transfer from 'seventh'.

4.2.8.2. Attested forms from B are: Singular masculine nominative B *oktante* (B 112 b 5) and *oktunte* (B 199 a 4), accusative B *oktañc(e)* (B 459.1); plural masculine accusative B *oktañceṃ* (B 603 b 3). The only form to survive in A is the accusative masculine plural A *oktäñces* (A 305 a 7).

A comment is required for the hapax B *oktunte*. Tempting as it may be to consider B *-u-* descended from PIE **-ō(w)-* (cf. A *oktuk* 'eighty'; see 4.1.18.1.), it seems wiser to assume that B *oktunte* was reshaped after B *ñunte* 'ninth'.

4.2.9. 'Ninth'

4.2.9.0. No form for 'ninth' has survived in A; the B entry is B *ñunte*.

4.2.9.1. The explanation offered in 4.1.19.1. for B *ñumka* and B *ñuṅka* is to be extended to B *ñunte* instead of B **ñwante**; the alternative offered

by van Windekens (1976: 328–329), in its turn, cannot be applied to the B forms for 'ninety' and hence is to be rejected.
4.2.9.2. The following forms can be listed: singular masculine nominative B *ñunte* (B 123 b 4), accusative B *ñuñce* (B 428 a 6); plural masculine instrumental B *ñuncen-tsa* (H 149 add 123 a 4).

4.2.10. 'Tenth'

4.2.10.0. The lead forms are B *śkante* (*śkänte*), A *śkänt*.
4.2.10.1. Common Tocharian **śəkəntV-* is the exact counterpart of Gk. *dékatos*, Lith. *dešim̃tas* < PIE **deḱm̥tos*.
4.2.10.2. Forms attested in B are: singular masculine nominative B *śkante* (H add 149.63 a 5), B *śkänte* (B 123 b 4), accusative B *śkäñce* (B 37 a 1); feminine nominative B *śkäñca* (B 131 frg. 4), accusative B *śkañcai* (PK NS 244 a 3).

From A, only one form can be cited: Singular masculine nominative A *śkänt* (A 291 b 6).

4.2.11. 'Eleventh' through 'nineteenth'

4.2.11.1. The ordinals referring to 'teens were formed in different ways in B and A: In B, we find asyndetic combinations of the type 'tenth' (plus) 'second'; in A, the ordinal suffix is attached to the complex cardinal, which means that A *-nt* occurs not after the digit proper, but after A *-pi*.
4.2.11.2. No etymological discussion is required.
4.2.11.3. Only a limited number of forms can be listed.

In B, the following have been preserved: B *ś(kä)ntewäte* 'twelfth' (H 149.291 b 5), B *śkäñce piṅkce* 'fifteenth' (B 37 a 1), B *śkänte ñunte* 'nineteenth' (B 123 b 4). All texts cited are from Ming-öy Qızıl or of MQ type; there is thus no reason to consider these forms compounds or juxtapounds; they are to be viewed as numeral phrases.

In A, the list includes: A *śäk-ṣapint* 'eleventh' (A 291 b 7), A *śäk-ṣäkpiñcäṃ* 'sixteenth' (A 303 b 8), A *śäk-ṣpätpi(nt)* 'seventeenth' (A 292 a 2), A *śäk-ñupint* 'nineteenth' (A 292 a 3). A type-3 form is found in the accusative plural masculine form A *śäk-ñupiñcinäs* 'nineteenth' (A 150 b 2).

4.2.12. 'Twentieth'

4.2.12.0. The entry for B is *ikante*, for A probably *wikiñci**.
4.2.12.1. A suggestion concerning the possible prehistory of B *ikante* has been made in 4.1.12.2.

A *-kiñci* as found in A *wikiñci** as well as in attested higher ordinals can be explained (cf. 4.2.0.2.1.) as reflecting an underlying Proto-Indo-European form **(d)ḱm̥t-yo-* with a Sievers-Edgerton variant **-iyo*. A *-kiñci* thus corresponds exactly to the constituent *-katio-* in Doric Greek *diakátioi* 'two hundred' (cf. Frisk 1960: 385); the difference in meaning is discussed elsewhere in this volume (cf. chapter 11).

4.2.12.2. In B, the following forms are found: Singular masculine nominative B *(ikä)nte* (B 135 b 2–3); plural masculine accusative B *ikañceṃ* (B 603 a 2).

4.2.12.3. Ordinals from 'twenty-first' through 'twenty-ninth' are fairly well attested in both languages:

B:	
'twenty-first'	(not found)
'twenty-second'	*(i)kañceṃ waceṃ* (B 603 a 1)
'twenty-third'	*ikañceṃ (tr)iceṃ* (B 603 a 2)
'twenty-fourth'	*ika(ñce)ṃ śtarceṃ* (B 603 a 3)
'twenty-fifth'	*ika(ñceṃ pi)ṅk(c)eṃ* (B 603 a 4)
'twenty-sixth'	*ikañceṃ ṣka(cceṃ?)* (B 603 b 1)
'twenty-seventh'	*(ikä)nte ṣuktänte* (B 135 b 3), *ikañceṃ (ṣu)ktañceṃ* (B 603 b 2)
'twenty-eighth'	*ikañceṃ oktañceṃ* (B 603 b 3)
'twenty-ninth'	(not found)
A:	
'twenty-first'	*(wiki ṣa)pint* (A 292 a 4), *wiki ṣapi(ñcinäs)* (A 151 a 1–2)
'twenty-second'	*wiki wepiñci* (A 226 b 4), *wiki (wepiñci)näs* (A 151 a 2)
'twenty-third'	*wiki täry(āpint)* (A 292 a 5), *wiki täryā(piñci)* (A 238.6)
'twenty-fourth'	*wiki (śtwarpiñcinäs)* (A 151 a 3)
'twenty-fifth'	*wiki päñpint* (A 292 a 6), *wiki päñpiñcinäs* (A 151 a 3)
'twenty-sixth'	*wiki ṣäkpiñci(näs)* (A 151 a 4)
'twenty-seventh'	*wiki ṣpätpiñcinäs* (A 151 a 4)
'twenty-eighth'	*wiki okätpiñcinäs* (A 151 a 5)
'twenty-ninth'	*(wiki ñu)piñcinäs* (A 151 a 5)

The forms in A *-pint* are from a single text, a manuscript of the Maitreyasamitināṭaka, the forms in A *-piñci*, from two different manuscripts. As all higher ordinals show A *-iñci* (the statement in Sieg – Siegling – Schulze 1931: 200 is misleading), it must be concluded that the forms in A 292 are deviant.

4.2.13. 'Thirtieth'

4.2.13.0. The ordinal is found in A *taryākiñci**.
4.2.13.2. The only form surviving is the accusative plural masculine, A *taryākiñcinäs* (A 151 a 6).
4.2.13.3. Ordinals for numbers between 'thirty-one' and 'thirty-nine' have survived in A *taryākk okätpiñc(i)///* 'thirty-eighth' (unpublished fragment, cf. Sieg – Siegling – Schulze 1931: 199) as well as in B *(täryā)ka śtarcce* (PK NS 245 b 5) 'thirty-fourth' and B *(tä)ryāka ṣkaśce* (PK NS 245 a 1) 'thirty-sixth' – cf. Bernhard (1958: 114).

The B forms are noteworthy: they seem to indicate that the multiple marking of the ordinal function in complex numerals did not extend beyond 'nineteenth'. Unfortunately, the data that have become available as of now, do not allow a more definitive statement.

4.2.14. 'Fortieth' and higher ordinals

4.2.14.0. The texts provide a basis for setting up A *śtwarākiñci** 'fortieth' and A *säkskiñci** 'sixtieth'.
4.2.14.1. The forms actually attested are A *stwarākiñci///* (A 203 a 3) and A *säkskiñciṃ* (accusative singular masculine) (A 18 a 2).
4.2.14.3. A higher ordinal containing a digit has been preserved in A *nmuk ṣapiñci///* 'ninety-first' (A 436 a 4).

4.3. Other numerals

4.3.0. Of other classes of numerals, only that of the distributives is relatively well attested (even this one, however, only in B). One term is available that can be used to express a fraction. While '*n*-fold' as a rule is designated by compounds or juxtapounds (cf. 4.1.3.3., 4.1.4.3., 4.1.5.3., 4.1.7.3.), a special term is available for 'double'. Derived forms exist for adjectives denoting 'fourfold' and 'eightfold'.

Finally, some words outside the number chains, but related semantically and distributionally deserve mention here: 'both', 'alone', 'other', 'each other'.

The arrangement of subtopics within 4.3. will follow the sequence of this enumeration. The sections 4.3.1. and 4.3.2., with their respective subsections, deviate only slightly from Winter (1987).

4.3.1. Distributives

4.3.1.0. Distributive numbers can be expressed phrasally or by means of a suffix added to a cardinal. The phrasal expression occurs in both A and and B, the suffix /-ar/ is limited to B (but note 4.3.1.2.1.).
4.3.1.1. As no retraction of the accent occurs, it is likely that B /-ar/ represents (morphophonemic) |-arə|. The shwa can be from various sources; no Indo-European parallels seem to be available.
4.3.1.2. The phrasal expression of the distributive function is commonly used for 'one each'; the expression is formed by a repetition of the required gender and case form of the numeral. Thus one finds in B:

Singular	masculine	nominative B	*ṣe ṣe* (B 548.2)
		accusative B	*ṣeme ṣeme* (B 270 b 2), *ṣeme ṣṣeme* (B 565 a 3)
	feminine	accusative B	*somo somo* (B 74 a 3), *sanai sanai* (B 366 a 4)

From A, one may list:

Singular	masculine	nominative A	*sas sas* (A 65 a 5)
		accusative A	*ṣom ṣom* (A 307 a 1)
		genitive A	*ṣomāp ṣomāp* (A 313 b 6)

With numerals higher than 'one', repetition is rarely found. Examples include: B *okt okt* 'eight at a time' (B 509 b 1), B *ñu ñu* 'nine at a time' (B 591 a 3).
4.3.1.3. The attestations of B *-ār* are distributed in such a way that one may assume that at least all noncomplex numerals could be so extended. The meaning 'one each', 'two each', etc., agrees closely with that of 'in groups of one, two, three, ...', so that the argument in Sieg – Siegling – Schulze (1931: 486), repeated without additional evidence by van Windekens (1979: 283), amounts to hair-splitting.

Forms surviving are:

'in groups of one'	masculine	B *ṣyār* (B 607 a 4; uncertain)
	feminine	B *somār* (B 28 a 5)
'in groups of two'		B *wyār* (B 497 b 4)
'in groups of four'		B *śwerār* (cf. Sieg – Siegling – Schulze 1931: 486)
'in groups of six'		B *ṣkāsār* (Paris text)
'in groups of seven'		B *ṣukar* (cited by Broomhead 1962 s. v. from Stein 3 b 5)
'in groups of eight'		B *oktār* (B 574 a 2; see below)
'in groups of nine'		B *ñᵘwār* (B 591 a 4)
'always in groups of ten'		B *śkarśkār* (B 41 a 8)

Forms derived from decads are B *pⁱśākar* (B 108 a 5), B *pśākar* (HW 4.4) 'by fifties', B *ṣuktakar* (HW 4.3) 'by seventies', and B *oktakar* (HW 4.2) 'by eighties'. A form derived from B *yaltse* is found in B *yiltsār* (PR 36.23) 'by the thousand'.

As for complex distributive numerals, B *wi(yā)r-känte pⁱśākar* (B 108 a 5) 'by two-hundred-and-fifties' indicates that the first member of the juxtapound B *wi-känte* 'two hundred' was extended by B /-ar/; this fact makes it likely that for B 574 a 2–3 a reading B *oktār-tma(ne)* or even B *oktār-tma(ne śtwārar-yältse)* 'in groups of eighty(-four) thousand' should be suggested (as against Sieg – Siegling 1953: 361; the metrical analysis of the lines in question is far from certain).

There is no accent retraction affecting B *-ār*; it is therefore proper to assume that the underlying form of the suffix was morphophonemic |-ar|. Details of the etymology are, however, in need of further clarification; the remarks found in van Windekens (1979: 283) are not helpful.

4.3.1.3.1. B *-âr* is also found in some expressions not derived from numerals, but semantically connected with counting or dividing processes.

B *kᵘśanār* 'in quantities of one *kᵘśāne*' (FW 19 a 6, 28 a 6, etc.) might be a replacement of B **ṣemār kᵘśāne*.

B *yästār*, supplied by Sieg – Siegling (1953) for the broken passage B 404 b 1, is rendered by 'je das Doppelte' in Thomas (1957: 119); the translation remains uncertain – there is no clear indication in the surviving text that the thief in question stole more than one item which then could be doubled. The attestation of B *yästār* in PK AS 17 D a 5, to which G. Pinault kindly called my attention, is in a very fragmentary context – line one of stanza two contains no more than *yästār* -- *snai-*

wace ñäkcye e - - - - (:), not enough even to attempt a translation. However, what is most disconcerting is the fact that there is no explanation available for B *y*- instead of *w*- as found in B *wasto* 'double' (for which cf. 4.3.2.); the proposal by van Windekens (1976: 596; 1979: 283) has nothing to recommend it. To be sure, it would be tempting to view B *yäst*- as a development from **y(n)-wäst*-; however, such an assumption must be considered falsified by forms with an onset B *ywār*- (see 4.3.1.4.).

B *ṣñār* has been translated in Sieg – Siegling – Schulze (1931: 486) by 'je sein, je für sich'; the passage containing this form (H 149.14 b 5) does permit an interpretation 'of each individual's own action', but the text is not clear.

The most interesting case in question is B *waiptār* / *waiptāyar* 'separate(ly)', derived, so it would seem, from B *waipte* 'apart' (the etymology of these forms will not be discussed here; for a recent treatment cf. Isebaert 1980: 114) inasmuch as here, and only here, B *-ār* is matched by A *-ār* in a semantically corresponding item, A *letkār* (: A *letäk* 'separate'). Unless the variant in B *-āyar* is the original form, so that A *-ār* could be the result of a fairly recent contraction, the absence of syncope in the second syllable of A *letkār* makes it likely that A *-ār* was borrowed from B, the more so as A *letkār* is a completely isolated form.

4.3.1.3.2. Tempting as it may seem, there is apparently no possibility of connecting B *-ār* with the nucleus of the first part of the compound form found in B *artsakauṃ*, A *ārts-koṃ* 'day by day' – B A |-tˢə| defies explanation.

4.3.1.4. The treatment of B and A forms for 'half' and 'between' provided by van Windekens (1976: 612–613, 1979: 283) contains some sound points, but has to be revised in all essentials.

The simplest form occurs as the first component of the designation of an official, B *ywārttaś* 'commander of the central region' (LP 3 a 1, 5 a 1, 29 a 1); for a similar title see B *ṣletaś* 'commander of the mountain(s)' (LP 1 a 1, 7 a 1, etc.). No analysis of the terms is offered by Pinault (1987: 76).

Van Windekens' reasoning can be accepted to the extent that B *y*- is a prefix (hardly an intensifier, but simply 'in') and that B *-wār* is taken to contain the element B *-ār* discussed here. B *-w*- I prefer not to derive from mere PIE **dw*-, but to take it to be the reflex of the masculine form of the numeral 'two', which otherwise has been lost in B (cf. 4.1.2.1.), and which in all probability should have been **u* (cf. B *ku* 'dog' < PIE **ḱwōn*, and the nominative singular masculine of the past participle in B *-u* < PIE **-wōs*).

If this analysis is correct (and this a point completely disregarded by van Windekens, although it would equally apply to what he suggests), B *ywār* would have to be interpreted as 'in (between) groups of two (parts) each'. This seems a strange way to express 'half, midway, between' until one remembers that another Tocharian expression for 'between, in between' also contained an indirect reference to 'four' and not to 'two' (cf. 4.2.5.3.).

The form B *ywārc* shows an extension which one may very tentatively identify as the dative marker shared by B *-ś-c*, A *-a-c*. For the cooccurrence of a prefix and a postposition or a case suffix see again 4.2.5.3.

By the time of our texts, B *-śc* had become established as the marker of the dative; hence B *ywārc* could no longer be analyzed properly. Therefore, the B form could be used as the first member of compounds, such as B *artsaywarcameñ* 'every half month' (H 149.5 a 2) or B *ywarcīṣi* 'at midnight' (B 65 b 8). Likewise, the instrumental B *ywār-tsa* was no longer interpreted as such, but used as an unchangeable adjective (e.g., in B 41 b 4).

As it had become unanalyzable, B *ywārc* could be extended by the particle B *-ka*, and the entire construct could be used as the nucleus of a postpositional phrase, B *ywārśka-ne* 'in the middle' (B 30 b 7; for a parallel, cf. B *enem̩* 'toward the interior' : B *eneṅka* 'in the interior' : B *eneṅka-ś* 'toward the interior'), and of a derived adjective, B *ywārśkaññe* 'middle' (B 393 frg. 1.2).

B *ywārcka* / *ywārśka* was borrowed by A; the resulting form A *ywārckā* / *ywārśkā* was reinterpreted as an instrumental case in A *-ā*, and a locative A *ywārckam̩* was created along with a derived adjective A *ywārckim̩* (A 295 b 2, 432 a 3).

B *ywārc* 'half' is also used as a constituent of a term denoting 'one and a half', B *śleywārc* (H 149.4 b 1).

Whether A *wäṣt ywārckam̩* (A 94 a 4) is the equivalent of B *śleywārc*, that is, whether it is to be interpreted as 'halfway to two' (cf. German *anderthalb*), cannot be decided.

4.3.2. The A form just cited contains a bound variant of the equivalent of a bound variant of 'two' in B, viz., *wästo-*, decomposed B *wasto*. Attestations are:

B *wästoyäkne* (B 44 b 4), *wasto-yä(kne)* (B 501.3–4) 'in two ways'
B *wasto* 'twice' (B 63 b 7)
B *wasto tot* (FW 9 b 1) 'twice that amount'
A *wäṣt-wäknā* (A 64 b 4) 'in two ways'
A *wäṣt ywārckam̩* (A 94 a 4), cf. 4.3.1.4.

Etymologically, B *wästo-*, A *wäṣt* present no problems: The Tocharian lexemes reflect a form PIE **dwistā* (< **dwi-steA*), a compound with a root noun of 'stand', a thematized variant of which is found in the adjective Skt. *dviṣṭha-* 'in two places; ambiguous'. The attempt at an explanation offered by van Windekens (1976: 565) disregards the absence of a reflex of palatalization in B *wästo-*, does not account convincingly for the *-t-*, and leaves the *-o* an underived entity.

4.3.3. For two digits, special adjectival derivatives have survived, which deserve comment.

A term for 'fourfold' occurs in B *śtwarātse**, A *śtwarāts**. The actually attested forms are:

B: Singular feminine accusative B *śtwarātsai* (B 153 a 6)
Plural feminine nominative/accusative B *śtwarātsana* (B 16 b 1)
A: Singular feminine accusative A *śtwarātsāṃ* (A 244 b 1)

While the B forms can be explained as regular adjectives containing, as their base, the bound form of the feminine stem of 'four' (cf. 4.1.4.0.), the adjective from A presents the same problem that was encountered in the case of A *śtwarāk* 'forty', but here only the first alternative mentioned in 4.1.14.1. is available: an earlier A **śtwārātsV-* is likely to have been reshaped under the influence of the cardinal 'four', A *śtwar*. There remains, however, the difficulty (as with 'forty') that one would have expected a reduction of presuffixal *-ā-* to *-a-* as a result of syncope.

'Eightfold' is B *oktatse**, A *oktats**; the following forms are found:

B:			
Singular	masculine	accusative	B *oktace* (B 17 a 7)
		genitive	B *oktacepi* (B 23 a 2)
	feminine	nominative	B *oktatsa* (B 30 a 6)
		accusative	B *oktatsai* (B 28 a 2)
A:			
Singular	feminine	nominative	A *oktatsi* (A 337 b 4), *oktasi* (B 392 a 5)
		accusative	A *oktatsāṃ* (A 251 b 3), *oktasāṃ* (A 386 a 2)

In spite of all overt similarity, B *-a-* and A *-a-* cannot be matched. B *-a-* represents stressed /ə/, A *-a-*, a phoneme /a/. The B form can be easily explained as a *-tse* extension of /oktə/, a form which would lose its final shwa before word boundary, but retain it in the interior of forms. Just as was the case with 'fourfold', the B form of 'eightfold' thus turns out to be quite regular. As for A *okta-*, the necessary comments have been made in 4.1.8.1.; attention should be called to the fact that A *-a-* in forms of 'eightfold' is not subjected to syncope.

4.3.4. The forms for 'both' agree in B, as far as their ending is concerned, with the forms for 'two'. One finds:

Nominative B	*antapi* (FY 2 b 4), *āṃtpi* (B 28 b 3), *āntpi* (B 23 b 4), *ātpi* (B 42 a 2)
Accusative B	*antapi* (B 5 b 5, 121 b 4), *āṃtpi* (B 84 b 4), *āntpi* (B 84 b 5), *ātpi* (B 25 a 1)
Dative B	*āṃtpi-ś* (B 20 b 6), *āntpi-ś* (H 149.294 b 5), *antpi-ś* (B 575 a 2), *āntpi-śc-o* (B 65 b 2)
Locative B	*antapi-ne* (LU 15 b 3)

Forms without B *-a-* occur only in metrical passages, while forms with B *-a-* are found both in prose and in poetry; therefore, B /antəpi/ is to be posited as the basic variant of the forms for 'both'. For a discussion of some other cases of variation between forms used in prose and poetry and others occurring in poetry only, see Thomas (1979).

In A, the situation is more complex. In Sieg – Siegling – Schulze (1931: 197), the following pattern is given:

	Masculine	Feminine
Nominative/'oblique'	*āmpi* (*āmpy*)	*āmpuk*
Genitive	*āmpe*?	*āmpine*

The description of the paradigm is repeated in Krause – Thomas (1960: 161). Viewed in connection with the numeral 'two' (cf. 4.1.2.0.), the distribution of the forms for 'both' over the two genders comes as a surprise, the more so as that for 'two' makes good sense in an Indo-European context (cf. 4.1.2.1.). It seems therefore proper to re-examine the data for clear cases of gender assignment for forms of 'both'.

A masculine nominative A *āmpi* is confirmed by A 144 a 2, with its reference to A *pratri* 'brothers'; a masculine accusative A *āmpi* can be identified in A 274 b 3, as A *tsaräṃ* 'hands' is shown to be masculine in A 23 b 5; A *āmpy esäṃ* 'both shoulders' in A 340 a 5 is modified by a masculine form of a past participle. A *āmpuk* is to be classified as a feminine form in A 248 b 3, where it occurs next to A *kapśiññāñ* 'bodies'. On the other hand, as pointed out by Sieg – Siegling – Schulze (1931: 198), A *āmpuk* in A 65 a 2 and A *āmpine* in A 64 b 6 have to be considered together. Now, while it is possible to assume that A *āmpuk* refers to the nonsingular of A *ṣurm* 'cause' (and hence to a noun form with feminine gender), A *āmpine* resumes a feminine plural form (A *pñintu* 'merits') and a masculine singular (A *niṣpal* 'property'); in a combination of masculine and feminine, one would expect the former to be generalized. Hence, the identification of A *āmpine* as a feminine form cannot be considered certain. As indicated by the question mark in the Sieg – Siegling – Schulze paradigm, an assignment of A *āmpe* to the masculine paradigm remains doubtful: if the feminine gender of A *ṣurmant* 'causes' (as against the masculine of the singular) offers sufficient reason for assuming that A *āmpuk* should be taken to be a feminine form, the fact that A *āmpe* modifies in two of its occurrences forms that must be taken not to be masculines, must make one utterly reluctant to accept the classification of A *āmpe* as a form of a masculine subparadigm of 'both'.

It then has to be noted that A *āmpe* and A *āmpine* belong to the same agreement class – both refer to nouns, the plural forms of which have feminine gender. The question arises as to what may have determined the choice of one or the other of the two apparent variants. Both forms occur in prose; the variation in the number of syllables thus cannot have been of importance. There is, however, one difference in the distribution of A *āmpe* and A *āmpine* that has not been noticed: as far as can be determined, A *āmpe* is used in attributive function, while A *āmpine* occurs as a nominalized form. This might be considered an accident, were it not for the fact that the forms maximally similar to A *āmpine*, that is, the dual genitives A *tine*, are also found not directly modifying a noun. It may thus be assumed that A *āmpe* and A *āmpine* were positional variants rather than forms differing in gender. If this assumption is justified, then the fact that A *āmpuk* in A 65 a 2 also fails to appear with a noun, may make one wonder whether the difference between A *āmpi* and A *āmpuk* likewise was one between bound (attributive) and free (nominalized) form. In this case A 248 b 3 would require an interpretation in which A *āmpuk* receives a high degree of independence, such as 'your bodies both'.

If the arguments offered here are based on facts, then the gender-oriented paradigm as found in Sieg – Siegling – Schulze and Krause – Thomas would have to be replaced by one in which gender was of no consequence, but for which nominalized or nonnominalized status of a form counted. A parallel for the state of affairs envisaged here is to be found in the use of two competing subparadigms of A *puk* 'all' (cf. Sieg – Siegling – Schulze 1931: 76–77).

The two subparadigms then would show different generalizations from the original inventory of forms for 'both' – the bound form would continue, in the nominative/accusative, the old neuter, the free one, the old masculine. In the genitive, two different oblique stems of the dual may have survived, one with, one without, the *-n-* extension of dual forms – cf. the genitive dual forms of the demonstrative B *tainaisäñ* / *tainaisi* vs. the corresponding nominative/accusative B *tai*.

4.3.4.1. The B form *antapi* (as well as its variants) differs from those forms in Indo-European languages which one would above all want to compare with the Tocharian words for 'both', viz., Gk. *ámphō*, Lat. *ambō*, in its onset. A *āmpi, āmpuk* presents no such problem, but it has to be kept in mind that the A forms can be derived by assuming a simple assimilation process from a Common Tocharian form with **ant-*, while no possibility appears to exist for positing a development CToch. **amp-* > B *antəp-* (the suggestion made by van Windekens 1979: 278 is not persuasive). The question then has to be asked whether the B form is more archaic in its onset not only than the A one, but also than its Greek and Latin counterparts. If so, the Tocharian, Greek, and Latin forms might be taken to be derivable from a Proto-Indo-European compound with 'both' as its second part and with a first element (in Brugmannian terms) **ant-*.

This necessary conclusion was first drawn by Jasanoff (1976), who posits a Proto-Indo-European root noun *H_2énts*, genitive *H_2ntés*, and compares Hitt. *ḫanz(a)*, Toch. B *ānte* (A *ānt*), Skt. *anti*, Gk. *antí*, all forms which may be taken to express binary, face-to-face, relationships in Indo-European languages. I find it impossible to accept Jasanoff's interpretation of the origin of **bh* in the forms for 'both', though; it seems simpler to consider **ant-bhô(w)*, etc., compounds containing the root noun mentioned and a dual form 'both'. PIE **ant-* may also be identified in forms denoting 'the other one (of two)': here an adjectival form **ant-ro-* / **ant-ero-* may have been reinterpreted as **an-tro-* / **an-tero-*, unless **antero-* (cf. Skt. *ántara-*, Goth. *anþar*, Lith. *añtras*) resulted from **ant-tero-* through a cluster reduction. Skt. *anyá-* 'another one (of many)' would then have originated from a transfer of Skt. *an-*, which was regular in the term for 'the other one (of two)' to the form that should have had a reflex of PIE **al-* (this interpretation of Skt. *anyá-* seems preferable to that referred to by Mayrhofer 1956: 37).

4.3.5. There can be no doubt that the Tocharian words for 'alone' are to be interpreted as extensions of 'one'. Surviving forms are:

B:			
Singular	masculine	nominative	B *ṣeske* (B 78 b 3), *ṣesky* (B 406 b 6)
		accusative	B *ṣemeske* (B 363 a 4)
		genitive	B *ṣemeskepi* (B 33 b 3–4)
A:			
Singular	masculine	nominative	A *sasak* (A 70 a 2)
		genitive	A *sasäkyāpä* (A 388 a 3)
	feminine	nominative	A *snāki* (A 381.3)
		accusative	A *snākyāṃ* (A 180 a 4)
		genitive	A *snākye* (A 126 a 5)
Plural	feminine	nominative	A *snākaṃ* (A 186 b 5)

The paradigms in the two languages show the results of various resegmentation and adaptation processes. In the prehistory of B, the following seems to have happened: After 'one' had, in the masculine, become B *ṣe*, *-s-* of 'alone' was attached to *-ke* to form the suffix complex *-ske*; this in turn could now be added to the full accusative form B *ṣeme*. As the masculine singular genitive B *ṣemepi* could be taken to be a mere extension of the accusative B *ṣeme* by a suffix *-pi*, B *ṣemeske* could receive the same suffix to yield B *ṣemeskepi*.

The regular equivalent of B *ṣeske* should be an A form ending in *-äk*, not in *-ak*. The likely source for the latter is the A term for 'other', A *ālak* (cf. 4.3.6.); note also van Windekens (1976: 416) in this respect. The accusative may have been A *sasakäṃ**, with absence of palatalization as in A *tsopats : tsopatsäm* 'great' (as against A *ālak : ālyakäṃ* 'other'); the genitive form A *sasäkyāp* lacks the nasal resumably found in the accusative, as do all genitives in A *-yāp* (cf. Sieg – Siegling – Schulze 1931: 160).

The forms of the feminine singular of 'alone' in A are best assumed to have come into existence when the masculine nominative singular still ended in A *-äk*. *-k* was added to the unreduced feminine nominative singular form of 'one'; the **sənāk-* resulting was extended by the feminine marker **-yā-* as found reflected, e. g., in A *āṣtri* (nominative), A *āṣtäryāṃ* (accusative) 'clear'; the relatively late date of the addition is indicated by the absence of palatalization of A *-k-* and by the stability of the embedded feminine stem A *snā-*.

The plural form A *snākaṃ*, too, is readily explained by the influence of adjectival subparadigms such as that of 'clear': A *snākaṃ* is to *snāki* as A *āṣtram* is to *āṣtri*.

4.3.5.1. An extension of B *ṣeske*, B *ṣesketstse* which seems to be attested only in B 331 b 2, apparently has the meaning 'quite alone'.

4.3.6. The paradigms for 'other' in B and A can be described in fairly great detail. Forms incurred are:

B:			
Singular	masculine	nominative	*allek* (B 4 a 7), *alek* (B 289 b 3)
		accusative	*alyek* (B 14 a 6), *allyek* (B 133 b 3), *alyeṅk* (B 346 a 4)
		genitive	*alyekepi* (B 23 a 5)
		instrumental	*aly(e)k-sa* (B 528 a 4), *alyek-tsa* (B 541 a 2)
		dative	*aly(e)kä-śc-o* (B 42 b 1)
		comitative	*(a)lly(e)kä-mpa* (B 144 b 3)
		ablative	*alyekmeṃ* (B 254 a 2)
		locative	*alyek-ne* (B 20 b 3)
	feminine	nominative	*alyāk* (B 123 b 7)
		accusative	*allok* (B 5 b 3), (?) *(a)lyok* (B 244 a 1)
	neuter	accusative	*allek* (B 5 b 6)
Plural	masculine	nominative	*alyaik* (B 31 b 8), *āllyaik* (B 273 a 1), (?) *alyaiṅk* (B 580 b 1)
		accusative	*alyeṅkäṃ* (B 31 b 3)
		genitive	*alyeṅkäṃts* (B 74 a 2), *alyeṅkäts* (B 22 a 4)
		dative	*aly(e)ṅkä(ṃ)-ś* (B 42 b 1)
		comitative	*(a)lyeṅkän-pa* (B 124 a 3)
	feminine	nominative	*alloṅna* (H add 149.77 a 6), (?) *alloykna* (B 200 a 1), *alloṅk* (B 379 b 2)
		accusative	*alloṅkna* (B 31 a 1), *alloṅna* (B 42 b 2)

A:

Singular	masculine	nominative	*ālak* (A 9 b 5)
		accusative	*ālakäṃ* (A 359.34), *ālyakäṃ* (A 217 b 4)
		instrumental	*ālaknā* (A 324 b 2), *ālyaknā* (A 244 b 4)
		locative	*āly(a)knaṃ* (A 73 b 5)
	feminine	nominative	*ālyāk-* (A 162 a 6)
		accusative	*ālyäkyāṃ* (A 5 a 5)
	neuter	accusative	*ālak* (A 102 a 6)
Plural	masculine	nominative	*ālyek* (A 66 a 3)
		accusative	*ālykes* (A 386 b 2), *ālyekäs* (A 226 a 6)
		instrumental	*ālyeksā* (A 69 a 3)
		dative	*ālyeksac* (A 58 b 4)
		ablative	*ālyeksäṣ* (A 360.12)
		locative	*ālyeksaṃ* (A 226 a 4)
	feminine	nominative	*ālkont* (A 226 a 1)
		accusative	*ālkont* (A 305 b 4)

4.3.6.1. The etymological connection of the Tocharian forms with Gk. *állos*, Lat. *alius*, etc., is obvious; it was pointed out as early as Sieg – Siegling (1908: 927). This fact, however, does not eliminate the need for a discussion of points of detail in the Tocharian paradigms and their forms.

To start with, one may take it for granted that the development PIE **-ly-* > B *-ll-*, A *-l-* is regular before old back vowels; the assumption by van Windekens (1976: 95) that PIE **-lyo-* > B *-lle-* was limited to spoken language, while in written language B *-lye-* resulted, has nothing to recommend it. The pair B *allek* : A *ālak* 'other' has a perfect match in numerous deverbal adjectives in B *-lle*, A *-l* (cf. Thomas 1952); there is no reason whatsoever for thinking (with van Windekens 1979: 81–82, 1982: 249) that B *-lle* derived from PIE **-lyo-* while A *-l* reflected PIE **-lo-*; note the remarks by Thomas (1985: 59). B *alyek* has been identified as an accusative ('oblique') by Winter (1962); later discussions, such as Thomas (1967), serve to confirm this observation.

While B *-lle-*, A *-la-* thus derive from PIE **-lyo-*, PIE **-lyā-* (stated in Brugmannian terms) yielded B *-llo-* in the feminine accusative singular B *allok* and the nominative/accusative plural B *alloṅkna*; matching A *-la-** has been reduced to mere *-l-* by syncope in A *ālkont*.

When B *-ll-*, A *-l-* was affected by palatalization, the result was B *-ly-*, A *-ly-*. Palatalization could have two sources – on the one hand the adaptation of the paradigm of 'other' to that of the demonstratives with their alternation between stem I with B *-e-*, A *-a-* (cf. B *seṃ* : A *saṃ*) and stem II with B *-'e-*, A *-'a-* (cf. B *ceṃ* : A *caṃ*), on the other, the addition of the feminine-marking suffix B *-ya-*, A *-yā-*. Forms such as the singular accusative B *alyek* and genitive B *alyekepi* and the plural nominative B *alyaik*, accusative B *alyeṅkäṃ*, genitive B *alyeṅkäṃts*, as well as the singular accusative A *ālyakäṃ* and the plural nominative A *ālyek*, are regular stem II formations, and the singular nominatives B *alyāk* and A *ālyāk-* < **aly-yə-* contain regular reflexes of a palatalization of B *-ll-*, A *-l-* by a following *-y-*.

In both languages, further changes affected the paradigms, thereby destroying part of their regularity. In B, the underlying form of the masculine accusative plural, B *ālyeṃ** (< PIE **alyons*), was extended not only by the [kə] shared by all forms of the paradigm, but also by an additional accusative-plural marker; the resulting form B *alyeṅkäṃ* then influenced the shape of the genitive plural. B *alloṅkna* must be viewed as the reshaping of an **allona**, itself an extension of an older collective formation deriving from PIE **alyā*. Once *-n-* had become established preceding the *-k-* of some forms, it could be transferred to others such as B *alyeṅk* and *alyaiṅk*, though the basic regularity of the B *alye-* pattern was never affected.

In A, more radical changes took place. There was, first of all, a tendency to transpose the case marking from the position before the *-k-* to that following it; when this happened, it became possible to have the unchanged nominative stem before the *-k-* also in oblique cases. Thus A *ālakäṃ,* A *ālyäkyāṃ* (syncopated from **ālyākyāṃ*), and A *ālyekäs* could come into existence. A *ālyakäṃ* is likely to reflect a mere extension of the old accusative form A *ālyak* *, the perfect match of B *alyek*. A *ālykes* seems to contain an adaptation to the masculine accusative plural forms of the demonstratives, viz., *ces-* in A *ces-äṃ, ces-äm, ces-äs*, or to A *ṣomes* 'the ones'. Finally, A *ālkont*, just as A *mätkont : mättak* '(one)self', may show the impact of A *pont*, the feminine nominative-accusative plural of A *puk* 'all'.

A late Common Tocharian paradigm of 'other' thus can be assumed to have had the basic properties of adjectival paradigms such as those of B *astare*, A *āṣtär* 'clear', combined with features of the demonstratives. Even at this point then, a reshaping would have had affected the inherited pattern of **alyo-* 'other'.

4.3.6.1.1. Both Sieg – Siegling – Schulze (1931: 192) and Krause – Thomas (1960: 168) include in their paradigm of A *ālak* a masculine genitive plural A *ālu*. The form is attested more than thirty times; the meaning 'of others; for the benefit of others' is assured by bilingual evidence as well as by occurrences in an opposition to A *ṣñi* 'of oneself; for the benefit of oneself' in, e. g., A 59 b 3, 65 a 3, 65 a 5, 262 b 6. The form A *ālu*, however, does not fit the paradigm to which it has been assigned, nor can it be easily explained. There is no genitive plural suffix A *-u* (one would expect to find A *-śśi* instead), nor are there any other A forms that invite comparison. It is tempting to equate A *ālu* with B *alo-* in B *alokälymi* 'leaving all other things aside (*ekānta*)' in view of the fact that we have an occasional match of B *o* and A *u*; however, these forms involve underlying **u*, and there seems to be no way of plausibly suggesting an extension by **-w-* in a paradigm of 'other'. As it is, one had better be content with a statement that *-u* in A *ālu* defies explanation. Furthermore, the identification of the function of A *ālu* is also best left open to a certain extent: it seems best to characterize it as an unchangeable form with a possessive-benefactive meaning; it may be advisable to include it among the not uncommon undeclinable adjectives (the fact that full-fledged nominal use can be observed in A 86 b 4 provides no counter-argument).

4.3.6.2. B *kälymiye* 'direction' is a feminine noun; hence B *alokälymi* could be taken to be a univerbalization of a nominal phrase '(toward) another direction', with the form of 'other' in the accusative singular feminine. PIE **alyām* should, however, have resulted in B *allo-** with *-ll-* and not just a single *-l-* (cf. B *allok* in 4.3.6.0.). As it happens, B *alokälymi* is not the only form in B with *-l-* instead of expected *-ll-*.

In most occurrences of B *aletstse** 'foreign; strange', single *-l-* is attested (B *alecce* B 128, H 149.37; B *aleccepi* B 142; B *alecce-meṃ* H 149.37; *aletsai* H 149.5; *(a)laits(ai)* B 315; *alecci* B 46, B 47; *alecceṃ* B 123); *-ll-* occurs in forms of one manuscript only (cf. Sieg – Siegling 1953: 208), viz., the accusative feminine singular B *allets(ts)ai* (B 332) and the de-adjectival noun form B *alletsñe* (B 327). The forms with single *-l-* thus have to be considered the usual ones.

One would not want to separate the adjective denoting 'strange' from PIE **alyo-* as reflected in B *allek*; thus there is the need to determine why B *alecce*, etc., and B *alokälymi* do not have *-ll-*. A possible reason may be suggested: both (groups of) forms contain additional morphological elements apart from endings in the position after the reflex of **-lyV-*; this does not apply to verbal adjectives in B *-lle*, nor can it be said to be the case for B *allek* (A *ālak*) if one considers B A *-k* a relatively late accretion. Morphological complexity as such probably would not suffice as a conditioning factor for a reduction of B *-ll-* to B *-l-*; however, forms of unextended B |allé-| would have in most cases undergone accent retraction from the final syllable, whereas forms containing B *-tstse*, etc., and B *-kälymi* would have preserved their accent on the reflex of PIE **-lyV-*. A parallel for a different treatment of a pre- and a postaccentual cluster is found in the variation of B *-CC'-* and B *-'Cw-* as discussed in Winter (1972).

4.3.6.3. The explanation proposed does not apply to B *āläṃ* 'elsewhere' (this translation seems to be more adequate than 'different(ly)', as was suggested by Sieg – Siegling 1949: 95 and repeated by Thomas – Krause 1964: 168). However, it is next to impossible to find a way in which B *āläṃ* could be connected with B *allek*, etc. B *āläṃ* cannot be equated with A *ālam-* (for which cf. 4.3.7.2.); unless one wants to view it as a fossilized form of an accusative plural of a consonant stem, one has to arrive for B *āläṃ* at a morphophonemic analysis |alnV|, with |V| not an old long vowel and not **a* **e* **o* or **ə* < **A*, **O*. In view of the local function of the lexeme, one may want to think of an underlying locative form in PIE **-i*. In any case, there is nothing that connects B *āläṃ* and the adjectival paradigm of 'other' except for the shared onset /al-/ and a similarity of meaning; this, however, does not suffice to make it necessary to posit anything but a thematic stem PIE **alyo-* as the ultimate source of all B forms related to 'other'.

4.3.6.4. Forms containing A *-l-* do not pose a problem if the comments in 4.3.6.1. are justified. Two forms have to be considered: A *ālaśi* (*ālaśī*) has been identified with B *aletstse** in Thomas – Krause (1964: 83); doubts are, however, in order regarding this alignment: the two passages in which the A form is found (A 62 a 4, 325 a 3) do not permit more than mere guesses about the meaning (note Couvreur 1955–1956: 70 for a reluctant statement, which was replaced by a less cautious claim in Thomas – Krause 1964: 83). Furthermore, the fact should not be overlooked that A does not have the coda *-ts* which one would expect to find in view of the inflection of B *aletstse**.

The suggestion by Sieg – Siegling – Schulze (1931: 193) that A *ynālek* 'elsewhere' might contain, apart from prefixed *yn-*, the reflex of a locative form, has much to recommend it, the more so as there are a few other terms with local reference ending in A *-e*: A *kātse* 'near', A *pärne* 'outside', A *pre* 'away'.

4.3.6.5. Forms of 'other' occur as antonyms of forms of 'one', as well as in combination with other forms of 'other', expressing the notion of '(the) one(s) ... (the) other(s)'. Cases in question are A 9 b 5 *ālak peke ālak pekant* 'one (thing is) the painting, another the painter', A 226 a 2–3 *ṣome ... ālyek*; a repetition of forms of 'one' may serve the same purpose, as, e. g., in A 288 a 8. Terms for 'other' are, however, not used as ordinals, not even in the process of building series from groups (cf. Winter 1954: 9–10).

4.3.7.0. The forms expressing the notion 'one another, each other' show parallel internal structures in A and B, but cannot be projected back toward a single Common Tocharian form.

4.3.7.1. The B paradigm consists of one form unextended by a suffix or postposition and a group of others showing the markings of the "secondary cases":

B *ālyewce* (B 407 b 3), *ālyauce* (B 27 a 5, H 149.223 a 2), *ālyoce* (B 526 b 4)
instrumental B *ālyauce-sa* (B 27 a 6), *ālyoce-sa* (B 196 a 4)
dative B *ālyauce-ś* (B 81 b 3, H 149.288 b 2)
comitative B *ālyewce-mpa* (B 245 a 3), *ālyauwce-mpa* (B 245 a 5), *ālyauce-mpa* (B 27 a 5, H 149 add 17 b 4)
ablative B *ālyeᵘcemeṃ* (B 275 b 5), *ālyauwcemeṃ* (B 255 b 4), *ālyaucemeṃ* (B 178 b 4).

The same general characterization applies to A:

A *ālamwäc* (A 338 a 1)
genitive A *ālamwcanis* (A 12 a 2)
instrumental A *ālamwcā* (A 73 a 2); *ālamwcanā* (A 186 a 3)
dative A *ālam wcac* (A 15 a 1); *(āla)mwcanac* (A 336 a 3)
comitative A *(ā)l(a)mwcaśśäl* (A 277 b 4)
ablative A *ālamwcäṣ* (A 347 a 3); *ālamwcanäṣ* (A 212 a 2)
locative A *ālamwcanaṃ* (A 262 b 7)

4.3.7.2. Any explanation of the forms for 'each other' has to take into account a number of facts:

a) The unextended forms in B and A end in a variant of the accusative masculine singular of 'second'.

b) In B, this variant is characterized as unaccented (as against the free form B *wace*); hence the term for 'each other' has to be identified as a juxtapound or compound in B.

c) B *ālye-* contains an accusative masculine singular form of 'other' unextended by B *-k*.

d) In Central and Eastern forms of B, the onset of 'each other' is consistently spelled with B *ā*- and not B *a*-.
e) A *ālam*- does not occur elsewhere.

Disregarding for the moment the onset *ā*-, the form B *ālyewce* (*ālyauce*) can be explained without residue as the equivalent, so to say, of Latin *alium secundum*, that is, as a sequence of two accusatives, and not, as one would be inclined to expect, as a combination analogous to Lat. *alius alium*. Hence no part of B *ālyewce* can be said to be in concord with the subject of its clause. Therefore, a passage like B 42 a 3 *kauṣträ ālyauce* 'you keep killing each other' is not a structural equivalent of Lat. *necātis alter alterum*, but requires a different analysis.

This analysis has also to account for fact (d). If 'each other' were a compound just of B |al'e| and B |wəce|, one would expect to find B *alyewce** with short *a*-. However, this is not the usual form incurred. There seems to be no other way but to assume that expected B *alyewce** was extended by a prefix, which then was fused with *a-** to yield *ā*-. This prefix can be easily identified: it recurs, in the shape B *e*-, in forms such as B *epiṅkte* 'in between', B *eraitwe* 'in combination', B *eweta* 'in conflict'. B *e*- is to be compared with Skt. *ā́* 'close to, towards' (for which cf. Mayrhofer 1956: 69); B *ālyewce* then would be an adverbial derived from B *e*- + *alye(k)* + *wace*, roughly equivalent to 'in (the situation of) one (doing something to) the other'.

The onset of A *ālamwäc* has no diagnostic value in determining whether here, too, a prefix was absorbed by the initial vowel of 'other'. However, there is a strong argument in favor of assuming that this was precisely what took place.

A *ālam*- cannot be directly equated with B *alye(k)*. An additional hypothesis is therefore called for: B *alyek* has been identified in 4.3.6.1. as the result of the reshaping of an adjectival accusative form under the influence of the accusative of demonstratives. The form to be expected as the regular reflex of PIE **alyom* should be B *alle(k)**. Its equivalent would be A *āla(k)*. If a loss of the reflex of PIE *-*m* was prevented by special conditions, such as the occurrence of 'other' in secondary nonfinal position, the regular development of PIE **alyom* should have been A *ālam* +, precisely the form found in A *ālamwäc*; hence, this word must be taken to have preserved a highly archaic accusative masculine singular form of 'other', more archaic than A *ālyakäṃ*, although it is this very form that is closest to B *alyek*. It seems necessary to ascribe the reshaping of adjectives after the pattern of demonstratives to Common Tocharian;

it is therefore the more remarkable that an old adjectival form proper should have survived in A *ālamwäc*, a fixed phrase turned compound.

A *ālamwäc* requires a rendering by Lat. *alium secundum*; it permits an extension of this rendering to (approximately) *ad alium secundum*; as its counterpart B *ālyewce*, in its turn, requires the extended interpretation, it seems reasonable to assume that A *ālamwäc*, too, should be analyzed as containing an underlying prefix (A *a*-) fused with the vocalic onset of the term for 'other'. It is this assumption that provides an explanation for the fact that A *ālamwäc*, too, never occurs in the nominative case – the underlying prefix necessitated the shift of the compound of 'other' and 'second' to the accusative; the resulting complex form was used adverbially – which did not prevent its being extended by postpositions or suffixes, a phenomenon that recurs with clear instances of prefixed expressions (cf. B *epiṅkte-ne*, A *opäntäṣ*; cf. Winter 1983: 322).

4.4. Conclusion

In the classical paper by Sieg – Siegling (1908) the presentation of Tocharian numerals served as a crucial point in their proof of the Indo-Europeanness of the two languages. The appraisal of a much larger body of data serves to confirm again that Tocharian numerals can be explained by recourse to a comparison with numerals from other Indo-European languages and, in their turn, provide substantial material for the reconstruction of the elements and the techniques that were used to form numerals in Proto-Indo-European.

Note

1. I am grateful to Georges Pinault for kindly providing me with the exact provenance of numerals attested in unpublished Paris texts. To those forms which had been referred to in print (and hence could be included in the present paper) he generously added several items which hitherto were altogether unavailable. I also appreciate his calling my attention to some relevant literature.

References

Bailey, Harald Walter
1951 *Khotanese Buddhist texts* (London: Taylor's Foreign Press).
Bernhard, Franz
1958 *Die Nominalkomposition im Tocharischen* (Göttingen) [dissertation].
Broomhead, J. W.
1962 *A textual edition of the British, Stein and Weber manuscripts with transliteration, translation, grammatical commentary and vocabulary* (Cambridge) [dissertation].
Couvreur, Walter
1955–1956 "Bemerkungen zu Pavel Pouchas *Thesaurus linguae tocharicae dialecti A*", *La Nouvelle Clio* 7–8: 67–98.
Fraenkel, Ernst
1932 "Zur tocharischen Grammatik", *Indogermanische Forschungen* 50: 1–20, 97–108, 220–231.
1965 *Litauisches etymologisches Wörterbuch* 2 (Heidelberg: Winter, Göttingen: Vandenhoeck & Ruprecht).
Frisk, Hjalmar
1960 *Griechisches etymologisches Wörterbuch* 1 (Heidelberg: Winter).
Hilmarsson, Jörundur
1984 "Reconstruction of a Tocharian paradigm: the numeral 'one' ", *Zeitschrift für vergleichende Sprachforschung* 97: 135–147.
1986 "Tocharian B *okt*, A *okät* '8' and the development of final Indo-European *-ō in Tocharian", in: Jörundur Hilmarsson, *Studies in Tocharian phonology, morphology and etymology, with special emphasis on the* o-*vocalism* (Reykjavík), 150–165.
Isebaert, Lambert
1980 *De Indo-Iraanse bestanddelen in de Tocharische woordenschat* [The Indo-Iranian component in the Tocharian lexicon] (Leuven) [dissertation].
Jasanoff, Jay H.
1976 "Gr. ἄμφω, [l]at. *ambo* et le mot indo-européen pour 'l'un et l'autre' ", *BSL* 71: 123–131.
Krause, Wolfgang
1952 *Westtocharische Grammatik* 1: *Das Verbum* (Heidelberg: Winter).
Krause, Wolfgang – Werner Thomas
1960 *Tocharisches Elementarbuch* 1: *Grammatik* (Heidelberg: Winter).
Lehmann, Winfred P.
1986 *A Gothic etymological dictionary* (Leiden: Brill).
Mayrhofer, Manfred
1956 *Kurzgefaßtes etymologisches Wörterbuch des Altindischen* 1 (Heidelberg: Winter).

1976 *Kurzgefaßtes etymologisches Wörterbuch des Altindischen* 3 (Heidelberg: Winter).

Meillet, Antoine

1912 "Remarques linguistiques", in: Sylvain Lévi — Antoine Meillet, "Les noms de nombre en Tokharien B", *Mémoires de la Société de Linguistique* 17: 281—294.

1913 "Le Tokharien", *Indogermanisches Jahrbuch* 1: 1—19.

Pedersen, Holger

1941 *Tocharisch vom Gesichtspunkt der indoeuropäischen Sprachvergleichung* (Det Kgl. Danske Videnskabernes Selskab, Historisk-filologiske Meddelelser 28.1) (København: Munksgaard).

Penney, J. H. W.

1976—1977 "The treatment of Indo-European vowels in Tocharian", *Transactions of the Philological Society* [1978], 66—91.

Pinault, Georges

1987 "Épigraphie koutchéenne. I: Laissez-passer de caravanes. II: Graffites et inscriptions", in: Chao Huashan et al., *Sites divers de la région de Koutcha. Épigraphie koutchéenne* (Mission Paul Pelliot. Documents archéologiques 8) (Paris: Collège de France), 59—196.

Pokorny, Julius

1959 *Indogermanisches etymologisches Wörterbuch* 1 (Bern — München: Francke).

Schmidt, Klaus T.

1986 "Bemerkungen zur tocharischen Umgangssprache", in: Annemarie Etter (ed.), *o-o-pe-ro-si. Festschrift für Ernst Risch zum 75. Geburtstag* (Berlin — New York: de Gruyter), 635—649.

Sieg, Emil

1952 *Übersetzungen aus dem Tocharischen* 2 (Abhandlungen der Deutschen Akademie der Wissenschaften zu Berlin, Klasse für Sprachen, Literatur und Kunst 1951.1) (Berlin: Akademie-Verlag).

Sieg, Emil — Wilhelm Siegling

1908 "Tocharisch, die Sprachen der Indoskythen", *Sitzungsberichte der Königlich Preussischen Akademie der Wissenschaften* 1908.39 (pp. 915—934).

1949 *Tocharische Sprachreste: Sprache B* 1 (Göttingen: Vandenhoeck & Ruprecht).

1953 *Tocharische Sprachreste: Sprache B* 2 (Göttingen: Vandenhoeck & Ruprecht).

Sieg, Emil — Wilhelm Siegling — Wilhelm Schulze

1931 *Tocharische Grammatik* (Göttingen: Vandenhoeck & Ruprecht).

Szemerényi, Oswald

1960 *Studies in the Indo-European system of numerals* (Heidelberg: Winter).

Thomas, Werner
1952 *Die tocharischen Verbaladjektive auf* -l (Deutsche Akademie der Wissenschaften zu Berlin, Institut für Orientforschung, Veröffentlichung Nr. 9) (Berlin: Akademie-Verlag).
1957 *Der Gebrauch der Vergangenheitstempora im Tocharischen* (Wiesbaden: Harrassowitz).
1967 "Besteht ein formaler Unterschied zwischen N. und Obl. Sg. m. bei den wtoch. Verbaladjektiven?", *Die Sprache* 13: 20–30.
1979 *Formale Besonderheiten in metrischen Texten des Tocharischen: Zur Verteilung von B* tane/tne *'hier' und B* ñake/ñke *'jetzt'* (Akademie der Wissenschaften und der Literatur Mainz. Abhandlungen, Geistes- und sozialwissenschaftliche Klasse 1979.15) (Wiesbaden: Steiner).
1985 *Die Erforschung des Tocharischen (1960–1984)* (Stuttgart: Steiner).
Thomas, Werner – Wolfgang Krause
1964 *Tocharisches Elementarbuch* 2: *Texte und Glossar* (Heidelberg: Winter).
Windekens, Albert Joris van
1976 *Le tokharien confronté avec les autres langues indo-européennes* 1: *La phonétique et le vocabulaire* (Travaux, Centre International de Dialectologie Générale, 11) (Louvain: CIDG).
1979 ... 2.1: *La morphologie nominale* (Travaux ... 12) (Louvain: CIDG).
1982 ... 2.2: *La morphologie verbale* (Travaux ... 13) (Louvain: CIDG).
Winter, Werner
1953 "Gruppe und Reihe. Beobachtungen zur Systematik indogermanischer Zählweise", *Zeitschrift für vergleichende Sprachforschung* 71: 3–14.
1962 "Nominal and pronominal dual in Tocharian", *Language* 38: 111–134.
1963 Review of Krause – Thomas 1960, *Deutsche Literaturzeitung* 83: 1066–1069.
1972 "Zur Vertretung von *w* nach Konsonant in Tocharisch B", *Orbis* 21: 385–390.
1983 "*A tentative English-Walapai dictionary* und *Etymologicum Tocharicum*: Unterschiede und Gemeinsamkeiten", in: Alfred Bammesberger (ed.), *Das etymologische Wörterbuch. Fragen der Konzeption und Gestaltung* (Eichstätter Beiträge 8) (Regensburg: Pustet), 313–327.
1987 "Distributive numbers in Tocharian", *Tocharian and Indo-European Studies* 2: 238–244.
forthcoming *Word accent in Tocharian B.*

Chapter 5
Old Indian

Ronald Emmerick

5.0. The earliest attestation of the Indian numerals[1] is in the R̥gveda, a collection of hymns generally considered by European scholars to have been composed c. 1200–1000 B.C. The linguistic position of a number of words, including numerals, attested earlier, in cuneiform texts of c. 1450–1350 B.C., has been disputed. According to Kammenhuber this material represents "(Ur-)arisch altindischer Dialektprägung" (1968: 142), that is, an Indian-type dialect of late Indo-Iranian rather than Indo-Aryan at an early date as advocated by Mayrhofer, *Die Indo-Arier im alten Vorderasien* (1966).

5.1. Cardinals

5.1.0. The cardinal numerals 'one' to 'ten' are attested in Old Indian as follows:

'one'	*éka-*	**oy-kó-*
'two'	*dvā́ dváu* (nom. masc.); *dvé* (nom. fem.-neut.)	**duwṓ(w)*
'three'	*tráyas* (nom. masc.); *tisrás* (nom. fem.); *trī́(ṇ)i* (nom. neut.)	**tréyes*
'four'	*catvā́ras* (nom. masc.); *cátasras* (nom. fem.); *catvā́ri* (nom. neut.)	*k^w*etwóres*
'five'	*páñca*	**pénk*^{w}*e*
'six'	*ṣáṣ-*	**kswéḱs*
'seven'	*saptá*	**septḿ̥*
'eight'	*aṣṭā́ aṣṭáu*	**oḱtṓ(w)*
'nine'	*náva*	**néwm̥/n̥*
'ten'	*dáśa*	**déḱm̥(t)*

5.1.0.1. All these numerals are declinable, but only 'one' to 'four' distinguish gender. 'Five' to 'ten' are used adjectivally like 'one' to 'four' but do not distinguish gender, and have no ending in the nominative and accusative except in the case of 'eight'. In the R̥gveda the use of inflected forms of 'five' to 'ten' is still optional: *páñca kṣitīnā́m* 'the five tribes' i. 7.9, i. 176,3, vi. 46,7, *páñca kr̥ṣṭíṣu* 'the five peoples' ii. 2,10, but *adhvar-yúbhiḥ pañcábhiḥ* 'the five Adh.-priests' iii. 7,7; *jáneṣu pañcásu* 'the five peoples' iii. 37,9, ix. 65.23. This state of fluctuation was considered by Wackernagel (1930: 352) to have obtained already in Proto-Indo-European, but others have regarded the inflection of 'five' to 'ten' as a late innovation.

5.1.0.2. The following oblique forms of 'five' to 'ten' are attested (R̥gveda forms in italics):

	instr.	dat.-abl.	gen.	loc.
5	*pañcábhiḥ*	pañcábhyaḥ	pañcānā́m	*pañcásu*
6	*ṣaḍbhíḥ*	ṣaḍbhyáḥ	ṣaṇṇā́m	ṣaṭsú
7	*saptábhiḥ*	*saptábhyaḥ*	*saptānā́m*	
8	*aṣṭābhíḥ*	aṣṭābhyáḥ	aṣṭānā́m	aṣṭāsú
9	*navábhiḥ*	navábhyaḥ	*navānā́m*	
10	*daśábhiḥ*	daśábhyaḥ	*daśānā́m*	*daśásu.*

According to Pāṇini vi. 180—1, the endings may optionally be accented in the instrumental, dative and locative (e. g. *pañcabhíḥ* beside *pañcábhiḥ*).

5.1.0.3. In the instrumental, dative, ablative and locative of 'seven', 'nine', and 'ten' the inflection accords with that of nasal stems, e. g., from *nā́man-* 'name': *nā́mabhiḥ, nā́mabhyaḥ, nā́masu.* This would suggest that the forms are old and show evidence of the Proto-Indo-European final nasal in **septm̥*, **newm̥/n̥* and **dek̑m̥. pañcábhiḥ* etc., would be analogical. The accentuation on the penult in these forms also points to their having been regarded as *an*-stems, according to Kuryłowicz (*L'accentuation des langues indo-européennes* (*PKJ* XXXVII) 1958: 34). And, according to Kuryłowicz (1968: 33) *aṣṭābhíḥ* continues the ancient accentuation. The contrast between *dáśa* and *daśábhiḥ* has been compared with that between *taíhun* and dative *tigum* in Gothic and regarded as evidence of antiquity (Wackernagel 1930: 352).

5.1.0.4. Despite the considerations just presented, it would seem most likely to me that the oblique inflection of 'five' to 'ten' is a purely Indian development. Certainly the genitive plural forms look late, as do their counterparts in Iranian. *ṣaḍbhíḥ* and *aṣṭābhíḥ* are clearly secondary, as are the other oblique forms of 'six' and 'eight', since they can only be explained as having the endings added to the nominatives *ṣáṭ* and *aṣṭā́* respectively. The shift of accent in *pañcábhiḥ* (< **pañcabhíḥ* [2], as would be expected if *páñca* was in fact treated as a root noun) may be due merely to *catúrbhiḥ*. This would not affect *ṣaḍbhíḥ* as it has a different number of syllables and would be regarded as in agreement with *tribhíḥ*. *aṣṭābhíḥ* would not have been affected since it alone had *-ā-*. *aṣṭānā́m* may have set the pattern for the genitive plurals, except in the case of 'six', where *trīṇā́m* would have been more closely associated.

5.1.1. *éka-* 'one' < **aika-*, attested as *aika-* in the Mitanni cuneiform material, contrasts with OIran. **aiwa-*. Both **aika-* and **aiwa-* are declined pronominally. An attempt to derive **aika-* (irregularly) from **aiwaka-* has been rightly rejected (Kammenhuber 1968: 202–203). Both **aika-* and **aiwa-* are probably to be ascribed to the Indo-Iranian period [3]. In Indian, **aika-* was specialised as 'one', while **aiwa-* was specialised as 'alone', two closely related concepts. **aiwa-* is continued by OInd. *evá* [4] adv. 'just so' and *iva* 'as, like'. The *-ka*-suffix may be that found in collectives.

5.1.2. *dvá-* 'two', in the R̥gveda also *duvá-*, is declined as a regular *a*-stem dual. Attested forms: nom.-acc. masc. *d(u)vā́, d(u)váu*; nom.-acc. fem. neut. *d(u)vé*; instr.-dat.-abl. *d(u)vā́bhyām*; gen.-loc. *d(u)váyoḥ*. Of these forms only *d(u)vā́* and *d(u)vé* have exactly corresponding counterparts in Iranian: Av. *duua* and *duuaē(ca)*. The alternative form of the nominative-accusative, *d(u)váu*, stands beside *d(u)vā́* as is usual in the Vedic *a*-declension. In the later language, *-au* is generalised although *-ā* survives in *dvā́daśa* 'twelve'. The dual ending is usually reconstructed as PIE *-ōw*, although only *-ō* is certainly indicated outside Indian by the forms continuing the thematic declension. *-ō*/*-ōw* are explained as sandhi-variants. PIE **d(u)wōw* is indicated, however, not only by OInd. *d(u)váu*, but also by Welsh *dau*, Breton *daou*. Cf. also 5.1.8.1.

In the R̥gveda *dv-* is found nine times, seven times after a short vowel; *duv-* thirty-five times, always after a long vowel or a consonant or initially in the line. This distribution is thought to reflect a Proto-Indo-European state of affairs (see F. Edgerton, *Language* xix, 1943: 86, 91). The question of the original accentuation (Greek δύω but OInd. *d(u)vā́*) must be considered in this connection. According to Hirt (1921–1937: v. 288). Old Indian shows the original accentuation, but according to Kuryłowicz (1968: 28) Greek does. The zero grade syllable is less likely to have borne the accent originally. The Greek forms probably follow the declensional pattern of monosyllables: δύο, δυοῖν like κύων, κυνός (but OInd. *ś(u)vā́, śúnaḥ*). Note also Greek δ(ϝ)ώ-δεκα like OInd. *dvā́-daśa*.

5.1.2.1. *d(u)vā́bhyām* contrasts with Av. *duuaēibiia*, which appears to be older in continuing the Proto-Indo-European diphthong *-oy-*. *d(u)vā́bhyām* and *d(u)váyoḥ* represent an Indian innovation: declension according to the *a*-declension.
5.1.2.2. As the first element of a compound as well as in derivatives, Proto-Indo-European used **dwi-* of uncertain origin. Compound: OInd. *dvi-pád-* 'two-footed', Sogdian δyβp'δ'kw, Khotanese *śivāa-* beside Greek δίπους, Latin *bipēs*. Derivatives: Oind. *dvitī́ya-* 'second', Av. *bitiia-*; OInd. *dvíḥ* 'twice', Av. *biš* beside Greek δίς, Latin *duis, bis*. *dvā́-* occurs as first element with the same distribution as *tráyaḥ* (5.1.3.4.). Its occurrence in *dvā́daśa* = OIran. **dvādasa*, cf. Greek δώδεκα, may reflect a need to avoid confusion with 'twenty' and 'two hundred'. *dvā-* is found also in two purely Indian compounds: *dvā-pára-* (and *dvā-pará-*), a technical term in dice-throwing, and *dvandvá-* 'pair' from the adverb *dvandvám* 'in pairs' based in turn on the āmreḍita *dvā́-dvā* 'by twos'.
5.1.3. *trí-* 'three' (fem. *tisṛ́-*) is represented by the following forms in the Ṛgveda:

	nom.	acc.	instr.	dat.	gen.	loc.
masc.	*tráyas*	*trī́n*	*tribhís*	*tribhyás*	*trīṇā́m*	*triṣú*
fem.	*tisrás*	*tisrás*	*tisṛ́bhis*	*tisṛ́bhyas*	*tisṛṇā́m*	*tisṛ́ṣu*
neut.	*trī́,*	*trī́ṇi*				

Of these few have exact counterparts in Iranian: *trī́n*, cf. Av. *θriš* (< Indo-Iran. **trinš*); *tribhyás*, cf. Av. *θribiiō; tisrás*, cf. Av. *tišrō; trī́*, cf. Av. *θrī. tráyas* is probably older than Iran. **θrāyah* and continues PIE **treyes* as in Greek τρεῖς, Latin *trēs*, but Av. *tišrąm* is older in form than OInd. *tisṛṇā́m*. The Avestan gen. pl. masc.-neut. *θraiiąm* can be explained in various ways but is based on an older principle than is *trīṇā́m. trī́ṇi* is based secondarily on the *i*-declension. Loc. pl. *triṣú*, absent by chance from Old Iranian, corresponds to Old Church Slavonic *trĭxŭ* and cf. Greek τρισί.
5.1.3.1. *tráyāṇām* (not *trayāṇā́m* as Macdonell 1910: 70; Whitney 1889: 181; implied by Renou 1961: 547; see Wackernagel 1930: 346–7), rarely pre-classical, replaced *trīṇā́m* in classical Sanskrit. It may represent a replacement of **tráyām*, possibly = Av. *θraiiąm*, under the influence of *pañcānā́m*, etc.
5.1.3.2. The Old Indian forms are all clearly based on stems *tri-* and *tisr-* corresponding to Av. *θri-* and *tišr-*. Further analysis would point to dissimilation[5] of an Indo-Iranian stem **tri-sr-* producing **ti-sr-* since **tri-*

seems basic to 'three'. Explanation of the *-sr-*element has been disputed, but it is probably no more than a feminine suffix. *tri-* was dissimilated to *ti-* before *-r-* as early as Indo-Iranian in *tisr-*, and the dissimilation is found also in Celtic where OIrish *teoir* has *-eoir* < *-esor(es)* (Thurneysen 1946: 246). Indo-Iran. *-sr-* beside forms in Celtic from *-sor-* (generalised) points to an old ablaut-variation. OInd. *tisráḥ, cátasraḥ* are therefore properly accusative forms as already seen by R. Meringer (IF xvi, 1904: 171–172).

5.1.3.3. PIE **tri-* was used as first member of a compound and in derivatives. Compound: OInd. *tri-pád-*, Av. *θripaδəm*, beside Greek τρίπους, Latin *tripēs*. Derivative: OInd. *trís* 'thrice', Av. *θriš*, beside Greek τρίς, Latin *ter*. From the earliest period (see 5.0.) we have *tri-* in **tri-vartana-* (in cuneiform spellings *ti-e-ru-u-ur-ta-an-na*, etc.) "Dreier-Runde", hippological technical term (Kammenhuber 1968: 203–4).

5.1.3.4. In expressing numerals consisting of decads plus three, *tri-* is often replaced by nom. pl. *tráyah*. With *tri-* only: *try-àśīti* 'eighty-three'. With *tráyaḥ* only: *tráyodaśa* 'thirteen', *tráyoviṃśati* 'twenty-three', *tráyastriṃśat* 'thirty-three'. With either *tri-* or *tráyaḥ*: 'forty-three', to 'seventy-three' and 'ninety-three' e. g. *tricatvāriṃśat* or *trayaścatvāriṃśat* 'forty-three'. For Iranian only 'thirteen' is attested and there both **θridasa* and **θrayaz-dasa* are represented.

5.1.4. *catúr-* 'four' (fem. *cátasr-*) is represented by the following forms (R̥gveda forms in *italics*):

	nom.	acc.	instr.	dat.	gen.	loc.
masc.	*catvā́ras*	*catúras*	*catúrbhis*	catúrbhyas	caturṇā́m	catúrṣu
fem.	*cátasras*	*cátastas*	*catasŕ̥bhis*	*catasŕ̥bhyas*	*catasŕ̥ṇā́m*	*catasŕ̥ṣu*
neut.	*catvā́ri*					

Of these only three have exactly corresponding counterparts in Old Iranian: nom. masc. *catvā́raḥ* = Av. *caθβārō*; acc. masc. *catúraḥ* = Av. *caturə̄*; acc. fem. *cátasraḥ* = Av. *cataŋrō*. Avestan gen. masc. *caturąm* is clearly older in form than OInd. *caturṇā́m* with secondary *-n-* as in *trīṇā́m* (5.1.3.); cf. Lesbian Greek πισύρων, Attic Greek τεττάρων.

5.1.4.1. The forms with a long vowel in the second syllable, *catvā́raḥ* and *catvā́ri* are discussed in 8.1.4.2.

5.1.4.2. As the first element of a compound, Old Indian used *cátur-*, which contrasts with Av. *caθru-*. It is Av. *caθru-* (Khot. *tcūra-*) which continues PIE **kʷetru-*, to be deduced from further comparison with

Latin *quadru-*, Gaulish *petru-*. But Avestan has also *caθβarə-*, with which OInd. *cátur-* can be equated if both continue PIE **k^{w}etwr̥r-*, that is, the antevocalic form beside anteconsonantal **k^{w}etru-* (so C. Bartholomae, *IF* xxi, 1907: 361–4; Wackernagel 1930: 348). Av. *caθβarə-* occurs before both vowels and consonants, but that may be the result of a later generalisation. Brugmann – Delbrück (1897–1916), however, separated OInd. *cátur-* from both Av. *caθβarə-* and Av. *caθru-*. According to them, OInd. *cátur-* continues PIE **k^{w}etur-*, originally antevocalic, while Av. *caθru-* continues PIE **k^{w}etru-*, originally anteconsonantal, beside which Av. *caθβarə-* continues PIE **k^{w}etwr̥-*, an analogical variant of **k^{w}etru-*. For this variation they cite (Brugmann – Delbrück 1897–1916: II. ii. 260; so also Kuryłowicz 1968: 201; see F. Edgerton, *Language* xix, 1943: 97) such forms as OInd. °*hvṛti* beside *hrutá-* to OInd. *hvárate* 'to go astray'. The chief advantage of Brugmann's reconstruction is that it enables us to explain the derivatives with the same form used in composition as is the case with **tri-* 'three' (5.1.3.3.). Thus, the old ordinal 'fourth', OInd. *turī́ya-*, Av. *tūiriia-* contains **k^{w}tur-* with a suffix, but a form with *-wr̥r-* would be expected to result in OInd. *-(v)ur-*, av. *-uuar-*.

5.1.4.3. OInd. *cátur-* was not only generalised for use as first member of compounds, but was treated on the analogy of original *s*-stems. Thus, the R̥gveda has such compounds as *cátuṣ-pad-* 'four-footed' and *cátuṣ-kaparda-* 'having four braids of hair', whereas *púr-* 'castle' retains its *r* in *pū́r-pati-* 'lord of the castle'. Similarly, from *tápus-* 'glow(ing)' it has *tápur-mūrdhan-* 'glowing-headed' and *tapuṣ-pā́-* 'protecting from the fire'. In derivation both treatments are found: *catur-thá-* 'fourth', but *cátuṣ-ṭaya-, catuṣ-ka-* 'consisting of four'. Classical *catvara-* 'square' and inscriptional *catvāraka-* (= *cátuṣṭaya-*) are based on the strong stem.

5.1.5. OInd. *páñca* 'five' agrees exactly with Av. *panca* and other Iranian forms. Comparison with Greek πέντε, Latin *quīnque*, etc., leads to the reconstruction of PIE **pénk^{w}e*. Beside *páñca*, Old Indian has *paṅktí-* fem. 'group of five' → 'group', with which Old Church Slavonic *pętĭ* (Russian *pjat'*, etc.) 'five' is usually compared, both from PIE **penk^{w}ti-*. Differently, Szemerényi connected *paṅktí-* rather with Old Church Slavonic *pęstĭ* 'fist', deriving both, as well as the Germanic cognates (Engl. *fist*, etc.), from PIE **p(e)nk^{w}sti-* (Szemerényi 1960: 107–114). For the suffix cf. OInd. *vítasti-*, Av. *vitasti-* 'span', from *tan-, taṃs-* 'stretch', and the parts of the body, *pr̥ṣṭí-* 'rib', *muṣṭí-* 'fist' and *śúpti-* 'shoulder'. It should, however, be noted that the spelling *paṅtí-* is often encountered and may be the older form (K. Hoffmann, *KZ* lxxix, 1965: 252). It may indeed even represent a PIE **peŋ-ti-* beside the numeral **péŋ-k^{w}e*, which may ultimately contain the enclitic *$k^{w}e$* 'and', as the two *e*-grade vowels would encourage further analysis (Hirt 1921–37: iii. 307 n. 1; Mayrhofer 1956–1980: 513; Burrow 1959: 542). Note further the ordinal forms in 5.2.5.2.

5.1.5.1. In later Indian there occur the derivatives *prapañca-* masc. 'diversity' and *prapañcana-* neut. 'detailed exposition', beside which a denominative verb *prapañcayati* is later attested. The semantic development is usually compared with that shown by Greek πεμπάζω 'count (with the five fingers)'.

5.1.6. The Iranian words for 'six' fall into two groups, **(x)šwaš* and **(x)šaš*. The latter may be merely a simplification of the difficult initial cluster of the former. Similar simplifications are found from the Iranian verbal base **xšwaip-*: Av. *xšuuiβi-* 'quick-moving' but Sogdian *xwšyp*, Parthian *'šyft*, Middle Persian *šyb-*, and cf. Khotanese *kṣäv-* (see Emmerick 1968: i. 25). Here the loss of the labial element of the cluster would be encouraged by the occurrence of a final labial. The same simplification occurs in OInd. *kṣip-* 'throw'. In Old Indian, *kṣv-* is not found in inherited words. In the R̥gveda only *kṣvíṅkā-* is found once (x. 87.7*d*) in a late book[6]. It is probably onomatopoeic in origin. Nor is *ṣv-* found initially in Old Indian. It is thus probable that an Indo-Iranian initial cluster **kšw-* would be simplified in Old Indian. In fact, Old Indian has simply *ṣ* in *ṣáṭ* 'six'. Nevertheless, Old Indian is in this case clearly not the same thing as Common Old Indian. For Prakrit *cha* 'six' indicates an initial *kṣ-* (see Hiersche 1964: 98–99), and many Modern Indian languages have forms implying *-v-* (see Turner 1966: no. 12803). It is clear therefore that, in Indian as in Iranian, we have to do with a number of simplifications of an original cluster, Indo-Iranian **kšw*. By further comparison with other Indo-European languages one is led to reconstruct for Proto-Indo-European, **ksweḱs*: Greek ἕξ, Latin *sex*, Gothic *saihs*, Welsh *chwech*, etc. The development of the final cluster *ḱs* to *š* in Iranian presents no difficulty, but in Indian the details are disputed. There are, however, two exact parallels for *-*ḱs* > OInd. *-ṭ*. PIE **wiḱ-* 'settlement', nom. sg. *wiḱs*, appears in Old Indian as *víś-*, nom. sg. *víṭ*, and PIE **speḱ-* 'spy', nom. sg. **speḱs*, appears in Old Indian as *spáś-*, nom. sg. *spáṭ* (cf. Av. *spas-*, nom. sg. *spaš*; Latin *-spex*). For a recent full discussion of the development PIE *-ḱs* > OInd. *-ṭ*, see F. B. J. Kuiper, *IIJ* x (1967: 103–125).

5.1.7. OInd. *saptá* 'seven' agrees exactly with OIran. **hafta* and regularly continues PIE **septḿ̥*: Greek ἑπτά, Latin *septem*, etc. The agreement in accentuation between OInd. *saptá* and Greek ἑπτά, Gothic *sibun*, points to an original Proto-Indo-European oxytone accentuation. That the Proto-Indo-European accentuation must itself be secondary (on a zero-grade syllable!) has been generally accepted since A. Fick, *GGA* (1881: 1449). Hirt (1921 – 37: v. 188) ascribed the shift of accent to the influence of PIE **oḱtṓw*.

5.1.8. Both *aṣṭā́* and *aṣṭáu* 'eight' are attested in the R̥gveda: *aṣṭā́* before a consonant (viii. 2.41*c*), *aṣṭā́v* before a vowel (i. 126.5*b*), and *aṣṭáu* before a consonant (i. 35.8*a*; x. 72.8*a*). *aṣṭā́* agrees exactly with OIran. **aštā* (Av. *ašta*). These forms in comparison with Greek ὀκτώ, Latin *octō*, etc., point to PIE **oḱtṓ*. The palatal *ḱ* is confirmed by OInd. *aśītí-* 'eighty' and by the satem languages in their words for 'eight': Lith. *aštuonì*, OCS *osmĭ*. On the possible origin, see 5.1.23.

5.1.8.1. *aṣṭáu* in Old Indian beside *aṣṭā́* recalls the alternation found for 'two': *duváu* beside *duvā́* (5.1.2.). That *aṣṭáu* reflects a Proto-Indo-European variant is made likely by comparison with such forms as Gothic *ahtau*, OHG *ahtowen*, Lith. *aštuonì* and with the ordinals Greek ὄγδοος (< *ὄγδοϝος), Latin *octāuus*. Hence it is usual to reconstruct PIE **oḱtṓw* and to explain the alternation with **oḱtṓ* as sandhi-variation: **oḱtṓw* originally before vowels, **oḱtṓ* before consonants. As in the case of *dváu* 'two', it is the form in *-au* which is later generalised: *aṣṭáu*. But beside *aṣṭáu* the classical language, and occasionally the pre-classical language, have *aṣṭa* with a short vowel (cf. also *áṣṭakā*, 5.2.8.1.) due to the influence of *saptá, náva, dáśa*. In classical Sanskrit *aṣṭā* survived in the numeral compounds: *aṣṭādaśa* 'eighteen', *aṣṭāviṃśati* 'twenty-eight', and *aṣṭātriṃśat* 'thirty-eight', and optionally in 'forty-eight', 'fifty-eight', 'sixty-eight', 'seventy-eight', 'ninety-eight'.

5.1.9. OInd. *náva* 'nine' agrees exactly with OIran. *nava*. Indo-Iranian provides no assistance in deciding whether the underlying Proto-Indo-European form was **néwm̥* or **néwn̥*. OInd. *náva* and OIran. *nava* are usually considered to be related to PIE **néwo-* 'new': OInd. *náva-*, Av. *nauua-*, Greek νέος, Latin *nouus*.

5.1.10. OInd. *dáśa* 'ten' agrees exactly with OIran. *dasa*. Indo-Iran. **dáśa* beside Greek δέκα, Latin *decem*, etc., leads to the reconstruction of PIE **déḱm̥*. Since, in the decads, 'ten' appears in the form *-*dḱm̥t-*, it is possible that **déḱm̥* is a sandhi-form of **déḱm̥t-* (continued in OInd. *daśát-*, apart from the shift of accent, 5.3.5.4.), probably influenced by **séptm̥*, **néwm̥*.

5.1.11. As in Iranian no special form is found as the first member of a compound for 'five' to 'ten', the unchanged cardinal being used. Examples from the R̥gveda are: *páñca-pāda-* 'five-footed'; *ṣáḍ-aśva-* 'having six horses'; *saptá-cakra-* 'having seven wheels'; *aṣṭā́-pad-* 'eight-footed'; *náva-pad-* 'nine-footed'; *dáśa-māsya-* 'ten months old'. In the cuneiform hippological text we have **panča-vartana-*, **sapta-vartana-*, and **nava-vartana-*, implied by cuneiform spellings such as: *pa-an-za-wa-ar-ta-an-na, ša-at-ta-wa-ar-ta-an-na, na-a-wa-ar-ta-an-na* (Kammenhuber 1968: 204–206). *nava-* here has been reduced to *na-* by haplology, cf. the reduction of *náva-* 'new' to *ná-* proposed by Oldenburg for RV *náviṣṭi-* (< **náva-viṣṭi-* 'new work') and *návedas-* (< **náva-vedas-* 'having new knowledge') – see Mayrhofer (1956–1980: s. vv.).

5.1.12. 'Eleven' to 'nineteen' had the following forms in Old Indian (Ṛgveda forms in italics):

'eleven'	*ékādaśa*	'sixteen'	ṣóḍaśa
'twelve'	*dvā́daśa*	'seventeen'	saptádaśa
'thirteen'	tráyodaśa	'eighteen'	aṣṭā́daśa
'fourteen'	*cáturdaśa*	'nineteen'	návadaśa
'fifteen'	*páñcadaśa*		

Inflected forms are found in pre-classical texts but not in the Ṛgveda. They show instr. *-ábhiḥ*, dat. *-ábhyaḥ*, loc. *-asu*, that is, they are declined like *dáśa* (5.1.0.2.–5.1.0.4.). All clearly contain a form related to the ordinals 'one' to 'nine' (5.1.0.) followed by *dáśa* 'ten' (5.1.10.). For the corresponding Iranian forms see 8.1.10.2. Exact counterparts are found in Iranian for *dvā́daśa* (= OIran. **dvādasa*), *tráyodaśa* (= OIran. **θray-azdasa*), *páñcadaśa* (= OIran. **pančadasa*), *saptádaśa* (= OIran. **haf-tadasa*), *návadaśa* (= OIran. **navadasa*). The forms were compounded in Indo-Iranian independently from the various other Indo-European languages.

5.1.13. OInd. *ékādaśa* 'eleven' probably owes its *-ā-* to the influence of *dvā́daśa* 'twelve'. OIran. **aivandasa* < **aivam dasa* would lead us to expect OInd. **ekaṃdaśa*, which is in fact thought to be behind Kati *yanīċ* and Ashkun *ċänīs* (G. Morgenstierne *NTS* xiii, 1945: 233; Turner 1966: no. 2526). Some Iranian forms, on the other hand, are based on **aivādasa*, which would similarly point to the influence of **dvādasa*.

5.1.14. OInd. *cáturdaśa* 'fourteen' shows the same *cátur-* as is found as first element of a compound and in derivation, and contrasts with Av. *caθru-* and *caθβarə-* (5.1.4.2.). Old Iranian had accordingly **čaθrudasa* and **čaθwardasa*.

5.1.15. OInd. *ṣóḍaśa* 'sixteen' may correspond exactly to OIran. **xšvaž-dasa*. The initial *ṣ-* against OIran. *xšv-* is as in *ṣáṭ* 'six': Av. *xšuuaš* (see

5.1.6.). No exact parallel is available for the Old Indian treatment of PIE *-ḱs-d-* (> *-ǵzd-*) but the group *-ḱ-s-dh* (> *-ǵzdh-*) resulted in OIran. *žd* in Av. *θβarōždūm* 'you fashioned' (see Narten 1964: 28 n. 38); corresponding to OIran. *žd* < PIE *ǵdh* in Av. *važdri-* 'travelling', OInd. had *voḍhar-* (see Brugmann – Delbrück 1897–1916: I. 560, 562, 734).

5.1.16. OInd. *aṣṭā́daśa* 'eighteen' corresponds to OIran. **aštadasa* except that the latter contains no long vowel. OIran. **aštā* was already shortened to **ašta* under the influence of **hafta* 'seven' etc. in the Old Iranian period.

5.1.17. It is clear that 'eleven' to 'nineteen' are not old compounds but fossilized collocations. OIran. **aivamdasa* and OInd. **ékaṃ dáśa* mean 'one (and) ten', not 'one-ten'. Hence *dvā́daśa* has the nominative-accusative dual and never **dvi-*, the proper derivational form: it represents *dvā́ dáśa* 'two (and) ten'. In the case of 'fifteen' to 'nineteen' the prior element was ambiguous, as it could represent either the nominative-accusative plural or the form used in derivation (see 5.1.11.). Once these forms came to be regarded as compounds the proper form for the prior element of a compound was expected, and accordingly *cáturdaśa* replaced **catvā́ro dáśa* and **catvā́ri dáśa*. In Iranian this process was extended to 'thirteen', where *θridasa* replaced **θrayaz dasa* and **θrī dasa*. In the higher numerals in Indian, a secondary distribution of the possible forms *dvā-* ~ *dvi-*, *tráyas-* ~ *tri-* and *aṣṭā-* ~ *aṣṭa-* took place (5.1.2.2., 5.1.3.4., 5.1.8.1.).

5.1.18. The decads 'twenty' to 'ninety' are attested in Old Indian (all in the R̥gveda) as follows (Avestan and reconstructed Proto-Indo-European forms are added):

20	*viṃśatí*	*vīsaiti*	**wīḱn̥tī*
30	*triṃśát*	*θrisatəm*	**trīḱont-*
40	*catvāriṃśát*	*caθβarəsatəm*	**kʷétwr̥ḱont*
50	*pañcāśát*	*pančāsatəm*	**pénkʷēḱont-*
60	*ṣaṣṭí*	*xšuuaštīm*	[**ksweḱsḱont-*]
70	*saptatí*	*haptāitīm*	[**séptm̥ḱont-*]
80	*aśītí*	*aštāitīm*	[**oḱtṓḱont-*]
90	*navatí*	*nauuaitīm*	[**néwn̥ḱont-*]

The Old Indian decads 'twenty' to 'ninety' are inflected as regular nouns in *-i* and *-t* respectively and are all feminine. From the R̥gveda on they are often construed with a genitive: *pañcāśátaṃ ... áśvānāṃ* 'fifty horses' (RV v. 18.5), but more commonly they are used adjectivally: *navatíṃ* *nāvyà ánu* 'along the ninety rivers' (RV i. 80.8). In the latter use even the plural is found: *puró ... náva ... navatī́* 'ninety-nine citadels' (RV iv. 26.3). From the earliest times there was a tendency to regard the decads as indeclinable. Thus the R̥gveda has: *pañcāśát kr̥ṣṇā́ ní vapaḥ sahásrā* (iv. 16.13) 'you cast down fifty thousand dark ones'; *catúrbhiḥ sākáṃ navatíṃ ca nā́mabhiś* (i. 155.6) 'with four and ninety names'. Here *pañcāśát* occurs for *pañcāśátaṃ* and *navatíṃ* for *navatíbhiḥ*.

5.1.19. As has long been recognised, the Indo-Iranian tens system appears to be analysable into two groups: (a) 'twenty' to 'fifty', (b) 'sixty' through 'ninety'. The former group is characterized by the presence of the morpheme OInd. *-śát-*, OIran. *-sat-*; the latter by the suffix *-ti-*. If the Old Indian forms are compared with their Old Iranian counterparts (see 8.1.3.0.), it will be seen that the most difference is in group (a), where three Old Indian forms have a nasal of which there is little trace in Old Iranian. The only important difference in group (b) is the disagreement between OInd. *aśītí* and OIran. **aštāti-*.

5.1.20. Unless the nasal in *viṃśatí* beside Osset. (Digor) *insäi* is old, as has been suggested, there seems no way of accounting for the OInd. *-iṃśat-*sequence in the decads. It is, however, difficult to accept that PIE **widk̑m̥tī́* should develop to **wink̑m̥tī́* only in Indo-Iranian but to **wīk̑m̥tī́* elsewhere. If therefore G. Schmidt is right (1970: 128) in seeing reflexes of *-nk-* also in Germanic, the argument is greatly strengthened. Certainly the old idea that the nasal of the strong form of PIE **-k̑ont-*, Indo-Iran. **-śant-*, was in some way anticipated seems not to be compelling, although Wackernagel's objection on account of *pañcāśát* (1930: 366) is weakened by the fact that this form already had a nasal in the first syllable. Szemerényi (1960: 55) suggests that the reason is that "*-śaṃt* would have resulted in *-śaṁ*, thereby losing the link connecting the decads '30–50 (–90?)' with **vīśati* and *śataṁ*, namely *-t-*". The most frequent form, however, would always have been *-sat*, as the nominative-accusative singular neuter of *-śant-*, until transition to the feminine gender occurred. The original neuter gender remains, of course, clear in **wīk̑m̥tī́*. It is clearly more convincing that a form **trīśat* < **trīśant-* should be replaced by *triṃśát* under the influence of *viṃśatí* than that **trīśant-* should be replaced by **triṃśát-* as a result of a not clearly motivated anticipation of the nasal.

5.1.21. OInd. *catvāriṃśát* 'forty' differs from Av. *caθβarəsat-*, OIran. **čaθwarsat-* both in respect of *-ār-* and of *-iṃ-*. From an original **kʷetwr̥̄-* we would expect **cat(v)ūr-*. That might have been regularized to *cátur-*, the compositional and derivational form discussed above

(5.1.4.2. – 5.1.4.3.). It cannot accordingly be explained as a directly inherited form like the Old Iranian one. It is generally thought to have been influenced by *triṃśát*. That could have happened in two stages. **trīśant-* may have been analysed as containing the neuter form *trī́*. Then **catvāri-śant-* would be formed analogically to it. The second stage depends for its formulation on the explanation adopted for *viṃśatí*. The short *-i-* in *catvāriṃśát* could have influenced the development of **trīṃśat* to *triṃśát* and this in turn that of **vīṃśati* to *viṃśatí* if one does not assume an ancient nasal here.

5.1.22. In order to account for the *-ī-* of *aśītí* 'eighty', Szemerényi (1960: 55, 61) assumed that **catvāri-śant-* developed to **catvārī-śant-*, under the influence of **vīśati*, **trīśant*, before ending up as *catvāriṃśát*. Because of its arithmetical relationship ('forty' to 'eighty') **catvārī-śant-* is held to have changed **aśtāśant-* to **aśtīśant-*. It is indeed difficult to explain *aśītí*, but its explanation is not greatly advanced by the postulation of such an improbable form as **catvārī-śant*.

5.1.23. OInd. *aśītí* 'eighty' has often been considered to be archaic (e. g. Sommer 1951: 83; Debrunner 1954: 370; Burrow 1959: 261), even though — or perhaps because — it has proved difficult to explain. It is in marked contrast with OIran. **aštāti-*, which is clearly a recent secondary formation, following the interpretation of *xšuuašti-* 'sixty' as *xšuuaš* 'six' + *-ti-*. Yet the *-ś-*, which is in striking agreement with the *ḱ* required by **oḱtṓ(w)* 'eight' (5.1.8.), would seem to confirm its antiquity. The *ḱ* in **oḱtō(w)* has itself caused a certain amount of difficulty (e. g., Szemerényi 1964: 399 – 400). But if we accept the etymology of **oḱtō(w)* that would connect it with the verbal base of OInd. *aṃś-* 'to extend', there is no more difficulty in the *ḱt* of **oḱtṓ(w)* than there is in the past participle of any verb in *-ḱ*, e. g., **derḱ-* 'to see', past participle **dr̥ḱ-tó-*, OInd. *dr̥ṣṭá-*. This etymology goes back at least to T. Benfey, *Griechische Grammatik* I: *Griechisches Wurzellexikon* (1939: 243 – 244): "so würde ich dasjenige aç als Wzf. betrachten, von welchem sskr̥ a(n)ça (mit eingeschobenem Nasal) *Theil*, kommt; heisst aç hiernach *theilen*, so würde aç + ta (im Sskr̥ ashṭa) *getheilt* heissen; ashṭau, *die beiden getheilten*, wäre: *die beiden Theile*". The accentuation of **oḱtṓ(w)*, which **septḿ̥* is considered to have followed, is also explained satisfactorily on this basis. Two new difficulties arise, however, as a result of the adoption of this etymology. First, the *o*-vocalism is unexpected in a past participle, and, secondly, the *-n-* which Benfey regarded as intrusive is nowadays usually considered to be inherent in the root. The *o*-vocalism could conceivably be explained as the result of the influence of a root noun **onḱ-*, dual **onḱī*, with a basic meaning similar to that of Av. *ašti-* (cf. also pre-classical *áṣṭi-* 'reaching'). Structurally the root noun would be like OInd. *akṣī́* 'the two eyes', Av. *aši*. It is, of course, inconvenient to have to posit **aṃśī* (< **onḱī*) instead of **aśī* for Old Indian, as the latter would suit *aśītí* admirably. If, alternatively, we posit a root noun **Hn̥ḱ* > OInd. **aś-* with zero grade like OInd. *diś-* 'direction', *viś-* 'settlement' or Greek νιφ-, Latin *nix* 'snow', the *o*-vocalism of **oḱtṓ(w)* remains difficult. OInd. *aśītí* therefore remains enigmatic, which is the more to be regretted, inasmuch as it is likely that a proper understanding of *aśītí* would shed much light on the whole system of decads.

5.1.24. In the decads after *pañcāśát* 'fifty' the weak form *-śat-* presumably prevailed over *-śant-* (see 5.1.20.). **ksweḱsḱont-* 'sixty' would therefore have developed to **ṣaṭ-śat*, which may have contracted to **ṣaṣṭ*. The development to **ṣaṭ-śat* would be more likely than Szemerényi's **ṣacchat* (1960: 58), cf. OInd. *ṣaṭ-śaḥ* 'in sixes' with a similar morpheme boundary. **ṣaṣṭ* would need a final vowel to prevent further development to **ṣaṣ* with consequent confusion with *ṣáṣ-* 'six'. For the extension to *ṣaṣṭí*, OInd. *paṅ(k)tí-* 'a group of five' may have provided the model. It is possible that the reduction of **ksweḱsḱont-* began in Indo-Iranian. The development may have been **kšwakš-śat* > **kšwakšt*. If *-ḱm̥tə* is reconstructed for Indo-European on the basis of Latin *-gintā*, etc., we can assume an original **ksweḱs-ḱm̥tə* developing to **ṣaṭ-śati* and contracting directly to *ṣaṣṭí* (cf. G. Schmidt, *KZ* lxxxiv, 1970: 134–135).

5.1.25. After the development of *ṣaṣṭí* the later decads will have been modified to take account of the analysis *ṣaṣ-* 'six' plus *-ti*-abstract suffix. Thus **saptāśat(i)* > *saptatí*, **aśīśat(i)* > *aśītí*, and **navaśat(i)* > *navatí*. The development was probably similar in Iranian, although there the later form of 'eight', OIran. **aštā*, was used for 'eighty': OIran. **aštāti*. In Iranian, however, the older accentuation on the prior element of the compound (like Greek εἴκοσι etc.) was retained or restored.[7] In Old Indian the oxytone accentuation of the abstracts in *-ti-* was generalised for the decads, spreading from *ṣaṣṭí* to *navatí* and then from *viṃśatí* to *pañcāśát*. The secondary shortening of *-tī* to *-ti* in *viṃśatí* may also be ascribed to the influence of *ṣaṣṭí*.

5.1.26. In the later language, 'thirty' to 'fifty' exerted further influence on *viṃśati*, which was often reduced to *viṃśat* (Epic, Purāṇas). Occasionally, however, we find *triṃśati* under the influence of *viṃśati* (cf. also 5.2.15.). The further reduction to *viṃśa-*, *triṃśa-* as prior elements of compounds in the later language is due to the influence of the ordinals.

5.1.27. OInd. *śatá-* 'hundred' corresponds exactly to Av. *sata-*, etc., in Iranian. Indo-Iran. **śatá-*, set beside Greek ἑκατόν, Latin *centum*, etc., continues a PIE **k̑m̥tó-*, which may earlier have been **dk̑m̥tó-* 'tenth (decad)'.

5.1.28. OInd. *sahásra-* 'thousand' corresponds exactly to Av. *hazaŋra-*, etc., in Iranian. Indo-Iran. **saźhásra-* is usually explained (so, for instance, Pokorny 1959: 446) as containing **sa-* < PIE **sm̥-* 'one' and **źhasra-* < PIE **ĝhéslo-*. With the latter is set Greek *χεσλ- (< **ĝhesl-*) in χείλιοι Ionic, χίλιοι Attic.

5.1.29. OInd. *śatá-* and *sahásra-* are neuter nouns, cf. Greek ἑκατόν, Latin *centum*. The following examples are typical: *sárvaṃ sahásram* 'a whole thousand'; *sahasra-sā́-* 'gaining a thousand'; *dvé śaté* 'two hundred' (cf. Av. *duuaēca saite*); *triśatā́(ḥ)* 'three hundred'. They may be construed with a genitive singular or plural in the R̥gveda: *sahásram vyátīnāṃ* (iv. 32.17) 'a thousand vyátis'; but *dvé ... śaté góḥ* (vii. 18.22) 'two hundred cows'. Instead of the genitive an adjective may be used: *gávyam áśvyam ... śatám* (viii. 21.10) 'a hundred cows and horses'. But, as in the case of the decads (5.1.18.), adjectival usage occurs already in the R̥gveda. Note three types:[8] (a) *śaténa háribhiḥ* (ii. 18.6) 'with a hundred bays'; (b) *śatáir ... vadháiḥ* (vi. 20.4) 'by a hundred blows'; (c) *śatá-pad-* (i. 116.4) 'having a hundred feet'. Again as in the case of the decads (5.1.18.), a tendency can be seen in the R̥gveda to regard *śatám* and *sahásram* as indeclinable: *śataṃ ... ūtíbhiḥ* (iv. 31.3, ix. 52.5) 'with a hundred aids'; *sahásraṃ pathíbhiḥ* (vi. 18.11, ix. 91.3, ix. 106.6) 'by 1000 paths'. *śatám* is accordingly found as a prior element of a compound in *śatám-ūti-* (attested seven times) 'having a hundred aids' (contrast *śatóti-*, bis). The R̥gveda hapax legomenon *śatád-vasu-* (i. 119.1) is usually explained as 'having a hundred goods' (H. Grassmann, *Wörterbuch zum Rig-Veda*, 1873: s. v.; Geldner (1951)) with *-ád-vasu-* for *-á-vasu-* after the analogy of *kr̥tád-vasu-* "Schätze sammelnd" (Geldner) and *pratád-vasu-*, of uncertain meaning, both RV (so Wackernagel 1930: 374; L. R. Renou, *Études védiques et pāṇinéennes* xvi, 20).

5.1.30. In the R̥gveda *ayúta-* is used for 'ten thousand' and higher numerals are found in the Atharvaveda: *nyàrbuda-* 'one hundred thousand' and *asaṃkheyá-* 'one million'. In the later language there is a great proliferation of expressions for higher numerals. OInd. *ayúta-* has, however, no counterpart in Iranian, and attempts to connect OInd. *bhū́ri-* 'many' (= Av. *būiri-* 'do.') with OIran. **baiwar-* 'ten thousand' (Av.

baēuuar-) are of doubtful validity. *asaṃkhyeyá-* is literally 'uncountable' and belongs to *saṃ-khyā-* 'count'. With *asaṃkheyá-*, Av. *ahąxšta-*, according to Bartholomae (1904: col. 280) "'unzählbar', als Ausdruck für 100000", has often been connected (see Wackernagel 1930: 375). Khot. *ahaṃkhiṣta-* 'innumerable' from privative *a-* + *haṃkhiṣṭa-* passive past participle to *haṃkhīś-* 'count' must also be considered nowadays. See Emmerick (1968: 63, 136). According to É. Benveniste, *Études sur la langue ossète* (1959: 85–6), a base **xīz-* was formed analogically to **xišta-*, which replaced **xšta-* (in Av. *ahąxšta-*) secondarily. But Khot. *pachīya-* 'to be called, considered' and *pachīś-* 'regard, consider' on the one hand, and Ossetic (Digor) *xincun, xinst* 'count' on the other, make this explanation less likely than the assumption of a base **khai-*, extended to *khyā-* in Old Indian, to **xaiz-* in Avestan and Khotanese, and to **xaig-* in Ossetic. OInd. *khyā-* is thus not to be considered a Prakritism with Hiersche (1964: 44–45). See F. B. J. Kuiper, *IIJ* ix (1966: 222), who, however, prefers the old theory that *khyā-* developed secondarily from the variant *kśā-*, with which Av. *xsā-* is usually equated. On the secondary nature of the aspiration in OInd. *khyā-* see further W. P. Lehmann, *Proto-Indo-European phonology* (1955: 82). Otherwise the expressions for higher numerals show no correspondence between Indian and Iranian.

5.1.31. 'Two hundred' to 'nine hundred' and 'two thousand' to 'nine thousand' could be expressed in Indo-Iranian by inflecting the units and *śatá-* or *sahásra-*. Thus RV vii. 18.22 *dvé śaté* corresponds exactly to AV *duiie saite*. In Indian, several other types of expression are found: (*a*) bahuvrīhi adjectives in the R̥gveda and later: *triśatā́(ḥ) ... śaṅkávaḥ* (i. 164.48) 'three hundred spokes'; (*b*) bahuvrīhi nouns in the classical language as a neuter collective in *-a-*: *triśatám*, etc.; or (*c*) as a feminine collective in *-ī-*: *triśatī́* etc. As is well known, only the accentuation distinguishes a bahuvrīhi such as *triśatám* 'three hundred' from a dvandva such as *tríśatam* 'one hundred and three'.

5.1.32. In the R̥gveda the analytical expression described in 5.1.31 readily admitted of addition. Thus, RV i. 164.11 *saptá śatā́ni viṃśatíś ca* 'seven hundred and twenty'. But the preference for composition in pre-classical prose led to complex expressions such as *saptá viṃśatí-śatāni* 'seven hundred and twenty' and *dvé dvā-pañcāśé śaté* 'two hundred and fifty-two' (ŚB vii. 3 1.43). With *ardha-* 'half' there is ambiguity: *ardha-sapta-śata-* 'three hundred and fifty' ($\frac{1}{2} \times 7 \times 700$) or 'seven hundred and fifty' ($\frac{1}{2}$ [$\times$ 100] + 7 $\times$ 100).

5.2. Ordinals

5.2.0. Overview

The ordinal numerals are attested in Old Indian (R̥gvedic forms in italics) as follows; Old Indian cardinals and Avestan cardinals are added in columns two and three:

1	*prathamá-*	*éka-*	*fratəma-*
2	*dvitī́ya-*	*dvā́*	*daibitiia-*
3	*tr̥tī́ya-*	*tráyas*	*θritiia-*
4	*turī́ya-*	*catvā́ras*	*tūiriia-*
5	pañcamá-[9]	*páñca*	*puxδa-*
6	ṣaṣṭhá-[9]	*ṣáṣ-*	*xštuua-*
7	*saptátha-*	*saptá*	*haptaθa-*
8	*aṣṭamá-*	*aṣṭā́*	*aštəma-*
9	*navamá-*	*náva*	*naoma-*
10	*daśamá-*	*dáśa*	*dasəma-*

5.2.1. 'First'

OInd. *prathamá-* 'first' does not agree exactly with Av. *fratəma-*. The latter may show the influence of the Indo-Iranian superlative suffix *-tama-*. Some Iranian forms have *-θama-*: Zorastrian Pahl. *pahlom*, **parθama-*, etc. But there is evidence for an Indo-Iranian form **prata-*, possibly represented in Old Iranian by the R̥gvedic form *pratádvasū* viii. 13.27 (of uncertain meaning). An Indo-Iranian *prathamá-* seems best explained as a conflation of **pratha-* (< **prata-* with *-tha-* as in 'fifth' and 'seventh') and **prama-* (as in Umbrian *promom*). The pre-classical adverb *pratamā́m* may be an Indian formation.

5.2.1.1. Other words derived from PIE **per-/*pro-*, which belong to this semantic sphere are discussed in 8.2.1.2.—8.2.1.4. From Old Indian we have *pū́rva-, pūrvyá-* 'prior', and *prātár* 'early in the morning'. As in Iranian, a variety of words tended to be substituted. Wackernagel (1930: 405) cites from the R̥gveda *agriyá-, agrimá- : ágra-* 'top', and, from the later language, *ādya-, ādimá- : ādí-* 'beginning'; *múkhya- : múkha-* 'mouth'.

5.2.2. 'Second'

OInd. *dvitī́ya-* 'second' is usually said to owe its suffix to *tr̥tī́ya-* 'third'. Old Iranian has forms such as Av. *bitiia-, θritiia-*, which indicate a Common Old Iranian **dvitĭ̄ya-* as well as forms such as Khot. *śäta-*, *dädda-*, which indicate a Common Old Iranian **dvita-*, **θrita-*. Traces of OInd. **dvita-*, **trita-*, have often been sought in the Ṛgvedic deity names *Dvitá-* and *Tritá-*. But *Dvitá-* is probably a secondary formation based on *Tritá-* just as *Ekatá-* was added later. *Tritá-* itself has been explained as short for **tri-tavana-* 'of triple strength' in order to connect it with Av. *θraētaona-*, son of *Āθβiia-*, which has long been identified with *Āptyá-*, epithet of *Tritá-* (for literature, see Mayrhofer 1956: s. vv). Both **θrita-* and **θritiya-* are likely to be old, as can be seen from the comparison with Greek τρίτος and Latin *tertius*. The reason for the lengthening of *-iya-* to *-īya-* in Old Indian is not clear. The Middle Indian forms implying **dvitiya-* (Pāli *dutiya-*) and **dvitya-* (Ardha-Māgadhī *docca-*) may be secondary developments rather than imply older forms, although **dvitya-* is implied by pre-classical *ditya-vā́h-* 'two-year-old steer' and **dvitya-* is the form to be expected according to Sievers-Edgerton phenomena. According to C. Bartholomae, *IF* xxiii (1908–1909: 80), a corresponding OIran. **dwiθya-* is continued by Gabrī *bih, beh* 'another' and Paštō *biyā* 'again'. But the latter is connected with Av. *apaya* by Morgenstierne (1927: 16). It is difficult to evaluate the former. A similar suffix variation occurs with the Old Indian forms for 'fourth': *turya-* as well as *turī́ya-*. Pressure to maintain *-iya-* may have come in Indo-Iranian from the word for 'prior', OInd. *pūrvyá-* (RV **pūrviyá-* metrically), Common Old Iranian **parviya-*. Lengthening to *-īya-* would regularize those forms where the suffix tended to be reduced (cf. Szemerényi 1960: 85).

5.2.3. 'Third'

OInd. *tṛtī́ya-* 'third' differs from OIran. **θriti̯ya-* in respect to its first syllable. Here *tṛ-* is not merely graphic for *tri-*, as Middle Indian forms such as Pāli *tatiya-* show. Since *tri-* could easily be explained as having replaced *tṛ-* under the influence of *tri-* used as first member of a compound (5.1.3.3.), and since *tṛ-* in OInd. *tṛtī́ya* agrees with *tṛ-* in Old Prussian *tīrts*, OInd. *tṛtī́ya-* is usually considered to contain a PIE **tṛ*, which has been replaced by **tri-* in forms like Av. *θritiia-*, Latin *tertius*, Gothic *þridja*, etc. (so Wackernagel 1930: 406; Mayrhofer 1956–1980: s. v.). But since *caturthá-* is probably an analogical secondary development from **catvṛthá-* (Wackernagel 1930: 407; Szemerényi 1960: 85; see 5.1.4.2.), it is possible that **tritīya-* became *tṛtī́ya-* under the influence of **catvṛthá-*. That would also account for the absence of **tṛti̯ya-* from Iranian, which had no **catvṛthá-*. Old Prussian *tīrts* may also have been formed under the influence of *kettwirts* 'fourth', which, like Lith. *ketviȓtas* and Old Church Slavonic **četvĭrtŭ*, goes back to PIE **kʷetwr̥to-* (see 5.2.4.1.). So Szemerényi (1960: 85).

5.2.4. 'Fourth'

OInd. *turī́ya-* 'fourth' corresponds to Av. *tūiriia-*, and points to an old form of the ordinal based on PIE **kʷtur-* with zero grade in both syllables. The initial consonant survives in protected position in the Avestan adverb *āxtūirīm* 'four times'. In classical Sanskrit both *turī́ya-* and *túrya-* are used. In pre-classical Sanskrit *turya-* occurs in *turya-vāh-* 'four-year-old steer'. For *-īya-* from *-ya-* see 5.2.2.

5.2.4.1. From the Atharvaveda onwards *caturthá-* 'fourth' is attested, and it tended to replace *tur(ī)ya-* because of its more evident connection with the cardinal. As noted already (5.2.3.), *caturthá-* is probably a secondary replacement of **catvr̥thá-*. For *-tha-* replacing older *-ta-* see 8.2.7. OInd. *caturthá-* thus belongs with other forms which indicate a PIE **kʷetwr̥to-*: Lith. *ketviȓtas*, Old Church Slavonic **četvĭrtŭ*, Greek τέτρατος (Brugmann – Delbrück 1897–1916: II. ii. 1,54; Wackernagel 1930: 407). The full grade of the first syllable is probably secondary and due to the use of **kʷetwr̥-* as prior element of a compound (5.1.4.2.). One expects **kʷtwr̥-* before a consonant, **kʷtur-* before a vowel as in *turī́ya-* (5.2.4.). Both zero and full grade of the prior element of a compound are found: Av. *fšū-šan-* beside OInd. *paśu-ṣā́-* 'gaining cattle' (Brugmann – Delbrück 1897–1916: II. ii. 1, 14). Moreover the zero grade form **tri-* in **tritī́ya-* (5.2.3.) was identical with the form used as prior element of a compound (5.1.3.3.).

5.2.5. 'Fifth'

OInd. *pañcamá-* 'fifth' first occurs in the Atharvaveda and is the only form used in pre-classical prose and in classical Sanskrit. It corresponds to MIran. **pančama-*. Both the Old Indian and the Middle Iranian forms are clearly secondary and show the influence of Indo-Iranian **saptama-* 'seventh', where the ancient ordinal was reanalysed as cardinal plus suffix *-ma-*. This influence was exerted on **panča* 'five' and not on *ṣáṣ-* 'six' because of the structural similarity of **panča* and **sapta*. In Iranian, where *-a* was early added in some languages to the word for 'six', *-ma-* is found in 'sixth' also: Khot. *kṣäta'* 'six', *kṣei'ma-* 'sixth'. **pančama-* may not be of Indo-Iranian date (Debrunner 1954: 753), but this is still possible, just as both *saptamá-* and *saptátha-* (5.2.7.—5.2.7.1.) go back to Indo-Iranian.

5.2.5.1. OInd. *pañcathá-* 'fifth' is confined to the pre-classical Kāṭhaka and is certainly secondary, although forms admitting of a reconstruction of PIE **penkʷe-to-* occur in Celtic also, e. g., Old Welsh *pimphet*. It is probably based on a reinterpretation of *ṣaṣṭhá-* 'sixth' as cardinal plus suffix *-thá-*.

5.2.5.2. Neither *pañcamá-* nor *pañcathá-*, which are clearly based secondarily on the full form of the cardinal, *páñca*, provides a form of comparable antiquity with OIran. **puxθa-*, continued by Av. *puxδa-* and Khot. *pūha-*. Such a form has been sought in RV *pakthá-* occurring x. 61.1 *pakthé áhan* 'on the fifth day' and as PN *Pakthá-* 'Quintus'. The meaning 'fifth' for RV *pakthá-* was rejected by Szemerényi (1960: 74), but it has been upheld again by K. Hoffmann, *KZ* lxxix (1965: 253). OInd. *pakthá-* would continue a PIE **pn̥kʷtó-* based on the zero grade of the cardinal and would correspond to OIran. **puxθa-* except that the latter has a secondary *-u-*. An OInd. *pakthá-* 'fifth' seems to have been refashioned to *paṣṭha-vā́h-* 'five-year-old steer' (L. Renou, *BSL* xliii, 1946: 38—42). Elsewhere the full grade due to the cardinal is found and indicates a PIE **pénkʷto-*: Greek πέμπτος, Latin *quīntus*, Lith. *peñktas*, etc.

5.2.6. 'Sixth'

OInd. *ṣaṣṭhá-* 'sixth' occurs first in the Atharvaveda, but it is the only form ever attested for this ordinal. It contrasts both with the clearly archaic form Av. *xštuua-* and with the later Iranian forms in *-ma-* (see 5.2.5.). OInd. *ṣaṣṭhá-* is evidently based on the cardinal *ṣáṣ-* in the same way as Latin *sextus* is on *sex*. OInd. *ṣaṣṭhá-* may have replaced an earlier **ṣuṣṭ(h)á-* under the influence of *pakthá-* 'fifth'. **ṣuṣṭhá-* could then be compared with Av. *xštuua-* < **xšušta-* (see K. Hoffmann, *KZ* lxxix, 1965: 254). The Indo-Iranian evidence would thus indicate an original PIE **ksuḱs-tó-*. For the development of PIE *ḱst*, cf. classical Sanskrit *apraṣṭa* (3rd sg. *s*-aor. middle): *praś-* 'to ask' (PIE **preḱ-*) and Gāthic Av. *fraštā* (3 sg. *s*-aor. inj.): *fras-* (Brugmann — Delbrück 1897—1916: I. 561; Narten 1964: 176; Vedic **apraṣṭa* 'expected').

5.2.7. 'Seventh'

OInd. *saptátha-* 'seventh' is the only form of the numeral occurring in the R̥gveda (*saptathá-*, Wackernagel 1930: 408, is a misprint). The form corresponds exactly to the only form found in Avestan, *haptaθa-*. Forms pointing to PIE **septḿ̥to-* are found elsewhere, as in Lith. *septiñtas*. As the older form *saptamá-* is found in Old Indian from the Atharvaveda and the Yajurveda on, it would seem likely that *saptátha-* is a secondary form based, like *pañcathá-* (5.2.5.1.), on a reinterpretation of *ṣaṣṭhá-* 'sixth' as cardinal plus suffix *-thá-*. Here a difficulty arises in that we should expect *saptathá-*, which occurs only later, although in a pre-classical text. Moreover, if the secondary **septḿ̥to-* was already formed in Indo-European, 'sixth' would then have had the form **ksuḱs-tó-* (5.2.6.). It is therefore likely that **septḿ̥to-* was based on **pénk*^{w}*to-* (5.2.5.2.), whose accentuation as well as full grade vocalism indicates the influence of the cardinal **pénk*^{w}*e* vis-à-vis older **pn̥k*^{w}*tó-*. PIE **septḿ̥to-* may likewise be regarded as a replacement of **s*$_{e}$*ptm̥tó-*.

5.2.7.1. OInd. *saptamá-* 'seventh', the only form in classical Sanskrit, is attested first in the Atharvaveda and Yajurveda, but, set beside such forms as Latin *septimus* and Greek ἕβδομος, it is evidently of Proto-Indo-European date, even though Iranian provides the corresponding **haftama-* only from Middle Iranian on. The Proto-Indo-European form will have been **septm̥mó-* for **s*$_{e}$*ptm̥mó-*.

5.2.8. 'Eighth'

OInd. *aṣṭamá-* 'eighth' corresponds exactly to OIran. **aštama-* as represented by Av. *aštəma-*. A thematicization of PIE **oḱtṓw* would be expected to result in **oḱtōwo-*, which may be continued by Latin *octāuus*. But since the older forms are based on the zero grade, an earlier **$_{o}$ḱt$_{o}$wó-* may be expected, to judge by Greek ὄγδοος. Such an **aštawa-* of Indo-Iranian has evidently been influenced by the surrounding **saptamá-* and **nawamá-*. If we are right in postulating an Indo-Iranian **aṃśī* or **aśī* for 'eight' (see 5.1.23.), a similarly influenced ordinal form **a(ṃ)śīma-* (with dissimilation?) may have been formed, but no trace survives unless in OInd. *aśītí* 'eighty'.

5.2.8.1. OInd. *áṣṭakā-* 'eighth day of the black fortnight' occurs from the Atharvaveda on. It is based on *aṣṭa* 'eight', whose final vowel was shortened early (5.1.8.1.). A great variety of *-ka-* formations with numerals is found in the later language (see Debrunner 1954: 529 and 5.3.2.3. below).

5.2.9. 'Ninth'

OInd. *navamá-* 'ninth' corresponds exactly to OIran. **nawama-*. Indo-Iranian **nawamá-* may either continue directly a PIE **newm̥mo-* from **néwm̥* or be a replacement of **nawana-* < PIE **newn̥no-* (Latin *nōnus*) due to nasal dissimilation and the influence of *_saptamá-_ and *_daśamá-_. PIE *_newm̥mo-_ or *_newn̥no-_ is evidently secondary, showing the influence of the cardinal, as the older forms are based on the zero grade. From PIE *_néwm̥_ we should expect *_numó-_ or *_nwm̥mó-_ according to the quantity of what precedes (Sievers-Edgerton phenomena) and likewise from PIE *_newn̥_ we should expect *_nunó-_ or *_nwn̥nó-_. With different suffix we find *_nwm̥-_ or *_nwn̥-_ continued in Greek ἔνατος.

5.2.10. 'Tenth'

OInd. _daśamá-_ 'tenth' corresponds exactly to OIran. *_dasama-_ and compared with Latin _decimus_, points to PIE *_dek̂m̥mo-_. If 'hundred' was originally *_dk̂m̥tó-_ 'tenth (decad)', *_dek̂m̥mo-_ must be a secondary formation. It is usually explained as a thematicization of *_dék̂m̥_ 'ten', which is itself a sandhi-form of *_dék̂m̥t_, attested in zero grade form in the decads as *_dk̂m̥t_.

5.2.11. Summary

The ordinals, according to the foregoing analysis, present the following picture:

1	*pr̥-mó-	*pró-mo-	*pró-to-
2	[*dwi-tó-]		
3	*tri-tó-	*tri-tyo-	
4	*k^{w}tur-ó-	*k^{w}etw?-to	
5	*pn̥k^{w}-tó-	*pénk^{w}-to-	[*penk^{w}-eto-]
6	*ksuk̂s-tó-	*kswék̂s-to-	
7	*s$_{e}$ptm̥mó-	*septḿ̥-to-	
8	*$_{o}$k̂t$_{o}$w-ó-	*ok̂tṓwo-	
9	*nwm̥mó-	*newḿ̥mo-	*n(e)wḿ̥-to-
10	*d$_{e}$k̂ḿ̥t-ó-	*dek̂ḿ̥-to-	*dek̂ḿ̥mo-.

The following are some of the forms on which this analysis is based:

1	[Lith. _pìrmas_]	[Umbrian _promom_]	Indo-Iranian *_prata-_
2	Indo-Iranian *_dwita-_		
3	Indo-Iranian *_trita-_	Indo-Iranian *_tritiya-_	
4	Indo-Iranian *_turiya-_	OInd. _caturthá-_	
5	Av. _puxδa-_	Av. _paŋta-_	OInd. _pañcathá-_
6	Av. _xštuua-_	OInd. _ṣaṣṭhá-_	

7	Indo-Iranian **saptama-*	Indo-Iranian **saptátha-*	
8	[Greek ὄγδοος]	[Latin *octāuus*]	
9		Indo-Iranian **navama-*	[Greek ἔνατος]
10	Indo-Iranian **śatá-*	[Greek δέκατος]	Indo-Iranian **daś-ama-*.

5.2.11.1. Basically, the ordinals were formed from the zero grade of the cardinal by thematicization except in the case of 'first' and possibly 'second'. For the formation of 'first' a different element was used from that for 'one', and Indo-Iranian **dwita-* 'second' may not be of Proto-Indo-European date. The three suffixes *-mo-, -to-, -yo-* used in the formation of some of the ordinals are all of Indo-European date. *-mo-* and *-to-* may have developed as a result of the alternation of **déḱm̥* and **déḱm̥t* standing beside thematicizations **d*$_e$*ḱm̥mo-*, **d*$_e$*ḱm̥tó-*. Hence the development of **septḿ̥to-* beside **septm̥mó-* and possibly of **newm̥to-* beside **newm̥mo-*. The origin of the suffix *-yo-* is, however, uncertain. It has been suggested that it is the result of thematicization of **tri-* to **triyo-* (Szemerényi 1960: 82–85; cf. Debrunner 1954: 816–817), but **triyo-* is not found except perhaps in Hitt. **tarryana-* (cf. Szemerényi 1960: 82–5, and 3.3.3.5. in this volume).

5.2.11.2. The most noticeable characteristic development of the ordinals besides the formation and spread of suffixes is the tendency to replace the zero grade forms with the full grade forms of the cardinals. For this the following reasons can be suggested: (a) the desirability of differentiating between 'ten' and 'hundred'; (b) the influence of such forms as **s*$_e$*ptm̥mó-*, where the zero grade would be unsyllabic; (c) the need to accent the distinctive element of the numeral rather than the thematic vowel; (d), associated with (c), the need to retain a clear relationship to the cardinal.

5.2.11.3. The ordinals are declined as *a*-stem adjectives in the masculine and neuter. In the feminine, 'first', 'second', 'third' follow the *ā*-declension, as does *turīya-* 'fourth', but the remaining ordinals have the feminine according to the *ī*-declension[10], e. g. *aṣṭamī* 'eighth', *pañcadaśī* 'fifteenth'. With this distribution Avestan accords except that *puxδa-* 'fifth' appears to have a feminine in *-ā*[11]. Thus, Avestan has *bitiiā-, θritiiā-* and *tūiriiā-*, but *xštuuī-* and **nawamī* (in *naomiiā-čit̰* Yt 14.33). In Khotanese the *ā*-declension prevails throughout. In related languages only the *ā*-declension is found.

5.2.12. In the older language the ordinals 'eleventh' to 'nineteenth' evidently followed the same pattern as in Avestan: Av. *panca.dasa*, OInd. *páñcadaśa* 'fifteen' beside Av. *panca.dasa-*, OInd. *pañcadaśá-* 'fifteenth'. In the Ṛgveda only *ekādaśá-* 'eleventh' is attested. It is also used idiomatically there: *devā́s tráya ekādaśā́saḥ* (ix. 92.4) 'the three groups of eleven gods'. There are attested in pre-classical Old Indian: *ekādaśá-, dvādaśá-, trayodaśá-, caturdaśá-, pañcadaśá-, ṣoḍaśá-, saptadaśá-, aṣṭādaśá-* and *navadaśá-*. Only the oxytone accentuation and the adjectival declension distinguish them from the corresponding cardinals (5.1.12.). This accentuation is probably old, or at least follows an ancient pattern, since this form of ordinal is not exactly paralleled outside Indo-Iranian. The oxytone accentuation of adjectives in contrast with barytone accentuation of nouns is characteristic of Proto-Indo-European (see Kuryłowicz 1968: 38 – 56). In the later language the ordinals were more clearly distinguished by the addition of the suffix *-ma-* : *dáśa* : *daśamá-* :: *ékādaśa* : *ekādaśama-*. This development has a clear parallel in Latin *ūndecimus*, etc.

5.2.13. The ordinals of the decads are of two types: (a) a short form in *-á-* e. g. *triṃśá-* 'thirtieth', and (b) a long form in *-tamá-* e. g. *triṃśattamá-*. The short form of 'twentieth' to 'fiftieth' ends in *-śá-*, that of 'sixtieth' to 'ninetieth' in *-tá-*. The short forms are thought to be secondary formations due to the ordinals 'eleventh' to 'nineteenth' : *dvā́triṃśat* : *dvā́daśa* :: *dvātriṃśá-* : *dvādaśá-*. Thematicization of the final member of a bahuvrīhi is common (see Renou 1961: 100 ff.). For 'twentieth' to 'fiftieth' *-śat-* will have been reduced to *-śá-* under the influence of *daśá-*. *viṃśá-* will have been due to *triṃśá-, catvāriṃśá-* and *pañcāśá-*. For 'sixtieth' to 'ninetieth' *-ti* will have been thematicized to *-ta-* according to such well-known models as *-akṣa-* for *akṣi-* 'eye' in bahuvrīhi compounds. According to Indian grammarians (see for instance Pāṇini v. 2.58; L. R. Renou, *La grammaire de Pāṇini*, 1966: ii. 42), the short form in *-ta-* was permissible only with a preceding unit, e. g., *ekaṣaṣṭá-* (or *ekaṣaṣṭitama-*) 'sixty-first' but only *ṣaṣṭitama-* 'sixtieth'. This, too, accords with the suggestion that the short forms originated in bahuvrīhi compounds. In the later language short forms are found without a preceding unit, e. g., *navata-* 'ninetieth'.

5.2.14. Only the ordinal in *-tamá-* is found with *śatá-* 'hundred'[12] and with *sahásra-* 'thousand', and these forms agree with Old Iranian: *śatatamá-* beside Av. *satō.təma-*, *sahasratamá-* beside Av. *hazaŋrōtəma-*. In the later language and in epic, forms with a secondary *-ka-*suffix are found: *śataka-, śatika-, sāhasrika-*. In the decads *-tamá-* is the older formation: OInd. *triṃśattamá-* like Latin *trīcēsimus* 'thirtieth'. OInd.

viṃśatitamá- is probably secondary for **viṃśattamá-*, under the influence of *ṣaṣṭitamá-*, etc., if *-i-* there is old (see 5.1.24.), or under the influence of the cardinal *viṃśatí*. Av. *vīsąstəma-* is comparable, apart from the nasalised vowel, with OInd. **viṃśattamá-*. They may continue a PIE **wīḱm̥t-tó-* (Greek εἰκοστός) with analogical *-ma-* as in Latin *uīcēsimus*.
5.2.15. In the later language and in epic the suffix *-ma-*, having first spread to the ordinals 'eleventh' to 'nineteenth', extended throughout the decads : *dáśa* : *daśamá-* :: *viṃśatí* : *viṃśatima-*. After *viṃśatima-* there was formed *triṃśatima-* etc. (cf. 5.1.26.).

5.3. Other numerals

5.3.1. Multiplicative adverbs

5.3.1.0. Cf. 8.3.1.0. The following types occur in Old Indian: (a) *sakŕ̥t, dvíḥ, tríh, catúḥ, ṣáṭ* (5.3.1.1.); (b) *prathamám, dvitī́yam*, etc. (5.3.1.2.); (c) *dvivat* (5.3.1.3.); (d) *ekadhā, dvidhā*, etc. (5.3.1.4. – 5.3.1.4.1.); (e) cardinals plus nouns (5.2.1.5. – 5.3.1.6.). Of these only (a), (b) and (e) are Indo-European types. Type (c) occurs also in Old Iranian in a similar form.
5.3.1.1. OInd. *sakŕ̥t* 'once' corresponds exactly to Av. *hakərəṯ*. OInd. *d(u)víḥ, tríḥ* correspond exactly to Av. *biš, θriš* and continue PIE **dwis, *tris* as seen in Latin *bis, ter*; Greek δίς, τρίς. OInd. *catúḥ* 'four times' beside Av. *caθruš* shows the same correspondence as seen above in composition (5.1.4.2.). Av. *caθruš*, like Latin *quater* may show a Proto-Indo-European development of **kʷetwr̥s* to **kʷetrus*, while OInd. *catúḥ* < **caturs* shows the originally antevocalic PIE **kʷetur-* generalised. OInd. *ṣáṭ* 'six times', attested in the pre-classical language (Wackernagel 1930: 427), corresponds exactly to Av. *xšuuaš*, which may derive from PIE **ksweḱs-s* with expected homonymity with the cardinal.
5.3.1.2. A common type of expression in Indo-European languages is the use of the accusative singular neuter of the ordinal as an adverb : Greek τὸ πρῶτον, Latin *prīmum, iterum, tertium*, etc. This type is found in Old Iranian and in Old Indian: *prathamáṃ ... dvitī́yaṃ ... tr̥tī́yaṃ* (RV ii. 18.2, x. 45.1).
5.3.1.3. The rare OInd. *dvivat*' 'zu zweien (?)' and 'dualisch'), opposed to *bahuvat* 'pluralisch' (Wackernagel 1930: 430) contrasts with Av. *bižuuaṯ, θrižuuaṯ*, which have the same suffix added to the forms in *-s*, already adverbs, discussed in 5.3.1.1. The same contrast between derivatives with and without *-s* appears in Germanic: OEng. *twiwa, þriwa*, but

OIcel. *tysuar, þrisuar* (cf. Brugmann – Delbrück 1897–1916: II. ii. 64). Cf. also **dwino-* beside **dwisno-* as in OHG *zwinal* 'twin' beside *zwirnôn* 'to twist' – Brugmann – Delbrück (1897–1916: II. ii. 78) and cf. 5.3.1.4.

5.3.1.4. Adverbs in *-dhā* to numerals are common in Old Indian, but are not found in Iranian. They are probably an Old Indian innovation. The following are found in the R̥gveda: *dvídhā, trídhā* and *tredhā́, caturdhā́, ṣoḍhā́, sahasradhā́.* The R̥gveda has also several words in *-dhā* whose meaning is closely associated with that of the numeral adverbs: *katidhā́* 'in how many ways?', *purudhā́* and *bahudhā́* 'in many ways', *viśvádhā* and *śaśvadhā́* 'at all times'. Of these only one has a counterpart in Iranian: *viśvádhā̆*, cf. OPers. *vi[s]padā* (DB IV. 92) 'everywhere'. Moreover, *viśvádhā̆* agrees in respect to its accentuation with *dvídhā, trídhā* against the remainder; *tredhā́* is clearly secondary. In nine out of eleven of its occurrences in the R̥gveda it is metrically trisyllabic, which would point to the influence of RV *trayá-* 'threefold', with contraction of *-aya-* to *-e-* as in *trétā-* 'triad', etc. From the Brāhmaṇas on there occurs *dvedhā́*, formed by analogy to *tredhā́.* After the R̥gveda the accentuation of *dvedhā́, tredhā́* prevailed also to produce *dvidhā́, tridhā́.* The evidence points thus to the creation within Old Indian of *dvídhā, trídhā* by analogy with inherited *viśvádhā̆*, rather than to an Indo-European formation. That Greek διχθά should be a contamination of δίχά and *διθα = OInd. *dvidhā́* (but older *dvídhā*!) is unlikely and cannot be demonstrated as long as the guttural forms remain unexplained. Nor can the Old Irish numeral forms with the adjectival suffix *-de* be compared directly. Beside *dvídhā* there may have been in Proto-Indian a *-dha*-adjective or *-dhā*-adverb formed to the *s*-adverb (cf. 5.3.1.3.) if Pāli *dveḷha-ka-* 'doubt' is correctly derived from **dviž-dha-* (see H. Smith, *BSL* xxx, 1929: xviii). RV *ṣoḍhā́* is sometimes replaced by *ṣaḍdhā, ṣaṭdhā*, or *ṣaḍḍhā* under the influence of *ṣáṭ* (either as cardinal or compositional form or as adverb, 5.3.1.1.).

5.3.1.4.1. In the later language, beginning from Vedic times, the numerals in *-dhā* proliferated. From the Atharvaveda we have *ekadhā́* 'singly' replacing an expected old form **sadhā́* from PIE **sm̥-* 'one' as seen in OInd. *sakŕ̥t*, Av. *hakərət̰*, Latin *semel* 'once', etc. In fact, **sadhā́* is continued by OInd. *sadha-* 'together with', *sahá* (preposition and adverb) 'with'. OInd. *sahá* 'with' already has *-h-* in the R̥gveda from older *-dh-* as also found in *ihá* 'here', the older form *idha* occurring in Pāli, corresponding to Av. *iδa*, Opers. *idā*. Cognate with OInd. *sahá* 'with' and having the same meaning in Iranian are Av. *haδa*, OPers. *hadā*, Parthian *'d*, Buddhist Sogdian *δnn, δ(')wn* (< **hada* + *awana-*, Gershevitch 1954: 234), Ossetic *äd-*.

5.3.1.5. As in Iranian and other Indo-European languages, there is an increasing tendency to employ the cardinal plus a noun meaning 'time(s)' instead of the types discussed in 5.2.1.1. – 5.3.1.4.1. The oldest of these words in Old Indian is *kŕ̥tvaḥ*, which occurs first in the R̥gveda: *bhū́ri kŕ̥tvaḥ* (iii. 18.4) 'many times' and *śáśvat kŕ̥tvaḥ* (iii. 54.1) 'at all times'. From the Atharvaveda on, *kŕ̥tvaḥ* occurs with cardinals either as a collocation with the uninflected numeral or as a compound: e. g., *dáśa kŕ̥tvaḥ* (AV xi. 2.9[b]) and *aṣṭa-kŕ̥tvaḥ* (AV xi. 2.9[a]). In pre-classical prose, *kŕ̥tvaḥ* occurs pleonastically with the multiplicative adverbs *dvíḥ, tríḥ, catúḥ*. OInd. *kŕ̥tvaḥ* has usually been connected with *-kr̥t* in OInd. *sakŕ̥t*, Av. *hakərəṯ*. This *kr̥t-* is further connected with Lith. *kar̃tas*, OCS *kratŭ* 'time', etc., from a Proto-Indo-European base *kert-* 'to cut'. But there is no reason to assume the same semantic development in Indo-Iranian as in Balto-Slavonic, and since *kr̥t* in *sakŕ̥t* has been more satisfactorily explained as containing *kr̥-* < PIE *k*ʷ*el-*, it is probable that *kŕ̥tvaḥ* is best explained as plural of **kr̥-tu-*, an abstract noun from the same verbal root. For *-kŕ̥t* beside **kŕ̥tu-* cf. RV *tri-vŕ̥t-* 'threefold' beside *tri-vártu-* < **tri-várt-tu-* (see L. Renou, *Études védiques et pāṇinéennes* xv, 1966: 113).

5.3.1.6. In the later language the cardinals are used with OInd. *vā́ra-* and *vélā-* either as a collocation or as a compound: *pañca vārān* or *pañca-vāram* 'five times'. OInd. *vā́ra-* may show parallel development with Zoroastrian Pahl. *bār*, Modern Persian *bār* in Iranian rather than an Indo-Iranian usage, as *vā́ra-* does not occur in this way in the older language. The word itself is no doubt of Indo-Iranian date. OInd. *vā́ra-* probably developed in meaning from an older **vāra-* 'choice' (so Mayrhofer 1956 – 1980: s. v.) as did Zoroastrian Pahl. *bār*, Modern Persian *bār* 'fois', cf. Ossetic (Digor) *bārä*, (Iron) *bār* 'will' < **vāra-* (Abaev 1958: 235; Miller 1903: 33). The origin of OInd. *vélā-* 'limit, time' is still disputed (see Mayrhofer 1956 – 1980: s. v.).

5.3.2. Multiplicative adjectives

5.3.2.0. Old Indian has the following types: (a) *-(t)aya-* (5.3.2.1.); (b) vr̥ddhi (5.3.2.2.); (c) *-ka-* (5.3.2.3.); (d) *-in* (5.3.2.4.); (e) *-vant-* (5.3.2.5.); (f) *-(i)ya-* (5.3.2.6.); (g) cardinals plus nouns (5.3.2.7.). There are no close correspondences with Iranian except for (e).

5.3.2.1. The type in *-aya-* is usually considered to be the oldest. RV *dvayá-, trayá-* are generally compared with Balto-Slavonic forms such as

Lith. *dvejì, trejì*, Old Church Slavonic *dĭvojĭ, trojĭ* and with Greek δοιός. Hence Proto-Indo-European forms **dweyó-*, **dwoyó-* and **treyó-*, **troyó-* are posited. Beside these forms there occur in the same sense derivatives in *-taya-*, of which the first is already found in the R̥gveda: *dáśataya-* 'tenfold'. Since *dáśa* 'ten' is originally only a sandhi-form of **dáśat* (5.1.10.), the form *dáśataya-* was probably the starting-point for the spread of the suffix *-taya-* as a result of re-analysis. What is not so clear is why *-aya-* should have been regarded as the suffix. Strict analysis of *dvayá-, trayá-*, would require thematicisation of the full grade: **daśatá-*. An analogical development such as *dvi-* : *dvayá-* :: *daśati-* : *dáśataya-* would meet the requirements, but *daśati-* is in fact only a late replacement of the abstract *daśát-*. Consequently Szemerényi (1960: 107) explained the suffix as an extension of the Proto-Indo-European material suffix *-eyo-*. But the development looks much more like a purely Indian one. Possibly *dáśataya-* : **daśatá-* is like *ubháya-* : *ubhá-* 'both'. Note also that *dáśataya-* and *ubháya-* agree also, against *dvayá-, trayá-*, in accenting the same syllable as the basic form *dáśa, ubhá-*. So also *saptátaya-*, etc. OInd. *ubháya-* and *ubhá-* are both attested from the R̥gveda and are Indo-Iranian. *-taya-* (*-ī-* fem.) spread after the R̥gveda to the following pre-classical forms: *ékatayī-, cátuṣṭaya-, cátuṣṭayī-, ṣaṭtaya-, saptátaya-, aṣṭā́taya-* (classical *aṣṭataya-*), *daśatayī-*, and *bahú-taya-* 'manifold'. In classical Sanskrit *-taya-* was allowed after any numeral by Pāṇini, v. 2.42. According to Pāṇini, v. 2.43, it was optional with *dvi-* and *tri-*, i.e., *dvítaya-* or *dvayá-*, *trítaya-* or *trayá-*.

5.3.2.2. In the R̥gveda derivatives in *-a-* with vr̥ddhi are already extremely common (Debrunner 1954: 111) and it is not therefore surprising to find there such a derivative from a cardinal as *sā́pta-* (i. 20.7, ii. 19.7) or *sāptá-* (vii. 55.5, viii. 59.5). According to Debrunner (1954: 135), the accentuation *sāptá-* in the Vālakhilya hymns is incorrect. *sā́pta-* in the R̥gveda is used as a collective noun, but it is clearly a nominalised adjective. The similarly formed adjective *sāhasrá-* occurs from the Atharvaveda on, whereas *sā́pta-*, according to Pāṇini, v. 1.61, is Vedic only. *sā́pta-* in the R̥gveda is of disputed meaning (see Geldner 1951 on ii. 19.7; L. R. Renou, *Etudes védiques et pāṇinéennes* vii, 1960: 29; xv 1966: 78) and may have nothing to do with *saptá* 'seven' originally. The contents suggest rather a derivative from *sápati* 'to honour'. *sāhasrá-* is used in several senses: 'counting one thousand', 'thousandfold', 'bought for one thousand', 'equipped with one thousand'.

5.3.2.3. Adjectives with a variety of meanings are found with the suffix *-ka-*, or with *-ika-* and vr̥ddhi. Some specialisations of meaning occur in the later language which are not listed here (see Debrunner 1954: 529). The older type in *-ka-* is attested in the pre-classical period in *áṣṭaka-* (Śatapathabrāhmaṇa), cf. *áṣṭakā-* (5.2.8.1.). Pāṇini (v. 2.77) allowed such a form as *dvíka-* beside *dvitīyaka-*. The latter type was evidently replacing the former. OInd. *dvíka-* has been compared with OHG *zwëho* 'doubt' (so for instance Brugmann – Delbrück 1897–1916: II. ii. 1,78; Pokorny 1959: 231), but, according to Mayrhofer (1956–1980): *dvikaḥ*, there is no ultimate connection. A connected form has also been sought in Greek τρικτύς, τριττύς (E. Schwyzer, *Griechische Grammatik* 1953: i, 597; H. Frisk, *Griechisches etymologisches Wörterbuch* 1960–72: τριττύς) set beside OInd. *tríka-*. The three oxytone adjectives, RV x. 59.9: *ekaká-, dvaká-, triká-*, are probably to be distinguished from the series under discussion. Their accentuation and usage indicate that the *-ká-*suffix is diminutive in function (Wackernagel 1930: 422; Debrunner 1954: 529). Mayrhofer (1956–80): *dvakáḥ* follows A. Meillet, *MSL* xii (1901: 431), in regarding *dvaká-* as an archaism continuing PIE **dwo-* in Arm. *erko-tasan* 'twelve'. The adjectives in *-ika-* with vr̥ddhi, e. g. *ṣāṣṭika-* 'sixty-year-old' (but *ṣaṣṭika-* 'ripening in sixty days') are an Indian development.

5.3.2.4. The suffix *-in-* is found in Old Indian both with cardinals and with ordinals. The latter usage is attested only late and is a consequence of the extensive use of the suffix in the later language. Thus, *daśamin-* 'counting ninety to one hundred years', i. e. in the tenth stage of (old) age (Atharvaveda *daśamī́-*). With cardinals the type is old; *śatín-* 'hundredfold' is frequent in the R̥gveda. From the Atharvaveda and Yajurveda we have *ṣoḍaśín-*, from the latter also *ekādaśín-*. Such forms as *pañcín-, daśín-, viṃśín-* are also pre-classically attested. The suffix *-in-* is Indo-Iranian and has a Proto-Indo-European basis. In Old Indian, the zero grade *-in-* was generalised: PIE *-ə̯en- : *-ə̯n (see K. Hoffmann, *MSS* vi, 1955: 35–40). The full grade suffix occurs in Old Iranian, in the same function as the suffix *-vant-* : *puθrān-* = *puθrauuant-* 'having a son' in Avestan just as the zero grade suffix occurs in Old Indian: *putrín-* (RV) = *putrávant-* (Vājasaneyisaṃhitā). Hence, the Old Indian forms in *-ín-*, e. g., *śatín-*, are indirectly comparable with the Old Iranian forms in *-vant-*, e. g. Av. *satauuant-*. Both formations occur in the interrogative adjective: OInd. *kíyant-* beside *kī́vant-* (cf. Av. *čuuant-*). OInd. *kíyant-* shows the full grade of the suffix with the same *-t-* extension as in *-vant-* (PIE *-wen-t-*). A comparable formation occurs in Latin in such forms as *quotiēns* (Sommer 1914: 277, 474; Brugmann – Delbrück 1897–1916: II. ii. 1,65) from *quot* (< *k*ʷ*oti*, cf. OInd. *káti*). The apparently similar form OInd. *ekākín-* (Atharvaveda Vājasaneyisaṃhitā) is of unclear formation (Debrunner 1954: 266, 542).

5.3.2.5. As in Old Iranian, there were, in Old Indian, multiplicative adjectives in *-vant-* (cf. 5.3.2.4.), which may represent a Proto-Indo-European type even though no exact parallel can be found outside Indo-Iranian. The R̥gveda has *śatávant-*, cf. Av. *satauuant-*, and *sahasrávant-*, cf. Av. *hazaŋrauuant-*. *-a-* is often lengthened before *-vant-* (Debrunner 1954: 885–6), hence **śatāvant-* could be expected. The vocative singular form *śatāvan* (RV vi. 47.9) may show this same secondary lengthening before the older suffix *-van-*. The hapax legomenon *śatasvín* (RV vii. 58.4) contains the secondary suffix *-vín-* (from *-van(t)-* + *-in-*, cf. Debrunner 1954: 919) added to *śatá-* under the influence of *sahasrín-*, in the same verse, and on the analogy of *-vín-* with *as*-stems, where the suffix is most frequent (so L. R. Renou, *Études védiques et pāṇinéennes* x, 1962: 103).

5.3.2.6. The Indo-European *-iy*-suffix for adjectives is found in Old Indian with *śatá-* and *sahásra-*. The R̥gveda has also, once only, *sáptya-* (viii. 41.4), which has usually been explained as an adjective from *saptá* 'seven'. According to Geldner (1951: viii. 41.4) it is equivalent to *sā́pta-*, on which see 5.3.2.2. Renou renders it by 'septuplicité' with the comment "la septuplicité est d'abord un « séjour » apte à servir de base au don ou à l'amitié" (*Études védiques et pāṇinéennes* v, 1959: 73, viii 1961: 29). The R̥gveda has twice *sahasríya-* (i. 168.2, vii. 56.14) 'thousandfold', where, according to Pāṇini, iv. 4.136, *-íya-* is used in the sense of *-vant-* (5.3.2.5.). *śatya-* 'bought for a hundred' is allowed by Pāṇini, v. 1.21. It is attested also at the end of a compound as in *ṣaṭtriṃśacchatya-* 'consisting of one hundred thirty-six', in which usage it has been compared with Greek -κοσιο- (Brugmann – Delbrück 1897–1916: II. ii. 1,44–45).

5.3.2.7. As in Iranian and other Indo-European languages, multiplicative adjectives are commonly formed by compounding the cardinals with a variety of nouns. The R̥gveda uses *-bhuji* (to *bhujáti* 'bends'), *-vr̥t-* and *-vártu-* (< **-várttu-* – L. R. Renou, *Études védiques et pāṇinéennes* xv, 1966: 113 – both to *vártate* 'turns'), *-vaya-* (probably to *vayā́-* 'twig, branch') and *-dhātu-* 'layer' (to *dádhāti* 'places'). In the later language the usual types are *-guṇa-* 'thread, quality' and *-vidha-* (to *vidhā-* 'kind, manner').

5.3.3. Fractions

5.3.3.1. As in Iranian, fractions may be expressed as ordinal plus noun meaning 'part, share': *ṣaṣṭho bhāgaḥ* 'one sixth'. So in other Indo-European languages: Latin *tertia pars*, Greek πέμπτον μέρος, etc. Attested at an earlier date than this type in Old Indian is the use of the ordinal alone as a neuter noun: *tṛ́tīya-m* 'one-third' (Yajurveda). In the pre-classical language this type contrasts with the use of a compound with *bhāgá-* to express a higher fraction: *dví-bhāga-* 'two-thirds' (literally 'two parts'), *trí-bhāga-* 'three-fourths' (literally 'three parts'). This usage is exactly like that in Modern Persian *do bahr* 'two-thirds' with *bahr*, which is cognate with OInd. *bhāgá-*. In Old Indian, *tṛ́tīya* 'one-third' was distinguished by its accentuation from *tṛtī́ya-* 'third'. In the pre-classical language *cáturtha-* 'one fourth' and *túrīya-* 'one fourth' are sometimes found accented like *tṛ́tīya-*, while in the classical language, according to Pāṇini, v. 3.49, accentuation of the initial syllable extended to all the ordinals in this function up to 'one tenth'. According to Pāṇini, v. 3.50, 'one sixth' and 'one eighth' optionally showed vṛddhi: *ṣáṣṭha-* or *ṣā́ṣṭha-*, *áṣṭama-* or *ā́ṣṭama-*.

5.3.3.2. As in Old Iranian, there are two ways in which 'half' is usually expressed: OInd. *ardhá-* = Av. *arəδa-* and OInd. *néma-* = Av. *naēma-*. Although both words may contain a Proto-Indo-European root, neither has an exact counterpart in another Indo-European language (see Mayrhofer 1956–80: s. vv., Pokorny 1959: 333). The Ṛgveda has both *ardhá-* and *árdha-* in about equal proportion. RV *ardhá-* may be adjective or noun while *árdha-* is exclusively substantival. In the Ṛgveda *néma-* is still pronominal, meaning 'some, many, another', but in some places the meaning 'half' is already beginning to emerge: *prathamáṃ ... némam* (ix. 68.5); *némo ... ardháḥ* (x. 27.18). An old word for 'half' survives in RV *ásāmi-* 'complete' (literally 'not half') containing *sāmí-*, cognate with Greek ἡμι-, Latin *sēmi-*.

5.3.3.3. Cardinal plus half is expressed in Old Indian by means of a compound of *ardhá-* (5.3.3.2.) and the subsequent cardinal: *ardha-tṛtīya-* 'two and a half' (having a half of the third (item)'). But instead of the expected **ardha-dvitīya-* for 'one and a half' *ádhy-ardha-* ('additional half') is found.

5.3.3.4. Already in the Ṛgveda two examples occur, both in viii. 47.17, of a type of numeral common later. These are *śaphá-* 'one eighth' (lit. 'hoof', cognate with Av. *safa-*, Khot. *saha-* 'hoof') and *kalā-* 'one sixteenth' (perhaps originally 'piece' to PIE *(s)kel-* 'cut' as in Lith. *skélti* 'split'; see Pokorny 1959: 923; Mayrhofer 1956–80: s. v.).

5.3.4. Distributives

5.3.4.1. Like Iranian (8.3.4.1.–8.3.4.2.), Old Indian used an inherited suffix added to the cardinals to form distributive adverbs: OInd. *-śáḥ*, OIr. **-sah*, Greek -κάς. The oldest forms attested are RV *sahasra-śáḥ*,

AV *śata-śáḥ, eka-śaḥ, dvi-śaḥ, tri-śaḥ*, etc. are later. According to Pāṇini, v. 4.43, *-śáḥ* may be added to any cardinal in distributive use.
5.3.4.2. Like later Iranian (8.3.4.4.), Old Indian used instead of *-śáḥ* (5.3.4.1.) a compound of the reduplicated cardinal (āmreḍita type): RV *ékaikā, dvā́-dvā, páñca-pañca, saptá-sapta*. In the R̥gveda *éka- eka-* is inflected as two words but accented as one. From the prose of the Brāhmaṇas on *ékaika-* is inflected only in the final member.
5.3.4.3. In the later language distributive compounds are found with prepositions as prior element, e. g., *prati-dvādaśa* 'each twelve'.

5.3.5. Collectives

5.3.5.0. Old Indian has the following types: (a) with abstract suffixes *-tā-, -tva-, -ya-* (5.3.5.1.); (b) nominalized multiplicative adjectives (5.3.5.2.); (c) *paṅktí-* (5.3.5.3.) and *daśát-* (5.3.5.4.).
5.3.5.1. The inherited Proto-Indo-European abstract suffixes were in Old Indian sometimes used with numerals, but none of the formations attested is likely to be of even Indo-Iranian date. Old Iranian has *-θβa-* used like OInd. *-tva-*. Examples of Old Indian collectives with abstract suffixes are: *triṃśat-tvá-* 'being thirty', *sāpta-daśya-* 'being seventeen', *trétā-* 'triad'. OInd. *trétā-* is probably implied by RV *tretínī-* used of the triple fire of the altar. *-e-* is an early contraction of *-aya-* as in *tredhā́* (5.3.1.4.). Common in the classical language is *pañcatva-* as in *pañcatvaṃ gacchati* 'he dies' (literally 'goes to the fivefold state', i. e., is resolved into the five elements).
5.3.5.2. Multiplicative adjectives in *-(t)aya-* (5.3.2.1.) and in *-ka-* (5.3.2.3.) are commonly used as neuter collective nouns. Thus, the R̥gveda has *dvayá-* ntr. 'duplicity' (i. 147.4,5; v. 3.7) and the later language *ṣaṭka-* ntr. 'hexad', etc. In the same way, the multiplicative adjectives in *-a-* with vr̥ddhi (5.3.2.2.) are occasionally used as neuter collective nouns. Of these types, that in *-(t)aya-* is the oldest: OInd. *dvayá-, trayá-* are of Proto-Indo-European date, while *ubháya-* and *ubhá-* 'both' are at least Indo-Iranian. Here also belong derivatives of the multiplicative adverbs in *-dhā* (5.3.1.4.) such as *aikadhyam, dvaidham, traidham*. These are rarely found before the classical period, when they occur as adjectives, adverbs and nouns.
5.3.5.3. OInd. *paṅ(k)tí-* fem. 'group of five' already occurs in the R̥gveda and continues PIE **penkʷti-* (see 5.1.5.). The only comparable abstract attested in Iranian is Av. *ašti-* 'four fingers' breadth' (cf. 5.1.23.) Whether *-ti-* abstracts lie behind the Indo-Iranian decads in *-ti-* remains

uncertain (cf. 5.1.24). A secondary derivative from *paṅ(k)tí-* is AV *pā́ṅkta-* 'fivefold'. For the formation cf. 5.3.2.2.

5.3.5.4. OInd. *daśát-* fem. 'decad' occurs from the Brāhmaṇas on. It is often merely a substitute for *dáśa* 'ten' in substantival use. It is usually considered to continue PIE **dék̂m̥t-* 'ten', for which the sandhi-form **dek̂m̥* was substituted as the cardinal (5.1.10.). The oxytone accentuation of *daśát-* cannot be original even though Greek δεκάς is in agreement. It is probably due secondarily to the influence of the decads (so G. Schmidt, *KZ* lxxxiv, 1970: 122). In the later language *daśati-* replaced *daśát-* perhaps under the influence of *paṅktí-*. At any rate its formal correspondence to Old Church Slavonic *desętĭ* is fortuitous. The collective *pañcát-*, known to Pāṇini, v. 1.60, is clearly analogical: *páñca* : *pañcát-* :: *dáśa* : *daśát-*.

5.4. Order of numerals

The normal order of composite numerals (as in Iranian) is digit preceding decad, but otherwise larger numbers precede. Thus *náva navatíṃ ca* 'ninety-nine' but *śatám ekáṃ ca* 'one hundred and one' (RV). In Old Indian, there was a tendency to compound even beyond 'one hundred', e. g., *cátuḥ-śata-* 'one hundred and four'. A common method of expressing composite numerals was the use of an adjective qualifying 'one hundred', etc.: *śatáṃ saptadáśám* 'one hundred and seventeen' (literally 'one hundred accompanied by seventeen'). In the classical language and in epic this method was improved by the use of *adhika-* or *uttara-* 'exceeding', e. g., *śatam ekottaram* 'one hundred and one' (literally 'one hundred with one exceeding it'). A somewhat similar expression with *paráḥ* 'beyond', found already in the R̥gveda: *triṃśáti tráyaḥ paráḥ* (viii. 28.1) 'thirty-three' (literally 'three beyond thirty'), led to the formation of compounds from the Atharvaveda on with *paraḥ* plus numeral in the sense of 'more than the number concerned': *paraḥ-sahasrá-* 'more than one thousand'. The subtractive type of expression, found also in later Iranian, occurs from the pre-classical period but not yet in the R̥gveda. In the pre-classical period there is a considerable variety of expressions mainly based on the principle: units to be subtracted precede in the instrumental or ablative case, plus *ná* 'not', plus higher numeral. Thus *dvā́bhyāṃ ná śatám* 'ninety-eight' (literally 'by two not one hundred'). In the classical language only one type remains: a compound with the ablative singular neuter (or masculine) of *éka-* 'one', plus *na* 'not', plus the higher numeral. Thus *ékān-na-viṃśati* 'nineteen'. Parallel with the use of *adhika-* and *uttara-*

'exceeding', there developed in the classical language a compound type with *ūná-* 'deficient'. It is occasionally found earlier, e. g., AV *ekona-viṃśatíḥ* 'nineteen'. The disjunctive use of numerals in ascending numerical order, e. g., *pañca ṣaṭ sapta* 'five, six, seven' was replaced by compounds, e. g., *catuṣ-pañca* 'four or five', later used as *-a*-adjectives, as taught by Pāṇini (ii. 2.25 with commentary).

Notes

1. The Indian numerals can be found in such standard grammars as Whitney (1889: 177–185); Renou (1961: 381–390); Macdonell (1910: 307–312). The fullest historical and comparative treatment is by Wackernagel (1930: 329–340). Burrow (1959: 257–262) is also useful.
2. The optional *pañcabhíḥ*, etc., of classical date (5.1.0.2.) is no doubt due to the influence of *ṣaḍbhíḥ* and *aṣṭābhíḥ*.
3. But **aina-*, which could be placed beside Greek οἰνός, cannot be postulated on the basis of OInd. *ena-* (pronominal stem), as this appears to have developed secondarily within Indian. See Mayrhofer (1956–1980: i. 560); Kuiper, *AO*, 213–20; Hauri (1963: 56, 87).
4. The oxytone accentuation of *evá* may be old. *éka-* may owe its accentuation to a tendency to stress the first syllable, a tendency resulting in the Middle Indian doubling of the consonant: *ekka-*. Cf. also, for the accentuation, Greek οἴνη, οἰνός. See Hirt (1921–1937: v, 288); Berger (*MSS* iii, 21).
5. A similar dissimilation has been proposed by Forssman, *KZ* lxxxii, 37–61, to account for Av. *tištriia-* and OInd. *tiṣyá-* 'star-name' (< **tri-str-iyo-*).
6. *āmā́daḥ kṣvínkās tám adantv énīḥ.* Translated by Geldner (1951): "Die aasfressenden, buntfarbigen Geier sollen ihn fressen", by Renou, *Études védiques et pāṇinéennes* xv (1966: 21): "Que les vautours, mangeurs de (viande) crue, (bêtes) bigarées, le dévorent"!
7. Differently Kuryłowicz (1968: § 60), according to whom the Proto-Indo-European accentuation was on the second element of the compound.
8. Wackernagel (1930: 373) cites also a type of adjectival usage where both elements are in the singular, e. g., *sahásrād yū́pāt* 'from a thousand sacrificial posts', but all the R̥gveda examples cited by him have been otherwise interpreted by Geldner (1951).
9. First attested in the Atharvaveda.
10. But according to the *ā*-declension as final member of a bahuvrīhi compound (rare).
11. Similarly, Avestan has *aparā-* 'posterior' but Old Indian *aparī́* (not as ordinal).
12. But a short form is sometimes found in composition in the later language, e. g., *triśata-* 'three hundredth'.

References

Abaev, Vasilij Ivanovič
1958 *Istoriko-ètimologičeskij slovar' osetinskogo jazyka* 1 (Moskva–Leningrad: Izdatel'stvo Akademii Nauk SSSR).
Bartholomae, Christian
1904 *Altiranisches Wörterbuch* (Strassburg: Trübner).
Benveniste, Émile
1935 *Origines de la formation des noms en indo-européen* (Paris: Maisonneuve).
Brugmann, Karl – Berthold Delbrück
1897–1916 *Grundriss der vergleichenden Grammatik der indogermanischen Sprachen*[2] (Strassburg: Trübner).
Burrow, Thomas
1959 *The Sanskrit language* (London: Faber & Faber).
Debrunner, Albert
1954 *Altindische Grammatik* II, 2 (Göttingen: Vandenhoeck & Ruprecht).
Emmerick, Ronald Eric
1968 *Saka grammatical studies* (London Oriental Series 20) (London: Oxford University Press).
Geldner, Karl Friedrich
1951 *Der Rig-Veda*, 1–3 (Cambridge, Mass.: Harvard University Press).
Gershevitch, Ilya
1954 *A grammar of Manichean Sogdian* (Oxford: Blackwell).
Hauri, Christoph
1963 *Zur Vorgeschichte des Ausgangs -ena des Instr. Sing. der A-Stämme des Altindischen* (Göttingen: Vandenhoeck & Ruprecht).
Hiersche, Rolf
1964 *Untersuchungen zur Frage der Tenues aspiratae im Indogermanischen* (Wiesbaden: O. Harrassowitz).
Hirt, Hermann
1921–1937 *Indogermanische Grammatik* i–vii (Heidelberg: Winter).
Kammenhuber, Annelies
1968 *Die Arier im Vorderen Orient* (Heidelberg: Winter).
Kuryłowicz, Jerzy
1958 *L'accentuation des langues indo-européennes* (Prace językoznawcze 17) (Wrocław-Kraków: Wydawnictwo Polskiej Akademii Nauk).
1968 *Indogermanische Grammatik* II: *Akzent. Ablaut* (Heidelberg: Winter).
Macdonell, Arthur Anthony
1910 *Vedic grammar* (Strassburg: Trübner).
Miller, Wsewolod
1903 *Die Sprache der Osseten, Anhang zum ersten Band*, in: *Grundriss der iranischen Philologie* (Strassburg: Trübner).

Mayrhofer, Manfred
1956–1980 *Kurzgefasstes etymologisches Wörterbuch des Altindischen* (Heidelberg: Winter).
Morgenstierne volume
1964 *Indo-iranica. Mélanges présentés à Georg Morgenstierne* (Wiesbaden: Harrassowitz).
Morgenstierne, Georg
1927 *An etymological vocabulary of Pashto* (Oslo: Hos Jacob Dybwad).
Narten, Johanna
1964 *Die sigmatischen Aoriste im Veda* (Wiesbaden: Harrassowitz).
Pokorny, Julius
1959, 1969 *Indogermanisches etymologisches Wörterbuch* i, ii (Bern–München: Francke).
Renou, Louis
1961 *Grammaire sanscrite*[2] (Paris: Maisonneuve).
Sommer, Ferdinand
1914 *Handbuch der lateinischen Laut- und Formenlehre* (Heidelberg: Winter).
1950/57; 1951 *Zum Zahlwort* (München: Bayerische Akademie der Wissenschaften).
Szemerényi, Oswald
1960 *Studies in the Indo-European system of numerals* (Heidelberg: Winter).
1964 *Syncope in Greek and Indo-European and the nature of Indo-European accent* (Naples: Istituto Universitario Orientale).
Thurneysen, Rudolf
1946 *A grammar of Old Irish* (Dublin: The Dublin Institute for Advanced Studies).
Turner, Ralph Lilley
1966 *A comparative dictionary of the Indo-Aryan languages* (London: Oxford University Press).
Wackernagel, Jacob
1930 *Altindische Grammatik* III (Göttingen: Vandenhoeck & Ruprecht).
Whitney, William Dwight
1889 *Sanskrit grammar*[2] (Cambridge, Mass.: Harvard University Press).

Journals

AO Acta Orientalia (Copenhagen)
BSL Bulletin de la Société Linguistique de Paris
GGA Göttinger Gelehrte Anzeigen
IF Indogermanische Forschungen
IIJ Indo-Iranian Journal
KZ Kuhns Zeitschrift: Zeitschrift für vergleichende Sprachforschung
MSL Mémoires de la Société Linguistique de Paris
MSS Münchener Studien zur Sprachwissenschaft

Old Indian texts

AV	Atharvaveda
RV	R̥gveda
SB	Śatapathabrāhmaṇa
VS	Vājasaneyisaṃhitā
YV	Yajurveda

Chapter 6
Middle Indo-Aryan

K. R. Norman

6.0. For the most part the numeral system of Middle Indo-Aryan is based upon that of Old Indian (see Chapter 5), and represents a phonological and morphological development of the earlier system. Such major differences as do exist are due to analogical extension in Middle Indo-Aryan from inherited forms, or to the retention of forms inherited from Proto-Indo-European or Old Indian which are not attested in the extant Old Indian material.

6.0.1. The existing studies of numerals in the dialects of Middle Indo-Aryan are scattered throughout a number of grammars and dictionaries. Only Sen (1960) aims to be comprehensive, and even that work makes no claim to completeness. The present study attempts to put together all the numerals under 'one hundred' known to the author from primary and secondary sources, together with a large selection of those above 'one hundred'.

6.0.2. Unless otherwise stated, the material quoted can be found in the following sources. Pāli: Geiger (1908, 1923–1927, 1956); Aśokan inscriptions: Hultzsch (1926); Ardha-Māgadhī: Pischel (1957); Jain Māhārāṣṭrī: Pischel (1957) or Jacobi (1886, 1914); Māhārāṣṭrī, Māgadhī, Śaurasenī, Jain Śaurasenī, Dākṣiṇātyā, Ḍhakkī, Deśī, and Cūlikā Paiśācī: Pischel (1957); Buddhist Hybrid Sanskrit: Edgerton (1953); Gāndhārī: Brough (1962); Niya: Burrow (1937); Western, Southern, Central, and Eastern inscriptions: Mehendale (1948); Kharoṣṭhī inscriptions: Konow (1929); Sinhalese Prakrit: Paranavitane (1970) or Karunaratne (1984); Apabhraṃśa: Pischel (1957) or Tagare (1948).

6.0.3. Frequently secondary sources give no references, and forms quoted in them can often not be checked. Where their correctness seems doubtful, comment has occasionally been made. Many texts from which forms are quoted, particularly in Ardha-Māgadhī, have not been critically edited, and there is frequently doubt about the correct spelling of such forms. No comment is normally made about these.

It must be remembered that in Gāndhārī, Niya, and in inscriptions generally, doubled consonants and long vowels are frequently not written, and, in the first two mentioned, idiosyncracies of orthography mean that the spelling is an inadequate guide to the pronunciation. A similar problem arises in all Middle Indo-Aryan verse texts, where single/double consonants may be written double/single, and long/short vowels may be written short/long respectively metri causa. Secondary sources do not usually make it clear whether quoted forms occur in verse or not.

6.0.4. The quotation of Buddhist Hybrid Sanskrit forms is restricted to those which are not found, or only rarely, in Classical Sanskrit.

6.1. Cardinals

6.1.0. As in Old Indian, the numerals 'one' to 'nineteen' (excluding the *ekūna-* type of 'nineteen') are adjectives, 'one' to 'four' having masculine/feminine/neuter forms in the nominative and accusative, 'five' to 'nineteen' being unchanged in these cases. In the earliest extant Middle Indo-Aryan sources, however, a confusion of gender in 'one' to 'four' is already observable, and by the time of Apabhraṃśa, gender in numerals is virtually lost, except for *éka-* 'one'.

6.1.1. 'One'

The forms for 'one' are all derived from OInd. *éka-*: Pāli *eka-*; Aś. *eka-*, *ika-* (presumably standing for *ikka* = *ĕkka*); AMg. *eka-, ega-*; JM *ĕkka-, ega-, ĕkkalliya-* (with *-ll-* and *-ya-*suffixes [Jacobi 1886]); BHS *eka-*, Gā. *eka-*; Niya *eka-* (probably implying *ĕkka-*), *eǵa-* (semel); Inscr. (W) *ekā* fem., (Kh.) *eka-*; SinPkt. *eka-;* Ap. *eka-, ega-* (Sanat.), *ĕkka-, ikka-, iga-* (with shortening *e-* > *i-*), *iya* (with change *-g-* > *-y-*), *ekalla* (with *-ll-* extension), *ĕkkalla-, ĕkkalliya* (feminine, with further *-ya-*extension [Bhav.]).

It is declined as a singular pronominal stem in *-a-* (in the plural it means 'some'), but occasional nominal forms are found, e. g. locative JM *ĕkke*, BHS *eke* (found in Classical Sanskrit too [Whitney 1889: §482]), *eki* (with shortening *-e* > *-i*, metri causa). Buddhist Hybrid Sanskrit also has loc. *ekahi* (cf. Ap. *ĕkkahĩ*), and instr. *ekinā* (possibly on the analogy of *iminā* 'by this').

All three genders are found. Pāli has fem. gen. *ekissā*, loc. *ekissā, ekissaṃ* (with *-i-* probably on the analogy of feminine adjective stems in *-ī*).

6.1.2. 'Two'

The forms of 'two' are all derived from OInd. *dva-*, with the change *dv-* > *duv-, d-*, or *b-* in the various dialects. Traces of the original dual endings are found only in developments from the nominative-accusatives, masculine *dváu* and feminine *dvé*. The use of *-o* < *-au* declines, and forms from *dvé* are used for all genders, although analogical neuter forms with *-ni* occur.

Relevant forms are: Pāli *dve, duve* (all genders); Aś. *duve* (Shah. *duvi*, with *-e* > *-i*), *dvo* (Gir. only, masculine), *dve* (Gir. only, feminine); AMg. *do, duve* (all genders); JM *do, duve, due* (all genders); Śaur. *duve*; Mg. *duve*; Mā. *be*; BHS *dve, duve, dvi* (with *-e-* > *-i-* metri causa) – all genders; Niya *dui, dvi, due, tui* (with confusion of voiced and unvoiced dental), *du*; Inscr. (W) *be, dve, ve, do*, (S) *be*, (C) *bo, du*, (E) *duve*; SinPkt. *duve, do*; Ap. *be, bi* (with shortening *-e* > *-i*), *ve, vi* (Paum.), *do* (Kp.), *du* (Sanat.), *dui* (Paum.), *duau* (with *-(y)a*-extension (Pp.), *bīhā* (formed to rhyme with *dīhā*, Pp.).

Neuter forms (used for all genders) with *-ni*, on the analogy of *tiṇṇi* (< OInd. *trī́ṇi*) occur: AMg. *doṇṇi*; JM *donni, dunni*; Mā. *doṇṇi*; Śaur. *doṇṇi*; Ap. *doṇṇi, duṇṇi, beṇṇi, biṇṇi, biṇṇa* (possibly a genitive plural in origin), *veṇṇi* (Hp.), *viṇṇi* (Bhav.), *venni* (Bhav.), *vinni* (Bhav.), *dunni* (Kp.).

The oblique case forms are made on the analogy of *-a-* and *-i-* stems by adding the thematic stem-endings to the stems *duve-, do-, dvi-, be-, bi-*:

Instrumental: Pāli *dvīhi*; Aś. *duvehi*; AMg. *dohiṃ*; JM *dohi, dohiṃ*; Mā. *dohiṃ*; Śaur. *duvehiṃ*; BHS *dvibhis, dvihi* (variant reading *dvehi*), *dvīhi, duvehi*; Inscr. (C) *dohi*; Ap. *dohĩ, dohiṃ, dohi, duhi* (Sanat.), *vihi* (Bhav.), *vihĩ* (Hp.), *behiṃ, bihiṃ*.

Genitive: Pāli *dvinnaṃ, duvinnaṃ* (from *dvi*-stem, with *-nn-* on the analogy of *tiṇṇaṃ* 'three', *catunnaṃ* 'four' and *sannaṃ* 'six'); AMg. *doṇha, doṇhaṃ* (with *-ṇh-* perhaps arising from a confusion between *-ṇṇ-* and *-h-* < *-s-* from the pronominal genitive plural ending *-saṃ* as Pischel 1957: § 436 suggests); JM *doṇha, doṇhaṃ*; Śaur. *duvenaṃ* (if correct, this probably represents the addition of the nominal genitive plural ending *-naṃ* to the stem *duve*), *doṇṇaṃ* (on the analogy of *tiṇṇaṃ* 'three' < OInd. *trīṇā́m*); Mg. *doṇṇaṃ*; Mā. *doṇha, doṇhaṃ*; BHS *dvinnāṃ* (cf. Pāli *dvin-*

naṃ), *duvinnaṃ* (with shortening of *-ā-* before *-ṃ*), *dvinnā* (with loss of *-ṃ*); Inscr. (W) *beṇa, dina,* (S) *donaṃ*; Ap. *doṇhaṃ* (Sanat.), *duṇhaṃ, doṇha, vihĩ* (Bhav.), *doha* (Hp.), *vihi* (Hp.), *bihū, beṇṇa* (used as a nominative).

Locative: Pāli *dvīsu* (from *dvi*-stem); JM *dosu*; Mā. *dosuṃ*; Śaur. *duvesu*; Ap. *dohi* (Hp.), *dosuṃ* (Sanat.), *vihi* (Bhav.), *behiṃ*.

6.1.3. 'Three'

Developments from OInd. *tráyaḥ* are found for the masculine (nominative and accusative) in several dialects, but developments from the Old Indian feminine stem *tisṛ-* are found only in Pāli. Neuter forms from OInd. *trīṇi* are found in most dialects; they are occasionally used for masculine and feminine also.

Nominative-accusative, masculine: Pāli *tayo, tayas* (in a fossilised sandhi position before the emphatic particle *su* 'indeed'); Aś. *trayo* (Shah.), *tī* and *trī* (Gir., where it is derived from the neuter *tīṇi* by dropping *-ṇi* on the analogy of the *-ā/-āni* masculine nominal ending variation; it is quite unconnected with the Vedic form *trī́*); AMg. *tao, tau* (used for all genders); JM *tao*; BHS *trayo* is used as an accusative as well as a nominative; Niya *treya* (with palatalisation of *-a-* to *-e-* before *-ya*), *tre* (either contracted from **traya*, or derived from *treya* with loss of *-ya*).

Nominative-accusative, feminine: Pāli *tisso* (< OInd. *tisraḥ*). Pāli (e. g. at Therīgāthā 518), Buddhist Hybrid Sanskrit, and some other dialects also use a neuter form for the feminine.

Nominative-accusative, neuter (but used for all genders in some dialects): Pāli *tīṇi*; Aś. *tiṃni* (with doubling of the nasal and compensatory shortening of the vowel), *tini* (with *-ṃ-* not written); AMg., JM, Mā., Śaur. *tiṇṇi, tinni*; BHS *trīṇī* (with *-ī* metri causa); Inscr. (W) *tini, trini, trīni*, (S) *tiṇi, tiṃṇi*, (C) *trini, tiṇṇā* (used as nominative masculine with *-ā* by analogy with masculine nominal stems); SinPkt. *tiṇi, tini*; Ap. *tīṇi* (Pp.), *tī* (with loss of *-ṇi* [Pp.]), *tiṇi* (Pp.), *tiā* (with *-(y)a-* added to *ti-* [Pp.]), *tiṇṇiā* (with *-(y)a-* added to *tiṇṇi* [Pp.]), *tinni* (Kp.), *tiṇṇa* (possibly a genitive plural in origin), *tiṇṇi, tiṃ* (with loss of *-i*, and replacement of resultant *-n* by *-ṃ*).

Instrumental: Pāli *tīhi* (with *-ī-* by analogy with *i*-stems); AMg. *tīhiṃ, tihiṃ*; JM *tihiṃ, tihi, tiṃhi* (by analogy with the singular of the *i*-stems), *tiṃhiṃ*; BHS *trīhi, trihi, trayebhi* (by analogy with the Old Indian genitive *tráyāṇām*); Gā. *trihi*; Inscr. (S) *tiṃhi*; Ap. *tihĩ* (Bhav.), *tīhi* (Hp.), *tihi, tihiṃ, tihime* (so Tagare 1948; misprint for *tihiṃ*?).

Genitive: Pāli *tiṇṇaṃ* (< Vedic *trīṇā́m*, with doubling of *-ṇ-* and compensatory shortening of the vowel); *tiṇṇannaṃ* (with double ending) for masculine/neuter and *tissannaṃ* (with *-nnaṃ* added to feminine stem *tissa-*) for feminine; AMg. *tiṇhaṃ* (cf. *doṇhaṃ* 'two'); JM *tiṇhaṃ, tiṇha*; Niya *trina*; Inscr. (S) *tina*; Ap. *tīha, tihū* (Bhav.), *tihĩ* (Bhav.).

Locative: Pāli *tīsu* (with *-ī-* by analogy with *i*-stems); Aś. *tīsu*; JM *tisu*; Mā. *tīsu, tīsuṃ*; Ap. *tisu*.

6.1.4. 'Four'

Masculine and neuter nominative/accusative forms are found from both the strong and weak Old Indian grades *catvār-* and *catur-*. Feminine forms from OInd. *catasr-* are found only in Pāli and Śaurasenī. In other dialects the genders are confused.

Nominative-accusative, masculine/feminine (except for Pāli and Śaurasenī): Pāli *cattarō* (from strong grade), *caturo* (from weak grade), *cattāri* (from neuter form); Aś. *catpāro* (Gir.), *cature* (Shah.), *catāli* (Kālsī); AMg. *cattāro, cauro, cattāri*; JM *cauro, cattāri*; Mā. *cattāri*; BHS *caturo, cature, caturi* (metri causa, all used as nominatives), *catvāra(ḥ), cature* (both used as accusatives); Gā. *catvari, cauri*; Niya *catu* (*-r-* lost from the stem *catur-*, which is then declined as a *u*-stem), *caura* (with the loss of *-t-*, which is unusual in the dialect), *cora* (with contraction *-au-* > *-o-* [Stein 1936]), *cohura* (if this means 'four', it is either a mistake for **cahura*, with glide *-h-* bridging the hiatus caused by the loss of *-t-*, or a confusion of *cora* and **cahura*); Inscr. (W) *catāri*, (S) *catāri, cāttāri*; SinPkt. *catara, catari, cara* (with loss of *-t-* and contraction *-aya-* > *-a-*); Ap. *cau* (cf. Niya *catu*), *caū, co* (contracted from *cau*), *cattāri* (Sanat.), *cāyāra* (with *-y-* < *-t-* replacing *-tt-* by analogy with *cattāro*/*caturo*, and compensatory lengthening of the preceding vowel [Paum.]), *cayāri* (with shortening of the vowel), *ceyari* (with palatalisation *-a-* > *-e-* by the preceding *c-* [Paum.]), *cāri* (with contraction *-ayā-* > *-ā-* [Pp.]), *cārī* (with lengthening of *-i* [Pp.]).

Nominative-accusative feminine: Pāli *catasso;* Śaur. *cadasso* (with voicing *-t-* > *-d-*).

Nominative-accusative neuter: Pāli *cattāri*; AMg. *cattāri*; JM *cattāri*; Gā. *catvari*.

Instrumental: Pāli *catubbhi* (< OInd. *catúrbhiḥ*), *catuhi, catūhi* (by analogy with *u*-stems); AMg. *cauhiṃ, caūhiṃ*; JM *cauhi, cauhiṃ*; BHS *caturhi, caturbhi, catuhi*; Ap. *cauhiṃ*.

Genitive: Pāli *catunnaṃ* (< OInd. *caturṇā́m*) for masculine-neuter, and *catassannaṃ* (with *-nnaṃ* added to the feminine stem *catassa-*) for the feminine; AMg. *cauṇhaṃ*; JM *cauṇha, cauṇhaṃ*; Mā. *cauṇhaṃ*; Inscr. (W) *catuṃnaṃ*, (S) *catuṇhaṃ*.

Locative: Pāli *catusu, catūsu* (by analogy with *u*-stems); AMg. *causu*; JM *causu*; BHS *catuṣu, catuṣū* (metri causa); Ap. *cauhi*.

6.1.5. 'Five'[1]

Nominative-accusative: Pāli *pañca*; AMg., JM, Śaur. *paṃca*; Gā. *paja* (= *paṃja*), *paje* (with palatalisation *-a* > *-e* after *-j-*); Niya *paṃca*; Inscr. (S) *pañca, paṃḍa* (probably a graphical error for *paṃca*), (C) *paca* (with *-ṃ-* not written); SinPkt. *paca*; Ap. *pañca, paṃcā* (with plural ending by analogy with *a*-stems [Pp.]), *paṃcau* (with *-(y)a*-suffix [Pp.]).

Instrumental: Pāli *pañcahi*; AMg. *paṃcahiṃ*; JM *pañcahi, pañcahiṃ*; Ap *pañcahĩ*.

Genitive: Pāli *pañcannaṃ* (with *-nn-* by analogy with *catunnaṃ* 'four' and *sannaṃ* 'six'); AMg. *paṃcaṇhaṃ*; JM *pañcaṇha, pañcaṇhaṃ*; Ap. *pañcanha* (Kp.), *pañcahã* (with the genitive plural ending *-ahã* from *-a*-stem nouns), *pañcana* (with loss of final nasalization).

Locative: Pāli *pañcasu*; Aś. *paṃcasu, paṃcaṣu* (with *-ṣ-* by analogy with the *a*-stem ending *-eṣu* (Shah.)); AMg. *paṃce* (by analogy with the locative singular ending of *-a-* nouns); JM *paṃcasu*; Gā. *pajaṣu* (for *-ṣ-* cf. the Aśokan form).

6.1.6. 'Six'

Forms with *s-* or *ṣ-* < OInd. *ṣaṭ-* occur in Middle Indo-Aryan only in the Aśokan inscriptions and Niya in the simple numeral, although they occur in other dialects in some compounds (see 6.1.16.). Most Middle Indo-Aryan dialects show forms with *ch-*, which probably arise from **kṣaṭ-* or **kṣvaṭ-*. The Niya form *ṣo* is perhaps from **ṣva(ṭ)-* (cf. Av. *xšvaš*), since *ṣaṭ-* would be expected to result in **ṣa* in that dialect. It is however possible that *ṣo* has been extracted from *ṣóḍaśa* 'sixteen'.

Nominative-accusative: Pāli *cha*; AMg. *cha*; JM *cha*; Niya *ṣo*; Inscr. (W) *cha*, (C) *cha*, (S) *cha*; Ap. *cha, chaa* (with *-(y)a*-suffix [Pp.]), *chau* (Pp.), *chaha* (probably from **kṣaṣa*, i. e. **kṣaṣ-* with a thematic vowel *-a* added, and the development *-ṣ-* > *-s-* > *-h-*, as Pischel (1957: § 263) suggests.

Instrumental: Pāli *chahi*; AMg. *chahiṃ*.

Genitive: Pāli *channaṃ* (with *-nn-* from OInd. *ṣaṇṇā́m*); AMg., JŚaur. *chaṇhaṃ, chaṇha*.

Locative: Pāli *chassu* (with *-ss-* from OInd. *ṣaṭsú*), *chasu* (by analogy with *pañcasu*, etc.); Aś. *sasu, ṣaṣu* (where retroflex *ṣ* is merely a scribal idiosyncracy); AMg. *chasu*; JM *chassu, chasu*; BHS *ṣaṭsū* (metri causa).

6.1.7. 'Seven'

All forms are derived from OInd. *saptá*.

Nominative-accusative: Pāli *satta*; JM, Mā. *satta*; Gā. *sata* (with *-t-* written for *-tt-*); Niya *sata*; Inscr. (S) *sata*; Ap. *satta, sattā* (with plural ending from *a*-stems added [Pp.]).

Instrumental: AMg. *sattahiṃ*; BHS *saptahi* (variant reading *saptehi*).

Genitive: Pāli *sattānaṃ, sattannaṃ* (with *-nn-* by analogy); AMg., JM, JŚaur. *sattaṇhaṃ, sattaṇha*; BHS *saptanām*.

Locative: AMg. *sattasu*, Ap. *sattihĩ*.

6.1.8. 'Eight'

All forms are derived from OInd. *aṣṭā́*.

Nominative-accusative: Pāli *aṭṭha*; AMg. *aṭṭha, aṭṭhaya* (with *-ya-* suffix), *aḍha* (with the development *-ṭṭh-* > *-ḍh-* without compensatory vowel lengthening); JM *aṭṭha*; Niya *aṭha, aṣṭi* (Stein 1936); Inscr. (W) *aṭha*; SinPkt. *aṭa* (with loss of aspiration); Ap. *aṭṭha, aṭha* (with simplification of the consonant-group without compensatory lengthening [Pp.]), *aṭṭhāā* (with *-(y)a*-suffix and plural ending *-ā* from the *-a*-stem nouns added [Pp.]), *aṭṭhaiṃ* (with *-aiṃ* borrowed from neuter plural *-a*-stem nouns).

Instrumental: Pāli *aṭṭhahi, aṭṭhāhi* (by analogy with *-ā*-stem nouns); AMg. *aṭṭhahiṃ*; Ap. *aṭṭhahiṃ, aṭṭhahĩ*.

Genitive: AMg., JM *aṭṭhaṇhaṃ, aṭṭhaṇha*; Inscr. (Kh.) *aṭhana*.

Locative: AMg. *aṭṭhasu*.

6.1.9. 'Nine'

All forms are derived from OInd. *náva*.

Nominative-accusative: Pāli *nava*; AMg. *nava, ṇava*; JM *nava*; Niya *no* (contracted from *nava*); Inscr. (W) *nava*, (E) *nava*; SinPkt. *nava*; Ap. *nava* (Sanat.), *ṇavalla* (with *-ll*-suffix [Bhav.]).

Instrumental: Pāli *navahi*; AMg. *navahiṃ*; JM *naveṇa* (by analogy with singular *-a*-stem nouns [Jacobi 1886]).

Genitive: Pāli *navannaṃ* (with *-nn-* by analogy); AMg. *navaṇhaṃ, navaṇha.*

Locative: Pāli *navasu.*

6.1.10. 'Ten'

All forms are derived from OInd. *dáśa.*

Nominative-accusative: Pāli *dasa*; AMg., JM, Śaur. *dasa*; Mg., Dh. *daśa*; Niya *daśa*; Inscr. (W) *dasaka* (with *-ka*-suffix), (C) *dasa*; SinPkt. *dasa, daśa, dhaśa* (with confusion of aspirated and unaspirated dental); Ap. *dasa, daha* (with change *-s-* > *-h*).

Instrumental: Pāli *dasahi, dasabhi*; AMg., JM *dasahiṃ*; Mā. *dasahi*; Mg. *daśehiṃ* (by analogy with *-a*-stem nouns); BHS *daśahi*; Inscr. (Kh.) *daśahi.*

Genitive: Pāli *dasānaṃ* (by analogy with *-a*-stem nouns), *dasannaṃ*; AMg. *dasaṇhaṃ, dasaṇha, -dasāṇaṃ* (by analogy with *-a*-stem nouns); JM *dasaṇha, dasaṇhaṃ*; Mg. *daśānaṃ* (by analogy with *-a*-stem nouns).

Locative: Pāli *dasasu*; AMg., Mā. *dasasu*; CuP. *tasasu* (with devoicing *d-* > *t-*); BHS *daśasū* (metri causa).

6.1.11. The numerals 'one' to 'ten' in compounds

6.1.11.1. 'One' in compounds

a) Numerical compounds: *eka- ega- eya- ĕkka- iga- ea- ekā- ikkā- ĕggā- eyā- eā- e- ĭ-*. The use of forms with *-ā-* in numerals other than 'eleven' represents an extension of its use in that numeral in OInd. *ékādaśa*, which in itself is based on the analogy of *dvā́daśa* 'twelve'.

b) Non-numerical compounds: *eka- ega- ĕgga-.*

6.1.11.2. 'Two' in compounds

a) Numerical compounds: *dvi- dvā- dbā- duvā- dve- du- bā- vā- be-*. In Old Indian, 'twelve', 'twenty-two', and 'thirty-two' have *dvā-*; 'forty-two' to 'seventy-two' and 'ninety-two' have *dvi-* or *dvā-*; 'eighty-two' has *dvi.*

b) Non-numerical compounds: *du- do- di- de- bi- be-.*

6.1.11.3. 'Three' in compounds

a) Numerical compounds: *ti- te- tri- tre- tro-*. The expected development *ta(y)o-* < OInd. *trayas-* occurs only in the title *tayodasa-rājako* 'the thirteen kings' given to Mahāvaṃsa chapter 36, where Sanskrit influence may be assumed. Niya *trodaśa* and Aś. *todaśa* (Shah.) may, if these readings are correct, be contractions from Skt. *trayodaśa*. The usual form in 'thirteen' is *t(r)e-*, which Turner (1966: no. 6001) suggests is to be derived from **traye-*, which would be a by-form of *trayo-*. A more likely explanation is to derive it from **traya-* (so Pischel 1957: § 153). This could have been extracted from OInd. *tráyāṇām* (cf. BHS *trayebhi*, and OInd. *tredhā́* 'thrice', which Wackernagel (1896: i. 53) derives from **tray-adhā*). The form *trai-* found in the Aśokan inscriptions (Girnār) is of no value for determining the etymology, since this merely indicates that the scribe at Girnār thought the pronunciation should be dissyllabic, perhaps having OInd. *tráyodaśa* in mind. AMg., Ap. *tāyattiṃsa* 'thirty-three' seems to show **trāyas-* (see Turner 1966: no. 5994 and the references there, and cf. Av. *θrāyo*). AMg. *tāvattīsaga-* and Pāli *tāvatiṃsa-* 'the thirty-three gods' seem to be based on the same form, with an Eastern glide *-v-* instead of *-y-*.

b) Non-numerical compounds: *ti-, te-, tre-*, Pāli *tīṇi-* (the neuter inflected form used in a compound [PTC]), BHS *tisra-* (the feminine stem), SinPkt. *tiṇi* (cf. Pāli *tīṇi-*).

6.1.11.4. 'Four' in compounds

a) Numerical compounds: *catur-, caur-* (with loss of *-t-*) before vowels; *catu-, cau-, co-, cu-* (with shortening of the vowel), *catu(r)-, cau(r)-, co(r)-, cu(r)-* (with assimilation of *-(r)-* to the following consonant) before consonants. The loss of *-t-* is already found in the Aśokan inscriptions, Gāndhārī, and Niya, so it was apparently earlier in numerals than elsewhere. There is therefore no need to follow Sen's suggestion (1960: § 52) of a base **cavur-*. Ap. *cāri-* is a declined form used in compounds. There also occur Pāli *cātur-*, Aś. *cāvu-* (with glide *-v-* replacing *-t-*), Ap. *cāur-*. OInd. *cātur-* occurs, but only in non-numerical compounds.

b) Non-numerical compounds: Pāli *catur-, catu(r)-* (with *-(r)-* assimilated to the following consonant), *catu-*; Aś. *catu-*; AMg. *caur-, cau(r)-, cau-*; JM *caur-, cau(r)-, cau-*; Mā. *co(r)-*; Gā. *cadu-*; Inscr. (W) *catu-*, (E) *catur-*; SinPkt. *catu-, cadu-*; Ap. *caur-, cau(r)-, cau-*. AMg. *cauro-* and Ap. *cāri-* are declined forms used in compounds. There also occur Pāli *cātu(r)-*, Aś. *cātuṃ-*.

6.1.11.5. 'Five' in compounds

a) Numerical compounds: *pañca-, paṃca-, pañña-* (with the assimilation *-ñc-* > *-ññ-*; cf. Pāli *pañña* 'wisdom' < *prajñā*), *panna-*, and *paṇṇa-* (especially in dialects which do not possess *-ñ-*). There is sometimes the later simplification of *-ṇṇ-* and *-nn-* to *-ṇ-* and *-n-*. Before *-v-*, final *-a* sometimes develops into *-u*. SinPkt., Ap. *paca-* shows loss of nasalisation.

b) Non-numerical compounds: *pañca-, paṃca-*.

6.1.11.6. 'Six' in compounds

a) Numerical compounds: all dialects agree in *so-* or *ṣo-* in the form for 'sixteen', although AMg. *chaddasahā* 'sixteen times' is quoted (Sheth 1963). The Aśokan inscriptions have *sa-* (probably for *sap-*) in *sapaṃnā* 'fifty-six' and *saḍ-* in *saḍuvīsati* 'twenty-six'. Inscriptional Prakrits (W) have *ṣaṇ-* in *ṣaṇuvisa* 'twenty-six'. Other dialects have *chaḷ-* before vowels and *cha-* before consonants, with the presence of original *-ṭ* sometimes shown by the doubling of the consonant or by compensatory lengthening of *-ā*. Apabhraṃśa has *chaha-* beside *cha-*.

b) Non-numerical compounds: Pāli *saḷ-* in the stereotyped technical word *saḷāyatana* 'the six sense-faculties' and possibly *sa-* in *samāna-* (Suttanipāta 18), if this is meant to be paralleled by *eka-* (ibid. 19); Aś. *saṃ-* in *āsaṃmāsika-* 'up to six months'; AMg. *saḍ* in the technical term *saḍaṃga* 'six constituent parts'. Elsewhere all dialects have *chaḍ-, chaḷ-* before vowels and *cha-* before consonants, with occasional doubling of the consonant. Apabhraṃśa has *chaḍa-* in *chaḍa-rasa* 'six flavours' (Bhav.).

6.1.11.7. 'Seven' in compounds

a) Numerical compounds: all dialects have *satta-* (Aś., SinPkt. *sata-* stands for *satta-*); Apabhraṃśa also *sata-*; AMg., JM *sī-* in *sīālīa* 'forty-seven', etc.

b) Non-numerical compounds: all dialects show *satta-*.

6.1.11.8. 'Eight' in compounds

a) Numerical compounds: all dialects have *aṭṭha-* (Inscr. (E) and (Kh.) *aṭha-* stands for *aṭṭha-*), *aṭṭhā-*; AMg., JM, Ap. also *aḍha-* (with simplification of *-ṭṭh-* and voicing to *-ḍh-*, without compensatory lengthening of the vowel); SinPkt. *aṭa-* (with loss of aspiration); Ap. *aṭha-* (with simplification of the consonant-group, without compensatory lengthening of the vowel).

b) Non-numerical compounds: Pāli, AMg., JM *aṭṭha-*; Aś. *aṭha-, aḍha-* (assuming that *aḍha-kosikyāni* in Pillar Edict VII means 'at every eight kos').

6.1.11.9. 'Nine' in compounds

a) Numerical compounds: Ap. *nava-* in 'nineteen', 'eighty-ninth', 'ninety-nine'. In the other dialects it is replaced by the *ūna-, ekūna-*, or *eū-* type of compound.

b) Non-numerical compounds: *nava-* or *ṇava-* in all dialects.

6.1.11.10. 'Ten' in compounds

a) Numerical compounds: Ap. *daha-*.

b) Non-numerical compounds: Pāli *dasa-*; Aś. *dasa-*, *daśa-*; AMg., JM, Śaur. *dasa-*; Mg. *daśa-*; Mā. *dasa-, daha-*; Gā. *daśa-*; Ap. *dasa-, daha-*.

6.1.12. The teens

6.1.12.0. General comments

In Middle Indo-Aryan, except for some innovations in Apabhraṃśa, the numerals in this group follow the Old Indian pattern of making compounds of 'one' to 'nine' with the numeral 'ten'. The form for 'ten' varies in the various dialects, with OInd. *-daśa* developing to *-daśa, -dasa, -ḍaśa*, and *-ḍasa* (with *-ḍ-* probably generalized from *ṣoḍaśa* 'sixteen', where it is historically correct), *-ḷasa* (in dialects where the development *-ḍ-* > *-ḷ-* is normal), *-lasa* (where *-ḍ-* > *-l-* is normal), *-daha* (where *-s-* > *-h-* is normal), *-raha* (where *-d-*/*-ḍ-* > *-r-* is normal). Already in Middle Indo-Aryan there are traces of the loss of *-ha* which becomes more widespread in Modern Indo-Aryan. Oblique case-forms and distinctions of gender are occasionally found.

6.1.12.1. 'Eleven'

Pāli *ekādasa, ekārasa*; AMg. *ekādasa* (Sūr.), *egārasa, ĕkkārasa, ikkārasa, ĕkkāra* (with loss of *-ha* [Viy.]); JM *egārasa, ĕkkārasa, egadasa*; Mā. *eāraha*; CuP *ekātasa* (with devoicing of *-d-* > *-t-*); Niya *ekadaśa* (used as an ordinal); Ap. *eyāraha, eāraha, ĕggāraha, gārehāiṃ* (with loss of *e-* and plural ending), *ĕkkādaha, ĕkkadaha, eadaha* (Pp.), *egāraha* (Pp.), *iggāraha* (Pp.), *eggārāhā* (with plural ending [Pp.]).

Instrumental: Pāli *ekādasahi*; Ap. *eārahahiṃ*.

Genitive: Pāli *ekādasannaṃ*.

6.1.12.2. 'Twelve'

Pāli *dvādasa, bārasa* (only in grammarians' and late texts); Aś. *duvadaśa, duvaḍaśa, duvāḍasa, duvādasa, duvāḷasa, dbādasa* (Upasak 1960: 98, reads *dvā-*, but the change *dv-* > *db-* at Girnār seems to be confirmed by the parallel change *-tv-* > *-tp-*), *badaśa* (Shah.; Hultzsch's reading *badaya* is incorrect; in the Kharoṣṭhī script *ya* and *śa* can be confused); AMg. *duvālasa, bārasa*; JM *duvālasa, bārasa* (fem. *-ī*); Mā. *bāraha*; JŚaur. *bārasa*; Niya *badaśa, badaśi* (used as an ordinal); Inscr. (W) *bārasa, bāra* (with loss of *-ha*), *bārasaka* (with the suffix *-ka-*); SinPkt. *dodośa, doḷasa* (Sen); Ap. *bārasa, bāraha, bārahā* (with plural ending [Pp.]), *bārāhā* (with plural ending [Pp.]), *bārahāi* (with plural ending (Pp.), *vārasa-* (at the beginning of a compound [Bhav.]), *vāraha* (Bhav.), *duvāraha* (Paum.).

Instrumental: Pāli *dvādasahi*; AMg. *duvālasehiṃ* (by analogy with *a-*stem nouns), *bārasahiṃ*; BHS *dvādaśehi* (by analogy with *a*-stem nouns); Ap. *bārahahiṃ*.

Genitive: Pāli *dvādasannaṃ*; AMg. *duvālasaṇhaṃ*.

6.1.12.3. 'Thirteen'

Pāli *terasa, telasa, teḷasa* (PTC), *tayodasa* (a late compound, doubtless in imitation of Sanskrit [Mahāvaṃsa 36]; Aś. *traidasa* (with *trai-* dissyllabic in imitation of Skt. *trayo-*? [Gir.]), *tidaśa* (possibly < OInd. **tridaśa*, but Hultzsch reads *todaśa* [Shah.]), *tedasa* (Kālsī, etc.), *treḍaśa* (Mānsehrā); AMg. *terasa* (fem. *-ī*); JM *terasa*; Mā. *teraha*; BHS *tridaśa* (allowed by the Sanskrit grammarians as a variant for *tráyodaśa*, but not attested in Classical Sanskrit); Gā. *tredaśa*; Niya *trodaśa* (although one editor reads *tredaśa* in Document No. 505); Inscr. (W) *terasa, tara* (probably mistake for *tera*, showing loss of *-ha*), (S) *teraṃ* (showing loss of *-ha*), *terasa*, (E) *terasa*; Ap. *terasa* (Bhav.), *teraha*.

Instrumental: BHS *tridasehi* (by analogy with *-a*-stems).

Genitive: Pāli *terasannaṃ*.

6.1.12.4. 'Fourteen'

Pāli *catuddasa, cuddasa* (= *cŏddasa*, with contraction *-au-* > *-o-* after loss of *-t-*); Aś. *codasa* (probably for *cŏddasa*); AMg. *cŏddasa, cauddasa, caudasa* (with *-dd-* > *-d-*, metri causa); JM *cŏddasa*; Mā. *cŏddaha*, fem. *cŏddasī*; Inscr. (C) *catudasa*; Ap. *cauddaha, cāuddāhā* (with plural ending), *cāridahā* (with plural ending), *cŏddaha, cāuddaha, caudaha* (Sanat.), *caudasa* (Kp.), *codaha* (Pp.), *dahacāri* (with reversed order of compound).

Instrumental: AMg. *cŏddasahiṃ*.

Genitive: AMg. *cauddasaṇhaṃ, cŏddasaṇhaṃ*.

6.1.12.5. 'Fifteen'

Pāli *pañcadasa, pannarasa, paṇṇarasa*; Aś. *paṃcadasā, paṃnaḍasā, paṃnaḷasā* (all used as ordinals); AMg. *pañcadasa* (Sūr.), *paṇṇarasa*; JM *paṇṇarasa, pannarasa, pannārasa* (with *-ā-* by analogy with *egārasa* 'eleven', *aṭṭhārasa* 'eighteen'); Niya *paṃcadaśa*; Inscr. (W) *panarasa* (used as an ordinal), (E) *paṃdarasa* (if this reading is correct, it shows a very early pronunciation **panrasa* for *pannarasa*, with the evolution *-ndr-* < *-nr-*; this is unparalleled in Middle Indo-Aryan so early, although common in Modern Indo-Aryan, but the corresponding development *-mr-* > *-mbr-* occurs, e. g. *āmra-* 'mango' > **ambra-* > *amba-*); Ap. *paṇṇaraha, paṇṇāraha, pannārasa* (Bhav.), *paṇṇarasa* (Paum.), *dahapaṃca* (with reversed order of compound), *dahapaṃcāi* (with plural ending).

Instrumental: Pāli *paṇṇarasahi*; AMg. *paṇṇarasahiṃ*.

Genitive: AMg. *paṇṇarasaṇhaṃ*.

Locative: Pāli *paṇṇarasesu* (by analogy with *-a*-stem nouns); AMg. *paṇṇarasasu*.

6.1.12.6. 'Sixteen'

Pāli *soḷasa, sorasa;* AMg. *soḷasa, soḷasaya* (with *-ya*-suffix), *solasa* (Sūr.), *sola* (with loss of *-ha* [Sūr.]), *solā* (Sūr.), *solāiṃ* (with plural ending [Sūr.]), *chaddasa-* (PSM); JM *solasa, solā*; Gā. *ṣoḍasa*; Inscr. (W) *sodasa, solasa, solasaka* (with *-ka*-suffix); Ap. *solasa, soḷasa, solaha, soḷaha, soḷā, solā* (Pp.).

Instrumental: Pāli *soḷasahi*; AMg. *solasahiṃ*; BHS *ṣoḍaśehi* (as variant reading for *ṣoḍaśahi*).

Genitive: AMg., JM *soḷasaṇhaṃ*.

6.1.12.7. 'Seventeen'

Pāli *sattadasa, sattarasa*; AMg. *sattarasa*; JM *sattarasa*; Inscr. (E) *satadasa* (Mehendale 1948 so, but Sircar 1965 has a different reading); Ap. *sattāraha* (with -*ā*- by analogy with *egāraha* 'eleven' and *aṭṭhāraha* 'eighteen' [Pp.]), *dahasatta* (with reversed order of compound).

Instrumental: Pāli *sattarasahi*.

6.1.12.8. 'Eighteen'

Pāli *aṭṭhādasa, aṭṭhārasa*; AMg. *aṭṭhārasa*; JM *aṭṭhārasa, aṭṭharasa*; Niya *aṭhadaśa* (used as an ordinal); Inscr. (W) *aṭhāra* (with loss of -*ha*); SinPkt. *aṭadaśa;* Ap. *aṭṭhārasa, aṭṭhāraha*.

Instrumental: Pāli *aṭṭhārasahi*; AMg. *aṭṭhārasahiṃ*.

Genitive: Pāli *aṭṭhārasannaṃ*; JM *aṭṭhārasaṇha*.

6.1.12.9. 'Nineteen'

Although Whitney (1889: § 476) quotes *návadaśa* for 'nineteen' in Old Indian, forms with *ekona*- are much more common. In Middle Indo-Aryan, *ṇavadaha* is found only in Apabhraṃśa (Pp.). All other dialects have *ekūna*-type forms. These are more conveniently dealt with later (see 6.1.40.).

6.1.13. Multiples of 'ten'

6.1.13.1. General Comments

In Classical Sanskrit 'twenty' is *viṃśatí* and 'thirty' *triṃśát*, but, by analogy, Buddhist Hybrid Sanskrit has also *viṃśat* and *triṃśati*, and the other dialects of Middle Indo-Aryan have forms derived from these. The -*a* forms, resulting from the loss of final -*t*, remain as -*a*, or become -*ā* (feminine declension) or -*aṃ* (neuter declension). The -i forms remain, or become -*ī* (feminine) or -*iṃ* (neuter).

6.1.13.2. 'Twenty'

Pāli *vīsati, vīsa, vīsā, vīsaṃ*; Aś. *vīsati*; AMg. *vīsaī, vīsaṃ*; JM *vīsaī, vīsaiṃ, vīsā, vīsaṃ*; BHS *viṃśat, viṃśa, viṃśa(ḥ), viṃśaṃ*; Niya *viśati, -viśa* (Stein 1936), -*viṃśa* (Stein 1936); Inscr. (W) *visa, vīsā*, (S) *vīsaṃ*, (E) *viṃśati*; SinPkt. -*visiti, -visiya* (with -*iya*-suffix); Ap. *vīsai* (Sanat.), *vīsa, vīsaiṃ* (with plural ending [Pp.]). The forms with *vīs-* instead of *viṃs-* are sometimes compared with certain unnasalized Indo-European forms, e. g. Latin *uīgintī*, but since this type of alternation is common in Middle Indo-Aryan, the resemblance is probably coincidental.

6.1.13.3. 'Thirty'

Pāli *tiṃsa, tiṃsaṃ, tiṃsā, tiṃsati*; AMg. *tīsā, tīsai* (Sūr.), *tīsaī*; JM *tīsaṃ*; BHS *triṃśa, triṃśaṃ, triṃśati*; Niya *triśa*; Ap. *tīsa, tīsā, tīsaṃ*.

6.1.13.4. 'Forty'

Pāli *cattārīsa, cattārīsā, cattārīsaṃ, cattālīsa* (with change *-r-* > *-l-*), *cattālīsā, cattālīsaṃ, tālīsa, tālīsā, tālīsaṃ* (the forms without *ca-* presumably being weak grade formations from PIE *k^{w}*tur-*, cf. OInd. *turī́ya-* and *túrya-*, MInd. **turtha* (see § 6.2.4.); AMg. *cattālīsā, cattālīsaṃ, cattāla* (with loss of *-sa*, cf. JM *pannā* 'fifty' [Sūr.]), *-yālīsa* (< *-cālīsa*, with *-c-* lost intervocalically), *cālī* (with loss of *-sa*), *cattā* (with loss of *-la*), *cattāiṃ* (with plural ending [Sūr.]), *-yāla* (< *-cāla*, with *-c-* lost intervocalically); JM *cattālīsaṃ, cāyālīsaṃ* (with *-y-* < *-t-* < *-tt-* and compensatory lengthening of the vowel), *cālīsa* (either contracted from *cāyālīsaṃ*, or with *c-* arising from contamination of *tālīsaṃ* by *cattālīsaṃ* [Jacobi 1886]), *cattā*; BHS *catvāriṃśaṃ*; Niya *capariśa* (with *-p-* for *-pp-* < *-tp-* < *-tv-*); Ap. *cālīsa, cālisa* (with shortening *-ī-* > *-i-*), *tālisa*.

6.1.13.5. 'Fifty'

Pāli *paññāsa* (with *-ññ-* < OInd. *-ñc-*), *paññāsā, paññāsaṃ, paṇṇāsa*; Aś. *-paṃnā* (with loss of *-sa*, cf. AMg. *cālī* 'forty'); AMg. *paṇṇāsa* (Sūr.), *paṇṇāsā, paṇṇāsaṃ*; JM *pannāsaṃ, pannā*; BHS *pañcāśati* (with *-i* added to *pañcāśat* by analogy with *viṃśati* 'twenty'), *pañcāśa, pañcāśaṃ*; Niya *paṃcaśa*; Inscr. (W) *pācasa* [read **pacāsa*?]; Ap. *paṇṇāsa, pañcāsa* (Sanat.), *pañcāsaya* (with *-ya*-suffix [Paum.]).

6.1.13.6. 'Sixty'

Pāli *saṭṭhi*; AMg. *saṭṭhi, saṭṭhiṃ*; JM *saṭṭhi, saṭṭhī, saṭṭhiṃ*; Śaur. *chaṭṭhiṃ* (either a wrong reading, or by analogy with *cha* 'six'); Ap. *saṭṭhi*.

6.1.13.7. 'Seventy'

Pāli *sattati, sattari* (with *-r-* < *-d-* < *-t-*); AMg. *sattari, sattariṃ, sayara* (= ordinal, with *-y-* < *-t-* < *-tt-*, without compensatory lengthening of the vowel [Sūr.]); JM *sattari, sayari*; Niya *satati*; Inscr. (W) *satari*; Ap. *sattari, sattara* (= ordinal).

6.1.13.8. 'Eighty'

Pāli *asīti*; AMg. *asīi, asīiṃ, asīā* (= ordinal, with plural ending [Sūr.]), *asīyā* (= ordinal, with plural ending [Sūr.]), *sīyāiṃ* (= ordinal, with loss of *a-* and plural ending [Sūr.]); JM *asīi, asīī, asīyāiṃ*, (= ordinal, with plural ending); Ap. *asiti* (with *-ī-* > *-i-*), *asii, asī* (with *-ī* < *-i-* + *-i-*), *asi* (with *-ī* > *-i*).

6.1.13.9. 'Ninety'

Pāli *navuti* (< OInd. *navatí*, with *-a-* > *-u-* after *-v-*); AMg. *naui* (Sūr.), *nauī, nauiṃ*; JM *nauī*; Niya *novati* (with *no-* by analogy with *no* 'nine'); Ap. *ṇavadi* (with voicing *-t-* > *-d-*), *ṇavai, navai* (Sanat.), *ṇaudi, nauya.*

6.1.14. The twenties

It is convenient to include with the following discussion of the twenties the *ekūna*-forms of 'nineteen'. Some of the Apabhraṃśa numerals in this group elide intervocalic *-v-*, and shorten *-ī-* to *-i-*.

6.1.14.0. 'Nineteen'. Pāli *ekūnavīsati, ekūnavīsa, ūnavīsati* (PED); Aś. *ekunavīsati*; AMg. *egūṇavīsaṃ, ekūnavīsa* (Sūr.), *eūṇavīsa* (Sūr.), *auṇavīsaī* (for *auṇa* < *aguṇa-* see Pischel 1957: § 444), *auṇavīsaṃ*; JM *auṇavīsaī, auṇavīsaṃ*; Inscr. (W) *ekunavīsa* (used as an ordinal); Ap. *egūṇaviṃsā, eūṇaviṃsā* (Pp.), *ĕkkūṇavīsa* (Paum.).

6.1.14.1. 'Twenty-one'. Pāli *ekavīsa, ekavīsati* (PTC); AMg. *egavīsā, ĕkkavīsaṃ, igavīsaṃ* (with shortening *e-* > *i-*), *ekavīsā* (Sūr.), *ĕkkavīsa* (Sūr.), *ĕkkavīsā* (Sūr.); JM *ĕkkavīsaṃ, egavīsā, eyāvīsa* (with *-ā-* by analogy with *egārasa* 'eleven' [PC 56.8]), *igāvīsaṃ*; Inscr. (W) *ekavisa*; Ap. *ekavīsati* (Pp.), *ĕkkavīsa, eāīsa* (Pp.).

6.1.14.2. 'Twenty-two'. Pāli *dvāvīsati, dvāvīsa, bāvīsati, bāvīsa*; AMg. *bāvīsā, bāvīsaṃ, duvīsaṃ* (Sūr.); JM *bāvīsaṃ*; Ap. *bāvīsa, vāvīsa* (Bhav.), *bāīsa* (Pp.), *bāīsā* (Pp.), *bāisa* (with shortening *-ī-* > *-i-*).

6.1.14.3. 'Twenty-three'. Pāli *tevīsati, tevīsa*; AMg. *tevīsā, tevīsaṃ*; JM *tevīsaṃ*; SinPkt. *tevisiti*; Ap. *teisa* (with shortening *-ī-* > *-i-*).

6.1.14.4. 'Twenty-four'. Pāli *catuvīsati* (PTC), *catuvīsa, catubbīsaṃ* (PTC); AMg. *cauvīsaṃ, cauvīsā* (Samav.), *cauvīsaya* (with -*ya*-suffix [Sūr.]); JM *cauvvīsaṃ*; Inscr. (W) *catuvisa,* (E) *catuvīsati*; Ap. *cauvīsa, covīsa, covisa, caubīsa* (Pp.), *cobisa* (Pp.).

6.1.14.5. 'Twenty-five'. Pāli *pañcavīsati, paññavīsati* (PTC), *pañcavīsa, paṇṇavīsati, paṇṇuvīsa* (with -*a*- > -*u*- before -*v*-); Aś. *paṃnavīsati*; AMg. *paṇuvīsā* (with the shortening -*ṇṇ*- > -*ṇ*- without compensatory lengthening of the vowel), *paṇuvīsaṃ, paṇavīsaṃ* (Samav.); JM *pañcavīsaṃ, pannavīsaṃ, paṇavīsaṃ, paṇuvīsā*; Niya *pacaviśa* (Stein 1936); SinPkt. *pacaviśati, pacavisiya* (with -*iya*-suffix); Ap. *pacīsa, paṇuvīsa, pañcavīsa* (Hp.), *paṃcavīsa, paṃcuttaravīsa* ('five beyond twenty').

6.1.14.6. 'Twenty-six'. Pāli *chabbīsati* (PTC); Aś. *saḍuvīsati* (with epenthetic -*u*- evolved between -*ḍ*- and -*v*-); AMg. *chavvīsaṃ*; JM *chavvīsaṃ*; Niya *ṣoviṃśa* (Stein 1936); Inscr. (W) *ṣaṇuvisa* (if this reading is correct it is presumably by analogy with **paṇuvisa* 'twenty-five'; it may, however, be a mistake for **ṣaḍuvisa*); Ap. *chavvīsaṃ, chabbīsa, chavvīsa* (Paum.), *chahavīsa.*

6.1.14.7. 'Twenty-seven'. Pāli *sattavīsati* (PED); Aś. *satavisati*; AMg. *sattavīsai, sattāvīsa* (with -*ā*- by analogy with *aṭṭhāvīsaṃ* 'twenty-eight' [Sūr.]), *sattāvīsaṃ* (Samav.); JM *sattavīsaṃ, sattāvīsā, sattāvīsaṃ*; Ap. *sattāīsa, sattāīsā* (Pp.), *sattāvīsa* (Paum.).

6.1.14.8. 'Twenty-eight'. Pāli *aṭṭhāvīsati* (PTC), *aṭṭhavīsa* (PTC); AMg. *aṭṭhāvīsai* (Sūr.), *aṭṭhāvīsaṃ, aṭṭhāvīsā*; JM *aṭṭhāvīsaṃ, aṭṭhavīsaṃ*; Inscr. (E) *aṭhaviṃśatihi* (instrumental plural ending); Ap. *aṭṭhāvīsa, aṭṭhāisa, aḍhāisa* (with the change -*ṭṭh*- > -*ḍh*-, without compensatory lengthening of the vowel).

6.1.15. The thirties

6.1.15.0. 'Twenty-nine'. Pāli *ekūnatiṃsa* (PTC); AMg. *egūṇatīsaṃ* (Samav.), *eūṇatīsaṃ* (Sūr.), *egūṇatīsai* (by analogy with -*vīsai* [Samav.]), *auṇatīsaṃ, auṇattīsaṃ*; JM *auṇattīsaṃ.*

6.1.15.1. 'Thirty-one'. Pāli *ekatiṃsa* (PTC); AMg. *ĕkkatīsaṃ* (Samav.), *ekatīsā* (Sūr.), *ĕkkatīsā* (Sūr.).

6.1.15.2. 'Thirty-two'. Pāli *dvattiṃsa, dvattiṃsā, battiṃsa*; AMg. *battīsa, battīsā, battīsaṃ, bātīsaṃ* (with retention of -*ā*- of *dvā*-, and shortening of -*tt*- > -*t*- [Sūr.]), *duvattīsaṃ* (Sūr.); JM *battīsaṃ*; BHS *dvātriṃśata-* (in compound); Ap. *battīsa, battīsā* (Pp.), *vattīsa* (Sanat.), *battisa* (Pp.).

6.1.15.3. 'Thirty-three'. Pāli *tĕttiṃsa* (PTC); AMg. *tĕttīsaṃ, tittīsaṃ, tĕttīsa, tĕttīsā, tetīsaṃ* (Sūr.), *tĕttisaṃ* (with shortening -*ī*- > -*i*- [Sūr.]),

tāyattīsā, tāvattīsā (with glide *-v-* replacing *-y-*), *tāvattīsaga* (with *-ga-*suffix); JM *tĕttīsaṃ, tittīsaṃ, tāvattīsaya* (with *-ya*-suffix); Ap *tĕttīsa, tĕttiya* (Tagare (1948) so; read **tĕttisa*?), *tāyatiṃsa*.
6.1.15.4. 'Thirty-four'. Pāli *catuttiṃsa* (PTC); AMg. *cauttīsaṃ* (Samav.), *cautīsaṃ* (Sūr.), *cŏttīsaṃ*; Ap. *cautīsa*.
6.1.15.5. 'Thirty-five'. Pāli *pañcatiṃsa* (Mahāvaṃsa 2.27), *pañcatiṃsā* (PTC); AMg. *pañcatīsaṃ* (Sūr.), *paṇatīsaṃ, paṇṇatīsaṃ* (Sūr.), *paṇṇatīsa* (Sūr.); JM *paṇatīsaṃ*; Inscr. (E) *panatīsă hi* (instrumental plural ending).
6.1.15.6. 'Thirty-six'. Pāli *chattiṃsa, chattiṃsati*; AMg. *chattīsaṃ, chattīsā*.
6.1.15.7. 'Thirty-seven'. Pāli *sattatiṃsa*; AMg. *sattatīsaṃ* (Samav.); Ap. *satatīsa* (with shortening *-tt-* > *-t-* [Pp.]).
6.1.15.8. 'Thirty-eight'. Pāli *aṭṭhatiṃsa* (PTC); AMg. *aṭṭhattīsaṃ, aṭṭhatīsaṃ* (Samav.); JM *aṭṭhatīsaṃ*; Inscr. (E) *aṭhātīsā* (Mehendale 1948 so; Sircar 1965 reads *aṭhatisā*); Ap. *aṭṭhatīsa*.

6.1.16. The forties

In some dialects *-tālīsa, -cālīsa, -cāla* become *-yālīsa, -yāla*. Numerals in Pāli marked with * are extracted from the corresponding ordinals.
6.1.16.0. 'Thirty-nine'. Pāli *ekūnacattārīsa*; AMg. *egūṇacattālīsaṃ* (Samav.), *egūṇatālīsā* (Sūr.), *eūyālīsai* (by analogy with *-vīsai*, with *eū-* < *eūṇa-* perhaps by analogy with *eūṇāuiṃ* 'eighty-nine' [Sūr.]), *ūyālīsaṃ* (with *ū-* < *ūna-*? [Sūr.]), *ūyālaṃ* (with *ū-* < *ūna-*? [Sūr.]).
6.1.16.1. 'Forty-one'. Pāli *ekatālīsa* (PTC); AMg. *egacattālīsaṃ* (Samav.), *igayāla* (with shortening *e-* > *i-*), *īālā* (with contraction of first two syllables to *ī-* [Sūr.]), *īālīsaṃ* (Sūr.), *īālīsaya* (with *-ya*-suffix [Sūr.]); Ap. *iālīsa* (with shortening of initial *ī-* to *i-*).
6.1.16.2. 'Forty-two'. Pāli *dvecattārīsa* (PTC), *dvācattālīsa* (PTC); AMg. *bāyālīsaṃ, ducattālīsa* (Sūr.), *bāyāla* (Sūr.), *bāyālaṃ* (Sūr.); JM *bāyālīsaṃ, bāyāla, bicatta*; Niya *ducapariśa*; Ap. *beāla* (Pp.), *bāālīsaṃ* (Pp.).
6.1.16.3. 'Forty-three'. Pāli *tetālisa* (PTC); AMg. *teālīsā, teyālīsaṃ* (Samav.), *tĕttālīsaṃ* (Sūr.); JM *teyālīsaṃ*.
6.1.16.4. 'Forty-four'. Pāli *catucattārīsa* (PTC), *catucattāḷīsa* (PTC); AMg. *cauyālīsaṃ, coyālīsaṃ, coyālīsā, cŏttālīsaṃ* (Sūr.), *cŏttāla* (Sūr.), *cŏttālaṃ* (Sūr.); Ap. *cauālīsa, coālīsa, cauāla* (Pp.).
6.1.16.5. 'Forty-five'. Pāli **pañcacattārīsa*; AMg. *paṇayālīsā, paṇayālīsaṃ, paṇatāla* (Sūr.), *paṇayāla* (Sūr.), *paṇṇayāla* (Sūr.), *paṇṇatālīsa* (Sūr.),

paṇṇayālīsa (Sūr.), _paṇṇayālīsaṃ_ (Sūr.), _paṇṇayālīsai_ (by analogy with _-vīsai_ [Sūr.]); Niya _paṃcacapariśa_ (Stein 1936); Ap. _pacaālīsa_.
6.1.16.6. 'Forty-six'. Pāli _*chacattārīsa_; AMg. _chāyālīsaṃ, chaccattāla_ (Sūr.), _chattālīsaṃ_ (Sūr.); Ap. _chāyālīsa, chahacālīsa_.
6.1.16.7. 'Forty-seven'. Pāli _*sattacattārīsa_; AMg. _sīyālīsaṃ_ (with _sī-_ < _se-_ < _saya-_ < _sata-_ < _satta-_?), _sīālīsā_ (Sūr.), _sattālīsaṃ_ (Sūr.), _sattacālīsaṃ_ (Samav.), _sattacattālīsaṃ_ (Samav.); JM _sīālā_ (Sheth 1963).
6.1.16.8. 'Forty-eight'. Pāli _aṭṭhacattārīsaṃ, aṭṭhatālīsa_ (PTC), _aṭṭhacattāḷīsa_ (PTC); AMg. _aṭṭhacattālīsaṃ, aḍhayālīsaṃ_ (texts often have _aḍa-_), _aḍhayāla_; JM _aḍhayālīsa_; Ap. _aṭṭhayāla, aṭṭhāyāla_ (Paum.), _aṭhatālīsa_ (with simplification _-ṭṭh-_ > _-ṭh-_ [Pp.]), _aḍhaālīsa_.

6.1.17. The fifties

In some dialects intervocalic _-p-_ becomes _-v-_, or is lost.
6.1.17.0. 'Forty-nine'. Pāli _ekūnapaññāsa, ekūnapaññāsā, ekūnapaṇṇāsa_ (PTC); AMg. _ĕkkūṇapaṇṇa, eūṇavaṇṇaṃ_ (Sūr.), _eūṇapaṇṇa_ (Sūr.), _eūṇapaṇṇāsā_ (Sūr.), _uṇāpaṇṇa_ (mistake for _ūṇā-_? [Sūr.]), _egūṇapannā_ (Samav.), _auṇāpanna_; Ap. _ĕkkūṇaīpaṇṇāsa_.
6.1.17.1. 'Fifty-one'. Pāli _ekapaṇṇāsa_ (PTC); AMg. _ĕkkāvannaṃ_ (with _-ā-_ by analogy with _ĕkkārasa_ 'eleven' [Samav.]), _ĕkkāvaṇṇa_ (Sūr.), _ekāvaṇṇa_ (Sūr.), _ekāvaṇṇā_ (Sūr.).
6.1.17.2. 'Fifty-two'. Pāli _dvāpaññāsa_ (Mahāvaṃsa 2.29); AMg. _bāvaṇṇa, bāvaṇṇaṃ_ (Sūr.), _bāvannaṃ_ (Samav.); Ap. _bāvaṇṇa_.
6.1.17.3. 'Fifty-three'. Pāli _*tepaññāsa_; AMg. _tevaṇṇaṃ, tevannaṃ_ (Samav.), _tepaṇṇa_ (Sūr.), _tepaṇṇaṃ_ (Sūr.); JM _tevannaṃ_.
6.1.17.4. 'Fifty-four'. Pāli _catupaṇṇāsa_ (PTC); AMg. _cauvaṇṇaṃ, cauppaṇṇa_ (Sūr.), _cauvannaṃ_ (Samav.), _caupaṇṇa_ (Sūr.), _caupaṇṇam_ (Sūr.); JM _caupannaṃ_; Ap. _cauaṇṇa_ (Pp.).
6.1.17.5. 'Fifty-five'. Pāli _pañcapaññāsa, pañcapaṇṇāsa_ (PTC); AMg. _paṇavaṇṇaṃ_ (with shortening _-ṇṇ-_ > _-ṇ-_), _paṇapannaṃ_ (Samav.), _paṇṇapaṇṇaṃ_ (Sūr.); JM _pañcavannaṃ, paṇapannaṃ_; Deśī _paṃcāvaṇṇa_ (with _-ā-_ by analogy with _aṭṭhā-_); Ap. _paṇapaṇṇāsa_.
6.1.17.6. 'Fifty-six'. Pāli _chappaṇṇāsa_ (PTC), _chappaññāsa_; Aś. _sapaṃnā_; AMg. _chappaṇṇaṃ, chappannaṃ_ (Samav.), _chappaṇā_ (misprint for _-ppaṇṇā_? [Sūr.]), _chappaṇṇā_ (Sūr.); JM _chappannaṃ_; Ap. _chappaṇṇa, chappaṇa_ (with shortening _-ṇṇ-_ > _-ṇ-_ [Pp.]).
6.1.17.7. 'Fifty-seven'. Pāli _*sattapaññāsa_; AMg. _sattāvaṇṇa_ (with _-ā-_ by analogy with _aṭṭhā-_ [Sūr.]), _sattāvaṇṇaṃ_ (Sūr.), _sattāvannaṃ_ (Samav.),

sattavaṇṇaṃ, sattāvannā; JM *sattavannaṃ*; Ap. *sattāvaṇī, sattāvaṇṇāi* (with plural ending).

6.1.17.8. 'Fifty-eight'. Pāli *aṭṭhapaññāsaṃ* (PTC), *aṭṭhapaṇṇāsa* (PTC: s. v. *paṇṇāsa*); AMg. *aṭṭhāvaṇṇam, aṭṭhāvannaṃ* (Samav.); Ap. *vahiṃ unī saṭṭhi* ('sixty less two', Sen 1960).

6.1.18. The sixties

In some forms in this group, *-s-* of *-saṭṭhi* is lost, presumably after the development to *-h-*. The resultant hiatus is either resolved by contraction, or avoided by the insertion of a *-y-* or *-v-*glide.

6.1.18.0. 'Fifty-nine'. Pāli *ekūnasaṭṭhi* (PED); AMg. *egūṇasaṭṭhiṃ, eūṇasaṭṭhi* (Sūr.), *eūṇasaṭṭha* (= ordinal [Sūr.]), *eūṇaṭṭha* (= ordinal [Sūr.]), *auṇaṭṭhiṃ*; JM *egūṇasaṭṭhi* (used as an ordinal), *auṇaṭṭhiṃ*; Ap *ĕkkuṇasaṭṭhi* (Paum.).

6.1.18.1. 'Sixty-one'. Pāli **ekasaṭṭhi*; AMg. *igasaṭṭhiṃ* (with shortening *e- > i-*), *egasaṭṭhi* (Sūr.), *egaṭṭhi* (Sūr.), *ekaṭṭha* (= ordinal [Sūr.]), *egaṭṭha* (= ordinal [Sūr.]); JM *egaṭṭhi.*

6.1.18.2. 'Sixty-two'. Pāli *dvāsaṭṭhi* (PTC), *dvaṭṭhi* (PTC); AMg. *bāsaṭṭhiṃ, bāsaṭṭhi* (Sūr.), *bāvaṭṭhiṃ* (Sūr.), *bāvaṭṭhi* (Sūr.); JM *bāsaṭṭhi, bāvaṭṭhi, bāvaṭṭhiṃ*; Ap. *bāsaṭṭhi* (Pp.).

6.1.18.3. 'Sixty-three'. Pāli *tesaṭṭhi* (PTC); AMg. *tesaṭṭhiṃ, tevaṭṭhi* (Sūr.), *tevaṭṭha* (= ordinal [Sūr.]), *tevaṭṭhāiṃ* (= ordinal, with plural ending [Sūr.]); JM *tevaṭṭhi, tevaṭṭhiṃ*; Ap. *tisaṭṭhi* (Paum.).

6.1.18.4. 'Sixty-four'. Pāli *catusaṭṭhi* (PTC); AMg. *causaṭṭhiṃ, causaṭṭhi* (Samav.), *cosaṭṭhī* (with contraction *cau- > co-*); JM *cauvaṭṭhi*; Mā. *caussaṭṭhi*; Inscr. (E) *coyaṭha* (= ordinal, but Sircar 1965 reads *coyaṭhi* (Ud.)); Ap. *causaṭṭhi* (Paum.).

6.1.18.5. 'Sixty-five'. Pāli **pañcasaṭṭhi*; AMg. *paṇasaṭṭhiṃ, paṇṇaṭṭhiṃ*; JM *pañcasaṭṭhi.*

6.1.18.6. 'Sixty-six'. Pāli *chasaṭṭhi* (PTC); AMg. *chāvaṭṭhiṃ* (with *-ā-* by analogy with *aṭṭhā-*), *chāvaṭṭhi* (Sūr.), *chāvaṭṭha* (= ordinal [Sūr.]), *chāvaṭṭhāiṃ* (= ordinal, with plural ending [Sūr.]); Ap. *chāvaṭṭhi.*

6.1.18.7. 'Sixty-seven'. Pāli **sattasaṭṭhi*; AMg. *sattasaṭṭhim, sattasaṭṭhi* (Sūr.), *sattasaṭṭha* (= ordinal [Sūr.]), *sattaṭṭhi* (Sūr.); Ap. *sattasaṭṭhi* (Bhav.).

6.1.18.8. 'Sixty-eight'. Pāli *aṭṭhasaṭṭhi* (PTC); AMg. *aḍhasaṭṭhiṃ* (some texts *aḍa-*), *aṭṭhasaṭṭha* (= ordinal [Sūr.]); JM *aṭṭhasaṭṭhi*; Inscr. (Kh.) *aḍhaṣaṭhi* (used as an ordinal); Ap. *aṭṭhāsaṭṭhā.*

6.1.19. The seventies

In some forms in this group *-s-* of *-sattati* becomes *-h-*, or is lost, the resultant hiatus being either resolved by contraction or avoided by the evolution of a *-v*-glide.

6.1.19.0. 'Sixty-nine'. Pāli **ekūnasattati*; AMg. *egūṇasattariṃ, auṇattariṃ.*

6.1.19.1. 'Seventy-one'. Pāli *ekasattati* (PTC); AMg *ĕkkasattariṃ, ekasattarī* (Sūr.); Ap. *ehattari* (with contraction *ea-* > *e-*).

6.1.19.2. 'Seventy-two'. Pāli *dvāsattati* (PTC), *dvesattati* (PTC); AMg. *bāvattariṃ, bāvattara* (ordinal [Sūr.]); JM *bisattari, bāvattari*; Ap. *bāvattari.*

6.1.19.3. 'Seventy-three'. Pāli *tesattati* (PTC); AMg. *tevattariṃ.*

6.1.19.4. 'Seventy-four'. Pāli *catusattati* (PTC); AMg. *covattariṃ*; JM *cauhattari.*

6.1.19.5. 'Seventy-five'. Pāli *pañcasattati* (PTC); AMg. *pannattari, paṇṇattarā* (= ordinal with plural ending [Sūr.]), *pañcahattari*; JM *paṇasayarī* (with *-y-* < *-t-* < *-tt-*); Inscr. (E) *panatariya* (Mehendale 1948 so, Sircar 1965 reads *pānatarīya*; this is the instrumental of a singular noun, so there is no need to emend to *-ihi* with Sen 1960); Ap. *paṃcasattari, paṃcasattara.*

6.1.19.6. 'Seventy-six'. Pāli **chasattati*; AMg. *chāvattariṃ* (with *-ā-* by analogy with *aṭṭhā-*), *chāvattara* (= ordinal [Sūr.]), *chāvattaraṃ* (= ordinal, with neuter singular ending [Sūr.]); Ap. *chāhattari.*

6.1.19.7. 'Seventy-seven'. Pāli *sattasattari*; AMg. *sattahattariṃ*; SinPkt. *satasatati.*

6.1.19.8. 'Seventy-eight'. Pāli *aṭṭhasattati* (PTC); AMg. *aṭṭhahattariṃ, aṭṭhahattari* (Samav.), *aṭṭhattariṃ* (Sūr.); JM *aṭṭhattari.*

6.1.20. The eighties

In some of the forms for 'eighty-three', 'eighty-four' and 'eighty-six', the second element of the compound is based upon **āsīti*, by analogy with the other numerals in the group where *-ā-* results from the contraction of the final vowel of the first element with the *a-* of *asīti.*

6.1.20.0. 'Seventy-nine'. Pāli **ekūnāsīti*; AMg. *egūṇāsīiṃ, egūṇāsīti* (Samav.), *egūṇāsiṃ* (either a misprint or with contraction *-īiṃ* > *-iṃ* [Samav.]), *eūṇāsīya* (= ordinal [Sūr.]), *eūṇāsīa* (= ordinal [Sūr.]).

6.1.20.1. 'Eighty-one'. Pāli **ekāsīti*; AMg. *ĕkkāsīi* (Samav.), *ĕkkāsīya* (= ordinal [Sūr.]); JM *ĕkkāsīī* (with *-i* > *-ī*).

6.1.20.2. 'Eighty-two'. Pāli *dvāsīti* (PTC), *dve-asīti* (PTC); AMg. *bāsīiṃ, bāsīi* (Samav.), *bāsīyaṃ* (= ordinal, with neuter singular ending [Samav.]); Ap. *beāsī* (with contraction *-īi* > *-ī-* [Pp.]).
6.1.20.3. 'Eighty-three'. Pāli **tiyāsīti* (with glide *-y-* evolved between *ti-* and *-āsīti*); AMg. *tesīiṃ, tesīi* (Sūr.), *tesīī* (with *-i* > *-ī* [Samav.]), *teyāsī* (with glide *-y-* and *-īi* > *-ī*), *tesīya* (= ordinal [Sūr.]); JM *tesīī*.
6.1.20.4. 'Eighty-four'. Pāli *caturāsīti* (PTC), *cullāsīti* (with *-ull-* < *-ŏll-* < *-ol-* < *-or-* < *-aur-* [PTC]); AMg. *caurāsīiṃ, corāsīiṃ* (with *caur-* > *cor-*), *corāsīi* (Samav.), *corāsī* (with *-īi* > *-ī*), *caurāsīi* (Samav.), *caurāsī* (Samav.), *caurāsīaṃ* (= ordinal, with neuter singular ending [Sūr.]), *culasīiṃ* (with shortening *cull-* > *cul-* [Sūr.]), *culasīaṃ* (= ordinal, with neuter singular ending [Sūr.]); JM *caurasīi, culasīi, caurāsī* (Jacobi 1886); BHS *caturāśīti, catvāri-āśīti*; Ap. *caurāsī, caurāsi* (with shortening *-ī* > *-i*).
6.1.20.5. 'Eighty-five'. Pāli *pañcāsīti* (PTC); AMg. *pañcāsīiṃ, pañcāsīi* (Sūr.), *paṃcāsīi* (Samav.), *pañcāsīya* (= ordinal [Sūr.]).
6.1.20.6. 'Eighty-six'. Pāli *chaḷāsīti* (PTC); AMg. *chaḷāsīiṃ, chalasīi* (Samav.), *chalāsīa* (= ordinal [Sūr.]), *chalasīya* (= ordinal [Sūr.]); BHS *ṣaḍāśīti*.
6.1.20.7. 'Eighty-seven'. Pāli **sattāsīti*; AMg. *sattāsīiṃ*.
6.1.20.8. 'Eighty-eight'. Pāli *aṭṭhāsīti* (PTC); AMg. *aṭṭhāsīiṃ, aṭṭhāsīi* (Samav.), *aṭṭhāsīya* (= ordinal [Sūr.]); JM *aṭṭhāsīi*; Ap. *aṭṭhāsi* (with *-i* < *ī* < *-īi*).

6.1.21. The nineties

6.1.21.0. 'Eighty-nine'. Pāli **ekūnanavuti*; AMg. *egūṇanaui* (Samav.), *egūṇaṇauī* (Samav.), *egūṇaṇauiṃ, egūṇaṇaua* (= ordinal [Samav.]), *ekūṇaṇauiṃ* (Sūr.), *eūṇāṇauiṃ* (Sūr.), *eūṇāuiṃ* (with loss of *-ṇa-* by haplography [Sūr.]).
6.1.21.1. 'Ninety-one'. Pāli *ekanavuta* (= ordinal [PTC]); AMg. *ĕkkaṇauiṃ, ĕkkaṇauī* (Samav.), *ekānaua* (= ordinal [Sūr.]).
6.1.21.2. 'Ninety-two'. Pāli *dvenavuti* (PTC), *dvenavuta* (= ordinal [PTC]); AMg. *bāṇauī* (Samav.), *bāṇauiṃ*; JM *bāṇauī*; Ap. *bāṇavai* (Paum.).
6.1.21.3. 'Ninety-three'. Pāli **tenavuti*; AMg. *teṇauiṃ, teṇauī* (Samav.), *teṇauā* (= ordinal with plural ending [Sūr.]); JM *teṇauī*.
6.1.21.4. 'Ninety-four'. Pāli *catunavuta* (= ordinal [PTC]); AMg. *cauṇauiṃ, cauṇaui* (Samav.), *caunauā* (= ordinal, with plural ending [Sūr.]), *caunavaiṃ* (Sūr.), *caunaua* (= ordinal [Sūr.]).

6.1.21.5. 'Ninety-five'. Pāli **pañcanavuti*; AMg. *pañcāṇauiṃ* (with *-ā-* by analogy with *aṭṭhā-*), *pañcāṇaui* (Samav.), *pañcāṇauī* (Samav.), *pañcāṇauya* (= ordinal [Samav.]), *pañcaṇava* (mistake for *-ṇavai*? [Sūr.]); JM *pañcāṇauī, paṇanauī, pañcānauiṃ*.
6.1.21.6. 'Ninety-six'. Pāli **channavuti*; AMg. *chaṇṇauiṃ, chaṇṇauī, chaṇṇaui* (Samav.), *chaṇṇauiya* (with *-ya*-suffix [Sūr.]), *chaṇṇauā* (= ordinal, with plural ending [Sūr.]); JM *channavaī, channauī*; Ap. *chaṇṇavai, channavai* (Paum.), *chānavai* (with *-ā-* by analogy, or as compensation for the shortening of *-nn-* > *-n-*), *chaṇṇāveā* (with plural ending [Pp.]), *chaṇṇaudi* (with voicing *-t-* > *-d-*).
6.1.21.7. 'Ninety-seven'. Pāli **sattanavuti*; AMg. *sattāṇauiṃ* (with *-ā-* by analogy with *aṭṭhā-*), *sattāṇaui* (Samav.), *sattānaua* (= ordinal [Sūr.]).
6.1.21.8. 'Ninety-eight'. Pāli *aṭṭhanavuti* (PTC), *aṭṭhānavuti* (CPD); AMg. *aṭṭhāṇauiṃ, aṭṭhāṇaui* (Samav.), *aṭṭhāṇauī* (Sūr.), *aṭṭhāṇauā* (= ordinal, with plural ending [Sūr.]); Ap. *aṭṭhāṇavai* (Paum.).
6.1.21.9. 'Ninety-nine'. Pāli *ekūnasata*; AMg. *ṇavaṇauiṃ, ṇavaṇaui* (Samav.); Ap. *ṇavaṇavai* (Paum.), *ṇavaṇauyaĩ* (with plural ending).

6.1.22. 'One hundred'

Pāli *sata*; Aś. *sata, śata, ṣata* (where *ṣ-* is a scribal idiosyncracy); AMg. *saya*; JM *saya*; Śaur. *sada*; Mg. *śada*; Gā. *śada*; Niya *śata*; Inscr. (W) *sata*; SinPkt. *śata*; Ap. *saya, saa, sau* (Pp.).

6.1.23. 'One hundred and one' to 'nine hundred and ninety-nine'

Numerals above 'one hundred' are not often found. The following represent a large proportion of those that do occur:
'one hundred and one': Ap. *ekkottarasaya*;
'one hundred and two': Ap. *duttarasaya*;
'one hundred and three': Inscr. (E) *ti(vasa)sata* (or 'three hundred'?);
'one hundred and four': Ap. *causaa* (or 'four hundred'?);
'one hundred and eight': Pāli *aṭṭhasatā*; AMg. *aṭṭhasayaṃ*; Ap. *aṭṭhuttarasaya, sau aṭṭhottaru* (Paum.);
'one hundred and ten': Niya *daśutara śata*; Ap. *dasa-uttara-saya* (Paum.);
'one hundred and eleven': Inscr. (Kh.) *ekadaśa⟨śa⟩ta* (extracted from the ordinal);
'one hundred and thirteen': Inscr. (E) *terasa(vasa)sata*;
'one hundred and twenty': Ap. *saubīsa* (Pp.);
'one hundred and thirty-eight': Ap. *aḍhayālīsauṃ sauṃ*;

'one hundred and seventy': Inscr. (S) *satari satam̥*;
'two hundred': Pāli *dve satāni dvisata*; Inscr. (W) *-satāni be* (Sen 1960);
'two hundred and fifty-six': Aś. *duve sapam̥nā satā*;
'three hundred': Pāli *tīṇi satāni, tisata*; Inscr. (E) *ti(vasa)sata* (or 'one hundred and three'?);
'three hundred and forty-six': Ap. *chāyālīsam̥ tiṇṇi sayaim̥* (Mp.);
'three hundred and sixty-three': Ap. *tesaṭṭhaim̥ tiṇṇi sayaim̥* (Mp.);
'four hundred': Ap. *causaa* (or 'one hundred and four'?);
'four hundred and ninety-nine': Pāli *ekūnapañcasatā* (PED), *ūnapañcas-atāni* (PED);
'five hundred': Pāli *pañcasata*;
'seven hundred': Ap. *sattasaa* (Pp.);
'seven hundred and ninety-nine': Pāli *ekūna-aṭṭhasatam̥* (PED);
'eight hundred': Pāli *aṭṭhasata*;
'nine hundred and ninety-eight': Pāli *dvīhi ūnam̥ sahassam̥* (PED).

6.1.24. 'One thousand'

Pāli *sahassa*; Aś. *sahasa, sahasra, ṣahaṣa* (where retroflex *ṣ* is a scribal idiosyncracy); AMg. *sahassa*; JM *sahassa*; Gā. *sahasa*; Niya *sahasra*; SinPkt. *sahasa, sahasaka* (with *-ka*-suffix), *śahaśa*; Ap. *sahassa, sahāsa, sahasa* (Sanat.).

6.1.25. 'One thousand and one' to 'ninety-nine thousand nine hundred and ninety nine'

'One thousand and eight': AMg. *aṭṭhasahassam̥*; Niya *sahasra aṣṭi* (Document No. 661); Ap. *aṭṭhottara sahāsa* (Paum.);
'one thousand two hundred and fifty': Pāli *aḍḍhatelasehi -satehi* (instrumental plural ending);
'two thousand': Pāli *dvisahassa* (PTC), *dve sahassāni*;
'four thousand': Inscr. (W) *-sahasrehi catuhi* (instrumental plural ending [Sen 1960]); SinPkt. *catarisahasaka*;
'five thousand': SinPkt. *pacasahasaka*;
'six thousand': Pāli *cha sahassāni*;
'eight thousand': Inscr. (W) *-sahasrāṇi aṭha* (Sen 1960); SinPkt. *aṭa sahasa*;
'eight thousand five hundred': Pāli *aḍḍhanavamasahassāni* (PTC);
'nine thousand': SinPkt. *navasahasaka*;
'nine thousand two hundred': JM *dasasahassāṇi aṭṭhasauṇagāṇi* (i.e. '10 000 less 800', Sen 1960);

'ten thousand': Pāli *dasasahassa* (PTC); JM *dasasahassa*; SinPkt. *daśa śahaśa*; also Pāli *nahuta* (PED); JM *ajuya*;
'thirty thousand': Ap. *dahaguṇiya tiṇṇi sahasa* (Mp.);
'seventy thousand': Inscr. (W) *-sahasrāni satari*;
'ninety thousand': Pāli *navutisahassa* (PTC).

6.1.26. 'Lakh'

'One hundred thousand': Pāli, AMg., JM, Ap. *lakkha*; SinPkt. *laka*. Also Pāli *satasahassa*; Aś. *satasahasra, ṣataṣahaśa* (where *ṣ* and *ś* are scribal idiosyncrasies), *satasahasa, śatasahasra, śatasahasa*; AMg. *sayasahassa*; JM *sayasahassa* (PC); Niya *śata sahasrani* (Stein 1936); Inscr. (E) *sata-sahasa*.

6.1.27. Large numbers below 'ten million'

'One hundred and twenty thousand': Pāli *dvādasanahuta* (PTC);
'one hundred and fifty thousand': Aś *diyaḍhamāte -satasahase*;
'three million five hundred thousand': Inscr. (E) *panatīsāhi satasahasehi* (instrumental plural ending, Ud.);
'three million eight hundred thousand': Inscr. (E) *aḍhatisāya satasahasehi* (instrumental, Ud.);
'seven million five hundred thousand': Inscr. (E) *paṇatariya satasahasehi* (instrumental, Ud.).

6.1.28. 'Crore'

'Ten million': Pāli *koṭi*; JM *koḍi*; Niya *koḍi* (Stein); Ap. *koḍi*;
'five hundred million': JM *paṇṇāsaṃ koḍīo* (Sen);
'one hundred and twenty billion': Pāli *dvādasakoṭisahassa* (PTC).

6.2. Ordinals

6.2.1. 'First'

Pāli *paṭhama*; AMg. *padhama, puḍhama, paḍhuma* (with metathesis of vowels), *puḍhuma* (with assimilation of vowels), *paḍhamilla* (with *-illa*-suffix), *paḍhamillaga* (with *-ga*-suffix); JM *paḍhama* (fem. *-ā*); Gā. *pra-dhamu, paḍhama*; Niya *prathama, pratama, paḍama*; Inscr. (W) *pathama*,

(S) *prathama, paḍama*, (C) *paṭhama, paḍhama*, (E) *padhama*, (Kh.) *praṭhama, praḍhama, padhaṃma*; Ap. *paḍhama, paḍhamĕlluya* (with -*ĕlla*- [= -*illa*-] and -*uya*-suffixes [Sanat.]), *pahila* (which probably results from the replacement of -*ma* by -*lla* (because of the confusion of -*imant* and -*illa*?) in Apabhraṃśa rather than from a development from **prathira* or **prathila*), *pahilaa* (with -*(y)a*-suffix), *pahilla, pahilliya* (with -*ya*-suffix), *pahilāraa* (with -*āra*- and -*(y)a*-suffixes), fem. *pahilārī*.

6.2.2. 'Second'

Pāli *dutiya*; Aś. *dutīya, dutiya*; AMg. *biīya, bīya* (with contraction -*iī*- > -*ī*-), *dŏcca* (< **dutya*), *ducca*; JM *biiya, bīya* (fem. -*ā*); Mā. *biijja* (with -*ijj*- < -*iyy*- < -*īy*-), *duiya, biia, bīa*; Mg., Śaur. *dudīa* (with -*t*- > -*d*-), *dudia*; Niya *dviti* (with loss of -*ya*), *biti, bhiti* (Stein 1936), *bitiya* (Stein 1936); Inscr. (W) *bitīya, bitiya*, (S) *bitīya, bitiya, bītiya* (mistake for *bitīya*?), (E) *dutiya*; Ap. *viijja* (Sanat.), *biijjaya* (with -*ya*-suffix [Kp.]) *bīya, bīa, bīyaya* (with -*ya*-suffix [Kp.]) *bīyaa* (with -*(y)a*-suffix), *bia* (with shortening -*ī*- > -*i*- [Pp.]), *vīya, vīyaya* (with -*ya*-suffix [Paum.]), *bīja* (Kp.), *viīya* (Paum.), *vijjaya* (with -*ya*-suffix [Paum.]), *bīja* (Kp.), *viīya* (Paum.), *vijjaya* (with -*ya*-suffix [Paum.]), *duiya, duijja*.

6.2.3. 'Third'

Pāli *tatiya*; AMg. *taīya* (Viy.), *taiya, tacca* (< **tṛtya*); JM *taiya* (fem. -*ā*); Śaur. *tadia* (with -*t*- > -*d*-); Mā. *taia*; Gā. *tridia*; Niya *triti* (with loss of -*ya*); Inscr. (W) *tatiya*, (E) *tatiya*; Ap. *taijja, taiya, taiyaa* (with -*(y)a*-suffix), *tīa* (Pp.), *tijjau* (with -*(y)u*-suffix), *taīya* (Paum.).

6.2.4. 'Fourth'

Pāli *catuttha*; AMg. *cauttha, cauṭṭha*; JM *cauttha* (fem. -*ī*); Mā. *cŏttha* (with contraction *cau*- > *co*-); Mg. *caduttha*; Śaur. *caduttha, caduṭṭha*; Gā. *cauṭha*; Niya *caturtha*; Inscr. (W) *cotha*, (S) *catutha*, (C) *cauttha*, (E) *cavutha* (with glide -*v*- replacing -*t*-); Ap. *cauṭṭha, cŏtthaa* (with -*(y)a*-suffix), *cauttha* (Sanat.), *cautha* (with simplification -*tth*- > -*th*- [Bhav.]), *cārima* (with the suffix -*ma* added to the nominative-accusative neuter of the cardinal [Pp.]), *turiya* and *turīya* (presumably learned memories of OInd. *túrya*- and *turī́ya*-, although Middle Indo-Aryan forms without *ca*- do occur, cf. **turtha* in *addhauṭṭha* 'three and a half' [Hp.]).

6.2.5. 'Fifth'

Pāli *pañcama, pañcamaka* (with *-ka*-suffix [PTC]); AMg. *paṃcama*; JM *pañcama* (PC), *paṃcama* (fem. *-ī*); Niya *paṃcama*; Inscr. (W) *paṃcama, pacama* (with *-ṃ-* not written), (S) *paṃcama, paṃcami*, (E) *paṃcama*, (Kh.) *paṃcama*; Ap. *paṃcama, paṃcava*.
6.2.5.1. From 'fifth' onwards Apabhraṃśa can make ordinals by adding the suffixes *-ma-* or *-va-* to the corresponding cardinals.

6.2.6. 'Sixth'

Pāli *saṭṭha, chaṭṭha, chaṭṭhama* (with *-ma* added by analogy with *sattama* 'seventh' etc.); AMg. *chaṭṭha*; JM *chaṭṭha* (fem. *-ī*); Niya *ṣodhama* (not the equivalent of Pāli *chaṭṭhama*, but the suffix *-tama* added to *ṣo* 'six'); Inscr. (W) *chaṭha*, (S) *chaṭha*; Ap. *chaṭṭha* (fem. *-ī*), *chaṭṭhaya* (with *-ya*-suffix), *chaṭṭhaga* (with *-ga*-suffix), *chaṭṭhama* (Paum.).

6.2.7. 'Seventh'

Pāli *sattama*; AMg. *sattama*; JM *sattama, satama* (with simplification *-tt-* > *-t-*); Niya *satama*; Inscr. (W) *satama, sātama* (with *-ā-* as compensation for the shortening *-tt-* > *-t-*), (E) *satama*; Ap. *sattama, sattava*.

6.2.8. 'Eight'

Pāli *aṭṭhama* (fem. *-ī*), *aṭṭhamaka* (with *-ka*-suffix [PTC]); AMg. *aṭṭhama*; JM *aṭṭhama*; Niya *aṭhama*; Inscr. (E) *aṭhama* (Kh.) *aṭhama*; Ap. *aṭṭhama, aṭṭhava*.

6.2.9. 'Ninth'

Pāli *navama*; AMg. *navama*; JM *navama*; Dā. *ṇavama*; Niya *navama*; Inscr. (W) *navama*, (E) *navama*; Ap. *ṇavama, navama, ṇavamaya* (with *-ya*-suffix [Paum.]).

6.2.10. 'Tenth'

Pāli *dasama* (fem. *-ī*); AMg. *dasama*; JM *dasama*; Niya *daśama, daśa* (= cardinal); Inscr. (W) *dasamiya* (fem.), (S) *dasama* (fem. *-ī*), (E) *dasama*, (Kh.) *daśama*; Ap. *dasama* (Sanat.), fem. *dasamī* (Paum.), *dasamaya* (with *-ya*-suffix [Paum.]), *dahama* (Hp.), *dahamaya* (with *-ya*-suffix [Paum.]).

6.2.11. 'Eleventh' to 'eighteenth'

The Old Indian cardinals 'eleven' to 'eighteen' can be used as ordinals merely by changing the accent, e.g. OInd. *ékadaśa-* 'eleven': *ekadaśá-* 'eleventh'. In Middle Indo-Aryan, devoid of accent, only the context enables the reader to detect a cardinal used as an ordinal.

6.2.11.1. 'Eleventh'

Pāli *ekādasa* (= cardinal), *ekādasī* (fem.), *ekādasama* (fem. -*ī*); AMg. *ekārasama, ĕkkārasama, ikkārasama*; JM *ekādasama*; Niya *ekadaśa* (= cardinal); Inscr. (E) *(ekā)dasama* (Mehendale 1948 reads so), (Kh.) *ekadaśa* (= cardinal); Ap. *eyārahama* (Mp.), *eyārahamaya* (with -*ya*-suffix [Paum.]), *egārahama* (Paum.).

6.2.12. 'Twelfth'

Pāli *dvādasa* (= cardinal), *dvādasī* (fem.), *dvādasama* (fem. -*ī*); AMg. *bārasama, bārahama* (Viy.), *duvālasama*; JM *bārasama*; Niya *badaśi* (= cardinal); Inscr. (E) *bārasama*; Ap. *duvālasama* (Sanat.), *bārahama* (Hp.), *vārahama* (Paum.), *vārahamaya* (with -*ya*-suffix [Paum.]).

6.2.13. 'Thirteenth'

Pāli *terasa* (= cardinal), *terasama* (fem. -*ī*); AMg. *terasama, terahama* (Viy.); JM *terasama*; Inscr. (W) *terasa* (= cardinal), (E) *terasama*; Ap. *terahama* (Hp.), *terahamaya* (with -*ya*-suffix [Paum.]).

6.2.14. 'Fourteenth'

Pāli *cuddasa* (= cardinal), *cuddasī* (fem.), *cuddasama* (fem. -*ī*), *cātuddasa* (fem. -*ī* [PTC]); Aś. *cāvudasā* (fem.); AMg. *cauddasama, cŏddasama;* JM *cauddasama* (PC), *cŏddasama*; Ap. *caudahama* (Paum.), *caudahamaya* (with -*ya*-suffix [Paum.]), *cŏddahama* (Mp.).

6.2.15. 'Fifteenth'

Pāli *pañcadasī* (= feminine of cardinal), *paṇṇarasa* (= cardinal), *pannarasa* (= cardinal), *pañcadasama, paṇṇarasama, pannarasama;* Aś. *paṃcadasā, paṃnadasā, paṃnaḷasā* (all feminines of cardinal); AMg. *pannar-*

asama, paṇṇarasama, paṇṇarasa (= cardinal); JM *pannarasama*; Niya *paṃcadaśa* (= cardinal); Inscr. (W) *panarasa* (= cardinal), (E) *paṃdarasa* (= cardinal), (Kh.) *paṃcadaśa* (= cardinal); Ap. *paṇṇarahama* (Paum.), *paṇṇārahamaya* (with *-ya*-suffix [Paum.]).

6.2.16. 'Sixteenth'

Pāli *soḷasa* (= cardinal), *soḷasī* (feminine), *soḷasama*; AMg. *soḷasama, solasama*; JM *solasama*; Inscr. (Kh.) *ṣoḍaśa* (= cardinal); Ap. *solahama* (Paum.), *solasamaya* (with *-ya*-suffix [Paum.]).

6.2.17. 'Seventeenth'

Pāli *sattarasama*; AMg. *sattarasama*; JM *sattarasama*; Ap. *sattarahama* (Paum.), *sattārahama* (Mp.), *sattārahamaya* (with *-ya*-suffix [Paum.]).

6.2.18. 'Eighteenth'

Pāli *aṭṭhārasa* (= cardinal [Mahāvaṃsa 20.1]), *aṭṭharasama*; AMg. *aṭṭharasama, aṭṭhārasama* (Viy.), *aṭṭhārasa* (= cardinal), *aḍhārasama*; JM *aṭṭhārasama*; Niya *aṭhadaśa* (= cardinal); Ap. *aṭṭhārahama* (Paum.), *aṭṭhārahamaya* (with *-ya*-suffix [Paum.]).

6.2.19. Higher ordinals: sources

Most of the higher ordinals are quoted from the chapter-numbers of texts, especially Mahāvaṃsa and Cūlavaṃsa for Pāli (up to 'one hundred and first'), Paumacariyaṃ for Jain Māhārāṣṭrī (up to 'one hundred and eighteenth'), Paumacariu and Mahāpurāṇa for Apabhraṃśa (up to 'ninetieth' and 'one hundred and second' respectively). Higher ordinals quoted without reference for these dialects may be assumed to be from these texts.

6.2.19.1. Ordinals 'nineteenth' to 'twenty-eight' forms

The ordinals for this group are formed by adding *-ma* to *vīsa-* or *vīsa(t)i*. Since the Middle Indo-Aryan equivalent of OInd. *viṃśá-* 'twentieth' is identical in form with the cardinal derived from **viṃśat*, there is an analogical use of cardinals in place of other ordinals.

6.2.19.2. 'Nineteenth'. Pāli *ekūnavīsatima*; AMg. *egūṇavīsatima, egūṇa-vīsaima* (Viy.), *eūṇavīsaima, egūṇavīsaitama* (with the suffix *-tama* by analogy with the sixties and eighties [Sūr.]); JM *egūṇavīsaima*; Inscr. (W) *ekunavīsa* (= cardinal); Ap. *eguṇavīsame, ĕkkuṇavīsama* (Mp.), *ĕkkuṇa-vīsamaya* (with *-ya*-suffix).
6.2.20. 'Twentieth'. Pāli *vīsa* (= cardinal), *vīsatima*; AMg. *vīsa* (= cardinal), *vīsaima*; JM *vīsaima*; Inscr. (S) *viṃsā* (= cardinal), (Kh.) *viśami*; Ap. *bīsama, vīsama*.
6.2.21. 'Twenty-first'. Pāli *ekavīsatima*; AMg. *ĕkkavīsaima, ĕkkavī-saiama* (with *-(t)ama*-suffix by analogy [Sūr.]); JM *ĕkkavīsaima*; Ap. *ĕkkavīsama*.
6.2.22. 'Twenty-second'. Pāli *bāvīsatima*; AMg. *bāvīsaima* (Viy.); JM *bāvīsaima*; Ap. *bāvīsama*.
6.2.23. 'Twenty-third'. Pāli *tevīsatima*; AMg. *tevīsaima*; JM *tevīsaima*; Ap. *tevīsama*.
6.2.24. 'Twenty-fourth'. Pāli *catuvīsa* (= cardinal [PTC]), *catuvīsatima*; AMg. *cauvīsa* (= cardinal), *cauvīsaima*; JM *cauvīsaima*; Ap. *cauvīsama*.
6.2.25. 'Twenty-fifth'. Pāli *paṇṇavīsati* (= cardinal [PTC]), *pañcavīsa-tima*; AMg. *paṇavīsaima* (Viy.); JM *pañcavīsaima* (PC), *paṃcavīsaima*; Ap. *pañcavīsama, paṃcavīsama* (Mp.).
6.2.26. 'Twenty-sixth'. Pāli *chabbīsatima*; AMg. *chavvīsaima* (Viy.); JM *chavvīsaima*; Ap. *chavvīsama*.
6.2.27. 'Twenty-seventh'. Pāli *sattavīsatima*; AMg. *sattāvīsaima* (Viy.); JM *sattāvīsaima*; Inscr. (S) *satavi⟨sati⟩ma* (Lüders 1912: no. 1340); Ap. *sattavīsama, sattāvīsama* (Mp.).
6.2.28. 'Twenty-eighth'. Pāli *aṭṭhavīsatima*; AMg. *aṭṭhāvīsaima* (Viy.); JM *aṭṭhāvīsaima*; Inscr. (Kh.) *aṭhaviśa, aṭhaviṃśati* (both identical with cardinal).

6.2.29. Ordinals 'twenty-ninth' to 'thirty-eight'.

The ordinals for this group are formed by adding *-ma* to *tiṃsa-* (*tīsa-*) or *tiṃsati-* (*tīsa(t)i-*). Since the Middle Indo-Aryan equivalent of OInd. *triṃśá-* 'thirtieth' is identical in form with the cardinal derived from OInd. *triṃśát-*, there is a formal identity between cardinal and ordinal for this numeral.
6.2.29.1. 'Twenty-ninth'. Pāli *ekūnatiṃsatima*; AMg. *egūṇatīsaima* (Viy.), *egūṇatīsaima*; Ap. *egūṇatīsama, ĕkkūṇatīsama* (Mp.).
6.2.30. 'Thirtieth'. Pāli *tiṃsa* (= cardinal), *tiṃsatima*; AMg. *tīsa* (= cardinal), *tīsaima*; JM *tīsaima*; Ap. *tīsama*.

6.2.31. 'Thirty-first'. Pāli *ekatiṃsatima*; AMg. *ĕkkatīsaima* (Viy.); JM *ĕkkatīsaima*; Ap. *ĕkkatīsama.*

6.2.32. 'Thirty-second'. Pāli *dvattiṃsatima*; AMg. *battīsaima* (Viy.); JM *battīsaima*; Ap. *battīsama* (Mp.), *vattīsama.*

6.2.33. 'Thirty-third'. Pāli *tĕttiṃsatima*; AMg. *tĕttīsaima* (Viy.); JM *tettīsaima*; Ap. *tĕttīsama.*

6.2.34. 'Thirty-fourth'. Pāli *catuttiṃsatima*; AMg. *cauttīsaima* (Viy.); JM *cautīsaima*; Ap. *cautīsama, cauttīsama* (Mp.).

6.2.35. 'Thirty-fifth'. Pāli *pañcatiṃsatima*; AMg. *paṇatīsaima* (Viy.); JM *peñcatīsaima* (PC), *paṃcatīsaima*; Ap. *pañcatīsama, paṃcatīsama* (Mp.).

6.2.36. 'Thirty-sixth'. Pāli *chattiṃsatima*; AMg. *chattīsaima* (Viy.); JM *chattīsaima*; Ap. *chattīsama.*

6.2.37. 'Thirty-seventh'. Pāli *sattatiṃsatima*; AMg. *sattatīsaima* (Viy.); JM *sattatīsaima*; Ap. *sattatīsama.*

6.2.38. 'Thirty-eighth'. Pāli *aṭṭhatiṃsatima*; AMg. *aṭṭhatīsaima* (Viy.); JM *aṭṭhatīsaima*; Ap. *aṭṭhatīsama.*

6.2.39. Ordinals 'thirty-ninth' to 'forty-eighth'.

The ordinals for this group are formed by adding *-ma* or *-(t)ima* (by analogy) to the cardinal. The formal identity of the Middle Indo-Aryan equivalents of OInd. *catvāriṃśá-* 'fortieth' and OInd. *catvāriṃśát-* 'forty', has led to the use of the cardinal as the ordinal for other numerals too.

6.2.39.1. 'Thirty-ninth'. Pāli *ekūnacattālīsatima*; AMg. *egūṇayālīsaima*; JM *egūṇacattāla* (= cardinal); Ap. *egūṇacālīsama, ĕkkūṇacālīsama* (Mp.).

6.2.40. 'Fortieth'. Pāli *cattārīsatima, cattālīsatima, cattārīsa* (= cardinal); AMg. *cattālīsaima*; JM *cattāla* (= cardinal); Ap. *cālīsama.*

6.2.41. 'Forty-first'. Pāli *ekacattārīsatima*; AMg. *ikkacattālīsaima* (Viy.); JM *egacattāla*; Inscr. (Kh.) *ekacapariśaa* (= cardinal, with *-(y)a*-suffix); Ap. *ĕkkacālīsama.*

6.2.42. 'Forty-second'. Pāli *dvecattārīsatima*; JM *bāyālīsaima*; Ap. *ducālīsama* (Mp.), *bāyālīsaima* (Paum.), *duyālīsama* (Sen 1960).

6.2.43. 'Forty-third'. JM *teyālīsaima*; Ap. *tiyālīsama.*

6.2.44. 'Forty-fourth'. Pāli *catucattārīsatima*; AMg. *coyālīsatima* (Samav.); JM *cauttālīsa*; Ap. *cauyālīsama.*

6.2.45. 'Forty-fifth'. Pāli *pañcacattārīsatima*; JM *paṇayāla* (= cardinal); Ap. *paṃcacālīsama* (Mp.), *pañcacālīsama* (Paum.).

6.2.46. 'Forty-sixth'. Pāli *chacattārīsatima*; JM *chāyālīsa* (= cardinal); Ap. *chāyālīsama.*

6.2.47. 'Forty-seventh'. Pāli *sattacattārīsatima*; JM *sattacattāla* (= cardinal); Ap. *sattacālīsama.*

6.2.48. 'Forty-eighth'. Pāli *aṭṭhacattārīsatima*; JM *aṭṭhacattāla* (= cardinal); Ap. *aṭṭhayālīsama* (Mp.), *aṭṭhacālīsama* (Paum.).

6.2.49. Ordinals 'forty-ninth' to 'fifty-eighth'.

Because of the formal identity of the Middle Indo-Aryan equivalents of OInd. *pañcāśát-* 'fifty' and OInd. *pañcāśá-* 'fiftieth', other ordinals in this group can, by analogy, be replaced by the cardinal. The ordinals are usually formed by adding *-ma* or *-(t)ima* to the cardinal.

6.2.49.1. 'Forty-ninth'. Pāli *ekūnapaññāsatima*; AMg. *egūṇapannāsaima*, *auṇāpaṇṇa* (= cardinal); JM *egūṇapannāsa* (= cardinal); Ap. *ĕkkūṇapaṇṇāsama*.

6.2.50. 'Fiftieth'. Pāli *paññāsatima*; JM *pannāsaima*; BHS *pañcāśima*; Ap. *paṇṇāsama*.

6.2.51. 'Fifty-first'. Pāli *ekapaññāsatima*; JM *egapannāsaima*; Ap. *ĕkkavaṇṇāsama*.

6.2.52. 'Fifty-second'. Pāli *dvāpaññāsatima*; JM *bāvanna* (= cardinal); Ap. *duvaṇṇāsama*.

6.2.53. 'Fifty-third'. Pāli *tepaññāsatima;* JM *tipañcāsaima* (PC), *tipaṃcāsaima*; Ap. *tivaṇṇāsama*.

6.2.54. 'Fifty-fourth'. Pāli *catupaññāsatima*; JM *caupannāsaima*; Ap. *cauvaṇṇāsama*.

6.2.55. 'Fifty-fifth'. Pāli *pañcapaññāsatima*; AMg. *paṇapaṇṇaima*; JM *pañcāvanna* (= cardinal [PC]), *paṃcāvanna* (= cardinal); Ap. *paṃcavaṇṇāsama* (Mp.), *pañcavaṇṇāsama* (Paum.).

6.2.56. 'Fifty-sixth'. Pāli *chappaññāsatima, chappaṇṇāsa* (= cardinal [PTC]); JM *chappanna* (= cardinal); Ap. *chappaṇṇāsama*.

6.2.57. 'Fifty-seventh'. Pāli *sattapaññāsatima*; JM *sattāvanna* (= cardinal); Ap. *sattavaññāsama*.

6.2.58. 'Fifty-eighth'. Pāli *aṭṭhapaññāsatima*; JM *aṭṭhāvanna* (= cardinal); Ap. *aṭṭhavaṇṇāsama*.

6.2.59. Ordinals 'fifty-ninth' to 'sixty-eighth'

Only Jain Māhārāṣṭrī has forms from *-ṣaṣṭa*. The remaining forms are made by adding *-ma* or *-tama* to the cardinal, by analogy with other groups.

6.2.59.1. 'Fifty-ninth'. Pāli *ekūnasaṭṭhima*; JM *egūṇasaṭṭha*; Ap. *ĕkkuṇasaṭṭhima*.

6.2.60. 'Sixtieth'. Pāli *saṭṭhitama*; JM *saṭṭhima*; Inscr. (Kh.) *ṣaṣṭihaa* (with *-ha* < *-tha*, cf. *caturtha*, and *-ya*-suffix; the reading is doubtful); Ap. *saṭṭhima*.

6.2.61. 'Sixty-first'. Pāli *ekasaṭṭhitama, ekasaṭṭhi* (= cardinal [PTC]); JM *egasaṭṭha*; Ap. *ĕkkasaṭṭhima.*
6.2.62. 'Sixty-second'. Pāli *dvāsaṭṭhitama*; JM *bāsaṭṭha*; Ap. *bāsaṭṭhima* (Paum.), *dusaṭṭhima* (Mp.).
6.2.63. 'Sixty-third'. Pāli *tesaṭṭhitama, tesaṭṭhima* (PTC); JM *tisaṭṭha*; Ap. *tisaṭṭhima.*
6.2.64. 'Sixty-fourth'. Pāli *catusaṭṭhitama*; JM *causaṭṭhima*; Ap. *causaṭ-ṭhima.*
6.2.65. 'Sixty-fifth'. Pāli *pañcasaṭṭhitama*; JM *pañcasaṭṭha*; Ap. *paṃca-saṭṭhima.*
6.2.66. 'Sixty-sixth'. Pāli *chasaṭṭhitama*; JM *chāsaṭṭha*; Ap. *chasaṭṭhima* (Mp.), *chāsaṭṭhima* (Paum.).
6.2.67. 'Sixty-seventh'. Pāli *sattasaṭṭhitama*; JM *sattasaṭṭha*; Ap. *satta-saṭṭhima.*
6.2.68. 'Sixty-eighth'. Pāli *aṭṭhasaṭṭhitama*; JM *aḍasaṭṭhima* (mistake for *aḍha-*); Inscr. (Kh.) *aḍhaṣaṭhi* (= cardinal); Ap. *aṭṭhasaṭṭhima.*

6.2.69. Ordinals 'sixty-ninth' to 'seventy-eighth'

Old Indian has *saptatimá-* for 'seventieth' and *-saptata-* for the other ordinals in this group. By analogy, *-ma* forms are extended throughout the group in Middle Indo-Aryan, while Jain Māhārāṣṭrī generalizes forms from *-saptata-*.
6.2.69.1. 'Sixty-ninth'. Pāli *ekūnasattatima*; JM *egūṇasattara*; Ap. *ĕk-kūṇahattarima* (Mp.), *ĕkkuṇasattarīma* (Paum.).
6.2.70. 'Seventieth'. Pāli *sattatima*; JM *sattara*; Ap. *sattarima.*
6.2.71. 'Seventy-first'. Pāli *ekasattatima*; JM *egasattara*; Ap. *ekahattar-ima* (Mp.), *ĕkkahattarima* (Paum.).
6.2.72. 'Seventy-second'. Pāli *dvāsattatima*; AMg. *bāvattara*; JM *bāv-attara*; Ap. *dusattarima.*
6.2.73. 'Seventy-third'. Pāli *tesattatima*; JM *tihattara*; Ap. *tisattarima.*
6.2.74. 'Seventy-fourth'. Pāli *catusattatima*; JM *cauhattara*; Ap. *cauhat-tarima* (Mp.), *causattarima* (Paum.).
6.2.75. 'Seventy-fifth'. Pāli *pañcasattatima*; JM *pañcahattara*; Ap. *paṃ-cahattarima.*
6.2.76. 'Seventy-sixth'. Pāli *chasattatima*; JM *chahattara*; Ap. *chahat-tarima* (Mp.), *chasattarima* (Paum.).
6.2.77. 'Seventy-seventh'. Pāli *sattasattatima*; JM *sattahattara*; Ap. *sat-tahattarima* (Mp.), *sattasattarima* (Paum.).

6.2.78. 'Seventy-eighth'. Pāli *aṭṭhasattatima*; JM *aṭṭhahattara*; Inscr. (Kh.) *aṭhasatatimaa* (with *-(y)a*-suffix); Ap. *aṭṭhahattarima* (Mp.), *aṭṭhasattarima* (Paum.).

6.2.79. Ordinals 'seventy-ninth' to 'eighty-eighth'

Some of the dialect forms in this group are based upon OInd. *-aśīta-*, which is used for ordinals other than 'eightieth'. The other forms are made with *-tama* (by analogy with OInd. *aśītitamá-* 'eightieth'), or *-ma* added to the cardinal. For the sake of completeness all variant readings from Harivaṃśapurāṇa are quoted.

6.2.79.1. 'Seventy-ninth'. Pāli *ekūnāsītitama*; JM *egūṇāsīya*; Ap. *ĕkkūṇāsīma*.

6.2.80. 'Eightieth'. Pāli *asītitama*; AMg. *asīima*; JM *asīima*; Ap. *asītima* (Mp.), *asīima* (Paum.).

6.2.81. 'Eighty-first'. Pāli *ekāsītitama*; JM *ĕkkāsīya*; Inscr. (Kh.) *ekaśitimaya* (with *-ya*-suffix); Ap. *ĕkkāsītima* (Mp.), *ĕkkāsīima* (Paum.).

6.2.82. 'Eighty-second'. Pāli *dvāsītitama*; JM *bāsīima*; Ap. *duvāsīma* (Mp.), *bāsīma* (Paum.), *duyāsītima* (Hp.), *duvāsītima* (Hp., variant reading), *duyāsīma* (Hp., variant reading).

6.2.83. 'Eighty-third'. Pāli *tiyāsītitama* (with glide *-y-*); AMg. *teyāsīima* (Samav.); JM *teyāsīima*; Ap. *teyāsītima* (Mp.), *teāsīma* (Paum.), *tīyāsītima* (Hp., variant reading), *teyāsīma* (Hp., variant reading).

6.2.84. 'Eighty-fourth'. Pāli *caturāsītitama*; AMg. *caurāsīima, caurāsīiṃ* (= cardinal); JM *caurāsīima, caurāsīiṃ* (= cardinal); Ap. *caurāsīma, caurāsītima* (Hp., variant reading).

6.2.85. 'Eighty-fifth'. Pāli *pañcāsītitama*; AMg. *paṃcāsīima*; JM *pañcāsīima*; Ap. *paṃcāsīma, pañcāsītima* (Hp., variant reading).

6.2.86. 'Eighty-sixth'. Pāli *chāsītitama*; JM *chāsīima*; Ap. *chāsītima* (Mp.), *chāyāsīma* (with glide *-y-*, Paum.), *chayāsīma* (Hp., variant reading).

6.2.87. 'Eighty-seventh'. Pāli *sattāsītitama*; JM *sattāsīima*; Ap. *sattāsītima* (Mp.), *sattāsīma* (Paum.).

6.2.88. 'Eighty-eight'. Pāli *aṭṭhāsītitama, aṭṭhāsīti* (= cardinal [PTC]); JM *aṭṭhāsīya*; Ap. *aṭṭhāsītima* (Mp.), *aṭṭhāsīma* (Paum.).

6.2.89. Ordinals 'eighty-ninth' to 'ninety-ninth'

The Jain Māhārāṣṭrī forms in this group are based upon OInd. *-navata-* (used for ordinals other than 'ninetieth'). The other forms are made with *-tama*, by analogy with OInd. *navatitamá-* 'ninetieth', or *-ma* added to

the cardinal. In this group the Apabhraṃśa numerals show the influence of Śaurasenī, with *-t-* voiced to *-d-*. For the sake of completeness all variant readings from Harivaṃśapurāṇa are quoted.
6.2.89.1. 'Eighty-ninth'. Pāli *ekūnanavutitama*; JM *egūṇanauya*; Ap. *ĕk-kūṇaṇavadima* (Mp.), *ekūṇavadima* (with loss of *-ṇa-* by haplography [Hp.]), *ṇavāsīma* (Paum.).
6.2.90. 'Ninetieth'. Pāli *navutima*; JM *nauya*; Ap. *ṇavadima* (Mp.), *ṇa-vaima* (Paum.), *ṇaudima* (Hp., variant reading).
6.2.91. 'Ninety-first'. Pāli *ekanavutima, ekanavuta* (PTC); JM *ĕkkāṇ-auya*; BHS *ekanavatima*; Ap. *ĕkkaṇavadima* (Mp.), *ĕkkāṇavadima* (Hp.), *ekaṇavadima* (Hp., variant reading), *ĕkkāṇaudima* (Hp., variant reading).
6.2.92. 'Ninety-second'. Pāli *dvānavutima*; JM *bāṇauya*; Ap. *duṇaudima* (Mp.), *duṇavadima* (Hp., variant reading), *duṇṇaudima* (with *-ṇṇ-* by analogy with *chaṇṇaudima* 'ninety-sixth' [Hp., variant reading]).
6.2.93. 'Ninety-third'. Pāli *tenavutima*; JM *teṇauya*; Ap. *tiṇavadima.*
6.2.94. 'Ninety-fourth'. Pāli *catunavutima*; JM *cauṇauya*; Ap. *cauṇau-dima.*
6.2.95. 'Ninety-fifth'. Pāli *pañcanavutima*; JM *pañcāṇauya*; Ap. *paṃca-ṇavadima.*
6.2.96. 'Ninety-sixth'. Pāli *channavutima*; JM *channauya*; Ap. *chaṇṇau-dima.*
6.2.97. 'Ninety-seventh'. Pāli *sattanavutima*; AMg. *sattāṇauya*; JM *sat-tāṇauya*; Ap. *sattaṇaudima.*
6.2.98. 'Ninety-eighth'. Pāli *aṭṭhanavutima*; JM *aṭṭhānauya*; Ap. *aṭṭha-ṇaudima.*
6.2.99. 'Ninety-ninth'. Pāli *ekūnasatama*; JM *navaṇauya*; Ap. *ṇavaṇa-vadima, ṇavaṇaudima.*
6.2.100. 'Hundredth'. Pāli *satama, satima* (PED); JM *sayayama*; BHS *śatima*; Ap. *sayama.*

6.2.101. Higher ordinals

From 'One hundred and first' onwards the Jain Māhārāṣṭrī forms are identical with the cardinals.
'One hundred and first': Pāli *ekasatama*; JM *ekottarasaya*; Ap. *ekottar-asayama.*
'One hundred and second': JM *duruttarasaya* (with *-r-* glide); Ap. *dut-tarasayama.*
'One hundred and third': JM *ti-uttarasaya*; Inscr. (Kh.) *tiśatimaa* (with *-(y)a*-suffix).

'One hundred and fourth': JM *caüruttarasaya.*
'One hundred and fifth': JM *pañcuttarasaya.*
'One hundred and sixth': JM *cha-uttarasaya.*
'One hundred and seventh': JM *sattuttarasaya.*
'One hundred and eighth': JM *aṭṭhuttarasaya.*
'One hundred and ninth': JM *navuttarasaya.*
'One hundred and tenth': JM *dasuttarasaya.*
'One hundred and eleventh': JM *egādasuttarasaya*; Inscr. (Kh.) *ekadaśa* < *śa* > *timaya* (with *-(y)a*-suffix).
'One hundred and twelfth': JM *bārasuttarasaya.*
'One hundred and thirteenth': JM *terasuttarasaya.*
'One hundred and fourteenth': JM *cauddasuttarasaya.*
'One hundred and fifteenth': JM *pañcadasuttarasaya.*
'One hundred and sixteenth': JM *solasuttarasaya.*
'One hundred and seventeenth': JM *sattadasuttarasaya.*
'One hundred and eighteenth': JM *aṭṭhadasuttarasaya.*
'Three hundred and ninety-sixth': Inscr. (Kh.) *ekuṇacaduśatimaa* (with *-(y)a*-suffix).
'One thousandth': Pāli *sahassima* (Edgerton 1953); BHS *sahasrima.*

6.3. Other numerals

6.3.1. Fractions less than one

'One thousandth': Aś. *sahasabhāga, ṣahaṣabhāga, sahasrabhaga.*
'One hundreth': Aś. *satabhāga, ṣatebhāga* (mistake for *ṣata-*), *śatabhaga.*
'One sixty-seventh': AMg. *sattaṭṭhi-bhāya* (Sūr.).
'One-eighth': Aś. *aṭhabhāgiya.*
'One-fourth': Pāli *catubbhāga*; Gā. *cadubhaka.* Also Pāli *pāda*; Niya *pata, pada* (Stein 1936); Inscr. (W) *pāya.* (OInd. *pā́da-* 'foot, quarter', reputedly because one foot of a quadruped is a quarter.)
'One-third': Pāli *tibhāga* (PTC); AMg. *tibhāga*; Ap. *tihāa* (all from OInd. *trí-bhāga-*, which can also mean 'three-fourths').
'One-half': Pāli *addha, aḍḍha*; Aś. *aḍha-* (in compounds); AMg. *addha, aḍḍha*; JM *addha, aḍḍha*; SinPkt. *aḍa*; Ap. *addha, aḍḍha.* See also AMg. *dubhāga* (Sheth 1963 so, but see next).
'Two-thirds': AMg. *dubhāga* (Sheth 1963 takes this as 'one-half'. In Old Indian *dví-bhāga-* means 'double portion or share'. In Ardha-Māgadhī it probably means 'having two portions (out of three)'; see next).
'Three-fourths': AMg. *tibhāga* 'having three parts (out of four)' – it can also mean 'one-third'. Also Inscr. (W) *pāyūna* '(one) less by a quarter'.

6.3.2. Fractions greater than one

'One and a half': Aś. *diyaḍha, diaḍha*; AMg. *divaḍḍha* (with glide *-v-* replacing *-y-*); Ap. *diyaḍḍha*.
'One and three-quarters': Inscr. (W) *pāonaduka* 'two less a quarter'.
6.3.2.1. Integers plus a half are expressed by compounding together *addha-* or *aḍḍha-* and the cardinal or ordinal of the next highest number. The Ardha-Māgadhī forms are quoted from Sūryaprajñapti, unless otherwise stated.
'Two and a half': Pāli *aḍḍhatiya, aḍḍhateyya*; Aś. *aḍhatiya, aḍhātiya*; AMg. *aḍḍhāijja*; BHS *aḍḍhatiya, aḍḍhātiya*; Ap. *aḍḍhāiya* (Bhav.).
'Three and a half': Pāli *addhacatuttha* (Jātaka v 418, n. 19), *aḍḍha-uḍḍha* (from *ardha-* + **turtha-* (cf. OInd. *túrya-* and *turī́ya-*) with voicing *-ṭṭh-* > *-ḍḍh-*); AMg. *addhauṭṭha*; Ap. *āuṭṭha* (with *ā-* < **ādha-* < *addha-*, with loss of *-h-*).
'Four and a half': AMg. *addhapaṃcama*.
'Five and a half': AMg. *addhachaṭṭha*; Ap. *addhachaṭṭha*.
'Six and a half': AMg. *addhasattama*.
'Seven and a half': Pāli *aḍḍhaṭṭha* (PTC so; PED translates 'half of eight', i.e. 'four'); AMg. *addhaṭṭhama*.
'Eight and a half': Pāli *aḍḍhanavama*; AMg. *addhanavama*.
'Nine and a half': AMg. *addhadasama*.
'Ten and a half': AMg. *addhĕkkārasa*.
'Eleven and a half': AMg. *addhabārasa*.
'Twelve and a half': Pāli *aḍḍhatelasa, aḍḍhateḷasa*; AMg. *addhaterasa*.
'Thirteen and a half': AMg. *addhacŏddasa*.
'Fourteen and a half': AMg. *addhapaṇṇarasa*.
'Fifteen and a half': AMg. *addhasolasa*.
'Sixteen and a half': AMg. *addhasattarasa*.
'Seventeen and a half': AMg. *addhaṭṭhārasa*.
'Eighteen and a half': AMg. *addheūṇavīsaṃ*.
'Nineteen and a half': AMg. *addhavīsaṃ*.
'Twenty and a half': AMg. *addhĕkkavīsaṃ*.
'Twenty-one and a half': AMg. *addhabāvīsaṃ*.
'Twenty-two and a half': AMg. *addhatevīsaṃ*.
'Twenty-three and a half': AMg. *addhacauvvīsaṃ*.
'Twenty-four and a half': AMg. *addhapaṇṇavīsaṃ*.
'Twenty-five and a half': AMg. *addhachavvīsam*.
'Forty-one and a half': AMg. *addhaducattālīsaṃ*.

'Forty-six and a half': AMg. *addhasīālīsaṃ*.
'Fifty-one and a half': AMg. *addhabāvaṇṇaṃ*.
'Fifty-eight and a half': AMg. *addha-eūṇasaṭṭhi*.

6.3.3. Aggregatives

The terms denote 'group of *n*'. Forms attested are:
'Two': Pāli *duka*; AMg. *duga, duya*; JM, JŚaur. *duga*.
'Three': Pāli *tika*; AMg., JM *tiya*.
'Four': Pāli *catukka*.
'Five': Pāli *pañcaka* (PTC):
'Six': Pāli *chakka* (PTC); AMg. *chakka*; SinPkt. *śaya* (with *s*- > *ś*-).
'Eight': Pāli *aṭṭhaka* (PTC).
'Nine': Pāli *navaka* (PTC).
'Ten': Pāli *dasaka* (PTC).
'Twelve': Inscr. (W) *bārasaka* (Sen 1960).
'Thirty-five': Inscr. (W) *pacatriśaka* (Sen 1960).
'One hundred': Pāli *sataka*.

6.3.4. Multiplicatives

These adverbs, except for 'once', are formed with the suffix Pāli -*khattuṃ*, AMg. -*(k)khutto*, Mā. -*huttaṃ* < OInd. *kṛ́tvaḥ*.
'Once': Pāli *saki, sakiṃ* (< OInd. *sakṛ́t*); AMg. *saiṃ*.
'Twice': Pāli *dvikkhattuṃ* (with -*kkh*- generalized from *tikkhattuṃ* 'three times' [PTC]); AMg. *dukhutto, dukkhutto* (< **dukṛtvas*).
'Three times': Pāli *tikkhattuṃ* (< OInd. *triṣ kṛ́tvaḥ* [Whitney 1889: § 1105]); so CPD); AMg. *tikhutto, tikkhutto*; BHS *tṛṣkṛtva*.
'Four times': Pāli *catukkhattuṃ*.
'Five times': Pāli *pañcakkhattuṃ* (PTC).
'Six times': Pāli *chakkhattuṃ*.
'Seven times': Pāli *sattakkhattuṃ* (PED); AMg. *sattakhutto, sattakkhutto*.
'Ten times': Pāli *dasakkhattuṃ* (PTC).
'Eighteen times': Pāli *aṭṭhārasaṃ khattuṃ* (PTC).
'Twenty-one times': AMg. *tisattakkhutto* ('thrice seven times').
'Twenty-five times': Pāli *pañcavīsatikkhattuṃ* (PTC).
'Twenty-nine times': Pāli *ekūnatiṃsakkhattuṃ* (PTC).
'Thirty times': Pāli *tiṃsakkhattuṃ* (PTC).

'Thirty-six times': Pāli *chattiṃsakkhattuṃ* (PTC).
'Fifty times': Pāli *paṇṇāsakkhattuṃ* (PTC).
'Fifty-one times': Pāli *ekapaṇṇāsakkhattuṃ* (PTC).
'Fifty-five times': Pāli *pañcapaṇṇāsakkhattuṃ* (PTC).
'Fifty-eight times': Pāli *aṭṭhapaṇṇāsakkhattuṃ* (PTC).
'Seventy-five times': Pāli *pañcasattatikkhattuṃ* (PTC).
'A hundred times': Pāli *satakkhattuṃ*; Mā. *saahuttaṃ*.
'A thousand times': Mā. *sahassahuttaṃ*.

6.3.5. Partitives

These adverbs give the idea of 'into *n* parts, in *n* ways', and are formed by the addition of the suffix *-dhā* > *-hā*.
'In two': Pāli *dvidhā, dvedhā* (there is no trace of the use of **dveḷhā*, which Smith (1930) derived from **dviž-dhā-*, in this sense, although Pāli *dveḷhaka* 'doubt' is clearly based upon it [PTC]); AMg. *duhā*.
'In three': Pāli *tidhā* (PTC); AMg. *tihā*.
'In four': Pāli *catudhā* (PTC); AMg. *cauhā*.
'In five': Pāli *pañcadhā* (PTC); AMg. *paṃcahā*.
'In six': Pāli *chaddhā* (< OInd. *ṣaḍdhā́* (PED)); AMg. *chahā*.
'In seven': Pāli *sattadhā*; AMg. *sattahā*.
'In eight': Pāli *aṭṭhadhā* (PTC); AMg. *aṭṭhahā*.
'In nine': AMg. *ṇavahā*.
'In ten': Pāli *dasadhā* (PTC); AMg. *dasahā*.
'In fourteen': AMg. *cauddasahā*.
'In sixteen': AMg. *chaddasadhā* (Sheth 1963).
'In twenty': AMg. *vīsahā*.
'In thirty-one': AMg. *ĕkkatīsahā* (Sūr.).
'In sixty-one': AMg. *egaṭṭhihā* (Sūr.).
'In one hundred': Pāli *satadhā*; JM *sayahā* (Sheth 1963).
'In one thousand': Pāli *sahassadhā*; JM *sahassahā* (Sheth 1963).

Note

1. The numerals from 'five' onwards make no distinction of gender, although the later grammarians teach (doubtless artificial) feminine forms, which are not listed here.

Abbreviations

Dialects, etc.

AMg.	Ardha-Māgadhī	(Kh.)	Kharoṣṭhī inscriptions
Ap.	Apabhraṃśa	Mā.	Māhārāṣṭrī
Aś.	Aśokan inscriptions	Mg.	Māgadhī
BHS	Buddhist Hybrid Skt	MIA	Middle Indo-Aryan
(C)	Central	NIA	New Indo-Aryan
CuP	Cūlikā Paiśācī	OIA	Old Indo-Aryan
Dā.	Dākṣiṇātyā	Pkt.	Prakrit
Ḍh.	Ḍhakkī	(S)	Southern
(E)	Eastern	Śaur.	Śaurasenī
Gā.	Gāndhārī	(Shah.)	Shābhāzgaṛhī
(Gir.)	Girnār	SinPkt.	Sinhalese Prakrit
IE	Indo-European	Skt.	Sanskrit
Inscr.	Inscriptional Pkts	Ud.	Udayagiri cave inscription of Khāravela
JM	Jain Māhārāṣṭrī		
JŚaur.	Jain Śaurasenī	(W)	Western

Texts, etc.

Bhav.	Bhavisatta Kaha (Jacobi 1918)
Clvs.	Cūlavaṃsa (Geiger 1926–27)
Erz.	Ausgewählte Erzählungen in Māhārāṣṭrī (Jacobi 1886)
Hp.	Harivaṃśapurāṇa (= Alsdorf 1936)
Kp.	Kumārapālapratibodha (Alsdorf 1928)
Mhvs.	Mahāvaṃsa (Geiger 1908)
Mp.	Mahāpurāṇa (Vaidya 1937–41)
Pp.	Prākṛta-paiṅgala (Vyas 1959–62)
Paum.	Paumacariu of Svayambhūdeva (Bhayani 1953–60)
PC.	Paumacariyaṃ of Vimala Sūri (Jacobi 1914)
Samav.	Samavāyaṃga (fourth aṅga of the Jain canon)
Sanat.	Sanatkumāracaritam (Jacobi 1921)
Sūr.	Sūryaprajñapti (Kohl 1937)
Viy.	Viyāhapannatti (fifth aṅga of the Jain canon)

Dictionaries, periodicals, etc.

BSL	Bulletin de la Société de Linguistique de Paris
BSOS	Bulletin of the School of Oriental Studies, London
CII	Corpus inscriptionum indicarum
CDIAL	Comparative dictionary of the Indo-Aryan languages (Turner 1966)
CPD	Critical Pāli Dictionary

Ep. Ind.	Epigraphia Indica
IHQ	Indian Historical Quarterly
MW	Sanskrit – English Dictionary (Monier-Williams 1899)
PED	Pāli – English Dictionary
PSM	Pāia-sadda-mahaṇṇavo (Sheth 1963)
PTC	Pāli Tipiṭakaṃ Concordance
PTS	Pali Text Society

References

Alsdorf, Ludwig
1928 *Der Kumārapālapratibodha* (Hamburg).
1936 *Harivaṃśapurāṇa* (Hamburg).
Barua, Beni Madhab
1938 "Hāthigumphā Inscription of Khāravela", *IHQ* XIV; 459–485.
Bhayani, Harivallabh C.
1953–1960 *Paumacariu of Svayambhūdeva* (3 vols.) (Bombay).
Boyer, A. M. – Rapson, Edward James – Senart, Émile – Noble, P. S.
1929 *Kharoṣṭhī inscriptions* (Oxford).
Brough, John
1962 *The Gāndhārī Dharmapada* (London).
Burrow, Thomas
1937 *The language of the Kharoṣṭhī documents from Chinese Turkestan* (Cambridge).
Childers, Robert Caesar
1874 *A dictionary of the Pāli language* (London).
Edgerton, Franklin
1953 *Buddhist Hybrid Sanskrit grammar* (New Haven).
Geiger, Wilhelm
1908 *Mahāvaṃsa* (London: PTS).
1925–1927 *Cūlavaṃsa* (2 vols.) (London: PTS).
1956 *Pāli literature and language* (second edition) (Calcutta).
Hare, E. M. – Norman, K. R. – Warder, Anthony Kennedy
1952– *Pāli Tipiṭakaṃ concordance* (London: PTS).
Hultzsch, E.
1926 *The Inscriptions of Asoka* (new edition), *CII* I (Oxford).
Jacobi, Hermann
1886 *Ausgewählte Erzählungen in Māhārāṣṭrī* (Leipzig).
1914 *Paumacariyaṃ of Vimala Sūri* (Bhavnagar).
1918 *Bhavisatta Kaha von Dhaṇavāla* (Munich).
1921 *Sanatkumāracaritam* (Munich).

Karunaratne, W. S.
1984 *Brāhmī inscriptions of Ceylon , Epigraphia Zeylanica* VII (Special Volume).
Kohl, J. F.
1937 *Die Sūryaprajñapti: Versuch einer Textgeschichte* (Stuttgart).
Konow, Sten
1929 "Kharoṣṭhī inscriptions" [with the exception of those of Aśoka], *CII* II, Part 1 (Calcutta).
Lüders, Heinrich
1912 "A list of Brāhmī inscriptions from the earliest times to about A. D. 400" [with the exception of those of Aśoka], Appendix to *Epigraphia Indica* X: 1–226.
Mehendale, M. A.
1948 *Historical grammar of inscriptional Prakrits* (Poona).
Monier-Williams, Sir Monier
1899 *Sanskrit-English Dictionary* (new edition) (Oxford).
Paranavitane, S.
1970 *Inscriptions of Ceylon* (Vol. I: *Early Brāhmī inscriptions*) (Colombo).
Pischel, Richard
1957 *Comparative grammar of the Prakrit languages* (Benares).
Sen, S.
1960 *A comparative grammar of Middle Indo-Aryan* (second edition) (Poona).
Sheth, H. D. T.
1963 *Pāia-sadda-mahaṇṇavo* (second edition) (Benares).
Sircar, Dines Chandra
1965 *Select inscriptions* Vol. I (second edition) (Calcutta).
Smith, Helmer
1930 "Procès-verbaux des séances, 23 March 1929", *BSL* 30: xviii.
Stede, William – Rhys Davids, T. W.
1925 *Pāli-English Dictionary* (London: PTS).
Stein, Otto
1936 "Numerals in the Niya inscriptions", *BSOS* VIII: 763–779.
Tagare, Ganesh Vasuder
1948 *Historical grammar of Apabhraṃśa* (Poona).
Trenckner, V. – Andersen, D. – Smith, Helmer – Hendriksen, Hans
1924 *Critical Pāli dictionary* (Copenhagen).
Turner, Ralph L.
1966 *Comparative dictionary of the Indo-Aryan languages* (London).
Upasak, Chandrika Singh
1960 *The history and palaeography of the Mauryan Brāhmī script* (Nalanda).
Vaidya, P. L.
1937–1941 *Maha-purāṇa of Puṣpadanta* (3 vols.) (Bombay).

Vyas, B. S.
1959–1962 *Prākṛta-paiṅgala* (2 vols.) (Benares).
Wackernagel, Jacob
1896–1957 *Altindische Grammatik* (3 vols.) (Göttingen).
Whitney, William Dwight
1889 *Sanskrit grammar* (second edition) (Harvard).

Chapter 7
Modern Indo-Aryan

Hermann Berger

Translated from the German by Susan Daugherty

7.0. Introduction

The Modern Indo-Aryan numerals deserve special attention within the framework of general historical linguistics because they seem to violate a psychological principle which, to the extent that one can generalize, applies in all natural languages, namely, that only the numbers from one to ten are formed from independent stems which are etymologically unrelated to each other; the numbers from ten to roughly twenty and the decads are more or less irregular, but nevertheless recognizable in their derivation; the units from twenty-one on, on the other hand, can be formed according to a recognizable pattern by anyone who has mastered the most important formation rules. When learning Hindī or another Modern Indo-Aryan language, however, one cannot form a higher number, say fifty-three, from *drei* and *fünfzig* as in German, or from *fifty* and *three* as in English, but rather must learn *tirpan* 'fifty-three', as a separate word. The connection with *tīn* 'three' and *pacās* 'fifty' is barely recognizable in the inital sounds, and even a comparison with numbers that have a component in common with 'fifty-three' reveals no regularity: although 'three' appears as *tir* also in *tirsaṭh* 'sixty-three', *tirāsī* 'eighty-three', and *tiranāve* 'ninety-three', it appears as *te-* in *teis* 'twenty-three', as *ten* in *tentis* 'thirty-three', and *tentālīs* 'forty-three', and as *ti-* in *tihattar* 'seventy-three'; *-pan* 'fifty' is also present in *pacpan* 'fifty-five' and *chappan* 'fifty-six', but the other units of fifty have *-wan*, as in *bāwan* 'fifty-two', *cauwan* 'fifty-four' and so on.

Since the earlier stages of the Indo-Aryan languages are well-documented, the causes of this irregularity can be investigated with some degree of confidence. They are not, as one would initially suspect, to be found exclusively in the rigorous implementation of Modern Indo-Aryan sound laws which have not been followed by analogical levelling, but also in the peculiar place of numerals within the linguistic system in general. The extremely abstract character of the numerals makes it likely that the series of natural numbers is subject to mechanical repetition more than any other series of words. The consequence of this is not only a tendency to increased phonetic erosion[1] extending beyond the "regular" sound changes, but often also an analogical change in the stem which is not, as with other words, based on an internal semantic relationship, but, rather, exclusively upon the external impetus of the neighboring items within the series of numerals. Very frequently phonetic traits of the next numeral are anticipated, as in Marāṭhī *bevīs* 'twenty-two' (beside the regular *bāvīs*) anticipating *teīs* 'twenty-three'. Assimilation to the preceding numeral, as, for instance, in Sinhalese *anū* 'ninety' for **nū*, from *asū* 'eighty' is much rarer. In some cases, an analogy based on one numeral has affected a whole series of numerals. For example, *tir-* for *ti-* 'three' from Hindī *tirāsī* 'eighty-three' (which is itself taken over from *caurāsī* 'eighty-four' < Sanskrit *caturaśīti*) is thus extended in many languages also to 'forty-three', 'fifty-three', 'sixty-three', and 'seventy-three' and, in Bengāli, also to *birāsi* 'eighty-two'; Marāṭhī *byāsyśi* 'eighty-two' < Sanskrit *dvyaśīti* via **dvyāśīti*) has passed on its *-yā-* to all other compounds with 'eighty'. But such serial analogies are often very inconsistent and incomplete; cf. the distribution of *aḍh-*, *aṛ-*, etc. for *aṭṭh-* 'eight' in compounds (see 7.1.8.), or the alternating *-y-*, *-c-*, *-t-* in compounds with 'forty' (Hindī *cālīs* etc., see 7.1.13.2.0.). Probably the only explanation here is the assumption of borrowing between related neighboring languages, to which the numerals, as the most important words of trade, are again more subject than other words.

The usual development, comparable to the European pattern, is shown by three language groups which, due to their early isolation, have followed their own course in other respects as well. Sinhalese today has old forms only for the numerals from 'one' to 'twenty' and the decads to 'hundred'; all other numerals are formed analytically. Turner (1966: 600, 7661, 12786) cites a few forms inherited from the earlier language (for example under 'thirty-three', 'thirty-five', 'thirty-six'). The Dardic-Kafiri languages in Northwest India have old forms for the numbers to 'twenty' and for 'one hundred' ('thirty' is an isolated case in Shina *c̣ī(h)*, Pashai *trīw*) and, beginning with 'thirty', form the decads analytically according to a vigesimal system (cf. e. g., Shina *c̣e-byo ga dái* 'seventy', i. e. $3 \times 20 + 10$). Lastly, the Gypsies count in Indian only to 'six', retain the words for 'ten' and 'hundred', and make up the rest of the numeral system with new analytical formations or borrowings.

The peculiar character of the Indian numeral system as described above implies that each of the numerals from 'one' to 'one hundred' must be treated individually. On the other hand, the large number of languages involved makes an exhaustive discussion of the topic impractical in view of the intended length of this study. I have attempted instead to work out the major lines of development and pointed out, above all, the analogical formations in language-specific changes, considering only those sound changes that are particularly striking. For the same reason, when individual languages show parallel development, only a selection of forms, predominantly from the better-known North Indian literary languages, are presented as examples: the remainder are all readily accessible in R. L. Turner's (1966) *Comparative dictionary of the Indo-Aryan languages.*[2]

Both the Sanskrit form and the corresponding Middle Indo-Aryan form are listed in each case, but this does not mean that the Modern Indo-Aryan form is always to be derived from the Middle Indo-Aryan. In its recorded form, Middle Indo-Aryan offers only a small selection of the actual range of variants, and indeed already exhibits strongly specialized forms itself in places. It is therefore often necessary to go back to the Sanskrit form for the source. Turner has even pointed out examples which show a closer affinity with forms from Iranian and other Indo-European languages (cf. the treatment of 'three', 'six', 'eleven', 'fourteen', 'forty', Turner 1966: 5994, 12 803, 2485, 4653, 4656).

7.1. Cardinals

7.1.0. 'One'

By far the greatest part of the Modern Indo-Aryan forms can be traced back to the form *ekka*, which first appears in Prakrit for Sanskrit, Pali *eka*: Sindhī *eku*, Hindī *ek*, Oṛiyā *eka*, etc. In Berger 1958 (p. 20 f.), I ascribe this gemination to the emphatic pronunciation to which the numeral 'one' is frequently subject. The *h* in Sindhi *heko* 'unique', Lahndā *hekk, hikk* 'one', Panjābī *hek*^{o}, *hik*^{o} 'single', is also certainly of emphatic origin. Burushaski *hik*, Yasin *hek* 'one', used only in measurements and counting, are borrowed from *hekh* in the Kohistānī dialect of Shina (overlooked by Turner).[3] The use of *i* for *e* in Panjābī *ikk* 'one', *ikkā* 'single', Lahndā *hikk* 'one' is also already present in Prakrit *ikka*. The *g* in Bhojpurī *ego* is an unusual isolated phenomenon, although we encounter it in 'eleven' in other languages as well; compare with this the Prakrit *igga* 'one'. The "regular" Prakrit form *ēa*, with loss of the *k*, is preserved in Oṛiyā *e* 'one, only', Assamese *eṭā*, Nepālī *yeuṭā* (with extension *-ṭā*, particularly well-known from Bengali) and in some Dardic and Kafiri forms such as Khowār *i*, Tōrwālī *ē*, Ashkun *ač*, etc.

7.1.2. 'Two'

The two forms which occur in Prakrit, *dō* < Sanskrit **duvau* (Rigveda metrical variant of Classical *dvau*) and *duvē* < Sanskrit **duvē* (Rigveda metrical variant of Classical *dvē*) are both represented in Modern Indo-Aryan in about equal proportions: from *dō*: Hindī *do*, Panjābī *do*, Māṛwāṛī *do*, etc.; from *duvē*: Nepālī *dui*, Assamese *dui*, Bengali *dui*, Oṛiyā *dui*, and so on. In addition, there are occasional descendents of a form with initial *b* in Prakrit *bē*, Apabhraṁśa *bi*, which goes back to *dv-* (via **db-*) and is also dominant in all compounds with 'two' (Hindī *bārah* 'twelve', *bāīs* 'twenty-two', etc.); cf. Oṛiyā *beni* (in poetry, beside *dui, di* elsewhere), Gujarātī *be*, Marāṭhī *be*, Sindhī *ḇa*. The *-ṇṇ-* taken over from 'three' of Apabhraṁśa *doṇṇi* reappears in Marāṭhī *don*, Koṅkaṇī *dōni*, Hindī *donõ* 'both'; the *h*-form of Prakrit *doṇha(ṁ)* (Pischel 1900: 436) is continued in Old Bengali *dō̃ha* 'two' (Chatterji 1926: 786). The Dardic and Kafiri languages have *dū* almost exclusively. The cerebral in Lahndā *ḍū* (— perhaps influenced by *ṭre* 'three'?, cf. 7.1.9.) is unusual. Turner (1966: 6648), following Morgenstierne (1957: 91), derives Khowār *jū* from **dyu* < **dui*.

7.1.3. 'Three'

In the purely Indian languages the convenient neuter form, Pāli *tīṇi*, Prakrit *tiṇṇi* < Sanskrit *trīṇi*, has become dominant almost everywhere; cf. Hindī *tīn*, Panjābī *tinn*, Assamese *tini*, Oṛiyā *tini*, etc. and, with preservation of the *r*, Old Gujarātī *triṇṇi*, Gujarātī *traṇ*[i]. Descendents of the masculine form, Sanskrit *trayaḥ*, Middle Indo-Aryan *tayo* are preserved in Sindhī *ṭrē*, Lahndā (Khetrānī dialect) *trē*, Panjābī *tare*, Old Sinhalese *te*, as also in many Dardic-Kafiri forms such as Waigalī *trē* Shina *ċē*, etc. Other forms of the same language-family, as in Dameli *trâ*, Tōrwālī *ċā*, Lahndā *trāe, trai*, Panjābī (Bhaṭĕālī subdialect of Ḍogrī) *trai* are derived by Turner (1966: 5994) from **trāyaḥ*, which is attested in Avestan (as *θrāyō*) but not in Sanskrit. In compounds, 'three' appears as the regular *te-, ti-*, and also as *tir-, tar-* as in Hindī *tirpan* 'fifty-three',

Panjābī *tarehaṭ* 'sixty-three', etc. Here it is not the *r* of Sanskrit *tri-*, *trayaḥ* which has been preserved, but rather there is a serial analogy based on Hindī *tirāsī* 'eighty-three' for **tiyāsī* (< Sanskrit *tryaśīti-*), which itself has taken over the *r* from Hindī *caurāsī* 'eighty-four' (< Sanskrit *caturaśīti-*).

7.1.4. 'Four'

Sanskrit *catvā́raḥ*, Middle Indo-Aryan *cattāro* is preserved only in Sinhalese *satara* and in a few northwestern forms, such as Ashkun *ċatā́*, Prasun *čpū*; the majority of the Dardic languages present variants which derive from the zero grade masculine plural accusative Sanskrit *caturaḥ*, Prakrit *caürō*, such as Ḍumāki *čaur*, Bashkarīk *čōr*, Phalūṛa *čūr*, etc. – also Indian as in Kashmiri *ċōr*, dial. *ċaur, ċāur*; Panjābī (Bhaṭĕālī) *caur*, Old Awadhī obl.pl. *cahuṁ*. The aspiration in Khowār *chor*, from *çhoi* 'six', is noteworthy. On the other hand, the majority of the purely Indian forms present an unrounded vowel, in part preceded by *i*/*y*, cf. Hindī *cār*, Lahndā *cār*, Panjābī *cār*, Kumaunī *cār*, Nepālī *cār*, Sindhī *cāri*, Old Awadhī *cāri*, Old Bengali *ciāri*, Old Gujarātī *cyāri*, Old Hindī *cyār*, Marāṭhī *cyār*, etc. Obviously Middle Indo-Aryan **cayāri* underlies these, and, with Turner (1966: 4655), we are faced with the choice of assuming either an alteration of Pali *cattāri*, Prakrit *cattāri* (< Sanskrit n.pl. *catvāri*) by analogy with *caturaḥ* or "abnormal phonetic development in a numeral".

7.1.5. 'Five'

Pali *pañca*, Prakrit *paṁca* < Sanskrit *páñca* has yielded regular descendents in all languages, without complications, cf. Hindī *pā̃c*, Māṛwāṛī *pā̃c*, Gujarātī *pā̃c*, Maithilī *pā̃c*, Bengali *pā̃c*, Marāṭhī *pā̃ċ*, etc., with regular *j* in Panjābī *pañj*, Lahndā *pañj*, Sindhī *pañja*, etc., with further reduction in Shumashti *pōn*, Shina (Gilgitī) *poĩ*, and other northwestern forms.

7.1.6. 'Six'

The Modern Indo-Aryan forms seem to indicate that Sanskrit *ṣaṣ*, nom. *ṣaṭ* 'six' was only one of several dialectal variants. Turner (1966: 12 803) distinguishes three groups: 1) Descendants of *ṣaṣ*/*ṣaṭ*, only in the northwest, cf. Kashmiri *śĕ, śĕh*, West Pahāṛī *śāh*, Shina (Gilgitī) *ṣa*, and others.

2) Forms with a rounded vowel or *u*/*v* before *a*, which indicate **ṣuvaṭ*, for which there is a correspondence in other Indo-European forms with *w*, cf. Gaulish *suexos* 'the sixth', Greek dial. ϝεξ, and others. These forms, too, are confined to the northwest, cf. Shina (Kohistan) *ṣva*, Gawar-Bati *ṣᵘō, ṣōᵘ*, Ashkun *ṣu*, etc. – in addition, European Gypsy (as a Dardicism?) *šov*. 3) Without exception the Indian languages have initial *ch-* or regular developments thereof, cf. Hindī *cha*, Sindhī *cha*, Marāṭhī *saha, sā*, etc. as do all dialects already in Middle Indo-Aryan, cf. Pali *cha* (*chaḷ-* in compounds), Prakrit *cha*, Apabhraṁśa *chaha*. Turner explains these forms, together with some northwestern forms with *ch-* (Pashai *ċha, ċhā*, Khowār *ċhoi*, and so on) from **kṣaṭ*/*kṣvaṭ* [4] which, again, shows correspondence with forms outside India, such as Avestan *xšvaš*, Welsh *chwech*. Turner omits a further variant 4) **kṣai* or **kṣvai*, suggested as early as his *Comparative dictionary of the Nepali language: chaiṭaũ*, but then abandoned in his etymological dictionary; from this are derived Bengali *chay*, Assamese *say*, Khowār *ċhoi*, Panjābī *che, chī*, Lahndā *chẽ, chī*, among others; cf. in Iranian Sakian *kṣai*. The form *che-*/*chi-* also appears beside *cha-* in many compounds with 'six' (from 'forty-six' onwards), but here there seems to be a purely phonological change, which has spread from 'forty-six'.

7.1.7. 'Seven'

Pāli *satta*, Prakrit *satta* (< Sanskrit *sapta*) is transmitted without complications in phonologically regular forms, cf. Hindī *sāt*, Gujarātī *sāt*, Marāṭhī *sāt*, Bengāli *sāt*, etc.; Panjābī *satt*, Lahndā *satt*, etc. In compounds (in 'twenty-seven' and 'ninety-seven' in all languages, in 'fifty-seven' and 'sixty-seven' in some), long *ā* appears (*satā-* for *sat(a)-*) by analogy with the succeeding numerals with 'eight' (*aṭhā-*).

7.1.8. 'Eight'

On the whole, 'eight' developed regularly in the simplex, cf. Hindī *āṭh*, Nepālī *āṭh*, Gujarātī *āṭh*, Marāṭhī *āṭh*, etc.; Panjābī *aṭṭh*, Lahndā *aṭṭh*; in the northwest, Dameli *aṣṭ*, Khowār *oṣṭ*, etc. (< Pāli *aṭṭha*, Prakrit *aṭṭha* < Sanskrit *aṣṭā* (RV), *aṣṭau*). On the other hand, in compounds in several languages (and as early as Prakrit), occasional forms occur which point to *ḍḍh* instead of *ṭṭh*, cf. Hindī *aṛtīs* 'thirty-eight', Gujarātī *aṛtālīs* 'forty-eight', Prakrit *aḍhārasaga* 'eighteenth' (not mentioned by Turner (1931, 1966)), *aḍhāisa* 'twenty-eight', *aḍhasaṭṭhi* 'sixty-eight' (Kharosthi Inscriptions *aḍhasaṭhi*). We have the following distribution (the plus-sign indicates a *ḍḍh*-form):

	Kashmiri	Sindhī	Nepāli	Bhojpurī	Awadhī	Hindī	Gujarātī	Marāṭhī	Prakrit
'eighteen'	+	+					+		+
'twenty-eight'									+
'thirty-eight'				+	+	+	+	+(dial.)	
'forty-eigth'	+			+	+	+	+	+(dial.)	
'fifty-eight'	+								
'sixty-eight'	+		+	+	+	+	+	+(dial.)	+

Even if the distribution is obscure in detail, the accumulation under 'sixty-eight' nevertheless shows that the voicing of *ṭṭh* and its partial simplification (as already in Prakrit *aḍhāisa* 'twenty-eight') and deaspiration (as already in Prakrit *aḍasaṭṭhi*) have arisen through dissimilation (*aṭṭhasaṭṭhi* > *aḍ(ḍh)asaṭṭhi*).

7.1.9. 'Nine'

Beside normal correspondences such as Hindī *nau*, Nepālī *nau*, Bengali *na*, Assamese *na*, Gujarātī *nav*, etc. < Pali *nava*, Prakrit *ṇava* < Sanskrit *nava*, there are also forms with *m*: Hindī (dial.) *nam*, Sinhalese *namaya*, Bashkarīk *num* (beside *nab*), Tōrwālī *nom*, Kashmiri *nam* (beside *nau, nav*). Since this *m* also occurs in the northwest in the homonymous word 'new' (cf. Ḍumāki *nama*, Bashkarīk *nam*, Tōrwālī *nam*), it is presumably to be explained purely phonetically, by assimilation of the nasality, and not analogically (by means, for instance, of the influence of the Sanskrit ordinal *navama*); in this connection, forms with the nasalized vowel only, such as Sindhī *nãvã*, Panjābī *naũ*, Shina (Palesī) *nãũ* and others, may be regarded as transitional forms. The 'nine' forms hardly ever occur in compounds; except in 'ninety-nine', almost everywhere, with few exceptions, combinations of the next higher decad with *ūna-, ēkōna-*, **ēkūna-* predominate, of which the first two are already used in this way in Sanskrit.

7.1.10. 'Ten'

Sanskrit *daśa*, Pāli *dasa*, Prakrit *dasa*, has yielded regular forms almost everywhere; cf. Hindī *das*, Nepālī *das*, Bengali *das*, Bihārī *das*, Gujarātī *das*, etc.; Gypsy *deš*, Kati *duċ*, Dameli *daš*, etc. In Kashmiri *dah*, Sindhī *ḏaha*, Lahndā *ḏāh*, Maithilī *dah* (beside *das*), Marāṭhī *dahā* (beside *das*) and already in Prakrit *daha, h* appears instead of the sibilant, taken over from the compound numerals from 'eleven' to 'eighteen' (for the compositional form see below). The *ǰ* of Khowār *ǰoš* is peculiar; according to Morgenstierne (1957: 91), it has arisen by assimilation to *š*. The recursive cerebral in Sindhī *ḏaha*, Lahndā (Ju.) *ḏāh, ḏah* probably originates in *coḏãhã* 'fourteen', which is, also in Sindhī, the only number between 'ten' and 'twenty' in which the *d* has not become *r* (for the change *-rd-* > *-ḏ-* in Sindhī, see Turner (1966: 4035, 5722, 7931). Apart from 'fourteen' and 'sixteen', where special conditions obtain, the compounds with *-daśa* have, since Middle Indo-Aryan times, *-raha*, cf. Hindī *igārah* 'eleven', *bārah* 'twelve', etc. In *d* > *r*, there seems to be dissimilation against *d/t* in the front element (as in Middle Indo-Aryan *sattadasa* 'seventeen', early Middle Indo-Aryan **dvādasa* 'twelve') with later analogical spreading; cf. Middle Indo-Aryan *tārisa* 'such' < *tādisa* (< Sanskrit *tādṛśa*) (Berger 1953); similarly, in the northwest, forms in **-laśa* occur in Kandia and Maiyā̃, as in Maiyā̃ (Kanyawālī) *agāleš* 'eleven', *duwāleš* 'twelve', etc., which have spread from **trelaśa* 'thirteen' (cf. Pali *telasa* 'thirteen' beside *terasa*), dissimilated from **treraśa* < **tredaśa* (for *trayodaśa*, see 7.1.13.; and Berger 1953: 375) – cf. also the Shina forms of 'fifteen'. Similarly, *h* for *s* in *-raha* could be dissimilated against *s* of the front element (in *sattarasa* 'seventeen'), but it may be nothing more than a case of phonetic reduction necessitated by the mechanical repetition. It is only in the northwest that descendents of forms with *-daśa* are also found, as in Tōrwālī *agāš* 'eleven', Gawar-Bati *bāš* 'twelve', etc.

7.1.11. 'Teens'

7.1.11.1. 'Eleven'

Some of the forms go back to Sanskrit *ēkādaśa*, Pali *ēkadasa*, Prakrit *ēgādasa, ēgārasa*, with simple *k* > *g* > Ø; cf. Panjābī *yārā̃*, West Pahāṛī (Bhadravāhī) *yāhrē*, in the northwest Waigalī *yāš, žāš*, etc. – all via the transitional stage **yāaśa*, **yāraha*, with *e* > *y* before a vowel. Other languages have the same form as in the simplex for 'one' in the front element, i. e., *k* > *kk*, e. g. Marāṭhī *akrā*, Savi *yakāš*, Shina *ăkāĭ*, Kashmiri *kāh*, etc. or *g* < Middle Indo-Aryan **gg* also known from the simplex, e. g. Tōrwālī *agāš*, Maiyā̃ (Kanyawālī) *agāleš*, Hindī *igārah*. dial. *gyārah*, Bengali *egāra*, Oṛiyā *egāra*, Gujarātī *agyār*, and others. It is interesting to note, in the northwest, Ashkun *čanīs, činís*, Kati *yanīč*. Morgenstierne (1926: 65) explains this as deriving from **ēkaṁdaśa* (cf. Avestan *aēvan-dasa*). The *n* in Panjābī (Bhaṭĕālī) *nyārā* is surprising.

7.1.11.2. 'Twelve'

Forms with initial *d* are preserved only in the northwest and in Sinhalese and Maldivian; they go back to **duvādaśa* (which is still to be read in the Rigveda instead of Classical Sanskrit *dvādaśa* cf. Prakrit *duvālasa*, Aśoka *duvādasa*); cf. Kati *dyīč*, Prasun *wūzu, üz*, Pashai *duwāi*, and others, Sinhalese *doḷasa, doḷaha*, Maldivian *doḷos*. All Indian languages and a great part of the northwestern languages have *b*-; cf. Hindī *bārah, bārā*, Kumaunī *bāra*, Assamese *bāra*, Nepālī *bāra*, Bengali *bāra*, Oṛiyā *bāra*; Gujarātī *bār*, and others < Prakrit *bāraha*; Dameli *bâš*, Ashkun *bäis, bās*, Shina *bāĭ*, and others < **bādaśa*. As the comparison with the descendents of *dvāra-* / **dvara-* 'door' shows (Turner 1966: 6663, 6651), the change *dv-* > *b-* (via *db-*) is regular.

7.1.11.3. 'Thirteen'

The Indian forms and some of the northwestern forms go back, not to Sanskrit *trayōdaśa*, but to Middle Indo-Aryan *terasa* (Pali, Prakrit), *teraha* (Prakrit), *tedasa* (Aśoka), **tredaśa*, with an earlier stage **trayadaśa* (or, according to Turner, **trayēdaśa*), cf. Hindī *terah*, Nepālī *tera*, Assamese *tera*, Bengali *tera*, Oṛiyā *tera*, Gujarātī *tera*, Marāṭhī *terā*, Koṅkaṇī *terā*, etc., in the northwest, Kati *trīč*, Tōrwālī *çeš*, Phalūṛa *trēš*, etc. Only some of the northwestern languages have representatives of Sanskrit *trayōdaśa*, cf. Dameli *trōš*, Shina *çōi*, Kashmiri *truwāh*, and so on. The *l*-form, Pali *telasa* < * *trelasa* < *trerasa*, which arose by dissimilation, and which we postulated as the starting-point of the northwestern *l*-teens (7.1.10.) does not survive anywhere in the Indian languages. Turner, somewhat obscurely, designates Kandia *ṭrigōlaš*, Maiyā̃ *čigōlaš* as "new compounds"; apparently the *g* is introduced from Kandis *agālaš* 'eleven, Maiyā̃ (Kanyawālī) *agā́leš* 'eleven', but, curiously, bypassing Kandia *dwālaš* 'twelve', Maiyā̃ *dwālaš* (Kanyawālī *duwāleš*).

7.1.11.4. 'Fourteen'

This is the only numeral with *-daśa* in which the *d* is retained throughout, because it has been doubled by assimilation to the preceding *r*. Pali *catuddasa, caddasa, cuddasa*, Prakrit *cauddasa, cuddaha, coddasa, coddaha*

(< Sanskrit *cáturdaśa*) yields regular Hindī *caudah*, Maithilī *caudah*, Bengali *codda*, Panjābī *caudā̃*, etc.; in the northwest, Tirāhī *čauda*, Shumashti *ċäudas*, Waigalī *čadēs, čadīš*, etc. (for the *ḏ* of Sindhī *coḏãhã*, see 7.1.10.). In the northwest, the frequent forms with nasalization, such as Dameli *čandīš*, Gauro *ċanduš*, Shina *čondai*, and so on, are easily explained by analogy to 'fifteen' (cf. Dameli *pančēš*, Gauro *pánjiš*, Shina *pănzaĭ*). The northwestern forms Kati *štruċ, štruiċ, štrēċ*, Prasun *čpulċ, čpluz* are curious; Turner derives them from **catrudaśa* (with which he compares Avestan *caθrudasa*) and thus, like certain forms of 'six' and 'eleven' already mentioned above, they are closer to Iranian than to Sanskrit.

7.1.11.5. 'Fifteen'

Of the Middle Indo-Aryan forms, Pali *pañcadasa, paṇṇarasa*, Prakrit *paṁcadasa, pannarasa, pannārasa, paṇarasa* (< Sanskrit *pañcadaśa*), it is the *c*-less ones, probably due to early dissimilation against the *ś* of *-daśa*, which are the basis for all the Indian forms. Most of the languages have inserted a *d* between *n* and *r*, as in the word for 'ape': Sanskrit *vānara-* > Hindī *bā̃dar*, Marāṭhī *vā̃dar*, etc. – cf. Hindī *pandrah*, Lahndā *pandrā̃*, Panjābī *pandrā̃*, Assamese *pondara*, etc., but also Bengali *panera, ponera*, Old Gujarātī *panara*. The *c*-forms survive in the northwest, most with regular voicing *c* > *j* after a nasal, cf. Dameli *pančḗš*, Bashkarīk *pānža*, Shina *pănzaĭ*, etc., and in Sinhalese, *pasaḷos, pahaḷos, pahaḷova, pahaḷaha*. Turner has explained the Shina dialect forms Gurēsī *panzuleĩ*, Koh *panziläĩ*, Jijelut *paziläĩ*, Palesī *panzəlaĩ* as due to contamination of the *l*-teens as in Kandia and Maiyā̃ (see 7.1.10.) with the regular forms Gilgitī *pănzaĭ*. A more complicated development must be assumed, in the course of which first the *l* of **trelaśa* spread to a part of the teens, and then the *l* was, by analogy with the forms which remained unaffected, in its turn replaced in all forms (including 'thirteen' but excepting 'fifteen') by *d*, which later disappeared.

7.1.1.11.6. 'Sixteen'

Pali *sōḷasa*, Prakrit *sōḷasa, sōlasa, sōlaha, sōlā* (< Sanskrit *ṣōḍaśa*) regularly yields Hindī *solah*, Bengali *sola*, Oṛiyā *soḷa*, etc.; in the northwest, Shumashti *ṣoṛās*, Bashkarīk *ṣōhr, ṣōr*. In the northwest, Dameli *ṣoyāš*, Chilīs *šouš*, and others point to **ṣōdaśa*, with early assimilation to the other *-daśa* forms, Kati *ṣeċ*, Tōrwālī *ṣē^i^š* and so on to an *ē*-form (cf. Turner 1966: 12812).

7.1.11.7. 'Seventeen'

Pali *sattadasa, sattarasa*, Prakrit *sattadasa, sattarasa, sattaraha, sattara* (< Sanskrit *saptadaśa*), yield regular Hindī *sattrah*, Bengali *satera*, Oṛiyā *satara*, etc.; in the northwest, Tōrwālī *sattāš*, Kati *satiċ*, Savi *satās*. In Dameli *sattâš*, with *-āš* instead of the regular *-ḗš*, there is assimilation to *aṣṭâš* 'eighteen'; in Lahndā (Khetrānī) *sattāra*, Panjābī *satārā̃*, West Pahāṛī (Bhalesī) *satāre* and so on, the long connecting vowel is taken over from 'eighteen' (cf. 7.1.11.8.).

7.1.11.8. 'Eighteen'

Beside the regular descendents of Pali *aṭṭhādasa, aṭṭhārasa*, Prakrit *aṭṭhadasa, aṭṭhadaha, aṭṭhāraha, aṭṭhāra* (< Sanskrit *aṣṭādaśa*), such as Hindī *aṭhārah*, Bengali *āṭhāra*, Marāṭhī *aṭhrā* etc. and in the northwest, Dameli *aṣṭâš*, Tōrwālī *aṭhā́ⁱš*, there is in Sindhī *arḍahā̃* and Gujarātī *aḍhār*, a voicing of the *ṭh*, which has been explained above (7.1.8.). Gujarātī also has a variant with metathesis, *arāḍh*, which also appears with displacement of the aspiration as *harāṛ*.

7.1.11.9. 'Nineteen'

The majority of the Modern Indo-Aryan forms go back to Sanskrit *ūnaviṁśati*, which is not recorded in Middle Indo-Aryan; cf. Hindī *unnīs, unīs*, Sindhī *uṇvīha*, Bengali *unis*, etc.; in the northwest, Dameli *uṇyḗš*, Tōrwālī *anbīš*, etc. The doubling in West Pahāṛī (Curāhī) *unnī̃h*, (Bhalesī) *unnī* has arisen from the assimilation *nv* > *nn*, as is clearly seen from Lahndā *unnī* beside *unvī*. The other languages have descendents of Pali *ēkūnavīsati*, Assamese *ekunavīsati*, Prakrit *iguṇavīsaṁ, iguṇīvīsaṁ, aüṇavīsaṁ* < **ēkūnaviṁśati* for Sanskrit *ēkōnaviṁśatí*, as Marāṭhī *ekuṇvīs, ekuṇīs, ekoṇīs* (with *o*!), Sinhalese *ekunvis*, and so on. Forms occurring only in some northwestern languages such as Kati *näċ*, Prasun *nālċ, nāliz*, Pashai (Lauṛowānī) *nawī́*, (Darrai-i Nīri) *nau* (Areti) *naweu* < **nevadaśa* are probably independent coinages, although old, and need not go back to Sanskrit *navadaśa*, Prakrit *ṇavadaha*.

7.1.12. 'Twenty' to 'twenty-nine'

7.1.12.0. 'Twenty'

All languages point to the nasal-less variants of Pali *vīsati, vīsaṁ*, Prakrit *viṁsadi, vīsaï, vīsaṁ, vīsā* (< Sanskrit *viṁśatí*); cf. Hindī *bīs*, Gujarātī *vīs*, Marāṭhī *vīs*, Nepālī *bis*, etc., in the northwest, Khowār *bišir*, Tōrwālī *bīš*, etc. The *h* of Panjābī *vīh, bīh*, Sindhī *vīha*, and so on, is no doubt taken over from compounds such as Sindī *ekīha* 'eleven' *ḇāvīha* 'twelve', in which it has arisen, as already in Middle Indo-Aryan, in *-daha* < *-daśa*, either by loss of accentuation in mechanical repetition, or by dissimilation against *s* of the front element (Sindhī *satāvīha* 'seventeen' < **satāvīsa*, etc.). In the compound numerals 'twenty-one' to 'twenty-eight', the *v* is very often lost; here, too, the general tendency toward the shortest forms possible has probably led to the generalization of occasional, phonologically regular loss (cf. 7.1.12.2.) For Bengali *kuṛi* 'twenty', see 7.1.15.3.

7.1.12.1. 'Twenty-one'

Of Prakrit *ēgavīsā, ekkavīsaï, ekkavīsaṁ* (< Sanskrit *ékaviṁśati*) only the forms with *kk* survive in Gujarātī *ekvīs*, Marāṭhī *ekvīs*, Lahndā *ikvī* (< **ikkavīsaṁ*). The lengthening of the connecting vowel in Nepālī *ekāis*, Hindī *ikkāis* (beside *ikkīs, ekīs*) from the next numeral, 'twenty-two' (Hindī *bāīs*, etc.) and the loss of *v* in these same forms and in Hindī *ekīs*, Awadhī *ekais*, and so on (see 7.1.0.) are already recognizable in Prakrit *ēgāvīsā* and *ēāisa* respectively. In Lahndā *ikkī*, the *v* is assimilated to the *k*; cf. Lahndā *ikvī* 'twenty-one' and *unnī* 'nineteen' beside *unvī*. In Bengali *ekus*, the *v* labialized the following *i* before it was lost.

7.1.12.2. 'Twenty-two'

Of Pali *dvāvīsati, bāvīsati* Prakrit *bāvisa, bāisa* (< Sanskrit *dvāviṁśati*) only the *b-* form has developed regularly, as in Sindhī *bāvīha*, Gujarātī *bāvīs*; without *v* in Hindī *bāīs*, Nepālī *bāis*, Bengali *bāis*, Panjābī *bāī*, and so on, perhaps by a very old dissimilation *dvāviṁśati-* > **dvāiṁśati*. In Marāṭhī *bevīs* (beside *bāvīs*), the *e* is anticipated from *teīs* 'twenty-three'.

7.1.12.3. 'Twenty-three'

Pali *tēvīsa*, Prakrit *tēvīsaṁ*, Apabhraṁśa *tēisa* developed regularly everywhere, cf. Hindī *teīs*, Nepālī *teis*, Bengali *teis*, Lahndā *trēvī*, etc.; only West Pahāṛī (Bhalesī) *ṭḷebbī* has anticipated the *bb* of *ċōbbi* 'twenty-four'. Moreover, the Middle Indo-Aryan forms (just as in *terasa* 'thirteen' < **trayadaśa*, see 7.1.11.3.) seem to go back to **trayaviṁśati* or **trayē-viṁśati* instead of Sanskrit *trayōviṁśati*.

7.1.12.4. 'Twenty-four'

Of Pali *catuvīsati*, Prakrit *caüvīsaï, caüvīsa, cauvvīsa* (< Sanskrit *caturviṁśati*) there survive both the form with *-vv-* (Modern Indo-Aryan *-bb-* > *-b-*), cf. Hindī *caubīs*, Bengali *cabbiś*, Marāṭhī *ċavvīs*, West Pahāṛī (Bhalesī) *ċöbbi*, and the form with *-v-*, cf. Sindhī *covīh*, Panjābī *cauvī*, etc.

7.1.12.5. 'Twenty-five'

While forms with loss of the *c* are dominant in Middle Indo-Aryan, except in Pali *pañcavīsati, pañcavīsa* (beside *paṇṇavīsati, paṇṇuvīsaṁ* < Sanskrit *pañcaviṁśati*), Apabhraṁśa *pacīsaṁ*, Niya *pacaviśa*, cf. Prakrit *paṇṇavīsa, pannavīsaī, pannavīsaṁ, pannuvīsa*, the *c* is everywhere preserved in Modern Indo-Aryan, cf. Hindī *pacīs* and *paccīs* (not mentioned by Turner [1966: 7672], the doubling is due to *chabbīs* 'twenty-six), Bengali *pãcis*, Nepālī *pacis*, Sindhī *pañjavīha*, etc. The loss of the nasal in Hindī *pacīs*, Nepālī *pacis*, Gujarātī *pacīś*, Oṛiyā *pacisa*, already to be seen in the Apabhraṁśa, is hardly more than a "numeral-abbreviation". From Hindī *pacīs* is derived the name of a board game, *pacīsī*, which passed into English as *Patcheesi* and later *Parcheesi*.

7.1.12.6. 'Twenty-six'

Of the Middle Indo-Aryan variants, Pali *chabbīsati*,[5] Aśoka (Delhi-Toprā) *saḍuvīsati*, Prakrit *chavvīsaṁ, chahavīsa* < Sanskrit *ṣaḍviṁśati*, it is the one with geminated *-vv-/-bb-* which has become dominant; cf. Hindī *chabbīs*, Bengali *chābbiś*, Gujarātī *chavvīs*, etc.

7.1.12.7. 'Twenty-seven'

In all languages there is a lengthening of the connecting vowel by analogy with 'twenty-eight', which is already present in Prakrit *sattāvīsaṁ* (against Pali *sattavīsati* < Sanskrit *saptaviṁśati*); cf. Hindī *satāīs*, Bengali *sātāis*, Gujarātī *sattāvīś*; cf. 7.1.7.

7.1.12.8. 'Twenty-eight'

The *-ḍh-* of Prakrit *aḍhāisa* (cf. 7.1.8.), which derives from 'sixty-eight' has not continued anywhere; all languages have regular developments of Pali *aṭṭhāvīsati*, Prakrit *aṭṭhāvīsaï, aṭṭhāvīsa, aṭṭhāīsa* < Sanskrit *aṣṭāviṁśati*; cf. Hindī *aṭhāwīs, aṭhāīs*, Bengali *āṭās* (*ṭ* instead of *ṭh* from *āṭ* 'eight'), Nepālī *aṭhāis*, etc.

7.1.12.9. 'Twenty-nine'

The basis is in part **ēkkōnatriṁśat* (**ek-*, **egg-*)/**ēkkūnatriṁśat*, cf. Kashmiri *kunatr*^{a}*h*, Awadhī *ontis*, Old Gujarātī *ugaṇatrīsa*, Gujarātī *ogaṇ-trīs*, Marāṭhī *ekuṇtīs*, in part Sanskrit *ūnatriṁśat*, as in Hindī *untīs*, Bengali *untrīs*, Panjābī *uṇattī*, and so on. In Middle Indo-Aryan, Prakrit *aüṇat-tīsaṁ* is the only form recorded; Nepālī *unantis* has its *-an-*, as in 'thirty-nine', from *unañcās* 'forty-nine' < Sanskrit *ūnapañcāśat*.

7.1.13. 'Thirty' to 'ninety-nine'

7.1.13.1. 'Thirty'

Beside the normal continuations such as Hindī *tīs*, Marāṭhī *tīs*, Panjābī *tīh*, Nepālī *tis*, and so on, from Pali *tiṁsa, tiṁsati*, Prakrit *tīsaṁ, tīsā, tīsaïṁ* < Sanskrit *triṁśat*, there also occur forms with preserved *tr-* as in Sindhī *ṭrīha*, Lahndā *trīh*, Gujarātī *trīś* (beside *tīś*), Bengali *tris*, Assamese *trix*, Oṛiyā *triśa*, which can be explained by Sanskrit influence in the eastern languages (Bengali, Assamese, Oṛiyā) and by association with 'three' (Gujarātī *traṇ*, etc.) in the western languages (Chatterji 1926).

7.1.13.1.1. 'Thirty-one'

Hindī *ikattīs, ektīs*, Bengali *ektris*, Panjābī *ikattarī, ikattī*, and so on < Middle Indo-Aryan **ekkattīsaṁ*, Sanskrit *ekatriṁśat*.

7.1.13.1.2. 'Thirty-two'

All forms except Kashmiri *dŏyĕtr*^{a}*h* have initial *b* (cf. 7.1.2.) as in Prakrit *battīsa, battisa*, Apabhraṁśa *batīsa* (as opposed to Pali *dvattiṁsa*) < Sanskrit *dvātriṁśat*, cf. Hindī *battīs*, Gujarātī *batrīs*, Bengali *battis*, etc.

7.1.13.1.3. 'Thirty-three'

Hindī *tetīs*, Bengali *tetris*, Gujarātī *tetrīś*, etc. < Pali *tettiṁsati, tettiṁsa*, Prakrit *tettīsaṁ* (beside *tittīsaṁ*, Old Sinhalese *tavutisā*, Ardha-Māgadhī *tāyattīsa*) < Sanskrit *trayastriṁśat*. The nasalization of Awadhī *tẽ̄tīs*, Hindī *tẽtīs* is, like that of *caũtīs* 'thirty-four', taken over in the first place from *paĩtīs* 'thirty-five', which, in turn, has been assimilated to 'forty-five' (see 7.1.13.2.5.).

7.1.13.1.4. 'Thirty-four'

Marāṭhī *ċautīs*, Gujarātī *cotrīs*, Sindhī *coṭrīha*, and so on < Prakrit **cauttīsa*, cf. Pali *catuttiṁsatima* 'thirty-fourth', Prakrit *cautīsa, cautisa.* Nasalization in Hindī *caũtīs*, Awadhī *cãũtis*, Nepālī *caũtis*, from 'forty-five' (see 7.1.13.1.2.).

7.1.13.1.5. 'Thirty-five'

The nasalized *i*-diphthong virtually throughout in Hindī *paĩtīs*, Bengali *pãĩtriś*, Panjābī *paĩtī*, and so on, is, like the nasalization in Oṛiyā *paãtisa*, taken over from 'forty-five' (Hindī *paĩtālīs*, etc.). Kashmiri *pānċatr*^{a}*h*, Sindhī *pañjaṭrīha*, Marāṭhī *pastīs* point to the regular form Prakrit **paṁ-cattīsa* < Sanskrit *pañcatriṁśat*, while Prakrit *paṇatīsaṁ* is to be found in Gujarātī *pā̃trīś, pā̃trī*, Sinhalese *pantis*.

7.1.13.1.6. 'Thirty-six'

Hindī *chattīs*, Marāṭhī *chattīs*, Gujarātī *chattrīs*, Panjābī *chattī*, Sinhalese *satisa*, etc. < Prakrit *chattīsaṁ, chattīsā*; Pali *chattiṁsati, chattiṁsa* [6] < Sanskrit *ṣaṭtriṁśat*.

7.1.13.1.7. 'Thirty-seven'

Beside the regular Sindhī *sataṭrīha*, Lahndā *satattrī*, Assamese *xātatris*, there are also forms which show influence of the word for 'thirty-five' (Hindī *paĩtīs*, etc.), bypassing 'thirty-six'; cf. Hindī *saĩtīs*, Bengali *saĩ̄tris*, Nepālī *saĩtis*, Panjābī *saĩtī* < Prakrit *sattatīsaṁ*, Sanskrit *saptatriṁśat*. On the other hand, in Gujarātī *sāṛtrīs*, the *ṛ* has been taken over from *āṛtrīs* 'thirty-eight'. The *d* of Marāṭhī *sadatīs* is peculiar; perhaps this represents partial assimilation from **sattatīsa* to **saddatīsa* from **aḍḍa-tīsa* 'thirty-eight (> *aḍtīs*?).

7.1.13.1.8. 'Thirty-eight'

The old *ṭh* of Pali *aṭṭhatiṁsā*, Prakrit *aṭṭhattīsa, aṭṭhatīsa* < Sanskrit *aṣṭātriṁśat* still appears in Sindhī *aṭhaṭrīha*, Lahndā *aṭhattrī*, Panjābī *aṭhattrī*, West Pahāṛī (Bhalesī) *aṭhɛttri*, while Hindī *aṛtīs*, Gujarātī *āṛtrīs*, Marāṭhī *aḍtīs*, among others, show a *ḍ/ṛ* taken over from 'sixty-eight' (cf. 7.1.8.). Bhojpurī *ā̃ṛā̃tis* (Tiwari 1960: 118, not listed by Turner), a dialect variant beside *artis*, has taken over the doubled nasalization of *saẽtis* 'thirty-seven', etc. (cf. 'thirty-four', 'thirty-five', 'thirty-seven'); it is perhaps to be interpreted as **ā̃ṛā̃*-, i. e. nasalization throughout.

7.1.13.1.9. 'Thirty-nine'

In part, the forms go back to Sanskrit *ūnacatvāriṁśat* as in Hindī *untālīs*, Assamese *unsallix*, Bengali *uncallis*, Panjābī *uṇtālī*, Nepālī *unañcālis* (for -*añ*- cf. 7.1.13.2.9.), in part to Prakrit *ēgūnacattālīsa*, Sanskrit *ēkōnacat-vāriṁśat*, as in Awadhī *ontālīs*, Gujarātī *ogaṇcāḷīs*, Marāṭhī *ekuṇċālis, ekuncālis*. For the *t* of Hindhī *untālīs*, see 7.1.13.2.0.

7.1.13.2. 'Forty'

All forms indicate Prakrit *cāālīsaṁ, cālīsa* < **catāriṁśat*, in which the -*tt*- has been simplified, apparently by analogy with **catāri* 'four' (Hindī *cār*, etc., see 7.1.4.); cf. Hindī *cālīs*, Bengali *callis*, Gujarātī *cāḷīs*, Panjābī *cālī*, etc.; only Kashmiri *ċatajih* and the compounded numerals based on it ('thirty-nine' and 'forty-one' to 'forty-eight') show -*tt*-, which also appears in Pali *cattārīsaṁ, cattālīsaṁ*, Prakrit *cattālīsaṁ, cattālīsā* < Sanskrit *catvāriṁśat*. The consistent *l* for *r* is unclear. Prasun *žibeze* is interesting; Morgenstierne (1926: 50) derives it from **čapuċa* < **catvarśat* and compares Avestan *caθwarəsatəm*. Niya *capariśa* < **catpariṁśa* shows related development. In Bengali, 'forty', appears with a double -*ll*-, which Chatterji (1926: 796) designates as "quite optional even now, and ... apparently recent in Bengali". One is reminded of the gemination of *s* and *v*/*b* in 'eighty' and 'ninety' (Hindī *assī, nawwe*, etc.), which is also spontaneous; perhaps this is the influence of the rhythmic recitation of the decads, reinforced by the decads with gemination, 'seventy' (Hindī *sattar*, etc.) and 'sixty' (Hindī *sāṭh* < **saṭṭh*)? Often *t* appears in the compounds with 'forty', apparently for the *c* of Hindī *cālīs*, etc.; cf. Hindī *ektālīs* 'forty-one', Bengali *titāllis* 'forty-three', etc. Actually there is here an echo of the *tt* of *cattārīsaṁ*; Hindī *ektālīs* can thus be traced back, via **ekkayatālīs, *eketālīs*, with exceptional shortening, to **ekkacattālīsa* (also, tentatively, by Chatterji 1926: 796) and the seemingly older forms with *c*, such as Nepālī *ekcālis*, Bengali *ekcallis* 'forty-one', etc., are secondary assimilations to the simplex Nepālī *cālis*, Bengali *callis*, etc.

The linking vowel *-e-*, derived from *-aca-*, is still preserved in Sindhī (*eketālīha* 'forty-one', etc., against Hindī *ektālīs*), and partially in Marāṭhī ('forty-four', 'forty-seven', 'forty-eight') and also in Hindī (among others) *paĩtālīs* 'forty-five' (see 7.1.13.2.5.). Beside *t* and *c*, the initial of the second element can appear as *y* or Ø as in Hindī *bayālīs* 'forty-two', *cauālīs* 'forty-four', and others; here we have, as in the simplex Hindī *cālīs*, etc., a protoform **catāriṁśat*, **catālīsa* or the like, with single *t*. In the individual languages, Sindhī, Panjābī and Lahndā have *t* consistently, and in the remaining languages the distribution is as follows:

	Nepālī	Bengali	Oṛiyā	Awadhī	Hindī	Marāṭhī	Gujarātī	Assamese
'forty-one'	*c*	*c*	*c*	*t*	*t*	*t*	*t*	*c*
'forty-two'	*y*	*y*	*y*	*y*	*y*	*c*	*t*	*c/y*
'forty-three'	*t*	*t*	*y*	*t*	*t*	*t*	*t*	*t/c*
'forty-four'	Ø	*y*	(*r*)	Ø	Ø	*t*	Ø	*c/y*
'forty-five'	*t*	*t*	*c*	*t*	*t*	*t*	*t*	*c*
'forty-six'	*y*	*c*	*y*	*y*	*y*	*t/ċ*	*t*	*c/y*
'forty-seven'	*t*	*c*	*c*	*t*	*t*	*t/ċ*	*t*	*c*
'forty-eight'	*c*	*c*	*c*	*t*	*t*	*t*	*t*	*c*
'forty-nine'	*c*	*c*	*c*	*t*	*t*	*ċ*	*c*	*c*

Why *y*/Ø should predominate in 'forty-two', 'forty-four', 'forty-six' in particular is not recognizable.

7.1.13.2.1. 'Forty-one'

Everywhere we have forms with *t*, as in Hindī *ektālīs*, Panjābī *aktālī*, etc., or with *c*, as in Nepālī *ekcālis*, Bengali *ekcallis*, Sindhī *eketālīha*, etc. (see above table) < Sanskrit *ekacatvāriṁśat*; Prakrit *igayāla, iālīsa* are not continued anywhere.

7.1.13.2.2. 'Forty-two'

Only Marāṭhī *beċāḷis* has *c*, otherwise we find *t* as in Panjābī *baitālī, bitālī*, Gujarātī *bɛtālīs* < Sanskrit *dvācatvāriṁśat*, or *y* as in Hindī *bayālīs*, Bengali *biyāllis*, corresponding to Prakrit *bayālīsa, biyāla* (see table).

7.1.13.2.3. 'Forty-three'

Sanskrit _trayaścatvāriṁśat, tricatvāriṁśat_, Prakrit _teyālīsaṁ, teyālīsā_ have yielded forms with _t_ (as in Hindī _tẽtālīs_, etc.) everywhere; _c_ (> _s_) only in Assamese _tesallix_, _y_ in Oṛiyā _teyālisa_. The _tir-/tar-_ found in Lahndā _tirtālī_, Marāṭhī _tirtāḷis_ (beside _tretāḷis_) and Panjābī _tartālī_ (beside _tittālī_) is based on 'eighty-three' (see 7.1.3.). The nasalization in Hindī _tẽtālīs_, Nepālī _tẽtālis_ for _*tetālīs_ (cf. Bengali _titālis_) is from 'forty-five'; cf. the same assimilation in the case of 'thirty-three'.

7.1.13.2.4. 'Forty-four'

We have _t_ < _tt_ (Prakrit _cauttālīsa_ < _*catucatvāriṁśat_, Sanskrit _catuś-catvāriṁśat_) in Kashmiri _čŏyĕtŏjih_, Sindhī _coetālīh_ (like Marāṭhī _cavetāḷ_, with preserved _e_, see 7.1.13.2.), analogical _c_ (> _s_) in Assamese _sausallix_, Old Sinhalese _sūsalis_; _y_ in Bengali _cauyāllis_; Ø (as already in Prakrit _cauālīsa_) in Hindī _cauālīs_, Old Gujarātī _ciūālīsa_ (with _i_ because of the palatal environment, cf. the same phenomenon in the case of the simplex 'four', Old Gujarātī _cyāri_ < _*ciyāri_ < _*cayāri_). For the remarkable Modern Gujarātī form _cummālīs_, one should perhaps start from a transitional form _*cĩūālīsa_ (> _*cĩvālīsa_, _*cĩmvālīsa_ with _*mv_ > _mm_, and labialization of the _i_?), which has, in turn, been influenced by Gujarātī _*pĩstāḷīś_ (protoform of _pistāḷīs_ 'forty-five'), which itself has taken its _i_ from 'forty-four'. The _r_ of Oṛiyā _caūrāḷiśa_ is from 'eighty-four' (see 7.1.13.6.4.).

7.1.13.2.5. 'Forty-five'

Apart from Oṛiyā _pañcāḷīsa, paĩcā ḷīsa_ and Old Sinhalese _pansālis_, there are everywhere forms with _t_, cf. Hindī _paĩtālīs_, Sindhī _pañjetālīha_, etc. The nasal of _pañca-_ has vanished as the result of exceptional shortening in Marāṭhī _pastāḷ_, Gujarātī _piśtāḷ_ (the latter for _paśtāḷ_, with _i_ from Old Gujarātī _ciūālīsa_ 'forty-four'). In other languages, a form with later dissimilation _*pãyacattāliīsa_, which has nothing to do with the earlier dissimilation in Prakrit _paṇayālīsa, paṇayāla_ (beside _pacaālīsa_ < Sanskrit _pañcacatvāriṁśat_), has, via _pãyayattālīsa_, yielded a _*pãetālīs_, which has in part preserved the disyllabic character of the first element, as in Bengali _pãyatāllis_, Bhojpurī _paẽtālis_, in part been contracted to a nasalized diphthong, as in Hindī _paĩtālīs_, Panjābī _paĩtālī_, Lahndā _pẽtālī_. The second form has penetrated into most of the forms for 'thirty-five' and 'sixty-five', and the nasalization also into compounds with 'three', 'seven', and 'four'; cf. 7.1.13.1.3.–7.1.13.1.5., 7.1.13.1.7., 7.1.13.2.3., and others.

7.1.13.2.6. 'Forty-six'

We have *t* < *tt* < Sanskrit *tv* in Panjābī *chitālī*, Gujarātī *chetālīs*, and so on; analogical *c* in Bengali *chacallis*, Marāṭhī *śeċāḷ*; *y* in Hindī *chiyālīs*, Nepālī *chiyālis*, Oṛiyā *chayālisa*. Since the *a* of *cha-* in this form originally always came to stand between two palatals, (*ch-* and *-c-* or *-y-*), it could become *i*/*e* in Panjābī, Gujarātī, Hindī, and Nepālī, and already in Prakrit *siyālīsa* (beside *chāyālīsaṁ, chāyāla*, Sanskrit *ṣaṭcatvāriṁśat*), which was then taken over in the following compounds with 'six'.

7.1.13.2.7. 'Forty-seven'

Sanskrit *saptacatvāriṁśat*, Prakrit *sīālīsa, sīāla* (with *ī* from *siyālīsa* 'forty-six', but oddly lengthened) yield regular forms with *t*, as in Sindhī *satetālīha*, Lahndā *satālī*; forms with *c* as in Bengali *sātcallis*, Oṛiyā *satacāḷisa*. Hindī *saĩtālīs*, Nepālī *saĩtālis* have been influenced by Hindī *paĩtālīs*, etc. 'forty-five'; in Panjābī *santālī* (beside *saĩtālī*), there is probably shortening from **saĩ-*. Marāṭhī *sattetāḷ, sattetāḷīs* (beside *satteċāḷ, satteċāḷīs* with analogical *ċ* < *c*) has retained the linking vowel *e*, as has Sindhī consistently (cf. 7.1.13.2.). Gujarātī *suṛtālīś* has been influenced in the consonantism by *aṛtālīs* 'forty-eight' (cf. the same anticipation in the case of 'thirty-seven'), but the *u* is obscure.

7.1.13.2.8. 'Forty-eight'

Sanskrit *aṣṭācatvāriṁśat*, Pali *aṭṭhācattārīsaṁ* yield everywhere forms with *t*, cf. Panjābī *aṭhtālī*, Sindhī *aṭhetālīh*. Instead of *aṭh-* in the first element, there is frequently *aṛ-*, cf. Hindī *aṛtālīs*, Gujarātī *aṛtālīs*, Kashmiri *aratöjih*, and already in Prakrit *aṛayāla* beside *aṭṭhayāla, aṭṭhatālīsa* (cf. 7.1.8.). For the nasalization in Bhojpurī (dial.) *ãṛatālis*, cf. 'thirty-eight' (*ãṛa-* instead of *ãṛã-* in *ãṛãtis* perhaps because of the greater length of the word). Marāṭhī *aṭṭhetāḷ* and Sindhī *aṭhetālīh* have retained the linking vowel *e*, cf. 7.1.13.2.

7.1.13.2.9. 'Forty-nine'

Sanskrit *ūnapañcāśat* with analogical *p* in Assamese *unpansāx*; more abbreviated in Bengali *unañcās*, Hindī *uncās*, Panjābī *unañjā*, Nepālī *unañcās*, etc.; with preserved *v* < *p* in Sindhī *unavañjāha*, Lahndā *unvañja*. The *-añ-* of Nepālī *unañcās* is analogically carried over into 'twenty-nine', 'thirty-nine', and 'ninety-nine'. Similarly, from Sanskrit *ēkōnapañcāśat* (Pali *ēkūnapaññāsa*, Prakrit *egūṇapaṇṇāsaṁ*), Gujarātī *oganpacās* and Marāṭhī *ekuṇvannās*, Kashmiri *kunawanzāh* beside Awadhī (Lakhīmpurī) *oncās*.

7.1.13.3. 'Fifty'

Sanskrit *pañcāśat*, Pali *paññāsa*, Prakrit *paṇṇāsa, paṇṇā*. The great majority of the Modern Indo-Aryan languages point to the fuller Sanskrit form with *-ñc-*; cf. Sindhī *pañjāha*, Gujarātī *pacās*, Hindī *pacās*, Nepālī *pacās*, Bengali *pañcās*, etc. Without *c*, we have only Marāṭhī *pannās*, Sinhalese *panas, panaha* (but Maldivian *fasās*!). In compounds, it is abbreviated to *-van, -pan*; only Kashmiri *-wanzāh*, Sindhī *-vañjāha*, Panjābī *-vañjā*, Lahndā *-vañja*, West Pahāṛī (Bhalesī) *-unzā*, preserve the longer form. If the first element ended originally in a vowel, a *-v-* regularly appears, as in Hindī *bāwan* 'fifty-two' < Sanskrit *dvāpañcāśat*, and a *-p-* if it ended in a consonant, as in Hindī *chappan* 'fifty-six' < Sanskrit *ṣaṭpañcāśat*; nevertheless *p* has analogically gained ground on the *v*-forms, cf. Hindī *pacpan* 'fifty-five' instead of **pacwan* or the like < Sanskrit *pañcapañcāśat*.

7.1.13.3.1. 'Fifty-one'

Sanskrit *ēkapañcāśat*, Prakrit *ēgāvaṇṇa* yield the regular *-v-* everywhere except in Bengali *ekpañcās*, in which the *p* of the simplex has been restored, cf. on the other hand Panjābī *ikvañjā*, Hindī *ekāwan*, dial. *ikyāwan*, etc. Nepālī, Oṛiyā, Awadhī (Lakhīmpurī), Hindī, Gujarātī and Marāṭhī have taken over the long *ā* of Sanskrit *dvāpañcāśat* 'fifty-two' (as has already Prakrit *ēgāvaṇṇa*); cf. Hindī *ekāwan*, Gujarātī *ekāvan*, Marāṭhī *ekāvan*, etc. from Hindī *bāwan* 'fifty-two', Gujarātī *bāvan*, Marāṭhī *bāvan*, etc. (cf. 7.1.12.1., 7.1.13.4.1.).

7.1.13.3.2. 'Fifty-two'

Sanskrit *dvāpañcāśat*, Prakrit *bāvaṇṇa, bāvaṇa* is regularly developed everywhere, cf. Hindī *bāwan*, Panjābī *bāvañjā*, etc. In Bengali *bāānna*, Oṛiyā *bāāna* (also contracted to *bāna*), the *v* has disappeared by dissimilation, and *-an-*, as in the simplex Bengali *pā̃c*, Oṛiyā *pāñca* 'five', is lengthened. Since the lengthening of Modern Indo-Aryan vowels in closed syllables (Middle Indo-Aryan *hattha* 'hand' > Hindī *hāth*, etc.) has not been sufficiently investigated, an accurate assessment of these two special forms is not possible. West Pahāṛī (Bhalesī) *biunǰa* points to Sanskrit *dvipañcāśat*.

7.1.13.3.3. 'Fifty-three'

Sindhī *ṭrevañjāha*, Kashmiri *trᵃvanzāh* with *-v-* point to a form **traya-pañcāśat* or the like, as does already Prakrit *tēvaṇṇaṁ* (< Sanskrit *trayaḥpañcāśat*), with early loss of the *ḥ*. On the other hand, in the *p*-forms such as Hindī *tirpan*, Nepālī *tirpana*, Bengali *tippānna* (for the *ā*, cf. 7.1.13.3.2.), Gujarātī *tepan*, and others, a Middle Indo-Aryan **tep-pañcāsaṁ* with *-pp-* from *-ḥp-* could be involved. Assimilation to phonologically regular *p*-forms is less likely, since the next one is not until 'fifty-six', and in the immediately following 'fifty-four', *-v-* is dominant. For the *r* of Hindī *tirpan*, Nepālī *tirpan*, Marāṭhī *tirpanna*, see 7.1.3.

7.1.13.3.4. 'Fifty-four'

We find *-p-* only in Gujarātī *cɔpan*, Marāṭhī *ċaupanna*, Old Sinhalese *sūpanäs*, otherwise *-v-*, cf. Hindī *cauwan*, Sindhī *covañjāha*, etc., which points to an early simplification **catupañcāśat* for Sanskrit *catuṣpañcāśat*. The Middle Indo-Aryan forms, Prakrit *cauṇṇa*, Pali *catupaṇṇasa*, beside Prakrit *caüpanna*, already reflect this change. The *r* of Panjābī *curañjā*, Lahndā *côrañja*, must derive from 'eighty-four', where it is regularly preserved in all languages.

7.1.13.3.5. 'Fifty-five'

We find regular *v* in Sindhī *pañjvañjāha*, Lahndā *pacvañja*, Oṛiyā *pañcā-wana*, among others; analogical *p* in Hindī *pacpan*, Nepālī *pacpanna*, Assamese *pā̃span, paspanna*, and others < Prakrit *paṁcāvaṇṇa, pa(ṇ)avaṇṇaṁ, paṇaaṇṇa*, Pali *pañcapaññāsa* < Sanskrit *pañcapañcāśat*. The *ā* of Oṛiyā *pañcāwana*, Gujarātī *pā̃cāvan*, Marāṭhī *pā̃ċāvanna*, which (as in the case of 'seventy-seven', q. v.) already exists in Prakrit *paṁcā-vaṇṇa*, is better ascribed to an anticipation of the *ā* of Marāṭhī *aṭṭāvan*, etc. 'fifty-eight' < Sanskrit *aṣṭāpancāśat* than to progressive influence of Marāṭhī *bāvan*, etc. 'fifty-two'.

7.1.13.3.6. 'Fifty-six'

We find regular *p* in Hindī *chappan*, Gujarātī *chappan*, Marāṭhī *chappanna*, and others, as in Prakrit *chappaṇṇa* < Sanskrit *ṣaṭpañcāśat*; analogical *v* in Kashmiri *śĕwanzāh*, Sindhī *chāvañjāh*, Lahndā *chivañja*. The *ā* of the Sindhī form is surprising since it is lacking in Sindhī *aṭhwañjāh* 'fifty-eight', which is the source of *ā* in other languages (see 7.1.13.3.5., 7.1.13.3.7.). The *i* in the Lahndā form is from *chitālī* 'forty-six', where it is old and phonologically regular (see 7.1.13.2.6.).

7.1.13.3.7. 'Fifty-seven'

The phonologically regular *v* is consistent, cf. Hindī *sattāwan*, Marāṭhī *sattāwanna*, Panjābī *satvañja*, Lahndā *satvañja*, etc. < Sanskrit *saptapañcāśat*, Prakrit *sattavaṇṇaṁ*. The long *ā* which is consistent except in Kashmiri, Sindhī, Lahndā, Panjābī, and West Pahāṛī, is taken over from 'fifty-eight'; see 7.1.7. The nasal of Bhojpurī *santāwani̇̆* (beside dial. *sattāwan*) also derives from 'fifty-eight'.

7.1.13.3.8. 'Fifty-eight'

Everywhere we find phonologically regular *v*, cf. Hindī *aṭṭhāwan*, Gujarātī *aṭṭhāvan*, Nepālī *aṭhāuna*, etc. ~ Sanskrit *aṣṭāpañcāśat*, Prakrit *aṭṭhāvaṇṇa*. Shortening or loss of the *ā*, as already in Prakrit *aṭṭhavaṇṇa*, can be seen in Kashmiri *arawanzāh*, Sindhī *aṭhwañjāh*, Lahndā *aṭhvañjā*, Panjābī *aṭhvañjā*, West Pahāṛī (Bhalesī) *aṭhunzā*. The *ṭ* instead of *ṭh* in Bengali *āṭannā* derives from the simplex *āṭ* 'eight'. The *n* of Bhojpurī *anṭhāwani̇̆* (beside dial. *aṭṭhāwan*) is doubtless from *onasaṭhi* 'fifty-nine'; cf. 7.1.13.7.8.

7.1.13.3.9. 'Fifty-nine'

Sanskrit *ūnaṣaṣti* yields such forms as Hindī *unsaṭh*, Nepālī *unsaṭh*, Oṛiyā *unasaṭhi, aṇasaṭhi*, and others; Sanskrit *ēkōnaṣaṣṭi*, Pali *ēkūnasaṭṭhi*; Prakrit *ēgūṇasaṭṭhi* in Gujarātī *ogaṇsāṭh*[i], Marāṭhī *ekuṇsāṭh*, and others. For the *h* of Panjābī *unāhaṭ*, etc. see 7.1.13.4.

7.1.13.4. 'Sixty'

Sanskrit *ṣaṣṭi*, Pali *saṭṭhi*, Prakrit *saṭṭhī, saṭṭhiṁ*, yield regular forms as in Hindī *sāṭh*, Marāṭhī *sāṭh*, Panjābī *saṭṭh*, Lahndā *saṭṭh*, and forms with -*i*, such as Sindhī *saṭhi*. Nepālī *sāṭhi*, Bengali (dial.) *sāiṭ* (with epenthesis) among others. Since old *-i* vanishes in Modern Indo-Aryan, Sanskrit *ṣaṣṭika* 'pertaining to sixty; the number sixty' must be considered for the second group. Turner (1966: 12805) derives only Marāṭhī *sāṭhī* 'aggregate of sixty' (as against *sāṭh* 'sixty') and Assamese *saṭhyo* 'having sixty' from this form. In compounds, Kashmiri, Sindhī, Lahndā, Panjābī, West Pahāṛī (Bhalesī) have *h* instead of *s*; cf. Panjābī *bāhaṭ* 'sixty-two', etc. This is due to transfer from the compounds with 'seventy', in which it is widespread also in other languages and already appears in Middle Indo-Aryan.

7.1.13.4.1. 'Sixty-one'

Sanskrit *ēkaṣaṣṭi*, Prakrit *ēgasaṭṭhi* > Hindī *iksaṭh*, Nepālī *eksaṭh*, Sindhī *ekahaṭṭhi*, etc. The *ā* of Panjābī *akāhaṭ*, Lahndā *ikāiṭh*, West Pahāṛī (Bhalesī) *ikāhaṭ* is from Panjābī *bāhaṭ*, etc. 'sixty-two'; cf. 7.1.12.1., 7.1.13.3.1.

7.1.13.4.2. 'Sixty-two'

Sanskrit *dvāṣaṣṭi*, Pāli *dvāsaṭṭhi, dvaṭṭhi* (!), Prakrit *bāsaṭṭhi, bāvaṭṭhi, bisaṭṭhi* > Nepālī *bāsaṭh*, Marāṭhī *bāsaṭ*, Panjābī *bāhaṭ*, etc. In Hindī (dial.) *bāyasaṭh* beside *bāsaṭh*, there has been influence from *bayālīs* 'forty-two', bypassing *bāwan* 'fifty-two'.

7.1.13.4.3. 'Sixty-three'

Pali *tēsaṭṭhi*, Prakrit *tēsaṭṭhiṁ* (beside *tisaṭṭhiṁ, tēvaṭṭhiṁ*) < Sanskrit *traya(ḥ)ṣaṣṭi*, are regularly developed in Gujarātī *tesaṭh*, Bengali *tesaṭṭi*, Oṛiyā *tesaṭhi*; with *h* (see 7.1.6.) in Kashmiri *tr^{a}haiṭh*, Sindhī *ṭrehaṭhi*, and others; the *tir-* of Hindī *tirsaṭh*, Nepālī *tirsaṭh*, Awadhī (Lakhīmpurī) *tirsaṭh^{i}* comes from 'eighty-three' (see 7.1.3.). The *r* of Lahndā *trēṭh* (< **trēhaṭh*), Panjābī *tarehaṭh*, Marāṭhī *tresaṭh*, Kashmiri *tr^{a}haiṭh* is hardly to be separated from this latter; the forms are probably based on a cross between **tiresaṭh/*tirehaṭh* (< **tirsaṭh/*tirhaṭh*) and *tesaṭh*. Only in Sindhī *ṭrehaṭhi* is the *r* certainly the same as in Sanskrit *trayaḥṣaṣṭi*.

7.1.13.4.4. 'Sixty-four'

Beside regular Gujarātī *cɔsaṭh*, Marāṭhī *ċausaṭ*, Sindhī *cohaṭhi*, etc. < Pāli *catusaṭṭhi*, Prakrit *caüs(s)aṭṭhi* (beside *cōvaṭṭhi*) < Sanskrit *catuḥṣ-*

aṣṭi, there is nasalization in Hindī *caũsaṭh*, Nepālī *caũsaṭṭhi*, Awadhī (Lakhīmpurī) *cā̃ũsaṭh*^{i}, which is taken over from Hindī *paĩsaṭh*, etc. 'sixty-five'.

7.1.13.4.5. 'Sixty-five'

Hindī *paĩsaṭh*, Panjābī *paĩsaṭh*, Nepālī *paĩsaṭh*, Gujarātī *pā̃saṭh*, Sindhī *pañjahaṭhi*, etc. < Prakrit *paṁcasaṭṭhi, paṇasaṭṭhiṁ* < Sanskrit *pañca-ṣaṣṭi*. The *paĩ-* in Hindī, Panjābī and Nepālī is by analogy with *paĩtālīs*, etc. 'forty-five'.

7.1.13.4.6. 'Sixty-six'

Sanskrit *ṣaṭṣaṣṭi*, Prakrit *chasaṭṭiṁ, chāvaṭṭhiṁ*. All languages except for Kashmiri *śihaiṭh* and Oṛiyā *chaasaṭhi*, have lengthening of the *a* of *cha-* of the first element, either as *chā-* as in Sindhī *chāhaṭhi*, Gujarātī *chāsɛṭ*, Marāṭhī *sāsaṭ*, or by the addition of a second syllable as in Hindī *chiyāsaṭh*, West Pahāṛī (Bhalesī) *chiāhaṭh*, influenced by 'eighty-six' (Hindī *chiyāsī*, etc.), whose *ā* is itself taken over from 'eighty-seven' (Hindī *satāsī* < Sanskrit *saptāśīti*), Awadhī (Lakhīmpurī) *chā̃chaṭh*^{i} has its nasalization from *paĩsaṭh*^{i} 'sixty-five'. Oṛiyā *chaasaṭhi* with disyllabic first element, but without lengthening of the *a*, seems to be formed on *satasaṭhi* 'sixty-seven'. For the *i* of Hindī, Nepālī, West Pahāṛī (Bhalesī), (see 7.1.6., 7.1.13.2.6.).

7.1.13.4.7. 'Sixty-seven'

Sanskrit *saptaṣaṣṭi* > Prakrit *sattaṭṭhiṁ* yields a regularly developed first element in Kashmiri *satahaiṭh*, Sindhī *satahaṭhi*, Lahndā *sataiṭh*, Panjābī *sataiṭh*, Bengali *sātsaṭṭi*; with analogical *-ā-* from 'eighty-seven' (cf. 7.1.7.) in West Pahāṛī (Bhalesī) *satāhaṭh*, Curāhī *satāhaṭ*; with *ṛ*/*r* from 'sixty-eight' (see 7.1.8., 7.1.13.4.8.) in Hindī *saṛsaṭh*, Gujarātī *saṛsaṭh*, Awadhī (Lakhīmpurī) *sarsaṭh*^{i}, Nepālī *sarsaṭh*.

7.1.13.4.8. 'Sixty-eight'

All Modern Indo-Aryan forms have short *a* as a linking vowel as already Pali *aṭṭhasaṭṭhi*, Prakrit *aṭṭhasaṭṭhi, aḍasaṭṭhi* (beside *aṭṭhāsaṭṭhi*) < Sanskrit *aṣṭāṣaṣṭi*, cf. Sindhī *aṭhhaṭhi*, Panjābī *aṭhahaṭ*, etc., except for Lahndā *aṭhāiṭ*. On the other hand, in West Pahāṛī (Bhalesī) *aṭhāhaṭh*, the long *ā* was probably reintroduced from *satāhaṭ* 'sixty-seven'. The *ḍh/ḍ/ṛ* in Hindī *aṛsaṭh*, Gujarātī *aṛsaṭh*, Nepālī *aṛsaṭh*, Marāṭhī *aḍsaṭh*, Awadhī (Lakhīmpurī) *araṭh*[i], Kashmiri *arahaiṭh*, already attested in Middle Indo-Aryan, has arisen from *ṭh* by dissimilation from the *ṭṭh* of *saṭṭhi*, and has spread analogically into many other forms, cf. 7.1.8. For the nasalization of Bhojpurī (dial.) *ā̃ṛsaṭh*, see 7.1.13.2.8.

7.1.13.4.9. 'Sixty-nine'

Some of the forms go back to Sanskrit *ūnasaptati*, as in Hindī *unhattar*, Nepālī *unhattar*, Bengali *unsattar*, and others, and some to Sanskrit *ēkōnasaptati*/**ēkūnasaptati* > Prakrit *ēgūṇasattariṁ*, *aüṇattariṁ*, as in Marāṭhī *ekuṇhattar*, Gujarātī *agṇoter*, and others.

7.1.13.5. 'Seventy'

Apart from Kashmiri *satath*, which seems to have its *th* from *aśīth*, Kashmiri Standard *śīth*, 'eighty' and Sinhalese *sätā̄*, *hätā̄*, *sättā̄va*, *hättā̄va*, all languages have the Middle Indo-Aryan *r* of Pali *sattari* (beside *sattati*), Prakrit *sattariṁ*, *sayari*, which has been dissimilated from the *tt* of *sattati* < Sanskrit *saptati*; cf. Hindī *sattar*, Marāṭhī *sattar*, Panjābī *sattar*, Bengali *sattar*. The final *-i* which is preserved in Nepālī *sattari*, Sindhī *satari*, and others, has caused assimilation of the penultimate syllable in Lahndā *sattir* and of the antepenult as well in Gujarātī *sitter*, *sīter* < **sittir*; see 7.1.13.7. In compounds, descendants of the *h*-form, *-hattari*, already attested in Middle Indo-Aryan, are dominant virtually throughout. Except in 'seventy-two', Gujarātī has *-oter* as second element throughout, which has spread from *sītoter* 'seventy-seven' (see 7.1.13.5.7.). In 'seventy-three', 'seventy-five', 'seventy-seven', and 'seventy-eight', Marāṭhī has *-yāhattar* as second element. The origin is *tiryāhattar* 'seventy-three', in which *-yā-* (like *tir-* of the other languages, cf. 7.1.3.) has been taken over from **tiryāśī* (today nasalized *tiryā̃śī*) 'eighty-three'.

7.1.13.5.1. 'Seventy-one'

Sanskrit *ēkasaptati* > Prakrit *ekkasattariṁ*, *ēkattari* > Hindī *ik-hattar*, Gujarātī *ikoter*, Bengali *ekāttar*, Oṛiyā *ekastari*, *ekasturi*, etc. Marāṭhī *ekehuttar*, with the *u* of the second element otherwise known only from

Gujarātī, is either the relic of a longer analogical series based on 'seventy-seven' (q. v.) which was later reduced, or an individual older borrowing from Gujarātī.

7.1.13.5.2. 'Seventy-two'

Sanskrit *dvāsaptati*, Prakrit *bāhattari, bahattari, bāvattari* (beside Sanskrit *dvisaptati*, Prakrit *bisattari, bisayari*) > Hindī *bahattar*, Nepālī *bahattar*, Awadhī *bahattar*[i], with remarkable shortness of the *a* as against Bengali *bāoyāttar* (orthographic for **bāwāttar*), Sindhī *ḇāhatari*, Gujarātī *bāter*, Marāṭhī *bāhattar* (beside *bahāttar*).

7.1.13.5.3. 'Seventy-three'

Sanskrit *trayaḥsaptati*, Prakrit *tēvattariṁ* > Hindī *tihattar*, Nepālī *tihattar*, Sindhī *ṭrēhattari*, etc. The *r* of Lahndā *tirhattar* comes from 'eighty-three' (cf. 7.1.3.); in Marāṭhī *tiryāhattar*, the *yā* is also introduced from *tiryāśī* 'eighty-three' (see 7.1.3., 7.1.13.6.3.). The nasalization of Gujarātī *tõter* is obscure.

7.1.13.5.4. 'Seventy-four'

Sanskrit *catuḥsaptati*, Prakrit *cōvattari, caühattari*, Hindī *cauhattar*, Nepālī *cauhattar*, Bengali *cuyāttar*, Sindhī *cohatari*, etc. In Marāṭhī *ċaurehattar*, West Pahāṛī (Bhalesī) *curhattar*, the *r* is taken over from 'eighty-four' (Marāṭhī *ċauryāśī*, Hindī *caurāsī*, etc.).

7.1.13.5.5. 'Seventy-five'

Sanskrit *pañcasaptati*, Prakrit *paṁcahattari, paṇṇattari* > Hindī *pachattar*, Bengali *pãcāttar, pãcātta*, Sindhī *pañjahatari*, Gujarātī *pãcoter*, etc.

7.1.13.5.6. 'Seventy-six'

Sanskrit *ṣaṭsaptati*, Prakrit *chassayariṁ, chāhattari*. The short *a* of the first element is partially replaced by the *i* of 'forty-six' (q. v.); cf. Hindī *chihattar*, Nepālī *chihattar*, Awadhī (Lakhīmpurī) *chiattar*[i], beside Lahndā *chehattar*, Marāṭhī *śehattar* and Assamese *sayhattar*, Sindhī *chāhattari*. For the *o* of Gujarātī *choter*, see 7.1.13.5.

7.1.13.5.7. 'Seventy-seven'

Beside *sattahattariṁ* < Sanskrit *saptasaptati*, which survives in Hindī *sat-hattar*, Sindhī *satahatari*, Assamese *xātxattar*, Bengali *sātāttar*, etc., Prakrit has also *sattahuttariṁ, sattuttari*, in which the second *-satta-* is replaced by *-sutta-* through a kind of dissimilation(?). The Gujarātī forms in *-oter*, such as *ikoter* 'twenty-one', *tõter* 'seventy-three', etc. (see 7.1.13.5.) are derived from the corresponding form Old Gujarātī *satahutari*, Gujarātī *sītoter*. The *ī* of Gujarātī *sītoter* < **sittahuttari* probably comes from *sitter, sīter* 'seventy'.

7.1.13.5.8. 'Seventy-eight'

Sanskrit *aṣṭāsaptati* > Prakrit *aṭṭhahattari, aṭṭhattari* > Hindī *aṭhattar*, Lahndā *aṭhattar*, Panjābī *aṭhattar*, Bengali *āṭāṭar*, etc. The *-yā-* of Marāṭhī *aṭhyāhattar*, which occurs also in other compounds with 'seventy' (q. v.) and derives from *tiryāhattar* 'seventy-three', occurs also in this numeral in Gujarātī *aṭṭhyoter*, **aṭṭhyāhuttari*. This could be the result of an older influence of Marāṭhī, or perhaps parallel analogical development, which was deleted again except in this word.

7.1.13.5.9. 'Seventy-nine'

Sanskrit *ūnāśīti* yields Hindī *unāsī*, Panjābī *unāsī*, Nepālī *unāsi*, Bengali *unāsi*; Sanskrit *ēkōnāśīti*, **ēkūnāśīti* > Prakrit *ēgūṇāsīiṁ* yields. Kashmiri *kunaśīth*, Awadhī (Lakhīmpurī) *onnāsī*, Gujarātī *agaṇyāśī*. On the *y* of Gujarātī, cf. 7.1.13.6.2.

7.1.13.6. 'Eighty'

Turner remarks that all the Modern Indo-Aryan forms derived from Sanskrit *aśīti*, Pali *asīti*, Prakrit *asīi*, Apabhraṁśa *asii* are phonologically irregular: Hindī *assī*, Lahndā *assī*, Panjābī *assī*, Bengali *āsi*, Sindhī *asī*, cf. point to geminated *-*śś*- (for this, cf. the remark on Bengāli *callis*, 7.1.13.2.); Gujarātī *ɛsi*, Marāṭhī *ēśī* presuppose an epenthesis **aiśīti*. The *ū* of Sinhalese *asū* is taken over from *anū* 'ninety'. In compounds, the initial *a* is always lengthened; Oṛiyā has, in addition, forms with reintroduced *a*, cf. *ekāaśī* beside *ekāśī* 'eighty-four'. In 'eighty-two, 'eighty-three', 'eighty-four', and 'eighty-six', there was already *ā* in Middle Indo-

Aryan, taken over analogically from other forms in which it was phonologically regular, for example, in Pali *chaḷāsīti* 'eighty-six' for Sanskrit *ṣaḍaśīti* by analogy with *pañcāśīti* 'eighty-five', etc.

7.1.13.6.1. 'Eighty-one'

Sanskrit *ekāśīti* > Prakrit *ekkāsīī* > Hindī *ikyāsī*, dial. *ekāsī*, Nepālī *ekāsi*, Bengali *ekāsi*, Oṛiyā *ekāsi*, Maithilī *ekāsi*, etc. On the *-y-* of Gujarātī *ekyāśī*, Marāṭhī *ekyāiśī*, Awadhī (Lakhīmpurī) *ekkyāsī*, cf. 7.1.13.6.2.

7.1.13.6.2. 'Eighty-two'

The Sanskrit form *dvyaśīti* (< Prakrit *bāsīī, bāsī, bēāsī*) has, via **dviyāśīti*, yielded Panjābī *biāsī*, Sindhī *b̲iāsī*, Gujarātī *byāśī*, Marāṭhī *byāyśī*, in which the long *ā* has been taken over from *pañcāśīti* 'eighty-five', and so on (see 7.1.13.6.). In Marāṭhī, *-yā-* is taken over into all the compounds with 'eighty' and (via 'eighty-three') in part also into those with 'seventy' and 'ninety' (q. v.); in Gujarātī in 'seventy-nine', 'eighty-one', 'eighty-five', 'eighty-seven', 'eighty-eight', and 'eighty-nine'. In Assamese *birāxi*, Bengali *birāsi*, the *r* of Bengali *curāśi* etc. 'eighty-four' is taken over, as it is in 'eighty-three'; Hindī *bayāsī*, Awadhī (Lakhīmpurī) *bayāsī*, Lahndā *beāsī*, Nepālī *bayāsi*, Oṛiyā *bayāasi* are influenced in their vocalism by analogy with other compounds with 'two', such as Hindī *bayālīs* 'forty-two', etc.

7.1.13.6.3. 'Eighty-three'

Much as in the case of 'eighty-two', for Sanskrit *tryaśīti*, Pali *tiyāsīti*, Prakrit *tēsīī, tēāsī* and for most of the Modern Indo-Aryan forms, one must assume **triyaśīti* > **tiyāśīti*, but, nearly everywhere, the *r* of 'eighty-four' is anticipated; cf. Hindī *tirāsī*, Panjābī *tirāsī*, Awadhī (Lakhīmpurī) *tirāsī*, Nepālī *tirāsi*, Bengali *tirāsi*, Marāṭhī *tiryā̃śi*, as against Gujarātī *tyāśī* and Oṛiyā *teyāasi*. The Oṛiyā form is assimilated to other forms with 'three', cf. Oṛiyā *teyālīsa* 'forty-three', *teyānau* 'ninety-three'. The *ā* is analogical, as in 'eighty-two'.

7.1.13.6.4. 'Eighty-four'

Sanskrit *caturaśīti* < Pali *cūḷāsīti*, *cullasīti*, Prakrit *culasī, cōrāsīī* > Hindī *caurāsī*, Bengali *curāśi*, Marāṭhī *ċauryāśī*, etc. The *ā* is analogical, as in 'eighty-two' and 'eighty-three'. The *r* which is preserved before the vocalic beginning of the decads reappears in all the Modern Indo-Aryan forms and, in addition, has spread analogically to 'eighty-three' and from there into other forms with 'three', and also into forms of 'ninety-for' (Hindī *caurānwe* and so on), in Oṛiyā into 'forty-four' as well (q. v.).

7.1.13.6.5. 'Eighty-five'

Sanskrit *pañcāśīti*, Prakrit *paṁcāsīiṁ, paṇasīiṁ* > Hindī *pacāsī*, Panjābī *pacāsī*, Nepālī *pacāsi*, with loss of the nasal by exceptional shortening; beside these, regular Bengali *pācāsī*, Sindhī *pañjāsī*, Lahndā *pañjāsī*, Gujarātī *pãcyāśī*, Marāṭhī *pãcyāsī*, and so on.

7.1.13.6.6. 'Eighty-six'

Sanskrit *ṣaḍaśīti* < Pali *chaḷasīti*, Prakrit *chalasīiṁ, chāsīiṁ*. The old sandhi-consonant *-ḍ-* is everywhere lost in favor of transparent new formations, in which the vocalism of other compounds with 'six' was the crucial factor (see 7.1.6., 7.1.13.2.6.); cf. Hindī *chiyāsī*, Panjābī *chiyāsi*, Bengali *chiyāsi*, Nepālī *chiyāsi*, Lahndā *cheāsī*, Gujarātī *chāsī*, etc.; the long *ā* is taken over from 'eighty-seven'. In Marāṭhī *śahā̃śī* (beside *śā̃yśī̃* < **śyāśī̃* and *śeāśī*) the *h* of simplex *saha* (cf. Apabhraṁśa *chaha*) eliminates the hiatus.

7.1.13.6.7. 'Eighty-seven'

Sanskrit *saptāśīti* > Prakrit *sattāsīiṁ* > Hindī *satāsī*, Sindhī *satāsī*, Panjābī *satāsī*, Lahndā *satāsī*, Bengali *sātāsi*, Gujarātī *satyāśī*, Marāṭhī *satyāyśī*.

7.1.13.6.8. 'Eighty-eight'

Sanskrit *aṣṭāśīti* > Prakrit *aṭṭhāsīi*, *aṭṭhāsi* > Hindī *aṭṭhāsī, aṭhāsī*, Bengali *āṭāsi*, etc. The Hindī dialect form *aṭheāsī* is formed on earlier **cheyāsī* 'eighty-six' (for present-day *chiyāsī*). Marāṭhī *aṭṭhyaśī* with short *a*, beside *aṭṭhyāẽśī, aṭṭhyāyśi*, is curious.

7.1.13.6.9. 'Eighty-nine'

Sanskrit *ūnanavati* in Hindī *unānwe*, Bengali *unanai*, Sindhī *ūṇāṇave*, etc., with nasal dissimilation in Oṛiyā *aṇāllau, aṇālabe*. Sanskrit *ēkōnanavati*, Prakrit *ēgūṇanaüiṁ* in Kashmiri *kunanamath*, Marāṭhī *ekuṇnavvad*. Beside this, Sanskrit *navāśīti* in Awadhī (Lakhīmpurī) *nawāsi*, Hindī *nawwāsī*, Gujarātī *navyāśī*, Marāṭhī *navyāyśī*. The *e* of the Gujarātī secondary form *nevyāśī* is taken over from *nevũ* 'ninety'.

7.1.13.7. 'Ninety'

Sanskrit *navati* > Pali *navuti*, Prakrit *ṇavaī, ṇaüiṁ*, besides its regular representation in Sindhī *nave*, Bengali *nai*, Assamese *nawai*, appears frequently with doubled *vv/bb*, cf. Hindī *nawwe, nabbe*, Panjābī *navve*, Bihārī *nabbai*, and so on; the reason is not clear, cf. the remark on Bengali *callis*, 7.1.13.2. In Oṛiyā *laü* (beside *naü, nabe*), the *l* of *aṇāllau* has had an effect. The *a*- of Sinhalese *anū* comes from *asū* 'eighty'. The *i* of Lahndā *nĩvve* and the *e* of Gujarātī *nevũ* have probably arisen, as in the case of Gujarātī *sitter, sīter* 'seventy' < **sittir* (cf. Lahndā *sattir*) < *sattari*, because of total vowel assimilation, **navvaï* > **navve* > **nevve* > Lahndā *nẽvve* (nasalization obscure); Gujarātī -*ũ* in *nevũ* must then have arisen by secondary labialization from **nevvẽ*. In the compounds with 'ninety', Marāṭhī has the -*yā*- taken over from the eighties (see 7.1.13.6.2.), and, in addition, gemination of the *ṇ*, which probably comes from *śāṇṇav* 'ninety-six' (q. v.); cf. *ċauryāṇṇav* 'ninety-four', *sayāṇṇav* 'ninety-seven', etc. Turner (1966: 6995) regards the Marāṭhī simplex *navvad* and Kashmiri *namăth* as borrowings from Sanskrit. In the compounds an *ā* appears before the *n* in all languages, which was generalized early from Sanskrit *aṣṭānavati* 'ninety-eight'.

7.1.13.7.1. 'Ninety-one'

Sanskrit *ēkanavati* > Prakrit *ekkāṇāuiṁ* in Hindī *ekānwe*, *ikānwe*, Bengali *ekānai*, Marāṭhī *ekyāṇṇav*, etc.

7.1.13.7.2. 'Ninety-two'

Sanskrit *dvinavati*, extended to **dviyānavati*, survives in Panjābī *biāṇvẽ*, and, assimilated to Hindī *bayāsi* 'eighty-two', etc. in its vocalism, in Hindī *bayānawe*, Nepālī *bayānnabe*. The form **dvānavati* (Pali *dvānavuti*, Prakrit *bāṇaüi, bāṇuvaī*) survives in Gujarātī *bāṇu*, Awadhī (Lakhīmpurī) *bānbe*, Nepāli *bānabe*, Panjābī *bānvẽ*. In Bengali *birānai*, the *r* of *curānabbai* 'ninety-four' is taken over, as in 'ninety-three'.

7.1.13.7.3. 'Ninety-three'

Sanskrit *trayōnavati*, Prakrit *tēṇavaïṁ, tiṇavaïṁ, tēṇaüiṁ*. Except in Oṛiyā *teyānaü*, the *r* of 'ninety-four' is taken over everywhere; cf. Hindī *tirānwe*, Panjābī *tarāṇvẽ*, Nepālī *tirānabe*, etc.

7.1.13.7.4. 'Ninety-four'

Sanskrit *caturnavati*, Pali *catunahutā*, Prakrit *cauṇaüi*. The *r* of *catur-* is preserved in all languages (except in Kashmiri *ċŏnamath*) and is therefore due either to a very old analogized formation **caturānavati* based on *aṣṭānavati* 'ninety-eight' (see 7.1.13.7.), or to a later remodelling on the Modern Indo-Aryan forms corresponding to Sanskrit *caturaśīti* 'eighty-four'; cf. Hindī *caurānwe*, Bengali *curānabbai*, Gujarātī *cɔrāṇũ*, Marāṭhī *ċauryāṇṇav*, etc.

7.1.13.7.5. 'Ninety-five'

Sanskrit *pañcanavati* > Prakrit *paṁcāṇaüi, paṁcaṇaüi, paṇaṇaüi, paṇaṇuvaï* > Hindī *pacānwe*, Bengali *pãcānaï, pacānabbaï*, Sindhī *pañjānave*, Lahndā *pañjānave*, etc.

7.1.13.7.6. 'Ninety-six'

The old Prakrit form *chaṇṇavaïṁ, chaṇṇauī* < Sanskrit *ṣaṇṇavati* is preserved in Marāṭhī *śāṇṇav*, Gujarātī *chaṇṇũ*; in Marāṭhī the *-ṇṇ-* was then extended to all other compounds with 'ninety' (cf. 7.1.13.7.). The other languages have analogical new formations on the model of the other compounds with 'six'; cf. Hindī *chiyānawe* (*i* from 'sixty-six', *-yā-* from 'eighty-six'), Oṛiyā *chayānabe*, in Sindhī *chahānve* with the *h* of the simplex *chīh* 'six', cf. Apabhraṁśa *saha* 'six'.

7.1.13.7.7. 'Ninety-seven'

Sanskrit *saptanavati*, Prakrit *sattāṇaüiṁ*, Hindī *satānwe*, Bengali *sātāṇaï*, Sindhī *satānave*, Panjābī *satānave*, Lahndā *satānave*, etc.; the *-ā-* is from 'ninety-eight', see 7.1.7. Bhojpurī *santānbē* has nasalization as in 'fifty-seven' (q. v.), which, as in 'ninety-eight', may well derive from *ninānbē* 'ninety-nine'.

7.1.13.7.8. 'Ninety-eight'

Sanskrit *aṣṭānavati* > Pali *aṭṭhanavuti,* Prakrit *aṭṭhānaüi* > Hindī *aṭhānwe*, Bengali *āṭānai* (*ṭ* instead of *ṭh* from *āṭ* 'eight'), Gujarātī *aṭṭhānũ*, etc. For the nasalization of Bhojpurī *anṭhānbē*, see 7.1.13.7.7.

7.1.13.7.9. 'Ninety-nine'

Sanskrit *ūnaśata*, which is unusual in its formation, survives in Hindī (dial.) *unsau*, Nepālī *unansai* (with *-an-* from 'forty-nine'), Assamese *unsaxa*. On the other hand, Sanskrit *navanavati* > Prakrit *ṇavaṇaüi* with the usual lengthening of the *a*, has regularly yielded Sindhī *navānave*, Gujarātī *navvāṇũ, navāṇũ*, Marāṭhī *navyāṇṇav*, and, with nasal assimilation, Kashmiri *namanamath*. The other languages show a curious extension by a prefix *nin(n)-*, cf. Hindī *ninānwe, ninānawe, ninānbe*, Awadhī (Lakhīmpurī) *ninnānbe*, Bhojpurī *ninānbē*, Lahndā *naṛinnave* (nasal dissimilated from **naṇinnave*, this last metathesized from **niṇannave*), Panjābī *nināṇvẽ*, Assamese *nirānawai*, Bengali *nirānaī* (both of the latter with dissimilated *r* from *n*). Since a phonological development *nin(n)-* < *nava-* seems out of the question, it is natural to think of the influence of another stem. One may consider Pali *ninna* 'low-lying, bent down', Prakrit *ṇiṇṇa* 'low' < Sanskrit *nimna-* 'deep, low', from which, in Modern Indo-Aryan, Turner (1966: 7244), derives Hindī *ninaunā* 'to make bend, lower'[7] in the sense of Sanskrit *ūna-* 'deficient' in the other numerals with 'nine' – but then one would have expected 'one hundred' in the second element, not 'ninety'.

7.1.14. 'One hundred'

Sanskrit *śata* > Pali *sata*, Prakrit *saya, saa* develop to forms with simple *a* only in Bengali *sa*, Assamese *xa*, Oṛiyā *sa* (beside *sae*); otherwise there are forms with an *i-* or *u*-diphthong, or forms derivable from these, throughout; cf. Kashmiri *sai*, Nepālī *sai*, Bihārī *sai*, Marāṭhī *śẽ*, and Hindī *sau*, Old Māṛwāṛī *sau*, Panjābī *sau, sai*, Sindhī *saü*, Lahndā *sô*, etc. The distribution in Awadhī (Lakhīmpurī) *sau*, pl. *sai*, and Old Gujarātī *saü*, pl. *saïṁ* < Middle Indo-Aryan *saaṁ* (Apabhraṁśa **saũ*) pl. *saāiṁ*, shows that, originally, the *u*-forms belonged to the singular, the *i*-forms to the plural.

7.1.15. Higher numbers

7.1.15.1. 'One thousand'

Sanskrit *sahasra*, ~ Pali *sahassa*, Prakrit *sahassa, sahāsa, sahasa* is replaced by Modern Persian *hazār* in most of the languages; it is preserved in Shina *sās, sā̃s*, Kashmiri *sās*, Sindhī *sahasu*, Maithilī *sahas*, Old Awadhī *sahasa*, Hindī (poetical) *sahas*, Old Gujarātī *sahassa*, Maldivian *hās, hāhe*. For the *d* of Old Sinhalese *jahasa, jahasaka* (*j* is a spelling for *d*), Sinhalese *dās, dāha*, Geiger (1900: 45–47) suggests assimilation to *daha* 'ten', whereas Bloch (1919: 224) also considers a contracted compound from *daha* 'ten' and *siya* 'hundred' possible.

7.1.15.2. 'One hundred thousand'

Sanskrit *lakṣa*, originally 'stake, prize; mark, sign', later also a numeral, survives in both meanings in Middle and Modern Indo-Aryan, cf. Pali *lakkha*, Prakrit *lakkha*, Hindī *lākh*, Māṛwāṛī *lākh*, Gujarātī *lākh*, Marāṭhī *lākh*, Kumaunī *lākh*, Nepālī *lākh*, Assamese *lākh*, Bengali *lākh*, Kashmiri *lach*, Sindhī *lakhu*, and so on. The *n* of Oṛiyā *nākha* (beside *lākha*) is striking.

7.1.15.3. 'Ten million'

Sanskrit *kōṭi*, Pali *kōṭi*, Prakrit *kōḍi*, is preserved in Old Bengali and Old Gujarātī as *koḍi*, in Sinhalese as *keḷa*; the other languages have inserted a second *r* after the *k*, before which, here and there, a partial vowel appears, cf. Hindī *kroṛ*, Bengali *kroṛ*, Panjābī *kroṛ*, Sindhī *kiroṛi*, Hindī *kiroṛ, karoṛ*, and others. The assumption of a hyper-sanskritism (Turner 1966: 3498) is probably unnecessary, cf. the same sporadic phenomenon in French *trésor* < Latin *thesaurus* (von Wartburg 1922–1929: 310 ff.). The word is, according to Przyluski (1929: 26),[8] to be taken as an Austro-Asiatic borrowing, to be compared with Bengali *kuṛi* 'twenty', Juang *koḍi* 'twenty', Birhor *kūṛī* 'twenty'; the original meaning would have been 'large number'.

7.2. Ordinals

7.2.0. Introduction

The ordinals are fully developed in the Modern Indo-Aryan languages, but compared to the cardinals they are of less general interest and can therefore be dealt with in a shorter survey. As is to be expected, the readiness to preserve direct descendents of Old and Middle Indian forms, which are in part rather irregular formations, is correspondingly greater the lower the number from which they are formed, whereas the higher numbers have consistently been subjected to analogical levelling, naturally not in the stem, since this is closely connected with the cardinal, but in the suffix. Old and Middle Indian *-ma* presents itself as a point of departure; it forms the ordinal of 'five', 'seven', 'eight', 'nine', and 'ten' in Sanskrit (cf. *pañcama* 'fifth' to *pañca* 'five' and so on) and must merge in Modern Indo-Aryan with *-tama*, which is used in competition with *-a* in the numbers from 'twenty' on (cf. *tryaśītitama* beside *tryaśīta* 'eighty-third' to *tryaśīti* 'eighty-three', etc.). Since *m* loses its labial closure in most languages, the most widespread ordinal ending is a simple vowel, in part nasalized, or preceded by a *v* (< *m*). The ordinal derived from 'ten' will serve as an example: Hindī *das-vā̃*, Old Awadhī *das-aũ*, Sindhī *ḏah-õ*, Marāṭhī *dahāvā*, Nepālī *das-aũ*, beside *m*-forms such as Kashmiri *dah-yum*[u], Gujarātī *das-mũ*, Panjābī *das-mā̃* (beside *das-vā̃*), and others. Bengali still has a suffix *-ai, ui* < *-amikā* in the written language, as in *daś-ai* 'tenth', *pā̃cui* 'fifth', but uses simply the genitive singular of the cardinal in the colloquial language, as in *daś-er* 'tenth'. Since the regular ending *-ma* appears in all languages from 'seven' (at the latest) on, only the ordinals up to 'six' need be discussed here, and otherwise only those words which, as the result of idiomatic specialization of the meaning, have continued the original forms. There is a very old and important idiomatic use of the feminine of the ordinals as date designations in the Hindu calendar, as, for example, in Sanskrit *caturthī* (i. e. *rātri* 'night') 'the fourth lunar day (*tithi*) of the first (or second) half of the lunar month'. The modern languages have, in this usage, some old fossilized forms such as Hindī *dūj* 'second day' beside the normal ordinal *dūsrā* 'second'; some otherwise normal ordinals in the feminine, as Hindī *cauth, cauthī* 'the fourth day', cf. *cauth, cauthā* 'fourth'; some partially levelled Sanskrit forms, as in Maithilī *doāsī, trodasī* (beside *terasi*) 'the twelfth, thirteenth day' for Sanskrit *dvādaśī, trayodaśī* (the normal ordinals are *bārahama, tērahama*); and some pure Sanskrit forms, such as Hindī *prathamā, dvitīyā* 'the first, second day', etc.

7.2.1. 'First'

Descendants of Sanskrit *prathama* are still widespread in Middle Indo-Aryan (Pali *paṭhama*, Prakrit *pathama, pudhama, paḍhuma*, etc.), in Modern Indo-Aryan, however, only in the first syllable of Shina *pumū́ko* and in Sinhalese *paḷamu*, of which the latter could be a borrowing from Pali. All other modern Indo-Aryan forms go back to a **prathila*, which is itself already present in Prakrit *pahila* (beside *paḍhamilla*), cf. Hindī *pahil* 'beginning', *pahilā, pahlī̃* 'first', Bengali *pahilā, paylā* 'first', etc. The suffix used here, which was already widely used in later Middle Indo-Aryan in the form *-(i)lla(ka)-* for the formation of adjectives from nouns and verb stems (Pischel 1900), occurs in modern Maithilī in the following numbers as well, in a peculiar idiomatic specialization for indicating the order in which pupils arrive at primary schools; *mīrā* 'first', *dolhā̃* 'second', *telhā̃* 'third', *cārillo* 'fourth', *pā̃cillo* 'fifth', *chabillo* 'sixth', *sātillo* 'seventh', etc. (Jhā 1958: 382). Of these, *dolhā̃* and *telhā̃* are old Prakrit formations, of which the latter appears, as *taïla*, already in the Old Bengali of the *caryāpadas*, while the others are regularly derived from the cardinals; *mīrā* 'first' belongs with Urdu *mīrī* 'leadership, chiefship; a winner at play; he that first comes to the teacher to say his lesson'.[9]

7.2.2. 'Second'

Turner (1966: 6676) derives the most widespread form, Hindī *dūsrā, dusrā*, Assamese *dosorā*, Bengali *dosrā*, Oṛiyā dial. *dusar*, and so on, from a formation **dviḥsara* 'twofold' (not attested in Sanskrit), which, except in Oṛiyā *disarā* 'two-stringed (of a necklace)', has taken over the *ō* or *ū* of the cardinal; whereas Schwarzschild[10] posits a later formation by analogy with Prakrit *ekkasaraka, ekāsara, egāsara* (> Nepālī *eksaro* 'single', Middle Bengali *ekasara* 'alone'; cf. Turner 1971: 2510). On the basis of Gujarātī *eksarī* 'necklace with one string', the connection is certainly clear, but the formation with 'one' has not developed into the ordinal like the following two; the same is true of Bengali *causar* 'fourth, square', Gujarātī *cɔsar* 'necklace with four strings' (Turner 1966: 4592). The old Sanskrit form *dvitīya*, with the exception of Sindhī *b̠i, b̠īo, b̠ījo* and Gujarātī *bījũ* 'second', survives only in a few special meanings, as in Tōrwālī *bī* 'again', Hindī (poetic) *biya, bīyā, biyā* 'second, other, enemy'; otherwise only forms which go back to Old Indo-Aryan **dutiya* (> Pali *dutiya*, Prakrit *duia, duijja*) are found, cf. Hindī *dūjā*, Gujarātī *dujũ* 'other, different', Oṛiyā *dui, duā, dujā* 'second', Bengali *doj-bare* 'a bridgeroom for the second time'; as a date designation in Panjābī *dūj*, Hindī *dūj*, Kashmiri *doy* 'second day of fortnight' < **dutīyā* (Sanskrit *dvitīyā*).

7.2.3. 'Third'

The third ordinal is also based, in large part, on a reconstructed form **triḥsara* corresponding to **dviḥsara* mentioned above. Turner also compares *trisara*, which, with the meaning 'triple string of pearls', is actually attested in Sanskrit. The Modern Indo-Aryan reflexes show more specialized idiomatic meanings than in the case of **dviḥsara*; cf. Old Hindī *tīsar, tesrī* 'third ploughing', Panjābī *tisrāt, tisrāit* 'third person, umpire', Oṛiyā *tisirī* 'necklace with three strings', beside Hindī *tisrā*, Oṛiyā *tisarā*, Marāṭhī *tisrā* 'third'; with *e* from the compounds of the cardinal in Nepālī *tesar*, Bengali *tesrā, tesar* 'third', and others. The old form survives in Panjābī *tīā, tījā*, Hindī *tījā*, etc. < Sanskrit *tṛtīya* > Pali *tatiya*, Prakrit *taïa, tēa, tiijja*, etc.; beside these, with the *-ma* of the higher ordinals (e. g. Sanskrit *pañcama* 'fifth'), Kashmiri *triyum*[u], *treyum*[u], *trayyum*[u], West Pahāṛī Bhadrahawāhī *ṭḷɛiyaũ, trẽã̄*. Of the numerous forms with special meanings, the following should be mentioned: the northwestern words for 'the day before yesterday', like Ashkun *nutrī́*, Kati *nutrī*, Waigalī *nútriäm*, Savi *nũλī*, etc., which are derived by Turner (1966: 5912) from **anutṛtīyam*; Sanskrit *tṛtīyaka* 'tertian (of fever)' in Assamese *tiyā* 'returning every third day', Sindhī *ṭriaṛu* 'tertian fever', and so on; Sanskrit *tṛtīyā* 'third day of the lunar fortnight' in Hindī *tīj*, Panjābī *tīj*, Gujarātī *tīj, trīj*, etc.

7.2.4. 'Fourth'

In no other cardinal is the old form better preserved. Forms which phonologically correspond exactly to Sanskrit *caturtha* > Pali *catuttha*, Prakrit *caüttha, cottha, caüṭṭha* are found in almost all languages, cf. Sindhī *cotho*, Hindī *cauth, cauthā*, Bengali *cauṭhā, cauṭhō*, etc., often in the meaning 'one quarter', as in Marāṭhī *ċaut*, Oṛiyā *cauṭha, cauṭhā*; 'the fourth lunar day' is formed from the feminine, cf. Hindī *cauth* f. or *cauthī*, Gujarātī *cɔth*[i], Marāṭhī *ċaut(h)*, f., and so on.

7.2.5. 'Fifth'

Sanskrit *pañcama* > Pali *pañcama, pañcamaka*, Prakrit *paṁcama*, from the point of view of the later languages the first ordinal which is 'regular', i. e., formed with the suffix *-ma*, is directly continued in all languages, cf. Hindī *pā̃cvā̃*, Marāṭhī *pā̃cvā*, Panjābī *pañjvā̃*, Nepālī *pā̃caũ*, etc.; 'the fifth day in the lunar month', Hindī *pā̃caĩ*, Sindhī *pañjāĩ*, Bengali *pā̃cui*, etc. < Sanskrit *pañcamī*.

7.2.6. 'Sixth'

Sanskrit *ṣaṣṭha* > Pali *chaṭṭha*, Prakrit *saṭṭha, chaṭṭha* is the last ordinal which is preserved without analogical alteration in the Modern Indo-Aryan languages, cf. Hindī *chaṭṭhā*, Gujarātī *chaṭṭhũ*, Maithilī *chaṭh*, and so on; the influence of the regular form is shown by Hindī *chaṭwā̃*, Nepālī *chaiṭaũ* (with *ai* from *chai* 'six', cf. 7.1.6.), Maithilī *chaṭvā̃, chaṭham, chaṭhama* (Kellogg 1893: 154), and so on; cf. *chaṭṭhama* already in Pali.

7.3. Fractions

7.3.0. Introduction

Among the special peculiarities of the Modern Indo-Aryan languages belong a series of fractions, which, according to present-day etymological consciousness, shows no connection either with the cardinals or with the ordinals.

7.3.1. 'Half'

7.3.1.1. 'One-half'

Sanskrit *ardha*, Pali *addha, aḍḍha*, Prakrit *addha, aḍḍha* are everywhere regularly continued, often extended by *-ā, -ō*, etc. < Sanskrit *-aka*. The forms with a dental are dominant, cf. Hindī *ādhā*, Marāṭhī *ādhā*, Maithilī *ādh*, Bengali *ādh, ād, ādhā*, etc. A cerebral is found, for example, in Oṛiyā *āṛa*, Bengali *āṛ-* (in compounds), Kashmiri *aḍ*, and so on. A special form for 'plus one half', Hindī *sāṛhe*, Panjābī *sāḍhe*, Bengali *sāṛe*, Gujarātī *sāṛā*, has developed from Sanskrit *sārdha* (< **sa-ardha* 'provided with a half').

7.3.1.2. 'One and a half'

Of Sanskrit *dvyardha*, which is preserved only in West Pahāṛī (Bhadrawāhī) *daḍḍh*, Turner (1966: 6698) postulates four subsidiary forms: **dviyardha* in Pali *diyaḍḍha*, Lahndā *ḍiḍḍh*, Marāṭhī *ḍīḍh, dīḍ, diḍh*; **dvaiyardha* in Panjābī *ḍeḍh*, Bengali *ḍeṛ, deṛ, deṛā, ḍeṛā*, Hindī *ḍeṛh* (the most common type); **duvardha* in Tirāhī *dowaḍī*, Kashmiri *ḍŏḍ*, Panjābī *ḍuḍḍhā, ḍūḍh*; **dauvardha* in Gujarātī *dɔḍh*. The consistent cerebralization in the group *-rdh-* (which has to a large degree affected also the first dental) is striking; it appears only sporadically in the reflexes of Sanskrit *ardha* 'half'. An old variant **ardhyardha* (cf. ŚPBr. *ardhyardhayaka* 'worth one and a half') seems to be evident in Sinhalese *yēḷa, yeḷa, yela*, with abnormal *ḷ* for *ḍ* in a numeral.

7.3.1.3. 'Two and a half'

Sanskrit *ardhatṛtīya* appears already abbreviated in Pali *aḍḍhatiya, aḍḍhateya*, Prakrit *aḍḍhāiya, aḍḍhāijja* (beside *addhataïya*), and is mutilated beyond recognition in the Modern Indo-Aryan languages, cf. Hindī *aṛhāī, ḍhāī*, Nepālī *aṛāi*, Bengali *āṛāi*, and so on.

7.3.2. 'Third'

Hindī *tihāī*, Bhojpurī *tihāī*, Bengali *tēhāī*, are derived by Turner from **tribhāgiya*, by Tiwari (1960: 124) and Chatterji (1926: 802) from **tribhāgika* (to *bhāga* 'part'). Turner also compares (with "?") West Pahāṛī (Bhalesī) *ṭlihāg* 'arbitrator, judge'. Maithilī *tek*[u]*rī* 'one third' is obviously the same word as Hindī *tiurī, teorī* 'brow, frown', Panjābī *tīuṛī* 'frown', Sindhī *ṭriurī* 'frown' < Sanskrit **tri-kuṭī*, originally 'triple fold/wrinkle' (cf. Sanskrit *bhṛkuṭi* 'frown').

7.3.3. 'Quarter'

7.3.3.1. 'One-quarter'

As early as Pali, Sanskrit *pāda* 'foot' has the meaning 'quarter of a verse, coin (worth one-quarter *kahāpaṇa*)', and, except for the northwest, is used in all Modern Indo-Aryan languages for 'one quarter'. Cf. Hindī *pāu*, Nepālī *pāu*, Bengali *po, pao, poā*, Gujarātī *pā, pāv*, and others. Beside this, the old compound **caturthapādikā* (to *caturtha* 'fourth') in Hindī *cauthāī*, Nepālī *cauthāi*, Gujarātī *cɔthāī*, and others.

7.3.3.2. 'Three-quarters'

As early as Sanskrit, the word for 'foot, quarter' appears with the stem *ūna*, which is known from the cardinals (cf. 7.1.9.) in the meaning 'less by a quarter' (*pādōna*, lexically also *pādūna*, cf. Turner 1966: 8078). But the majority of Modern Indo-Aryan forms indicate short *a* in the first syllable; cf. Hindī *paun, paunā*, Panjābī *pauṇe*, Bengali *paune*, and so on; *pādōna*, with *ā*, underlies only Oṛiyā *pāuṇā*, Marāṭhī *pāuṇ-* (in compounds), Koṅkaṇī *pāuṇ*. Kashmiri *dūn*[u] is strangely abbreviated.

7.3.3.3. 'One and a quarter'

Sanskrit *sapāda* 'provided with one foot' is already attested in the meaning 'a quarter' in the *Manusmṛti*. The Modern Indo-Aryan forms are completely regular; cf. Hindī *sawā*, Nepālī *sawā*, Bengali *saoyā*, and so on.

7.4. Multiplicatives

7.4.0. Introduction

In multiplication, Hindī and closely related languages (Bhojpurī, Maithilī, Magahī, Mārwāṛī) use special forms for the multiplicand, as, for example, in Hindī *tīn pãje pandrah* 'three times five (is) fifteen', where the derived form *pãje* stands for *pā̃c* 'five' as used elsewhere. In whole-number multiplication, the forms are especially variable and irregular,[11] which is due to the fact that a multitude of methods of formation have contributed to their formation, viz: a) the old collective suffix *-ka*/*-aka* (with 'three to eight'); b) composition with *-guṇa* 'fold' (with 'two', 'three'); c) an *m*-suffix (with 'one and a quarter', 'two and a half', 'ten'), perhaps identical with that of the old ordinals, cf. the use of the ordinal *chaṭṭhā* for 'times six' in Magahī; d) the old Sanskrit formation in *-vāra* '-fold, times' (only Maithilī 'two' to 'ten'); e) an *-āī*-suffix (with 'one', 'three', 'nine', 'ten'), also nasalized, which has been secondarily abstracted from 'two and a half' (Hindī *aṛhāī*, etc.); f) the plural of the ordinal (in Magahī *chaṭṭhā* 'times six'); g) the simple cardinal (with 'three', 'five', 'seven', 'eight', 'nine'), which is consistently used with numbers greater than 'ten'; h) a suffix *-aũcā, -õcā*, and the like, abstracted from 'four and a half' (with 'five and a half', 'six and a half', 'seven and a half'). There are also mechanical assimilations to neighboring forms, as in the case of the cardinals (Magahī *saṭṭhe* 'times eight' instead of *aṭṭhe*, from *sate* 'times seven', Mārwāṛī *chãj* 'times six' from *pãje* 'times five'). The fractional multiplicatives are essentially identical with the expressions for the improper fractions; but, while the latter go only as far as 'two and a half', the multiplicatives preserve forms up to 'four and a half' through the system of multiplication tables; on the other hand, those for 'five and a half', 'six and a half', 'seven and a half' depend partially on more recent analogical formations and partially on the introduction of stems from outside the numeral system (Bhojpurī *bichiyā* 'times six and a half', *calausā* 'times seven and a half').

7.4.1. 'Times one'

Kellogg expressly gives *ekam, kam* as the pronunciation of Hindī *ekã, kã*, so that the *m* can be taken as identical with that of 'one and a quarter', 'two and a half', 'nine', 'ten'; correspondingly also in the forms Mārwāṛī *ekū̃*, Magahī *ekkā̃*, Maithilī *kā̃*. The *-ā* of Maithilī *kā*, Bhojpurī *ekkā, kā* turns up in other multiplicatives also ('two' to 'nine' in various languages) and is, no doubt, like its plural *-e*, to be traced to forms with Sanskrit *-aka-* (beside *-ka-* in *catuṣka* 'set of four') as in *pañcaka* 'set of five' (see 7.4.5.). The *-āī* of Bhojpurī *ekāī* derives from *aṛhāī* 'two and a half', nasalized in Maithilī *kā̃i*.

7.4.2. 'Times two'

Hindī *dūnā*, Māṛwāṛī *dūnī*, Bhojpurī *dūni, dugunī*, Magahī *dūnī, dūgunā*, Maithilī *dunnā, dūn*, and so on, go back to Sanskrit *dviguṇa* 'twofold, double', while the Old Indo-Aryan formation in *-vāram* survives in Magahī *dōbarī*, Maithilī *dōbarā, dōbar*.

7.4.3. 'Times three'

Magahī *tīnā*, probably also the basis for the nasalized *tīyā̃* in Bhojpurī, is, because of its isolation, more probably formed by analogy to *dūnā*, etc., 'times two' than a descendent of Sanskrit *triguṇa* 'threefold, triple'. It is no longer possible to determine whether Bhojpurī *trikā, tirikā, trike, tirike* is to be derived from an older **trikka* (as by Turner 1966: 6019), or has taken over its *k* only secondarily from *cauk*, etc., 'times four'; striking is the *r*, which suggests Sanskrit influence. On the other hand, Magahī *tīyā*, Maithilī *tiyā* is certainly the old *trika* 'triple' of Sanskrit, cf. Pali *tika*, Prakrit *tiga, tiya* 'triple' and Panjābī *tīā* 'the number three'. Bhojpurī *tiyāī*, Maithilī *tiyāi* are, like 'times one', assimilated to 'times two and a half' (Bhojpurī *arhāī*, see 7.4.13.). Maithilī *tebarā*, like *dobarā* 'times two', contains old *-vāram*. In Hindī *tī, tīn*, Bhojpurī *ti, tin*, Maithilī *tī*, there is probably nothing more than the old cardinal.

7.4.4. 'Times four'

All forms can be traced back to the old noun, Sanskrit *catuṣka* n., Pali *catukka*, Prakrit *caükka* 'set of four, quadrangular courtyard', cf. Hindī *cauk, caukā*, Bhojpurī *cauk, cauke*, and so on. The ending in Maithilī *cauc* is assimilated to 'times four and a half' (Maithilī *chaũcā*, etc.); for Maithilī *caubarā*, cf. *dōbarā*, 7.4.2. In Bhojpurī *car*, there is probably only the cardinal, Hindī *cār*, Bhojpurī *cāri* 'four', in abbreviated form.

7.4.5. 'Times five'

Hindī *pāje*, Bhojpurī *pac, pāc, pācā, pace*, Magahī *pace, pāce*, Maithilī *pace, pājā, pāje* are probably old plural forms of a stem corresponding to Sanskrit *pañcaka* 'set of five', in Bhojpurī *pac, pāc* probably also just the abbreviated cardinal. Striking is the *j* – for *c* in Hindī *pāje*, Maithilī *pājā, pāje* – influence of the northwestern dialects (Panjābī *pañj*, etc.)?

7.4.6. 'Times six'

Hindī *chakkā*, Māṛwāṛī *chak, chakē*, Bhojpurī *chāk, chak, chakā*, etc., regularly from Pali *chakka*, Prakrit *chakka* < Sanskrit *ṣaṭka* 'consisting of six'. Māṛwāṛī *chāja* is partially assimilated to Māṛwāṛī *pāje* 'times five'. Magahī *chaṭṭhē* (beside *chak, chakkā*) is the old ordinal, cf. Hindī *chaṭṭhā* 'sixth'.

7.4.7. 'Times seven'

Hindī *satte*, Māṛwāṛī *satā*, Bhojpurī *sāt, satē, sat*, etc., old plural form or ordinal as in 'times five'.

7.4.8. 'Times eight'

Hindī *aṭṭhē*, Bhojpurī *āṭh, āṭhē, aḍhē*, Maithilī *aṭṭhē*, and so on – as in 'times seven' and 'times five'. In its initial, Magahī *saṭṭhē* is assimilated to *satē* 'times seven'.

7.4.9. 'Times nine'

The *m* of Hindī *nam, nammā*, Māṛwāṛī *nammā*, Mēwāṛī *namā̃*, Maithilī *nam, namā* is already present in the cardinal, Hindī *nam*, etc.; *v*-forms also occur in Bhojpurī *navā̃*, Maithilī *navẽ*, abbreviated in Māṛwāṛī *ne*; with the *-āī* of 'two and a half' in Bhojpurī *navāi*, Magahī *navā̃ī̃*; with the *k* of 'times four', 'times six' in Bhojpurī *naukā*.

7.4.10. 'Times ten'

In striking contrast to the cardinal, almost consistently with *h* for *s*, cf. Hindī *dahām*, Bhojpurī *dahā̃, dahā̃ī̃*, Maithilī *daham, dahāi* and others, with extrusion of the first vowel through mechanical recitation, Māṛwāṛī *dhām*, Maithilī *dhā̃*. Whether the suffixal *m* is identical with that of 'two and a half' (see 7.3.1.3.) or whether it is to be ascribed to assimilation to 'times nine' (Hindī *nam*, etc.) cannot be decided.

7.4.11. 'Times one and a quarter'

The cardinal 'one and a quarter', which appears only slightly or not at all altered in Bhojpurī *sawā*, Magahī *sawā, sawaiyā*, Mēwāṛī *śawāyā*, is, in Hindī *sam*, Maithilī *sama, samā̃*, extended by the suffixal *m* usual in 'times one' and the other multiplicatives mentioned in 7.4.1., with simultaneous loss of *w* by contraction.

7.4.12. 'Times one and a half'

In contrast to the forms of the cardinal with simple *ē* (Hindī *ḍēṛh*, etc.), forms with *ō/u/eō/ēu* dominate in the multiplicatives, cf. Hindī *ḍēōṛhā, ḍauṛhā*, Mēwāṛī *ḍōḍā*, Magahī *ḍyoḍhā*, Maithilī *ḍĕuḍhā, ḍeōḍha*, and so on, beside Bhojpurī *ḍēṛhā, ḍēḍhĕ*. For this, Turner (1966: 6698) assumes a contamination of the *ē*-forms with descendents of **duvardha*, **dauvardha* (see 7.3.1.2.), which seems problematic.

7.4.13. 'Times two and a half'

The cardinal Hindī *aṛhāī, aḍhāī* appears hardly or not at all altered in Mēwāṛī *ḍhiyā*, Bhojpurī *aḍhā̃, aḍhāī*, Magahī *aḍhāī*, and so on, or extended by *m*, as in 'times one', in Hindī *ḍhām, ḍhāmā*, Maithilī *ḍhām*.

7.4.14. 'Times three and a half'

Sanskrit *ardhacaturtha* 'three and a half', already heavily abbreviated in Pali *aḍḍhuḍḍha*, Prakrit *aḍḍhuṭṭha*, appears in the multiplication tables regularly with forms with *h* or initial vowel or even *g* (in Bhojpurī), all of which have arisen by dissimilation: **ḍh...ṭh* > *h/g/Ø...ṭh*, cf. Hindī *ū̃ṭhā, hū̃ṭhā, hū̃ṭā, hõṭā*, Old Gujarātī *uṭh, uṭhā̃*, Panjābī *ū̃ṭā*, Bengali *āhuṭhā*, Marāṭhī *āū̃ṭ, auṭ*, Bhojpurī *ăgūṭhā*; in Bhojpurī *ăgūṛhā* an assimilation *ḍh...ṭh* > *ḍh...ḍh* must have taken place earlier, and in Hindī *hū̃ṭā, hõṭā*, a dissimilation *ḍh...ṭh* > *ḍh...ṭ*.

7.4.15. 'Times four and a half'

Sanskrit **ardhapañcama*, Prakrit *addhapaṁcama* 'four and a half' becomes, via an unrecorded **aḍḍhavãcama*, through the Middle Indo-Aryan sound-change *ava* > *ō*, Hindī *ḍhõcā, ḍhaũcā*, Maithilī *ḍhaũcā, ḍhõcā*, and so on. In Bhojpurī *ḍhãgucā, ḍhãgūcā*, the *g* is analogically taken over from *ãgūṭhā, ãgūṛhā* 'times three and a half'; the *m* of Bhojpurī *dhamūcā* (only in Kellogg) is not clear.

7.4.16. 'Times five and a half'

With this multiplicative there begins a new type of formation, as Kellogg (1893: 166), following Hoernle, has correctly seen; these multiplicatives are no longer derived, like the Old Indo-Aryan type **ardhapañcama* 'four and a half', from the next whole number, but depend clearly on the preceding one for their initial. Hindī *põcā*, Maithilī *põcā* contain the initial *p* of Hindī *pā̃c* 'five' and a "suffix" *-õcā* abstracted from *ḍhõcā* 'times four and a half', which also appears in 'times six and a half' and 'times seven and a half'. The secondary forms Maithilī *pahũcā, pahũce*, Bhojpurī *pahũcā*, Magahī *pahũcā* are difficult to explain; popular etymological assimilation to Maithilī *pahũc-*, Bhojpurī *pahũc-* 'to arrive'?

7.4.17. 'Times six and a half'

Hindī *khõcā*, Magahī *khaũcā*, Maithilī *khõcā, khaũcā, khaũce* have doubtless arisen by dissimilation from **chõcā, *chaũcā* (with the initial *ch* of Hindī *chah*, etc. 'six'); the assumption of the usual substitution of *kh* for Sanskrit *ṣ* specifically by Maithilī (cf. Sanskrit *ṣaṣ* 'six'), is less attractive. Bhojpurī *bichiyā* is an extraneous stem, which cannot be explained without a detailed knowledge of the traditional system of computation.

7.4.18. 'Times seven and a half'

Hindī *satõcā*, Maithilī *satõcā* to Hindī *sāt*, Maithilī *sāt* 'seven' according to the new system of formation beginning with 'times five and a half'. Bhojpurī *calausā* is hard to explain; like *bichiyā* 'times six and a half', it is an extraneous stem.

Notes

1. Cf. Turner's observation cited in 7.1.4.
2. Turner has not included the numerals from Kumauni, Maithili, Bhojpuri, Māṛwāṛī, probably because they do not offer much original material compared to the major languages, and probably also often borrowed from the latter; there are considerable gaps in West Pahari, Assamese, Sinhalese; smaller ones in Bengali, Panjabi, etc.
3. Cf. Lorimer (1938). Yasin *-ek* (in the form *-ik*) is also used to mark the double plural; see Lorimer (1938).
4. In Berger (1953: 70), I explained the *ch-* as arising in certain Sandhi positions *ṣ-*. It is thus much easier for me to recognize the superiority of Turner's interpretation because it offers evidence for the change *kṣv-* > *ch-* that I (1953: 81) suspected on the basis of the analogy of Old Indo-Aryan *kṣr-, kṣm-, kṣṇ-, kṣy-* > Middle Indo-Aryan *cch-* but could not definitively substantiate. In the meantime there is a second example, Middle Indo-Aryan *chīra* 'milk' < **kṣvīra*, cf. Avestan *xšvīd-* 'milk'. (Sanskrit has *kṣīra*; see Mayrhofer 1956–1976.)
5. Turner has *chabīsati*, apparently misunderstanding the somewhat clumsy citation style of *The Pali Text Society's Pali–English dictionary,* p. 106.
6. By error, Turner has *chatiṁsa*; see note 5.
7. He prefers the connection to Sanskrit *nirṇāmayati*, however.
8. Not available to me; citation is from Mayrhofer (1956–1976), under *koṭiḥ*.
9. Cf. Ferozsons, *Urdu–English dictionary* (1960), under *mīrī*; according to Jhā (1958) "of unknown origin".
10. L. A. S. Schwarzschild, "'First', 'second', and 'third' in Middle Indo-Aryan", *JAOS* 82 (1962: 517–522).
11. The data are taken from Kellogg (1893: 152–163) (who calls them, not very aptly, "denominatives"), where the subtleties of usage are also listed. Turner's dictionary is incomplete in this respect.

References

Berger, Hermann
1953 *Zwei Probleme der mittelindischen Lautlehre* (München: Kitzinger).
1958 "Der Akzent von *εἶς, πᾶς* und *ἔγωγε* ...", *MSS* 3: 5–26.
Bloch, Jules
1919 *La formation de la langue Marathe* (Paris: Champion).
Chatterji, Suniti Kumar
1926 *Origin and development of the Bengali language* (Calcutta: University Press Calcutta).

Davids, T. W. Rys – W. Stede
1925 *The Pali Text Society's Pali-English dictionary* (Chipstead).
Geiger, Wilhelm
1900 "Litteratur und Sprache der Singhalesen", in: *Grundriß der indo-arischen Philologie* (Straßburg: Trübner).
Hoernle, A. F. Rudolf
1916 *Manuscript remains of Buddhist literature found in eastern Turkestan* (Amsterdam: Philo Press).
Jha, Subhadra
1958 *The formation of the Maithili language* (London: Luzac).
Kellogg, Rev. Samuel Henry
1893 *A grammar of the Hindi language* (London: Routledge & Kegan Paul).
Lorimer, David
1938 *The Burushaski language* I (Oslo: Aschehoug).
Mayrhofer, Manfred
1956–1976 *Kurzgefaßtes etymologisches Wörterbuch des Altindischen* (Heidelberg: Winter).
Morgenstierne, George
1926 *Report on a Linguistic Mission to Afghanistan* (Oslo: Aschehoug).
1957 "Sanskrit words in Khowar", in: *Dr. S. K. Belvalkar Felicitation Volume*, 84–98 (Benares: Motilal Banarsidas).
Pischel, R.
1900 *Grammatik der Prakritsprachen* (Straßburg: Karl J. Trübner).
Przyluski, Jean
1929 *Pre-Aryan and Pre-Dravidian in India* (Calcutta: University of Calcutta).
Schwarzschild, Louise A.
1962 "'First', 'second', and 'third' in Middle Indo-Aryan", *JAOS* 82: 517–522.
Stede, William – Rys Davids, T. W.
1925 *The Pali Text Society's Pali-English Dictionary* (London: PTS).
Tiwari, B. N.
1960 *The origin and development of Bhojpuri* (Calcutta: The Asiatic Society).
Turner, Ralph Lilley
1931 *A comparative and etymological dictionary of the Nepali language* (London: Routledge & Kegan Paul).
1966 *Comparative dictionary of the Indo-Aryan languages* (London: Oxford University Press).
Wartburg, Walter von
1922–1929 Französisches etymologisches Wörterbuch (Bonn: Klopp usw.).

Chapter 8
Iranian

Ronald Emmerick

8.0. Introduction

The Avesta is the main source for the Old Iranian numerals.[1] Most of them are found in its later strata. A very few numerals are attested in the Old Persian inscriptions.[2] These have been somewhat augmented in recent years by the discovery and interpretation of Old Persian loanwords occurring in Elamite.

Already the Old Persian inscriptions of the fifth and sixth centuries B. C. refer to other Iranian groups such as the Medes (*Māda-*), Sogdians (*Suguda-*), and various branches of Sakas (*Saka-*). There is reason to believe that these groups were already linguistically differentiated. But we have no direct evidence in the form of texts or inscriptions for the Old Iranian period apart from the Avesta and the Old Persian inscriptions. The other Iranian linguistic groups are attested first in the Middle or Modern Iranian periods. The Middle Iranian languages and dialects already show signs of considerable evolution, which makes their use for comparative historical purposes difficult, especially in view of the fact that our knowledge of these languages is still in its early stages. Sure results, however, are being steadily obtained thanks largely to the extensive use of bilingual texts. A further difficulty presented by the Iranian material is caused by the fact that the Modern Iranian languages do not on the whole continue directly the languages attested in the Middle Iranian period.

8.1. Cardinals

8.1.0. Overview of the lower cardinals

The cardinal numbers from 'one' to 'ten' are attested in Old Iranian as follows:

	Avestan	Old Persian	Proto-Indo-European
'one'	*aēuua-*	*aiva*	**oy-wo-*
'two'	*duua* (nom. masc.)		**d(u)wṓ*
'three'	*θrāiiō* (nom. masc.)		**tréyes*
'four'	*caθβārō* (nom. masc.)		**kʷetwóres*
'five'	*panca*		**pénkʷe*
'six'	*xšuuaš*		**kswéks*
'seven'	*hapta*		**septḿ̥*
'eight'	*ašta*		**oḱtṓ*
'nine'	*nauua*		**newm̥/n̥*
'ten'	*dasa*		**deḱm̥(t)*

These numerals are indeclinable except for 'one' to 'four' and three genitive plurals. These are in *-anąm* : *pancanąm, nauuanąm, dasanąm*, and occur in three places in the Avesta (Y. 10.16, V. 22.20, Yt. 8.24). These forms are usually compared with OInd. *pañcānā́m, navānā́m* and *daśānā́m*. The inflection in these forms is not an Indo-European development but is due to the influence of the *a*-declension: 'five' and 'seven' to 'ten' all end in *-a*. Thus we have in Yt. 8.24: *dasanąm aspanąm aojō* 'the strength of ten horses'.

8.1.0.1. Lower cardinals in Khotanese

In Khotanese[3] a fully developed inflectional system for 'five' to 'ten' has been evolved as follows:

	'five'	'six'	'seven'	'eight'	'nine'	'ten'
Nom.-acc.	*paṃjsa*	*kṣäta'*	*hauda*	*haṣṭa*	*nau*	*dasau*
Gen.-dat.	*paṃjinu*	*kṣei'ṇu* [4]		*haṣṭänu*		*daśśänu*
Instr.-abl.	*paṃjyau*	*kṣätyau*	*haudyau*	*haṣṭyau*	[*nauya*][5]	*daśyau*
Loc.	*paṃjuvo'*	*kṣvo*		*haṣṭuvo'*		*daśvo'*

It is hard to see how the starting-point for this development could have been "the gen. *paṃjinu*, being formed after the analogy of *drrainu* < **trayānam*, of three" (Konow 1932: 33). The oblique forms of *all* the Khotanese numerals after 'three' (which cannot itself show palatalization because of *-y-*) are characterized by palatalization preceding the terminations. The inflection follows the *i*-declension and must have spread originally from the decads 'sixty' to 'ninety'.[6] In Khotanese even 'hundred' and 'thousand' were affected, e. g. nom.-acc. *satä*, loc. *sītuvo*' 'one hundred'; nom.-acc. *ysāre*, loc. *yseruvo*' 'one thousand'.

8.1.1. 'One'

The Avestan form is *aēuua-*. The Indo-European numerals for 'one' differ except that there is considerable agreement concerning the initial syllable **oy-*. OIran. **aiwa-* is usually said to represent an Indo-European **oywo-*, found also in Greek *οἶος* 'alone'. But from the Indo-Iranian side it is surprising to find such a distinctive contrast with OInd. *éka-* 'one', whose great age is known from the occurrence of *aika-* in the Mitanni hippological text. The attempt to reconcile OIran. **aiwa-* and OInd. *aika-* with one another by deriving the latter irregularly from **aiwaka-*[7] has been rightly rejected (A. Kammenhuber, *Die Arier im Vorderen Orient* 1968: 202–203), even though **aiwaka-* is commonly found in later Iranian: Zoroastrian Pahl. *ēk*[8], Middle Persian (Turfan)[9] *yk*, Modern Persian *yek*, Sanglēčī *wok* 'one', but Parthian *'ywg* 'alone'[10]. On the other hand, *εw* 'one' in the Dardic languages Katī and Waigalī is, rather, from *éka-*[11]. Nevertheless, **aiwa-* is represented in OInd. *evá* (adverb) 'just so' and in *iva* 'as, like', so that the most likely hypothesis is that Indo-Iranian had both **aiwa-* and **aika-*.[12]

8.1.1.1. The suffix *-wo-* seen in OIran.* *aiwa-* < **oy-wo-*, in contrast with PIE **oy-no-*[13] in Greek οἰνός 'one (on dice)', Latin *oinos* > *ūnus* 'one', etc., is found in other words[14] from the same semantic sphere in Iranian. In particular, one of the ordinals to **aiwa-* is based on an OIran. **par-wa-* 'prior' (Av. *paouruua-*, OPers. *paruva-*; cf. OInd. *pū́rva-*), namely **parwya-* 'first', seen in GAv. *paouruiia-*, Yav. *paoiriia*, OPers. *paruviya-* (cf. OInd. *pūrvyá-*) – see 8.2.1.2. Note further Indo-Iranian **wiśwa-* 'all': Av. *vīspa-*,[15] OPers. *viça-*, OInd. *viśva-*, and **sárwa-* 'whole, all': Av. *hauruua-*, OPers. *haruva-*, OInd. *sárva-* (cf. Greek ὅλος). See further 8.3.3.1.

8.1.1.2. While OIran. **aiwa-* is clearly continued in most of the Middle Iranian languages (*'yw* in Middle Persian and Parthian, *'yw* in Sogdian[16] and Chorasmian), difficulty is presented by Khot. *śśau* 'one'. According to Konow (1932: 50), "the base is apparently *sya, si*, Indo-Eur. *k̑io, ki*. In the nom. *va* has been added, cf. Av. *aēva*". Khotanese inflects in the singular as follows:

Nom. masc.-fem.	*śśau*
Acc. masc.-fem.	*śśau*
Gen.-dat. masc.-fem.	*śśye*
Instr.-abl. masc.	*śśäna*
fem.	*śśiñi*
Loc. masc.	*śśäña*

The oblique cases show pronominal inflection of a stem **śśa-*. Morgenstierne (1929: 407) compared Ormuṛī *šē* 'one' from the Proto-Indo-European pronominal stem **ḱyo-*. But note Ormuṛī *šăndas* 'eleven' (8.1.11.1.). Other forms in the modern languages which are thought to continue **aiwa-* are: Paštō *yau* (Morgenstierne 1927: 99), Parāčī *žŭ̄* (Morgenstierne 1929: 304), Yidgha-Munjī *yū* (Morgenstierne 1938: 271), Ossetic (Digor) *yeu*, (Iron) *yu* (Miller 1903: 47). With further reduction we find in the Southern Tati dialects *i* 'one', fem. *ya, ia.*[17] It is probable that Ormuṛī *šē* also developed from **aiwa-*, perhaps with secondary devoicing of an earlier initial **ž-*. It is known too now that **aiwa-* developed to *-yū-* in Khotanese as in *byūrru* 'ten thousand' < **baiwarnam* (8.1.33.), and Khotanese has *śśū-* 'one' in *śśūjäta-* 'one another', *śśūvarebistä* 'twenty-one', etc., and probably in *śśūka-* 'alone', cf. Parthian *'ywg* 'alone'. In view of the close connection between the concepts 'one' and 'alone' (i. e. 'all one', Modern Engl. *alone* < OEngl. *eall-āna*; cf. Gonda 1953: 76–80), it is tempting to propose that the puzzling initial *śś-* is what remains of *biśśa-* 'all' from Indo-Iranian **wiśwa-*, but it remains possible that it is nothing more than a secondarily devoiced **ź-* (cf. Parāčī *žŭ̄*). The *-au* in the nominative-accusative forms may reflect an emphatic form **aiwakam*, perhaps influenced by *dasau* 'ten', itself apparently affected by *nau* 'nine' < **nawa*.

8.1.2. 'Two'

Av. *duua* 'two' (fem. *duuā-*) is declined like a regular *a*-stem as is its counterpart in Old Indian (5.1.2.). The only exception is the form *duuaēibiia* for the dative (instrumental-ablative), which was thought by Bartholomae, *Grundriss der iranischen Philologie* (1895: 128), to have been based on the nominative dual neuter, but which is more likely to be old, cf. OCS *dŭvěma*, Lith. *dviẽm*, etc.; for the *i*-diphthong see Wackernagel (1930: 341) and cf. 8.1.2.1.

8.1.2.1. The spelling *duua* in Avestan continues PIE **duwō* (OInd. *d(u)vā́*, Greek *δύω*). The original length of the final vowel in Iranian is confirmed by **dwādasa* 'twelve' (8.1.12.). The Avestan spellings *duuaē(ca), duiiē*, and *baē* all represent the Old Iranian nominative feminine-neuter dual **d(u)wai* = OInd. *dvé*. This is continued in Khot. *dvī*[18], which contrasts with Khot. *d(u)va*. In view of Av. *duuaēibiia* (8.1.2.), the Khotanese gen.-dat. *dvīnu* probably represents **dw-oy-* + *-nu* from the genitive-dative plural (Emmerick 1968: 249), cf. Greek *δυοῖν*, but it could have been reinterpreted as **duvänu* (since in Khotanese, spellings *uvä, uī* and *vī* alternate) with the general genitive-dative plural ending *-änu* of numerals. Similar forms surviving elsewhere are Middle Persian (Turfan) *dw'(')n*, Balōčī *dun*, and Šughnī *δīō*[w]*n* (cf. J. Elfenbein, *BSOAS* xxiv, 1961: 92). Here also belongs Sogdian *δ(y)βnw* rather than as a collective (8.3.5.3.). It is oblique in all passages known to me.

8.1.2.2. As the first element of a compound a special form in *-i* was used for 'two' in Proto-Indo-European. This *dwi-* is said by Wackernagel (1930: 343) to owe its *-i* to **tri-*, but it is probably merely the zero grade of PIE **dw-ey-/-oy-* (cf. Gonda 1953: 43–44). PIE **dwi-* is represented in Avestan as *bi-*, e. g. *bi-zangra-* 'two-footed'. With further phonetic development Sogdian has *δiv-* (< **δvi-* < **dwi-*, Gershevitch 1954: 65), e. g. *δyβp'δ'kw* 'two-footed'. Khotanese had *śi-* (regularly < **dwi-*), e. g. *śivāa-* 'two-footed' (Bailey 1967: 333). Ossetic has Digor *du-*, Iron *dy-* (Miller 1903: 47–48), which shows the influence of Ossetic *duvä* 'two'. Middle Persian (Turfan) *dwp'y* 'two-footed' simply contains the cardinal, Middle Persian (Turfan) *dw* (Parthian *dw*), cf. Modern Persian *do-pāye*. **dwi-* was also used in derivatives (see 8.2.2., 8.2.2.1., 8.3.1.2., 8.3.1.6.–7.) as in Old Indian (5.1.2.2.).

8.1.3. 'Three'

The Avestan nominative masculine *θrāiiō*. Its declension is based on the two stems masc.-neut. *θri-* and fem. *tišr-*, which correspond to OInd. *tri-, tisr-*. Similarly, in the declension of 'four', Avestan contrasts nom. masc. *caθβārō* with nom. fem. *cataŋrō* like OInd. *catvā́raḥ* beside *cátasraḥ*. By assuming that Indo-Iranian **tisr-* derives by dissimilation from **tri-sr-*, several scholars long ago proposed to see in these feminine formations a PIE **sor-* 'woman' found also in PIE **swe-sor-* 'sister', Latin *uxor* 'wife', etc. More recently a number of scholars have attempted to abolish PIE **sor-* 'woman' altogether[19]. The most attractive explanation so far advanced is that of W. H. Snyder, *KZ* lxxxiv (1970: 2–4), who argues in favour of an Indo-Iranian innovation based on **tris-* (in **trisno-* etc., see 8.3.1.1.2., 8.3.5.3.). The feminine stem **tris-r-* would be like OInd. *usr-*

fem. 'dawn' (beside *uṣas-*). An original nominative **tisáras* in Old Indian (like *usáras*) would have been replaced by accusative *tisrás* (like *usrás*), and *cátasras* would by analogy have replaced **cátaras*.

8.1.3.1. There are some differences of detail in the inflection of Av. *θri-* compared with that of OInd. *tri-*; for agreements see 5.1.3. Thus nominative masculine *θrāiiō* contrasts with OInd. *tráyaḥ*[20]. The *-ā-* is subject to secondary shortening in *θraiias-ča* (Y. 1.10) just as we find *caθβarasca* (Yt. 19.7) beside *caθβārō* (= OInd. *catvā̆raḥ*). In fact, *θrāiiō* may have been formed to *θraiiasca* after *caθβārō*: *caθβarasca*, etc. (cf. W. Caland, *KZ* xxxiii, 1893: 594). Bartholomae, however, claimed the support of Modern Iranian languages in favour of the antiquity of *-ā-*[21] (*Grundriss der iranischen Philologie [GIP]*, Strassburg, 1895–1901: i. 111, 131; *ZDMG* xlviii, 1894: 143) but the evidence of Bal. *sai* and Wakhī *trūi* (Morgenstierne 1938: 489) is insufficient to let us decide. On the other hand, where a short vowel form occurs later, as in Khot. *drai, draya*, the influence of the genitive (Av. *θraiiąm*, Khot. *draiṇu* < **drayänu*) may account for it (but see 8.1.3.4.).

8.1.3.2. It is unlikely that Modern Persian *sih* 'three' goes back to a form corresponding to the Avestan accusative neuter *θrī* (= OInd. *trī́* [RV]), as Bartholomae wanted, rather than to **θrā̆yah* as Horn and others (Geiger – Kuhn, *GIP*, Strassburg, 1895–1901: i. 34) suggest. The spelling *sh*[22] for the Middle Persian of Turfan gives no indication of the vowel length as the spelling was clearly devised to distinguish it from *syh* 'thirty'. In Parthian, however, where 'three' and 'thirty' are distinct already for other reasons, the spelling with *-y* is found: *hry* 'three', but *hryst* 'thirty'. Moreover, the Middle Persian of Turfan has *sy-* in *syzdh* 'thirteen', Modern Persian *sīzdah* (see 8.1.13.). The spellings with *-y* in Sogdian (*'δry*; cf. É. Benveniste, *Essai de grammaire sogdienne*, 1929: 141) and in Chorasmian (*šy*)[23] will also reflect **θrā̆yah*.

8.1.3.3. It is possible that the Middle Persian of Turfan preserves a reflex of Avestan *tišrō* 'three' in the word for 'three hundred': *tyryst* or *tylyst*. A continuation is found also in early Modern Persian *tīrist* (Lazard 1963: 217). It was proposed by É. Benveniste, *BSL* xxxii, 1931: 88–91, that *tyryst* may represent the late Avestan *tišrō sata* 'three hundred' (V. 2.30, 4.11). A further survival may be Paštō *tēr sū* (Benveniste, against Morgenstierne 1927: 21). But Parthian *hrysd* 'three hundred' contains merely *hry* 'three' just as Christian Sogdian *šyst* contains Christian Sogdian *šy* 'three'.

8.1.3.4. The Avestan genitive masc.-neuter *θraiiąm* contrasts with OInd. *trīṇā́m* (RV) and *tráyāṇām* (classical). Theoretically, *θraiiąm* could stand graphically for **θriiiąm* (the attested spelling *θriiąm* is probably defective) and be compared with Greek *τριῶν*. Such a **θriiiąm* would accord well with the Avestan gen. *caturąm* 'four', but it seems difficult to reconcile with Khot. *draiṇu* and Middle Persian (Turfan) *sn'n*. Bartholomae, *Grundriss der iranischen Philologie* (1895–1901: 135) regarded *θraiiąm* as related to *tráyāṇām* as is *vaiiąm* (radical *i*-stem) to *vaiianąm* 'of birds'. The expected **θraiianąm*, created under the influence of *pancanąm*, etc. (8.1.), could in fact be continued by Khot. *draiṇu* and Middle Persian (Turfan) *sn'n*. Av. *θraiiąm* and *vaiiąm* probably owe their full grade to their monosyllabic stem under the influence of such forms as the nominative-accusative plural (so Brugmann – Delbrück 1897–1916: II. ii. 242–243). Association with the Old Indian nom. masc. *tráyaḥ* is clear in the accentuation of OInd. *tráyāṇām* (see 5.1.3.1.) by contrast with *pañcānā́m*, etc. But both Middle Iranian forms are unfortunately able to be explained in various ways. Both may simply reflect patterning of 'three' on 'two' (cf. Khot. *dvīnu* and Middle Persian (Turfan) *dwn'n* (8.1.2.1.)). Khot. *draiṇu* is particularly ambiguous because it may relate to either *drai* or *draya* in the nominative-accusative. These I take to represent respectively **θrăyah* and **θrăyā(h)*, the latter with nominative-accusative masculine ending of the a-declension (see Emmerick 1968: 264). Thus *drai* : *draiṇu* :: *dvī* : *dvīnu*, and *draya* : **drayänu* (> *draiṇu*) :: *haṣṭa* : *haṣṭänu*, are both possible analogical proportions. For *-änu*, see 8.1.0.1.

8.1.3.5. The Avestan feminine genitive *tišrąm* also shows an older form than OInd. *tisr̥̄ṇā́m*. Similarly, Avestan has a masculine genitive *caturąm* beside OInd. *caturṇā́m*. The influence of the *n*-declension is seen in Avestan only through the "thematicized" feminine genitive *tišranąm*.

8.1.3.6. PIE **tri-* as the first member of a compound and in derivation is continued by Av. *θri-*, corresponding to OInd. *tri-* (5.1.3.3.). Avestan has such compounds as *θri-aiiar-* 'period of three days', *θri-kamərəδa-* 'three-headed', *θri-māhiia-* 'lasting three months', etc. OIran. **θri-* is probably regularly continued in Khotanese as *dri-* in *drri-bāḍua-* 'belonging to the three times' and *drrä-haṣkalia-* 'pertaining to the three spheres'. From still later Iranian note Paštō *dərbalaī* 'tripod' < **θri-pad-* (Morgenstierne 1927: 21).

8.1.4. 'Four'

In Avestan, the masculine nominative form is *caθβārō*. Its declension is based on the two stems *caθβar-* (masc.-neuter) and *cataŋr-* fem., which correspond to OInd. *catvar-, catasr-*. Exactly equivalent to Old Indian forms are: masculine nom. *caθβārō* = OInd. *catvā́raḥ*, acc. *caturə̄* = OInd. *catúrah*, feminine acc. *cataŋrō* = OInd. *cátasraḥ*.

8.1.4.1. The *-ā-* of OIran. **čaθwārah* is widely confirmed: Middle Persian (Turfan) *čh'r*, Zoroastrian Pahl. *čh'r*, Parthian *cf'r*, Chor. *cf'r*, Sogdian *čtf'r*,[24] Modern Persian *čahār*, Ossetic (Digor) *cuppar*, (Iron) *cyppar*. Less direct confirmation is afforded by Khot. *tcahora* and Paštō *calōr* (Morgenstierne 1927: 17). Already in the Late Avestan of the Vendidad, *caθβārō* is generalized (as nominative feminine, accusative neuter), and that is the only form that is usually represented in Iranian.

8.1.4.2. Whether one postulates a corresponding long vowel for Proto-Indo-European depends on one's views concerning the ablaut variation. Thus Brugmann — Delbrück 1897—1916: 12) posited **k*^{w}*etwor-es* in line with Greek τέτορες (Doric; Attic τέτταρες), while Hirt (1921—1937: iii. 308) adopted **k*^{w}*ъtwṓres* in line with Indo-Iranian and Germanic (Gothic *fidwor*). Both *-or-* and *-ōr-* may represent secondarily contrasted grades in relation to an old Indo-European accusative **k*^{w}*etur̥ns* represented directly in Indo-Iranian (8.1.4.3.); see now R. Schmitt-Brandt, *Die Entwicklung des indogermanischen Vokalsystems* (*Wissenschaftliche Bibliothek* VII) (1967: 24 n. 28).

If one accepts H. Pedersen's reformulation (*KZ* xxxvi, 1900: 74—110) of Brugmann's Law (as does, for instance, Lehmann, *Proto-Indo-European Phonology*, 1955: 30), the *-ā-* in **čaθwārah*, etc., will continue regularly PIE **-ŏ-*. But the *-ā-* can be explained as an Indo-Iranian innovation. See Kuryłowicz (1968: 282, 286), who suggests the influence of the long grade in strong stems of root-nouns. According to older scholars the accent was originally on the first syllable as in Greek τέτορες (so H. Møller, *PBB* vii, 1880: 499, 547; A. Fick *Göttingische gelehrte Anzeigen* [GGA] 1880: 428), but, since A. Meillet, *BSL* xxiii (1922: 35) (so also Hirt 1921—1937: v. 288), it has been accepted as having the second syllable accented (cf. Latin *quattuor*, Arm. *čʻorkʻ*).

The Indo-Iranian long grade may have been secondarily imported from the neuter, attested by OInd. *catvā́ri*. The expected Avestan counterpart, nom.-acc. *caθβārə**, is, probably only by chance, unattested. The Avestan accusative neuter *catura*, found once only, in a late text (V. 19.22) is certainly a secondary thematic form. The *-ā-* of OInd. *catvā́ri* follows a Proto-Indo-European type (see Brugmann — Delbrück 1897—1916: II. ii. 1, 235—236). The Germanic forms could also represent the neuter.

8.1.4.3. The Avestan masculine acc. *caturə̄* occurs once only (Yt. 5.129) but is indirectly confirmed by the thematic neuter acc. *catura* (see 8.1.4.2.). The form corresponds exactly to OInd. *catúraḥ* < PIE **k*^{w}*etur-n̥s*.

8.1.4.4. The Avestan masculine gen. *caturąm* (once only (Nīrangistān 65 [J. W. Waag 1941: 70, l. 8]), is older than the partially corresponding OInd. *caturṇā́m* (see 8.1.3.5.). Av. *caturąm*, set beside Greek (Lesbian) πισύρων, (Attic) τεττάρων, continues a PIE *k^wetur-ōm.*

8.1.4.5. The Avestan feminine acc. *cataŋrō* is a regular development from OIran. **čatahrah* [25] which corresponds exactly to OInd. *cátasraḥ*. For *-sr-* see 8.1.3. Hirt (1921–1937: iii. 308), reconstructed **k^weto-sres*. This feminine formation is otherwise found only in Celtic e. g., OIrish *cethéoir*, where *-eoir* derives from *-esor(es)* (cf. R. Thurneysen, *A grammar of Old Irish*, 1946: 246). Just as in the case of the feminine stem Av. *tišr-*, OInd. *tisr-*, dissimilation of *r* – *r* seems certain (8.1.3. and 5.1.3.2.), so here too dissimilation seems probable as *r* is essential to 'four' in all its forms (PIE **k^wetwor-* : **k^wetur-*). In the case of Indo-Iranian it appears that *w* was lost by dissimilation as elsewhere too (cf. Szemerényi 1960: 20). Thus PIE **k^wetwor-sr-es* > **k^wetosres*.

8.1.4.6. Khotanese also preserves inflected forms of PIE **k^wetwor-*: nom.-acc. *tcahauri, tcohaurä*, etc., and *tcahora, tcohora*, etc.; gen.-dat. *tcuīrnu, tcuīnu*; instr.-abl. *tcūryau*; loc. *tcūruvo'*. Nom.-acc. *-ä* in Old Khotanese continues the ancient consonant-stem declension while *-a* shows thematicization (cf. 8.1.3.4.). The *-o-* in the first syllable shows assimilation to the second syllable. The form *tcuī(r)nu* is from **tcuīränu*, where *-änu* is the generalized termination (see 8.1.0.1.). The palatalization (*uī* < *$ū^i$*) will also be that generalized from the decads. The *ū* in the instrumental-ablative and locative is not surprising, as *ū* does not always admit palatalization. *tcūra-*, which serves as the stem for these oblique forms, is also found as the first element of a compound and as the basis of the ordinal *tcūrama-* 'fourth'. This *tcūra-* must derive from **čaθru-* (8.1.4.7.).

8.1.4.7. As the first element of a compound, 'four' appears in Avestan in three forms according to Bartholomae (*GIP*, 1895–1901: i. 150): *caturə-* in *caturə.zīzanatąm* (Yt. 5.129 only; acc.masc. *caturə̄* given in Bartholomae 1904: 577) 'quattuor parientium'; *caθru-* in *caθru.yuxtəm* (V. 7.41) 'mit vieren bespannt'; *caθβarə-* in *caθβarə.zangra-* (V. 18.38, Y. 9.18) 'vierfüssig'. The first, whether in a compound or not,[26] is probably the accusative plural masculine (8.1.4.3.). *čaθru°*[27] is no doubt the Proto-Indo-European form **k^wetru°* seen in Latin *quadru°*, Gaulish *petru-*. It is continued also in Khot. *tcūra-*. Already Salemann – Shukovski (1899: 128) recognised OIran. *čaθru-* in Middle Persian (Turfan) *ts-* as in *tsb'y* 'four-footed' < **čaθru-pāda-*[28]. *caθβarə° probably continues PIE *k^wetwr̥* (regular variant of **k^wetru-* as suggested by Brugmann – Delbrück

1897–1916: II. ii. 1,15 against Bartholomae). *-arə* (not *-ərə-*) may be due to such forms as *caθβarasca* (8.1.3.1.) and *caθβarəsat* 'forty' (see 8.1.23.) reanalyzed after *θrisat-* 'thirty' beside *θri-* (8.1.3.6.). See further 8.1.14. and 5.1.4.2.

8.1.5. 'Five'

OIran. **panča* 'five' presents no problems and can be compared exactly with OInd. *páñca* < PIE **penkʷe*: cf. Greek πέντε, Latin *quīnque*, etc. Iranian examples: Av. *panca*, Sogd. *pnč*, Chor. *pnc*, Middle Persian (Turfan) *pnz*, Parth. *pnǰ*, Modern Persian *panǰ*, Khot. *paṃjsa*, Paštō *pinja*, Oss. *fonj*. See further 5.1.5.

8.1.6. 'Six'

The Iranian words for 'six' fall into two groups: those continuing **(x)šwaš* and those continuing **(x)šaš*. To **(x)šwaš* belong Av. *xšuuaš*, Parth. *šwh*, Buddhist Sogd. *wγwšw*, Paštō *špaẓ̌*. To **(x)šaš* belong Zoroastrian Pahl. *šaš*, Modern Persian *šeš*, Chor. *'x*, Khot. *kṣäta'*, Oss. *äxsäz*. It is probable that **(x)šaš* is merely a simplification of **(x)šwaš* (cf. 5.1.6.). The Chorasmian, Khotanese, and Ossetic forms are accordingly said to represent Av. *xšuuaš*. Certainly in the case of Chorasmian and Khotanese we have one instance of a different result to set beside Av. *xšuu-*. Thus, where Avestan has *xšuuipta-* 'milk', Chorasmian has *xwfc* and Khotanese *ṣvīda-*. But in Modern Persian, where *šeš* developed, *š-* is found for *xšw-* in *šēb* 'whip', cf. Sogd. *xwšyp*, **xšwaipa-* (cf. Av. *xšuuiβi-*). From the base **xšwaip-* Khotanese has *kṣäv-* (Emmerick 1968: 25). A. S. C. Ross, *Transactions of the Philological Society* (1944: 57) proposed to explain Khot. *kṣäṣa'* as derived from a form **xšaš* which, according to him, is based on a contamination of **xwaš*, which he sees in Buddhist Sogd. *wγwšw*, with a form **š(w)aš*. However, PIE **sw-* results in Khot. *hv-*, as in *hvī* 'sweat' (cf. OInd. *sveda-*), so that it is difficult to see how **hvaṣ* and **ṣ(v)aṣ* would result in **xšaš*. Moreover, the attempt to find in Buddhist Sogd. *wγwšw* a continuation of PIE **sweḱs* without assimilation of the sibilants cannot convince, as it is contrary to what the Iranian evidence leads us to expect, namely, dissimilatory loss of one *š* (cf. 8.1.6.2.). The variety of treatment of the group *xšw-*, not only in the word for 'six', but also in other words, is the result of different resolutions of a complicated cluster, rather than an indication of a variety of underlying forms.

8.1.6.1. Strictly speaking, the Iranian evidence could be explained on the basis of an original **swaxš* < IIran. **šwakš* by assimilation from **swakš*, as the development of an initial *x-* could be secondary. But an initial **ks-* is required for Indian (5.1.6.), which also confirms the palatal nature of *ḱ* in the final group. If a single form is to be reconstructed as the Proto-Indo-European antecedent of Indo-Iranian, it must be **ksweḱs*. Such a form is included by Pokorny (1959: 1044). An original PIE **ksweḱs* has often been posited, e. g. by Hirt (1921 – 1937: iii. 308); A. Vaillant, *BSL* xliv (1948: 129).

8.1.6.2. In Iranian the final *š* tended to cause difficulty, which was variously resolved. In Khotanese and Sogdian, a final short vowel was added early under the influence of the other disyllabic numerals ending in *-a*. This may have happened also in the case of Middle Persian *šaš*, Paštō *špaẓ̌*, etc. (see R. Gauthiot, *MSL* xvii, 1911 – 1912: 152 – 153), where the retention of final *-*š* is not expected. In Khotanese, where intervocalic *-*š*- was lost, the *-*š*- was accordingly dropped (OKhot. *kṣäta'*) with eventual contraction of the juxtaposed vowels (*kṣei'*). In other cases, the second *š* may have undergone dissimilation: Oss. *äxsäz* (< **äxsäs*), Parth. *šwh*, Waxī *šāδ*.

8.1.7. 'Seven'

OIran. **hafta* 'seven' presents no difficulties and corresponds exactly to OInd. *saptá* < PIE **septḿ̥*, cf. Greek ἑπτά, Latin *septem*, etc. (cf. 5.1.7.). Some examples are: Av. *hapta*,[29] Middle Persian (Turfan) *hpt*, Parth. *hft*, Zoroastrian Pahl. *haft*, Modern Pers. *haft*. In East Iranian, *-*ft*- was voiced to *-*βd*-: Sogd. -*'βt*, Chor. *'βd*, Khot. *hauda* (< **haβda*), Oss. *awd*. For the loss of *h* in some forms see 8.1.8.2.

8.1.8. 'Eight'

OIran. **aštā* 'eight' corresponds exactly to OInd. *aṣṭā́* (5.1.8. – 5.1.8.1.). IIran. **aštā* continues PIE **oḱtṓ*, cf. Greek ὀκτώ, Latin *octō*, etc. Iranian examples are: Av. *ašta*, Zoroastrian Pahl. *hašt*, Modern Pers. *hašt*, Chor. *'št*, Sogd. *'št*, Khot. *haṣṭa*, Oss. *ast*. For the initial *h-* in some forms see 8.1.8.2. The original length of the final vowel in Old Iranian is confirmed by the form taken by 'eighty': Av. *aštāiti-*, etc. (see 8.1.2.7.). But it was shortened under the influence of **hafta* already in the Common Old Iranian period: Av. *aštadasa-* 'eighteenth' *aštahuua-* 'eighth part', etc.

8.1.8.1. Although the ending of **oḱtṓ* has long been recognized as the dual and hence the existence of a quartal system of reckoning in Indo-European was suspected (see A. S. C. Ross, *Transactions of the Philological Society* [TPS], 1941: 12), an important confirmation was provided by W. B. Henning, *TPS* (1948: 69), from Av. *ašti-*, a measure of length, which he had shown (*Journal of the Royal Asiatic Society* [JRAS], 1942: 235) meant 'four fingers' breadth, palm. According to Szemerényi (1964: 399–400, n. 5), the connection was disputed by H. W. Bailey, *Asia Major* (1959: 23, n. 21). But Bailey is there merely specifying the underlying verbal base in Av. *ašti-* without committing himself concerning *ašta* 'eight'. See further 5.1.23.

8.1.8.2. The words for 'seven' and 'eight' have had considerable influence on each other in Iranian owing to their structural similarity, which is especially clear when one bears in mind the weakness of initial *h-* in Iranian. *h-* is normally used for both 'seven' and 'eight'; see, for instance, Zoroastrian Pahl. *haft, hašt*; Modern Pers. *haft, hašt*; Khot. *hauda, haṣṭa*; Waxī *hūb, hat*; or for neither, for instance, Chor. *'βd, 'št*; Sogd. *'βt, 'št*; Oss. *awd, ast*; Paštō *ōwa, at*; Yidgha *avdo, aščo*. Avestan has the original distribution in *hapta, ašta*, but even there the finals have been assimilated (8.18.).

8.1.9. 'Nine'

OIran. **nawa* 'nine' presents no difficulty and can be compared directly with OInd. *náva* (5.1.9.). Whether Proto-Indo-European had final *-*n̥* or *-*m̥* (see Brugmann – Delbrück 1897–1916 II. ii. 1,20; Szemerényi 1960: 171–173) cannot be decided from the Indo-Iranian side. Iranian examples: Av. *nauua*; Khot. *nau*; Sogd. *nw'*; Zoroastrian Pahl. *noh*, Modern Pers. *noh* (with *-h* from *dah* 'ten').

8.1.9.1. In later Iranian, two languages show a notable divergence at 'nine', although there is evidence that **nawa* was inherited: Ossetic has *farast* and Chorasmian *š'δ*. Miller (1903: 48) very plausibly derived *farast* from **para* (cf. Av. *parō*, Greek πέρα 'further') and *ast* 'eight' [30]. **nawa* is attested, however, in Ossetic (Digor) *näudas*, (Iron) *nudäs* 'nineteen'. Chor. *š'δ* was derived by W. B. Henning, *Togan Fs.* (1950: 433) from **frād-* 'to increase' (Av. *frād-*, etc.). Chorasmian has **nava* in *nw'δ(y)s* 'nineteen' *nw(y)c* 'ninety' and *nwsd* 'nine hundred'.

8.1.10. 'Ten'

Indo-Iranian had **daśa* for 'ten': Av. *dasa* beside OInd. *dáśa*. An OIran. **dasa* is represented by Sogd. *δs'*, Chor. *δ(y)s*, Parth. *ds*, Oss. *däs*. OPers. **daθa* is represented in an Elamite loan (Brandenstein – Mayrhofer 1964: 116) and is continued in Middle Persian (Turfan) *dh*, Zoroastrian Pahl. *dah*, Modern Pers. *dah*. Khot. *dasau* probably has *-au* from *nau* 'nine' rather than from **-akam* as suggested by Konow (1932: 51), since the oblique cases do not admit **-aka* (gen. *-änu*, not *-ānu*, see 8.1.0.1.). The Indo-Iranian evidence set beside other languages, e. g., Greek δέκα, Latin *decem*, leads to the reconstruction of PIE **deḱm̥*. But see 8.1.31.1., 8.2.11.2., and 8.1.15., n. 35.

8.1.10.1. No special form is found as the first element of a compound for the numerals 'five' to 'ten', the unchanged cardinal being used. Examples from Avestan: *panca.māhiia-* 'lasting five months', *xšuuaš.aši-* 'six-eyed', *hapta.māhiia-* 'lasting seven months', *ašta.māhiia-* 'lasting eight months', *nauua.xšapar-* 'period of nine nights'. *dasa.māhiia-* 'lasting ten months'.

8.1.10.2. The 'teens'

'Eleven' to 'nineteen', indeclinable in Old Iranian, are attested in Avestan as follows: 'eleven' *aēuuandasa**; 'twelve' *duuadasa*; 'thirteen' *θridasa**; 'fourteen' *caθrudasa**; 'fifteen' *pancadasa*; 'sixteen' *xšuuaš.dasa**; 'seventeen' *haptadasa**; 'eighteen' *aštadasa**; 'nineteen' *nauuadasa**. The forms with an asterisk added are attested only as ordinals. All forms are from non-Gāthic Avestan. All are clearly related to the cardinals 'one' to 'nine' (8.1.0.) and have *dasa* 'ten' as their second component. The forms were compounded already in Indo-Iranian but probably independently in the various Indo-European languages. For the corresponding Old Indian forms see 5.1.12. For additional remarks on the underlying structure see 5.1.17.

8.1.11. 'Eleven'

Av. *aēuuandasa** was thought by Bartholomae (*GIP* 1895–1901: i. 112) to continue PIE **oiwondeḱm̥*, from which he also derived Latin *ūndecim*. He regarded the *-n-* as due to the influence of PIE **sendeḱm̥* seen in

Greek ἕνδεκα. Brugmann — Delbrück's explanation (1897—1916: II. ii. 1,24—25) is more probable: *aēuuan-* from nom.-acc. sg. ntr. *aēuuam*. Greek ἕν is also a nominative-accusative singular neuter and Latin *ūndecim* is from **ūnundecim* < **oinom-decem*, where **oinom* is also nominative-accusative singular neuter.

8.1.11.1. An OIran. **aiwandasa* is directly continued by Parth *'ywnds*, Chor. *'ywnd(y)s*, Christian Sogd. *ywnts*,[31], Ossetic (Digor) *yevändäs*, (Iron) *yuändäs*,[32] Parāčī *žuuns*, Zaza *žūendäs* (Morgenstierne 1929: 304), Ormuṛī *šǟndas* (Morgenstierne 1929: 408). In Khotanese, 'eleven' has been found only in the late language, where *śūdasa*[33] may represent an OKhot. **śśūndasu*. As in Khotanese *-d-* is usually lost and is so in 'twelve' to 'nineteen', while **-nd*, when secondary, remains, often written *-d-*, there is a strong presumption in favour of **śśūndasu*.

8.1.11.2. OIran. **aiwandasa* differs from the usual Indian *ékādaśa* (5.1.13.), not only in respect of the choice of **aiwa-* as against **aika-* (8.1.1.—8.1.1.1.), but also in the composition. OInd. *ékādaśa* shows the influence of *dvā́daśa* 'twelve'. A similar **aiwādasa* may be represented in Iranian by Waziri Paštō *ywōlas, ywēlas* (Morgenstierne 1927: 100). The length of the vowel in the first syllable of Modern Persian *yāzdah* 'eleven' (cf. Middle Persian (Turfan) *y'zdhwm* 'eleventh') could be accounted for in this way. The *-z-* is usually said to have spread from *pānzdah* 'fifteen' (P. Horn 1898—1901: 144), but it can be explained as old in the nearer *sīzdah* 'thirteen' (see 8.1.13.1.), and even in *yāzdah* it may represent a survival of the old nominative singular masculine ending: *yāzdah* < **aiwaz-daθa* (P. Tedesco, *JAOS* xlii, 1922: 296). On the other hand, the Dardic forms, Kati *yanīċ* and Ashkun *ċänīs* may represent an older **ekaṁdaśa* (G. Morgenstierne, *NTS* xiii, 1945: 233; Turner 1966: no. 2526) structurally like OIran. **aiwandasa*.

8.1.12. 'Twelve'

Av. *duuadasa*, with *duuă-*, may be secondary, perhaps due to the influence of nom. masc. *duua*, as a Common Old Iranian compound **dwādasa* seems to be indicated by the concordance of Middle Persian (Turfan) *dw'zdh*, Zoroastrian Pahl. *dwāzdah*, Modern Pers. *davāzdah* (for *-h* see 8.1.11.2.), Parth. *dw'dys*, Chor. *'δw's*, Sog. *δw'ts*, Khot. *dvāsu*, Paštō *d(w)ōlas*, Parāčī *duwās*, Ormuṛī *dwâs*, Ossetic (Digor) *duvadäs*, (Iron) *dyvvadäs*[34]. With this OIran. **dwādasa*, OInd. *dvā́daśa* can be equated (5.1.12.).

8.1.13. 'Thirteen'

Av. *θridasa** is characterized by the use of **θri-*, the form for 'three' used as first element of a compound and in derivation (8.1.3.6.), instead of the masculine nom. *θrāiiō* (8.1.3.). See 5.1.17. *θridasa** is continued by Chor. *hrδ(y)s*, Ossetic (Digor) *ärtindäs*, (Iron) *ärtyndäs* (with intrusive *-n-* due to 'eleven' and 'fifteen' – see Tedesco 1922: 296; Szemerényi 1960: 53).

8.1.13.1. OInd. *tráyodaśa* 'thirteen' has its Iranian counterpart in Middle Persian (Turfan) *syzdh*, Modern Pers. *sīzdah*, which represent an Old Persian dialect form **s̭sayaz-daθa* (cf. P. Tedesco, *JAOS* xlii, 1922: 296). **s̭sayaz-* is the Old Persian equivalent of an Av. *θraiiaz-**, which would be the sandhi-form corresponding to voiceless *θraiias-* in Av. *θraiias-ca* (8.1.3.1.). The preservation of **-az-* in such a position in some cases in Old Iranian is well-known: Av. *aogaz-dastəma-* 'der am meisten Kraft gibt', Old Persian *Vahyaz-dāta-*. Khot. *draisu* and Paštō *dyā̆rlas* (Morgenstierne 1927: 21), on the other hand, represent a form **θrā̆yah-dasa* with no trace remaining of the ancient sandhi.

8.1.14. 'Fourteen'

Av. *caθrudasa** contains **caθru-*, a form of 'four' used in derivation and composition (8.1.4.7.). **čaθrudasa* is continued in Chor. *cwrδys* (W. B. Henning, *Togan Fs.*, 1950: 433); possibly also in Paštō *swārlas* (Morgenstierne 1927: 17). A corresponding Indian **catrudaśa* is found only in Dardic, Kati *štruċ* and Prasun *čpulċ* (Turner 1966: no. 4605). The alternative compositional form **čaθwar-* is also represented in forms for 'fourteen' based on **čaθwar-dasa* such as Khot. *tcahaulasa* and Ossetic (Digor) *cuppärdäs*, (Iron) *cyppärdäs*. In Khotanese, **-rd-* > *-l-*, but an intervocalic **-d-* would simply be lost. In other cases, although a form like **čaθwar-dasa* may have been the starting-point, the influence of the cardinal 'four' has prevailed: Parth. *čf'rds*, Zoroastrian Pahl. *čahārdah*, Modern Pers. *čahārdah*; for *čār-* in *čārdah* see 8.1.4.7., n. 28. On the relationship of OInd. *cáturdaśa* to OIran. **čaθwardasa* see 5.1.4.2.; 5.1.14.

8.1.15. 'Fifteen'

Av. *pancadasa* corresponds exactly to OInd. *páñcadaśa*. Iranian examples are: Middle Persian (Turfan) *p'nzdh*, Modern Pers. *pānzdah*, Chor. *pnṣ* (W. B. Henning, *Handbuch der Orientalistik* IV, 1958: 118), Sogd. *pnčts-*, Khot. *paṃjsūsi*[35], Ossetic (Digor) *findtäs*, (Iron) *fyndtäs*.

8.1.16. 'Sixteen'

An OIran. **xšwaž-dasa*, to which OInd. *ṣóḍaśa* would correspond exactly (5.1.16.), is represented in Avestan by *xšuuaš.dasa** 'sixteen'. The spelling is analytical, influenced by the component cardinal *xšuuaš* 'six'. In most Iranian languages **xšwaž-dasa* developed further to **xšwar-dasa*: Chor. *'xrδys* (W. B. Henning, *Handbuch der Orientalistik* IV, 1958: 118), Christian Sogd. *xwšrts* [36], Ormuṛī *ṣ̌ūlēs* (Morgenstierne 1929: 347), Oss. *äxsär-däs*, Paštō *špāṛas* (Morgenstierne 1927: 76). Khot. *kṣasu* may rather have developed via **xšaštsu*. Middle Persian (Turfan) *š'zdh*, Modern Pers. *šāndzah* show progressive influence of *p'nzdh* 'fifteen'.

8.1.17. 'Seventeen'

Av. *haptadasa** corresponds exactly to OInd. *saptádaśa*. Iranian examples are Chor. *'βd-δ(y)s*, Zoroastrian Pahl. *haftdah*, Modern Pers. *haf(t)dah*, Oss. *äwdtäs*, Ormuṛī *awēs* (Morgenstierne 1929: 347). Khot. *haudūsu* probably continues **haftadasam* (8.1.15., n. 35). Christian Sogdian probably had **btts*. The ordinal is given as *bbtsmyq* by Hansen (1954: 898 [107]), but comparison with *btmyq* 'seventh' (Hansen, 1954: 897 [77]) and *šttsmyq* 'eighteenth' (cf. 8.1.18.) would lead one to expect **bttsmyq*. M. Schwartz, *Studies in the texts of the Sogdian Christians* (1968: 60) suggested a misprint but the reading is confirmed by N. Sims-Williams, *The Christian Sogdian Manuscript C 2* Berlin (1985: 104).

8.1.18. 'Eighteen'

Av. *aštādasa** corresponds to OInd. *aṣṭā́daśa* apart from the vowel quantity in the second syllable. The short vowel in Iranian is to be expected from the treatment of **aštā* 'eight'; cf. 8.1.8. It is not necessary to assume with Reichelt (1909: 214–215) that **aštādasa* was influenced by 'fifteen', 'seventeen' and 'nineteen'. OIran. **aštādasa* is continued by Chor. *'št-δ(y)s*, Christian Sogd. *štts* [37], Zoroastrian Pahl. *haštdah*, Modern Pers. *haštdah, hiždah, hiǰdah* (see Lazard 1963: 216–217), Ossetic (Digor) *äst(d)äs*, (Iron) *(ä)stäs*. On Khot. *haṣṭūsu* < **aštadasam* see note 35 (8.1.15.).

8.1.19. 'Nineteen'

Av. *nauuadasa** corresponds exactly to OInd. *návadaśa*. The form is continued in Iranian by Chor. *nw'δ(y)s*, Christian Sogd. *nwts* (attested in Ordinal *nwtsmq*, Hansen 1954: 898 [112]), Ossetic (Digor) *näudäs*, (Iron) *nudäs*, Modern Pers. *nūzdah, nuvāzdah* (with *-z-* from *pānzdah* 'fifteen'). Khotanese has *nausu* < **nawadasam* (cf. note 35).

8.1.20. The decads

'Twenty' to 'ninety' are attested in Avestan as follows:

	Avestan	Old Indian
'twenty'	*vīsaiti*	*viṃśatí*
'thirty'	*θrisatəm*	*triṃśát*
'forty'	*caθβarəsatəm*	*catvāriṃśát*
'fifty'	*pancāsatəm*	*pañcāśát*
'sixty'	*xšuuaštīm*	*ṣaṣṭí*
'seventy'	*haptāitīm*	*saptatí*
'eighty'	*aštāitīm*	*aśītí*
'ninety'	*nauuaitīm*	*navatí*

These forms all belong to the later Avesta and, after 'twenty', are all in the accusative. Other forms will be discussed in the appropriate paragraphs. On 'twenty', 'thirty', 'forty', see C. Bartholomae, *IF* xlii (1924: 133–142).

8.1.21. 'Twenty'

An OIran. **wīsati* as seen in Av. *vīsaiti* is continued by forms in many Iranian languages, e. g., Parth. *wyst*, Christian Sogd. *wyst* (attested in the ordinal *wystmyq*, Hansen 1954: 898 [117]), Zoroastrian Pahl. *wīst*, Modern Pers. *bīst*, Balōčī *gīst*, Ormuṛī *jīst*, Yidgha *wīšt*, Sanglēčī *wīšt*, Waxī *wīst*, Paštō *wīšt* (and *šil*[38]; see Morgenstierne 1927: 73). A secondary shortening of *-ī-* seems to have taken place in Parāčī *ušt* (Morgenstierne 1929: 25, 59), Chor *'wsyc* and Khot. *bistä*. Ossetic (Digor) *insäi*, (Iron) *ssäj*, may continue an OIran. **winsati* that corresponds exactly to OInd. *viṃśatí* (Henning, *Annali, Istituto orientale di Napoli* [AION] vi (1965: 43, n. 3)). OIran. **wīsati* would then be a later development from **winsati*, which would represent PIE **winḱm̥tī́* (see 5.1.20.).

8.1.21.1. Av. *vīsąs* 'twenty', invented by Bartholomae, has been discussed at length, notably by Szemerényi (1960: 121–123), who has transformed it into an "archaizing" *vīsąsta*. The word in question is a hapax legomenon at Yt. 1.19, where Bartholomae read *vīsąs tāča* for manuscript readings *vīsąstača* (adopted by K. F. Geldner, *Avesta, the sacred books of the Parsis*, 1895), *vīsąstasča, vīsąsčasča, vīsąstisča*. Szemerényi has pointed out the improbability of Bartholomae's *tā*. Moreover, verses 12–15 contain more than twenty names. I suspect that F. Justi, *Handbuch der Zendsprache* (1864: 282), was correct in seeing here *vi-sąh-* = RV *vi-śaṃs-* 'to recite'. The past participle *visąsta-*, against *frasasta-* 'famed', etc., and OInd. *viśasta-*, will owe its *-ą-* to the present stem. It may also have been early associated with *vīsąstəmō* 'twentieth' in Yt. 1.8. The passage thus reads: *vīsąstaca imą̊ nāmə̄nīš parštasca pairiuuārasca vīsənte* 'and when they have been recited these names will serve as a bulwark and a protection'.

8.1.21.2. Av. *vīsata-* 'twenty' in *vīsata.gāiia-* 'a length of twenty paces' (V. 17.4) is clearly based on analogy with *θrisata.gāiia-* 'a length of thirty paces' (Bartholomae 1904: 1458). Here *θrisata-* is itself a thematicization of *θrisat-*.

8.1.22. 'Thirty'

Av. *θrisatəm* is nominative-accusative singular neuter of *θrisata-* seen in *θrisata.gāiia-* (8.1.21.2.) and *θrisataθβəm* (8.3.5.2.) 'thirty times'. The earlier athematic form is attested by *θrisaθ-βant-* 'thirtyfold' (Yt. 10.116). The later Iranian forms imply an old athematic stem.

8.1.22.1. Av. *θrisat-* 'thirty' could be purely graphic for **θrīsat-* as the quantity of the *i* is not reliably indicated in the Avestan tradition. The Middle Iranian languages mainly attest **θrīsat-*: Chor. *šys*, Zoroastrian Pahl. *syh*, Middle Persian (Turfan) *syh*, Modern Pers. *sī*, Parth. *hryst*, Manichaean Sogd. *šys* (cf. Gershevitch 1954: 199). The modern languages are in general too remote to provide evidence. The long vowel of Ormuṛī *ṣ̌īstu* could be due to *jīstu* 'twenty' (Morgenstierne 1929: 347). The *-u-* in Parāčī *šus* 'thirty' (Morgenstierne 1929: 60) could be due to vowel assimilation (Szemerényi 1960: 50). The same explanation must apply to Sanglēčī *rʊs, rɜs* 'thirty' (Morgenstierne 1938: 328). The vowel of Ossetic Digor *ärtin*, Iron *ärtyn* 'thirty' (a form from the shepherds' dialects, cf. Frejman, "Zabytye osetinskie čislitel'nye", *Ol'denburg Fs*; 1934: 561–564) is ambiguous.

8.1.22.2. Parth. *hryst* 'thirty', according to Szemerényi (1960: 50), represents 'an earlier **hrīs* (from **θrīsat*) which assumed the final *-t* of *wīst* 'twenty')'. Parth. *hryst* 'thirty' contrasts with *hrysd* 'three hundred', which shows the expected development of intervocalic *-t-* to *-d-*. But *wyst* 'twenty' in Parthian must itself be secondary. In the similar case of Zoroastrian Pahl. *wīst*, Modern Pers. *bīst*, C. Bartholomae assumed that the *-t* was from the ordinal (*GIP* 1895–1901: i. 111). But it is clear that *st* was maintained or restored in secondary contact, e. g., Middle Persian (Turfan) *tyryst* 'three hundred' (8.1.3.3.), Modern Pers. *astar* 'mule' < OPers. **asa-tara-* (P. Horn, *GIP*, 1898–1901: i. 2. 80; OInd. *aśvatará-*, Chor. *sptyr, spdyr*). Parth. *hryst* could thus equally well represent **θrīsata-* or **θrīsat-*.

8.1.22.3. Khot. *därsä* 'thirty', according to C. Bartholomae, *IF* xliii (1924: 141–142), shows the following development: **θris-* > **dris-* > **dr̥s-* or **dərs-* under the influence of 'forty'. But this explanation depends upon an unsatisfactory understanding of Khot. *tcaholsä* 'forty', which must represent **čaθwărsat* (cf. 8.1.4.1., 8.1.4.6.–7., 8.1.14.). Moreover, from **dr̥sat* a form **dälsä* would be expected in Khotanese. The most likely development is **θrīsat* > **drīsä* > **dīrsä* > *därsä* by analogy with *bästä* 'twenty' < **bīstä*.

8.1.22.4. In two places (Y. 1.10, V. 14.9 bis), Avestan has *θrisą̄s* 'thirty', which led Bartholomae (*GIP*, 1895–1901: i. 111) to assume an inherited nasal stem **θrisant-*. *θrisatəm, caθβarəsatəm*, and *pancāsatəm* are irregular to a nominative *θrisą̄s*. Hence Bartholomae then assumed (*GIP*, 1895–1901: i. 117) that *-santəm* was replaced by *-satəm* under the influence of *satəm* 'hundred'. Szemerényi (1960: 121) used the same analogy to explain the replacement of older *θrisat-* (8.1.22.). But it seems difficult to assume that in a phrase like *panca vā* **pancāsat vā satəm vā* 'five or fifty or a hundred', *satəm* should have induced *pancāsatəm*, which looks dangerously like *panca sata* 'five hundred'. Moreover it did not induce *pancāsata-*, even in the case of the formula in V. 7.53: *pancasaɣnāi ... sataɣnāi ... hazaŋraɣnāi ... baēuuarəɣnāi ...*[39] The thematicization must be part of the general Avestan process of thematicisation to avoid consonant-stem declension. Even so, Sommer (1951: 55) is right of course to emphasize that such forms in Iranian cannot be used to establish an Indo-European thematic inflection.

8.1.22.5. Av. *θrisą̄s* has been explained away by Szemerényi (1960: 123–124). Starting from Y. 1.10 he explains *θrisą̄s* as substituted for **θrisas* (comparing *-as* beside *-ą̄s* in the nominative singular of present participles, etc.) and **θrisas* as the Avestan sandhi-form (before *ca*) of **θrisat̰*. The other occurrences he passes over with the words: "The other two instances in the *Vidēvdāt* (14.9), in which *θrisą̄s* functions as an 'instrumental', are ungrammatical and the interpretation hardly final".

In fact, there can be no question of dismissing these perfectly clear occurrences. In a list of weapons we have *akana maṯ θrisąs aiiō.aγrāiš* 'quiver with thirty metal-pointed (arrows)' and *fradaxšana ... maṯ θrisąs fradaxšaniiāiš* 'a sling ... with thirty sling(-stones)'. *θrisąs* is clearly only "ungrammatical" in the sense that it shows a nominative singular masculine form generalized instead of a "grammatical" instrumental plural **θrisaṯbīš*, or, thematic, **θrisatāiš*. Such generalizations are not uncommon in the later Avesta and, of course, the nominative-accusative singular neuter forms in *-satəm* were similarly generalized. In any case, a tendency to generalize case-forms of the decads can be seen very early in Old Indian (5.1.18.). *θrisąs* could in fact be old, < PIE **trīḱonts*, if compared with Bret. *tregont*, OIrish *trícho* (see G. Schmidt, *KZ* lxxxiv, 1970: 122).

8.1.23. 'Forty'

Av. *caθβarəsatəm* is nominative-accusative singular neuter to **caθβarəsata-*, thematicization of *caθβarəsat-* seen in *caθβarəsaθβant-* 'fortyfold' (Yt. 10.116). The Avestan writing of the word is wholly ambiguous, as recognized by Bartholomae, who suggested four possible interpretations (1924: 138–140): 1) shortening of **caθβārəsatəm* like *caθβarasca* beside *caθβārō* (8.1.3.1.); 2) *ar* < PIE **r̥̄*, cf. Latin *quadrāgintā*, Greek τετρώκοντα; 3) **caθβar-* is the form used as first element of a compound (8.1.4.7.); 4) *-arə-* may be graphic for *-ərə-* so that **caθβərə-* represents PIE **k^w^etwr̥-*. Khot. *tcaholsä* 'forty' (cf. *tcahaulasa* 'fourteen', 8.1.14.) must represent **čaθwăr°* and probably excludes the fourth possibility. Christian Sogd. *štfrs* (Hansen 1954: 897) could also represent **čaθwar-*. This **čaθwar-* could be secondary (first element of a compound) or original (< PIE **r̥̄*).

8.1.23.1. The much-discussed Paštō word for 'forty', *calwēṣ̌t*, has been variously explained (cf. B. Geiger, *ABAW* XX, 1897: 208; Bartholomae *IF* xlii, 1924: 141; Morgenstierne 1927: 17, 1948: 70; Szemerényi 1960: 52). Morgenstierne changed from seeing **čaθwr̥sata-* to seeing **čaθwr̥sat-* behind it. Szemerényi wishes to see **čaθwarsat-* and writes of "the parallel development of *wēṣ̌t* 'hair' < OIr. *warsa-*", referring to Morgenstierne (1948: 70). The Khotanese and Sogdian forms would incline one to expect **čaθwarsat(a)-*. The *-ē-* in *calwēṣ̌t* points to a palatalised *-a-* as in *špēta* 'sixty' < **xšwašti-* (Morgenstierne 1927: 76).

8.1.23.2. The Ossetic shepherds' dialects (cf. A. A. Frejman, *Ol'denburg Festschrift*, 1934: 561–564) have Digor *cuppor*, Iron *cyppor* 'forty', which differ only in respect of the final vowel from the standard words for 'four', Digor *cuppar*, Iron *cyppar*. Szemerényi (1960: 53) compares the treatment of **hwar-* 'sun' in Ossetic (Digor) *xor*, (Iron) *xūr*. But in the case of *cuppor, cyppor*, we have *-o-* in both dialects, which is characteristic of the treatment of OIran. *ă̄* before nasals (Miller 1903: §§ 10.1, 20). Nevertheless, this is hardly enough to justify Frejman's derivation from **čaθwārinsat-*. Moreover, the numeral 'forty' survives in a much more archaic form in Ossetic in the name for Christmas, which was no doubt originally preceded by a forty-day fast: Digor *cäpporse*, Iron *cyppūrs* (Abaev 1958: 323, 1970: 5, cf. chapter 5). Here the expected alternation *o/ū* occurs and the *s* survives.

8.1.23.3. Zoroastrian Pahl. *čh(h)l*, Modern Pers. *čehel* 'forty' have generally been regarded as continuing an OPers. **čaθwr̥θat-* — for literature see C. Bartholomae, *IF* xlii (1924: 140). But Szemerényi (1960: 51–52) has attempted to show that they could be derived from **čaθwarθat-*, which would correspond to the OIran. **čaθwarsat-* proposed for the forms discussed above (8.1.23.–8.1.23.2.). He suggests that the secondarily palatalized vowel of the first syllable may have prevented the expected development of the second syllable by causing vowel assimilation. Thus, as he puts it, "**čahwahl* > **čihahl* > **čihihl*" instead of **čahwahl* > **čihahl* > **čihāl* (as Modern Pers. *x^vāl* 'food' beside Av. *x^varəθa-*). But the vowel assimilation must have worked in the opposite direction, as has traditionally been understood: *i(h)l* < *r̥θ*. There is no *-i-* in *čahār* 'four'. The reason for the replacement of **čaθwarθat-* by **čaθwr̥θat-* remains unclear. One is reminded, of course, of the Old Indian antecedent of *caturthá-* 'fourth', namely **catvr̥thá-* (5.2.41.), but this seems not to be reflected in Iranian.

8.1.24. 'Fifty'

Av. *pancāsatəm* is nominative-accusative singular neuter to *pancāsata-* seen in *pancāsata.gāiia-* 'length of fifty paces' (V. 17.4). *pancāsata-* is a thematicization of *pancāsat-* found in *panca.saθβant-* 'fiftyfold' (Yt. 10.116) and instr. masc. pl. *pancăsat̰bīš* (Visprat [Visperad] 8.1). *pancasaγnāi*, V. 7.53, (see 8.1.22.4.) can hardly be compared with OInd. *pañcāśá-* 'fiftieth', which is itself secondary, but must represent a simplification of *-δγn-*.

8.1.24.1. Av. *pancāsat-* 'fifty' corresponds exactly to OInd. *pañcāśát-*. Iranian examples are: Parth. *pnǰ'st*, Sogd. *pnč's*, Chor. *pnc's*, Khot.

paṃjsāsä, Modern Pers. *panǰāh*, Paštō *panjōs*, Ormuṛī *panjāstu*. Ossetic *fänjai* 'fifty' (shepherds' dialects) owes its final to *äwdai* 'seventy' and *ästai* 'eighty' (Abaev, 1958: 445; cf. chapter 5).

8.1.25. 'Sixty'

Av. *xšuuaštīm* is accusative singular feminine to *xšuuašti-* seen in *xšuuaštiuuant-* 'sixtyfold' (Yt. 10.116). *xšuuašti-* corresponds to OInd. *ṣaṣṭí-* 'sixty' as does Av. *xšuuaš* 'six' to OInd. *ṣáṭ* (*ṣáṣ*); cf. 8.1.6, 5.1.6. An OIran. **(x)š(w)ašti-* is continued by Parth. *ššt*, Middle Persian (Turfan) *šst*, Zoroastrian Pahl. *šast*, Modern Pers. *šašt*, Chor. *'xyc*, Khot. *kṣaṣṭä*, Paštō *špēta*, Ossetic *äxsai* [40], Ormuṛī *ṣ̌ūṣ̌tu* [41]. Baločī *šastād* 'sixty' owes its final to *haftād* 'seventy' and *haštād* 'eighty'.

8.1.26. 'Seventy'

Av. *haptāitīm* is accusative singular feminine to *haptāiti-* seen modified in *haptaiθiuuant-* 'seventyfold' (Yt. 10.116). The *-ā-* is shortened secondarily in the latter as in *aštaiθiuuant-* 'eightyfold' (C. Bartholomae, *GIP*, 1895–1901: i. 171; 1904: col. 261). The *-θ-* is probably due to the analogy of such forms as *θrisaθβant-* beside *θrisata-* and *panca.saθβant-* beside *pancāsata-* (8.1.22., 8.1.24.). Av. *haptāiti-* contrasts with OInd. *saptatí-* in respect of the medial vowel, but an OIran. **haftāti-* [42] is universally guaranteed in later Iranian: Manichaean Sogd. *'βt't*, Chor. *'βd'c*, Khot. *haudātä*, Middle Persian (Turfan) *hpt'd*, Zoroastrian Pahl. *haftād*, Modern Pers. *haftād*, Paštō *awiā*, Ossetic *äwdai* (shepherds' dialect), Ormuṛī *awaitu*.

8.1.27. 'Eighty'

Av. *aštāitīm* is accusative singular feminine to *aštāiti-* seen modified in *aštaiθiuuant-* 'eightyfold' (Yt. 10.116, see 8.1.26.). *aštāiti-* contrasts with OInd. *aśītí-* (see 5.1.23.), but an OIran. **aštāti-* is continued everywhere in later Iranian: Christian Sogd. *'št't*, Chor. *'št'c*, Zoroastrian Pahl. *haštād*, Modern Pers. *haštād*, Khot. *haṣṭātä*, Paštō *atiā*, Ossetic *ästai* (shepherds' dialects), Ormuṛī *haštāī*. The distribution of initial *h-* accords with that for 'seven' and 'eight' (8.1.8.2.).

8.1.28. 'Ninety'

Av. *nauuaiti-* 'ninety' is found in the accusative singular feminine *nauuaitīm* Yt. 5.82, accusative plural feminine *nauuaitiš* V. 22.2, Yt. 13.59+, accusative dual feminine *nauuaiti* V. 14.17 ter, and in *nauuaitiuuant-* 'ninetyfold' (Yt. 10.116). Similar forms of OInd. *navatí-* are attested already in the R̥gveda: *navatís, navatím, navatyā̀, navatī́, navatī́s, navatīnā́m*. Szemerényi's attempt (1960: 124–125) to dismiss the Avestan forms seems without justification, as it is clear that they are at least Indo-Iranian. The *i*-declension is still found in Khotanese (cf. 8.1.0.1.). Thus, from *nautä-* 'ninety', Khotanese has the locative plural feminine *nvetuo* and *nvevo'*.

8.1.28.1. OIran. **nawati-* 'ninety', as in Av. *nauuaiti-*, agrees with OInd. *navatí-* and is continued in many Iranian languages: Chor. *nw(y)c*, Khot. *nautä*, Zoroastrian Pahl. *nawad*, Modern Pers. *navad*, Ormuṛī *niwē*, Paštō *nawē*. Since the normal treatment of *-awa-* in Middle and Modern Persian was reduction to *-ō-*, C. Bartholomae, *IF* xxxviii (1917–1920: 21–26), explained *navad* as based on **nōt* refashioned to **nōat* under the influence of *sat* 'hundred'. But it is simpler to assume that **nawat* was maintained because of pressure in the opposite direction, that is, towards **nawāt* (cf. Buddhist Sogd. *nw't*), exerted by *haftāt* 'seventy' and *haštāt* 'eighty'. Buddhist Sogd. *nw't* 'ninety' may owe its final to *'βt't* 'seventy' and *št't* 'eighty', but the spelling may be only a device to show that *nawat* and not *nōt* was intended. Three forms, without dialect information, are given by Frejman, *Ol'denburg Fs*. (1934: 562), for the Ossetic shepherds: *nauäjä, näuäj, näu*. These must all represent **nawati-*. Since *näu* 'nine' was not in use, *näuäj* could safely be reduced to *näu*.

8.1.29. The vigesimal system

The forms discussed above (8.1.20.–8.1.28.1.) clearly indicate an inherited Old Iranian system of decads. Nevertheless, over a wide area, there was a tendency to adopt a vigesimal system (see D. I. Ėdel'man, *Jazguljamskij jazyk*, 1966: 33 n. 11), either side-by-side with the ancient system or as a (partial) replacement of it. A vigesimal system is found also in the neighbouring Dardic languages such as Gawar-bati (C. Morgenstierne 1950: 17) and Shina (T. G. Bailey 1904: 25). In many cases numerals above 'twenty' are borrowed from Modern Persian or Turkish[43]. 'Forty', 'sixty', 'eighty' and sometimes 'hundred', '120', '140', '160', '180' are expressed as multiples of twenty. The intervening tens are expressed either by the addition of ten, or as 'n + '½'+ × 20'. Some examples are:

thirty	= '10' + '20'	Ossetic (Digor) *däs äma insäi*
	'20' + '10'	Yaghnobi *bíst-at das* (cf. Andreev – Peščereva 1957)
	'1 [×] 20' [+] '10'	Yidgha *yūwistolos* (cf. Morgenstierne 1938: 125)
'forty'	= '2' [×] '20'	Ossetic (Digor) *duvinsäji*
		Yaghnobi *dŭ bist*
		Baločī *dō gīst*, cf. W. Geiger, *GIP* (1898–1901: i. 2. 240); G. W. Gilbertson, *The Balochi language* (1923: 39); V. A. Frolova, *Beludžsky jazyk* (1960: 38))
		Yidgha *luwist*
'fifty'	= '10' + '2' [×] '20'	Ossetic (Digor) *däs äma duvinsäji*
	'2½' [×] '20'	Yaghnobi *dŭ níma bist*
	'2' [×] '20' [+] '10'	Yidgha *luwistolos*
	'2' [×] '20' + '10'	Yazgulami *δow wast-a δůs* (cf. D. I. Ėdel'man, *Jazguljamskij jazyk*, 1966: 33 n. 11)
'sixty'	= '3' [×] '20'	Ossetic (Digor) *ärtinsäji*
		Yaghnobi *tĭráy bist*
		Baločī *sai gīst*
		Parāčī *šī γuštak* (cf. Morgenstierne 1929: 59)
		Waxī *trūbīst*
		Tātī *säbíst*
		Yazgulami *cůy wast*
'seventy'	= '10' + '3' [×] '20'	Ossetic (Digor) *daš äma ärtinsäji*
	'3' [×] '20' + '10'	Baločī *sai gīst u dah*
	'3' [×] '20' + '10'	Tātī *säbistdäh*
	'3' [+] '½' [×] '20'	Parāčī *šīnīm γuštak*
		Paštō *drē nīm šəla*
		Yaghnobi *tĭráy níma bist*
'eighty'	= '4' [×] '20'	Ossetic (Digor) *cupparinsäji*
		Paštō *calōr šəla*
		Baločī *čīār gīst*
		Tātī *čarbist*
		Yaghnobi *tĭfór bist*
		Ormuṛī *čâr jīstu*
		Parāčī *čōr γuštak*
		Waxī *cəbür bist*
'ninety'	= '10' + '4' [×] '20'	Ossetic (Digor) *däs äma cupparinsäji*
	'4' [×] '20' + '10'	Baločī *čīār gīst u dah*
	'4' [×] '20' [+] '10'	Tātī *čarbistdäh*
	'4' [+] '½' [×] '20'	Paštō *calōr nīm šəla*
		Yaghnobi *tĭfór níma bist*
'one hundred'	= '5' [×] '20'	Ossetic (Digor) *fonjinsäji*

		Parāčī *pōnž γuštak*
		Yidgha *pānžwist*
'one hundred and twenty'	= '6' [×] '20'	Ossetic (Iron) *äxsäzyssäjy* (Abaev, cf. chapter 5, 1964: 21)
		Baločī *šaš gīst*
'one hundred and forty'	= '7' [×] '20'	Ossetic (Iron) *awdyssäjy* (Abaev, cf. chapter 5, 1964: 21)
		Baločī *hapt gīst*
'two hundred'	= '2' [×] '5' [×] '20'	Ossetic (Iron) *dyvvä fonjyssäjy* (Abaev 1964: 21)

8.1.30. Common Iranian decadic numerals

The Common Iranian decads with their Old Indian counterparts and underlying Proto-Indo-European forms are as follows:

'twenty'	**wīsatī*	*viṃśatí*	**wīḱm̥tī*
'thirty'	**θrīsat-*	*triṃśát*	**trīḱont-*
'forty'	**čaθwarsat-*	*catvāriṃśát-*	**kʷetwr̥̄ḱont-*
'fifty'	**pančāsat-*	*pañcāśát-*	**penkʷēḱont-*
'sixty'	**xšwašti-*	*ṣaṣṭí-*	**ksweḱsḱont-*
'seventy'	**haftāti-*	*saptatí*	**septm̥̄ḱont-*
'eighty'	**aštāti-*	*aśītí-*	**oḱtōḱont-*
'ninety'	**nawati-*	*navatí*	**newn̥̄ḱont-*

For the analysis into groups see 5.1.19. The Proto-Indo-European reconstructions for 'sixty' to 'ninety' are only in part supported by Indo-Iranian data, as a different system was developed there.

8.1.30.1. Iranian provides little evidence (cf. Av. *θrisąs*, 8.1.22.5.) for an ancient nasal in the second component of the decads. In Old Indian, the nasals of *triṃśát-* and *catvāriṃśát-* are in the wrong place when set beside other languages e. g. Latin *trīgintā, quadrāgintā*, Greek τριάκοντα, τετταράκοντα. They were probably transposed secondarily under the influence of *viṃśatí* 'twenty' (see 5.1.20.).

8.1.30.2. It is probable that 'twenty' to 'fifty' were structurally similar in having a long vowel before the second element. In this respect 'sixty' would provide a natural break in the system as 'six' is the only numeral between 'two' and 'nine' that does not end in a sonant and is therefore not capable of being lengthened. In Latin and Greek the problem was solved by the insertion of a long vowel: Latin *sexāgintā*, Greek *heksēkonta*.

It is perhaps surprising that this way out was not adopted in Indo-Iranian as the pressure of **pančāsat-* (to use Iranian reconstructions) followed by **haftāsat-*, **aštāsat-* and **nawāsat-* must have been considerable.

8.1.30.3. The Indo-Iranian decads 'sixty' to 'ninety' have therefore usually been explained as *-ti-* abstracts (Brugmann – Delbrück 1897–1916: II. ii. 21; Hirt 1927: 313; Sommer 1951: 82; T. Burrow, *The Sanskrit Language*, 1955: 261; etc.). Thus **xšwašti-* is really 'a hexad [of tens]. The reason given for the departure from the ancient forms at this point is the phonetic and morphological complications that would result from such a form as PIE **ksweḱsḱont-* in Indo-Iranian. There would of course have been no difficulty if a long vowel had been inserted analogically (cf. 8.1.30.2.). An Old Iranian form **xšwašāsat-* would follow **pančāsat-* and be followed by **haftāsat-*. But unless this solution were adopted, the formal difficulties would be considerable. One has only to recall the difficulties caused in the ordinal 'sixth', Av. *xštuua-* (8.2.6.). There the result is contraction and that is what one would expect here too. Whatever the antecedent of **xšwašti-* it may well have contained *-sat-*. A form like **xšwašsat-*[44] would undoubtedly have resulted in **xšwašt-*. The final *-i-* may be accounted for in a number of ways (see 5.1.24.) not mutually exclusive.

8.1.30.4. The resulting **xšwašti-* would certainly have been later analysed as **xšwaš* 'six' plus *-ti-*, and *-ti-* may then have replaced *-sat-* in **haftāsat-, *aštāsat-* and **nawāsat-*. *-ti-* may also have seemed to hold the advantage of keeping the decads more distinct from the hundreds.

8.1.30.5. Part of the difference between the forms for 'seventy' to 'ninety' in Iranian and Indian can be accounted for on the basis of a difference in accentuation. In Indian, the oxytone suffix *-tí-* prevailed to induce oxytone accentuation throughout the decads (5.1.25.), whereas in Iranian the older accentuation on the prior element of the compound was retained or restored. Thus **haftā́ti, *aštā́ti, *náwāti* resulted in **haftā̆ti*, **aštā̆ti* and **náwăti*.

8.1.31. 'One hundred'

The Indo-Iranian form was **śatá-* as seen from Av. *sata-*, OInd. *śatá-*. OIran. **sata-* is continued in Av. *sata-*, Christian Sogd. *stw*, Chor. *syd*, Khot. *sata-*, Zoroastrian Pahl. *sad*, Modern Pers. *sad* (usually spelled with *sad* but early and rare with *sīn*; cf. Lazard 1963: 217), Parth. *sd*, Ossetic *sädä*, Paštō *sal*. Old Persian has the usual variant **θata-* attested in the province-name *θata-gu-* and in Elamite spelling representing **θata-xnpati-* 'centurion'. **θata-* is continued in Modern Pers. *hadba* 'centipede'

(Morgenstierne 1932: 55; I. Gershevitch, *Transactions of the Philological Society* 1964: 13 n. 2).

8.1.31.1. Indo-Iran. **śatá-* goes back without difficulty to PIE **ḱm̥tó-* (cf. Latin *centum*, Greek ἑκατόν, etc.). Recently E. Risch (*IF* lxvii, 1962: 129–141) has convincingly confirmed previous suggestions that this was earlier **dḱm̥tó-*, an adjective meaning 'tenth (decad)'. **dḱm̥tó-* was the older form of the ordinal beside **deḱm̥tó-*, which shows the influence of the cardinal **deḱm̥t-* 'ten' (see 8.2.11.2.). The reduced form of 'ten' appears as *-ḱm̥t-* < *-dḱm̥t-* as the second element of the decads, OIran. *-sat-* (8.1.30). Thus Proto-Indo-European originally had for 'twenty' **dwi-dḱm̥tī* > **widḱm̥tī* (dissimilation) > **wīḱm̥tī́* (simplification with compensatory lengthening)[45]. See also 5.1.20.

8.1.32. 'One thousand'

Indo-Iran. **saźhasra-* 'one thousand' is continued regularly by OInd. *sahásra-* and Av. *hazaŋra-*. Other Iranian examples are: Zoroastrian Pahl. *hazār*, Modern Pers. *hazār*, Parth. *hz'r*, Chor. *hz'r*, Sogd. *z'r*, Khot. *ysāru*, Ossetic *ärzä, ärjä* (epic only), Paštō *zər*. The loss of the first syllable in some later Iranian forms can be explained by reference to other developments within those languages and cannot justify the assumption of a form **źhasra-*.

8.1.32.1. There seems to have been no Common Indo-European form for 'one thousand'. Attempts have been made (Brugmann – Delbrück 1897–1916: II. ii. 1,46 ff. and *IF* xxi, 1907: 10–13) to bring together Greek χείλιοι Ionic, χίλιοι Attic < χεσλ-, Latin *mīlle*[46] and Indo-Iran. **saźhasra-* but without great success. Indo-Iran. *°*źhasra-* and Greek χεσλ- could however continue without difficulty a PIE **ǵhesl-*. Indo-Iran. **sa-* would then be PIE **sm̥-* 'one' (8.3.1.1.).

8.1.33. 'Myriad'

OIran. **baiwar/n-* is widely attested for 'ten thousand' in Iranian: Av. *baēuuar/n-*, Zoroastrian Pahl. *bēwar*, Modern Pers. *bēwar*, Middle Persian (Turfan) *bywr*, Parth. *bywr*, Sogd. *βrywr*, Khot. *byūrru*, Ossetic (Digor) *be(u)rä*, (Iron) *bīrä*, Alan *baior-* in names, e. g., *Baioraspos*. The Iranian word was borrowed into Armenian as *biwr* (H. Hübschmann, *Armenische Grammatik*, 1897: 121) and into Georgian as *bevr-i*. In Ossetic, the meaning is 'much, very' as in Georgian, where the meaning 'ten thousand' is said to be obsolete (E. Cherkesi, *Georgian–English dictionary*, 1950:

17). The Ossetic form was borrowed by Circassian as *beurə* 'beaucoup, longtemps' (N. S. Trubetskoy, *MSL* xxii, 1922: 249).

8.1.33.1. No clear cognate of OIran. **baiwar/n-* has been found. Attempts have been made (for literature cf. Mayrhofer 1958–80: *bhū́riḥ*) to connect it with OInd. *bhū́ri-* 'many' (= Av. *būiri-*). If this connection could be established it might be possible to link these forms further with Gk. *mūríos* 'measureless', *múrioi* 'ten thousand', and OIrish *múr* 'great number'[47], by assuming an alternation **m* ∼ **bh*. But at present all is obscure.[48]

8.1.34. Multiples of 'hundred' and 'thousand'

The numerals 'two hundred' to 'nine hundred' and 'two thousand' to 'nine thousand' could be expressed in Indo-Iranian by inflecting the units and the word for 'hundred' or 'thousand'. Thus Avestan has *duuaēca saite duuaēca hazaŋre* (Yt. 19.7) 'both two hundreds and two thousands'. Av. *duiie saite* 'two hundred' (V. 16.12) corresponds exactly to OInd. *dvé śaté* (RV vii.18.22). In Old Indian, other types of expression are also found (5.1.31.). The type of compound found in OInd. *triśatám* 'three hundred' seems not to occur in Old Iranian. Av. *θrisatanąm* in Yt. 5.129 is the genitive plural of *θrisata-* 'thirty' (8.1.22.) (see R. Hauschild, *MIO* xi, 1965: 35–37). Av. *θrisatō.zəma* '300 years' (V. 2.8) should be read as **θrī satō.zəma* 'three centuries' (H. Humbach, *MSS* xxvii, 1970: 69–71).

8.1.34.1. OIran. **dwai satai* 'two hundred' is continued in Khot. *dvī satä*. Here *dvī* is identical in form with the nom. fem.-neuter *dvī* (8.1.2.1.). The genitive-dative *dvī satänu* is to be understood as showing the usual type of group-inflection and thus represents *dvīnu satänu*. Elsewhere this type has been secondarily compounded: Chor. *'δwysd*, Christian Sogd. *dwyst*, Parth. *dwysd*, Modern Pers. *diwist*, early *duwēst* (Lazard 1963: 217), Pāzand *duēst*. For 'three hundred' see 8.1.3.3.

8.1.34.2. 'Four hundred' to 'nine hundred' in Chorasmian and early Modern Persian:

	Chorasmian	Early Modern Persian
'four hundred'	*cf'rzd*	*čahārṣaδ*
'five hundred'	*pnṣd*	*pānṣaδ, panǰsaδ*
'six hundred'	*'x̌zd*	*šašṣaδ, šaṣṣad, šanṣaδ*
'seven hundred'	*'βdzd*	*haftṣaδ, hafṣaδ*
'eight hundred'	*'štzd*	*haštṣaδ, hašṣaδ*
'nine hundred'	*nwsd*	*nuhṣaδ*

8.2. Ordinals

8.2.0. Overview of the lower ordinals

The following table shows the Avestan ordinals 'first' to 'tenth' beside their Old Indian counterparts and the Avestan cardinals:

		Avestan	Old Indian		Avestan	
'first'	(a)	*fratəma-*	*prathamá-*	:	*aēuua-*	'one'
	(b)	*pouruiia-*	[*pūrvyá-*]	:		
'second'		*daibitiia-*	*dvitī́ya-*	:	*duua*	'two'
'third'		*θritiia-*	*tr̥tī́ya-*	:	*θrāiiō*	'three'
'fourth'		*tūiriia-*	*turī́ya-*	:	*caθβārō*	'four'
'fifth'		*puxδa-*	*pañcamá-*	:	*panca*	'five'
'sixth'		*xštuua-*	*ṣaṣṭhá-*	:	*xšuuaš*	'six'
'seventh'		*haptaθa-*	*saptátha-*	:	*hapta*	'seven'
'eight'		*aštəma-*	*aṣṭamá-*	:	*ašta*	'eight'
'ninth'		*naoma-*	*navamá-*	:	*nauua*	'nine'
'tenth'		*dasəma-*	*daśamá-*	:	*dasa*	'ten'

On 'first' and 'second' see C. Bartholomae, *IF* xxii (1907 – 1908: 95 – 116; 1908 – 1909: 43 – 92, 331 – 336).

8.2.1. 'First'

An OIran. **fratama-* 'first' is continued by the following: Av. *fratəma-*, OPers. *fratama-*, Zoroastrian Pahl. *fradom*, Parth. *'frdwm* (W. B. Henning, *BSOS* ix, 1937: 80), Middle Persian (Turfan) *prtwm'yn* (with additional suffix), Khot. *hatäma-*[49]. OIran. **fratama-* is also continued by various Sogdian forms: Manichaean Sogd. *ftm-*, Christian Sogd. *'ftm*, Manichaean Sogd. *'ftm-*, Sogd. *'βtm-*, Buddhist Sogd. *(')prtm-* (Gershevitch 1954: 49). These are also found extended by a further suffix in Manichaean Sogd. *'ftmyk*, Buddhist Sogd. *'prtmyk*, and in Manichaean Sogd. *(')ftmčyk*, Sogd. *'prtmčykw* (Gershevitch 1954: 200). In Chorasmian, *frd(y)m* is 'best', while, with a suffix similar to that of Sogd. *ftmčyk*, Chor. *ftmyck* (Muq. 40^6) is 'first'. Paštō *wr̥umbai* 'first' (Morgenstierne 1927: 93) is thought to be related in some way to Av. *fratəma-* (see G. Morgenstierne, *BSOAS* xxxiii, 1970: 127).

8.2.1.1. OIran. **fratama-* does not exactly match OInd. *prathamá-* 'first'. OInd. *pratamā́m* 'especially' cannot be compared directly as it is an Indian formation like *anutamā́m* 'most' to *ánu* 'according to' (C. Bartholomae, *IF* xxii, 1907–1908: 97). Moreover, an OIran. **parθama-* is implied by a number of later Iranian forms[51]: Zoroastrian Pahl. *pahlom* [50], Parth. *Parthama-* in names. If Indo-Iranian had **prathama-*, the Iranian development could be explained as a replacement of **-θama-* by *-tama-* from the closely related superlatives, whereas a secondary development of **-tama-* to **-θama-* would be difficult to explain. Indo-Iranian **prathama-* may represent a conflation of **pratha-* (with *-tha-* as in 'fifth' and 'seventh') and **prama-* (as in Um. *promom*).

An Indo-Iranian **prata-* seems to have existed. In Old Indian, the hapax legomenon *pratádvasū* (RV viii.13.27) is of disputed interpretation (Mayrhofer 1956–1980, s. v.) but may belong with the OIran. **frata-* attested in such names as *Eufrátas, Frataférnēs* (see I. Gershevitch, *Pagliaro Fs.*, 1969: 143) and *Fratagoúnē* (É. Benveniste, *Titres et noms propres en iranien ancien*, 1966: 122). G. Cameron, *Persepolis treasury tablets* (1948: 7 n. 41) recognized **frata-* in the Elamite *Upirda*. The old explanation of *Frataférnēs* and *Fratagoúnē* as containing an Iran. **frāta-* 'fire' attested in Arm. *hrat* 'fire' (so F. Justi, *Iranisches Namenbuch*, 1895: 105) has had considerable popularity; so still for *Fratagoúnē*. An Iran. **frāta-* 'fire' has also been sought in a commonly misread Iranian title *frataraka-* (8.2.1.6.).

8.2.1.2. Av. *fratəma-* is not found in a sequence such as 'first ... second ... third ...' where *paoiriia-* is regularly used. Yav. *paoiriia-*, GAv. *paouruiia-* represent OIran. **parwiya-*, attested also by the Old Persian adverb *prᵘuvⁱiyt*. OIran. **parwiya-* is a derivative of **parwa-*, which is also found in Avestan and Old Persian. Av. *pauruua-*, OPers. *prᵘuv-* < **parwa-* correspond in form and meaning to OInd. *pū́rva-* 'prior'. But Av. *paoiriia-* 'first' contrasts both with Av. *pauruua-* 'prior' and with OPers. *prᵘuvⁱiy-*, OInd. *pūrvyá-* in meaning. Old Church Slavonic *prŭvŭ* 'first', cognate with Av. *pauruua-* 'prior', shows a development similar to that of Av. *paoiriia-* 'first', which originally meant 'prior'. Cf. also Tocharian B *pärweṣṣe* 'first' and see 8.2.1.6.

8.2.1.3. The later Iranian forms which C. Bartholomae, *IF* xxii (1907–1908: 112–115) thought continued OIran. **parwa-* and **parwiya-* are better otherwise explained; see Gershevitch (*Indo-Iranica, Mélanges ... Georg Morgenstierne,* Wiesbaden 1964: 78–88). **parwa-* survives with the addition of a suffix *-īčk* in Buddhist Sogd. *prw'yčk'* 'former' (Gershevitch 1954: 154).

8.2.1.4. In Khotanese *paḍāa-* is used for 'first' (Emmerick 1968: 310). This is derived by Bailey (1943: 179 n. 1) from **partāka-*. He compares Zoroastrian Pahl. *fradāg*, Modern Pers. *fardā* 'early, next morning'. For **par-* beside **fra-* he adduces **parθama-* beside **fratama-* (8.2.1.1.). In fact all the above words are derivatives of PIE **per-* ~ **pro* 'in front'. Other words with the meaning 'early, next morning' are based on the lengthened form PIE **prō* (OInd. *prātár-*; Greek *prōí*, OHG *fruo*): Buddhist Sogd. *βr''k*, Manichaean Sogd. *fr'k*, Ossetic (Digor) *raǵi*, (Iron) *raǰy* (Gershevitch 1954: 248); Waxī *vərōk* (Morgenstierne 1938: 547; Benveniste, *Vessantara Jātaka*, 1946: 91). For their semantic connection with 'first', cf. AV 6.47.1 ff., 9.1.11 ff.: *prātaḥsavané* beside *dvitī́ye sávane* and *tṛtī́ye sávane* 'at the morning Soma pressing, at the second, at the third'.
8.2.1.5. A variety of words tends to be used in place of derivatives of PIE **per-/*pro-*. C. Bartholomae, *IF* xxii (1907 – 1908: 101 n. 1) cites some of these. Thus Zoroastrian Pahlavi has analogical *ēkom* (to *ēk* 'one'), cf. Modern Pers. *yekom*, and *nazdist*, cf. Av. *nazdišta-* 'nearest'. The Turfan texts use Middle Persian (Turfan) *nxwst(yn), nxwyn*, Parth. *nxwšt, nxwyn*, derivatives of a word meaning 'beginning', Parth. *nwx* as in *'c nwx, pd nwx* 'in the beginning' and *nwxz'd* 'first born'. These words are probably to be connected (see R. E. Emmerick, *Asia major*, 1971: 61 – 63) with Khot. *nūha-* 'point, tip', which renders Sanskrit *ágra-* 'top' (cf. *agrimá-* 'first'). Many modern languages use Arabic *awwal*, sometimes adapted with analogical suffixation, e. g., Modern Persian *avvalīn*, Balōčī *aulī*. *p'ēšī* is also used in Baluchi, cf. Zoroastrian Pahl. *pēš*, Modern Pers. *pīš* 'before'[52]. Similarly Ossetic (Digor) *fitcag*, (Iron) *fytcag* 'first' probably derives from **patišāka-*, cf. Parāčī *pač* 'before, in front of'[53].
8.2.1.6. Another derivative of PIE **pro-* is **pro-tero-* with the comparative suffix: Av. *fratara-*, Greek *próteros* (C. Bartholomae, *IF* xxii, 1907 – 1908: 115 – 116). Possibly inherited also are the Old Indian adverbs *pratarám, pratarā́m* 'further'. Av. *fratara-* developed in addition to the original meaning 'prior' a superlative meaning (e. g., 'besonders gut' in H. 2.14) giving rise to a secondary comparative *fratarō.tara-*. Old Persian has *fratara-* in a difficult passage DNb 38. The adverb *frataram* in DB 3.26 and A[1]Pa (Persepolis inscription of Artaxerxes I) 21 seems clearly to mean 'previously'. Comparison of the use of *fratara-* in XPg 11 with that of *fraθara-* in XPf makes it likely that the two words should be equated and mean 'excellent', but there is no agreement among scholars on this matter (see Brandenstein – Mayrhofer 1964: 120; W. Wüst, *Altpersische Studien*, 1966: 207 – 208). As a title, *frataraka-* was used of

an administrative head under the Achaemenids and also under the Seleucids (see P. Naster, *Archaeologia iranica* viii, 1968: 74–80).
8.2.1.7. OIran. **fratara-* is continued in Sogdian, where both comparative ('before', 'better') and superlative ('special', 'first') meanings are found: Manichaean Sogd. *frtr*, Christian Sogd. *frtr*, Buddhist Sogd. *prtr* (Gershevitch 1954: 66). Khotanese has the adverb *hatäro* 'formerly' (Bailey 1967: 381; R. E. Emmerick, *JRAS*, 1969: 71). In Chorasmian *frdr* is 'better' (W. B. Henning 1956: 432). Secondary comparatives are common: Parth. *'frdrystr* (W. B. Henning, *BSOS* ix, 1937: 80), Sogd. *frtrstr*, Khot. *hatäḍara-* 'former'.

8.2.2. 'Second'

OIran. **dwitī̆ya* is attested by GAv. *daibitiia-*, YAv. *bitiia-* (on *b-* see Hoffmann, *Handbuch der Orientalistik*, 1958: 11–12), OPers. $d^{u}uv^{i}itiy$-. In Middle Iranian **dwitī̆yaka-* is common: Middle Persian (Turfan) *dwdyg*, Parth. *bdyg*, Manichaean Sogd. *δβtyk*, Christian Sogd. *dbtyq*. Unextended **dwitī̆ya-* is also attested in Sogdian: Manichaean Sogd. *δβty-*, Buddhist Sogd. *δ(y)βty-*. To this is added a generalized ordinal suffix in Chor. *δβcym*. Unextended **dwitī̆ya-* is used in a compound with **kara-* 'time' (cf. Ossetic (Digor) *karä*, (Iron) *kar* 'age') Zoroastrian Pahlavi *dudīgar* (cf. early Modern Pers. *duδīgar* – Lazard 1963: 220)[54], Modern Pers. *dīgar* 'second'. The Iranian material provides no evidence concerning the original length of *-i-* in the suffix, and the long vowel in the Indian tradition may be secondary (see 5.2.2.).
8.2.2.1. An OIran. **dwita-* 'second' is attested in Parth. *byd*, Zoroastrian Pahl. *did*, Khot. *śäta-*. It is probably also implied by the adverb Middle Persian (Turfan) *dwdy* 'ferner, dann'. An OIran. **dwita-* may be contained in OPers. $d^{u}uv^{i}taprnm$ (DB 1.10 only), of which the meaning is disputed[55]. GAv. *daibitā(nā)*, also of disputed meaning, may contain **dwita-*. Paštō *bəl* may be more simply derived from **dwita-* than from **dwitī̆ya* (so Morgenstierne 1927: 14). No certain reflex of Indo-Iran. **dwita-* is preserved in Old Indian.
8.2.2.2. As in the case of 'first' (8.2.1.5.), other words are sometimes substituted for **dwitī̆ya-*, **dwita-*. Thus Avestan has *antara-*, lit. 'other', and *apara-*, lit. 'posterior'. Common later are secondary forms based on the cardinal plus a generalized suffix: Modern Pers. *dovvom, doyyom* (see further Lazard 1963: 220), Paštō *dwayam*, Balōčī *duhmī* (like *nuhmī* 'ninth'), Sarīkolī *δɛwinči* (like *cavurinči* 'fourth').

8.2.3. 'Third'

OIran. *θritiya- is attested by Av. θritiia- and OPers. çitiy-, in Middle Iranian by Buddhist Sogd. *'šty-, 'tδrty-, čšty-*. In Chorasmian, *šym* 'third' is secondary to *šy* 'three' with generalized suffix, but ancient *θritiya- survives in the fraction *'rcy 'd(y)k* 'third part' < *θritiya-yāta- (W. B. Henning, *Handbuch der Orientalistik*, 1958: 109–110). In Middle Iranian, *θritiyaka- is continued by Parth. *hrdyg*, Middle Persian (Turfan) *sdyg*, Manichaean Sogd. *(')štyk*. Zoroastrian Pahl. *sidīgar* is a compound like *dudīgar* (8.2.2.). On the suffix *-iya-* see 8.2.2.

8.2.3.1. OIran. *θrita- is attested in Avestan only in the proper names *θrita-* and *θritī-*. This latter is the name of Zaraθuštra's second daughter and third child. In Old Persian, *çita- 'third' is not to be restored at DB 5.3; see R. Schmidt, *Orientalia* n.s. xxxii, 1963: 437 ff.). An OIran. *θrita- is continued by Khot. *dädda-*[56]. *θrita- may be compared directly to Greek *trítos*. Concerning the Old Indian divine name *Tritá-* see 5.2.2.

8.2.4. 'Fourth'

Av. *tūiriia-* must clearly continue a very ancient form, standing as it does against the cardinal *caθβārō* and in agreement with OInd. *turiya-* (in compounds *turya-*). It is to be derived from a PIE *k^wtur-, with zero grade in both syllables. In addition, Avestan has an adverb *āxtūirīm* 'four times', where *-x-* continues PIE *k^w because of its protection in a non-initial position[57]. Initial *xt-* is not found in Avestan, nor is *kt-* in Old Indian.

8.2.4.1. An OIran. *čaθruma- 'fourth' is continued by Parth. *čwhrm*, Zoroastrian Pahl. *tswm*, Middle Persian (Turfan) *tswm* (on *ts-* see 8.1.4.7.), and Khot. *tcūrama-*. O. Szemerényi, *ZDMG* ci (1951: 197–199) proposed to restore at DB 5.3 a corresponding Old Persian form *čaçuma-, but further examination of the inscription has made it unlikely (see G. Cameron, *JCS* v, 1951: 53; K. Hoffmann, *KZ* lxxix, 1965: 250 n. 1) that such a restoration should be adopted.

8.2.4.2. Elsewhere, secondary forms more closely related to the cardinal are found: Buddhist Sogd. *čtβ'rm(y)k*, Chor. *cf'rym*, Zoroastrian Pahl. *čahārom*, Modern Pers. *čahārom*.

8.2.5. 'Fifth'

Av. *puxδa-* 'fifth' has been variously explained. It is probably old, as its relation to the cardinal *panca* is not clear and an analogical form was at hand (8.2.5.1.). Bartholomae, *GIP* (1895–1901: i. 113) explained the *-u-*

as due to **turθa-* 'fourth', but this form did not exist in Iranian. It was based on a false interpretation of Zoroastrian Pahl. *tswm* (8.1.4.7., 8.2.4.1.). The genuineness of Av. *puxδa-* (A. Meillet, *MSL* ix, 1896: 379, suggested a misreading for **pą̇xδa-*) is confirmed by Khot. *pūha-* 'fifth'. Szemerényi's attempt (1960: 76 n. 42) to dispose of Khot. *pūha-* is altogether unsatisfactory. Thus his concluding comment "*pūha-* continues **panxta-* or **paxta-*; it certainly cannot prove **paxθa-* or **puxθa-*" is completely at variance with the phonology of Khotanese. **-(n)xt-* results in Khot. *-t-* (often *-y-* after *-ī-*, *-v-* after *-ū-*). Thus Khotanese has *thaṃj-*, past participle *thīya-*, corresponding to Av. *θanjaya-*, past participle *θaxta-* 'to pull'. With an initial labial we have a good parallel in Khot. *būta-* 'distributed' < **baxta-* (see Emmerick 1968: 103). Moreover if the labialisation of the vowel is secondary (later), the resultant vowel is short: Khot. *huto* 'thigh' beside Av. *haxti-*. Szemerényi's explanation "Its *-h-* probably represents an earlier *-θ-* from *-χt-*, with transfer of the aspiration, cf. *pamuha-* 'garment' from **-muxta-* (not *-θ-*, Konow 1949: § 18)" is also untenable. Khot. *pamūha* — the evidence points to *-ū-* — undoubtedly supports just the opposite with *mūha-* < **muxθa-*, as we have *pamäta-* < **pati-muxta-* (see Emmerick 1968: 66), past participle to *paṃjs-* 'to put on (clothing)' < **pati-muča-*. The development **-xθ-* > *-h-* is probable also in Khot. *paha-* 'cooked' < **paxθa-* (cf. RV *pakthín-* and Av. *-puxδa-*). Derivation of *paha-* from **paxva-* (cf. OInd. *pakvá-*) is less likely, as **pūha-* would be expected. As, however, Av. *-puxδa-* 'cooked' shows, the *-u-* could replace *-a-* secondarily under the influence of the labial. There should thus be no doubt that Old Iranian had **puxθa-* 'fifth' from an earlier **paxθa-*. A corresponding *pakthá-* may occur RV x.61.1 (see 5.2.5.2.). The Old Iranian form **puxθa-* may, however, owe its *-u-* not simply to the preceding labial but to the influence of **xšušta-* 'sixth' (K. Hoffmann, *KZ* lxxix, 1965: 254).

8.2.5.1. Middle Iranian forms other than Khotanese continue a Common Iranian **pančama-* 'fifth': Zoroastrian Pahl. *panǰom*, Modern Pers. *panǰom*, Middle Persian (Turfan) *pnzwm*, Parth. *pnǰwm*, Chor. *pncym*, Buddhist Sogd. *pnčm(yk)*, Ossetic (Iron) *fänjäm*. Old Indian had a parallel form *pañcamá-*; see 5.2.5.

8.2.6. 'Sixth'

Av. *xštuua-* is the only ancient form of this ordinal found in Iranian. Bartholomae's explanation (*GIP*, 1895–1901: i. 113) is complex, and, as in the case of his explanation of *puxδa-* (8.2.5.), involves his assumption of **turθa-* 'fourth', which is no longer tenable. It is difficult to see why an earlier form **xšwašta-*, as proposed by Szemerényi (1960: 77 n. 46) should not have been maintained, since the relationship to the cardinal *xšuuaš* would have remained clear. The logical assumption of an original form **xšušta-*, as proposed by K. Hoffmann (*KZ* lxxix, 1965: 254), meets with the difficulty that the development from **xšušta-* to *xštuua-* remains unclear, although consideration of the development of Av. *xšma-* (pronoun of the second person plural) < **ušmá-* goes some way towards clarifying the process. See further 8.2.11.1.

8.2.6.1. Later Iranian forms are based on the cardinal plus generalized suffix: Zoroastrian Pahl. *šašom,* Modern Pers. *šešom*, Parth. *šhwm*, Chor. *'xtm* [58], Khot. *kṣei'ma*, Buddhist Sogd. *wγšmy(k)*.

8.2.7. 'Seventh'

An OIran. **haftaθa-* is attested by Av. *haptaθa-* only, but the form corresponds exactly to OInd. *saptátha-* (5.2.7.). The suggestion made by Szemerényi (1960: 88) that an original **haftata-* became **haftaθa-* under the influence of the derivative *haptaiθiia-* 'consisting of seven parts' is in itself implausible. Moreover **-θa-* is certainly attested in 'fifth', Av. *puxδa-* (8.2.5.) and may have occurred early in Indo-Iran. **pratha-* 'first' (8.2.1.1.). In Old Indian it spread to *caturthá-* 'fourth', *pañcathá-* 'fifth' and *ṣaṣṭhá-* 'sixth'. Nevertheless Indo-Iran. *-tha-* may have been replacing a PIE **-to-*, if, as seems likely, *-tho-* is not to be considered of Indo-European date[59]. Indo-Iran. **-tha-* indicating the specific as opposed to *-ta-* indicating the general (so P. Thieme, *Der Fremdling im Ṛgveda*, 1938: 65), e. g., OInd. *uktám* 'was gesprochen ist' (Av. past participle *-uxta-*) beside OInd. *ukthám* '(feierlicher) Spruch' (Av. *uxδəm*), would seem more appropriate as the ordinal suffix.

8.2.7.1. Later Iranian forms continue an OIran. **haftama-*, corresponding exactly to OInd. *saptamá-* (5.2.7.1.): Zoroastrian Pahl. *haftom*, Modern Pers. *haftom*, Parth. *hftwm*, Chor. *'βdym*, Khot. *haudama-*, Buddhist Sogd. *'βtmy(k)*.

8.2.8. 'Eighth'

Indo-Iran. **aštama-* is continued directly by OInd. *aṣṭamá* and by OIran. **aštama-*, Av. *aštəma-*, Zoroastrian Pahl. *haštom*, Modern Pers. *haštom*, Parth. *hštwmyg*, Buddhist Sogd. *'štmy(k)*. The secondary initial *h-* in some Iranian forms comes from the corresponding cardinal (8.1.8.2.). On the underlying Proto-Indo-European form see 5.2.8.

8.2.9. 'Ninth'

Indo-Iran. **nawama-* is continued directly by OInd. *navamá-* and OIran. **nawama-*: Av. *naoma-*, OPers. *navama-*, Khot. *nauma-*, Buddhist Sogd. *nwm'y*, *n'wmyk*. The generalized suffix is added to the cardinal in Zoroastrian Pahl. *nohom*, Modern Pers. *nohom*, Middle Persian (Turfan) *nwwm*, Parth. *nhwm*, Chor. *š'δym* (cf. 8.1.9.1.). On the underlying Proto-Indo-European form see 5.2.9.

8.2.10. 'Tenth'

Indo-Iran. **daśama-* is continued directly both by OInd. *daśamá-* and by Av. *dasəma-*. Later Iranian forms include: Khot. *dasama-*, Buddhist Sogd. *δsmy, δsm'yk*, Chor. *δsym*, Parth. *dswm*, Zoroastrian Pahl. *dahom*, Modern Pers. *dahom*. For the underlying Proto-Indo-European forms see 5.2.10.

8.2.11. Summary

The Old Iranian ordinals 'first' to 'tenth' beside the corresponding cardinals were thus as follows:

		Cardinal	Ordinal
1	(a)	**fratama-* / **parθama-*	**aiwa-*
	(b)	**parwiya-*	
2		**dwitī̆ya-* / **dwita-*	**duwā*
3		**θritī̆ya-* / **θrita-*	**θrā̆yah*
4		**(x)turī̆ya-* / **čaθruma-*	**čaθwārah*
5		**puxθa-*	**panča*
6		**xštwa-*	**xšwaš*
7		**haftaθa-* / **haftama-*	**hafta*
8		**aštama-*	**aštā*
9		**nawama-*	**nawa*
10		**dasama-*	**dasa*

The ordinals are clearly — for the most part — related to the cardinals (except for 'first') by the addition of a limited number of suffixes: *-ta-*/ *-θa-* (see 8.2.7.), *-ī̆ya-* and *-ma-*. The correspondence between ordinal and cardinal is clearest in the case of 'seventh' to 'tenth'.

8.2.11.1. Apart from the words for 'first', which are based on a different morpheme from the word for 'one', it must be assumed that the ordinals were at some stage methodically derived from the cardinals. The original principle of derivation is most likely to be deducible from those ordinals which least resemble their cardinal counterparts and hence are most archaic, namely *(x)turīya-*, **puxθa-* and **xštwa-*. These forms seem best explained as the zero grade of the cardinal plus suffix. The suffixes PIE **-mo-*, **-to-*, **-yo-* are all of Proto-Indo-European date but probably originated secondarily (see 5.2.11.1.).
8.2.11.2. That the original principle of formation was suffixation added to the zero grade of the cardinal is confirmed by the explanation of the Indo-European word for 'hundred' as **dḱm̥tó-* 'tenth (decad)' (8.1.31.1.). PIE **deḱm̥to-* as seen in Greek *dékatos* 'tenth', etc., will then have the full grade under the influence of the cardinal. Since 'ten' was originally **-dḱm̥t-* in the decads, it seems likely that the ordinal was formed simply by thematicization of PIE **déḱm̥t* 'ten'. PIE **deḱm̥*, required by Indo-Iran. **daśá*, Greek *déka*, etc. (8.1.10.), is therefore explained as a secondary form, a generalized sandhi-variant. The influence of PIE **séptm̥*, **néwm̥* may have been the reason that the final was lost only in the numbers below 'twenty' (cf. G. Schmidt, *KZ* lxxxiv, 1970: 108 n. 63).
8.2.11.3. The above analysis of the ordinal system as seen in Iranian shows that, from the point of view of Iranian, there can be no objection to the traditional view (Brugmann – Delbrück 1897–1916: II. ii. 50; Szemerényi 1960: chapter IV) that the original principle that obtained in the formation of the ordinals 'third' to 'tenth' was thematicization of the zero grade of the corresponding cardinal. For the Proto-Indo-European background to the Indo-Iranian system see 5.2.11. Only **dwita-* 'second' causes difficulty, and it remains uncertain whether this form is of Proto-Indo-European date. An expected **du-tó-* to **duwṓ* may have been influenced by **tri-tó-* 'third'. On the other hand, **dwi-*, and even the full grade **dwoi-*, must be ascribed to Proto-Indo-European (8.1.2.–8.1.2.2.).

8.2.12. 'Eleventh' to 'nineteenth'

These ordinals have in Old Iranian the same form as the corresponding cardinals (8.1.10.2.), but they are declined as *-a*-declension adjectives with feminines in *-ī*[60] as in Old Indian (5.2.11.3.). Thus Avestan has *panca.dasa* 'fifteen' (indeclinable) beside *panca.dasa-* 'fifteenth' (*-a*-declension adjective). The forms may originally have been distinguished by a difference of accentuation as in OInd. *páñcadaśa* 'fifteen' beside *pañcadaśá-* 'fifteenth'.

8.2.12.1. In later Iranian the ordinals 'eleventh' to 'nineteenth' have everywhere been distinguished from the cardinals by the addition of a generalized ordinal suffix, usually *-(a)ma-*. Thus Khotanese has *śūdasama-*[61] 'eleventh', *dvāsama-* 'twelfth', *draisama-* 'thirteenth', *tcahaulasama-* 'fourteenth', *paṃjsūsama-* 'fifteenth', *kṣasama-* 'sixteenth', *haudūsama-* 'seventeenth', *haṣṭūsama-* 'eighteenth', *nausama-* 'nineteenth'. Christian Sogdian has *ywntsmyq* 'eleventh', *xwšrtsmyq* 'sixteenth', **bttsmyq* (see 8.1.17.) 'seventeenth', *šttsmyq* 'eighteenth', *nwtsmyq* 'nineteenth'. Ossetic has Digor *-äimag*[62], Iron *-äm*, e. g. Digor *yevändäsäimag*, Iron *yvändäsäm* 'eleventh'. Zoroastrian Pahlavi has *-(w)m*, Parthian *-wm*, Modern Persian *-om* and optionally *-omīn*, differently construed (Lazard 1963: 221). This is found in Parāčī as *-umī* (Morgenstierne 1929: 60), Balōčī *-amī, -umī*, Iškāšmī *-ьm*, Yazgulami *-əm*, Paštō *-am*. Kurdish has the dialect variants *-am(īn), -amē, -ē* (D. N. MacKenzie, *Kurdish dialect studies*, 1961: 72, 170). Waxī retains the old ordinal suffix as *-ьıng* for 'second' to 'tenth' but .otherwise uses borrowed forms in *-əm* (A. L. Grjunberg – I. M. Steblin-Kamenskij, *Vaxanskij Jazyk*, Moscow 1976: 646). Sarīkolī has *-inči* from Turkish.

8.2.13. Ordinals of the decads

8.2.13.1. 'Twentieth'

Av. *vīsąstəma-* occurs once only, in a late passage (Yt. 1.8). Here *-ą-* is probably to be ascribed to a nominative singular **vīsąs* to be inferred from *θrisąs* (8.1.22.4.), since the attested *vīsąs* is to be otherwise explained (8.1.21.1.). Av. *vīsąstəma-* would correspond, apart from the nasalized vowel, to an OInd. **viṃśattamá-*, which has been secondarily replaced by *viṃśatitamá-* (5.2.14.). The Indian and Iranian forms thus represent PIE **wīḱm̥t-tó-* (Greek *eikostós*) with analogical *-ma-* as in Latin *uīcēsimus*.

8.2.13.1.1. The later Iranian forms continue an OIran. **wīsastama-* rather than a secondary form like Av. *vīsąstəma-*. The contraction of **wīsastama-* to **wīstama-*, found in all the later Iranian forms, may have taken place very early if I. Gershevitch, *JNES* xxiv (1965: 183–184) is correct in deducing **vīstama-* 'twentieth' for Old Persian from Elamite spellings (cf. 8.3.3.2.). In this case the ordinal may have induced the contraction of **wīsatī* 'twenty' (8.1.22.2.). Examples from later Iranian: Khot. *bistama-*, Christian Sogd. *wystmyq*, Parth. *wystwm* in M 728 (unpublished; Boyce), Zoroastrian Pahl. *wīstom*, Modern Pers. *bīstom*.

8.2.13.2. 'Thirtieth', etc.

According to Bartholomae, Avestan had for 'thirtieth' *θrisastəma-* (1904: col. 810) or *θrisąstəma-* (1904: col. 1914) – his emendation of Nirangistan 51, which he gives as *θrəstəməmcaṯ*. The passage was not rendered by J. Darmesteter, *Le Zend-Avesta* (1892–1893: iii. 113), and was not used by A. W. Waag, *Nīrangistān* (1941: 64). *θrəstəməmcaṯ* occurs on p. 107, lines 2–3, of *Nirangistan*, ed. P. Sanjana (Bombay 1894). No variant is cited from ms TD on p. 44. The Pahlavi does not appear to correspond and no sense has yet been made of the passage[63]. Such a form as *θrisąstəma-* would be expected for Avestan in the light of *vīsąstəma-* 'twentieth' (8.2.13.1.), but it cannot yet be considered established. Later forms of 'thirtieth' and the higher ordinals are based secondarily on the corresponding cardinals. 'Thirtieth' is also attested in Parthian: *hrystwm* M 728 (unpublished; Boyce).

8.2.14. 'Hundredth'

Av. *satō.təma-* occurs once only, in a late text (Vištāsp Yt. 19) but agrees with OInd. *śatatamá-*. In later Iranian the expected **satama-* is found: Khot. *satama-*, Modern Pers. *sadom*. With the contraction to **wīst* for 'twenty' in Middle Iranian (8.1.21.), perhaps induced by the earlier contraction of **wisastama-* to **wīstama-* for 'twentieth' (8.2.13.1.1., 8.3.3.2.), it was possible to generalize *-ma-* for the decadic and higher ordinals. Cf. the similar development in later Old Indian (5.2.15.).

8.2.15. 'Thousandth'

Av. *hazaŋrōtəma-* occurs once only, in a late text (Vištāsp Yt. 19) but agrees with OInd. *sahasratamá-*. In later Iranian the expected analogical forms (cf. 8.2.14.) are found: Khot. *ysārama-*, Modern Pers. *hazārom*.

8.3. Other numerals

8.3.1. Multiplicative adverbs

8.3.1.0. Overview

Avestan provides the following (cf. 5.3.1.0.).

	Types: I	II	III	IV	V
1	*hakərat̰*			*paoirīm*	
2	*biš*	*bižuuat̰*	*bisarəm*	*(āt̰)bitīm*	
3	*θriš*	*θrižuuat*	*θrisarəm*	*(ā)θritīm*	
4	*caθruš*			*(āx)tūirīm*	
6	*xšuuaš*			*xštūm*	*xšuuažaiia*
9				*naoməm*	*naomaiia.*

Of these, types I and IV are in principle Indo-European. The examples of type IV are complete only for those forms which have *ā-*.

8.3.1.1. Av. *hakərat̰* 'once' corresponds exactly to OInd. *sakŕ̥t*. The word is usually explained as containing PIE **sm̥-* 'one' and **kr̥t* from PIE **kert-* 'cut' (OInd. *kr̥ntáti*, Av. *kərəntaiti* 'cut'). This *ha-* is found also in Av. *ha-* 'with' and Av. *haδa*, OPers. *hadā* 'with', etc. = OInd. *sa-, sadha-* and *sahá* (see 5.3.1.4.). Avestan has also *hakat̰* 'at the same time' explained by Bartholomae (1904: col. 1742) as a contamination of **hakam* and *hakərat̰*.[64] He compared **hakam* with OInd. *sākám* 'at the same time'.

**kr̥t* has usually been connected with Lith. *kar̃tas* and OCS *kratŭ* 'time(s)'. OPers. *hakaram* 'once' is connected with Av. *hakərat̰* by assuming thematicization after the loss of final *-t*. The same explanation is given for OPers. *čiyăkara-* 'quantus', but it is surely not convincing in view of the variety of **kara-* forms in later Iranian (see Gershevitch 1954: 171 and 8.2.2. above), which no doubt belong, like OInd. *kālá-* 'time', to PIE **kʷel-* 'to turn, move'. Indo-Iran. **sakŕ̥t* should therefore be explained as **sa-kr̥-t*, where *-t* is the Indo-European determinative (Hirt 1921–1937: iii. 120 ff.). OInd. *kŕ̥tvaḥ* 'times' may be explained as the plural of **kr̥-tu-*, an abstract from the same verbal root (5.3.1.5.). For the use of PIE **sem-* 'one' for the multiplicative adverb beside **oy-* for the cardinal, note the occurrence in Latin of *semel* 'once' beside *ūnus* 'one'.

8.3.1.1.1. Zoroastrian Pahl. *hk(w)lč* [65], Modern Pers. *hargiz* continue an OIran. **hakr̥t-čid*, cf. OPers. *hakaram-čiy* (DN 34–35); Zoroastrian Pahl. *hklc* [66] means 'ever' in negative sentences, Modern Pers. *hargiz* 'never'.

8.3.1.1.2. Khot. *hatärra, hatärro* 'once', presumably derived from **sakr̥tna-*.[67] The suffix *-no-* was commonly used to form adjectives from Indo-European multiplicative adverbs e.g. Latin *trīnī* < PIE **tris-no-* (Brugmann – Delbrück 1897–1916: II. ii. 1,77–78; etc.). Such a derivation is unlikely to be far wrong. Khot. *hatärra, hatärro* 'once' must, however, be distinguished from *hatäro* 'formerly' > **fratara-* (8.2.1.7.).

8.3.1.2. Av. *biš* 'twice' corresponds exactly to OInd. *dvíḥ* and continues PIE **dwis*: Greek *dís*, Latin *duis, bis*.

8.3.1.3. Av. *θriš* 'three times' corresponds exactly to OInd. *tríḥ* and continues PIE **tris*: Greek *trís*, Latin *ter*.

8.3.1.4. Av. *caθruš* 'four times', like Latin *quater*, may show Proto-Indo-European development **k^{w}etwr̥s* > **k^{w}etrus* (Hoffmann, *KZ* lxxix, 1965: 251 n. 1). On OInd. *catúḥ* 'four times' see 5.3.1.1. Av. *caθruš* has been thematicized in *caθruša-* 'side of a square' (V 2.25+).

8.3.1.5. Av. *xšuuaš* 'six times' occurs beside other multiplicative adverbs in V. 7.15, 75. It could continue PIE **ksweḱs* directly, with the expected homonymity with the cardinal. No comparable form has been noted elsewhere except in Old Indian (see 5.3.1.1.).

8.3.1.6. Av. *bižuuat̰* 'twice' and *θrižuuat̰* 'three times' have caused unnecessary difficulty. *-uuat̰* is clearly due to *čuuat̰* 'how often?'. This itself is an adverbial accusative singular neuter to *čuuant-* 'quantus', cognate with OInd. *kī́vant-*. The *ž* which caused Bartholomae (*GIP*, 1895–1901: i. 143; 1904: 812) so much difficulty, can scarcely be separated from *-š-*/*-ž-* in the prefix *duš-* (*dušmata-* 'übel gedacht', *dužuuacah-* 'des Reden übel ist') and elsewhere (*aršuxδa-* and *ərəžuxδa-* 'truly spoken') at a morpheme boundary. Av. *bižuuat̰* and *θrižuuat̰* simply contain *biš* and *θriš* (8.3.1.2.–8.3.1.3.) with suffix *-uuat̰* as in *cuuat̰*. A similar explanation of Av. *bižuuat̰* was given by J. Scheftelowitz (*ZDMG* lix, 1905: 700). He read *bižavat̰* 'zweimal soviel' with C. Bartholomae against K. Geldner ("gegen die NA", Bartholomae, *GIP*, 1895–1901: i. 1. 143). See further 5.3.1.3.

8.3.1.7. Av. *bisarəm* 'twice' and *θrisarəm* 'thrice' occur once only, in a late Avestan fragment (see J. Darmesteter, *Le Zend-Avesta*, 1892–1893: 65). Bartholomae offered no etymology (1904: s. vv.). With *-s-* (not *-š-*) the analysis must be **bi-sar(a)-* with *-s-* < PIE *ḱ*. Theoretical connection with Av. *sarah-* 'head' or *sari-* 'fragment' is possible. In the former case cf. Balōčī *do sar* 'double', *sai sar* 'threefold' (G. W. Gilbertson, *The Balochi language*, 1923: 41).

8.3.1.8. A common type of expression in the Indo-European languages is the adverbial use of the accusative singular neuter of the ordinal: OInd. *dvitī́yam* 'secondly', Greek *tò prôton*, Latin *prīmum, iterum, tertium*. Av. *paoirīm* 'firstly', etc. is of this type. The use of the preposition *ā-* is paralleled by OInd. *ādvādaśám* (RV x. 114.6) 'bis auf zwölf' (Bartholomae 1904: col. 310), but the meaning has developed further in Avestan.

8.3.1.9. Av. *xšuuažaiia* 'six times' and *naomaiia* 'nine times' each occur once only, in late Avestan, at V. 8.17 and 8.18 respectively. Both have attached the enclitic particle *ciṯ* (cf. 8.3.1.1.1.). Bartholomae saw an ancient compound with **aya-* 'Gang', 'Mal' (1904: s. vv.). But *naomaiia* (Geldner *nāumaiiā*) looks much more like an instrumental singular feminine to the ordinal *naoma-*, cf. GAv. the locative singular *paouruiiē* 'at first'. Possibly, therefore, *xšuuažaiia* is an analogical replacement of **xštuuaiia* due to *xšuuaš* 'six times' (8.3.1.5.; *-ž-* as 8.3.1.6.).

8.3.1.10. As in other Indo-European languages, there is an increasing tendency to employ the cardinal plus a noun meaning 'time(s)' instead of types I – III. A great variety of words is found, of which a few examples follow.

Zoroastrian Pahl. *bār*, Modern Pers. *bār*; cf. OInd. *vā́ra-* (see 5.3.1.6.);

Middle Persian (Turfan) *j'r* (= Zoroastrian Pahl *y'wl*), Kurdish *jār*, Buddhist Sogd. *y'wr*; cf. Av. *yauua* 'always';

Manichaean Sogd. *prwrtyy* 'turn' < **pari-wart-*;[68]

Khotanese has *gyūna-* (< **yauna-*, see H. W. Bailey 1967: 91), *tcīra-* (< **čarya-* to PIE **kʷel-*, cf. 8.3.1.1.), and *rrāyä* (< **rāti*, see Bailey 1967: 302);

Ossetic (Digor) *xadt*, (Iron) *xat*; Digor *xatun*, Iron *xatyn* 'to turn', see É. Benveniste, *Études sur la langue ossète* (1959: 57 – 58).

8.3.2. Multiplicative adjectives

8.3.2.1. Avestan provides the following: *vīsaitiuuant-* 'twentyfold' *θrisaθβant-* 'thirtyfold', *caθβarə.saθβant-* 'fortyfold', *panca.saθβant-* 'fiftyfold', *xšaštiuuant-* 'sixtyfold', *haptaiθiuuant-* 'seventyfold', *aštaiθiuuant-* 'eightyfold', *nauuaitiuuant-* 'ninetyfold', *satauuant-* 'hundredfold', and *hazaŋrauuant-* 'thousandfold'. The formation is cardinal plus *-want-* suffix (< PIE **went-*). For similar forms in *-vant-* and *-in-* in Old Indian see 5.3.2.4. – 5.3.2.5. No exact parallel is found elsewhere: Greek *tetrâs* and

Latin *quadrāns* adduced by Brugmann – Delbrück (1897–1916: II. i. 464–465; II. ii. 72), are now considered to be secondary formations (see E. Schwyzer, *Griechische Grammatik*, 1939: 528; A. Ernout – A. Meillet, *Dictionnaire étymologique de la langue latine*, 1967: ii. 554).

8.3.2.2. In later Iranian, multiplicative adjectives are variously formed compounds as in other Indo-European languages.

In early Modern Persian they appear to be related to the distributives: *dugān* 'in pairs' but *dugānah* 'two' (Middle Persian (Turfan) *dwg'ng*) – see Lazard (1963: 222 f.). The origin of these forms is uncertain (see B. Geiger – A. Kuhn, *GIP*, 1895–1901: i. 1. 290; *GIP*, 1898–1901: i. 2. 116, and cf. 8.3.4.3.). In Modern Persian *tā* (< Zoroastrian Pahl. *tāg* 'piece') is also found in this use: *dō-tā* 'twofold'. Ossetic has *-c'ar* (literally '[tree-]bark), *-daγ* (possibly connected with Zoroastrian Pahl. *tāg* 'piece' – cf. Abaev 1958: 342), *-wazug* (from OIran. **baz-* 'extend' – cf. Benveniste 1959: 65). Sogdian (cf. Gershevitch 1954: 199; W. B. Henning, *Ein manichäisches Bet- und Beichtbuch*, 1937: 140) has *-zng'n* : *δw'zng'n* 'twofold', *pnčzng'n* 'fivefold', etc. Khotanese has *-ysania-* in *tcūrysania-* 'fourfold', *haṣṭä-ysania-* 'eightfold' (see Bailey 1967: 287). These are extended forms of OIran. **zana-* (< PIE **ǵen-* 'to be born') in Old Pers. *vispa-zana-* 'of all kinds' (Sogd. *wyspzng'n*), etc.

8.3.3. Fractions

8.3.3.1. Avestan provides five fractions with what looks like an Indo-Iranian suffix **-swa-* : *θrišuua-* 'third', *caθrušuua-* 'quarter', *paŋtaŋhuua-* 'fifth', *haptaŋhuua-* 'seventh' and *aštaŋhuua-* 'eight'. In fact, *θrišuua-* and *caθrušuua-* were probably based on the multiplicative adverbs *θriš* and *caθruš* (8.3.1.3.–4.8.3.1.4.) with the addition of the suffix **-wa-*. These forms were reanalyzed as comprising the compound form (8.1.3.6., 8.1.4.7.) plus *-suua-*. Hence *haptaŋhuua-* and *aštaŋhuua-* were formed with the cardinal (8.1.10.1.). It remains difficult however to account for *paŋtaŋhuua-* 'fifth'[69]. The expected Old Iranian form **pančahwa-* is implied by an Elamite spelling for Old Persian (see 8.3.3.2.). It is probable, therefore, that *-taŋhuua-* has spread from *haptaŋhuua-* and *aštaŋhuua-* (Szemerényi 1960: 75). The replacement of **panč-* by *paŋ-* may be due to **paŋti-* 'group of five' = OInd. *paṅtí-* (K. Hoffmann, *KZ* lxxix, 1965: 253).

8.3.3.2. Fractions of the kind discussed in 8.3.3.1. have been discovered in Old Persian loanwords found in Elamite texts (see I. Gershevitch, *JNES* xxiv, 1965: 182–186; K. Hoffmann, *KZ* lxxix, 1965: 247–254; W.

B. Henning, *Kahle Fs.*, 1968: 138–145). The following forms have been reconstructed for Old Persian on the basis of Elamite spellings:

'one-third'	**çišuva-*	= Av *θrišuua-*
'one-quarter'	**čaçuva-*[70] < **caçušuua-*	= Av *caθrušuua-*
'one-fifth'	**pančauva-*	: Av *paŋtaŋhuua-* (8.3.3.1.)
'one-eighth'	**aštauva-*	= Av *aštaŋhuua-*
'one-ninth'	**navauva-*	
'one-tenth'	**daθauva-*	
'one-twentieth'	**vīstauva-* (< **vīsa(s)tauva-*?)	

To the above can be added OIran. **haftahwa-*, recognized in the title *hptḥpt'* in an Old Aramaic text by W. B. Henning, *Kahle Fs.*, (1968: 138–145). He drew attention in the same place (see also C. Salemann, *GIP*, 1895–1901: i. 1. 290), to the following fractions from Middle Persian: 'one-third' *sriśwadag*[71], 'one-quarter' *časruśwadag*[72] (Middle Persian (Turfan) *tswg*[73]), 'one-fifth' *panǰwadag* (Middle Persian (Turfan) *pnǰwg*), 'one-seventh' *haftwadag*, 'one-eighth' *aštwadag*. Among the Old Persian forms there are two instances of haplology which are noteworthy: **čaçuva-* and **vīstaava-*. According to I. Gershevitch, *JNES* xxiv (1965: 183), the latter "was built on an ordinal of the form **vīstama-*" according to the proportional analogy: **aštama-* 'eighth', etc. : **aštahva-* 'one-eighth', etc. :: **vīstama-* 'twentieth' : **vīstahva-* 'one-twentieth'. It remains unclear to me why the ordinal need be invoked. The fractions were clearly understood as comprising the compound form (i. e., in most cases, the cardinal) plus suffix (8.3.3.1.). The compound (and derivational) forms of 'twenty' and 'thirty' were in Avestan *vīsata°* and *θrisata°* (8.1.21.2.–8.1.22.), to which OP **vīsata°* and **çīsata°* would correspond. These are the forms which may have been contracted even if under the influence of the contracted ordinal. Two further fractions of a slightly different form have recently been found in Elamite: *mišduya* 'one-twentieth' and *šišduyaš* 'one-thirtieth'. These are derived by I. Gershevitch *TPS* (1969: 174–175) from **wīstahwya-* and **ṣistahwya-* (*-ya-* derivatives of *-hwa-* fractions based on ordinals).

8.3.3.3. Just as the ordinals could be used as neuter nouns to indicate a fraction in Old Indian, so in Chorasmian after 'third' the ordinals also had this function: *cf'rym* 'quarter', *pncym* 'fifth', *'xtm* 'sixth' etc. The adjective *haptaiθiia-* 'consisting of seven parts', occurring once only in Avestan (Yt. 19.26), was explained by Bartholomae (1904: 1766) as a derivative of the ordinal *haptaθa-* 'seventh' used like the Old Indian ordinals to indicate a fraction. *haptaθa-* is not itself found in this usage, nor are the other ordinals in Avestan (see K. Hoffmann, *KZ* lxxix, 1965: 247 and n. 1), but it is difficult to explain *haptaiθiia-* satisfactorily in any other way.

8.3.3.4. Av. *θrižat̰* occurs once only, in late Avestan (V. 2.23). Bartholomae (1904: 812) explained it as a derivative of *θriš* 'three times' with the suffix of Latin *trientis* : *θrižant-* 'third'. In this case we should expect in Iranian the meaning 'three times', as in *θrižuuat̰* (8.3.1.5.). The Pahlavi rendering of *θrižat̰* in V. 2.23 is *az 3 gyāgān* 'from three places', i. e. presumably the three places mentioned in the stanza. The Pahlavi translator apparently took *-at̰* to be the ablative termination of consonant-stems.[74] Such an interpretation is also indicated by the readings of those manuscripts which have *aδa-* instead of *-at̰*. It is not however clear what an ablative of *θriš* 'thrice' should mean. If we compare the use of the ablative of the cardinal as a distributive in Oss. *ärtäyä* 'by, in threes', a distributive usage is conceivable, but the interpretation of the passage is not clear.

8.3.3.5. In Iranian, as in Old Indian, there are two ways in which 'half' is usually expressed, namely, by use of words continuing Indo-Iranian **ardha-* and **naima-*. Av. *arəδa-* (adj., noun) = OInd. *ardhá-* and Av. *naēma-* (adj., noun) = OInd. *néma-*. OIr. **arda-* is continued by Khot. *hala-* (Bailey 1967: 412) and, with *-ka*-suffix, by Khot. *hālaa-* (adj., noun), Oss. (DI) *ärdäg*, Zoroastrian Pahl. *ālag*, Middle Persian *''rg*. OIr. **naima-* is continued by Sog. *nym*, Chor. *nym(yk)*, Zoroastrian Pahl. *nēm(ag)*, Modern Persian *nīm(e)*, Pashto *nēmai*.

8.3.3.6. Except for 'half' it is possible in later Iranian to express fractions as ordinal plus noun meaning 'part': Chor. *'rcy'd(y)k* < **θritiya-yāta-* (W. B. Henning, *Handbuch der Orientalistik*, 1958: IV. i. 109–110); Oss. (D) *ärtikkag xai*[75]. An archaism is Modern Persian *do bahr* (common in the Šāhnāme) 'two-thirds', literally 'two parts (out of three)', where *bahr* 'share' is cognate with Av. *baxəδra-* < **baxθra-* to **bag-* 'to distribute'. But, with the ordinal, *bahr* is used in the regular way in Baluchi: *gīstumī bahr* 'one-twentieth' (V. A. Frolova, *Beludžskij jazyk*, Moscow 1960: 40).

8.3.3.7. Fractions may also be expressed by means of two cardinals e. g. Zoroastrian Pahl. III *-ēvag(ē)*, Modern Persian *seyek(ē)* 'one third', literally 'three-one', Bal. *čīār-sai* 'three-quarters', literally 'four-three'.

8.3.4. Distributives

8.3.4.1. Avestan provides only one distributive: *nauuasō* 'by nines'. It occurs twice only (Yt. 13.59, V 22.2) in the same phrase: *nauuasəsca baēuuąn* 'and nine times ten thousand'. The use as a multiplicative may be poetical. It is at any rate secondary. °*sō* (sandhi-form °*sə̄s-ca*) corresponds exactly to OInd. °*śaḥ* and to Greek °κάς, which are used distributively. Brugmann — Delbrück (1897—1916: II. ii. 1,75) proposed to see behind it PIE **k̑n̥s*, which he connected further with Latin *cēnsēo*, OInd. *śáṃsati*, Gāthic *sənghaitī* 'proclaim solemnly'.

8.3.4.2. OIr. *°*sah* (8.3.4.1.) may be continued in one place in Sogdian according to I. Gershevitch (*Central Asiatic Journal* vii, 1962: 95). The Mugh document Nov. 4 V 1 has *XXII sw pr wrtw δ'r'm k'm*, according to him, 'I shall hold it subject to interest at the rate of twenty per cent'. *XXIIsw* he explains as *δas δas δwa-su* 'at the rate of two for each ten'. Apart from the fact that we should expect *δiv-* (cf. OInd. *dviśáḥ* and 8.1.2.2. above), the normal result of OIr. *-ah* in Sogdian is *-y*. It is therefore difficult to see how this interpretation can be maintained on formal grounds. It is perhaps better to seek a solution on other lines. V. A. Livšic, *Sogdijskie dokumenty s Gory Mug*, Moscow (1962: ii. 43), suggested that *s* was an abbreviation for *stryk* 'stater', but it remains difficult to account for the *-w*.

8.3.4.3. In later Iranian a great variety of distributives is found, mainly characterized by *k*-suffixes (see I. Gershevitch, *Transactions of the Philological Society*, 1948: 63—65). These may be related to the *-ka-* multiplicatives in Old Indian. Examples are: Sogd. *-ky* in Buddhist Sogd. **z'rky* (written ILPWky), Manichean Sogd. *z'rkyy* 'by the thousands'. Yaghnobi *īki īki* 'one by one' shows the same *-ki* as in Sogdian. In Chorasmian the whole series of distributives from 'one' to 'ten' is listed: *'ywc, 'δwc, šyc, cf'rc, pncc, 'xc, 'βdc, 'štc, š'δc, δsc*. The formation is cardinal plus *-c* suffix < *-*ki*, perhaps further from **kiya-* or even **kaya-*, but hardly from **kāya-* as H. W. Bailey[76] wanted for Oss. (DI) °*gai* in Digor *yeugai* 'by ones', *radugai* 'in turns' etc. A *k*-distributive is probably to be recognized in a number of forms that have not yet been adequately explained. On °*gān* in Modern Persian *yagān* 'one by one' (now obsolete), etc. see 8.3.2.1. Similar are Wakhī *īgōn īgōn* 'one each' (Morgenstierne 1938: 513), Pashto *salgūnah* 'hundreds', Yazgulami °*gén* (D. I. Ėdel'man, *Jazguljamskij jazyk*, Moscow 1966: 35).

8.3.4.4. In later Iranian, instead of a distributive adverb of the kinds discussed in 8.3.4.1.—8.3.4.3., the cardinal may be repeated in distributive sense. Examples: Zoroastrian Pahl. *ēk ēk*, Modern Persian *yek yek*, Parthian Sogd. *'yw 'yw*, Khot. *śśau śśau* 'one each'.

8.3.4.5. Proto-Indo-Iranian **anya-* 'other' is similarly repreated to express 'one another': OInd. *anyonya-*, Av. *aniiō.aniia-*, Chor. *nywny*, Wakhī *yoman*. More usual in Iranian is the expression of 'one another' by 'one second' (cardinal plus ordinal): Khot. *śśūjäta-*, Buddhist Sogd. *'yw δyβty*, Modern Persian *yek dīgar*.

8.3.5. Collectives

8.3.5.1. As is to be expected in a language family characterized by three numbers (singular, dual, plural), the oldest collective is that for two, i. e. 'both'. Indo-Iranian **ubha-* and **ubhaya-* 'both' have, however, an initial vowel that is difficult to explain when these forms are set beside those of other languages e. g. Gothic *bai*. Possibly it is merely Indo-Iranian **u* 'and'. **ubha-* is found in various spellings in Avestan: GAv. *uba-*, YAv. *uua-*, *auua-*. OPers. *uba-* = OInd. *ubhá-*. Khot. *hūduva-* 'both' appears to be a compound of "both" and "two" with prothetic *h-* (Bailey 1967: 425). For such a compound note It. *ambedue* 'both' with the same order. **uba-* has also been sought in Parāčī *huddī* (Morgenstierne 1929: 258). Indo-Iranian **ubhaya-* is continued in Av. *uuaiia-*. Sogdian has it as *'wβy* (W. B. Henning, in Gershevitch 1954: 245) and Manichean Sogd. *wβyw*, Buddhist Sogd. *wβyw*, Christian Sogd. *byw* (Gershevitch 1954: § 101).
8.3.5.2. The Indo-European *-two-* abstract suffix (Brugmann — Delbrück 1897—1916: II. ii. 450) is found in two Avestan numeral derivatives: *darəyō.fratəmaθβa-* (Y 60.2) 'langdauernder Prinzipat, lange Gebieterschaft' (Bartholomae 1904: 695) and *θrisataθβəm* 'thirty times', accusative singular neuter as adverb (twice V 8.98). Both forms are secondary: on **fratama-* see 8.2.1.1., on *θrisata-* 8.1.22.
8.3.5.3. Manichean Sogd. *δyβnw*, Buddhist Sogd. *δyβnw* 'both' may continue the Indo-European suffix *-no-* in Latin *bīnī* etc., (Brugmann — Delbrück 1897—1916: II. ii. 1,77—78) according to R. Gauthiot, *Essai de grammaire sogdienne* (Mission Pelliot en Asie centrale 8: I, III), Paris (1914—23: 120); Gershevitch (1954: § 1320); cf. also 8.3.1.1.2. But a different explanation has been proposed above (8.1.2.1.). Shugni *δiō*[u]*n* 'two' was connected with Sogd. *δyβnw* by G. Morgenstierne, *NTS* v, (1932: 343).

8.4. Order of numerals

The normal order of composite numerals (as in Old Indian) is unit preceding ten, but otherwise larger numbers precede. Thus Avestan has *pancāca vīsaiti* 'twenty-five' (lit. 'five and twenty'), *nauuaca nauuaitīmca* 'ninety-nine', etc. Buddhist Sogd. *nw' nw't* 'ninety-nine'. Khot. *puspare-bästä* 'twenty-five' has *paṃjsa* 'five' + **parah* 'beyond' (so already E. Leumann, *ZDMG* lxii, 1908: 95 n. 1) + *bästä* 'twenty'. Khot. *nauvar-enautä* 'ninety-nine'. In the modern languages, where it is usual to express a number consisting of a ten and a unit simply by juxtaposing the respective cardinals usually linked by 'and', the unit sometimes precedes e. g. Pashto *yau wīšt* 'twenty-one', Ossetic (D) *yau äma insäi*, (I) *yu ämä ssäj* 'twenty-one', but more often follows e. g. Bal. *gist o yak* 'twenty-one', Modern Persian *bist o yek* 'twenty-one', Yazgulami *bīst-ə-čōr* 'twenty-four', Parāčī *γušt u žū* 'twenty-one', Sarīkolī *wīst-at iw* 'twenty-one', Tati *bīsti panǰ* 'twenty-five', Kurdish *sīh ô sē* 'thirty-three', Shugni *δu δīs-at yīw* 'twenty-one'. In some languages the analytical method has penetrated even the teens e. g. Shugni *δīs-at yīw* 'eleven', Tati *dähyäk* 'eleven', Wakhī *δas-yiw* 'eleven'. Some examples of larger numbers are: Buddhist Sogd. *ILPW 'δwy C 50nw* 'one thousand two hundred and fifty', Khot. *ysārä drrai se haudā* 'one thousand three hundred and seventy', *satä śśūvarebistä* 'one hundred and twenty-one', Modern Persian *hazār o sad o bist o yek* 'one thousand one hundred and twenty-one'. In some cases subtractive numerals are found: Manichean Sogd. *ii qmbyy xxx* 'twenty-eight' (lit. 'thirty less two'), Buddhist Sogd. *'yw knpy L* 'forty-nine' (literally 'fifty less one'), Tati *hästād säta käm* 'seventy seven' (literally 'eight less three').[77] The related Avestan *kamna-*, OPers. *kamna-* 'few' is not so used, but it seldom occurs. Early Modern Persian also used *kam* in this way (Lazard 1963: 220): *hazār kam panǰāh* 'nine hundred and fifty' (lit. 'one thousand less fifty').

Notes

1. For the Avestan numerals see C. Bartholomae, *Grundriss der iranischen Philologie* (1895–1901: i. 111–113), H. Reichelt, *Awestisches Elementarbuch* (1909: 213–217), A. V. W. Jackson, *An Awesta grammar* (1892: 106–108).
2. For the Old Persian numerals see R. G. Kent, *Old Persian* (1953), Brandenstein – Mayrhofer (1964: 65–66).
3. For the Khotanese numerals see S. Konow (1932: 50–52; 1949: 44–45; 1941: 50–52); L. G. Gercenberg, *Chotano-Sakskij jazyk* (1965: 88–89). Additions and corrections are here made from an unpublished volume of my *Saka grammatical studies*.
4. Contracted from **kṣätä'ṇu*. Cf. Buddhist Sogdian gen. pl. *wγwšw-nw* (Gershevitch 1954: 251).

5. Once only (P4099.27, Bailey 1951: 114) in a badly written late Khotanese text, no doubt for **nauyau*.
6. Cf. the extension of *-tĭ* to 'five' to 'ten' in Old Church Slavonic, where 'five' to 'ten' are treated as collective feminine *i*-stems (see G. Nandriş, *Old Church Slavonic grammar*, 1959: 120).
7. So Mayrhofer, *IIJ* iv (1960: 146, n. 75).
8. The Pahlavi spelling *'ywk'* is read as *ēvak* by H. S. N. Nyberg, *Hilfsbuch des Pehlevi* (1931: 68–69) but as *ēk* by D. N. M. MacKenzie, *A concise Pahlavi dictionary* (1971: 30), presumably as a hypothetical intermediate form between *ēvak* and *yek*. The development to *yek* is in any case phonologically exceptional. See further W. B. Henning, *Handbuch der Orientalistik* IV (1937: 70, n. 2).
9. For Middle Persian of Turfan and Parthian numerals see C. Salemann, *Manichaeische Studien* (St. Petersburg, 1908: 160). The numerals occur in various texts chiefly published in the following works: F. C. Andreas – W. B. Henning, *Mitteliranische Manichaica aus Chinesisch-Turkestan* i–iii (*SPAW* 1932.X, 1933.VII, 1934.XXVII); M. Boyce, *The Manichaean hymn-cycles in Parthian* (*LOS* III, 1954); W. Sundermann, *Mittelpersische und parthische kosmogonische und Parabeltexte der Manichäer* (Berliner Turfantexte IV, Schriften zur Geschichte und Kultur des alten Orients 8), Berlin 1972. I am grateful to Professor Mary Boyce for information from unpublished texts.
10. Zoroastrian Pahl. *'yw'č* (MacKenzie, *A concise Pahlavi dictionary* 1971, *ēwāz*) 'sole, only' is a compound of *aiwa-* 'one' and the particle **čit* (Av. *cit̰*); so Nyberg (1931: 73; cf. above).
11. See Morgenstierne, *NTS* xiii (1945: 233; 1954: 234); Turner (1966: nos. 2472, 2525–2526).
12. So P. Thieme, *JAOS* lxxx (1960: 301–302).
13. The suffix *-no-* may here originally have been that found in collectives (8.3.5.3.) according to Gonda (1953: 75). Similarly *-ko-* in OInd. *éka-* is no doubt collective (cf. 8.3.4.3.).
14. The suffix indicates "la position spatiale" according to É. Benveniste, *Le vocabulaire des institutions indo-européennes* (Paris, 1969: 262).
15. Av. *vīspa-* 'all' and *aēuua-* 'one' both have pronominal inflection.
16. For the Sogdian numerals see Gershevitch (1954: 197–201). On 'one' to 'ten', see R. Gauthiot, *MSL* xvii (1911–1912: 137–161).
17. See E. Yar-Shater, *A grammar of southern Tati dialects* (*Publications in Near and Middle East Studies* B. III), The Hague (1969: 144).
18. Hence the Sogdian spellings with *-y* (*(')δwy*) probably continue the old feminine rather than a collective **dvaya-* as proposed by R. Gauthiot, *MSL* xvii (1911–1921: 143).
19. See the bibliographical references given by Emmerick (1966: 21, n. 5) and the discussion of Av. *hāirišī-* (1966: 21–22). Add now O. Szemerényi, "Indo-

European **sor-*", *Kratylos* xi (1966: 206–221). But I find it impossible to accept his "Middle Iranian" explanation of Av. *hāirišī-* (1966: 217). It occurs already in Yt. 5, which such an authority as W. B. Henning would ascribe to c. 400 B.C. (Henning, *TPS*, 1945: 162, n. 1). Szemerényi's procedure would allow us to treat virtually all non-Gathic Avestan as Middle Iranian. On **sor-* see again É. Benveniste, *Le vocabulaire des institutions indo-européennes*, Paris (1969: 214–215); O. Szemerényi, *Studies in the Kinship Terminology of the Indo-European Languages, with special reference to Indian, Iranian, Greek and Latin* (*Acta Iranica* 16, *Varia 1977*) Leiden etc. (1977: 1–240), on **sor-* pp. 34 ff.

20. Some later Indian languages show forms implying **trāyaḥ* (Turner 1966: no. 5994), but they are probably secondary as their forms for 'thirteen' have **-ă-* (Turner 1966: no. 6001).
21. I. Gershevitch, *The Avestan hymn to Mithra*, Cambridge (1959: 209) sees support for its antiquity in his etymology of Av. *θrāiiauuan-*, a type of priest, from **θrāya-* 'a triple course of studies'. But the etymology is uncertain, cf. R. Hauschild, *MIO* xi (1966: 500, n. 69). Av. *θrāiia-* 'protection' is attested.
22. The final *-h* is probably due to the influence of Zoroastrian Pahl. *dh*, Middle Persian (Turfan) *dh* 'ten' (see C. Bartholomae, *Zum altiranischen Wörterbuch*, 1900: 69–70).
23. The Chorasmian (Khwarezmian) numerals are found mainly in Zamaxšarī, *Muqaddinat al-Adab*, (Benzing (ed.) 1968: 28 ff.). For a bibliography of Chorasmian see Benzing (ed.) 1968: ix–xii and H. Humbach, 'Choresmian', pp. 193–203 in *Compendium Linguarum Iranicarum*, ed. R. Schmitt, Wiesbaden 1989.
24. Also Christian Sogdian *štfr* (É. Benveniste, *JA* ccxliii, 1955: 319) and Yaghnobi *tïfór* (Andreev – Peščereva 1957: 334).
25. Perhaps continued in Paštō *cūṇ(-sū)* 'four hundred'; see Morgenstierne, *NTS* xii (1942: 67).
26. Cf. Bartholomae "čaturə̄ (Akk. plur.) zīzan° zu lesen" (*IF* xxi, 1907: 352 n.). So in (1904: col. 577) against K. Geldner.
27. É. Benveniste, *Titres et noms propres en iranien ancien*, Paris (1966: 92) proposed to see the numeral 'four' in some Elamite personal names. Against this proposal see Gershevitch, *Pagliaro Festschrift*, Rome (1969: 232). On the other hand Gershevitch, *Journal of Near Eastern Studies* xxiv (1965: 177) proposes to see in an Elamite title a Median loanword **čaθru-pati-* 'chief of four'.
28. For the phonology involved see P. Tedesco, *Le monde oriental* xv (1921: 209), and I. Gershevitch, *Pagliaro Fs.* (1969: 251). Modern Persian *čārpāy* 'four-footed' thus probably contains *čār* 'four', which early stands beside *čahār* (Lazard 1963: 168) as does *čahārpāy* beside *čārpāy*. *čh'lp'd* is found already in Pahlavi (see Nyberg, *Hilfsbuch des Pehlevi*, 1931: 41). *čār* is thus a contraction of *čahār* and does not continue OIran. **čaθru-* as suggested by C.

Bartholomae, *Grundriss der iranischen Philologie* (1898–1901: i.111, 150), and P. Horn (1896–1901: 115 n. 1). Compare also Modern Persian *čel* beside *čehel* 'forty' (both already in Šāhnāme, etc.). In Modern Persian, *tas-* survives only in *tasū* (8.3.3.2.) 'a quarter' (gold weight), borrowed into Chorasmian as *cswy* (Muq. 35[2]), into Arabic as *ṭassūǰ* (Horn 1898–1901: 116 n. 2), and into Armenian as *t'asu* (Hübschmann 1895: 266). Note further Modern Iranian *tašpūč* 'quarter' in Kermānī and Behdīnānī (Gershevitch, *Pagliaro Fs.*, 1969: 251).

29. Av *-pt-* is merely graphic for [ft]. After the change of **-pt-* to **-ft-*, the graph *-pt-* could have indicated only [ft] until the development of secondary *-pt-*, which is not found in Avestan. See also G. Morgenstierne, *NTS* xii (1942: 70).
30. Cf. Waziri Paštō *tā̄r pa wōta* 'nine', where Morgenstierne explains *tēr* as 'passed' < **tarya-* (1927: 51–52).
31. In the ordinal *ywntsmyq* (Hansen 1954: 897 [89]).
32. See Szemerényi (1960: 53 n. 58); É. Benveniste, *JA* ccxxviii (1936: 196).
33. Note however the spelling *śūṃdasa* at Or 6400.2.2 5 (Bailey 1963: 10).
34. Miller (1903: 48) gives the Iron from as *duvädas*, which I have not seen elsewhere. It would be a simple juxtaposition of *duvä* 'two' and *däs* 'ten'. Such a secondary formation occurs in Paštō *dwǟlas* (Morgenstierne 1927: 23) and perhaps in Sanglēčī *dīδuš* (Morgenstierne 1938: 344).
35. *paṃjsūsi* is probably late Khotanese for **paṃjsūsu* (cf. *dvāsu*, *draisu*, etc.), but the ending has not yet been explained. Konow (1949: 51) may be correct in assuming that the teens contain as a second element **dasam*, which can hardly be accounted for except as an old sandhi-form of **dasa*, that is, a pre-vocalic **deḱm̥m* beside pre-consonantal **deḱm̥*, to put it in Proto-Indo-European terms, although it need not be older than Indo-Iranian. It remains, however, difficult to account for the *-ū-* in 'fifteen', 'seventeen', and 'eighteen'. From **panča-dasam*, we should expect an intermediate stage **paṃjsā̆su*, and similarly from **hafta-dasam* and **ašta-dasam* respectively **haudā̆su* and **haṣṭā̆su*. These forms seem to have undergone *u*-umlaut although this is not expected as a result of *-u* < *-am*. Perhaps it began in **paṃjsāsu* in order to keep the form distinct from *paṃjsāsä* 'fifty' – *-ä/-u* are interchanged early – and then spread to the other trisyllabic teens.
36. Attested in the ordinal *xwšrtsm[yq]* (Hansen 1954: 898; cf. É. Benveniste, *JA* ccxliii, 1955: 320–321). I see no reason to follow Szemerényi (1960: 52 n. 51) in his rejection of Benveniste's explanation of *xwšrts* (apparently accepted by Henning op.cit. (1958: 118 n. 4). Szemerényi's difficulty may be the *-t-*, but *-ts* has been generalized, at least in the spelling, in the Sogdian numerals 'eleven' to 'nineteen' ('thirteen' and 'fourteen' are still missing).
37. Attested in the ordinal *šttsmyq*, Hansen (1954: 898 [110]). Christian Sogd. *šts* (F. W. K. Müller, *Soghdische Texte* [*SPAW*], 1912: 41.3) shows further simplification, perhaps only graphic.

38. Assuming two different treatments of **wīsati*, with Morgenstierne, rather than seeing in *šil* an original collective connected with OInd. *kṣiti-* 'abode' with Bartholomae, *IF* xlii (1924: 136–137) (followed by Mayrhofer: *kṣitíḥ*).
39. The precise rendering has been hotly disputed. For literature on the formula see Hauschild, *Orbis* xviii (1969: 561–572); J. Haudry, *BSL* lxxii (1977: 129–168).
40. So A. A. Frejman, 'Zabytye osetinskie čislitel'nye', *Ol'denburg Festschrift* (1934: n. 53). The phonological development of *äxsai* I take to be **äxsästi* > **äxsäti* (by dissimilation) > **äxsati* (by analogy with 'seventy' and 'eighty') > *äxsai*. It is unnecessary to assume with Frejman an analogical **xšvašati* (!) as his **äxsäzáj* implies.
41. On the difficulty presented by the maintenance of the final vowel in the Ormuṛī and Pašto forms see Morgenstierne, *NTS* xxvii, 65.
42. For *ft* represented by *pt* in Avestan see 8.1.7. n. 33.
43. So 'sixty' to 'ninety' in Sarīkolī, see T. N. Paxalina *Sarykol'skii jazyk* (1966: 30): *oltmiš, yatmiš, saksan, tuqsan*.
44. Not **xšvasat*, as Szemerényi (1960: 58) suggests, who cites PIE **pr̥ḱ-sḱo-* giving Av. *pərəsa-* 'ask'. There the morpheme boundary differs. Cf. also 5.1.24.
45. Cf. H. L. Ahrens, *KZ* viii (1859: 349): "Aus dvi-dçati, δϝι-δκατι entstand einerseits vinçati, indem das d in den bequemeren laut überging, anderseits ϝῑκατι, indem es ausgestossen, dafür aber dem vorhergehenden vocale die ersatzdehnung gegeben wurde".
46. Most recently on Latin *mīlle*, E. P. Hamp, *GL* xlvi (1968: 274–278); H. Frisk, *Griechisches etymologisches Wörterbuch* (1960–1972): s. v. *khilioi*. No connection was given by A. Ernout – A. Meillet, *Dictionnaire étymologique de la langue latine* (1967: s. v.).
47. For the Greek and Irish connection see W. Stokes (*Beiträge zur Kunde der indogermanischen Sprachen* xix, 1893: 97; *KZ* xl, 1907: 249); H. Frisk, *Griechisches etymologisches Wörterbuch* (1960: 12) gives μῦρίος; R. Thurneysen, *A grammar of Old Irish* (1946: 42) μύριος, *baēvarə* and *bhū́ri-* were set together by W. Prellwitz, *Etymologisches Wörterbuch der griechischen Sprache* (1892: 206).
48. On Av. *ahąxšta-* 'one hundred thousand' see 5.1.30.
49. Uncertain: Suvarṇaprabhāsottamasūtra 34*r*1, (H. W. Bailey 1963: 112) only.
50. In Konow (1932: 50) there is cited *paḍauysa-* and *prrauda-*. The former is 'leading, chief' from *paḍā* + **vaz-* (Khot. *bays-*), lit. 'going first'. *prrauda-* means 'obtained' and is past participle passive to *prev-* 'to obtain' (Emmerick 1968: 89). It is thus irrelevant to the discussion of numerals.
51. On the spellings of this word in Book Pahlavi, inscriptions and Pāzand, see H. W. Bailey (1943: 179).
52. The etymology of *pēš* is disputed; see I. Gershevitch (1964: 86–87).
53. So H. W. Bailey, *TPS* (1945: 8). Abaev's derivation (1958: 487 n. 56; cf. chapter 5) from Digor *finz(ä)*, Iron *fynz* 'nose' seems arbitrary.

54. See Gershevitch (1954: 171). Bartholomae's explanation of *ditīkar* i. e. *dudīgar* (*IF* xxiii, 1908–1909: 72–73) is untenable.
55. See O. Szemerényi, *Die Sprache* xii (1966: 209–211), with bibliography. His own bold interpretation (to Hittite *tapar-* 'rule') will not convince.
56. **tritya-* (Konow 1932: 50), is impossible. For Indo-Iran. *-*ty*- cf. the development of **satya-* 'true' (Av. *haiθiia-*, OInd. *satya-*) as seen in Khot. *haṭhṭhā-* 'truth'. The Khotanese development of **θrita-* I assume to have been to **drida-* > **dirda-* > *dädda-*. This will be after original **rd* > *l* (*salī* 'year', Av. *sarəd-*) and after secondary **rt* > *ḍ* (*baḍe* 'to ride' < **baratai*). For the secondary movement of *r* cf. *därsä* (8.1.22.3.) and see R. E. Emmerick, *JRAS* (1969: 73).
57. Szemerényi's suggestion (1960: 81) that Av. *āxtūirīm* "is a misreading for *ātūirīm*" can hardly be taken seriously.
58. Read *'xtm* (not *'xyym* with J. Benzing) with D. N. MacKenzie, *BSOAS* xxxiii (1970: 545). *'xtm* probably owes its *-t-* to the influence of *'štym* 'eighth'.
59. For the relevant literature see Szemerényi (1960: 87 n. 97), R. Hiersche, *Untersuchungen zur Frage der Tenues Aspiratae im Indogermanischen*, Wiesbaden (1964: 258); Kuryłowicz (1968: 340–341).
60. Forms such as *panca.dasaiiå* (H. 2.9) 'of a fifteen-year-old (girl) may not show a transfer to the *ā*-declension but represent **panca.dasiiå* in the same way as *aspaiiąm* (Yt. 8.19, acc. sg. fem. from *aspaiia-* 'pertaining to horses') corresponds to OInd. *aśv(i)yām.*
61. Late Khotanese probably for older **śśūndasama-* (see 8.1.11.1.).
62. Digor *-äimag* appears to have spread from *insäimag* 'twentieth' (: *insäi* 'twenty').
63. S. J. Bulsara, *Aêrpatastân and Nîrangastân*, Bombay (1915: 256) emends and translates valiantly but unsuccessfully.
64. In my opinion *hakaṯ* is to be explained rather as the athematic present participle nominative-accusative singular neuter of *hak-* 'to accompany', used as an adverb.
65. Literature: H. S. Nyberg, *Hilfsbuch des Pehlevi* (1931: ii. 92); Brandenstein – Mayrhofer (1964: s. v.): *hakaram.*
66. Read as *hagriz* by MacKenzie, *A concise Pahlavi dictionary* (1971: 39), on account of Middle Persian (Turfan) *hgryč.*
67. Cf. E. Leumann, *Das nordarische (sakische) Lehrgedicht des Buddhismus*, Leipzig (1933–1936: 517).
68. Sogdian terms: Gershevitch (1964: 199). But note that *znk'n* is not 'times' but 'ways'; see the parallels in Bailey (1967: 306). It belongs to 8.3.2.2.
69. Even if it is accepted that *-wa-* is the result of hypostatization of locative plurals, it remains difficult to see why just in this particular instance the locative of an abstract noun instead of the cardinal should be used: **paŋtā* 'in einer Fünfheit' from **paŋti-* 'Fünfheit' (= OInd. *paṅtí-*); cf. K. Hoffmann, *KZ* lxxix (1965: 252–253).

70. -*ç*- here instead of -*š*- (with Gershevitch) is indicated by the Middle Persian forms (so W. B. Henning, *In memorian Paul Kahle* (i. e. *Kahle Fs.*), 1968: 144 n. 40).
71. Pahlavi *slyšwtk'* is interpreted as *srišwadag* by MacKenzie (1971: 76).
72. Some manuscripts have *čtr*- instead of *čsr*-. It is in any case a learned form based on Av. *caθrušuua*-, which it glosses.
73. On *tswg* see also 8.1.4.7. n. 28. Note *tswkw* on Sassanian seals (R. Frye, *Beiträge zur alten Geschichte und deren Nachleben: Festschrift für Franz Altheim zum 6. 10. 1968*, Berlin, 1970: 80–81).
74. J. Darmesteter, *Le Zend-Avesta*, Paris (1892–1893: ii. 25 with n. 27) followed him, rendering "de ces trois lieux" and commented on *θrižat̰* "sorte d'ablatif de *thrish*".
75. On *xai* 'share' see I. Gershevitch, *Central Asiatic Journal* vii (1962: 91); *Studia classica et orientalia Antonino Pagliaro oblata* [*Pagliaro Fs.*] (1969: ii. 192); É. Benveniste, *Titres et noms propres en iranian ancien* (1966: 84) and *JA* ccxlii (1954: 306); H. W. Bailey, *Transactions of the Philological Society* (1945: 9).
76. *Transactions of the Philological Society* (1945: 9). Bailey proposed to see in Oss. °*gai* an OIr. **kāya*- 'heaping up' but that seems unlikely in view of the wider context of *k*-distributives.
77. A. L. Grjunberg, *Jazyk severo-azerbajdžanskix Tatov*, Leningrad (1963: 45).

Abbreviations

Av.	Avestan	OInd.	Old Indian
Bal.	Baluchi	OIr.	Old Iranian
Chor.	Chorasmian	OP	Old Persian
Christian Sogd.	Christian Sogdian	Oss.	Ossetic
D	Digor	Par.	Parthian
I	Iron	PIE	Proto-Indo-European
Ind.	Indian	RV	R̥gveda
Ir.	Iranian	Sogd.	Sogdian
Khot.	Khotanese	V	Vidēvdāt
Man.	Manichean	Y	Younger (of Avesta)
Mn Pers.	Modern Persian	Yt.	Yašt
MPT	Middle Persian (Turfan)	ZP	Zoroastrian Pahlavi

References

Abaev, Vasilij Ivanovič
1958–1989 *Istoriko-ètimologičeskij slovar' osetinskogo jazyka*, I–IV vols (Leningrad: "Nauka" Leningradskoe otdelenie).

Andreev, Mixael Stepanovič S. – Elena Mixaelova Peščereva
1957 *Yagnobskie teksty* (Moskva-Leningrad: Izdatel'stvo Akademii Nauk SSR).
Bailey, Harold Walter
1943 *Zoroastrian problems in the ninth-century books* (Oxford: Clarendon), reprinted 1971.
1945 *Khotanese texts 1* (Cambridge: Cambridge University Press).
1951 *Khotanese Buddhist texts* (= *Cambridge Oriental Series No. 3*) (London: Taylor's Foreign Press).
1954 *Indo-Scythian studies* (= *Khotanese texts 2*) (Cambridge: Cambridge University Press).
1956 *Indo-Scythian studies* (= *Khotanese texts 3*) (Cambridge: Cambridge University Press).
1961 *Indo-Scythian studies* (= *Khotanese texts 4: Saka texts from Khotan in the Hedin Collection*) (Cambridge: Cambridge University Press).
1963 *Indo-Scythian studies* (= *Khotanese texts 5*) (Cambridge: Cambridge University Press).
1967 *Indo-Scythian studies* (= *Khotanese texts 6: Prolexis to the Book of Zambasta*) (Cambridge: Cambridge University Press).
Bailey, Thomas Grahame
1904 *Panjabi grammar* (Lahore).
Bartholomae, Christian
1904 *Altiranisches Wörterbuch* (Straßburg: Trübner).
Benveniste, Émile
1959 *Études sur la langue essète* (Paris: Klincksieck).
Brandenstein, Wilhelm – Manfred Mayrhofer
1964 *Handbuch des Altpersischen* (Wiesbaden: Harrassowitz).
Brugmann, Karl – Berthold Delbrück
1897–1916 *Grundriß der vergleichenden Grammatik der indogermanischen Sprachen* (Straßburg: Trübner).
Debrunner, Albert – Jacob Wackernagel
1930 *Nominalflexion – Zahlwort – Pronomen* (Göttingen: Vandenhoeck & Ruprecht), volume 3 in: Jacob Wackernagel (ed.), *Altindische Grammatik*.
Emmerick, Ronald Eric
1968 *Saka grammatical studies* (*London Oriental Series 20*) (London: Oxford University Press).
Gershevitch, Ilya
1954 *A grammar of Manichean Sogdian* (Oxford: Blackwell).
Gonda, Jan
1953 *Reflections on the numerals "one" and "two" in ancient Indo-European languages* (Utrecht: N. V. A. Oosthoek's uitgevers-mij.).

Hansen, Olaf
1954 *Berliner sogdische Texte II* (*Abhandlungen der geistes- und sozialwissenschaftlichen Klasse Jahrgang 1954, Nr. 15*) (Wiesbaden: Verlag der Akademie der Wissenschaften und der Literatur in Mainz).
Henning, Walther Bruno
1956 "The Khwarezmian language", *Z. V. Togan'a Armağan,* (Istanbul), 421–436. Reprinted in *W. B. Henning, Selected Papers II* (*Acta Iranica* 15) (Leiden Téhéran-Liège: E. J. Brill/Bibliothèque Pahlavi), 1977: 485–500.
Herzenberg, Leonard Georgievič
1965 *Xotano-sakskij Jazyk* (Moskva: Izdatel'stvo "NAUKA") (Series: *Jazyki narodov Azii i Afriki*), edited by T. P. Serdjučenko.
Hirt, Hermann
1921–1937 *Indogermanische Grammatik*, 1–7 vols. (Heidelberg: Carl Winter).
Horn, Paul
1898–1901 *Neupersische Schriftsprache* in: W. Geiger – E. Kuhn (eds.), *Grundriß der iranischen Philologie* (Straßburg: Trübner), 1,2.1: 1–20.
Konow, Sten
1932 *Saka studies* (*Oslo Etnografiske Museum Bulletin 5*) (Oslo: Oslo Etnografiske Museum).
1941 *Khotansakische Grammatik* (Leipzig: Harrossowitz).
1949 *Primer of Khotanese Saka* (Oslo: Aschehoug [W. Nygaard]), reprinted from *Norsk Tidsskrift for Sprogvidenskap, Vol. XV.*
Kuryłowicz, Jerzy
1968 *Indogermanische Grammatik, 2: Akzent Ablaut* (Heidelberg: Winter).
Lazard, Gilbert
1963 *La langue des plus anciens monuments de la prose persane* (Paris: Klincksieck).
MacKenzie, David Neil
1971 *A concise dictionary of Pahlavi* (London: Oxford University Press).
Mayrhofer, Manfred
1956–1980 *Kurzgefaßtes etymologisches Wörterbuch des Altindischen* (Heidelberg: Winter).
Miller, Wsewolod
1903 "Die Sprache der Osseten", in: W. Geiger – E. Kühn (eds.), *Grundriß der iranischen Philologie 1* (Straßburg: Trübner).
Morgenstierne, Georg
1927 *An etymological vocabulary of Pashto* (Skrifter utgitt av Det Norske Videnskaps-Akademi II. Hist.-Filos. Klasse 1927 No. 3) (Oslo: Det Norske Videnskaps-Akademi).
1929 *Indo-Iranian Frontier Languages 1: Parachi and Ormuri* (Oslo: Aschehoug [W. Nygaard]).

1938 *Indo-Iranian Frontier Languages 2: Iranian Pamir languages* (*Yidgha-Munji, Sanglechi-Ishkashmi and Wakhi*) (Oslo: Aschehoug [W. Nygaard]).

Müller, Friedrich Wilhelm Karl
1913 *Soghdische Texte 1* (Abhandlungen der Königlichen preußischen Akademie der Wissenschaften vom Jahre 1912) (Berlin: Verlag der königlichen Akademie der Wissenschaften).

Pokorny, Julius
1959 *Indogermanisches etymologisches Wörterbuch* 1 (Bern and Munich: Francke Verlag).

Reichelt, Hans
1909 *Awestisches Elementarbuch* (Heidelberg: Carl Winter).

Salemann, Carl — V. Shukovski
1889 *Persische Grammatik mit Literatur Chrestomathie und Glossar* (Berlin usw.).

Sommer, Ferdinand
1951 *Zum Zahlwort* (*Sitzungsberichte der Bayerischen Akademie der Wissenschaften, Philosophisch-historische Klasse, Jahrgang 1950, Heft 7*) (München: Verlag der Bayerischen Akademie der Wissenschaften).

Szemerényi, Oswald
1960 *Studies in the Indo-European system of numerals* (Heidelberg: Winter).
1964 *Syncope in Greek and Indo-European and the nature of Indo-European accent* (ΑΙΩΗ, Quaderni della sezione linguistica degli annali, edited by W. Belardi) (Naples: Istituto universitario orientale di Napoli).

Turner, Ralph Lilley
1966 *A comparative dictionary of the Indo-Aryan languages* (London: Oxford University Press).

Chapter 9
Armenian*

Werner Winter

9.0. Introductory comments

Etymological work on Armenian numerals is beset with the same difficulties all etymological study of the Armenian lexicon is faced with: only a relatively small number of items is clear in all respects; many more can be said to differ only as to their place on a scale of increasing opaqueness. The reason for such a state of affairs is that the number of lexical forms which can be classified as "inherited" with a high degree of certainty is fairly small; as a consequence, it is sometimes hard, sometimes even impossible, to provide precise parallels for sound changes posited to explain a given form. Matters are further complicated by the fact that Classical Armenian appears to have incorporated material from more than one dialectal source (cf. Winter 1966).

Unter the circumstances, no full agreement is to be expected among scholars dealing with the same set of problems; at certain points, decisions made will be based on personal preference, with the arguments adduced often not better than those used to support a conflicting hypothesis. In

* The paper printed here appears in the version submitted to A. S. C. Ross when he first asked for contributions to this volume. It thus reflects one person's state of knowledge at the beginning of the 1970s. While my own views have of course changed on a number of points (see in particular the general chapter in this book), I still find the summary as given then useful and defensible. One special comment, though, seems called for: In a paper read at Austin, Texas, in 1986 and to be published under the title "Armenian, Tocharian, and the 'glottalic' theory" (which will hopefully appear in print soon), I reviewed the claims made of late concerning the particularly archaic character of the system of Armenian obstruents; I found these claims insufficiently supported by the data. Hence I see no reason to delete references to the "Great Armenian Soundshift" from the present paper. For 9.1.6., the discussion in Olsen (1981) now is to be compared.

a survey article like the present one, no plausible alternative exists to a basically eclectic approach: only in a few instances will it be possible to give reasons for rejecting an explanation other than the one incorporated, or for not adopting an explanation at all. Also, for the sake of economy, reference will be made to basic works whenever possible, rather than to special studies evaluated for these books. Only publications referred to in the text are listed in the bibliography.

The transcription used is that of Hübschmann as modified by Meillet, except that aspiration is marked consistently by (raised) ʿ.

9.1. Cardinals

9.1.0. Inflected forms of the cardinal numbers will be discussed only in exceptional cases (cf. 9.1.3., 9.1.9.; for details cf. Jensen 1959: 70–71).

9.1.1. Arm. _mi_ 'one' reflects PIE *_sm-yA_ (cf. Gk. _mía_). Confirmation for this derivation from the Proto-Indo-European feminine form is to be found in Arm. _metasan_ 'eleven' and Arm. _mekin_ 'single': there is no indication in the lexical paradigms of either of these forms that they should be derived from _mi-_ plus connecting vowel _-a-_ plus _-tasan/-kin;_ _me-_ is therefore to be taken to be the unstressed variant of *_mea-_ < *_miya-_ < *_smiya-_.

9.1.1.1. If Arm. _mēn_ 'each one' stands for older *_myayn_ (for a parallel, note Arm. _tēr_ 'lord' < *_tyayr_; cf. Meillet 1936: 45), it can be interpreted as *_miya-_ plus _-in_ (for the suffix cf. Jensen 1959: 41, 65, 78, 84). If so, the alternant form Arm. _min_ 'one' may reflect the masculine-neuter stem *_sem-_ (which in Armenian would be represented by *_im-_ and, in unstressed position, *_m-_) plus the same suffix _-in_. That a feminine and a masculine-neuter form should be used in identical function is not really surprising, since the gender distinction was lost in Armenian nouns, adjectives, and pronouns.

9.1.1.2. Arm. _mu_ 'one' and _ez_ 'one' remain obscure.

9.1.2. Arm. _erku_ 'two' derives from PIE *_dwō_; initial _er-_ appears to be due to transfer from the numeral 'three' – the expected onset _k-_ is found, inter alia, in Arm. _krkin_ 'twofold'. Regular loss of unstressed _-u-_ occurs in compounds such as Arm. _erkbay_ 'doubtful', _erkban_ 'deceitful'. _erko-_ in Arm. _erkotasan_ 'twelve', _erkokʿean_ 'both' matches Gk. _dúo_ 'two'. The old feminine-neuter form of the numeral is preserved in Arm. _erkeriwr_ 'two hundred'; _-e-_ is the unstressed variant of *_-ea-_, which in turn is to be derived from *_-iya-_ for earlier *_-eya-_.

9.1.2.1. The explanation just offered for _erkeriwr_ seems preferable to that usually given (cf., e. g., Brugmann 1911: 46), since the higher numerals of the Armenian 'hundred' set clearly contain cardinals as their first members. Moreover, the insertion of the connecting vowel _-a-_ after a bound prefix would be strange. This argument, by the way, applies also to Arm. _erkeam_ 'two years old' and _eream_ 'three years old' (cf. Brugmann 1911: 10–11), which can also be interpreted as containing cardinal numbers as their first components: _erkeam_ < _*dwo-yE-..._, _eream_ < _*triyA-..._; if correctly analyzed, the forms would lead us to identify _am_ 'year' as an old neuter. It is important to note that in compounds with safely recognizable _-a-_, 'three' appears as Arm. _eṙ-_ and not _er-;_ _eṙatʿiw_ 'consisting of three numbers' (: _tʿiw_) is a sure example. For a discussion of _eṙ-_ cf. 9.3.1.
9.1.3. Arm. _erekʿ_ 'three' reflects PIE _*treyes_; the accusative form Arm. _eris_ is a close match of Skt. _trī́n_. For a continuation of the Proto-Indo-European neuter form, cf. 9.1.14.
9.1.4. Arm. _čʿorkʿ_ 'four' corresponds to either Skt. _catvā́ras_ or Doric Greek _tétores_; while no certainty can be reached, the assumption of an early loss of _*-w-_ has some advantages (cf. 9.2.2.). Initial _čʿ-_ of the Armenian form derives from a combination of the reflex of _*k^w-_ with _*-y-_ (from intervocalic _*-t-_ or _*-tw-_) after the loss of unstressed _*i_ from _*e_ (cf. Winter 1955: 6); contrary to what Szemerényi (1960: 19–21) maintains, PIE _*k^we_ does not yield Arm. _čʿe_: note forms like _elikʿ_ 'he left', _hing_ 'five', _hngetasan_ 'fifteen'.
9.1.4.1. In a number of compounds, the longer form _čʿorekʿ-_ is found; cf. _čʿorekʿtasan_ 'fourteen', _čʿorekʿkin_ 'fourfold', _čʿorekʿkerp_ 'in four shapes'; possibly, _-ekʿ_ instead of _-kʿ_ is due to the influence of _erekʿ_ 'three'.
9.1.4.2. In other compounds, 'four' is rendered by Arm. _kʿaṙ-_; examples are _kʿaṙajikʿ_ 'team of four horses', _kʿaṙapatik_ 'fourfold'. For an explanation of _kʿaṙ-_, cf. 9.2.2.
9.1.5. Arm. _hing_ is a regular equivalent of Gk. _pénte_; final _*-e_ is preserved in the compound form _hngetasan_ 'fifteen' as well as in the ordinal _hingerord_ 'fifth'. For further comments, cf. 9.1.15.
9.1.6. Arm. _vecʿ_ 'six' can neither be derived from _*seḱs_ nor from _*sweḱs_: _*s-_ would have yielded initial zero (or perhaps _h-_), _*sw-_ could have resulted in _kʿ-_. It seems therefore reasonable to compare related forms without _*s-_, notably Old Prussian _uschts_ 'sixth' (though of course a common innovation is out of the question). The vexing problem of what the conditioning factors for the development of either _v-_ or _g-_ as a reflex of PIE _*w_ in Armenian were, cannot be discussed here; even if _*weḱs_

'six' (later transformed to **s(w)eḱs* under the impact of **septm̥* 'seven'; cf. Szemerényi 1960: 78) is to be connected with PIE **Aweḱs-* 'grow' (Szemerényi 1960: 79), Arm. *v-* cannot be explained as the regular reflex of **Xw-* (cf. Winter 1965: 106–108).

9.1.6.1. For the variants of 'six' found in the Armenian forms for 'sixteen' and 'sixty', cf. 9.1.16.

9.1.7. Arm. *ewtʿn* 'seven' corresponds to Gk. *heptá*, Lat. *septem*, etc., and like these forms, derives from PIE **septm̥*.

9.1.7.1. The variant *eōtʿn* may be viewed as a contamination of *ewtʿn* and a dialect form **awtʿn* (cf. Winter 1966: 22).

9.1.8. Arm. *utʿ* 'eight' is based on an underlying form with *-*pt*- and reflects thus the influence of 'seven' in the same way as Elean *optō* does beside normal Greek *oktṓ*.

9.1.9. Arm. *inn* 'nine' poses considerable problems of detail. PIE **Enewn̥* should have resulted, through the various stages of internal Armenian development, in **enewan* > **inowan* > **inown*. It is just possible that this **inown* survived in the variant of 'nine' marked for plural, viz., *inunkʿ*; note that the presence of *-u-* in the genitive-dative-ablative plural form *inuncʿ*, quite unusual in *-n-* stems, seems to support an argument in favor of the existence of *inun-* outside the marked nominative plural form (and, of course, its accusative counterpart). Considering that after the syncope of the vowel of the last syllable, marked *tasúnkʿ* 'ten' was paired with unmarked *tásn*, it seems no unlikely that this pattern served as the basis for a reshaping of *inúnkʿ* 'nine' : **inún* resulting in *inúnkʿ : ínn*.

9.1.9.1. *inn-* in *innsun* 'ninety' can be derived equally well from **inun*, as posited in the preceding section, as from attested *inn*; the same applies to the ordinal 'ninth', *innerord*.

9.1.10. Arm. *tasn* 'ten' developed from earlier **tasan* < **tesan*, a form which corresponds closely to Gk. *déka*, Lat. *decem*, etc. (cf. Szemerényi 1960: 21).

9.1.11. The numerals form 'eleven' to 'sixteen' are compounds, the second part of which is *-tasan*. Szemerényi (1960: 104) proposes to interpret *-san* as due to the influence of *kʿsan* 'twenty'; there is little likelihood that this view is correct, as the numerals with *-tasan* are separated in the number chain from 'twenty' by a whole string of forms which do not contain *-tasan*, but *tasn: ewtʿn ew tasn* 'seventeen', *utʿ ew tasn* 'eighteen', *inn ew tasn* 'nineteen'. It seems necessary to assume that *-an* was preserved in the *tasan* forms because it was followed, at an earlier stage in the history of Armenian, by a syllable lost later; in view of the fact (not conclusive in itself, to be sure) that *tasan* forms are inflected as *-i-* stems, *-tasan* may represent earlier **deḱm̥ti-*.

9.1.11.1. *me-* in *metasan* 'eleven' has been discussed in 9.1.1. (note also the remarks in Brugmann 1911: 24), *erko-* in *erkotasan* 'twelve' in 9.1.2. For *č'orek'tasan* 'fourteen' (*erek'tasan* 'thirteen' requires no further comment) cf. 9.1.4.1., for *hngetasan* 'fifteen', 9.1.5. For *veštasan* 'sixteen', cf. 9.1.16.

9.1.12. Arm. *k'san* 'twenty' clearly belongs with Lat. *vīgintī*, Doric Greek *wīkati*, Toch. B *ikäṃ*, etc. The initial *k'-* is usually explained as due to assimilation (cf. Hübschmann 1897: 504, Meillet 1936: 40, Szemerényi 1960: 126), but serious difficulties remain, and the alternative derivation of Arm. *k'-* < **Xw-* (Winter 1965: 106–107) deserves to be kept under consideration.

9.1.13. Arm. *eresun* 'thirty' is best derived from earlier **erea-* < **eriya-*; as in the case of Arm. *metasan* 'eleven' (cf. 9.1.1.), **-a-* should not be taken to be the vowel connecting the two elements of a compound, but should be interpreted as part of the first element. *ere-* would then be, in Brugmannian terms, derived from **triyə-*; this form would be the neuter plural of 'three', and the entire form *eresun* would be analyzed as **triyA-ḱomtA*. What cannot be decided on the basis of the Armenian data is whether a secondary lengthening of *-a-* occurred as in Gk. *triā́konta* 'thirty'.

9.1.14. That part of *k'ar̄asun* 'forty' which denotes 'four' differs sharply from the cardinal *č'ork'*; it therefore requires a special interpretation. As a first step toward analysis, a decision has to be made as to how *k'ar̄asun* should be cut: both a segmentation *k'ar̄a-* + *-sun* and *k'ar̄-* + *-a-* + *-sun* deserve to be considered. The second alternative, chosen by Brugmann (1911: 33), depends, after *eresun* has been explained differently (cf. 9.1.13.), solely on the validity of the assumption that *-a-* preceding *-sun* in *ewt'anasun* 'seventy' can only be explained as a connecting vowel *-a-*; this not being the case (cf. 9.1.17.), Brugmann's suggestion need not be pursued any further. For *k'ar̄a-sun*, either Gk. *tettarákonta* or Gk. *tetrṓ-konta* could be adduced as the closest match. In the first case, the compound would begin with a neuter plural form, in the second, with a bound form transcribable, in Brugmannian terms, as **k^wet(w)r̥̄-*. As it happens, the difference between the two forms is sharply reduced once laryngealist conventions are adopted: both can be subsumed under a generalized formula **k^wet(w)rX*, and only the question remains whether the laryngeal **A* which serves as a marker of the neuter plural, can also be posited for the form underlying Gk. *tetrō-*. As for the Armenian form for 'forty', it can be said that if *eresun* 'thirty' derives from a juxtaposition of two neuter plural forms, it clearly would be advantageous to be in a position to explain *k'ar̄asun* as a strictly parallel formation. Unfortunately, it seems impossible to determine the ablaut relationship originally existing between the masculine and neuter forms of 'four' in Proto-Indo-European by strictly comparative methods; if 'three' can be used as a parallel, a basic pattern masculine full grade vs. neuter zero grade appears to deserve preference. If this assumption is justified, Arm. *k'ar̄a-* would be derivable from PIE **k^w et(w)rA*; in order to explain the retention of the unpalatalized onset *k'-* (in contrast to *č'-* in *č'ork'*), one must assign the assimilation **-e-ar-* *-a-ar-* to a time prior to the change of the reflex of intervocalic **-t-* to **-y-*. Szemerényi's analysis (1960: 21) can thus be essentially adopted.

For a parallel to the development **-rX-* > *-ar̄a-* in Arm. *k'ar̄asun*, cf. 9.2.1.

9.1.15. On the basis of Gk. *pentēkonta*, Skt. *pañcāśát-*, and possibly Toch. B *piśāka*, a form PIE **penk^w ē-ḱomtA* 'fifty' can be posited with some confidence. Arm. *yisun* has to be compared with this reconstructed form. Initial *y-* for PIE **p-* recurs in Arm. *yawray* 'stepfather' (cf. Winter 1966). *-i-* in *yisun* cannot reflect PIE **e*; syncope would have led to *ə*/Ø. Adopting the view of the Great Armenian Soundshift as expressed in Winter (1955) and incorporating findings from Winter (1966), the following chain of developments from PIE **penk^w ē-ḱomtA* to Arm. *yisun* can be posited (steps of no immediate concern for the argument are omitted):

**penk^w ēḱomtA* > **finxisun* > **fixisun* > **fiyisun* > **yiyisun* > **yəyəsun* > *yisun*

For a largely parallel derivation of Arm. *tēr* 'lord', cf. Winter (1970: 52).

9.1.16. Arm. *vat'sun* 'sixty', with its reduction of [t'ss] to [t's], shows a strikingly different treatment of the final consonant of 'six' from that found in *veštasan* 'sixteen'. Rather than consider *-š-* a particularly archaic feature (cf. Meillet 1936: 40), it seems more appropriate to classify *vat'sun* and *veštasan* as forms from different dialects (cf. Winter 1966: 207). As for the underlying Proto-Indo-European form, *vat'sun* can be derived from **(s)weḱs-ḱomtA* and therefore resembles especially Toch. B *ṣkaska*, A *säksäk*, and OIr. *sesca*.

9.1.17. A Proto-Indo-European form **septm̥-ḱomtA*, matching **sweḱs-ḱomtA* 'sixty', would lead to Arm. **ewt'an-sun* and, with loss of nasal before spirant, Arm. **ewt'asun*. It can be assumed that from the word for 'seven', *-n-* was introduced after *-t'-*, and the cluster **-wt'n-* (or perhaps even earlier **-fθn-*) was reduced in complexity by the insertion of *-a-* before *-n-*; for a parallel, note the numerous verbs in *-a-nam, -a-nem*, and *-a-nim*. Thus, in order to account for Arm. *ewt'anasun*, neither an identification of *-a-* before *-sun* with the connecting vowel *-a-* (Brugmann 1911: 33) nor the reconstruction of a Proto-Indo-European form with **-m̥̄-* (Szemerényi 1960: 11) appears to be necessary.

9.1.18. Arm. *ut'sun* 'eighty' presents no problems whatsoever; **u* from **ō* in final position of 'eight' is regularily lost in unstressed syllable.

9.1.19. For Arm. *innsun* 'ninety', a modification of Szemerényi's explanation (1960: 15) can be adopted: **inunsun* was reduced, by loss of nasal before spirant, to **inusun* and, by syncope of unstressed **-u-*, to **insun*; this form was reshaped after *inn* 'nine'. However, since the reflex of **nX* should be *-ana-* and not *-an-* (cf. Winter 1965: 103–104), there is very little likelihood that 'ninety' is to be reconstructed with "*n̥̄*", as Szemerényi thinks; rather, all available data point to the fact that the forms underlying the Armenian words for 'sixty' to 'ninety' contained as their first part the plain cardinal numbers 'six' to 'nine'. In this respect, Armenian is closely matched by Tocharian (B *ṣkaska*, B *ṣuktaṅka* [if *-aṅka* was not transferred, by way of 'eighty', from 'ninety'], A *oktuk*, B *ñumka*).

9.1.20. Arm. *hariwr* 'hundred' remains obscure. The use of the neuter form of 'two' in *erkeriwr* 'two hundred' may indicate that *hariwr* was originally neuter or replaced a neuter noun. The reflex to be expected for PIE **k̑m̥tóm* would be, depending on the dialect, **sat'*, **sand*, or **san*; one is tempted to speculate whether the fact that words with precisely these shapes do exist in Armenian (*sat'* 'amber', *sand* 'mortar', *san* 'bowl' and 'godchild') contributed to the replacement of the inherited term.

For all attempts at analyzing *hariwr* (cf., e.g., Hamp 1955), one probably has to keep in mind that *ha-* could have been introduced under the impact of the word for 'thousand'.

9.1.21. Arm. *hazar* 'thousand' and *biwr* 'ten thousand' are loanwords from Iranian (Hübschmann 1897: 174, 121). While West Iranian origin seems certain for *hazar* (cf. Persian *hazār*), the source of *biwr* is not quite clear (cf. Abaev 1958: 262).

9.2. Ordinals

9.2.0. In terms of form, three groups can be distinguished among the Armenian ordinals:

a) a totally isolated item, *aṙaǰin* ‘first’;
b) a small set of short forms for ‘second’ to ‘fourth’;
c) a full set of forms extended by *-ord*.

9.2.1. It seems reasonable to assume that Arm. *aṙaǰin* ‘first’ is not unrelated to words for ‘first’ found in other Indo-European languages; these words share, as their first part, the sequence *prX- (cf. Skt. *pū́rva-*, Doric Greek *prâtos*, Lith. *pìrmas*), and Arm. *aṙa-* can be derived from precisely this sequence.

While the onset poses no particular problem, the remainder of the Armenian form is far from fully understood. In view of *aṙaǰ* ‘before’, *-in* may be isolated as a suffix (of uncertain function, cf. the references given in 9.1.1.1.). It is tempting to speculate whether *-ǰ-* can be connected with the (genitive-dative-)locative singular ending *-ǰ* found in a few Armenian noun classes; if the connection is warranted, one may further wonder whether Arm. *aṙaǰ* may be equated with Lat. *prae* or Old Latin *prī*, both semantically nearly identical with the Armenian word. The exact origin of Arm. *-ǰ* needs, however, further clarification (cf. Meillet 1936: 73); the explanation proposed here for *aṙaǰin* must, therefore, remain most tentative.

9.2.2. The short forms attested are Arm. *erkir* ‘second’, *erir* ‘third’, and *č‘orir* ‘fourth’. *č‘orir* appears to be an innovation after the pattern provided by *erir*; it therefore need not concern us here any further. From a variant of the long form for ‘fourth’, an older short form can be extracted: beside *č‘orrord*, the regular extension of *č‘orir*, we find *k‘aṙord*, which allows us to posit with great confidence an earlier *k‘aṙ ‘fourth’.

This *k‘aṙ can readily be analyzed. Arm. *ṙ* derives, inter alia, from PIE *rs. Assuming that the very same sound changes that led to the development of *k‘aṙasun* ‘forty’ (cf. 9.1.14.) affected also the preforms of *k‘aṙ, the following derivation of *k‘aṙ can be proposed:

*k^wet(w)rs > *xeθarr > *xaθarr > *xayarr > *xarr > *k‘aṙ

The development sketched here depends on an early loss of *-w-*; if it survived till the time of the Great Soundshift, a slight modification would be due.

*k^wetwrs > *xexarr > *xaxarr > *xayarr > *xarr > *k‘aṙ

No definitive decision between the two alternatives seems possible at this time.

If correctly identified, Arm. **k'aṙ* corresponds closely to Skt. *catúḥ* 'four times'; Avest. *čaθruš* differs slightly.

The juxtaposition of 'fourth' and 'four times' requires some additional comment. The transfer of a term for '*n* times' to a use 'for the *n* th time' is not unheard of. Thus, Lat. *bis consul* refers not only to a person who has been consul twice, but also to a man who holds this office for the second time (conversely, Gk. *tríton* and Lat. *tertium* were secondarily used to denote 'three times'; cf. Buck 1949: 944). Likewise, Arm. *eric's* (cf. 9.3.3.) does not only mean 'three times', but also 'for the third time' (cf. Jensen 1959: 75–76).

Strong support for the derivation of **k'aṙ* from PIE *k^w*et(w)rs* comes from Arm. *erir*.

For PIE **i* to survive as Arm. *i* in a form like *erir*, one of two conditions had to be met: either *i* had to occur in a syllable which was penultimate before the time of the loss of post-stress vowels, or the form in which it was preserved was monosyllabic at that time. Szemerényi, who proposes to derive (1960: 94–96) the troublesome *-ir* from a form for 'third' which was reshaped after a form for 'fourth', considers only the first alternative; since the transfer pattern required by Szemerényi's argumentation is extremely involved and thus does not immediately carry conviction, the second alternative deserves at least equal attention.

There seems to be good reason to state that under conditions still requiring further clarification, PIE **s* is reflected by Arm. *r* after **r*, **u*, **i* (cf. Winter 1970: 51–52). If so, Arm. *erir* can be said to be a perfect match of Skt. *tríḥ*, Gk. *trís*, Lat. *ter*, and, like these forms, to derive from PIE **tris*.

By the same token, *-kir* in Arm. *erkir* 'twice' can be explained on the basis of PIE **dwis; er-* then would be due to transfer either from *erku* 'two' (which in turn owes its *er-* to *erek'* 'three') or from *erir* 'three times'. For a reflex of **kir* without *er-* cf. 9.3.1.

9.2.3. The long forms belong to two subclasses, one characterized by *-ord*, the other, by *-erord*. *-ord* is used as an extension of the short ordinals *erkir, erir*, **k'aṙ, č'orir* (*aṙajnord* means 'head, leader'; cf. Jensen 1959: 72) and of the cardinal 'hundred'; the unreduced form of the cardinal 'ten' occurs in *tasanord* 'tithe' which is to be mentioned here as ordinals are used to express fractions. *-erord* is attached to cardinal numbers from 'five' upwards, including *hariwr* in *hariwrerord*, and to the ordinal *aṙajin* in *aṙajnerord* 'first'.

Repeatedly, attempts have been made to regard the form for 'fifth', *hingerord*, as highly archaic (cf. the discussion of Meillet's views by

Szemerényi 1960: 95–97); however, as it seems that *hingerord*, with its absence of syncope in the first syllable, must have undergone at least some reshaping, one should be reluctant to attach too much importance to the form. Szemerényi is probably right in accepting (1960: 94) Meillet's suggestion (1936: 101) that *-e* spread from the form for 'fifth' to the higher ordinals; if so, **hnger* as reflected in *hingerord* would be a short ordinal like *erir*, etc., and both *-ord* and *-erord* forms would be analyzable as containing an ordinal nucleus extended by an element *-ord*. Support for this analysis can be found in the existence of a term like *tasnereak* 'one tenth' which seems to be based on an ordinal **tasner* 'tenth' without *-ord*.

This leaves *-ord* still to be accounted for. Szemerényi's suggestion (1960: 95) that a **č'ord* (< **k*ʷ*etortos*) merged with *č'orir* to yield *č'orrord*, and that this form then influenced all other ordinals, is quite improbable if the old short ordinal 'fourth' was **k'aṙ*. Rather, the view of Pisani (1944: 174), rejected by Szemerényi (1960: 95), deserves to be revived in a slightly modified version: *-ord*, compared by Pisani with Skt. *-kṛt-* in *sakṛ́t* 'once', is to be equated with Lith. *kar̃tas*, OCS *kratŭ* 'times'; for a parallel to the development of PIE **k-/k*ʷ*-* > Arm. Ø, cf. Arm. *o* 'who?': Lith. *kàs*, etc. (cf. Hübschmann 1897: 481). Semantically, no problem seems to exist once adverbial use is taken as a starting point: *tasnerord* would at first mean 'for the tenth time' and then be employed also for 'tenth'.

9.3. Other numerals

9.3.0. For an enumeration of types of derivation and compound formation as well as of sundry syntactic usages, cf. Jensen (1959: 73–76). Only a few selected items will be treated in the following sections; attempts at striving for exhaustiveness seem pointless as long as numerous morphological details remain obscure.

9.3.1. Arm. *krkin* 'double' has attracted considerable attention; for a brief discussion of earlier views, cf. Szemerényi (1960: 96). It seems quite improbable that Pisani's argument to the effect that *krkin* derived from **krukin*, a form which was supposedly reshaped from **kukin* under the influence of the word for 'three', is justified: If metathesis affected alleged **kru* 'two', why did **krukin* not become **erkkin*? There is no alternative to the assumption that *k-* and *-r-* were originally separated by a vowel, and that this vowel, reduced as it was to [ə] in unstressed position, can only have been **i* or **u*. Of the various possibilities theoretically available for the derivation of [kər-], only one ties in with rich data from other Indo-European languages: only **dwis* 'twice' is a genuine choice; for further details, cf. 9.2.2.

Arm. *krkin* would thus be a compound with a reflex of **dwis* as its first member (for *-kin* cf. 9.3.1.1.). **dwis* in this position is matched by **tris* in Arm. *eṙatʿiw* 'consisting of three numbers' (: *tʿiw*), *eṙanun* 'having three names' (: *anun*), etc., and by **k^{w}et(w)rs* in *kʿaṙajikʿ* 'team of four horses' (: *ji*), *kʿaṙameay* 'four years old' (: *am*), etc. It is to be noted that in forms other than *krkin*, the connecting vowel *-a-* is found.

Once **ku* 'two' had been transformed into *erku*, the connection between 'two' and 'double' became totally obscured; it is therefore not surprising that beside the derivative *krknaki* 'doubly' a new form *erkaki* arose with the same meaning. Likewise, not *kr-*, but *erk-* appeared as the first member of compounds matching *eṙ-* and *kʿaṙ-*; cf. 9.1.2.

Finally, *krkin* itself lost its precise meaning when a clear connection with 'two' ceased to exist: beside *čʿorekʿkin* 'fourfold', itself a relatively recent formation, a new form *čʿorekʿkrkin* developed with an identical meaning (cf. Jensen 1959: 74). Perfect parallels for a use of 'double' for '-fold' in other Indo-European languages are listed in Buck (1949: 946).

9.3.1.1. The observation just made about the use of a form originally denoting 'double' for '-fold' seems to open up a way toward explaining Arm. *-kin*. If Arm. *k-* is the regular reflex of PIE **dw-*, then *-kin* can be derived from either PIE **dwinV-* or PIE **dwisnV-*, both of which can be supported by parallels from other Indo-European languages (cf. Pokorny 1959: 231); the meaning of the forms is roughly 'two each', 'twofold', 'paired items'.

If the suggestion made concerning Arm. *-kin* is appropriate, the following development would have taken place:

a) The meaning 'double' of *-kin* is changed to '-fold', and 'twofold' is explicated by the addition of **kir-* 'twice';
b) the meaning 'double' of *krkin* is changed to '-fold', and new compounds using *-krkin* instead of *-kin* are created.

9.3.2. The possibility should be mentioned that Arm. *kēs* 'half' is also to be connected with the word for 'two'. *kēs* can be derived from PIE **dwoyḱo-*; parallels with **k* instead of **ḱ* may be found in Russ. *dvojka* 'pair' and perhaps Skt. *dviká-* 'consisting of two parts' (cf. Pokorny 1959: 231); for an etymological tie between a word for 'half' and that for 'two' in Tocharian, cf. 9.3.2.

9.3.3. A productive formative for the expression of 'times' is Arm. *-icʿs* (*erkicʿs* 'two times', *ericʿs* 'three times', etc.; cf. Jensen 1959: 75). *erkicʿs* has been compared with **dwisko-* as found in some Germanic forms meaning 'twofold; both' (cf. Pokorny 1959: 231) by Brugmann (1911: 64, 78). The extension of **-isko-* to higher numerals would be an internal Armenian development, likewise the addition of the suffix *-s* (from **-ns* of the accusative plural?).

9.3.3.1. Again a regular reflex of **dwisko-* seems to have survived in a form which became separated semantically from 'two' and its derivatives before **ku* was adapted to *erekʿ* 'three': It seems possible to derive *kicʿ* 'partner' (cf. Jensen 1959: 32) and possibly also *kicʿ* 'next to' from PIE **dwisko-*.

9.3.4. Arm. **kir, -kin, kēs*, and *kicʿ*, if correctly interpreted, all offer strong support for the assumption that *k-* and not *erk-* was the regular reflex of PIE **dw-* in Armenian (cf. Pedersen 1906: 398; Szemerényi 1960: 96), an assumption that has the advantage of being perfectly natural in view of the fact that PIE **tw-* leads to Arm. *kʿ-* (cf. Meillet 1936: 51). None of the examples listed in favor of Arm. *erk-* < PIE **dw-* by Mann (1963: 92–93) require a revision of the statement just made.

References

Abaev, Vasilij Ivanovič
1958 *Istoriko-ėtimologičeskij slovar' osetinskogo jazyka* 1 [Historical-etymological dictionary of Ossetic 1] (Moskva/Leningrad: Izdatel'stvo Akademii Nauk SSSR).

Brugmann, Karl
1911 *Grundriss der vergleichenden Grammatik der indogermanischen Sprachen* II.2^{2} (Strassburg: Trübner).

Buck, Carl Darling
1949 *A dictionary of selected synonyms in the principal Indo-European languages* (Chicago: University Press).

Hamp, Eric P.
1955 "Armenian *hariwr*", *KZ* 72: 244–245.

Hübschmann, Heinrich
1897 *Armenische Grammatik* 1: *Armenische Etymologie* (Leipzig: Breitkopf & Härtel).

Jensen, Hans
1959 *Altarmenische Grammatik* (Heidelberg: Winter).

Mann, Stuart E.
1963 *Armenian and Indo-European (Historical phonology)* (London: Luzac).
Meillet, Antoine
1936 *Esquisse d'une grammaire comparée de l'arménien classique*[2] (Wien: Imprimerie des Mekhitharistes).
Olsen, Birgit
1981 "IE *Vwe/i = ARM. Vwe/i (Vve/i)?", *Arbejdspapirer* (Institut for Lingvistik, Københavns Universitet) 2: 1–9.
Pedersen, Holger
1906 "Armenisch und die nachbarsprachen", *KZ* 39: 334–484.
Pisani, Vittore
1944 "Armenische Studien", *KZ* 68: 157–177.
Pokorny, Julius
1959 *Indogermanisches etymologisches Wörterbuch* 1 (Bern/München: Francke).
Szemerényi, Oswald
1960 *Studies in the Indo-European system of numerals* (Heidelberg: Winter).
Winter, Werner
1955 "Problems of Armenian phonology II", *Language* 31: 4–8.
1965 "Armenian evidence", in: Werner Winter (ed.), *Evidence for laryngeals* (The Hague: Mouton), 100–115.
1966 "Traces of early dialectal diversity in Old Armenian", in: Henrik Birnbaum – Jean Puhvel (eds.), *Ancient Indo-European dialects* (Berkeley/Los Angeles: University of California Press), 201–211.
1970 "Some widespread Indo-European titles", in: George Cardona – Henry M. Hoenigswald – Alfred Senn (eds.), *Indo-European and Indo-Europeans* (Philadelphia: University of Pennsylvania Press), 49–54.

Chapter 10
Thraco-Phrygian

Edgar C. Polomé

10.0. The nature of the linguistic evidence extant in Thraco-Phrygian accounts for the scantiness of the data which the materials provide for the numerals. Thracian is known only through proper names and glosses, which have been carefully studied by a number of scholars[1] since W. Tomaschek compiled them some eighty years ago.[2] Very little has emerged from this work as regards Indo-European numerals in Thracian.
10.1.1. The toponym *Anádraimos* (Dečev 1957: 17) is supposed to mean *ennéa hodoí* in Greek; this would imply an analysis of the term into *ana-* 'nine' and *draimos* 'road'.[3] Thracian *ana-* is then supposed to reflect **enwa-* and is compared with Greek (Hom) *einάetēs* 'for nine years', Boeotian *enakēdématos*, etc., but Greek **enwa-* hardly gives support to this interpretation if Szemerényi (1974: 107–118) is right in assuming that this form reflects a recent (post-Mycenaean) development in Greek. Moreover the initial *a* is not properly accounted for.[4] The interpretation of Thracian *ana-* (also found in the place name *Anagonklí*) as a reflex of the Proto-Indo-European numeral for 'nine' remains, accordingly, rather dubious.
10.1.2. The element *kentho-* found in a number of personal names (with variants *kent-, kint-, kend-, kind-*)[5] provides a remarkable Celto-Thracian isogloss as it corresponds neatly with Gaulish *cintu-*, as for instance in *Cintugnātos* 'first born', Old Irish *cétnae, cét-* 'first', Welsh *cyn(t)* 'before', *cyntaf* 'the first', etc.[6]
10.1.3. The initial *di-, zi-*, in onomastic compounds like *disuros, zisuros* (Dečev 1957: 143, 192) is sometimes interpreted as a reflex of the Proto-Indo-European numeral for 'two',[7] but this remains purely conjectural.[8]
10.2.1. As regards Phrygian, for which we have only a few short inscriptions from the seventh and sixth centuries BC, reflecting an older stage of the language, as against less than a hundred much later inscriptions of the Christian era, often mixed with Greek,[9] the situation is somewhat better insofar as we have an apparently unimpeachable attestation of a numeral in the phrase *otuwoi wetei* (15 a 1) meaning 'in the

eight year', in which Phrygian *otuwoi* would reflect the locative **oḱtuwoi* of the Proto-Indo-European ordinal. It is, however, not excluded that the inscriptional sequence *otuwoiwetei* ... can be split differently.[10]

10.2.2. The name of the Phrygian god *Doías*, the brother of *Ákmōn*, has been interpreted by Fick (1907: 347), as 'twin' < PIE **dwoyn̥-t*; it is, however, also possible that the term was borrowed from Greek (cf. the gloss *doiás* 'duality').[11] If the term were genuinely Phrygian, one would expect initial *t*-, but as Haas (1966: 162) suggests, the cluster *dw* may have remained unshifted. The equation of Modern Phrygian *tou* with Greek *dúō*, suggested among others by Bonfante (1946: 88), is hardly cogent; the Phrygian form is better explained as a reflex of the Proto-Indo-European pronominal dative **tōi* (> Greek *tōi*).

10.2.3. As for the assumed Phrygian numeral **thidra*- 'four' posted by Haas (1960: 41) to account for the plant-name *thidrax* 'lettuce', alleged to mean originally 'square' < *k^{w}*itr̥*- 'four' + **aḱ*- 'sharp (angle)', it is merely due to a misunderstanding based on the folk-etymology of Hipponax *thidrakínē* = *tetrakínē*.[12] It does not accordingly confer any credibility to the interpretation of Greek *dithurambos* 'dithyramb' – originally 'four-step' – as a Phrygian loan (Haas 1960: 56) by assuming that *dithur*- reflects a metathesis of Phrygian **thidur*- < *k^{w}*itwr̥* (Haas 1966: 164).[13] Similarly, there is no cogent evidence that Greek *thríambos* 'hymn to Dionysus' would originally be Phrygian with initial *th* from *t* in PIE **tri*- 'three'.

10.3. Consequently, with only one or two possible exceptions, the reflexes of Indo-European numerals in Thraco-Phrygian are based on more or less disputable etymologies, so that evidence from this branch can only contribute very little to the study of the Indo-European system of numerals.

Postcript

Since this short note was prepared some years ago, a number of new Phrygian inscriptions have been discovered (cf. besides the article of O. Haus "Neue phrygische Sprachdenkmäler" in *Zeitschrift für vergleichende Sprachforschung* 83 [1969], more recent research by M. Lejeune, Cl. Brixhe, G. Neumann, R. Gusmani, and others), and several new studies on Thracian have appeared (such as V. Georgiev's *Trakijskijat ezik* [Sofia, 1977] or V. P. Neroznak's *Paleobalkanskie jazyki* [Moscow, "Nauka", 1978]). These do not appear, however, to have brought new evidence for the reflexes of the Indo-European numerals in Phrygian or Thracian:

Aná-draimos in southeastern Macedonia or southwestern Thracia is still interpreted as 'nine roads' (= *ennéa hodoí*, i. e. *ana* 'nine' < **enwn̥* + *-draimos* 'road' < **dr̥m-yo-s*), but considered as "of Macedonian origin" by Vladimir I. Georgiev in his *Introduction to the History of the Indo-European Languages* (Sofia: Publishing House of the Bulgarian Academy of Sciences, 1981: 120). In his survey of the *Ancient Languages of the Balkans* (The Hague—Paris: Mouton, 1976: 145), Radoslav Katičić merely quotes Thrac. *Kíntos* in connection with the "affrication" in *Tzinto*, without venturing an etymology.

10.4. Addendum to "Thraco-Phrygian" (as published in the Journal of Indo-European Studies, vol. 14: 1—2 [1986], pp. 185—189, under the title "Note on Thraco-Phrygian Numerals")

Thracian and Phrygian are commonly considered as constituting a minor subgroup of the Indo-European languages (thus, e. g., still in Philip Baldi's *Introduction to the Indo-European Languages*, Carbondale: Southern Illinois University, 1983: 1670), but Warren Cowgill is presumably right in doubting the traditional approach by indicating that Phrygian is not any closer to Thracian than to Greek or Armenian (*Indogermanische Grammatik. I.1. Einleitung*, Heidelberg: Carl Winter, 1986: 54) — though Thracian, Phrygian, Armenian and Greek apparently share a number of important features (cf. I. Diakonoff, *The Pre-History of the Armenian People*, Delmar, N. Y.: Caravan Books, 1984: 110, 188—189).

Most of the data listed in the "Note on Thraco-Phrygian Numerals" were disputable etymologies. In his revised German edition of his work on the Thracian language (*Die Sprache der Thraker*, Bulgarische Sammlung, vol. 5; Neuried: Hieronymus, 1985), Ivan Duridanov does not mention any of the examples quoted in the "Note": Thrac. *an(a)-* appears only in the place-name *Anasamus*, designating a stronghold (*castellum*) at the mouth of the river Asamus, and represents the preposition **an(a)* 'on, near' in this toponym (Duridanov 1985: 21, 74). As for the element *-kenthos* in anthroponyms, Duridanov (1985: 78) rightly interprets it as a reflex of IE **ken-to-s* with the meaning 'child, offspring', related with Lat. *re-cens* 'fresh, newly come', and with another suffix, with OCS *čędo* 'child'. He identifies, however, a new numeral stem in the Thracian personal names *Ketriporis, Kedrēpolis, Cetrilas*, in which the first element would reflect IE *$*k^{w}etr$-* 'four' as in Greek *tetra-*, Welsh *pedry-*, Latin *četri*, etc. (Duridanov 1985: 60, 78).

As for Phrygian, the publication of the *Corpus des inscriptions paléo-phrygiennes*, edited by Claude Brixhe and Michel Lejeune (Paris: Recherche sur les Civilisations, 1984), and of *Phrygian*, by I. M. Diakonoff and V. P. Neroznak (Delmar, N. Y.: Caravan Books, 1985) has provided us with better sources to check the alleged attestations of numerals in Phrygian: only *otuvoi* deserves further consideration, but it could also consist of two words; besides, as Brixhe and Lejeune indicate (1984: 237), if οτνϝοιϝετει means 'octavo anno", the change of *-*kt*- to *-*t*- needs to be accounted for. Nevertheless, Neroznak (1985: 65, 128) accepts the identification of the term as an ordinal numeral.

Ultimately, it accordingly appears that only one numeral can be identified with some plausibility in Phrygian and Thracian each: "eighth" is **o(t)tuos* in Phrygian, and "four" as first part of a compound is **ketr(e/i)-* in Thracian.

Notes

1. E. g. Kretschmer (1896: 171–243), Jokl (1929: 284–296), Georgiev (1957), Dečev (1957, 1960), Russu (1959), Vlahov (1963: 219–372). An exhaustive bibliography has been compiled by Velkova (1967: 1972).
2. *Die alten Thraker, SKAWW* CSSVII.vi, CXXX.ii, CXXXI.i.
3. *draimos* < **dramjos* (as to the diphthong, see Dečev 1960: 182), with *d* for *t* as a result of voicing in contact with *r*; if so, the term can be derived from PIE **dr-em-* 'run' (OInd. *dramati*, Greek δρόμος 'course, race', etc.).
4. Cf. the rather ad-hoc rule of Dečev (1960: 185).
5. Cf. Dečev (1960: 171, 183): note that *Kintos* (Dečev 1957: 240) may be Celtic. Duridanov (1969: 78–80) connects Thracian *Cintis* with Baltic **kint-* in Old Prussian and Lithuanian personal names (e. g. Old Prussian *Dan-kinte, Kyntinne*; Lith. *Bar-kintis, Kinti-butas* etc.) which Fraenkel (1956: 246) compares with Lith. *kę̃sti* 'suffer, endure'.
6. Cf. Pokorny (1959: 564). For a different view, see also Duridanov (1976: 60, 94, 102).
7. E. g., by Georgiev (1957: 70).
8. Dečev (1957: 126) prefers to derive *di-* from PIE **dey-* 'shine', but the initial *d-* (instead of **t*) forces him to consider the element as borrowed from Greek (1960: 152–153).

9. The inscriptions have been conveniently assembled by Friedrich (1932: 123–140); supplemented by Masson (1954). On the language cf. for instance Kretschmer (1896: 217–240), Jokl (1927), Friedrich (1941), Gusmani (1958, 1959), Haas (1960, 1966), for which see Dressler (1968: 40–49).
10. Haas (1966: 180–181) reads *otu voi vetei* 'Otys sibi ipsi', in which *Otu* is considered as a nominative without *s*, *voi* corresponds to Greek *woĩ* < **swoi* and *vetei* < **swetei* can be compared with Alb. *vetë* < **sweti-* 'self'.
11. Cf. Haas (1966: 162).
12. Dressler (1968: 48).
13. Dressler (1968: 42). On this difficult word of which the Phrygian origin is purely hypothetical, see Hester (1965); see also Puhvel (1954), who posits a Mycenean Greek $*k^{w}ituragg^{w}os$.

References

Beer, Hildegard (translator) – see also Russu, I. I.

1969 *Die Sprache der Thrako-Daker* (Bucureşti: Editura ştiinţifică) [= German translation of Russu 1967 (1st edition, 1959)].

Bonfante, Giuliano

1946 "Armenians and Phrygians", *Armenian Quarterly* 1: 82–97.

Dečev, Dimitri

1952 *Charakteristika na trakijskija ezik* [A characteristic of Thracian] (Sofija: Bŭlgarska Akademija na Naukite).

1957 *Die thrakischen Sprachreste* (Wien: Österreichische Akademie der Wissenschaften. Schriften der Balkankommission, Linguistische Abteilung. Vol. 14) (Wien: Rudolf M. Rohrer [in Kommission]).

1960 "Charakteristik der thrakischen Sprache", *Linguistique balkanique* 2: 147–213. [German translation of Dečev 1952]

Dressler, Wolfgang U.

1968 "Die phrygischen Sprachdenkmäler. Zu einem neuen Buch von Otto Haas", *Die Sprache* 14: 40–60.

Duridanov, Ivan

1969 "Thrakisch-dakische Studien I: Die thrakisch- und dakisch-baltischen Sprachbeziehungen", *Linguistique balkanique* 13. 2 (Sofia: Académie bulgare des sciences).

1976 *Ezikŭt na Trakite* [The language of the Thracians] (Sofia: Izdatelstvo "Nauka i izkustvo").

Ebert, Max (ed.)

1929 *Reallexikon der Vorgeschichte* (Berlin: Walter de Gruyter).

Fick, August

1907 "Die Indogermanen", *Zeitschrift für vergleichende Sprachforschung* 41: 336–355.

Fraenkel, Ernst
1956 *Litauisches etymologisches Wörterbuch* (Heidelberg: Carl Winter).
Friedrich, Johannes
1932 *Kleinasiatische Sprachdenkmäler* (Berlin: Walter de Gruyter).
1941 "Phrygier, Sprache", in: A. F. von Pauly – G. Wissowa (eds.), *Realencyklopädie der classischen Altertumwissenschaft* 39 (Stuttgart: Metzlersche Verlagsbuchhandlung), col. 882–891.
Georgiev, Vladimir
1957 *Trakijskijat ezik* [The Thracian Language] (Sofia: Izdanie na Bŭlgarskata Akademija na Naukite).
Gusmani, Roberto
1958 'Studi frigi', *RIL* 92: 835–929.
1959 'Studi frigi', *RIL* 93: 17–49.
Haas, Otto
1966 *Die phrygischen Denkmäler* (Sofia: Izdanie na Bŭlgarskata Akademija na Naukite).
Hester, D. A.
1965 "Pelasgian – A new Indo-European language?", *Lingua* 13: 335–384.
Jokl, Norbert
1927 "Thraker", in: Ebert (ed.) 13: 284–296.
1929 "Phrygier", in: Ebert (ed.) 10: 141–153.
Kretschmer, Paul
1896 *Einleitung in die Geschichte der griechischen Sprache* (Göttingen: Vandenhoeck & Ruprecht).
Masson, Olivier
1954 "Épigraphie asianique. Bibliographie relative aux inscriptions lyciennes, cariennes, lydiennes et phrygiennes", *Or.* XXIII; 439–442.
Pokorny, Julius
1959 *Indogermanisches etymologisches Wörterbuch* (Bern: A Francke).
Puhvel, Jaan
1954 "A propos Greek *δῑθύραμβος*", *Glotta* 34: 37–42.
Russu, I. I.
1967 *Limba traco-dacilor*, Ediţia a II-a revăzută şi adăugită (Bucureşti, Editura Academiei Republicii Populare Romîne) [The language of the Thraco-Dacians] (see also Beer 1969).
Szemerényi, Oswald
1964 *Syncope in Greek and Indo-European and the nature of the Indo-European accent* (Napoli: Istituto universitario orientale di Napoli. Quaderni della Sezione linguistica degli Annali, 3).
Tomaschek, Wilhelm
1893 *Die alten Thraker* (Sitzungsberichte der kaiserlichen Akademie der Wissenschaften zu Wien, 128.4) (Wien: F. Tempsky [in Kommission]).

Velkova, Ž.
1967 "Die thrakische Sprache: Bibliographischer Anzeiger 1852–1965", *Linguistique Balkanique* 12: 155–164; 16.1: 55–63.
Vlahov, K.
1963 "Nachträge und Berichtigungen zu den thrakischen Sprachresten und Rückwörterbuch", *Godišnik na Sofijskija Universitet filologičeski fakultet* 57.2: 219–372.

Chapter 11
Greek

Frederik M. J. Waanders

11.0. Introduction

Whoever deals with Greek has to deal with a large number of dialects over a long span of time; the decipherment of Linear B in 1952 meant a further increase of the available data. On the one hand, this variety from different times and regions is helpful to etymologists, as they can apply the comparative method to closely related speech-forms; on the other hand, interdialectal discrepancies other than such as can be explained by sound-laws sometimes create additional problems. On the average, however, scholars of Greek historical linguistics have the advantage of an early start (written sources from the second half of the second millennium B.C.), a steady flow of linguistic data (even up to the present day), many competent predecessors in the field; moreover, the development of the morpho(phono)logical system of Ancient Greek from Indo-European is relatively perspicuous (as far as that goes), especially in respect of its vocalism which has not been obscured by a merger of, say, *a* and *o*, or by 'weakening' of unstressed vowels (as in Latin or Germanic; Ancient Greek had a pitch accent).

These general remarks of course also apply to Greek numerals; in the following paper, I shall present the Attic data, augmented by those from Mycenaean, and supplemented by such from other dialects as are of special interest.

11.1. Cardinals

11.1.1. Of the two competing Indo-European roots that in the daughter-languages lie at the base of the cardinal 'one', **sem-* and **oi-* (undoubtedly *H_3ey-), Greek uses the first one: **sem-s* > ἕνς > ..., *$sm\text{-}iH_2$ > *μ(h)ίᾰ* [1], **sem* > ἕν. Through analogical spread of *ν* < *μ* (regular in nominative masculine, nominative/accusative neuter; originally only singular, of course), masculine and neuter are inflected as *ν*-stems; in Mycenaean, however, we still find the form *e-me hεμεί* (dat.), from the older *μ*-stem. The root *sem- further underlies ἁ̆- in ἅ-παξ 'once', ἁ-πλοῦς (-πλός) 'single', 'simple', ἅ-τερος 'one' or 'the other' (of two) (Att.-Ion. → ἕτερος, with the ε of ἑν-); through Grassmann's law a. o. ἀ-δελφός 'brother' and ἄ-λοχος 'partner of one's bed', i. e., 'wife'; from Epic-Ionic (with psilosis) ἄ-κοιτις 'wife', ἀτάλαντος 'equal (in weight)', etc.; all these forms have (h)ᾰ- < *sm̥-. The same first element, but with a different (regular) reflex, is usually assumed for μῶνυξ 'with a single (i. e., uncloven) hoof' < *sm̥-H_3nog^{w}h- (the original stem-form of the second element is somewhat problematic), rather than haplologically ← *μονῶνυξ.

Also derived from *sem- are ἅμα 'together', 'at once' < *smeH$_2$? (disyllabic 'Lindeman-form'[2]; the sandhi-variant with shortened final vowel has been generalized in most Greek dialects, but we also have Doric ἁμᾶ; for such sandhi-variants, cf. δύω [Hom.]/δύο [Hom. +] 'two'), and ὁμο- 'same' + derivatives < *som-o- (*somHo- according to Beekes 1982/1983: 203). It is a plausible assumption that *sēmi-*/ἡμι- 'half-' derives from *sem- as well (old loc. *sēm, later recharacterized as a locative by means of the ending -i).

The root *oi- also occurs in Greek, in οἴ-νη 'one (on a die)' and οἶ-(ϝ)ος 'alone'.

The question concerning the semantic difference between *sem- and *oi- is not easy to answer. It is often assumed that *sem- was a neutral 'one', as against *oi- 'one alone', 'a single one'; semantically marked *oi- + suffix could then have replaced the neutral term *sem- in a number of daughter-languages (Latin, Germanic *oi-no-, OIndian *oi-k^{w}o-, OIranian *oi-wo-, etc.) — the priority of *sem-* is indirectly evidenced by the various suffixations in the case of *oi-. Nevertheless, *sem- need not have been strictly neutral; Gonda (1953: 38) assumes the value 'one of a natural pair', other scholars prefer 'several things taken together as one', see e. g. Anttila (1972: 366 f.). I think that association with a plurality can safely be assumed for *sem-, but the data could just as well be interpreted as pointing to a "partitive", rather than a "collective" sense, i. e. 'one element of a set of countable entities', and this sense would make *sem- especially apt for use as a counting word. However, the problem is hard to solve, each language having taken its own direction.

11.1.2. The Greek numeral 'two' is a disyllabic 'Lindeman-form' δύω/δύο (cf. n. 2), as against δ(ϝ)ω- in the polysyllabic form δ(ϝ)ώ-δεκα 'twelve'. In Homer, δύω/δύο is uninflected (δύο once as genitive, δύω once as genitive, once as dative), as is also sometimes the case in later Greek.

In some dialects we find a genitive/dative form of the dual type, e. g. Att. *δυοῖν* (later *δυεῖν*, probably resulting from dissimilation), but plural inflection is not uncommon (frequently gen. *δυῶν*; dat. Cret. *δυοῖς*, late Att. *δυσί(ν)*; acc. Thess. *δύας*); the gradual decline of the dual as a grammatical category, starting early at the colonial periphery of the greek world, but eventually also in evidence on the mainland (from about the fourth century B.C.), may be partly responsible for the instances of plural inflection. A third declension nominative/accusative dual ending *-ε* is found sporadically (Aetol. *δύϝε*, Lac. *δύε*). The Mycenaean form nominative/accusative is *dwo*, which to my mind should equally be interpreted as a disyllabic form; the phonological interpretation of the instrumental form *du-wo-u-pi* is very uncertain.

In compounds, the allomorph *δ(ϝ)ι-* is used (cf. Lat. *bi-*), as also in the adverb *δ(ϝ)ί-ς* 'twice' (possibly zero-grade of the neuter form **dwoi* – not found in Greek –, if not influence of **tri-*, zero grade of **trey-*).

11.1.3. The Greek forms of 'three' are fairly straightforward: in Cretan (Gortys) uncontracted nom. m./f. *τρέες* (analogical preservation of the nominative plural ending *-ες*, as in *πόδες*), otherwise contracted, as Att.-Ion. *τρεῖς* (i. e. [tre:s]), Dor. (Thera) *τρῆς* (also Lesbian, according to ancient grammarians), from **treyes*. Genitive and dative show the expected zero-grade of the stem: usually *τριῶν, τρισί* (with isolated local variants). The acc. m./f. *τρῖς* (< **trins*; Cretan [Gortys] has the surprising form *τρίινς*, disyllabic like *τρέες* [see above], for expected *τρίνς*, with dialectal preservation of final *-νς*) has in a number of dialects (a. o. Attic) been replaced by *τρεῖς* [tre:s], the same form as the nominative, according to Buck (1955: 95) "under the influence of the indeclinable numerals"; reversely, the accusative form *τρῖς* is also used as nominative in some dialects (Heraclean, Delphian, Troezenian). As for Attic, since this dialect invariably has an accusative plural in *-εις* [-e:s] whenever the nominative plural ends in *-εις*, I am not quite convinced by Buck's assumption that acc. *τρεῖς* is simply the nominative used as accusative – besides, under the influence of indeclinable numerals, one would also expect *τρεῖς* to be used as a genitive or dative once in a while, which is not the case[3]. However, (additional) influence of *δύο* is possible, as this also shows accusative = nominative.

The neuter nominative/accusative is *τρίᾰ* < **triH*$_2$.

In compounds, the zero-grade *τρι-* is used (also in the adverb *τρί-ς* 'three times').

11.1.4. The Greek dialects show a variety of forms for the cardinal 'four': m./f. Att. *τέττᾰρες*, Ion. and Arc. *τέσσερες* (Homeric *τέσσᾰρες* shows Attic influence), Lesb. *πέσσῠρες* (gloss in Hesychius; cf. Hom. *πίσῠρες*), Boeot. *πέττᾰρες*, West Gk. *τέτορες*. The neuter form has *-ᾰ* for *-ες* in the corresponding masculine/feminine form (*τέττᾰρα, τέσσερα*, etc.). Initial *τ-* is the regular reflex of *k^w- before e-vowel in most dialects, but *π-* is regular in Aeolic; *-ττ-* (Att., Boeot.)/*-σσ-* (elsewhere) is the regular reflex of intervocalic **-tw-*. Some of the aforesaid forms can thus be explained as continuing *k^w*etw(e)r-*[4]. However, Lesb. *πέσσυρες* may have either analogical *-σσ-* for *-σ-* (? — or *-τ-*?), or analogical *-υ-* for *ε/ο/α*; the Homeric Aeolism *πίσυρες* points to a pre-form *k^{we}*tures*.

Apparently, this confused state of affairs must be ascribed to the use of different ablaut-forms outside their original domains. Moreover, West Gk *τέτορες* shows early loss of *-w-*, which must also be assumed for *τετρᾰ-/πετρο-*, and *$κ^w$ετρο-* in Myc. *qe-to-ro-po-pi* (instr. case form *$κ^w$ε-τρόποπφι* 'quadrupeds'), allomorph of the stem in compounds, and also for yet another (shorter) allomorph *τρᾰ-* in *τράπεζα* 'table' ('four-legged', originally; *τορ-* in Myc. *to-pe-za* 'table', perhaps with *τορ-* for *τρο-* under the influence of *τυρ-*, see below). The conditioning factors for the distribution of *k^{we}*t(w)r-* : **t(w)r-* are unclear to me (analogy may play a role). Influence of **tri-* may explain *τρυ-* in *τρυ-φάλεια* 'helmet (with four *φάλοι* 'crest-holders')' instead of the expected form *τυρ-* < *(k^w)*tur-*, which is found in the name *Τυρταῖος* ('of [i. e., born on] the fourth day [**τύρτᾱ*]', viz. of the month); the ad hoc assumption of **twr̥-* > *τρυ-*, or regular (i. e. not analogical) metathesis **tur-* > *τρυ-*, fails to convince me[5].

11.1.5. The Greek forms for 'five', *πέντε* (most dialects)/*πέμπε* (Aeolic), regularly derive from **penk*^{w}*e* and require no special comment. The same forms are also used in compounds originally; the regular form before *a/o* is *πεμπ-* in all dialects, e. g. *πεμπώβολον* 'five-pronged fork' in Homer, likewise in derivatives like *πεμπάς* 'the number five', 'group of five' (Att.), *πεμπάζω* 'count (by fives)'. The form *πεμπ-*, however, was generally replaced by *πεντ-* in the '*πέντε*-dialects': e. g., *πεντ-ώβολος* 'of/worth five obols', likewise *πεντάς* (Aristotle and others) = *πεμπάς*. Moreover, *πεντα-*, with *ᾰ* after *ἑπτᾰ(-), δεκᾰ(-), τετρᾰ-*, is frequent from Homer onwards (e. g., *πεντά-δραχμος* 'of the weight/price of five drachmas', Herodotus etc.).

11.1.6. For 'six', we find *ϝέξ* (i. e. *ϝhέξ*) in some dialects; in those where *ϝ* was regularly lost the result is *ἕξ*. As sandhi-forms before consonant we find *ἑκ-* and *ἑσ-*, e. g. in Att. *ἑκκαίδεκα* 'sixteen', Boeot. *ἑσκηδεκάτη* 'sixteenth' (dative singular feminine); one or the other — or both? — must be old, as shown by Mycenaean *we-pe-za* *ϝhέσ-πεζα* (or *ϝhέπ-πεζα*, with assimilation of -κ|π-??) 'six-legged' (said of a table). The Greek forms thus derive from **sweks*. On the model of *ἑπτᾰ(-), δεκᾰ(-)*, etc., the form *ἑξᾰ-* (before *C*) is not uncommon in compounds.

11.1.7. The Greek cardinal 'seven' is *ἑπτᾰ́*, the regular reflex of **septm̥*. As first member of compounds, *ἑπτᾰ-* (together with *δεκα-*, etc., cf. 11.1.5.) influenced the first members based on *πέντε, ἕξ*, and others.

11.1.8. Greek 'eight' *ὀκτώ* < **H_3ektoH$_1$* (?) has undergone a modifying influence from the neighbouring numeral 'seven' in some dialects: Heraclean *hοκτώ* with *h-* after *ἑπτά*; Elean *ὀπτό* (quantity of final *-ο* unknown, as the inscription does not indicate vowel-length) with *-πτ-*. Boeotian has *ὀκτό*, Lesbian *ὄκτο*, with short final vowel (influence of *δύο*, or just parallel development?). Beside *ὀκτω-* as a first member of compounds, we also find *ὀκτα-*, with analogical *ᾰ*, cf. *πεντα-* (q. v.), etc. (and *hοκτα-* in Heraclean, with *h-* like *hοκτώ*).

11.1.9. Greek 'nine' *ἐννέα* presents an (insoluble) problem: the origin of the geminate *-νν-*; from **H_1newn̥*, the regular form should present only one *-ν-*[6]. In a few dialects, *-εα* is contracted: *ἐννῆ* in Delphian, Rhodian, Coan, Cyrenaean. Heraclean *hεννέα* again shows influence of *ἑπτά* (cf. *hοκτώ*, 11.1.8.). In compounds, *ἐννεα-/ἐννη-* is found, but also local reflexes of the zero-grade form *ἐνϝᾰ-*. This *ἐνϝᾰ-* must be a relatively late Greek creation: from **H_1nwn-*, one expects *†ἐνυν-*.

Mycenaean has the descriptive adjective *e-ne-wo(-)pe-za* 'nine-legged' (said of tables), i.e., *ἐ(ν)νεϝό-πεζα* (also the dual form *e-ne-wo pe-zo -πέζω*). As the *-o-* of *ἐ(ν)νεϝο-* cannot come from the syllabic nasal (which yields *ᾰ* in all Greek dialects), influence of, say, *κʷετρο-* must be assumed (with *-ρο-* regularly < **r̥*); or, if an independent *ἐ(ν)νέϝο* also existed, there may have been influence of a form *ὀκτό* for 'eight' (which is attested in Aeolic, see 11.1.8., but even if it were found in our Mycenaean texts, could not be *proved* to have short final vowel there, as the spelling does not permit us to distinguish long and short vowels).

11.1.10. The all but Panhellenic form of the numeral 'ten' is *δέκα*, the regular reflex of **dekm̥*. For Arcadian, the form *δέκο* is attested, and also *δυό-δεκο* 'twelve' (commonly interpreted as = *δυώδεκο* – the inscription does not indicate vowel-length; however, since Arcadian has unambiguous *δύο*, in inscriptions where vowel-length *is* indicated, *δυόδεκο* may well have short internal *-ο-*). The *-ο* of *δέκο* possibly betrays influence of (putative, not attested) Arc. *ὀκτό* (and *ἐννέο*?), cf. 11.1.9., Myc. *e-ne-wo(-)*. In view of the ordinal *δέκοτος*, which is found not only in Arcadian, but also in Lesbian *πεμ[π]εκαιδέκοτος* 'fifteenth', *ὀκτοκαιδέκοτος* 'eighteenth', we may suspect *δέκο* for Lesbian as well. Further confirmation for the spread of *-o(-)* beyond its original domain in Lesbian may be found in Lesb. *ἔνοτος* 'ninth' besides *ἔνατος*.

11.1.11. For the Greek teens, I shall first give the Attic forms. 'Eleven' to 'twelve': these forms are indeclinable dvandva-compounds: *ἕνδεκα, δώδεκα*. 'Thirteen' to 'fourteen': *τρεῖς* (*τρία*, etc.) / *τέτταρες* (etc.) *καὶ δέκα*, later (from the third century B.C. onwards) indeclinable *τρεισκαίδεκα* etc., in view of the single accent (on *-καί-*) to be valued as an innovative type of compound (called "Zusammenrückung" in German literature). The numerals 'fifteen' to 'nineteen' are of the "Zusammenrückung"-type: *πεντεκαίδεκα* etc. 'Sixteen' is *ἑκκαίδεκα*, with allomorph *ἑκ-* for *ἕξ*, cf. 11.1.6. An alternative type *δέκα τρεῖς, δέκα πέντε*, etc. (Attic already fifth century B.C.), especially *after* the counted objects, has become increasingly common. For 'eighteen' to 'nineteen' one also finds the expressions *δυοῖν/ἑνὸς δέοντες* (*-α*, etc.) *εἴκοσι*, lit. 'twenty lacking [participle] two/one', 'twenty minus two/one'.

Similar types are in use for 'twenty-one' etc.: *εἷς καὶ εἴκοσι* or *εἴκοσι εἷς* (also *εἴκοσι καὶ εἷς*), etc., and expressions like *δυοῖν δέοντες τριάκοντα* 'thirty minus two' = 'twenty-eight'.

Local variants show disyllabic *δυω-* in *δυώδεκα* (prevalence of the Lindeman-form of the numeral 'two', see 11.1.2., over the monosyllabic alternative *δϝω-*), sometimes *δυο-* (possibly Arc. *δυόδεκο*, cf. 11.1.10.; indirectly in Boeot. *δυοδέκοτος* 'twelfth'); *τρισ(-)* for *τρεισ(-)*, cf. 11.1.3.; epichoric forms for 'four-', cf. 11.1.4.; *ἑσ-* as allomorph of *ἕξ* in the Boeotian ordinal *ἑσκηδέκατος* 'sixteenth', presupposing *ἑσκήδεκα* 'sixteen', cf. 11.1.6.; *-δεκο* for *-δεκα*, cf. 11.1.10.

Since the use of *καί* (+ local variants) in the function of connector 'and', Panhellenic from the first alphabetic sources onwards, appears to be post-Mycenaean (Myceanean uses $κ^wε$), those of the above types which use *καί* can hardly date back to Mycenaean times. However, Mycenaean data are lacking for the higher numerals in general (*e-ne-wo(-)* being the highest item attested; see 11.1.9.). This is due to the circumstance that numbers are noted by means of numeric signs (strokes, circlets) when objects are counted; therefore, we are fortunate to find any data at all in the tablets.

11.1.12. For the explanation of Greek *εἴκοσι* etc., the glottalic theory can be adduced; in the framework of this theory, Kortlandt (1983: 100) explains *ἐϝῑκ-* from **'twi-'tkm̥-t-*, which through dissimilatory processes became **'wi'km̥t-*; the preglottalization (') eventually merged with H_1 the result being the form *ἐϝῑκ-*; total dissimilation of **'t-* explains West Gk *ϝῑκᾰτι*. The *-o-* of *ἐϝῑκοσι/εἴκοσι* is due to influence of the higher decads, which have -*κοντα*. Homeric *ἐείκοσι* conceals older *ἐ(ϝ)ῑ́κοσι*; it is a case of *diektasis* (*εει* for contemporary [contracted] *ει*, to restore the original rhythmic pattern). The original -*ᾰ*- < *-*m̥*- is preserved in West Greek and Mainland-Aeolic *(ϝ)ῑ́κᾰτι*, Pamphylian *φῑ́κᾰτι* (with [f] or [v] < [w]); these dialects also preserve original -*τι*, which in Arcado-Cyprian (and already Mycenaean), Attic-Ionic, and Lesbian (under Ionic influence) regularly became -*σι*.

11.1.13. The Greek decads 'thirty' to 'ninety' end in -*κοντᾰ*. According to Szemerényi and others, the final -*ᾰ* is not original; see Kortlandt (1983: 98 ff.). Certain peculiarities of the first parts of the -*κοντα*-forms can again be accounted for in the framework of the glottalic theory. Thus, the -*η*- of *πεντ-ή-κοντα* shows the same kind of compensatory lengthening as -*ῑ*- in **(ἐ)ϝ-ῑ́-κᾰτι*, cf. 11.1.12. Kortlandt's explanation of *πεντή-κοντ(α)* from **penk^{w}e-H$_1$kont* (< **penk^{w}e-'tkomt*) (ibid.) is, therefore, very attractive. The -*η*- of **πενκ^w-ή-κοντα* was then introduced into **ϝhεξέκοντ(α)* (? < **sweks-H$_1$kont*) to yield *(ϝ)hεξήκοντα*.

In Kortlandt's opinion, final -*ᾰ* spread from 'thirty', where it was introduced on the analogy of 'twenty': **(H)wi-H$_1$kn̥t-i* → **triHa-H$_1$kont-a* (with influence from free-standing *τρία*; from **triH$_2$-H$_1$kont-*, however, we may expect **triHa-Hkont-* as the regular reflex in Greek; Kortlandt's notation differs slightly from the one offered here); again, the final vowel of the first part of 'thirty' shows compensatory lengthening. The same is also assumed for 'seventy': **septm̥-H$_1$kont* > **ἑβδμήκοντ(α)* (with voicing of the [Greek] cluster *-*ptm*-[7]), later re-shaped into *ἑβδομήκοντα*, with -*o*- from the ordinal *ἕβδομος* (which in its turn seems to owe its -*o*- to *ὄγδο[ϝ]ος*; for the problems connected with these ordinals, see 11.2.7., 11.2.8.). Along the same lines, *ὀγδοήκοντα* was formed (Ionic *ὀγδώκοντα*, with contraction), replacing the expected form **ὀκτώκοντα*.

The first member of 'forty' is *τεττᾰρᾰ-* in Attic (*τεττᾰρᾰ́-κοντα*), formally the neuter form of 'four'; other dialects exhibit similar formations (*τεσσερά-*/*τεσσαρά-κοντα*; Boeot. *πετταράκοντα*; cf. 11.1.4.). The West Ionic form *τετράϙοnta* (from a Chalcidian colony in Sicily) may betray influence from 'four hundred' (*τετρᾰ-κό σιοι*). More problematic is the West Greek form *τετρώκοντα*; in this case, I feel little inclination to accept Kortlandt's (1983: 100) view, viz. that in its pre-form, *'t (*d) "apparently merged with *H$_3$". Perhaps an old form **k^{w}etur-H$_1$kont-* was (at a still early date) replaced by **k^{w}etru-H$_1$kont-*, under the influence of **triH$_2$-H$_1$kont-* (see above), before the latter form developed into **triHa-Hkont-*. In that event, the expected result is **κ^{w}ετρῠ́-κοντα*, which could have undergone influence of the -*o*- of *κ^{w}έτορες* (later West Gk. *τέτορες*,

11.1.4.), or of the -*ω*- of **ὀκτώκοντα* ('two times forty'), before 'eighty' was subjected to reshapings itself (see preceding paragraph). Or *k^{w}*etōr-Hkont-* (with loss of -*w*- [cf. *τέτορες*] for *k^{w}*etwōr*, the old neuter; cf. Lat. *quattuor*, Gothic *fidwōr*) was replaced by *k^{w}*etrō-Hkont* under the influence of *k^{w}*etr-* in compounds. However, I do not want to insist on these speculations, as a bundle of hypotheses verges on the gratuitous.

Ἐνενήκοντα 'ninety' probably also owes its -*η*- to *πεντήκοντα* etc.; again, Kortlandt's explanation (1983: 99) fails to convince me. The evidence, I think, indicates that the regular outcome of *H_1*newn-'tkomt* would be **ἐνευνέκοντ(α)*, rather than **ἐνεϝνήκοντ(α)*. Another explanation is therefore called for. I think it possible that we have to start from *H_1*nun-'tkomt*, from which I expect **ἐνυνέκοντ(α)*; influence of *ἐ(ν)νέϝα* 'nine' explains the replacement of -*υ*- by -*ε*-, and *ἐνενε-* was further modified to *ἐνενη-* through the influence of the lower decads (from 'fifty' upwards).

In the preceding lines, zero grade of the first element was assumed for some of the decads (**dwi-*, *tri*H_2-, perhaps k^{we}*tur-*, H_1*nun-*), and this may well reflect the original situation. However, influence of the corresponding freestanding allomorphs with full grade has to be accepted for a very early, possibly still Proto-Indo-European date.

In Heraclean, the initial *h*- of 'seventy' (with aberrant -*ε*-: *hεβδ-ε-μήκοντα*) was transferred to 'eighty': *hογδοήκοντα*, and to 'ninety': *hενε-νήκοντα*, cf. *hοκτώ, hεννέα* in the same dialect (11.1.8., 11.1.9.).

11.1.14. The Greek form for 'hundred' is *ἑκᾰτό ν*, but Arcadian has *hεκοτόν*, with the -*ο*- of the decads in -*κοντα* (cf. the -*ο*- in *εἴκοσι*, 11.1.12.). The form *ἑκατόν* has been variously explained as the result of **se[m]-k̥m̥tom* 'one hundred', with dissimilatory loss of the first -*m*-, or as a refection of *ἁ̊κᾰτό ν* < **sm̥-k̥m̥tom*, with *ε*- for *α*- under the influence of *ἕν* 'one' (n.). In the framework of the glottalic theory again, Kortlandt (1983: 98) convincingly backs the derivation of **dkm̥-tom* (*'*tkm̥tom*) from **dekm̥* (*'*tekm̥*) 'ten'; this became *H_1*km̥tom* > **ἐκᾰτό ν* in Greek, which then acquired the initial aspiration of *ἕν*, and was re-analyzed as *ἑ-κατό-ν* (and appreciated, I suppose, as a maimed **ἓν κατόν* 'one hundred' by way of popular etymology).

For the hundreds, Greek has the morpheme -*κᾰτιοι* (declinable) in a number of dialects (West Greek, Mainland Aeolic), apparently drawn from – reanalyzed – *ἑ-κατόν*; this regularly became -*κᾰσιοι* in Arcadian, and in Cyprian *ti-wi-ya-ka-si-a-se* = *δϝιᾱκᾰσία*^{n}*ς* (acc. pl. fem.) according to Neumann (1980), with -*τι*- > -*σι*-. Influence of the -*κοντα*-decads explains the further change to *-κόσιοι* in Attic-Ionic, and in Lesbian Aeolic (under Ionic influence).

Counting of the hundreds is done in Attic-Ionic with the first members *διᾱ-* (Ion. *διη-*), *τριᾱ-* (Ion. *τριη-*), *τετρᾰ-, πεντᾰ-, ἑξᾰ-, ἑπτᾰ-, ὀκτᾰ-, ἐνᾰ-* (Ion. *εἰνᾰ-*, < **ἐνϝᾰ-*). This situation is best explained by the assumption that *διᾱ-κόσιοι* 'two hundred' was made on the model of *τριᾱ-κόσιοι* 'three hundred', which in its turn took over the first part of *τριᾱ́-κοντα* 'thirty' (11.1.13.); and that the *-ᾰ-* of *τετρᾰ-, ἑπτᾰ-, ἐν(ϝ)ᾰ-* was extended to the remaining hundreds. From the other dialects, we can quote a few deviant local forms. Thessalian has *ἑξει-κάττιοι* 'six hundred'[8] (*ει* = [eː]), with *ἑξει-* after **ἑξεί-κοντα* 'sixty'. Lesbian *ὀκτω-κόσιοι* 'eight hundred' shows direct influence of *ὀκτώ* 'eight' (before this was ousted by *ὄκτο*). Heraclean has *hοκτα-κάτιοι* 'eight hundred', with the *h-* of *hεπτα-κάτιοι* 'seven hundred' – cf. *hοκτώ* (11.1.8.), *hογδοή-κοντα* (11.1.13., last paragraph).

Secondarily, we find singular forms of the hundreds with collective nouns (especially *ἡ ἵππος* 'cavalry').

11.1.15. The Greek forms for 'thousand' are based on **gheslio-*, itself an *-io-*derivative (adjective) of **gheslo-*, also known from e. g. Indo-Iranian. In most dialects, the regular reflex shows loss of *s* before *l*, with compensatory lengthening of the preceding vowel (thus Ion. *χείλιοι*, with [eː]; Laconian *χήλιοι* with [ɛː]); the Aeolic reflex of **-sl-* is *-λλ-*, because of which Lesbian and Thessalian have *χέλλιοι*. Attic has *χῑ́λιοι*, with unexpected *-ῑ-* in the first syllable (assimilation of [eː] to the *-ι-* of the next syllable?).

The usual manner of expression for 'two thousand' to 'nine thousand' is by means of multiplicative + *χῑ́λιοι* (etc.), the two forming a (recent type of) compound: (Att.) *δισ-χίλιοι* "twice thousand", *τρισ-χίλιοι* "three times thousand", etc. Alternatively, the noun *χιλιάς* 'a thousand' is used: *δύο* [etc.] *χιλιάδες* (+ genitive) 'two [etc.] thousands (of ...)'. For the singular of (-)*χίλιοι* with collective nouns, cf. 11.1.14., last paragraph.

For 'ten thousand', Greek has *μῡ́ριοι* (first in Hesiod: *τρὶς μύριοι* 'thrice ten thousand'), a specialized application of the adjective *μῡρίοι* 'countless', 'innumerable'; the difference in accent is secondary, perhaps even artificial. Both the numeral and the adjective can be used in the singular with collective nouns; cf. 11.1.14., last paragraph. The etymology of *μῡριο-* has not been established with any degree of probability.

Multiples of 'ten thousand' are expressed by means of multiplicatives, e. g. *δισμύριοι* "twice ten thousand", or as "so-and-so many *μυριάδες*";

cf. 'two thousand' to 'nine thousand', above. As 'ten thousand' is the highest basic numeral in Ancient Greek, 'one hundred thousand' is *δεκακισμύριοι* "ten times *μύριοι*".

11.2. Ordinals

11.2.0. In the formation of the Greek ordinals, the suffix *-το-* plays a prominent part; only few ordinals are formed by different means. According to some scholars, the origin of *-το-* in *τρί-τος* 'third' and higher ordinals must be looked for in the re-analysis of **dekm̥t-os* as **dekm̥-tos*; see, e. g., Szemerényi (1980: 209 f.). If the supposition concerning **dekm̥t-os* (older than **dekm-os*, Lat. *decimus*) should not be correct – though it may be –, we are probably dealing with the 'completive' ("superlative") suffix **-to-* (cf. 11.2.1.).

The first two ordinals are not derivationally related to the corresponding cardinals.

11.2.1. 'First' is *πρῶτος* in Attic-Ionic, Arcado-Cyprian, and also in a part of Aeolic: Lesbian has *πρῶτος* like the aforesaid dialects, Thessalian the local form with close [o:]: *προῦτος*. Boeotian, however, agrees with West Greek in having the form *πρᾶτος*. *Πρῶτος*/*πρᾶτος* are derived, probably with the 'completive' suffix *-το-*, from an element (elements) which is (are) evidently connected with the preposition *πρό*. The latter may continue an old adjectival stem with spatial meaning ("front-ish", or the like), and the element preceding *-το-* can then be considered an old instrumental form ("by the frontside"), neuter *proH_1 in *πρῶτος* (cf. *ἄνω – ἀνώ-τερος*, etc.), fem. **pre*$H_2(e)H_1$ in *πρᾶτος* (cf. Lat. *citrō*/*citrā*, etc.). Some scholars have proposed an analogical explanation for *πρῶτος*, viz. that it has supplanted *πρᾶτος* (**pr̥*H_2*-to-s*) in several dialects under the influence of *πρό-τερος*; see, e. g., Chantraine (1974 s. v. *πρῶτος*), Rix (1976: 73).

Contrary to what has often been assumed, the two forms cannot be reconciled as different results of contraction. It is possible that *πρωτο-* is represented in the Mycenaean personal names *po-ro-to* (*Πρῶτος*?), *po-ro-te-u* (*Πρωτεύς*?). When only two persons/objects are involved, Greek uses the "binarily contrasting" form *πρότερος*. Occasionally, superlative forms ('very first') are found: *πρώτιστος* (Attic-Ionic) / *πράτιστος* (West Greek).

11.2.2. The Panhellenic word for 'second' is *δεύτερος*. This word has been convincingly explained by Ruijgh (1972: 445 ff.) as a *-τερο-*derivative of *δεῦ 'here'; the suffix again expresses a binary (spatial) contrast (cf. *πρό-τερος*, 11.2.1.), so that we can reconstruct a spatial meaning 'situated rather on this side' (but not in front position), as against what is farther away.

11.2.3. 'Third' is *τρί-τος*, formed from the zero-grade stem form of *τρέ(y)ες* 'three'. The Lesbian form *τέρτος* (in glosses and proper names) has perhaps developed from *τρίτος* by the way of an intermediate stage with palatal syllabic *r* (*$^{*}t\mathring{r}^{y}tos$*). The Homeric alternative form *τρίτᾰτος* has the outward appearance of a superlative, though this is hard to accept from a semantic point of view (*πρώτιστος* [11.2.1.] is quite a different case) – perhaps it is just a matter of superficial influence of the coda of *τέτρατος* 'fourth', *εἴνατος* 'ninth', *δέκατος* 'tenth'.

11.2.4. West Gk *τέτρᾰτος*, Att.-Ion. *τέτᾰρτος* (Homeric both *τέτρατος* and *τέταρτος*), and Arc. *τέτορτος* 'fourth' point to *$^{*}k^{w}et\mathring{r}\text{-}to\text{-}$*; the regular reflex of *-r̥-* is *-ρᾰ-* (Arc. *-ρο-*), but the position of *e/o* in the full grade has often had an analogical effect on the zero-grade, whence *-ᾰρ-/-ορ-* in some dialects. Boeotian *πέτρατος* is a little awkward, as one would rather expect †*πέτροτος*, with Aeolic *-ρο-* < *-r̥-*. If not influenced by a neighbouring dialect (Attic, or more likely West Greek), Boeotian could have taken the unexpected *-ᾰ-* in *πέτρατος* from the cardinal *πέττᾰρες*. A more archaic zero-grade base lies behind *Τυρταῖος* from *τύρτᾱ 'the fourth [day]', feminine of *τύρτος < *$^{*}(k^{w})tur\text{-}to\text{-}$* (cf. 11.1.4.).

One might be tempted to explain Att.(-Ion.) *τέταρτος* as a remodelling of *τέ-τυρτος (cf. *τε-τρᾰ-* beside *τρᾰ-*: 11.1.4.) under the influence of *τέτταρες*; however, this expedient is impossible in the case of Arc. *τέτορτος*, as this dialect has *τέσσερες*, and not a form †*τέσσορες* (or *τέτορες*, like West Greek) which could explain the *-o-* in the ordinal. Note that Mycenaean already has *$\kappa^{w}\varepsilon\tau\rho o\text{-}$* in compounds; in Arcadian, therefore, *$^{*}\kappa^{w}\acute{\varepsilon}\tau\rho o\text{-}\tau o\varsigma$* may well have preceded *τέτορτος* (cf. also *τετρᾰ-* in compounds: *τέτρᾰ-τος* ordinal ≈ *τέτᾰρτος*).

11.2.5. *Πέμπτος* 'fifth' is the regular outcome of *$^{*}penk^{w}\text{-}to\text{-}$*. With zero-grade of the base, we should expect †*πάπτος* < *$^{*}p\mathring{n}k^{w}\text{-}to\text{-}$*; apparently, the cardinal has influenced the ordinal. *Πέντος* in Gortynian and in the Central Ionic dialect of Amorgos shows renewed influenced of the cardinal. Arcadian *πέμποτος* is best explained by influence of *δέκοτος* 'tenth' (11.2.10.), 'five' being 'half of ten', cf. my remark on the possibility of influence of *ὀκτώκοντα 'eighty' to explain *τετρώκοντα* 'forty' = 'half of eighty' (11.1.13.), and of *$^{*}\kappa^{w}\acute{\varepsilon}\tau\rho o\tau o\varsigma$* (the forerunner of *τέτορτος*, cf. 11.2.4.).

11.2.6. Greek *ἕκτος* 'sixth' (one example of *ϝέκτος*, in a Cretan inscription) is the outcome of **swek(s)tos*; unless we assume very early absence of the internal *-s-*, the Greek form is irregular from a diachronic point of view, as *-kst-* should have resulted in *-χθ-*. However, compare *ἑκ-* in compounds (e. g. *ἕκ-πους* 'six-footed', in an early Attic inscription). The postulated Proto-Indo-European form **suk(s)-to-s* must again have been influenced by the cardinal.

11.2.7. Most Greek dialects have *ἕβδομος* 'seventh', but West Greek has *ἕβδ-ε-μος* (Delphian, Cyrenaean, Aetolian; indirectly attested by derivatives in Heraclean and Epidaurian). As it has been demonstrated in recent research[9] that Sievers' Law should not operate in **septmos*, the internal *o/ε* cannot be regarded as an analogical replacement of earlier *-ᾰ-* (*†septm̥-mos* > *†ἕπτ-ᾰ-μος*); moreover, *-βδ-* can most easily be accounted for if *pt* was followed (in Proto-Greek?) by non-syllabic *m*; cf. 11.1.13. The *-o-* in *ἕβδ-ο-μος* is, to my mind, due to influence from *ὄγδο(ϝ)ος* 'eighth', which in its turn owes the voicedness of its stop-cluster to *ἕβδομος*. The West Greek form still puzzles me.

For the Homeric alternative form *ἑβδόμ-ατος*, cf. *τρίτ-ατος*, 11.2.3.

11.2.8. Instead of the expected (?) form for 'eighth', **ὄκτο(ϝ)ος* < **H_3okto-wo-s* (???), Greek has *ὄ-γδ-οϝος*. The irregular voicing arose under the influence of *ἕβδομος*, see 11.2.7.

For the Homeric alternative form *ὀγδό-ατος*, cf. *τρίτ-ατος* and *ἑβδόμ-ατος* (11.2.3., 11.2.7.).

11.2.9. From **ἕνϝᾰτος* 'ninth' come Att. *ἔνατος*, Ion. *εἴνατος*, Argolic/Cretan/Cyrenaean *ἥνατος*, the different dialect forms showing the respective local treatments of *ἐνϝᾰ-*. As stated above (11.1.9.), *ἐνϝᾰ-* is a recent (Greek) zero-grade allomorph of *ἐ(ν)νεϝᾰ-*. The form *hένατος*, found in Delphian and Theran, probably got its *h-* from *ἕβδεμος* 'seventh'; cf. the spread of *h-* from 'seven' in Heraclean (11.1.8, 9, 13 fin., 14).

Lesbian *ἔνοτος* may point to a cardinal *ἔννεο*, with *-o* under the influence of *ὄκτο*, cf. 11.1.8. – 11.1.10; influence of the *-κοντα*-decads (trickling down via *εἴκοσι* 'twenty' and *δέκο(-τος)* 'ten(th)) is less likely, to my mind.

11.2.10. The majority of dialects have *δέκᾰτος* 'tenth' < **dekm̥#to-s* (*dekm̥t#o-s*, according to some scholars, cf. 11.2.0.; the result is the same, of course). For the explanation of Arcadian and Lesbian *δέκ-ο-τος*, see 11.1.8. – 11.1.10.; 11.2.9.

11.2.11. The Attic forms of 'eleventh' and 'twelfth' are *ἑνδέκατος* and *δωδέκατος*, i. e. cardinal + *-το-*; instead of *δω-* from monosylabic *δϝω-*, we find *δυω-/δυο-* in agreement with the cardinal in other dialects, cf. 11.1.11.

'Thirteenth' to 'nineteenth': the Classical Attic type is *τρίτος (τέταρτος, πέμπτος*, etc.) *καὶ δέκατος*, which indirectly shows the relative recentness of the "Zusammenrückung"-type, not only for 'thirteen', 'fourteen', but also for 'fifteen' to 'nineteen' (11.1.11.). In later Attic, and very frequently in other dialects from old times, the type *τρεισκαιδέκατος* (with local variants like *τρισ-*, etc.) is in vogue.

For °-*δέκοτος*, cf. *δέκο(-τος)*: 11.1.10.; 11.2.10.

11.2.12. Att.-Ion. *εἰκοστός* 'twentieth' has the same analogical *-ο-* as *εἴκοσι*; it replaced earlier *ἐ(ϝ)ῑκᾰστό ς* < **dwi-dkm̥t-to-s* (for the development of **d* (= **'t*), see 11.1.12.). For Boeotian, the form *ϝῑκᾰστό ς* has been attested; this was doubtless also the West Greek form. The form *ἰκοστός*, attested for Thessalian, must have been created after the other *-κοστός*-forms see 11.2.13.), in spite of the fact that the cardinal *ἴκατι* has not undergone the influence of the *-κοντα*-decads. Lesbian *εἴκοιστος* has *-κοιστος* from the ordinals of the higher decads (11.2.13.).

Homeric *ἐεικοστός* is a diektasis-form; cf. *ἐείκοσι*, 11.1.12.

11.2.13. The ordinals of the higher decads end in *-κοστός*. Again, the older forms undoubtedly were in **-κᾰστό ς*, but here, influence of the cardinals (*-κοντα*) seems to be a pandialectal phenomenon. In Lesbian, the **-καστός*-ordinals took over not only the *-ο-*, but also the *-ν-*, of the *-κοντα*-cardinals: *-καστος* → *-κονστος* > *-κοιστος*, with the regular Lesbian treatment of nasal before strong sibilant.

11.2.14. The final part *-οστός* of the ordinals 'thirtieth' to 'ninetieth' was quite simply taken over for the formation of the ordinals of the hundreds, thousands, and ten-thousands: *ἑκατ-οστός* ≈ *ἑκατ-όν; διᾱκοσι-οστός* ≈ *διᾱκόσι-οι (-α* etc.), *τριᾱκοσι-οστός* ≈ *τριᾱκόσι-οι*, etc.; *χῑλι-οστός* ≈ *χίλι-οι; μῡρι-οστό ς* ≈ *μύρι-οι*. It goes without saying that these forms are rather recent Greek creations.

11.3. Fractions

11.3.0. For the expression of fractions, Greek has no uniform pattern; one expedient is the use of the noun *μοῖρα* (fem.) 'part', another the expression by means of a substantivized ordinal, feminine (sc. *μοῖρα* or *μερίς*) or neuter (sc. *μέρος*). I shall deal with the expression of 'a half' first; next, the different types of designation of further fractions will be discussed.

11.3.1. For 'a half', Greek has a prefixed morpheme *ἡμι-* ("in (for) one part", a locative form of the root **sem-*, see 11.1.1.), as in *ἡμι-τάλαντον* 'half a talent'. *Ἡμι-* is sometimes preceded by another numeral morpheme, so as to express a certain number of halves, as in *τρι-ημί-γυον* "three-half-*γύης*" = 'a *γύης* (measure of land) and a half'. For 'X + a half', we also find expressions of the type *τέταρτον ἡμιτάλαντον* "the fourth (is) a half talent", i. e. 'three and a half talent'.

Alternatively, the adjective *ἥμισυς* (+ local variants) is used, in a number of different ways: a) *ἡμίσεες λαοί* (Hom.) 'half the people', *τὸ ἥμισυ τεῖχος* (Thuc.) 'half the wall', etc.; b) (prose) *οἱ ἡμίσεις τῶν ἄρτων* (Xen.) 'half of the loaves', *αἱ ἡμίσειαι τῶν νεῶν* (Thuc.) 'half of the ships' – the adjective agrees in gender with the noun in the partitive genitive; c) substantivized *(τὸ) ἥμισυ* (sc. *μέρος* 'part'): [c1] + partitive genitive, [c2] ⟨cardinal⟩ *(καὶ) ἥμισυ*, either with case agreement between ⟨cardinal⟩ and *ἥμισυ*, or *ἥμισυ* indeclinable; d) substantivized *ἡ ἡμίσεια* (sc. *μοῖρα* 'part') + partitive genitive.

The word *ἥμισυς* is believed by many (or most) scholars to be a substantive originally; *-συ-* (older *-τυ-*; the development *-τυ-* > *-συ-* is problematic, cf. Lejeune 1972: 65 f.) is not usually found as an adjectival suffix.

11.3.2. "One + a fraction" is often expressed in the following way: *ἐπί-τριτος* "having a third in addition" = 'one and a third', *ἐπιτέταρτος* 'one and a quarter', etc.

For 'x/y', one finds expressions of the type *τῶν πέντε αἱ δύο μοῖραι* (Thuc.) "two parts on the five" = 'two-fifths'. 'Two-thirds' is sometimes expressed by *τὰ δύο μέρη (αἱ δύο μοῖραι)* 'the two parts', without the genitive of the whole (*τῶν τριῶν* 'of the three').

11.4. Multiplicatives; divisionals; proportionals

11.4.1. To answer the question "How many times?", Greek employs the multiplicative adverbs *ἅπαξ* 'once', *δίς* 'twice', *τρίς* 'three times', *τετράκις* 'four times', *πεντάκις* 'five times', etc.

Ἅ-παξ is an adverbial compound, the first part of which is the zero grade of **sem-*, cf. 11.1.1.; the second member ends in "adverbial *s*", whatever its origin may be (I have difficulty in accepting the hypothesis that *ἅπαξ* is an old nominative). The *-πᾰK*-part is usually explained as belonging with *πᾱ́γνῡμι* (Att.-Ion. *πήγνῡμι*) 'to fix in/on', 'to fasten together', etc.; **sm̥-pH₂g-s* is thus believed to mean literally something like 'in one blow'. However, I am not quite convinced that this is the correct etymology; one might for instance envisage a connection with **bhn̥gh-u-s* (Skt. *bahuḥ* 'much', Greek *πᾰχύ-ς* 'thick'), provided that this connection was still felt when by Grassmann's Law **φαχύς*, became *παχύς*.

The forms *δίς* and *τρίς* appear to be old: cf. Skt. *dviḥ, triḥ*, Lat. *bis* (Old Lat. *duis*), *ter* (< **tr̥s* < **tris*). Their structure is zero-grade of the cardinal + *s* (unless **dwi-* owes its *-i-* to **tri-*). *Τρίς* is found already in Mycenaean, in the name of a (semi-)divine being *ti-ri-se-ro-e Τρισ(h)ήρωhει* 'Thrice-Lord' (dative; probably the designation of an ancestral hero who enjoys divine worship). For 'four times', one might expect **(τε)τύρς* (or, with influence of *τρίς*, **(τε)τρύς*), or **(τε)τράς* (with loss of *-w-*), cf. Skt. *catuḥ* (< **-turs* or **-tr̥s*), Lat. *quater* (< **-tr̥s* < **-trus* ← **-turs*). The actually attested forms in *-κις* (dialectally also *-κι, -κιν*) from 'four times' onwards are explained as remodellings after **πολύ-κι* < **pl̥H₃u kʷid*, with the indefinite pronoun (≈ Skt. *purūcid* 'often'); *k* < **kʷ* is regular after *u*, and the *-ς* has been taken over from *δίς, τρίς* in part of the dialects. **Πολύκι*(-) has later been replaced by *πολλάκι(ς)*. See Rix (1976: 173). The forms in *-κιν* (Laconian) can be explained, I believe, by the influence of *πάλιν* 'again'.

11.4.2. The Greek adverbs *δίχᾰ, τρίχᾰ, τέτρᾰχᾰ*, etc., answer the question 'In(to) how many parts?'. The elements *δ(ϝ)ι-, τρι-, τετρᾰ-* need not be discussed any more; the origin of the *-χα*-suffix is disputed, and the problem seems as yet insoluble. From *τέτραχα* (and perhaps *ἕπταχα, δέκαχα*, if sufficiently old) the *-ᾰ-* preceding *-χα* spread to *πένταχα, ἕξαχα*. In Homer, we find *διχθά, τριχθά, τετραχθά* as alternative forms; these are equally difficult to explain[10]. Interpreting the divisional adverbs in *-χα* as adverbial neuter plural forms, the Greeks created further adverbial forms with case-like endings, e. g. *διχοῦ, διχῇ* = *δίχα*, and with the adverbial morpheme *-ως*, e. g. *διχῶς, τριχῶς*; the difference in place of accent is, however, embarrassing.

11.4.3.1. For 'single', 'double', 'triple', etc. ('*n*-fold', '*n* times as much/many') Greek has a variety of compounds, the first member of which is of the type *ἁ-, δ(ϝ)ι-, τρι-, τετρᾰ-, πεντᾰ-*, etc. As second members are used: *-πλόο-ς*, contracted *-πλοῦ-ς; -πλᾰ́σιο-ς* (Att.), *-πλήσιο-ς* (Ion.); *-φᾰ́σιο-ς* (Ion.) – the plurals *διφάσιοι* (etc.), *τριφάσιοι* (etc.) are used much like the cardinal numbers *δύο, τρεῖς* by Herodotus; occasionally *-φυιος, -φυής, -πτυχος*, and the like. In Hellenistic Greek, the forms *ἁ-πλό-ς, δι-πλό-ς* (poetic) are found. The general rule that Greek compound adjectives do not have separate feminine forms is not observed in the case of the thematic amongst the above-mentioned proportional adjectives.

For the second members with *-πλ-*, connection with the Indo-European root *pel- 'to fold' is usually assumed. The forms with *-πλό-ς*, though attested only rather late, agree fairly well with Lat. *duplus* 'double', *triplus* 'triple'; considering that Homer already has forms like *διπλῆν* (acc.), with the outward appearance of a contracted form (though the masculine forms are uncontracted), and not †*διπλόη*, I wonder whether behind such "contracted" forms we may not suspect *-πλή* as straightforward feminine of *-πλό-ς*. A form like *δι-πλ-ό-ς* would be of the same type as *δί-φρ-ος* 'chariot(-board)', 'couch' (on which two people could stand/sit; *-φρ-* zero-grade of *φερ-* 'to bear, carry'), apart from the accent. If *-πλό-ς* is old, the forms with *-πλόο-ς* may be the result of morphological innovation, albeit unexplained (*πλό[ϝ]ος* 'sailing', 'voyage' is an unlikely source for analogical change, from a semantic point of view). Note that etymological connection with *$pleH_1$- 'to fill' is unlikely, as *-$pl̥H_1o$- should have yielded *-*πελο-* in Greek, and not *-πλο-*, whereas *-$ploH_1w$-*o-* (thematization in a compound adjective of a neuter noun *$ploH_1$-u from *$pleH_1$-, type Gk *γόνυ, δόρυ*) would have become *-*πλω(ϝ)ο-ς*. It is safest, therefore, to abide by the etymology which connects *-πλόο-ς* with **pel-* 'to fold', notwithstanding the morphological problems.

The element *-πλᾰ́σιο-ς* can also be connected with **pel-*, if one is prepared to derive it in the following manner: *-πλᾰσιο-* < *-*πλᾰτιο-*, the latter based on (Att.-Ion.) **πλᾰτό -ς* 'folded' (verbal adjective) < **pl̥-tó-*.[11] One would have to assume that, e. g., **δϝί-πλᾰ-το-ς* (*-ν*) could denote an object folded in two, and that an adjective in *-ιο-ς* could be derived therefrom to express 'belonging to the class of objects folded in two', admittedly a somewhat abundant manner of word-formation (*δ(ϝ)ίπλᾰτος* itself would do just as well), but not without parallel in natural language. In Ionic, *-πλήσιος* in the proportional adjectives has supplanted *-πλάσιος* under the influence of *παραπλήσιος* 'nearly equal' (in number, size, age) etc. — cf. Frisk (1960 s. v. *διπλάσιος*).

In the same manner, *-φᾰ́σιος*, is derived from (-)*φᾰτο-ς*; in fact, *δίφατος* (in Hesychius' lexicon) and *τρίφατος* (in the *Theriaca* of Nicander) tell us as much. These forms derive from the Indo-European root *$bheH_2$- 'to shine' or 'to show'.

Of the other elements mentioned as the beginning of this section, *-φυιος* and *-φυής* belong with the verbal stem *φυ-* 'to grow', and *-πτυχος* with the stem *πτυχ-* 'to fold' (cf. *-πλός, -πλόος* above!).

11.4.3.2. Another type of proportional adjective is based on the adverbs mentioned in 11.4.2., without their final *-α*: from early sources onwards *δισσός* 'double', *τρισσός* 'threefold' (Att. *διττός, τριττός*) < **διχ-yός, τριχ-yός*; much later also *τετρασσός, ἑξασσός*, etc. The Ionic equivalents are *διξός, τριξός, τετραξός, πενταξός*, etc. < **διχθ-yός, τριχθ-yός*, etc.

It would be going too far to sum up all further bits and pieces of evidence for numerical adjectives and adverbs; for these, the reader is referred to (e. g.) Schwyzer (1939: 597–599).

11.5. Survey of Mycenaean data

In concluding this paper, I give a survey of the oldest data for numerical elements in the Greek language: those which have been found on the clay tablets from the Mycenaean archives. Some of these data have already been mentioned above.

'One.' From cardinal **sem-: e-me* dat. *ἑμεί*; derived: *a_2-te-ro ἅτερος* 'every second ...'. From **oiwo-: o-wo-we οἰϝ-ώϝης* 'with a single ear (handle)'. The man's name *po-ro-to* may be identical with the ordinal *πρῶτος*, cf. Latin names like *Quintus, Sextus*. Another man's name, *po-ro-te-u*, could well be *Πρωτ-εύς*.

'Two.' The cardinal *dwo δύω* or *δύο* is found, and also the instrumental case form *du-wo-u-pi* (morphological interpretation uncertain). The man's name *du-wo-jo/dwo-jo* stands a good chance of being *Δϝοῖος* 'Twin' (cf. *Δίδυμος*), onomastic application of the adjective *δ(ϝ)οιός* 'twofold'.

'Three.' The zero-grade stem *τρι-* is found in a number of compounds: *ti-ri-jo-we τρι-ῶϝες* (neuter) 'with three handles'; *ti-ri-po τρί-πος* (*τρίπως*?) 'tripod cauldron'; *ti-ri-po-di-ko τριποδίσκοι* (nom. pl.) 'small tripod cauldrons'; perhaps in the personal names *ti-ri-da-ro* and *ti-ri-jo-ko-so*, but this is very uncertain. The adverb *τρίς* is used in the 'divine' name *ti-ri-se-roe Τρισ-(h)ήρωhει* 'Thrice-Hero'.

'Four.' The zero-grade stem *$κ^w$ετρ(ο)-* is found in the compounds *qe-to-ro-we $κ^w$ετρ-ῶϝες* (neuter) 'with four handles', and *qe-to-ro-po-pi $κ^w$ε-τρό-ποπφι* (instr.-loc.) 'four-footed animals'. It is no more than a remote possibility that the same element is part of the personal names *qe-ta-ra-je-u* and *qe-te-re-u*. The shorter zero-grade allomorph *τορ-* (for *τρο-*, < **(k^w)r̥-*) is found in *to-pe-za τόρπεζα* 'table' (cf. Att.-Ion. *τράπεζα*).

'Five.' The element *πεγ$κ^w$-* might be present in the personal names *pe-qe-u* and *pe-qe-ro-jo* (genitive in *-οιο*).

'Six.' *Fhεσ-*, morphophonological variant of *(ϝ)ἕξ*, is found in the compound adjective *we-pe-za* *ϝhέσ-πεʒα* (fem.) 'with six legs' (?, description of a table).
'Nine.' *'E(ν)νεϝο-* is found in the adjective *e-ne-wo-pe-za* (fem.) 'with nine legs' (?, description of a table).

Notes

1. $*smiH_2$ ($*smyH_2$), being a vowel-less form from the Proto-Indo-European point of view, cannot, I deem, be original; one expects it to have replaced older $*sem\text{-}yH_2$.
2. Cf. Lindeman (1965); for *ἅμα*, this means $*s\mathring{m}^{m}eH_2$; alternatively, separating *ἅμα* from *ἁμᾶ*, one might reconstruct the Lindemanform $*s\mathring{m}^{m}\mathring{n}$ for the former.
3. I think that in Attic analogical spread of the ε-stem allomorph of ι-, υ- and σ-stems is responsible for the accusative plural in [-e:s]. If early, then e. g. (pre-contractional) nom. pl. *πόλε-ες* (< **πόλεy-ες*) 'cities', acc. *πόλε-νς* > *πόλεις* (cf. gen. *πόλε-ων*, dat. *πόλε-σι*), like nom. pl. *ἰχθύ-ες* 'fishes', acc. *ἰχθύ-νς* > *ἰχθῦς*; similarly, nom. pl. *βό-ες* (< $*\gamma^{w}$*όϝ-ες*) 'cattle', acc. *βό-νς* > *βοῦς*, nom. pl. *ταχέ-ες* (< **θαχέϝ-ες*) 'fast', acc. *ταχέ-νς* > *ταχεῖς*, nom. pl. *ἀλǣθέ-ες* (< **ἀλᾱθέσ-ες*) 'true', acc. *ἀλǣθέ-νς* > *ἀληθεῖς*. If the analogical reshaping under discussion is more recent, the accusative plural ending of vowel stems (including *πολε-*, *βο-*, etc.) is no longer *-νς*, but "lengthening (of preceding vowel) + ς"; cf. Ruijgh (1975: 353 ff.). Even if acc. *τρεῖς* should not be old enough to be explained as *τρε-* + *-νς* or "lengthening + ς", after nom. *τρέ-ες*, the type *πόλεις* nom./acc. pl., *ταχεῖς* nom./acc. pl. may at least have served as a model for *τρεῖς* = accusative as well as nominative (in spite of the stem *τρι-* in gen. *τρι-ῶν*, dat. *τρι-σί*). The fact that this explanation cannot be applied to the reverse case of *τρῖς* = nom./acc. does not, I think, invalidate the argument.
4. $\text{-}tw\mathring{r}\text{-}$ instead of *-tur-* cannot be old, *pace* Szemerényi (1964: 288; repeated 1980: 205): On the scale of "vocalization ability", the semivowels (y, w) appear to rank higher than the liquids (r, l) and nasals (n, m); in **twr*, therefore, it is *-w-* that becomes syllabic, whether the cluster stand before vowel or consonant. The (Greek) forms with syllabic $\text{-}\mathring{r}\text{-}$ must be dated fairly late, perhaps when **tw* had already become ^{t}ss. At that time, $*k^{w}e^{t}ss\mathring{r}\text{-}$ (-/C) / $*k^{w}e^{t}ss\mathring{r}r\text{-}$ (-/V) could have been created as zero-grade allomorphs of $*k^{w}e^{t}s\text{-}ser\text{-}$.
5. Cf. Szemerényi (1964: 302 f.); he seems willing to accept $*tw\mathring{r}$ > *tru*. To this I cannot subscribe, see n. 4.
6. Ruijgh (1967: 357 f.) thinks that *-νν-* can be explained by the assumption that the first syllable of *ἐ-νέ-ϝα* has been replaced by that of *ἐν-ϝα-*.

7. Note that a *single* unaspirated voiceless stop does not undergo voicing before *m* in Greek; perhaps there were different degrees of tenseness as between a single unaspirated voiceless stop, and two unaspirated voiceless stops, before non-syllabic sonants (or between T/V-N and T/C-N).
8. -ττ- in -*κάττιοι* is due to Aeolic gemination of consonants before semivocalic *i̯*: [katioi] → [kattyoi] (cf. the parallel phenomenon in some Germanic languages).
9. See Ruijgh (in press), who gives an elaboration for Greek of the refinements of Sievers' Law as proposed by Lindeman (1965) and Schindler (1977).
10. -*χα* ≈ -*χθα* reminds one of *χαμαί* ≈ *χθών*, with an original initial sequence **dhgh*-. However, this does not take us much further, as -*χα*/-*χθα* can hardly be semantically connected with **dh(e)ghom*: there are no indications for a semantic development **part* → *piece of land* → *land, earth* (only the meaning 'earth, land' can be reconstructed, with the derivatives *earthling* = 'man', Lat. *homo*, etc.).
11. Gothic *ain-falþs, fidur-falþs* contain the deverbal substantive **pól-to*-, not the adjective **pl̥-tó*-; the Gothic words are bahuvrīhi-compounds, whereas the Greek ones are not.

References

Anttila, Raimo
1972 *An introduction to historical and comparative linguistics* (New York: Macmillan).
Beekes, Robert S. P.
1982–1983 "On laryngeals and pronouns", *ZVS* 96: 200–232.
Buck, Carl D.
1955 *The Greek Dialects* (Chicago & London: The University of Chicago Press).
Chantraine, Pierre
1974 *Dictionnaire étymologique de la langue grecque. Histoire des mots III: Λ – Π* (Paris: Klincksieck).
Frisk, Hjalmar
1960 *Griechisches etymologisches Wörterbuch 1: A-Ko* (Heidelberg: Winter).
Gonda, Jan
1953 *Reflections on the numerals 'one' and 'two' in ancient Indo-European languages* (Utrecht: Oosthoek).
Kortlandt, Frederik H. H.
1983 "Greek Numerals and PIE glottalic consonants", *MSS* 42: 97–104.
Lejeune, Michel
1972 *Phonétique historique du mycénien et du grec ancien* (Paris: Klincksieck).

Lindeman, Fredrik O.
1965 "La loi de Sievers et le début du mot en indo-européen", *NTS* 20: 38–108.
Neumann, Günter
1980 "Beiträge zum Kyprischen, VII", *Kadmos* 19: 149–160.
Rix, Helmut
1976 *Historische Grammatik des Griechischen. Laut- und Formenlehre* (Darmstadt: Wissenschaftliche Buchgesellschaft).
Ruijgh, Cornelis J.
1967 *Études sur la grammaire et le vocabulaire du grec mycénien* (Amsterdam: Hakkert).
1972 "A propos de *de-we-ro-a$_3$-ko-ra-i-ja*", in: M. S. Ruipérez (ed.), *Acta Mycenaea.* Proceedings of the Fifth International Colloquium on Mycenaean Studies, held in Salamanca, 30 March–3 April 1970. Vol. II (= *Minos* 22): 441–450.
1975 "Analyse morphophonologique de l'attique classique. La seconde et la première déclinaison. II. Esquisse d'une méthode d'analyse morphophonologique pour l'attique. III. Analyse de la seconde déclinaison", *Mnemos.* IV 28: 337–379.
In Press "Chronologie relative: le grec", to appear in the Proceedings of the Eighth Conference of the Indogermanische Gesellschaft, Leyden 31 Aug.–4 Sept. 1987.
Schindler, Jochem
1977 "Notizen zum Sieversschen Gesetz", *Die Sprache* 23: 56–65.
Schwyzer, Eduard
1939 *Griechische Grammatik* I: *Allgemeiner Teil. Lautlehre, Wortbildung, Flexion* (Munich: Beck).
Szemerényi, Oswald
1964 *Syncope in Greek and IE and the nature of the IE accent* (Naples: Istituto Universitario Orientale di Napoli).
1980 *Einführung in die vergleichende Sprachwissenschaft* (2nd, revised edition) (Darmstadt: Wissenschaftliche Buchgesellschaft).

Chapter 12
Italic[1]

Robert Coleman

12.0. Introduction

The data are divided into six sections: 12.1. Cardinals, 12.2. Ordinals, 12.3. Adverbs, 12.4. Distributives, 12.5. Numerals in composition, and 12.6. Fractions. They are drawn from Latin, Faliscan, Oscan, Central Italic (Paelignian, etc.) and Umbrian. It is assumed throughout that these languages once formed a single speech-community (Proto-Italic) which did not include Venetic or Sicel, neither of which in any case has much to offer as far as the numerals are concerned. Most of the material is from Latin, but the inclusion of a separate section on compositive formations enables a number of relevant words from other areas of Italic to be taken into account. For Latin itself epigraphic forms are preferred where they are available, as being more authentic than those offered by manuscript traditions of ancient authors.[2] The Latin material itself is often nullified by the use of numeral signs[3], which are themselves without linguistic significance.

12.1. Cardinals

12.1.1. 'One'

The Italic forms reflect **oino-*, which is also attested in OIrish *óen*, Gothic *ains*, and, outside the numeral system, Greek *οἰνή* 'the ace at dice'.The Sanskrit and Avestan cardinals exhibit different suffixes, *éka-, aēva-*; cf. Greek *οἶος* (Cyprian dat. sg. *οἰϝωι*), OPers. *aiva-*, both meaning 'alone'. The semantic connection is obvious, and we may perhaps infer that **oi-no-* itself combines a lexical root signifying 'isolation, separateness'[4] with the suffix signifying 'completeness of a state', which is attested in Latin *dignus*, Greek *στυγνός*, Skt. *pūrṇá-* 'full'. This suffix appears in the Latin distributives (see 12.4.1.), whence we may infer that **oino-* was originally the first member of that series.

Latin *oinos*, represented by the accusative *oino*[5] in *CIL* 1.9, > *ūnus* some time before 150 B.C. The occasional spelling *oenus*, e. g. Cic. *Leg.* 3.9, is a spurious archaism, due to analogy with the replacement of earlier /ai/ by /ae/, and is irrelevant to the phonological diachrony of the word.

The normal pronominal declension of *ūnus*, with gen. *-ius*, dat. *-ī* in all genders, seems to be due to the quasi-pronominal use of *ūnus ... alter* 'one ... the other' (cf. *hic ... ille*)[6] and was extended to *alter*, to *ūllus* (see 12.5.1.), where it was no doubt helped by the association with *quisquam* etc., and even to *solus* 'alone'. Substantival case morphs of *ūnus* are sometimes found, e. g. gen. sg. masc. *uni* beside *unius*, Cat. 17.17, 5.3, dat. sg. fem. *unae* beside dat. sg. masc. *uni* Cato *Agr.* 19.1, 58.

unus occurs at all periods of Latin in adjectival function meaning 'alone' and as such is found in the plural, e. g. *unos ex omnibus Sequanos* Caes. *Gal.* 4.16.5. In its rare use as a distributive (for the normal *singuli*, 12.4.1.) it also has plural morphology, e. g. *ex unis geminas mihi conficies nuptias* (Ter. *An.* 674), *una castra* (Caes. *Gal.* 1.74.4).

The development of *unus* as an indefinite article is derived from such usages as *una aderit mulier lepida* (Pl. *Ps.* 948), *sicut unus pater familias ... loquor* (Cic. *De Or.* 1.132), where the numeral meaning is already somewhat attenuated. However, unequivocal examples of articular meaning do not occur till late in the post-classical period, e. g. *insurgunt contra eum in una conspiratione* (Greg. Tur. *H.F.* 2.1), and *propheta unus* for Greek *προφήτης τις* Vulg. *Luc.* 9.19; *una ancilla* for *μία παιδίσκη* Vulg. *Mat.* 26.29, where the latter shows the parallel extension of the numeral in Greek.

Proto-Italic **oino-* > Umbrian acc. sg. *unu* (Ig. 2A6), corresponding to a ns. **uns*, **us*.[7]

12.1.2. 'Two'

12.1.2.1. Of the allophonic variants[8] of the Proto-Indo-European cardinal, **dwōu*, **duwōu* (masc.), **dwoi*, **duwoi* (fem.-ntr)[8a] and **dwōu*, **dwoi*, both are reflected in Vedic *duvā́, dvā́*, Greek *δύο* and *δύω* (Ionic), *δώδεκα*;[9] only the latter in Gothic *twai, twos, twa*, OIrish *dóu dáu, dí*; only the former in Italic[10].

Although Proto-Italic probably had a distribution **duōw* before vowels, **duō* before consonants, cf. Skt. *d(u)vā́u, d(u)vā́*, the former was quickly lost, as in Greek, and the general loss of the dual paradigm in Italic led to extensive morphological remodelling.

Masculine nominative: Latin *duō* < Proto-Italic **duō* rather than **duōu*, which would probably have given **duou* > **duū* > **dū* (cf. *noctū* < **noktōu*, if the reconstruction with the long diphthong is correct, and *nūdiūs* < **nū-diēus*; **g^{w}ōus* > *bōs* is inconclusive for Latin in view of its dialectal origin). *duō*, attested Pl. *Mil.* 1394 (and, no doubt through Homeric influence, Prud. *Perist.* 11.89), > *duŏ*, which is already the regular Plautine form, occurring indeed in the same line as *duō*. The change is partly a generalization of correption before a following vowel, as in Greek *δύο* for *δύω*, but chiefly due to the specifically Latin phenomenon of iambic shortening ◡́ – > ◡́ ◡.[11] *duī* with the regular *o*-stem nominative plural morph is mentioned as an old form[12] by the seventh century grammarian Virgilius (*Epitomae* 6 p. 46.11); it must have been widespread in Vulgar Latin, since it is reflected in mediaeval French and Italian.

A similar normalization occurs in Umbr. *dur* reflecting (*Ig.* 6B50), with the addition of *-s* to **dū* (< **duō* or **duōu*) through the influence of nom. pl. *-s* in nouns, *iiouinur, ikuvinus* 'Iguvines' etc.

Masculine accusative: Latin *duōs* < **duō* + *-s* or *-ns* (cf. *o*-stem acc. pl. *agrōs* < **agrons*). For Umbr. *tuf* see feminine nominative.

Neuter nominative-accusative: Latin *duo* < **duō*, replacing **duoi* reflected in Skt. *dvé*. The distinction made by the imperial grammarian Charisius (*GL* 1.35.24–25) between masc. *duō* and ntr. *duo* is not supported by the extant data. A form *dua*, analogical with *o*-stem nouns and perhaps with *tria*, occurs regularly in the compound *duapondō* 'two pounds in weight', which is censured as a barbarism by Quintilian (1.5.15), and once perhaps in a line of Accius cited by Cicero (*Or.* 156), where the manuscripts vary between *dua* and *duo*. It is not infrequent in imperial inscriptions, e. g. *CIL* 3.138, 4.1990, 5.1102, 13.3487. Umbr. *tuva* (*Ig.* 2A27) shows a similar analogical extension from the substantival paradigm.

Masculine-neuter genitive: The Indo-European form on which Skt. *dváyoḥ*, Old Church Slavonic *dŭvoju*, Greek *δυοῖν* are all ultimately based is remodelled in Latin to the *o*-stem substantival genitive plural morph *-ōm* (cf. Ionic Greek *δυῶν*) to produce *duom* and, with the replacement of *-om* by *-ōrum, duōrum*. Both forms occur in Plautus, e. g. *duom nummum* (*Men.* 542), *duorum adfinium* (*Trin.* 626). From the phrase *duom uirum* (e. g. *CIL* 5.971) was formed a regular compound *duomuir* (*CIL* 1.1225), subsequently *duumuir* (*CIL* 1.992) 'a member of the board of two'; cf. *duouir* (*CIL* 1.788) from *duo uiri.*

Masculine-neuter dative-ablative: **d(u)wōbhōm* (cf. Skt. *dvā́bhyām*) or whatever else the Proto-Indo-European form had been was remodelled to the athematic noun form in *-*bhos*, cf. *ignibus* beside Skt. *agníbhyaḥ* and Latin *duābus* below. Umbr. *tuves* (*Ig*. 3.19), *duir* (*Ig*. 5B10) < **dueis* < **duois*, the regular Italic thematic noun plural morph.

Feminine nominative: PIE **d(u)woi* (or less probably *-ai*), reflected in Skt. *dvé*, Old Church Slavonic *dŭvě*, was replaced in Latin by a form with the *ā*-stem noun nominative plural (originally pronominal) *-ai* : **duai* > *duae*. For the probability that Umbr. *dur* was used, like Greek *δύο*, for both masculine and feminine, see on *tuf* below.

Feminine accusative: PIE **d(u)woi* was replaced by the *ā*-stem acc. pl. *-āns*, to give Latin *duās*. The pattern *duai* : *duās* may have provided a model for *duō* : *duōs*. Umbr. *tuf* (*Ig*. 1B41) < **dū* < **duō* + *-ns* as in the Latin masc. *duos*. It is unlikely to reflect **duāns*, which, on the evidence of *kumiaf* < **gomiāns* 'pregnant', *purka* **purkaf* < **porcāns* 'sow', would have yielded **tuvaf*, **tuva*. Hence *tuf* can be regarded as of common gender.

Feminine genitive Latin *duārum* shows the regular *ā*-stem substantival form.

Feminine dative-ablative. There is no trace in Latin of the extension of the pattern *duae, -ās, -ārum* to produce **duīs*. The regular form *duābus* is probably due to the replacement of the inherited form, perhaps identical with the masculine-neuter, viz *-*ōbhōm* or the like[13] by the inherited *ā*-stem substantival dative-ablative morph *-*ābhos*.[14] In fact **duai* for **duoi*, **duābos* for **duōbos* were probably the starting-points for the new feminine paradigm. Umbr. *tuvere* (Ig. 2A33) viz. *tuver* + *e(n)* 'in', must be taken as feminine, if its concordant noun *kapiřus* has the same gender as the Latin cognate *capis* 'sacrificial bowl'. Phonologically *tuver* could reflect **duais*, but in view of *tuf* above it is better taken as the reflex of **duois* with common gender.

An indeclinable Latin *duo* is attested as nominative feminine in Avien. *Arat*. 1535, as accusative masculine Pl. *Epid*. 373, Verg. *A*. 11.285, *CIL* 6.2027.11, as dative-ablative masculine-neuter Nov. *apud* Non. 500, *CIL* 6.2785, 10.7658.

12.1.2.2. 'Both'

Latin *ambō* 'both' < **ambhō*, cf. Greek *ἄμφω*, with *am-* as in Latin *ambi-*, Oscan *am-fret* 'they surround', Umbr. *an-ferener* 'being surrounded', Greek *ἀμφί* and **bhō* < *-*bhōu*, as in Skt. *u-bháu*, Lith. *a-bù*.

The declension of *ambo* is on the whole parallel to that of *duo*, save that -*ō* is regular. *ambŏ*, no doubt on the analogy of *duŏ*, is not attested before Stat. *Theb.* 6.374, Val. Fl. 7.693. *ambō* occurs as an accusative Pl. *Am.* 470, Ovid *Met.* 7.792, cf. *ambōs* Pl. *Mo.* 330, Ovid *Met.* 10.685. A rare dat.-abl. *ambīs* occurs at *CIL* 6.11687, 9.3358, cf. the regular *ambōbus ambābus*.

In Italic there is no trace of a separate feminine paradigm comparable to that of Old Irish or Sanskrit, and the inherited masculine forms are employed in both genders, as in the Italic *i*-stem nouns and adjectives.

12.1.3. 'Three'

Masculine-feminine nominative: PIE **treyes* (cf. Skt. *tráyaḥ*, Greek *τρεῖς*) > Latin *trēs*, Oscan *trís* (fem., Vetter 1953: no. 81).

The replacement of the *i*-stem nominative by the accusative morph, on analogy with consonant-stems (-*ēs* : -*ēs* :: -*īs* : -*īs*), which is occasionally found in nouns, occurs in nom. *tris, CIL* 3.10190.

Masculine-feminine accusative: PIE **trins* (masc.) > Latin *trīs*, Umbr. *trif* (*Ig.* 1B24), *tref* (*Ig.* 1A7), *tre* (*Ig.* 1A3). The frequency of *tres* as an accusative in imperial Latin is symptomatic of the general tendency for *i*-stem morphs to be replaced by those of consonant-stems.

Neuter nominative-accusative: PIE **trī* (< **tri*$ə_2$) was replaced by **triā*[15] in Italic, with -*ā* from the thematic paradigm,[16] whence Umbr. *triia* (*Ig.* 4.2) and probably *triiuper* (*Ig.* 1B21) from **triā-pert* 'thrice',[17] Latin *tria*. Analogical with *tres* is Latin *trea CIL* 3.13917.

Genitive (all genders): PIE **triyom* (masc.-ntr) > Latin *trium*. From the phrase *trium uirum* (Cato *Or.* 40.3), corresponding to nom. *tres uiri*, a regular compound *triumuir* was formed, e. g. Plin. *Ep.* 2.11.12.

Dative-ablative (all genders): PIE **tribhos* (masc.-ntr.) beside **tribhyos* (whence Skt. *tribhyáḥ*) > Latin *tribus* and Umbr. **trifos* > **trifs* > *tris* (*Ig.* 3.18). Undeclined Latin *tres* for *tribus* occurs *CIL* 8.8637.

12.1.4. 'Four'

For the last of the certainly declined numerals in Indo-European, two theoretical stem-patterns may be established: [a1] **k*^{w}*etwor*- with weak-case forms: [a2] **k*^{w}*etwr̥*, **k*^{w}*etwr̥r*-; [b1] **k*^{w}*tuwor*- with weak-case forms; [b2] **k*^{w}*tuwr̥*, **k*^{w}*tur*.[18] These did not of course constitute actual doublet paradigms, but the distribution of the various patterns within one paradigm is unclear from the reflexes. Thus form [a1] is reflected in Skt. nom.

masc. _catvā́raḥ_ and, generalized through the paradigm, in Gothic _fidwor_ (with _f-_ from _fimf_), Old Church Slavonic _četyre_ (< _-wer-_) and Doric Greek _τέτορες_, [a2] is similarly generalized in Attic Greek _τέσσαρες_, [b2] in Aeolic Greek _πίσυρες_ (*_πισυρας_ < *_k_^{w}_turn̥s_) and _πεσσυρες_ with _πε-_ from *_πεσσορες_, the [a1] form. [b2] seems also to have been generalized in Sanskrit from acc. *_turaḥ_ (< *_k_^{w}_turn̥s_, cf. _turī́yaḥ_ 'fourth' < *_k_^{w}_tur-_) to give *_turbhis_, etc., subsequently remodelled on _catvā́raḥ_ to give _catúraḥ, catúrbhiḥ_.

It may be that Latin _quattuor_ < *_quatworr_ < *_quatwors_ < *_k_^{w}_two-res-_.[19] However, there are no certain reflexes elsewhere[20] of *_k_^{w}_twores_. Indeed we should expect *_k_^{w}_tuwores_ as the inherited [b1] pattern, which is itself difficult to reconcile with the gradation reflected in Doric Greek _τέτορες_, Skt. _catvā́raḥ_. The distribution of [a] and [b] forms might suggest an Indo-European paradigm *_k_^{w}_etwores_, *_k_^{w}_turn̥s_, etc., though it is equally possible to postulate the [a] pattern as original: *_k_^{w}_etwores_, *_k_^{w}_etwr̥rn̥s_, etc., and explain the presence of the [b] forms as due to the influence of the ordinal (see 12.2.4.). Either way the surprising appearance of _a_ in _quattuor_ must be due to the influence of a form reflecting *_k_^{w}_tur-_, whether in the original paradigm or in other parts of the numeral system.

That *_k_^{w}_etwores_, inflected, was indeed the Proto-Italic form is confirmed by the evidence of Oscan. P. Festus 226, after glossing _petoritum_ as _Gallicum uehiculum_, so called _a numero quattuor rotarum_, continues _alii Osce quod hi quoque 'petora' uocant_ (the manuscript reading _i quoque pitora_ is obviously due to misunderstanding after the corruption of _hi_ to _i_). For the dissimilatory loss of _w_ in *_k_^{w}_etwor-_ prior to the change of _k_^{w} to _p_, cf. Doric Greek _τέτορες_. Final _-ā_ is proved for Oscan by _petiru_ (see below) and the fact that the _o_-stem neuter plural was generalized through all substantive paradigms in both Oscan and Umbrian. It is probable that this extension took place in Proto-Italic and the regular Latin substantival ntr pl. _-ă_ is due to a subsequent and specifically Latin change. It follows that Proto-Italic *_k_^{w}_etworā_ rather than *_k_^{w}_etwor(a)_ (< _-rə_$_2$) should be postulated for the neuter plural of this word.

Oscan _petiru_ in _petirupert, petiropert_ (Vetter 1953: no. 2.14, 15) 'four times' < *_petiryu_, with the characteristic Bantian change of _ryV_ > _rV_, cf. _herest_ 'he will wish' beside Umbr. _heriest_. *_petiryu_ with anaptyctic _i_ < *_petriā_, a replacement of *_petorā_ by the influence of *_triā_, cf. Umbr. _triiuper_.[21] Alternatively *_petiriu_ < *_petriā_ (ablative with omission of _-d_ in sandhi) < *_peturiā-_ < *_k_^{w}_eturiā-_, remodelled on the cardinal, < *_k_^{w}_turiā-_ 'group of four' (cf. _triiuper_, 12.1.3.).

The absence of declension in Latin *quattuor* resulted, no doubt, from the loss of inflectional distinctiveness in the nominative following the Proto-Latin change *-*ores* > *-*ors* > *-*orr*. Both trisyllabic and disyllabic values are attested, e. g. Virg. *E.* 5.43, Hor. *S.* 1.3,8 and Enn. *Ann.* 92, Pl. *Mo.* 630 respectively. That the latter, in spite of their earlier date, are significant for the spoken language is suggested not only by the consistent -*tt*-spelling at all periods but also by such epigraphic variants as *quattor* (*CIL* 3.1860.6), *quator* (*CIL* 8.8573, 10.5939), *qator* (*CIL* 8.8789), which all presuppose earlier *quattwor* (cf. *quattbor* in *CIL* 3. p. 805) and also indicate the transitional stages to the Romance reflexes.

12.1.5. 'Five'

PIE **penkʷe* > Proto-Italic **kʷenkʷe* by anticipatory assimilation, influenced also no doubt by **kʷetwores*. For assimilation between successive numerals, cf. Old Church Slavonic *devętĭ* after *desętĭ*, Gothic *fidwor* 'four' after *fimf* 'five' (which itself shows the assimilatory replacement of Proto-Gmc. -*xʷe* by -*fe* in the final syllable).

**kʷenkʷe* > Oscan-Umbrian **kʷonkʷe* > **pompe* (cf. 12.2.5. and 12.5.5.).[22] For Latin **quinque*, cf. the change *eŋ* to *iŋ* in *lingua, inquit*, etc. *quīnque*, with *ī* attested in *quInque* (*CIL* 1.988, etc.), and required by the Romance reflexes, is due to ord. *quīntus* (12.2.5.). Dissimilation produced *cinque* (*CIL* 6.17508, 10.5939), which is the direct starting-point for the Romance forms. *quique* is occasionally found, e. g. *CIL* 6.25962, 10.4407.

12.1.6. 'Six'

Of the Indo-European forms reconstructed for this numeral, original **weks*, reflected in Arm *veç*, and secondary **sweks* and **seks*, with *s*- from **septm̥*,[23] reflected in Welsh *chwech* and Gothic *saíhs* respectively, only the last can be established for Proto-Italic. **sweks* would have given Latin **sox*, not *sex*, cf. *socer* < **swekuro*-. An isolated *six* occurs *CIL* 7.80. For Oscan **sehs*, see 12.5.6.

12.1.7. 'Seven'

PIE **septm̥* can be postulated on the basis of Latin *septem*. Cognates with -*n* are inconclusive, e. g. Arm. *ewtʻn*, OIrish *secht n*-, which could reflect either -*m̥* or -*n̥*, Gothic *sibun* with -*n* from the ordinal **sibunda* after the Proto-Germanic loss of _*-m_ and _*-n_. Although the possibility _septem_ < _*septen_ < _*septn̥_ is supported by the parallel replacement of the final nasal in _nouem_ < _*nouen_ < _*newn̥_, the originality of _-m_ here is confirmed by the contrast between the corresponding ordinals _septimus_ and _nonus_ (12.2.7., 12.2.9.). _septe_, attested _CIL_ 2.4331, 8.1040, 10.4407, > _*sette_, whence the Romance forms.

12.1.8. 'Eight'

PIE _*oktōu_ (the dual of a complex reflecting _*ə$_3$ek-_, which is attested in Av. _ašti_ 'palm') > OInd. _aṣṭáu, aṣṭā́_, declined, and Gothic _ahtau_, Latin _octō_, both indeclinable. _octŏ_ Manil. 5.340, Mart. 2.57,8, is probably due to _duŏ_ (cf. _ambŏ_ in 12.1.2.2.), though by Martial's time _-ŏ_ for _-ō_ was beginning to appear even in non-iambic words, cf. _respondētŏ_ Mart. 3.4.7, _estŏ_ Juv. 8.79.

12.1.9. 'Nine'

Of the two Indo-European variants _*newn̥, *enwn̥_ (< _*ə$_1$n-ew-n̥_, _*ə$_1$en-w-n̥_)[24] reflected in Skt. _náva_, Arm. _inn_ respectively, only the former has Italic reflexes: Latin _neuen_, on an early inscription from Ardea[25] > _nouem_, with _-m_ from _decem_. Imperial Latin shows rare _nouim_, e. g. _CIL_ 6.25058, by analogy with _decim_ (see 12.1.10.) and _noue, CIL_ 6.11590, 8.8573 (cf. _nobe, CIL_ 5.1652), which is the starting-point for the Romance forms.

12.1.10. 'Ten'

PIE _*dekm̥_, with _-m̥_ not _-n̥_, is confirmed by the contrast between the Latin ordinals _decimus_ and _nonus_ and by the retention of _m_ in Lith. _dẽšimt_,[26] ord. _dešim̃tas_ 'ninth'. The Latin reflex is _decem_, whence _decim, CIL_ 12.942, with _-i-_ from _decimus_, and _dece, CIL_ 8.1040, which is the starting-point for the Romance forms. For Umbr. _*desem_ see 12.1.11.

12.1.11. 'Eleven' to 'nineteen'

12.1.11.1. In Latin 'eleven' to 'seventeen' are all indeclinable compounds of 'one', 'two', etc. and 'ten', which appears as _-decim_. By normal vowel weakening _*-decem_ > _*-dicem_, cf. _auspicem_ < _*auispecem_ acc. sg. to _auspex_. The metathesis must have been due to the combined pressure of _decem_ and the ordinals, viz. _decimus : decem :: undecimus : undecim_ in place of **undicimus* : **undicem* (cf. *decim*, 12.1.10.). The inclusion of the ordinal in this analogical process[27] would make the change relatively recent, since *decumus* was still the regular spelling in the middle of the first century B.C. and comparable *-imus* forms are not attested at all before the last quarter of the second century, e. g. *infimo* beside *proxumo* (*CIL* 1.584). Although there is apparently no epigraphic evidence for the numerals 'eleven' to 'seventeen' for the relevant period, it is remarkable that none of the grammarians of the Empire seem to have known **undicem*, etc., if these forms were so recent.

All these are dvandva compounds. Thus Latin **oinos-decem* > **oins-dicem* > **ūndicem* > *undecim* which, with the loss of final *-m*, e. g. *undeci* (*CIL* 5.1666), is the form reflected in Romance. *duodecim* appears as *duodecem* (*CIL* 5.6214); *du̯odecim* (Pl. *Epid.* 675), whence *dodece* (*CIL* 12.7645), which is the starting-point for the Romance forms. **trēs-decem* > *trēdecim* or *trĕdecim* with *-ĕ-* by the influence of *duŏdecim* and *trĕcenti*. *quattuordecim* is clear. **quīnque-decem* > *quīndecim*, whence *quindeci* (*CIL* 6.9162), which is reflected in Romance, as is *sedeci* (*CIL* 6.7260) (cf. *sedece* (*CIL* 10.3148)) < *sēdecim* < **sex-decem*. *septemdecim* and *septendecim* are both well attested.

The Umbrian acc. *desenduf* (*Ig.* 7B2) < **dekem duōns*, which is possibly symptomatic of the Umbrian ordering of the two components throughout the teens. However, the Latin components often occur as free forms, e. g. *decem et una* (*CIL* 3 p. 864.5), *decem trisque* (Manil. 4.452), *quinque decemque* (Mart. 14.192.2), *decem et quinque* (*CIL* 3 p. 855.6), *decem septe* (*CIL* 3.2283). The last of these represents a type that became general for the later teens in Vulgar Latin, cf. Ital. *sedici* but *diciasette*, Fr. *seize* but *dix-sept*, Span. *quinze* but *diez y seis*.

12.1.11.2. The formation of Latin *duo dē uīgintī* 'eighteen' seems to be extended from *undēuīgintī* 'nineteen' (cf. OEngl. *twā lǣs twentiġ* from *ān lǣs twentiġ*), which may have been an inherited variant, if Skt. *ekonaviṃśati-* beside *návadaśa* is older than its attestation suggests. The pattern occurs occasionally elsewhere in the cardinal series, e. g. *undeoctoginta* 'seventy-nine' (Hor. *S.* 2.3.117–8). The variants *decem et octo* (Caes. *Gal.* 4.19.4) and *dece et octo* (*CIL* 9.2272), *decem ac nouem* (Caes. *Gal.* 2.4.9), *decem nouem* (Caes. *Gal.* 1.8.1; *CIL* 5.4370), are the basis of the Romance exponents.

12.1.12. 'Twenty'

We may conjecture two types of formation in Indo-European: Type I **dwi-dkm̥t-*,[28] a neuter collective of 'ten', with *t*-suffix, preceded by the compositional form of the numeral 'two', viz. 'a double decad'; type II the dual of the same collective, i. e. **dkm̥ti*, or, less likely in the first place at least, **dkm̥tī*,[29] preceded optionally by the free form **d(u)woi*,[30] viz. 'two decads'.

Type I **dwidkm̥t-* > **widkm̥t-* with dissimilatory loss of initial *d-* > **wīkm̥t-*[31] with compensatory lengthening from the reduction of the cluster *-dk-*. This is reflected, with remodelling to the animate declensions, in OIrish *fiche* 'twenty' (< **wĭ-*, perhaps influenced by **dwi-*, but compare the short vowel reflected in the Old Irish tens after *trícho* 'thirty', Greek *ἰκάς, εἰκάς* (< **e-wīk-ad-*, perhaps transferred from the *t*-suffix type, cf. 12.1.10.).

The simple Type II with **dkm̥ti* appears not to be directly reflected, though the lexical pattern 'two decads' is preserved in Gothic *twai tigjus*, OCS *dŭva desęti*, with the second member remodelled to **dekm̥t-*. Latin *ueiginti* (*CIL* 1.1570.6) might be from PIE **woi-*, reflecting **dwoi-*, but this would presuppose that the loss of *d-* here, as in type I, had already taken place in Proto-Indo-European; the Latin example is in any event too late to prove an authentic diphthong, as are Laconian Greek *βείκατι* Heraclean Greek *ϝείκατι* beside general West Greek and Thessalian *ϝῑκατι*.[32]

A conflation of the two types, **wīkm̥t-* and **dkm̥ti*, to give **wīkm̥ti*, lit. 'two double decads', is directly reflected in Greek *ϝῑκατι*, Av. *vīsaiti*. Skt. *viṃśatí*, with unexplained *-ṃ-*, has been attracted into an *i*-stem substantival paradigm. The fact that Greek certainly shows reflexes of both types (*εἰκάς, ϝῑκατι*, etc.) supports the hypothesis that both coexisted in Indo-European and were not simply dialectal variants.

Latin **uikentī* reflects this conflated form, with the final long vowel either arising in Latin itself by analogy with the pattern of *trī-gintā* etc. or inherited from a possible dialectal innovation **wīkm̥tī* within Proto-Indo-European. The latter alternative is perhaps supported by the fact that the long vowel seems also to be required for British **wikantī*, reflected in OWelsh *uceint*, Middle Bret. *ugent*, for which no obvious analogy can be cited.[33] **uīkentī* > *uīgintī*, with *-g-*, as in *triginta*, from *quadraginta* and *septuaginta* and the assimilation of *-e-* to the surrounding *i*-vowels (cf. the normal phonological development *m̥* > *n̥* > *en* in *ducenti* < **dukm̥t-*). *βειεντι* (Marini, *Papiri diplomatici* 122.82 [sixth century]), *uinti* (*CIL* 6.19007.4, 8.8573), are probably due to palatalization viz. [g] > [ʒ] > [j] > Ø.[34] Thus *uīginti* > *uiịnti* > *uịnti*, the starting-point for the Italian, French and Provençal formations. Span. *veinte* presupposes *uịinti*, with the shift of accent required for the later decads generally in Romance (see 12.1.13.1., 12.1.13.2.).

12.1.13. 'Thirty' to 'ninety'

12.1.13.0. General

Corresponding to 'twenty' we may postulate two types of formation in Indo-European for 'thirty' to 'ninety'.[35] Type I, a neuter collective with the prefixed compositional form of the units, **tridkm̥t* 'triple ten', **kʷetwr̥-dkm̥t* 'quadruple ten', etc. whence **trikm̥t*, **kʷetwr̥̄km̥t-*, etc., with simplification of the cluster *dk* and compensatory lengthening of the preceding vocalic. Type II, a phrase **triə₂ dkomtə₂* 'three tens', **kʷetworə₂ dkomtə₂* 'four tens', etc., with the full-grade suffix of **dkm̥t-*, etc., whence either (a) **triyəkontə*,[36] **kʷetworəkontə*, etc., or (b) **trīkontə*, **kʷet-worəkontə*, etc., forming new compounds. It is assumed here that both modes of formation were available in Proto-Indo-European for the entire decadic series from 'twenty' to 'ninety', but they need not of course have been equally operational as free variants throughout the series. Indeed it is likely that for each decad there was a single preferred form, the preferences differing from dialect to dialect in Indo-European, and that what is reflected in the attested data is the generalization of the predominant pattern belonging to that particular linguistic area.

Type I is represented by OIrish *trícho, cethorcho* etc. with the introduction of the full grade (**kont-*) accompanying the shift of gender. The shortening of the vocalic reflected in *cethorho* (< **kʷetru-*[37] < **kʷetwr̥-* < **kʷetwr̥̄-*) is due to the influence of the ordinary form of the compositional, cf. Middle Bret. *tregont* < **trĭ-*.

Type II is represented by OCS *tri desęti, četyri desęti*; Gothic *þreis tigjus, fidwor tigjus*, etc., with the second member remodelled to the reflex of **dekm̥(t)*.

Forms representing both types are found in Av. *θrisą̊s* and *θrisatəm, pančāsatəm* (type I), with thematic declension from *satəm*, beside *čaθwarəsatəm* < **kʷtwr̥̄-kn̥t-* (or **kʷetwr̥ə-*), a conflation of types I and II, cf. Skt. *triṃśát-, pañcāśát-* beside *catvāriṃśát-*, with *ṃ* as in *viṃśatí* and animate gender.

Similarly Greek has *τριᾱ́κοντα* (indeclinable, as all the Greek decads) < **tria konta* (type IIa) or less probably **trikonta* (type IIb), with *-ā-* by analogy with *τετρώκοντα*, **τετρᾱ́κοντα* and *πεντήκοντα*; also *τριᾱκάς* reflecting type I (see 12.1.12. on *εἰκάς*) with similar intrusion of *-ā-*. Beside East Greek *τεσσαράκοντα* (type IIa), West Greek *τετρώκοντα* reflects a conflation of **τετρωκάς* (type I) and *τεσσαράκοντα*. Once again the indications are that both types were inherited from Proto-Indo-European, where they may be assumed to have coexisted in free variation rather than as dialectally or diachronically distinct formations.

12.1.13.1. 'Thirty'

Latin *trīgintā* may reflect either type. **trīkm̥t-* (type I) > **trīkent-* with the subsequent addition of the pluralising *-ā*. Alternatively **triə kontə* (type II) > **trīkonta* or **trīkont* (depending on what the Proto-Italic reflex of *-*ə* was – see note 15), if this was not the inherited IIb form, > **trīkentā* with *-kent-* by analogy with **uīkenti* and the replacement of *-a* by *-ā*, > **trīgentā*, with *-g-* from *quadraginta* or *septuaginta*, as in the other decads, > *trīgintā* with *-i-* from *uiginti*.

trīgintă is occasionally guaranteed by the metre in later Latin, e. g. *Anth. Lat.* (Riese) no. 28.5, Iuvenc. 4.639. The shift of accent, *tríginta* for *trigínta*, reported by Consentius (*GL* 5.392.4), is probably to be assumed before the change to *trienta* found *CIL* 12.5399, which is clearly parallel to *uiginti* > *uinti* (12.1.12.), with the further dissimilation of [íi] to [íe].[38] Dissyllabic *trinta* or *trenta* on *CIL* 11.711, implies the origin of It. *trenta* etc.

12.1.13.2. 'Forty'

Latin *quadrāginta* is difficult. It may be derived in two ways. Firstly **kʷetwr̥km̥t-* (type I) > **kʷetwr̥gn̥t-* by assimilation of *k* to the surrounding sonants. This would provide a starting-point for the spread of *g* through the decads. **kʷetwr̥gn̥t-* > **kʷedrāgent-* by simplification of the emergent consonant-cluster in *-twrā* through the loss of [w] and the transfer of its resonance to the preceding stop.[39] *quadrāgintā* with *qua-* from *quattuor* (see 12.1.4., 12.5.4.), the addition of the pluralising *-ā* and the development to *-gintā* as in *triginta* (12.1.13.1.). Alternatively **kʷetwr̥kont*, the conflation of types I and II reflected in West Greek, > **kʷedrākentā*, with subsequent introduction of *-g-* from the ordinal (12.2.4.) and the remainder of the development as outlined above. *quadracinta* (*CIL* 8.8642, 10.5939), is presumably not an archaic survival, but due to the analogy of *centum*.

A rare *quadragintă* is guaranteed by the metre in Iuvenc. 2.170. An assimilatory change *dr* > *rr* is indicated by *quaraginta* (*CIL* 13.11032), *qaragita* (*CIL* 8.12200). *qarranta* (*CIL* 13.7645) shows a change [a:gi] > [a:ʒi] > [a:ji] > [a:i] > [a:], with the initial stages parallel to *uinti, trienta* and the final loss of [i] perhaps influenced by the pattern of *trienta*. It is the starting-point for the Romance forms.

12.1.13.3. 'Fifty'

Latin *quinquāgintā* may reflect either type of Indo-European formation. **penk^{w}ēkn̥t* (type I) > **k^{w}enk^{w}ēkentā*, with the addition of pluralising *-ā*, > *quīnquāgintā*, with *-ā-* for *-ē-* from *quadraginta*, the change of *-kent-* to *-gint-* by analogy with the other decads and *ī* in the first syllable from *quīnque*. Alternatively, from type II, either a) **penk^{w}e kontə* > **k^{w}en-k^{w}ekont(a)*, or b) **penk^{w}ēkontə*, > reflected in Greek πεντήκοντα, **k^{w}en-k^{w}ēkont(a)*, whence *quīnquāgintā* with *-ā-* for *-ē-* from *quadrāginta* and the replacement of *-kont(a)* by *-gintā* as in the other decads generally (see 12.1.13.1.).

quinquacinta (*CIL* 3.2234, 11.1411) is again by analogy with *centum*, not an archaic survival. *cinquaginta* (*CIL* 10.5939) shows the dissimilation of initial *qu-* presupposed by the Romance reflexes. *quinquagenta* (*CIL* 12.482) shows the influence of the 'hundreds'.

12.1.13.4. 'Sixty'

Latin *sexāgintā* may reflect the type I formation **sekskn̥t-*, cf. OIrish *sesco* < **swekskont*, with the full grade accompanying the shift to masculine gender. For the development from *-kn̥t-* to *-gintā*, see 12.1.13.1. Alternatively the starting-point may be **seks kontə* (type II), which is ultimately reflected in Gothic *saíhs tigjus*, with the subsequent development from **kontə* to *-gintā* as outlined also in 12.1.13.1. The normal Latin resultant would have been **sēgintā* with **sēg-* from **seksg-*, cf. *sēdecim*. The insertion of *-ā-* to give *seksāg-* is again by analogy with *quadrāgintā*.[40]

12.1.13.5. 'Seventy'

Latin *septuāgintā* may reflect type I: **septm̥̄kn̥t-* > **septm̥̄gn̥t-*, which, with its assimilation of *k* to the surrounding resonants would provide another plausible starting-point for the spread of *-g-* throughout the decads, > **septmāgent-*, with subsequent development to *-gintā* as outlined in 12.1.13.1. **septm̥ kontə* (type IIa) would normally have produced Latin **septingintā*, unless an early intrusion of *-ā-* from the preceding decads is envisaged, to give **septm̥māk ont(a)* or the like. But that would presuppose that the change *r̥̄* > *rā*, on which the spread of *-ā-* would have to depend, preceded that of *m̥* > *em*, which, though not impossible, may seem a little arbitrary. The compound form, type IIb, **septm̥̄kontə* would, however, be reflected as **septmākont(a)*, with subsequent development to *-kenta* as outlined in 12.1.13.1. and the introduction of *-g-* from *septingenti* or the ordinal (see 12.2.12.). On the whole the first derivation proposed, from type I, seems the more probable.[41] Thereafter **septmā-*[42] > **septumā-* > **septuwā-*.[43] The widely-held view[44] that *septuaginta* is remodelled on *octuaginta*, reflecting an inherited **okto-uākont*, cf. Greek *ὀγδοήκοντα*, is unacceptable in view of the late attestation of *octuaginta* (12.1.13.6.).

The isolated *septuazinta*[45] shows the palatalization assumed for the transitional stages to *uinti, trienta, qarranta*.

12.1.13.6. 'Eighty'

Latin *octōgintā* may reflect either **oktōk̥n̥t-* (type I) or **oktōu kontə* (type II), > **oktō(u)kont(a)*, with the development to *-gintā* in either case as in 12.1.13.1., save that here *-g-* could have been introduced directly from *septuaginta* or *nonaginta*.

octaginta (*CIL* 3.810, 7.39, 50, etc.) shows *-ā-* from the same source, and a further analogical extension from *septuaginta* produced the late *octuaginta*,[46] attested Greg. Tur. *H. F.* 5,15 and in some manuscripts of classical authors, e. g. Colum. 3.3.9, Gell. 3.10.8.

12.1.13.7. 'Ninety'

Latin *nōnāgintā* may be derived from either type. **new̥n̥k̥n̥t-* (type I), where the surrounding resonants would again provide favourable conditions for the change *k* > *g*, > **neunāgent-* > *nōnāgintā*, with the change of *neun-* to *nōn-* as in *nonus* (12.2.9.), and of *-gent-* to *-gintā* as in *quadraginta, septuaginta*. Alternatively, of the type II formations we have a choice between a) **newn̥ kontə* > **nōnginta*, with the development from *-kont(a)* to *-gintā* as in 12.1.13.1. and the insertion of *-ā-* from the decads before 'eighty'; b) **new̥n̥kontə* > **neunākont(a)* with the development to *-gintā* again as in 12.1.13.1.

nonanta (*CIL* 8.27985) presupposes the same development as *qarranta*.

12.1.13.8. Summary

The correspondence between the sequence **septum-ā-, octu-ā-, non-ā-* and Greek *ἑβδομ-η-, ὀγδο-η-, ἐνεν-η-*, which on the above analysis is purely coincidental, has been used to support the view that these three forms are in both languages based on a compound of the ordinal unit and the collective decad, as if from, for instance, **septm̥mom dkm̥t-*, **oktowom dkm̥t-*, **neunom* or **enwn̥nom dkm̥t-*, with subsequent remodelling at least in Greek to type II.[47] However, Latin *octoginta* has strong chronological priority over *octuaginta*, there are no clear parallels for such a pattern even in the great variety of decad-formations attested outside the Latin and Greek forms in question, and the latter can all be satisfactorily explained without recourse to this hypothesis.[48]

To sum up the Latin decads: (i) *uiginti* clearly reflects an inherited conflation of the two PIE types postulated. (ii) *quadraginta* certainly, *triginta, septuaginta, nonaginta* probably, reflect a remodelling of Type I; (iii) the remainder can be equally well derived from either Type.

12.1.14. 'Twenty-one', etc.

Combinations of 'twenty plus unit' are denoted by such patterns as *sex et uiginti* (*CIL* 5.4091), *(ui)ginti et duo* (*CIL* 5.8635), and later *uiginti quattuor* (e. g. Aur. Vict. *Vir. Illustr.* 49.7). Similarly for the rest of the decads, e. g. *quinque et triginta* (*CIL* 6.909), *duo et octoginta* (Aug. *R. G.* 20.4), *triginta et quinque* (ibid. 21.3), *quinquaginta septem* (Tac. *Hist.* 1.48).

12.1.15. 'Hundreds'

12.1.15.0. 'One hundred'

PIE **kn̥tom* < **dkm̥tom* may be analysed in one of two ways. First as the genitive plural of the neuter collective noun **dkm̥t-* postulated above for the decads. The gradation pattern *-km̥t-* (dual), *-komt-* (nom.-acc. pl.), *-km̥t-* (gen. pl.) would correspond to the Sanskrit ntr. *-nt*-paradigm: *adát* 'eating' (nom.-acc. sg.), *adatī́* (nom.-acc. dual), *adánti* (nom.-acc. pl.), *adatā́m* (gen. pl.). **dkm̥tom* would then be elliptical for **dkm̥t dkm̥tom* 'a decad of decads' (cf. Szemerényi 1960: 139 – 140), the terminal member of a series of which the lexico-syntactic pattern is reflected either in OCS *pętĭ desętŭ* 'a pentad of decads' and the elliptical Skt. *ṣaṣṭí-* 'a hexad of decads' and in Gothic *sibuntēhund* 'a decad of sevens'.

Alternatively **dkm̥tom* could be the neuter of a quasi-ordinal form, again used elliptically for **dkm̥t dkm̥tom* 'tenth ten'.[49] That the suffix *-to-* was already a productive ordinal formant at this date in PIE is very doubtful (see 12.2.10.), as is the alternative ordinal analysis **dkm̥t-o-*, viz a thematic derivative from the collective form.[50] However, the isolated use of adjectival *-to-* signifying the limiting point in a series[51] 'that which marks the limit of decads' might well have predated, and in fact provided one of the starting-points for, its use as an ordinal in place of the simple thematic suffix.

Whatever the original analysis, **kn̥tom* had come to be regarded already in Proto-Indo-European as a thematic neuter singular.[52]

Latin *centum* is its normal phonological reflex. It is used as an invariable adjective, e. g. *centum uiri, centum oppida*, cf. Skt. *śatám púraḥ* 'a hundred castles' beside *śatám purā́m*. As in other languages, it is sometimes used for an indefinitely large number, e. g. *centum puer artium* (Hor. *C.* 4.1.15).

12.1.15. 'Hundreds'

Corresponding to the decads, we may postulate for the hundreds two separate formations for Proto-Indo-European: type I **dwi-kn̥tom* 'double hundred', **tri-kn̥tom* 'triple hundred' etc. In contrast to the decads there is no trace of compensatory lengthening of the vowel in the compositional unit form, which suggests that the compound was based, not on the older form PIE **dkm̥tom* but on its later reflex **kn̥tom*. Type II **d(u)woi kn̥toi* 'two hundreds' **triyə kn̥tā* 'three hundreds' etc., with the thematic neuter paradigm appropriate to the more recent substantival status of **kn̥tom* in Proto-Indo-European.

Type I is represented in Greek, e. g. Doric *τετρακάτιοι*, Attic *τετρακόσιοι* with *-o-* from *τεσσαράκοντα*,[53] an adjectival derivative in *-yo-* of **k^w^etwr̥-kn̥to-* (cf. **k^w^etwr̥̄-* in Doric *τετρώκοντα*, 12.1.13.2.). Type II is reflected in Av. *duye saite, tišəro sata*, Old Church Slavonic *dŭvě sŭtě, tri sŭta*; Gothic *twa hunda, þrija hunda*, Middle Irish *dá cét, trí chét*. Both types are attested in Skt. *dviśatám* and *dvé śaté, triśatám* and *trī́ṇi śatā́ni*, and perhaps in Latin, though the majority of forms here are best treated as remodelled reflexes of type I, declined in the *o/ā*-stem adjectival paradigm.

12.1.15.2. 'Two hundred'

Latin *ducentī* reflects either **dwi-kn̥to-* + plural morphs,[54] with the replacement of **dwi-* (> Latin *bi-*) by *du-* from the cardinal (cf. compositional *du-* in 12.5.2.) or less probably a contamination of this form by **duō kentā*, the remodelled reflex of **duwoi kn̥toi*. *ducentum* in the phrases *milia dūcentum* and *centum ac dūcentum ... milia* (Lucil. 555,

1051–1052) may be an archaic survival (with *ū* for *ŭ*) of the singular type I, but is just as likely to be on analogy with *centum. bis centum* occurs as a variant exponent, e. g. Ovid, *Met.* 5.208.

12.1.15.3. 'Three hundred'

Latin *trecentī* shows the intrusion into **tri-kn̥to-* of the *e* from the cardinal *trēs*, shortened by the influence either of the *tri-* which it replaced or of *du-* in the preceding hundred. The Romance reflexes indicate Vulgar Latin *trē-*. The variant exponent *ter centum* occurs, e. g. Verg. *A.* 1.272.

12.1.15.4. 'Four hundred'

Latin *quadringentī* shows the intrusion of *-in-* from *quīngentī, septingentī*. The earlier form may have had *quadru-*,[55] but this cannot be directly related to any of the possible reconstructions (cf. § 12.5.4.). The most likely one, type I **kʷetwr̥kn̥to-* (cf. the initial component of Greek *τε-τρακάτιοι* Av. *čaθwarəsat-* 'forty') might yield a) **quatrukento-*, with metathesis of *wr̥* and the spread of *a* from *quattuor*,[56] > **quadrukento-* > *quadringentī* by the successive analogical pressures of *quadraginta* and *quīngentī*, or b) **kʷetwr̥gn̥to-*, with assimilation of *k* to the surrounding resonants, > **quetworgento-*, which would surely have been remodelled to **quattuorgenti*, or c) **kʷedr̥gn̥to-*, with loss of *w* and transfer of its resonance to the preceding dental stop, whence **quedorgento-*. This with the successive analogies of *quattuor, quadraginta* and *quingenti* as in a) above, would yield the required reflex. None of these analyses seems decisive and the matter remains obscure. Dative-ablative *quadragentis* is found *CIL* 3. p. 811.40.

12.1.15.5. Five hundred'

Latin *quīngentī* may reflect either type I **penkʷekn̥tom*, pluralised, or type II **penkʷe kn̥tā*, remodelled to adjectival declension. Either way **penkʷ-ekn̥t-* > **quenquekent-* > **quenkent-* > **quīncent-* (cf. 12.1.5.). *-gent-* may have resulted either from dissimilation within **quenquekent-* or by analogy either with *quadringenti*, if this already had *-g-*, or with *septin-genti*; for *-ncV-* does not normally yield *-ngV-* in Latin. According to P. Festus p. 254M (338Th.) *"quincentum" et producta prima syllaba et per c litteram usurpant antiqui, quod postea leuius uisum est ita ut nunc dicimus pronuntiari.* If the latter part of this statement is not just an inference from the use of *C* for /g/ which was still common in the third century B.C. and survived sporadically thereafter, then the replacement of *quincent-* by *quingent-* must be relatively recent and therefore presumably analogical. The implication of the first part seems to be that *quīn-*, with *ī* by analogy with *quīnque*, was obsolete in Festus' time, which is hard to reconcile with the Romance reflexes. The invariable *quingentum* attested Gell. 16.10.10: *mille quingentum aeris* is more likely to be by analogy than by archaizing retention of an original type I form.

12.1.15.6. 'Six hundred'

Latin *sescentī* reflects either a pluralized version of type I **seks-kn̥tom* or the adjectivalized version of type II **seks kn̥tā*. In *sescentum ac mille* (Lucil. 1053), *sescentum* may be an archaic survival of the pure type I but is more likely an ad hoc analogical singular, cf. *sescenta* (ntr pl.), Pl. *Au.* 320.

12.1.15.7. 'Seven hundred'

Latin *septingentī* reflects **septn̥-kn̥tom* (type I) or **septm̥ kn̥tā* (type II), remodelled to adjectival declension with the assimilation of *k* to the surrounding resonants. Dative-ablative *septigentis* occurs *CIL* 3 p. 809.51, probably influenced by the compositional *septi-* (12.5.7.).

12.1.15.8. 'Eight hundred'

Latin **oktōkent-*, reflecting **oktō(u)kn̥t-* from either Proto-Indo-European type has been remodelled by analogy with *septingentī* to give *octingentī*.

12.1.15.9. 'Nine hundred'

**newn̥kn̥t-* from either PIE type again provides a plausible environment for the voicing of *k*,[57] whence **newngn̥t-* > **noungent-* > Latin *nōngentī* with *ō* for *ou* as in *nōnus* (12.2.9.). The imperial forms *nongentum* (*CIL* 4.1136), *noncentos* (Caper *GL* 7.104.1), are too late to be archaic survivals and represent differing analogical influences from *centum*. The spread of *-in-* from *septingenti* is further illustrated by *noningenti* reported by Priscian (*GL* 3.413.1).

12.1.15.10. Combinations

Typical combinations of hundreds with lower numerals are *centum triginta* (Cic. *Ver.* 2.119); *trecentos septem* (Liv. 7.15.10); *quinquaginta et ducenta, trecentis et uiginti* (Aug. *R. G.* 15.1,2).

12.1.16. Thousands

12.1.16.1. 'One thousand'

Latin *mīlle* is normally, like *centum*, an invariable adjective in the singular; the plural *mīlia, mīllia* is normally declined as a neuter noun and constructed with a dependent genitive. Usages like *mille annorum* (Pl. *Mil.* 1079), *hominum mille* (Cic. *Mil.* 53), *mille passuum* (Caes. *Gal.* 6.7.4), though not infrequent, tend to disappear in the classical and post-classical language. It is merely question-begging to explain them by analogy with the construction of *milia*, and in view of the rare and exclusively early evidence for a declined singular form constructed with a genitive, e. g. *milli nummum ... uno, milli passum*, cited from Lucilius by Gellius (1.16.10), it is probable that *mille*, like *milia*, was originally a neuter *i*-stem and owes its invariable adjectival status to the influence of *centum*.

The earlier Latin form of *mille*, apart from the probable final -*ĭ* is uncertain. *meilia* (*CIL* 1.638) is too late (132 B.C.) to guarantee the authenticity of the diphthong, cf. *miliarios* 'milestones' on the same inscription. Similarly obscure is the significance of the *l*/*ll* variation; *mille* is the regular form in the singular, and, although *millia*, etc. are often found, e. g. Aug. *R. G.* 3.3, *CIL* 3.3200, 5.2482, *milia*, etc. are the more frequent, e. g. *CIL* 3.3198, 5.121; and Pliny's doctrine that *in numero plurali unum i ponere debemus* is cited with approval by later grammarians, e. g. Pompeius (*GL* 5.185.16).

Attempts have been made to relate the Latin forms to PIE *_ghes-lo-_, which is thought to be represented by Skt. *sahásra-*, Av. *hazaŋra-*, reflecting *_sm̥-gʰ̣eslo-_, and Greek (Lesb.) *χέλλιοι*, (Lac.) *χηλιοι*, (Ion.) *χέιλιοι*, (Att.) *χῑλιοι*, reflecting *_gheslyo-_.[58] Thus one might establish a PIE *_smiə_$_2$ _ghsliə_$_2$ 'one thousand', whence *_smīghslī_[59] > Latin *_mīl(l)ī_, with the replacement of the anomalous nom. sg. fem. -*ī* by the regular *i*-stem neuter -*i*[60] to form a neuter noun *_mīl(l)ĭ_ (> *mīlle*) and the innovation of a full plural paradigm *mīl(l)ia* etc.[61]

The chief stumbling-block in all this is the postulation of a free form *_smī_ to provide the first element of a compound. There is no other evidence for this unit form in Italic; Greek, which uniquely exhibits reflexes of both **gheslyo-* and **smiə₂* in *χέλλιοι* etc. and *μία*, does not have them in combination; Skt. *sahásra-*, if it does reflect **sm̥-gheslo-*, provides evidence only for the compositional form of the *sem* root in this connection. Indeed the true Latin cognate to the Old Indian form on this analysis would be **singēlum*. When so much remains in doubt, it is best to record a verdict of 'etymology unknown' on *mīlle*, as on *mīles* 'soldier', with which the ancients, e. g. Var. *L.* 5.89, Lyd. *Mens.* 4.72, perhaps rightly connected it.

12.1.16.2. Combinations

Of the larger numerals, the following are typical samples: *pedes quattuor millia et octingentos* (Colum. 5.1.10) '4,800 feet', *capita centum quattuor milia septingenta quattuordecim* (Liv. 3.3.9) '104,714 persons', *capitum quadragiens centum millia et n[onge]nta triginta et septem millia* (Aug. *R. G.* 8.4) '4,937,000 persons'. The genitive construction of the counted noun is in fact much the more frequent.

12.2. Ordinals

12.2.1. 'First'

No single Common Italic form can be established. The extant data all reveal roots signifying 'before' with suffixes used elsewhere in Italic for grades of adjectival comparison.

Latin *prior* 'first of two' < **pri-yos-*, with the regular Latin comparative suffix and a root meaning 'before', attested in adv. *pri*, which according to P. Festus 252.25 *antiqui pro 'prae' dixerunt*, and in Greek *πρίν*.

Latin *prīmus*, Paelignian nom. sg. fem. *prismu* < **pri-is-mo-* with the same root and a superlative suffix.[62]

For Umbr. **prōmo-*, see 12.3.1.

12.2.2. 'Second'

No single Common Italic form can be established. Proto-Italic **alitero-* 'the second of two' has the root **ali-* 'some' (**ə₂el-i-*) attested in Latin *aliquis*, Greek *ἄλλος* (< **alyo-* viz. **ali-o-*), OIrish *aile* 'other, second', and the adversative suffix *-tero-* reflected in Latin *uter* 'which of two?',

Gothic *anþar* 'other', Lith. *añtras* 'second', Greek *ἕτερος*. From it are derived Oscan acc. sg. fem. *alttram* (Vetter 1953: no. 1B 27), loc. sg. masc. ntr *alttrei* (ibid. no. 147.17), abl. sg. fem. *atrud* (ibid. no. 2.24). In Latin **aliteros* > **aliters* > *aliter*, which, like *fortiter* etc., survived as an invariable adverb. **aliterom*, etc., by contrast became *alterum* etc., whence a new paradigm was formed, *alter, altera*, etc. It normally has pronominal declension (see 12.1.1.). Syncopated variants *altrum, altram*, etc. comparable to the Oscan forms may have been widespread already in early Latin;[63] they are certainly implied for imperial Latin by, for instance, Priscian (*GL* 2.228.7), and are the basis for the Romance reflexes of the word.

The same suffix is reflected in Umbr. acc. sg. fem. *etru* 'other, second' (*Ig*. 6A35), *etrama* (acc. sg. fem. + **ad; Ig*. 3.34). The root here may be **e*-, reflected in Skt. *asya* etc. in the paradigm of the pronoun *ayám, idám* 'this', or *ei*- attested in Umbr. *eaf* (< **eians*), accusative plural feminine of the pronominal **i*-, **eyo*-, represented by Latin *is, eas*, etc. The spread of *ei*- at the expense of *i*- in the Umbrian pronominal system is seen in nom. sg. masc. *erek* 'he' < **eis-ek*, which replaced **is-ek*, reflected in Oscan *izic* 'he', and was the basis for the development of a new paradigm **eiso*-. It is possible that *etr*- < *eitr*-, which similarly replaced **itr*-, so that *etru* is ultimately cognate with Latin *iterum*. For the latter and for Umbr. **dutio*- 'second' see 12.3.2.

The commoner Latin ordinal is *secundus* < **sequondos* 'following', the -*nd*- verbal adjective which seems to have been, for a time at least, employed as active imperfective participle to *sequor* and perhaps to all deponent verbs, cf. *oriundus*. The introduction of the -*ns* form in the latter function and the restriction of -*ndus* to gerundival use, both the product of influence from the non-deponent system (*sequens* : **sequondos* :: *agens* : **agondos*), belong to the prehistoric period. Being dissociated in its numeral function from the verbal system, **sequondus* was not affected by the analogical pressure from *sequens* that produced the classical form of the gerundive *sequendus*, nor was its phonological reflex in the late Republic, *secundus*, subject to the paradigmatic levelling from *sequitur, sequimur* that later replaced *secuntur* by *sequuntur*. The isolated *secus* (*CIL* 6.3176) is either an abbreviation or by assimilation to *primus*.

12.2.3. 'Third'

PIE **tritios* is required for Av. *θritya*-, Goth. *þridja*, Welsh *trydydd*. It is presumably a contamination of **tri-tos* (cf. Greek *trítos*) and an older **triyos*, as **tr̥tios* (cf. Skt. *tr̥tī́yaḥ*) is of **tritos* and **tr̥yos*, the allophonic variant of _*triyos_. _*tritio-_ may be reflected in _*tr̥tio-_, perhaps attested in Praenestine Latin _Trtia_ (_CIL_ 1.289) > Latin _tertius_ [64] and Umbr. _tertiama_ viz. _tertiam a(d)_ (_Ig_. 4.2), loc. sg. ntr _tertie_ (_Ig_. 2B 14). The expected palatalization is attested in late Latin _tercium, tersio, tesia_ (_CIL_ 12.5347, 2081, 2187).

12.2.4. 'Fourth'

Both the [a2] and [b2] forms of the numeral postulated in 12.1.4. are represented in Indo-European: _*k^wetwr̥-tos_, reflected in Old Church Slavonic _četvrĭtŭ_ (cf. _četyre_ < _*k^wetwer-_), Greek _τέτρατος, τέταρτος_ (cf. _τέτορες_ < _*k^wet(w)or-_, _τέσσαρες_ < _*k^wetwr̥r-_); _*k^wtur-_, reflected in Av. _tūirya-_, Skt. _turī́ya-_, with the _-yo_-suffix, mediated via _tr̥tī́ya-_, perhaps replacing an original thematic type _*k^wtur-o-_, and probably Greek _τυρταῖος_ with _τυρτ-_ < _*k^wtur-to-_, cf. Skt. _caturthá-_, also with the _-to_-suffix and with the root remodelled to the cardinal. The [b2] form _*k^wtur-_ may perhaps be preferred as original for the ordinal, the [a2] form being due to the influence of the cardinal.

Latin _quārtus_ with the vowel-length guaranteed epigraphically by, for instance, Aug. _R. G._ 16.1, _CIL_ 3.4939, _CIL_ 12.3851, is not easily derived from either form.

*k^wetwr̥tos would give _*quetwortos_, which with dissimilatory loss of the first _t_ > _*quewortos_ > _*quowortos_ > _quōrtos_,[65] attested perhaps in the Praenestine dialect form _Quorta_ (_CIL_ 1.328), > _quārtus_ by the influence of _quattuor_. _*k^wturtos_ would give either _*turtos_ or _*quaturtos_. The former may be reflected, with metathesis of _-ur-_ in Oscan acc. sg. _trutum_ (Vetter 1953: no. 2.15), acc. pl. fem. _trutas_ (ibid. no. 6.12), if this does mean 'fourth'.[66] But it cannot be reflected by _quartus_. _*quaturtos_ might be, on the somewhat implausible assumption of a dissimilatory loss of _-tu-_ or better, since that would among other things leave _quortos_ unaccounted for, of _-t-_, to give _*quaurtos_ with the rustic _-ō-_ for _au_ at Praeneste and the replacement of _au_ by _ā_ in standard Latin, due to the combined pressure of _quattuor_ and _quīntus_.[67] Both derivations presuppose that _quattuor_ already had _a_, which can only have arisen from a Primitive Latin generalization of the zero grade in the initial syllable of certain forms within the cardinal paradigm, viz. _*k^wt-_ > _quat-_ (see 12.1.4.). They leave much to be desired; in particular the assumed loss of the first _t_, in itself phonologically unconvincing,[68] is even more difficult in the presence of a cardinal _*quet-_ or _quat-_.

The most widely accepted derivation[69] is from *$k^w tw\r{r}tos$. This at first sight provides an easier diachrony: > **twortos* > *quortos*, the Praenestine form, > **quartus*, the last two stages by progressive influence from *quatttuor*, > *quārtus* by analogy with *quīntus*. However, we should expect the inherited form to be *$k^w tuw\r{r}tos$. Nor is it easy to see how *$k^w tuw\r{r}tos$ would have arisen in Proto-Italic. An inherited *$k^w tuw\r{r}tos$ might have produced **tuwortos*, whence possibly **tuortos* > **twortos* etc., but given the change $k^w t$- > Latin *quat-*, which must be assumed to account for the *a* of *quattuor*, it is much more likely to have produced **quatuwortos*. The latter would require even more ad hoc phonology than the other derivations discussed, if it is to yield *quārtus*. The whole question remains obscure.

12.2.5. 'Fifth'

The Italic forms might reflect phonologically either *$penk^w tos$ or *$p\r{n}k^w tos$ in Proto-Indo-European, but in the absence of any unequivocal reflexes of the latter,[70] we can prudently postulate only *$penk^w tos$. This gives Latin **quenqutos* > *quīnctus* (*CIL* 1.1215, 6.873), with lengthening of the vowel (as in *sānctus,* etc.) guaranteed by *[Q]ueinctius* (*CIL* 1.1547) > *quīntus*, with the vowel length retained, as is clear from Greek transliterations *Κοεῖντος*, etc., and from the Romance reflexes.

In Oscan and closely related dialects *$k^w enk^w tos$ > **pomptos*, whence the gentile name, corresponding to Latin *Quinctius*, Oscan nom. sg. *Púntiis* (Vetter 1953: no. 8), nom. sg. *pompties* (ibid. no. 196), Paelignian *Ponties* (ibid. no. 202).

12.2.6. 'Sixth'

Corresponding to the cardinal **seks* the only form that can be established for Primitive Italic is **seks-to-*, which is paralleled by Sanskrit *ṣaṣṭhá-*, Gothic *saíhsta*, Venetic *sextio*. Latin *sextus* > *sest-* in imperial popular Latin[71] e. g. *sestum* (*CIL* 5.5583). For Oscan and Umbrian *sest-* see 12.5.6.

12.2.7. 'Seventh'

Latin *septimus*, earlier *septumus*, e. g. *septumo* (*CIL* 1.2519), < *$sept\r{m}mo$-, which may be analysed morphologically as *$sept\r{m}$ + *-mos* or *-os*. The latter is the more probable. For of the Latin ordinals from 'second' to 'tenth' the only two that have *-mos* are those that seem to have had *-m* in the cardinal. **septm̥m-os*, **oktō̆w-os*, **newn̥n-os*, **dekm̥m-os* would thus form an inherited homogeneous group.[72]

12.2.8. 'Eighth'

The thematic stem of **oktōu* is recognisable in Skt. *aṣṭa-má-*. Here as for the other thematic cardinal unit **d(u)wōu* it is impossible to recover the original mode of ordinal formation. It may be that these were the two points at which the thematic mode of formation postulated in 12.2.7. was first broken, e. g., by the use of *-yos* in the one (extended from **triyos*, originally **tr̥y-os*, to give **duyos*, **dwiyos*) and of *-wos* in the other, which must have been based on the re-analysis of *-u* in the nominative-accusative form *-ōu* as part of the root itself. Thus Greek *ὄγδοος* < **oktowos* < **oktō̆wos* or **oktuwos*, cf. Phrygian dat. loc. sg. *οτυϝοι*, Gothic dat. *ahtudin*, Old High German *ahtodo* < **axtū-*[73] or more probably **axtŭ-* < **oktu-*.[74] Gaulish *oxtumeto(s)* is ambiguous as between **oktu-* and **oktō-*.

The origin of Latin *octāuus* is obscure and two different base-forms have been postulated: 1) PIE **oktowos*,[75] presumably reflecting *$ə_3$ektе$ə_3$-os* > **oktowos* > **oktawos*[76] > *octāuus* with the long vowel by the influence of *octō*; 2) **oktōwos*,[77] also reflecting *$ə_3$ekte$ə_3$-os* but with the *o* from *e* before intervocalic $ə_3$ lengthened by analogy with *ō* in the cardinal, > **octōuos* > *octāuus*, with the change *ō* > *ā* as in *flāuus, grāuus, prāuus*.[78]

Oscan *Úhtavis* (Vetter 1953: no. 4), corresponding to the Latin gentile name *Octauius*, may be evidence for *ă̄* in the Oscan ordinal, but the independence of the Oscan word cannot be established. The Latin variants *octabo, octaum* (*CIL* 12.4083, 2143) show familiar Vulgar Latin phonological developments.

12.2.9. 'Ninth'

**newn-os*, formed with thematic suffix from the cardinal **newn̥*[79], > Proto-Italic **neunos*, still surviving in Lat. dat. sg. fem. *neuna* at Lanuvium[80] > **nounos*. *nounos* (*CIL* 10.2381, fifth century A.D.), is not relevant here, representing rather the close articulation of /o:/ that had become general in imperial Latin. The normal reflex of **nounos* would be **nūnus*, cf. *noundinum* (*CIL* 1.581), > *nondin[um]* (*CIL* 1.582), where

-o- = [ọ:], > *nūndinum*. In *nōnus*, however, the influence of *nouem* kept the root-vowel within the boundaries of /o:/[81], hence *nōnus* in classical Latin.

Faliscan **nouno-* is guaranteed by the proper name *Nounis* (Vetter 1953: no. 216) 'Nonius'. In Umbr. *Noniar* (*Ig*. 6A14) 'of Nonia', the *o* may be the close reflex of *ō*, or the open reflex of *ou*, and therefore correspond to either Latin *nōn-* or *noun-*. The meaning of Umbr. *nuvime* (*Ig*. 2A26) is uncertain. If it is 'for the last time', then the word reflects **new-* 'new' + *-m̥mo-* in place of *-mo-* as the superlative, employed in the locative (< *-oi*) or instrumental (< *-ē*) case, for which cf. Latin *nouissimē*. If it is 'for the ninth time', the word is a replacement of earlier **neunos*, reflected in *noniar*, by **newn̥-mo-* or even **nowumo-*, reformed from the initial syllable of the cardinal, with *-umo-* from **dekumo-* and the change of *-umo-* to *-imo-* as in Latin.

12.2.10. 'Tenth'

Latin *decimus*, earlier *decumus* (*CIL* 1.1482, 10.3956), may be by anaptyxis from **dekmo-* (*decmus* in *CIL* 1. 1014 is too late to represent this stage and is better taken as a syncopated form of *decumus*). PIE **dekmos* would be the thematic derivative from the cardinal, viz. **dekm̥* + *-os*. If *decumus* < **dekm̥mos*, then the latter is either due to the influence of **septm̥mos* on **dekmos* or else a derivative in *-mos* (see n. 72) from the cardinal, viz. **dekm̥* + *mos*; cf. Skt. *daśamáḥ* < **dekm̥mo-*.[82] *decema* occurs *CIL* 12.1501, by analogy with *decem*.

12.2.11. 'Eleventh' to 'nineteenth'

12.2.11.1. A break in the pattern of formation of 'eleventh' to 'nineteenth' occurs after 'twelfth'.[83] Thus Latin *undecimus* and *duodecimus*, whence *dudecema* (*CIL* 12.2654) and *dodecimus* (*CIL* 5.1751) (with *do-* < *dwo-* < *duo-*, reproducing the trisyllabic shape of *undecimus*) are both based directly on the cardinals. Thereafter however *tertius decimus, quartus decimus*, etc. A few analogical formations are found in later Latin, e. g. *primus et decimus* (*Grom*. 278.13), *secundus et decimus* (Amm. Marcell. 30.6.6), *tredecimus* (*Anth. Lat*. [Riese] no. 680*a*.13).
12.2.11.2. The normal forms in Latin are *duodēuīcē(n)simus* 'eighteenth', *undēuīcē(n)simus* 'nineteenth', based on the cardinals. The pattern

of the preceding ordinals is sometimes extended; e. g. *octauus decimus* (Tac. *Ann.* 13.6), *nonus decimus* (Tac. *Dial.* 34); cf. the Sanskrit variants *navadaśá-, ekonaviṃśá-*.

12.2.12. 'Twentieth' to 'ninetieth'

The Latin formations are comparable to those of the cardinals, with the long final vowel of the unit component reflecting the change of the following *-dk-* to *-k-* within PIE. However, the decad component itself probably had the zero grade *-dkm̥t-* in contrast to the cardinal with *-dkomt-*; thus ordinal **trīkn̥t-*, cardinal **trīkont-* etc. The Latin suffix reflects **-tm̥mo*, which, as in the Sanskrit superlative *-tamaḥ*, is best analysed as the allophonic variant of **-t-mo-*. It is also represented in Skt. *triṃśattamá-* etc. in contrast to the *-to-* reflected in Greek τριᾱκοστός, analogically remodelled from *τρῑκαστος, cf. Boeotian ϝικαστος beside Attic εἰκοστός.

**-kn̥ttm̥mo- > -censumo- > -cēnsumo-*, e. g. *uicensumam* (*CIL* 1.584), > *-cēnsimo*, e. g. *uicensimus, tricensimo* (*CIL* 6.7872, 751B). The comparative rareness of *-g-* in these two ordinals, e. g. *uigesimus* (*CIL* 5.1693), *trigesimus* (Colum. 11.2.11), confirms that it is not organic here, but analogical. The source may be any one of the forms 'fortieth', 'seventieth' or 'ninetieth'. Thus **kʷetwr̥̄kn̥ttm̥mo- > *kʷedwr̥̄gn̥ttm̥mo- > *quedrāgenssumo- > quadrāgēnsimo-* (cf. 12.1.13.2.); **septm̥̄kn̥ttm̥mo- > *septm̥̄gn̥ttm̥mo- > septuāgēnsimo-* (cf. 12.1.13.5.); **newn̥̄kn̥ttm̥mo- > *newn̥̄gn̥ttm̥mo- > nōnāgēnsimo-* (cf. 12.1.13.7.).

Likewise *-ā*-spread from *quadrāgensumo-, septuāgensumo-* to the intervening tens, *quinquāgensumo-, sexāgensumo-*, replacing **quinquēcensumo-, *sexcensumo-* respectively.

For *-ēnsumo- -ēnsimo-* the variants *-ēsumo- -ēsimo-*, frequent in manuscripts, are found occasionally also in inscriptions, e. g. the syncopated *uicesma* (*CIL* 1.37), *septuagesimo* (*CIL* 5.6738), beside the commoner *quadragensimum, septuagensu[mum]* (Aug. *R. G.* 8.2, 35.2), *quinquagen[simae]* (*CIL* 2.5064), etc.

Typical examples of the combinations of tens and units are *uice(n)simo octauo, nono et uice(n)simo* (Gell. 10.12.1, 15.17.3).

12.2.13. 'Hundredth'

The regular Latin reflex of **kn̥t-tm̥mo-*, viz. **censumo-*, was replaced by a form based on the cardinal *cent-* with *-ensumo-* from the tens, giving *centē(n)sumus*, later *centē(n)simus*; cf. Skt.*śatatamá-* in place of **śattama-*, Greek ἑκατοστός replacing *ἑκαστός.

12.2.14. 'Two hundredth' to 'nine hundredth'

Normally *ducentē(n)simus, trecentē(n)simus*, also formed from the stem of the cardinal by the addition of *-ensumo-* (later *-ensimo-*) from the tens. The analogy of *uice(n)simus* : *uiginti* seems to have led to *duce(n)simus* : *ducenti*, and Priscian (*GL* 2.412.16 ff.) reports a whole series of such variants, *tricesimus, quingesimus, sescesimus* etc. It is unlikely that these are archaic survivals **dukn̥t-tm̥mo-*, etc.; for among them are *quadrigesimus, septigesimus, octigesimus*, which imply late cardinal forms of the type *septigenti* (see 12.1.15.7.).

Typical examples of combinations of hundreds with smaller numbers are *trecente(n)simus alter, quingente(n)simum quinquage(n)simum octauum* (Liv. 3.33.1, 34.54.6), *septimum et quinquage(n)simum atque cente(n)simum* (Plin. *Nat.* 7.175).

12.2.15. 'Thousandth'

mille(n)simus is formed likewise from the cardinal stem by the addition of *-ensumo-* (later *-ensimo-*) from the decads and hundreds.

12.3. Adverbs

12.3.1. 'Once'

Latin *semel* 'once' clearly contains the root *sem̥* (or *sm̥*), reflected also in Latin *sem-per* 'always' and the compounds *simplus, simplex* 'single', as well as in the Greek and Armenian cardinals (see 12.1.1.). For the contrast of root between the adverbial and cardinal forms cf. Sanskrit *sakṛ́t, éka-*.

The further analysis of *semel* is uncertain. It may be derived from the neuter singular of the adjective reflected in *similis* 'similar'.[84] The reconstruction of the latter is not undisputed, but the neuter singular of an adjective **sem-li-* or **sm̥-li-* could easily yield an adverb **semli* > **seml̥* > *semol* (cf. *CIL* 1.1531) > *simul* (with *-i-* by analogy with *similis*, where it is due to anticipatory assimilation). The last two forms both mean 'at the same time', so we should have to assume that **seml̥* or, better, **semli*[85] itself acquired *-s* from **dwis*, **tris*, whence **seml̥s* > **semels* > *semel*. Although *sem-per* indicates the possibility of a lexical root **sem* or **sm̥-* in Latin, the relevant forms in other Indo-European languages show the compositional **sm̥-* affixed to a verbal root; thus Sanskrit *sak;ṛ́t*, cf. *kṛ̥ṇóti* 'he makes' or *kṛntáti* 'he cuts', Greek *ἅπαξ* cf. *πήγνυμι* 'I fix'. Both

OIrish *oenfecht* an Gothic *ainamma sinþa*, meaning literally 'at one go', show a similar lexical patterning. Hence Latin *-el* may be a reflex of the root **ə$_1$el-*, represented by Greek ἐλθεῖν Latin *ex-il-ium, amb-ul-are* (ultimately from **ə$_1$l-*). *semel* then < **semals* with *-s* from **duis*, < **sm̥m-ə$_1$el-* or **sem-ə$_1$l*[86] 'a going together in one'. This would leave open the possibility of deriving *similis* likewise, < **sm̥-ə$_1$(e)l-i-* or **sem-ə$_1$(e)l-i-* (also Greek ὁμαλός < **som-ə$_1$l-o-*, OIrish *samail* < **sm̥m-ə$_1$l-yā*) and Umbr. *sumel* 'at the same time' (*Ig.* 1A27) < **som-ə$_1$el-s* or **sm̥m-ə$_1$el-s*. But all this is very speculative.

Latin *prīmum, prīmo* 'at first' are case-forms of the ordinal. Similarly Umbr. *prumum, promom* (*Ig.* 3.15, 7A52) either from **pro-mo-*, as in Greek πρόμος 'chief', Gothic *fruma* 'first' or from **prō-mo-*, based on the adverbial form attested in Latin *prō*, Oscan *pru*.

12.3.2. 'Twice'

Latin *bis* 'twice' < **dwis*, perhaps represented by the archaic *duis*, cited Cic. *Or.* 153. However, the coexistence of *bellum* and *perduellio*, reflecting **dwel-* and **duel-* respectively, confirms that there could have been a free variation between *dwis* and *duis* in prehistoric Latin, reflecting the originally allophonic variation between **duis* and **duwis* in Proto-Indo-European; cf. Skt. *dvíḥ, duvíḥ* (see the discussion of *duo* in 12.1.2.).

For Latin *iterum* 'a second time' see 12.2.2. *secundum, secundo* 'secondly', are rare. Umbr. *duti* 'a second time' (*Ig.* 6B63) < **dutim* < **dutiom*, the neuter accusative singular of an ordinal **dutio-* formed analogically with *tertio-*. An alternative analysis of **dutim* as the accusative of a *-ti-*collective noun 'a pair' is also possible (see on *pomtis* in 12.3.5.1., on *puntes* in 12.5.5.).

12.3.3. 'Three times'

**tris* 'thrice', reflected in Greek τρίς, Sanskrit *tríḥ*, > Latin **tr̥s* > *terr* (Pl. *Ba.* 1127) > *ter*, if this does not reflect an unsuffixed PIE *ter* beside *tr-i-* (see n. 65). For Umbr. *triiuper* 'three times', see 12.1.3.

Umbr. *terti, tertim* (*Ig.* 2A28, 6B64) 'a third time' < **tertiom*, the neuter accusative singular of the ordinal, also reflected in Latin *tertium*; cf. on *duti* above. The remainder of the Latin series is similarly formed, *quartum* 'a fourth time', *decimum* 'a tenth time', etc.

12.3.4. 'Four times'

Latin *quater* 'four times' is best derived from PIE *k^wturs*, the [b2] form of the root postulated in 12.1.4., with *-s* as in the preceding numeral adverbs. In Sanskrit the reflex of *k^wturs* was remodelled to the cardinal: **turs* > **caturs* > *catúḥ*. So too Avestan, but with metathesis in the final: *caθrus*. A similar metathesis in Latin would give *k^wturs* > **quaturs* > **quatrus* > **quatr̥s* > *quater*. Alternatively **quaturs* > **quatur*, with *-er* from *ter*, if this already existed. For Oscan *petiropert* see 12.1.4.

12.3.5. 'Five times' to 'nine times'

12.3.5.0. The remeaining Latin multiplicatives have *-iē(n)s*. This is usually analysed as *-ient-* + *s*, reflecting *-(i)yn̥t-*, ntr sg. of an adjectival suffix *-(i)yont-* attested in Skt. *íyant-* 'so great', *kíyant-* 'how great?'; cf. Latin *quotiens, totiens* from **quoti*, **toti* (Skt. *káti* 'how many?', *táti* 'so many') + *-ients*.[87] That the Latin type is relatively recent is indicated by the form of the numeral root in, for instance, *sept-iens, oct-iens, dec-iens*. Palatalization is attested in *sepsies, hocsies* (*CIL* 12.2086, 2087).
12.3.5.1. Oscan *pomtis* (Vetter 1953: no. 2.15) is usually taken to mean 'five times'. It cannot be derived from **pompients*, corresponding to Latin *quinquiē(n)s*, and is best regarded as an adaptation of the ordinal **pompt-*, perhaps specifically from **pomptom* 'for the fifth time' by the transfer of *-is* from **dwis*, **tris* (so Pisani 1964: 58). The alternative is to relate the word to **pompti-* 'a group of five' (see 12.5.5.), but neither acc. pl. **púntiss* nor abl. pl. **púntifs* is semantically plausible and it is unlikely that the nominative singular was adapted to adverbial use on the analogy of **dwis*, **tris*.
12.3.5.2. Umbr. *nuvis* 'nine times' (*Ig*. 2A25) may be *nou-is*, with the numeral stem as in Latin *nouiē(n)s* and *-is* extended from **dwis*, **tris*. That it could represent a remodelling of **nouif* (< **nouief*, cognate with *nouiens*) on **dwis* is very doubtful.

12.3.6. 'Ten times' to 'nineteen times'

12.3.6.1. Latin *decis* (*CIL* 12.2087) for the regular *deciē(n)s* 'ten times' shows the confusion of /i/ and /e:/ that was widespread in the imperial period. The change of *-ciē-* to *-cē-*, more clearly exhibited in *deces* (*CIL* 12.2086) may be synizesis or an early instance of palatalization, viz. [ki] > [kj] > [c].

12.3.6.2. As in the ordinals, *undeciē(n)s, duodeciē(n)s*, then *terdeciē(n)s, quaterdeciē(n)s*, etc., and probably *duodēuīciē(n)s, undēuīciē(n)s* beside the forms *octiē(n)s deciē(n)s, nouiē(n)s deciē(n)s* cited by Priscian (*GL* 2.415.21).

12.3.7. 'Twenty times' to 'ninety times'

12.3.7.1. Latin *uīciē(n)s* is by haplology from **uīkentients*, reflecting **uikn̥t-yn̥t-*. *uices* (*CIL* 12.2187) represents either synizesis of *ie* or palatalization (cf. on *deces* above).

Typical instances of combinations of 'twenty' with units are *semel atque uicie(n)s* (Tac. *Ann.* 1.9), *sexiens et uiciens* (Aug. *R. G.* 22.3), *uicie(n)s quinquie(n)s* (Cic. *Ver.* 1.92), *duodetricie(n)s* (Cic. *Ver.* 3.163). Similar patterns occur for the remaining terms.

12.3.7.2. *Trīciē(n)s, quadrāgiē(n)s* etc. are also by haplology. The forms *quadragesies*, etc. that are occasionally transmitted in classical manuscripts are analogical: *quadrages-ies : quadrages-imus :: decies : decimus*. They have no certain ancient attestation, and even the most plausible example, *quinquagesies* (Pl. *Men.* 1161), is textually suspect. *quatragies* (*CIL* 12.1045) shows the influence of *quattuor, quater*.

12.3.8. 'A hundred times' to 'a thousand times'

12.3.8.1. *centiē(n)s, ducentiē(n)s*, etc. are formed by the addition of *-iēns* to the cardinal stem; see Priscian (*GL* 2.415.22).

12.3.8.2. *milliē(n)s, miliē(n)s*, with the same variation as in the cardinal *millia, milia*. Augustus has *milliens* consistently, e.g. *bis mill[ie]ns, sexsiens milliens* (*R. G.* 16.1).

12.4. Distributives

12.4.0. Introduction

This semantic category, denoting 'one at at time, in ones', 'two at a time, in twos' etc., seems to have been inherited, since its characteristic Latin suffix *-no-* is paralleled in Lith. *dvynù* 'twins', OIcel. *tvennr* 'double'. There is, however, no evidence to suggest that there was, as in Latin, a complete series of *-no-* numeral derivatives in Proto-Indo-European parallel to the cardinals.

Besides the inherited distributive and multiplicative meanings, e. g. Hor. *S* 1.4.86: *saepe tribus lectis uideas cenare quaternos* 'you would often see them dining on three couches, four to a couch'; Verg. *A.* 1.43: *bis senos cui nostra dies altaria fumant* 'in whose honour the smoke rises from our altars on twice six days', where *bis senos*, not *bis sex*, is employed for the unmetrical *duodecim*, Latin employs these forms in cardinal meanings with nouns that have no singular, e. g. *binae nuptiae* 'two weddings', or else have a distinctive meaning in the plural, e. g. *duae litterae* 'two letters of the alphabet', *binae litterae* 'two epistles'.

12.4.1. 'One'

12.4.1.0. The suffix of *unus* (see 12.1.1.) suggests that it was originally the first member of the distributive series, and this perhaps is confirmed by the occasional use of *uni* rather than the normal *singuli* in the second of the two functions indicated above (see the examples cited in 12.1.1.).
12.4.1.1. Latin *singulī* is usually derived from **sm̥-gno-* 'born together' (for which cf. *bignae* 'twins' reported by Festus) either by dissimilation of the second nasal[88] or by the addition of the diminutive *-lo-* suffix, as in *paruolus* and *ullus* (see 12.5.1.1.).[89] The word is sometimes used both in the singular and the plural to mean simply 'separate, individual' and this is probably its original sense. Like the rest of the distributives it has the full adjectival plural paradigm in numeral usage.
12.4.1.2. Umbr. abl. pl. masc. *prever* 'one at a time' (*Ig.* 5A13) < **prei-wo-* with the same root as *prior, prīmus* (see 12.2.1.). It is cognate with Latin *prīuus* 'individual, peculiar', the plural of which, according to Gellius (10.20.4) and P. Festus (252.30), was earlier used for *singuli*, though it is not clear whether this refers to the numeral or more general meaning of the latter word.

12.4.2. 'Two'

Latin *bīni* < **dwisno-* (analysed as either **dwis-no-* based on the adverbial form, or **dwi-sno-* the compositional form with a suffix *-sno-*), cf. Old High German *zwirnen* 'to twist', OIcel. pl. *tvenner*, or < **dwei-no-* (cf. Old High German *zwein (-zng)* 'twenty'); alternatively < **dwī-no-* (cf. Lithuanian *dvynù*). The first derivation seems the more plausible.[90]

12.4.3. 'Three'

It is not clear whether Latin _ternī_, e. g. Pl. _Mer._ 304, or the rare _trīnī_, e. g. Pl. _Ps._ 704, is the regular Latin reflex of _*trisno-_, which is represented elsewhere by OIcel _þrenner_, sg. _þrennr_. If the former, then _trini_ is by analogy with _bini_; if the latter, then _terni_ would represent the assimilation of the pattern _*trisno-_ : _*dwisno-_ to _ter : dwis._

12.4.4. 'Four'

Latin _quaternī_ may reflect an inherited _*k^{w}etrusno-_, itself from _*k^{w}etwr̥-sno-_ or _*k^{w}etwr̥s-no-_, with the same development as in adverbial _quater_ (see 12.3.4.). Alternatively _*k^{w}etur-sno-_ > _*quaturno-_ > _quaterno-_ by the influence of _quater_. However, _quaterni_ may be a recent formation, extending the sequence _*dwisno-, terno-_ on the model of _duis, ter, quater._ The rare _quadrīnī_, e. g. Cato, _Agr._ 18.1, is almost certainly recent, representing an extension of _bini, trini_ on the model of the compositional series _bi-, tri-, quadr-_ (see 12.5.2., 12.5.3.).

12.4.5. 'Five' to 'nine'

quīnī, sēnī, octōnī could reflect either _-sno-_ or _-no-_ suffixed to _*penk^w-_ (or _*penk^{w}e-_, subsequently syncopated), _*seks-_, _*oktō-_, the respective cardinal forms.[91] _septēnī, nouēnī_ cannot be directly related to _-no-_, since _*septm̥-no-_, _*newn̥-no-_ would give _*septemno-_, _*nouenno-_, and we should then have to assume replacement of _-emn-_, _-enn-_ by _-ēn-_ through the influence of _seni, octoni._ This is not impossible, but it is simpler to derive both from _-sno-_ suffix forms: _septēnī_ < _*septensno-_ < _*septm̥-sno-, nouēnī_ < _*nouensno-_ < _*newn̥-sno-_. The question remains open whether _-sno-_ was inherited or abstracted from _*dwis-no-_, _*tris-no-_.

12.4.6. 'Ten' to 'nineteen'

The preceding pattern would give: _*dekm̥-sno-_ > _*decēnī_; _*dekm̥-no-_ > _*decemnī_ or possibly _*decennī._ Whether _dēnī_ is due to the influence of _seni_ or reflects rather an original _*dek-(s)no-_ (cf. _*penk^w-(s)no-?_) we cannot say. As in the ordinals, there is a break after 'twelve': _undēnī, duodēnī_ but _ternī dēnī, quaternī dēnī_, etc. Both _octōnī dēnī_ and _duodēuīcēnī_ occur, e. g. Liv. 38.38.15, 21.41.6; also _nouēnī dēnī_ and _undēuīcēnī_, e. g. Prisc. _GL_ 2.413.33, Quint. 1.10.44; but all four forms are in fact very rare.

12.4.7. 'Twenty' to 'ninety'

Latin *uīcēnī* < **uīkent-(s)no-* from **wīkm̥t-*[92] + *-(s)no-*. Similarly *trīcēnī, quadrāgēnī* etc.

12.4.8. 'Hundred'

12.4.8.0. Latin *centēnī* shows the spread of *-ēnī*, replacing **cēnī*, the reflex of **kn̥t-* + *-(s)no-* which is attested in the following hundreds.
12.4.8.1. *ducēnī, trecēnī* < **dukn̥t-(s)no-*, **trikn̥t-(s)no-* etc. are the regular Latin forms, but the pattern already established in *centeni* is extended occasionally in imperial texts, e. g. *quadringentena* (Plin. *Nat.* 8.63.170) beside *quadringenos* (Aug. *R. G.* 15.10), *ducenteni* and even *duocenteni* (*Grom.* 153.29, 110.4), *trecenteni* (Amm. Marcell. 18.2.11).
12.4.8.2. Latin *millēnī* is reported by Priscian (*GL* 2.414.3) but there appear to be no certain examples elsewhere and Aug. *R. G.* 3.18 has *millia nummum singula.*

12.5. Numerals in composition

12.5.1. 'One'

12.5.1.0. The data are classified as complexes if the numeral root is combined with derivational affixes, and as compounds if it is combined with other lexemic roots. The examples discussed, though selective, are intended to be representative.
12.5.1.1. A number of complexes with **oino-* (see 12.1.1.) are attested. *ūnicus* 'unique' reflects either **oin-ikos*, with *-ikos* as in *pudicus* etc., or **oine-kos* with *-kos* as in *priscus, ciuicus*. The latter derivation is supported by Gothic *ainahs* (cf. Old Church Slavonic *inokŭ*), assuming that the thematic vowel employed in Latin compounds (*agricola, signifer* etc.) was *-e-* not *-o-*.[93]

ūllus 'any' < **oino-los*, with the diminutive suffix, whence, with the negative prefix *ne-, nūllus* 'no'. Both have pronominal declension.

ūnitās 'unity, singularity', first attested in Varro, is apparently calqued on Greek *ἑνότης*.

Compounds with **oino-* include *ūniuersus* < **oinouorsus*, cf. *oinuorsei* (*CIL* 1.581), < **oino-wr̥t-tos* 'turned into one'.
12.5.1.2. Among complexes with **prismo-* (see 12.2.1.) are *prīmānus* 'belonging to the first legion' and probably *prīmor* 'first member or part',

with the suffix *-or* perhaps first established from a division of *prīm-ōrum*, genitive plural of *primus* (masc.) *primum* (neuter), as *primōr-um.*[94]

Compounds include *prīnceps* 'leading', < **prismo-kaps* 'one who takes first', *prīncipium* 'a beginning or principle' < **prismo-kapiom* 'a first taking'. Beside *princeps*, Varro (*L.* 5.50–54) reports old compounds *terticeps, quarticeps, quinticeps* and *sexticeps* based on the corresponding ordinals.

12.5.2. 'Two'

12.5.2.1. The inherited compositional form **d(u)wi-* > Latin *bi-* is attested in a number of compounds.

bipēs 'biped' is an exact cognate of Skt. *dvi-pád-*, Greek *δίπους*.

biennium 'a period of two years' is the reflex, with normal vowel-weakening, of **dwi-atnyo-*, cf. *annus* < **at-no-*.

biceps 'two-headed' < **dwi-kaps* or by syncope of the final syllable **-kaputs*; cf. *bicipit-* in the oblique cases. *triceps* 'three-headed' is similarly derived, cf. *terticeps* 'taking third place' in 12.5.1.1.

bīduum 'a period of two days' < **dwi-diwo-* and *bīgae* 'a two-horse cart, pair' < **dwi-yugā-*, cf. adj. *biiugus* (Lucr. 2.602). The long vowel in both is probably due to the influence of *bīni dies, bīni equi*, etc. rathen than to derivation from *dwis-*.[95]

bīmus 'two years old' < **dwi-himo-* 'of two winters', cf. *trīmus, quadrīmus*.

bessis, bēs 'two-thirds of an as, a coin' (cf. *binae partes* 'two-thirds') < **dui-assis* by vowel-weakening and synizesis of *-i-*. By contrast *dussis* 'two asses', reported by Priscian (*GL* 3.416) < **du-assis*.

Umbr. acc. sg. *difue* (*Ig.* 6B4) 'double, in two parts' < **difuim* < **dwi-bhū-yo-* with a dissimilatory loss of *w*.[96] The word is cognate with, rather than borrowed from the Greek *s*-stem *διφυής*.

12.5.2.2. Italic *du-* is either by syncope from **dui-* < **duwi-* (see 12.1.2.), or more probably the stem of the cardinal *duo*. It is represented by a number of Italic forms.

Latin *dubius* 'doubtful', probably the thematic adjective derived from **dubhi* 'on two sides' with *-bhi* as in Skt. *abhítaḥ* 'around', Greek *ἀμφί*.[97]

Umbr. dat.-abl. pl. *dupursus* 'bipeds, men' (*Ig.* 6B10) < **dupodufs* (< **dupodbhos*, cf. Prakrit (Aśoka) *dupada-* but Latin *bipedibus*.

Latin *duplus* 'double', Umbr. acc. pl. fem. *dupla* (*Ig.* 6B18), abl. pl. masc. *tupler* (*Ig.* 5A19) 'in a pair, two' < **du-pl-o-* 'twofold', cf. Greek *διπλός*, Gothic *tweifls*, where the first components must be referred to **dwi-*; see 12.5.2.1.

Faliscan *dupes* (Vetter 1953: no. 241) 'double weight' (a coin-name corresponding to Latin *dupondium*) < **du-pend-s* or **du-pendens*.

Umbr. acc. sg. ntr *tuplak* (*Ig*. 3.14) is usually rendered 'two-pronged (fork)' and equated with Latin *duplex*, Greek *δίπλαξ* 'double, twofold'. The Greek word may reflect **pl̥k-*, cf. *πλέκω* < **pl-ek-*. The Latin may contain the same root, viz. PIE **pel-* + *-k*-suffix, cf. *-plicare* 'to fold'. On Martinet's theory of the $ə_2$-reflexes in Latin,[98] it may also be derived from **pel-*$ə_2$, as Greek *διπλάσιος* < **dwi-pl*$ə_2$*-tyos* (if this and not **dwi-pl̥-tyos* in the right reconstruction). This would related *duplex* to Latin *plānus*. Greek *πλατύς*. The semantic affinity between **pel-*$ə_2$ 'flat' and **pel-k-* 'to fold' is obvious enough in such compounds. Now *tuplak* is unlikely to reflect **plek-* or **pl̥k-*, so a laryngal origin for the *-a-* is attractive, whether it is long or short[99]. This would suit, though it is not demanded by, Vetter's interpretation (1953: 213) of the word as 'ein zweiter Boden'.

Latin *bellum* 'war', earlier *duellum*, may belong here, if the derivation is from **du* + **el-no-* 'a going apart into two'. (For *-el* see on *semel* in 12.3.1.)

12.5.3. 'Three'

Compounds with *tri-* include a variety of formations. Latin *tripēs* 'three-footed' is straightforward, cf. Greek *τρίπους*, OInd. *tri-pád-*. See on *bipes*, in 12.5.2.1.

For Latin *triplex* 'threefold' and the rare *triplus*, paralleled in Umbr. abl. pl. masc. *tripler* (*Ig*. 5A21), with the same meaning, see on *duplus, duplex* 12.5.2.2.

Perhaps Latin *tribus* 'tribe', Umbr. acc. sg. *trifu* (*Ig*. 1B16), gen. sg. *trifor* (*Ig*. 6B54)[100] belong here, **tri-bhu-* indicating a threefold division of the Primitive Italic communities.

Latin *trīduum* 'a period of three days' < **tri-diwom*, with *-ī-* by analogy with *bīduum* (see 12.5.2.1.) and perhaps *trīnī*. By contrast *trimēstris* < **tri-mēns-tri-* 'lasting three months', like *bimēstris*.

Latin *tressis* 'three asses' (Var. *L* 5.169) < **tri-assis*; cf. *bessis* in 12.5.2.1. For *trepondo* 'three pounds in weight' cf. *dupondo*, and for the short *e, trecenti* in 12.1.15.3.

Umbr. nom. sg. *tribriçu* (*Ig*. 5A9), abl. sg. *tribrisine* (*Ig*. 6A54) 'group of three' < **tri-pedik-iōn* or **tri-plek-iōn*.

12.5.3.1. Latin *testis*, also attested in Sabine (Vetter 1953: 376), 'witness' is usually derived from **terst-* < **tr̥st-* < **tri-st-* 'standing as third person to the disputants', with the earlier stages of the development supported by Oscan nom. pl. *trstus* (Vetter 1953: no. 5C10). The reflexes of the original laryngeal-stem declension of **-steə₂s* (cf. Skt. *ratheṣṭhā́-* 'warrior') or **-stə₂s* (with zero-grade as in *dŭx*) have been remodelled to the thematic stems in Oscan and to the *i*-stems in Latin[101]; cf. Latin *testāmentum*, Oscan abl. sg. *tristaamentud* (Vetter 1953: no. 11) 'testimony, will', with *-ā-* < *-eə₂-*. However, the phonetic interpretation of *trstus* is by no means certain[102], and the assumed Latin change of *-ris-* to *-r̥s-* in accented position is difficult, cf. *crista, crīnes* (< **kris-ni-*) and see 12.2.3., 12.3.3. So it would perhaps be better to regard **terst-* as a replacement of **trist-* under the influence of *tertius*, for instance in such contexts as *ne quis esset testis tertius* (Pomponius *Com.* 143). The difficulty, however, is obviated entirely if both Latin **tr̥st-* and Oscan *trst-* < **tr̥tio-st-* < **trityo-stə₂s* by syncope of the second syllable.[103]

12.5.4. 'Four'

**kʷetur̥*, derived probably from **kʷtur-* by the influence of **kʷetwor-* (respectively the [b2] and [a1] forms of 12.1.4.), is reflected in the Umbrian compound *peturpursus* (*Ig.* 6B 11) 'quadrupeds' (dat. pl.); cf. the first component of Sanskrit *caturakṣá-* 'four-eyed', *caturvarga-* 'collection of four things', Gothic *fidurfalþs* 'fourfold'.

The gentile name Latin *Petrōnius*, Faliscan *Petrunes*, a matronymic from **Petrōnyāī* + *-s*, clearly belongs in origin to one of the *p*-areas of Italic. It is in fact attested both in Paelignian *ptruna* (Vetter 1953: no. 215q) < **petrōnya*, Umbr. *petruniapert* (abl. sg. fem. + *pert: Ig.* 2A21) and perhaps nom. sg. masc. *ptrnio* (Vetter 1953: no. 234). *petr-* in all these may be by syncope from the [a2] form **kʷetwr̥* or it may reflect **kʷetru-* (paralleled in Av. *čaθrušva-* 'a quarter' and the Gaulish proper name *Petrucorius*), which is itself derived either by metathesis from **kʷtur*, with subsequent influence of the cardinal, or from **kʷetwr̥* represented in Av. *čaθwarəzaŋgra-* 'four-footed', Greek *τετράπους*.

Latin *quadru-* is difficult. The antiquity of *-u-* here is by no means certain. *quadriiugus, quadriuium* 'cross-roads' may be analogical with *biiugus, triuium*[104], *quadriennis* 'lasting four years' with *biennis, triennis, quadrīduum*[105], *quadrīgae*, with *bīduum, bīgae*; but the most securely attested *u*-spellings all occur before labials, e. g. *quadruplus, quadrupes*, where the vocalic quality may have been assimilative. Moreover, none of the base-forms noted above could yield *quadru-*. *k^wtur* > Latin **quatur-*, or with metathesis **quatru-*, *k^wetwr̥* + *C* > **quedor-* and *k^wetwr̥r* + *V* > **quedar-* (if we accept a change *-etwr̥r-* > *-edr̥r-*, etc. comparable to that outlined in 12.1.13.2.). The evidence of the Avestan forms cited above and of Greek *τρυφάλεια* [106] beside *τετράφαλος* indicates the possibility of more than one variant of the compositional numeral existing within the same language, so we might derive *quadru-* from the contamination of **quatru-* and a syncopated **qued(a)r-* **qued(o)r-* (see 12.1.4., 12.1.13.2., 12.2.4.).

From *quadr-* is formed the verb *quadrāre* 'to quarter, shape into a square'.

The complex *quartānus* 'quartan, of the fourth day' is formed from the ordinal stem.

12.5.5. 'Five'

The Latin compound *quīncunx* 'a pattern of five, five-twelfths (for instance, of an as)' clearly contains the cardinal stem *quinqu-*. The second component may be connected with *uncia* (12.5.1.1.), as the ancients believed, cf. Var. *L* 5.171: *septunx a septem et uncia conclusum.*

In the Latin compound *quincuplex* the *-u-* may be anaptyctic in *k^wenk^w-plek-* or by assimilation to the surrounding labial articulations in *k^wenk^{w}e-plek-*. However it is probable that either form would normally have developed to **quinplek-*, whence **quimplex*; so the influence of the preceding *quadruplex* should be assumed. The authenticity of the imperial spelling *quinquiplex* (e. g. Martial 14.4.2), need not be challenged, since by this time the change of unchecked *u* to *i* before labial was complete.

The complexes Oscan nom. pl. *pumperias* (Vetter 1953: no. 77A), loc. abl. pl. *púmperiaís* (ibid. no. 87), Umbr. *pumpeřias* 'grouped in fives', adj. nom. pl. fem. (*Ig.* 2B 2), with *ř* from the adjacent *fameřias* 'families', suggest a reconstruction *k^wenk^{w}eriā-*. But a suffix *-ryā-* seems improbable in spite of Latin *decuria* (on which see 12.5.10.), and it is preferable to reconstruct *k^wenk^w-yā-*, [107] whence Oscan-Umbrian **pompiā-*, and to explain the suffix by analogy with **peteriā-* (< **petriā-* < **peturiā-*; for *petiro* see 12.1.4.) or with **peturiā-* itself, with *e* for *u* from **pompe*. A parallel for the analogical spread of the suffix occurs in the Lithuanian distributives, *dvejì, trejì, ketverì*, whence *penkerì* etc.

Umbr. nom. pl. *puntes* 'groups of five' (*Ig.* 3.9), abl. pl. *puntis* (*Ig.* 3.4) and perhaps Oscan *pomtis* (see 12.3.5.) are from *k^wenk^w- + *ti-*. The suffix, which can hardly be the inherited PIE verbal noun formant, [108] must have developed from **wīkn̥ti*, spreading first to replace the collective **dkn̥t-*, as it seems also to have done in Sanskrit, which offers an exact parallel here in *paṅktí-*, with the same full grade from the cardinal, in contrast to the zero-grade in the inherited verbal noun formation; cf. also Old Church Slavonic *pętĭ*.

12.5.6. 'Six'

Among Latin compounds *seks-* is preserved in prevocalic position, e. g. *sexennis* 'lasting six years', but reduced to *sē-* before consonants, e. g. *sēuirī* 'the committee of six', whence *sēuir* 'a member of such a committee', and *sēmēstris* from **sex-mēnstri-* 'lasting six months'.

Oscan *sehsímbriịs* (Vetter 1953: no. 25) 'born in the sixth month' < **seksēmbrios* with *-embri-* from **septēmbri-* (see 12.5.7.). For 'the sixth month' viz. August in the old calendar, Latin has originally *Sextilis*, a complex based on the ordinal, cf. *Quintilis* 'the fifth month' viz. July.[109]

Umbr. fem. gen. plur. *sestentasiaru* (*Ig*. 3.2) 'pertaining to a sixth, two-monthly' resembles the Latin ordinal compound *sextantārius* < **sekst-ānt-āsyo-* (cf. *sextans* 12.6.6.) 'pertaining to a sixth (of an as)'. The Umbrian *e* in the second syllable may be due to an unattested cognate of Latin *trientarius* 'pertaining to a third (of an as)' or to progressive assimilation.

12.5.7. 'Seven'

Various forms of the numeral 'seven' are attested in Latin compounds.

septemplex (Verg. *A*. 12.925), *septemfluus* (Ovid *Met*. 15.753)) 'with seven streams' are perhaps recent formations: But *septentriōnēs*[110] 'the seven oxen (Great Bear), North' seems early, since it occurs Pl. *Am*. 273, and the archaizing tmesis *septem* ... *triones* (Cic. *ND* 2.105) may have been adopted merely for metrical reasons.

septuennis 'lasting seven years', which is guaranteed by the metre in Pl. *Ba*. 440, appears to be older and more frequent than *septennis* with *sept-* (cf. the late attested *octennis*; both apparently influenced by *sexennis*). It is perhaps derived from **septumannis*, with the assimilatory change of *m* to *w* assumed for *septuāginta* in 12.1.13.5., < **septm̥m-atni-*, **septm̥-* in prevocalic composition. *septimontium* 'group of seven hills' may also be from *septu-* reflecting **septm̥* before *m*. However, it could result from regular vowel-weakening in **septemontium* with *septe-* from *septem* as in *septeṛ[esmom]* 'with seven banks of oars' (*CIL* 1.2.25), if this is not a false restoration of the early imperial *septi-* (< *septu-* as in *septimus* etc.).

September, originally 'pertaining to the seventh month' is either from **septumomēmbri-*, from **septm̥mo-*, the ordinal stem, + **mēns-ri-* (cf. *membrum* < **mēmsro-*), or less probably **septe(m)mēmbri-*, in either case by haplology. *settembris* occurs *CIL* 11.2885.

12.5.8. 'Eight'

Latin compounds have both *octō-* and *octu-* for 'eight', the latter probably reflecting **oktŏ-*, cf. Sanskrit *aṣṭā́pād-* but *aṣṭapāda-* 'eight-footed', though the *-u-* may be a residue from the cardinal (see 12.1.8.).

octu- is exemplified by *octuplus* and *octipēs* (< **octuped-*) and probably *octussis* 'eight asses' < **octūessis* < **octouessis* with *w*-glide, reflecting **octo-assis*. On *octussis* appear to be modelled *nonussis, decussis, centussis* (Var. *L.* 5.169).

octō- is represented by *octōiugis* 'in a team of eight'. *Octōber* is by analogy with *September*, as *octō : septem*. *ottobres* occurs *CIL* 11.2537.

12.5.9. 'Nine'

Among Latin compounds with 'nine' are *Nouember*, either from **nō ọmembris* < **nou(no)mēmbris* < **neuno-mēnsri-*, with **nọ̄mem-* replaced by *nouem-* on the analogy of *September : septem*, or from **noue(m)mēmbri-* by haplology. *nobebres* occurs *CIL* 10.1342.

nouendiālis 'taking place on the ninth day, within nine days, *nouem dies*' is straightforward. *nūndinus* 'taking place once every nine days', whence *nūndinae* 'market day' and *nūndinum* 'the interval between market days' < **nowen-di-n-o-*.[111] The normal phonetic development is represented by *noundinum* (*CIL* 1.581), whence *nondin[um]* (*CIL* 1.582.31) with *ọ̄*. The resultant shift to /ū/ was not subject to analogical pressure from the numeral, since the word was semantically dissociated, in contrast to *nonus* (see 12.2.9.).

12.5.10. 'Ten'

The Latin cardinal compound *decemuir* is formed, as *duumuir* etc., from the phrase *decem uiri*.

decuplex owes its *-u-* to the influence of *duplex, quadruplex* etc. and perhaps also *decumus*.

December, < **decumomēmbri-* or less probably **dece(m)mēmbri-*, has been syncopated, or else remodelled to the cardinal on the analogy of *September : septem*.

Oscan nom. pl. *degetasiús* (Vetter 1953: no. 115), dat. sg. *deketasiúí* (ibid. no. 1.5), the title assigned to a magistrate *meddix*, is of uncertain interpretation but seems to mean 'for a tenth part (of the year? of the community?)', < **dekentāsio-* (for *sestentasiaru* see 12.5.6.).

The two Umbrian complexes, nom. pl. *tekvias* (*Ig*. 2B 1) and abl. pl. *tekuries, decurier* (*Ig*. 2B 1, 5B 11), are obscure as to meaning and composition[112]. *Tekvias* may be a noun or an adjective in the context, and its sense may be collective, '(comprising) a group of ten', or fractional, '(comprising) a tenth part'. The collective sense would suggest a connection with the series of nouns in *-yā-* assumed for *pumpeřias* in 12.5.5. If the sequence originally ran **nowi*$^{o}/_{a}$- **deki*$^{o}/_{a}$- (cf. perhaps the Latin gentile names *Nouius, Decius*, Oscan *Dekis*), it is possible that the latter was remodelled by analogy with the former to **dekwi*$^{o}/_{a}$-. On the other hand, the fractional sense would suggest a formation from the ordinal. An original **dekumi*$^{o}/_{a}$- based on the ordinal **dekumo-* might then have been replaced by the influence of the reflex of **oktō̆wi*$^{o}/_{a}$-, the corresponding 'eight', form, to give **dekuwio-* > **dekṷia*.[113] The chief difficulty here is the intervening ordinal *nuvime* < **nowumo-* (see 12.2.9.), which would surely have acted as a barrier against such an analogy. A more drastic solution would be to assume syncope of **dekumia*, giving **dekmia*, whence, with assimilatory loss of nasalization, viz. [m] > [β] > [w], **dekwia*; but the phonology would be very ad hoc. The formation must remain obscure.

From *dekwiā-* is formed the Oscan complex adjective **dekwiā-rio-* attested in acc. sg. fem. *dekkviarim* (Vetter 1953: no. 8) '(the street) of the *decvia*'. The *-rio-* suffix, beside *-sio-* in *degetasiús* above, is very puzzling.

It is difficult to avoid the equation of *tekuries* with Latin *decuria* 'group of ten'. The formation in both languages is usually taken as an extension of *-uriā-* from *k^w*eturyā-* (for Oscan-Umbrian **peturiā*, Latin **quaturia*, see 12.5.5.).[114] But whereas Latin **quincuria* can be set up as a possible parallel, the only actually attested parallel in Latin is *centuria*, and the relevant Umbrian form *pumpeřias* (see 12.5.5.) shows no trace of the crucial *-u-*; so the development remains uncertain.

Although the meaning of Oscan *dekmanniúís* (Vetter 1953: No. 147B 23) is doubtful – it may be 'for those who have been tithed' (dat.) or 'at the December festival' (loc.)[115] – it is clearly a complex from the ordinal: **dekum-ān-io-*; cf. Latin *decumānus* 'tithed, belonging to the tenth division', < **dekum-ān-o-*.

Faliscan *decimātrus* 'the tenth day after the Ides of the month' is reported by P. Festus 306, together with Latin *quinquātrus* and (from Tusculum) *triatrus, sexatrus, septematrus*. It may be a compound of the ordinal **decimo-* (< **decumo-* as in Latin) or, if the spelling of the other forms cited is reliable, of the cardinal, **decem-*.[116]

From the distributive **dek-(s)no-* (see 12.4.8.) is formed the Latin complex *dēnarius* 'ten asses'.

12.5.11. 'Hundred'

Among Latin compounds with 'hundred' are *centumuir* (cf. *duumuir*, 12.5.2.), *centumpondium* 'hundred-weight', *centumplex*, later *centuplex* probably on the analogy of *duplex, quadruplex*, as *decuplex* in 12.5.10, and *centiceps* 'hundred-headed' < **kente-kaputs* (cf. *biceps* in 12.5.2.1.). *centussis* may be by internal prodelison from **centumassis* (partial parallels occur in *actumst, circuire*), but more probably owes its *-u-* to analogy with *decussis* etc. (see 12.5.8.).

12.5.12. 'Thousand'

Latin *millennium* 'period of a thousand years' < **mill(e)-anniom*, cf. *biennium* in 12.5.2.

12.6. Fractions

12.6.1. General

The absence of a term for e. g. 'one-fifth', taken with the positive evidence set out below, points to an original duodecimal system of division in Latin.

12.6.2. 'Half'

12.6.2.1. Latin *dīmidius* (adj.), *dīmidium* (noun) < **dis-medius* 'divided medially', whence the denominative verb *dīmidiāre*. For *dis-* see 12.5.2.1., n. 96 *demedium*, perhaps by analogy with *dē-* compounds occurs *CIL* 10.3428.

12.6.2.2. The compositional form is *sēmi-*, cf. Greek *ἡμίβιος*, Latin *sēmiuīuus* 'half-alive', and the Sanskrit adv. *sāmí* 'too soon'.

An apocopated form is found for instance in *sēmēsus* 'half-eaten', *sēmis, sēmissis* 'half an as' < **sēmiess* < **sēmi-ass; sē-* < *sēmi-* by haplology occurs in *sēmodius* 'half a peck', from **sēmi-modio-*, whence analogical *sēlibra* (*sĕ-* Martial 4.46.7), and in *sēmestris* 'twice monthly' < **sēmi-mēns-tri-*, a rare homonym of the reflex of **sex-mēns-tri-* (see 12.5.6.).

A form *sēs-* appears in *sēstertius*, from **sēmis-tertio-* 'half the third', i.e., 'two and a half asses', and in the rare *sēsque* (e.g. Cicero *Or.* 188) 'more by a half', by syncope from **sēmis-que* 'and a half', which is commonly used as a prefix, e.g. *sēsquioctāuus* 'containing one and one-eighth, in the ratio nine to eight', *sēsquipēs* 'a foot and a half'.

sinciput 'half a head, brain' < **senceput* < **sēmi-kaput.*

12.6.3. 'Third'

Latin *triēns* (masc.) is commonly analysed as the participle of a verb **triēre* 'to divide in three', but we should expect a factitive **triāre* here, cf. *quadrāre*. It may be a semantic adaptation of **tri-yn̥t-* 'a group of three' from the series that formed the adverbs *quinquiē(n)s*, etc., or alternatively, like the latter, based directly on *totiens, quotiens* (see 12.3.5.0.). For the shift of gender cf. Greek *τριάς*, stem *τριάδ-* (generalized from the reflex of, for instance, acc. sg. **triyn̥tm̥*, replacing the original neuter form **triyn̥t*).

tertia (*pars*) is more commonly used, except in the sense 'third of an as'. So also for the remaining fractions, *quārta, quīnta* etc.

For 'two-thirds' a variety of exponents was current, *duae* or *binae partes, dimidia et sexta* and even *bēs, bessis*, originally 'two-thirds of an as' (12.5.2.). Similarly *tres partes* 'three-quarters', *quattuor partes* 'four-fifths' etc.

12.6.4. 'Quarter'

Latin *quadrāns* (masc.) appears to be the participle of *quadrāre* (see 12.5.4.). However it may represent an analogical remodelling of the reflex of **kʷtwr̥-yn̥t-* or the like (see above on *triens*). The phonology of *dōdrāns* 'three-quarters' (*dempto quadrante*: Var. *L.* 5.172), said to be derived from **dēquadrāns* [117], 'minus a quarter', is wholly obscure. The former word occurs in various phrases, e.g. *terni quadrantes* 'three-quarters', *quadrans cum triente* 'seven-twelfths'.

12.6.5. 'Sixth'

Latin *sextāns*, unlike the preceding, is based on the ordinal stem; cf. *sexta pars*. The word occurs in various phrases, e. g. *sextans cum quadrante* 'five-twelfths', *quini sextantes* 'five-sixths'. *dextans* 'five-sixths' is by syncope from **dē-sextāns* 'minus a sixth'.

Notes

1. I am grateful to W. Sidney Allen and Calvert Watkins for reading a draft of this chapter in 1971, when it was written, and making valuable comments and criticisms. Their advice has not always been heeded, so they must not be incriminated in what is left.
2. For which see the lists in Neue — Wagener (1902: 275—343). Latin citations follow the usual conventions; for Italic texts, Vetter's numbering is employed.
3. I for the 'unit' is self-explanatory; V for 'five' seems to have originated as a pictogram of the open hand, X for 'ten' as a pair of crossed hands; L for 'fifty', C for 'one hundred', M for 'one thousand' have developed from the three redundant letters of the Western Greek alphabet, L from ѱ, C from Θ, through the influence of *centum*, M for Φ through the influence of *mille*. D 'five hundred' is in origin a half of Φ. For further details see Neue — Wagener (1902: 343—345).
4. In contrast to **sem-* signifying 'inclusion, togetherness', which provided the Greek and Armenian cardinals and is reflected in the Latin adverbial and distributive forms. A possible connection with the pronominal **i- *eyo-* reflected in Latin *is, eum*, is suggested by the comparison of Skt. *éka-* with the defective deictic pronoun *ena-* 'this', and by the use of the feminine *ἰά* of the pronominal *ἰός* attested in Central Cretan, to form the cardinal numeral in Aeolic Greek (Homeric examples are ambiguous, e. g. *ἰοῖ ἤματι Il.* 6.422 could mean 'on that day' or 'in one day'). The connection would accord with an analysis of **i-* as *$ə_1$*i-*, **eyo-* as *$ə_1$*ey-o-* and **oi-* as *$ə_1$*oy-*.
5. Often interpreted as *oino(m)*, but it is probable that vowel weakening was already complete and that *oino*, **oinum*, were in free variation, the former indicating a retention of the open vowel in final unchecked position.
6. Cf. Skt. *éka-* with pronominal declension (except in nom.-acc. sg. ntr. *ékam*) and pronominal usage in *ékaḥ ... ékaḥ, éke ... ápare* 'some ... others', etc.
7. Although the derivation of *unu* from **ouinom* 'victim', proposed by Pisani (1964: 195), cf. *AGI* xxvii (1935: 165—166) and adopted by Vetter (1953: 190), is phonologically satisfactory, it presupposes an improbable Proto-Italic *-ĭno-*, cf. *-īno-* in Latin *ouīnus*, Umbr. gen. sg. *cabriner* 'goat-meat' (< **kaprīneis*); see Poultney (1959: 173).

8. Treatment of the continuants in Proto-Indo-European throughout this chapter follows largely the version of the Sievers — Edgerton rules set out in W. P. Lehmann, *Proto-Indo-European phonology* (Austin, 1952) pp. 10—11. However it is difficult to see how considerations of word-juncture can be integrated into a consistent view of the Indo-European phenomena, and in the present chapter these are ignored altogether.

8a. If this and not *-ai* is the correct vocalism. For the possibility that these inflected forms were themselves derived from an earlier PIE **d(u)wo*, which they may not have entirely ousted, see n. 11.

9. For the possibility that *δώδεκα*, like OIrish *da*, reflects PIE **do-* beside **dwo-* (cf. Hitt. *tān, tāyuga-*) see É. Benveniste, *Hittite et Indo-Européen* (1962: 85—86).

10. Occasional instances of monosyllabic *duo*, e.g. Pl. *Epid.* 344, are probably insignificant in this connection, representing rather the free but rare variation between *CuV* and *CwV* sequences seen in *t̯uam* (Pl. *Trin.* 185), *genu̯a* for *genua* (Verg. *A* 5.432), *soluit* for *solu̯it* (Cato 2.13).

11. For the phonological conditions in which this change occurred see W. S. Allen, *Vox Latina* (1978: 86); *JL* v (1969: 193—203). It is possible that Latin *duŏ*, Greek *δύο*, Arm *erko-* in *erkotasan* 'twelve' are not due to independent shortening but rather reflect a PIE **duŏ*, viz. the lexical stem without inflection.

12. Welsh fem. *dwy* < **dwei* would support its antiquity, if this is not just a parallel independent development.

13. If this was indeed the inherited form; fem. *duobus* (*CIL* 9.2151A) is probably an analogical innovation rather than an archaic survival.

14. Cf. Skt. *áśvābhyaḥ* 'mares', Gaulish *namausicabo*. Latin *dextrabus* (Liv. Andr. ap. Non. 493), *filiabus* (Cato ap. Prisc. *GL* 2.293 ff.), *gnatabus* (Pl. ap. Prisc. *ibid.*) can be regarded therefore as archaisms rather then innovations, retained, no doubt, beside the normal Latin feminines *dextrīs, gnatīs, filiīs* (< *-eis* < **ais*) to distinguish them from the masculine homophones with *-īs* (< *-eis* < **ois*).

15. The assumed distribution of neuter plural morphs in Proto-Italic *-*a* or *-∅ (< *$ə_2$) in athematic stems and *-*ā* (< *-*e*$ə_2$) in thematics, is, of course, very conjectural. The latter was certainly generalised in Oscan and Umbrian, e.g. *petiropert* 'four times', *teremenniú* 'boundary-stones' and *sakreu* 'sacred', *pequo* 'animals'. It is difficult to account for *-ā* in the Latin decads except on the assumption of a similar extension in Proto-Latin, unless of course one assumes the influence of an inherited *-ī* in *uīgintī*. However, if **trīkent(ă)* gave **trīkentā* etc. in Proto-Italic, or at least in Proto-Latin, and this provided the model for the replacement of **uīkenti* by **uīkentī*, as proposed in 12.1.12., the combined influence of this *-ī* in turn and the indeclinable character of the tens in Latin would have sufficed to protect the *-ā* from the general Latin change *-ā* > *-ă*. All this would be easier if we could

assume that the *-ā* of the tens was the nominative singular of a collective *-ā*-stem or the neuter plural of a thematic formation **-konto-*, but both these hypotheses raise more difficulties at the level of Indo-European comparison.

16. The isolated Greek *τριᾱ́κοντα*, if it is not an independent parallel, would suggest that the generalization of *-ā* began still earlier.
17. Alternatively *triiu* might be the ablative of **tri-yā* 'a group of three' (for the suffix see 12.5.5.), though the oblique cases of *ā*-stems in Umbrian normally have *-a*, e. g. nom. sg. *muta, mutu* 'penalty', but *asa* 'altar', abl. sg. *tota* 'community'.
18. For the syllabifications here and throughout see 12.1.2.1., note 8.
19. Cf. the derivation from **kʷъtwores* adopted by Leumann – Hofmann (1926: § 206).
20. Meillet, *Esquisse d'une grammaire comparée de l'armenien classique* (1936) 54, derived Arm. *č̣ork῾* 'four' from **ktwores*. Szemerényi (1960: 19–21) revives an older derivation (Brugmann – Delbrück 1897–1916: I. 619): **kʷetwores* > **kʷetores* (cf. Greek *τέτορες*) > **č̣eyor*; but PIE **kʷe* > Arm. *k῾e* not *č̣e*; cf. *elīk* < **elikʷet* and indirectly *hngetasan* < **penkʷe -dkn̥ni*.
21. See Buck (1928: §§ 81, 100.3*c*, 192.2). Pisani's derivation (1964: 58 n. 14), of *petiru* by metathesis from **petiur-*, reflecting **kʷetur-*, is unlikely, since in forms like *últiumam* 'last' (< **oltumam*) the *i* is consonantal and there is no parallel for the further shift of *-tyu-* to *tiu-*.
22. The change *e* > *o* is perhaps more likely in the labio-velar environment (cf. **swen-* > Umbr. *sonitu*, as Latin *sonitō*; in Oscan *sverrunei* the following liquid has impeded the change, cf. Latin *uorsus* > *uersus*) than after the replacement of the labio-velar by the labial stop, cf. Umbr. *pelmner* 'meat' (< **pelp-men-eis*), *peperscust* 'to place', etc., with *e*, not *o*. In Latin the presence of the following nasal in **kʷenkʷe* seems to have impeded the assimilatory change to the back vowel attested in *coquō* (< **quoquō* < **kʷekʷō* < **pekʷō*) and *colō* (< **kʷelō*).
23. So Szemerényi (1960: 78–79). If however **weks* < *ə$_2$*weg-s* 'increase, enlargement', cf. *ə$_2$*ew-g-* reflected in Latin *augere*, Greek *αὔξω* etc., then the addition of *s-* would have to postdate the loss of the laryngal or we should expect **sə$_2$ewgs* > **sawks*, etc.
24. For arguments in favour of *-m* here see Szemerényi (1960: 171–173).
25. Vetter (1953: no. 364 b). The change of *-n* to *-m* may have already taken place, the *n* here possibly being due to sandhi before the following word *deiuo* (genitive plural).
26. The use of the *t*-suffix to form (originally neuter) collectives may plausibly be attributed to Indo-European. In addition to the Lithuanian forms in *-t-* and *-ti-*, Vedic *daśát-* (later Sanskrit *daśati-*) beside *dáśa*, and perhaps Greek *δεκάδ-* with *-δ-* generalised from, for instance, acc. pl. *δεκάδας* < **dekn̥dn̥s* < **dekn̥t-n̥s*, with animate declension, all reflect PIE **dekm̥tə$_2$* or **dekomtə$_2$*

(ntr pl.; see Szemerényi (1960: 30–31)). That *$dek\mathring{m}t$* was not the only Indo-European cardinal form is proved by the survival of *m* in Latin. For *$dek\mathring{m}t$* would have given Latin **decent*. Moreover Skt. *dáśa* would have to be explained as an analogical remodelling of **daśat* (< *$dek\mathring{m}t$*) after *náva* 'nine'. This does not rule out a connection between *$dek\mathring{m}$* and PrGmc. **xandu-* 'hand', as suggested by R. Thurneysen, *KZ* xxvi (1883: 310 n. 1); cf. Szemerényi (1960: 69), since the latter could be from **kem-* + *-tu*-suffix.

27. So J. Wackernagel, *KZ* xxxiii (1890: 10–11).
28. For other reconstructions of the initial syllable see below, especially notes 30, 31. Although there is no evidence whatever for *d-* in either component, it is *a priori* probable that the words for 'twenty' and 'ten' contained a common lexical item, and *-$dk\mathring{m}t$-* has the advantage of providing a cluster of which the simplification could account for the long vowel of the preceding syllable in this and subsequent tens. The relation between *$dk\mathring{m}t$-* here and *$dek\mathring{m}t$-* in 12.1.10. is admittedly obscure. The zero grade of the initial syllable in the former is unlikely to be the result of syncope in the latter. Although it might represent a paradigmatic variation as between dual-plural and singular, it seems best on the whole to treat *$dek\mathring{m}t$-* as a remodelling of *-$dk\mathring{m}t$-* on the cardinal *$dek\mathring{m}$*.
29. The reconstruction of the Proto-Indo-European nominative-accusative dual neuter in the consonant declension is very uncertain. Skt. *bṛhatī́* 'high', OCS *imeni* 'name', etc. < *-ī, which looks like a borrowing from the *i*-stems, Greek *γένεε* has *-ε* from the animate paradigms. The first of the above Indo-European forms is based, without much conviction, on an extrapolation of *-i* from the thematic declension, e. g. Skt. *yugé* 'yokes', OCS *idzě* (< *-oi). It is possible that *-i* was already replaced in some dialects of Indo-European by *-ī* (see below). *-tī*, being identical with the dual of *-tis* would then be the starting-point for the otherwise puzzling intrusion of what is normally a verbal noun formant into the numeral system in many areas of extant Indo-European.
30. Sommer's **dwī* (*KZ* xxx, 1912: 404) and (1913: 468)) is an improbable dual, since the abundant evidence points clearly to masc. **d(u)wōu*, fem.-ntr **d(u)woi* (or less probably, fem. **d(u)wai*).
31. **wī̆-* has sometimes been taken as the original form (e. g. Brugmann – Delbrück 1897–1916: II. ii. 11; Kent 1946: 325.3). Skt. *ví-* 'separated', *vitarám* 'further', Gothic *wiþra-* 'against' indicate a basic meaning 'apart' for this root, which would give for *$widk\mathring{m}t$-* a meaning 'a decad apart, the other decad'. But the pattern of the latter decads, formed with the normal unit-compositives, favours **dwi-* here. Toch. (A) *wu we*, (B) *wi* are irrelevant, showing simply the normal phonological reflex of PIE **dw-*.
32. East Greek *εἴκοσι*, with *-o-* from subsequent decads, might seem to provide surer evidence for *$weik\mathring{m}ti$*, but the change of **woi-* to **wei-*, easy enough in Latin, is hard to explain for Greek, and it is better to derive *εἴκοσι* from

ε-ϝīκατι with *e* < **he-*, transferred from *ἑκατόν* 'hundred' or from some other source.

33. The assumption that **wīkm̥tī* was the only Proto-Indo-European form and *-ĭ* a specifically Indo-Iranian and Greek innovation (see J. Wackernagel – A. Debrunner, *Altindische Grammatik* 1930: 145; F. B. J. Kuiper, *Lingua* iii, (1956: 332) is less attractive. Apart from the problem of an Indo-European consonant-stem dual in *-ī* noted above, neither Indo-Iranian nor Greek shows a normal change *-ī* > *-i*, and the special case of correption in Greek *δύω* > *δύο* does not seem a compelling parallel; cf. note 11.
34. Cf. *maester* for *magister* (*CIL* 3.14730). The alternative assumption of a weakening by loss of occlusion in pre-accentual position, viz. [g] > [γ] > [h] > ∅ is less likely, since the change occurs only before front vowels (see C. H. Grandgent, *Introduction to Vulgar Latin*, 1963: § 259).
35. The clue to this reconstruction, which obviously owes much to the distinction between a *τριᾱκάς*-Reihe and a *τριᾱ́κοντα*-Reihe made by Brugmann – Delbrück (1897–1916: II. ii. 30, 32–37), lies in the fact that a PIE pl. **tri-dkomtə* or the like ought to mean not 'triple decad' but 'triple decads' viz. 'sixty', 'ninety', etc., cf. **wīkm̥ti* 'two double decads', 12.1.12.
36. I originally assumed that the assimilatory change **mt* > **nt* postulated here for PIE would also have affected *m̥t*, giving, for instance, *-km̥t-* > *-kn̥t-* in 12.1.12. But, as Professor Allen points out, **m̥* in such cases marks a syllabic peak and is therefore less likely to have been assimilated; cf. the distinct reflexes of PIE **-m̥t-*, **-n̥t-* in Lith. *rim̃ti* 'to be quiet', *giñti* 'to drive' (Skt. *ráti-* 'rest', *háti-* 'blow').
37. Cf. Gaulish *petru-* in composition. The normal development of PIE **r̥* to Celtic *ri* (Thurneysen 1946: § 215) is here disrupted by the preceding *w*, as by preceding labio-velars (ibid. § 223).
38. *uigenti* (*CIL* 5.1645) is, by contrast, merely a graphic confusion of *ē* and *i*, representing the Vulgar convergence of earlier /e/ and /i/ at [ẹ].
39. The sequence *-twr-*, though it emerged too late to be bound by the relevant Sievers – Edgerton formula, is nevertheless patently unstable. For the change assumed here, admittedly a very ad hoc bit of phonology, cf. Szemerényi (1960: 69) and Leumann – Hofmann (1926: § 143 a), where, however, the relation between **kʷъturā* and the **kʷetwr̥* set up in § 206 is not discussed. Yet the alternatives, *twrā* > *trā*, would yield sequences that appear to be stable in Latin (if not in West Romance, e. g. *petra* > Sp. *piedra*, Fr. **pedre* > *pierre*; cf. It. *pietra*, Rum. *piatra*). Professor Allen points out that ad hoc phonology is sometimes required to account for the later forms of Indo-Aryan numerals, e. g. Hindi *bārah* 'twelve' with *r* not *ā* < OInd. *dvā́daśa*, dialectal *gyārah* 'eleven' with intrusive *y* < OInd. *ékodaśa*, *cālīs* 'forty' with *l* not *r* < OInd. *catvāriṃśát*.
40. Cf. Greek *ἑξήκοντα*, with *-η-* from *πεντήκοντα*, replacing the type II reflex **hekskonta* which would have given **heskonta*. The loss of distinctiveness

in the morphemic structure resulting from phonetic changes that **-ksk-* would have undergone in Sanskrit and Avestan may have been the reason for the adoption of the elliptical *ṣaṣṭí-*, *xšvašti-* 'hexad (of decads)', which provided the model for 'seventy', etc. That the latter lexico-syntactic pattern was inherited is suggested by Old Church Slavonic *pętĭ desętŭ, šestĭ desętŭ*, etc., where the first items had in fact become the normal unit forms: 'a group of five' etc., cf. Germanic **funxstiz* 'first'. However, it is doubtful whether the development of a collective numeral suffix *-ti-* from **wīkn̥ti* or any other source should be attributed to Proto-Indo-European.

41. Greek *ἑβδομήκοντα* may reflect either type IIb viz. **hebdmākonta* – IIa would give **heptakonta* – or a conflation of type I **hebdmākat-* and type II. The *-η-* is by analogy with preceding decads.
42. The sequence *-ptm-* here, as in Greek, where the stops have been assimilated to the sonority of the following nasal, would have emerged too late to be subject to the Sievers – Edgerton formulations (cf. Sommer 1950: 17), though the anaptyxis in both languages illustrates the instability of such a cluster.
43. Or even **septmā-* > **septwā-* > *septuā-*. The change *-umā-* > *-uwā-*, first proposed by S. Bugge, *BB* xiv (1889: 71), cf. S. Pieri, *RFC* xxxv (1907: 312 f.), was attributed by him to a dissimilatory impulse before the nasal of the following syllable; see most recently Szemerényi (1960: 7). There seems to be no parallel for this phonetic change in Latin, though an interchange between [m] and [w] is sometimes attested in other languages; see for instance, M. Bloomfield and F. Edgerton, *Vedic variants* (1932: 115–124), and cf. Hindī *sātwā̃*, Mar. *sātvā* 'seventh' < Pali, Pkt. *sattama-*, Skt. *saptamá-* (Turner, *Comparative dictionary of the Indo-Aryan languages* 1966: no. 13151).
44. For instance by J. Wackernagel, *KZ* xxv (1881: 281); Meillet – Vendryes (1960: § 748) Leumann – Hofmann (1926: § 206 f.).
45. Diehl, *Christ*. 1428.
46. Cf. OIrish *sechtmogo*, which reflects a remodelling of **septm̥̄kn̥t-* (type I) to **septm̥kont-*, as in the earlier decads, whence **sechtm̥mukont* (with *-u-* from **kʷetrukont-*, **ochtūkont-*), and *ochtmoga* with *-m-* from *sechtmogo*.
47. Cf. Brugmann – Delbrück (1897–1916: II. ii. 35) Walde – Hofmann (1938: 518).
48. Cf. Sommer (1950: 37 ff.); Szemerényi (1960: 2–3).
49. So E. Risch, *IF* lxvii (1962: 136), who relates it to the ordinal analysis of the first component in Latin *septuaginta*, Greek *ἑβδομήκοντα*, rejected in 12.1.13.5. There is in fact no necessity to assume that **dkm̥tom* on this analysis was in origin a member of a sequential pattern rather than a sui-generis formation.
50. For objections to **dekm̥t* (and *a fortiori* **dkm̥t*) as the original form of the cardinal, see 12.1.10., 12.2.10.

51. A meaning reflected in *-to-* verbal adjectives, ordinal and superlative formations, e. g. Greek *ῥυτός, δέκατος, ἥδιστος*; see E. Benveniste, *Noms d'agent et noms d'action en indo-européen* (1948: § 11).
52. This has been held to be the original analysis of the form, e. g. by Brugmann – Delbrück (1897–1916: II. ii. 40), Meillet – Vendryes (1960: § 749); but a parallel gradation-pattern in thematic and athematic formations (**dkm̥t-* in both) is implausible, unless one is a derivative of the other, as proposed above.
53. The influence of the decad-form is also seen in *τριᾱκάτιοι, τριᾱκόσιοι* for **τρικατ-*, whence also *διᾱκάτιοι, διᾱκόσιοι.*
54. Cf. Classical Sanskrit *ṣaṭśataiḥ padātibhiḥ* 'with six hundred infantry' for the older constructions *ṣaṭśatám p., ṣaṭśaténa p., ṣaṭśaténa padātīnām.*
55. So Brugmann – Delbrück (1897–1916: II. ii. 15, 46). This may be the correct reading in Pl. *Ba.* 934, *Ru.* 1324 where the manuscripts have *quadringenti.*
56. The *a* might be derived phonologically from a base **kʷturkn̥to-* which would normally have yielded **quaturcento-* or perhaps **quaturgento-*, but the assumption of a Latin reflex of this form of the compositional unit is problematic (see 12.4.5.4.).
57. Indeed R. Thurneysen, *KZ* xxvi (1883: 312–313) regarded this as one of the starting-points for the general extension of *-g-* throughout the hundreds and the decads.
58. The Attic form must on this analysis reflect an assimilatory change of *-ηλι-* (cf. Ion. *χέιλιοι*) to *-ῑλι-* (see J. Wackernagel, 1909: 326 ff.). The alternative would be to derive *χῑλιοι* < **χισλιοι* < **ghslyo-*, a thematic-suffix adjective from **ghsli-*, an *i*-stem doublet of **gheslo-*, the *-yo*-adjectival derivative of which would, presumably, provide the reflexes exhibited in the other dialects.
59. So E. W. Fay, *AJPh* xiii (1892: 226–227); *IF* xi (1900: 320–322). Cf. Sommer, *IF* x (1899: 216 ff.). The gradation pattern of the second component here cannot be established with any certainty. O. Szemerényi, *Archivum linguisticum* vi (1954: 38–41), operates with **smī gheslī*, assuming an assimilatory change **mīhēlī* > **mīhīlī* in the penultimate stage of the Latin development.
60. By contrast, the feminine *-wī* of *u*-stem adjectives was attracted to the *i*-stem animate paradigm in *-is*, which subsequently ousted the masculine forms; cf. *gurvī́, mr̥dvī́, svādvī́* (< **-wiə₂* beside masc *-us*) with *grauis, mollis, suāuis.*
61. E. Hamp, *Gl* xlvi (1968: 275–277) has suggested **smī ghesliyă̄* as the starting-point, with *mīlia* as its direct reflex, treated as a neuter plural, and a singular **mīl(l)i* formed from it. There are difficulties here. Whereas **smī gheslī*, **smī gheslīā* (< *-ieə₂*) might be postulated as free forms within the same synchronic structure, Hamp's *-iă̄* beside *-ī* begs a large question. Moreover the diachrony proposed by him: **smīgheslia* > **mīheslia* >

**mīhehlya* > **mīhlia* > *mīlia* entails too much ad hoc phonology. Moreover it is hard to see why the outcome was not a Latin feminine sg. **mīlia*, pl. **mīliae*.

62. *-is-mo-* may also lie behind *maxumus* (usually derived from **mag-sm̥mos*): viz. **magsumos* < **magsmos* < **magismos*; cf. *maior* < **mag-ios-* and *magis*.
63. It is debatable whether in *alterum quadrimum* (Pl. *Cap*. 8), the pronoun should be scanned as – ∪ ∪ (so W. M. Lindsay, *Early Latin Verse*, 1922: 146) or as --.
64. The phonological conditions for this change are difficult to define; cf. Sommer (1913: § 55.1), Leumann – Hofmann (1926: § 102.1a). The emergence of *r̥* must postdate the change of inherited *r̥* to *or* reflected for instance in Latin *transuorsus* Umbr. *trahuorfi* 'crosswise', which prevents the equation of *tertius* with *tr̥tīyaḥ*. It may have been helped by the change **tris* > **ters* (> *ter*, see 12.3.3.) and **tri-stā̆s* 'standing third', > **terst-* (see *testis* 'witness', 12.5.3.), but these developments are themselves unclear. Aeolic Greek *τέρτος* is insufficient to justify setting up PIE **ter* without *-i*, though the latter is not in itself impossible.
65. Somewhat unlikely, but remarkably paralleled in Germanic: **fedwurda-* > OHG *fiordo*, OE *fēorþa* 'fourth'.
66. It can hardly mean 'second' as Vetter proposes, following J. Untermann, *Kratylos* i (1956: 65).
67. For sporadic evidence of a tendency for vowels to be lengthened before *r* + consonant, see Sommer (1913: § 83.5).
68. Though it has been assumed by many scholars (see Leumann – Hofmann 1926: § 207.4) including, most recently, Szemerényi (1960: 79), who operates with **quat(t)uor-tos*, which he explains by the influence of the cardinal. This form could, however, reflect an inherited ordinal formation. See below.
69. See Brugmann – Delbrück(1897–1916: II. ii. 54), Sommer (1913: § 299.4), Leumann – Hofmann (1926: § 207).
70. On Old High German *funfto* see Szemerényi (1960: 71–73).
71. The gentile name *Sestius*, however, occurs earlier beside *Sextius*, the doublets being specialized for different families, e. g. *C. Sextius Caluinus* (*Fast. Triumph*. 122 B.C.), *L. Sextius* (*Fast. Cons*. 366 B.C.) but *P. Sestius* (*Fast. Cons*. 452 B.C.), *L. Sestius Quirinalis* (*Fast. Cons*. 23 B.C.).
72. That this group originally included the whole sequence from at least 'third' to 'tenth' – **triy-os*, **kʷtur-os* etc. – is very probable. See Szemerényi (1960: 67–114), who, however, postulates **dekm̥t-os* for 'tenth'. It is possible that the introduction of *-mo-* into the ordinal system, as reflected in Skt. *pañcamá-, aṣṭamá-, navamá-*, began precisely from a redivision of **septm̥-m-o-*, **dekm̥m-o-* (see Brugmann – Delbrück 1897–1916: II. ii. 50). Kuryłowicz's attempt (1964: 235–239 to relate both *-mo-* and *-to-* to the bare thematic suffix by exclusively phonological procedures does not carry

much conviction). If *-mo-* outside the numeral system originally had a semantic field relevant to its late Indo-European use as a superlative, this would provide an overlap with *-to-* marking the completion of a series or state (see 12.1.15.0. and note 51), and so explain the rivalry of the two suffixes in ordinal function, as revealed in Skt. *daśamá-, ṣaṣṭhá-, śatatamá-*, cf. *adhamá-* 'lowest', *svā̆diṣṭa-* 'sweetest', *uttamá-* 'highest', with subsequent specialisations of one or the other, as in Latin *primus, decimus, suauissimus* and Greek *πρῶτος, δέκατος, ἥδιστος*, Gothic *frumists* 'first', *taíhunda* 'tenth', *sutists* 'sweetest'.

73. So Brugmann — Delbrück (1897—1916: II. ii. 56), deriving *-u-* from *-ōu-*, transferred from the cardinal, which however shows *-au* in Gothic; also Szemerényi (1960: 89), deriving *-ū-* from *-ō-*. The phonology is a little askward in both cases.
74. So Sommer (1950: 25), who reconstructs Proto-Gmc. **axtuwaz* (< **oktu-wos*).
75. So Ernout — Meillet (1951: 663).
76. The alternative assumption of the normal phonological development of *-owo-* to *-ūo-* to *-uo-* would give **octuus*, which has sometimes been held to be reflected in *octuaginta* (see 12.1.13.6.). For the obscure conditions of the shift from *-ou-* to *-au-* attested, for instance, in *lauo, caueo*, see Sommer (1913: § 77.1—2).
77. So Sommer (1913: § 299), Walde — Hofmann (1956: 200), following R. Thurneysen, *KZ* xxviii (1887: 154).
78. For this change see Thurneysen, *KZ* xxviii (1887: 154), Meillet — Vendryes (1960: § 163), Szemerényi, *KZ* lxx (1951: 51—52). If it is recent, as these scholars assume, then the laryngeal origins of some at least of these Latin long vowels are irrelevant. If it is early, then the phonology is difficult. Martinet's account (cf. *Word* ix, 1953: 253—267; *Phonetica* i, 1957: 20, etc.) raises almost as many problems as it solves. Thus the derivations ***$ə_3$*ekteəʒ* > **oktō(u)*, ***$ə_3$*ekteə*$_3$*os* > **oktāwos* assume not only a different colouring of the ablaut vowel by the following laryngeal in each case but also an improbable lengthening of the preceding vowel on the loss of the laryngeal in the latter form, viz. *eə*$_3$ # > *ōw*, *eə*$_3$*C* > *ōC* but *eə*$_3$*V* > *eə*^{w}*V* > *āuV*. It would be possible to derive **octăuos* from ***$ə_3$*ektə*$_3$*-os*, treating *-u-* as the residue of a labio-velar component of $ə_3$, *or even from **$ə_3$*ektə̥*$_3$*ə̥* $_3$*os*, though the assumption that the laryngeal allophones followed the same distributional pattern as the continuants (see n. 8) is admittedly disputable, and the reflex of such a sequence as *-tə̥ʒ*$_3$*əʒ*$_3$*o-* is highly uncertain. The chief objection, however, is that the replacement of the original thematic stem of ***$ə_3$*ekto-* by a stem incorporating the laryngeal of the dual case-form would then have to be put back into the full laryngeal stage of PIE. The whole question remains obscure.
79. A parallel formation **enwn̥nos* from **enwn̥* (see 12.2.9.), which seems to have coalesced with *newn̥* to produce the Greek cardinal, viz. *εννέα* < **en-*

newn̥, probably lies behind Greek *ἔνατος*, with **enwanos*, reflecting inherited **enwn̥nos*, remodelled after *δέκατος* (cf. Germanic **newunda-*).

80. See Vetter (1953: no. 364b, note).
81. Cf. **co-uentio* > **countio* > **cọ̄ntio* > *cŏntio*, influenced by *conuentus* etc., in contrast to *nūntiare* < *nọ̄ntiare* (*CIL* i.586: *nontiata*) < *nountiare* (cf. Marius Victorinus, *GL* 6.12.18) < **nouentiare*.
82. Greek *δέκατος* would then reflect the allomorph in *-to-*, viz. **dekm̥-tos*. This seems preferable to a Proto-Indo-European analysis **dekm̥t-os*, since it is hard to see why the corresponding Sanskrit and Latin reflexes **daśatá-*, **decentus* should have been displaced; cf. 12.1.10., n. 26 on the cardinal. Celtic shows a combination of both allomorphs: OIrish *dechmad*, Gaulish *decametos* < **dekm̥mo-* + *dekm̥to-*.
83. Reminiscent of the break that occurs in the cardinal series of certain other languages, though not in Latin itself; e. g. Gothic dat. *ainlibim, twalif*, but *fidwortaíhun*, etc.; Greek *ἕνδεκα, δώδεκα* but *τρεῖς καὶ δέκα*, etc.
84. So Kent (1946: § 342), Walde – Hofmann's (1956: 512) citation of the obscure Gothic *simle* 'once upon a time' does not, however, guarantee the reconstruction.
85. See Walde – Hofmann (1956: 512). The different reflexes of *l̥* in final unchecked position and before *-s* present no difficulty. The regular phonological development **semlis* > **seml̥s* > *semel* was of course counteracted in the adjective by paradigmatic analogy.
86. The precise phonology is uncertain; both **sem-ə*$_1$*l* and **sm̥m-ə*$_1$*l* (> **sum-*, replaced by *sem-* analogically) are possible. Among other analyses are Brugmann – Delbrück's (1897–1916: II. ii. 65–66) from **sem- uēlom*, which includes a root found in parallel function in Skt. *ekavāram*, cf. *vā́ra-* 'time', but not otherwise attested in Latin; Wackernagel's (*KZ* xxx, 1890: 316) from **sm̥-mēli*, presumably with analogical *sem-* for **sum-*, but again with a root attested only elsewhere, in Gothic *mel* 'time', Old High German *z'einemo mâle*.
87. The attested contexts of this suffix might suggest that the *i* is a glide and that its original form was *-n̥t-*: *quinquiens* replacing **quinquens* < **penk*^{w}*n̥ts* 'a group of five' by analogy with **quotients*, **totients*. But *-n̥t-* is not attested elsewhere as a collective-numeral formant, except indirectly in Greek *πεντάς, πεντάδ-*, etc., where it seems rather to have spread from *δεκάς* < **dekn̥-ts*, reflecting PIE **-t-*, not **-n̥t-*; so we should have then to assume that Latin *-ent-* spread from **dekents*, which was itself subsequently replaced by **dekients*.
88. So Leumann – Hofmann (1926: § 171.1B.2b), who explain Gothic *ainakls* 'alone' in the same way.
89. An alternative derivation is from **sm̥-g*^{w}*olo-* 'thrown together, running together into one' compounded of the zero grade of *sem-* and the root reflected in Greek *βάλλω, βόλος*, Skt. *gálati* 'he vanishes', OHG *kuëlan* 'gush' and perhaps Latin *uolāre*; viz. > **semguolo-* > **singuulo-* > *singulus*.

90. Leumann – Hofmann (1926: § 208) suggest a falling together of a distributive **dwis-no-* and a collective **dwī-no-*, but the status of the assumed distinction in Indo-European is very dubious.
91. For the change after 'four' from the use of the compositional to that of the cardinal forms cf. the similar break between *quater* and *quinquiē(n)s*.
92. For this reconstruction see 12.1.12.
93. The derivation of *uncia* 'ounce', also 'inch' or 'twelfth part of anything' from **oinicia* (cf. Varro *L.* 5.171: *uncia ab uno*) is improbable if the early Sicilian Greek *ὀγκία* 'a measure of weight', cited by Photius, and the Himeran coin *οὐγκία*, cited by Pollux from Aristotle, are cognates. A loan from Sicel or some similar source seems possible for both the Latin and Greek forms, though the Latin one may have been influenced by *unus*. See H. B. Rosén, *Language* xl (1964: 21–22). It is of course conceivable that there were two homonyms, the one a loan-word, the other a *-yā-* derivative of **oineko-*, but *uncia* is certainly not as straightforward as it once seemed.
94. See F. Sommer, *IF* ix (1900: 64 ff.). Ernout – Meillet (1951: 947) suggest a contamination of *primus* with *prior*; W. Prellwitz, *BB* xxvi (1901: 46 ff.) and M. Leumann, *Gl* xiii (1924: 32) derive the word somewhat implausibly from the phrase *primo ore* meaning 'an der Vorderseite'.
95. Wackernagel's suggestion, *Gl* ii (1913: 1–2), that *bīduum* has been influenced by *postrīdiē* 'on the next day' seems unlikely.
96. A similar dissimilation in such compounds as Latin **dwis-wertō*, **dwis-weidō*, **dwis-weldō*, reflected ultimately in *dīuerto, dīuīdo, dīuello*, could have produced the common verbal prefix *dis-* 'apart'; but this would perhaps entail rejecting the cognateness of Gothic *dis-*, Old High German *zir-*. For the remote possibility of PIE **dis-* beside **dwis*, cf. 12.1.2.1., n. 9.
97. The semantic association of 'two/doubt/fear', attested in Fr. *doute, redouter*; Gothic *tweifls* 'doubt', *twai* 'two'; Greek *δείδω, ἐν δοιῇ* (cf. *Iliad* 9.229–30), are already in PIE **dwei-* 'to fear', **dwōu*. See É. Benveniste, *Word* x (1954: 255).
98. For a plausible suggestion as to how *-eə₂s* could give *-āx* in *audāx*, *-ăx* > *-ex* in *senex*, see C. Watkins (Winter 1965: 186–187). Professor Watkins himself now disowns this analysis.
99. A laryngeal account of the *-k*-suffix generally in Umbrian is supported by the consistent appearance of *-a-* preceding it, e. g. acc. sing. *curnaco* 'crow', nom. sing. *huntak* 'earthernware jar'.
100. For the possibility of an Etruscan origin see C. Watkins (Birnbaum – Puhvel pp. 45–48).
101. Where the regular phonology would in any case give *-stə₂s* > *-stas* > *-stes* > *-stis*, though the remodelling may have predated the completion of vowel-weakening.
102. E. Goldmann's suggestion, *Zeitschrift der Savigny Stiftung für Rechtsgeschichte, Romanistische Abteilung* li (1921: 22–34), that it is a loan-word from Latin, merely transfers the problem from Oscan to Latin, but the thematic declension certainly suggests independent origin.

103. F. Skutsch, *Beiträge zur Kunde der indogermanischen Sprachen* xxiii (1897: 100) suggested **trito-sti-*, but this is perhaps less likely for Italic, where an ordinal **trito-* is unattested.
104. *quadruuiis* is in fact a manuscript variant at Catullus 58.4.
105. The isolated *quatriduum* (*CIL* 2.21) is clearly influenced by *quattuor, quater*.
106. Although Greek *τρυφάλεια* is usually derived from *k^wtru-*, this pattern cannot be inherited, any more than that of *k^wtwr̥* which at first sight appears to be reflected in Greek *τράπεζα*.
107. The series may even be represented by *triiuper* (see 12.1.3.).
108. Cf. Szemerényi (1960: 113–114), whose derivation from PIE **pn̥k^wstis* 'fist' leaves open the question of how this form itself is to be analyzed.
109. Umbr. *semeniar* (gen. sg. or nom. pl. fem., *Ig*. 1B 42), dat.-abl. pl. *sehmenier* (*Ig*. 5B 11) is interpreted by Conway (1897: 482) as 'six-monthly', as if from **seks-mēn-yo-*, but the context is obscure and a wide variety of alternative interpretations of the words have been offered. The most plausible connect the word with Latin *sēmen*, making it a festival-name comparable to Latin *feriae sementiuae* (Buck 1928: 188) 'pertaining to sowing' or 'to the god Semo', with *semeniar dequriar* paralleled in *CIL* 6.568: *Sanco Sancto Semoni deo fidio sacrum decuria sacerdotum bidentalium* (Poultney 1959: 190, 293, following Pighi and Pisani). For other analyses see Devoto (1937: 301), Vetter (1953: 187).
110. *-trio* is obscure; it seems to be a deverbative *-iōn-* suffix, as in *legio, dicio*, and is perhaps formed on *terere* 'to rub', viz. **terio* 'a trampling', or less likely on *trahere* 'to haul' viz. **trahio* 'a hauling', whence *-*trehio* > *-*treio* > *-*trīo* > *-trio*. Var. *L*. 7.14 reports that *triones* was actually used in rustic dialect for *boues* and connects it with *terra*, though Gellius (2.21.8) credits him with the suggestion that in *Septentriones* it is related to *tres, ternae*. For a derivation from *-*sterio-* see Szemerényi, *Trends and tasks in comparative philology* (1961: 17).
111. Calvert Watkins points out that there is a parallel in OIrish *noínden* and evidence for a PIE *-*n*-stem in Old Church Slavonic *dĭnĭ*, gen. sg. *dĭne*, with thematic extension, as in Latin, in Vedic *su-dína-* 'brightness of the day'.
112. For *tekvias* the connection with the numeral is doubted by Vetter (1953: 205).
113. Cf. Poultney (1959: 106–107), Devoto (1937: 353). The latter assumes, however, an unlikely **ogduwos* for the ordinal. Buck (1928: § 191) suggested that **deku-* was by analogy with *k^wetru-*, but there is no evidence that the latter was reflected in Umbrian, and Latin *decussis, decuplex*, are inadequate support for a productive *deku-* in Italic. The reconstruction of an inherited **deku-* (e.g. by Pisani 1964: 202, n. 1) is improbable. It is based on the evidence for PrGmc *-u-* in forms like Gothic *tigjus*; but these ultimately

reflect not *_teʒus_ but *_teʒun-_ < PIE *_dekn̥-t-_; see Brugmann – Delbrück (1897–1916: II. ii. 37) and most recently Szemerényi (1960: 41–43).

114. Cf. Poultney (1959: 107), Leumann – Hofmann (1926: § 172.II.B.1).
115. See Buck (1928: 255–256), Vetter (1953: 107).
116. For an ingenious interpretation, connecting the second component with Latin _āter_ 'dark', see J. Wackernagel, _Archiv für Religionswissenschaft_ xxii (1923–24: 215).
117. So Ernout – Meillet (1951: 323), Walde – Hofmann (1938: 363).

Abbreviations

_A_	_Aeneid_
_Ad._	_Adria_
Agr.	_De agri cultura_
_Am._	_Amphitruo_
Amm. Marcell.	Ammianus Marcellinus
Anc.	_Monumentum ancyranum_
Andr.	Andronicus
Ann.	_Annales_
Anth.	_Anthologia Latina_ (A. Riese)
Ar.	Aristophanes
Arm.	Armenian
Att.	Attic
_Au._	_Aulularia_
Aug.	Augustus
Aur. Vict.	Aurelius Victor
Av.	Avestan
Avien. _Arat._	Avienus _Aratus_
Ba.	Bacchides
Bret.	Breton
_C._	_Carmina_
Caes.	Caesar
Cat.	Catullus
Cic.	Cicero
Cic. _Mil._	Cicero _Pro Milone_
CIL	_Corpus inscriptionum latinarum_
Colum.	_Columella_
Com.	_Commentaries_
Dial	_Dialogus de oratoribus_
Enn.	Ennius
_Ep._	_Epistulae_
Epid.	_Epidicus_
Epit.	_Epitomae_
Gal.	_De bello gallico_
Gell.	Gellius
_GL_	_Grammatica Latina_
Greg. Tur.	Gregory of Tours
Grom.	_Gromatici_
_H. F._	_Historia Francorum_
Hist.	_Historiae_
Hor.	Horae
Icel.	Icelandic
_Ig._	_Igurium_
_Il._	_Ilias_
Ind.	Indian
Ion.	Ionian
Iuvenc.	Iuvencus
_L._	_De lingua latina_
Leg.	_De legibus_
Lesb.	Lesbian
Liv.	Livy
Luc.	Lucas
Lucil.	Lucilius
Lucr.	Lucretius
Lyd.	Lydus
Manil.	Manilius
Mar.	Marāṭhī
Mart.	Martial

Mat.	Matthaeius	Plin.	Pliny
Men.	*Menaechmi*	Prud.	Prudentius
Mens.	De mensibus	Ps.	Pseudolus
Mer.	*Mercator*	*Ru.*	*Rudens*
Met.	*Metamorphoses*	*S.*	*Sermones*
Mil.	*Miles gloriosus*	Skt.	Sanskrit
Mo.	*Mostellania*	Span.	Spanish
Nat.	*Naturalis historia*	Stat.	Statius
ND	*De natura deorum*	Tac.	Tacitus
Non.	Nonius	Ter.	Terence
O	Old	Toch.	Tocharian
OCS	Old Church Slavonic	Trin.	Trinumus
OHG	Old High German	Umbr.	Umbrian
Or.	*De oratore*	Val. Fl.	Valerius Flaccus
Ov.	Ovid	*Ver.*	*In verrem*
Perist.	*Peristephanon*	Verg.	Virgilius
Pkt.	Prakrit	*Vir. Illustr.*	*De viris illustribus*
Pl.	Plautus	Vulg.	Vulgar

References

Brugmann, K. – B. Delbrück
1897–1916 *Grundriss der vergleichenden grammatik der indogermanischen Sprachen* (2nd edition) (Strassburg).

Buck, C. D.
1928 *A Grammar of Oscan and Umbrian* (Boston).

Conway, R. S.
1897 *The Italic dialects* (Cambridge).

Devoto, G.
1937 *Tabulae Iguuinae* (Rome).

Ernout, A. – A. Meillet
1951 *Dictionnaire étymologique de la langue latine* (3rd edition) (Paris).

Ihm, M.
1892 "Vulgärformen lateinischer Zahlwörter auf Inschriften", *All* 7: 65–72.

Kent, R. G.
1946 *The forms of Latin* (Baltimore).

Kuryłowicz, J.
1964 *The inflectional categories of Indo-European* (Heidelberg).

Leumann, M. – J. B. Hofmann
1926 *Lateinische Grammatik* (5th edition of F. Stolz and J. H. Schmalz's Grammar) (München).

Meillet, A. – J. Vendryes
1960 *Traité de grammaire comparée des langues classiques* (3rd edition) (Paris).
Neue, F. – C. Wagener
1902 *Formenlehre der Lateinischen Sprache* (3rd edition) (Leipzig).
Pisani, V.
1964 *Le Lingue dell'Italia Antica oltre il Latino* (*Manuale Storico della Lingua Latina* IV) (Torino).
Poultney, J. W.
1959 *The bronze tablets of Iguvium* (Baltimore).
Sommer, F.
1913 *Handbuch der lateinischen Laut- und Formen-lehre* (3rd edition) (Heidelberg).
1950 *Zum Zahlwort*, Sitzungsb. Bay. Ak Wiss. (Phil.-Hist. Kl.) Heft 7.
Szemerényi, O.
1960 *Studies in the Indo-European system of numerals* (Heidelberg).
Thurneysen, R.
1946 *A grammar of Old Irish* (tr. D. A. Binchy – O. Bergin) (Dublin).
Vetter, E.
1953 *Handbuch der italischen Dialekte* I (Heidelberg).
Walde, A. – J. B. Hoffmann
1938–1956 *Lateinisches Etymologisches Wörterbuch* (3rd edition) (Heidelberg).
Winter, W. (ed).
1965 *Evidence for laryngeals* ('s Gravenhage).

Chapter 13
Romance

Glanville Price[1]

13.0. Introduction

The material is organised as follows: 13.1. cardinals, 13.2. ordinals, 13.3. collectives, 13.4. approximatives, 13.5. adverbs, 13.6. distributives, 13.7. multiplicatives, 13.8. fractions, 13.9. latinisms, 13.10. Greek elements, 13.11. Slavonic elements.

A distinction is made between Franco-Provençal and Provençal; the latter term is used in its strict sense, with reference to the dialect of Provence – the term *Occitan* is used with reference to the *langue d'oc* in general, which has as its other principal varieties Gascon, Languedocian and northern Occitan. Romansh includes Engadinish, Surselvan and a variety of other dialects. The term *Arumanian* is used instead of *Macedo-Rumanian*.

13.1. Cardinals

The cardinals from 'one' to 'ten' in all the major Romance languages and dialects are – with some slight analogical remodelling in certain cases – reflexes of the corresponding Latin forms.

13.1.1. 'One'

Masculine forms generally reflect the accusative *ūnum* (the nominative *unus* survived in OFr. *uns*, OOc. *uns*), which in some languages has given two different forms, the fuller of the two used when the numeral stands alone, the other when it determines a following substantive: Span. *uno*, but *un dedo* 'one finger'; Ital. *uno, un dito*;[2] Rum. *unu, un deget*; Fr. *un, un doigt*; Oc. *un, un det*; Port. *um, um dedo*; Cat. *un, un dit*; Surs. *in, in det*; Engad. *ün, ün daint*. In Sardinian, *unu* serves not only as an independent form but also as a preconsonantal determinant (e.g. *unu fidzu* 'one son', but *un' amiku* 'one friend'). Dalmatian has [jojn] in both functions, *jojn jájne e jojn mis* [3] 'one year and one month' (Bartoli 1906, 2: 15). Catalan has *u* which is used instead of *un* as an ordinal (*la pagina u, l'u d'abril*, etc.) and may be used as an alternative to *un* when the numeral stands (expressly or implicitly) in opposition to other numerals *u* (or *un*), *dos, tres; u (un) i dos fan tres* 'one and two make three' (Badia Margarit 1962: § 124).

Reflexes of fem. *ūna* fulfil both functions, except in Rumanian, which has for example *numai una* 'only one' but *numai o carte* 'only one book':[4] Fr. *une*, Oc. *una* [yno], Span. *una*, Port. *uma*, Cat. *una* [unə], Ital. *una*, Sard. *una*, Surs. *ina*, Engad. *üna*, Dalm. *jojna*.

The indefinite article in all the Romance languages derives from *ūnus* etc., and, in general, has the same form as the numeral: Fr. *un, une*; Span. *un, una*; Cat. *un, una*; Oc. *un, una*; Ital. *un, una*; Port. *um, uma*; Sard. *unu, una*; Surs. *in, ina*; England *ün, üna*; Dalm. *jojn, jojna*; Rum. *un, o*. In some Italian dialects, however, the numeral and the indefinite article are phonetically distinct, particularly in northern dialects e. g. western Ligurian [yŋ] 'one' but [in dɛnte] 'a tooth', Ticinese [vyŋ] but [un dɛɲ], Romagnol [ɔ̃] but [un dɛnt] and occasionally also in southern dialects e. g. Barese [junə] but [nu dɛndə] (Rohlfs 1966 – 1969: § 971). The same is true of the Franco-Provençal dialects of Savoy, the most widespread forms being *ĭon* masc., *ĭënă* fem. for the numeral, and *on* m., *onnă* fem. for the indefinite article.[5] An adjective meaning 'sole, only' is sometimes used to avoid ambiguity and make it clear that the numeral and not the indefinite article is intended, e. g. Fr. *j'ai un seul frère*, Ital. *un solo fratello*, Rum. *un singur frate*; the same procedure may even be used when there is no ambiguity, e. g. Fr. *Combien de frères avez-vous? – Un seul* 'one'.

The origins of the use of *ūnus* as an indefinite article are already to be seen in Latin. In this function it could have a plural which is still so used in the Ibero-Romance languages, Span. *unos, unas* 'some' (e. g. *unos libros* 'some books'), Port. *uns, umas*, Cat. *uns, unes*. Though the corresponding form in Rumanian in the nominative-accusative case is *nişte* (< *nescio quid*), the form of the genitive-dative case is *unor*; the nom.-acc. pl. fem. *une* remains in the one word *uneori* 'sometimes' < *une* + *ori* (plural of *oară* 'time'). Plural forms also remain in Old French but only with reference to objects considered in pairs or collectively, e. g. *uns solers, uns esperons, uns ganz, unes botes, unes brayes* 'a pair of spurs, gloves, boots, breeches'; *unes joes* 'cheeks', *uns dras* 'sheets, clothing', *unes noveles* 'news', *unes armes* 'armour'; this usage remains in Modern

Occitan, e. g. Provençal *ùni cisèu, ùni braio* 'a pair of scissors, breeches', *ùni biasseto* 'a double wallet', *ùnis ouro* 'a book of hours'.

13.1.1.1. In Old and Middle French there exists a curious form *empreu* 'one' used in counting as follows (the pattern is frequently attested): *empreu et deus et trois et quatre* ... It has been suggested that this may be an abbreviated form of *en pre(mier)* but Nyrop, who points out that the word remains in Switzerland in the form *emprô* "qui est à la fois le début et le nom d'une formulette de jeu usitée à Genève", proposes a different explanation (1960: 481.1° n. 1):

> Quant à l'origine, *preu* est probablement le substantif ordinaire *pro, preu* (de prode), profit; *empreu* est donc une sorte de souhait de bonheur, une parole de bon augure prononcée au moment où l'on commence à compter: on sait que selon des croyances superstitieuses très répandues, compter porte malheur.

13.1.2. 'Two'

Whereas the Classical Latin forms in the nominative are masc. *duo*, fem. *duae*, ntr. *duo*; and in the accusative masc. *duos*, fem. *duās*, ntr. *duo*, Vulgar Latin developed analogical nom. masc. *dui*, nom.-acc. ntr. *dua*.

The two-case system characteristic of masculine nouns in Old French and Old Occitan retained the nominative form *dui* [6], which has since disappeared with the loss of the two-case system.

Only three of the modern literary languages retain distinct forms for masculine and feminine: Port. *dous* (*dois*),[7] *duas*; Cat. *dos, dues*; Rum. *doi, două.*[8]

In Catalan, masc. *dos* is used instead of *dues* as an ordinal (e. g. *la cadira dos* 'the second chair'); the widespread use of *dos* for *dues* in other contexts (e. g. *son les dos* for *son les dues* 'it is two o'clock') is a castilianism (Badia Margarit 1962: §§ 124–125).

Distinct masculine and feminine forms are still found in non-literary dialects in many widely-scattered parts of the Romance-speaking area; e. g. western Leonese masc. *dos*, fem. *duas duyas dues* (Menéndez Pidal 1962a: 91–92); Gascon masc. *dus*, fem. *dues duas* (e. g. *dus òmis* 'deux hommes', *dues hémnes* 'deux femmes' (Rohlfs 1970: § 512); Franco-Provençal, e. g. masc. [du], fem. [dave] in Savoy[9], masc. *du* [du:], fem. *dāwe* (da:wə] at Bagnes (Bjerrome 1957: 67), masc. *düi*, fem. *dua* in the Vaud (Meyer-Lübke 1895: § 68); Italian dialects, e. g. Ligurian (*dui òmi, due dòne*) and Piedmontese (*düi omni, due fumne*) in the north, Latian (*doi muli, doe donne*) in the centre, Calabrian (*dui cavalli, due fímmine*) and Lucanian (*dui òmminə, dò fèmminə*) in the south; Sardinian masc. *dúos*, fem. *dúas*. The distinction was also made in Old Occitan (*dos, doas*), Old Spanish (*dos, duas dues*, the feminine forms having been replaced by *dos* in literary usage since the thirteenth century) and in Old French, where fem. *doues* occasionally occurred, in eastern dialects only, though in most texts the originally masculine form *dous* is usual in the feminine also.

Though modern literary Italian has adopted the invariable form *due*, Old Italian had in addition *duo* (e. g. *le duo nature* Dante), *dua* (e. g. *dua mesi, dua cose* Machiavelli), *dui* and *duoi*; these various forms seem to be used without respect to the gender of the nouns they qualify. *Due* may finally have been preferred as providing in its ending a parallel to *tre, cinque, sette* and *nove.*[10] Rohlfs (1966–1969: § 971) suggests that the form *dua*, which is still widespread in some Tuscan dialects before a pause, e. g. *ne ho trovato dua* 'I have found two of them', is more likely to derive from the proclitic development of *due* (cf. *le tua* [= *tue*] *sorelle* 'your sisters' in Tuscan vernaculars) than from Latin ntr. *dua*.

There is now no distinction of gender in Spanish (*dos*), French (*deux*) or Romansh (e. g. Surs. *dus*, Engad. *duos* – for *dua* see 13.1.3.). Dalm. [doj] seems to have been invariable for gender.

Popular French occasionally has the pronunciation [døs] for *deux*. This may be an archaism, cf. the prepausal pronunciation of *six, dix* as [sis], [dis] in standard French.[11]

13.1.3. 'Three'

Latin *trēs* survives in Span. *tres*, Cat. *tres*, Oc. *tres*, Sard. *tres*, Port. *três*, Fr. *trois*, Surs. *treis*. The nominative forms OFr. *troi*, OOc. *trei*, and OItal. *trei*, Rum. *trei* are probably formed on the analogy of the corresponding forms for 'two' (*dui, doi*, etc.). Ital. *tre* was probably originally a proclitic form. The history of Dalm. *tra* is uncertain.

The only literary language to make a distinction of gender is Rumanian, and then only in the various forms for 'all three' viz. fem. *toate trele, tustrele, cîteşitrele*[12] corresponding to masc. *toţi trei, tustrei, cîteşitrei*. Elsewhere, a distinction between masculine and feminine forms exists in some Italian dialects, e. g. Lombard and Romagnol masc. *tri*, fem. *tré*, the feminine form apparently deriving, like the comparable *tree* in Old Ligurian, Old Venetian and other dialects, from **trēae* (Rohlfs 1966–1969: § 971).

Relics of Latin ntr. *tria* occur in Old Lombard and Old Paduan *trea*, in some Modern Italian vernaculars, e. g. *trea* in parts of Tuscany, southern Latium and elsewhere, *tria* at Cosenza (Rohlfs 1966–1969: § 971), and in OFr. *treie* > *troie*, signifying a throw of three at dice (preserved as Engl. *trey* 'three' [at cards, dice and dominoes]).

Both *dua* and *tria* remain in Romansh, as *dua* and *trei* (Surselvan)[13] or *traia* (Engadinish), in the numerals 'two thousand' and 'three thousand' (Surs. *duamelli, treimelli*; Engad. *duamilli, traiamilli*) and (by analogy with the thousands) 'two hundred' and 'three hundred' (Surs. *duatschien, treitschien*; Engad. *duatschient, traiatschient*), with the word *per* 'pair' (Surs. *dua, trei pèra*; Engad. *dua, traia pera*) and with a small number of words denoting units of measurement, viz. Surs. *bratsch* 'ell', *det* 'finger's breadth', *ster* (unit of dry measure): *dua, trei bratscha, detta, stera.*

Forms with paragogic *-ne, -ni, -de, -di* occur, in most cases only before a pause, in various Italian dialects, e. g. Tuscan *trene*, Sicilian *trini*, Salentine *trede*, Calabrian *tridi* (Rohlfs 1966–1969: § 971). For Popular French [trwas] occasionally found instead of [trwa], cf. [døs] for *deux* 12.1.2.

13.1.4. 'Four' to 'ten'

The principal forms to be considered are the following:

	Latin	Spanish	Portuguese	Catalan
'four'	*quattuor*	*cuatro*	*quatro*	*quatre* [kwatrə]
'five'	*quīnque*	*cinco*	*cinco*	*cinc* [siŋ]
'six'	*sex*	*seis*	*seis*	*sis* [sis]
'seven'	*septem*	*siete*	*sete*	*set* [sɛt]
'eight'	*octō*	*ocho*	*oito*	*vuit* [bujt]
'nine'	*nouem*	*nueve*	*nove*	*nou* [nɔw]
'ten'	*decem*	*diez*	*dez*	*deu* [dɛw]

	French	Occitan	Italian	Sardinian
'four'	*quatre*	*quatre* [katre]	*quattro*	*battor*
'five'	*cinq*	*cinc* [siŋk]	*cinque*	*kímbe*
'six'	*six*	*sièis* [sjɛjs]	*sei*	*sès*
'seven'	*sept*	*sèt* [sɛt]	*sette*	*sètte*
'eight'	*huit*	*uèit* [wɛjt], [bɛjt]	*otto*	*òtto*
'nine'	*neuf*	*nòu* [nɔw]	*nove*	*nòbe* [nɔβe]
'ten'	*dix*	*dètz* [dɛts]	*dieci*	*dèke*

	Surselvan	Rumanian
'four'	*quater* [kwatər]	*patru*
'five'	*tschun* [tʃun]	*cinci*
'six'	*sis* [sis]	*şase*
'seven'	*siat* [sjat]	*şapte*
'eight'	*otg* [ɔtç]	*opt*
'nine'	*nov* [nɔf]	*nouă*
'ten'	*diesch* [diəʃ]	*zece*

The Occitan forms noted in phonetic script are only some of the most typical and widespread of the multifarious forms that occur in the various dialects. Gallo-Romance reflexes of the various numerals are quoted in von Wartburg (1922–): *quattuor* (2: 1440–1441); *quinque* (2: 1480–1481); *sex* (6: 554–556); *septem* (6: 478–480); *octo* (7: 305–308); *novem* (7: 207–209); *decem* (3: 23–24). See also Gauchat – Jeanjaquet – Tappolet (1922–, 4: 72–73): *cinq*, where a wide range of forms is listed.

The attested forms for Dalmatian, some of which may have been influenced by Venetian or other Italian dialects and so not be fully authentic, include [kwatro] [kwatri] 'four', [tʃiŋk] [tʃɛŋk] 'five', [si] [sis] 'six', [sjapto] [sapto] 'seven', [vapto] [wat] [gwapto] 'eight', [nu] 'nine', [dik] 'ten'.

The Romance forms for 'four' and 'five' reflect not the Classical Latin forms but Vulgar Latin *quattor, cinque*, both of which are attested in inscriptions. At later periods, various analogical and other influences have been at work.

Span. *cinco*, Port. *cinco*, with irregular *-o*, has presumably been influenced by a reflex of *quattor* (> Span. *cuatro*, Port. *quatro*).

The *-e* of Rum. *şase* is probably due to the influence of *şapte*.

Various Upper Italian forms for 'six', e. g. *seže, seš, ses*, seem not to derive directly from *sex* (or **sexem*), but to have been partially remodelled on the basis of reflexes of *decem* (> *deže, deš, des*; Schmid 1964: 210–212).

In various north Italian dialects, forms for 'eight' have been influenced by those for 'seven', e. g. Bergamo, Novara, western Lombardy *(v)ot*, Piedmontese *öt* < *octō*, which do not show the effects of palatalization characteristic of forms such as *noč* < *noctem, lač* < *lacte* (Schmid 1964: 209–210).

Wagner (1957–1964, 1: 188) gives *battor* as an Old Logudorese form and comments: "Il log. moderno *báttoro* è la stessa forma colla solita vocale d'appoggio: la zona mista fra log[udorese] e camp[idanese] ha *bátturu*, e solo più verso Sud compaiono forme come *kwátturu, kwáttru* (la quale ultima è rifatto sulla forma italiana e spagnola)". And under *kímbe*, given as Logudorese, there appears (Wagner 1957–1964, 1: 337) the following comment: "Il camp[idanese] dice *činku* ... e a volte *čínkwi* ... L'ultima forma è senz' altro l'ital. *cinque*, e *činku* avrà il suo *-u* dallo spagn. *cinco*". *Nòbe* and *dèke* are characteristic of the very conservative central dialects; other forms are Logudorese *nòe* and *dege*, Campidanese *nòi* and *dèži* (Wagner 1957–1964, 2: 173; 1: 458–459).

Dalm. *guapto, vapto* 'eight' may indicate the same phonetic development [kt] > [pt] that is characteristic of Rumanian (e. g. *octō* > *opt, noctem* > *noapte*), but, on the other hand, this may be a further instance of the analogical influence of 'seven' (*sapto*).

The phonetically irregular stem of Rum. *zece* (for **zace* < **dzieace*, cf. Arumanian *dzatse*) is perhaps to be attributed to plural *zeci* as in *douăzeci* 'twenty', *treizeci* 'thirty', etc. (Schmid 1964: 213).

The final *-i* of Ital. *dieci* and of such forms as Old Veronese *quatri* 'four', Old Lombard *zinqui* 'five', Old Genovese *seti* 'seven', Old Umbrian *nuovi* 'nine', is plausibly attributed (Rohlfs 1966–1969: § 972) to the adoption in these forms of the characteristic masculine plural ending *-i*.

A similar analogical plural ending may occur in Popular French in the liaison form *quatres*; Nyrop (1960: 481.4) refers to sixteenth-century attestations of *quatres amours* and *les quatres éléments*, and points out that this liaison form is allowed by the Académie française in the expression *entre quatre yeux* [ɑ̃trəkatzjø] (often written *entre quatre-z-yeux* or *entre quat'z yeux*) 'between you and me'; on the other hand this may be not a plural form but merely a liaison form on the analogy of *deux, trois, six, dix* (pronounced [døz], [trwaz], [siz], [diz] in liaison). Nyrop also quotes the notary in Balzac's *Eugénie Grandet* who pronounces *Il est neuf heures* as *Il est neuffe-s-heures*;[14] liaison forms in [z] for 'four', 'five', 'seven', 'eight', are also quoted for the Franco-Provençal dialects of Savoy by Désormaux (1904: 106–108), who transcribes them as *càtro-z* 'four', *fin-z* 'five' (e. g. *fin-z òmo* 'cinq hommes'), *sà-z* 'seven', *wi-z* 'eight'.

-que (instead of *-che*) of Ital. *cinque* is surprising; Rohlfs wonders (1966–1969: § 972 n.) whether, like the *-que* in *ovunque* 'wherever', *chiunque* 'whoever', it could be a latinism.

Rum. *cinci* for **cince* has not been satisfactorily explained.

Fr. *cinq, six, huit* and *dix* illustrate a feature of pronunciation that was characteristic of the language from about the thirteenth to the sixteenth century, when words that had ended in a pronounced consonant in Old French (e. g. *lit* [lit], *drap* [drap], *vif* [vif], *duc* [dyk]) lost the consonant when followed without a pause by a word beginning with a consonant, but retained it before a pause. One or other form has since been generalized in most words, either the prepausal form with final consonant (as in *duc* [dyk], *vif* [vif], *net* [nɛt], *ours* [urs], *mer* [mɛ:r]), or the preconsonantal form without consonant (as in *lit* [li], *drap* [dra], *blanc* [blɑ̃], *pas* [pa], *parler* [parle]). The earlier dual pronunciation remains however in, for instance, *cinq* (*six, huit, dix*) *jours* [sɛ̃] ([si], [ɥi], [di]) [ʒu:r]) as opposed to *j'en ai cinq* (*six, huit, dix*) [ʒɑ̃ne sɛ̃:k] ([sis], [ɥit], [dis]); furthermore *six* and *dix* have a third pronunciation as a liaison form before words beginning with a vowel, e. g. *six enfants* [sizɑ̃fɑ̃], *dix hommes* [dizɔm]. The prepausal pronunciation [sɛ̃k] *cinq* now occurs frequently before consonants, e. g. [sɛ̃k li:vr] for [sɛ̃ li:vr] *cinq livres*; in this respect *cinq* is following along the same path as *sept* [sɛt] and *neuf* [nœf] whose original preconsonantal forms [sɛ] and [nœ], which are still recommended in some old-fashioned works, have now disappeared from normal Parisian usage;[15] *neuf* however retains a liaison form [nœv] before the words *heures* and *ans* [nœvœ:r], [nœvɑ̃] (but *neuf arbres* [nœfarbr], etc.).

Finally it must be mentioned that, according to Meyer-Lübke (1895: § 70), where the source of the information is not quoted, the Franco-Provençal dialect of the Forez – and in this respect it would appear to be unique amongst Romance languages and dialects – makes a distinction of gender for 'four' between masc. [katru] and fem. [katrə]. Von Wartburg (1922–), however, does not list these forms among the reflexes of *quattuor* (2: 1440).

13.1.5. 'Eleven' to 'sixteen'

The principal forms to be considered are the following:

	Latin	Spanish	Portuguese
'eleven'	*ūndecim*	*once*	*onze*
'twelve'	*duodecim*	*doce*	*doze*
'thirteen'	*trĕdecim*	*trece*	*treze*
'fourteen'	*quattuordecim*	*catorce*	*catorze*
'fifteen'	*quīndecim*	*quince*	*quinze*
'sixteen'	*sēdecim*	OSpan. *seze*	OPort. *seze*

	Catalan	French	Occitan
'eleven'	*onze* [onzə]	*onze*	*onze* [ũnze]
'twelve'	*dotze* [doʒə]	*douze*	*dotze* [dudze]
'thirteen'	*tretze* [treʒə]	*treize*	*tretze* [trɛdze]
'fourteen'	*catorze* [katorzə]	*quatorze*	*catòrze* [katɔrze]
'fifteen'	*quinze* [kinzə]	*quinze*	*quinze* [kĩnze]
'sixteen'	*setze* [sɛʒə]	*seize*	*sètze* [sɛdze]

	Italian	Sardinian	Surselvan
'eleven'	*undici*	*úndiki*	*endisch* [ɛndiʃ]
'twelve'	*dodici*	*dóiki*	*dudisch* [dodiʃ]
'thirteen'	*tredici*	*tréiki*	*tredisch* [trɛdiʃ]
'fourteen'	*quattordici*	*battórdiki*	*quitordisch* [kwitɔrdiʃ]
'fifteen'	*quindici*	*bíndiki*	*quendisch* [kwindiʃ]
'sixteen'	*sedici*	*séiki*	*sedisch* [sɛdiʃ]

The Engadinish forms (see below) do not differ significantly from the Surselvan ones.

Sardinian forms quoted are those of the central dialect (Nuorese). For Logudorese and Campidanese forms see Wagner (1957–1964): *úndiki* (2: 561); *dóiki* (1: 475); *tréiki* (2: 513); and *séiki* (2: 402). Note in particular that in various dialects, forms for 'thirteen' and 'sixteen' occur having [ɛ] instead of [e] (e. g. *trèiki, sèiki*) under the influence of *très* 'three', *sès* 'six'.

The authentic Dalmatian forms appear to have been something like [joŋko], [dɔtko], [trɛtko], [kwatwarko], [tʃɔŋko], [sɛtko] (Bartoli 1906: § 521). The last remaining speaker of Dalmatian, who died in 1898, used [joŋko] but had apparently forgotten the others and used the suppletive forms *dikdoi* (= 'ten' + 'two') 'twelve', *diktra* 'thirteen', *dikčink* 'fifteen', *diksis* 'sixteen' (Bartoli 1906: § 146).

In Spanish and Portuguese, the old form *seze* 'sixteen' has long since been replaced by Span. *diez y seis*, Port. *dezasseis* (see 13.1.6.).

Rumanian has completely abandoned the Latin system (see 13.1.7.).

The digraph *ei* of Fr. *treize, seize* has never represented a diphthong; the usual spelling in Old French was *treze, seze*.

The Gallo-Romance and Ibero-Romance forms for 'eleven' presuppose a Vulgar Latin form in *ŭn-* (Classical Latin *ūndecim*), and the forms for 'twelve' derive, not directly from *duodecim*, but from *dodece*.

In Latin, the forms for 'eleven' to 'sixteen' are transparent, in that the origin of the two elements of each compound can clearly be seen (e. g. *trēdecim* = *trēs* + *decem*). The same is true of Italian. In Sardinian, the identity of the first element is nowhere obscured but the loss of intervocalic [d] must render the reflex of *-decim* unrecognisable to the uninitiated in *dóiki, tréiki* and *séiki*, though the second element of *úndiki, bíndiki* (in both of which there is a cacuminal allophone of /d/) and *battórdiki* (where there is a fricative allophone [ð]) is clearly cognate with *dèke*. The various Romansh dialects have, except for the first element of 'fifteen', fairly transparent forms, viz.:

Surselvan	
'one' to 'six', 'ten':	*in, dus, treis, quater, tschun, sis, diesch.*
'eleven' to 'sixteen'	*endisch, dudisch, tredisch, quitordisch, quendisch, sedisch.*
Lower Engadinish	
'one' to 'six', 'ten'	*ün, duos, trais, quatter, tschinch, ses, desch.*
'eleven' to 'sixteen'	*ündesch, dudesch, traidesch, quattordesch, quindesch, saidesch.*

But Schmid (1964: 217–219) shows that many of these Romansh forms have been subject to considerable analogical remodelling. In Lower Engadinish, where the unstressed penultimate syllable regularly disappears, we should have expected **ündsch* < **undece* etc., and the whole series *ündesch* to *saidesch* can only be explained as having been remodelled on the basis of *desch* 'ten'. In Surselvan, where the unstressed penultimate syllable remains, analogical remodelling of the second element need necessarily be supposed only for *dudisch, tredisch, sedisch*, for which, with the loss of intervocalic [d], one would have expected **dusch* < **dodece*, etc.; the model on which the existing forms are based is *endisch, quitordisch, quendisch*, in which the [d], not being intervocalic, remains.

In the various Ibero-Romance and Gallo-Romance forms, the reflexes of *-decim* have become uniformly unrecognizable, having been reduced to [θe], [zə], [ʒə], [dze], [z], etc. Similar forms occur in some Italian dialects, e. g. Romagnol-Emilian *onč, doč* (Schmid 1964: 217), Ligurian *ünśe* (*ś* = [z]), *duśe, trèśe, quatorśe, chinśe, sèśe* (Rohlfs 1966–1969: § 973). If reflexes of the first element remain fairly transparent in the various forms for, say 'thirteen' and 'fourteen', this is probably merely fortuitous, as those for 'eleven' and 'fifteen' in particular are comparatively or totally opaque.

What is common to both groups (i. e. the Italo-Romance and Rhaeto-Romance group on the one hand and the Ibero-Romance and Gallo-Romance group on the other) is a high degree of uniformity among the endings: [θe] in Spanish, [zə] in Portuguese, [z] in French, [ditʃi] in Italian, [diʃ] or [dəʃ] (according to dialect) in Romansh; at most we have variations of the order of [zə], [ʒə] in Catalan; [ze], [dze] in Occitan; [iki], [diki] in Sardinian. This regularity within each language suggests that structural links within the group of numerals under discussion are stronger than links either with the numerals 'one' to 'six' or with 'ten'.[16]

Fr. *onze* is normally – and quite contrary to the usual conventions of the language – treated as if it began with a consonant, and so causes neither elision (*le onze janvier* rather than *l'onze; un enfant de onze ans*) nor liaison (*les onze* [le ɔ̃:z] not *[lez ɔ̃:z]). This is perhaps due to analogy with other numerals. There was fluctuation in the medieval period. Vaugelas (1647) condemns *le onzième*, the Academy's dictionary hesitates (1718: *le onze* or *l'onze du mois*; 1762: *l'onzième* or *la onzième page*), and occasional deviations from the normal practice still occur, particularly it would seem with the expression *onze heures*, e. g. *aux environs d'onze heures* (Simenon).

13.1.6. 'Seventeen' to 'nineteen'

The Classical Latin form for 'seventeen' which followed the same pattern as 'eleven' to 'sixteen', viz. *septemdecim*, and those for 'eighteen' and 'nineteen' which were formed by subtraction from 'twenty' viz. *duo dē uīgintī, un dē uīgintī*, have left no trace in the Romance languages. Instead, we find a variety of forms, all however conforming to the basic pattern 'ten' plus 'seven', etc. and, in particular, to the three types *decem nouem, decem et nouem, decem ac nouem.*

The asyndetic construction *decem septem* is reflected in Catalan: *disset* [disɛ́t] 'seventeen', *divuit* [diβújt] 'eighteen', *dinou* [dinɔ́w] 'nineteen'.[17]

The type *decem et septem* is most clearly reflected in Spanish: *diez y siete, diez y ocho, diez y nueve* (which are also written *diecisiete, dieciocho, diecinueve*); these are remodelled from OSpan. *diz y siete* etc., which show the countertonic development of *decem.* Until the sixteenth century. French had forms (here given in their usual Old French spellings) *dis e set, dis e uit, dis e nuef*, since replaced by *dix-sept, dix-huit, dix-neuf.*[18] Similarly Old Portuguese had *dez e sete, dez e oito, dez e nove*, since supplanted by *dezassete, dezaoito* > *dezoito, dezanove*, which first appeared in the fifteenth century; it is uncertain whether the *-a-* of these forms is the preposition *a* or whether it reflects *ac*, in which case it must be assumed that reflexes of *decem ac septem*, etc. (see below) had, though not recorded in writing, always existed in Portuguese alongside reflexes of *decem et septem*. *et* is probably also the origin of the [d] of various Italian dialectal forms, e. g. Venetian [dizdɔto], Calabrian [ditʃedwɔtto], Sicilian [ditʃidɔttu], Lucchese [ditʃennɔve] ([nn] < [dn]), etc. (Rohlfs 1966–1969: § 973); of Dalm. *dikidápto* 'eighteen' ('seventeen' and 'nineteen' are *dikisápto* and *dikinú*); and of Engad. *deschdot* 'eighteen' (*deschset* 'seventeen' and *deschnouv* 'nineteen' may represent an asyndetic construction or the loss of [d] in the middle of a consonant-cluster).

Decem ac septem etc. are reflected in Ital. *diciassette* 'seventeen' and *diciannove* 'nineteen' (perhaps also *diciotto* 'eighteen').

Sardinian has both forms in *-a-* and apparently asyndetic forms: Wagner (1957–1964) gives under *a* (1: 458–459) central *dekaṡette* (*ṡ* = [z]) and *dekanòe* (but for the central dialect of Núoro, Pittau (1972: § 130) gives *dekessette, dekeotto, dekennobe*) and Logudorese *deg̨esètte, deg̨eòttu, deg̨enòe*.

Schmid (1964: 228–233) discusses at some length the curious Surselvan forms *gissiat* [dʒisiát] 'seventeen', *schotg* [ʒɔtç] 'eighteen' and *scheniv* [ʒɛ́nif] 'nineteen'. His suggestion for these forms is as follows. *decem septem* > *[diʃsiát] which, by assimilation, becomes *[dissiát], the loss of the palatal element being compensated for by palatalization of initial [di] to [dʒi], whence *[dʒissiát] > [dʒisiát]; in this connection Schmid draws attention to a similar development in Rumanian where the loss of the final syllables [zetʃe] of *doisprezece* etc. is partly compensated for by the substitution of [ʃ] for [s] in the popular form *doişpe* etc. *decem octō* > *[diʒɔ́tç] > *[dʒɔtç] > [ʒɔtç], cf. *dicebat* > *dschaiva* [dʒ] but Surs. *scheva* [ʒ-]. **decém novem* > *[diʒɛ́nif] > *[dʒɛ́nif] > [ʒɛ́nif] (cf. 'eighteen'); the postulated stress pattern *decém nŏuem*, found only in the Romansh dialects of the Rhine Valley and nowhere else in the Romance-speaking world, is conditioned by the short *ŏ* of *nŏuem* and may be compared with that of, for instance, *septémdĕcim, ádmŏdum, rénŏuo*, etc. The particular interest of these Surselvan forms is that, whereas the formation of the reflexes of *decem (et) septem* etc. remains transparently clear in other languages, here the kind of development that in many languages and dialects has obscured the origins of reflexes of *undecim*, etc. came into play again and produced completely opaque reflexes of the analytic forms for 'seventeen', 'eighteen' and 'nineteen'. It is on the face of it strange that the very dialects that have witnessed this type of development should be those that have remodelled 'twelve', 'thirteen' and 'sixteen' (*dudisch, tredisch, sedisch*) on the basis of 'eleven' (*endisch*), 'fourteen' and 'fifteen' (see 14.1.5.), the more so since the lower numerals, being more frequently used, are more likely to be regarded as independent forms rather than as compounds. Schmid (1964: 236) suggests that the reason for the remodelling of *[duʃ] and *[trejʃ] to *dudisch* and *tredisch* may have been the near-homonymy of the unattested forms with *dus* 'two' and *treis* 'three' (and if this is so, then presumably *[sejʃ] 'sixteen', which would be well enough differentiated from *sis* 'six', was brought into line). Schmid further points out that Surselvan is in general very tolerant of considerable divergences in forms of the same word brought about by phonetic change (e. g. *tgiern* 'horn', pl. *corns; créscher* 'to grow', ppart. *carschiu; encurir* 'to seek', *enquera* 'seeks', etc.).

In Spanish and Portuguese, analytic forms are also employed for 'sixteen' and 'seventeen': *diez y seis* (*dieciséis*) for OSpan. *seze; diez y siete* (*diecisiete*); Port. *dezasseis* (for OPort. *seze*), *dezassete.*

In Old Spanish, similar forms are also attested for other numerals, e. g. *diez e dos* and *dizedós* 'twelve' (Menéndez Pidal 1962b: § 89.2); *dizetrés* (1252) 'thirteen', *diez y quatro* (1219) 'fourteen' (Corominas 1954, 2: 171) and, according to R. Menéndez Pidal, *Antología de prosistas castellanos,* (1917: 172), also occur in some modern dialects.

Bearnese appears to be unique in having a form *trés-chéys* (= 'three' × 'six') for 'eighteen' (Palay 1961: 983).

13.1.7. The Rumanian teens

In Rumanian, the traditional forms have completely disappeared and have been replaced by an analytic system of the type 'one on ten', using prep. *spre* < *super* : *unsprezece* 'eleven'; masc. *doisprezece*, fem. *douăsprezece* 'twelve'; *treisprezece* 'thirteen'; *paisprezece* 'fourteen'; *cincisprezece* 'fifteen'; *şaisprezece* 'sixteen'; *şaptesprezece* 'seventeen'; *optsprezece* 'eighteen'; *nouăsprezece* 'nineteen'. The following comments on these forms are called for:

1) Though the opposition *doi : două* 'two' is reflected in distinct masculine and feminine forms for 'twelve', *unsprezece* 'eleven' is invariable and there is no corresponding form based on fem. *o* 'one'.

2) The forms *paisprezece* 'fourteen', *şaisprezece* 'sixteen' (perhaps formed by analogy with *doisprezece* and *treisprezece*) and now accepted in the literary language in place of *patrusprezece* and *şasesprezece.*

3) Through the full form of *cincisprezece* is retained in writing, it is pronounced as though written *cinsprezece*.
4) A vowel is often introduced in speech in the medial consonant-cluster of *optsprezece*, which is then pronounced as though written *optusprezece* or *optîsprezece*.
5) Reduced forms *unsprece, doisprece*, etc. and even more reduced forms *unşpe, doişpe, treişpe, paişpe, cinşpe, şaişpe* occur widely in the spoken language; these are interesting in that they provide further illustrations both of the tendency to create a uniform pattern within a sequence of numerals and also of the ease with which transparent, analytic forms can give way to opaque or semi-opaque synthetic forms (in *paişpe* 'fourteen', for example, none of the three elements of *patru/spre/zece* is clearly identifiable).

The origin of these forms has given rise to much debate turning particularly on the question whether or not this formation is to be attributed to Slavonic influence. There is certainly a parallel with the typical Slavonic construction (cf. Old Church Slavonic *jedĭnŭ na desęte* 'one on ten' = 'eleven', etc.), but it does not of course necessarily follow from this that the construction is borrowed from Slavonic. In *Istoria limbii române* 1969, 2: 325, attention is drawn to the existence of similar formations in Albanian (e. g. *një-mbë-dhjetë* 'eleven'), Armenian and the Baltic languages, and it is suggested that we have to do with "un fenomen autohton". Another theory is that the construction originated in Latin in the type *nouem et/ac decem* but in the east was extended to 'eleven' and 'twelve', the influence of Slavonic or of a substratum having affected only the use of the preposition (*spre*) instead of a conjunction.[19]

13.1.8. 'Twenty' to 'ninety'

13.1.8.1. Reflexes of the Latin forms

13.1.8.1.1. 'Twenty' and 'thirty'

Though the etyma of the various Romance forms (except those of Rumanian,[20] see 13.1.8.1.3.) are clearly Latin *uīgintī* and *trīgintā*, with loss of intervocalic *-g-*, the precise relationship of the Romance forms to the Latin ones is far from certain. There are numerous and widely-varying views as to, first, vowel quality and the position of the tonic stress in the corresponding Vulgar Latin forms, and, secondly, the extent to which these or their reflexes may have been subjected to later analogical remodelling.[21] The modern forms are the following: – Span. *veinte, treinta*

< OSpan. *veínte, treínta*; Port. *vinte, trinta* < OPort. *viinte, triinta*; Cat. *vint* [bin], *trenta* [trɛntə]; Oc. *vint* [vĩ], [bint] etc., *trenta* [trɛ̃nto] [trɛ̃nta]; Fr. *vingt* (OFr. *vint*), *trente*; Ital. *venti, trenta*; Sard. *binti, trinta*; Surs. *vegn* [veɲ], *trenta* [trɛnta]; Engad. *vainch* (vajntç], *trenta* [trɛnta].

The unexpected stem vowel [e] of Ital. *venti* is probably to be attributed to the influence of *trenta; vinti* exists in Old Tuscan and in modern dialects in many parts of the peninsula. For Dalmatian the form [ventʃ] is attested. Though Daco-Rumanian has abandoned *uīgintī* together with all the other Latin forms for the tens (see 13.1.8.1.3.), a reflex of it remains in Arumanian *yig'i(n)ţi.*[22] Piedmontese *tranta* has doubtless been influenced by *quaranta* etc.

13.1.8.1.2. 'Forty' to 'ninety'

The principal forms to be discussed are the following:

	Latin	Spanish	Portuguese
'forty'	*quadraginta*	*cuarenta*	*quarenta*
'fifty'	*quinquaginta*	*cincuenta*	*cinquenta*
'sixty'	*sexaginta*	*sesenta*	*sessenta*
'seventy'	*septuaginta*	*setenta*	*setenta*
'eighty'	*octoginta*	*ochenta*	*oitenta*
'ninety'	*nonaginta*	*noventa*	*noventa*

	Catalan	French	Occitan
'forty'	*quaranta*	*quarante*	*quaranta*
'fifty'	*cinquanta*	*cinquante*	*cinquanta*
'sixty'	*seixanta*	*soixante*	*seissanta*
'seventy'	*setanta*	*septante*	*setanta*
'eighty'	*vuitanta*	*huitante*	*oitanta*
'ninety'	*noranta*	*nonante*	*nonanta*

	Italian	Sardinian	Surselvan
'forty'	*quaranta*	*baranta*	*curonta*
'fifty'	*cinquanta*	*kimbanta*	*tschunconta*
'sixty'	*sessanta*	*sessanta*	*sissonta*
'seventy'	*settanta*	*settanta*	*siatonta*
'eighty'	*ottanta*	*ottanta*	*otgonta*
'ninety'	*novanta*	*nobanta*	*navonta*

Spanish and Portuguese differ from the other languages in having the ending *-enta*. It is generally accepted that this derives from Latin *-ĭnta*. In Old Spanish and Old Portuguese there occur forms such as *quaraenta, cinquaenta, sessaenta, setaenta*.

The ending *-anta* that is characteristic of Gallo-Romance and Italo-Romance generally is assumed to derive from forms in which the intervocalic *-g-* was lost and the tonic stress shifted, e. g. *quadragínta* > **quadráinta* > **quarranta*. This type of ending is also attested in those parts of the Iberian peninsula that had close relations with Gaul and Italy (Lapesa 1950: 72 – 73), not only in Catalan but also in Old Leonese *cinquanta, sexanta* (now rare or unknown) and Old Aragonese *cinquanta, sixanta, setanta, huitanta*, all attested in the fourteenth century (Zamora Vicente 1966: 166, 252). The [ɔnta] ending of Surselvan is a regular phonetic development (cf. *plonta* 'plant' < *planta, tonta* 'so much' fem. < *tanta*), corresponding to [awnta] in some other Romansh dialects and [anta] in Lower Engadinish (*quaranta, tschinquanta, sesanta, settanta, ottanta, novanta*).

There has been considerable remodelling of the stem:

'Forty': Span. *cuarenta*, Port. *quarenta* are remodelled on *cuatro, quatro* – [kw] + pretonic [a] normally gives [k] (as in *catorce, catorze*). It may be noted that an older Portuguese form *corenta* survives in popular speech (Williams 1938: § 40.7); the Campidanese dialect of Sardinian has *kwaranta, koranta*, the latter being either a development of *kwaranta* or else a catalanism (Wagner 1957 – 1964, 1: 176) (the town of Alghero has been Catalan-speaking since the fourteenth century).

'Fifty': By dissimilation *quīnquāgintā* gave *cinqua-*, cf. *quinque* > **cinque*.

'Sixty': The single intervocalic *-s-* of Engad. *sesa(u)nta* and of Sard. *sesánta* (some dialects – others have regular *sessanta*) is due to the influence of Engad. *ses*, Sard. *ses* 'six'; the *-x-* of Fr. *soixante* (for OFr. *soissante*) is a learned graphy based on *sexāgintā* (cf. *six* for OFr. *sis*) that has had no influence on pronunciation.

'Seventy': The "learned" *p* of Fr. *septante* (for OFr. *setante*) has influenced pronunciation [sɛptɑ̃:t] in those areas where the form is used (see 13.1.8.2.).

'Eighty': The Romance forms derive not from Classical Latin *octōgintā* but from *octaginta* (which is attested); Fr. *huitante* (now only dialectal) for OFr. *oitante* is remodelled on *huit*; the "learned" from *octante* appears to have gone out of use.

'Ninety': Though the stem of *nonaginta* is reflected in dialectal French *nonante,* Oc. *nonanta*, Upper Engad. *nonaunta*, Venetian *nonanta* and *nonanta* in the Sardinian dialect of Baunei [Wagner 1957–1961, 2: 171), the evidence of *noventa, novanta, nobanta* [-β-], and other such forms in Spanish, Portuguese, Italian, Surselvan, Lower Engadinish and Sardo-Nuorese seems to indicate that an unattested form with a stem *nova-* must have been well established in Vulgar Latin. Further, the existence of *noranta* in Catalan, Genovese, Lombard, Campidanese and some Logudorese dialects of Sardinian, and of similar forms in some extreme south-eastern varieties of Occitan (i. e., in areas bordering on Italy, see von Wartburg (1927–, 7: 186), points, in Elcock's words (1960: 74) "to yet another Vulgar Latin creation, for which *quarranta* may have served as model", though Lausberg (1962: § 770) considers that the *-r-* results from the dissimilation of the second *n* of *nonāgintā* (or a reflex thereof).[23] For various Gallo-Romance forms, see von Wartburg (1922–, 7: 186).

13.1.8.1.3. Rumanian has developed new forms all based on the pattern 'two tens', 'three tens', etc.: *douăzeci* 'twenty', *treizeci* 'thirty', *patruzeci* 'forty', *cincizeci* 'fifty', *şaizeci* 'sixty', *şaptezeci* 'seventy', *optzeci* 'eighty', *nouăzeci* 'ninety'. The reduced form *şaizeci* is now adopted in the literary language instead of *şasezeci*, and *cincizeci* is pronounced as though written *cinzeci* – and is indeed sometimes so written. *Optzeci* is often pronounced [obzetʃ].

It is widely held that these forms may be due either to an unidentified pre-Romance substratum (cf. Alban. *tridhjetë* 'thirty', *pesédhjetë* 'fifty', etc.) or to a Slavonic adstratum (cf. Old Church Slavonic *dŭva desęti* 'twenty', *pętĭ desęti* 'fifty', etc.), but, as Elcock (1960: 75) points out, "their exact resemblance to multiples of a hundred in the west ... makes the assumption of 'substratic' influence appear unnecessary".

13.1.9. The vigesimal system

13.1.9.0. Rumanian stands alone in having entirely abandoned the Latin forms for the decads. However, although the Rumanian forms do not reflect their Latin equivalents, the decimal system itself remains intact. A more radical change is the partial adoption in some western Romance dialects of a vigesimal system, which is clearly represented in the Modern French decads from 'seventy' to 'ninety': *soixante-dix* (= 'sixty' + 'ten'), *quatre-vingts* (= 'four' × 'twenty'), *quatre-vingt-dix* (= 'four' × 'twenty' + 'ten'). The other French decads, as we have seen, reflect the Latin forms: *vingt, trente, quarante, cinquante, soixante.* This mixed but apparently stable pattern represents a compromise between the more usual decimal system and a more thorough-going vigesimal system, both of which can be seen in operation in different historical and geographical varieties of French.

13.1.9.1. The decimal system is in current use, not only in various patois, but also in French as spoken in Belgium and Switzerland, where the most usual forms for 'seventy' and 'ninety' are *septante* [sɛptɑ̃:t] (OFr. *setante*, the "learned" *p* having been introduced not only in spelling, as in *sept* [sɛt], but also in pronunciation) and *nonante*; 'eighty' is usually *quatre-vingts* in both Belgium and Switzerland though *huitante* also occurs in some parts of Switzerland – the archaic latinizing form *octante* appears to be no longer in use in either country.

On the other hand, vigesimal forms not now found in Standard French occur at earlier periods. Nyrop (1960: § 490) quotes the following attested Old French forms: 'thirty' *vint e dis*, 'forty' *deus vins*, 'sixty' *trois vins*, 'seventy' *trois vins e dis*, 'eighty' *quatre vins*, 'ninety' *quatre vins e dis*, 'one hundred and twenty' *sis vins*, 'one hundred and forty' *set vins*, 'one hundred and sixty' *huit vins*, 'one hundred and eighty' *neuf vins*, 'two hundred and twenty' *onze vins*, 'two hundred and forty' *douze vins*, 'two hundred and eighty' *quatorze vins*, 'three hundred' *quinze vins*, 'three hundred and twenty' *seize vins*, 'three hundred and forty' *dis set vins*, 'three hundred and sixty' *dis huit vins*. Of these, *six-vingts* is well attested in the seventeenth century (Nyrop quotes two examples from Molière viz., *Vous passerez les six-vingts* in *L'avare* and *Une autre fois, six vingts* in *Le bourgeois gentilhomme*, and one from Racine viz., *Six-vingt productions* in *Les plaideurs*); such sixteenth-century examples as *Que ne suys-je roy pour cinq ou six vingts ans* (Régnier) and *Environ sept vingts faisans* (Rabelais), also quoted by Nyrop, may be no more than ephemeral usages. The form *quinze-vingts* survives in the name of the *hospice des Quinze-Vingts*, founded by St. Louis in 1260 as an asylum for three hundred blind people. There is also a *rue des Quinze-Vingt* in Troyes.

In Walloon, only *quatru-vints* remains, and the form *quatru* betrays the influence of Standard French[24] ('four' in Walloon is *cwète*); however, Remacle reports that some old people at La Gleize remembered hearing their grandparents use forms like *cwète vint-èt-doze* 'ninety-two' (now *nonante-deûs*) and *sî vints* 'one hundred and twenty', and J. Haust, *Dictionnaire liégeois*, gives as archaisms *on pourcê ki peûse ût vingts* (= *un pourceau qui pèse huit-vingts*) 'a pig weighing one hundred and sixty pounds', and *noûv vingts* (= *neuf vingts*) 'one hundred and eighty [pounds]'. Archive material quoted by Remacle provides numerous examples from the regional French of Belgium (as distinct from the Walloon dialect), e. g. *troys vingts, trois vint et XVI, six vingt*, in various sixteenth-century documents, *neuf vingts douze et demy verges* 'one hundred and ninety two and a half verges [a measure of land]' (1658).

In Franco-Provençal, Maps 1239 and 1240 of the *ALF* give forms corresponding to *trois-vingts* ([tre vɛ̃] etc.) and *trois-vingts-dix* for some points in Savoie, with the comment that this usage is "vieilli". With reference to the patois of Bagnes, one of the best preserved Franco-Provençal dialects in Switzerland, we are told (Bjerrome 1957: 68) that some vigesimal forms were maintained until recently "pour indiquer le nombre de vaches d'un alpage", e. g. *wī vẽ vàtse* (= *huit vingts vaches*), *sà vẽ vàtse e demyï* (= *sept vingts vaches et demi*, i. e. 'one hundred and fifty cows').

In Occitan, though forms corresponding to *quatre-vingts* (e. g. [katre vĩ], [katre bins]) are found over most of the area (*ALF* Map 1113), the normal forms for 'seventy' (*ALF* Map 1240) and 'ninety' (*ALF* Map 1114) are generally of the types represented by Provençal [sɛtãnto] and [nɔnãnto] (Gascon [nabãntə]) with forms corresponding to *huitante* at some points (especially in the extreme south-west and the extreme south-east). In other words, Occitan generally retains a decimal system. However Palay gives *trés-bints* (= *trois-vingts*) as well as *chichante* for 'sixty' and, under *cén(t)*, comments: "On emploie souvent, au lieu de *cén*, le comp. *cinq bints*". Various other Gallo-Romance forms (including *deux-vingts* in Haute-Marne, and a parallel form *düvẽ* in Savoie (*ALF* Map 1110, Point 965)) are quoted in von Wartburg (1922–, 14: 443–444).

13.1.9.2. Outside the Gallo-Romance area elements of a vigesimal system are well established in Southern Italy (see Rohlfs 1966–1969: § 975–976), particularly in Sicily (*du vintini* 'forty', *du vintini e ddèci* 'fifty', etc., up to *cincu vintini* 'hundred'), but also in parts of the southern mainland, e. g. *dua/tri/quattro vintini* in various Calabrian dialects and parallel forms as far north as the Abruzzi. In some cases the system is used for numerals up to 'fifteen times twenty' = 'three hundred', e. g., *quínnici vintini* (Cosenza) and *diecentine* 'two hundred' and *quindice intine* 'three hundred' at Vernole. These forms are of course based on collectives (corresponding to Fr. *vingtaine*), but forms corresponding exactly to the French type are found in Salentine dialects (*quattro vinti*). Widespread though the vigesimal system is in southern Italy, the decimal system coexists with it, and the use of the vigesimal system is restricted to specific functions, e. g. for stating a person's age or for counting eggs, fruit, etc.

Sporadic forms occur in Ibero-Romance, viz. *tres vent medidas de farina* 'sixty measures of flour' in Berceo (c. 1180–c. 1246) and *quatro vezes vinte* 'four times twenty' beside *oitenta* in Tras os Montes. The forms *dous veintes* 'forty' and *cuatro veintes* 'eighty' occur in the Leonese dialect of Sanabria.[25]

Various theories have been put forward in explanation of the vigesimal system in Romance. It has often been suggested that its occurrence in French is perhaps to be attributed to the influence of a Gaulish substratum,[26] on the grounds that a vigesimal system is found in the Modern Celtic languages of both branches (e.g. 'twenty' is Welsh *ugain*, Irish *fiche*; 'forty' is Welsh *deugain*, Irish *daichead* 'two times twenty', 'sixty' is Welsh *trigain*, Irish *trí fichid*, etc.). Rösler (1909, 1929), however, argued against this view, for the following reasons:
a) that a vigesimal system exists in the Modern Celtic languages is no proof that such a system existed in Gaulish; indeed, not only is there no evidence at all that Gaulish ever had a vigesimal system, but the only known relevant Gaulish form, *tricontis* 'thirty', fits clearly into the decimal system, and there are indications that the vigesimal system developed comparatively late in the other Celtic languages;
b) even if Gaulish had a vigesimal system, it is inherently improbable that Latin, as the language of a highly developed culture and of trade, would have taken over the numerical system of a subjugated and culturally less advanced people.

On the other hand, she argues, a vigesimal system was well established at an early date in Norse, and it seems clear that it was from the Viking invaders that the system passed into Anglo-Saxon.[27] It is significant, she suggests, that vigesimal forms occur in English monastic Latin (e.g. *quinquies viginti oves* and *octies viginti agri* as equivalents of *V scora scæp* and *VIII score æcere* in the inventory, ca. 1100, of the abbey of Bury St. Edmunds, i.e., an area where there had been much Norse influence, and others in later texts from various parts of England) at a time when parallel forms seem not to be attested in Latin documents from France and Germany. Further, the earliest French forms are in twelfth-century Anglo-Norman texts, and it is not until the thirteenth-century that such forms are attested in Central French dialects. Rösler suggests then that the vigesimal system passed from Norse into Anglo-Saxon and thence, via English monastic Latin, into Anglo-Norman and then into other French dialects.[28]

Rösler's view is supported by Rohlfs (1943) who argues, on the basis of an examination of the forms for 'seventy', 'eighty' and 'ninety' in the

Gallo-Romance area, that we have to do with a relative neologism that, originating (as far as French is concerned) in the west or northwest of the French-speaking area, has since fanned out along the main river systems (Somme, Seine, Loire and Garonne).

It is almost universally agreed – by Rohlfs among others – that the vigesimal forms occurring in Sicily and parts of the southern mainland of Italy also derive from Norman French, and first entered the dialects of these areas in the twelfth century when they were under Norman rule.[29]

Rösler suggested that *tres vent medidas de farina* in Berceo and *quatro vezes vinte* in Tras os Montes, the latter being frequently used with reference to measures of corn, could perhaps be ascribed to the influence of the French merchants who, for a long period of time, handled the corn trade in the Peninsula, though Berceo's use could be a literary gallicism. Rohlfs argues that the forms from Tras os Montes and northern Spain (Leonese *dous, cuatro veintes*) are probably to be attributed to the influence of a Basque substratum, Basque having a coherent and well-established vigesimal system.[30]

As early as 1925, L. Spitzer had already argued that vigesimal systems occur in widely separated parts of the globe and that the vigesimal forms occurring in France, Spain and southern Italy should be considered as the result of independent and spontaneous developments. An actual illustration of this was by coincidence provided, at about the same time as Spitzer's article appeared, by Alcover (1925–1926), who, during his linguistic investigations in various parts of the Catalan-speaking area, discovered that, in some places, the young people especially tended to count in twenties, at least up to 'forty-nine', though occasionally up to 'sixty', e. g. *vint y deu* 'thirty', *vint y onze* 'thirty-one', *dos vints* or *vint y vint* 'forty', *dos vints y tres* 'forty-three', etc. This seemed to him to be a spontaneous development that never succeeded in establishing itself, for, wherever he came across the system, he found that the young people who had adopted it were laughed at by their elders and corrected by their teachers and in the end they abandoned it.

The hypothesis of spontaneous origin for the various vigesimal forms in Romance was taken up much later by Reichenkron (1952). He argues that Rohlfs' article leaves too much unexplained, for instance: why do decimal and vigesimal systems coexist in Savoy and elsewhere?; why, if the vigesimal system in French is attributable to Norman influence, is it not characteristic of Channel Islands French?; why, if the sporadic vigesimal forms in Spanish and Portuguese are to be ascribed to an Ibero-Basque substratum, do such forms not occur in the Pyrenean dialects?

More fundamentally, a doubt subsists as to whether the Normans in fact had a vigesimal system. It may be that factors other than the influence of substrata or adstrata were decisive.

Sixteenth-century evidence seems to indicate that, whereas *septante, octante* and *nonante* were characteristic of cultivated usage, the common people (including farmers and traders) employed a vigesimal system ranging from *soixante-dix* to *dix-neuf vingts*. Taken in conjunction with the fact that the use of the decimal system in the South of France is characteristic of an area that corresponds exactly to the Provincia Narbonensis, which Reichenkron thinks cannot be due to mere coincidence, this suggests that the distinction between the two systems has sociological origins. His hypothesis is that, for reasons to be discussed below, a vigesimal system arose in the rural north of Gaul, but was inhibited from spreading to the Provincia Narbonensis where romanization had radiated to the country districts from the Graeco-Roman towns and where the influence of the literary language was strongest. Consequently the vigesimal system could in time have come to be associated with rural and uncouth speech, and the decimal system with urban and cultivated usage. Later, however, when the North became politically dominant and northern forms of speech were acceptable, the rôles were reversed. The fact that Artois, Flanders, Wallonia, Lorraine, Franche-Comté, *la Suisse romande* and the Channel Islands have a decimal system reflects the fact that these areas lay for several centuries outside the political frontiers of France (as some still do) and were consequently unaffected by the spread of the vigesimal system. The vigesimal elements found in Savoy and Sicily and parts of the southern mainland of Italy cannot be plausibly attributed to Norman influence,[31] and, as also the vigesimal forms in the Iberian peninsula, must be considered as being unrelated.

It is an essential part of Reichenkron's argument that, in various Middle French documents, vigesimal forms are used in particular with reference to sums of money and measures and that the vigesimal forms attested in Italian and Ibero-Romance have a similarly restricted currency, having reference principally (though not exclusively) to rural products (eggs and sheaves in Italy, flour, corn and farm animals in Spain) or (in Italy) age. Reichenkron thinks therefore that vigesimal systems of reckoning arise independently in various areas, both for sociological reasons (when rural products are offered for sale or reckoned in scores) and for linguistic reasons (numerals up to 'twenty' frequently follow a particular rhythmic pattern, whereas those above 'twenty' are often too long for the speedy reckoning that is necessary for trading purposes – one may therefore tend to count up to twenty, then begin on a second twenty, and so on). Depending on other sociological and cultural factors, the system may become generalized or may remain restricted to the reckoning up of observable objects while the decimal system persists for more abstract and arithmetical purposes.

In the present state of our knowledge, it does not seem possible to come to any firm conclusions regarding the origin or origins of the vigesimal forms attested in various Romance languages and dialects. The evidence adduced in support of the various substratum or adstratum theories – Celtic, Norman or Basque – seems too slender and the counter-indications, though perhaps not conclusive, too telling for these theories to carry conviction. Reichenkron's view that elements of a vigesimal system arose independently but in similar sociological contexts in a number of areas, though consistent and well argued, and not inherently implausible, is not however supported in all respects by a substantial body of evidence and can only lead to a verdict of "not proven".[32]

13.1.10. Decads and digits

The order of the two elements in the intermediate stages within each decad is invariably decad + digit, i. e., constructions of the type 'one and twenty' do not occur. There is, however, some variation in the way in which the two elements are linked.

Asyndetic constructions are constant in literary Italian and in Sardinian (with loss of the final vowel of *venti, trenta*, etc. before *uno* and *otto*), Ital. *ventuno, ventidue, ventitre, ventiquattro, ventotto*, etc.; *trentuno, trentadue, trentotto*, etc.; *quarantuno, quarantadue*, etc.; Sard. *bintunu, bintitres*, etc. The same construction is employed in Romansh, except that here the form for 'twenty' takes an *-a* (by analogy with *trenta*, etc.) before a consonant and, in Surselvan, takes the form *ventg(a)* [ventç(a)] as opposed to the simple form *vegn* [veɲ] 'twenty': Surs. *ventgin, ventgadus, ventgatreis, ventgaquater, ventgotg; trentin, trentadus, trentotg; curontin, curontadus*, etc.; Engad. *vainchün, vainchaduos, vainchatrais, vainchot; trentün, trentaduos, trentot; quarantün, quarantaduos*, etc.

Spanish, Portuguese and Rumanian are characterized by the use throughout of the conjunction 'and': Span. *veinte y uno, veinte y dos, veinte y tres;*[33] *treinta y uno, cuaranta y cuatro*, etc.; Port. *vinte e um, vinte e dois, trinta e um, quaranta e três*, etc. Rum. *douăzeci şi unu, treizeci şi cinci*; Ştefănescu-Drăgăneşti – Murrell, *Teach yourself Romanian* (1970: 176) say "in 21 to 99 the element *-zeci şi* is colloquially reduced to *-zăş* or *ş* (*-j* before a voiced consonant): *două(ză)şunu* (21), *două(ză)jdoi* (22), *patruştrei* (43), *şaijdoi* (62), etc.".

Catalan and Occitan use the conjunction from 'twenty-one' to 'twenty-nine', but elsewhere an asyndetic construction: Cat. *vint-i-un, vint-i-dos,* etc.; *trenta-un, trenta-tres*, etc.; Oc. *vint-e-un, vint-e-dos*, etc.; *trenta un, trenta tres*, etc. Modern French uses the conjunction only with *un*, e. g. *vingt et un, vingt-deux, vingt-trois; trente et un, trente-deux*, etc., but *quatre-vingt-un.*[34] In older French, however, *et* is found with other numerals, e. g. *vint et quatre, vint et sis, nonante et nuef* in the *Couronnement de Louis* (twelfth century), and *quarante et deux, soixante et trois* as late as Molière (Nyrop 1960: § 487). The pronunciation [vɛ̃t] that is regular in all compounds of *vingt* – e. g., *vingt-cinq* [vɛ̃tsɛ̃:k] – may represent a relic of the pronunciation of the [t] in liaison with a following *et* in *vingt et cinq*, etc., or else have spread to the other numerals by analogy with *vingt et un.*

Williams (1938: § 133.2) remarks that "as in the group from sixteen to nineteen in standard Portuguese [*dezasseis*, etc.] the preposition *a* is used instead of the conjunction *e* in the cardinals from twenty-one to twenty-nine in dialectal Portuguese, e. g. *vinta um*", whereas Rohlfs (1966 – 1969: § 974) thinks that Old Umbrian *vintadoi, vintacinque* probably contain a reflex of the conjunction *ac*. However it is at least equally likely that these forms illustrate the analogical influence of the higher decads ending in *-a* (Port. *trinta, quarenta*, etc.) – cf. Romansh *ventgadus*, etc. (see above).

Abbreviated forms of numerals ending in *sei* or *sette* are attested in Italian from the fourteenth to the early nineteenth centuries, e. g. *venzei* 'twenty-six' (for *ventisei*), *venzette* 'twenty-seven', *quaranzei* 'forty-six', *quaranzette* 'forty-seven', *cinquanzei* 'fifty-six', *cinquanzette* 'fifty-seven'.[35]

It remains to be mentioned that, at Amaseno in south Latium, C. Vignoli (*Il vernacolo di Veroli*, 1925) discovered that the numerals from 'eighty' to 'ninety-nine' are expressed by subtraction from 'one hundred', e. g. *centə menə quínici* 'one hundred minus fifteen' = 'eighty-five' (Rohlfs 1966 – 1969: § 975).

13.1.11. Hundreds

13.1.11.1. 'One hundred'

Except in Rumanian (see below) reflexes of *centum* remain: Span. *ciento* (but *cien* before a noun), Port. *cento* (but *cem* before a noun), Cat. *cent*, Oc. *cent*, Fr. *cent*, Ital. *cento*, Sard. *kéntu*, Surs. *tschien* [tʃɪən], Engad.

tschient. Franco-Provençal has forms corresponding to Fr. *cent*, Oc. *cent*; before a vowel, various liaison forms in plural [z] or [j] instead of [t] occur, e. g. *ṣan-z-óji* (*ṣ* = [θ]) 'cent oiseaux' (Gauchat – Jeanjaquet – Tappolet 1924–, 4: 200–202).

Rumanian has the form *sută* (used with the indefinite article, viz. *o sută* 'a hundred') which is generally considered to be of Slavonic origin, though Meyer-Lübke (1895: § 560) asserted that it is not Slavonic and may be of Dacian origin.[36] The reason for the elimination of *centum* may perhaps be, as argued by Iordan and Manoliu (1965: 157), that its reflex would, in the plural, have been a near-homonym of that of **cinque* (< *quinque*), viz. **cinţi* (cf. *cinci* 'five') and indeed in Arumanian there would have been total homonymy, viz. **ţinţi*.

13.1.11.2. Multiples of 'hundred'

The Latin multiples *ducentōs*, etc., have tended to become decomposed. There are however a number of relics, particularly in Ibero-Romance and in Sardinian:
'two hundred': *ducentōs* > OSpan. *dozientos*, Leonese *ducientos*, Port. *duzentos*, Sard. *dukkentos* (for variants in different dialects see Wagner (1957–1964, 1: 328);
'three hundred': *trecentōs* > OSpan. *trezientos*, Leonese *trecientos*, Port. *trezentos*, Sard. *trekkentos* (see also Wagner (1957–1964, 1: 328);
'five hundred': *quīngentōs* > Span. *quinientos*, Port. *quinhentos*.

Tuscan *dugento, duegento* 'two hundred' are considered by Rohlfs (1966–1969: § 976) to be borrowings from northern dialects (cf. Ligurian [dudzɛntu], Emilian [duʒɛnt]). There are also there cited various relics in Italian place-names e. g. *Quarzenti* (Veneto) < *quadringentī, Quingentole* (Mantua) < *quīngentī, Stienta* (Roviga) < *septingentā*. Some of these illustrate the now lost plural ending *-ī* that is also attested in Old Genoese *duxenti* 'two hundred', Old Pugliese *novicenti* 'nine hundred'.

Old Occitan had relics of the Latin nominative in *dozent* 'two hundred' and *trezent* 'three hundred' (but *quatre cens* 'four hundred', etc.).

Apart from *quinientos* 'five hundred', Spanish now uses analytical forms *dos cientos, tres cientos*, etc. and similar forms (*dois, tres, cinco centos*) occur in popular spoken Portuguese. On the other hand Sardinian has evolved an almost complete series of forms (here quoted after Pittau 1972: § 130) in which the ending of the first element differs slightly from the form of the simple unit: *battokentos* 'four hundred' (: *battor* 'four'), *kimbikentos* 'five hundred' (: *kimbe* 'five'), *settikentos* 'seven hundred'

(: *sette* 'seven'), *ottikentos* 'eight hundred' (: *otto* 'eight'), *nobikentos* 'nine hundred' (: *nobe* 'nine') – but note *seskentos* 'six hundred' (: *ses* 'six'); *settekentos, ottokentos, nobekentos* also occur.

A distinction of gender is made in Ibero-Romance and Sardinian: Span. *doscientos, -as; quinientos, -as*, etc.; Port. *duzentos, -as; quatrocentos, -as*, etc.; Cat. *dos-cents* masc., *dues-centes* fem.; *tres-cents, -centes* etc.; Sard. *dukkentos, -as*, etc.

Rum. *sută* has the plural *sute* (e. g. *două sute* 'two hundred').

For Surs. *duatschien, treitschien*; Engad. *duatschient, traiatschient*, see 13.1.3.

13.1.12. Hundreds, decads and digits

Numerals of the type 'one hundred and two', 'three hundred and forty', are most frequently expressed asyndetically, e. g. Span. *ciento dos*, Cat. *cent-dos*, Oc. *cent dos*, Fr. *cent deux*, Ital. *centodue*, Surs. *tschien dus*, Rum. *o sută doi*; and 'three hundred and forty': Span. *trescientos cuarenta*, Cat. *tres-cents quaranta*, Oc. *tres cents quaranta*, Fr. *trois cent quarante*,[37] Ital. *trecentoquaranta*, Surs. *treitschien curonta*, Rum. *trei sute patruzeci*.

Portuguese however uses the conjunction *e*, e. g. *cento-e-dois, trezentos e quarenta*, as does Walloon e. g. *cint-èt-deûs* 'one hundred and two', *cwète cint èt vint'-deûs* 'four hundred and twenty-two' (Remacle 1952, 3: 273).[38]

13.1.13. Thousands

Latin *mílle* remains in Ital. *mille*, Span. *mil*, Port. *mil*, Cat. *mil*, and also in Fr. *mil*, which now survives only in dates (e. g. *mil neuf cent trente*), having been ousted as a free form by learned *mille*. Sard. *milli*, Surs. *melli*, Engad. *milli*, Oc. *mila* are not regular reflexes of *mīlle*. Rum. *mie* – a noun, i. e., *o mie* 'a thousand' – derives from Latin plural *mīlia*.

The word for 'thousand' is normally invariable for number in Ibero-Romance (Span. *tres mil*, Cat. *tres mil*, Port. *três mil*), French (*trois mille*), and Romansh (for special forms for 'two' and 'three' in Surselvan, *duamelli, treimelli*, see 13.1.3.). Latin pl. *mīlia* is reflected in Sard. *duamidza* 'two thousand', *tremidza* 'three thousand', *battomidza* 'four thousand', etc. and in OFr. *milie*, which, in the Chanson de Roland for example, is used only as a plural (e. g. *plus de vint milie humes* 'more than twenty thousand men'). A form *milia* which may have been subject to learned influence is found, for instance, in Old Tuscan *dumilia, tremilia*,

Old Neapolitan *quindici milia*, and survives in Calabrian *duimilia, trimilia, cientumilia* (Rohlfs 1966–1969: § 976). *Milia* also occurs in Old Catalan, e.g. *quatre milia bèsties* 'four thousand animals' (1309) (Badia Margarit 1951: 262). Ital. pl. *mila* (e.g. *duemila, tremila*) is not a regular reflex of *milia*.

Though Cat. *mil* is invariable in multiples of 'thousand', pl. *mils* is used in expressions such as *té moltes mils pessetes* 'I have thousands of pesetas' (Badia Margarit 1962: § 124 n. 3).

13.1.14. Higher numerals

13.1.14.0. None of the simple forms for numerals higher than 'thousand' are inherited directly from Latin numerals.

13.1.14.1. 'Million'. Fr. *million* (first attested in the thirteenth century), Span. *millón* (fourteenth century) and parallel forms in other Romance languages (e.g. Port. *milhão*, Cat. *milió*, Surs. *milliun*, Rum. *milion*) are usually considered[39] to derive directly or indirectly (i.e., via another Romance language) from Ital. *milione*, an augmentative of *mille*. Devoto (1968) however, gives Fr. *million* as the etymon of Ital. *milione*.

Port. *conto* and Span. *cuento* < late Latin *computus* acquired the value 'ten times one hundred thousand', i.e. 'a million'.

13.1.14.2. 'Milliard'. This form is of French origin (attested 1544) and has spread to certain other languages including Italian (*miliardo*) and Rumanian (*miliard*), but not Spanish, which expresses 10^9 by *mil millones*.

13.1.14.3. 'Billion', 'trillion', etc. *Billion, trillion, quadrillion* (now *quatrillion*) are first attested in Middle French, *quintillion* not until 1877. These forms have passed into the other Romance languages, e.g. Span. *billón, trillón, quatrillón, quintillón*; Port. *bilhão, trilhão, quatrilhão, quintilhão*; Ital. *bilione, trilione, quadrilione, quintilione*; Rum. *bilion, trilion, cvadrilion, cvintilion*.

The value of these terms has not been constant. In sixteenth-century French, each denomination represented the preceding one multiplied a millionfold, as in current British and German (but not American) usage, i.e. *un billion* '10^{12}', *un trillion* '10^{18}'. However, in the Romance languages, as in American usage, each denomination came to represent the preceding one multiplied a thousandfold, i.e. *un billion* '10^9' = *un milliard, un trillion* '10^{12}' (= *un billion* in the other system). Since 1948, however, official mathematical terminology in French again affects to each denomination the value of the preceding one multipled a millionfold.

For forms and datings of higher multiples (some of them introduced twice into French, first in the sixteenth and then again in the nineteenth century), see von Wartburg (1922–): *sextillion* (11: 559); *septillion* (11: 479); *octillion* (7: 307); *nonillion* (7: 189).

13.2. Ordinals

13.2.1. 'First'

The only major Romance language to retain a reflex of *prīmus* in current usage is Italian (*primo*). Other reflexes are found in Romansh (e. g. Engad. *prüm* and prefixed forms such as Surs. *emprem*) and Dalmatian (the most authentic of the attested forms is probably *prein*, see Bartoli 1906, 1: § 146). Relics in French include OFr. *prin* (of limited currency) and such words and expressions as *printemps, primerose* 'hollyhock', *de prime abord* 'at first sight' (the feminine adjective here is due to the analogy of *de prime face*) – for other Gallo-Romance reflexes see von Wartburg (1922–, 9: 381–389). Rum. *prim* is a learned form, though relics of an inherited form occur in *primăvară* 'spring' and Old Rumanian and dialectal *de-a-primă* (Iordan – Manoliu 1965: 157) and in the Arumanian and Megleno-Rumanian adv. *prima* (Densuşianu 1901: 113–115).

Reflexes of *prīmārius* are widely distributed: Span. *primero*, Port. *primeiro*, Cat. *primer* [prime], Fr. *premier*, OItal. *primaio* (e. g. Dante, Inferno 5.1 *dal cerchio primaio*, Rohlfs 1966–1969: § 977). Relics in Rumanian include *cale primară* 'the first visit paid by a young bride to her parents eight days after the wedding', *văr primar* (Megleno-Rumanian *prima ver*) 'first cousin'. Sardinian has *ermánu brimárdzu* (Logudorese), *ĝermanu primálvu* (Bitti) 'second cousin' (Wagner 1930: 19). Old French also had a further derivative, *premerain* < **primarianus*, cf. OItal. *premeran* (Tekavčić 1972: 263–264). For other Gallo-Romance reflexes of *prīmārius* see von Wartburg (1922–, 9: 377–378).

The usual Rumanian form is *întîi* < **antaneus*, perhaps originally a military term, indicating the first in a rank of soldiers (Iordan – Manoliu 1965: 157 n. 1).

For 'twenty-first' etc., French uses *vingt et unième, trente et unième*, etc.; cf. Oc. *vint-e-unième*, etc.; Cat. *vint-i-unè* (fem. *-unena*) etc.; and Ital. *ventunesimo* (or *ventesimo primo*); but Span. *vigesimo primo* (a learned form), Port. *vigesimo-primeiro*.

13.2.2. 'Second'

Secundus remains in Span. *segundo*, Port. *segundo*, Cat. *segon* [səγon], OFr. *sëont*, Engad. *seguond*, etc. Fr. *second* [səgɔ̃] and Ital. *secondo* are learned borrowings. The more usual form in French is *deuxième* (for *-ième* see 13.2.6.), which is also used to the total exclusion of *second* in 'twenty-second' etc.: *vingt-deuxième*. In Old French *altre, autre* < *alter* was the most usual form for 'second'. For Rumanian forms see 13.2.7.

3.2.3. 'Third'

Tertius remains in Ital. *terzo*, Surs. *tierz*, Engad. *terz*, Cat. *terç* (the more usual form is *tercer*, see below), OFr. *tiers* (fem. *tierce*), OOc. *tertz*. Though *troisième* has largely ousted the inherited forms not only in French but also in Occitan, relics remain in French, as the fraction *un tiers* 'one-third', and in various fixed expressions such as *le tiers état* 'the Third Estate', *une tierce* 'third' (music), *fièvre tierce* 'tertian ague' and various legal expressions, e. g. *en main tierce* 'in the hands of a third party', *tierce caution* 'contingent liability'. For other examples of *tiers, tierce* in Modern French see von Wartburg (1922–, 3.1: 266–267).

Span. *tercero*, Port. *terceiro*, Cat. *tercer* reflect *tertiārius*. Relics of *tertius* remain in Cat. *terç* (used primarily as a fraction, 'one-third'), in the Spanish and Portuguese forms for the fraction, viz. Span. *tercio*, Port. *têrço*, and in Port. *têrça-feira* 'Tuesday'. For Rumanian forms see 13.2.7.; a relic of *tertius* remains in the expression *an ţărţ* 'two years ago' (i. e., the third year counting backwards from the present).

13.2.4. 'Fourth' to 'tenth'

Reflexes of the Latin forms (some inherited, some learned) occur as follows:

	Latin	Spanish	Portuguese	Old French	Italian
'fourth'	*quārtus*	*cuarto*	*quarto*	*quart*	*quarto*
'fifth'	*quīntus*	*quinto*	*quinto*	*quint*	*quinto*
'sixth'	*sextus*	*sexto*	*sexto*	*siste*	*sesto*
'seventh'	*septimus*	*séptimo*	*sétimo*	*se(d)me*	*settimo*
'eighth'	*octāuus*	*octavo*	*oitavo*	—	*ottavo*
'ninth'	*nōnus*	*nono*	*nono*	—	*nono*
'tenth'	*decimus*	*décimo*	*décimo*	*disme*	*decimo*

In addition, Catalan has *quart* (kwərt] and *quint* [kin] (coexisting with *cinquè*) and Romansh has *quart* (coexisting in some dialects with forms such as *quartavel*) and *quint* (coexisting with forms in *-avel*, see below). Old Occitan had *quart, quint, sest.*

Span. *sexto, séptimo, nono, décimo*; Port. *sexto, sétimo, nono, décimo* and Span. *octavo* are learned or semi-learned forms. *sietmo* < *septimum* remained in Old Spanish.

Old Portuguese had a number of forms for 'sixth', viz. *seisto* < *sextus* but influenced by *seis*, and a derivative thereof *seistimo* (influenced by OPort. *seitimo* < *septimum*), and *seismo sesmo* < **seximum* (formed analogically on *septimum*). Relics of *sexta, octavus, nona, decimus* are seen in Span. *siesta*, Port. *sesta* (originally 'the sixth hour'), Span. *ochavo* 'something octagonal in shape', Port. *nôa* 'nones'; Span. *diezmo*, Port. *dízimo* 'tithe'.

OFr. *siste* perhaps represents a generalization of the feminine form by analogy with *se(d)me* and other masculine ordinals in *-e*. The regular **sist* is not attested.[40].

Old French also had *ui(d)me* 'eighth', and *nuefme* 'ninth', formed analogically on the model of *se(d)me* and *disme*.[41] All of the Old French and Old Occitan forms have now been ousted by forms in *-ième* (see 13.2.6.5.), though relics remain e. g. Fr. *un quart; la fièvre quarte* (*quinte*) 'quartan (quintan) ague', *Charles-Quint* '(the Emperor) Charles V', *une quarte* '(musical) fourth', *une quinte* '(musical) fifth', *la díme* 'tithe'. *neume* < *neufme* survived in Brittany till the eighteenth century as a substantive denoting a priest's right to one-ninth of a deceased parishioner's furniture (Nyrop 1960: § 492).

Ital. *quinto, nono, decimo* are learned forms; alternative forms having the learned ending *-èsimo* occur in various Tuscan dialects, e. g. *settèsimo, ottèsimo, novèsimo, decèsimo*, while a relic of *decimum* is found in Tuscan PlN *Diécimo* (Rohlfs 1966–1969: § 977).

13.2.5. Numerals above ten

Elcock (1960: 76) characterizes the situation neatly as follows:

> From 'eleventh' onwards the Latin ordinals seem to have fallen largely out of use. When a need for them was felt in Romance, they were recreated with the help of literary Latin. Thus in Italian the learned suffix *-esimo* was attached to the cardinals, e. g. *undicesimo,*

> *ventitreesimo*, &c., while modern Spanish employs purely learned forms, e. g. *undécimo, vigésimo, cuadragésimo*, &c.

Portuguese likewise uses *undécimo, vigésimo, quadregésimo*, etc. Other examples are Span. *décimo sexto*, Port. *décimo sexto* 'sixteenth'; Span. *centésimo*, Port. *centésimo* 'hundredth'; Span. *quingentésimo*, Port. *quingentésimo* 'five hundredth'; Span. *milésimo*, Port. *milésimo* 'one thousandth'; Span. *septengésimo*, Port. *septingentésimo* 'seven hundredth'; Span. *octogentésimo*, Port. *octingentésimo* 'eight hundredth'.

While the dominant forms in Italian are those derived from the cardinal by means of the learned ending *-esimo* (*ventunesimo* 'twenty-first', *trentesimo* 'thirtieth', etc.), latinizing forms such as *ventesimo primo* 'twenty-first' and pure latinisms such as *vigesimo* 'twentieth', *trigesimo* 'thirtieth', etc. also occur (Rohlfs 1966–1969: § 977). Tekavčić (1972: 264) comments as follows:

> I numerali ordinali *decimo primo, decimo secondo, vigesimo terzo,* nonché *undecimo, duodecimo* ecc., sono netti latinismi. La coesistenza delle forme popolari e dei latinismi può venir sfruttata per specializzazioni semantiche o stilistiche di vario genere : per un corridore si dirà che è arrivato *ventitreesimo*, per il Papa si dice *vigesimo terzo*.

Other languages have extended to the higher numerals the various ordinal endings adopted for the lower numerals (see below).

Relics of two of the Latin higher ordinals, viz. *quadragesima* 'fortieth' and *quinquagesima* 'fiftieth' survive, the former as a widely distributed term for 'Lent': Span. *cuaresma*,[42] Cat. *coresma*, Fr. *carème*, Surs. *cureisma*, Engad. *quaraisma*, Rum. *păresimi*; and the latter with reference to Whitsunday (celebrated fifty days after Easter, cf. Greek πεντηκοστή: OSpan. *cinquaesma*, Old Picard *ciunkesme*, Walloon *cinqüème* [sẽkwem], Surs. *tschuncheismas*, Engad. *tschinquaisma*; and also, in Romansh, as a unit of measurement of length (= German *Klafter*), Surs. *tschuncheisma*, Engad. *tschinquaisma*.

13.2.6. Suffixation

13.2.6.0. In those languages that have not adopted learned formations, the ordinals are derived from the cardinals by means of one or other of a number of suffixes.

13.2.6.1. *-ānus*. OFr. *-anum* (nom. *-ains* < *-anus*) was used to derive new forms either from the inherited lower ordinals viz. *premerain* (from *prīmārius* + *-anum*), *tierçain* (from *tiers*), *quartain*, *quintain*; or, in the case of the higher numerals, from the cardinals: *sisain, setain, uitain, dizain, unzain, douzain, trezain, quatorzain, quinzain, vintain* (Nyrop 1960: § 496). These forms did not outlast the medieval period as ordinals, though many survived in the feminine form as collective nouns (*une huitaine, dizaine, douzaine, quinzaine, vingtaine, centaine*, etc.).

It must be noted however that Meyer-Lübke (1908–1921; § 178) considered that, in spite of the spelling with *-ai-*, the origin of *-ain* is to be sought in the distributive *-ēnī* which gave the Old Occitan ordinals in *-en* (see 13.2.6.4.). Mr. J. R. Wheatley, of the University of Queensland, who is preparing a thesis on the Romance ordinals, draws my attention to the use of *-ēnus* as an ordinal suffix in medieval Latin, e. g. *vicenus, tricenus* in Paulus Diaconus (K. Sittl, *ALL* vi, 1889: 108–109), and observes that these are in fact more common than ordinals in *-ānus* in medieval Latin, except in medical terminology (and even there *quārtānus*, for example, as in *febris quārtāna*, is strictly speaking not an ordinal).

13.2.6.2. *-ārius*. In addition to reflexes of *prīmārius* (13.2.1.) and *tertiārius* (Span. *tercero*, Port. *terceiro*, Cat. *tercer*) there are OPort. *quarteiro, quinteiro*. However *-ārius* has nowhere become the basis of a complete ordinal system.

13.2.6.3. *-āuus*. The only Latin ordinal having a stressed suffix was *octáuus* (contrast *séptimus, décimus*, etc.) and this has served as the basis for new ordinal systems in Gascon and Romansh.

Gascon has forms based on *-āuus* for the ordinals from 'second' upwards: *dusàu, tresàu, quatàu, cinquàu, cheysàu, setàu, oeytàu, nabàu, dètzàu, ounzàu, doudzàu, tredzàu, quatourzàu, quinzàu* ... *bintàu* 'twentieth', *trentàu* 'thirtieth', etc. These forms are invariable for gender (e. g. *la dètzàu gouyate* 'the tenth girl'), as a consequence of confusion of *-au* < *-auum* with *-au* < *-ale*, which explains Old Gascon variants such as *septal, nabal, detzal* (Rohlfs 1970: § 512 n. 334). The native Gascon forms are nowadays tending to be ousted by French forms in *-ième*.

Romansh has ordinals in *-avel, -evel*, a suffix that seems to go back to a derivative of *octāuus* viz. **octavilis*: Surs. *tschunavel* 'fifth', *sisavel* 'sixth', *siatavel, otgavel, novavel, dieschavel, endischavel, dudischavel* ... *vegnavel* 'twentieth', *trentavel* ... *trentasisavel* 'thirty-sixth' ... *tschienavel* 'hundredth' ... *melliavel* 'thousandth', etc. Lower Engad. *terzavel* (beside *terz*) 'third', *quartavel* (beside *quart*), *tschinchavel* (beside *quint*), *sesavel, settavel, ottavel, nouvavel, deschavel, ündeschavel, dudeschavel* ... *vain-*

chavel 'twentieth' ... *tschientavel* 'hundredth' ... *milliavel* 'thousandth', etc. Upper Engad. *tschinschevel* 'fifth', *sesevel* 'sixth', *novevel* 'ninth', *deschevel* 'tenth' *vainschevel* 'twentieth', etc.

13.2.6.4. *-enus.* This suffix, which originated in the Latin distributives *septēni, nouēni, undēni, uicēni*, etc., has been widely used, either sporadically or systematically, as an ordinal suffix (see also above).

Spanish now has only *noveno* (beside learned *nono*), but Old Spanish also had *cuatreno, cinqueno, seiseno, seteno, ocheno, dezeno, onzeno, trezeno, dizesseseno, veynteno* (Menéndez Pidal 1962: 246–247), and in the thirteenth-century Aragonese *Fuero General de Navarra* the forms *quarteno, cinqueno, seyseno, seteno* are usual (Zamora Vicente 1966: 252). Some forms remain in Spanish as collectives, e. g. *decena, docena, cuarentena.* Old Portuguese also had *noveo* < *noveno, onzeno, dozeno.* In Catalan, on the other hand, *-è* (from earlier *-èn*), fem. *-ena*, is the basis of a complete system of ordinals from 'fifth' to 'thousandth': *cinquè/cinquena* (beside *quint, -a*), *sisè, setè, vuitè, novè, desè, onzè, dotzè, vintè, vint-i-unè, centè, milè*, etc.

Old Occitan had similar forms from 'sixth' upwards: *seizen, seten, ochen, noven, detzen, onzen, dotzen, vinten, centen, millen*, etc. These have now been ousted by forms in *-ième* borrowed from French. Forms in *-en* also predominated in Old Italian in northern dialects, e. g. Old Ligurian *unzén* 'eleventh', *diseptén* 'seventeenth', Old Lombard *zinquén* 'fifth', *sexén, setén, ogén, novén, dexén, tredesén* 'thirteenth', *quindesén* 'fifteenth', *dexsetén* 'seventeenth', *dexnovén, trentén, cinquantén* (Rohlfs 1966–1969: § 977).

13.2.6.5. Fr. *-ième.* The origin of this suffix, which is used to form all the ordinals from *deuxième* upwards (e. g. *huitième, dix-septième, vingt-et-unième, quatre-vingtième, centième, millième, millionième*), is obscure. It occurs in Old French in the forms *-ime -isme -ieme -iesme*. It is generally held[43] that *-i(s)me* drives from *-ecimum*, i. e. either from *di(s)me* < *decimum*[44] or from reflexes of *undecimum* and *duodecimum* (> OFr. *onzime, dozime*).[45] Walloon still has *-îme* or *-inme* [ẽ:m] according to dialect, e. g. *deûzîme, deûzînme* 'second'; *vint-onîme, -înme* 'twenty-first', *cintîme, -înme* 'hundredth' and forms in [i:m] also survive in various eastern dialects of French (see for example *ALF* Map 589: *la troisième fois*). However, as early as the thirteenth century the ending *-ie(s)me* had become general in the literary language. It is possible that this originated in the reflex *diesme* < *decimum* that is characteristic of south-western dialects of French (Anjou, Maine, etc.) and that it later spread "par on ne sait quel hasard" as Nyrop (1960: § 493) puts it,[46] to other areas, including the Île-de-France. P. Fouché (1942: 11–19) after surveying various previous views as to the origin of *-ième*, all of which he considers impossible or implausible for one reason or another, argues that *-ième* could represent a Central French reflex of *-dĕcimum* (as in *undĕcimum*, etc.); his suggested phonetic development, though doubtless theoretically valid, rests on so many unattested stages, some of them depending on a certain amount of special pleading, as not to carry conviction.

-ième has not only become generalized in French but has almost entirely supplanted the indigenous ordinal forms in the Occitan-speaking area, except in Gascony (see *ALF* Map 589). Even in Gascon however the forms in *-àu* suffer competition from forms in *-ième* – Palay, for example, makes such comments as the following: s. v. *dètsàu* 'tenth' "on dit aussi, mais à tort, *dètsième*", s. v. *ounzàu* 'eleventh' "on dit aussi *ounzième*"; s. v. *tredzàu* 'thirteenth': "sous l'influence du fr., on dit aussi *tredzième*"; s. v. *trentàu* 'thirtieth': "on francise, aujourd'hui, et on dit *trentième*".

13.2.7. Rumanian ordinals

Rumanian has constructed a regular ordinal system on the pattern: possessive article (masc. *al*, fem. *a*) + cardinal + enclitic definite article (masc. *-le*, fem. *-a*) + (in the masculine) adverbial suffix *-a*, e. g. *al doilea, a doua* 'second'; *al treilea, a treia* 'third'; *al patrulea, a patra* 'fourth'; *al cincilea, a cincia* 'fifth'; *al zecelea, a zecea* 'tenth'; *al douăzeci şi unulea, a douăzeci si una* 'twenty-first'; *al o sutălea, a o suta* 'hundredth'. The reasons for the adoption of *-le* rather than *-lu* in the masculine (contrast Arumanian *doilu, treilu, paturlu*, etc. and Old Daco-Rumanian *patrul, optul*) are unclear (see *Istoria Limbii române* 1969: 238).

13.2.8. Sardinian ordinals

Sardinian has no synthetic forms for the ordinals (other than italianisms such as *primu, sikundu, tertzu, kuartu*, etc.) but uses analytical forms *su 'e unu* 'first', *su 'e duos* 'second', *su 'e binti* 'twentieth', *su 'e kéntu* 'hundredth', etc., which could be literally translated into Italian as *quello d'uno, quello di due*, etc.[47] Similar forms are attested in Lombard viz. *quel di düü* 'second' (masc.), *quela di trè* 'third (fem.)' (see Salvioni 1899: 234–235).

13.3. Collectives

13.3.1. 'Both'

Latin masc. *ambō* (Vulgar Latin masc. nom. **ambi*, acc. **ambos*), fem. nom. *ambae*, acc. *ambās* is reflected in the following forms: Span. *ambos, ambas* (the same forms in Portuguese and Sardinian); OFr. fem. *ambes* [48] (Nyrop 1960: § 488); OOc. masc. obl. *ams*; OItal. *ambi, ambe* (also Mod. Ital. *ambo*); Rum. *îmbi, îmbe*. In combination with various forms for 'two' we find, inter alia[49]: Cat. masc. *ambdós* [əmdós], fem. *ambdues*; OFr. masc. nom. *andui*, obl. *ansdous*, fem. *ambesdues*; OOc. masc. nom. *andui*, obl. *ansdos*, fem. *amdoas*; Ital. *ambedue*; Engad. *amenduos*; Rum. masc. *amîndoi*, fem. *amîndouă*. Italian also has various prepositional forms (the first element reflecting *intra*) e. g. *entrambi*, Tuscan *tramendue*, Corsican *tremendui*, Old Florentine *intradue*, Old Milanese *intrambidù* (Rohlfs 1966–1969: § 980).

13.3.2. 'All three', etc.

Arumanian has a series of forms showing the influence of *amindo(i)l'i* 'both' (corresponding to Daco-Rum. *amîndoi*) viz. *amintreil'i* 'all three', *aminţinţile* 'all five', etc. (*Istoria limbii române* 1969: 237).

The pattern 'all three' occurs a) with the definite article in French, e. g. *tous (toutes) les deux, trois, seize, vingt*, etc.;[50] b) without an article in Catalan, e. g. *tots dos, tots tres, tots quatre*, etc., and Rumanian (from 'three' upwards) e. g. *toţi trei* (fem. *toate trele*), *toţi patru* 'all four', etc.;[51] and c) with the conjunction *e* 'and' in Italian, e. g. *tutti* (fem. *tutte*) *e due, tutti e tre, tutti e quattro*.

13.4. Approximatives

13.4.0. A variety of suffixes have been used to form collective numerals having, normally if not invariably, an approximative value.

13.4.1. *-āna*. Fr. *-aine* occurs in the feminine nouns *huitaine* (especially in the sense of 'eight days', i. e. 'a week'), *neuvaine* (exclusively in the religious sense of 'novena'), the approximatives *dizaine, douzaine* (also, like its English borrowing *dozen*, used with the precise value of 'twelve'), *quinzaine* (also in the sense of 'fifteen days', i.e. 'a fortnight'), *vingtaine, trentaine, quarantaine, cinquantaine, soixantaine, centaine.*[52]

13.4.2. *-ēna.* Reflexes of *-ena* occur in the Ibero-Romance languages, in particular, though not necessarily exclusively, to form derivatives of 'ten', 'twelve' and the tens (including 'hundred'): Span. *decena, docena, veintena, centena*, etc.; Port. *dezena, dozena* (also *duzia*), *vintena, centena* etc.; Cat. *desena, dotzena, vintena, trentena*, etc. (but *centenar*). Occitan has similar forms not only for the corresponding numerals (*desena, dotzena, vintena, centena*, etc.) but also for the other numerals from 'five' (*cinquena*) to 'sixteen' (*setzena*). Further reflexes of *-ena* occur in Franco-Provençal, e.g. *wĭtḗna* 'eight', *diyzḗna* 'ten', *trẽtḗna* 'thirteen' at Bagnes (Bjerrome 1957: 68), and some northern Italian dialects, e.g. Lombard [dundzεna], Milanese *deśèna, vintèna, sesantèna* (Rohlfs 1966–1969: § 979).

13.4.3. *-īna.* Italian has *decina, dozzina* (a northern borrowing), and corresponding forms for each of the tens from *ventina* to *novantina.*

13.4.4. *-ārium.* Reflexes occur in Ital. *centinaio* 'approximately a hundred', *migliaio* 'approximately a thousand', and learned forms such as Span. *millare,*[53] Port. *milheiro*, Cat. *miler*, Fr. *millier*. Other forms include Port. *milhento*, resulting from a contamination of *milheiro* and *cento* (Williams 1962: § 138), Cat. *milanta*, defined by Moll (1952: § 263) as a "numeral indefinido para significar una inmensa cantidad"; and Ital. *millanta*, referred to Rohlfs (1966–1969: § 976), as a "forma scherzosa (in particolare nell'espressione *millantanove*)" serving to express "un numero grandissimo".

13.5. Adverbs

13.5.1. A relic of Latin *semel* remains in Old Milanese *sema* 'once', which survives in certain pre-Alpine dialects, e.g. *sema* in the Valtellina and *sem'* in the Valle Anzasca.

13.5.2. Otherwise the adverbial function is expressed by means of a variety of substantives, the most typical of which in the modern languages include Span. *vez*, Port. *vez* (Span. *dos veces*, Port. *duas vezes*), Cat. *cop, vegada* (*dos cops, dues vegadas*), Fr. *fois* (*deux fois*), Oc. *cop* (*dos cops*), Ital. *volta* (*due volte*) and *via* (as in *tre via quattro* 'three times four'), Rum. *o dată* 'once', *două ori* (plural of *oară*) 'twice'. *Coup* is used in Popular French in addition to *fois*, and in Walloon *côp* is more frequent than *fî* 'fois', e.g. *deûs côps* 'deux fois'.[54]

13.6. Distributives

Elcock (1960: 77) considers, doubtless correctly, that, though the Latin distributives from *singuli* to *seni* persisted in popular speech, "to judge from their sporadic occurrence in Romance, and from the specialized usages in which they appear, it would seem that their meaning was often misunderstood and obscured". He instances the following:
a) *singuli*, which generally acquired the meaning 'single' – to Elcock's example of OFr. *sangle* 'alone' (also *bière sangle* 'small beer'), one might add. OOc. *sengle*, Span. *sendos*, Port. *sendos* 'each of two, one for each' < *singulos*, Rum. *singur* 'single'.
b) *bini* > OFr. *bin et bin* 'two by two'.
c) *quatern(i)* > Fr. *cahier*, Span. *cuaderno*, Ital. *quaderno*, the meaning 'note-book' deriving from 'four-fold sheet'.
d) Gambling terms, such as *ternes* 'double-three', *quaernes* 'double-four', *quinnes* 'double-five' and *sines* 'double-six' in the Picard *Jeu de Saint Nicolas* (ca. 1198). With reference to these, Elcock comments that "in view of the age-old popularity of dice-throwing there seems no reason to doubt that these are genuine survivals of Vulgar Latin; they may be feminines, agreeing with an implied *vĭces*".

The functions of the Latin distributives are expressed in the Romance languages by a wide variety of lexical and analytic means, e. g. (to quote from only two languages), Fr. *ils ont dix francs chacun, un à un* 'one by one'; OFr. *par un e un* 'one by one'; Port. *a dois e dois* or *dois a dois* 'two by two'; *de três em três horas* or *cada três horas* 'every three hours'.

13.7. Multiplicatives

Duplum survives as Span. *doble*, Cat. *doble,* Oc. *doble*, Port. *dobre*, Fr. *double*, Ital. *doppio*, Romansh *dubel*, some of which may well be learned or semi-learned forms. Rum. *dublu* is a borrowing of Fr. *double*.

The higher multiplicatives are learned borrowings and, in general, not characteristic of popular usage, e. g. Span. *triple, cuádruple, quíntuplo, décuplo, céntuplo*, etc.; Port. *triple, cêntuplo,* etc.; Fr. *triple, quadruple, quintuple, sextuple, centuple*, etc.; Ital. *triplo, quadruplo, quintuplo, sestuplo*, etc.; Rum. *triplu, cvadruplu, cvintuplu* (probably via French) – but *însutit* from *sută* for 'hundredfold', see below. Ital. *duplice, triplice, quadruplice* also occur. Rumanian also has a number of participles of para-synthetic verbs derived from certain cardinal numerals, e. g. *îndoit* 'double' from the verb *a îndoi* (= *în* + *doi* + *i*), *întreit* 'threefold', *împătrit* 'fourfold', *încincit* 'fivefold', *înzecit* 'tenfold', *însutit* 'hundredfold', *înmiit* 'thousandfold'.

13.8. Fractions

13.8.1. 'Half'

As nouns, most Romance languages use derivatives of *medietatem*, viz. Span. *mitad*, Port. *metade*, Cat. *meitat*, Fr. *moitié*, Oc. *mitat*, Ital. *metà*. Rum. *jumătate* is generally considered to be a derivative of *medietātem*, influenced in its first part by Alban. *giymës* 'half'.[55]

As adjectives, derivatives of *medium* include Span. *medio* (e. g. *media hora* 'half an hour'), Port. *meio* (*meia hora*), Cat. *mig* (*mitja hora*), Oc. *mieg*, Ital. *mezzo*, Sard. *mésu*, Surs. *miez*, Engad. *mez* – these Romansh forms are also used as nouns. Fr. *mi* < *medium* now remains only in a few words (*midi, milieu, minuit* for earlier *mienuit*, etc.) and fixed expressions such as *à mi-chemin, mi-temps, à mi-voix, paupières mi-closes, la mi-août*, etc., having been supplanted as a free form by *demi* < *dimedium* (for *dimidium*), which also gives OOc. *demeg*.

A form *mitan(t)*, which is clearly related etymologically to *medium, medietātem*, etc., but whose precise origin is uncertain, occurs widely in the various Gallo-Romance dialects (e. g. Walloon *lu mitant*, Prov. *lou mitan*).

13.8.2. Other fractions

The ordinal forms are widely used also to express fractions, e. g. Span. *un cuarto, un décimo*; Port. *um sexto, um nono*; Fr. *un cinquième, un dixième*, etc.; Ital. *un quarto, un dodicesimo*. In some cases forms that are no longer – or not normally – used as ordinals survive as fractions (e. g. Span. *un tercio*, Port. *um terço*, Cat. *un terç* 'one-third'; Fr. *un tiers, un quart*).

The following call for special mention.

13.8.2.1. Spanish and Portuguese use *-avo* (from *octavo, oitavo* 'eight') to derive fractional forms from the cardinals from 'eleven' to 'ninety-nine'; e.g. Span. *un onzavo, catorzavo, dieciseisavo, veintavo*; Port. *um onze avo, cinco vinte avos* 'five-twentieths'; Spanish, but not Portuguese, also has *un centavo* 'a hundredth'.

13.8.2.2. The word *part(e)* is widely used in the Ibero-Romance languages in conjunction with the ordinals, e.g. Span. *la tercera parte de ellos* 'one-third of them'; Port. *duas quintas partes* 'two-fifths'; Cat. *quatre quinzenes parts* 'four-fifteenths'; similar constructions also occur in other languages, e.g. Rum. *a treia parte* 'the third part.

13.8.2.3. Rumanian has adopted *un sfert* 'quarter' from Slavonic, cf. OCS *četvrŭtŭ*, but otherwise the literary languages forms its fractions by means of the suffix *-ime*, e.g. *o treime* 'third', *o pătrime* 'quarter' (less widely used than *sfert*), *o cincime* 'fifth', *o zecime* 'tenth', *o sutime* 'hundredth', *o miime* 'thousandth' (also *o doime* 'half', as a technical term).

13.8.2.4. Sardinian expresses fractions analytically, e.g. *dessu tres unu* (literally 'of the three, one') 'third' (Pittau 1972: § 132).

13.9. Latinisms

The extensive use of Latin elements in the formation of learned terms, not only in the Romance languages, will not be discussed in detail here. It will suffice to mention that the most frequently occurring Latin prefixes are (in their French forms) *uni-* (e.g. *unicellulaire*), *bi-* (e.g. *biréacteur*), *tri-* (e.g. *trilingue*), *quadr(i)-* (e.g. *quadrimoteur*). Some of these Latin prefixes are occasionally combined with a non-Latin second element, e.g. *unijambiste, bicéphale, centibar, millimicron.*

13.10 Greek elements

The widespread use of Greek elements in the formation of technical terms is not limited to the Romance languages and will not be discussed at any length here. The most productive Greek prefixes are (in the forms in which they are used in French) *mono-, di-, tri-, déca-, kilo-*, though *tetra-, penta-, hexa-, hepta-, octa-, ennéa-, hendéca-, dodéca-* also occur. It is worthy of note that the Greek prefix *mono-* is nowadays frequently combined with a non-Greek second element in hybrids such as Fr. *monolingue, mononucléaire, monoplace, monorail*; Ital. *monodattilo*, Rum. *monobrăzdar* 'having a single plough-share (*brăzdar*)', etc.; *kilo-* is also so used, but only in such highly technical terms as Fr. *kilocalorie, kilotonne, kilovolt, kilowatt.*

13.11. Slavonic elements

The use in Rumanian of *un sfert* 'quarter' and *o sută* 'hundred' have already been noted (13.8.2.3., 13.2.11.1.), as also the (not universally accepted) view that the formation of the teens, *unsprezece* 'eleven' etc. and tens, *douăzeci* 'twenty', etc. may have been influenced by Slavonic patterns.

The numerical system of Istro-Rumanian, which survives in two small areas in north-west Yugoslavia, has been extensively contaminated by the Slavonic (more specifically, Croatian) speech of the surrounding areas. This topic has been most recently studied by H. A. Hurren in his unpublished D. Phil. thesis, *A linguistic description of Istro-Rumanian* (Oxford 1972), from which the following information is taken. The numerals 'one' to 'four' are virtually identical with those of Daco-Rumanian, viz. *un, doi, trei, patru.* For 'five', 'six' and 'seven' (also 'twenty-five' to 'twenty-seven', 'thirty-five' to 'thirty-seven', etc.), both Rumanian forms, *cinci, şase, şapte*, and forms derived from Croatian, [pet], [ʃest], [sédəm], are in use. For 'eight' the northern area uses both Rum. *opt* and Croatian [ósəm], and the southern area this latter form only; for 'nine' both use Croatian [dévet]; for 'ten', the north uses Croatian [déset] and the south Rum. *zece.* The teens, decads and hundreds are uniformly of Croatian origin, e. g. [jedənájst] 'eleven', [tʃetərnájst] 'fourteen', [dvájset] 'twenty', [pedesét] 'fifty', [sto] 'hundred', [dvisto] 'two hundred', etc.[56]

The ordinals up to 'tenth' are formed from the cardinal with the addition of *-ile* masc. and *-a* fem., regardless of whether the cardinal is of Rumanian or Slavonic origin; the only major exception – there are some other minor differences between cardinal and ordinal – is 'first' which, in contrast to the cardinal, has a stem of Slavonic origin; the following forms are those of the northern dialect: [pərvile], [pərva] 'first'; *dovile, doua* 'second'; *treile, treia* 'third'; [osmile], *opta*/[osma] 'eighth'; *devetile, deveta* 'ninth'; *desetile, deseta* 'tenth'. Also *patrile* 'fourth', *cincile* 'fifth', *şasile* 'sixth', *şaptile* 'seventh' and corresponding feminine forms.

Abbreviations

Alban.	Albanian	O	Old
Cat.	Catalan	Oc.	Occitan
Daco-Rum.	Daco-Rumanian	OCS	Old Church Slavonic
Dalm.	Dalmatian	Port.	Portuguese
Engad.	Engadinish	Rum.	Rumanian
Fr.	French	Sard.	Sardinian
Istro-Rum.	Istro-Rumanian	Span.	Spanish
Ital.	Italian	Surs.	Surselvan
Megleno-Rum.	Megleno-Rumanian		

Notes

1. The author is grateful to the late Professor R. C. Johnston and to Professor P. T. Ricketts for reading through a draft of this chapter and for their helpful comments. Lack of space has meant that not all their suggestions have been followed, and they are in no way responsible for any errors or omissions that remain.
2. *uno* is used before *z* ([dz] or [ts]) and before "impure *s*" i. e. *s* + consonant : *uno zio* 'an uncle', *uno specchio* 'a mirror'.
3. For typographical reasons, Dalmatian non-syllabic *i* is rendered *j* in the present chapter.
4. *o* – which can now be stressed – seems to derive from unstressed *una* perhaps via a form **uă* with unexplained loss of *-n-*; Arumanian has the one form *ună* corresponding to Daco-Rum. *o* and *una*. Rumanian also has the genitive-dative case *unui* (masc.), *unei* (fem.) or, as substantives, *unuia, uneia*.
5. Désormaux. The method of transcription used is that adopted by A. Constantin – J. Désormaux, *Dictionnaire savoyard* (*Études philologiques savoisiennes* I 1902), see especially Chapter 2, 'Système graphique'; the exposition given therein is far from clear but the pronunciations represented by the forms quoted above would seem to be something like *ĭon* [jɔ̃], *ĭënă* [jëna], *on* [ɔ̃], *onnă* [ɔ̃na] ([ë] represents a sound "intermédiaire entre l'*e* muet et l'*è* ouvert"). For a wide range of Gallo-Romance forms see von Wartburg (1922–, 14: 54).
6. Later Old French also had an alternative form *doi*, which Pope (1952: § 822) regards as being modelled on the oblique case *dous* (> *deux*), not as a reflex of Latin *dui*.
7. On the alternation between *ou* and *oi* in Portuguese generally, Williams (1962: § 92.7c) comments as follows:

   The development of *-oct-* in some regions to *-oit-* and in others to *-out-*, followed by interdialectal influence, may have been the origin of the confusion of *ou* and *oi* ... As a consequence of this early confusion, the use of *oi* spread in the sixteenth century to words which originally had *ou*, e. g. *coisa* (for *cousa* < *causam*).

He notes however that the change *ou* > *oi* has also been explained as due to dissimilation of the two elements of *ou*.

8. *două* < *doauă* (attested in the sixteenth century and still occurring in dialects – Rosetti 1968: 144): these forms may reflect a Latin **doae* (*Istoria limbii române* 1969: 237), though the possible influence of *nouă* < *nouem* 'nine' cannot be excluded.
9. Désormaux. For other Gallo-Romance forms see von Wartburg (1922–, 3: 181).
10. This suggestion is put forward (Meyer-Lübke 1927: 168) alongside an alternative view that the reason may be that "*due* era la forma più indifferente rispetto al genere e al numero", insofar as the ending *-e* may be masculine singular (as in *piede*), feminine singular (as in *voce*) or feminine plural (as in *rose*), whereas the endings *-o, -i* and *-a* of *duo, dui, dua* are associated specifically with masculine singular, masculine plural and feminine singular respectively.
11. For Sard. *dua* see 13.1.13. Reflexes of *ambō* 'both' are discussed in 13.3.1.
12. The origin of *trele* is uncertain. It has been variously suggested that it is formed on the analogy of the plural possessive adjectives masc. *mei*, fem. *mele*, or of such nouns as *stea* 'star', pl. *stele*, or that it incorporates the feminine plural postposed article *-le*.
13. *trei* is defined by Lausberg (1962: § 765) as a "satzphonetische Variante" of *treis* acting as a suppletive form for vanished *treia*.
14. I heard a guide at the château de Vaux-le-Vicomte, when describing a ceiling depicting the Muses, refer to Clio and *les huits-z-autres sœurs* [le ɥi z otrə sœ:r].
15. Nyrop (1960: § 481.5) quotes the following view expressed by Remy de Gourmont in his *Esthétique de la langue française* (1899): "On entend à Paris des gens ornés de gants et peut-être de rubans violets dire: *sette sous, cinque francs*: le malheureux sait l'orthographe, hélas! et il le prouve".
16. For fuller discussion see Schmid (1964: 216–228). For Gallo-Romance forms see von Wartburg (1922–): *undecim* (14: 34–35); *duodecim* (3: 182–183); *tredecim* (13.2: 234–236); *quattuordecim* (2: 1441); *quindecim* (2: 1478–1479); *sedecim* (11: 391–392).
17. Badia Margarit (1951: 261) explains that the [i] of the first syllable of these forms arises from dissimilation in **desset* > *disset*, and then spreads by analogy to the other two forms. It is also noted that in Valencian, where in 'seventeen' and 'nineteen' the stress is on the first syllable, the vowel [ɛ] is retained; [dɛ́sət], [dɛ́nɑw] but [diwít].
18. The [z] of [diznœf] may reflect the liaison that occurred in *dis e nuef* or alternatively it may have come about by analogy with *dix-huit* [disɥit].

19. Iordan – Manoliu (1965: 155) – a footnote refers also to Iordan's view (expressed in a lithographed work of 1957) that, as far as Rumanian is concerned, the construction could be of Thracian origin but reinforced later by Slavonic influence.
20. Désormaux (1904: 111) quotes a form *trê dié* (= 'trois dix') 'thirty' at Manigod; other Savoyard patois have derivatives of *trīgintā*, e. g. *trênta*. For other Gallo-Romance forms see von Wartburg (1922–): *viginti* (14: 442–446) and *triginta* (13.2: 270–272).
21. The problem has been discussed at length by the following: d'Ovidio 1884; "I reflessi romanzi di *vīgĭntī, trīgĭntā* ...", *ZfrPh* viii (1884: 82–105); Rydberg 1896 "*Víginti, tríginta*, ou *vigínti, trigínta*", *Mélanges de philologie romane dédiés à C. Wahlund à l'occasion du cinquantième anniversaire de sa naissance*, (1896: 337–351) (reviewed by Gaston Paris 1897) *Romania* xxvi (1897: 107–108); J. Jud 1905 "Die Zehnerzahlen in den romanischen Sprachen", *Aus romanischen Sprachen und Literaturen: Festschrift Heinrich Morf zur Feier seiner fünfundzwanzigjährigen Lehrtätigkeit von seinen Schülern dargebracht*, (1905: 233–270); largely devoted to *viginti* and *triginta*. Among more recent assessments, different conclusions are reached, for example, Elcock (1960: 73–74) and Lausberg (1962: § 773).
22. This is the form in which the word is quoted in *Istoria limbii române* (1969: 325); *g'* represents a voiced, palatal stop.
23. R. Posner, *Consonantal dissimilation in the Romance languages* (*PPS* XIX) (1961: 154) quotes *nonanta-* > *nor-* as an example of the dissimilation of the second of three nasal consonants. Wagner (1957–1964, 2: 171) suggests that Sard. *noranta* is due either to dissimilation or to the influence of forms for 'forty', but that in Campidanese at least it is probably a catalanism.
24. See Remacle (1952, 1: 273–274). Professor Léon Warnant (Liège) informs me that in the Liège dialect of Walloon the form for 'eighty' is [katrəvɛ̃].
25. After this chapter had been completed, I came across a further example in Penny (1969), a study of the present-day speech of the Valle del Pas. The expression quoted (p. 102, using the *Revista de filología española*'s system of phonetic transcription) is *cuando tengas cuatro veintes* 'when you are eighty [years old]'. In answer to a query, Dr. Penny reports that the phrase is used "in familiar-jocular" tone and adds: "although I recorded the phrase only in the second person singular, and in the future tense, I have no reason to believe it is restricted to that person and tense".
26. See, for instance, Ewert (1943: § 220); Bourciez (1967: § 220); Dauzat (1950: 220); Elcock (1960: 74); also J. Vendryes, *Revue de linguistique romane* (1925: 274).
27. The Norse word *skor* 'twenty' was all the more easily adopted into English in that the cognate form *scoru* in the earlier sense of 'notch on a tally-stick' already existed in the language.
28. She also wonders whether the vigesimal system of the Modern Celtic languages may not derive from Norse, but leaves it to the Celticists to decide.

29. Alessio (1955: 68), while stating the Norman hypothesis, adds the comment that the possibility of a Liguro-Sicanian origin cannot be excluded, but adduces no evidence to support this suggestion.
30. e. g. *ogei* 'twenty', *ogeitamarr* 'thirty' ('twenty plus ten'), *berrogei* 'forty' ('two times twenty'), *berrogeitamarr* 'fifty' ('two times twenty plus ten'), *irurogei* 'sixty' ('three times twenty'), etc. Entwistle (1936: 18) suggests that the Basque vigesimal system "may be of Celtic provenance", but there is no evidence to support this and, if Gaulish in fact had no vigesimal system and the vigesimal system of Welsh, Irish, etc., is a comparatively recent innovation, then of course Entwistle's suggestion lacks any foundation at all.
31. The Norman Kingdom of Sicily lasted from 1016 to 1198 and there is no evidence that, by that time, a vigesimal system prevailed in Norman French.
32. In his article entitled "Zum Zwanzigersystem der Zahlwörter" (1968), G. Colón expresses the view that Reichenkron's article marks an important step forward in the search for the origins of the vigesimal system. As a further argument against the Norman origin of the system in French, as advanced by Rösler and Rohlfs, Colón quotes the form *cen e quatre vint e vueit* 'one hundred and eighty-eight' in William of Poitou (1071–1127), and two other – later – Old Occitan examples, which seem enough to call in question this hypothesis. Otherwise, Colón's article contains little that is new.
33. The numerals from 'twenty-one' to 'twenty-nine' are now more commonly written *veintiuno, veintidós*, etc.
34. Note that the two forms that, according to the vigesimal system, involve the use of *onze* behave differently from one another: *soixante et onze* but *quatre-vingt-onze*. In Walloon, the asyndetic construction is used throughout, e. g. *vint-onk* 'twenty-one', *cinkante-onk* 'fifty-one' in Remacle's orthography (1952, 1: 273).
35. Rohlfs (1966–1969: § 974); Migliorini – Griffith (1966: 146, 184, 325, 360, 376).
36. Iordan – Manoliu (1965: 156) suggest that *sută* is of Slavonic or "rather" (*mai curînd*) of "native" (*autohtonă*) origin.
37. The convention in standard Modern French orthography is that *cent* varies for number only for round hundreds, e. g. *deux cents*, but: *deux cent trois; cent* is also always invariable as the equivalent of an ordinal, e. g. *la page deux cent*.
38. For 'one hundred and forty four' nouns derived from the Latin feminine adjective *grossa* 'thick, bulky' exist in the western Romance languages but not in Rumanian: Span. *gruesa*, Port. *grosa*, Cat. *grossa*, Fr. *grosse*, Ital. *grossa*.
39. See for example Bloch – von Wartburg (1968: s. v.) *mille*, and Corominas (1954: s. v.) *mil*.
40. In two notes in *Romania* 47 (1921: 388–389, 633), Antoine Thomas quotes three rare examples in Old French of *sisme, sipme, sime*.

41. Pope (1952: § 825) and Bourciez (1967: § 220) prefer to postulate etyma **octimum* and **novimum*, formed analogically on *septimum*. The *-s-* of *disme* is due to analogy with *dis*.
42. Port. *quaresma* is stated by Williams (1962: § 135.12A), on account of its phonology, to be an early borrowing from Spanish.
43. E. g. Nyrop (1960: § 493); Pope (1952: § 825); Bourciez (1967: § 304c); Lausberg (1962: § 785.4); Elcock (1960: 76). For a well-documented, if now rather outdated, discussion, see P. Marchot (1897), reviewed by G. Paris, *Romania* xxvi (1897: 326); Staaff (1898); Vising (1899, a rejection of Staaff's attempt to explain *-ième* as a phonetic development of *-ime*); Rydberg (1899–1901, reviewing the articles by Marchot and Staaff).
44. The regular reflex of *decimum* is *dime*; the *-s-* of *disme* is due to the analogy of *dis* (> *dix*).
45. The stem of these forms has been remodelled on the basis of the cardinals; the phonologically regular reflexes of *undecimum, duodecimum* would have been something like **ondime*, **douime*. Gilliéron (1921: 5) quotes (from information supplied to him by L. Clédat) a number of fourteenth-century Liégeois reflexes of **tredecima* denoting the Epiphany (i. e. the thirteenth day after Christmas) viz. *treme, treisme, treyme*.
46. There may or may not be any justification for the theory that, whether or not it originated in the south-west, the spread of *-iesme* was facilitated by the influence of learned *-esimum* (as in *uīcēsimum, trīcēsimum*, etc.) – see for example Bourciez (1967: § 304c), Elcock (1960: 76), Lausberg (1962: § 785.4). Gilliéron (1920: 102–119) suggested that *-i(s)me* < *di(s)me* became adopted as an ordinal suffix under the influence of learned *-isme* < *-issimum*, arguing that ordinals have a certain latent superlative value; there was also *-esme* < *-esimum* (*centēsimum*, etc.) and *-ie(s)me* resulted from a "compromise" between *-i(s)me* and *-e(s)me*.
47. Pittau (1972: § 131). *su* < *ipsum* functions both as the definite article, e. g. *su kane* = Ital. *il cane*, and as a determinative pronoun (cf. Span. *el*, etc.), e. g. *su ki ti naro* = Ital. *ciò che ti dico, sa 'e mama* = Ital. *quella di mamma*.
48. A relic of this is still found in *ambesas* [ɑ̃bza:s] '(a throw of a) double ace' (at backgammon).
49. Badia Margarit (1962: 261 n. 1) comments that Cat. *ambdós, -dues* are "reservados para la lengua literaria culta" and "no tienen existencia popular", whereas they did occur in popular usage in the medieval period. Old Occitan had a variety of forms in addition to those listed here, e. g. masc. obl. *amdos, abdos, ambedos*. In earlier periods Italian had a variety of forms including *ambodue ambidui amendue*. Note also OFr. *ambure* (< *amborum et*), OItal. *amburo*, etc., which, by contamination with *ambidue* etc., gave a variety of forms, e. g. Old Umbrian *ammendoro*, Old Neapolitan *ambendora* (Rohlfs 1966–1969: § 980).
50. The language has also retained the earlier construction without the article in *tous deux, tous trois, tous quatre* (but not with higher numerals), and then

only when there is no accompanying noun (e. g. *tous les trois enfants* not **tous trois enfants*).

51. With the lower numerals Rumanian also has forms based on *tus-* < *toţi*, viz. *tustrei* (fem. *tustrele*), *tuspatru, tuscinci, tusşase*, and an alternative series *cîteşi trei*, etc. (*cîte* = neuter plural of *cît* < *quantum* + *şi* 'and' < *sic*).
52. Remacle (1952: 281) points out that Walloon *-inne* [ẽ:n], which generally indicates approximation but sometimes has a more precise value (e. g. *fé one noûvinne* 'faire une neuvaine') is not only the basis of *dîhinne* 'dizaine', *dozinne* 'douzaine', *vintinne, cintinne*, etc., but can also be applied to certain numerals that do not take *-aine* in French, viz. *one treûzinne du saminnes* 'trois semaines environ', *cwètrinne* 'four', *dj'arè one cinkinne du cokès* 'j'aurai environ cinq poulets (dans une couvée)', *sîhinne* 'six', *sètinne* 'seven', *trazinne* 'thirteen'. Various Franco-Provençal forms are listed in Gauchat – Jeanjaquet – Tappolet (1924–, 4: 73) *cinquaine*.
53. A popular reflex of *milliarium* is found in Span. *mijero* 'mile'.
54. Tobler (1921) discusses the replacement of the Latin proportionals and numeral adverbs by analytical forms, in particular those involving *tanz* or *doubles* for the proportionals and those involving *voie* (> *fois*), *ore* (> *heure*), *tens, coup* and various other less common nouns for the adverbs. The discussion is taken further by Rickard (1961) in an article that deals mainly but not exclusively with the gradual replacement of *tanz* by *fois*.
55. Cioranescu (1958–1961: 456–457), however, rejects this view and suggests that *medietātem* may have been metathesised to **diemetātem*.
56. The south uses *patrusto* and similar forms with a Romance first element as alternatives to [tʃetírasto], etc. for 'four hundred' to 'seven hundred'.

References

Academia Republicii Socialiste România
1965–1969 *Istoria limbii române* 2 vols. (Bucharest: Editura Academiei).
Alcover, A. M.
1925–1926 "Lo sistema de contar per vints a Catalunya", *Bolletí del Diccionari de la llengua catalana* 14: 279–288.
Alessio, Giovanni
1951–1955 *Grammatica storica francese* 2 vols. (Bari: Leonardo da Vinci).
ALF = Gilliéron – Edmont 1902–1912.
Badia Margarit, Antonio M.
1951 *Gramática histórica catalana* (Barcelona: Noguer).
1962 *Gramática catalana* 2 vols. (Madrid: Gredos).
Bartoli, Matteo G.
1906 *Das Dalmatische* 2 vols. (Vienna: Hölder).

Bjerrome, Gunnar
1957 *Le patois de Bagnes (Valais)* (Stockholm: Almqvist & Wiksell).
Bloch, Oscar — W. von Wartburg
1968 *Dictionnaire étymologique de la langue française* (5th ed.) (Paris: P. U. F.).
Bourciez, Édouard
1967 *Éléments de linguistique romane* (5th ed.) (Paris: Klincksieck).
Cioranescu, Alejandro
1958—1961 *Diccionario etimológico rumano* (La Laguna: Universidad de La Laguna).
Colón, Germán
1968 "Zum Zwanzigersystem der Zahlwörter", *Verba et Vocabula: Ernst Gamillscheg zum 80. Geburtstag* (Munich: Fink), 127—133.
Corominas, Joan
1954 *Diccionario crítico etimólogico de la lengua castellana* 4 vols. (Bern: Francke).
Dauzat, Albert
1950 *Phonétique et grammaire historiques de la langue française* (Paris: Larousse).
Densuşianu, Ovid
1901 "*Primus* et **antaneus* en roumain", *Romania* 30: 113—115.
DES = Wagner 1957—1964.
Désormaux, J.
1904 "Contribution à la morphologie des parlers savoyards: les noms de nombres cardinaux", *Mélanges de philologie offerts à Ferdinand Brunot* (Paris: Société nouvelle), 103—114.
Devoto, Giacomo
1968 *Avviamento alla etimologia italiana* (2nd ed.) (Florence: Le Monnier).
d'Ovidio, Fr.
1884 "I reflessi romanzi di *vīgĭntī, trīgĭntā, quadrāgĭntā* [etc.]", *ZRPh* 8: 82—105.
Elcock, W. D.
1960 *The Romance Languages* (London: Faber) (2nd ed., revised by John N. Green, 1975).
Entwistle, William J.
1936 *The Spanish Language* (London: Faber).
Ewert, Alfred
1943 *The French Language* (2nd ed.) (London: Faber).
FEW = Wartburg 1922—
Fouché, Pierre
1942 "La terminaison ordinale, ancien français *-iesme*, fr. mod. *-ième*", *FM* 10: 11—19.
Gauchat, Louis — Jules Jeanjaquet — Ernst Tappolet
1924 *Glossaire des patois de la Suisse romande* (Neuchâtel: Attinger).

Gilliéron, Jules

1920 "Patologie et térapeutique verbales. La fonétique artificielle. II. Suffixe ordinal *-ième*", *Revue de philologie française et de littérature* 32: 102–119.

1921 [Appendix to Gilliéron, 1920], *Revue de philologie française et de littérature*, 33: 1–19.

Gilliéron, Jules – Edmond Edmont

1902–1912 *Atlas linguistique de la France* (Paris: Champion).

GPSR = Gauchat – Jeanjaquet – Tappolet 1924–

ILR = Academia Republicii Socialiste România 1965–1969.

Iordan, Iorgu – Maria Manoliu

1965 *Introducere în lingvistica romanică* (Bucharest: Editura Didactică şi Pedagogică). Spanish translation: *Manual de lingüística románica* (Madrid: Gredos, 1972). Italian translation: *Linguistica romanza* (Padua: Liviana, 1974).

Jud, Jakob

1905 "Die Zehnerzahlen in den romanischen Sprachen", *Aus romanischen Sprachen und Literaturen: Festschrift für Heinrich Morf* (Halle: Niemeyer), 233–270.

Lapesa, Rafael

1950 *Historia de la lengua española* (2nd ed.) (Madrid: Gredos) (8th ed., 1980).

Lausberg, Heinrich

1962 *Romanische Sprachwissenschaft* 3 vols. (Berlin: de Gruyter). Spanish translation: *Lingüística románica*, 2 vols. (Madrid: Gredos, 1964–1965). Italian translation: *Linguistica romanza* 2 vols. (Milan: Feltrinelli, 1971).

Marchot, Paul

1897 "La numération ordinale en ancien français", *ZRPh*, 21: 102–111.

Menéndez Pidal, Ramón

1962a *El dialecto leonés* (Oviedo: Instituto de estudios asturianos).

1962b *Manual de gramática histórica española* (11th ed.) (Madrid: Espasa-Calpe).

Meyer-Lübke, Wilhelm

1890–1906 *Grammaire des langues romanes* 4 vols. (Paris: Welter). Originally published as *Grammatik der romanischen Sprachen* (Leipzig: Fues, 1890–1902).

1908–1921 *Historische Grammatik der französischen Sprache* 2 vols. (Heidelberg: Winter).

1927 *Grammatica storica della lingua italiana e dei dialetti italiani* 3rd ed. by M. Bartoli and G. Braun (Turin: Loescher). Originally published as *Italienische Grammatik* (Leipzig: Reisland, 1890).

1966 *Historische Grammatik der französischen Sprache* II (2nd ed.), revised with a supplement by J. M. Piel (Heidelberg: Winter).

Migliorini, Bruno – T. Gwynfor Griffith
1966 *The Italian Language* (London: Faber).
Moll, Francisco de B.
1952 *Gramática histórica catalana* (Madrid: Gredos).
Nyrop, Kristoffer
1899–1930 *Grammaire historique de la langue française* 6 vols. (Copenhagen: Gyldendalske Boghandel).
1960 *Grammaire historique de la langue française* II (2nd ed.) (Copenhagen: Gyldendalske Boghandel).
Palay, Simon
1961 *Dictionnaire du béarnais et du gascon modernes* (2nd ed.) (Paris: CNRS).
Penny, Ralph J.
1969 *El habla pasiega* (London: Tamesis).
Pittau, Massimo
1972 *Grammatica del sardo-nuorese* (Bologna: Pàtron).
Pope, Mildred K.
1952 *From Latin to Modern French* (2nd ed.) (Manchester: Manchester University Press).
Posner, Rebecca
1962 *Consonantal Dissimilation in the Romance Languages* (Oxford: Philological Society).
Reichenkron, Günter
1952 "Einige grundsätzliche Bemerkungen zum Vigesimalsystem", *Festgabe Ernst Gamillscheg* (Tübingen: Niemeyer), 164–184.
Remacle, Louis
1952–1960 *Syntaxe du parler wallon de La Gleize* 3 vols. (Paris: Les Belles Lettres).
Rickard, Peter
1961 "*Tanz* and *fois* with cardinal numbers in Old and Middle French", *Studies in Medieval French presented to Alfred Ewert* (Oxford: Clarendon), 194–213.
Rohlfs, Gerhard
1952 "Die Zählung nach Zwanzigern im Romanischen", *An den Quellen der romanischen Sprachen* (Halle: Niemeyer), 238–244. Originally published in *ASNS* 183 (1943): 126–131.
1966–1969 *Grammatica storica della lingua italiana e dei suoi dialetti* 3 vols. (Turin).
1970 *La gascon* (2nd ed.) (Tübingen: Niemeyer).
Rosetti, Alexandru
1968 *Istoria limbii române* (Bucharest: Editura Academiei) (3rd ed. 1986).
Rösler, Margarete
1909 "Das Vigesimalsystem im Romanischen", *Prinzipienfragen der romanischen Sprachwissenschaft* (= *ZRPh*, Beiheft 26), 187–205.

1929 "Auf welchem Wege kam das Vigesimalsystem nach Frankreich?", *ZRPh* 49: 273–286.

Rydberg, Gustav
1897 "*Víginti, tríginta,* ou *vigínti, trigínta*?", *Mélanges de philologie romane dédiés à Carl Wahlund* (Macon: Protat), 337–351.

Salvioni, Carlo
1899 "Giunte italiane alla *Romanische Formenlehre* die W. Meyer-Luebke", *Studi di filologia romanza,* 7: 183–239.

Schmid, E.
1964 "Zur Entwicklungsgeschichte der romanischen Zahlwörter", *VR* 23: 186–238.

Spitzer, Leo
1925 "Urtümliches bei romanischen Zahlwörtern", *ZRPh* 45: 1–27.

Staaff, Erik
1898 "Le suffixe *-ime, -ième* en français", *SMSpr* 1: 101–132.

Ştefănescu-Drăgăneşti, Virgiliu – Martin Murrell
1970 *Romanian* (London: Teach Yourself Books).

Tekavčić, Pavao
1972 *Grammatica storica dell'italiano* (Bologna: il Mulino).

Tobler, Adolf
1921 "Ersatz für lateinische Proportionalia und Zahladverbia", *Vermischte Beiträge zur französischen Grammatik* 1st series (3rd ed.) (Leipzig: Hirzel), 181–195.

Vising, Johan
1899 'Le suffixe *-ime, -ième* en français', *Romania,* 28: 293–294.

Wagner, Max Leopold
1930 *Studien über den sardischen Wortschatz* (Geneva: Olschki).
1957–1964 *Dizionario etimologico sardo* 3 vols. (Heidelberg: Winter).

Wartburg, Walter von
1922–1929 *Französisches etymologisches Wörterbuch* (Bonn: Klopp, Basle: Helbing & Lichtenhahn, Basle: Zbinden).

Williams, Edwin B.
1938 *From Latin to Portuguese* (Philadelphia: University of Pennsylvania Press).

Zamora Vicente, Alonso
1966 *Dialectologia española* (2nd ed.) (Madrid: Gredos).

Chapter 14
Celtic

David Greene

14.0. Introduction

14.0.1. The Celtic languages fall into two geographical divisions, Continental and Insular. Continental Celtic ranges between Gaul and Galatia; outside Gaul and northern Italy, where short inscriptions are found, the evidence consists entirely of onomastic material and words recorded by ancient writers as Celtic. It may be taken that all forms of Continental Celtic were dead or moribund by the end of the third century A.D. Insular Celtic comprises the Celtic languages of the British Isles, of which Irish and Welsh are still spoken in areas which they have occupied for well over two thousand years, at the most conservative estimate. Scottish Gaelic, Manx and Breton are the results of colonisations which took place around the time of the break-up of the Roman power in Britain. Scottish Gaelic and Manx, which first emerge as written norms in the seventeenth century, are historically dialects of Irish, though their latest forms show sufficient divergence for them to be regarded as separate languages; Scottish Gaelic is still spoken, but Manx died out early in the twentieth century. Breton has diverged a good deal more from South-East British, which survived up to the eighteenth century as Cornish. Literary evidence for Irish begins in the sixth century A.D. and three centuries later for British, which by this time is differentiated into Breton, Cornish and Welsh. There is no possibility of establishing a Common Celtic numeral system, since only the merest fragments of evidence are available from Continental Celtic, mainly Gaulish; these are discussed in 14.1.1.14., 14.1.2.4., 14.5.1.2. – 14.5.2.5. Such archaic features of Insular Celtic as feminine forms of the numerals 'three' and 'four' (see 14.1.1.3.) or the completive use of the ordinal (14.1.2.0.) presumably existed in Continental Celtic also, but this cannot be proved.

14.0.2. The common features of the numeral systems of the Insular Celtic languages may either be inherited from Common Celtic, or innovations after separation. The numeral 'one' is originally marginal to the systems, since simply unity is indicated by the substantive, which can also be used pronominally (Old Irish *fer dinaib feraib* 'one of the men'); the developments of PIE **oinos* are, in the earliest documents, emphatic, with meanings such as 'single', 'same', 'self'. An inflected dual is preserved only in Irish, and even there dual forms are compulsorily preceded by proclitic forms of the numeral 'two'; on the other hand, the original function of the dual to indicate natural pairs is continued in British by the development of a special category of compounds, and in Irish by the use of a word meaning 'side' to indicate one member of a natural pair, and the generalization of this word in the meaning 'half'. The division of the numerals into adjectives and substantives is carried out to the fullest extent in Irish, but syntactic traces of such a division exist in all the Insular languages. An important development of this division is that numerals treated as substantives may qualify not only nouns in the genitive plural, which is the older construction, but also indefinite nouns preceded by a partitive preposition (Mid. Welsh *mil o wyr* 'a thousand men'). When numerals are combined (14.0.3.) the digit comes first and is followed by the decads and hundreds. Although the place of the qualifying adjective is normally after the noun in all the Insular languages, all the cardinal numerals and all the ordinals (except, in a few cases, those derived from 'one' and 'two') precede the noun they qualify.

14.0.3. Above 'ten', Insular Celtic continues a number of inherited formations such as Old Irish *trícho* 'thirty', Welsh *cant* 'hundred', etc. Apart from these, the types mentioned in 14.0.3.1. – 14.0.3.4. exist.

14.0.3.1. *Compound* numerals based on addition, contain two numeral elements stressed as a single word. These were restricted to compounds of 'one' to 'nine' with 'ten': Welsh *deuddeg*, cf. Latin *duodecim*.

14.0.3.2. *Combinatory* numerals consist of an adjectival numeral qualifying a substantival, or substantivized, numeral. The former case is familiar from many languages, e. g. Old Irish *trí chét* 'three hundred' is similar in formation to English *three hundred'*. In Old Irish, however, we also find *trí chóic* 'fifteen', where *cóic* is an adjectival numeral substantivized by being qualified by neut. *trí L.*[1] In Irish, combinatory numerals where the second element was not a substantive have always been marginal to the numeral system. In British, however, *dou nau* 'eighteen' and *pem nau* 'forty-five' are attested from Old British and we seem to be justified in assuming that a combinatory system made some penetration into Insular Celtic at a distant date. Combinatory numerals may become either secondary or composite numerals.

14.0.3.3. *Secondary compounds* are the result of treating combinatory numerals as single words: Old Irish *da ḟichet* 'two twenties' = 'forty' > Mod. Irish *daichead* 'forty'. The latter is the only example quotable from Irish but the procedure is very common in the British languages, cf. Modern Breton *triwec'h* 'eighteen'. It may be old there; the most likely explanation of the anlaut of Old Welsh *unceint* is that it is an abstraction from *douceint* 'forty', which would be a secondary compound derived from the combinatory numeral *dou *uiceint*.

14.0.3.4. *Composite numerals* consist of adjectival numerals from the series 'one' to 'nine' plus a substantival numeral either in the genitive case or preceded by a preposition or conjunction; the substantival numeral is normally 'ten' or a multiple of 'ten', but later Welsh also uses 'fifteen'. The use of the genitive is found only in Irish, e. g. Old Irish *a ocht fichet* 'twenty-eight', were *fichet* is the genitive of *fiche* 'twenty'; such a formation is unknown in other Indo-European languages, but has a distant parallel in Finnish, where 'twenty-eight' is expressed by the numeral 'eight' plus the partitive of the ordinal 'three': *kahdeksan kolmatta* 'eight of (the) third (decad)'. The use of a preposition is found in all the Insular Celtic languages; thus Welsh has replaced the original compound 'thirteen' (cf. Breton *trizek*) with *tri ar ddeg*, where *ar L* is a preposition to which the meaning 'on' may be assigned. Here there are Indo-European parallels, but no nearer than Balto-Slavic, cf. Old Church Slavonic *dŭva na desęte*, Latvian *divpadesmit* 'twelve'. When composite numerals qualify a noun they are discontinuous, the noun being placed immediately after the adjectival numeral: Old Irish *ocht mbaí fichet* 'twenty-eight cows', Welsh *tri gwr ar ddeg* 'thirteen men'.

14.0.4. Insular Celtic offers an exceptionally clear picture of the penetration of the vigesimal system into languages which had inherited a decimal system. Old Irish, which is usually the most archaic of these languages, has preserved the full decimal series, and combinatory equivalents are only just beginning to make their appearance. British, even in its earliest documents, has already a mixed system and the explanation of Old Welsh *uceint* 'twenty' offered above involves us in supposing that a combinatory numeral had displaced the inherited decad 'forty' at a very early period. Yet the decads 'thirty' and 'fifty' still exist in the early documents, and Breton has preserved 'thirty' to the present day, while modern Breton and Welsh both continue 'fifty' with the new formation meaning 'half-hundred', a formation found also in Modern Irish, which is otherwise entirely vigesimal. The rise of the vigesimal system has resulted in a proliferation of the composite numerals, e. g. for 'ninety-nine' Modern Irish has *naoi déag is ceithre fichid*, where *naoi déag* is a genitival composite numeral linked to the combinatory *ceithre fichid* 'four twenties' by the conjunction *is* 'and'. For the same numeral Modern Welsh has *pedwar ar bymtheg a phedwar ugain*, with the composite *pedwar ar bymtheg* 'four' on 'fifteen' linked to the combinatory *pedwar ugain* 'four twenties' by the conjunction *a S* 'and'.

14.0.5. All speakers of the surviving Celtic languages are more or less bilingual, the second language being English for speakers of Irish, Scottish Gaelic and Welsh, and French for speakers of Breton. Up to recent times, the medium of education has been the second language; this is still the case for Breton and, to a large extent, for Scottish Gaelic. It is well known that it is very difficult for an adult to change the linguistic code in which he was first taught to manipulate numbers. Since educationalists and language planners in Ireland and Wales had invariably learned arithmetic through the medium of English, divergencies between the English numeral system, on the one hand, and those of Irish and Welsh, on the other, were perceived as deficiencies in the latter; the English system was seen as a norm to which the systems of the others should be aligned. The ridiculous consequences of the application of this principle to Welsh have been described by Iorwerth Peate in his article "Bilingualism and the Welsh society" (Pilch – Thurow 1972: 143–149). A form such as *un deg tri* 'thirteen', now taught in the schools, violates several basic principles of the native Welsh system, in that the combinatory *un deg* 'ten' introduces *un* 'one' which is never used in combination with other numerals (cf. *cant* 'hundred'), that the digit is not in initial position, and that it is not linked to the decad by either preposition or conjunction (cf. *tri ar ddeg* 'thirteen' of literary and spoken Welsh). Similar attacks have been made on the numeral system of Modern Irish. The most explicit statement of motivation came from Peadar Ó Laoghaire, famous for his insistence on the authority of the spoken language, who, in a pamphlet entitled *Irish numerals and how to use them* (1922), said: "The method of counting with which I have been familiar, in spoken Irish, during my life, is not at all suitable for any lengthened arithmetical work". The revisions he proposed, while much less drastic than those of the current Welsh system, had the same aim in view: to provide a set of Irish calques for the English numerals. That the underlying assumption was that only the English system was suitable for computational purposes is clearly seen in his plea that the inherited forms should be preserved in all other domains; in other words, his own diglossia should be continued in another form. It does not appear necessary to describe here the official revisions of the Irish and Welsh numeral systems, since they are so clearly artificial. Breton and Scottish Gaelic are seldom used in arithmetical instruction; in conditions of increasing bilingualism, this has the result that their speakers tend to use the numeral systems acquired at school, those of French and English respectively, except for the lower numbers. The numeral systems described for the modern languages are, therefore, often those of the nineteenth century, when monoglots were still plentiful, rather than those of the present day.

14.1. Old Irish

14.1.0. Old Irish is copiously attested for a period of about three hundred years, 600–900 A.D.; no references will be given here for forms cited by Thurneysen (1946), or by the *Dictionary of the Irish language* (*DIL*) under numeral headwords.

14.1.1. Cardinals

14.1.1.0. General considerations

14.1.1.0.1. The cardinal numerals 'two' to 'ten' are essentially adjectival, 'two' to 'four' showing distinction of gender as well as of case. When they do not qualify a noun they are substantivized by one of the following procedures:

(i) By the prefixing of another cardinal of the same series: *trí chóic* 'three fives' = 'fifteen' where, as the lenition shows (14.1.13.1.), the second numeral is treated as a neuter plural; similarly, *da ndeich* 'two tens' = 'twenty' shows the nasalization appropriate to a neuter dual. These substantivized numerals are normally invariable, but they occasionally show the dative plural ending *-(a)ib*, as in *ar thríb deichib*, which occurs in verse as the equivalent of *ar thríchait* 'plus thirty'.

(ii) By the prefixing of the plural article, which is definite: *inna secht* 'the seven (specified things)'. The nominative plural masculine of the article, *ind L*, was already giving way to the feminine-neuter form *inna h-* in the Old Irish period, and the latter is regular before numerals followed by a masculine noun: *na trī recte* 'the three laws' (*Thesaurus* 1: 687.14). It is therefore not possible to say what gender is involved here; in the noteworthy case *inna dáu-sa* 'these two' (*Thesaurus* 1: 68.34), the two referred to are persons and the masculine is the expected gender.

(iii) In dates, by being qualified by a definite noun-phrase: *ó ocht calne apréile* 'from the eight day before the Kalends of April'.

(iv) By the prefixing of the particle *a*, which is indefinite (Irish has no indefinite article): *a ocht fichet* 'twenty-eight'. The deficiencies of the Old Irish orthographical system did not permit the indication of the mutations following this particle, which is normally *a h-* in later Irish, but C. H. Borgstrøm, *Scottish Gaelic Studies* v (1938: 35–44), has demonstrated that the original situation was *a L* before *ďau* 'two' and *a h-* before the rest of the set, 'three' to 'ten'. This is still the case in Scottish Gaelic and Manx, and is continued in Modern Irish in the phrase *nó dhó* 'or two', Old Irish, *no a dáu*. This suggests a demonstrative with vocalic auslaut in the dual and consonantal auslaut in the plural. Borgstrøm's identification of it with the **sen* which provides the nominative-accusative neuter singular of the article must, however, be rejected; the substantivizing particle is never definite, and it shows no trace of an *s*-anlaut in sandhi: *ina dáu* 'in two things', but *issa tech* 'into the house'.

14.1.1.0.2. The decads 'twenty' to 'ninety' inclusive, *cét* 'hundred' and *míle* 'thousand' are fully declined nouns and are never preceded by the substantivizing particle: *it a deich* 'they are ten', *is fiche* 'it is twenty' (*Thesaurus* 2: 15.43). The nouns they enumerate are in the genitive plural, as are those which are enumerated by the substantivized numerals described in 14.1.1.0.1. (i): *fiche blíadnae* 'twenty years', *trí chóic blíadnae* 'fifteen years'. Combinations such as *trí fichit* 'sixty', *trí coecait* 'one hundred and fifty' are common as stylistic variants, but the replacement of *sesco* 'sixty' by *trí fichit* as the normal form belongs to a later period of the language.

14.1.1.0.3. *oen* 'one' occupies an anomalous position. In Old Irish simple unity does not require the use of the numeral: *bó* 'a cow', 'one cow'; even in Modern Irish the usage is demonstrated by the fact that currency notes have *Punt* as the Irish equivalent of *One Pound*. Similarly, at no period of the languages can Irish *cét*, Welsh *cant*, Breton *cant* 'hundred' have the numeral 'one' prefixed to them when they are part of the numeral system. 'One' is not, therefore, a member of the adjectival set 'two' to 'ten' and its declined forms occur only substantivally: *cuid inna oíne ocus inna aile* 'part of the one (fem.) and of the other (fem.)'; *in oena focerddar* 'it is cast into units' (*Thesaurus* 2: 127.32). Substantival *oen* is not preceded by the substantivizing particle when followed by a partitive: *oen di archinnchib Assiae* 'one of the leaders of Asia'. It may be preceded by the neuter singular article, as in the example *a n-oen ar fichet it tri secht són* 'the twenty-one, they are three sevens' – see *Thesaurus* 1: 9.26, which is most instructive. The editors emend *ar fichet* to *ar fichit*, which is the appropriate form for a combinatory numeral the first element of which is not an adjectival numeral (14.1.1.0.6.): *oen ar fichit* 'twenty-one' is the counting form corresponding to *bó ar fichit* 'twenty-one'. But, since we know that *oen fichet* was possible in later Irish, as *oen* began to enter, partially at least, the class of the adjectival numerals, it may be that we have here a hesitation between the older and the later forms.

14.1.1.0.4. The remaining numerals between 'twenty' and 'hundred', are, apart from those where the digit is 'one', formed by joining one of the adjectival numerals 'two' to 'nine' with the appropriate decad in the genitive cases: *a ocht fichet* 'twenty-eight'; *ocht mbaí fichet* 'twenty-eight cows'. When the digit is 'one', the combinatory numeral is formed with *ar L*, as shown in the last paragraph.

14.1.1.0.5. Since *deich* 'ten' belongs to the adjectival set of numerals, it cannot be used as a substantive in the genitive singular; the numerals 'eleven' to 'nineteen' are formed by adding an element *deëc, deäc*, which is functionally equivalent to the genitive of the decads, insofar as it may be used only with the adjectival numerals, here, however, with the addition of *oen* 'one' in *oen deëc* 'eleven'. Synchronically, this usage can be explained by the fact that there is no corresponding dative to the genitive *deëc*, so that the construction with *ar L* was not available. It may be conjectured that the use of the genitive of the decads to form combinatory numerals is an innovation in Irish; the British languages originally used composition, which may well be reflected in Old Irish *coícthiges* 'fifteen days', cf. Welsh *pythef-nos* 'id.'. Such considerations are relevant to the discussion of the etymology of *deëc*, which has long been taken as a highly archaic formation from **dwei-penk^{w}-*, and they tend to reinforce the scepticism expressed by W. C. Cowgill (in Cardona *et al.* 1970: 145 n. 1) about this explanation. Cowgill's alternative solution, of **deankos* by metathesis from **dekanos* is, however, far from convincing.

14.1.1.0.6. In numerals above hundred, the appropriate form of *cét* 'hundred' is preceded by the preposition *ar L*, which in this construction takes the dative. This preposition is cognate with Skt. *pári*, Gk. *péri* and its commonest meaning in Old Irish is 'in front of'; for a full discussion see J. E. Caerwyn Williams, *Celtica* ii (1954: 305–324). In so far as it is possible to translate prepositions, those used in Balto-Slavic (14.0.3.4.) are roughly equivalent to 'upon', and this is the usual meaning of *war S*, which appears in Breton in the form *warn* before the decads; we even find the mixed form *dec super LXXX*, showing that *warn* was identified with Lat. *super*, with which it is cognate. The Old Irish cognate of *warn* and *super* is *for* 'on', which is not used in the numeral system of Old Irish; it does occur before numerals, however, in the meaning 'in excess of': *forsind ochtmugait bliadnae* 'in excess of the eighty years' (*Thesaurus* 1: 376.24). Irish, therefore, is unique in using a preposition meaning 'in front of' as part of the numeral system. Examples of its use with *cét* are: *fiche ar chét* 'one hundred and twenty' and *cóic míli ochtmugat ar chét* 'one hundred and eighty-five thousand', where the noun qualified (*míli* 'thousands') comes immediately after the adjectival numeral *cóic* 'five'. The same preposition with the dative singular of the noun qualified replaces the genitive in composite numerals which do not contain an adjectival numeral: *bó ar ḟichit* 'twenty-one', *diäs ar ḟichit* 'twenty-two people', where *diäs* is a numeral substantive (14.1.3.0.). A corollary is that, since *deëc* functions only as genitive, and *ar L* requires a following dative, the construction with the proposition does not occur in the range 'eleven' to 'nineteen'.

14.1.1.1. 'One'

The inflected forms of *oen, oín* 'one' show that, like Latin *unus*, it is in origin an adjective of the *o/ā*-declension; we can assume Proto-Celtic **oinos*, etc. It never occurs, however, as an independent adjective meaning 'one'; in the latter sense it forms a compound with the noun it qualifies: *fer oínṡétche dunar ructhae acht oentuistiu* 'a man of one wife to whom only one child has been born'. As this example suggests, the meaning is always emphatic; rather 'only one, single' than 'one', with further developments to 'same'. The derivative *oenán* appears once glossing *ullus*, no doubt because the latter word was taken to derive from *unulus*; elsewhere, however, *oenán* is used adverbially in the meanings 'alone' and 'in the same way', both of which can be accounted for by usages of the prefix *oen-*. It is marginal to the numeral system in Old Irish, but penetrates into it in Scottish Gaelic and Manx; the British counterpart *unan* is also marginal to the numeral system in Welsh, but an integral part in Breton and Cornish.

14.1.1.2. 'Two'

14.1.1.2.1. The stressed numeral *dóu, dáu* is indeclinable and must always be substantivized: *ina dáu* 'in two things'; the declined forms of 'two' are proclitic to the nouns they qualify. The proclisis of 'two' to the noun is qualifies clearly derives from the old category of the dual denoting natural pairs; in Breton the numeral 'two' forms a secondary compound with the noun in such cases, but not elsewhere: Vannetais *dehorn* 'pair of hands' but *deu zorn* 'two handles'. In the Breton dialect of Batz, now extinct, the development had reached a stage very similar to that of Old Irish; the numeral 'two' before nouns not denoting natural pairs was unstressed *do* (*do vrèr* 'two brothers'), while the stressed substantive was *déo* see E. J. M. Ernault, *Mémoires de la société d'histoire et d'archéologie de Bretagne* (1928: 7). While *dóu* is normally indeclinable in Old Irish, it is likely that the stressed genitive is preserved in the *de* which occurs in bound forms such as *cia de, ci pé de*, 'whichever of the two', *cechtar de* 'each of the two', *nechtar de* 'one of the two' and is formally identical with the conjugated preposition *de* 'of him, of it'. This is strongly suggested by such cases as *cia de do-gega* 'which of them I shall choose' (*Thesaurus* 1: 645.22), which glosses *coartor autem e duobus*, and *a dó ... ci pé de* 'two things ... whichever of the two' (*Apgitir Chrábaid* 72.3). It is likely that the original form was **dé*, which was then assimilated to the conjugated preposition; in later Old Irish it became unstressed, but some Middle Irish forms, as well as Manx *jeh* (14.2.1.2., 14.4.2.2.) show that this was not the invariable treatment. As well as this archaism, it should be noted that there are a few examples of new substantival forms such as fem. *a dí* (*Apgitir Chrábaid* 28), dat. *ónaib dib* 'from the two' (*Thesaurus* 1: 12.24); as will be shown below, these can be explained only as secondary developments.

14.1.1.2.2. The unstressed forms of the numeral 'two' are followed by the dual forms of the noun; the dual article, which is invariable, is *(s)in.*

Nominative-accusative masculine *da L*:
Stressed *dóu, dáu* is from PIE **dwōu*. The unstressed *da-* shows the same treatment as that of *-cuala* 'I heard' from **kuklowa, *kuklow*. It is possible that we have an analogical accusative in *im da ndil* 'about two dear ones' (*The Poems of Blathmac*, ed. J. Carney, line 1807), where the formation would be the same as that of the neuter.

Nominative-accusative feminine *di L*:
This does not match Welsh *dwy*, from Proto-Celtic **dē*, which suggests an original **-ei*, against **-oi* in Sanskrit *dve* and **-ai* in Latin *duae*; perhaps there was an assimilation to the form of the prefix **dwei-*. The unstressed forms of **dē* would be *de, di* cf. *ce, ci* 'though' from *cía* (Welsh

pwy). If we assume that **dē* was both feminine and neuter, there was a distribution of *di* to the feminine and *de*, later *da*, to the neuter. In fact, we have two archaic examples of fem. acc. *de: i nde rainn* 'into two portions', and *eter de notlaic* 'between two Christmases'.

Nominative-accusative neuter:
The nasalization is secondary, in accordance with the tendency in Old Irish to generalization of nasalization after the nominative-accusative neuter. We have the stressed form preserved in the bound phrase *i ndé* '(breaking) in two' and unstressed *de N* in *mo de n-ó* 'my two ears'.

Genitive *da L*:
The stressed form **dé* has been discussed above; perhaps **dwēyu*, cf. Old Church Slavonic *dŭvoju*.

Dative *deib N, dib N*:
The form *deib N* occurs in only one source, but would be consistent with **dwēbyen*, thus allowing us to postulate a vocalism **d(w)ē-* for all forms except the nominative-accusative masculine.

14.1.1.2.3. The only certain case of the compositional form **dwei-* is *díabol* 'double' from **dweiplos*, but this compound is inherited from Proto-Indo-European. This prefix has been lost in all branches of Insular Celtic; on the analogy of the secondary compounds indicating natural pairs, the British languages form compounds with the masculine or feminine form of the numeral, according to the gender of the substantive involved. Continental Celtic is no help here; *di-* in this meaning is rejected by J. Whatmough, *Grammar of the dialects of Ancient Gaul* (1970: 79, 82) and *vo-*, whether it means 'two' or not (see D. Ellis Evans, *Gaulish personal names*, Oxford: Oxford University Press [1967: 289 n. 12] and É. Benveniste, *Vocabulaire des institutions indo-européennes* [1969, 1: 111]) has no parallel in Insular Celtic. The normal Old Irish form is *de-*, in spite of Thurneysen's attempt (1946: 242) to distinguish between *dé-* 'two' and *de-* 'in two'; the same prefix occurs in *dethriub* '(the) Two Tribes' and *debide* 'cut in two'. Thurneysen's authority has tended to obscure the evidence; the headword *déthriub* is given in the *Dictionary of the Irish language* in spite of the fact that not one of the five examples from the Old Irish glosses shows a length-mark in the manuscript. Whatever the process may have been, there has clearly been a levelling of *de-* and *tre-*, the composition form of 'three', which is also unhistorical.

14.1.1.3. 'Three'

14.1.1.3.0. All the remaining cardinal numerals are fully stressed words. 'Three' and 'four' are fully declined; the feminine form, which must be related to those of Indo-Iranian, present some difficulty. The history of the discussion was summarised by W. C. Cowgill, *Language* 33 (1957: 341–345), who also offered a new solution based on the assumption that the cluster **-sr-* fell together with **-dr-* in Insular Celtic, and perhaps in Continental Celtic also. The following review takes into account the revision of Cowgill's solution by E. P. Hamp, *Ériu* xxiv (1973: 177–178).
14.1.1.3.1. The forms of 'three' are:

Nominative-accusative masculine *trí h-*:
From accusative **trins* see C. W. Watkins, *Ériu* xviii (1967: 97); the **tre h-*, from **treyes*, which Watkins gives there as the old nominative is not in fact attested.

Nominative feminine *teüir, téoir*:
The former is clearly from **tesores*, which would be a regular development from earlier **tisores*. In that case it is hardly likely that there was a competing form **tesres*, giving monosyllabic *téoir*; the latter is an early reduction of the disyllabic form, cf. Old Irish *soer* 'freeman' for archaic *soër*. Though the origin of the similar word *treöir, tréoir* 'guidance, direction' is not clear, it shows that the raising of *-e-* to *-i-* before *-o-* in hiatus is not a general rule.

Accusative feminine *téora h-*:
PIE **tisr̥ns* would regularly develop to **tesrās*, which, following Cowgill's theory, would give **téra h-* in archaic Old Irish. The diphthong would then be a penetration from the new nominative *téoir*.

Nominative-accusative neuter *tre L, trí L*:
tre L is the regular development of **triya*, but is found only in archaic sources. Otherwise *trí*, modelled on the masculine form, but keeping the mutation of *tre L*.

Genitive masculine-neuter *tre N, trī N*:
tre N represents original **triyon*; again there has been assimilation to *trí*, with preservation of the appropriate mutation.

Genitive feminine *téora N*:
An analogical formation, consisting of the feminine accusative form plus the appropriate mutation.

Dative masculine-neuter *tríb*:
Original **tribis* would have given **trib*; the long vowel has been introduced from *trí*.

Dative feminine *téoraib*:
Probably an analogical form.

As has already been seen, the normal composition form of 'three' is *tre-* even before palatalized consonants, where the variant *tri-* might be expected. The older form is preserved in a few compounds such as *trimse*, later *treimse*, 'period of three months', *trilis* 'plait of hair', *triphne* 'having three teats', etc.

14.1.1.4. 'Four'

14.1.1.4.1. The forms of 'four' are:

Nominative masculine *cethair*:
From *k^wetwōres*, cf. Gothic *fidwor*. The *-ō-, giving Celtic *-ā-, is assumed to account for *-ā-* rather than *-o-* in the second syllable, and thus diverges from the form assumed for British (14.5.1.3.).

Nominative feminine *cethoir, cethéoir*:
cethoir, found only in *Apgitir Chrábaid*, represents the immediate post-syncope [*k^weθ'or'*] from *k^wetesores*, while *cethéoir* shows the penetration of the diphthong of *téoir* into the second syllable.

Nominative-accusative neuter *cethair L*:
From *k^wetwōri*, cf. Sanskrit *catvā́ri*.

Accusative masculine *cethri h-*:
Probably from *k^wetworins*, remodelled on **trins*.

Accusative feminine *cethora h-, cethéora h-*:
The first form would represent *k^wetesorn̥s*, with penetration of the full grade into the accusative; it is found only in *Apgitir Chrábaid*. Otherwise *cethéora h-*, with the diphthong of *téoir*.

Genitive masculine neuter *cethre N*:
Probably from *k^wetwōriyon*, remodelled on **triyon*.

Genitive feminine *cethéora N*, dative masculine-neuter: *ceithrib* and dative feminine *cethéoraib* are all analogical.

The composition form of 'four' is *cethar-L* (*cethr-* before vowels); it has thus been assimilated to the usual composition pattern, as *k^wetwaro-*. It is to be identified with the *k^wetor-* attested in Gaulish *petor-ritum* 'four-wheeled vehicle'.

14.1.1.5. 'Five'

14.1.1.5.0. The remaining adjectival numerals are not normally inflected. However, all of them are capable of taking the dative plural ending when substantivized by the definite article: *isnaib sechtaib* 'in the seven things'. Similarly, when 'five' and 'six' qualify a noun in the genitive plural they substitute nasalization for their normal mutation: *inna sé mbó* 'of the six cows'.

14.1.1.5.1. It is customary to give the Old Irish forms of 'five' as *cóic L* (gen. *cóic N*, see above). This is not absolutely certain, for the length mark over *-oi-* in Old Irish orthography is not used consistently, and may indicate either a long vowel followed by a palatalized consonant or a diphthong followed by a consonant of unspecified colouring; it is now customary to indicate these two cases by *-ói-* and *-oí-* respectively. The distribution in the later language is that *-ói-* is found in the cardinal and in the ordinal and numeral substantive derivatives, while *-oí-* is found in the composition form of the cardinal as well as in *coíco* 'fifty'. According to the general view, PIE *k^wenk^{w}e* should have given *céic L* in Old Irish; the problem is well summarized by Thurneysen (1946: 246 f.), and no satisfactory solution has been advanced since then. Any explanation must also embrace the isolated pret. pass. 3 sg. *-goít* 'wounded, killed' from earlier *g^went*, cf. Welsh *gwant*; here again *gét* is expected, cf. Old Irish *cét*, Welsh *cant* 'hundred'. The element which these two forms have in common is an initial labio-velar; it may be speculated that the long vowel which arose from *-en-* and *-an-* before *-k* and *-t* in Proto-Irish (Thurneysen 1946: 126) had an allophone [oi] after labio-velar consonants, which fell together with the /oi/ inherited from Proto-Indo-European. Even such an assumption, however, fails to account for *cóic*; variants such as *fáilid, faílid* 'joyful' exist in Old Irish and the Scottish Gaelic *tòiseach*, beside Old Irish *toísech* 'chieftain', may well be old, but in no form of the language are the variants functionally distributed.

14.1.1.6. 'Six'

sé h- (gen. *sé N*) 'six' is the regular development from **sweks*. Its original composition form is found only in the numeral substantives *sess-er* 'six men' and *mórfess-er*; 'seven men' otherwise *sé L*, with the usual generalization of lenition after the first element of a compound.

14.1.1.7. 'Seven'

secht N 'seven' is the regular development of **sexten* from **septm̥*; the cluster *-xt-* resists palatalization. The old composition form *secht N* is found as well as the innovation *secht L*.

14.1.1.8. 'Eight'

ocht N 'eight' derives from a form with final nasal, on the pattern of 'seven', 'nine' and 'ten'; that this is an old development is shown by *ochtmogo* 'eighty'. The composition form *ocht L* is therefore more likely to be an innovation than an archaism.

14.1.1.9. 'Nine'

noí N 'nine' is a regular development from **nowen*; the composition form is *nói L*, except in the numeral substantive *nónbar* 'nine men'.

14.1.1.10. 'Ten'

Similarly, *deich N* is the reflex of earlier **deken*; the composition form is *deich L*, except in the numeral substantive *deichenbor* 'ten men'.

14.1.1.11. 'Eleven' to 'nineteen'

The formation of the numerals 'eleven' to 'nineteen' has already been discussed (14.1.1.0.4.). The only trace of a compound numeral of the British type is *coícthig-* in the word *coícthiges* 'fortnight'; the treatment of the second element is regular for Old Irish, except for the unvoicing to *-th-*, which may be due to the influence of *cóicthe* (or *coícthe*?) 'period of 5 days' (14.1.4.2.).

14.1.1.12. 'Twenty'

fiche 'twenty' is a masculine noun, declined for the most part like *carae* 'friend' from *karants. The starting point must have been the interpretation of *wikenti (Old Irish *fichit*), the regular reflex of PIE *wikm̥tī, as the dative of a *-nt*-stem noun; the aberrant dual *fichet*, however, suggests the treatment of *wikentī as the nominative plural of a masculine *-o*-stem, and a nominative *fichet* occurs sporadically in the later language. It seems likely that the transforming of the decads into fully declined nouns began with 'twenty', since the original ending *-konta of the others does not correspond to that of any case in the Proto-Irish *-nt*-stems.

14.1.1.13. 'Thirty' to 'ninety'

14.1.1.13.1. *trícho* 'thirty' is a masculine noun of the *nt*-declension, based on a Proto-Celtic *tríkonta. The evidence of Old Irish, together with that of Gaulish *trIcontis*, suggests strongly that the vowel of the first syllable was long; Breton *tregont* is secondary (14.5.1.8.). For the view that the vowel was long in Proto-Indo-European see Szemerényi (1960: 136). All the rest of the decads are declined like *trícho*.
14.1.1.13.2. *cethorcho* 'forty' is derived by Thurneysen (1946: 247) from *k^{w}etru-kont-; by Szemerényi (1960: 18) from *k^{w}etrākont from PIE *k^{w}etwr̥̄kont-. The former solution assumes that the composition form *k^{w}etru- had penetrated into the system of the cardinal numbers; Gaulish *petrudecametos* 'fourteenth' shows that this happened in the ordinal series. Either will account for the Old Irish form, which must have been *cethrcho in the immediate post-syncope stage, with the cluster later expanded to *cethorcho*.
14.1.1.13.3. It has already been suggested that *coíc-* is the Old Irish reflex of *k^{w}enk^{w}e. It is clear that, whatever the Proto-Indo-European form may have been, Proto-Celtic had a syncopated *k^{w}enk^{w}ont- for 'fifty', cf. French *cinquante* from *quinquaginta*; this will adequately account for *coíco*, as well as for the British form. On the other hand, *sesco* 'sixty' must derive from *sweksu-/sweksā-kont- rather than *wekskont-, which might be expected to give *secco, cf. *ecrae* 'enemy' from *eks-karants. A connecting vowel has also been lost in *sechtmogo* 'seventy' and *ochtmogo* 'eighty'; the voicing of the spirant between unstressed vowels is regular in Old Irish. But *nócho* 'ninety' has no trace of the nasal, and must derive from *nowu/nawa-kont-.

14.1.1.14. 'Hundred' to 'thousand'

14.1.1.14.1. *cét N* 'hundred' is a neuter *o*-stem, from **kṃtom* through **kenton*. Nouns of this declension have both the inherited nominative-accusative plural *cét L* and a secondary formation *céta h-*. Only the former is found in numerals: *trí chét* 'three hundred' beside *inna céta* 'the hundreds'. As the genitive plural is *cét N*, only the dative *cétaib* has an ending in the plural.
14.1.1.14.2. *míle* 'thousand', a feminine *-iā* stem, is the only loanword, being borrowed from the Latin pl. *milia*.

14.1.2. Ordinals

14.1.2.0. It has been shown by É. Benveniste, *Noms d'agent et noms d'action en indo-européen* (1948: 145–160), that the original function of the ordinal in Indo-European and other languages was *completive*; that is, that it marked the final member of a series. C. W. Watkins, *Lochlann* iii (1965: 287 ff.) has collected a number of examples from Insular Celtic, such as Old Irish, *ro bátar da apstal deac apud Dominum et hesom fessin in tres deac* 'the Lord had twelve apostles, and he himself the thirteenth'. A development of this function is the use of the ordinal as *selective*; that is, to indicate one member of a group of *x*, e. g. Old Irish *is sí sin in chóiced bruden ro boí i nÉrinn* 'that is the fifth palace which was in Ireland' = 'one of the five palaces'. It is hardly necessary to say that Old Irish also has the ordinal in *enumerative* function, as in modern European languages, e. g. *cétnae accuis* ... ... *accuis aile* ... ... *tris accuis* ... ... *in chethramad accuis* 'first cause ... ... second cause ... ... third cause ... ... the fourth cause' (*Thesaurus* 1: 402.19–22); the introduction of the definite article to mark completion of the series is noteworthy.
14.1.2.0.1. The normal place of the qualifying adjective in Insular Celtic is after the noun qualified, but the ordinals, together with a few other adjectival words, regularly precede the noun (the position of *aile* in the example above is exceptional and is discussed below). This class of adjectival words sometimes shows lack of inflection in Old Irish.

14.1.2.1. 'First'

Neither 'one' nor 'two' can produce completive derivatives; ordinals are formed from them only at the stage where the system becomes enumerative, and the forms always display anomalies. All the Celtic languages use an element which appears in Gaulish as *cintu-* to form an ordinal to 'one'; we have Gaulish *cintu*[ ], the suffix of which is uncertain, Old Welsh forms such as *cysefin*, which seems to derive from **kintsamos* (14.5.2.1.), Welsh *cintam*, Breton *cintam*, Cornish *cintam*, from **kintu-samos*, and Old Irish *cétnae*.[2] The latter form is derived by Thurneysen from **kentonyos*, with a suffix which obviously contains two elements, **-on-* and **-yo-*. The second of these is found elsewhere in the Celtic ordinal system, e. g. Old Irish *aile*, Welsh *eil*, cognate with Latin *alius*. The first is not, but it inevitably recalls the Hittite ordinal suffix *-anna-* reconstructed by C. W. Watkins as **eno-*, *International Journal of Slavic Linguistics and Poetics* iv (1961: 7–12). The word *cétnae* has already a double function in Old Irish: when it precedes its noun in the usual ordinal position it means 'first', but when it follows the noun it means 'same'. There can be no doubt that the function as ordinal is the older and that the extension of usage has arisen from the double function of *oen* 'one' as both 'one' and 'same'. In later Irish *cétnae* has only the latter meaning and ceases to be an ordinal; that it was moving in this direction during the Old Irish period is shown by its sporadic use in the meaning 'same' *before* the noun as early as the eighth century (*co cétnu chórus* 'with the same allowance' *Críth Gablach* 438), and by the fact that substantival *in cétnae* always means 'the same (person)', never 'the first (person)'. There are two other ordinal formations corresponding to 'one' in Old Irish, both of them innovations. Somewhat marginal is the adjectival formation *toísech* from *tuùs* 'leading, beginning', itself the verbal noun of *do-fed* 'leads'; this is the exact cognate of the Welsh noun *tywyssawg* 'leader, prince', and *toísech* when used as a noun has these meanings; one is reminded of the relation between English *first* and German *Fürst*. Thurneysen does not list *toísech* as an ordinal at all, and it is true that it most commonly contrasts with *dédenach* as 'first' and 'last', but cases such as *forsing í toísech* 'on the first (letter) *í*' (*Thesaurus* 2: 58.29) clearly establish its status. This example shows that it keeps its adjectival position after the noun even when used as an ordinal, and the same is true of its counterpart *tánaise* 'second', which Thurneysen accepts as an ordinal. Much commoner than *toísech* is the prefix *cét-*: in *cétṡíans* and *in cétnae síans* 'the first sense' are completely equivalent. This use of *cét-* is a specialization of the meaning of the prefix seen in Gaul. *Cintug-natos* 'first-born', rather than that of Old Irish *cétlongad* 'fasting', literally 'pre-eating'. It was, of course, favorized by the parallelism with the compounded form of the cardinal: *int oenḟer* 'the one man'; *in cétḟer* 'the first man'; it is the normal form of the ordinal in all the later stages of the language.

14.1.2.2. 'Second'

The distinction between 'second' and 'other (of two)' is not found in all languages: Old Norse *annarr* has both meanings. Celtic disposed of two related words, **allos* and **alyos*, to serve these functions, the distribution being different from one language to another. In Old Irish the form which belongs to the ordinal 'second' rather than to 'other' derives from **aliyos*, the regular Irish reflex of **alyos*, and is the unstressed indeclinable *ala*; this is the only unstressed ordinal in Old Irish, just as adjectival *da, di* 'two' is the only unstressed cardinal and it is reasonable to deduce that the detoning of the ordinal is taken over from the cardinal. However, indeclinable *ala*, with the article *indala*, is almost completely confined in Old Irish to the selective function, 'one of two': *indala fer* ... *alaile* 'the one man ... the other'; *indala n-aí* 'one of them' (with unexplained nasalization); *dondala lucht* ... ... *dond lucht ailiu* 'to the one group ... ... to the other group'; *li ala lecuinn Saul* 'by one of Saul's cheeks'. (The last example shows that *leth-* (14.1.5.1.) is not compulsory for denoting one member of a natural pair; cf., however, *do errisem dia lethlaim fuir ocus lorc isind laim aili* 'to rest one hand on it and (to have) a staff in the other hand', *Thesaurus* 1: 133.25.) The stressed *aile* almost always follows the noun and means 'other'; such cases as *aile máthir*, glossing *altera mater*, may be Latinisms, but *aile blaí* '(the) second immunity' (*Audacht Morainn* § 29) suggests that the usage can be native. Similarly, substantivized *aile* always means 'other', as in *inna oíne* ... *inna aile* (14.1.1.0.3.). In Old Irish, the normal enumerative ordinal corresponding to 'two' is *tánaise*, which is an adjective of the *yo*/*yā-* declension following its noun in the same way as *toísech* 'first', to which it is the complement. Both words derive from the Irish legal system, in which the king was *toísech* 'leader', cf. Latin *primus inter pares*, and the man who had already been elected to succeed him was the *tánaise* 'the expected one', the latter words being formally the verbal adjective of **do-ánat* 'expects'. To what extent this was a purely literary usage is hard to say; it is normal in the Old Irish material, but has left no trace in the later langage, where forms based on *indala* take over the enumerative ordinal function.

A quite marginal ordinal formation in Old Irish was the use of the prefix *aith-* 'again' with verbs and verbal nouns, so that *aithbéimm* meant not only 'striking again', but 'the second stroke'; it had little or no extension in the literary language, but is the source of Manx *yn nah* 'the second': *yn nah cheayrt* 'the second time', corresponding to Old Irish *in aith-chuaird*.

14.1.2.3. 'Third'

The ordinal 'third' is *triss, tress* which, like *toísech* and *tánaise*, comes from outside the numeral system proper; the two forms represent **tristis* and **tristos* and are cognate with Latin *testis* and Oscan *trstus*, meaning 'the third standing by'. No doubt it was originally an *o*-stem, as suggested by the dat. sg. *triuss*, which is the only old inflected form attested; the gen. sg. fem. *tresi* (*Thesaurus* 2: 311.29) is isolated. This form also points clearly to the substantival origin of the ordinal, for the construction *et héseom triuss* 'and he himself as the third' is never found with the other ordinals; it is entirely parallel with *at-recht Mongán mórfessiur* 'M. arose as one of seven men' (14.1.3.1.2.). Apart from this example, it is normally undeclined in Old Irish and in the later language.

14.1.2.4. 'Fourth' to 'tenth'

cethramad 'fourth' is an innovation, based on an ending *-*ametos* which is shared by the ordinals formed from 'seven', 'eight', 'nine', 'ten', all the decads and 'hundred'. The ending also appears in Gaulish and in British, and is clearly based on 'seven', 'nine' and 'ten'. Presumably the first stage was the formation of the ordinals **sextamos*, etc., cf. Latin *septimus*, and the next the adding of the element *-et-* abstracted from *k^w*enk*^{w}*etos* 'fifth', which is Proto-Celtic, cf. Gaulish *pinpetos*, Welsh *pymhed*, and Old Irish *cóiced*. The same ending has spread to 'sixth' in Insular Celtic: Old Irish *seissed*, Welsh *chweched*. For Old Irish, therefore, all the ordinals from 'fourth' onwards are formed with the ending *-*etos*; for all except 'fifth' and 'sixth' it has the extended form *-*ametos*. A. Meillet (*Bulletin de la Société de Linguistique de Paris* xxix, 1928: 34) has recognised the Gaulish ordinal *suexos* 'sixth' as an archaic survival of the procedure of thematicizing the ordinal, which is otherwise attested in Celtic only as an earlier stage of the formation in *-*ametos*. All these ordinals in *-ed* and *-(a)mad* are declined as *-o/ā* stems in Old Irish.

14.1.2.5. 'Other ordinals'

The ordinal 'eleventh' introduces the analogical formation *oenmad deäc*, and 'twelfth' has *ala* as its first element: *ala rann deäc* 'twelfth part', with a corresponding substantive *aile deäc* 'a twelfth'. In composite numerals only the series 'one' to 'nine' has the ordinal; the structure is otherwise that of the cardinal: *isin fichetmad blíadain ar chét* 'in the one hundred and twentieth year'. The isolated *in trisdécdi* 'of the thirteenth (psalm)', glossing *tertii decimi*, is calqued on the Latin; it is identical in structure with the technical term *noídécde* 'decennoval' – see 14.1.4.1.; *míle* 'thousand' does not form an ordinal at any period of the Irish language.

14.1.3. Numeral substantives

14.1.3.0. Corresponding to the adjectival numerals 'two' to 'ten' Old Irish has evolved numeral substantives, so that beside *a trí* 'three things', which is a neuter plural, we find also the singular nouns *tréide* 'three things' and *triar* 'three persons'. The first two of these formations appear to be semantically identical; thus, in the archaic text *Apgitir Chrábaid, a trí* occurs (68) in exactly the same context as *tréide* (137), and both are to be translated as 'three things'. This is in keeping with the neuter formation of the substantivized numerals (14.0.3.); although the same text provides us with the quite exceptional example of a substantivized feminine numeral (*a dí diib* ... *a dí aili* 'two of them ... two others'), it refers to the feminine abstract noun *ícc* 'salvation'. In the nature of things, neither of these formations can be used to enumerate a noun at any period of the language. When persons are referred to, the 'personal' series appears to be required (but see the possible exceptions mentioned in 14.0.3.), and, in later Irish, this series is used to enumerate nouns. This usage must have begun with cases such as *in triar maith* 'the good trio', where the adjective *maith* could also be understood as the genitive plural of the substantivized form; the only certain example from an Old Irish text is *cona thriur dedblén* 'with his three weaklings' (*Félire Oengusso Céli Dé*, Oct. 11), where there can be no doubt that *dedblén* is a noun formed from *dedbol* 'puny'. The personal numeral substantives are also the starting point for a development of considerable importance in the later language: the transformation of what was originally a partitive construction into an alternative plural formation. The normal partitive construction in Old Irish is with the preposition *di L*, as in *a dí ddib* 'two of them' above; this has superseded the construction with the genitive, cf. *for oín aí* 'on one of them' (*Zeitschrift für Celtische Philologie* xii, 1921: 364). In a case such as *fácab morfesser lais dia muintir* 'he left with him seven of his community' (*Thesaurus* 2: 241.17), the sense is clearly partitive. But when we come to a text in late Old Irish, we find the construction losing its partitive force: *íar n-órdned do deichinbair ar dib fichtib ar tríb cétaib do* [= *di*] *epscopaib* 'after he had ordained ten and two score and three hundred of bishops' (*Bethu Phátraic* 3103). The plural noun is here indefinite, and the construction is precisely the same as that of Medieval Welsh. In the latter, the construction is normal with *mil* 'thousand', and the text quoted above has also *téora míli do* [= *di*] *ṡacartaib* 'three thousand priests' (3105), which represents a shift from the older usage illustrated by *for dib milib ech* 'on two thousand horses' (*Thesaurus* 1: 121.36). The personal numeral substantives tend, therefore, to develop along the same lines as the older substantival numerals. As will be seen, however, the division into 'personal' and 'non-personal' is not entirely watertight at any period of the language, and there are remnants of a third series which has no such division. This contains the element *-ceng* in *decheng* 'two people' (see *Dictionary of the Irish language* s. v. *dechenc*) and *trecheng* 'three people or things, triad' (see *DIL* s. v. *trecheng*). The same element appears in Old Irish *coceng* (see *DIL* s. v.? *cocung*) which, following Cormac, I take to mean 'two animals leashed together', from **com* + *ceng*; it is continued in modern Scottish Gaelic *caigeann*, with precisely the same meaning. The etymology offered by Marstrander in *DIL* is impossible; the element *-ceng* is almost certainly identical with that found in Modern Welsh *rhaff deircainc* 'rope of three strands', but whether *cainc* here is identical with the common word meaning 'branch' must be left for further discussion.

14.1.3.1. The personal numeral substantives are, with the exception of *diäs* 'two persons', formed with a suffix which is synchronically *-er, -ar*. Thurneysen's view (1946: 243) that they are compounds of *fer* (**wiros*) 'man' is by no means generally accepted; Pedersen held that they were collectives formed with the suffix *-ero-* and that the association with *fer* was "volksetymologisch" (1913: 136). More recently, Szemerényi (1960: 98) has revived the theory that these substantives, like similar formations in Italic and Balto-Slavic, are based on a suffix abstracted from the substantivized **k^{w}eterom* 'foursome'; like Pedersen, he would ascribe the forms in *-bor* to popular etymology. In favour of Thurneysen's view, however, it must be said that, in Old Irish, the series refers overwhelmingly not only to persons but precisely to men; furthermore, that in Old Irish, as in other Indo-European languages, the formation of collectives from numeral + noun is a common procedure. Just as Latin has *biduum, trivium*, etc., so we can quote from Old Irish *dedartaid* 'pair of male calves', *dethriub* 'The Two Tribes', *cetharech*, 'four horses', *noínden* 'period of nine days', *deichthriub* 'The Ten Tribes'. The specifically Irish factors support the derivation from **wiros*, and it will be followed here.

14.1.3.1.1. Although Thurneysen begins the list of the personal numerals with *oenar* 'one man', this form is found only in the construction described in the next paragraph. Elsewhere we find the spelling *oenfer*; this is the normal way of expressing emphatic unity (*rethit huili et is oínfer gaibes búaid diib inna chomalnad* 'they all run and it is *one* man that gets victory from them in the end', *Thesaurus* 1: 565.26), and has nothing to do with the numeral substantves). For 'two', we have *diäs*, a feminine *ā*-stem with no generally accepted etymology. Brugmann in "Die distributiven und die kollektiven Numeralia der indogermanischen Sprachen" (*Sächsische Abhandlungen* xxv, 5, 1907: 66) rejected Stokes's old comparison with Latin *bēs* and very tentatively suggested **dweyo-st-*, parallel with *triss, tress*, but it is not clear why the collective **dweyo-* should appear here and nowhere else in the Celtic numeral system, or why the second element should be a feminine *ā*-stem. Perhaps Pedersen's suggestion (1913: 136) that we have here the same suffix as in *coícthiges* (14.1.1.11.), is correct; the fact that *diäs* has a derivative *deisse* (14.1.4.2.) meaning 'two days' may indicate that it did not originally belong to the category of personal numerals. For 'three' and 'four' *triar* and *cethrar* [3] are both regular compounds of the numerals with (presumably) **widron*; the neuter gender is certain only for the derivatives of 'nine' and 'ten'. *cóicer* 'five men' is also regular, except for the difficulty that *coíc-*, the usual composition form, would be expected (14.1.1.5.1.). *seisser* 'six men' is the expected form for an old compound, and it forms the basis for *mórfesser* 'seven men', literally 'big six'; such a formation is unparalleled in the Celtic languages, but Calvert Watkins informs me that Sanskrit *mahāpaṅkti-* 'big five' means 'seven verse line'. *ochtar* 'eight men' shows no trace of a nasal; in view of *ochtmogo* 'eighty' this is hardly likely to be an archaism. *nónbar* 'nine men' is not the regular development of **nowenwiron*, which might be expected to give **noínber*, cf. the undoubtedly old compound *noínden* 'nine days', Old Latin *noundinum*; it may perhaps have been influenced by the ordinal *nómad*. The non-palatal quality of *-nb-* in *deichenbor* 'ten men' is also hard to explain.

14.1.3.1. The dative singular of all the personal numerals can be used in apposition to a noun in the meaning 'as one of a number x': *at-recht Mongán mórfeissiur* 'M. arose as one of seven'. When preceded by the appropriate possessive particle these datives are equivalent to a numeral and pronoun in apposition: *táncammar ar triur* 'we three, three of us, came'; *táncatar a triur* 'they three, three of them, came'. The analogical *oenur* appears in the phrase *meisse m'oenur* 'I alone', and can be extended to the other persons and even to the plural: *fuirib for n-oenur* 'on you (pl.) alone'. These appositional datives can be used to denote things as well as persons; thus, referring to three Latin words, *biit a triur do anmaim* *ind éiuin* 'they are all three (used) for the name of the bird'. The dative plural of the personal numeral can be used without preposition in the meaning 'in groups of': *dessib ocus tririb* 'by twos and threes'.

14.1.3.2. The non-personal collective numerals formed from 'one' to 'ten' are the neuter forms of *yo/yā*-stem adjectives in *-de*, a highly productive suffix in Old Irish (Thurneysen 1946: 220 f.); from *deichde a buar* 'his cattle is tenfold' is derived *deichde* (noun) 'group of ten things'. Although the first member of the series *oendae* is not, of course, a collective, it has the expected meaning of 'single object'; cf. *oindae, bís a oinur* 'single, which is alone' (*Thesaurus* 1: 345.26), *inna oindai* 'sola' (*Thesaurus* 1: 410.28); as I have shown elsewhere (*Ériu* xxii, 1971: 178–180), Thurneysen is wrong in allotting the meaning of 'single object' to *úathad.* Forms such as *sechtae, noíde, deichde*, with no trace of the expected nasal, suggest that these adjectives, and the nouns derived from them, are comparatively late formations. The vocalism of *déde* 'group of two' and *tréde* 'group of three' is not easy to explain, since we have seen that **dé-* from PIE **dwei-* was hardly productive in Old Irish; there has clearly been mutual influence, just as in the composition forms *de-* and *tre-*. On the other hand, *cethardae* could be an old form and so could *cóicde*, apart from the usual problem of the vocalism.

14.1.4. Periods of time

14.1.4.1. Another highly productive suffix, *-ach*, is used with the decads 'twenty' to 'hundred' to form adjectives denoting periods of time, usually years: *cétach Abracham, noíchtech Sarra* 'Abraham (was) one hundred years old, Sarah ninety'. The form *noíchtech* is the only Old Irish example of the adjective formed from 'ninety' and it cannot be the regular formation from *nócho*. It must arise from the learned coining *noíchtech* 'having twenty-nine days', in which the composite numeral *noí fichet* 'twenty-nine' is treated as a compound with lenition of the second element and then has the adjectival ending attached. Another learned coinage is found in the phrase *in cicul noidécde* 'the decennoval cycle', where again a composite numeral is treated as a compound, this time having the *-de* suffix: from this the masculine noun *noídécde* 'period of nineteen years' is derived. The regular adjectives in *-ach* form feminine abstracts in *-(a)ige: fichtige* 'period of twenty years'. At *Críth Gablach* 67 we should probably read *co fichtig[i]* and delete the noun *fichtech* 'period of twenty years' from the *Vocabulary* (*Críth Gablach*, ed. Binchy, 1941).

14.1.4.2. In legal texts, periods of time are indicated by the feminine form of the cardinal *oen* and of the ordinals of other numerals; for a full discussion see Greene, *Ériu* xxii (1971: 176–178). In the latter contribution I noted three examples of *oena* or *oenu* to indicate a period of one day but could offer no explanation; it now seems to me that these may be late spellings of Old Irish *oendae* (14.1.3.2.). An objection is that none of the other non-personal numeral substantives in *-de* is used to indicate periods of time, but *oendae* differs from the rest of the series sufficiently to make the conjecture worth putting forward.

14.1.5. Fractions

14.1.5.1. As the collection of Old Irish forms in *Dictionary of the Irish language* (DIL), s. v. *leth*, shows, Thurneysen's distinction (1946: 250) between *leth o* neuter 'half' and *leth s* neuter 'side' cannot be maintained; the comparison with Latin *latus* suggests that the latter is the original declension and meaning. The word has extended its semantic field to 'one of a pair', 'half', in a way strikingly similar to the Finno-Ugric words of which Finnish *puoli* and Hungarian *fél* are representatives; see B. Collinder, *Finno-Ugric vocabulary* (Uppsala, 1955: 48). This extension is confined to Irish among the Celtic languages; while the Welsh prefix *lled-* can mean 'partly', 'somewhat', it cannot indicate the fraction (for which the word is *hanner*), still less 'one of a pair'. That this extension is of comparatively recent date in Irish may perhaps be indicated by the maintenance of the prefix *oen-* in the formula *for oenchois ocus for oenṡúil* 'one-legged and one-eyed', describing the stance of a satirist, which must be very old. But *for lethchois ocus for lethsúil* also occurs, and *lethlám* 'one hand', *lethchlúas* 'one ear', etc., are attested from the Old Irish period. So are further extensions, such as *lethchosmailius* 'one member of a comparison' (*Thesaurus* 1: 67.24) and *ledcholbe flatho* 'one of the two pillars of the kingdom' (*Thesaurus* 1: 649.22). In this meaning *leth-* is always a prefix, as it often is in the meaning 'half': *lethchosgarthai* 'semirutas' (*Thesaurus* 1: 437.24); *lethbairgen* 'half a loaf'. But the fraction 'half' can also be expressed as a noun followed by a genitive: *leth ind orpi-so* 'half of this heritage'. The phrase *co lleuth, co lleith* expresses the meaning 'and a half'.

14.1.5.2. *triän* 'a third' is a neuter *o*-stem; taken with Welsh *traean* it suggests an original **triyanon*, and some doubt must attach to the interpretation by R. Thurneysen (*Zeitschrift für Celtische Philologie* xv, 1925: 350–351), of Gaulish *tidres trianis* as 'three thirds'. It is tempting to compare *triän* with the Hittite ordinal *triyana-* 'third', but this derives from **triy-ono-* which would not account for the *-a-* of the Celtic forms; the formation remains isolated.

14.1.5.3. *cethramthu* 'quarter' is a feminine *n*-stem which superficially resembles the large class of verbal derivatives in *-tiu, -tu* (Thurneysen 1946: 451). Since, however, the *-t-* in these is part of the suffix, *cethramthu* would be difficult to explain as an old form, and it is more likely to be a late differentiation of the ordinal *cethramad*, earlier **cethramath*; the British group has the undifferentiated ordinal here. In Irish the neuter ordinal is used from 'five' onwards to denote the fractions: *sé sechtmad* 'six-sevenths'. Fractions can also be expressed with the ordinal and the feminine noun *rann* 'part'; it is no doubt for this reason that *aile deäc* 'twelfth', in the technical sense of 'judge's fee', is feminine.

14.1.6. Multiplicatives

It has already been noted that the adjectival numerals 'two' to 'ten' can be substantivized by having another numeral placed before them; they can also be placed before the comparative of adjectives: *secht trummu* 'seven times heavier'. Otherwise, multiplication is expressed by the particle *fo L* : *fo thrí* 'thrice'; *fo chóic sechtmogat* 'seventy-five times'. There is no example in Old Irish of this particle being used with *oen* 'one'; 'once' is expressed as *oenḟecht* (cf. Welsh *unwaith*), *oenúair*, etc., and *ind oíndid* 'semel' (*Thesaurus* 1: 60.35; 79.23). For 'twice' we have *fo dí*, where Thurneysen (1946: 250) would see the feminine; the formal correspondence of *dí* with Sanskrit *dvíḥ*, Latin *bis*, etc., together with the secondary nature of stressed *dí* (14.1.1.2.2.), make it more likely that we have here an inherited Proto-Indo-European form which has been assimilated to the rest of the series by the prefixing of the particle *fo L*. This particle is usually taken to be the preposition meaning 'under', cognate with Sanskrit *úpa*, etc., but, apart from semantic considerations, the fact that it can be preceded by the preposition *co h-* in such cases as *confitebimur du ebert cu fu dí* 'to say *c.* twice' makes this somewhat doubtful, for doubling of prepositions is foreign to Old Irish.

14.1.7. Distributives

cach 'each' is used before cardinals, *cach oen* 'every single one', *cach da dorus* 'every two entrances'; numeral substantives, *cach cóicer* 'every five men'; and ordinals, *cach ala blíadain* 'every second year', *cach nómad n-aidchi* 'every ninth night'.

14.2. Middle Irish

14.2.0. By the end of the ninth century A.D. the breakdown of the social structure of Ireland made the maintenance of the standardised Old Irish language impossible, and it was not until the end of the twelfth century that a new standard was evolved; for the intervening period, which we call that of Middle Irish, all texts show a mixture of archaizing and innovating forms.

14.2.1. Cardinals

14.2.1.0. General considerations

The basic system of the cardinals is not essentially changed from that of Old Irish. In verse dealing with history and chronology we find a proliferation of multiplicative numerals: *da n-ocht mbliadan* 'eighteen years' (*The Book of Leinster* [*LL*] 14958); *trí secht mbliadan* 'twenty-one years' (*LL* 14877). A new development is the placing of the preposition *ar L* before numerals preceded by the substantivizing particle: *blíadain ar a deich* 'eleven years', analogous to Old Irish *blíadain ar fichit* 'twenty-one years'. Sometimes the preposition *for* replaces *ar L* in composite numerals: *triar for tríchait* 'thirty-three men' (*Lebor na Huidre* [*LU*] 3789); since *for* and *ar L* fall together during the Middle Irish period this is of no special significance. It is likely that a construction such as *blíadain for a deich fa dó* 'twenty-one years' (*LL* 14833) was evolved solely for metrical purposes, and the same is probably true of *fiche acht sé bliadna* 'fourteen years', literally 'twenty save six years', for numerals formed by subtraction are rare in Irish (though see 14.4.1a.3.). None of these innovations continues in the later language. The introduction of the conjunction *ocus, is, 's* 'and' into composite numerals is, on the other hand, a penetration of the modern Western European system which is well established in Modern Irish. So is the use of *ar L* where Old Irish required the genitive of a decad: *da staid ar ḟichit* 'twenty-two stadia' for earlier *da stait ḟichet*. Composite numerals can, therefore, be made in three ways: with the genitive of the decad, with the preposition *ar L*, or with the conjunction *ocus*, and all three formations are found in the modern language; in the case of the numerals 'eleven' to 'nineteen', however, *ar L* and *ocus* occur only marginally in Middle Irish and the formation with *deäc* is the invariable rule in the later language.

14.2.1.1. 'One'

Independent *oen* 'one' is commonest when followed by a partitive construction; the use of the genitive plural is very rare, and we find *ó L* as well as *di L*: *cech oen uainn* 'each one of us'. It is in the Middle Irish period that the phrase *ar oen fri, mar oen fri* 'together with' first appears. The view that it derives from *imma roen fri*, containing *roen* 'path', by no means excludes the possibility that *ar oen* was an independent development, *co tísad ar oen fri Ultu* 'that he should come together with the Ulaid' (*LU* 5943). The composition form *oen-* continues to be used as in Old Irish; at least as early as the twelfth century the diphthong had been simplified to [e:], and spellings such as *énrand* 'one part' (*LL* 34899) appear, though only in the composition form.

14.2.1.2. 'Two'

The independent form of the cardinal 'two' now appears as *dó*, the reduction of the diphthong to a simple vowel being regular. The *de* which was interpreted as the genitive of the independent form in Old Irish (14.1.1.2.1.) occurs as a stressed word preceded by *indara* in a few examples: *masa dligthech indara de ocus indligthech a cheile* 'if one of the two be lawful and his fellow unlawful' (*The Ancient Laws of Ireland* 2: 342.17); for the continuation of this *de* in Manx see 14.4.2.2. The declension of the unstressed form used with nouns is gradually eliminated during the Middle Irish period, by the end of which the old masculine nominative-accusative form *dá L* has been generalized; as the spelling indicates, the vowel has been lengthened and the numeral was presumably stressed in the same way as the other adjectival numerals, though it is not reckoned as a stressed word for metrical purposes. The feminine *dá L* occurs sporadically, as does the neuter *dá N*, especially in such bound phrases as *dá cét* 'two hundred'. There are also occurrences of the dative *díb N*; a stage just after its elimination is reflected by *for da n-echaib díana* 'on two shift horses' (*LU* 6486), where the nasalization is carried over from the older *for dib n-echaib díana*. A difficulty is raised by the constant use of the plural article with the numeral, *na dá L* usually replacing the *in da L* of Old Irish for *an dá L* is regular in Classical Modern Irish and the modern spoken language (but see 14.4.1a.2.). The same is true of the compounds seen in *adam láim* 'my two hands', *bás mo dam ingen* 'the death of my two daughters', *adad láim* 'your (sg.) two hands', *adar n-ainm* 'our two names'; here, as O. Bergin, *Ériu* xi (1970:

146), showed the possessive particle follows *da*, and may precede it as well, and there is a parallel in *indana athair* 'the two fathers', where the old singular form of the article precedes *da* and the Middle Irish plural follows it. These constructions occur only in Middle Irish but they are closely connected with a usage which began in early Middle Irish and continued into the modern spoken language, whereby the appropriate mutations of the possessive particles are transferred from the following numeral to the noun, so that for Old Irish *a nda araid* 'their two charioteers' we find Middle Irish *a dá n-ara*, or even *a ndá n-ara* with double nasalization. Composition forms of 'two' are rare in Middle Irish but *de-choste* 'two-legged' is attested.

14.2.1.3. 'Three'

The numeral 'three' is also simplified during the Middle Irish period, the old masculine *trí h-* becoming the normal form in all cases, except for a small number of old neuters where *trí L* is retained, such as *trí chét* 'three hundred'. The feminine *teóra h-* occurs sporadically as an alternative form without distinction of gender: *teóra catha* 'three battles' (masculine) and *teóra anmi* 'three names' (masculine), as well as *teóra mná* 'three women'. The composition form *tre-* is still productive.

14.2.1.4. 'Four'

The available evidence would seem to show that the Old Irish masculine accusative *cethri h-* 'four' became generalized in the function of qualifying nouns, while the old masculine nominative *cethair, ceithir* survived only in substantivized position; the mutation, though not the form, of the old neuter survived in *cethri chét* 'four hundred'. Against this, however, is the fact that the Classical Modern language recognizes *caethair* as an adjectival form with certain restrictions, and that Scottish Gaelic has only *ceathair*, with lenition in *ceathair cheud* 'four hundred'. Since we know that the standard of Classical Modern Irish recognized a certain number of variants occurring only in Scottish Gaelic, we are entitled to assume that the Scottish Gaelic forms derive directly from the Old Irish nominative masculine and neuter and must have existed in the Middle Irish period. The feminine *cetheóra*, is used sporadically in Middle Irish in much the same way as *teóra*.

14.2.1.5.0. 'Five' to 'nineteen'

cóic 'five' has in the Middle Irish period an unambiguous alternative *cúic*, and it is likely that *cóic-*, *cúic-* were the composition forms also. The numerals from 'six' to 'ten' continue their Old Irish forms. The numerals 'eleven' to 'nineteen' continue to be formed on the Old Irish pattern, the element *deäc* being reduced to *déc* by a regular Middle Irish sound-change.

14.2.1.6. Other cardinals

fiche 'twenty' continues its Old Irish form and declension. During this period the vigesimal system begins to be normal, although all the decads up to and including 'ninety' are still attested. There are signs that the precision of the Old Irish system was breaking down. Thus we find *sechtmoga sé passe ar chét* 'one hundred and seventy-six paces', where Old Irish would demand *sé passe sechtmogat ar chét*, and *fiche ar chét míli caírech* 'one hundred and twenty thousand sheep' for earlier *fiche míle caírech ar chét*.

14.2.2. Ordinals

toísech is eliminated from its ordinal function early in this period, being replaced by *cét-; cétnae* seems to have survived a little longer in ordinal function, but was ultimately restricted to the meaning 'same', *tánaise* continues to be the normal ordinal 'second', *indala* usually meaning 'one (of two)'; an early example of the shift of the latter to the meaning 'second' is *isindara blíadain* 'in the second year' (*Saltair na Rann* 3437). The more usual meaning is illustrated by *in dara n-aí* 'one of them' (*Saltair na Rann* 19) and C. J. S. Marstrander (*Dictionary of the Irish language*, s. v. *darna*) is no doubt right in suggesting that the variant *indarna* for *indala* has incorporated the nasalization (perhaps through an intermediate form **indarna haí*?). This variant shows considerable extension in the modern dialects of Ireland and Scotland, but is very rare in texts of the Classical Modern period, where (*an*) *dara* is the rule. Late Middle Irish texts, in which the letter *h* is to be interpreted as [h] rather than a hiatus marker; regularly show *dara h-, darna h-*, and this is also the usage of the modern spoken language. Since *indala* caused the appropriate mutations for gender and case in Old Irish, and to some extent at least, in Middle Irish (cf. *dindara chur* 'for the second time', *The* *metrical Dindsenchas* 3: 4.33), the generalization of the nominative masculine form is an instance of the tendency towards the loss of declension of the ordinals of which there are many other examples: *co dorus in chúced nime* (*Lebor na Huidre* 2111, 'to the door of the fifth heaven'). It should be noted that the selective function of the ordinals is maintained: *Matha ... indara fer déc ro thog Ísu ... in cethramad fer ro scríb in soscela* '... one of the twelve men ... one of the four men ...' (*Lebor na Huidre* 2313).

14.2.3. Numeral substantives

The two series of numeral substantives continue in Middle Irish. The personal substantives now begin to function as simple numerals when followed by a noun in the the genitive plural, so that *días ḟer* may be used as an alternative to *da ḟer* 'two men', no doubt on the pattern of *fiche fer* 'twenty men'; in line with this we begin to find a plural verb in agreement with them. The non-personal numerals are still treated as singulars and do not take a genitive of this kind: *tréide gobann* means 'the three things pertaining to a smith', not 'three smiths'. The boundary between the two series is somewhat blurred. Thus, in the series of personal substantives, we find *días ḟidchrand* 'two wooden shafts', *ro tirchanait in tríar sin* 'those three things were prophesied', etc. Similarly, we have several examples of *déide* in the meaning 'two people', and of *tréide* denoting the Trinity. On the whole, the non-personal series is disappearing; we have no Middle Irish examples of *séde* or *noíde*, and *deichde* survives only with its original adjectival meaning of 'tenfold'.

14.2.4. Other forms

The terms relating to periods of time (14.1.3.1. – 2.) still occur in Middle Irish texts. Fractions are expressed as in Old Irish. Multiplication is expressed by *fo L* or *co fo L*; the *fo dí* of Old Irish is found, as well as the innovation *(co) fo dó*.

14.3. Classical Modern Irish

14.3.0. This term is used to describe the literary norm which came into use of the end of the twelfth century and remained essentially unchanged until the collapse of the native Irish social system in the seventeenth century. Not only do we possess a vast corpus of verse with rigid metrical patterns which make it easy to establish the precise structure of words, but also grammatical and metrical tracts which were composed in the fifteenth and sixteenth centuries for students whose vernaculars were by this time divergent from the literary norm. It should be noted that the orthographical system is also new; e. g. Old Irish *cét* and Classical *céad* represent exactly the same sound [kʽe:d]. The outstanding feature of the numeral system of this period is the development of the use of the singular form of nouns qualified a) by the adjectival numerals 'three' and 'four' and b) by the substantival numerals 'twenty', 'hundred' and 'thousand'.

14.3.0.1. The contrast between *trí chét* 'three hundred' and *céta* 'hundreds' in Old Irish (14.1.1.14.) is an early example of a general feature of the Insular Celtic languages: the restoring of the distinction between nominative singular and nominative plural where phonetic evolution might otherwise have blurred it, in the case of these neuter *o*-stems by adopting the nominative plural *-a* of the feminine *ā*-stems. The falling together of all short unaccented final vowels as [ə] in the Middle Irish period resulted in the almost complete loss of the declension of the *yo*- and *yā*-stems except for following mutations and the dative plural ending *-(a)ibh*; thus to *bile* 'tree' (nom. sg.) corresponded *bile L* (gen. and dat. sg., nom. pl.), *bile N* (acc. sg. and gen. pl.), *bilibh* (dat. pl.). While, as in Old Irish, the near identity of the forms *bile* 'tree' and *trí bile L* 'three trees' presented no difficulty, plurality being already marked, a nominative plural *bile L* 'trees' was otherwise unacceptable and, again, forms from another declension were incorporated, thus offering a choice between *bile* and *bileadha*, both of which could be used after numerals. (It may be remarked in passing that there are traces both in Middle Irish and in the modern spoken language of the alternative solution of using the distinctive dative plural form as nominative plural, but this does not concern us here.) The final elimination of the category of the neuter had taken place during the Middle Irish period and *céad* 'hundred' was now a masculine noun, but 'three hundred' was still *trí chéad*, with the original mutation appropriate to neuter *trí L*. This was the case for all dialects, as shown by Scottish Gaelic *trì cheud* and Manx *three cheead*; outside Ireland itself this break in the regular pattern did not bring about any significant analogical change and most nouns show new plural formations after numerals above 'two': Scottish Gaelic *trì bileachan*, Manx *three biliyn* 'three trees'. In Irish, however, *trí bile* assimilated itself to *trí chéad* and became *trí bhile*, while *trí bileadha* continued with the inherited lack of mutation; it is laid down as a rule in the grammatical tracts that, where a noun has a nominative plural identical in form with the nominative singular, it must have its initial consonant lenited after *trí*, while no lenition takes place when a distinctive plural is used. The rules relating to *ceithre, ceathra, ceithir, ceathair* 'four' are also historically determined: the former two derive from the old masculine accusative *cethri h-* and never lenite, while the latter two lenite plurals which are identical with their singular, as in *ceathair bhile* (cf. 15.2.1.4.). The process did not stop there: the rule was then extended to other nouns, regardless of their original declension, so that from *marg* 'mark (monetary unit)', nominative plural *marg*, can be derived either *trí mharg* or *trí mairg* – significantly enough, the tract adds that the latter is the correct form but that the former is justified by usage. Thus, for the first time in the history of the Irish language, a form which is inherently only a singular follows a numeral.

14.3.0.2. In the early language, the genitive plural was used after numerals which were either inherently substantive, or had been substantivized (14.1.1.0.1. – 2.) and this is still the rule in Classical Modern Irish. Even in Old Irish, the genitive plural of *o-, yo-, ā-* and *yā*-stems was, except for the following mutation, identical in form with the nominative singular and this pattern later spread to some other declensions as well. Once an undoubted singular could be used after a numeral, as in *trí mharg*, the interpretation of the noun in *céad fear* 'a hundred men' as a nominative singular rather than a genitive plural became a possibility. We find *fiche ban* (gen. pl.) 'a hundred women' given as the correct form in the grammatical tracts and *fiche bean* (nom. sg.) condemned as faulty. Since these tracts were normative, it is legitimate to assume that forms described as faulty were already in common use; the construction condemned here has become the rule in the modern spoken language. However, this must have been a more recent development than *trí mharg* which, although known to be unhistorical, was accepted as justified by usage; *fiche bean* was excluded, and no certain examples of this construction occur in Classical verse.

14.3.1. Cardinals

14.3.1.1. 'One'

Independent *aon* continues to exist. It is preceded by the substantivizing particle *a h-* in counting, and when used as the equivalent of an enumerative ordinal: *a haon díbh* 'number one of them' = 'the first of them'.

The particle is not used otherwise: *aon díbh* 'one of them', *aon na leabhar* 'one of the books', *aon acu* 'one of them'; the use of the conjugated preposition in the last example (never *ag* + noun) seems to derive from the use of *oc* in the meaning 'among'; see *Dictionary of the Irish language* O 85.25–33. Independent *aon* is always treated as a masculine noun, genitive singular *aoin*, regardless of the gender of the referent. *Gach aon* is the usual equivalent of 'everybody', cf. English *everyone*; it is gradually displacing *cách*, of which *gach* is historically the unstressed form. In a negative sentence *aon* usually means '(not) any': *ní mholaim d'aon* ... 'I do not advise anybody'; this is the beginning of the process whereby *aon* comes to mean simply 'any' in later Irish, and 'one' is expressed by the discontinuous morpheme *aon* ... *amháin* (14.4.1a.1.). The adjectival form is still a prefix: *aon-, éan-*.

14.3.1.2. 'Two'

From 'two' onwards the adjectival numerals when used independently require the substantivizing particle, which is now *a h-* in all cases except the bound phrase *nó a dhó* 'or two'; note the difference between *aon díbh* 'one of them' and *a dó dhíbh* 'two of them'. There is no longer any trace of the article used with these numerals, except in such derived meanings as *an dó* 'the deuce (at dice)', etc. The adjectival form has been generalized as *dá L*; there is no longer any feminine form, but a trace of the neuter remains in *dá dtrian* 'two thirds' and of the dative in *i ndíbh leithibh* 'in two halves'. No example is found of a composition form.

14.3.1.3. 'Three'

trí h- is the invariable form of 'three', with the exception of *trí L* before nouns which are singular in form, and *trí N* in the genitive. The old feminine form *teóra* has become a masculine numeral substantive, followed by the genitive plural: *an teóra crann* 'the three trees'; it seems likely that this was a purely literary usage. No composition form is found.

14.3.1.4. 'Four' to 'ten'

The treatment of the numeral 'four' has already been discussed (14.3.0.1.); a composition form *ceathar-* is well attested.

The rest of the adjectival numerals seem to preserve their old forms and syntax during the classical period; the composition forms *cóig-, seacht-, ocht-* and *eich-* are well attested.

14.3.1.5. 'Twenty' to 'ninety'

As has been noted above (14.2.1.6.), *fiche* 'twenty' plays an increasingly important part in the system. It retains its original declension, except that *fichit*, the old nominative plural, is specialized as a nominative-accusative plural after *trí h-* and the remaining adjectival numerals. Since *fiche* was masculine in Old Irish, and has remained so to the present day, it is puzzling to find *fiche fhear* prescribed by the tracts as the correct form, with *fiche fear* tolerated on grounds of current usage; since no examples of *fiche fhear* have been found in verse of the period, the rule may be artificial, and based on the undoubted shift of gender of *tríocha* 'thirty', *ceathracha* 'forty', *caoga* 'fifty' and *seasca* 'sixty', though lenition after these is seldom or never marked. The rest of the decads remain masculine, but become *seachtmhoghad, ochtmhoghad* and *nóchad*, with a new declension, genitive singular *seachtmoghaid*, etc.; it has been suggested that, in the spoken language, *seachtmhogha*, and *ochtmhogha* would have been easily confused with the ordinals *seachtmhadh* and *ochtmhadh* and that their old genitive singular was adopted to avoid confusion, while *nócha* followed the other two. All these shifts arise from a tension between the literary standard, which tried to preserve the decads, and the spoken language, which had undoubtedly gone over to the vigesimal system by this time; no modern Irish dialect has preserved any of the decads above 'twenty', nor is there any trace of them in Scottish Gaelic or Manx. For the artificial formation *dóchad* 'twenty', see B. Ó Cuív, *Éigse* xiii (1970: 10).

14.3.1.6. 'Hundred' to 'thousand'

céad 'hundred' and *míle* 'thousand' show no inflection when used as numerals; otherwise *céad* is a masculine noun with plural *céada* and *míle* feminine with plural *mílte*.

14.3.2. Ordinals

céad- 'first' is still a composition form. *dara h-* 'second' is invariable, as is *treas* 'third', and none of the rest of the ordinals is normally declined. All other ordinals are formed with the ending *-amhadh*.

14.3.3. Numeral substantives

The non-personal numeral substantives have largely disappeared. There is no example of *déidhe*, and *tréidhe*, which originally meant 'three things, triad', has become a *pluralis tantum* meaning 'characteristics', from the

Irish custom of grouping these in triads; on the other hand, a new substantive has been evolved from *teóra* (14.3.1.3.). *ceathardha* continues as an adjective in the phrase *an chruinne cheathardha* 'the world of four quarters', and occasionally as a numeral substantive: *ceathardha d'fhoir-ceadluibh* 'four teachings', but this is an isolated case. The personal numerals are, on the other hand, well preserved; beside *dias* 'two peoples' emerges a new personal numeral *beirt* in the same meaning, which seems to have had a semantic development similar to that of English *brace, couple*, though the process is not entirely clear; for a discussion see B. Ó Cuív, *Éigse* viii (1956: 101 ff.). When used without a qualifying genitive these 'personal' numerals can also apply to inanimate objects: *ina dtriúr* 'the three of them (gifts)' (*Aithdioghluim Dána* 37.11); *cóig tréidhe* ... ... *cóigear* 'five characteristics ... ... (the) five', (*Ériu* xvi, 1952: 135). When a genitive plural follows, however, these substantives are always personal: *beirt bhráithreach* 'two brothers', *triar mac* 'three sons', etc., though *dá bhráthair, trí meic*, etc., are commoner constructions.

14.3.4. Other forms

The numeral derivatives denoting periods of time have disappeared, except *caoicdhigheas* 'fortnight'. The system of fractions is as in the earlier language; *ceathramha* 'quarter' is still distinguished from the ordinal *ceathramhadh* 'fourth', and the fraction *deachmhadh* 'tenth, tithe' is declined as a feminine noun, while the ordinal *deachmhadh* is indeclinable. Multiplication is expressed by *fa L: fa thrí* 'three times', *fa chéad* 'a hundred times'.

14.4. Modern Irish and Scottish Gaelic

14.4.0. From the beginning of the seventeenth century, after the break-down of the classical norm, the dialects of Ireland, Man and Scotland begin to appear in writing. Manx was written in an orthography largely based on that of English, while Irish and Scottish Gaelic continued to use modifications of the classical orthography. The Manx linguistic community died out early in the twentieth century; the numeral system had been penetrated by that of English from the beginning of the written records, and Manx forms are cited in this study only for purposes of comparison. Although Irish and Scottish Gaelic must synchronically be regarded as distinct languages (14.0.1.), their numeral systems diverge mainly in the cardinals which, accordingly, are treated separately below.

14.4.1. Cardinals: Scottish

14.4.1.0. Scottish Gaelic has been more conservative than Irish in this area. The substantivizing particle retains the dual form *a L* and the plural *a h-* (14.1.1.0.1. [iv]), and is used in the same way as in the earlier language: *a dhà dhiùbh* 'two of them'. The adjectival numerals 'three' to 'ten' are not affected by the development described for Classical Irish in 14.3.0.1.; the only nouns which show singular forms after these numerals are the substantival numerals *fichead* 'twenty', *ceud* 'hundred', and *mìle* 'thousand', together with the enumerators *dusan* 'dozen', *duine* 'person', *latha* 'day' and *bliadhna* 'year'. A few nouns have two plural forms, one historically older and used only after adjectival numerals, the other an innovation and used in all other contexts, e. g. in Lewis Gaelic *bó* 'cow', *cóig ba* 'five cows', but *an crodh* 'the cows'. On the other hand, the substantival numerals are followed by the singular form of the noun rather than by the genitive plural, an innovation condemned by the Classical norm (14.3.0.2.): *fichead cù* 'twenty dogs'. In the composite numerals the conjunction *agus (is, 's)* 'and' does not precede indeclinable *fichead*; it can, however, follow it: *fichead cù is a trì* 'twenty-three dogs', beside the more usual *trì coin fhichead* or *trì coin air fhichead*. The partitive plural is well established, so that a fourth possibility here is *a trì air fhichead de choin*, and this construction is likely to be selected when the noun is qualified by an adjective.

14.4.1.1. 'One'

Adjectival *aon* 'one' has followed the general trend of prefixes in modern Irish and Scottish and become a proclitic: *aon bhó* 'one cow'; when preceded by the article, the feminine form is generalized: *an aon chù* 'the one dog'. It is not usually preceded by the substantivizing particle, which is no doubt an archaism (14.1.1.0.3.). Instead, the substantives *aonan* (14.1.1.1.), *fear* (masc.) and *té* (fem.) are used, the latter two when the partitive preposition *dhe* follows: *fear dhiùbh, té dhiùbh*, 'one of them'; *fear* is simply the word meaning 'man', while the derivation of *té* is obscure.

14.4.1.2. 'Two'

The adjectival numeral *dà* 'two' is still followed by the dual which, as a result of the breakdown of declension, is usually identical with the nominative singular; where, however, a dative singular distinct from the nominative singular survives, the dual is identical with the dative singular: *cas* 'foot'; *mo dhà chois* 'my two feet'. As the latter example suggests, the use of the dual to refer to natural pairs is maintained, although *mo chasan* 'my feet' is an acceptable alternative. The substantivized form *a dhà* has taken over the vocalism of the adjectival *dà*.

14.4.1.3. Other cardinals

All decads above *fichead* 'twenty' have been eliminated, though the innovation *leith cheud* (with a secondary compound variant *leithchead*) 'half hundred' provides a new equivalent of 'fifty'. The vigesimal system is strongly established, to the extent that 'one hundred and twenty' is normally expressed as *sia fichead* rather than as *ceud is fichead*; above 'three hundred and ninety-nine', however, hundreds must be expressed, since **fichead fichead* is not acceptable.

14.4.1a. Cardinals: Irish

14.4.1a.0. Here the substantivizing particle has lost most of its former functions. It is used in counting, in giving the time of day (*a hocht of chlog* 'eight o'clock', where Scottish has *ocht uairean* 'eight hours', and hence *bus a hocht* 'the eight o'clock bus') and in certain quasi-ordinal contexts: *Hannraoi a Ceathair*, like French *Henri Quatre*, compared to English *Henry the Fourth*; this latter usage no doubt continues the Classical usage *a haon díbh* 'the first of them' (14.3.1.1.). It occurs in the partitive plural only when two adjectival numerals are connected by *nó* 'or': *a trí nó a ceathair de bhlianta* 'three of four years', though it is often deleted in this construction. It is not deleted in counting, however, and in this context has even spread to the substantival numerals: *a fiche, a céad*. It must also be noted that the form *ceathair* 'four' quoted above is used only with the particle, *ceithre* being the adjectival form. Apart from the cases mentioned above, the adjectival numerals are substantivized by the use of the appropriate form of the noun *ceann* 'head'; thus, in reply to the question 'How many (non-human)?' the reply will normally (but see 14.4.3.) be *cúig cinn* 'five' rather than the *a cóig* of Scottish Gaelic, and of the earlier language. Similarly, in the partitive plural construction where only one numeral is involved, we find *cúig cinn de bha* 'five cows' and, as in Scottish (14.4.1.0.) this construction will normally be selected when the noun is followed by an adjective. When the partitive construction is not used, most dialects tend to generalize the tendency noted for Classical Irish in 14.3.0.1., that is, to use the lenited form of the singular after the adjectival numerals 'three' to 'ten'. In all dialects, however, there are some nouns where the singular is compulsory (*cúig lá* 'five days', *cúig mhí* 'five months') and others where the plural is compulsory (*cúig seachtaine* 'five weeks', *cúig bliana* 'five years'); in the latter case there is often a new plural formation which is used in all other contexts (*na seachtainí* 'the weeks', *na blianta* 'the years'). In the composite numerals *fiche* is still declined, but may also be preceded by the conjunction *agus, is, 's* 'and'. 'Twenty-three dogs' can therefore be expressed as:

trí coin }	{ *fhichead*
	ar fhichid
trí chú }	*is fiche*

as well as by the partitive plural construction.

14.4.1a.1. 'One'

Adjectival *aon* 'one' has, as in Scottish, become a proclitic but, except in a few fossilized phrases (*aon mhac Dé* 'God's only son', etc.), it functions as a numeral only when the noun it qualifies is followed by *amháin* 'only', and the latter may even function by itself; thus for 'one cow' we have *bó, aon bhó amháin* and *bó amháin*, with the latter two stressing unity more strongly than the first. When *aon* is preceded by the article, the masculine form is generalized: *an t-aon bhó amháin* 'the one cow'. The substantivized forms are: *ceann, aon cheann amháin, ceann amháin.*

14.4.1a.2. 'Two'

In Irish, adjectival *dhá* 'two' is lenited except when preceded by the article, while the substantival *a dó* shows no lenition except in the bound phrase *(ceann) nó dhó* '(one) or two'; this represents a switch of the earlier mutations (14.1.1.0.1. [iv]). As in Scottish, adjectival *dhá* is followed by the dual, which is synchronically identical with the dative singular when such a form is distinct from the nominative singular: *cos* 'foot', *mo dhá chois* 'my two feet', with the same variation between *mo dhá chois* and *mo chosa* as noted for Scottish (14.4.1.2.). The introduction of the loanword *péire* 'pair' as the equivalent of *dhá cheann* 'two (things)' is clearly recent; whether the sporadic occurrence of the plural article in western dialects (*na dhá chois* rather than *an dá chois*) continues the Middle Irish development (14.2.1.2.) is very uncertain.

14.4.1a.3. Other cardinals

All decads above *fiche* have been eliminated, but the secondary compound *daichead* 'forty' (from *dá fhichead*) is used in all dialects, as is *leithchéad* 'fifty'. In some dialects the loanword *scór* 'twenty' is part of the numeral system; it is noteworthy that in such cases composite numerals derived from it use only the conjunction *agus, is, 's* 'and' and reverse the order of the elements; thus, to *dhá cheann fhichead, dhá cheann ar fhichid, dhá cheann is fiche* 'twenty-two' corresponds *scór is péire*. It is also mainly with *scór* that subtracting numerals are found: *sé scóir ach trí cinn* 'one hundred and seventeen'; this would suggest that these are innovations rather than continuations of the Middle Irish constructions noted in 14.2.1.0. Again, while the old numeral substantives *fiche* 'twenty', *céad* 'hundred' and *míle* 'thousand' are followed by the nominative singular (14.3.0.2., 14.4.1.0.), *scór* takes the genitive plural: *fiche duine, scór daoine* 'twenty people'. With these exceptions, the vigesimal system is used in much the same way as in Scottish (14.4.1.3.).

14.4.2. Ordinals

14.4.2.0. The ordinals began to lose their declension at an early period; in the modern language that process has been completed. The loss of the distinction of gender, seen in the opposite generalization of the article before *aon* in Scottish (14.4.1.1.) and Irish (14.4.1a.1.), also takes place. In Irish, Manx and Scottish, the ordinal 'first' (14.4.2.1.) is treated as feminine; in Irish and Scottish, the rest of the ordinals are treated as masculine, while in Manx those after 'second' are treated as feminine.

14.4.2.1. 'First'

Just as *aon* 'one' has become proclitic to the following noun, so has the corresponding ordinal *céad L* 'first'; in Irish, Manx and Scottish it is preceded by the feminine article: Irish *an chéad lá*; Scottish Gaelic *a' cheud latha*; Manx *yn chied laa*. The generalization of feminine gender may be due to the need for distinguishing between the new proclitic ordinal and *céad* 'hundred' (taking the nom. sg.); the Classical contrast between *an céadlá* 'the first day' and *an céad lá* 'the hundred days' was converted into that between *an chéad lá* and *an céad lá* respectively.

14.4.2.2. 'Second'

Irish *(an) dara h-, (an) darna h-, (an) tarna h-*; Scottish Gaelic *(an) tàrna* 'second' all ultimately derive from an abstraction from some Middle Irish form such as *indarna haí* (14.2.2.). In Irish the ordinal is purely enumerative, while in Scottish it still has selective function: *an tàrna fear* 'one of the two men' or 'the second man'. Both Irish and Scottish have vestiges of the prefix *ath-* in the meaning 'next, second' (14.1.2.2.), but in Manx *yn nah L*, generalized as feminine, is the regular ordinal: *yn nah vraar* 'the second brother'. The reflex of Old Irish *indara* occurs only in the bound phrases *yn derry yeh ... ... y jeh elley* 'one (of the two) ... ... the other (of the two)'. The first of these continues directly Middle Irish *indara de* (14.2.1.2.); with the re-interpretation of *jeh* as a pronoun, *y jeh elley* replaced the *a chéile* of Middle Irish.

14.4.2.3. Other ordinals

treas 'third' survives only marginally in the modern languages, though it seems to have been the only form in Manx. It is normally replaced by a formation obtained by adding the later reflex of the ending *-amhadh* of Classical Irish: Irish *tríú*, Scottish Gaelic *tritheamh* 'third'; Manx *kiaroo* 'fourth'. In numerals above 'ten' this ending is generalized in Irish: *an t-aonú lá déag, an dóú lá déag* ... 'the eleventh, twelfth day'.

14.4.3. Personal numerals

As has been seen (14.3.3.) the non-personal numeral substantives were eliminated in the Classical period; only *péire* (14.4.1a.3.) represents an innovation in this category. The personal numerals corresponding to the series 'two' to 'ten' are well preserved in both areas, and Irish has added the secondary compound *dáréag* 'twelve people', from *dá fhear dhéag* 'twelve men'. In Ireland, however, *dias* 'two people' has largely been replaced by *beirt* (14.3.3.), while Scottish continues a form older than *dias* in *dithis*, formally identical with *diïs*, the accusative-dative singular of Old Irish *diäs*. In Irish there is a large area in the Northwest and a smaller one in the South where the personal numerals without a qualifying genitive refer to inanimate objects (14.3.3.); this is not permitted elsewhere in Ireland, nor in Scotland. Only a small number of nouns (denoting sex, relationship, nationality, etc.) can be enumerated by personal numerals: Irish *beirt bhan* 'two women', *triúr Sasanach* 'three Englishmen'; Scottish Gaelic *deichnar dhaoine* 'ten men'. The general rule, that the noun enumerated by a personal numeral must be in the genitive plural, is maintained in Scottish. In Irish, however, it has been breached by the existence of a number of nouns where an old genitive plural identical in form with the nominative singular is maintained after the personal numerals, while a new genitive plural identical with the nominative plural replaces it in other contexts; thus, from *leanbh* 'child' we have *scoil na leanaí* 'the children's school' but *beirt leanbh* 'two children', with what is synchronically a singular form. An interesting innovation is the use of *claigeann* 'skull' in Northwest Irish to form the equivalent of personal numerals; since *ceann* is used of non-human objects (14.4.1a.0.), there is therefore a contrast between *cúig claigne déag* 'fifteen people' and *cúig cinn déag* 'fifteen things'.

14.4.4. Other forms

The fractions *leath* 'half', *trian* 'third' and *ceathrú* 'quarter' are maintained; otherwise the ordinal is used with *cuid* 'portion' or *rann* 'part'. The use of the prefix *leath-* 'half' to denote one member of a natural pair is maintained and extended; thus we find not only *leathchos* 'one of two feet', but *leathbhróg* 'one of a pair of shoes' and *leathlaí* 'shaft of a cart', where the simplex *dlaí* from which it was formed has been lost. Sometimes the noun combined with *leath-* does not denote one of a natural pair, as in Irish *leathbhádóir* 'partner in a boat', from *bádóir* 'boatman' or Scottish Gaelic *leithbhreac* 'equal, match, equivalent' from *breac* 'trout' perhaps through 'one of a pair of trout'? An adjectival formation is *leathlámhach* 'short-handed, in need of assistance', from *leathlámh* 'one of two hands'.

14.5. Common British

14.5.0. The evidence of the earliest records of Breton, Cornish and Welsh indicates that all three languages had substantially the same numeral system at, say, the end of the sixth century A.D., and in this section an attempt will be made to reconstruct it, using the orthography of Old Welsh, which is known from the ninth century onwards; this orthography is based on that of Old Irish.

14.5.1. Cardinals

14.5.1.0. The distinction between adjectival and substantival cardinals is not formally expressed; since declension had been lost before our oldest documents were written there can be no contrast between following nominatives and genitives. Combinatory numerals show no inflection: *pem nau* 'five nines' = 'forty-five'; *teir trigont* 'three thirties' = 'ninety'; on the other hand, all cardinals can have plural forms when used independently: *ir nauou* 'the nines'; *ucentou* 'twenties'.

14.5.1.1. 'One'

un 'one' is etymologically identical with Old Irish *oen*; mutations are not written in the Old Welsh orthographical system, but the evidence of the later language shows that the feminine form is *un L*. It is more freely used than Old Irish *oen*, but examples from the later language such as Middle Welsh *oed blwydd* 'age of (one) year'; Middle Breton *bloaz ha tregont* 'thirty-one years' shows traces of the older system. It is likely that the original substantival form was simply *un*, but in Old Breton the derivative *unan* has already penetrated into the numeral system as the substantive corresponding to adjectival *un*, a striking parallel to the development of Scottish Gaelic *aonan*, Manx *unnane* from Old Irish *oenán* (14.1.1.1., 14.4.1.1.). In spite of phonological difficulties (see Jackson 1953: 461), there can be no doubt of the etymological equivalence of *unan* and *oenán*. The latter does not belong to the numeral system in Old Irish (14.4.1.1.) nor does *unan* in Welsh, where it occurs only when preceded by a possessive particle in the function of a reflexive pronoun: Middle Welsh *fy hunan* 'myself', like Middle Breton *ma hunan*; here Welsh, but not Breton, has an alternative formation, *fy hun*. (The sandhi *h-* in these words is, as so often in British, difficult to account for historically.)

14.5.1.2. 'Two'

The etymology of *dou L* 'two' (masc.) and *dui L* (fem.) has already been discussed (14.1.1.2.2.). That British, like Irish, had at one time a neuter form ending in a nasal is shown by the irregular mutations of Middle

Welsh *deucant*, Modern Breton *daou c'hant*. It is not possible to recover the original composition form of this numeral, because of a special development of British, whereby secondary compounds are formed with 'two' from nouns denoting natural pairs (cf. 14.1.1.2.1., 14.1.5.1., 14.1.4.); Middle Welsh *glin* 'knee', pl. *glinieu*, but *deulin* (from **deu lin*) '(the) knees (of one person)', *fy neulin* 'my knees'; *bronn* 'breast', *dwyvron* '(woman's) breasts'. In these cases the form of the numeral is determined by the gender of the noun, and the same procedure has spread to all compounds containing 'two'; Welsh *deublyg* 'two-fold' but *dwybig* 'two-pronged', from *plyg* masc. and *pig* fem. respectively.

14.5.1.3. 'Three'

The oldest mutation after masc. *tri* 'three' appears to be the spirant, Welsh *tri pheth* 'three things'; it is therefore identical in origin with Old Irish nom.-acc. *trí h-*. The fem. *teir* is most easily explained by taking it to be from **tisres* through **tedres*, (W. Cowgill, *Language* 33, 1957: 341–345), or perhaps rather from acc. **tisr̥ns* (14.1.1.3.1.). Whether Gaulish *tidres* (read by some scholars as *tidrus*) should be compared is quite uncertain, in spite of Thurneysen, *Zeitschrift für Celtische Philologie* xv (1925: 379–383). The composition form is *trĭ-*, Middle Welsh *try-*, Middle Breton *tre-*, cf. Middle Breton *trywyr* 'three men', Breton *Treger* from **Tricorios* (Jackson 1953: 587).

14.5.1.4. 'Four'

Masc. *petguar* 'four' derives from **petwores*, and fem. *peteir* from **petesres*. The composition form seen in Continental Celtic *Petru-corii* is continued in Middle Welsh *pedry-*.

14.5.1.5. 'Five' to 'ten'

The mutations after the numeral from 'five' onwards are too varied for any reconstruction of them to be possible, and they will not be marked here. *pimp* 'five' shows a vowel shift already seen in Gaulish *pinpetos* 'fifth', beside the composition form *pempe-* (and even *pompe-*) found in Gaulish words quoted by classical writers. The expected form of 'six' is **hue* from **sweks*, but forms with a final spirant (Middle Welsh *chwech*, etc.) are regularly attested. Jackson (1953: 637–638) suggests that *chwech* is a generalization of the sandhi form; it is also possible that it derives from a **swekse* which had patterned on *pempe*, cf. the ordinal **sweksetos* modelled on *$k^{w}enk^{w}etos$ in all the Celtic languages. *seith* 'seven' from **sektan* has irregular treatment of the anlaut, since Celtic **s-* normally gives *h-* in British; *s-* in Latin loanwords, however, continues as *s-* in British, and the *s-* of *seith* may derive from Latin *septem*. The vocalism of Middle Welsh *wyth*, Old Breton *eith* shows that it must derive from **oxtī* < **oxtū* < **oḱtō*, though elsewhere in the numeral system it has acquired a final nasal, cf. Old Breton *eithnec* 'eighteen' (14.4.1.6.). *nau* 'nine' and *dec* 'ten' represent **nawan* and **dekan* respectively.

14.5.1.6. 'Eleven' to 'nineteen'

In the formation of the teens, British and Irish diverge completely. It has been demonstrated by H. Lewis (*Bulletin of the Board of Celtic Studies*, 5: 93 ff.) that the original system in British was composition of the cardinals 'one' to 'nine' with **dekan* 'ten'. Survivals of this system are Welsh *deuddeg* 'twelve', *pymtheg* 'fifteen' and Old Welsh *naunec-* 'nine-teen'; Breton *trizek* 'thirteen', *pevarzek* 'fourteen', and *eitek* 'eighteen', as well as Old Breton *eithnec* 'eighteen', which, as Jackson (1967: 358) suggests, may derive from **oxtūndekan*. Our one piece of evidence from Continental Celtic shows a similar system in the ordinal *petrudecametos* 'fourteen' where, however, the composition form of the numeral has replaced the **petwar-* suggested by Breton *pevarzek*.

14.5.1.7. 'Twenty'

Old Welsh *uceint*, Cornish *ucent* 'twenty' must derive from **wikantī*, but the treatment of the initial presents serious difficulty. The most attractive solution is to assume that there has been an abstraction from the form attested as Cornish *douceint*, Old Welsh *douceint* 'forty', presumably a secondary compound from **dou uiceint*. This implies an early penetration of the vigesimal system into British, but it is to be noted that there is no trace of any form corresponding to Old Irish *cetharcho* 'forty', nor to *sesco* 'sixty', where **triuiceint* could easily be reduced to *triceint* and thus strengthen the new form *uceint*. If this explanation is correct, the devel-opment is insular and renders very doubtful the suggestion made by A. Tovar (*La lengua vasca*, 1950: § 13) and other scholars that Basque *hogei* 'twenty' is a loanword from Celtic; the fact that Basque is the only European language in which the vigesimal system appears to be original would suggest rather that *ogei* is inherited. The numerals 'one' to 'nine' were connected with the decads by the preposition *gwar(n)* 'on', occasionally expressed by Latin *super* in Old Breton documents; as the vigesimal system spread, this was extended to the numerals 'ten' to 'nineteen' when connected with scores, cf. Old Breton *dec super LXXX* 'ninety'. This is parallel to the use of the preposition *ar L* in Old Irish, although the two have different origins (14.1.1.0.6.). The penetration of the conjunction *(h)a* 'and' into the numeral system began early, but it is probably and innovation, as in Middle Irish (14.2.1.0.).

14.5.1.8. 'Thirty' to 'ninety'

Old Breton *tricont*, Middle Breton *tregont* 'thirty' points to earlier **trĭ-*, in contrast to Old Irish *trícho*, which agrees with Gaulish *trIcontis* if the evidence of the *i longa* is accepted. As Old Breton shows, the obviously secondary Old Welsh *trimuceint* 'thirty' is not necessarily evidence for *-ī-*; Old Welsh orthography is ambiguous here. The weight of the evidence is in favour of the assumption that the Common Celtic form was **trīkont-* and that the Breton shortening of the first vowel arose from assimilation to the composition form of 'three', cf. Gaulish *petrudecametos* 'fourteenth'. Szemerényi (1960: 22, n. 106) is almost certainly right in rejecting the view that the *trychon* of an early Welsh poem should be interpreted as **trycwnt*, corresponding to Old Breton *tricont*. No trace of a form for 'forty' appears in any British language. Welsh *pymhwnt* and Old Breton *pimmont* point to **pimpont* from **pempont*; the latter is the precise equivalent of the **k^{w}enk^{w}ont-* assumed for Irish (14.1.1.13.3.).

14.5.1.9. 'Hundred' to 'thousand'

cant 'hundred' is the British equivalent of *cét* (14.1.1.14.1.) and is uninflected after numerals, as is the feminine loanword *mil* 'thousand'.

14.5.2. Ordinals

14.5.2.1. 'First'

Middle Welsh *cyntaf*, Middle Breton *quentaff*, which follow the noun they qualify, represent an earlier **cintam*. This derives from the adding of the superlative ending to the element **kintu-* (14.1.2.5.), and a similar form may lie behind the Gaulish name *Cintusmus*. Old Welsh has one example of *cisemic*, glossing *primus*, which would point to another superlative formation, **cisam* from **kintsamos*; another derivative of this **cisam* is Middle Welsh *cysefin*, which can also mean ‘first’. The evidence, therefore, points to **cisam* and **cintam* as alternative forms in British, with the latter generalized in the later stages.

14.5.2.2. ‘Second’

Middle Welsh *eil* ‘second’ is the exact British equivalent of Old Irish *aile* from **alyos*. In the Insular Celtic languages the variant **allos* is restricted to the meaning ‘other’; in Gaulish, however, *all*[ ] ‘second’ is probably to be interpreted as *allos*.

14.5.2.3. ‘Third’

Old Welsh *tritid* ‘third’ derives from an earlier **tr̥tiyos*, while Gaulish *trit*[ ] may represent either *tritos* or *tritios*. It is to be noted that the British form implies an ending *-*tiyos*, as opposed to the *-*yos* of **alyos*, though admittedly Szemerényi (1960: 83) would analyse the latter as **ali-os*.

14.5.2.4. ‘Fourth’

Middle Welsh *pedwerydd* ‘fourth’ continues a British **petwariyos*, cf. the British place-name *Petuaria* (Ptolemy); the reconstruction of Gaulish *petuar*[ ] must remain uncertain. E. P. Hamp (*Indogermanische Forschungen* 74: 153–154) has discussed the alleged Gaulish *tartos* ‘fourth’, but D. Ellis Evans (*Gaulish personal names* pp. 377–378) rejects it as an ordinal.

14.5.2.5. ‘Fifth’ to ‘tenth’

With Middle Welsh *pymhed*, Middle Breton *pempet*, Gaulish *pinpetos* we have a clear case of the *-*to*- suffix. Reinterpreted as *-*eto*- this suffix also gives the ordinals ‘sixth’ to ‘tenth’, with ‘eighth’ showing a nasal even in Gaulish *oxtumeto*[ ]. Gaulish *namet*[ ] ‘ninth’ is explained by Szemerényi (1960: 90) as **nametos*, contracted from **nawametos*, though the motivation is not clear; it may well be, however, that **nametos* was also the British form, since the attested forms for ‘ninth’ in those languages (Middle Welsh *nawved*, Middle Breton *navvet, naovet*) look like later reconstructions.

14.5.2.6. Other ordinals

The ending *-ved* obtained from the series 'seventh' to 'tenth' spread to all the ordinals above 'ten', exactly as did the equivalent *-mad* in Irish; it may be taken to be an Insular Celtic development.

14.5.3. Other forms

14.5.3.1. *hanter* 'half' is from Celtic **santero-*; the first element is found in Irish *sain* (from **sanis*) 'separate', cf. Latin *sine*, Old High German *suntar*, etc. The element Welsh *lled-*, Breton *let-*, which is cognate with Irish *leth* 'half' (14.1.5.1.), can occur in compounds with the meaning 'partly', cf. Welsh *lledwag* 'partly empty', Breton *led-enez* 'peninsula', but it cannot be regarded as being part of the series of fractions. Welsh *traean*, Breton *troian* 'third' are the cognates of Old Irish *triän* (14.1.5.2.). Otherwise the ordinals are used, sometimes with the introduction of Welsh *rhann*, Breton *rann* 'part', cf. the use of the cognate word in Irish (14.1.5.3.).
14.5.3.2. As in Irish (14.1.6.), numerals can be placed before the comparative of adjectives to indicate multiplication: Welsh *pum mwy* 'five times more'. Otherwise the word Welsh *gweith*, Breton *guez* is used: Welsh *teir gweith* 'three times', Breton *mil guez* 'a thousand times'. Distributives are formed with *pop* 'each', cf. Irish *cech* (14.1.7.).

14.6. Middle Welsh

14.6.0. The Middle Welsh period, extending from the twelfth century, is the earliest form of a British language for which we have extensive documentation. Some features of its numeral system should no doubt be allotted to the previous section, as Common British; however, only those which can be shown to be common to all branches were listed there. It is clear, for example, that the completive and selective uses of the ordinal (14.1.2.0.) must be Common Celtic, but no examples for British survive outside Middle Welsh. Turning to innovations, it may well be that the generalizing of singular forms after numerals was already well advanced in the Common British period, but the uneven rate of the generalization in Breton and Welsh makes it better to consider them separately. Middle Cornish exhibits the same system as Middle Breton and is not considered separately.

14.6.1. It has already been noted (14.5.1.0.) that the distinction between adjectival and substantival numerals is not formally expressed. Any numeral may be used as a noun: *y pedwar* 'the four', *y pedwar hynny* 'those four', *yn pedwar* 'our four' = 'the four of us', *yll pedwar* 'the four of them'; the origin of *yll* in the last phrase is uncertain, but it is probably related to Irish *uile* 'all'. A curious development is the use of the plural of the substantivized numeral after *yll: a'e ddwylaw yll dwyoedd* 'with both his hands'. A definite plural noun governed by the preposition *o L* may follow a numeral, and has the function of a partitive genitive: *deuddeg o'r gwyr* 'twelve of the men'; when the noun is indefinite, the construction is no longer felt as partitive: *deuddeg o wyr* means simply 'twelve men' (cf. 14.0.2., 14.1.3.0., 14.4.1.0., 14.4.1a.0.). It is expecially common when dealing with large numbers, and is the normal construction with *mil: pym mil o wyr* 'five thousand men'.

14.6.2. Middle Welsh still shows many examples of the use of the plural after numerals (*pump wragedd* 'five women', *ugein ychen* 'twenty oxen'), but mainly in cases where this plural is historically justified. The loss of final syllables which took place in prehistoric times left the British languages with a very large number of words in which the singular and plural forms were homophonous. Just as in Old Irish, where a different phonological development had produced a much smaller number of such words (mainly neuter *o*-stems, cf. 14.1.1.14.), the undifferentiated plural form continued to be used after numerals, while new plurals were evolved for other environments: Old Irish *trí chét* 'three hundred' but *céta* 'hundreds' shows exactly the same process as Welsh *tri chant* 'three hundred' but *cannoedd* 'hundreds'. There are even cases where an inherited and differentiated plural is restricted to use after numerals, while a new plural is used in other environments: *deunaw weis o weisson culyon cochyon* 'eighteen lean red-headed youths', shows the old plural *(g)weis* of *gwas* after the numeral, but the new plural in the construction with *o L* described above (14.6.1.). These represent a transition stage: already in Middle Welsh the majority of examples show the singular after numerals, but plural formations in other environments. The evidence from Breton and Cornish would seem to indicate that the process took place earlier in those languages; it is certainly completed by the Middle Breton period. In Irish, on the other hand, it was a much slower process (see 14.3.0.1., 14.4.1a.0.), and it is still restricted to a very small number of nouns in Scottish Gaelic (14.4.1.0.). It may be laid down as a general principle that, except after numerals, the Insular Celtic languages did not tolerate undifferentiated plurals of the type English *fish, sheep*, etc., while in

British, and to a lesser extent in Irish, the existence of such undifferentiated plurals after numerals was generalized into a synchronic rule that numerals must be followed by the singular.

14.6.3. The most striking innovation of the Middle Welsh numeral system is the introduction of composite numerals for 'eleven', 'thirteen', 'fourteen', 'sixteen', 'seventeen' and 'nineteen' and of a secondary compound for 'eighteen'; only *deuddeg* 'twelve' and *pymtheg* 'fifteen' continue the old compounds (14.5.1.6.). The linking element in the new composite numerals is the preposition *ar L*; since, by the Middle Welsh period, this represents both the *war(n)* used to link other numerals with the decads (14.2.1.4.) and the cognate of Old Irish *ar L* (14.1.1.0.6.), there is no way of deciding which we have here. For 'eighteen' we have the secondary compound *deunaw*. Only *un ar ddeg* 'eleven', *tri ar ddeg* 'thirteen' and *pedwar ar ddeg* 'fourteen' are built on 'ten'; *un ar bymtheg* 'sixteen', *dau ar bymtheg* 'seventeen' and *pedwar ar bymtheg* 'nineteen' are built on 'fifteen'. Such a procedure is not known from other Indo-European languages; it is obviously a reminiscence of a system where 'five' rather than 'ten' is the base, but there is otherwise no trace of such a system in Celtic or Indo-European. See, however, 14.10.1.

14.6.4. The *ar L* used in the series described above can hardly be identical with the prepositional element in *ar hugein*, which combines with 'one' to 'nineteen' to form the numerals 'twenty-one' to 'thirty-nine'; in spite of the formal difficulties, *ar h-* here must derive from the *(g)war(n)* preserved in the other British languages. It occurs only with *ugein* 'twenty'; elsewhere, linking is realised by *a(g)* 'and': *tri ar ddeg a deu ugein* 'fifty-three'.

14.6.5. The survival of the completive and selective functions of the ordinal in Middle Welsh has already been mentioned (14.6.0.). They are illustrated by the sentence *ymgeiraw a orug Teirnon ar y drydydd marchawg, a'r mab yn bedwyrydd y gyd ag wynt* 'Teirnon and two other horsemen equipped themselves, and the boy as a fourth along with them'. Here we have the prep. *ar L* 'on' + poss. particle 3rd sg. masc. + ordinal: 'T. on his third (horseman)' = 'as one of three horsemen', which is selective, while the ordinal preceded by the predicative particle *yn L* shows the completive usage. An example of the selective without *ar L* is *honno oedd trydydd prif rieni yn yr ynys hon* 'she was one of the three [literally 'the third'] ancestors in this island'. This is entirely parallel with the Irish usage (14.1.2.0.), while the construction with *ar L* is found only in Middle Welsh.

14.7. Modern spoken Welsh

14.7.0. The written norm of Modern Welsh is based on the Bible translation of 1588, and is in many ways much closer to Middle Welsh than to the spoken language, which seldom appears in writing except to represent dialogue. As has already been noted (14.0.5.), the numeral system taught in the schools is an invention of comparatively recent origin. Only the usage of the spoken language is considered here.

14.7.1. The use of *un* 'one' remains unchanged. The numerals 'two', 'three' and 'four' maintain their feminine forms. The secondary compounds of 'two' which denoted natural pairs (14.5.1.2.) have been completely eliminated; the only survival is *dwylo* 'hand' which, however, does not function as a dual but as the plural formation from *llaw* 'hand'. Other secondary compounds such as *deugain* 'forty', *deufis* 'two months', *dwyfil* 'two thousand', *dwywaith* 'twice' are regular in the spoken language but constitute a closed category. Already in the literary language some subtracting numerals had appeared, such as *cant namyn un* 'one hundred less one' = 'ninety-nine'; in the spoken language phrases such as *mewn tair i bedwar ugain* 'in three to four twenties' = 'seventy-seven years old' are found. (It should be noted here that the fem. *tair* refers to *blwydd* fem. 'year', a singular used only when stating the age of an animate object; *blwydd* (*oed*) 'one year (of age)' is an example in Welsh of the old Celtic system of using the simple noun to express unity.) The vigesimal system is used up to 'three hundred and ninety-nine', which is expressed as *pedwar ugain ar bymtheg a phedwar ar bymtheg* 'nineteen twenties and nineteen', but, just as in Irish and Scottish Gaelic (14.4.1.3.), **ugain, ugain* is not acceptable and hundreds must be expressed from this point onwards. Again as in Irish and Scottish Gaelic (14.4.1.3., 14.4.1a.3.) 'fifty' is expressed as *hanner cant* 'half hundred'.

14.7.2. Numerals are regularly followed by the singular noun, as in all the modern British languages, and this construction is compulsory when the following noun is a unit of measurement: *pum munud, milltir* 'five minutes, miles'. In other cases, however, with numerals above 'two', the construction with *o L* and the plural (14.6.1.) is much commoner: *pump o ddynion* 'five men'. It will be noted that in this case adjectival *pum* has been formally differentiated from substantival *pump*, which is the pausa form and that used in counting, so that in this case at least Modern Welsh has reconstituted a distinction which goes far back in the history of Insular Celtic. The substantival numerals preceded by possessive par-

ticles (14.6.1.) have been strengthened by prefixing the pronouns: *ni 'n dau* 'the two of us', and there are many variants, e. g. *yni ill trioedd* 'we three', *nwch tri* 'they three' from different dialect areas.
14.7.3. The ordinals in Modern Welsh, both literary and spoken, have lost their completive and selective functions (14.6.5.) and, as in later Irish, are purely enumerative. In the spoken language the composite numerals tend to form ordinals as though they were secondary compounds; to literary *unfed ar ddeg* 'eleventh' corresponds spoken *un-ar-ddegfed*. Distributives are formed with *fesul*, from *mesur* 'measure': *fesul dau* 'two by two', and *bob* survives only in the phrase *bob yn ail* 'alternately'.

14.8. Middle Breton

14.8.0. Middle Breton is known to us from a number of texts, largely religious, from the fifteenth and sixteenth centuries; the orthographical system is based on that of medieval French. While French loanwords constitute a high percentage of the vocabulary, no penetration of the French numeral system had taken place at this period.

14.8.1. Cardinals

14.8.1.1. In Middle Breton the numeral 'one' has split into adjectival *un* and substantival *unan*; as has been seen (14.5.1.1.), the derivative *unan*, Old Irish *oenán*, has had a tendency to penetrate into the numeral system. Furthermore, the adjectival *un* now functions as an indefinite article as well as a numeral. K. Jackson's view (1967: 143) that this is 'unquestionably' a borrowing from French seems too strong; for a discussion of this problem see W. U. Dressler, "A propos de la grammaire du discours breton", *Études Celtiques* 13 (1972: 153–170). The substantival *unan* varies in gender according to the object referred to; since gender in Celtic is normally marked only by mutations, this simply means that *unan* has taken over the mutations of *un* masc., *un L* fem. (14.5.1.1.). It is also *unan* which appears in the meaning 'self'.
14.8.1.2. The other cardinals maintain the system which has been described for Common British, except that the vigesimal system has eliminated all the decads except *tregont* 'thirty' and the innovation *hanter cant* 'fifty'. The linking element *warn* is now restricted to the phrase *warnugent* 'plus twenty'; we have *unan ha tregont* 'thirty-one', etc. This is precisely the same development as in Middle Welsh (14.6.4.). All the numerals are

followed by the singular; traces of the older system, such as *tri nyet* 'three nephews' are very rare, and one of them, *rouanez tri* 'three kings', shows poetic inversion. Plural forms are not, as in Welsh, re-introduced through a development of the partitive construction; the preposition *a L*, corresponding to W, *o L*, has always partitive force in phrases such as *unan ... ... a pevar requet* 'one of four requests'. However, traces at least of the partitive plural occur in the later language (14.9.1.3.).

14.8.2. Ordinals

Quentaff, corresponding to Middle Welsh *cyntaf*, is the only form of the ordinal 'first'. The ordinals form 'three' and 'four' have lost the gender distinction as *trede, pevare*, but in the latter case a new feminine form *pedervet* has been evolved from the feminine cardinal *peder* and the generalized ordinal ending *-vet*. Fractions and multiplicatives are treated as in Common British.

14.9. Modern Breton

14.9.0. Modern Breton is spoken by something under a million persons; no census figures are available, and the number of children being brought up as Breton speakers seems to be small. Breton has almost no place in the educational system and, although a literary language has been evolved, a reliable authority has estimated that not more than five hundred people can use Breton as a means of written intellectual expression or communication. Purely literary forms will, therefore, not be discussed here. Later Cornish is not well enough known to be described separately; some forms are cited below for purposes of comparison.

14.9.1. Cardinals

14.9.1.1. 'One'

In most dialects the separation of *un* 'one' into numeral adjective and indefinite article has taken place, with the numeral retaining the form *un* [y:n] and the indefinite article becoming *eun* [ön], *eul, eur*, the two latter variants being sandhi forms based on those of the definite article. 'Twenty-one' may therefore be expressed as *bloaz war n-ugent*, continuing the original system of Insular Celtic, or *un bloaz war n-ugent*, with the numeral *un* expressed, or, as in the Vannetais dialect, *ur blai ar n-ugent*, where *ur* is identical in form with the indefinite article. In all dialects *unan* is the substantival form; as well as *unan* with feminine mutation, the feminine form *unannes* has been recorded in the phrase *unan hag unannes* 'a man and a woman'. There is also an expressive diminutive *unanik: da unanik* beside *da unan* 'thyself'.

14.9.1.2. 'Two'

All surviving dialects maintain the distinction between masc. *daou* and fem. *diou* 'two'. The Common British treatment of natural pairs has, in contrast to the Welsh development (14.7.1.), been maintained and expanded, and plurals can be formed from both singulars and from pair forms; thus, from *lagad* 'eye' are derived *lagadou* 'eyes', *daoulagad* 'pair of eyes' and *daoulagadou* 'pairs of eyes of a number of people', with the last two having the expressive variants *daoulagadik* and *daoulagadigou* respectively. In some cases, the pair form has a different meaning from that of the plural; thus *dorn* 'hand' has the reduced pair form *daourn*, while the plural *dornou* means 'handles' or 'handfuls'. There are, however, a few dialects where *daourn* has been lost and *dornou* is used both as pair form and as plural; in most areas the plural *treid* 'feet' has ousted the pair form, and the numeral 'two' is prefixed to *troad*, without forming a secondary compound, in the emphatic phrase *war e zaou droad* '(he came here) on his own two feet'. From 'two' onwards the possessive particles prefixed to numerals have the force of apposition: *hon diou* 'the two of us (fem.)'.

14.9.1.3. 'Three' to 'ten'

The masculine and feminine forms of 'three' and 'four' are well preserved. It may be noted here that there are sporadic examples of the numerals 'three' to 'five' in the partitive plural construction so common in Welsh (14.6.1., 14.7.2.); they are usually followed by nouns denoting persons (*tri a vugale* 'three boys'), but cf. [pwa:r ə-benew] 'four heads', from the Vannetais of the Ile de Croix. There are a few examples of the partitive plural from later Cornish also, again usually in the case of nouns denoting persons. The construction must be regarded as marginal for the southwest British area.

14.9.1.4. 'Eleven' to 'nineteen'

Both Breton and Cornish continued to use compound numerals in the series 'eleven' to 'nineteen', but Modern Breton has broken the series by the introduction of the secondary compound *tric'hwec'h* 'eighteen', formed on the same principle as the Welsh equivalent *deunaw* (14.6.3.), but with a different factorization. This form goes back at least to the seventeenth century and has completely ousted *eizdek*; Cornish, on the other hand, preserved *eatag* up to the end.

14.9.1.5. Other cardinals

The vigesimal system resembles strongly that of the other surviving Insular languages, with the exception that the old decad *tregont* 'thirty' remains the normal form in all dialects; some dialects still retain the vigesimal system up to 'three hundred and ninety-nine' (cf. 14.4.1.3., 14.4.1a.3., 14.7.1.), but others have adopted a system patterned on that of French, in which 'one hundred and twenty' is expressed as *kant ugent* rather than as *c'hwec'h ugent*.

14.9.2. Ordinals

The ordinal 'first' is now often spelled *kentañ*, which represents the same form as Middle Breton *quentaff*; in some dialects it has followed the pattern of the other ordinals and is placed before the noun it qualifies, a process which may have been assisted by the similar position of French *premier*. The general ordinal ending *-vet* has spread even to the ordinal 'second'; while *eil* continues in some dialects, others have masc. *daouvet*, fem. *divet*, and others the contaminated *eilvet*. Similarly, beside inherited *trede* 'third' and *pevare* 'fourth', some dialects have masc. *trivet*, fem. *teirvet*; masc. *pevarvet*, fem. *pedervet*; this may be extended through the rest of the series: *pempvet, c'hwechvet* ... ... *dekvet*. On the other hand, some Vannetais dialects have generalized *-et*: masc. *triet*, fem. *teiret* ... ... *deket*. The composite numerals show a very wide variety of forms. 'Twenty-first' is expressed as *unanvet warn-ugent*, and 'twenty-second' as *eilvet warn-ugent, daouvet warn-ugent, divet warn-ugent*, etc. After 'thirty', where *ha* 'and' replaces *warn* as the connective, there are examples of double expression of the ordinal: *daouvet ha tregontvet* 'thirty-second' beside *eilvet ha tregont*. The ordinal 'fiftieth' is expressed as *hanter-kantvet*. Over 'one hundred', the older usage *daou c'hantvet pemp ha* *tregont* 'two hundred and thirty-fifth', has been largely replaced by *daou c'hant pemvet ha tregont.* There is a strong tendency to generalize the feminine mutation after the article (*an drivet den* 'the third man', rather than *an trivet den*) except in the case of *kentañ* 'first', where some dialects generalize the masculine *ar c'hentan*; this tendency has also been observed in the Irish, Manx and Scottish ordinals (14.4.2.0.).

14.9.3. Fractions

The only fractions for which special words exist are *hanter* 'half' and *kart* 'quarter'. From *hanter* is formed the singulative *hanterenn*, and on this analogy are formed *karterenn* and *trederenn* 'third'.

14.10. Exotic counting systems in England and Wales

14.10.0. A study of the numeral systems of the Celtic languages would not be complete without a mention of the counting systems which have been recorded among English and Welsh speakers and which clearly derive respectively from the British and Irish numeral systems. None of these can now be studied at first hand, but the mass of material collected by field workers in the past, together with general resemblances of structure, show that they are not mere fabrications. They usually comprise no more than the numerals 'one' to 'twenty' and are said to have been used for counting sheep, stitches in knitting, etc., as well as in children's games.

14.10.1. The so-called 'North-Country Score' has been exhaustively studied by M. Barry ("Traditional enumeration in the North Country', *Folk Life* 7, 1969: 75–91). A typical example of this 'score' is:

1. yan	6. sethera	11. yan-a-dik	16. yan-a-bumfit
2. tan	7. lethera	12. tan-a-dik	17. tan-a-bumfit
3. tethera	8. hovera	13. tethera dik	18. tethera bumfit
4. pethera	9. covers	14. pethera dik	19. pethera bumfit
5. pimp	10. dik	15. bumfit	20. figgit

The resemblance to the Welsh system set out in 14.6.3. is obvious, in spite of the revisions brought about by turning the elements 'one' – 'two', 'three' – 'four', 'six' – 'seven', 'eight' – 'nine' into minimally differentiated pairs. But that Welsh system, as was shown there, is innovatory, since British did not use composite numerals in the series 'eleven' to 'nineteen', still less composite numerals with a base 'fifteen'. It does not seem possible, therefore, to regard these numerals as an ancient inheritance from the time of the Saxon invasions; though it is not easy to explain the methods of transmission and reception, the weight of the evidence is strongly in favour of regarding them as deriving from contacts between Welsh and English speakers within the last few hundred years.

14.10.2. A quite different score has been reported from Welsh-speaking areas in Mid-Wales, mainly Cardiganshire, of which a specimen is:

1. în	6. sîch	11. inde	16. sichde
2. tô	7. soch	12. tode	17. sochde
3. târ	8. nîch	13. tarde	18. nichde
4. câr	9. noch	14. carde	19. nochde
5. cŵi	10. dê	15. cwide	20. wichi

Again, in spite of heavy revisions, this clearly derives from Irish, but of what period? Sommerfelt, who published two papers on these numerals, was convinced that they were based on forms anterior to 600 A.D., thus going back to the Irish colonies in Wales, one of the main arguments being that *wichi* showed an older anlaut than that of Old Irish *fiche* 'twenty'. This evidence must be reviewed, however, and it can be demonstrated that, as in the case of the North Country Score, the weight of the evidence favours importation within the last few hundred years. Neither of the scores, therefore, can be regarded as a contribution to our understanding of the Celtic numeral systems.

Notes

1. All the Insular Celtic languages have morphophonemic variations of anlaut, usually called mutations; the full specification of a word must include the mutation which follows it. They will be noted here as L = lenition, N = nasalization, S = spirantization, and *h-* = prefixing of [h] to vowels.
2. The long vowel *-é-* here has not been adequately explained either, since the reflexes of **-in-*, **-on-*, **-un-* in this position are short vowels. It may be noted that there is a group of words in Scottish Gaelic (*faodaidh* 'is able', *taod* 'cord' etc.) which shows the reflex of Old Irish *-oí-* instead of the *-é-* of Irish (*éta* 'obtains', *tét* 'cord', etc.).

3. It should be noted that the dat. pl. *cethrairib* quoted by Thurneysen does not belong to the numeral substantive, but to the hapax **cethraire* used to translate *quaternio* which was taken by some medieval exegetists to be a formation like *centurio* and thus to mean 'officer in charge of four men', cf. the further Latin gloss: *quaternio dúx .iiii. virorum et ipse quintus* (*Thesaurus* 1: 497.16) – itself providing a good example of a Hiberno-Latin completive ordinal.

References

The Ancient Laws of Ireland (*Laws*)
1865–1901 (Dublin).

Aithdioghluim Dána
1939 edited by Lambert McKenna (Dublin).

'Apgitir Chrábaid'
1968 edited by Vernam Hull, *Celtica* viii: 44–89.

Audacht Morainn
1975 edited by Fergus Kelly (Dublin).

Bethu Phátraic; the tripartite life of Patric (Trip.[2])
1939 edited by Kathleen Mulchrone (Dublin).

The Book of Leinster (*LL*)
1954–1967 edited by Richard I. Best, Osborn Bergin and Michael A. Brian (Dublin).

Cardona, George – Henry Hoenigswald – Alfred Senn
1970 *Indo-European and Indo-Europeans* (Philadelphia).

Críth Gablach
1941 edited by Daniel A. Binchy (Dublin).

Dictionary of the Irish language and *Contributions to a dictionary of the Irish language* (*DIL*)
1913–1974 (Dublin: Royal Irish Academy). [In spite of the differences of titles these are complementary, and together constitute a dictionary of Old and Middle Irish.]

Félire Oengusso Céli Dé
1905 edited by Whitley Stokes (London).

Jackson, Kenneth
1953 *Language and history in early Britain* (LHEB) (Edinburgh).
1967 *A historical phonology of Breton* (HPB) (Dublin).

Lebor na Huidre (*LU*
1929 edited by Richard I. Best and Osborn Bergin (Dublin).

The metrical Dindsenchas
1903–1935 edited by E. J. Gwynn (Dublin).

Pedersen, Holger
1909–1913 *Vergleichende Grammatik der keltischen Sprachen* (Göttingen).

Pilch, Herbert – Joachim Thurow (eds.)
1972 Indo-Celtica. Gedächtnisschrift für Alf Sommerfeldt [Commentationes Societatis Linguisticae Europae II] (München).

Saltair na Rann (SR)
1883 edited by Whitley Stokes (Oxford).

Szemerényi, Oswald
1960 *Studies in the Indo-European system of numerals* (Heidelberg: Winter).

Thesaurus Palaeohibernicus (*Thesaurus*)
1901–1903 edited by Whitley Stokes and John Strachan (Cambridge).

Thurneysen, Rudolf
1946 *A grammar of Old Irish* (OIG) (Dublin).

Chapter 15
Germanic*

Alan S. C. Ross – Jan Berns

15.0. Introduction[1]

15.0.1. Sources[2]

Some of the Germanic languages have standard orthographies – as, for instance, most of the modern ones. For these – thus, for example, for Færoese – it is only necessary to give the forms, without reference. But many Germanic languages are not at all homogeneous – Middle English is perhaps the paramount example – and, for these, it is customary to refer to the texts. Clearly space and time prevent us from doing this here, at least as normal practice. But many of the Germanic grammars, dictionaries, and other philological works contain excellent lists of numeral forms. Forms given here from such Germanic languages without reference are, the reader may assume, to be found in the relevant one of the works listed below. But, in the case of forms occurring only twice, or once, in a language, we often refer to the texts.

- *Gothic*: Streitberg (1965).
- *Crimean Gothic*: Streitberg (1920: 280–282).
- *Old West Norse*: Noreen (1923).

Old and Modern Icelandic differ but little in orthography. We therefore follow the common practice of giving one form for both stages of the language; we use the prefix "Icel." and the orthographic conventions customary in England;[3] thus Icel. *áttungr* means OIcel. *ǫ́ttongr*, Mod. Icel. *áttungur*. We prefix specifically Old Icelandic forms with OIcel. and give them in the standard German orthography (as in Noreen 1923); we

* The original draft of this chapter was prepared by the late Professor Ross. It has been updated and revised for publication by Dr. J. B. Berns.

prefix forms specific to Modern Icelandic (which has, of course, a standard orthography) with "Mod. Icel.".

- *Shetlandic*: the few numeral forms that survive will be found in Hægstad (1900: 75–98).
- *Modern Norwegian*: Standard Landsmål forms from: Torvik (1966). We have naturally also made use of Torp (1919).
- *Old Swedish and Old Gutnish*: Noreen (1904).
- *Old Danish*: Brøndum Nielsen (1950–1957).
- *Modern Danish*: Some dialect forms from the collections of the *Institut for dansk dialektforskning*.
- *Old High German*: Braune – Mitzka (1967); Schatz (1927), and the *Althochdeutsches Wörterbuch*.
- *Middle High German*: In many of the higher numerals a great number of different forms are theoretically possible; thus, for instance, those produced by combining each possibility for each of the two parts of the decads. We give only forms actually recorded in Mausser (1932), Paul – Mitzka (1966), and the *Mittelhochdeutsches Handwörterbuch* (Lexer 1872–1878).
- *Old Saxon*: Gallée (1910); Sehrt (1925).
- *Middle Low German*: Lasch (1914) and the *Mittelniederdeutsches Wörterbuch*.
- *Salic Law*: van Helten (1900).
- *Old East Low Franconian*: van Helten (1902).
- *Middle Dutch*: Franck (1910) and the *Middelnederlandsch Woordenboek*.
- *Old Frisian*: van Helten (1890).
- *Modern Frisian*: Århammar (1968); Möllencamp (1968); Löfstedt (1933) and Spenter (1968).
- *Anglo-Saxon*: Campbell (1959); Cosijn (1872–1873); *An Anglo-Saxon dictionary* (Bosworth – Toller 1889–1892) and *Supplement* (Toller 1921); *Oxford English dictionary*.
- *Middle English: Middle English dictionary* (MED) and *Oxford English dictionary* (OED). Surprisingly, as yet no comprehensive accidence of Middle English has been written. We have found it useful to quote, where possible forms from the *Ormulum*,[4a] *the Ayenbite of Inwyt* and the *Language AB*, for these three different types of Middle English are standardized.[4b]
- *Middle Scots*: We have made use of *A dictionary of the older Scottish tongue* (Craigie 1931).

In the case of numeral derivatives, if a Modern English form descends regularly from a quoted Old English form, we sometimes omit the corresponding Middle English form. We may note here that many pronunciations of numeral forms which differ in origin from those of present-day English are attested in earlier periods of Modern English. For the most part we do not discuss these here; they may be assembled from Dobson (1957: index of words).

– *Modern dialects*: We have been able to make but little use of these. With labour, the numeral forms of many Germanic dialects could be extracted – for instance, from the very numerous High German dictionaries and studies, but often such forms cannot be safely related to earlier ones. It may indeed be a generation or so before the numeral forms of the modern dialects can be comprehensively treated. But one modern Germanic language would have been entirely left out of consideration, if we had not taken some account of modern dialects. We refer to Modern Low German. This has, of course, no standard form, but is constituted by a conglomerate of dialects. In his little book *Plattdeutsche Mundarten* (1922), H. Grimme gives, throughout, forms from four selected dialects – those of Assinghausen, Ostbevern, Heide in Dithmarschen, and Stavenhagen, and we often use numerals forms from these dialects here. For Modern English dialects we have used *English dialect grammar* (Wright 1905: index), and for Scots *Scottish national dictionary*.

15.0.2. In most of the later Germanic languages the nominal flexion has been greatly reduced. In English, gender has been lost; in some other later Germanic languages (e. g., Danish and Dutch), the three original genders have been reduced to two, common and neuter. These processes have their effects on the numerals.

15.1. Cardinals

15.1.0. 'One' is essentially a normal adjective. 'Two', 'both', and 'three' have special declensions. Before a noun, 'five' to 'twelve' do not decline; in other positions they usually do – originally, according to the *i*-declension.[5] 'Four' has a special declension in Norse, but belongs to the indeclinable 'five' to 'twelve' class in Gothic and West Germanic. 'Thirteen' to 'nineteen' also belong essentially to this class. The decads 'hundred', 'thousand', 'million', etc., are, by origin, nouns, but for the most part these numerals have, in attributive function, become indeclinable adjectives, though they decline – as nouns – in non-attributive function. 'Eleven' and 'twelve' are special formations. In 'thirteen', 'fourteen', 'twenty', 'thirty' and 'forty', the first element was originally inflected,[6] and various cases have crystallized out. In 'fifteen', 'nineteen', the first element is the normal uninflected cardinal.

15.1.0.1. *i*-inflection

In non-attributive use the cardinals 'five' to 'nineteen' were originally *i*-stems, and this state of affairs is attested in Gothic: *ainlibim* 'eleven', *fimftaihunim* 'fifteen'. When it became indeclinable (see 15.1.4.2.), 'four' was added to this group in Gothic *fidworim*.

In Norse, the inflection of this *i*-group has vanished;[7] this is no doubt simply due to the influence of the uninflected attributive forms. In West Germanic, 'four' is, as in Gothic, added to this *i*-group. The *i*-inflection – which, naturally, causes umlaut – remains at first, but, in the later languages, as is normal with *i*-nouns, is not distinct from that of *a*-nouns. A nominative-accusative plural neuter is added, on the model of the adjectives. Hence, for instance, the Old High German and Middle Dutch paradigms of 'four':

	Old High German masc.-fem.	Old High German neuter	Middle Dutch all genders
nom.-acc	*fiori*	*fioriu, fioru*	*viere*
gen.	*fioreo, fioro*		*vierre*
dat.	*fiorim, fiorin*[8]		*vieren*[9]

With the Old High German paradigm compare the plural of the masculine and feminine *i*-stems; nom. acc. *gesti*; gen. *gesteo, gestio, gesto, gestim, gestin, gesten* to *gast* 'guest'; and nom. acc. *ensti*; gen. *ensteo, enstio, ensto*, dat. *enstim, enstin, ensten* to *anst* fem. 'favour'; with the nominative-accusative plural neuter, cf. nominative-accusative neuter *blintiu, blintu* to adj. *blint* 'blind'. The Middle Dutch paradigm is the same as that of old *i*-stems, masculine and feminine, except for the genitive, which is adjectival (*-re*).

Naturally, there was much analogical interaction between the uninflected attributive forms and the *i*-inflected non-attributive forms. Thus we have the type **siƀun* (uninflected) 'seven' from **seƀun* (uninflected)[10] + **siƀuni* (*i*-inflected). Cross-influencing of this type is prominent in Middle High German. Here there are three kinds of short *e*, distinguished in the grammars as *e* (closed), *ë* (open) and *ä* (very open). The first, *e*, is the normal umlaut of *a* (nom.-acc. plural *geste* < OHG *gesti*); *ë* derives from PGmc. *e* (*gëben* = *gefa* 'to give'); *ä* is a later *i*-umlaut of *a* which took place under special conditions – only one of these is relevant to the numerals and that is the case of first-syllable *a* umlauted by third-syllable *i* (*ärze* 'ore' < OHG *aruzzi* – Paul 1901: § 40 n. 2.2), *e* often appears instead of *ë* when followed by *i* in the next syllable (Paul 1901: § 43 n. 3.1). In the manuscripts *e* and *ë* are not kept distinct, while *ä* sometimes appears as such, sometimes as *e*. The distinction between the three *e*s made in the grammars is based on this last feature, on rhymes, and on the developments in the modern dialects.[11] In the numerals we have *sehs* 'six' (beside *sëhs*) from inflected OHG *sëhsi* (> MHG *sehse*) – as against *sëhzëhen* 'sixteen', *sëhzec* 'sixty' (but *sehste* 'sixth'); and *zehen* 'ten', *-zehen* '-teen' (beside *zëhen, -zëhen*): inflected OHG *zëheni* (< **zehani*). It is not possible to decide whether Mod. HG *sechs, zehn, -zahn* derive from forms with *ë* or *e*, or, as is more probable, from both. Note further inflected MHG *ähte* 'eight', OHG *ahtouui*.

Originally *i*-inflected non-attributive forms can occur in attributive function, replacing or standing beside the original uninflected forms. The occurrence of these is somewhat sporadic. The use is not uncommon in Middle Low German (as *sesse* 'six'); see Lasch (1914: § 397 n.2.). It also occurs – with normal adjectival endings – in Old English, in the dialects of Northumbria and Rushworth (*fīfo* 'five' Lindisfarne Gospels); see Campbell (1959: § 683). Also, Modern English *five* descends from inflected OEngl. *fīfe*, not from the uninflected OEngl. *fīf*. Cf., further, Crimean Gothic *sevene* 'seven', *nyne* 'nine', and *thiine* 'ten'.[12]

15.1.1. 'One'

In the main, the Germanic forms descend from PGmc. **aena/ō* Gothic *ains*;[13] Icel. *einn*; Færoese *ein*; Mod. Norw. *ein*; OSwed. *ēn, en æn* (Noreen 1904: § 80.II.2), *in* (Noreen 1904: §§ 103.1, 146.1); OGut. *ann* (Noreen 1904: § 124.1); Mod. Swed. *en*; ODanish *ēn*, with dialectal diphthongization *ien, iæn* (Brøndum Nielsen 1950–1957: § 186.1) – also *ĕn æn* (Brøndum Nielsen 1950–1957: § 163.2), *in* (Brøndum Nielsen 1950–1957: § 145.2); Mod. Danish *en*; OHG *ein*; MHG *ein*; Mod. HG *ein*; OSax. *ēn*; MLG *ên*; LG *ę^{i}n* Assinghausen – *ę^{i}n* Ostbevern, Heide

(Dithmarschen), *aⁱn* Stavenhagen; MDutch *een*, very rarely *ein*; Mod. Dutch *een*; OEngl. *ān*. In Middle English this last form is shortened to *ăn* (Ormulum *ann*) in unstressed position (Luick 1921–1940: § 354.1); under stress, it remains for a time (Ormulum *an*), and this form persists in the north – hence Mod. Scots *ane* (also regionally *een* and *yin*)[14] – while in the south it becomes *ǭn* (Ayen. *on*). In late Middle English this last gives *wǭn* (Luick 1921–1940: § 435.1), which later becomes *wō̹n*; from the former there derives the Midland Standard pronunciation of the numeral, [*wʌn*] etc. (see Wright 1905: index: *one*), from the latter Mod. Engl. *one* [*wʌn*] (so Dobson 1957: §§ 37, 429). There is loss of *n*, both in stressed and unstressed position (Jordan 1925: § 172), the former in Middle English *ǭ*, Middle Scots *ā*, Mod. Scots *ae* (also, regionally, *yae*), the latter in MEngl. *a*,[15] Mod. English *a*.

15.1.1.1. There is also evidence of apparent *i*-inflection. This is perhaps clearest in Old English acc. sing. masc. *ĕnne* < *ǣ̆nne* < *ǣnne* (Campbell 1959: § 193d) < **aininō* or **ainjanō*.[16] In North Northumbrian, *ĕnne* is also used as a nominative (Ross 1937: n. 280).

This is also the case in Frisian. On the mainland and in the north we have the development *ă* < *ǣ̆i* < PGmc. *ai* with umlaut and shortening (Löfstedt 1933: 23), whereas in Old East Frisian the shortening of the unumlauted form yields *ănne*. The feminine and neuter is **ǣn*, **ēn*. The distinction between masculine and feminine-neuter is preserved in *aen'een* Upgant, *aan'een* Saterland, *ohn'eyhn* Harlingen, *ân'ain* Wangeroog,[17] *åån'iin(j)* in all mainland north Frisian dialects, *ään/ian* Föhr and Amrun. In West Frisian the feminine-neuter form has been generalized: *ien*; similarly *iaan* Helgoland, *jen* Sylt.

In Gothic the compositional vowel of both *a*- and *ō*-stems is normally *-a-*: *figgra-gulþ* 'ring' to *figgrs* 'finger', *aírþa-kunds* 'of earthly nature' to *aírþa* 'earth'. In this respect the *i*-stems with long root-syllable alternate between *-i-* and *-ø-*: *naudi-bandi* 'fetter' to *nauþs* 'compulsion', *brūþ-faþs* 'bridegroom' to *brūþs* 'bride'. There are however occasional examples of *-ø-* for normal *-a-*: *wein-drugkja* 'wine-bibber' (beside *weina-basi* 'grape') to *wein* 'wine' and *laus-handja* (weak) 'empty-handed' (beside *lausa-waurdei* κενοφωνία) to *laus* 'empty' (see Carr 1939: 275 ff.), *ainfalþs* 'simple', *ainfalþei* 'simplicity' – as well as dative *ainlibim* 'eleven' (15.1.11.0.) – might suggest a stem **aini-*, though *aina-baúr* 'only begotten' and *aina-mundiþa* ἑνότησ must represent **aina/ō-*. But *ain-* could be explained from this last as exactly parallel to *laus-* in *laus-handja*.

In Old English, the first element of 'eleven' must be taken as **aini-* (15.1.11.5.). There are other Anglo-Saxon compounds of 'one' with *ǣn-*

as the first element and with parallel forms in *ān-: ǣnlic, ānlic* 'peerless', *ǣn-liēpe, ān-liēpe* (also *ǣn-liēpig, ān-liēpig*) 'solitary'.[18] But we cannot take the *ān*-forms (as if from **ana/ō-*) as original and the *ǣn*-forms as analogical because there are not enough suitable forms in the normal paradigm of 'one' to account for the analogy – only acc. sing. masc. *ǣnne* (above) and instr. sing. *ǣne* (< **ainī*, a form normal in the *a/ō*-paradigm). The *ǣn*-forms must therefore be original – they are satisfactorily explained from **aini-* – and the *ān*-forms analogical.[19] In Modern Frisian compounds the feminine-neuter form is the rule[20] (and cf. OFrisian *ênfald* 'simple') – but these are late formations.[21] It is natural to consider another anomalous form in conjunction with PGmc. acc. sing. masc. **aininō*; just as this exists beside the normal **ainanō*, so, too, does acc. sing. masc. **mīninō* 'mine' beside the normal **mīnanō*. The first form is attested by Runic Norse (Kjølevig) acc. sing. masc. *minino* (Jóhannesson 1923: no. 33). And it is the case that, while some Germanic forms of this part of the two words must derive from those with ending *-anō* (e.g., Gothic *ainana, meinana*; OHG *einan, mînan*), others could as well derive from those with ending *-inō*, e.g., Icel. *einn, minn*; OSwed. *ē̆n, min*; ODanish *ēn, min*; OSax. *ênna*; OEnglish *mīnne*.

Clearly **aini-*, **mīni-* cannot be of Proto-Indo-European age; for the formation of **mīna/ō*, see Brugmann – Delbrück (1897–1916: II.i.274, 277). Further, there is clearly no reason to suggest that 'one' influenced 'mine' or vice versa. The *i*-forms thus remain entirely obscure.

15.1.1.2. In Germanic, 'one' is, essentially, a normal *a/ō*- adjective. The details of its paradigm are well discussed in the grammars, so here we only observe upon a few points. The word is very generally declined weak in the sense 'alone'; for instance, in Scandinavian. Here, too, it can, in this sense, form a superlative: Icel. *einasta* adverb 'solely' (Modern Icelandic also has an indeclinable adjective 'only'); Færoese *einasta*; Mod. Norwegian *einaste*; Færoese *einastur* 'sole'; OSwed. *ēnaster*; ODanish *ēnastær* (Brøndum Nielsen 1950–1957: § 541 n. 3); Mod. Danish *eneste*.

In some of the later Germanic languages the paradigm has been considerably altered by sound-change. Thus, in the genitive and dative singular feminine, there is sometimes the assimilation *nr* > *rr* (> *r*, with lack of stress); shortening of the vowel, due to this same cause, is also common. Hence MLG *êre, erre, er* (Lasch 1914: § 242); Middle Dutch *êrre, erre, ere* – also *erer* with additional adjectival *-er*;[22] Middle English dat. sing. fem. *āre ǭre* (< OEngl. *ānre*). Similarly, in Middle Low German, with assimilation *nm* > *mm*, dat. sing. masc. *ênem(e)* > *emme*.[23]

15.1.2. 'Two'

15.1.2.0. Preliminary note

The nominative-accusative plural – and, possibly, the dative plural – of the definite article are, in many respects, parallel to 'two' and the second element of the compounded forms of 'both' and, indeed, may have influenced the former. It will therefore be convenient to discuss here – very briefly – these parts of the paradigm of the definite article in the earlier Germanic languages. See Streitberg (1896: § 187), van Helten (1906: 87 ff.), Brugmann – Delbrück (1897–1916: II.ii.355 ff.), and cf. Noreen (1913: § 204).

15.1.2.0.1. Nominative masculine PGmc. **þae* > Gothic *þai*; Runic Swedish *þai*; OSwed. *þē* (in part – Noreen 1913: § 204.11); OHG *dê*, OSax. *thê*; OFrisian *thâ*; OEngl. *þā*. In Scandinavian, *R* is added from the adjectives: Runic Swedish *þaiR*; OIcel. *þeir*; OSwed. *þēr* > *þē*;[24] OGut. *þair*; Runic Danish *þeR*; ODanish *thē* (Brøndum Nielsen 1950–1957: § 399 n. 5). OHG *dea, dia, die* < *dê*, by diphthongization (see Sievers 1876: 116 ff.). OSax. *thie* from *thê* + nom. acc. pl. fem. *thia*, nom. acc. pl. neuter *thiu*; OSax. *thia* from *thie* with adjectival *-a*; then *thea* beside this *thia* because *thea* exists beside *thia* in the nominative-accusative feminine Old East Low Franc. *thia* similar to OSax. *thia*.

15.1.2.0.2. Accusative masculine PGmc. **þanz* > Gothic *þans*; OIcel. *þá* (Noreen 1923: § 299.5 and cf. §§ 277.c, 122); OSwed. *thā* (Noreen 1904: §§ 249.6, 86). This case has been replaced by the nominative form in West Germanic, and by those of the dative and nominative in Old Danish (Brøndum Nielsen 1950–1957: § 574.B.1.6).

15.1.2.0.3. Nominative-accusative feminine[25] PGmc. **þōz* > Gothic *þos*. The vowel is shortened to *ă* in the rare Old Saxon form *tha*, and this same development has taken place in Norse: Runic Norse (Einang) acc. fem. *þaR* (Jóhannesson 1923: no. 16); then lengthening of the vowel under suitable stress-conditions (Noreen 1913: §§ 46d, 38b), hence OSwed. *þār þā*, and, with *R*-umlaut, OIcel. *þǽr*. A similar development took place in Anglo-Frisian: **þōz* > **þă* (cf. OSax. *tha*) > **þā*; hence OFrisian *thâ*; OEngl. *þā*.

Noreen (1913: § 204.12) tentatively suggests that Runic Norse (Istaby) acc. fem. *þaiaR* (Noreen 1923: appendix 31) should be brought into connection with nom.-acc. fem. dat. OInd. *tē* (< PIE **tai*); that is, then, nom.-acc. fem. *þaiaR* from **þae* (< PIE **tai*) + *þāR*. This suggestion receives support from Old Saxon. Here the normal nominative-accusative feminine form is *thê*, and there is no reason to suppose that this is, by origin, merely the masculine form. It could, however well derive from this dual form, **þae*. Norse nom. acc. fem. *þaiaR* continues; it gives Old East Norse **þēar*, whence, with contraction (cf. Noreen 1913: § 167b),[26] OSwed. *þēr þē*, ODanish *thē*; OIcel. nom. fem. *þeir* < **þæi* (< **þae*) + *þāR*, doubtless reinforced by nom. masc. *þeir*.

From PIE **tyo* (cf. OInd. *tyá*, 'that', Pokorny 1959: 1087): nom.-acc. sing. fem. **þiōz*, whence by analogy with *e*-forms in the main paradigm (such as dat. sing. masc. neuter OHG *dëmu*, OSax. *themu*), **þeōz* > OHG *deo, dio*, and, with adjectival *-a*, OSax. *thea, thia*; OSax. *thie* because this exists beside *thia* in the nominative plural masculine; Old East Low Franc. *thia*, similarly to OSax. *thia*.

15.1.2.0.4. Nominative-accusative neuter PGmc. **þō* > Gothic *þo*. The Scandinavian forms have not been satisfactorily explained. Noreen (1913: § 204.13) seeks their origin in the nominative-accusative masculine dual PIE **tow* (> OInd. *tắu*) > PGmc. **þau*, taken, in Norse, as nominative-accusative plural neuter because of the *-u* in this case of the adjecives. And this view is surely right. The long diphthong can develop in two ways — to PGmc. *ō* before a consonant, elsewhere to *a* (Streitberg 1896: §§ 85–86). Hence PGmc. **þō* (anteconsonantal), indistinguishable from nominative-accusative neuter **þō* just mentioned, and **þau*. From this latter: OIcel. *þau*; Runic Swedish *þau*; OSwed. *þō̄* (cf. Noreen 1904: § 123.2); Runic Danish *þau*.

Noreen mentions Runic Swedish *þa* but does not explain it. However, he does explain (Noreen 1913: § 215.2) the apparently parallel form of 'two', nominative-accusative neuter OIcel. *tuá*, OSwed. *twa*, as equal to Gothic *twa*. But his explanation is obviously quite untenable (see below).[27] Van Helten (1906: 87–88) unites OIcel *þau* and Runic Swed. *þa* (which he takes as *þā*) by deriving the latter directly from PGmc. **þō* — and **þā-u* (> OIcel. *þau*) with adjectival *-u*. But his postulated derivation **þā* < **þō* is in complete opposition to the accepted views as to the development of such as PGmc. *ō* in Norse.

The Norse difficulties may be considered to centre in Runic Swed. *þa*; this is reinforced by the 'this'-form, Runic Swed. nominative-accusative neuter *þasi*, and, indirectly, by the certainly parallel OIcel. *tuá*, OSwed. *twā* already mentioned.

There is really no doubt about the development of *ō* in Norse. When stressed, final *-ō* gives *-ū*: Icel. acc. sing. *kú* 'cow' = OSax. *kô* (Brøndum Nielsen 1950–1957: § 98). Unstressed *ō* develops in two different ways according to its situation: to *ă*, as in nom.-acc. fem. *þaR* already considered, or to *ŭ*, and it is certain that, in the final position, it is the *ŭ*-

development that takes place; under suitable stress-conditions this *u* may be lengthened (Noreen 1913: § 38). The equation nominative-accusative singular feminine Gothic *so* (definite article) = OIcel. *sú*, Runic Danish *sū* may thus be interpreted in two ways: either PGmc. **sō* > ON **sū* under stress; or PGmc. **sō* > ON **sŭ* in unstressed position, then **sū* by lengthening.

We suggest the following solution of the Norse forms. **þōu* > **þău*, with *a*-development of the unstressed *ō*; **þō* > **þŭ*, with *u*-development of unstressed *ō*. The **þŭu* from **þŭ* with added adjectival *-u*. Then **þă* by the analogy **þă*: **þŭ*: **þău*: **þŭu*. By contraction **þŭu* > **þŭ* (cf. Noreen 1923: § 130); by lengthening under stress (cf. Noreen 1913: § 46a) **þă* > **þā*, **þŭ* > **þū* – which last is thus identical with both the end-product of **þŭu* and a possible development **þō* > **þū*. OIcel. *þau*, Runic Swed. *þau*, OSwed. *þȫ*, Runic Danish *þau* < **þau*. Runic Swed. *þa* as *þă* or *þā*. **þū* and/or **þŭ* may survive in the 'this'-forms nominative-accusative neuter Runic Swed. *þusi*, Runic Danish *þusi*,[28] but has otherwise died out.

15.1.2.0.5. The Old High German nominative-accusative neuter *dei* occurs only in early texts (see Schatz 1927: § 421). This is clearly to be brought into connection with the Old Indic nominative-accusative neuter dural *té̆*. But OHG *dei* cannot be derived directly from PGmc. **þae* < PIE **tai*, for **þae* must give an OHG **dê*; cf. OHG *wê* = Latin *uae* (see Braune – Mitzka 1967: § 43 n. 3). A form **þaeu*, with adjectival *-u*, is therefore suggested by van Helten (1905–1906: 90); the *-u* would of course be lost after the long syllable in West Germanic, but OHG *dei* would then be regular. **þaeu* could also account for the nominative-accusative neuter OSwed. *þē*, ODanish *thĕ* (shortened from **thē*); OFrisian *thâ*; OEngl. *þā* – though all these could as well be derived from the unextended **þae*.

OSwed. *þōn, þēn*, Runic Danish *þaun*, with the nominative-accusative plural article (OSwed. *-in -en*, ODanish *-in -en*) must be added to the forms discussed above.[29]

From *a*-stem **tyo-* (above): PGmc. **þiō* > **þiu* > OSwed. *þȳ* (cf. Noreen 1904: § 122.2a); OHG *diu*; OSax. *thiu*, and *thia* with adjectival *-a*, then, because *thea, thie* exist beside *thia* in both the nominative-accusative plural masculine and the nominative-accusative plural feminine, these two forms came to be used in the neuter also. Old East Low Franc. *thia* is to be explained similarly to OSax. *thia*.

15.1.2.0.6. Dative OFrisian *thâ* = Old Indian instrumental masculine neuter plural *tā́iḥ* (van Helten 1889: 280). PGmc. **þaimiz* > OEngl. *þǽm*;

PGmc. *_þaemuz_, *_þaemaz_ [30] > OFrisian _thâm_, Hunsiger Laws (Hoekstra 1950), Rüstringen (Buma 1954: § 11e); OEngl. _þām_. From any or all of these protoforms: Gothic _þaim_; OIcel. _þeim_; OSwed. _þēm_; OGut. _þaim_; ODanish _thēm_; OHG _dêm, dên_; OSax. _thêm, thên_; Old East Low Franc. _thēn_.

15.1.2.1. Proto-Indo-European nom.-acc. masc. *_dwow_ > PGmc. *_twau_; *_twō_ (15.1.2.0.4.); Proto-Indo-European nom.-acc. fem.-neuter *_dwoy_ > PGmc. *_twae_.

In view of the nom.-acc. pl. neuter PGmc. *_þō_, PGmc. *_twō_ must have appeared to be a nominative-accusative plural neuter; in North and West Germanic, PGmc. *_twau_ must also have appeared to be this case – with, as it were, an added adjectival _-u_ – and this phenomenon will have been reinforced by the situation of PGmc. *_þau_ (15.1.2.0.4.). On the other hand, in view of the nom. masc. PGmc. *_þae_, PGmc. *_twae_ must have appeared to be a nominative plural masculine. Hence, then, the resulting distribution Proto-Germanic nom. masc. *_twae_, nom.-acc. neuter *_twau_, *_twō_. But the transference just described was not absolute, for PGmc. *_twae_ also survived in its feminine and neuter function – as a nominative-accusative plural, no doubt reinforced as to the neuter by the Proto-Germanic nom.-acc. pl. neuter *_þae_ (15.1.2.0.4.). In Proto-Germanic the dative of 'two' was undoubtedly *_twaimiz_, *_twaemuz_, *_twaemaz_ (see Ross 1954: 118).

The paradigm nom. masc. *_twae_, nom.-acc. neuter *_twō_ dat. *_twaimiz_, etc., was thus exactly similar to that of the definite article: nom. pl. masc. *_þae_, nom.-acc. pl. neuter *_þō_, dat. pl. *_þaimiz_, etc. – and also to that of the adjective: Gothic nom. pl. masc. _blindai_, nom.-acc. pl. neuter _blinda_ < *_blindō_, dat. pl. _blindaim_ 'blind'. It is therefore not surprising that two new case-forms were created on the analogy of the definite article and the adjectives, namely acc. masc. *_twanz_ (cf. Gothic acc. pl. masc. _þans, blindans_) and nom.-acc. fem. *_twōz_ (cf. Gothic nom.-acc. pl. fem. _þos, blindos_). There remains the genitive: PIE *_dwoyous_ with the ending replaced by that of the genitive plural, hence *_dwoyōm_ > PGmc. *_twajǭ_ (see Ross 1954: 119).

We are now in a position to discuss the individual forms.

15.1.2.2. Nominative masculine. PGmc. *_twae_ > Gothic _twai_. With Norse development exactly parallel to that of PGmc. *_þae_ set out in 15.1.2.0.1., which latter development no doubt influenced that of *_twae_: Icel. _tveir_; Færoese _tveir_;[31] Modern Norwegian _tveir_ Nordhordland, _tvei_ (15.1.2.0.4.) Setesdall; Runic Swedish _tuaiR_; OSwed. _twēr, twē_ (15.1.2.0.4.); OGut. _tueir_;[32] ODanish _twē_ (15.1.2.0.4.). The form survives in Modern Dutch dialects: Goeree *twie*, Overflakkee *twji*, Maastricht *twie* (Weijnen 1966: 297).

15.1.2.3. Accusative masculine. PGmc. **twanz*, with a development exactly parallel to that of PGmc. **þanz* set out in 15.1.2.0.2.: Gothic *twans*; OIcel. *tuá*; Mod. Icel. *tvo* (Þórólfsson 1925: XI–XII); (Brøndum Nielsen 1950–1957: § 155) > *tō* (Brøndum Nielsen 1950–1957: § 384) > Mod. Danish *to* (> Mod. Norw. *to*).

15.1.2.4. Nominative-accusative feminine. PGmc. **twōz* > Gothic *twos*. The orthography of the Old High German forms causes some difficulty. Schatz (1927: § 408.2.) gives the following written forms: *zo, zwo, zuuô, zuo, zuuo*. Of these the first two can only mean *zô* and *zwô*, respectively. The third must mean *zwô*, too. But, at first sight, the fourth could mean either *zwô* or *zuo* (no [*w*] and diphthong) and the fifth either *zwô* or *zwuo* ([*w*] and diphthong). At first sight, then, there are four possible spoken forms: *zô, zwô, zwuo, zuo* (the last two with diphthong). The first two are certain – the second continues as MHG *zwô*. Schatz (1927: §§ 26, 408.2) makes it clear that the diphthong appears nowhere in these Old High German forms. We thus have to explain only OHG *zô* and *zwô* – the latter gives, in part, MHG *zwuo* (> *zwue*, cf. Mausser 1932: 245, and also *zwuu*, cf. Mausser 1932: 859). OHG *zwô* is developed from **twōz* with no diphthongization because of lack of stress (cf. Braune – Mitzka 1967: § 38 n. 1 and n. 2); *zô* shows loss of *w* before *ô* (Schatz 1927: § 284). Forms of the same development: OSax. *twô*; MLG *tô* with loss of *w*, then *twô* from this last + nom.-acc. masc. *twêne*, nom.-acc. neuter *twey, twê* (so Lasch 1914: § 299.2.); *tu, twu* are, essentially, orthographic variants (see Lasch 1914: § 160).

There is another development of PGmc. **twōz*, namely one similar to that of PGmc. **þōz* set out 15.1.2.0.3.: Icel. *tvær*; Færoese *tvær*; Mod. Norw. *tvær, tvæ*; OSwed. *twār, twā*; ODanish *twār, twā* > *twō, tō*, as the accusative masculine above; OHG *zwâ*; MHG *zwâ*; OSax. *twâ*; MLG *twâ*; Saterland *tuâ*; OFrisian *twâ*; OEngl. *twā*.

PGmc. **twae*, with a Norse development exactly parallel to that of PGmc. **þae* set out in 15.1.2.0.3. Old Icel. nom.-acc. fem. *tveir* (reinforced by nom. masc. *tueir*; Old Swed. nom. fem. *twēr*).

15.1.2.5. Nominative-accusative neuter. PGmc. **twō* > OIcel. *tú*; OSwed. *tū*;[33] Mod. Swed. *tu*: ODanish *tū*; Mod. Danish *tu* in *itu* 'in pieces' – *tu* survives in the dialect of Als (Bennike – Kristensen 1898–1912: 165).[34] In Anglo-Saxon, there are two developments of Proto-Germanic final stressed *ō*; the normal one is to *ū* – cf. OEngl. *cū* 'cow' = OSax. *kô*; but in OEngl. *tō* 'to' = OSax. *tô* (cf. Latin *donec*), the *ō* remains (see Campbell 1959: § 122). Hence, with the first development: OEngl. *tū*;[35] MEngl. *tu tow*; early Mod. English *tow*. And, with the second development: OEngl. **twō*[36] (cf. Lindisfarne Gospels *tuoge*, 15.1.2.8.).

PGmc. **twau*, with Norse development exactly parallel to that of PGmc. **þau* set out in 15.1.2.0.4.: OIcel. *tuau*;[37] Mod. Icel. *tvö* (Þórólfsson 1925: XX); Færoese *tvey*; Mod. Now. *tvau*. There is another development of PGmc. **twau* – to ON **twă* or **twā*, because of the analogies **twă* (or **twā*): **twău* : **þă* (or **þā*)[38]: **þău* – hence, from ON **twā*, or lengthened from ON **twă*, we have OIcel. *tuá*.[39]

PGmc. **twaeu*, exactly parallel to **þaeu* (15.1.2.0.5.) > OHG *zwei*; MHG *zwei*; Mod. High German *zwei*.[40] From this protoform and/or PGmc. **twae* (cf. 15.1.2.0.5. **þae*): OSax. *twê*; MLG *twe^i*;[41] Mod. LG *twę^i* – Assinghausen *twe^i*; Ostbevern, Heide (Dithmarschen) *twa^i*; Stavenhagen Saterland *tue*; MDutch *twee* (> *twie*, cf. Franck 1910: § 75); Mod. Dutch *twee*; OFrisian *twâ*; Mod. Frisian *twa* [*tva*:] West; OEngl. *twā*. Gothic *twa* (Crimean Gothic *tua*), instead of the expected **two* (cf. *þo*), is due to analogy with the adjectives: *twa* beside nom. masc. *twai*, acc. masc. *twans*, nom.-acc. fem. *twos*, dat. *twaim*, just as nom.-acc. pl. neuter *blinda* beside nom. pl. masc. *blindai*, acc. pl. masc. *blindans*, nom.-acc. pl. fem. *blindos*, dat. pl. *blindaim* to *blinds* 'blind'.[42]

15.1.2.6. Genitive. PGmc. **twajǭ*: Gothic *twaddje*, which is recorded as masculine (*twaddje manne δύο ἀνθρώπων* John 8, 17) and has the normal genitive plural *-e*, found in the masculine and neuter of many nouns, adjectives and pronouns.[43]

The protoform yields further: Icel. *tveggja*; Færoese *tveggja*; Old Norw. *tuæggia*; OSwed. *twæggia*[44] (which survives in Mod. Swed. *tveggehanda* 'of two kinds'); ODanish *twæggia*; OHG *zweiio*[45] *zweio*; OSax. *tweio*.

By analogy with the adjectives: OHG *zweiero*; MHG *zweier, zweiger*; Mod. HG *zweier*; MDutch *tweere*; OFrisian *twera*, Hunsinger Codex: III/153 (Hoekstra 1950: 153).

By analogy with the genitive of 'three': MHG *zwîer* (*drîer* – so Weinhold 1883: 336); MLG *twîger* (from **drîger*);[46] MDutch *twier* (from *drier*), *twijer* (from *drier*);[47] OFrisian *twira* (from *thrira*).

PGmc. **twōjǭ* from **twajǭ* + nom.-acc. neuter **twō* (above), nom.-acc. masc. **twōjinō* (below): OEngl. *twoega* (Vespasian Psalter Hymn 6/2); *twēga, twēgea*.

By analogy with the adjectives: OEngl. *tuoegra* (Rit. 115/28); *twoegera* (Lindisfarne Gospels 18va10); *twēgra twēgera*; MEngl. *tweire*.

15.1.2.7. Dative. PGmc. **twaimiz* > OEngl. *twǣ-m*, PGmc. **twaemuz* and/or **twaemaz* > OFrisian *twâm* (van Helten 1890: § 22x); OEngl. *twām twǭm*. The remaining Germanic forms can derive from any or all of these three protoforms: Gothic *twaim*; Icel. *tveimr, tveim* (Noreen 1923: § 277 n. 5); Færoese *tveimum* from **tveim* and adjectival *-um* (cf. definite article dative plural *teimum*); OSwed. *twēm*; OGut. *tuaim*;[48] ODanish *twēm* (with *tuœm* as an orthographic variant – Brøndum Nielsen 1950–1957: § 163 n. 1); OHG *zweim, zwein*;[49] MHG *zwein*;[50] OSax. *twêm, twên*; MLG *twên*; MDutch *tween*.

15.1.2.8. We turn next to the most difficult 'two'-form in Germanic – the West Germanic nominative-accusative masculine.[51] It is clear, first, that this is compounded, and, secondly, that OEngl. *twǣgen* is an umlauted form. Van Helten (1906: 91) suggests that this last is formed on OEngl. **þǣgen* 'both' (15.1.2.11.0.), and that this is from **þō-junu*: he regards the second element as OEngl. *geon*[52] (1906: 92) and proposes a development *-ju-* > *-jie-* > *-je-* > *-ji-* in it – the umlaut being due to the *j*. As the origin of OHG *zwêne* (instead of **zweine*, see below) the suggests **twaenae*, a mixture of nom. masc. **twae* and **aena/ō-*. Neither of these explanations is satisfactory, and, furthermore, they make OHG *zwêne* and OEngl. *twǣgen* unconnected – though this is not necessarily against them.

We now put forward an explanation which keeps these two forms connected, namely, that, ultimately, they derive from PIE nom.-acc. masc. dual **dwōw enōw*, in which the second word is the pronoun **eno/ā* (> Icel. *inn*, Greek ἕνη- Pokorny 1959: 319–321). In semi-stress, *ĕ* of this pronoun must have given PGmc. *ĭ*; cf. Runic Norse *ik* (beside *ek*) 'I' < PIE **eǵ* (Pokorny 1959: 291): Latin *ego*; see Streitberg (1896: § 65.1c). The dual form will give PGmc. **twau inau*; from this, **twō inau* (because of **twō* beside **twau*, 15.1.2.1.) and, then, **twō inō*, nom. pl. **twai inae* beside it will be a natural enough formation. We have no control for the phonology of this form. However, we suggest that, in part, **twaiinae* remained – as **twajinae*, while in part, the group *aii* was replaced by the phoneme PGmc. *aei* – no doubt by the route *aii* > *aī* > *ai* – hence **twaenae*. Then **twōjinae* from **twajinae* + **twō inō*; further **twaijinae* from **twōjinae* + **twaenae*. Hence also **twōjinō*, **twaijinō* from **twō-jinae*, **twaijinae* + **twō inō*.

We can now derive the actual forms.

In Proto-English, **twōjinō, *twaijinō* > *twǣjinu*, **twǣjinu* > **twǣjin*, **twǣjin* with loss of final *-u* postulated by van Helten (1906: 92–93).

PEngl. **twǣjin* > OEngl. *twǣgen*[53] > *twēgen*. PEngl. **twǣjin* > OEngl. *twǣgen* Ru^{1}.[54]
From either or both of these last two: MEngl. *tweien* (Ormulum *twezzenn*), *twein, twayn*; Mod. Engl. *twain*; and, with loss of final *-n* (Jordan 1925: § 170), MEngl. *tweie, twei* (Ayen *tuaye tuay*) *twie* (Jordan 1925: § 97); early Mod. Engl. *tway*.
PGmc. **twaenae* > Old East Low Franc. *tuēne*; OSax. *twêna* (with adj. *-a*); MLG *twêne*[55]; OFr. *twêne* (apocopated *twên* – van Helten 1890: § 233); Mod. Fr.: East *twäin* Saterland, *twain* Wangeroog; North: *tween* Hattstedt, Halligen. From OFr. *twên(e)* + gen. *twiro*, we have OFr. *tweer* > Mod. Fr. North Coast *twäär, twäir, tweer.*[56] The protoform could only give an OHG **zweine*; OHG *zwêne* is, then, from this latter + **zwê* (< **twae*); cf. the discussion above. Hence, directly, MHG *zwêne*; early Mod. HG *zween*; Bavarian *tswę̄n*. MHG nom.-acc. fem. *zwône* by analogy with nom.-acc. fem. *zwô* MHG *zweine* does not represent OHG **zweine* above, but is, rather, by analogy with gen. *zweier* (and nom.-acc. neuter *zwei*).

15.1.2.9. Further developments in Scandinavian

15.1.2.9.1. By sound change

1) Nom.-acc. fem. OIcel. *tueir* (15.1.2.4.), *tuér*.
2) Nom.-acc. neuter MNorw. *tuau* > *tuaug*, OSwed. *tū* > *tūgh* (15.1.7.4.).
3) Gen. ODanish *twæggia* > *twiggia.*[57a]
4) Forms of the genitive with weakened ending (Noreen 1904: § 144; Brøndum Nielsen 1950–1957: § 213): OSwed. *twæggæ, twæggie, twægge*; ODanish *tweggæ; twiggiæ, tuiggæ, twigge, twiggi.*[57b]
5) Gen. OSwed. *twiggia* (15.1.2.6.) > *tiggia*; the loss of *w* started in compounds such as *hwār-tiggia* 'neither' (Noreen 1904: § 252 n. 1).

15.1.2.9.2. By analogies within the paradigm

1) In Old Icelandic, because of nom.-acc. fem. *tuær* beside nom.-acc. fem. *tueir* (15.1.2.4.), nom.-masc. *tuær* came into being beside nom. masc. *tueir*. Similarly Mod. Norw. *tvær* (Nordhordland).
2) OIcel. acc. masc. *tuáa* from adjectival forms such as acc. masc. *gráa* to *grár* 'grey' (Jónsson 1925: 85).
3) OSwed. nom. masc. *twǣr, twǣ* from nom. masc. *twēr, twē* + gen. *twæggia*[57c] – so Noreen (1904: § 480 n. 1).

4) OSwed. nom. masc. *tuĕr* from nom. masc. *twēr* + dat. **tuæm* (= OGut. *tuem*, 15.1.2.7.).
5) OSwed. acc. masc. *twē* from acc. masc. *twā* + nom. masc. *twē*, dat. *twēm* (so Noreen 1904: § 480 n. 1).
6) In Old Swedish, because of nom. masc. *twǣ* (15.1.29.2.) beside nom. masc. *twē*, acc. masc. *twǣ* came into being beside acc. masc. *twē* (15.1.29.2.).
7) Gen. OEN **tuggjo* from **twaggjo* (> OSwed. *twæggia*) + nom. acc. neuter *tū*;[57c] hence OSwed. *annat-tyggia* 'either'; OGut. *tyggia* – so Noreen (1913: § 215.4).
15.1.2.9.3. In Old Swedish and Old Danish, because of the conflation of *twā* (> ODanish *twō tō*) as accusative masculine and nominative-accusative feminine, this form became dominant; it thus occurs also for the nominative masculine and nominative-accusative neuter and later (15.0.2.) for the other cases. So it is the parent of the modern forms, Mod. Swed. *två* and Mod. Danish *to*. The situation is somewhat similar in Norwegian; hence Mod. Norw. *tvo*, the form normal in most dialects.

15.1.2.10. Further developments in West Germanic

In the nominative-accusative there was conflation – of the feminine and neuter in Anglo-Frisian, and, as we suggest, of the masculine and neuter in Dutch. This, together with the decay of inflection in the later languages (15.0.2.), led to the dominance of certain forms.

OEngl. nom.-acc. fem. neuter *twā* remained in early Middle English (Ormulum *twa*, AB *twa*) and survived in the north; hence Mod. Scots *twae* and *twa* over a large part of northern and western Scotland, in which the *w* has prevented the fronting of the vowel (cf. *awa* 'away' and *wha* [beside *whae*] 'who'). In the south, *twā* gave *twǭ* (Ayen *tuo*) > *twǭ* (Luick 1921–1940: § 370) > *tǭ* (Jordan 1925: § 162.3) > Mod. English *two*. The loss of *w* was evidently not quite complete, for Bullokar has *twoo*,[58] which means [*twu*:] (Dobson 1957: § 421).

In Modern Frisian OFr. nom.-acc. fem. neuter *twâ* survives, beside the masculine (15.1.2.2.) as West: *twa* [*twa:*]; *twoo* Saterland; *two, twa* Harlingen, *twô* Wangeroog *towéh, twa* Wursten; North: *tuu(ch), tau(e)* Coast, *tau* Islands.

In Dutch, the position is somewhat different: *twee, twie* is invariant in the nom.-acc. – hence Mod. Dutch *twee* – and Franck (1910: § 232.2.) states that this is, by origin, the form of the neuter. But there must have been some reason why this became dominant.

The West Germanic *n*-form or the nominative-accusative masculine (15.1.2.8.) does not occur in Dutch;[59] there must have been something instead, and we suggest that this was the descendant of nom. masc. PGmc. **twae* (= Gothic *twai* (15.1.2.2.); this must have given Mod. Dutch **twee*, identical with the neuter. Hence, we may suppose, the dominance under discussion.

In High German the position is different again, for, in some dialects – west and south Oberdeutsch – the three genders are preserved distinct to this day; cf., f. i. Swabian masc. *tswēⁿ*, fem. *tswuo, tswō*,[60] neuter *tswǫe*; see further Schirmunski (1962: 348). In Swiss there are some dialects with three genders (masculine *zwē*, fem. *zwō*, neuter *zwei*), others with two (masculine fem. *zwē*, neuter *zwei*), others with no gender (Hotzenköcherle 1971: 304). Nom.-acc. neuter *zwei* begins to be used for the masculine and feminine as well as the neuter from the twelfth century (Mod. HG *zwei*); see Schirokauer (1923: 66).

A similar spread of the neuter is found in Low German; cf. late MLG *twey, twê* used for masculine and feminine (Lasch 1914: § 396, n. 4); some relevant Low German forms are given, as neuter, in 15.1.2.5.[61]

15.1.2.11. Both

15.1.2.11.0. The development is, in many respects, parallel to that of 'two'.

Nominative masc. PGmc. *ƀae* (cf. **twae*) > Gothic *bai.*

Acc. masc. **ƀanz* (cf. **twanz*) > Gothic *bans.*

Nom.-acc. fem. PGmc. **ƀōz* (cf. **twōz*) > OEngl. *ba.*

Nom.-acc. neuter PGmc. *ƀō* (cf. **twō*) > OEngl. *bū*; Gothic *ba*, cf. *twa.*

PGmc. **ƀaeu* and/or *ƀae* (cf. **twaeu*, **twae*) > OEngl. *bā.*[62]

Genitive. PGmc. **ƀajō* (cf. **twajǭ*) > Icel. *beggja*; Færoese *beggja*; ONorw. *beggia*; Mod. Norw. *beggje*; OSwed. bæggia > *bægge* (Noreen 1904: § 144) > Mod. Swed. bägge; ODanish *bæggia*;[63] Mod. Danish *begge.*

PGmc. **ƀōjǭ* (cf. **twōjǭ*) > OEngl. *bǣga* (Sweet 1885: charter no. 37/12) > *bēga, bēgea*. By analogy with the adjectives: OEngl. *boegera* (altered from *boegra*) Rit. 61/35;[64] *bēgra*; MEngl. *beire, beier.*

Dative. PGmc. **ƀaimiz* (cf. **twaimiz*) > OEngl. *bǣm*; PGmc. **ƀaemuz* and/or **ƀaemaz* (cf. **twaemuz* **twaemaz*) > OEngl. *bām*. Gothic *baim* can derive from any or all of these three protoforms.

Nom. masc. PEngl. **bæjin* (cf. **twæjin*) > OEngl. **bǣgen*[65] *begen*; MEngl. *beien* (Ormulum *beȝȝenn*) *beie.*

15.1.2.11.1. Compounded forms: Gothic

bajoþs, dat. *bajoþum*. Bartholomae (1890–1891: i, 61) suggests that this originates in a nom.-acc. masc. dat. *ƀajō þō*, the latter word being the definite article. Van Helten (1906: 93) says: "Dieser Fassung widersetzt sich der konsonantische Stamm des Wortes." He is right as to the consonantal inflection: dat. *bajoþum* points to this or *u*-inflection, and the latter is eliminated by neuter *bajoþs* (not **bajoþus*). He then suggests that the form derives from a **bho-iōtēs*, the latter element being from the root *ei* 'to go' (Pokorny 1959: 293 ff.). This is, however, a very unattractive suggestion.

bajoþs is reminiscent of Gothic *menoþs* 'month', for both words have an athematic *-oþ*-suffix. *Menoþs* derives from PIE **mēn-ōt-* (Pokorny 1959: 731–732), cf. Gothic *mena* 'moon', but the nature and function of the suffix is obscure. Indeed it seems to have little function, for the root itself can mean 'month' – OInd. *mās* means this as well as 'moon' (cf. Brugmann – Delbrück: 1897–1916: II.i.427). Is it possible that nom.-acc. fem. neuter *b^hoy* (cf. **dwoy*, 15.1.2.1.) was extended by a virtually meaningless suffix *ōt-* to give **ƀaēōþ-* > **bajōþ-*, and hence the Gothic form?

15.1.2.11.2. Compounded forms: Scandinavian

The definite article is used as the second element to form, originally, a loose compound. In the relevant parts PGmc. *ae^i* can develop in three ways:

a) To Icel. *ei*, ONorw. *æi*, OSwed. *ē*, OGut. *ai*, ODanish *ē* – the development normal in stress,

b) To PN *ā* in the pretonic position; cf. OIcel. *nakkuarr* 'some' (< **nākkwarR*); OSwed. *nākwar*; ODanish *nākuark* < **ne-wait-ek-hwáriR*.[66] We must suppose then that, in 'both', the main stress was originally on the definite article, but, after this development, was retracted to the first element.

c) To PN *ē* > *i* in unstressed position.[67]

We must also assume that, in the first element, *R* must have been lost before *þ* in the nominative-accusative feminine – a development for which there is no control – and this before the time of *R*-umlaut in West Norse, unless, with Brøndum Nielsen (1950–1957: § 608A), we assume that this case is a reformate (as the dative certainly is – see below). In concluding this introductory section, we may note that, to a considerable extent, unstressed *i* > *e* in "vokalbalanz" in Old Swedish (cf. Noreen 1904: § 142), and there is this, and also weakening (*a* > *e, æ*) in Old Danish (Brøndum Nielsen 1950–1957: §§ 204, 206 ff.).

Nominative masc. PN **ƀae þaeR* (in the event **ƀ-aeR þaeR*) > **bāþeR* (...) > Icel. *báðir*; Færoese *báðir*, OSwed. *bāþir, bāþi*;[68] ODanish *bāthi, bāthe*.

Acc. masc. PGmc. **ƀanz, þanz* (β) > Icel. *báða*; OSwed. *bāþa*; ODanish *bātha, bāthæ, bāthe*.

Nom.-acc. fem. PGmc. **ƀōz, þōz* > PN **bāþōR* (β) > Icel. *báðar*; Færoese *báðar*;[69] OSwed. *bāþar, bāþa*;[70] ODanish *bātha, bāthæ, bāthe*.

Nom.-acc. neuter[71] PGmc. **ƀae þiu*[72] > PN **bāþiu* > Icel. *bæði*; Færoese *bæði*, OSwed. *bǣþi*; OGut. *bēþi* (cf. Noreen 1904: § 105); ODanish *bǣthi, bǣthe*; further, with (a) OIcel. *beiþe*.

PGmc. **ƀō þiu* > OIcel. *bøþe*; Mod. Norw. *bøþe*.

OEN **bā þēn*[73] (βγ) > OSwed. *bāþen*[74] (by analogy ONorw. *báðen*); OGut. **bāþin*; ODanish (Skånsk) *bāthen*; from the first two + OSwed. *bǣþi*, OGut. *þēbi*, respecively, OSwed. *bǣþin* (ONorw. *bæðen*); OGut. *bēþin*.

Dative. This has been reformed in consonance with the declension of adjectives, on a stem *bāþ-* extracted from the relevant forms of the nominative and accusative: Icel. *báðum*, Færoese *báðum*, OSwed. *bābom*, ODanish *bāthum*.

Genitive. The uncompounded type (above) survives, but there is also an adjectival reformate, ONorw. *báðra*.

15.1.2.11.3. Further developments

15.1.2.11.3.1. By sound change

In late Old Danish, *ā* gives *o* and *aa* by rounding (Brøndum Nielsen 1950–1957: § 138); hence acc. masc., nom.-acc. fem. *bothæ*, acc. masc. *bothe*, nom.-acc. masc. *bodhæ*; acc. masc., nom.-acc. fem. *bodæ bode*; nom.-acc. masc., nom.-acc. fem. *baade*. Examples of the corresponding Swedish rounding (Noreen 1904: § 110) are not given for 'both' (Noreen 1904: § 481).[75]

15.1.2.11.3.2. Analogical changes in North Germanic

1) OEN nom.-acc. neuter **bāþi* from **bǣ-þi* + nom. masc. **bāþir* and other cases: OSwed. *bāþe* (by analogy ONorw. *báðe*); OGut. *bāþi*; ODanish *bāthi, bathe*.

2) OGut. nom. masc. *bēþir*, acc. masc. *bēþa*, nom.-acc. fem. *bēþar* – from **bāþir*, **bāþa*, **bāþar* (corresponding to the Old Swedish forms) + OGut. nom.-acc. neuter *bēþi, bēþin*.
3) Because, in Old Swedish, *bāþen* (< **bāþin*) exists beside *bāþi* in the nominative-accusative singular neuter, *bāþin* came to be used in the nominative masculine also.
4) OSwed. acc. masc. *bādan* from *bāþa* + nom. masc. *bāþin* (and nom.-acc. neuter *bāþen, bǣþin*?).
5) In Later East Norse *s* occurs in the genitive plural of nouns – it is borrowed from the singular (Noreen 1904: § 383 n. 11; Brøndum Nielsen 1950–1957: § 430.8). This feature is also found in 'both': OSwed. *bæggias, bægges*;[76] ODanish *bæggias, bægges, beggæs, begges, bæggis, beggis.*[77] Cf. also MNorw. *beggias* (a. 1429), *beggæs* (a. 1450), *beggis* (a. 1413).[78]
6) In late Old Swedish, a singular form is occasionally developed analogically: nom. masc. *bāþær*, dat. neuter *bādho*, nom. neuter *bāþe*, acc. neuter *bādhe* (weak, with *-e* for *-a*, cf. Noreen 1904: § 459.1).
7) In late East Norse, there is, naturally, some confusion of cases (15.0.2.); cf. OSwed. acc. masc. *bægge*, acc. fem. *bæggiaa* and *bæggiæ* (Noreen 1904: § 144); dat. *bāþe*, and, for Old Danish, see Brøndum Nielsen (1950–1957: § 608 n.1).
In Scandinavian, the nominative-accusative neuter is used as a conjunction ('both ... and'; see Brøndum Nielsen (1950–1957: § 608 n. 2). Hence, in this sense, Icel. *bæði* (ONorw. also *báðe*);[79] Færoese *bæði*; OSwed. *bæþe, bāþe*[80] (> *bādh*, Noreen 1904: § 156.1b), *bāþen*, also *bāþa*; ODanish *bǣthe, bāthe* (later, cf. § 15.1.2.11.3.1.: *boþe, bodhæ, bodæ, baadhe, baade*). In Modern Danish – except in some Jutland dialects – the numeral and conjunctional uses are morphologically distinct: the old genitive (*begge*) is used for the former, while *baade*, deriving from a generalized *bāthe*, is used for the latter. In Modern Norwegian, *både* and *beggje* are more or less synonymous, except that only the former can be used as a conjunction. In Modern Swedish, the old genitive (*bägge*) is purely numeral, while *både* is a conjunction. The form *båda*[81] can also be used for the numeral.

15.1.2.11.3.3. Analogical changes in West Germanic

Here, as in Norse, there is compounding with the definite article. The flexion of this latter can be said to remain to some extent in Old Saxon: nom.-acc. masc. *bedie, bedea*, nom.-acc. fem. *bedea, bethia*. Otherwise the whole word is declined as an adjective. The starting point is doubtless

PGmc. nom.-acc. neuter *ƀae þae, taken as nominative masculine plural. Hence nom.-acc. masc. OHG *beide* with *bêde* from this + **bê* > **ƀae* — see above; MHG *beide, bêde*; Mod. HG *beide*, OSax. *bêđia*; MLG *bêde beide*; MDutch *bêde, beide*;[82] Mod. Dutch *beide*. OFrisian *bêthe*, and also *beithe*, whose first element van Helten (1906: 93) derives from **ƀājō-* (cf. Gothic *bajoþs*). In Modern Frisian we have: *beide* West, *bee* Saterland, *baiδ* Wangeroog, *biise* East Moringen, *bial* Föhr, *bias* Amrum, *biir* Sylt, *beed* Helgoland.[83]

English has two sets of compounded forms. From 'both' + 'two': nom.-acc. fem. neuter *bātwā* (> MEngl. *bǭ twǭ*), nom.-acc. neuter *būtū*; from these two, also *būtā*, which is used for all three genders — the extension is parallel to that of *twā* and *bā* in later English (15.1.2.10., 15.1.2.11.); dat. *bām twām*.

From 'both' + the definite article: MEngl. *bāthe, bǭthe* (> Mod. Engl. *both*); *bāthen, bǭthen; bēthe* (> early Mod. Engl. *beath*) *beoth*; gen. *bāther*,[84] *bǭthere, bēthere, beithere, beither, bǭthes, bǭthens, bǭtheres.*[85] MED: *bǭthe* regards the word as exclusively English — from OEngl. *bā þā*; it is suggested that the forms with *-en* are due to the influence of *beien*, the genitival *r*-forms to that of gen. *beier*. The latter explanation is, in any case, not necessary, for the forms may simply be due to the paradigm of the normal adjective.[86]

MEngl. *bēthe* is not explained in MED; surely, as Björkman (1900—1902: 108) points out, it must be of Scandinavian origin (: Icel. nom.-acc. neuter *bæδi*, etc.). Indeed the whole English word could well be Scandinavian (so *OED*: *both*) — Icel. nom. masc. *báδir*, etc. Björkman (1900—1902) mentions ONorw. *báδra* in connection with the Middle English *r*-genitives — but, again, there is no necessity for this explanation. For *bāthen, bōthen*, cf. ODanish nom.-acc. neuter *bāthen.*[87] MEngl. gen. *beithere, beither* may well be due to analogy with gen. *beier*. It is of course very possible that the origin of the word may be in part English (as suggested by MED), in part Scandinavian — so d'Ardenne (1936: glossary) *bade*.

15.1.3. 'Three'

15.1.3.1. Nominative masc.[88] PIE **treyes* > PGmc. **þrīz* > Icel. *þrír*;[89] Mod. Norw. *tre*, pronounced *tri* (the spelling is Danish); OSwed. *þrīr þrī* (see note 24); Runic Danish *þrīR*; ODanish *thrī*; OHG *drî*; MHG *drî*; Mod. HG *drei*; MLG *drî*, LG *drą^i^* Assinghausen, *dra^i^* Ostbevern, Stav-

enhagen, *dre*[i] Heide (Dithmarschen); MDutch *dri*; Mod. Dutch dial. *drij* (many places) – Weijnen (1966: 296).
With adjectival ending: OHG *drîe*; MHG *drîe*; OSax. *thria* (also *threa, thrie* because of *thea), thie* beside *thia* in this case of the definite article (15.1.2.0.1.); MLG *dre* (so Lasch 1914: § 396 n. 6); MDutch *drie*[90] *dre* (van Loey 1964–1965, 1: § 46, 2: § 53); Mod. Dutch *drie*.

In early West Saxon *ī̆e* appears monophthongized to *ī̆* – and therefore *ie* appears for *ī̆* by inverted spelling; *ī̆e* is monophthongized to *ȳ̆* before a labial consonant and *r* (Campbell 1959: § 300). In late West Saxon, *ī̆e* appears as *ī̆* before palatal consonants, but as *ȳ̆* in all other positions (Campbell 1959: § 301). In some areas this *ȳ̆* becomes *ī̆* (Campbell 1959: § 317). In late West Saxon, *ī̆* often becomes *ȳ̆* in the neighbourhood of labials and before *r* (Campbell 1959: § 318). In Middle English there is an area in the south-west in which *ȳ̆* early becomes *ī̆*, but in the rest of the old West Saxon area *ȳ̆* remains, written *u* (Luick 1921–1940: § 287), until it, too, is unrounded to *ī̆* (Luick 1921–1940: § 397). There can thus be confusion with [*œ*:] < OEngl. *ēo*, for this too was written *u* (as well as *ue*) by some scribes – though it is not likely that it actually became [*y*:] (Luick 1921–1940: § 357).[91] For the case under discussion early West Saxon has *þrīe* (Cosijn 1883–1886, 2: § 67), later West Saxon this form, and also *þrī, þrȳ*. It is clear that we cannot decide whether we have here original *þrī* (= Icel. *þrír*) or analogical *þrīe* (= OHG *drîe*). In Middle English, Ayen *þri, þry* can represent OEngl. *þrīo* (15.1.3.4.) – see Luick (1921–1940: § 359.2).

15.1.3.2. Acc. masc. PIE **trins* > PGmc. **þrinz* > Gothic *þrins*; ON **þrē* (Noreen 1913: § 29b), with added adj. *-a*, ON **þrēa*. In West Norse, final *-ē* remains, but *ēa* > Icel. *já* (Noreen 1923: § 133b 2).
In East Norse, *ē* > *ǣ* except before a vowel (Noreen 1904: § 114.1); hence OIcel. *þré*;[92] ODanish *thrǣ*; Icel. *þrjá*; Mod. Norw. *trjå*; OSwed. *thrēa*.

15.1.3.3. Nom.-acc. fem. PGmc. **þrijōz* > Runic Norse (Tune – Jóhannesson 1923: no. 72) *þrijoR*; Icel. *þrjár*;[93] Mod. Norw. *trjå* (also used as masc.) Set, *treå* Voss;[94] OHG *drîo*[95] (> MHG *drîe*);[96] OSax. *threa*;[97] MLG *drê*; Saterland *thrio* (-stund) – van Helten (1900: § 193); OFr. *thria*;[98] Mod. Frisian: East *trjoo* Saterland; *triau, triah* Harlingen; *thrîû* Wangeroog;[99] *tĕrjáh, tria* Wursten; North *trii(e), träi* Coast; *trii* Föhr and Amrum Sylt; *tree* Helgoland; for West *trije* (*trooi* Schiermonnikoog) and Old West Frisian Charters *treija*, see Spenter (1968: 295); OEngl. *þrīo* > *þrēo*.[100]

15.1.3.4. Accusative fem. PIE **trins* > PGmc. **þrinz* > Gothic *þrins*; OWN **þrē*; OEN **þrǣ* (> OSwed. *þrǣ*). From this + nom.-acc. fem. PN **þrijoR* (15.1.3.3.), we obtain PN **þrējoR* > ONorw. *þréar*; OSwed.

þrēar, þrēa; ODanish *thrēa*[101] – the phonology being exactly parallel to that of the accusative masculine. Since PN **þrijoR* was used for both nominative and accusative, the last-mentioned forms came to be used for the nominative also.

15.1.3.5. Nom.-acc. neuter PIE **tri(y)ā* > PGmc. **þrijō* > Gothic *þrija* (> Crimean Gothic *tria* – von Grienberger 1897: 131–132); Icel. *þrjú*;[102] Mod. Norw. *trju* (on *trjug* see 15.1.7.4.); OSwed. *þrȳ* (Mod. Norw. *tríj* > Mod. Norw. *try*); ODanish *thrȳ*;[103] OHG *driu*; MHG *driu, dreu*; Mod. HG dial. *droi, drui* (Mausser 1932: 860) Bavarian, *drû̂* Swiss; OSax. *thriu, thrio, thria* (see Gallée 1910: § 68b) *thru* (Gallée 1910: § 103 n. 1); MLG *drû̂, drê, drie, dri*;[104] OFr. *thriu*; OEngl. *þrīo þrēo*.[105]

15.1.3.6. Genitive. PIE **tri(y)ōm* > PGmc. **þrijǭ*: – Gothic *þrije*;[106] ICel. *þriggja*; Færoese *tríggja* (from **triggja*, with long vowel from nominative-accusative, all genders); OSwed. *þrigjja*; ODanish *thriggia*; OHG (Tatian) *thriio* and *drîo*; OFr. *thria*.

By analogy with the adjective: OHG *drîero*; MHG *drîger, drîer*; Mod. HG *dreier*, MLG *drîger*, Mod. Dutch *drier*, (rare) *drierre, driere*, OFr. *thrira*; OEngl. *þrīora, þrēora* – by further analogy with nom.-acc. fem. neuter *þrīo, þrēo*.[107]

15.1.3.7. Dative. PGmc. **þrimaz* > *þremr, þrem*; from this protoform, together with PGmc. **þrimuz, *þrimiz* (Ross 1954: 118): Gothic masc. neuter *þrim*; OIcel. *þrimr, þrim*;[108] OSwed. *þrim*; ODanish *thrim*; OHG *drim, drin*; MHG *drin*; OSax. *thrim*; MLG *drin*;[109] OFr. *thrim* (*thrium* from this + nom.-acc. neuter *thriu*); OEngl. *þrim* (MEngl. *þreom* from this + MEngl. *þreo*).

MHG *drîn*[110] is usually explained as by analogy with nom.-acc. masc. *drî* – similarly MLG *drin*. But OEngl. *ðriim* Lindisfarne seems to point to a reformate, PGmc. **þrijim* – hence also Lindisfarne *ðrim* (Ross 1937: 110–111), and the High and Low German forms just mentioned could be explained as from this too. There is the further possibility that some of the Germanic forms usually regarded as with short vowel may, in whole or in part, have this long vowel; so, perhaps, in Anglo-Saxon texts other than the Lindisfarne Gospels, the spelling *þrim* may mean *þrīm* instead of, or beside, *þrĭm*.

15.1.3.8. Further developments in Scandinavian

15.1.3.8.0. By the influence of 'two'

1) Nominative-accusative neuter OSwed. *þrū* from *þrȳ* + nom.-acc. neuter *tū*.

2) Genitive OSwed. *thræggia* from *þriggia* + gen. *twæggia*.
3) Dative OEN **þrēm* from **þrim* + dat. *twēm*: OSwed. *þrēm*, ODanish *thrēm*.

15.1.3.8.1. By sound change

1) *þ* > *t* (see Noreen 1904: § 260; Brøndum Nielsen 1950–1957: § 297); ODanish nom.-acc. neuter *try*; gen. OSwed. *træggia* (15.1.3.8.); ODanish *triggi* (15.1.3.8.2.).
2) Nom.-acc. fem. OSwed. *þrēa* > *þrēia* (Noreen 1904: § 328.1a).
3) Genitive OSwed. *trigge* (15.1.3.8.2.); ODanish *thriggiæ, thriggie, thriggæ, thriggi*; cf. the corresponding weakened forms of 'two' (15.1.2.9.1.).
4) Dative. OEN **þrēm* (15.1.3.8.) > **þrĕm* > **þrǣm* (Brøndum Nielsen 1950–1957: § 159 n. 2): OSwed. *þrǣm*, ODanish *thrǣm*.
5) Dative. OSwed. *þrim* > *þrym* (Noreen 1904: § 108.1) > *thrøm* (Noreen 1904: § 116).

15.1.3.8.2. By analogies within the paradigm

1) From OEN acc. masc. **þrēa* (> OSwed. *þrēa*) and nom.-acc. fem. **þrēar* (> OSwed. *þrēar*, ODanish *thrēa*) + OEN nom. masc. **þrīr* (> OSwed. *þrīr*, ODanish *thrī*): acc. masc. OEN **þrīa* > OGut. *þrīa*; OSwed. **þrīa* > *þrīæ* (Noreen 1904: § 96); and OEN nom.-acc. **þrīar* > OGut. *þrīar*; OSwed. *þrīa*.[111]
2) OEN nom. masc. **þrēr* (> OSwed. *þrē*, ODanish *thrǣ*) by the analogy: nom. masc. **þrēr*: acc. masc. **þrēa*, nom.-acc. fem. **þrēar*: nom. masc. **þrīr*: acc. masc. **þrīa*, nom.-acc. fem. **þrīa* (15.1.3.8.2.).
3) OEN acc. masc. **þrē* (> OSwed. *þrē*, ODanish *thrē*) from **þrǣ* (15.1.3.2.) + **þrēa*.
4) OEN acc. fem. **þrē* from **þrǣ* (15.1.3.4.) + nom.-acc. fem. **þrēar*; hence nom.-acc. fem. OSwed. *þrē*, ODanish *thre*; further, OSwed. *þrēr*.
5) OSwed. acc. fem. **þrǣa* from *þrǣ* (15.1.3.4.) + *þrēa*; hence also OSwed. nom. fem. *þrǣa*, because OSwed. *þrēa* is used in both cases.
6) OSwed. gen. **þryggia* (> *þryggiæ*, 15.1.3.8.1.) from *þriggja* + nom.-acc. neuter *þrȳ*. Similarly ODanish *thrygge* (neuter).
7) From the foregoing it is clear that, in Old Swedish and Old Danish, *þrē, thrē* was used in the nominative masculine and the nominative-accusative feminine; it therefore came to be used in the nominative-accusative neuter also.[112] It is thus seen that, in the nominative-accusative

of this paradigm, gender was no longer distinguished. So it is not surprising that the modern forms, Mod. Swed. *tre* and Mod. Danish *tre*, descend from the invariant *þrē, thrē.*[113]

15.1.4. 'Four'[114]

15.1.4.0. The original Indo-European inflection continues, in some form, in Norse – in Old Danish this survives only in Skånsk – but in Gothic and West Germanic it has been eliminated, so that the numeral belongs to the uninfluenced category, which, in Indo-European begins with 'five'. There is every reason to suppose that the elimination of the inflection in Gothic is entirely distinct from its elimination in West Germanic, and so these two branches of Germanic must be discussed separately. There is however one point in common: in neither case is there any morphological reason why the genitive and dative should have been eliminated. In both, then, the process must have originated in the reduction of the nominative and accusative to one form for all genders. This was evidently sufficient to transfer the numeral into the uninflected category.

15.1.4.1. Norse

15.1.4.1.0. The entire Norse system can be explained on the basis of **feðura/ō-* and a form with *i*-inflection, **feðuri-*. Two sporadic Proto-Norse sound changes are required.
(α) Between a back-vowel and *u*, *ð* > *ʒ*:[115] ONorw. PN *Augun* = OIcel. *auðonn*; PGmc. **euðura-* 'udder' (> OFrisian *iâder*) > OSwed. *iûgher*, ODanish **iūghær*, **iūvær* > early Mod. Danish *jyffr*.
(β) *ð* is lost before *r*[116] with lengthening of the preceding vowel or diphthong:[117] OIcel. neuter pl. masc. *huárer* < **huaðrer* to OIcel. *huaþarr* (= Gothic *aþar*); similarly OSwed. *hwār*; PN ODanish *Gūrith* = OIcel. *Guþríþr*. Other sound changes are also involved.
(γ) The normal rules of syncope.
(δ) *ū*-breaking of *ĕ*. In Old West Norse this results in (1) *iǫ*, in part – in Old Norwegian – in (2) *iu*; later *iǫ* > *io* (if this is not only a spelling) (Noreen 1923: § 89 and n. 1); the result of lengthening is *ió* (not *iǫ́*) (Noreen 1923: § 123). In Old East Norse the result of the breaking is (3) *iu*, which (4) in Old Swedish remains before a preserved *u* or *i* of the next syllable otherwise (5) becoming *io* (Noreen 1904: § 75.2) and in Old Danish

(6) remains before labials, *g, k (k)* (in part also before *l*) otherwise (7) becoming *io* (Brøndum Nielsen 1950–1957: §§ 93, 94 n. 1).
(ε) By *i*-umlaut, OEN *iū* > *ȳ* (Noreen 1904: § 59.11; Brøndum Nielsen 1950–1957: § 78) which, in part (ε 1), yields *ī* in Old Danish (Brøndum Nielsen 1950–1957: § 140).

The phonologies are of three kinds.

15.1.4.1.1. (I) nom. masc. PN. **feδurēR* > OWN **fiǫδrir* (γ, δ 1); OEN **fioδrir* (γ, δ 5) > (β) Icel. *fjórir*;[118] Mod. Norw. *fjore* Set; OSwed. **fiō ŏrir* [119] *fiōri*; ODanish **fiōrir* (cf. δ 7).

With the same phonology:
Acc. masc. PN **feδuranR* > Icel. *fjóra*; OSwed. *fiōra*; ODanish **fiōra* (cf. δ 7). Nom.-acc. fem. PN **feδurōR* > Icel. *fjórar*; OSwed. *fiōrar, fiōra*; ODanish **fiōrar* (cf. δ 7).
Dat. PN **feδurumR* > Icel. *fjórum*; Færoese *fjórum*; OSwed. *fiūrom* [120] (cf. δ 4); ODanish **fiōrum* (cf. δ 7).

15.1.4.1.2. (II) Nom. masc. PN **feδuriR* > OEN **fiuδrir* (γ, δ 3) > **fiūrir* (β) > (ε) OSwed. *fȳrir, fȳri*; ODanish (Skånsk) *fȳri, fīri* (ε 1).

With the same phonology:
Accusative masc. PN **feδurinR* > OSwed. **fȳri*; ODanish (Skånsk) *fiūri, fȳri, fīri* (15.1.4.1.2.).
(III) Nom.-acc. neuter PN **feδurō* > **feδuru* > **feδur* (c) > **feʒur* (α) > OEN **fiǫʒur* (δ 1), **fiuʒur* (δ 2); OEN **fiuʒur* (δ 3); > OIcel. *fiogor* (Mod. Icel. *fjögur*); ONorw. *fiogor, fiugur* (δ 2); Mod. Norw. *fjogo*; OSwed. *fiughur* (δ 4); OGut. *fiugur*; ODanish *fiughur* (δ 6) > *fiūr* (Brøndum Nielsen 1950–1957: § 392.2).

With similar phonology:
Genitive. PN **feδureRō* > **feδurrō* > **feʒurrō* > OEN **fiǫʒurra, *fiuʒurra*; OEN **fiuʒurra*; > OIcel. *fiogorra* (Mod. Icel. *fjögurra*); ONorw. *fiogorra, fiugurra*; OSwed. *fiughurra*; ODanish (Skånsk) *fiūra*.

15.1.4.1.3. Some analogies are discussed in the following.
i) Accusative masc. PN **feʒuranR* (from **feδuranR* + nom.-acc. neuter **feʒur*) > ODanish (Skånsk) **fiugra* (> *fiugræ* with weakening, 15.1.4.1.5.2.) > **fiūra* (so, essentially, Brøndum Nielsen 1950–1957: § 95).
ii) In Old Swedish, from nom.-acc. neuter *fiughur*, gen. *fiughurra* + nom. masc. **fiōrir*, acc. masc. *fiōra*, nom.-acc. fem. *fiōrar, fiōra*, reinforced by dat. *fiūrim*, we have nom. masc. *fiūrir, fiūri*, acc. masc. *fiūra*, nom.-acc. fem. *fiūrar, fiūra*.
iii) In Skansk, by analogy with acc. masc. *fiūra* (ι), we have nom. masc. *fiūrur, fiūri*, dat. *fiūrum*.

iv) Acc. masc. OSwed. *fȳra*, from *fiōra, fiūra* + **fȳri*; and, because *ȳ*-forms exist in the nominative-accusative masculine beside those with *iu io*, they come into being in the nominative-accusative feminine (*fȳrar, fȳra*) and the dative also (*fȳrom*). Similarly accusative masculine Skånsk *fȳra, fīra* from **fiōra, fiūra* + *fȳri, fīri*, and hence nom.-acc. fem. *fȳra, fīra*, dat. *fȳrum, fīrum*.

15.1.4.1.4. It may be mentioned here that, in the Old East Norse languages, there are undoubtedly forms with a short vowel. These surely arise in 'forty' (15.1.24.); thus OSwed. **fȳritighi* 'forty' > **fy̆ritighi* > *fĭritighi* (Noreen 1904: § 101);[121] ODanish *fȳritiughu* > *fīritiughu* (15.1.4.1.2.); hence *fy̆ritiughu, fĭritiughu*. Now acc. masc. OSwed. *fĭri* from the analogy **fȳritighi: fĭritighi:* acc. masc. **fȳri* (15.1.4.1.2.): acc. masc. *fĭri*. Since *fyri* can be used for the nominative as well, so also can *fĭri* – hence, then, also *fĭrir* (by analogy MNorw. *fĭrir* – Hægstad 1914–1915: 198, n. 399 – > Mod. Norw. *fire*). Similarly in Skånsk: *fȳritiughu, fīritiughu: fy̆ritiughu, fĭritiughu:* acc. masc. *fȳri, fīri*: acc. masc. *fy̆ri *fĭri* – from which last, by weakening (15.1.4.1.5.1.), *fĭre*,[122] used also as the nominative.

15.1.4.1.5. Further developments

15.1.4.1.5.1. By sound change

1) The weakening of final vowels in Old Danish is relevant here, for earlier *-i, -a* can appear as *-e, -æ*. The phenomenon is fairly complicated; see Brøndum Nielsen (1950–1957: §§ 200–215).
2) Syncope: gen. OSwed. *fiughra* < *fiughura* (15.1.4.1.5.1.) – cf. Noreen (1904: § 157).
3) ODanish nom. masc. *fiūri* > *fiyræ*; nom.-acc. neuter *fiūr* > *fyur* (Brøndum Nielsen 1950–1957: § 179.5).
4) OGut. *fygura* < *fiugura* (15.1.4.1.5.1.). – Noreen (1904: § 100).[123]
5) Nom.-acc. neuter OSwed. *fiughur* > *fiuwur* (Noreen 1904: § 279.1), written *fiuwr* > *fiūr*.
6) *-rr-* > *-r-* in unstressed position (cf. Noreen 1904: § 242.2): gen. OSwed. *fiughura* < *fiughurra*; similarly OGut. *fiugura*.

15.1.4.1.5.2. By analogies within the paradigm

1) OSwed. nom.-acc. *fioghor*, gen. *foighora*, from *fiughur, fiughura* (15.1.4.1.5.1.) + nom. masc. *fiōrir*.

2) OSwed. nom.-acc. neuter *fighur*, gen. **fighura* (MNorw. *figura* – Hægstad 1914–1915: II.1.84 n. 153), from *fiughur, fiughura* (15.1.4.1.5.1.) + nom. masc. *fīrir, fīri*.
3) OSwed. nom.-acc. neuter *fiur* (Södermannalag, Collin – Schlyter 1827–1877, 4: 228): nom. masc. *fiurir*: nom.-acc. neuter *gōþ*: nom. masc. *gōþir*. Cf. also *fiuwr* from the beginning of the Dalalag (Noreen 1892–1894: § 100).
4) OGut. gen. *fiaugura*, from *fiugura* (15.1.4.1.5.1.) + dat. *fiaurum*.
5) Gen. OSwed. *fiūra, fȳra, fīra*, ODanish *fiūra, fȳra, fīra*, reformed on nom. masc. OSwed. *fiūrir, fiūri, fȳrir, fīrir*, ODanish *fiūri, fȳri, fīri* and corresponding forms with *iū, ȳ, ī* in other parts of the paradigm.
6) OSwed. dat. *fiugrum* from gen. *fiughra* (15.0.2.) + dat. *fiūrum*, etc.
7) In the Old East Norse languages, invariant forms gradually emerge. In each of the two languages, the starting point seems to be the accusative masculine: because OSwed. **fȳri*, ODanish *fȳri, fīri* could be used for both nominative and accusative masculine OSwed. *fiūra, fȳra*, ODanish **fiugra, fȳra, fīra* came to be used for the nominative also. In both languages *fȳra, fīra* could thus be used in the nominative and accusative of both the masculine and feminine; they therefore came to be used in the corresponding neuter case too. The genders were thus no longer distinguished in the paradigm. Hence, essentially, the invariance (15.0.2.). Even in Middle Swedish, *fȳra* is used for the dative, and Mod. Swed. *fȳra* derives from this invariant form. In non-Skånsk Danish the invariants are of two sorts: **fiugra* > *fiughræ* ≥ *fiuræ, fyuræ*; secondly *fira* (which survives as *fīra* in the modern dialects of Skåne and Bornholm) > *fīre* with weakening (15.1.4.1.5.) > Mod. Danish *fire*.[124]

15.1.4.2. Gothic

Nom.-acc. neuter PIE **petwórə* (a form replacing ***k^{w}*etwora* under the influence of *penk^{u}e 'five') > PGmc. **feδwōr* > Gothic *fidwor*. Nom. masc.-fem. PIE **petwṓres* (from nom. masc.-fem. **petwṓres* + nom.-acc. neuter **petwṓrə*) > PGmc. **feδwōriz*. This last would give Gothic **fidwors* or *fidwor* according to whether the final *-s* has been lost after *r* or not. There is some variation here. In monosyllables *-s* would appear to be lost after a short syllable (Gothic *waír* = Lith. *výras* 'man'), preserved after a long one (Gothic *skeirs* 'clear'). But Gothic *ga-faúrs* 'honourable' goes against this rule. After a short unstressed syllable, *-s* is certainly lost (Gothic *anþar* = OInd. *ántara-* 'other') but there is no control for the position after a long unstressed syllable (Jellinek 1926: § 75.2). We must suppose then either that *-s* was correctly most in nom. masc.-fem. *fidwor*, or that, beside a **fidwors*, there existed a **fidwar* < **fidwars* < PGmc. **feδwariz* < PIE nom.-acc. fem. **petwṓres* – in this case the loss of *-s* in Gothic would be certain – and then *fidwor* from **fidwors* + **fidwar*. But this is argumentum in vacuo. The elimination of the gender distinction in the nominative-accusative required above (15.1.4.) has thus taken place. *Fidwor* is recorded in congruence with masculine, feminine and neuter nouns (cf. Forshall – Madden 1850: *fidwor dagans* 'four days', John 11, 17; *fidwor þusundjos* 'for thousand' Mark 8, 9; *jere ahtautehund jah fidwor* 'eighty-four years' Luke 2, 37). It is not certain whether Crimean Gothic *fyder* derives from *fidwor* of *fidur-* (15.3.2.4.); cf. von Grienberger (1897: 131).

15.1.4.3. West Germanic

15.1.4.3.0. Nom.-acc. fem. PIE **pekwóres* > PGmc. **feʒwariz* > **fewariz*. Acc. masc.-fem. PIE **pekwórn̥s* (from **pekúrn̥s* + nom. masc.-fem. **pekwóres*) > PGmc. **feʒwurunz* > **feʒurunz*; from this last + nom.-acc. fem. **fewariz*, we have **fewurunz*, in part **fiwurunz.*[125]
Nom.-acc. neuter PIE **pekwórā* from **pekwórə* (from **pekwṓrə* + nom. masc.-fem. **pekwóres* > PGmc. **feʒwurō* > **feʒurō*; from this last + nom. masc.-fem. **fewariz*, we have **fewuru*, in part **fiwuru.*[126] Then, with loss of ending: **fewuru*, **fiwuru*, **fewariz* > **fewur*, **fiwur*, **fewar*.

We must suppose that the difference nom. masc.-fem. **fewar*, nom.-acc. neuter **fewur* was eliminated, so that either form could be used as an invariant – hence, also, **fiwur* in this role. It is this invariant which has given rise to the indeclinability. In **fewur*, **fiwur*, loss of *w* before *u* took place, but the *w* was in part analogically restored from **fewar*. The final set of forms is thus **fewur*, **feur*, **fiwur*, **fiur*, **fewar*; to these must be added **feuwar*, from **fewar* + **feur* (so van Helten 1906: 95).

15.1.4.3.1. Hence the following actual forms: **feur* > OHG *feor, fior, fiar, fîer*; MHG *vier*; Mod. HG *vier*, OSax. *fior, fiar, vier*;[127] MLG *vêr, vir*; LG *fe^i^r* Assinghausen, *fe^ir^* Ostbevern, Heide (Dithmarschen), *fīr* Stavenhagen; MDutch *vier*; Mod. Dutch *vier*; OEngl. *feor* **feuwar* > OSax. *fiuwuar, fiuuar*.

15.1.4.3.2. The Frisian forms are of some complexity and are discussed in van Helten (1906: 95).
**feur* > **fior* > **fiar* > *fiar-, fyaer-* (*fôte*) 'four-footed', **feuwar* > **fiûwer*, **fiower* (from **fior* + **fiûwer*) > **fiower* > *fiôr* and also *fiouwer, fiouwr, fiour*.

OFrisian *fiôwer* > Mod. Fr. West *fjouwer*, Wursten *veijóhr, viower* (Schiermonnikoog *fjeur* < **fi̯ōur* – Spenter 1968: 313); OFrisian *fiûwer* > Mod. Fr. East: *fjauer* Saterland, Wangeroog; North: *fjau(w)er*; Coast: *fjauer, fjāwer* Föhr and Amrum (recent *sjauer*), *fjuur* Sylt and Helgoland (recent *schtjuur*).[128]

15.1.4.3.3. In Old English, **fewar* > PEngl. **fewar* > **feuwær* (breaking) > *fĕower*; and *feuwar* > PEngl. **fēuwær* > *fēower*.[129] The two unstarred forms would of course be indistinguishable in writing, but the scansion shows that the long diphthong at least existed (Sievers 1885: 223). The spelling *feower*, indicating a pronunciation with long or short [*oe*] (15.1.3.) survives into early Middle English. But the main development is OEngl. *fĕower* > *fouer* by "akzentumsprung"[130] (Ormulum *fowwerr*, AB *fouer*), then *ou* > *ū* after the labial (Luick 1921–1940: § 373d), hence *fuwer, fūr* (> Mod. Engl. *four*) – cf. Jordan (1925: § 102, n. 2).

Both the diphthongal and monophthongal forms (that is, then, those with MEngl. *ou* and *ū* respectively) are represented in the Modern English pronunciations of the word (Dobson 1957: § 173). In two areas, namely Kent and the north-west Midlands (with, possibly, an adjoining stretch of the North), there is the development *fouer* > *faur* (infl. *fawre*) (Luick 1921–1940: § 408.2), though the Ayenbite has *uour* with *ū* (Wallenberg, 1923: 271, n. 3).

15.1.5. 'Five'

15.1.5.0. PIE **penk^{w}e* > **penpe* > **pempe* > PGmc. **fimf*. PGmc. **fimf* or **fimfi-* – the forms are not in general distinguishable > Gothic *fimf*; OHG *fimf, finf*; MHG *finf*; OSax. *fīf*; MLG *vîf*; LG *ve^{i}f* Assinghausen, *fīf* Ostbevern, Dithmarschen, Stavenhagen; Saterland *fīf*; MDutch *vîf*; Mod. Dutch *vijf*;[131] OFr. *fīf*; Mod. Fr. *fiif* West (*fiiw, fiu* from the inflected form); OEngl. *fīf*; MEngl. *fīf* (Ormulum *fif*; AB *fif*; Ayen *uif, uyf*) and, from the inflected forms, *fīve* (> Mod. Engl. *five*).[132]

15.1.5.1. Von Grienberger (1897: 132) takes Crimean Gothic *fyuf* as a genuine form with loss of nasal. He refers to Gothic *fif hundam* 'five hundred' (I Corinthians 15,6) as if the form were straightforward; in fact *m* is written above the line, so *fimf* is normally read. Others have emended *fyuf* to **fynf* (so, essentially, Massmann 1841: 363).

From **fimf* + ordinal **fumftan/ōn-* (15.2.5.), we have **fumf* > OHG *funf* Notker (Piper 1895); MHG *vumf, funf*; from **fumf* + **fimfi-*, we have **fumfi-* > MHG *fümf, fünf* (> Mod. HG *fünf*). But it has been suggested (e. g. van Helten 1906: 98) that *funf, fünf* derive from **fimf* by simple sound change. So, most recently, Hotzenköcherle (1971: 307 ff.), who discusses the Swiss variants *föif, füüf, fuuf, fünf,* MHG *viumf, fiunf, feunf* (> allgäuisch *fainf*) from *fümf, fünf* + *fimf, finf*; with MHG *vouf,* cf. dat. sing. masc.-neuter *vouffzigstem* 'fiftieth' (15.1.25.), and, from this + *fiumf, feunf,* also MHG *fiuf, feuf*; with MHG *vonf* cf. MHG *vomfzên* 'fifteen' (15.1.15.).

15.1.5.2. The Scandinavian forms are difficult and are well discussed in Brøndum Nielsen (1950–1957: § 159 n. 1). The following development is suggested there. Ordinal PGmc. **fimftan-* (15.2.5.) > OWN **fēfte,* OEN **fǣfte* with loss of *m* before a following consonant, whereas cardinal PGmc. **fimf* > **fimm* with assimilation. Hence Icel. *fimm* (and OIcel. *fim* with simplification of the double consonant) and Færoese *fimm.* Then, from **fimm* + **fǣfte,* OEN *fǣm,* which is attested in Old Swedish and Old Danish by the spelling *fææm* in the former, and by this spelling and *feem* in the latter. OEN **fām* > **fǣ̆m* > OSwed. *fem*[133] (> Mod. Swed. *fem*) and ODanish *făm* (> Mod. Danish *fem*).[134]

15.1.6. 'Six'

PIE **seḱs* > PGmc. **sexs* > Gothic *saíhs*; Crimean Gothic *seis* (von Grienberger 1897: 132); Icel. *sex*; Færoese *seks*; Mod. Norw. *seks*; OSwed. *sæx*;[135] Mod. Swed. *sex*; ODanish *sæx, sex*;[136] Mod. Danish *seks*; OHG *sëhs*; MHG *sëhs*;[137] OSax. *sehs, ses* (Gallée 1910: § 289); MLG *ses, sees, seis,*[138] LG *säs* Assinghausen, *sęs* Ostbevern, *ʃüs* Heide (Dithmarschen), *ʃös* Stavenhagen – also *soss* (van Helten 1906: 90); Saterland *sechs*; MDutch *ses* (Franck 1910: § 111.1); Mod. Dutch *zes*; OFrisian *sex.*[139]

In English, PGmc. **sexs* > **seox,* by breaking; as such, this form does not survive. In West Saxon, *eo* > *i* before the palatal (Campbell 1959: § 305), and this can also be written as *ie* and *y* (cf. 15.1.3.). Hence early WSax. *siex,* Cosijn (1883–1886, 2: § 67.6), later *six and syx* as well.[140] In Kentish, **seox* > *sex,* later **six* (Ayen.) *zix, zyx*) – Campbell (1959: § 307). In Anglian, **seox* > *sex* with smoothing, which later gave **six* before the Middle English period (Luick 1921–1940: § 274). Hence MEngl. *sex* (Ormulum infl. *sexe,* AB *six) six* (> Mod. Engl. *six*).[141]
OEN **siax* from **sæx* + ordinal **siaxtan-* (15.2.6.) > OSwed. *siatte*; hence OSwed. *siæx,*[142] ODanish *siax* (*siahs,* Brøndum Nielsen 1950–1957: § 302), *siæx* (Brøndum Nielsen 1950–1957: § 177), *siex.*[143a]
OSwed. *sax* from *sæx* + *saxtān* 'sixteen'; OSwed. *six* from *sæx* + *sixtighi* 'sixty'.

15.1.7. 'Seven'

15.1.7.0. PIE **septm̥* > **sepm̥* > PGmc. **seƀun*;[143b] hence **siƀuni-*, and, from this + **seƀun*, also **siƀun*.

15.1.7.1. PGmc. **seƀun is preserved in Scandinavian: ƀ* > *w* before *u*,[144] and this *w* is then lost;[145] contraction takes place (Noreen 1923: § 133a; Brøndum Nielsen 1950–1957: § 117.2), the hiatus is early eliminated, and there results a diphthong identical with that from PGmc. *eu*; this latter gives PN *iǫu* (Noreen 1923: § 56), which, in this position, must appear as *ió* in Old Icelandic and can appear as *iú* in Old Norwegian (Noreen 1923: § 101.2 and n. 2); in East Norse it gives *iū* (> OGut. *iau*) (Noreen 1904: § 122; Brøndum Nielsen 1950–1957: § 114). Hence OIcel. *sió*; Mod. Norw. *sju*; OSwed. *siū*;[146] Mod. Swed. *sju*; OGut. *siau*; ODanish *siū* (> *syū* – Brøndum Nielsen 1950–1957: § 179.4); Skansk *ʃy, ʃu*.

15.1.7.2. In Gothic, PGmc. **seƀun* and **siƀun* must be indistinguishable because of the change *e* > *i*; and this is also the case over much of the West Germanic areas, because of the change *e* > *i* before a following *u*. This change took place in High and Low German (Braune – Mitzka 1967: § 30c; Gallée 1910: § 65; Lasch 1914: § 25) and in Old East Low Franconian (van Helten 1902: 2. I § 5); it is evidenced in the Salic Law (van Helten 1900: 425 ff.). It should be noted that *i* is lengthened to *e* in the open syllable in Middle Dutch; a similar "zerdehnung" takes place in Middle Low German (see Lasch 1914: §§ 39–41).

From **seƀun* and/or **siƀun*: Gothic *sibun*; Crimean Gothic *sevene* (infl.); OHG *sibun*;[147] MHG *siben, siven* ("unverschoben"), *seben*, also *suben, söben, süben*;[148a] Mod. HG *sieben*; OSax. *sibun, sivon*; Saterland *sifun*; OELFranc. *sinuolualdun* [? read *siuonualdun*] 'septuplum', Lipsius Glosses: 631 (van Helten 1902: 1: 58–89).[148b]

Van Helten (1902: 100–101) derives MLG *söven*;[149] LG *säoven, söven*;[150] MDutch *söven*[151] from **seƀun* and MLG *seven*; LG *seven*; MDutch *seven*[152] (> Mod. Dutch *zeven*) from **siƀün-* < **siƀuni-*. This last also accounts for OHG *sibin siben*; OSax. *siven*.

15.1.7.3. Van Helten (1906: 99–100) suggests that *e* > *i* before a following *u* in Anglo-Frisian also. But the evidence for this is weak, and, in any case, in our context the point is an academic one, for **siƀun* (see above) must certainly have existed beside **seƀun* there. He explains the *g* of most of the Frisian forms of 'seven' as due to a sound change: *ƀ* > *ʒ*; he compares, e. g., *progost* 'provost'; cf. further Mod. Frisian *jûgel* Wangeroog, *djigel* Helgoland, *jügel* Sylt, Halligen < OFrisian **jûgel* < **jiuvul-* < **ʒiƀula-* 'gable' (van Helten 1890: § 117x). But van Helten later (1906: 100) renegues on this view and explains **sigun* as by analogy with *nigun* 'nine'. His earlier view is surely to be preferred. We have then **siƀun* > **siʒun* > OFr. (East) *siugun* (*u*-breaking – van Helten 1890: § 36), but also OFr. (East) *sigun* under the influence of **siʒyn* < **siʒuni-*. Further **seƀun* > **seʒun* > **siōgun* > **siōgon*; OFr. (East) *sôgun, sôgon* from these last two + *sex* 'six' – i.e. initial *s-* instead of *si-* (so van Helten 1906: 100). OFr. (East) *sôgin* (> *sôgen*) from *sôgun* + **seʒin* < **seʒyni-*. Without the change *ƀ* > *ʒ*: OFr. *sowen, sauwen, sawen* (van Helten 1906: 100). The Modern East Frisian forms regularly descend from those of Old Frisian: *soogen* Saterland, *soggen* Harlingen, *sjûgen* Wangeroog, *tsiăgún* Wursten.[153] Old West Frisian *sawen, sowen* and Mod. Frisian *sawn* West (cf. Spenter 1968: 310); North *sääwen* Hattstedt, Halligen *sööwen* Föhr and Amrum, Helgoland (recent *seeben*), *soowen* Coast, *soowen* Sylt are probably borrowed, with or without "lautersatz„ from MLG *söven*.

15.1.7.4. The English forms are complicated by many factors.[154] Final *-n* is lost in Old Northumbrian (Campbell 1959: § 472), but in 'seven' it is in large part restored from the inflected form. Here, too, adjectival forms (Lindisfarne Gospels *-o -a -e*) frequently appear beside the normal uninflected one.

We have the following developments:

**seƀun* > early WSaxon *seofon*; Ru[1] *seofun*; Lindisfarne Gospels *seofo*.[155]

**siƀun* > *sifun* (*-sterri*) 'pliadas'; *sifu* (Napier 1901: 290); Ru[1] *siofun*; Ru[2] *siofu* – *siofo* (Luke 17,4 [bis]); late WSaxon *syfon* > **siofon* (Campbell 1959: § 299c) < **siuƀun*.

**seuƀun* and/or **siuƀun* > **suƀun* ("akzentumsprung") > Irish WSaxon *sufon*.

From *æhta eahta* 'eight' + *seofon, siofon*: Lindisfarne Gospels *seofa*; early WSaxon *seofan, siofan* (> Irish WSaxon *syfan*).[156] *Vespasian Psalter seofen* < PE **seuƀoni-* from **seuƀuni-* (from **seuƀun* + **siuƀuni-*) + **æhto* (> *æhta*) 'eight'.

In Middle English, the loss of *-n* is extended to areas other than Northumbria. The reduction of unstressed vowels and the change *ĭo* > *ĕo* caused all the Old English forms[157] to coalesce in **sĕove(n)* in the transition period between Old and Middle English. Hence *söve(n)* > *seve(n)*. Lengthening in the open syllable took place – to *sę̄ve(n)* – but the short vowel was, for the most part, restored from infl. *sevne*. This last gave *sę̄ne* with loss of *v* (Luick 1921–1940: § 428.3), whence *sen* (cf. early Mod. Engl. *sennight*). Hence the forms *seoven, seove, soven, sove, seven* (> Mod. Engl. *seven*), *seve*,[158] MScots *sewin* (with *w* written for *v*,

Luick 1921–1940: § 761); early Mod. Engl. *seaven* (cf. Dobson 1957: § 8.1b) < *sę̄ven*.

15.1.7.5. From PN **siǫu* + the nominative-accusative neuter of 'two' (OIcel. *tuau*):[159] OIcel. *siau*; MIcel. *siø*; Mod. Icel. *sjö* (Kock 1891: 252 ff., Þórólfsson 1925: XX); Færoese *sjey*; Mod. Norw. *sjau*.

Mod. Danish *syv* and its forerunners have been considered difficult, but in fact they can readily be explained if we postulate the following sound change: sporadically in Scandinavian, final *ū̆* (whether or not in a diphthong) develops *g* after it. The examples are: MNorw. nom.-acc. neuter def. art. *þaug* < *þau*; nom.-acc. neuter Mod. Norw. *tuaug* (Mod. Norw. *tveug* Nordhordland, Voss, Hardanger) < *tuau*;[160] MSwed. *tūgh* < *tū* (15.1.2.5.); Mod. Norw. *trjug* 'three' (: Icel. nom.-acc. neuter *þrjú*), to which we must now add ONorw. *siaug* (> Mod. Norw. *sjaug*) < *siau*, OSwed. *siūg, siūgh* < *siū*; ODanish *sivgh* (> Mod. Danish *syv*) < *siū*.[161]

15.1.8. 'Eight'

PIE **oḱtō(w)* > PGmc. **axtau* > Gothic *ahtau*; Crimean Gothic *athe* (von Grienberger 1897: 131); Icel. *átta*; Færoese *átta*; Mod. Norw. *åtta*; OSwed. *ātta*;[162] Mod. Swed. *åtta*; ODanish *ātta*; Mod. Danish *otte*; OHG *ahto*; MHG *ahte*; Mod. HG *acht*; OSax. *ahto, ahta*; MLG *achte*; LG *acht* Assinghausen, Ostbevern, Stavenhagen, *ach* Heide (Dithmarschen); Saterland *achto*; MDutch *achte, acht*; Mod. Dutch *acht*; OFrisian *achta, achte* (*acht* before *and*, van Helten 1890: § 234); Mod. Frisian, West: *acht*; East: *oachte* Saterland, *acht* Wangeroog; North: *aacht* Coast (EMoringen *ǫǫcht* from this + *sǫǫwen* 'seven'?), *aacht* Islands[163] (Helgoland *ach*, loanword from Low German).

In English: WSaxon *eahta*, OKentish **eahta* > *ehta* (Luick 1921–1940: § 278) > MEngl. *eghte* (Ormulum *ehhte*, Iul *eahte*, Ayen. *eȝte*) > *eighte* (Luick 1921–1940: § 403.1a; Jordan 1925: § 63) > Mod. Engl. *eight*; Anglian **æhta* > MEngl. *aghte* (AB ahte) > *aughte* (Luick 1921–1940: § 403.1d) > MScots *aucht*, Mod Scots *aucht, aught*.

The modern dialect forms descend, in some part, from MEngl. *eight* in the south and *aught* in the north, but Dobson (1957: § 139) says: "modern Northern (and Midland) dialects have pronunciations descended from MEngl. *ī*, as if from OEngl. **ĭhta*"[164] – this last is of course impossible, and the explanation is perhaps to be sought in the ordinal (15.2.8.).

Inflected: PGmc. **axtawi-* > OHG **ahtouui* (emended from *hatouui* Steinmeyer – Sievers 1879–1922: 1,732,62), dat. *ahtowen* Notker (Piper

1895); MHG *ehtewe, ähtewe;*[165] OEngl. *æhtowe* Ru^2, *ehtuwe* Riddle 36/4 (see Krapp – van Kirk Dobbie 1936: 198).

15.1.8.1. Analogies

(i) OEngl. *æhto* Lindisfarne Gospels, from **æhta* + *seofo* 'seven'.
(ii) OHG *ahtu* Tatian, from *ahto* + *sibun* 'seven' and **ni-un* 'nine'; similarly OSax. *ahte* from *ahto* + *siven* and *nigen*; MLG *achten* from *achte* + *seven* and *negen*.
(iii) MSwed. *otto* < **ātto* (Noreen 1904: § 110), from *ātta* + *nio* 'nine' and *tīo* 'ten'.

15.1.9. 'Nine'

15.1.9.0. PIE **newn̥* > PGmc. **newun*[166] > **neun* and **neʒun*; hence **niwuni-* (> **niuni-*), **niʒuni-*; thus **niwun* (> **niun*), from **newun* + **niwuni-*, and **niʒun* from **neʒun* + **niʒuni-*.
15.1.9.1. In Scandinavian, several different developments are evidenced, and these are somewhat similar to those found in the case of 'ten' there (15.1.10.1.). The difference between these developments of 'nine' seems in part to be due to the carrying-over of the accentual difference between barytone PIE **néwn̥* and oxytone PIE **newń̥* – whatever exactly the cause of this difference may have been.[167]
(1) PIE **néwn̥* yielding PGmc. **niwun* > ON **niwu* > **ni-u* (loss of *w* before *u*) > **nī* (syncope of *-u* and lengthening of preceding vowel), Icel. *ní(tján)* 'nineteen' (15.1.19.) and ODanish *nī* (> Mod. Danish *ni*). Cf. PGmc. **tixun* 'ten' > ODanish *tī*.
2) PIE **newń̥* > PGmc. **newun* > ON **newu* < **ne-u* (loss of *w* before *u*) > **neu* (early elimination of the hiatus) > OWN **niō* (in part **niū* – cf. Noreen 1923: § 101, n. 2), OEN **niū*. This development is similar to that of OIcel. *sió*, OSwed. *siū* < PGmc. **seƀun* 'seven' (15.1.7.). Cf. PGmc. **texun* 'ten' > OWN **tiō*, **tiū*, OEN **tiū*.
3) PIE **newń̥*, yielding PGmc. **niwun* > ON **niwu* > **ni-u*[168] (loss of *w* before *u* and early preservation of the hiatus). Cf. PGmc. **tixum* 'ten' > ON **ti-u*.
4) From **ni-u* (3) + **nī* (1), we have **nīu* > Mod. Icel. *níu*, Færoese *níggju* (15.1.10.1.), and with normal development of unstressed *-u* (as in *-ōn*-stem obl. *-o*), OSwed. *nīo*[169] (> Mod. Swed. *nio*); ODanish *nīo* (> North (-East) Skånsk *ni̥ę*). Cf. **tīu*, 'ten' > Mod. Icel. *tíu*, OSwed. *tīo*, etc.

5) From **nīu* (4) + OWN **niō* (2), we have OIcel. *nīo*, Mod. Norw. *nie* (*nio* Voss, Hardanger). Cf. OIcel. *tío* 'ten'.
6) From **nīu* (4) with unshifted *-u* and/or from this + OEN **niū* (2), we have OSwed. **niū* (> *nyu* – cf. Noreen 1904: § 270, n. 3); ODanish *niū* (whence *niə* in modern dialects).[170] Cf. ODanish *tīu* 'ten'.
15.1.9.2. **Neun* and/or *niun* > Gothic *niun*; Crimean Gothic *nyne*;[171] OHG *niun*; MHG *niun* (> *nûn*, Mausser 1932: 259); Mod. HG *neun*; Saterland *niun* (van Helten 1900: § 186).
**neʒun*, **niʒun* are exactly parallel to **seƀun*, **siƀun* 'seven' (15.1.7.2.): OSax. *nigun, nigon, nigen*, like *siƀun, sivon, siven*; < LG *negen*, like *seven*; MDutch *neghen*[172] (> Mod. Dutch *negen*),[173] like *zeven*.
The old Frisian forms are parallel to those of 'seven' too: *nigun*, like **siʒun; niûgun*, like *siûgun; niôgen* (van Helten 1894: 385) < **niogin*, from **niogun* (like **siogun*) + **niʒin* (like **siʒin*); *niûgin* (> *niûgen*) from *niûgun* + **niogin*. OFrisian *niôgen* > Mod. Frisian *njoggen* West (*njyəgən* Schiermonnikoog, Spenter 1968: 282); OFrisian *niûgun* > Mod. Frisian, East: *njûgen* Saterland, Wangeroog; North: *njügen* (East Moringen *njöögen*); OFrisian: *nigun* > Wursten *nigúhn* (Helgoland *neägen*, loan-word form, Low German).
15.1.9.3. The English forms are rather diverse.
(**neun* in Lindisfarne gospels *hundneontig* 'ninety' [15.1.29.]) **niuni-* > Ru^2 infl. *nione*. **Niʒun* > OEngl. *nigon* (also *nygon*, cf. 15.1.3.);[174] **niʒuni-* > OEngl. *nigen*.[175]

In Middle English there is, to some extent, loss of final *-n* (cf. 'seven' 15.1.7.3.): OEngl. *nigon, nigen* > MEngl. *niʒen* (Ormulum *niʒhenn*), *niʒe* (AB *nihe*) > *nīen* (> Mod. Engl. *nine*) *nīe*. In the North, *niʒen* > nę̄ghe, nę̄ghen > *nę̄n* (> Mod. Scots *neen*); infl. **niʒene*, **niʒne* > **nīne* > *nīn*.[176a] OHG *niuuan* (> MHG *niwen*) from *niun* + *zëhan* 'ten'. (Similarly OEngl. Lindisfarne Gospels *hundneantig* 'ninety' (15.1.29.) with *-nean-* = **nean*, from **neun* + **texan*.)

15.1.10. 'Ten' and '-teen'

15.1.10.0. *Ten* 'ten' and the second element *-teen* of *(thir)teen* 'thirteen' to *(nine)teen* 'nineteen' may be considered together. We distinguish them by prefixing a hyphen to the *-teen* forms.
PIE **déḱm̥* > PGmc. **texun*,[176b] PIE **déḱom* > PGmc. **texan*, PIE **dḗḱom* > PGmc. **texan*; hence, then, **tixuni-*, **texani-*, **tēxani-*; further, **tixun* from **texun* + **tixuni-*.
**tixuni-* > Crimean Gothic *thiine* (cf. von Grienberger: 1897: 132).

15.1.10.1. In Scandinavian, several different developments are evidenced, and these are somewhat similar to those found in the case of 'nine' (15.1.9.). The difference between these developments of 'ten' seem again to be due in part to the carrying-over of the accentual difference between barytone PIE **déḱm̥* and oxytone PIE **deḱḿ̥* – even though the latter (i. e., a PGmc. **teʒun*) is not attested.

Intervocalic *x* is of course lost.

1a) PGmc. **tixun* > ON **tixu* > **ti-u* > **tī*: OSwed. *tī-*, ODanish *tī* (> Mod. Danish *ti*). Cf. PGmc. **niwun* > Icel. *ní(tján)* 'nineteen', ODanish *nī* 'nine'.

1b) PGmc. **texun* > ON **texu* > **te-u*: OIcel. *té(-rœbr)* 'in the nineties' (of age) (see 15.3.2.2.). The development is parallel to (1a).

2) PGmc. **texun* > ON **texu* > **te-u* > **teu* > OWN **tīo* (in part **tiū*), OEN **tiū*. Cf. PGmc. **newun* 'nine' > OWN **niō*, **niū*, OEN **niū*.

3) PGmc. **tixun* > ON **tixu* > **ti-u*. Cf. PGmc. **niwun* 'nine' > ON **ni-u*.

4) From **ti-u* (3) + **tī* (1), we have **tīu* > Mod. Icel. *tíu*, Færoese *tíggju*;[177] OSwed. *tīo*[178] (> Mod. Swed. *tio*); ODanish **tīo* (> *tyo* – cf. Brøndum Nielsen 1950–1957: § 176 n. 3) > North (-East) Skånsk *tie̯*. Cf. **nīu* 'nine' > Mod. Icel *níu*, OSwed. *nīo*, etc.

5) From **tīu* (4) + OWN **tiō* (2), we have OIcel. *tío*, Mod. Norw. *tie*. Cf. OIcel. *nío* 'nine'.

6) From **tīu* (4) and/or from this + OEN **tiū* (2), we have OSwed. *tīu*; ODanish *tīu* (whence *tiə* in the modern dialects).[179] Cf. ODanish *nīu* 'nine'.

15.1.10.2. **tixun* and/or **texun* > Gothic *taíhun, -taíhun*.

**texan* > Icel. *-tján*; Færoese *-tjan*; OEN *-*tiān* (15.1.10.); OHG *zëhan -zëhan*; MHG *zëhen -zëhen*; OSax. *tehan* > **tean* > *tian, ahtetian* 'eighteen' (Wadstein 1899: 21(75); MLG *tien, tin* (Lasch 1914: § 397, n. 1); Saterland *tehan* (van Helten 1900: § 11); MDutch *tien -tien*;[180] Mod. Dutch *tien, -tien*; OFrisian *tiân* (van Helten 1890: § 65) *tîen, -tîen* (van Helten 1899: 421). Mod. Frisian: West *ts(j)ien*; East *tjoon* Saterland, *tjôen* Wangeroog, *tjahn* Wursten; North: *tiin* Coast, Sylt; *tjiin* Föhr and Amrum (Helgoland: *täin*, loan-word form, Low German).

15.1.10.3. Both Old English and Old Frisian show a form of '-teen' with final *-e*. Van Helten (1906: 110) suggests that in 'thirteen' this form represents **texani-* and derives from **þrī texanī*, in which the second *ī* is due to the first; he considers that this *-i* then spread to the corresponding forms of 'fourteen' to 'nineteen'. This explanation is far-fetched, but no other has been suggested. It is, however, possible to explain these forms in *-e* from nom. pl. masc.-fem. **texanīz* to **texani-* – cf. nom. pl. Gothic *gasteis, ansteis* to the *i*-stems *gasts* masc. 'guest', *ansts* fem. 'grace'. *-iz* should of course vanish after a long stem or after one consisting of two short syllables, but, in fact, in the feminine, it remains in the first case in two early Old English examples: *maecti* 'mighty deeds' (Cædmon's Hymn, v. 2)[181] and *hyfi* 'alvearia' (Sweet 1885: 133).[182] The irregularity is no doubt due to some overlength in the vowel of the ending; see Campbell (1959: § 605, p. 242, n. 1). If we assume this origin for and this development in this Old English form of '-teen' – and a precisely similar state of affairs for Frisian – then, with the vowel-shift *j* > *e*, the forms are explained.

15.1.10.4. **texani-* > OHG infl. *zehini* (Braune – Mitzka 1967: § 27, n. 4) *zëhen*; MHG *zehen -zehen*;[183] OSax. *tehin(fald)* 'tenfold' Hêliand, *tein, -tein* (van Helten 1906: 105); MLG *tein -tein*[184] *-tên* (> *-tîn*, Lasch 1914: § 145) LG *tein, -ten* Assinghausen, *ta^{i}n, -ta^{i}n* Ostbevern, *ta^{i}n, -ta^{i}n* Heide (Dithmarschen), *ta^{i}ə* (*ta^{i}dn*), *-ta^{i}n* Stavenhagen; OELFranc. *ten* (< **tehen*); OFrisian *-tên* (< **teen* < **tehen*), *-tîn* (< **ti-en*, from **ti-an* + **te-en* – van Helten 1906: 110); further *-têne, -tîne.*[185]

15.1.10.5. Ross (1971: 59) treats of the Old English and, after some discussion, puts forward a solution, which is amplified here.
(**texun*: WSaxon *hundtēontig* 'hundred' [15.1.29.1.].)
**tixuni-* > **tiuxuni-* > **tiexyni* > WSaxon *tīen, tȳn, tīn* (cf. 15.1.3.), further *-tīene, -tȳne, -tīne.*
**texan* > **texan* > **teoxån* > **teaxan* > **tēan* > Lindisfarne Gospels *tę̄a*, Ru^2 *tēo.*[186] **teoxyni* (from **tiuxyni* (< **tiuxuni*) + **teoxån*) > **texyni* > Ru^1 *tēn*, Vespasian Psalter *tēn*, further non- WSaxon *-tēne*; MEngl. *tēn* > *tĕn*[187] (> Mod. Engl. *ten*), *-tēne* > *-tēn* (> Mod. Engl. *-teen*).[188]

15.1.10.6. **texan* > Icel. *-tán*; Færoese *-tan*; Mod. Norw. *-tan*; OSwed. *-tān*; ODanish *-tān.*

In West Norse length is preserved in '-teen' in Icelandic (*-tján, -tán*) and in Mod. Norw. *nikjas* 'nineteen' (15.1.19.); in Færoese (*-tjan, -tan*) and Mod. Norw. generally (*-tan*, and *saukjan* 'seventeen', 15.1.17., *nikjan* 'nineteen', 15.1.19.), there has been shortening.

In East Norse, the second element *-tān* appears to have had secondary stress in 'thirteen' to 'sixteen', but not in 'seventeen' to 'nineteen' (Noreen 1904: § 57.II.B.2a). When this was lost, shortening took place; hence OSwed. *s(i)æxtăn* 'sixteen' against OSwed. *siūtan̄* 'seventeen'. Later, both long and short forms could be used in any numeral of the group.

The shortened *-tăn* survives in Modern Swedish dialects, the standard language has *-ton* < **tån* < *-tăn* (Brøndum Nielsen 1950–1957: § 198); hence, with weakening (Brøndum Nielsen 1950–1957: § 214.2), *-tæn* Mod. Danish *-ten* (by analogy Mod. Norw. *-ten*). A similar shortening is evidenced in West Norse: Færoese *-tan*, Mod. Norw. *-tan*, and, here, the form with *j* is also affected: Færoese *-tjan*, Mod. Norw. *-kja(n)*.

Both *-tiān* and *-tān* exist in both Old West Norse and Old East Norse. In the former *-tán* is normal in 'thirteen' to 'sixteen', *-tián* in 'nineteen'; in 'seventeen' and 'eighteen' there is considerable variation; *-tián* is also found as a rare form in 'thirteen' to 'sixteen'.[189] In Old East Norse *-tā̆n* is invariable, but that *-tiān* also existed is shown firstly by the Modern Swedish dialect Dalecarlia *tiå*, and secondly by OSwed. *sixtān* 'sixteen', which must be derived from **siaxtiān*, with dissimilatory loss of the first *i* because of the second (15.1.16.).

It could be suggested that only *-tiān* is old, and that *-tan* is thus not from PGmc. **tēxan*, as stated above. For in Old West Norse, *-tán* could arise in 'seventeen': OIcel. *siautián* > *siaután*, with dissimilatory loss of the second *i* because of the first; cf. OIcel. *sautián*, with dissimilatory loss of the first *i* because of the second (15.1.17.). In Old East Norse, *-tān* could arise similarly in both 'sixteen' and 'seventeen' (OSwed. **siaxtiān*, 15.1.16., **siūtiān*, 15.1.17.). From 'seventeen' in Old West Norse, from this and 'sixteen' in Old East Norse, *-tān*, it might be suggested, could have spread to all the other numerals of the class. But more probably *-tān* did exist in its own right (> **tēxan*), and originally it existed beside *-tiān* in all the numerals of the class. But, for the reason just given, *-tān* became dominant in 'seventeen' in Old West Norse, and in this and 'sixteen' in Old East Norse; its spread in Old West Norse, and its dominance in Old East Norse, took place because of this fact.

15.1.11. 'Eleven'[190]

15.1.11.0. Gothic dat. *ainlibim* attests **aini-* not **aina-* as the first element. The former has thus – tacitly – been accepted as that of the Germanic prototype. Yet the latter form must be the earlier one; see the discussion in 15.1.1.1. **aini-* is of course necessary to explain many of the umlauted forms. In some forms, however, the umlaut is due to an *i* in the second element. In others it could either be due to this latter or have originated in **aini-*. And, in these, this second explanation must be considered to hold good (in neglect of the first for we can never disprove the existence of **aini-* in a particular context). In large part **aini-* and

**aina*- will be indistinguishable; see the discussion in Carr (1939: Part 2, Chapter 3, "The composition vowel"). Noreen (1923: § 66, n. 2) derives OIcel. *ellifo* precisely from **aina-liƀ*.

It is usual to interconnect the *u*/*o*-vocalism of the second syllable found in Scandinavian and Anglo-Frisian. Thus van Helten (1906: 107) postulates a special sound change *i* > *u* before *b*.[191] It may indeed be that the rare OHG *éinlúften* (acc. sing. masc. ordinal) (Notker, Piper 1895: 546/19), beside normal *einlif*, does attest this change. But, we suggest, the great majority of the relevant *u*/*o*-forms are better explained separately and otherwise (see below). In Dutch in part (Franck 1910: § 232.11), and in later English wholly (Jordan 1925: b § 21 n.), the stress of the word has been shifted to the second syllable; the reason for this is not apparent.

15.1.11.1. The word is widely subject to a number of sound changes and to one analogy. These developments are not of Proto-Germanic age, but have operated independently in the various branches. The changes are the following.

(α) *i*-umlaut.
(β) Assimilation *nl* > *ll*, which (β′) yield *l*.
(γ) Shortening before *nl* or *ll*.
(δ) Insertion of *d* between *n* and *l*.
(ε) Analogy with 'ten' – with (ε*¹*) **texun* **tixun* or (ε²) **texan* – or their descendants.
(ʒ) *a*-umlaut – in Low German and Frisian.

15.1.11.2. We can now proceed to the discussion of the individual forms.
**aini-liƀa*: Gothic dat. *ainlibim*.
**aina-lifą* > OHG *einlif*; MHG *einlif, einlef, eilif, eilef, eilf*[192] (> Mod. HG *elf* – Paul – Mitzka 1966: § 23 n.).

The main cause of the complexity of the Scandinavian forms is the Proto-Norse change *ƀu* > *wu* > *u*, which has already been discussed in respect of 'seven' (15.1.7.). In respect of 'eleven' the change is only partial, that is, forms unchanged by it survive beside changed ones.[193]

We have then **aina-lifu*, **aina-liƀu*, **aini-lifu*, **aini-liƀu* (ε*¹*)[194] > **anli-ƀu*[195] > **ālliƀu*[196] (β) > **ālliu*. From this + **ālliƀu* we obtain **ālliuƀu*. Next **ālliƀu*, **ālliuƀu* > **ǣlliƀu*, **ǣlliuƀu* (α) and **ālliu* > **ǣllu* (α – with loss of *i*). From **ǣllu* + **ǣlliƀu* we obtain **ǣlluƀu*. Then **ǣlliƀu*, **ǣlliuƀu*, **ǣlluƀu* > **œlliuƀu*, **œlliuƀu*, *œlluƀu* (γ). **œlliƀu* > Icel. *ellefu*; Færoese *ellivu*; ONorw. *œllifu* (Noreen 1904: § 127.6); Mod. Norw. *elleve*; OSwed. *œllivu* (and *œllevo* by "vokalbalanz" – see Noreen 1904: § 140 ff.); ODanish *œllivu*,[197] *œllefue*,[198] *elløfuœ,ølloff* (cf. Brøndum Nielsen 1950–1957: § 135.1); Mod. Danish *elleve*.[199]

*ælliuƀu > ONorw. ælliufu; OSwed. *ælliuwu.
*ælluƀu > early Færoese edluvu (Svabo, ed. Matras, 1943);[200] OSwed. ællovo; ODanish ællufhæ, ællowæ; and, with change ƀ > ʒ (Noreen 1923: § 256), ONorw. ællugu, then with u-umlaut of æ (Noreen 1923: 77.7), *ølluƀu > *ølluʒu > Mod. Norw. øllug.

Noreen (1904: § 148, n. 1) explains -a of Mod. Swed. elva (< OSwed. ællova) as due to analogy with fyra 'four' and åtta 'eight'; a similar – somewhat far-fetched – analogy could account for Mod. Norw. ælluva (: ONorw. átta 'eight').

15.1.11.3. *aina-lefan, *aina-leƀan, *aini-lefan, *aini-leƀan (3, ε^2) > OSax. elleƀan (β, γ) (Gallée 1910: §§ 89, n. 5, 212.1) elevan, eleven; MLG elven, elve (Lasch 1914: § 274); LG elf Assinghausen, elmn̥ Ostbevern, ölm̄ Heide (Dithmarschen), elm̄ Stavenhagen. MDutch elleven (β, γ) (Franck 1910: §§ 112.3, 42)[201a] may represent these protoforms or the corresponding ones with i in the second syllable (weakening i > e); elf (> Mod. Dutch elf) is apparently modelled on tweelf, etc. 'twelve'.

15.1.11.4. The Frisian forms[201b] have, in addition, been affected by the loss of final -n (van Helten 1890: § 107a) – which is partially restored from the inflected forms – and by the sporadic change eƀ > oƀ (cf. OFrisian iova = Icel. gefa 'to give' – van Helten 1890: § 7b). Hence, then, *aina-lefan, *aina-leƀan, *aini-lefan, *aini-leƀan, (3, ε^2) > êleve; (β, γ) andlova, (δ) elleva, allewa, (β, γ) elleve; infl. elvene, allewene, alwene, alven; and elleven, uninflected, -n restored. Modern Frisian: West alve, alf (some dialects also forms with e); East alwen Saterland, anelf Wangeroog, Wursten (metathesized from *anlef), elff, eylff Harlingen; North alwen Coast (Halligen elew), elwen Föhr und Amrum, elev Sylt, el(e)wen Helgoland (now ölm, influenced by Low German).[202] The East and North forms with e are probably borrowed from Low German, but Sterdebüll aalfä is native.

15.1.11.5. The West Saxon forms have been affected by back-umlaut: i > iu (> io > eo) before a labial followed by u and å (< PGmc. a) in the next syllable (Campbell 1959: § 212). We have then: *aini-lifą, *aini-liƀą > Lindisfarne Gospels 23vb3, ællef; Matthew 28,16; (hundændlæftig (α, γ, δ) 'one hundred and ten', 15.1.29.2.); *aini-lifan, *aini-liƀan (ε^2) > Ru^2 ællefne Luke 24,33; Lindisfarne Gospels ællefno (inflected – the latter with late adjectival ending). From these last two protoforms with weakening of i to e (Campbell 1959: § 372) – rather than a-umlaut, cf. 3: early WSaxon enlefan (α, γ);[203] Ru^1 enlefan 28,16; OEngl. endlefan (α, γ, δ); with back-umlaut, WSaxon endleofan[204]; *aini-lifun, *aini-liƀun (ε^1) > WSaxon endlufon[205] (α, γ, δ), with "akzentumsprung" iu > u.

The various forms continue in later English: MEngl. *alleven, aleven:* Ru[2] *ællefne*; MEngl. *endleven, endleve* < *endlefan*; MEngl. *enleven, enleve* < *enlefan*; MEngl. *endlufan* < *endlufin* (and MEngl. *enlufan* from a parallel **enlufon*); MEngl. *elleoven* (> Mod. Engl. *eleven*), *elleove* < **enleofan* (parallel to *endleofean*) with assimilation (β).

15.1.12. 'Twelve'

15.1.12.0. **twa-liƀą* > Gothic[206] *twalif*, dat. *twalibim*. **twa-lifą* > OHG *zwelif*; MHG *zwelif, zwelef, zwelf.*

In Scandinavian, the word is affected by a change *ua* > *ua* > *uo* > *o*. In West Norse, this change is almost completely carried out (Noreen 1923: §§ 77.10, 235. 1a), but, in East Norse, only the first stage takes place in stressed syllables, though in those with lesser stress the whole series can eventuate (Brøndum Nielsen 1950–1957: § 103 n. 3); here, then, there is variation in 'twelve' according to the stressing. Hence **twa-lifą*, **twa-liƀa* > OIcel. *tolf*;[207] Mod. Icel *tólf*;[208] Færoese *tólv*;[209] Mod. Norw. *tolv*; OSwed. *tolf*,[210] Mod. Swed. *tolv*; ODanish *tolf* (> *tølf*, Brøndum Nielsen 1950–1957: § 126); Mod. Danish *tolv*.

15.1.12.1. From the same two protoforms: OSax. *tuuelif*; MLG *twelf*; LG *twiẹlf* Assinghausen, Ostbevern; Saterland *tualif*; MDutch *twelef* (> **twelf* > *twellef*, Franck 1910: § 52), *tweelf* (Heeroma 1939: 207); OFrisian *twelif, twelef, twelf*; Mod. Frisian: East *tweel(i)f* Saterland, *twolfe*[211] Harlingen, *twüllef* Wangeroog, *tweliff* Wursten;[212] North *tweelew, twilew* (also *-wen*)[213] Coast; OEngl. *twelf*[214] (> North Northumbrian *tuoelf*, Campbell 1959: § 319); MEngl. *twelf*,[215] infl. *twelve* (> Mod. Engl. *twelve*).

15.1.12.2. A Dutch form and an Anglo-Saxon one have been especially noted. Cf. Franck (1910: § 33 n.): "*Twalef* neben *twēlef* aus *twalif* beruht wahrscheinlich auf einer sächsisch-friesischen Umbildung von *twalif* mit *twâ* für *twai*". And Campbell (1959: § 197): "Ru[1] *twǣlf twelve*, perhaps contains the mutation of the *ā* of *twā*". Clearly, neither of the suggested analogies is satisfactory. And the forms can be otherwise – and independently – explained. Cf. van Helten (1906: 108): "Mittelniederländisch *twalef, twaelf* ... die Form geht wohl zurück auf **tualìb-*, worin mitteltoniges *i* das *a* nicht beeinflußte"[216]. And Ru[1] attests a change *we* > *wæ* (Campbell 1959: § 328) so that *twælf*[217] can be derived from the normal OEngl. *twelf* (so Campbell 1959: § 197 n. 3 as an alternative explanation).

The change *we* > *wæ* occurs over a wider area, for it is evidenced in North Northumbrian also (Britton 1970: 12 ff.). Cf. further Mod. Frisian *twaalew* Föhr and Amrum – Helgoland *tuálow* may be parallel (cf. *hualow* 'half' = OEngl. *healf*) or from *twelf* (cf. *salow* 'self' = OEngl. *seolf*). Sylt *twelev* influenced by *elev* 'eleven', or from Low German? The forms just discussed continue: MDutch *twaelf* > Mod. Dutch *twaalf*; OEngl. *twælf* > MEngl. *twalf*, Mod. Scots *twall* (with loss of *f*).

In MHG *zwilf*,[218] OSax. *tuilif*, OFrisian *twilif* (van Helten 1890: § 26 n. 3), the *i* of the second syllable has caused the *e* of the first syllable to become *i*. Change of this *e*, to *ö*, *o* and even *u*, under the influence of the preceding consonant is widespread: MHG *zwelf* > *zwolf* > *zwölf* (> Mod. HG. *zwölf*, Paul – Mitzka 1966: § 27.4), *zwulf*;[219] OSax. *tuuelif* > *tuulif* and MLG *twölf* (Lasch 1914: § 169b) (> LG *twölf* Heide [Dithmarschen], *twölf* Stavenhagen), *twolf* (Lasch 1914: § 177) (> LG *twolf*, Bremer Wörterbuch s. v.); OFrisian *twelef* > *tolef*;[220] OEngl. *twelf* > MEngl. *tweolf* (*eo* representing *ö* – Jordan 1925: § 33, n. 3 – cf. AB *tweolf*); MEngl. *twolf*, Mod. Scots *twoll*.

'-teen' has already been discussed (15.1.10.0. ff.), so that, in the ensuing sections on 'thirteen' to 'nineteen', only the first elements are treated. Constant reference to the discussion of the cardinals 'three' to 'nine' is desirable. We do not give individual references.

15.1.13. 'Thirteen'[221]

15.1.13.1. Nom. masc. PGmc. **þrīz*; (ordinal Runic Swed. [Rök] *þrītaunti* [15.2.13.]); OHG *drîzëhen*; MHG *drîzëhen*, *drîzên*; Mod. HG *dreizehn*. Acc. masc. fem. PGmc. **þrinz*: OIcel. *þréttán*,[222] *þrétián* (Jónsson 1925: 87): Mod. Icel. *þrettán* (cf. Noreen 1923: § 127), Færoese *trettan*; Mod. Norw. *trettan*, *tretten*; OSwed. *þrǣtān*,[223] OGut. *þrētān* (Noreen 1904: § 105) > OSwed. *þrættǟn*,[224] Runic Gut. *þrettān* (Noreen 1904: § 105); Mod. Swed. *tretton*; ODanish *thrætǟn*[225] (> *thrættǟn*, Brøndum Nielsen 1950–1957: §§ 99, 111.1, 162), *thretāan*; further *thrætæn*, *thrættæn*; Mod. Danish *tretten*.

OSwed. *brittan* from *þrættān* + the descendant of **þrītaun* (cf. ordinal *þrītaunti*, above),[226a] OSwed. *þrattān* from *þrættān* + *atẹrtān* 'eighteen'.[226b]

Nom.-acc. neuter PGmc. **þrijō*; MHG *driuzehen*, *drizên*; OSax. *thriutein*, *thrûtein*; OEngl. *þrēotīene*.[227a]

15.1.13.2. In the West Germanic forms of this word there is a widespread change of long vowel or diphthong + single consonant to short vowel or diphthong + double consonant. Van Helten (1906: 112) suggests that this is due to short vowel + double consonant (*dd*) in the ordinal 'third' (15.2.3.). But this is surely very far-fetched. The change in fact seems to be fairly general and to apply to many words (Franck 1910: §§ 42, 100; Campbell 1959: § 287).

We have, then, OSax. *thrûtein* > MLG *drüttein* (cf. Lasch 1914: § 173); MLG *drittein* is due to the influence of *drittich* 'thirty'; *drettein* from *drüttein* + *drê*[227b] whence, by metathesis, *dertein* (Lasch 1914: § 231). The Middle Low German forms survive into Modern Low German and van Helten (1906: 111) discusses some of the forms of the latter: *dertein* > *dertein* (Schambach 1858 s. v.), *dortein, drüttaaijen* (Berghaus 1880–1884), *dörtein* (Danneil 1859); *drüttein* > *drüttein* (ibid.), *drytáen* (Holthausen 1886: § 395), *drytīn* (Holthausen 1886: 552) and *dörtein* (Schütze 1800–1806: *dörde*, and as for *dortein*). MDutch *dertien* (> Mod. Dutch *dertien*) < **þrittexan* (Franck 1910: § 232) < nom. masc. **þrītexan*. OFrisian *threttên* < **thrêtên*, with *thrê*. Mod. Frisian: West *trett(s)jin*; East *trättien* Saterland; *thretthyan, trettyhn* Harlingen, *threttîn* Wangeroog; North *tratäin, trotain, tretain* Coast, *trataanj* Föhr and Amrum (*tretanj* WFöhr), *tretain, trötain* Sylt (Helgoland *dötain* < Low German).

OEngl. *þrĕottyne* < *þrēotīene* (above); OEngl. *þryttēne*,[228a] with *y* written for *i*, < nom. masc. **þrītēne*. In Middle English *ĕo* > *ö* > *e*, and in the later periods, this *ĕ* can give *ĭ* between *r* and the dental (Luick 1921–1940: § 379); towards the close of the period metathesis takes place (Jordan 1925: § 165). With the exception of Ormulum's *þrittene* (< OEngl. **þrittēne* above), all the Middle English forms can be explained from Old English ones in *þrĕott-*: AB *þreottene*; further *þrottene, þrettene, þretene, þritten, þirtene* (> Mod. Engl. *thirteen*).

15.1.14. 'Fourteen'

15.1.14.1. Norse

Nom.-acc. neuter OWN **fiǫʒur*, **fiuʒur*, OEN **fiuʒur*: OIcel. *fiogortán*; ONorw. *fiugurtán*; OSwed. *fiughurtān*; ODanish *fiughurtăn*.

Various analogies affected this nominative-accusative neuter form. (1) It was remodelled on OWN **fiǫðr*, OEN **fiuðr* to give OWN **fiǫʒr* **fiuʒr*, OEN **fiuʒr*, and it was (2) replaced by (a) OWN *fiōr-* and (b) OEN *fiūr-*; in addition, from OWN **fiuʒur* + (2a) *fiōr-*, we have[228b] (2aa) OWN *fiūr-*; and, from OEN **fiuʒur* + (2b) OEN *fiūr-*, we have (2ba) OEN *fiur-*. Hence: 1) OWN **fiǫʒr*, **fiuʒr*; OEN **fiuʒr*; OIcel.

fiogrtán; ONorw. *fiugrtán*; with svarabhakti (Noreen 1904: § 160.2b; Brøndum Nielsen 1950–1957: § 221); OSwed. *fiughęrtān*;[229] ODanish *fiugghærtăn* (> *figertă̄n, fygerten*) > Mod. Danish dialectal *fjaurtan* (Espersen 1908: § 24).
2a) OWN *fiōr-*: Mod. Icel. *fjórtán*; ONorw. *fjórrtán*; Mod. Norw. *fjortan, fjorten*.
2aa) OWN *fiūr-*: ONorw. *fiúrtán*; Mod. Norw. *fjurten* Numedal, Sunnmøre, Hallingdal; Færoese *fjúrtan*.
2b) OEN *fiūr-*: OSwed. *fiurtān*; ODanish *fiūrtă̄n* > *fȳrtă̄n* (Brøndum Nielsen 1950–1957: § 180.A4).
2ba) OEN *fiŭr-*: OSwed. *fiūrtān* > *fiŏrtān* (Noreen 1904: § 120): ODanish *fiŭrttăn* > *fiŏrtăn*; from this + *fiūtă̄n*, we have *fiōrtă̄n*, cf. Brøndum Nielsen (1950–1957: § 546.4); he there renegues on explanations of the forms that he has given earlier (§§ 140 n. 1, 183).
Mod. Swed. *fjorton* < OSwed. *fiūrtān* or *fiŏrtān*, Mod. Danish *fjorten* < ODanish *fiōrtă̄n* or *fiŏrtă̄n*.

15.1.14.2. Gothic

Fidworthaíhun – as *fidwor*.

15.1.14.3. West Germanic

**feur*: OHG *fiorzëhan*; MHG *vierzëhen, vierzên*; Mod. HG *vierzehn*; OSax. *fiertein*; MLG *vertein* (*vêrtein* from this + *vêr*); LG *feirten* Assinghausen, *fettain* Ostbevern, *feirtain* Heide (Dithmarschen), *firtain* Stavenhagen; MDutch *viertien* (> *veertien*, Franck 1910: § 76 > Mod. Dutch *veertien*).
**feuwar*: OFrisian: *fiuwertîn, fiwertîn, fiuertên, fiurtên, fiowrtên*. Mod. Frisian: East *fjaurtien* Saterland, *viaurthyn* Harlingen; North *fjauertäin*, etc.; *fîrtîn* (*fîrtennacht* 'fortnight') Wangeroog < **fiwertine*? Spenter (1968: 279) considers West *fjirt(s)jin* (Schiermonnikoog *fjitsien*) as modelled on ordinal *fjirde* (Helgoland *feartain*, loan-word form; Low German).
**feuwar* or **fewar*; OEngl. *feowertīene, feowertȳne, feowertēne*; MEngl. *feowertene, feowertyne, fourtene* – AB *fowrtene* – (> Mod. Engl. *fourteen*) *faurten*.

15.1.15. 'Fifteen'

Gothic dat. *fimftaíhunim*; OIcel. *fimtán, fimtián* (Jónsson 1925: 87); Mod. Icel. *fimmtán*; Færoese *fimtan*; OSwed. *fǣmtăn* > *fǣmptān* (Noreen 1904: § 332.2); Mod. Swed. *femton*; ODanish *fæmtă̄n* (> *fæmptă̄n*, Brøndum

Nielsen 1950–1957: § 351, and *fæntăn*, Brøndum Nielsen 1950–1957: § 320.1); also *fæmtæn, femten* (> Mod. Danish *femten*, adapted as Mod. Norw. *femtan, femten*), *fæntæn*; OHG *finfzëhan*; MHG *finfzëhen, vinfzên, funfzëhen* (> *funzëhen*, cf. Mausser 1932: § 129) *vunfzên, fumfzëhen, fünfzëhen, fünfzên, fümfzëhen, fiunfzëhen, viumfzehen* (vomfzên unexplained); Mod. HG *fünfzehn* (dialectal *funfzehn*); OSax. *fīftein*; MLG *vîftein* > *veftein* (Lasch 1914: § 68.2) > *vöftein* (Lasch 1914: § 398, n. 1). The Middle Low German forms survive into Low German; van Helten (1906: 113–114) mentions *feftein*, Schambach (1858) *föftein, föftein* (as preceding, also Schütze 1800–1806: *fief*, and cf. *föfftein*, Danneil 1859: *fīw*), *föfteijen* (Dähnert 1781: s. v., Berghaus 1880–1884: *foftein*), *föften* (cf. Schambach 1858: *föftên*, s. v. *föftein*), *foftein* (as for *föftein*, and Berghaus 1880–1884: s. v., Bremer Wörterbuch: *fofte*). MDutch *viftien* (Franck 1910: § 41) and *vichtien* (Franck 1910: § 110) – *vijftien* (> Mod. Dutch *vijftien*) in analogy with the cardinal; OFrisian *fīftîn, fīftên*; Mod. Frisian: *fyft(s)jin* West, *fūftîn* Wangeroog, *füftien* Saterland, *füftäin* EMoringen, *fiftaanj* Föhr and Amrum (*füftanj* WFöhr), *föftain* Helgoland (loan-word form, Low German): OEngl. *fīftȳne, fīftēne*; MEngl. *fīftēne* > *fĭftēne* [230] (shortening, Luick 1921–1940: § 352) *fĭftēn* (> Mod. Engl. *fifteen*) and [*fīvetēne*] (cf. Mod. Scots *fyveten*) – analogy with the inflected cardinal.

15.1.15.1. Some of the forms in the southern and middle dialects of High German been much discussed, *fuchzehn* has been held to derive ultimately from an ordinal OHG **fûhto* = OInd. *Pakthá-* 'Quintus'. But not only is there no old trace of this ordinal in Germanic, but there is no trace of a form with the original PIE k^w instead of the assimilated *p*. The explanation is to be rejected. Van Helten (1906: 133) plausibly suggests that *fuchzehn* is based on *sechszehn* 'sixteen'; whence further *fufzehn* from *fuchzehn* + *funfzehn*. See, most recently, Hotzenköcherle (1971: 311).

15.1.16. 'Sixteen'

Icel. *sextán*, OIcel. *sextián* (Jónsson 1925: 87); Færoese *sekstan*; Mod. Norw. *sekstan, seksten*. In Old East Norse, **sexstān* > **siaxstān* (breaking); from this + **sexstiān*, we have **siaxstiān* > **saxstiān* (dissimilatory loss of first *i*); **siaxstān, *siaxstiān* > **siæxtān, *siæxtian* (Noreen 1904: § 96, Brøndum Nielsen 1950–1957: § 177) > **sæxtiān* (dissimilatory loss of first *i*); from this + **siæxtān*, we have **sæxtān*, and, from **saxstiān* + **sæxtān*, we have **saxtān*. Hence, then, OSwed. *siæxtān, sæxtăn* (>

Mod. Swed. *sexton*), *saxtān* (see Noreen 1892–1894: 331–332); ODanish *siæxtăn, siextăn, siæxtæn, siextæn,*[231] *sæxtān* (> *seyxtan*, Brøndum Nielsen 1950–1957: § 312.2), *sexten* (< Mod. Danish *seksten*[232]). OHG *sëhszë-han*; MHG *sëchszëhen* (> *sëhzëhen*, cf. Mausser 1932: §129), *sechzên*; Mod. HG *sechszehn, sechzehn*; OSax. *sehstein, sestein*, MLG *sestein*;[233] MDutch *sestien*; Mod. Dutch *zestien*; OFrisian *sextîn, sextên*; Mod. Frisian: *sextîn* Wangeroog, *säkstien* Saterland, *seekstäin* EMoringen, *sääkstaanj* Föhr and Amrum, *sech(s)t(s)jin* West; OEngl. *sixtȳne, syxtȳne*; MEngl. *sextēne, sextēn, sixtēne* (Ormulum *sextene*, AB *sixtene*) > Mod. Engl. *sixteen.*

15.1.17. 'Seventeen'

OIcel. *siaután*, Mod. Norw. *sjauttan*; OIcel *siautián* (> *sieytián*, with umlaut), Mod. Norw. *sjaukja*[234] Set; from this type, with dissimilatory loss of first *i̯*, Icel. *sautján* (> *seytján*, with umlaut), Færoese *seytjan*,[235] Mod. Norw. *saukjan, saukja*[236]; MIcel. *siøtián*; ONorw. *siótián*; OSwed. *siūtān* > *siuttăn* (Noreen 1904: § 297.2) > Mod. Swed. *sjutton*; ODanish *siūtān* > *siuttăn* (Brøndum Nielsen 1950–1957: §§ 416, 197.2) > *siytten* > *sytten* (Brøndum Nielsen 1950–1957: §§ 180a.4, 386.2) > Mod. Danish *sytten* – also > *søttæn* (Brøndum Nielsen 1950–1957: § 164) *søtten.*[237] MHG *siebenzëhen*, early Mod. HG *siebenzehn*; Mod. HG *siebzehn*; OSax. *sivontein*; MLG *seventein*; LG *siwn̥tęn, sībnten* Assinghausen, *sieb̥mtaⁱn* Ostbevern, *söm'aⁱn* Heide (Dithmarschen), Stavenhagen; MDutch *seventien, söventien*; Mod. Dutch *zeventien*; OFrisian *sogentîn*; Mod. Frisian *sjûgentîn* Wangeroog, *soogentien* Saterland, *soowentäin* EMoringen, *sööwentaanj* Föhr and Amrum, *sawnt(s)jin* West; OEngl. *seofontīene(wintre)* 'seventeen years old' *seofontȳne, seofentȳne*;[238] Mod. Engl. *seventeen*, early Mod. Engl. also *seauenteene.*

15.1.18. 'Eighteen'

There is a widespread "irregular" loss of the medieval vowel.[239]
OIcel. *áttián* > Icel. *átián* (Noreen 1923: § 267); Færoese *átjan*; Mod. Norw. *attan, atten*; OSwed. **ātttān* > *ăttan* (Noreen 1904: § 90.1); from **āttatān* + **fiuʒrtān* 'fourteen', we have **āttrtān*, and with still further analogy, **āʒrtān* (> Mod. Swed. dialect *åkurta, agärta,*[240] *arton*[241]; **āttrtān* > **ātrtān* (Runic Gut. *atrt* ...); from this + *ăttan*, we have *atęrtān* > *aþęrtān* (Noreen 1904: § 266) (> Mod. Swed. *aderton*); from *atęrtān* + *ātta*, we have *atartān, attartān, attẹtān.* ODanish **āttan* >

attān (Brøndum Nielsen 1950–1957: § 115), *attæn*;[242] Mod. Danish *atten* (also dialectal *atan*). OHG *ahtozëhan*; MHG *ahtzëhen* (> *ahzëhen*, cf. Mausser 1932: § 129) *achzên*; Mod. HG *achtzehn*; OSax. *ahtetein, ahtetian, ahtetein*; MLG *achtein*; LG *achtẹn* Assinghausen, *achtaⁱn* Ostbevern, Heide (Dithmarschen), Stavenhagen; MDutch *achtien*; Mod. Dutch *achttien*; OFrisian *achtatîn, achtetên, achtên*; Mod. Frisian *achtîn* Wangeroog, *achttien* Saterland, *oochtäin* EMoringen, *aagitaani*[243] Föhr und Amrum (*achtaanj* OFöhr), *achtt(s)jin* West; OEngl. *eahtatiene, eahtatyne, ehtatyne, ehtatene*;[244] MEngl. *eightetene, eightene* (> Mod. Engl. *eighteen*) *aghtene, aughtene*.

15.1.19. 'Nineteen'

Icel. *nítján*; Færoese *nítjan*; Mod. Norw. *nikjan, nikjaa*;[245] OSwed. *nītān* > MSwed. *nittăn* (Noreen 1904: § 297.2) (> Mod. Swed. *nitton*); ODanish *nītān* > *nittăn* (Brøndum Nielsen 1950–1957: §§ 197.2, 416) *nittæn*[246] (> Mod. Danish *nitten*[247]); OHG *niunzëhan*; MHG *niunzëhen*; Mod. HG *neunzehn*; OSax. *nigentein*; MLG *negentein*; LG *nīʒn̩tẹn* Assinghausen, *niᵉʒn̥taⁱn* Ostbevern, *niəˈaⁱn* Heide (Dithmarschen, *nēətaⁱn* Stavenhagen; MDutch *negentien*; Mod. Dutch *negentien*; OFrisian *niûgentên*; Mod. Frisian *njûgentîn* Wangeroog, *njuugentien* Saterland, *njöögentäin* EMoringen, *njügentaanj* Föhr and Amrum, *njoggent(s)jin* West; OEngl. *nigantīene, nigontȳne, neogontȳne*; MEngl. *niȝentēne, neȝentēne, ninetēne, nintēne* (> Mod. Engl. *nineteen*) *nēnteyn*.

15.1.20. 'Twenty'

15.1.20.0. -ty

There are four main formations, typified by: (A) Gothic acc. *fimf tiguns* 'fifty'; (B) Gothic *sibuntehund* 'seventy'; (C) OEngl. *hundseofontig* 'seventy'; (D) OHG *sibunzo* 'seventy'. Less important formations are typified by: (E) OIcel. *tuítian* 'twenty'; (F) OIcel. *fimtíu* 'fifty'; (G) Mod. Danish *tresindstyve* 'sixty'; (H) Crimean Gothic *furdeithien* 'forty'.

15.1.20.1.[248] Type A

Ross (1954: 116–128) discusses this formation. What follows here is in part a quotation from, in part an expansion of, this discussion. We begin by enumerating certain endings which are postulated by Ross for the *u*- and consonant-paradigms in Germanic.[249]

ŭ	Maculine	Neuter
nom.-acc. sing.		[+ 01]-*u*
nom. pl.	[+ 02] -*iwiz*	[+ 04] -*ū* (> -*u*)
acc. pl.	[+ 03] -*unz*	
nom.-acc. dual	[+ 05] ≡ [+ 04]	([+ 06?] ≡ [+ 04]), [+ 07] -*iwī* (> -*iwi*)
gen. pl.-dual	[+ 09] [+ 12] -*iwǫ* [+ 102] Gothic -*iwe*, [+ 12] N & W Gmc -*ǭ*	
"dat." pl.-dual.	[+ 08] -*um*-	

Consonant (neuter)		
nom.-acc. pl.	**teʒunðō*	[cf. + 14]
nom.-acc. dual	**teʒunði*	[cf. + 15]
gen. pl.-dual	**teʒunðǭ*	[cf. + 17]
dat. pl.-dual	**teʒunðm-*	[cf. + 16] > *teʒum(m-.

In Old Indian, *dáśa* 'ten' has gen. *dáśanā́m*, instr. *daśábhiḥ*. Declining **dékm̥* as a neuter consonant-stem, including the uninflected form as nominative-accusative singular and making allowance for alternation in Verner's Law, we obtain the Proto-Germanic paradigm [+ 21]:

nom.-acc. sing.	**texu*	**teʒu*	
nom.-acc. pl.	**texumō*	**teʒumō*	[cf. + 14]
nom.-acc. dual	**texumi*	**teʒumi*	[cf. + 15]
gen. pl.-dual	**texumǭ*	**teʒumǭ*	[cf. + 17]
dat. pl.-dual	**texum-*	**teʒum-*	[cf. + 16]

It will be seen that paradigm [+ 21] coincides in two cases, nominative-accusative singular and dative plural and dual, with the neuter portion of the *u*-paradigm set out above; we may reasonably suppose that this would have been sufficient to transfer **texu*, **teʒu* to the *ŭ*-declension. Moreover a Proto-Germanic reflection of Benveniste's Lemma will have been alternation between neuter *ŭ*-stem with [V –] (original barytone) and masculine *ŭ*-stem with [V +] (original oxytone). Now in paradigm [+ 21] we have just this alternation between [V –] and [V +] in what is now, by transference, a *ŭ*-stem. Ross suggests: a) that this was sufficient to bring into being a masc. *ŭ*-stem beside the neuter one; b) that at some later period the ʒ-forms with [V +] were generalized; c) that the decads now conformed to these [V +] *ŭ*-paradigms, with concord. We thus have two paradigms, one neuter and one masculine. Before setting them out we may note that in some Germanic types a different ablaut-grade of 'ten', viz. **deḱm̥t* appears, e. g., in OIcel. *tottogo* 'twenty' and OHG *-zug*. This vowel would here give the bipartite phoneme PGmc. o^u; this will materialize as *u* before *i* or *u* in the next syllable, otherwise as *o*, e. g. as *o* in the replacement gen. pl. *-o* [+ 11]. Further PIE *e* > *i* before *i* of the next syllable generally, and before *u* of the next syllable in, at least, Old High German (cf. 15.1.7.2.). There will thus be variations *u* ~ *o*, *i* ~ *e* (e. g. nom.-acc. pl. neuter **teʒu* ~ nom.-acc. pl. masc. **tiʒiwiz*) – variations well reflected in OIcel. *tegr, tigr, togr, tugr*. The decads paradigm may now be assembled as follows:

	Masculine	Neuter
nom. pl.	[+ 22] **tiʒiwiz* [+ 23] **tuʒiwiz*, [cf. + 02]	(= [+ 27] **teʒu* [+ 28] *tiʒu [+ 29] **tuʒu*, [cf. + 04]
acc. pl.	[+ 24] **teʒunz* [+ 25] **tiʒunz* [+ 26] **tuʒunz*, [cf. + 03]	
nom.-acc. dual	≡ [+ 27] [+ 28] [+ 29], [cf. + 05]	[+ 27] [+ 28] [+ 29], [cf. + 06])?; [+ 30] **tiʒiwi* [+ 3] **tuʒiwi*, [cf. + 07]
gen. pl.-dual	[+ 32] **tiʒiwǫ* [cf. + 09] [cf. + 12]; Gothic [+ 33] **tiʒiwē*, [cf. + 10] N & W Gmc. [+ 34] **teʒǭ* [+ 35] **tʒǭ* [cf. + 11]	
dat. pl.-dual	[+ 36] **teʒum* [+ 37] **tiʒum* [+ 38] **tuʒum*, [cf. +08]	

In Gothic, the masculine inflection of **tiʒiwiz* [+ 22], [+ 24], [+ 33], [+ 36] is apparently preserved intact: acc. *þrins tiguns*. The Scandinavian forms are difficult. The usual explanation of OIcel. *tottogo* as a fossilized form corresponding to a Gothic **twans tiguns* (Noreen 1913: § 231) is not acceptable, for it offers no reason why the form was fossilized. And OSwed. *tiughu* can hardly be explained, with Noreen, as identical with Gothic acc. *tiguns*, for there appears to be no reason why a word originally meaning 'ten' should suddenly come to mean 'twenty'. Ross begins by postulating nom.-acc. neuter dual [+ 39] **twae tiʒiwi*, [+ 40] **twae tuʒiwi*, the second elements being [+ 30], [+ 31], the first nom.-acc. neuter **twae*; further nom.-acc. neuter dual [+ 41] **two teʒu*, [+ 42] **twō tiʒu*, [+ 43] **twō tuʒu*; for the second element, see the discussion in Ross (1954); the first is nom.-acc. neuter **twō*, which, in Scandinavian, gives **tū*; hence

[+ 41] **tūteʒu*, [+ 42] **tūtiʒu*, [+ 43] **tūtuʒu*. In the Scandinavian decads above twenty we have the masculine paradigm of **tiʒiwiz*, **tuʒiwiz*.

In West Norse a paradigm congruent to a Gothic **twai tigjus* also appears and the accusative of this, a Gothic **twans tiguns*, shows a special phonological development to [+ 44] **tott-* (Noreen 1923: §§ 266.2, 77.10). Having in mind [+ 43] **tūtuʒu* and [+ 44] **tott-*, all the West Norse forms of 'twenty' can be satisfactorily explained: OIcel. *tottogo*; Icel. *tuttugu*; ONorw. *tottogo, tuttugu, tut(e)gu, tutigu*; Orkney *tuttv* (< **tut-tugu*) (see Hægstad 1900: 63); ONorw. *tuittugu* (Hægstad [1906–1942] 1915: 23), analogy with prefix OWN *tuí-*, > *tyttugu* (Noreen 1923: § 77.12), *tugtugu* (Hægstad [1906–1942] 1915: 23), assimilation *tyktugu* (Hægstad 1914–1915: 23), from the last two. The higher West Norse decads have as a rule preserved the masculine inflection of **tiʒiwiz*, **tuʒiwiz* intact: OIcel. *þrír tiger, teger, toger, tuger, toger,*[250] etc.[251] – '-ty' survives here as a normal noun, OIcel. *tigr, tegr* 'group of ten'.

In Old Swedish, matters are more complicated. PGmc. **teʒu-* survives here as a normal noun (both masculine and neuter). By the ordinary rules of Swedish breaking (Noreen 1904: § 75), we have the following paradigm:

	Singular PN	OSwed.	Plural PN	OSwed.
nom. masc.	**teʒuR*	**tioghẹr*	**teʒiR*	**tighir*
acc. masc.	**teʒu*	**tiogh*	**teʒu̯*	**tiughu*
nom.-acc. neuter			**teʒu*	**tiogh*
gen.	**teʒōR*	**tiaghar*	**teʒō*	**tiagha*
dat.	**tiʒiu*	**tighi*	**teʒum*	**tiughum*

With generalization: *-i-*, OSwed. *tighẹr*; *-ia-* (> *-æ-*, Noreen 1904: § 96), Modern Swedish dialectal (Dalecarlia) *tiæg; -io-*, Mod. Swed. *tjog; -iu-*, OSwed. *tiughẹr, tiugh* neuter.

The neuter dual forms [+ 30] **tiʒiwi*, [+ 31] **tuʒiwi* appear fossilized, and, to judge by the development PIE loc. sing. **sunewei* (cf. OInd. *sūnáve*, Greek *phḗkhei*) > PGmc. **suneu* > PN **suniu* – cf. Stentofta[252] dat. sing. *maʒiu* – OIcel. *syne*, OSwed. *syni*, ODanish *syni*, we may safely assume a development **tiʒiwi*, **tuʒiwi* > **tiʒi*, **tuʒi*; hence from [+ 39] **twae tiʒiwi* + [+ 42] **twō tiʒu* on the one hand, and [+ 40] **twae tuʒiwi* + [+ 43] **twō tuʒu* on the other, we obtain [+ 45] **tutiʒi* and [+ 46] **tutuʒi*. We next assume that, in Proto-Norse, [+ 43] **tutuʒu* >

[+ 47] **tuȝu* with haplological loss of the first syllable; hence by analogy, [+ 48] **tuȝi* and [+ 49] **tiȝi*; further, by analogy between [+ 49] **tiȝi* and [+ 47] **tuȝu*, also [+ 50] **tiȝu*. In the higher decads Old Swedish should have neuter *tighir* (= Gothic *tigjus*), acc. *tiughu* (= Gothic *tiguns*) and, with analogical accusative plural of the *ŭ*-stems (Noreen 1913: § 194.8), *tighi*; by further analogy, *tiughi*. We should thus finally arrive at the following system:

'twenty'	higher decads	
(uninflected)	nom.	acc.
**tiȝi*	*tighir*	*tighi*
**tuȝi*		*tiughi*
**tuȝu*		*tiughu*
**tiȝu*		

Since *-tiughu* existed beside *-tighi* in the higher decads, it came to be used beside **tiȝi* for 'twenty' and became dominant. Hence *tiughu* 'twenty' > *tyughu* (Noreen 1904: § 270, n. 3) > MSwed. *tyūgho* (Noreen 1904: § 130.2) > Mod. Swed. *tjugo, tjugu*; from *tiughu* + **tiȝi*, we have *tiughi* 'twenty' > *tyghi* (Noreen 1904: § 59.10), and, from this + *tiughu*, we have *tyghu* 'twenty'. In the higher decads we have, from the forms given above, *-tigi, -tighi* (> *-tȝ*, Noreen 1904: § 311,2c), *-tiughi*[253] (> *-tyghi*), *-tiughu*. The nom.-acc. pl. neuter **teȝu* (above) survives in the higher decads as *-*tiogh*; from this + *-tiughu*, we have *-*tiugh* > **tyugh* (Noreen: 1904: § 270, n. 3).[254] Since *-*tiugh* could thus be used beside *-tiughu* in the higher decads, *tiugh* could be used beside *tiughu* for 'twenty'. Forms of similar development are found in Danish and West Norse – it is possible that some of these latter are due to Swedish influence.

In Danish,[255] all the forms of 'twenty' correspond to OSwed. *tiughu*, namely *tiughu, tyugho, tiwgho, tiughæ, tyughæ* and *tiyghu, tiyghæ, tiwo* (> Modern Danish dialectal *tjuð* North Skåne). The corresponding form is also found in '-ty': *-tiughu* and *-tiuwæ, -tyghæ* (Brøndum Nielsen 1950–1957: § 180.4) – the penultimate form came to be used for 'twenty' also, hence Mod. Danish *tyve*. Two other types certainly occur for '-ty', namely *-tiugh* (= OSwed. *-*tiugh*) and *-tighi* (= OSwed. *-tighi*) > *-tighæ* (> *-tīæ*) > *-tigh*, or > *-tī*. There is also some slight evidence for yet another type, *-tughu* (cf. OIcel. *-tugu*) > *-tue*.

OIcel. *tiogo*, ONorw. *tiugu* (Noreen 1923: § 89, n. 1) (> Mod. Norw. *tjugo, tjuge, tjue*), Færoese *tjúgu* 'twenty' = OSwed. *tiughu*. In the higher decads we have *-*tiʒi* > OIcel. -*tigi*; Shetlandic -*tige*; ONorw. -*tigi*; Mod. Norw. -*ti*. Since both **tuʒu* and **tiʒu* can be used beside **tiʒi* in 'twenty', they are introduced in the higher decads also; hence OIcel. -*tugu* and ONorw. -*tigu* (OIcel. -*togo* from *togr* + **tiʒu*, **tuʒu*).[256]

It will be convenient to subdivide the Scandinavian A-forms of the higher decads according to be following types: (A1) Icel. *tighir*, etc.; (A2) OSwed. -*tiughu*; (A3) OSwed. -*tiugh*; (A4) OSwed. -*tighi*; (A5) OSwed. -*tiughi*; (A6) OIcel. -*tugu*; (A7) ONorw. -*tigu*; (A8) OIcel. -*togo*. In Old Danish, type A3 is not entirely distinctive because loss of the final vowel can cause type A2 to coalesce with it. The existence of A6 is somewhat doubtful in Old Danish; forms apparently due to it could be explained as due to a loss of *i* (*iugh* > *ugh* > *u(w)*, Brøndum Nielsen 1950–1957: §§ 179 n. 4, 387.4). In respect of Old Danish, then, the markings "A3" and "A6" are to be understood in this sense.

The most striking problem concerning the West Germanic decads is the question of why they have lost inflection; for instance, why do we not find an OHG genitive **drio zugo*? The fact that OHG *zweinzug* is a fossilized dative may perhaps give the clue.

In West Germanic there appears to be no evidence for forms other than the original neuter paradigm (above); further, for at least some part of West Germanic, PGmc. **twae* remains a neuter (15.1.2.5.). We seek the origin of the fossilization in the fact that, in paradigm [+ 21], nominative-accusative and dative will fall together as **teʒum*, **tiʒum*, **tuʒum* owing to the loss of final -*i* in West Germanic in the trisyllable nom.-acc. dat. **teʒumi*, etc.; only genitive plural-dual **teʒumo*, **tiʒumo*, **tuʒumo* will be outstanding and we assume that this has been eliminated in favor of an invariant **teʒum*, **tiʒum*, **tuʒum*. We shall then have the paradigm [+ 51]:

nom.acc.	**twaiteʒum*, **twaitiʒum*, **twaituʒum*
gen.	**twajoteʒum*, **twajotiʒum*, **twajotuʒum*
dat.	**twaimteʒum*, **twaimtiʒum*, **twaimtuʒum*

But equivalent to this (having in mind the loss of final -*u* in the trisyllable, exactly comparable to that of final -*i*, above), we shall have (from the paradigm above), paradigm [+ 52]:

nom.-acc.	**twaiteʒ*, **twaitiʒ*, **twaituʒ*
gen.	**twajotego*, **twajotogo*
dat.	**twaimteʒum*, **twaimtiʒum*, **twaimtuʒum*

It seems very possible that an invariant **twaimteʒ*, **twaimtiʒ*, **twaimtuʒ* (in addition to an analogical **twaimtoʒ*) was generalized from the two equivalent paradigms [+ 51] and [+ 52].

In 'thirty' and 'forty' the same process seems to have taken place, except that here the forms of the nominative-accusative plural neuter have become dominant, with old forms of the first elements, viz. nominative-accusative neuter **þrī* and **feur*, **fiur* (15.1.4.3.).[257] Hence the equivalent pair of paradigms [+ 53], [+ 54] for 'thirty':

[+ 53]	nom.-acc.	**þrīteʒum*, **þrītiʒum*, **þrītuʒum*
	gen.	**þrijoteʒum*, **þrijotiʒum*, **þrijotuʒum*
	dat.	**þrimeteʒum*, **þrimtiʒum*, **þrimtuʒum* – from [+ 21],

with *-ō* > WGmc. *-u* lost in the trisyllable in nominative-accusative;

[+ 54]	nom.-acc.	**þrīteʒ*, **þrītiʒ*, **þrītuʒ*
	gen.	**þrijoteʒo*, **þrijotogo*
	dat.	**þrimteʒum*, **þrimtiʒum*, **þrimtuʒum* ~

whence, finally, an invariant **þrīteʒ*, **þrītiʒ*, **þrītuʒ* (and **þrītoʒ*).

And for 'forty', the equivalent pair [+ 55] and [56]:

[+ 55]	nom.-acc.	**feurteʒum*, **fiurtiʒum*, **feurtuʒum*, **fiurtuʒum*
	gen.	**fewaroteʒum*, **fewarotiʒum*, **fewarotuʒum*
	dat.	**feurumteʒum*, **fiurumtiʒum*, **feurumtuʒum*, **fiurumtuʒum*
[+ 56]	nom.-acc.	**feurteʒ*, **fiurtiʒ*, **feurtuʒ*, **fiurtuʒ*
	gen.	**fewaroteʒo*, **fewarotoʒo*
	dat.	**feurumteʒum*, **fiurumtiʒum*, **feurumtuzum*, **fiurumtuʒum* –

whence an invariant **feurteʒ*, **feurtuʒ* (and **feurtoʒ*).

For the decads higher than 'forty' the state of affairs is much simpler, for the first elements do not decline. Thus for 'fifty' the first paradigm reduces to an invariant **finfteʒum*, **finftiʒum*, **finftuʒum*, the second to nom.-acc. **finfteʒ*, **finftiʒ*, **finftuʒ*; gen. **finfteʒo*, **finftoʒo*; dat. **finfteʒum*, **finftiʒum*, **finftuʒum*; whence an invariant **finfteʒ*, **finftiʒ*, **finftuʒ* (and **finftoʒ*).

For the higher decads the forms with *-toʒ* are not preserved – OHG *-zog* is clearly from -zug + *-zo* (type D). But the variant *-teʒ* × *-tiʒ* is, in some part, preserved – OHG *-zig -zeg*, MHG *-zic -zig -zec -zeg*. In the individual languages these forms have suffered considerable change. Final *-g* > *-ch* in Low German, Dutch, and Frisian.[258] In Middle Low German *i* is generally not weakened before *ch* (Lasch 1914: § 212 n.). In Middle Dutch *-tech* > *-tach* in part (Franck 1910: § 64). In Old Frisian *-tich* > *-tech* in large part (van Helten 1890: § 82, and cf. Steller 1928: § 22 n. 5).[259]

In Anglo-Saxon *-teg* > *-tig* (Campbell 1959: § 376), in part *-ig* > *-i* (Campbell 1959: § 267);[260] this latter change is completed in Middle English (Luick 1921–1940: § 401a) and *-i* is shortened (Luick 1921–1940: § 443).

15.1.20.2. Type B

Gothic *-tehund* < PIE **dĕḱm̥t-*. *Taíhuntaíhund* L 16,6; L 16,7; *taíhuntaí-hundfald* 'a hundredfold' L 8,8 is curious. Were it not for the fact that Gothic orthography is very careful, it might well be suggested that *ai* of the second element is an error due to *ai* of the first – perhaps with "scribal preference". *-taíhund* could of course be from **déḱm̥t-*, but it would be difficult to explain why it should only appear when the first element was *taíhun*.

15.1.20.3. Type C

This formation is type A prefixed by PGmc. **xunda*, identical with 'hundred' (15.1.30.); hence OEngl. *hund-*. In Old Saxon, and sometimes in Anglo-Saxon, the prefix is reduced and assimilated to various other prefixes: OSax. *ant- at-*, OEngl. *un-*. In Middle Low German and Middle Dutch it is reduced to *t-* (from *-ds* > *-ts* in 'seventy'), and this survives in Low German and Modern Dutch.[261]

15.1.20.4. Type D

OHG *-zo* constitutes a celebrated problem. The forms are rare and occur only in early texts. Schatz (1927: § 409) and Frings (1962: 43) give enumerations: Isidor *sibunzo* (quater), *zehanzo* (Hench 1893: Glossary s. vv); Monsee Fragments: *sibunzo, zehanzo, zehanzofalt* (bis) (Hench 1890: Glossary s. vv); Keronisches Glossar: *ahttozo* 1,262,19 (Kögel 1879: 177) – in all three manuscripts, a, b, and c; Hrabanisches Glossar *zehanzo-hêrosto* 'ciliarcus' (Steinmeyer – Sievers 1879–1922: 1,88,15): *hêrosto* superlative to *hêr* 'great'; see also Ottmann (1886): *zehanzo* (Steinmeyer – Sievers 1879–1922: 1,412,27; *cehanzo* 1, 426, 69); further *hahtozo* (Steinmeyer – Sievers 1879–1922: 1,735,39); *zehanzo-hêrosto* 'decurio' (Steinmeyer – Sievers 1879–1922: 1,820,14).

There are three principal theories as to the origin of the form. (α) Osthoff – Brugmann (1878–1910: v, II ff.) suggest that it is a genitive plural, corresponding to a Greek formation and that the end of the word is omitted; thus essentially, OHG *sibunzo* [262] (> *sibunzohunt) = Greek *heptádōn dékas*. They further suggest that Gothic *sibuntehund* (on which see above) is an exact parallel, with the normal Gothic genitive plural *-e*. (β) Schmidt (1889: 32) takes *-zo* as congruent to a Gothic word of which only the dat. sing. *tewai* τὰγματί (Pokorny 1959: 190, 218) is recorded (I Corinthians 15,23) – and cf. dat. *taíhuntewjam*. (γ) The view of Osthoff and Brugmann has been modified by H. F. Rosenfeld in a series of articles;[263] he would make the first element an ordinal – in this connection, he naturally discusses the distribution of the voiced and unvoiced dentals of the ordinals. Rosenfeld fails to point out that his view could well receive support from the Crimean Gothic decads, type H (below).

Van Helten (1906: 118) rejects Schmidt's theory on phonological grounds; he denies that a Gothic **tew* could appear as OHG *-zo*. This is however not entirely right. Admittedly, if the form is stressed, we must have had *-*zâo*; cf. *blâo* 'blue' (< **blēwa/ō*- > OEngl. **blǣw*, cf. *blǣ-hǣwen* 'blue-coloured'), *grâo* 'grey' (< **grēwa/ō* > OEngl. *grǣw*). Suppose however, that *-*zâo* was shortened to *-*zao* in unstressed position. Then this *ao* would have developed to *ô*; cf. *strao* (< **strawa*- > OEngl. *streaw*, Campbell 1959: § 120.3 and n. 7) > *strô* (Braune – Mitzka 1967: § 45 n. 3). The resulting *-*zô* may of course well have been shortened, again in unstressed position to *-zo*.

It seems then, that nothing of the above entitles us to reject the theories of either Osthoff and Brugmann, or Schmidt or Rosenfeld. But they can all be rejected on the simple grounds that, in its own way, each of them separates these Old High German decads from those of the rest of Germanic. We suggest a much simpler explanation of *-zo*, namely that it represents an originally barytone PGmc. *-*tox* exactly parallel to the originally oxytone *-*toʒ*, and that, though final *-x* normally remains in Old High German (Braune – Mitzka 1967: § 154), as in *hôh* 'high' (cf. Lith. *kaukas* 'a boil'), it is here exceptionally lost in unstressed or semi-stressed position.

Mahlow (1879: i,48) takes the *-o* of *-zo* as long, but Schmidt regards it as short, and on any of the three theories set out above, it must be short. It is of interest to see whether the textual occurrences determine the quantity of the *-o*. In the Isidor, length is often indicated in closed syllables by doubling, but not in open ones (Hench 1893: 63); original *ô* is however, for the most part, diphthongized to *uo* (Hench 1893: 66). In the Monsee Fragments, *oo* does not appear (though *aa* does); original *ô* appears as *o*, or is diphthongized to *uo* (Hench 1890: 100–101). In the *Keronisches Glossar*, in MS A original *ö* is in general diphthongized to *oa* (occasionally, *ua*); for the long vowel, *o* is rare (once it appeared as *oo*); in MS b, *o* and *oo* are not very disparate in frequency; there are occasional examples of *ua*; see Kögel (1879: 102). In the *Hrabanisches Glossar*, diphthongization of original *ô* has not yet begun – there is only one example (of *oa*); length is indicated – as *oo* or *ó* – rather frequently; see Wüllner (1882: 9). In "Rb", original *ô* is already completely diphthongized – nearly always to *ua* (Ottmann 1886: 14–15); *ô* < *ao* is already present, written *oo* (Ottman 1886: 17; Braune – Mitzka 1967: § 38 n. 2). Unstressed original *ô* appears as *o* (unmarked) in all the five texts considered above (see Hench 1893: 75, 1890: 106; Kögel 1879: 24 ff.; Wüllner 1882: 34–36; Ottmann 1886: 22–23). It will thus be seen that the textual evidence for the quantity of *o* of *-zo* is entirely indecisive.

Corresponding to the *-o* of OHG *-zo*, we should expect OSax. *-o*; instead we find *a*, but this can be explained as due to a dialectal change *-o* > *-a* (Gallée 1910: § 114 n. 1). *-e* of *nichonte* 'ninety' can be explained as a weakening of *-o* (Gallée 1910: § 114 n. 1).[264] The "correct" OSax. *-o* survives indirectly in *ahtodoch* 'eighty', from **ahtodo* + **-tiʒ*, **teʒ*. Gallée (1910: § 269) mentions *d* for *t* in this form (and in *ahtedeg* 'eighty') in connection with the occasional voicing of *t* before voiced consonants. Were is valid, his remark could also apply to *antahtoda ahtoda* 'eighty'. But, clearly, it is not valid. The explanation may lie in a dissimilation *t* – *t* > *d* – *t* (cf. Mod. Ind. *aṭṭhasaṭṭhi* 'sixty eight' > *a(ḍ)ḍ(h)asaṭṭhi*. A similar phenomenon is attested in Italian dialects; cf. It. *sanitade* beside *sanitate; parentado*;[265] Battisti (1912) also calls attention to the common ending *-tádo* for It. *-táto* in Florentine and Umbro-Aretino. In Old Saxon, we thus have the correspondent of OHG *-zo* indirectly preserved in *ahtodoch* 'eighty', as *-ta* in *antsiōunta, atsiƀunta* 'seventy' (with weakening in *nichonte* 'ninety'), as *-da* in *antahtoda, ahtoda* 'eighty' and analogically introduced in *nigonda* 'ninety'.

15.1.21. Marginal forms

15.1.21.1. Type E

OIcel. *tuítán* 'twenty' may be an even more archaic relic than OGut. dat. *fiaurum* 'four' (15.1.4.1.). Of it, Ross (1954: 124 n. 6) says: "OIcel. *tuítián* 'twenty' is an interesting form; PIE **wī-dkm̥tī* (Latin *uīginti*, etc. – see Brugmann 1902: § 443.1) would have appeared as **wī-hund* in Germanic, and the **wī-* may well have been folk-etymologised to **twĭ-* ... > ON **twī-* [15.3.1.]. The second element would then have had to be replaced by a word meaning 'ten'; *-tián* of the Icelandic 'teens' lay at hand."

15.1.21.2. Type F

Icel. *-tigi* > *-tíi*; from this + *tíu* 'ten', we have *-tíu.*[266] OSwed. *-tighi* > *-tī* (Noreen 1904: § 311.2c); from this + -tio 'ten', we have *-tīo* (> MSwed. *-tīe*, Noreen 1904: § 149.4), Mod. Swed. *-tio.*[267]

15.1.21.3. Type G

The formation of Mod. Danish *tresindstyve* 'three time twenty' and the like is fairly straightforward; it is the *raison d'être* that is difficult. The vigesimal forms develop in Old Danish and are dominant in Modern Danish. In the relevant formations the second element is, naturally, always 'twenty' – in the forms A2, A3 or A6. The first element is of the following different types: (1) the cardinal; (2) the ordinal; (3) 'twice' and 'thrice'; (4) a part of Danish neuter *sin*[268] 'time' viz.: (a) nom.-acc. sing. *sin*; (b) dat. sing. *sinni*; (c) dat. pl. *sinnom* (see Brøndum Nielsen 1950–1957: § 443); (d) the form *sins, sinz, sindes, sinnes*, for which see Brøndum Nielsen (1950–1957: § 547 n. 3). The odd decads have the ordinal coupled with ODanish *half* 'half' in the idiom *half-third* = 'two-and-a-halfth', etc. The even decads have the cardinal, and occasionally the adverb (type G3).

The G-forms are very diverse and cannot all be enumerated below; Brøndum Nielsen (1950–1957: § 547C. 3 ff.) gives a very full account.

15.1.21.4. Type H

Crimean Gothic *treithyen* 'thirty' and *furdeithien* 'forty' are obscure. Von Grienberger (1897: 132) takes the second element as Gothic *taíhun* 'ten' and the first elements as the ordinals (15.2.3., 15.2.4.). If he is right, the *raison d'être* of the formations ('third ten', 'fourth ten') is not clear; they are not Turkic or Iranian calques, for such formations are not found in either of these groups of languages.

The second elements of the decads have already been discussed, so that in the ensuing only the first elements are treated. constant reference to the discussion of the earlier cardinals is desirable; we do not give individual references.

15.1.22. 'Twenty'

(A) Gothic dat. *twaim tigum*;[269] for the Scandinavian forms see above; **twaimteȝ*, **twaimtiȝ*, **twaimtuȝ*: OHG *zweinzug*; MHG *zweinzëc*, *zweinzic*;[270] Mod. HG *zwanzig*;[271] OSax. *twentig, twentich, twentech, twenteg*; MLG *twintich*; LG *twintich* Assinghausen, Ostbevern, *twinti* Heide (Dithmarschen), *twintich* Stavenhagen. MDutch *twintich*; Mod. Dutch *twintig*; OFrisian *twintich, twintech*; Mod. Frisian *twintîg* Wangeroog, *twintich* Saterland, *twunteg* EMoringen, Föhr, and Amrum, *tweintich* West.[272] In Old English, from **twāmteȝ*, **twāmtiȝ* + dat. *twǣm* 'two', we have **twæmteȝ*, **twæmtiȝ* > *twĕntig*[273] (Lindisfarne Gospels 7vb10 *tuoentig*, cf. Campbell 1959: § 319);[274] MEngl. *twenti* (Ormulum), *twenntiȝ*, AB *twenti* (Ayen. *tuenti*)); Mod. Engl. *twenty*.[275]

15.1.23. 'Thirty'

(A) Gothic acc. *þrins tiguns*, gen. *þrije tigiwe*.
In Scandinavian, it is the Danish forms are particularly complex and diverse; they are enumerated by Brøndum Nielsen (1950–1957: § 547C.2). They are affected by a change of the medial *t* to *d* (Brøndum Nielsen 1950–1957: §§ 301 n. 2, 416 n. 4), and by shortening of the vowel of the first syllable, but the orthography does of course in general not make it plain when this has happened.
(A) OIcel. *þrír tiger*, etc.; Mod. Icel. *þrír tigir, þrír tugir*.
Acc. masc. (i) PGmc. **þrinz*: (A2): OSwed. *þrǣtiughu*; ODanish *thrætiughu, thrætiugo, thrætyughæ, thrætiwo*; (A3): ODanish *trætiugh, trædiugh*; (A4): ONorw. *þræthigi* (Hægstad 1914–1915: ii 34, 111 n. 331) – > *þrættigi* > Mod. Norw. *tretti*; Shetlandic *þrǽtige* (in a charter of 1355);[276] OSwed. *þrǣtighi*; ODanish *thrætighe* (A5): OSwed. *þrǣtiughi*.
(ii) Icel. *þrjá*, OSwed. *þrēa*, OGut. *þrīa*, ODanish *thrē*; (A4): OIcel. *þriátigi*; early Færoese *tríati* (*í* from nom.-acc. fem. **trī̯ar*, 15.1.10.0.);

Runic Gut. *þriatihi*. From (i) + (ii) we obtain (iii) (A2): OSwed. *trētiughu* (> *trĕttiughu*, cf. Noreen 1904: § 297); ODanish *thretiughu, thrediogho, thrediwghe, thrediwæ, trediwe*; (A3): ODanish *trediugh*; (A4): OSwed. *þrētighi*; ODanish *thretti*; (A6): ODanish *threthwge, tredwge, tredhwe* (> Mod. Danish *tredive*, Bornholm, *træδua*).

In late Old Danish, *e* occurs for *æ* (Brøndum Nielsen 1950–1957: § 54.2), so that (i) and (ii) are not distinct. It is possible that from ODanish **thrȳ-tugh* (nom.-acc. neuter), (A3) **thrȳ-tiugh* (above) is indirectly preserved, with change *thrȳ̆-* > *thrø-* (Brøndum Nielsen 1950–1957: § 165) in *trødug, trødwe* (cf. Mod. Danish dialectal *trödə* Jutland), but this may be (iii) and show the change *thre-* > *thrø* (Brøndum Nielsen 1950–1957: § 134 n. 1).

Mod. Norw. *trædeve* (some parts of the South) is a borrowing from Danish, as is also Færoese *tretivu* (pronounced with medial [*d*]),[277] with *-u* from *thúgu* 'twenty'[278] (earlier *treduvu*, with vowel-harmony). **þriteȝ* **þritiȝ* **þrituȝ*: OHG *drîzzug, drîzug* (cf. Braune – Mitzka 1967: § 160); MHG *drîȝȝëc, drîȝëc, drîȝȝic, drîȝic*; Mod. HG *dreissig*; OSax. *thrîtig, thrîtich, thrîtic*; OFrisian *t(h)rîtich, t(h)rîtech*;[279] Mod. Frisian *tritich* West, *trüttich* Saterland: OEngl. *þritig* > *þrittig* (Campbell 1959: § 287); MEngl. *þrittiȝ, þritti*, (Ormulum) *þrittiȝ*, AB *þritti*, (Ayen *þritti*) > *thyrty* (Jordan 1925: § 165) > Mod. Engl. *thirty*, early Mod. Engl. *thurty* (Luick 1921–1940: § 432). In later Low German and Dutch 'thirty' in part shows the same development as 'thirteen', to which it has in parl been assimilated (so, essentially, van Helten 1906: 118): MLG *drüttich, drittich, dertich, dortich*; LG *dertig*[280] *dartig, dortig, dörtig*,[281] *drüttig* (Danneil 1859: *dörtein*), *drittig* (Schambach 1858: s. v.); MDutch *dertich, dartich, dortich* (Franck 1910: § 48); Mod. Dutch *dertig*. (MEngl. *þretti* influenced by 'thirteen', as is also *þrutti* "Robert of Gloucester" MS B, W. A. Wright 1887) v. 7055 – by **þruttene* < OEngl. *þrĕottyne*. (F) Icel. *þrjátíu* (first element as in OIcel. *þriátigi*); OSwed. *thrǣtīo* (first element as in *þrǣtighi*) > Mod. Swed. *trettio* (cf. Noreen 1904: § 297).
(H) Crimean Gothic *threithyen* – first element, ordinal Gothic *þridja* (cf. 15.1.21.4.)?

15.1.24. 'Forty'

(A) Gothic acc. *fidwor tiguns*; OIcel. *fiórer tiger*, etc.; Mod. Icel. *fjórir tugir*.
Accusative masculine (A4): OSwed. *fiūratighi*,[282] *fȳratighi, fiōratighi*; ODanish *fīratighi*.

Nominative masculine (A4) – in large part with weakening *-i* > *-e* (Noreen 1904: § 149.3): OSwed. **fiūritighi* > *fiūretighe*. OSwed. **fȳritighi*[283] > (i) **fȳritighi* > MSwed. *firitighi* (Noreen 1904: § 101 n. 2), and (ii) MSwed. *firtighi* (cf. Noreen 1904: § 297). OSwed. *fīrætī* with first element from *fĭri-* + *fȳri-*.
Nominative-accusative neuter (A2): ODanish *fivghærtiughæ, fiurthygæ*; (A3): OSwed. dat. *fiūrum tiughum* and *tiughum fiūrum* (also *tighiom*); ODanish *fiurtiugh, fiyrtivgh*.
Nominative-accusative masculine. The great majority of the Old Danish forms belong here; they are even more complex and diverse than those of 'thirty' – too many to be completely enumerated (cf. Brøndum Nielsen 1950–1957: § 547C.3). In section A of this paragraph the possible first elements are given as *fȳri-, fȳ̆ræ, fyr, føræ, fyrre, førræ-*, to which – from the more detailed references – there must be added *firi-, fire-, fir-, fere-*; references for the sound change involved in these forms are given. Some examples: (A2): *fyritiughu, fyretiwæ, fyretywe, fyrtiughæ, føretiugho, føretywgho, førethywæ, førrætyuæ, firitiughu, firetiuo, feretiwe*, MDanish *fyrretyve* (abbreviated *fyrre*); (A3): *fyrætiugh, fyrtiugh, firætiugh, firtiugh*; (A4): *fyrætighæ, firitighe, firætighe, fyrætij, firæthii* – and, as a loanword, Mod. Norw. *fyrti*; (A6) *fyrtwghæ*.

There remain the curious forms OIcel. *fiorutigi*, Færoese *fjøruti*,[284] OSwed. *fiurutighi*. The first element exists as the simplex OSwed. *fyuru* 'four', but it is more probable that this is extracted from 'forty' (so 15.1.4.1.4.), than that *-u* is an inflectional ending of 'four', for such an ending would be essentially without a parallel and hard to explain. We suggest that the form is due to the influence of the F-type (Mod. Icel. *fjörutíu*) in which the first element can, we think, be explained.
**feurteʒ*, **fiurtiʒ*, **feurtuʒ*, **fiurtuʒ*: OHG *fiorzug*; MHG *vierzëc, vierzic*; Mod. HG *vierzig*; OSax. *fiortig, fiartig, viarteg, vierteh, fiertich, fiertihc*; MLG *vertich, vêrtich* (cf. *vertein, vêrtein* 'fourteen'); LG *fęrtich* Assinghausen, *fettich* Ostbevern, *fe^irt^i* Heide (Dithmarschen), *fīrtich* Stavenhagen; MDutch *viertich, veertich* (cf. *veertien* 'fourteen'); Mod. Dutch *veertig*; Mod. Frisian *fjirtich* West, *fjautich* Saterland; OEngl. (North Northumbrian) *feortig*.[285]

There is Ingvaeonic assimilation to 'four': OSax. *fiwartig*; OFrisian *fiuwertich, fiovrtich, fiortech*; OEngl. *fē̆owertig*; MEngl. *feowerti, fowerti, fuuerti, fourti, furty, forty* (Dobson 1957: § 14) (> Mod. Engl. *forty*) *faurty*, (Ormulum) *fowwerrtʒ*, AB *fowrti* (Ayen. *uourti*).
(C) Mod. Dutch dialectal *tfirtig* Oudenard (Weijnen 1962: 15).

(F) Nom. masc. OSax. *fȳretīo, fȳrætiō, fȳretīghio*, MSwed. *fȳritīo* (Noreen 1904: § 149.4), Mod. Swed. *fyrtio*.

Acc. masc. OIcel. *fjórutíu* from **fióratíu* (with acc. masc. *fióra*) and assimilation of *-a-* to *-u-*? Mod. Icel. *fjörutíu* shows a shortening of the diphthong (due to analogy with gen. *fjögurra* 'four'?). If this view is correct, a similar form is to be postulated for Færoese and Old Swedish in order to explain Færoese *fjøruti* and OSwed. *fiurutighi* (above): first element acc. masc. OWN **fiōra*, OSwed. *fiūra* (15.1.4.1.1., 15.1.4.1.3.), second element **tīu* > Færoese *tiggju* and OEN **tīu* (15.1.4.1.5.2.). These last two forms also have shortening, as does OIcel. *fiorutighi*.

(G) ODanish *thuswartywghæ* (G3, A2), *tysuærtiugh* (G3, A3).

(H) Crimean Gothic *furdeithien* – first element, the ordinal (cf. 15.1.21.4.)?

15.1.25. 'Fifty'

(A) Gothic acc. *fimf tiguns*; OIcel. *fimm tiger*, etc.; Mod. Icel. *fimm tugir*; (A2): ODanish *fæmtiughæ*; (A3): OSwed. *fæmtyugh*; ODanish *fæmtiugh*; (A4): OIcel. *fimtigi*; OSwed. *fǣmtighi* (> *fǣmtighi*, Noreen 1904: § 272.1) *fǣmtyghi, fǣmtī*; ODanish *fæmtighi, fæmtii, fæmti*;[286] OHG *funfzug, fimfzuc*; MHG *vinfzic, vumfzëc, funfzëc, funfzic, fumzic, vunzic* (cf. Mausser 1932: § 129) *fümfzëc, fünfzic, fiunfzëch, veunfzëh*; Mod. HG *fünfzig, funfzig*; OSax. *fīftich, vîftech*; MLG *vîftich* > *veftich* > *vöftich*[287] *vuftich* (see Lasch 1914: § 169b); LG *föftig*[288] *foftig*;[289] MDutch *viftich* (Franck 1910: § 41) > *vichtich* (Franck 1910: § 110); *vijftich* (reanalogy with *vijf*); Mod. Dutch *vijftig*; OFrisian *fīftech*; Mod. Frisian *fyftich* West, *fiiftich* Saterland; OEngl. *fīftig* (dat. *firtegum* Cura Pastoralis 9/1; MEngl. *fifti* (Luick 1921–1940: § 352 – Ormulum *fifftiȝ*, AB *fifti*); Mod. Engl. *fifty*.

In the southern and middle dialects of Modern High German we have *fuchzig, fuchzg, fuchzk* (Saxon *fauchzk*) from *fuchzehn* (15.1.15.);[290] hence also *fufzig, fufzg, fufzk* like *fufzehn* 'fifteen'. See Hotzenköcherle (1971: 311).

(C) Mod. Dutch dialectal. *tfijftig* Oudenard (Weijnen 1962: 15).

(F) OIcel. *fimftíu*; Mod. Icel. *fimmtíu*; OSwed. *fǣmtīo* (> Mod. Swed. *femtio*), *fǣmtīghio*.

(G) ODanish: G2/A3: *halfthrithiætiugh, halfthretyætywgh*; G4a/A2: *halffthrithiætywghe*; G4a/A3: *halfthrithiæsintiugh*; G4b/A2: *halfthridiæsinnetiughu, halffthrediesynnetiwffue*; G4c/A2: *halfftrediesynnontyughe* (Mod. Danish G4d/A2: *halvtredsindstyve*, abbr. *halvtreds*);[291]

G4D/A2: *halfthridiasinstiwo, halftrediæsinztyuæ, halffthridiasinztiugha, halfftrediesindstiwe, halffthrediesindztiwghe*; G3/A4 with admixture of G4b: *halffthrøswendhetiugh.*

15.1.26 'Sixty'

(A) Gothic dat. *saíhs tigum*; OIcel. *sex tiger*, etc.; Mod. Icel. *sex tugir*; (A2): ODanish *sextiuge, sextyue*; (A3): ODanish *siextiw*: (A4): OIcel. *sextigi*; Mod. Norw. *seksti*; OSwed. **sextighi* (> *sixtighi*, Noreen 1904: § 164) and *sæxtighi, siæxtighi* (cf. *siæx*); also *sæxtyghi*; ODanish *sextii,*[292] *sæxti*; (A6): OIcel. *sextugu*; (A7): ONorw. *sextigu* (Hægstad 1914–1915: 197 n. 398); (A8): OIcel. *sextogo.*
OHG *sëhszug* > *sëhzug* (Braune – Mitzka 1967: § 99 n. 3); MHG *sëhzec, sëhzic* > Mod. HG *zechzig*; LG *söstig*[293] (as *söstein* 'sixteen'); MDutch *sestich*; Mod. Dutch *zestig*; OFrisian *sextich, sextech*; Mod. Frisian *sech(s)tich* West, *säkstich* Saterland; OEngl. *sextig, siectig, syxtig*[294] MEngl. *sexti* (Scots *sexte*), *sixti*[295] (> Mod. Engl. *sixty*).
(C) MDutch *tsestich*;[296] Mod. Dutch dialectal. *tsestig.*[297]
(F) Icel. *sextíu*; OSwed. *sæxtīo* (> Mod. Swed. *sextio*), *siæxtīo.*
(G) ODanish – the cardinal form is mostly nom.-acc. neuter *thry*, but later its replacement *thrē* (15.1.3.5.) – we mark these last forms with an asterisk: G1/A3: *thrytiugh*; G3/A2: *tryswertyue, thrysætiughæ*, abbreviated or with further loss of vowel: *thrystiughæ, thrustyughæ,*[298] G4/A2: *tresintiuge*; G4b/A2: *thrysinnetiwe, thresinnetiwffuæ* *; G4d/A2: *thrysinstiwo, trysinstiwe, thrysinztiwe, trysinztywe, trysindstiwe* (Mod. Danish *tresindstyve* *; abbreviated *tres*)[299] *trysinnestiwe*; mixed forms with G3: G4a/A2: *tryssyntywe*, G4d/A2: *tryssinstywe*; further mixing: *tryswersintywe.*

15.1.27. 'Seventy'

(A) OIcel. *siau tiger*, etc.; Mod. Icel. *sjö tugir*; (A2): ODanish *siutiughæ*; (A3): ODanish *siutiugh, syutiugh, syutywff*; (A4): Mod. Norw. *sjautti* (*sytti*, Diocese of Bergan, loan-word form, Danish); OSwed. *siutighi*; ODanish *siutighe, sywti*; OHG *sibunzug, sibinzig*; MHG *sibenzëc, sibenzic, sivenzich* ("unverschoben"), *subenzich, söbenzëg, sübenzëch*; Mod. HG *siebzig*; OSax. *sibuntig, sibontig*; LG *ſömti* Heide (Dithmarschen), *ſömtich* Stavenhagen[300] MDutch *seventich, soventich*; Mod. Dutch *zeventig*; OFrisian *siuguntich, sogentich*; Mod. Frisian *sawnntich* West (*soogentich* Saterland, loan-word form, Low German); MEngl. *seventi, seventy* (> Mod. Engl. *seventy*), *senty*;[301] early Mod. Engl. *seaventy.*

(B) Gothic *sibuntehund.*
(C) MLG *tseventich*; MDutch *tseventich*; Mod. Dutch dialectal. *tseventig* (Weijnen 1962: 15); OEngl. *hundseofontig, hundsiofontig*; Ru^2 *hundsifuntig* L 10, 17; *hundsifontig* L 10, 1; *hundsiofantig* Cura Pastoralis, 317/145; dat. *hundseofentigu* Vespasian Psalter, lxxxix, 10.[302]
(D) OHG *sibunzo.* (C + D) OSax. *antsibunta, atsibunta.* (F) Mod. Icel. *sjötíu*; OSwed. *siutio* > Mod. Swed. *sjuttio* (cf. Noreen 1904: § 131.1).
(G) ODanish G2/A2: *halffyærthætiwo*; G2/A3: *halffiærthætiwgh*; G4a/A2: *halffierdesintyughe*; G4b/A2: *halffierdesindetiuge; halffiærdæsindætiwæ, halffierdesinnetiwe*; G4b/A3: *halffiærdesynnetiwgh*; G4d/A2: *halffierdsinstiwge, halffiærdhasinztiwo, halffierdhæsinztyuæ*; Mod. Danish *halvfjerdsindstyve* (abbreviated *halvfjerds*).[303]

15.1.28. 'Eighty'

There is the same widespread loss of the medial vowel as in 'seventy'. In some West Germanic forms *-n-* is introduced from 'seventy' and 'ninety'.
(A) OIcel. *átta tiger*, etc.; Mod. Icel. *átta tugir*; (A3): OSwed. dat. *tiughum āttæ* (also *tighiom*); (A4): Mod. Norw. *åtteti, åtti*, OSwed. *āttatighi, āttighi*; ODanish *attatige, attati, atteti* (adapted as early Færoese *áttati*); OHG *ahtozug, ahzech* (cf. Mausser 1932: § 129); MHG *ahtzëc, ahzëc, ahzic*; Mod. HG *achtzig*; OSax. *ahtedeg*; MLG *achtich, achtentich* (< **achtetich*); LG *achtich*[304] Stavenhagen, MDutch *achtich*; OFrisian *achtantich* (< **achtatich*); MEngl. *eighteti, eighti* (> Mod. Engl. *eighty*), *aghti*; Mod. Scots *auchty.*
(B) Gothic *ahtautehund.*
(C) Mod. HG dialectal *dachzig* Carinthia; *tachzig, dochtsk* Tyrol (Weijnen 1962: 15); MLG *tachtentich* (< *tachtetich*); LG *tachnti* Heide (Dithmarschen), MDutch *tachtetich* > *tachtich, tachetich* (Franck 1910: § 117), *tachtentich* > *tachentich*; also *tachtentech, tachtech, tachtach*; Mod. Dutch *tachtig*; OEngl. *hundeahtatig*, dat. *hundehtatigu* (Earle – Plummer 1892–1899: 5/43); gen. *hundaehtatiges* (Vespasian Psalter, lxxxix, 10).
(D) OHG *ahtozo*; OSax. *ahtoda.*
(A + D) OSax. *ahtodoch.*
(C + D) OSax. *antahtoda.*
(F) Icel. *áttatíu*; OSwed. **āttatīo* (MSwed. *āttatīe* > *ottotīe*); Mod. Swed. *åttio.*
(G) ODanish G1/A2: *fivghærtivghæ* (with nom.-acc. neuter), *firætiughæ*;[305] G4a/A2: *fiyrsintiughæ* (with nom.-acc. neuter), *fyresintywe, firesintiwgho*; G4a/A3: *fyræsintiugh*; G4b/A2: *fyræsinnitiughæ, firesinnetiughæ,*

firæsynnætywæ; G4d/A2: *firasinstiwgho, firesinstiwgho, fyræsinstywge, firesindstiufwe, firesindstiwe, firesindztiwe; firsinstiwo*; Mod. Danish *firsindstyve* (abbr. *firs*).[306]

15.1.29. 'Ninety'

(A) OIcel. *níu tiger* etc.; Mod. Icel. *níu tugir*; (A4): OSwed. *nīotighi, nīghiotighi*; ODanish *niotighi, niotigh, nitigh* (Mod. Norw. *nitti*, loan-word form, Danish), *nytii* (cf. Brøndum Nielsen 1950–1957: § 36 n. 1); OHG *niunzug*; MHG *niunzëc, nûnzic*; Mod. HG *neunzig*; LG *ninti* Heide (Dithmarschen), *nentich* Stavenhagen[307], *niuntich* Saterland; MDutch *neghentich, negentach*; Mod. Dutch *negentig*; Mod. Frisian *njoggentich* West, *njuugentich* Saterland; OEngl. dat. *nigontigum* Anglo-Saxon Gospels: L 15,7; MEngl. *niȝenti, nēnty, nīnty* (> Mod. Engl. *ninety*).
(B) Gothic *niuntehund*.
(C) MLG *tnegentich*; MDutch *tneghentich*; Mod. Dutch dialectal *tnegentig*;[308] OEngl. *hundnigontig, hundnygontig*; Ru² *hundniontig* Luke 15,4, Luke 15,7; Lindisfarne *hundneantig* Matthew 18,13; Luke 15,7; *hundneontig* Luke 15,4; dat. *hundnigentigon* (Earle – Plummer 1892–1899 a. 993); dat. *hundnigantigan*.
(D) OSax. *nichonte, nigonda*.
(F) Mod. Icel. *níutíu*; OSwed. *nīotīo* > **nītīo* (dissimilatory loss of first *o*) > **nĭttīo* (cf. Noreen 1904: § 131.1) > Mod. Swed. *nittio*.
(G) ODanish G2a/A2: *halffæmtæsintyughe, halffemtesintywghe*; G4a/A3: *halffæmtsintiygh*; G4b/A2: *halffæmtæsinnetywghe, halffemtesindetiuge, halfæmtesynnetiwæ*; G4c/A2: *halfemtesynnomthyue*; G4d/A2: *halffæmtesinstywæ, halffæmptæsinstiughæ, halffemtesindstiwe, halffemtesindetiuffue*; Mod. Danish *halvfemsindstyve* (abbr. *halvfems*).[309]

15.1.29.1. 'Tenty'

(A) OIcel. *tío tiger*, etc.; OHG *zëhanzug, zênzech*; MHG *zëhenzëc, zëhenzic, zênzëc, zênzich*.
(B) Gothic *taíhuntehund, taihuntaihund* (see 15.1.20.2.).
(C) OEngl. *hundtēontig*, North Northumbrian *hundtēantig* (cf. Britton – Ross 1960: 154), dat. *hundteontegu'* (Liebermann 1903–1916; Ælfred 15: (i, 58))).
(D) OHG *zëhanzo*.
(F) Mod. Icel. *tíutíu*.
(G) ODanish G4b/A2: *femsynnætyffwæ femsindetiuge*; G4c/A2: *femsynnomtiwffwe*.

15.1.29.2. 'Eleventy'

(A) OIcel. *ellefo tiger*, etc.
(C) OEngl. *hundændlæftig* (Birch 1885–1893: ii. 282/1).

15.1.29.3. 'Twelvety'

(C) OEngl. *hundtwelftig; hundtwentig* from this + *twentig* 'twenty'.[310]

15.1.30. 'Hundred'

There are several different formations.
(A) PIE *k̑m̥tóm* > Gothic *hund*; OHG *hunt*; MHG *hunt*; OSax. *hund*; OEngl. *hund*; MEngl. *hund, hun* (cf. Jordan 1925: § 200 n. 3).
(B) A compound consisting of PIE **k̑m̥tóm* and a noun cognate with Gothic *ga-raþjan* 'to count' (Pokorny 1959: 59). This noun is generally taken as a PGmc. **rađa- nta* (so for instance Torp 1919: *hundrad*) but van Helten (1890: § 82e) explains OSax. *hunderod* from an *ō*-grade from (i. e. **rođa-* neuter),[311] and indeed it is difficult to see what other explanation of the OSax. *o* there can be. It is thus seen that, in fact, whereas the Anglo-Saxon form demands **rađa-*, the Scandinavian and the other West Germanics forms can as well be explained from **rođa-* as from **rađa-*. We then have: Icel. *hundreδ*; Færoese *hundraδ*;[312] Mod. Norw. *hundrad*; OSwed. *hundraþ, hundrat* (cf. Noreen 1904: § 260 n. 7); Mod. Swed. *hundra*;[313] ODanish *hundrath, hundrætth, hundret, hundrith, hundrit*, and with loss of *δ* in unstressed position (cf. Brøndum Nielsen 1950–1957: § 390 n. 5), *hundra (*early Færoese *hundra,* Svabo), *hundræ*;[314] Mod. Danish dialectal *hunreδ, hunre* Zealand, *hondRa, honRa* Skåne, *huñər* Jutland, *hunrə, hunv* in the Islands;[315] MHG *hundert*; Mod. HG *hundert*; OSax. *hunderod*; MLG *hundert*; LG *hundr̥t* Assinghausen, *hunnr̥t* Ostbevern, *hunʳt* Heide (Dithmarschen), Stavenhagen; MDutch *hondert*[316] (> *hondart*, Franck 1910: § 19); Mod. Dutch *honderd*; OFrisian *hundred* (> *hondred*, van Helten 1890: § 13) *hunderd, hunder* (van Helten 1890: § 122E) *hundert, hondert* (van Helten 1890: § 120); Mod. Frisian *hön'ert* Sylt, *honert* Helgoland[317] MEngl. *hundred* (Ormulum *hunndredd*, AB *hundret*, Ayen. *hondred*) > Mod. Engl. *hundred,* also *honred, hunderd* (Jordan 1925: § 290 n. 2) > *hunder* (Jordan 1925: § 200 n. 3).[318]
(C) Saterland **chunn* is by origin a distributive; see van Helten (1900: § 186) and 15.4.6. below.
(D) Crimeon Gothic *sada*, loan-word form: Iranian; cf. Ossete *sädä* Scytho-Sarmatian *Sadmanos.*[319]

15.1.31. 'Thousand'

The Germanic forms do nothing to resolve the much-discussed question: is this a compound of PIE **ḱm̥tóm* 'hundred', or a derivative of PGmc. **þūs-* by means of various suffixes? If the latter hypothesis is accepted, an apparent variable suffixation can be explained by suffix-interchange. In this connection it may be observed, first, that Saterland **thuschund*, at one time extracted from the relevant corrupt glosses, has now been abandoned in favor of a reading *thusund* (so van Helten 1900: § 186), and secondly, that OIcel. *þúshund* is, for the most part, late (Noreen 1923: § 453), but in form, it could of course be archaic. Neither the Salic Law nor the Icelandic form can thus be taken as definitely supporting the first hypothesis mentioned above – and, for convenience, an opposite view will be taken below of the Icelandic form.

From Germanic we may thus write the following interconnected forms: (1) **þūsundjō-*, (2) **þūsunda-* neuter, (3) **þūsanda-* neuter, (4) **þūsandja-* neuter, (5) **þūsinda-* neuter. These types cannot always be distinguished. The actual forms are the following.

Gothic[320] (1) *þūsundi*; OIcel. (1) *þúsund*;[321] (2) Mod. Icel. *þúsund*; (3) OSwed. *þūsand*[322] (> *þūsæn*, Noreen 1904: § 292.2, > Mod. Swed. *tusen*, Mod. Norw. *tusen*); ODanish *thusand, thusænd, thusend*; (5) Runic Swed. *þūsind*; ODanish *thusind, tusind, tusin*; Mod. Danish *tusind*;[323] (1) and (2) OHG *dûsent, thûsent*, later *tûsent* (Braune – Mitzka 1967: § 167 n. 8); MHG *tûsent, tûsunt*, also *tûsant* neuter (Mausser 1932: 525);[324] Mod. HG *tausend* neuter; MLG *dûsent* neuter; LG *deūʃn̥t* Assinghausen, *dūʃn̥t* Ostbevern, Stavenhagen, *dūʃn* Heide (Dithmarschen); (1) and (2) Saterland *thusund*; OELFranc. *thûsint* (see van Helten 1890: § 81); MDutch *dûsent* (> duust, Franck 1910: § 16.4); Mod. Dutch *duizend*; (1) + (2) OEngl. *þūsend* neuter;[325] MEngl. *þousend*[326] Laȝamon; the Frisian form may also be (1) + (2): OFrisian *thûsend*; Mod. Frisian West *tûzen* – see further Spenter (1968: 250 n. 968).[327] OSax. *thûsundig* from **þūsund* + *-tig* of the decads – and, precisely, from *-*dig* of *'eighty'* (cf. *ahtedeg*, 15.1.20.4.). So also MLG *dûsentich*, MDutch *dûsentech*.

15.1.32. 'Million', etc.

The numeral entities above 'thousand' in Germanic are all borrowed from French.[328]

Mod. Icel. *milljón* neuter; Færoese *miljón* fem.; Mod. Norw. *million* masc.; Mod. Swed. *million* cardinal; Mod. Danish *million* cardinal; Mod. HG

million fem.; Mod. Dutch miljoen cardinal; Mod. Frisian *miljoen* neuter West; Mod. Engl. *million* – Mod. French *million* '10^6'.
Mod. Icel. *miljarður*; Mod. Swed. *milliard* cardinal; Mod. Danish *milliard* cardinal; Mod. HG *milliarde* fem.; Mod. Dutch *miljard* neuter; Mod. Frisian *miljard* neuter West; Mod. Engl. *milliard* – Mod. French *milliard* '10^9'. Mod. Icel. *biljón*;[329] Mod. Danish *billion*; Mod. HG *billion*; Mod. Dutch *biljoen*; Mod. Frisian *biljoen* West; Mod. Engl. *billion* – Mod. French *billion*. The meaning varies between '10^9' (the American meaning) and '10^{12}' (the English one).
Mod. Swed. *trillion*; Mod. Danish *trillion*; Mod. HG *trillion*; Mod. Dutch *triljoen*; Mod. Frisian *triljoen* West; Mod. Engl. *trillion* – Mod. French *trillion* '10^{12}' and '10^8'.
Mod. Swed. *kvadrillion*; Mod. Danish *kvadrillion*; Mod. HG *quadrillion*; Mod. Engl. *quadrillion* – Mod. Engl. *quadrilion* '10^{15}' and '10^{24}'.
Mod. HG *quintillion*; Mod. Engl. *quintillion* – Mod. French *quintilion* '10^{18}' and '10^{30}'.
Mod. Engl. *sextillion* – Mod. French *sextilion* '10^{21}' and '10^{36}' – and so on.[330]

15.2. Ordinals[331]

15.2.0. In many cases the ordinals show the same development as, or have been remodelled on, the corresponding cardinals. We often denote these states of affairs by the indicators "c̄" and "c̄′" respectively, sometimes adding the relevant cardinal form if this makes the matter clearer. Some languages have developed "standard" ordinal suffixes for some part – occasionally a large part – of the range of numbers. That is to say, in the relevant portion of the range the ordinal is simply formed by affixing the standard suffix to the cardinal, or inserting it in ordinal forms already existing. The origin of these standard suffixes is obvious. We denote any standard suffix by the indicator.

In Old High German, a suffix identical with one of the two superlatives of adjectives (*-ôsto*) is used to form the ordinals of the decads. This form continues into later High German (MHG *-ost, -est, -ist, -st*;[332] Mod. HG *-st(er)* and a corresponding suffix occurs elsewhere in West Germanic: MLG *-(e)ste*, MDutch *-(e)ste*;[333] OFrisian *-uste, -oste, -(e)ste*; the forms can be either strong or weak. From the decads, this suffix often spreads to the lower ordinals. The corresponding form is found, in the decads, in later Icelandic (*-tugasti*) and, occasionally, in later English (*-tiest*).

This latter is certainly directly borrowed from Dutch, and the former is doubtless a modification of the Middle Low German type;[334] the borrowing must have been felt to be a superlative and thus replaced by the Icelandic superlative, *-asti*.

In all of later West Germanic except English there is another suffix which can be considered standard, namely *-de* ~ *-te*; in large part the variation is due to the character – voiced or unvoiced – of the preceding consonant. This suffix derives, in a neutral manner, from the low ordinals 'fourth', 'fifth', 'sixth', etc. In later High German, *-te* tends to be generalized, in Modern Dutch *-de* is generalized as the written form; the Low German forms with *-t* are from High German.

In Modern Norwegian, *-ande* is developed as a standard; it originates in *åttande* 'eight', spreads thence to *sjuande* 'seventh' and *niande* 'ninth', and thence to *tiande* 'tenth'; from *trettande* 'thirteenth' onwards, it takes the place of *-ende* in the ordinals. In Færoese the situation with regard to *-ndi* is rather similar; this occurs in *níggjundi* 'ninth', *tíggjundi* 'tenth', and spreads to *ellindi* 'eleventh'; cf. also *hunddrandi* 'hundredth'. In spoken Færoese there is a tendency to pronounce [*indi*] whether the ending is *-andi, -indi* or *-undi*.[335]

In Middle Low German the suffix PGmc. **-iȝa/ō-* appears in *negenech* 'ninth', *elevenich* 'eleventh' and *twelvich* 'twelfth'.

In Middle English the standard suffix originates in *-eþe*, which derives from OEngl. *seofoþa* 'seventh', *eahtoþa* 'eight' and *teogeþa* 'tenth'. Later, a twofold development takes place. First, final *-e* is lost, hence *-eþ*; this frequently appears as *-ith* in the North, and, in the course of time, also in other areas (Luick 1921–1940: § 460. 2a). Secondly, the medial *-e-* is lost, hence *-þe*, which, with loss of final *-e*, gives *-þ* (Mod. Engl. *-th*); *-eþ -þ* often appears as *-et -t*, no doubt originally under the influence of 'fifth' (OEngl. *fīfta*) and 'sixth' (OEngl. *siexta, sexta*).

15.2.0.1. Finally we may mention here the Middle English ordinal form in *-ende*, etc., although this is not standard in the sense that it is analogically extended from one numeral to another. This ending is identical with that of the present participle, and in some respects shares its development. In the South (and south-west Midlands), this latter frequently appears as *-ind(e)*,[336, 337] while in the North *-end* is very usual. While this may be of native origin (cf. the remarks in Ross 1937: 144), its spreading is certainly due to Scandinavian influence[338] (Icel. *-andi*).[339] Further, *-nd* can yield *-nt*; this was at first apparently a peculiarity of the West Midlands, but in later Middle English it has a wider distribution (Luick 1921–1940: § 440 n. 4; Jordan 1925: § 9).

In the Middle English ordinals, *-and* is found only in the decads *-end(e)*, and its developments occur in the teens – very occasionally in the decads and in 'seventh' to 'tenth'. In these last four this ending is surely in the main of native origin,[340] whereas *-and* of the teens must be considered to be of Scandinavian provenience – the relevant Norwegian and Danish ending (*-undi*) has been assimilated to that of the present participle in its "Norse" form *-and*. The question of how far Scandinavian influence has played a part in the use of these ordinals for the teens and for 'seventh' to 'tenth' remains to be discussed. Only a detailed study of the distribution can resolve the point.

The ordinals are of course in general weak adjectives; note that in these, Old Danish gradually replaces the original endings (including the nominative singular masculine) with the oblique *-a*; see Brøndum Nielsen (1950–1957: § 523).

15.2.0.2. In conclusion we may first call attention to a curious phenomenon unique in Germanic, in the modern Frisian dialect of Wangeroog; here there are ordinal-stems distinguished by gender for 'second' and 'third': masc. *twainst*: fem. neuter *twôst* and masc. *thrêst*; fem. neuter *thrîûst* – all are new formations (the older *twôd* and *thräd* are used for all genders). We may point out, secondly, that there are no old ordinals for 'hundred' (when not expressed as 'ten decads') and 'thousand' – the recent formations are thus, naturally, standard (as are those of 'million', etc.). We may note, thirdly, that almost all the words for 'first' and most of those for 'second' are suppletives. The other ordinals run parallel to the cardinals; constant reference to the discussion of these is desirable; we do not give individual references.

15.2.1. 'First'

Several types, some of them with subtypes, are to be distinguished.

15.2.1.1. Comparative subtype. Gothic *fruma* (Pokorny 1959: 814); OSax. *formo*; OFrisian *forma, furma*; OEngl. *forma*;[341] MEngl. *forme* (Ormulum *forrme*, AB *forme*); with comparative suffix because of the superlative suffix in *formest*, we have *former* (> Mod. Engl. *former*).

Superlative subtype. Gothic *frumists*; OFrisian *formest* (by analogy with *forma*); OEngl. **furmist* (> *fyrmest*, MEngl. *firmest, furmest*); from this + (i) *forma, first* **formist* > Ru² *foermest* Mark 9,35; Luke 13,30 (and from this + *forþ* 'forth', Ru² *foerðmest*), and, secondly, **formest* > *formest* (further *formāst*, *formast* by analogy with *fāst, mǭst* 'most' (cf. OED: *most*), Mod. Engl. *foremost)*, and similarly to Ru[2] *foerδmest*, we have *forδmest* Lindisfarne Gospels; Ru[1] 23,6 – and MEngl. *forthmǭst* similarly to MEngl. *formǭst*.

15.2.1.2. OIcel. *fyrstr* (Pokorny 1959: 812); Icel. *fyrsti*; Færoese *fyrstur, fyrsti*; Mod. Norw. *fyrste*; OSwed. *fyrster, fyrste*;[342] Mod. Swed. *först*; ODanish *fyrstær, fyrsti*;[343] Mod. Danish *forste* (> Mod. Norw. *förste*); OHG *furisto*; OSax. *furisto*; OFrisian *ferist, ferst*; Mod. Frisian *foarste* West; OEngl. *fyrest, fyrst*; MEngl. *first* (> Mod. Engl. *first*), *furst* (Ayen. *uerst*), *frist, frust, frest* (metathesis, Jordan 1925: § 165).

15.2.1.3. Comparative subtype. OEngl. *ærra* (Pokorny 1959: 12); MEngl. *erre, earre, arre* and *erer, errur*, reshaped after *er* and *erre* respectively.

Superlative subtype. OHG *êristo*; MHG *êreste* > *êrste*; MHG *erster*; OSax. *êrista*; MLG *êrst*; LG *ẹiste* Assinghausen, *ērste* Ostbevern, *eirste* Heide (Dithmarschen) *ī̃rst* Stavenhagen, MDutch *eerste*; Mod. Dutch *eerste*; OFrisian *êr(e)st(a* > Mod. Frisian *eerste* Saterland, *êrst* Wangeroog; North *jarste* East Moringen, *iarst* Föhr and Amrum, *jest* Sylt, *iaars* Helgoland, OFrisian *ârst(a* > *earste* West, *aist* Schiermonnikoog; OEngl. *ǣrest*, MEngl. *ē̆rest, erst, arst* (AB *earest, earst*); early Mod. Engl. *erst*.

15.2.1.4. We have further Mod. Swed. *ende, enda* 'single', sup. *endaste* 'single', adv. *endast* 'only'.

15.2.2. 'Second'

15.2.2.1. Of the types not based on the cardinal 'two', the first mentioned is the most important.

15.2.2.1.1. PGmc. **anþara/ō-* (Pokorny 1959: 3) > Gothic *anþar*; Icel. *annarr*; Færoese *annar*; Mod. Norw. *andre*; Shetl. *arar* (see Hægstad 1900: § 42 n. 1); OSwed. *annar*,[344] inflected *aþr- andr-* (Noreen 1904: § 229); Mod. Swed. *andre*; ODanish *annar* and *annan* (> Mod. Norw. *annan*) – originally accusative singular masculine, inflected *andr-* (see further Brøndum Nielsen 1950–1957: § 554); Mod. Dutch *anden*; OHG *ander*; MHG *ander*; Mod. HG *ander*; OSax. *ôthar, âthar, andar*; MLG *ander*; MDutch *ander*, OFrisian *ôther*; Mod. Frisian *ôr* Wangeroog, and with standard suffix added, *oarde* West, *ourde* (*uurde*) Saterland, *ousere* East Moringen; *ööder öler* Föhr and Amrum, *üđer* Sylt, *uur* Helgoland; OEngl. *oþer*; MEngl. *ōþer* (Ormulum *oþerr*), AB *oδer*, Ayen. *oþer*; Mod. Engl. *other*.

15.2.2.1.2. Comparative OEngl. *æfterra* (Pokorny 1959: 53); MEngl. *after*.
15.2.2.1.3. Comparative OFrisian *letera* (Pokorny 1959: 666); Mod. Frisian *lääsere* East Moringen, *leeder* Föhr and Amrum.
15.2.2.1.4. Mod. Frisian *naaist* OFöhr (= OHG *nâhister*, Mod. Engl. *next*; cf. Gothic *neþa*, 'near' – Pokorny 1959: 317).
15.2.2.2. Three types are based on the cardinal 'two'.
15.2.2.2.1. Mod. HG *zweiter*; LG *twedde* Assinghausen, Ostbevern *tweide* Heide (Dithmarschen), *twait* Stavenhagen; MDutch *tweede*; Mod. Dutch *tweede*.[345]
15.2.2.2.2. MDutch *tweeste*; Mod. Frisian *twôst* (*tweinst* masculine, see 15.2.0.2.) Wangeroog, *taust* Sylt.
15.2.2.2.3. Mod. Engl. (dialectical) *twoth* Devon.
15.2.2.3. Finally a borrowing is found, MEngl. *secounde* (Ayen. *seconde*), Mod. Engl. *second*, from OFrench *second*.

15.2.3. 'Third'

PGmc. **þridjan/ōn-*: Gothic *þridja*;[346] OIcel. *þriþe*; Færoese *triði*; OSwed. *þriþi*;[347a, 347b] ODanish *þriþi*. In Scandinavian the oblique cases must regularly have *-j-* in the stem (OSwed. oblique masc. *þriþia*), and this *-i-* is often introduced into the nominative singular masculine also. Hence Mod. Icel. *þriðji*; Mod. Norw. *tridje*; OSwed. *þriþie* (Mod. Swed. *tredje*).

ODanish *thrithia* (*thrythia* Brøndum Nielsen 1950–1957: § 133), *thridhie* (> *thredhie* – Brøndum Nielsen 1950–1957: § 159.4 – > Mod. Danish *tredie*,[348] Mod. Norw. *tredje*). OHG *drittio, dritto*; MHG *dritte* > *dritt* (Mod. HG *dritter*) > **dirtte* (Mausser 1932: 9 ff.) > *dirte* (> *drite* and *derte*);[349] OSax. *thriddio*; MLG *dridde* (> LG *dridde*, Schambach 1858: s. v., also Assinghausen), *dirde, derde* (> LG *derde*), *darde* (> LG *darde*), *dorde, dörde* (> LG *dörde* – Schambach 1858: s. v.; Berghaus 1880–1884: s. v.), *dürde, drüdde* (Lasch 1914: § 173) – LG *drüdde*[350] – *dröde, dredde* (from *dridde* + *drê*) > LG *dredde* (Schambach 1858: s. v.), *drede*; MDutch *dridde* > *derde* (Franck 1910: § 234) > Mod. Dutch *derde*; OFrisian *thredda, tredda* (as MLG *drådde* Hindeloopen); *trääde* Saterland, *thräd* Wangeroog; *treede* East Moringen, *traad* Föhr and Amrum, *träär* Sylt, *dör* Helgoland, loan-word form, Low German,[351] OEngl. *þridda* > North Northumbrian *ðirdda, ðirda*, Ru^2 *ðirda* (Campbell 1959: § 459.2); MEngl. *þridde*[352] (> Mod. Engl. dialectal [*θrid*]), *þirde* (Jordan 1925: § 165) (Mod. Engl. *third*) > *þerdde therd* (Jordan 1925: § 271) – from this + *þridde*, we have also *thredde*.

15.2.4. 'Fourth'

15.2.4.0. Norse

PIE **petwúrto/ā-* > PGmc. **feđurþan/ōn-*.

In Proto-Norse, the nominative singular masculine was thus **feourþǣ* and many of the oblique cases were **feδurþan* (Noreen 1923: § 399 ff.). Hence, in West Norse nom. sing. masc. **fioδrδe* (Noreen 1923: § 89), oblique **fiaδrδa* (Noreen 1923: § 88). The first form is generalized; the first *o* is lost in it, but the diphthong is kept short (cf. 15.1.4.1.2.) because of the influence of comp. **feδur-* (15.3.2.4.); hence OIcel. *fiorþe*, then *fiórþe* (c̄′) – Mod. Icel. *fjórδi*; similarly Færoese *fjórδi*, Mod. Norw. *fjorde*. This development is also found in East Norse (OSwed. *fiorþe*), but in the main, the oblique form is generalized: OSwed. *fiarþe* (Noreen 1904: § 75.1), ODanish *fiarthi fiarþæ* [353] (*fyarthæ*, Brøndum Nielsen 1950–1957: § 176 n. 3), OSwed. *fiærþe* (Noreen 1904: § 96)[354] > Mod. Swed. *fjärde*; ODanish *fiærdhe* (Brøndum Nielsen 1950–1957: § 177), *fierdhe* (> Mod. Danish *fjerde*, Mod. Norw. *fjerde*).[355]

15.2.4.1. Gothic

Von Grienberger (1897: 132) takes the first element of Crimean Gothic *furdeithien* 'forty' as ordinal Gothic "**fidurda*" – read **fidurda* (cf. 15.3.2.4.).

15.2.4.2. West Germanic

PGmc. **feurþan/ōn-* (c): OHG *feordo, fiordo*; MHG *vierde, vierte*; Mod. HG *vierter*; OSax. *fiordo, fiorda*; MLG *verde* (*vêrde* from this + *vêr*); LG *feirte* Assinghausen, *feirte* Ostbevern, *feirte* Heide (Dithmarschen), *firt* Stavenhagen, MDutch *vierde* (> Mod. Dutch *vierde*), *vierste*; OFrisian *fiarda* (cf. **fiar*, 15.1.4.2.3.3.); Mod. Frisian *fjirde* West; *fjoode* Saterland (*fjädde* Strücklingen), *fiäd* Wangeroog (beside later *fiaurst*), *fiirde* East Moringen, *fjuard* Föhr, *sjuard* Amrum (earlier *fjuard*), *fjaard, fjaart* Sylt (beside later *fjaarst*), Helgoland *fear*, loan-word form, Low German; OEngl. *fēorþa*,[356] late WSaxon *fēowerþa* (c̄′); MEngl. *feorδe, fērthe, furþe* (cf. 15.1.3.), *firþe* (Luick 1921–1940: § 429.3); with *d* from 'third', *ferde, furde*; late MEngl. *fourthe* [357] (c̄′) (*fourt*); Mod. Engl. *fourth* has the spelling of MEngl. *fourthe*, but Dobson (1957: § 173) derives its pronunciation from MEngl. *fǭrþe* (cf. MEngl. *forδe, forδ*), by "akzentumsprung" from OEngl. *fēorþa*;[358] MEngl. *fort*.[359]

15.2.5. 'Fifth'

PGmc. **fimftan/ōn-*: OWN **fefte*, from which + **fimm* we have OIcel. *fimte* (Mod. Icel. *fimmti*, c̄′), Færoese *fimti*; and OEN **fæfte*, from which + **fǣm*, we have OSwed. *fæmte* (> Mod. Swed. *femte*), *fæmpte* (Noreen 1904: § 332.2), ODanish *fæmtæ, fæmte* (> Mod. Danish *femte*), *fempta* (Brøndum Nielsen 1950–1957: § 351); OHG *fimfto, finfto*; MHG *finfte*; OSax. *fīfto, fīfta, vîfthe*; MLG *vefte, vöfte*; LG *föfte*,[360] *fofte*;[361] MDutch *vijfte, vifte* (Franck 1910: § 41) > *vichte* (Franck 1910: § 110), *vijfste*; Mod. Dutch *vijfde*; OFrisian *fīfte*; Mod. Frisian *fiifde* (*fyfte*) West, *füfte* Saterland, *fīfst* Wangeroog (but *tum fīften* 'fifthly'), *füfte* East Moringen, *fift fiift* Föhr, *fifst* Amrum, Sylt (obsolete *fift*), *füfs* Helgoland; OEngl. *fīfta* > MEngl. *fīfte* (Ormulum *fĭfte*) and *fifte* (AB *fifte*, Ayen. *uifte, uyfte*) – Luick (1921–1940: § 352); early Mod. Engl. *fift*; Mod. Scots *fift, fifth* (> Mod. Engl. *fifth*), *fivethe* > *fivet*.
PGmc. **fumftan/ōn* (< PIE **pm̥pto/ā-*): OHG *funfto*; MHG *funfte*; Mod. HG dialectal *fufte* (see van Helten 1906: 113).
i- and *u-*forms mixed: MHG *viumfte, viunfte, veunfte*.
c̄′: MHG *fümfte, fünfte*; Mod. HG *fünfter*.

15.2.6. 'Sixth'

PIE **seḱto/ā-*: PGmc. **sextan/ōn-*: Icel. *sétti* (Mod. Icel. also *sjötti*, from this + *sjöundi* 'seventh'); Færoese *sætti*; Mod. Norw. *sette*; OSwed. *sætte* and, with *a*-breaking in the oblique cases, **siatte* > *siætte* (Noreen 1904: § 97) > Mod. Swed. *sjätte*; hence also *sǣte, siǣte* (Noreen 1904: § 304, n. 3); similarly (cf. Brøndum Nielsen 1950–1957: § 177), ODanish *sætti, sættæ, sette, siatti, siatta, siattæ, siætti, siættæ, siette* (> Mod. Danish *sjette*, Mod. Norw. *sjette*), *sietta, sætæ*,[362] *siata, siate, siatæ, siæta, siætæ*,[363] OHG *sëhto*; MHG *sehte*.[364]
PGmc. **sextan/ōn-* (c̄′):[365] Gothic *saihsta*; ONorw. *sexte*; Mod. Norw. *sekste* Sogn; ODanish *sæxte*; Mod. Danish dialectal *sæjst* South Jutland; OHG *sëhsto*; MHG *sëhste* (c̄′ *sehste*); Mod. HG *sechster*, OSax. *sehsto, sehsta*; MLG *seste, söste* (c̄); LG *säste* Assinghausen, *sęste* Ostbevern, *ſüste* Heide (Dithmarschen), *ſüst* Stavenhagen; MDutch *seste* (c̄); Mod. Dutch *zesde*; OFrisian *sexta*; Mod. Frisian *seisde* (*sech[s]te*) West, *säkste* Saterland, *sext* Wangeroog, *seekste* East Moringen, *säākst* Föhr and Amrum, *soks* Sylt, Helgoland *sös*, loan-word form, Low German; OEngl. *sexta, siexta, syxta*,[366] *sixta* (c), Northumbrian *sesta* (Campbell 1959:

§ 417) – North Northumbrian also *seista*;[367] MEngl. *sexte* (Ormulum *sexte*), *sext, sixte* (Ayen. *zixte zyxte*), *sixt, seste* (AB *seste*) – from the last and penultimate forms; early Mod. Engl. *sixt*; Mod. Engl. *sixth*.

15.2.7. 'Seventh'

PIE **sepm̥to/ā-*: PGmc. **seƀunþan/ōn-*; PIE **sepm̥tó/ā́-*: PGmc. **seƀundan/ōn-*. PGmc. **seƀundan/ōn-*: OIcel. **siōnde*, Old Norwegian in part also **siūnde*; then, with shortening before the two consonants (Noreen 1923: § 133 n.), *sionde*, and, beside this, also OIcel. *siunde*, because of OIcel. **niŭnde* 'ninth', **tiŭnde* 'tenth' beside **niŏnde*, **tiŏnde* (15.2.9., 15.2.10.); Old Norwegian, by the phonology, **siŏnde*, in part also **siŭnde*; OEN **siunde*, with similar shortening > OSwed. *siunde*; c̄′: OIcel. *siaunde*[368] (Mod. Icel. *sjöundi*, cf. Þórólfsson 1925: XX) – for *sionde*, cf. MIcel. *sio*; Færoese *sjeyndi*; OSwed. *siūnde* (> Mod. Swed. *sjunde*); OGut. *siaunde*; ODanish *siūndi*[369]; cf. OIcel. *siau*, Færoese *sjey*, OSwed. *siū*, OGut. *siau*, ODanish *siŭ*, respectively.

The West Germanic forms, in the main, developed as did the cardinals, that is, they are c̄: OHG *sibunto*; MHG *sibente, sivente, subende, suvente*; Mod. HG *siebenter, siebter*; OSax. *siƀunda, sivondo*; MLG *sevende*; LG *sīwn̥te* Assinghausen, *ſömte* Heide (Dithmarschen); OFrisian *sigunda, siugunda, sogunda, sogenda, soginda*; Mod. Frisian *sawnde* West, *soogende* Saterland, *soowente* East Moringen, *sjûgenst* Wangeroog, *sööwenst* Föhr and Amrum (*sövende* sixteenth century), *soowenst* Sylt, *seebens* Helgoland, loan-word form, Low German: OEngl. Ru² *siofunda*[370] (c′) John 4, 52; Lindisfarne Gospels *seofonda* 8*va* 25; *seofunda*; MEngl. *sevende*,[371] *sevend, seyvend, sevind, sevente, sevint, sewint, sente*. PGmc. **seƀunþan/ōn-* > OSax. *sivotha*; MLG *sevede*; LG *siewete, siefte* Ostbevern, *ſöwt* Stavenhagen; OEngl. *seofoþa, seofeþa* (Campbell 1959: § 385), *siofþa* (c̄′); MEngl. *seovethe* (AB *seoueðe*), *sevethe*,[372] *sevenethe, seuoenþe, seventhe* (> Mod. Engl. *seventh*), *senthe*; early Mod. Engl. *sevinth, seaventh*.
From either or both of the Proto-Germanic forms: MDutch *sevende* (*sevenste*); Mod. Dutch *zevende*.

15.2.8. 'Eighth'

PIE **oḱtṓto/ā-*: PGmc. **axtṓþan/ōn-*; PIE **oḱtōtó/ā́-*: PGmc. **axtōðan/ōn-*. Further, from **seƀunþan/ōn-*, **seƀundan/ōn-* 'seventh' and **newunþan/ōn-*, **neȝunþan/ōn-*, **newundan/ōn-*, **neȝundan/ōn-* 'ninth', we have **axtunþan/ōn-*, **axtundan/ōn-*.

PGmc. **axtōdan/ōn-* > Gothic dat. sing. masc. *ahtudin* Luke 1, 59, with *u* written for *o* (Streitberg 1920: § 23A). In Scandinavian, the Proto-Germanic form gives **attuðe* > **ąttðe* > **ąttte* > **ątte*, thus (c̄′) OIcel. *átte*, OSwed. *ātte* in *attaluta, attunger* 'an eight of an eight'. Further OSax. *ahtodo*; MLG *achtede*.

PGmc. **axtōþan/ōn-*: OHG *ahtodo* (or *ahtôdo*? – Braune – Mitzka 1967: § 278 n. 1); MHG *ahtede, ahtode*. From either or both of these Proto-Germanic forms: MLG *achtede*; MDutch *achtede*.

And further, with irregular sincope similar to that found in 'eighteen' and 'eighty' and assimilation *xtd* > *xtt* > *xt*: MHG *ahte*; Mod. HG *achter*; MLG *achte*; LG *achte* Assinghausen, Ostbevern, *achte* Heide (Dithmarschen), *acht* Stavenhagen, MDutch *achte* (Mod. Dutch *achtste*); OFrisian *achta*; Mod. Frisian *oachte, aachte* East, *oochte* East Moringen; *achtste* West, *achst* Wangeroog, *aachst* Föhr and Amrum (*aechte* sixteenth century), *aachst* Sylt, *achs* Helgoland MEngl. *eighte, egh t, aght* (> Mod. Scots *aucht, aught*).

PGmc. **axtundan/ōn-*: Icel. *áttundi*; OSwed. *āttunde* [373] > *ātunde* (Noreen 1904: § 304 n. 3); ODanish *āttundi* (oblique *attonda*) > *attende* (Brøndum Nielsen 1950–1957: § 200 n. 2) – *attænde* – > *ottende* (Brøndum Nielsen 1950–1957: § 138) – *ottinde* (Brøndum Nielsen 1950–1957: § 146 n. 2);[374] Mod. Danish *ottende* (dialectal *åtənə* Skåne, Bornholm); c̄′: OIcel. *áttande*, Færoese *áttandi*; Mod. Norw. *attande*; OSwed. *āttande* (< *ātande*); ODanish *āttandi*.

From this Proto-Germanic form, further, MLG *achtende*; OFrisian *achtunda, achtanda* (c̄′); Mod. Frisian *áchtende* Saterland; MEngl. *eightend*,[375] "pres. part." *aghtand, aughtand*; before a following consonant, *eghten, eighten, aghten, aughten*; MScots *auchtende, achtand, achtend, auchten, auchtan, auchen, achen*; Mod. Scots *auchten*.

From either or both of PGmc. **axtundan/ōn-* or **axtunþan/ōn-*: MDutch *achtende*.

From either or both of PGmc. **axtōþan/ōn-* or **axtunþan/ōn-*: OEngl. *eahtoþa eahteþa* (Campbell 1959: § 385) – late WSaxon *eahtēoþa*, MEngl. *eahtuðe* AB from this + *-tēoþa* 'teenth'; MEngl. *eightethe, eightthe* (> Mod. Engl. *eighth*), *aghthe*.[376]

15.2.9. 'Ninth'

PIE **newń̥to/ā-*: PGmc. **newunþan/ōn-* > **neunþan/ōn-* and **neȝunþan/ōn-* (c̄); PIE **newn̥tó/ā́-*: PGmc. **newundan/ōn-* > **neundan/ōn-* and **neȝundan/ōn-*; further PGmc. **niunþan/ōn-*, **niundan/ōn-* and **niȝunþan/ōn-*, **niȝundan/ōn-*.

PGmc. **newundan/ōn-* > OIcel. **niŏnde*, and from this + **ni-u*, also **niŭnde*; Old Norwegian, by the phonology, **niŏnde*, in part also **niŭnde*;[377] OEN **niŭnde* – similarly to OIcel. *sionde*, ONorw. **siŏnde*, **siŭnde*, OEN **siŭnde* 'seventh'; c̄′: OIcel. *níonde*; Mod. Icel. *níundi*; Færoese *níggjundi*;[378] OSwed. *nīonde* (Mod. Swed. *nionde*); cf. OIcel. *nío*, Mod. Icel. *níu*, Færoese *níggju* (< **nīu*), OSwed. *nīo*; OSwed. *nīunde* from **niŭnde* + *nīo*; ODanish *nīundæ* (from **niŭnde* + *nīu*) > *niændæ*, *niende* (Brøndum Nielsen 1950–1957: § 555. 7), Mod. Danish *niende*, dialectal *nięnę* North Skåne, Halland, but generally *nīnde* (c̄′).
PGmc. **niunþan/ōn-* > OEngl. *nioδa* Lindisfarne Gospels.
PGmc. **niundan/ōn-* > OHG *niunte*, MHG *niunte, niunde* ("unverschoben"), Mod. HG *neunter*.
PGmc. **niȝunþan/ōn-* > OEngl. *nigoþa, nigeþa* (Campbell 1959: § 385); MEngl. *niȝeþe* (AB *niheδe*), *nȳeþe* (Luick 1921–1940: § 372), *nīþe*[379].
PGmc. **niȝundan/ōn-* > OFrisian *niûgunda* (c̄), c̄′: *niûgenda, niôgenda*; Mod. Frisian *njoggende* West, *njuugende* Saterland, *njöögente* East Moringen, *njûgenst* Wangeroog, *njügenst* Föhr and Amrum (*njüggende* sixteenth century), *niigenst* Sylt, *neägens* Helgoland (*neägen*, loan-word form, Low German); MEngl. *niȝende*,[380] c̄: *nīend, nēghend, nēnd, nīnd, nēghent, neent, nīnte* (*nigenδe, nȳnþe, nīnþe* [> Mod. Engl. *ninth*]).
PGmc. **neundan/ōn-* and/or **niundan/ōn-*: Gothic *niunda*.
PGmc. **neȝunþan/ōn-* and/or **niȝunþan/ōn-*: OSax. *nigûđa*; MLG *negende*.
PGmc. **neȝundan/ōn-* and/or **niȝundan/ōn-*: OSax. *nigunda*; MLG *negende* (also *negenech*, 15.2.0.); LG *niȝn̥te* Assinghausen, *nieȝn̥te* Ostbevern.
From one or more of the four Proto-Germanic forms last mentioned: MDutch *neghende* (*neghenste*); Mod. Dutch *negende*.

15.2.10. 'Tenth' and '-teenth'

PIE **déḱm̥to/ā-*: PGmc. **texundan/ōn-*; PIE **deḱḿ̥to/ā-*: PGmc. **teȝunþan/ōn-* – from these two, PGmc. **texunþan/ōn* and **teȝundan/ōn-*; PIE **déḱomto/ā-*: PGmc. **texandon/ōn-*, PIE **déḱm̥to/ā-*: PGmc. **texundan/ōn*.
PGmc. **texundan/ōn-* > Gothic *taíhunda, -taíhunda*. In Scandinavian we obtain OIcel. **tiŏnde*, and from this + **ti-u*, also **tiŭnde*; Norwegian, by the phonology, **tiŏnde*, in part also **tiŭnde*;[381] OEN **tiunde* – similarly to OIcel. *sionde*, ONorw. **siŏnde*, **siŭnde*, OEN **siŭnde* 'seventh'. The c̄: OIcel. *tíunde*, Mod. Icel. *tíundi*, Færoese *tíggjundi*,[382] OSwed.

tiōnde (> Mod. Swed. *tionde*), cf. OIcel. *tío*, Mod. Icel. *tíu*, Færoese *tíggju* (< **tīu*), OSwed. *tīo*; OSwed. *tīunde* from **tiŭnde* + *tīo*; ODanish **tīundi* > *tiunæ* (Brøndum Nielsen 1950–1957: § 341. 2) Lucidarius[383] (from **tiunde* + *tiu*) > *tiendæ* (> Mod. Danish *tiende*, dialectal. *tiẹnẹ* North Skåne, Halland), but generally *tīndi* (c̄′) *tīndæ*.[384]
PGmc. **teʒunþan/ōn-* > OSax. *tegotho*; MLG *tegede* (> *teide*, cf. Lasch 1914: § 342B. 1) *-tegede* (*-tegeste*); OFrisian *tegotha, tegetha, tegatha*; OEngl. **tegoþa* > *tegeða* (Campbell 1959: § 385), **-tegeða* > *-tegða* in the polysyllable, hence also **tegða* > Lindisfarne Gospels *teigða* John 1, 39, and *teiða* 5rb7, 8vb5 (also *-teiða* – Britton – Ross 1960: 146 n. 4); Mercian *teogeða* (AB *teoheðe*) *-teogeða* from *tegeða* + *teoþa*,[385] hence, similarly *-teogða* (and thus acc. *teogoan*, Herzfeld 1900: 80/13). OEngl. *-tegeba, -tegba, -teba*, and in unstressed position (Campbell 1959: § 376), *-tigeþa*, **tigþa*, hence **tigeþa*, **tigþa* > MEngl. *tiʒeðe, tiʒðe* 8> *tīþe* (Luick 1921–1940: § 372, *-tīþe*).
PGmc. **teʒundan/ōn-* > MLG *teinde*,[386] *tengde* (c); *tengede* from this last + *tegede* (also *-tengede*).[387]
PGmc. **texunþan/ōn-* > OEngl. *tēoþa* (> MEngl. *tēoþe, tēþe*), *-tēoþa* (> MEngl. *-tēoþe, -tēþe*).
PGmc. **texandan/ōn-* > Icel. *-tjándi* (c̄), OEN **-tiande* (see below); OHG *zëhanto, -zëhanto*; MHG *zëhente, -zëhente, zehente, -zehente* (> *-zênte*) ("unverschoben"): *zëhende, -zëhende, zehende, -zehende* (> *zênde, -zênde*).[388]
Mod. HG *zehnter, -zehnter*; OSax. *tehando*; MDutch *tiende, -tiende* (c̄), *tienste, -tienste*; Mod. Dutch *tiende, -tiende*; OFrisian (c̄) *tîanda, tîenda, -tînda, -tênda, -tîndosta, -tîndusta, -têndesta, -têndista, -tênsta*; Mod. Frisian *tsiende* West, *tjaande* Saterland, *tiinjde, tiinte* East Moringen; *tjôenst* Wangeroog, *tjiinst, tjinst* Föhr and Amrum (*tjiende* sixteenth century), *tiinst* Sylt, *tains* Helgoland; MEngl. *tende* (Ormulum *tende*, Ayen. *tende*) *teynd, -tende, -tend, -teind, tent, -tent, tenðe* (> Mod. Engl. *tenth*), *-tenþe, -tenth*; Mod. Engl. *-teenth*.
PGmc. **texundan/ōn-* > Icel. *-tándi*; Færoese *-tandi*; Mod. Norw. *-tande*; Runic Swed. *þritaunti* 'thirteenth'; OSwed. *-tānde*,[389] Mod. Swed. *-tonde*; ODanish *-tā̆nde*;[390] Mod. Danish *-tende*. In respect of shortening, the ordinal forms are thus seen to be very similar to the cardinals. They are also similar in respect of the distribution of the *-j-* and *-j*-less forms (15.1.10.5.); thus for instance OIcel. *fimtánde* against *nítiánde*, with *-tā̆nde* invariable in Old East Norse – this is however not to say that **-tiande* did not once exist there.

In concluding this section we may note that, in the teens 'thirteenth' to 'nineteenth', the old system by which both parts are ordinals survives in Gothic (*fimftataíhunda* 'fifteenth') and early Old High German (*drittozëhanto* 'thirteenth', etc.); elsewhere the first part is cardinal, the second ordinal.

'Tenth' as a special life of its own in that, by substantivization, it has in large part yielded the Germanic words for the ecclesiastical concept *decima* 'tithe'. In some languages the words for *'tenth'* and *'tithe'* are not distinct – Mod. Danish *tiende* means both;[391] in others there has been differentiation of form – Mod. Engl. *tenth: tithe.*

In Middle Low German, ordinal *tegede* is chiefly used in the sense *'tithe'* (Lasch 1914: § 399.1). In English, two forms of the ordinal are specialized in this sense, namely those which eventuate as Mod. Engl. *tithe* and Mod. Scots *teind.*[392] There is, further, a derivative -*ō*-verb (which, naturally, can also be used in the sense 'decimate') and occasionally, an -*ingō*- -*ungō*- abstract thereto. Verb: Mod. Icel. *tíunda*; Færoese *tíggjunda*; Mod. Danish *tiende*;[393] MHG *zëhenden*; Mod. HG *zehnten*; MDutch *tienden*; OEngl. *tèogoþian, tēoþian*; MEngl. *teoþeȝen, teþeȝen, teoþe* (> early Mod. Engl. *teethe*), *tīþen* (> Mod. Engl. *tithe*); Mod. Scots *teind.* Abstract: Mod. HG *zehntung*; MEngl. *tiþing* (> Mod. Engl. *tithing*[394]); Mod. Scots *teinding.*

15.2.11. 'Eleventh'

PGmc. **aina-liftan/ōn-* **aini-liftan/ōn-* > OIcel. *ellepte* (cf. Noreen 1923: § 240.2); Mod. Icel. *ellefti*; Færoese *ellivti* – *ellindi* from *tíggindi* 'tenth', *níggindi* 'ninth' and -*ndi* of '-teenth'; ONorw. *ælliufti* (c̄′ – cf. *ælliufu*), *øllyfti* (c̄′ – cf. **øllub̄u* and see Noreen 1923: § 85); *øllepti* from this last + **ellepti* (= OIcel. *ellepte*); *øllykti* from *øllyfti* + **ølluȝu* (*ȝt* > *kt*); *ærlipti* (c̄′ – cf. *ællifu* and *ll* > *rl*, cf. Noreen 1923: § 254); Mod. Norw. *ellevte* < **ellepti*. The East Norse forms run exactly parallel to those of the cardinal: OSwed. *ællipte* (cf. Noreen 1904: § 259. 2), *ælliufti, ællofte*; Mod. Swed. *elfte*; ODanish *ælliftæ, ællipte* (cf. Brøndum Nielsen 1950–1957: § 296), *ællefte, ellifte, ellefte* (> Mod. Danish *ellevte*), *ellufte, elløftæ, ølluffte.*[395] Further: OHG *einlifto*; MHG *einlift, einleft, eilft*; Mod. HG *elfter*;[396] OSax. *ellifto, ellefta*; MLG *elfte*;[397] LG *elfte* Assinghausen, Ostbevern, *ölfte* Heide (Dithmarschen), *elft* Stavenhagen; MDutch *ellefte* (*elfste, ellevenste*); Mod. Dutch *elfde*; OFrisian *andlofta, allefta, ellifta, ellefta*; Mod. Frisian *alfde, alfte* West, *alfte* Saterland, *alefte* East Moringen; *ánlefstst* Wangeroog, *elwenst* Föhr and Amrum, *elefst* Sylt, *ölms* Helgoland, *aalftä* Sterdebüll (native).

The English forms are diverse. OEngl. *ællefta* Ru[1] 20, 6; Lindisfarne Gospels: Matthew 20, 6; Matthew 20, 9 (c – cf. Lind. *ællef*). Ru[1] *elleftan* 'undecimam' 20, 9 (c – cf. **ellef*, with development comparable to that of Lindisfarne *ællef*, but *e* as in acc. sing. masc. *ĕnne* beside *ǣnne*, 15.1.11.) > MEngl. *ellefte* (*ellefthe*), Irish WSaxon *endlyfta* = **endlifta* (15.1.3.); WSaxon *enlefte* (c̄ – cf. *enlefan*); MEngl. *enlefte* (*enlefthe*); OEngl. *endlefta* (c̄ – cf. *endlefan*) > MEngl. *endlefta* (*endlefthe*); MEngl. *enleofte* (cf. OEngl. **enleofan*); OEngl. *endleofta* (c̄ – cf. *endleofan*) > MEngl. *endleofte*. Middle English standards: *enlevethe* (c̄ – cf. *enleve*), *ellevetth* (c̄ – cf. *elleove*),[398] *enleventhe* (c̄′ – cf. *enleven*), *endleventhe*[399] (c̄ – cf. *endleven*), *elleventhe* (c̄′ – cf. *elleoven*), *eleventhe* (c̄′ – cf. *eleven*) > Mod. Engl. *eleventh*.

Almost all the ensuing ordinal-forms show the same development as the corresponding cardinals (c̄), or are remodelled on these (c̄′) – it is not generally possible to distinguish the two. "c̄" and "c̄′" are omitted from now on, and unless there is a statement to the contrary, one or the other is to be understood.

15.2.12. 'Twelfth'

PGmc. **twa-liftan/ōn-* > OIcel. *tolfte*; Mod. Icel. *tólfti*; Færoese *tólvti*; Mod. Norw. *tolfte* (*tôvte* – cf. Indrebø 1951: 132 – "Twelfth Night" Set); OSwed. *tolfte* (Runic Swedish – Rök *tualfte* = *twǫlfte*); Mod. Swed. *tolfte*; ODanish *tolfte* (*tolthe*, Brøndum Nielsen 1950–1957: § 366); Mod. Danish *tolvte*; OHG *zwelifto*; MHG *zwelefte, zwelfte*; Mod. HG *zwölfter*; MLG *twęlfte*;[400] LG *twięlfte* Assinghausen, Ostbevern, *twölfte* Heide (Dithmarschen), *twölft* Stavenhagen; MDutch *twelefte, twaelfte* (*twelefste, twaelfste*); Mod. Dutch *twaalfde*; OFrisian *twelefta, twelfta, twilifta, tolifta, tolefta*; Mod. Frisian *tolfde, tolfte* West, *tweelfte* Saterland, *tweelefte* East Moringen *twüllefst* Wangeroog, *twaalewst* Föhr and Amrum, *twelefst* Sylt, *twalows* Helgoland; OEngl. *twelfta*; MEngl. *tweolfte*,[401] *tuelfte* (Ormulum *twellfte*), *tuelft*; with loss of *f* (Jordan 1925: § 216 n. 4) *tuelt-*, *twelfþe* (> Mod. Engl. *twelfth*), with loss of *f*, *tweolþe, twelfthe* (also *twolthe*); further *twellifth, twelveth*; with loss of *t*, originally before a following consonant, *twelf*.

15.2.13. 'Thirteenth'

OIcel. *þréttánde*; Mod. Icel. *þrettándi*; Færoese *trettandi*; Mod. Norw. *trettande*; Runic Swedish (Rök) *þritaunti*;[402] OSwed *þrǣtānde, þrættānde, þrāttānde, þrættundi* (15.2.10.); Mod. Swed. *trettonde*; ODanish *þrætandæ, thrættandæ, trættinde, trettende*; Mod. Danish *trettende*;[403] OHG *dritto-zëhanto*; MHG *drîzëhente, drîzëhende, drîzênte, drîzênde, driuzëhende* (*drî-zëhenste*); Mod. HG *dreizehnter*; MLG *drütteinde, drüttegede, drüttengede* (*drütteingeste*); LG *drüttęnde* Assinghausen, *dięttainste* Ostbevern, *dör-tainste* Heide (Dithmarschen), *dürtaist* Stavenhagen; MDutch *dertiende* (*dertienste*); Mod. Dutch *dertiende*; OFrisian *threttînda* (*threttêndesta, threttênsta*);[404] Mod. Frisian *trett(s)jinde* West, *trättienste* Saterland, *thréttînst* Wangeroog, *tratäinste* East Moringen, *trataanjst, tratanjst* Föhr and Amrum, *trötainst* Sylt, *dörtains* Helgoland; OEngl. *þreoteoba, þre-otteoba* (Campbell 1959: § 287), *þrytteoδan* Old English + dat. sing. Gospels: Matthew 11,20 (margin), dat. *þrēotegoan* (Herzfeld 1900: 38/24), acc. *þreottegoan* (Herzfeld 1900: 181), *þrīetēoba* (OED: *Thirteenth*, without reference); MEngl. *þretteþe, þritteþe, thrittende* (Ormulum *þrit-tennde, þrittende*), *thrittend, thretende, thretend, þrettende, þrettend, thri-tend, thritteind, threttent, þrittenþe, þritteneþ, threttenethe, þirttenth* (Mod. Engl. *thirteenth*), *thertenst*.

15.2.14. 'Fourteenth'

OIcel. *fiogrtánde*; Mod. Icel. *fjórtándi*; Færoese *fjúrtándi*; ONorw. *fiu-grtánde, fiórtánde*; Mod. Norw. *fjortande*; OSwed. *fiūrtande* (> *fyūrtānde*, Noreen 1904: § 270 n. 3), *fiughartānde* [? read *fiughertānde*],[405] *fyghurtāndi* (cf. genetive *fygura* < *fiugura*, 15.1.4.1.5.), *fiortunde* (15.2.10.); MSwed. *fiortānde* (> Mod. Swed. *fjortonde*); ODanish *fiūrtandæ, fyrtandæ, fior-tende* (> Mod. Danish *fjortende*), *fiortennæ, fiortinde*; OHG *fiordozë-hanto, fierzêndo*; MHG *vierzëhente, vierzëhende, vierzëhentest, vierzëhend-est*; Mod. HG *vierzehnter*; LG *fęįrtęnde* Assinghausen, *fettainste* Ostbev-ern, *feirtainste* Heide (Dithmarschen), *firtaist* Stavenhagen; MDutch *vier-tiende, veertiende, viertienste, veertienste*; Mod. Dutch *veertiende*; OFrisian *fiuwertînda, fiuwertîndosta, fiuwertîndusta, fiuwertêndista, fiwertêndesta, fiurtîndesta, fiartêndista, fiortênsta*; Mod. Frisian *fjirt(s)jinde* West; OEngl. *feowertēoþa*, dat. *feowerteogeδan, feowertegeδan* (Schipper 1898: 48/1045), acc. *feowertegoδan* (Herzfeld 1900: 118/22), MEngl. *fourteoþe* (AB *fowrtuδe*), *fourteþe, fourtithe, fourtende, bourtend, faurtend, four-tenthe* (> Mod. Engl. *fourteenth*).

15.2.15. 'Fifteenth'

Gothic *fimftataíhunda*; OIcel. *fimtánde*; Mod. Icel. *fimmtándi*; Færoese *fimtandi*; Mod. Norw. *femtande*; OSwed. *fămtande, fæ̆mptande*; Mod. Swed. *femtonde*; ODanish *fæmtande, femtande, femtende* (> Mod. Danish *femtende*) *femtennæ*; OHG *finftazëhanto, funfzêndo*; MHG *fünfzëhente, vünfzëhende;* Mod. HG *fünfzehnter*; LG *feiftęnde* Assinghausen, *füftainste* Ostbevern, *föftainste* Heide (Dithmarschen), *föftaist* Stavenhagen; MDutch *vijftiende, vichtiende, vijftienste, vichtienste*; Mod. Dutch *vijftiende*; OFrisian *fîftînda, fîftêndesta, fîftênsta*; Mod. Frisian *fyft(s)jinde* West; OEngl. *fīftēoþa*, dat. *fifteogeðan, fiftigeðan, fifteþan* (Schipper 1898: 430/2239); Ru^2 *fiftegða* Luke 3,1; Lindisfarne Gospels *fifteiðe* 'quinto decimo' Luke 3,1; *fifteiðo* 132rb3; MEngl. *fifteoþe, fifteþe, fiftende* (Ormulum *fiftende*), *fiftenthe* (> Mod. Engl. *fifteenth*).

15.2.16. 'Sixteenth'

Icel. *sextándi*; Færoese *sekstandi*; Mod. Norw. *sekstande*; OSwed. *sæxtānde, siæxtānde*; Mod. Swed. *sextonde*; ODanish *sæxtandæ, siextande, sextende* (> Mod. Danish *sekstende*), *sextennæ, sextinde*; OHG *sëhzêndo*; MHG *sëhzëhente, sëhzëhende, sëhszëhende*, sëhzëhdendest; Mod. HG *sechzehnter*; LG *sästende* Assinghausen, *sestainste* Ostbevern, *süstainste* Heide (Dithmarschen), *söstaist* Stavenhagen; MDutch *sestiende*; Mod. Dutch *zestiende*; OFrisian *sextînda, sextêndesta, sextênsta*; Mod. Frisian *sech(s)t(s)jinde* West; OEngl. *sixtēoþa, syxtēoþa, sextēoþa, sextegða*; MEngl. *sixteoþe, sixteþe*; MScots *sextend* (Mod. Scots *saxteent*), *sixtendðe* (> Mod. Engl. *sixteenth*), *sextenþe, syxtenethe*.

15.2.17. 'Seventeenth'

OIcel. *siautiánde*; ONorw. *seytiánde*; Mod. Icel. *sautjándi, seytjándi*; Færoese *seytjandi*; OSwed. *siūtānde* (> *sȳutānde*, Noreen 1904: § 270 n. 3);[406] Mod. Swed. *sjuttonde*; ODanish *sīutānde* (> *siuttande*, Brøndum Nielsen 1950–1957: § 197.2), *syttende* (> Mod. Danish *syttende*, Mod. Norw. *syttande*), *syttennæ, søttendæ*;[407a] OHG *sibuntozëhanto*; MHG *sibenzëhente, sibenzëhende, sibenzëhentest, sibensëhendest*; Mod. HG *siebzehnter*; LG *sīwn̥tende* Assinghausen, *siebmtainste* Ostbevern, *ſömtainste* Heide (Dithmarschen), *ſömtaist* Stavenhagen; MDutch *seventiende, seventienste*; Mod. Dutch *zeventiende*; OFrisian *siuguntînda, sogentêndesta, sogentênsta*; Mod. Frisian *sawnt(s)jinde* West; OEngl. *seofontēoþa, seofonteogeþa, seofontegδa, seofontigeþa*; MEngl. *seventeþe, sevintende, seventenþe* (> Mod. Engl. *seventeenth*), *seventenyth.*

15.2.18. 'Eighteenth'

OIcel. *áttiánde*; Icel. *æátjándi*, Færoese *átjandi*; Mod. Norw. *attande*; OSwed. *attertānde, atertānde*; MSwed. *adhęrtānde*; Mod. Swed. *adertonde*; ODanish attende, attenæ; Mod. Danish *attende*; MHG *ahtzëhente, ahzëhende*; Mod. HG *achtzehnter*; MLG *achtegede*; LG *achtende* Assinghausen, *achtainste* Ostbevern, *achtainste* Heide (Dithmarschen), *achtaist* Stavenhagen; MDutch *achtienste*; Mod. Dutch *achttiende*; OFrisian *achtatînda, achtêndesta, achtênsta*; Mod. Frisian *achtt(s)jinde* West; OEngl. *eahtatēoþa, eahtategeþa, eahtateogþa, eahtategþa*; MEngl. *eighteteothe, eightetethe, eightetenthe, eightenthe* (> Mod. Engl. *eighteenth*).

15.2.19. 'Nineteenth'

Icel. *nítjándi*; Færoese *nítjandi*; OSwed. *nītānde* > Mod. Swed. *nittande* (> Mod. Swed. *nittonde*); ODanish *nittende* (> Mod. Danish *nittende*, Mod. Norw. *nittande*), *nittennæ, nyttende* (cf. Brøndum Nielsen 1950–1957: § 36 n. 1); OHG *niuntazëhanto*; MHG *niunzëhende, niunzëhentest, niunzëhendest*; Mod. HG *neunzehnter*; LG *niʒntende Assinghausen, nieʒntainste* Ostbevern, *nintainste* Heide (Dithmarschen), *nentaist* Stavenhagen; MDutch *negentiende, negentienste*; Mod. Dutch *negentiende*; OFrisian *niuguntînda, niugentêndesta, nioghentêndesta, niugentênste*; Mod. Frisian *njoggent(s)jinde* West; OEngl. *nigontēoþa, neogontēoþa, nygentegþa*; MEngl. *nienteþe, nientend, nintenth* (> Mod. Engl. *nineteenth*).

15.2.20. '-tieth'

Formally, many of the Proto-Germanic prototypes are identical with two of those given under 'tenth', namely **teʒunþan/ōn-* and **teʒundan/ōn-*. From the latter, OIcel. *-tegonde*, OSwed. **-tegundi*, **-tegonde*, ODanish **-tegundi*, **-tegonde*, with no breaking because of lack of stress (Noreen 1923: § 94; Brøndum Nielsen 1950–1957: § 96). Hence then, from OIcel. *-tegonde* + nom. pl. *toger, tuger, tøger*, we have also *-togonde, -tugunde* (*-tugande* from this + *-ánde* of the teens[407b]) and *-tøgonde*. In Færoese, *tjúgundi* 'twentieth' from *tjúgu* + OWN **teʒunde; -ndi* from this is added to *tretivu* 'thirtieth' and *fjøruti* 'fortieth'. Mod. Norw. *tjuande* 'twentieth' from *tjue* + *-ande*. From OSwed. **-tegundi*, **-tegonde* + *tiughu* 'twentieth', *-tiughu*, *-tighi*, we have *tiughunde*, *tiughonde* (> Mod. Swed. *tjugonde*), *tyūvende* (Noreen 1904: §§ 270 n. 3, 279.1) – *tiūvande* with *-ande* from the teens – *tyūnde* (Noreen 1904: § 324.2), *-tiughunde, -tighinde*. Similarly in Old Danish, with *-u-* > *-æ-*, *-e-*, *tiugende, tiuende, tiwende* (> Mod. Danish *tyvende*), *tyuuennæ* (Brøndum Nielsen 1950–1957: § 341.2) 'twentieth', *-tiughænde, -tiwende, -tywende, -tyuennæ* (> Mod. Danish *-tyvende*) – also in type G, in the Færoese adaptation, it is replaced by *-tjúgundi* because of the equation Færoese *tjúgundi* = Mod. Danish *tyvende* 'twentieth'.

In Old Swedish, in type F, we have *-tiūnde, -tiōnde* [408] (> Mod. Swed. *-tionde*) > *tīęnde* (Noreen 1904: § 149.4), exactly as *tīunde, tīonde* 'tenth'. Curiously, type F admixed with type G appears in occasional Old Danish ordinals (though type F does not appear in the Old Danish cardinals) e. g. *fæmtæsyntyænde aar* 'annum quinquagesimum' ÆB 271[2] and thus meaning *'fiftieth'* and not *'hundreth'* (*-tyænde* exactly as *tyænde* 'tenth'). Type E: OIcel. *tuítiánde* from *tuítián* 'twenty' because of *siautiánde, áttiánde, nítiánde* beside *siautián*, 'seventeen', *áfftián* 'eighty', *nítián* 'ninety'.

OIcel. *-ti* in *-tugti, -tygti* is puzzling. It can hardly be old, for it is impossible to envisage an old ordinal form without a nasal; *-ti* must in fact be taken from its appearance in OIcel. *ellepte* 'eleventh', *tolfte* 'twelfth' – though the distance is considerable.

15.2.21. PGmc. **teʒunþan/ōn-* appears in the English '-tieths'; in some part it shares the fact of this form in the '-teenths', giving **-teʒuþa* > *-tegoþa* > *-tegþa* (> Lindisfarne Gospels *-teigδa*), also **-teuʒuþa* > *-teogoþa*; hence, by "akzentumsprung" (Luick 1921–1940: § 266.2; Campbell 1959: § 302), **-tuʒuþa* (> *-tugoþa*)[409] and *-togoþa*.

But, in its main development, it shows analogy with *-tig* of the cardinals, hence **-tiʒuþa* > *-tigoþa*, and *-tiogoþa* from *-tig* + *-teogoþa*. This analogy is no doubt reinforced by **-tiʒeþa* (> **-tigþa*) of the '-teenths'. We also have *-tigþa* < *-tigeþa* < *-tigoþa*, just as *-tegþa* < *-tegeþa* < *-tegoþa*. Even in Old English there is analogical replacement of the true '-tieth' form by *-tēoþa* of the '-teenths', and later this analogy is widely spread.

The Middle English forms in the main descend regularly: *-teogeδe* > *-tugeδe*, *-tēoþa* > *-tuδe*, *-tēδe* 8> *-tēth*), *-tīgþa* > *-tīþe*, *-tīth*; further *-tieth* and *-tiand* from Scandinavian.[410]

West Germanic, other than English, has the standard "superlative" suffix added to the cardinal. Modern Icelandic has a similar formation.

15.2.22. 'Twentieth'

Some of the Scandinavian forms have been discussed immediately above. Cf. also OIcel. *tuttugonde, tottogonde, tuttugti, tugtugti*; ONorw. *tyttugti, tyktukti* (Hægstad 1914–1915: 170); Mod. Icel. *tuttugasti, tvítugasti* (by analogy with OIcel. *tuítián* 'twenty'). Further: OHG *zweinzugôsto*; MHG *zweinzigest, zweinzegest*; Mod. HG *zwanzigster*; MLG *twintigeste, twintigeste*; LG *twintichste* Assinghausen, Ostbevern, *twintichste* Heide (Dithmarschen), *twintichst* (Stavenhagen; MDutch *twintichste*; Mod. Dutch *twintigste*; OFrisian *twintigosta, twintegosta, twintegasta*;[411] Mod. Frisian *tweintichste* West, *twintichste* Saterland, *twíntîgst* Wangeroog, *twuntigste* East Moringen, *twuntegst* Föhr and Amrum, *twuntichst* Sylt, *twintis* Helgoland, OEngl. *twentiogoδa, twenteogoδa, twentigoδa, twentugoδa, twentigδa, twentegoδa*; MEngl. *tventuδe* AB, *twenteth, twentiþe, twentythe* (early Mod. Engl. *twentith*), *twentide, twentiest*; Mod. Engl. *twentieth*; with Scandinavian ending, MEngl. *twentiande, tuentiand, tuentende.*

15.2.23. 'Thirtieth'

The Old West Norse forms are diverse: OIcel. *þréttogonde, þréttugande*; ONorw. *þrétugti* (analogy with *þréttán* 'thirteen'); OIcel. *þrítogonde*; ONorw. *þrítugti* (analogy with *þrír tiger*); ONorw. *þriátygti* – cf. *þriátigi*. Mod. Icel. *þrítugasti* (analogy with *tvítugasti* 'twentieth'); Færoese *tretivundi*; Mod. Norw. *trettiande*; OSwed. *þrætiughunde* > *þrætiunde* (Noreen 1904: § 324.2); MSwed. *thrætighindi*; Mod. Swed. *trettionde* (type F); ODanish *thrætiughændæ, thrædiwghende, tretiwende, trediuende, trætyuennæ* > *träynð* West Fyn (and islands south of Fyn); OHG *drîzugôsto*; MHG *drîȝȝegest, drîȝegest, drîȝȝigist, drîȝigist*; Mod. HG *dreissigster*; MLG *dortigeste, drittegeste, drüttigeste*; LG *di̧ertichste* Assinghausen, *di̧ettichste* Ostbevern, *dörtichste* Heide (Dithmarschen) *dürtichst* Stavenhagen; MDutch *dertichste, dartichste* (Franck 1910: § 46), *dortichste*; Mod. Dutch *dertigste*; Mod. Frisian *tritichste* West; OEngl. *þrītogoδa, þrittogoδa, þrittigoδa, þritteogoδa, þritegoδa, þritegoδa*; MEngl. *þrittuδe* AB, *þritteþe, thyrteth* (early Mod. Engl. *thirteth*) *þrittiþe, threttithe, thirtith, thretyd, thrittyde, thryydtyþe, thryddyþ* (dative from *þridde* 'third'), *thyrthyest, therttieth*; Mod. Engl. *thirtieth* (Ayen. *þrittaȝte*).

15.2.24. 'Fortieth'

OIcel. *fertugande, fertugti*, Mod. Icel. *fertugasti* – compositional first element (15.3.2.4.); ONorw. *fiórtugti* (analogy with nom. masc. *fiórer* 'four'); Færoese *fjørutindi*; Mod. Norw. *førtiande*; OSwed. *fȳretighinde, firitighinde*; Mod. Swed. *fyrtionde* (type F); ODanish *føretiughende, føretiwende, fyretywende, fyretiwende*; Mod. Danish *fyrretyvende*; OHG *fiorzugôsto* (dat. sing. *fiarzegusten*, Otfrid: Hartmuat v. 90); MHG *vierzegest, vierzegist, vierzegost, vierzigist*; Mod. HG *vierzigster*; LG *fęrtichste* Assinghausen, *fettichste* Ostbevern, *feirtichste* Heide (Dithmarschen), *firtichst* Stavenhagen; MDutch *viertichste, veertichste, viertechste, veertechste*; Mod. Dutch *veertigste*; Mod. Frisian *fjirtichste* West; OEngl. *feē̆owertēoða, fē̆owertigoða, fē̆owertigeða*; MEngl. *fowertuða, fourteoþe, fourtithe, fowertiðe, fuwertiðe, fourtide, fourtyd* (MScots), *fourtied* (Mod. Engl. *fortieth*), *fourtiand* from Scandinavian.[412]

15.2.25. 'Fiftieth'

OIcel. *fimtugande*; Mod. Icel. *fimmtugasti*; Mod. Norw. *femtiande*; OSwed. *fǣ̆mtighinde*, type F: MSwed. *fǣ̆mtighiande, fǣ̆mtīęnde* (cf. Noreen 1904: § 149.4) *fǣntīænde*, Mod. Swed. *femtionde*; type G: ODanish *halffuetrydiesynnetywende, halftredyæsinztyuennæ*; Mod. Danish *halvtredsindstyvende* (Færoese *hálvtrysinstjúgundi*). Further: OHG *finfzugôsto*; MHG *vinfzegist, fumfzigist, funfzigist, funfzegest, fümfzigist, fünfzigist*;[413] Mod. HG *fünfzigster*; LG *fiftichste* Assinghausen, *füftichste* Ostbevern, *fofttichste* Heide (Dithmarschen), *föftichst* Stavenhagen; MDutch *vijftichste, vijftechste, vichtichste, vichteste*; Mod. Dutch *vijftigste*; Mod. Frisian *fyftichste* West; OEngl. *fīfteogoða, fīftigoða, fīfteogoða, fīftiogoða*; MEngl. *fīftugeoða, fīftuða, fīftīthe, fīftīth*; Mod. Engl. *fiftieth*.

15.2.26. 'Sixtieth'

OIcel. *sextugande*; Mod. Icel. *sextugasti*; Mod. Norw. *sekstiande*; type F: OSwed. *siæxtiōnde*; Mod. Swed. *sextionde*; type G: ODanish *thrysinstywændhe, trysinztywenne, trisinztyuendæ*; Mod. Danish *tredsindstyvende* (Færoese *trýsinstjúgundi*). Further: OHG *sëhszugôsto*; Mod. HG *sechzigster*; LG *sekstichste, sästichste* Assinghausen, *sestichste* Ostbevern, *ſüstichste* Heide (Dithmarschen), *ſöstichst* Stavenhagen; MDutch *sestichste*; Mod. Dutch *zestigste*; Mod. Frisian *sech(s)tichste* West; OEngl. *sixteogoða, syxtigeða*; MEngl. *sixtīthe, sixtēth, sextid* (Ayen. *zixtiaȝte*); Mod. Engl. *sixtieth*.

15.2.27. 'Seventieth'

OIcel. *siautugti*; Mod. Icel. *sjötugasti*; Mod. Norw. *syttiande*; Mod. Swed. *sjuttionde* (type F); type G: Mod. Danish *halvfjerdsindstyvende* (Færoese *hálvfjerðsinstjügundi*). Further: OHG *sibunzugôsto, sibunzogôsto, sibinze-*

gôsto; Mod. HG *siebzigster*; LG *sīwn̥tsichste* Assinghausen, *siebmsichste* Ostbevern, *ſöm̥tichste* Heide (Dithmarschen), *ſǫ̈mtichst* Stavenhagen; MDutch *seventichste*, type C: *tseventichste, tseventechste*; Mod. Dutch *zeventigste*; Mod. Frisian *sawntichste* West; type C: OEngl. *hundseofontigoδa, hundsiofantiogoδa, hundsiofantigoδa* (MEngl. *hundseofonteoδe*); MEngl. *seventēþe, sevetēþe, seventīþe, seventyth*; *seventiand, seyvintand* from Scandinavian; Mod. Engl. *seventieth* (early Mod. Engl. also *seaventieth*).

15.2.28. 'Eightieth'

OIcel. *áttugande*; Mod. Icel. *áttugasti*; Mod. Norw. *åttiande*; type F: OSwed. *attatiiande*; Mod. Swed. *åttionde*; type G: Mod. Danish *firsindstyvende* (Færoese *fyrsinstjúgundi*). Further: OHG *ahtozugôsto*; Mod. HG *achtzigster*; LG *achtsichste* Assinghausen, Ostbevern, *tachntichste* (type E) Heide (Dithmarschen), *achtsicht, achtichst* Stavenhagen; type C: MDutch *tachtichste*; Mod. Dutch *tachtigste*; Mod. Frisian *tachtichste* West; OEngl. *hundeahtatigoδa*; further: MEngl. *eightetīthe, eightīthe*; Mod. Engl. *eightieth*.

15.2.29. 'Ninetieth' and '-tieth'

15.2.29.1. OIcel. *níotogande*; Mod. Icel. *nítugasti*; Mod. Norw. *nittiande*; OSwed. *nīotighindhe*; type F: *nīotīǫnde*; Mod. Swed. *nittionde*; type G: ODanish *halffemtesintywende, halffæmtæsinætiwghende*; Mod. Danish *halvfemsindstyvende* (Færoese *hálvfemsinstjúgundi*). Further: OHG *niunzugôsto, niunzogôsto*; MHG *niunzegest, niunzigist, nûnzigist*; Mod. HG *neunzigster*; LG *niȝntsichste* Assinghausen, *nieȝntsichste* Ostbevern, *nintsichste* Heide (Dithmarschen), *nentichst* Stavenhagen; MDutch *negentichste, negenstichste*; Mod. Dutch *negentigste*; Mod. Frisian *njoggentichste* West; OEngl. (type C) *hundnigontigoδa, hundnigontēoþa*; further: MEngl. *nintēth, nyntīthe*; Mod. Engl. *ninetieth*.

15.2.29.2. 'Tenth'

OHG *zëhanzugôsto*; MHG *zëhenzigest*; OEngl. (type C) *hundtēontigeδa, hundtēontigoδa*; Lindisfarne Gospels *hundteanteig* 'centensimo' 136*ra* 21.[414]

15.2.29.3. 'Eleventh'

OEngl. (type C) *hundælleftiogoδa*.

15.2.29.4. 'Twelfth'

We have not found this in Old English, although it must have existed.

15.2.30. 'Hundredth'

As stated above (15.2.0.1.), the ordinals for 'hundredth' and higher numeral units are recent, and, therefore, in large part standard. Where the ordinal does not exist, the corresponding cardinal is often used for it (e. g. in Middle English). In East Norse the cardinals are in part inflected adjectivally to form the new ordinals.[415]

15.2.31 Mod. Icel. *hundraðasti*; East Færoese *hundraði* (Svabo *hundraï*), Færoese *hundrandi* (with *-ndi* from *hálvfemsinstjúgundi* 'ninetieth', etc.); Mod. Swed. *hundrade*; Mod. Danish *hundrede* (by analogy. Mod. Norw. *hundrede*); Mod. HG *hunderster*; MLG (oblique case generalized) *hunderdesten, hundertesten, hundertsten* (> *hundersten*, Lasch 1914: § 310); LG *hundr̥tste* Assinghausen, *hunnr̥ste* Ostbevern, *hunr̥tste* Heide (Dithmarschen), *hunr̥tst* Stavenhagen; MDutch *hondertichste* (cf. *hondertich*); Mod. Dutch *honderdste*; Mod. Frisian *hûnderste* West, *hunnerste* Saterland, *hunnerst* Wangeroog, *hunertste* East-Moringen, *hunertst* Föhr and Amrum, *hön'erst* Sylt, *honderts* Helgoland; MEngl. *hundredethe*[416] (> Mod. Engl. *hundredth*).

15.2.32 'Thousandth'

Mod. Icel. *þúsundasti*; Mod. Swed. *tusende*; Mod. Danish *tusende*[417] (Mod. Norw. *tusende*, Færoese *túsundi*); MHG *tûsentiste, tûsenteste, tûsentste* (Mausser 1932: 512 ff.); Mod. HG *tausendster*; MLG (oblique case generalized) *dûsentsten* (> *dûsensten*, Lasch 1914: § 310, > *dûsesten*, Lasch 1914: § 274); also with suffixes reversed,[418] *dûsentesteghen* (cf. *dûsentich*), *dûsenstenghen* (ending from the teens); LG *deūʃn̥tste* Assinghausen, *dūʃn̥tste* Ostbevern, *dūʃn̥ste* Heide (Dithmarschen), *dūʃn̥tst* Stavenhagen; MDutch *dûsentichste, dûsentechste* (cf. *dûsentech*); Mod. Dutch *duizendste*; Mod. Frisian *tûzenste* West; Mod. Engl. *thousandth*.

15.2.33. 'Millionth', etc.

Mod. Icel. *milljónasti*; Mod. Swed. *millionde, millionte*; Mod. Danish *millionte* (loan-word form, German; Mod. Norw. *millionte*, Færoese *miljónti*); Mod. HG *millionste, millionte*; Mod. Dutch *millioenste*; Mod. Engl. *millionth*. Mod. Icel. *billjónasti*; Mod. Engl. *billonth*; Mod. Engl. *trillionth, quadrillionth, quintillionth, sextillionth* – and so on.[419]

15.3. Other numerals

15.3.1. Forms with a *-*k*-suffix

'Two'

PIE **dwey-k-no/ā-* > PGmc. **twīxna/ō-* > Gothic nom. pl. masc. *tweihnai* 'two each'; cf. also *miþ tweihnaim markom ἀνά μέσου τῶν ὁρίων* Mark 7,31. In Scandinavian, PN **twēxnR*[420, 421] > **twēnR* > OIcel. *tuénn* (Noreen 1923: § 277.1) 'double',[422] OEN **twēn* (Noreen 1904: § 295; Brøndum Nielsen 1950–1957: § 258.2) > **twǣn* (Noreen 1904: § 114.1; Brøndum Nielsen 1950–1957: § 162); hence OSwed. nom. pl. masc. *twǣni* 'two' (*twēni* from this + nom. masc. *twē* 'two'); OFrisian *twîne* (van Helten 1890: § 147) 'two, of two kinds, double'; OEngl. *be ... twēonum* (< **twīonum*, Campbell 1959: § 461, < **twīuxnum*, Campbell 1959: § 153), Mod. Engl. *between.*

'Three'

From PGmc. **twixna/ō-* + comp. **þri* (15.3.2.3.) and forms of the cardinal, we have PGmc. **þrīxna/ō-*[423] (in part) > OIcel. *þrénn* 'triple'[424] (as *tuénn*), OEN **þrǣn* (as '*twǣn*); hence OSwed. nom. masc. *þrǣni*[425] 'three', ODanish nom. masc. *thrǣnæ* 'thirty-eight'; OFrisian *thrîna* (cf. van Helten 1890: § 147). In English the form appears in the derivatives *þrīnen* (Kluge 1926: § 201); *þrīnlic* (Kluge 1926: § 237), both meaning 'triple'.

15.3.2. The compositional form

15.3.2.1. As a special old form, this exists only in 'two', 'three' and 'four'.[426] For the higher numerals the cardinal was used in composition (OHG *sibunfalt* 'sevenfold'),[427] and this cardinal use was gradually extended also to the lower numerals mentionend.
15.3.2.2. PIE **dw-* > PGmc. **twi-*. Where this survives in Norse it is treated as if it were a final syllable and the vowel is lengthened,[428] thus **twī-* in West Germanic; there is often lengthening because of the stressing (cf. Campbell 1959: § 282). We have then: Icel. *tví-*; Færoese *tví-*; Mod. Norw. *tvi-*; OGut. *twī-*; ODanish *twī-*; OHG *zwi-*; MHG *zwi-*,[429] MLG *twî-* (and *twê-* cardinal); MDutch *twi-* and *twê-* (< *twi-*), regarded as *twee-* cardinal (Franck 1910, § 66); Mod. Dutch *twee-*; OFrisian *twi-*; Mod. Frisian *twî-* Saterland, Wangeroog, *twii-* Föhr and Amrum (*twa-*

West cardinal); OEngl. *twī-* (and *twa-* cardinal); Mod. Engl. *twy-, twi-* (as in *twilight*), also *two-* cardinal.[430]
PN **twē-* from **twī* + **tew̄nR* (above); *ē* remains here in West Norse (OIcel. *tué-*,[431] Mod. Norw. *tve-*); in East Norse, **twē-* > **twǣ-* except before a vowel, when *ē* remains (Noreen 1904: § 114.1; Brøndum Nielsen 1950–1957: § 162); hence alternating forms OSwed. *twǣ-* × *twē-* (*twā-* cardinal); Mod. Swed. *tve-*; ODanish *twǣ-* × *twē-*; Mod. Danish *tve*.
15.3.2.3. PIE **tri-* > PGmc. **þri-*; hence as **twī-*, we have PN **þrī-*, and in West Germanic, often **þrī-* also – this last is not distinguishable from the old nominative masculine of the cardinal; this fact is naturally a particular cause of other nominal forms of the cardinal, too, being used in composition. We have then: Icel. *þrí-*; Færoese *trí-*; Mod. Norw. *tri-*; OGut. *þrī-*; ODanish *thrī-*; OHG *dri-*;[432] MHG *dri-*; Mod. HG *drei-*; OSax. *thrî-*; (Saterland *thrio-stunt* 'three times', cardinal, nominative-accusative feminine); MDutch *drie-*; Mod. Dutch *drie-* (cardinal); OFrisian *thri-*; Mod. Frisian *trije-* West (cardinal); OEngl. *þrī-* (cardinal, *þrīe-, þrēo-*]
PN **þrē-* from **þrī-* + **þrēnR* (above). Hence OIcel. *þré-* (as *tué-*); OSwed. *þrǣ* × *þrē-* (as *twǣ* × *twē-*); Mod. Swed. *tre-*; ODanish *þrǣ* × *þrē-* (as *twæ-* × *twe-*); Mod. Danish *tre-*.

There are some anomalous English forms. OEngl. *þrīness* 'Trinity' is correctly formed; hence also *þrĭnness* (Campbell 1959: § 287) > MEngl. *þrĭnness*.[433] But in Middle English there is also the form *þrimness*, apparently by association with the descendant of OEngl. *þrymm* 'flory' (cf. MEngl. *þrum* and *þrimsetles*, Morris 1867–1873 : 219/10). If we suppose the *m*-form already to have existed in Anglo-Saxon, this could account, by analogy, for OEngl. *þrimfeald* 'threefold' (> MEngl. *thrinfals*) beside *þrifeald*.[434]
15.3.2.4. PGmc. **feδur-* > Gothic *fidur-*. The *u* is sometimes marked long (e. g. Feist 1936: s. v.), which would make the form hard to explain. The reason for the marking is that PGmc. *u* is considered always to have broken to *aú* before *r*, and this is certainly the case for stressed *u* (Jellinek 1926: § 83 and cf. OCS *četyre*). There is but little control for PGmc. *u* before *r* in unstressed syllables; *aú* appears in *undaúrni-mat* ἄριστον L 14, 12, but here there may have been secondary stress.

On the basis of *fidur-* it may be assumed then, that truly unstressed PGmc. *u* was not broken before *r*, just as it was not broken before *x* in the enclitic *-uh*.

In Old Norwegian, **feδur-* > **fiaδur* (*u*-breaking, Noreen 1923: § 98) > **fiaδr-* > **fiæδr-* (Noreen 1923: § 70.1) > **fiǣr-* (loss of *δ* and lengthening, cf. 15.1.4.1.0.) > *fiǣr-* (shortening in unstress).

The main West Norse development is, however, from **feður-* in unstressed position, hence no breaking (Noreen 1923: § 94) and the vowel kept short after the loss of *ð*; hence **feðr-* > *fer-*, Færoese *fer-*.[435] In Old Swedish **feður-* > **fioþur-* (*u*-breaking, Noreen 1904: § 75.2) > **bioþr-* > *fioþe̜r*; from this + cardinal nom. acc. neuter *fiughur*, we have *fiuþæ̜r-* ; from *fioþe̜r-* + ordinal *fiærþe*, we have *fiæ̜þer- fiæþr-*. In unstressed position – with similar development to that of Icel. *fer-*: **feður-* > **feðr-* (no breaking, Noreen 1904: § 76.2) > **fæðr-* (Noreen 1904: § 113) > **fǣr-* > *fær-*; from this + *fiæþe̜r-*, we obtain *fiær-*. Many forms of the cardinal (15.1.4. ff.) are used instead of the compositional form, particularly in Middle Swedish: *fiughur-*, *fygher-*, *fiur-*; MSwed. *fiugher-*, *fioghir-* (vowel syncopated by analogy with *fioþe̜r-*) *fȳr-*, *fȳra-*, *fȳre-*, *fīra-*; Mod. Swed. *fyr-*.
PGmc. **feður-* > Saterland *fither-* (*e* > *i* before *a* following *u*, 15.1.7.2.); OEngl. *feoþor*,[436] MEngl. *feðer-* (Lindisfarne Gospels *fē̜arfald* 'quadruplum' Luke 19, 8, by analogy with ordinal *fē̜arða*).

15.3.3. Extensions of PIE **dwis*, etc.[437]

15.3.3.1. *-n-*[438]

PIE **dwis-nó/ā́* > PGmc. **twizna/ō-*, whence in part **twezna/ō-* (*a*-umlaut, so Noreen 1904: § 163.1). From the *i*-form, PN nom. sing. masc. **tuinnR* (Noreen 1923: § 224.2; Brøndum Nielsen 1950–1957: § 254.1), oblique **tuinn-*; in Old Icelandic the former gives *tuiþr* (Noreen 1923: § 261), with *tuinnr*[439] by analogy with the latter, which remains unchanged[440] (OIcel. *tuínn* from this + *tuénn* above), PN **tuinnR*: nominative plural masculine.[441] OSwed. *twinni* 'two', ODanish *twinnæ*.[442] Similarly PGmc. **twezna/ō-* > OIcel. *tueþr*; Icel. *tvennr*; Mod. Norw. pl. *tvenne* 'two' Hadanger, Gudbrandsdal; OSwed. *twænne*;[443] Mod. Swed. *tvenne* 'of two kinds', 'two'; ODanish *twænni* 'two'; Mod. Danish *tvende* < PN **twennR* (Noreen 1904: § 113; Brøndum Nielsen 1950–1957: § 161).

Substantivized weak nouns: Icel. *tvinni* masc. 'binding-thread'; Mod. Swed. *tvinna*; Mod. Danish *tvinde*, also 'instrument for winding'; further Mod. Danish dat. *øretvinde* 'earwig'.

The West Germanic forms derive from **twizna/ō-*, and three developments of *-zn-* are evidenced.
(1) The resulting *-rn-* remains: masc. *a*-stem: MHG *zwirn* 'double thread'; Mod. HG *zwirn*; MLG *twern*[444] 'twine'; LG *twēr̥n* Assinghausen, *tweirn*

Heide (Dithmarschen), *twīrn* Stavenhagen; MDutch *twern*[445] 'twine'; Mod. Dutch *tweern*.
(2) *z* is lost with lengthening of the preceding vowel: *a*-stem: masc. MDutch *twijn*; Mod. Dutch *twijn*; neuter OEngl. *twīn*[446] 'linen'; Mod. Engl. *twine*.
(3) *zn* > *nn*: adjective:[447] OEngl. *ge-twinn*; 'twin'; and in plural 'two'; Mod. Engl. *twin*; masc. *a*-stem: OEngl. *ge-twinn* 'twin'; Mod. Engl. *twin*.[448]

The derivative verb, PGmc. **twiznōþ* is also attested: Icel. *tvinna* 'to double'; Mod. Icel. *tvinna* 'to twist'; Færoese *tvinna*; Mod. Norw. *tvinna*; OSwed. *tvinna*; Mod. Swed. *tvinna*; Mod. Danish *tvinde*; OHG *zwirnôn*;[449] MHG *zwirnen*; Mod. HG *zwirnen*; MLG *twernen* 'to twine'; MDutch *tweernen, twînen*; Mod. Dutch *tweernen, twijnen*; Mod. Frisian *twine*; MEngl. *twinen twinnen*; Mod. Engl. *twine*[450] *twin*.

There are, in addition, a number of extensions to the word, as, for instance, the following:
(a) Kluge (1926: § 55): Icel. *tvenning* 'duality' (> *tvening*, Noreen 1923: § 285.2).
(b) Kluge (1926: § 1959): Færoese pl. *tvinningar* 'two parts'; ODanish *tvinning* 'twin' (Mod. Frisian *twaning* 'doppelgänger', loan-word form, Danish?).
(c) Kluge (1926: § 55): Mod. Norw. *tvinnling* 'twin' Mandalen, Telemark, OSwed. *tvinlinger* (> Mod. Swed. *tvilling*; ODanish *tvinling*; > Mod. Danish *tvilling*, Brøndum Nielsen 1950–1957: § 251);[451] Mod. Frisian *twenling* (and *twanling*, cf. *twane*, above) North, *twineling* East (*twilling* Saterland, *twöllung* Helgoland, assimilated to the Dutch or German form); MEngl. *twinling*; Mod. Engl. dialectal *twinling* 'a twin', especially one of twin lambs (also *twindling*, with paragogic *d*, cf. Jordan 1925: § 202).
(d) Mod. Norw. *tvinla* 'to twine', 'entangle'; Mod. Swed. dialectal *tvinnäl* 'to whirl around' (intr.).
(e) Mod. Norw. *tvinta* 'to reel', 'walk dizzily', 'stumble'; Mod. Swed. dialectal *tvinta* 'to hit' (someone).[452]

'Three'

PIE **tris-nó/ā́-* > PGmc. **þrizna/ō-* and **þrezna/ō-* (with *a*-umlaut). Hence OIcel. *þribr, þrinnr, þrebr*; Icel. *þrennr* 'triple', 'three'; Færoese *trinnur*; Mod. Norw. *trinn* (*trenn* Hallingdal) 'threefold', 'three'; OSwed. *þrinni, þrænne*[453] 'three'; Mod. Swed. *trenne* 'three'; ODanish *thrinnæ*,

thrænni[454] 'three'; Mod. Danish *trende* 'three' – exactly as the corresponding 'two'-forms. (OEngl. *þrinna*, Liebermann 1903–1916: III Æthelred, 13/i, 230, MEngl. *þrinne*,[455] loan-word form, Scandinavian, Björkman 1900–1902: 173.)
Extensions – as in the corresponding 'two'-forms: Icel. *þrenning* (> *þrening*), *þrinning* 'threeness'; Mod. Norw. *i trinungå* 'in parts', Nordhordland;[456] Mod. Norw. *trinnling* 'triplet' Magdalen, Nordhardland; Mod. Swed. *trilling*; Mod. Danish trilling;[457] Mod. Frisian *trenling* North (also *tranling*, cf. *trane*).

'Four'

PGmc. **feδurzna/ō-* > OWN **feðrRnR* > **feRnR*, with essentially the same development as comp. *fer-* (15.4.6.); hence Icel. nom. pl. masc. *fernir* 'in sets of four'.

15.3.3.2. ***-k-***

PIE **dwis-ko/ā-* (and **dwis-ko/ā-*) > PGmc. **twiska/ō-* **twiskja/ō-*: OHG *zwisk zwiski* 'twofold', 'two'; also in *zwiskên* 'between', *untar zwiskên*; MHG *zwischen, zwüschen*; Mod. HG *zwischen*; OSax. *under twisk*; MLG *twisk* 'twofold', *twischen* (> *tüschen*, Lasch 1914: § 172, *twöschen*, Lasch 1914: § 174) 'between'; MDutch *twisschen, tusschen* (van Loey 1969: II § 23); Mod. Dutch *tussen*;[458] *twiska, twisk*; Mod. Frisian *tuske, tusken* West, *twiske* Saterland, *tusken* Wangeroog, *twasche* East Moringen, *tesk* (preposition), *tesken* (adverb) Föhr and Amrum.

In English **twisk* remains in Mod. Engl. dat. *twish*, Mod. Scots *a-tweesh, be-tweesh*. But in general, the form is metathesized to **twihs* (Campbell 1959: § 460); from this + **twixn* (15.3.1.), we obtain **twiksn*; hence OEngl. *be-twix*, **be-twixn* (> *bi-tuixen*); from these + the relevant forms of **twīh* (15.4.8.) – so Campbell (1959: § 440 n. 2) – *be-twēox, be-twēoxn, be-twux, be-tux*. Hence MEngl. *bi-twix, bi-twux, bi-twuxen, bi-tux, bi-tuxen, bi-twex*. Further, with added *-t* (cf. Jordan 1925: § 199), OEngl. *be-twuxt, be-twyxt* (*y* written for *i*), MEngl. *bi-twixt* (> Mod. Engl. *betwixt*), *bi-twuxt, bi-tuxt*.[459]

Spenter (1968: 67–93) explains OFrisian *tusk*; OEngl. *tusch, tux*; Mod. Engl. *tusk, tush* from **twis-ku-*, of this provenance. He adduces forms with *w* such as Schiermonnikoog *twesk, twisk*, and OEngl. *twuxan*.
PIE **tris-ko/ā-* (and **triskyo/ā-*) > PGmc. **þriska/ō-*, **þriskja/ō-* > *drisk, driski*.[460]

15.3.3.3. Twice, thrice

The older view of these is that they represent extensions of PIE **dwis*, **tris* by means of a *w*-suffix (so Brugmann – Delbrück 1897–1916: II. ii. 64), and it is the case that a PIE gen. loc. dual **dwiswows* > PGmc. **twiswauz* will apparently explain OIcel. *tysuar* – similarly for OIcel. *þrysuar*. ONorw. *tysuár, þrysuár*, however, cannot possibly be explained in this way, for they have a long vowel in the second syllable (they are given, so accented, by Noreen 1923: § 463[461] – the forms are supported by MSwed. *tisvår*, Noreen 1904: § 110). These forms must by origin have been compounds, and it is for this reason that Loewe (1916: 98 ff.) postulates compounds of **dwis* and **tris* with a **wēro-* (> OInd. *vā́ra-*, cf. *pañca-vāram* 'five times').

The difficulty here is that the Old Indic form is now usually taken to derive **wel-*,[462] which would, of course, eliminate Loewe's suggestion. The coincidence between the Old Indian and Germanic forms is however so striking that we should perhaps reconsider the accepted etymology of the Old Indic word and connect it with a root *wer-* (perhaps that found in OInd. *vartati* 'to turn', OEngl. *weorþan* 'to become' [Pokorny 1959: 1152]; **wert-* would then have to be considered extended). On the other hand, a compound with **wero-* cannot possibly explain West Germanic forms such as OHG *zwiro*, despite Loewe's (1916: 98 ff.) discussion. Therefore, what we have here seems to be a mixture of the two types **dwiswous* and **dwis-wero-* (and similarly for 'three'). We begin by discussing the development of the suffixed type.

PIE gen. loc. dual. **dwis-wóws*[463] > PGmc. **twizwaus*, PIE **dwís-wows* > PGmc. **twiswauz*; from these two, **twiswaus* and **twizwauz* also have to be recognized. The two endings must have developed in the following way; *-auz* > PN *-oR* (Noreen 1923: § 140) > OIcel. *-ar*, OSwed. *-ar*; ODanish *-ar*; cf. gen sing. OIcel. *sonar*; OSwed. *sonar, sunar*; Runic Danish *sunaR*; *-aus* > early OHG *-ô* (*fridoo*, Benediktinerregel: 194/1 = Icel. *friðar*); OFrisian *-a* (genitive sing. *suna*, Rüstringer Codex, Buma 1961); OEngl. *-a* (genitive sing. *suna*, cf. Walde 1900: 54–55).[464] We have no control for the development of *-auz* in Old High German, but it might well have given *-or*.

The medial consonant cluster develops differently in the various Germanic domains. In Norse, *-sw-* is generalized, and remains. in West Germanic *-zw-* is generalized, but does not remain: in High German *w* is lost, in Ingvaeonic *z* is in general lost, and after this, *w* too is in part lost by dissimilation from the preceding *tw-*; here too, there is later analogy with 'once', the adverbial genitive singular masculine neuter of 'one'.[465] Hence the following developments.

'Two'

Norse. PGmc. **twiswauz* > PN **twiswōR* > OIcel. *tysuar* (Noreen 1923: § 82. 10); OSwed. *tyswar* (Noreen 1904: § 69. 9) > *tøswar* (Noreen 1904: § 116), also MSwed. *tyswer* (Noreen 1904: § 149. 1), *tyswa*; ODanish *tyswar* (Brøndum Nielsen 1950–1957: § 92) > *tøswar* (Brøndum Nielsen 1950–1957: § 164), also with loss of *w, tyssær* (> Mod. Danish dialectal *tysser*), *tøssær*, sometimes with loss of *r* as well, *tyssæ* (Brøndum Nielsen 1950–1957: § 388, n. 9).[466] From this type + comp. **twī-*:[466a] Icel. *tvisvar*; OSwed. *twiswar* (*tweswar* by analogy with nom. masc. *twē*).[466b]
High German. PGmc. **twizwaus* > **twizaus* > OHG *zwiro*; MHG *zwire, zwir, zwier* (Mausser 1932: 95); early Mod. HG *zwir, zwier*.[467]
PGmc. **twizwauz* > **twizauz* > OHG *zwiror*.
Ingvaeonic, PGmc. **twizwaus* > **twiwō* > **twiwo* > **twio*, which in part gives **twijo* (Luick 1921–1940: § 97), which again in part yields **twīo*. Hence then **twiwo* > OEngl. *twuwa* (Luick 1921–1940: § 221. 2) > *tuwa* (Campbell 1959: § 470), and if *"gesteigerter"* back-umlaut did not take place (Luick 1921–1940: § 224 n. 1), **twiwa* > **twiowa* > **tweowa*.
**Twio* > OFrisian *twia*; Mod. Frisian *twäie* Saterland, *twaie* East Moringen.
**Twio* > OSax. *twîo*.
**Twijo* > OFrisian *twiia*; OEngl. *twiga, twigea*, and *twīga, twīgea* by analogy with **twīa* (< **twīo*); MEngl. *twīȝe, twīe*, and *tweie* from this + *tweȝen* 'two', and further, from this latter, MEngl. *twīȝen, twīen, tweien* (AB *twie twien*); similarly MLG *twîge*.
With adverbial *-es*: – MLG *twîges* – *tweyes* from this + *twey* 'two'; early Mod. Fr. *tweis* Föhr and Amrum;[468] MEngl. *twīȝes*,[469] *twīes* (Ayen. *tuyes, tuies*); Mod. Engl. *twice*.[470]

'Three'

The developments are, in large part, similar to those of 'twice'.
Norse PGmc. **þriswauz* > PN **þriswōR* > OIcel. *þrysuar* (Icel. *þrisvar* from this + comp. **þrī-*;[470a] OSwed. *þriswar, þriswa*; ODanish *thriswar*.[471] From this type + the descendants of PN **twiswōR*, we have OSwed.

þryswar (MSwed. *thrø-suar*), *þryswa*; ODanish *thryswar* (> *thrøswar*), *thryssæ* (*thrissæ*, Brøndum Nielsen 1950–1957: § 140), *thruswar* from this type + *tuswar*.
High German. PGmc. **þrizwauz* > **þrizauz* > OHG *driror* Sievers 1874).
Ingvaeonic. PGmc. **þrizwaus* > **þriwō* > **þriwo*; hence also **þrio*, **þrijo*, **þrīo* because of **twio*, **twijo*, **twīo* beside **twiwo*. Hence then **þriwo* > OEngl. *þriwa, þriowa, þreowa* (> MEngl. *þreoue*). OSax. *thrîwo* from **þriwo* + **þrīo*.
**Þrio* > OFrisian *thria*; Mod. Frisian *traie* Saterland, *traie* East Moringen;[472a] OEngl. *ðria* Lindisfarne Gospels.
Þrīo > OSax. *thrîo*.
Þrijo > OSax. *thriio* (MLG *drîge* as *twîge*); OFrisian *thriia*; OEngl. *þriga*; MEngl. *þrīe* (*þreie, þrien, þreoien* – AB *þrie, þrien*) by analogy with the relevant forms of 'twice'.
With adverbial *-es*: MLG *drîges*; MEngl. *þrīes* (Ormulum *þriȝȝess, þriȝess*, Ayen. *þries*), *threies* from this + *þreie*; Mod. Engl. *thrice*.

We turn now to the **wēro*-type. The second element will give PN *-*wār*; since this will have been inflected we must also obtain – for instance in the dative plural – umlauted forms with OIcel. *ó* (Noreen 1923: § 77. 11), OSwed. *ō* (Noreen 1904: § 67. 7), ODanish *ō* (Brøndum Nielsen 1950–1957: § 88), and, with restitution of the *w* from the unumlauted forms, also OWN *uó*, OSwed. *wō*, ODanish *wō*. Then shortening occurs in the second syllable due to lack of stress; *-*war* here will thus not be different from the *-*war* of the suffixal type. As the remaining forms we then have: ONorw. *tysuor, tuisuor, þrysuor* (*þesuor* by analogy with *þré-* in various cases of the cardinal),[472b] *þrysor* – also *þrissuor*,[473] and from this + *þrysor*, also *þrissor*; OSwed. *tyswor*; MSwed. *tysa* from **tyssor* + *tyswar; trøsa* from **trysor* + *thrøswar*.

We may mention finally two – clearly archaic – High German forms, namely OHG *zwiron* Tatian, MHG *zwiren, zwirn* and OHG *zwiront* Notker (ed. Piper 1895),[474] MHG *zwirent, zwirnt, zwirunt, zwürunt* (cf. Mausser 1932: 550); Mod. HG (Swiss) *zwirund*. These must surely be brought into connection with **dwis-went-* and have the development PIE *-sw-* > OHG *-r-* discussed above. The endingless nom.-acc. sing. neuter **dwis-went* would then give OHG **zwirin* with loss of the completely final *-t-*[475] – hence, from this + *zwiro*, we obtain *zwiron*.

In *zwiront*, we must suppose the *-nt* (< PGmc. *-nd*) to be restored from the other cases, otherwise with precisely similar development.[476]

15.3.4. The Norse *-ti*-abstracts

'Five'. PIE **pémpti-* > PGmc. **finfti-* > Icel. *fimt* 'set of five', 'five days'; Færoese *fimt* 'five days'; ODanish *fimt* (> *fymt* Brøndum Nielsen 1950–1957: § 135) *fimpt* (Brøndum Nielsen 1950–1957: § 351); OSwed. *fæmt* 'five days', 'meeting after five days'; Mod. Swed. *femt* 'set of five'; ODanish *fæmt, femt*, c̄′.

'Six'. PIE **sek̑ti-* > PGmc. **sixti-*, then **sexti-* from ordinal **sextan/ōn-* > OIcel. **sétt* (cf. *séttareiþr* – genitive singular + *eiþr* 'oath') 'denial which a defendant makes with one or two others from twelve chosen men (six on either side of him)'.[477]

'Seven'. PIE **sepm̥tí-* > PGmc. **siƀundi-*; this may well have given **seƀundi-* by remodelling an ordinal **seƀundan/ōn-*; the forms actually appearing are c̄: OIcel. *siaund* 'set of seven'; 'the seventh day after a death, when the funeral and wake took place'; Orkney *schone, schound* 'division of a deceased person's property made on the seventh day after death' (Marwick 1929: s. v.); Mod. Norw. *sjaund* (*sjund* Nordland) 'wake'.

'Eight'. PIE **ok̑tṓti-* > PGmc. **axtoʒþi-* > **āttuði-* > **ǫtti-* (cf. the development of the ordinal) > OIcel. *ætt* (and c̄′ *átt*) 'one third of the Runic alphabet, that is, originally, eight runes' (in middle Icelandic also 'an octant of the horizon': *útsuorsætt*).[478]

'Nine'. PIE **newn̥tí-* > PGmc. **niundi-*; the resulting mutated form is c̄′: OIcel. *níund* 'set of nine'.

'Ten'. In some respects, the Scandinavian word for 'tithe' (cf. 15.2.10.) belongs here. Noreen (1923: § 461) takes OIcel. *tíund* as a *-ti*-abstract, but it may be doubted whether PGmc. **texundi-* (< PIE **dek̑m̥ti-*) would in fact have yielded this form. It is no doubt for this reason that Torp (1919 sv: *Tie*) takes the word as nominative singular feminine of the ordinal, substantivized. Clearly, he must mean – though he does not state it – that the case is strong.

Stromg forms of ordinals do occur in Scandinavian, though very rarely; cf. OSwed. acc. sing. fem. *þriþia*, dat. sing. neuter *þriþiu* to *þriþi* 'third'; Noreen (1904: § 491 n. 1) regards these as due to the influence of *annar* 'second', strong.[479] It will then be seen that Torp's suggestion, as it stands, is not very probable. The explanation is, surely, that the word started as a *-ti*-abstract, PGmc. **texundi-*, in the event, **tixundi-*, but that the forms actually occurring have all been analogized to the ordinal, which is sometimes in aberrant form: Icel. *tíund* (to OIcel. **tíunde* from **tionde* + **tiu*); Færoese *tíggjund* (normally pronounced as if spelled *tíggind*, cf. 15.2.0.); Mod. Norw. *tiend* (< ONorw. **tīond* to *tíonde*); OSwed. *tīund* (and *tīond* from this + *tīo*) and *tīunde* which actually is the ordinal. We have further OSwed. *tīnde* < *tīunde* in the common compound *hovoþtīnde* – cf. *Tīndaland* (see Noreen 1904: § 492 n. 3). OGut. *tīunt* and *tīont* (to **tīonde* with *īo* from **tiŭnde* + *tīo*) has perhaps been influenced by *hælft* 'half' – so, tentatively, Noreen (1904: § 497) – (*tīunta* from this + oblique ordinal *tīunda*). The word is borrowed into Finnish and Lappish: Fi. *tihunti, tiunti, tivunti, tiuni*; Lappish *tivod, tijod* (Russian), *tivut* (Lule), *divâd, divâg, divât, diddo* (Norwegian), *tievod* (Inari).[480] Karsten (1943–1944: 545) says of the Finnish word (we translate) "the Finnish *h* derives from the Germanic *"tehun"*, and this view is essentially followed by Collinder (1932–1941: 73). But it is not possible that a Christian word should preserve a PGmc. *x* lost in pre-Christian times; and the absence of the word in the other Balto-Finnic languages also lends support to the view that the Finnish word is indeed a comparatively late borrowing. Wiklund (1903: 27) is surely right in supposing the *h* of *tihunti* to be a purely Finnish insertion (is *v* of *tivunti* another such case?). We may thus regard *tiunti* as the basic Finnish form – and this is certainly a borrowing of OSwed. *tīund, tīundi.*[481] The Lappish forms require investigation; they are presumably borrowed, at different times, from Norwegian, Swedish and Finnish.

'Twelve'. The forms are difficult and clearly cannot derive from the expected PGmc. **twalifti-*. Brøndum Nielsen (1950–1957: § 81 n. 4) plausibly suggests a fairly late reshaping after the cardinal. OIcel. *tolf*, OSwed. *tolf*, ODanish *tolf* because of the "systemzwang" of unmutated *o*: mutated *y* in pairs such as Icel. *folk* 'people' x *fylki* 'troop'. Hence then: Icel. *tylft* 'dozen' (OIcel. also 'twelve days', 'voyage'); Færoese *tylft* 'dozen'; Mod. Norw. *tylft* (> *tyllt*, cf. Indrebø 1951: 235); OSwed. *tylpt* (cf. Noreen 1904: § 259, 2a) 'dozen', 'twelve men who swear an oath' (> *tilpt*, Noreen 1904: § 101. 1, and *tylt*, Noreen 1904: § 309); cf. also *tólft* (Noreen 1904: § 116); ODanish *tylft* 'dozen' (> *tylt*, Brøndum Nielsen 1950–1957: § 366); Mod. Danish *tylvt, tylt.*[482] With further remodelling on the cardinal: OIcel. *tolft*; Mod. Swed. *tolft*; ODanish *tolft.*[483]
'-*ty*'. PIE **dekm̥tí-* > PGmc. **tiʒundi*, (c') **teʒundi-*: OSwed. *brætiughend.* OIcel. *tuíøgt* 'the age of twenty', Mod. Icel. *tvítugt*; OIcel. *þrítøgt* 'thirty years', 'prayer for the decad in the first thirty days after death'; Mod. Icel. *þrítugt* 'age of thirty'; OSwed. *thrætiught* 'thirtieth day after a

person's death', are not *-ti*-abstracts; the form is in fact the nominative-accusative singular neuter of a bahuvrihi. These bahuvrihi compounds exist in Icelandic, Old Norwegian, and, rarely, in Old Swedish. The second element is PGmc. *-teʒu-*; cf. Gothic *laus-handus* 'empty-handed' to *handus* 'hand'; the forms naturally agree with those of '*-ty*', discussed above.[484]

Correctly, the first element is the compositional form in the case of 'two', 'three', 'four': Icel. *tví-, þrí-, fer*; OSwed. *þrǣ-, fioþer* etc.; in the cases above 'four', the cardinal is used.

Originally, the *-teʒu*-formations went no higher than 'six'; after this point there correspond compounds with OIcel. *-røþr*, Mod. Icel. *-ræður*; but there has been some analogy so that a *-teʒu* form is found for 'seven' in both Old and Modern Icelandic, and one for 'nine' in Old Icelandic.

The meaning of the 'two'-bahuvrihi is essentially 'in the third decade'; this can refer to various measurements (e. g., in Modern Icelandic, of length) but, especially, to age (so that a man aged twenty-seven might be referred to by this bahuvrihi). And so on for the higher bahuvrihis.[485] We thus have: 'two': OIcel. *tuítøgr*, Mod. Icel. *tvítugr*; 'three': OIcel. *þrítøgr*, Mod. Icel. *þrítugur*;[486] 'four': OIcel. *fertøgr*, Mod. Icel. *fertugur*; OSwed. *fioþęrtiogher, fiæþęrtiugher, fiuþætigęr* 'comprising forty'; 'five': OIcel. *fimtør*, Mod. Icel. *fimmtugur*; 'six': OIcel. *sextøgr*, Mod. Icel. *sextugur*; 'seven': OIcel. *siautøgr* (also *siótugr*), Mod. Icel. *sjötugur*; 'eight': OIcel. *att-røþr*, Mod. Icel. *áttræður*, etc.; 'nine': OIcel. *nítøgr* – as against 'seven': OIcel. *siau-røþr*.

In conclusion we may note first that, in Icelandic, 'half' is used as in OIcel. *halffertøgr*, Mod. Icel. *hálf-fertugur* 'thirty-five years old' to the 'four'-formation: Mod. Icel. *hálf-áttræður* 'seventy-five years old' to the 'eight'-formation and so on. And, secondly, that in Old Swedish, comparable bahuvrihi forms are made from the 'twelve' *-ti* abstract: *twǣtylfter, twǣtylter, twǣtolfter* 'concerning two dozen people' (with OSwed. compound *twǣ-*, 15.3.2.2.); *þrǣtylftęr, þrǣtyltęr, þrǣtølftęr*[487] 'concerning three dozen people', also *þrænnetylftęr* (with *þrænne* 15.3.3.1.). Cf. further, *twǣtyltæbęr, þrætylftaþęr* with added accusative feminine suffix as in Mod. Swed. *baramad* 'bare-armed'.

15.4. Some numeral derivatives

15.4.1. *-a(n)*[488]

PIE **dwey-o-* > PGmc. **twīa-* neuter > OHG *zwî* 'branch'; MHG *zwî*. Derivative verb: Swiss *zwien* 'to graft' (and *zweien* by "hiatusdiphthong-

ierung").[489] PIE **dwoy-o-* > PGmc. (*n* +)[490] **twaian-* > **twajjan-* > PIcel. *Tuegge*, one of Odin's names.[491]
PGmc. **twisa(n)-* (: PIE **dwis*): OEngl. *ge-twis* 'germanus'; OHG *gi-twiso* 'twin'; OSax. *gi-twiso*; MLG *twese*; OEngl. *ge-twisa*. Further, PGmc. **twisalinga-* (Kluge 1926: § 55) > MLG *tweseling* and **twisakan-* (Kluge 1926: § 61a) > MLG *twēseke*; LG pl. *twīskes* 'twins', Ostbevern.

15.4.2. *-ō-*

PIE **dwey-ā-* > PGmc. **twīō-* > **twījō-* > OIcel. *týja* (cf. Noreen 1923: § 77. 13) 'doubt' Edda, *atlaqviδa in grenlenzca*, Stanza 27, v. 1.[492]

15.4.3. *-ārja-*

'Hundred' PGmc. **xundārja-* > OHG *huntâri* (gender not determined)[493] 'hundred (of land)', OSwed. *hundare* neuter, Mod. Swed. *hundare* neuter.

15.4.4. *-ōđja-*

'One' PGmc. **aenōdđja-* neuter > OHG *einôti*; MHG *einôte, einœde, einœte*; Mod. HG *einöde*; OSax. *ênodi*; MDutch *ênode*; OEngl. *ānad*. The word received its feminine gender and its *d* in High German by association with MHG *œde*, Mod. HG *öde*.

15.4.5. *-itja-*[494]

'One' PGmc. **ainitja-* neuter > OEngl. *ǣnett* 'solitude' (c̄′: *ānett*).

15.4.6. *-inga-, -unga-*

'One'. Adverb, PGmc. **ainingō*, **aeningō*:[495] OEngl. *ǣninga, ānunga* (and *āninga* by mixture of the two) 'at once', 'of necessity', 'by all means'.[496]
A set of masculine derivatives to the ordinals belongs here (Kluge 1926: § 100a).[497] They are predominantly Scandinavian. The meaning is that of the relevant fractions ('one-third', 'one-quarter', etc.)[498] and the senses are readily derivable from these.[499]

'Three'. OIcel. *þriþongr* 'specifying a territorial division'; Færoese *triδingur*; Mod. Norw. *tridjung* (c′: *triung, treung*, reshaped after the ordinal); OSwed. *þriþungẹr*; ODanish *thrithung*. By analogy with oblique cases of the ordinal (Icel. *priðja*, OSwed. *þriþia*, ODanish *thrithia*): OIcel. *þriþiongr*; Mod. Icel. *þriojungur*; OSwed. *þriþiungẹr*; ODanish *thrithiung*; late MSwed. *trediunge*; ODanish *thrediwng* (cf. ordinal Mod. Swed. *tredje*, Mod. Danish *tredie*); OSwed. *þriþinger*; late MSwed. *tridinge*; ODanish *thrithing*; Mod. Danish *treding* 'specifying measure of capacity, area or district'.[500]

'Four'. OIcel. *fiorþongr* 'specifying a quarter of a mile, territorial division, measure of weight, unit of currency', *fiórþongr*; Mod. Icel. *fjórðungur*; Færoese *fjóðingur, fjórðungur*; Mod. Norw. *fjordung* 'specifying a quarter of a mile'; OSwed. *fiærþungẹr* 'specifying a quarter of a carcase, a year, a mile, and in liquid measure; quarter of a silver mark; territorial division, part of a parish, town'; *fiorþongẹr, fiurþongẹr* (c̄′), *fiorþiungẹr* (analogy with *þriþiungẹr*);[501] Mod. Swed. *fjärding* 'specifying a measure of area, district, kind of cask'; Mod. Danish *fjerding* 'specifying a measure of capacity, weight, time, area – also quarter-carcase, and district'; OHG *vierdung* 'specifying a quarter of a weight or measure; particularly of a pound (money)'; MHG *vierdinc*; MLG *vêrdink* (*vêrdink* (c̄′)) 'specifying a measure of weight, coin'; MDutch *vierdinc, vierdonc* 'measure of weight'; OFrisian *fiardeng* 'quarter of a mark'; Mod. Frisian *fiirding*.

For 'farthing' the *-linga* derivative (Kluge 1926: § 55) is usual in Anglo-Saxon: *fēorþling*, except for Lindisfarne *feorðung*. In later English the type without *l* is wide-spread (MEngl. *ferþing*, Mod. Engl. *farthing*). The Lindisfarne form and some of the later ones could be of Scandinavian origin (so, tentatively, OED: *Farthing* sb.) but the distribution in Middle English (MED: *Farthing*) shows that not all of them are like this (cf. especially Ayen. pl. *uerbinges*, 193/30); the word must be in part native.

'Five'. Mod. Icel. *fimmtungur*; Færoese *fimtingur*; OSwed. *fæmtunger* 'specifying a fifth part of a farm'; MSwed. *fæmtinger*; Mod. Swed. *femting* 'fifth part of a farm; set of five people'.

'Six'. Mod. Icel. *sjöttungur*; Færoese *sættingur*; Mod. Norw. *settung* 'specifying a sixth of a quarter of a mile'; OSwed. *sǣttungẹr* 'specifying a tax-unit', *sǣtungẹr, siǣttungẹr, siǣtungẹr, settiung* (analogy with *þriþiunger*), *sǣttinger*; OGut. *sēttungr* (Noreen 1904: § 105); early Mod. Danish *sjetting* (and *sæting*) 'specifying a administrative division'.

'Seven'. Færoese *sjeyndingur* – no doubt a recent formation.

'Eight'. Mod. Icel. *áttungur*; Færoese *áttingur*; Mod. Norw. *åttung* 'specifying an eighth of a parish'; OSwed. *āttungęr* 'specifying an eighth of a barrel, land-division, tax-unit'; *ātungęr, āttingęr, āttangęr* (c̄′, *ātta*); ODanish **ātting* > *atyng* (Brøndum Nielsen 1950–1957: § 133).[502]

'Twelve'. Mod. Icel. *tólfungur*; OSwed. *tolftunger* 'specifying a tax-unit';[503] ODanish *tolfting*; early Mod. Danish *tolvting, tolting* 'specifying a twelfth of a farm'.

'Thirty'. OSwed. *thrǣtiunger* (type F) 'period of thirty days'.

15.4.7. *-welle-*

'Hundred'. *húnduelle* 'centesimum' Lindisfarne Gospels, Matthew 13, 8. For a suggestion as to the origin of this curious suffix, see Jordan (1906: 104–105).

15.4.8. *-x(ʒ)a/ō*

'One'. PIE **oynó-ko/ā-* PGmc. ***aenaxa/ō-* > Gothic *ainahs* (weak). There are two oxytone forms, PGmc. *aenaʒa/ō* and PGmc. *ainiʒa/ō* (cf. Kluge 1926: § 202 ff.); the variation may in part be due to **aena/ō-* beside **aini-* (15.1.1.2.). Originally the basic sense 'only' seems to have been attached to the *aʒ*-form, 'some, any' to the *-iʒ*-form. But there has been some confusion and in some of the later West Germanic languages the two suffixes are not kept distinct. A third sense, 'at one', appears in the later languages.

In the following sets the suffixes are clear:
PGmc. **aenaʒa/ō-* > OIcel. *einga* (indecl.) 'only'; Mod. Norw. *einga* 'single (of thread)'; OSwed. *ænge, ænga* (Noreen 1904: § 80. II. 2) 'only'; OHG *einag*; OSax. *ênag*; OFrisian *êng, âng* 'any'; OEngl. *anga* (weak) 'only'.

The form has been borrowed into Baltic Finnic and thence secondarily into Lappish: Fi. *ainoa, ainova, ainoo, aino, ainua, ainuva, ainut* (gen. sing. *ainuvan*), *ainuo, ainuu, ainu* 'alone'; Karelian *ainuo, ainova*; Annus *ainavo*; Vot *ainago, ainago, ainô*; Estonian *ainuv, ainua, ainukens*; Livonian *âinagi*; Lappish *a'inεs* (Vefsn), *aiena, aienu* (Lule), *aîdnâ, aîdno* (Norwegian), *aiho* (Inari) (see a. o. Toivonen 1955: *ainoa*).

PGmc. ***ainʒa/ō-* > OIcel. *einigr* 'some'; OSwed. *ēnig* 'only'; ODanish *ēnighær* 'only'; OHG *einîg* 'some, any'; OSax. *ênig*; OFrisian *ênich* 'any';

Mod. Frisian *ien(n)ich* 'unique, alone' West, *ianig* Föhr and Amrum – but many of the forms are borrowed from German (e. g. *eenige* Saterland, or made up on a German model); OEngl. *ēnig, ānig* (c̄′) – the two types survive in later English: MEngl. *ę̄ni, ǭni*; with shortening in trisyllabic inflected forms (Luick 1921–1940: § 353), *ĕni* (> Mod. Engl. *any*) and *ăni* (> *āni*, lengthening in open syllables, Dobson 1957: II § 70).[504]

With some confusion of the two suffixes: MHG *einig* 'only, alone, some'; Mod. HG *einig* 'at one' (Mod. Swed. *enig*; Mod. Danish *enig*), early Mod. HG also 'only'; pl. *einige*; MLG *einich* 'unique, alone, any'; MDutch *ênich* 'alone, lonely, constituting a unit'; Mod. Dutch *eenig* 'only', pl. *eenige* 'some, any'.

'Two'. PIE **dwei-ko-* > PGmc. **twīxa-* > PEngl. **twīux*. This develops in three ways – with smoothing to **twīx* (Campbell 1959: § 229), with change due to low stress to **twux* (Campbell 1959: § 338 n. 1), or with straightforward non-Anglian development to **twīox* > OEngl. *-twēoh*. Hence OEngl. *betwīh, betwēoh, betwuh* (> *betuh*, Campbell 1959: § 470) 'between'.

PIE **dwi-ko-* > PGmc. (*n* +) **twixan-*, and with a-umlaut, **twexan-*. Hence OHG *zwëho* 'doubt'; OSax. *tweho*; OEngl. *twēo* (< **twīun* < **twiuxan-*. Campbell 1959: § 235, < **twixan-*).

Further the derivative verb PGmc. **twixōþ * twexōþ*, with similar developments: OHG *zwëhon* 'to doubt'; OSax. *twehon*; OEngl. *tweogan* (see Ross 1961a: 291–293).

Extension: PIE **twik-nā-* (cf. Kluge 1926: § 151) > PGmc. **twixnō* > PGmc. **twīxnu* > **twīuxnu* > **twīunu* > **twīon* > OEngl. *twēon* 'doubt'.

The derivative verb PGmc. **twixnōþ* > OEngl. *twēonian* 'to doubt' (with similar development); MEngl. *tweonien* 'to doubt', 'be in doubt'.

15.4.9. *-k-*

PIE **oyno-go/ā* > PGmc. **aenaka/ō-* > Icel. *einka* (indeclined) 'only'; Færoese *onka* (indeclined); Mod. Norw. *einka*; OSwed. *enka, ænka* (cf. Noreen 1904: § 80. II. 2), indeclined; Mod. Swed. *enka* 'a few'; ODanish *ænkæ* 'only'; Mod. Danish *enke*.

The dative plural is used as an adverb: Icel. *einkum* 'especially'; Mod. Norw. *einkom* 'alone'; South-East Mod. Swed. *enkom* 'especially'; Mod. Danish *enkom* – hence, somewhat obscurely, Mod. Danish *enkomst*.[505]

Derivative verb PGmc. **aenakōþ* > OIcel. *einka* 'to select'.

Extensions: PGmc. **aenakjōn-* (Kluge 1926: § 38) > PN **æinkjo* > **ænkja* (cf. Noreen 1913: § 41b) > Icel. *ekkja* (Noreen 1923: § 266.3) 'widow' (= Færoese *einkja*; Mod. Norw. *ekkja*;[506] OSwed. *ænkia* [Mod. Norw. *enkja*]; Mod. Swed. *änka*; ODanish *ænkia*[507]; Mod. Danish *enke*) (Mod. Swed. dialectal *änker, änk* 'widower'; Mod. Danish dialectal *enk* is formed on this last; cf. also Mod. Swed. dialectal *änkeman*; Mod. Danish *enkemand*, earlier *enkjemann*).

PGmc. **aenakla/ō-* (Kluge 1926: § 63) > Gothic *ainakls* 'alone'.

PGmc. **aenakila/ō-* (cf. Kluge 1926: § 190) > Mod. Icel. *ekkill* 'widower'; OSwed. *ænkil*; MLG *enkel* 'single' (by analogy Mod. Swed. *enkel*; Mod. Danish *enkel*); MDutch *enkel*; Mod. Dutch *enkel*.

A dental is sometimes added in Low German (cf. Lasch 1914: § 308): MLG *enkelt*[508] and in colloquial and regional Modern Dutch.

PGmc. **aenakilinga-* (cf. Kluge 1926: § 55) > OSwed. *ænklinger* 'widower'; Mod. Swed. *änkling* (Mod. Norw. *enkling*, Innherad).

PGmc. **twikila-* or **twikilō/n-* (Kluge 1926: §§ 90–91) > EDD: *twitchell* 'a narrow footpath between hedges', 'a narrow passage', 'a blind alley', 'a short cut'.

The suffix of OEngl. *twicen* feminine 'fork in a road' (to which *twicene* is a parallel weak form), MEngl. *twychen* (in place-names, Smith 1956: ii, 199) is not clear; perhaps **twikunnjō-* or **twikinnjō*.[509]

Mod. Norw. *tvika* 'to be in doubt' – also reflexive 'hesitate' (in speech), 'grope for words', Hardanger – must derive from **twik-*; the original verb-class is uncertain; early Mod. Swed. *tvika* is the same verb; early Mod. Swed. *tväka*; Mod. Swed. *tveka* 'to hesitate', 'be doubtful', is a dialect form (Noreen 1904: § 130. 2). Mod. Swed. *tvekel* 'doubt' could be similarly from a **twikilō-*, but it may represent a mixture of the types represented by Mod. Swed. *tveka* and *tvivel* (15.5.1.).

'Four'. Dat. instr. masc. *-kan-* (Kluge 1926: § 61a): Mod. Icel. *fjarki* 'four' (at cards), from oblique ordinal **fiaðrða* (15.2.4.), with simplification of the consonant-group. This is only superficially reminiscent of the Helgoland-Frisian card-names: *seebenk* [*se:mk*] 'seven', earlier *sööfk, achtk* [*axk*] 'eight', *neägenk* 'nine', *taink* 'ten' (Krogmann 1957–1967: 378). Cf. also *poork of inpoork* 'Paar oder Unpaar; 'even and uneven'. These are reshaped after **esk*, **esken* 'ace', of now vanished ordinals in *-t* (*sööft* etc.). These ordinals are borrowed from Low German;[510] cf. *söft* 'seven' (at cards), *teint* 'ten' (at cards) (Mensing 1927–1935: iv, 699; v. 37). Similar forms are found in Modern West Frisian for the number of eggs in a nest – *twake* 'two', *trijke* 'three'.

15.4.10. *-ʒa-*

PIE **dweyg^h^o-* > PGmc. **twīʒa-* > OHG *zwîg* neuter; MHG *zwîc* masculine; Mod. HG *zweig* masculine; MLG *twîch*[511] neuter 'branch'; LG *twich* masculine Stavenhagen; MDutch *twîch* masculine; Mod. Dutch *twijg* (common gender) 'twig'; Mod. Frisian (common gender) *twiich* West, *twiech* Saterland, *twîg* Wangeroog, *twich* East Moringen or OFöhr, *twiich* Föhr, *twiig* Amrum, Helgoland.
PIE **dwi-gho-* > PGmc. **twiʒa-*, (*n* +) **twiʒan-*: early Mod. Danish *tvige* 'branch'; Mod. Danish[512] *tvege* 'forked branch'; OEngl. *twig* neuter 'twig', *twige.*

c̄′: *zuog* (< **zôg*) masculine-neuter 'branch' (see Schatz 1927: § 371), cf. nom.-acc. fem. *zuo*; and OSax. *tôg*. In order to explain this latter form, we must suppose that nom.-acc. neuter **two* existed in the parent language and that this became POSax. **tū*, cf. OSax. *hû* < **xwō* (= OEngl. *hū* 'how') (Gallée 1910: § 189); hence, then, **twōg* 'branch', on the analogy of **twō*, and when *w* was lost in **tū* it was also lost — analogically — in *tôg*; this latter gives MLG *tôch*; LG *toch* Ostbevern; (*n* +) OHG *zuogo* 'branch'.

There is a further form which should be mentioned here: OEngl. *twigge* fem. (> MEngl. *twigge, twig* > Mod. Engl. *twig*) < PGmc. **twiʒjōn-* (cf. Kluge 1926: §§ 81–82), or (*n* +) PIE **dwighnā-* (cf. Kluge 1926: § 87); by an analogy similar to that mentioned above, OHG *zuocko* 'branch' (see Schatz 1927: § 237), with masculinization on *zuogo.*

15.4.11. *-t-*

'One'. PGmc. **aenatja/ō- *ainitja/ō-* > OHG dat. pl. *einazêm, einigên* Otfrid, *einzên* Notker (ed. Piper 1895) 'singulatim' (Kluge 1926: § 214). Extension: MHG *einzec*, Mod. HG *einzig.*[513]

'Two'. Mod. Norw. *tvita* 'to be in doubt', Hardanger 'wander about' singular nominative masculine (original verb-class not certain).

A number of other forms may, rather doubtfully, be assigned here; for several of them, the suffix is not clear.
PGmc. **twitina-* (Kluge 1926: § 57): EDD: *Twitten* Sussex 'narrow path between two walls or hedges' (also *twitting*); LG *twite* 'alley', Assinghausen.
Mod. Engl. *twit* 'fault or entanglement in a thread' (with adjective *twitty*).

PGmc. **twitrōþ* > Mod. Engl. *twitter* 'to spin or twist unevenly', and (as noun) 'the part of a thread that is unequally spun', 'shred', 'fragment', 'entanglement', 'complication'; further *twittery* 'slender', 'spun very small'.[514]

15.4.12. 'Two'. PIE **dwis-thō/a-:*

PGmc. **twista-* masculine: Mod. Danish dialectal *øre(n)tvist* 'earwig'; MHG *zwist*; Mod. HG *zwist* 'dissension' (in Bavarian also 'branch', in Oberlausitzisch also 'double thread'); MLG *twist* 'dissension' (Mod. Norw. *tvist*, Mod. Swed. *tvist*, Mod. Danish *tvist*); MDutch *twist* 'dissension' (also *'twine'*); Mod. Dutch *twist* 'dissension';[515] OFrisian *twist*; OEngl. *mæst-twist* 'parastates' (Wright – Wülcker 1884: i, col. 182); *candel-twist* 'emunctoria' (Wright – Wülcker 1884: i, col. 165/29, and col. 19/18); Mod. Engl. *twist.*[516] (MEngl. *twist* also used with 'line and rope to designate some part of the tackle of a vessel'; OED: *Twist*? sb^2.[517] With *kw-*:[518] Icel. *kvistr* 'branch'; Færoese *kvistur*; Mod. Norw. *kvist*; Mod. Swed. *kvist* 'twig'; Mod. Danish *kvist*; further Mod. Swed. *på morgenkvisten* 'in the early morning' (i. e. 'morning-twilight'); Mod. Danish *på morgenkvisten*;[519] Mod. Frisian *kwes* Helgoland 'hole in the wood of a three where there has been a branch' (also, transferred, 'obstinate person'); *dan quist kôl* (= *dan krop kôl*) 'head of cabbage' Wangeroog (so Ehrentraut 1849: 386) or perhaps better 'cabbage-plant'.

Both the Frisian meanings could be developed from 'branch'. Jensen (1927) has *kwest* 'Astmal', 'Knorren im Holz'. There is certainly the possibility that the Frisian word is a Scandinavian borrowing.

n +: PGmc. **twistan-: Tuisto* (Tac Germania 2.2; see Schönfeld, 1911: s. v., where further literature).

PGmc. **twistō-*: Mod. Norw. *tvist* 'fault in the web' (weaving) Hallingdal; with extension, *tvisma* (< **tvistma*)[520] 'tangle in thread' – hence the verb *tvismast* 'to dispute'.

Derivative verb PGmc. **twistōþ*: Mod. Norw. *tvista* 'to separate' (fat from the intestines), 'fritter'; MLG *twisten* 'to contend' (by analogy Mod. Swed. *tvista*, Mod. Danish *tvistes*); MDutch *twisten*; Mod. Dutch *twisten*; MEngl. *twisten*; Mod. Engl. *twist.*

Extension: OIcel. *tvistra* 'to separate'; Mod. Icel. *tvístra.*

15.4.13. -đ-

PIE **dwoy-d^{h}yo/ā-* > PGmc. **twaiđja/ō-* > OSax. *twêdi* 'one-half'; MLG *twêde* 'two-thirds'; OFrisian *twêde* 'two-thirds', and also 'one-half'; OEngl. *twǣde* 'two-thirds' (noun).[521a]

15.4.14. *-f-*

PGmc. **twīfan* (cf. Kluge 1926: § 105) > OHG *zwîfo* 'doubt'.
PGmc. **twaifjiþ* > OEngl. *ge-twǣfan* 'to separate'.

15.4.15. -m-

PGmc. **twaimjiþ* > OEngl. *ge-twǣman*; MEngl. *tweme*.

15.4.16. -nan-

PGmc. **xundnan-* (Brugmann — Delbrück 1897—1916: II. i. 303) > OHG *hunno* 'centurion'; MHG *hunde* (c̄′: *hunt*).[521b]

15.4.17. *-na-la-*

PGmc. **twinala-* masculine and **twenala-* (*a*-umlaut) > OHG *zwinal, zwenel* 'twin' (verb: Mod. HG — Swiss — *zwinle, zwindle* 'to bear twins'); EDD: *twinnel, twindle* (cf. Jordan 1925: § 202) Lancashire 'a twin' (and as verb 'to bring forth twins'). Further: **twinilinga-* masc. (Kluge 1926: § 25) > OHG *zwiniling*, MHG *zwilling* (Paul — Mitzka 1966: § 71 n. 4), Mod. HG *zwilling*; c̄′: Mod. HG (Swiss) *zweiling*; MLG *twêling*; MDutch *twêling*; Mod. Dutch *tweeling*. **twinilina* — (Kluge 1926: § 59) neuter > MHG *zwinilîn* 'twin'. OHG **zwileni* (> *zwileni* Macugnaga); verb: Swiss *tswillinun* 'to bear twins' (Henzen 1940: 283).[522]

15.4.18. *-nassu-*[523]

OHG *drînissa* 'Trinity', OEngl. *þrīness* (and see 15.3.2.3.), formed from the respective nominative-accusative masculine of the cardinal.

15.4.19. *-ra-*

'Five'. PIE **penkʷ-ró-* > PGmc. **fingra-* masc. 'finger' > Gothic *figgrs*; Icel. *fingr*; Færoese *fingur*; Mod. Norw. *finger*; OSwed. *finger* (also neuter); Mod. Swed. *finger*; ODanish *fingær*; Mod. Danish *finger*; OHG *fingar*; MHG *finger*; Mod. HG *finger*; OSax. *fingar*; MLG *vinger*; MDutch *vinger*; Mod. Dutch *vinger*; OFrisian *finger*; Mod. Frisian *finger* West Saterland, Wangeroog, Sylt, Helgoland, *fainj(g)er* East Moringen,[524] *fanger* Föhr and Amrum; OEngl. *finger*; Mod. Engl. *finger*.

15.4.20. *-la- -lo-*[525a]

PGmc. **twisla-* masc. > Mod. Norw. *tvisl* 'unstable person', *morgen-kvisl*[525b] 'early morning' (cf. 15.4.12.); *n* +: OEngl. *twisla* 'confluence'; cf. also "Scinodens, twiseltode" (Wright – Wülcker 1884: i, col. 108/15); early Mod. Engl. *twisel, twissel* 'fork', 'double twig'; Mod. Engl. dialectal *twizzle* 'the part of a tree where the branches divide from the stock'; EDD: *tweezel-nut* western Yorkshire (also *tweezeled-*) 'a double nut'. The word survives in place-names (Smith 1956: ii. 200).
PGmc. **twizla-* > MLG *twil* 'branch split into a fork'; Mod. Dutch *twil*.
PGmc. **twislō-*:[526a] Icel. *kvísl* 'fork', 'branch'; Færoese *kvísl* 'manure-fork'; Mod. Norw. *kvisl* (*kviksl, kveksl* Larvik, Østfold) 'fork'; Mod. Swed. dialectal *kvisl* 'confluence', 'manure-fork'.
PGmc. **twizlō-*[526b] > Mod. Swed. dialectal *kvill* 'branch'.[527]
PGmc. **twizlōn-* > LG *twile* 'fork' Assinghausen, *twiele* 'branch' Ostbevern, *twel* Heide (Dithmarschen), *twelt* Stavenhagen; Mod. Frisian *twille* 'fork-like', 'bit of a branch' Saterland, *twilt* 'forking' Sylt, *twill* 'fork of a branch' Wursten. PGmc. **twisilan-* (Kluge 1926: § 90) > OHG *zwisila* 'fork'; MHG *zwisel*; Mod. HG *zwiesel*; Swiss *zwisel* 'something double' (cf. *zwiselen* fem. 'double fruit'), also 'branch'; *Zwieselberg*[528] (name of a hill); PN *Twisselbach.*[529]
Derivative verbs: PGmc. **twislōþ* > Icel. *kvísla* 'to put forth branches'; Mod. Norw. *tvisla* 'to vacillate' Sunnmøre, Nordfjord; *tvislast* 'to vanish'; *kvisla, kvislast*; MHG *zwiselen* 'to fork'; Mod. HG (Swiss) *zwislet* 'double', OEngl. *twislian* 'to fork', 'split'; MEngl. *twiselen* (perhaps also Mod. Engl. *twizzle,* different sense).
PGmc. **twizlōþ*: Mod. Norw. *tville* 'stir together',[530] 'envelop'; *tvillast burt* 'to vanish away' Telemark; Mod. Engl. *twirl* (verb-class not certain).
PGmc. **þrisli-* > OEngl. *þrisel-lic* (*þreosellices hiwes* 'tripartite colore').

15.4.21. *sti-*

PIE **pn̥kʷ-s-ti-* > PGmc. **funxwsti-* 'fist' > **fuxsti-* > **fusti-* (cf. Streitberg 1896: § 129. 1): OHG *fûst*; MHG *fûst*; Mod. HG *faust*; MLG *vûst*; MDutch *vûst*; Mod. Dutch *vuist*; OFrisian *fêst*; Mod. Frisian *fest(e)* Saterland, *fest* Wangeroog, *feest* East Moringen, *fist* Föhr and Amrum, *fest* Sylt (West *fûst*; *fyst* Schiermonnikoog, Terschelling) and probably Helgoland *füs(t)* from Low German and/or Dutch; OEngl. *fyst*; MEngl. *fist* (Luick 1921–1940: § 352b); Mod. Engl. *fist*.

15.5. Some compounds

15.5.1. PIE **dwey-plo-* > PGmc. **twīfla-* 'doubt': Gothic *tweifl(s)*;[531] OHG *zwîfal* masculine and neuter; MHG *zwîfel* masculine; Mod. HG *zweifel* masculine; MLG *twîfel*[532] masculine and neuter; MDutch *twîvel, twîfel* (see Franck 1910: § 100) masculine and neuter; Mod. Dutch *twijfel* (common gender); OFrisian *twîfel* masculine; Mod. Frisian *twivel* (common gender) West, *twiuel* (common gender) Saterland, *twiwel* masculine East Moringen, *twiiwel* (? gender) Föhr and Amrum, Sylt, *twiibel* (common gender) Helgoland.
Derived verbs: PGmc. **twifljiþ*; Gothic *tweifljan*; OHG *zwîfalen*; OSax. *twîflian*; PGmc. **twifloþ* > OHG *zwîfalôn*; MHG *zwîveln*; Mod. HG *zweifeln*; OSax. *twîflon*.
From one or both of these protoforms: MLG *twîvelen*; MDutch *twîfelen twîvelen*; Mod. Dutch *twijfelen*; Mod. Frisian *twivelje* West, *twiuelje* Saterland, *twîvel* Wangeroog, *twiwele* East Moringen, *twiiweli* Föhr and Amrum, Sylt, *twiibele* Helgoland.[533]

15.5.2. *-lika/o*[534]

PGmc. **ainlīka/ō-* > OEngl. *ǣnlic* (MEngl. *enle*, Pearl: v. 849); c′: OEngl. *ānlic*; MEngl. *ānli, ǭnli*; Mod. Engl. *only*. From this protoform and/or **aenalīka/ō-* (15.1.1.): OSwed. *ēnlīker* 'alone'; Mod. Swed. *enlig* 'in agreement with' (and nominative-accusative singular neuter *enligt* 'according to'); Mod. Danish *enlig* 'single', 'solitary'.

15.5.3. *-sama/o*[535]

Mod. HG *einsam* is a late formation; it is adapted in Scandinavian as a modification of what was Icel. *einn saman* 'alone': Mod. Swed. *ensam* 'lonely'; Mod. Danish *ensom*. Cf., further dissimilated, OIcel. *einn samall*; Færoese *einsammallur*; Mod. Norw. *eismall*.[536]

15.6. Borrowings and adaptations from other Indo-European languages

15.6.1. Greek

In the modern Germanic languages, as in others, these borrowings are very numerous; they are in fact for the most part "international" words. In recent times there have been borrowings directly from Greek; there have also been very many creations on Greek models, especially in science and medicine, but also in other fields (cf. e. g. Mod. Engl. *dodecaphonic* 'twelve-tone' (*δώδεκα, θων ή*).

In earlier times the Greek words for the most part entered Germanic from Latin or French; there was also interborrowing between the Germanic languages, as, for instance, from German into Danish. Since these words are of little linguistic interest, just a few examples will suffice.
Nom. acc. neuter *ἕν* Mod. Engl. *henotic*; Mod. French *hénotique*; Greek *ἑπτά* Mod. HG *heptateuch*; Mod. Engl. *heptateuch*; Mod. French *heptateuque*; Greek *επτάτευχος*.
ἐννέα: Mod. Engl. *ennead*; Mod. French *ennéade*.
ἕνδεκα: Mod. Engl. *hendecasyllable*; Mod. French *hendécasyllable*.
Nom.-acc. neuter *εἰκοσάεδεος*: Mod. Swed. *ikosaeder*; Mod. HG *ikosaeder*; Mod. Engl. *icosahedron*; Mod. French *icosahèdre*.
ἑκατόμβη: Mod. Swed. *hekatomb*; Mod. HG *hekatombe*; Mod. Engl. *hecatomb*; Mod. French *hécatombe*; Latin *hecatombe*.

Various Greek numeral prefixes each give rise to many borrowings:
δι- Mod. Swed. *di-*; Mod. Danish *di-*; Mod. Engl. *di-*; Mod. French *di-*.
τρι- Mod. Swed. *trigon-*; Mod. HG *trigon-*; Mod. Danish *trigon-*; Mod. Engl. *trigon*; Mod. French *trigono-*.
τετρα- Mod. Swed. *tetra-*; Mod. HG *tetra-*; Mod. Engl. *tetra-*; Mod. French *tetra-*; Latin *tetra-*.
πεντα- Mod. Swed. *penta-*; Mod. HG *penta-*; Mod. Engl. *penta-*; Mod. French *penta-*; Latin *penta-*.
δεκα Mod. Icel. *deka-*; Mod. Swed. *deka-*; Mod. Danish *deka-*; Mod. HG *deka-*; Mod. Dutch *deca-*; Mod. Engl. *deca-*; Mod. French *déca-*; Latin *deca-*.
μύρια Mod. HG *myria-*; Mod. Dutch *myria-*; Mod. French *myria-*.
πρωτο- Mod. Swed. *proto-*; Mod. HG *proto-*; Mod. Dutch *proto-*; Mod. Engl. *proto-*; Mod. French *proto-*; Latin *proto-*.
δευτερο Mod. Engl. *deutero-*; Mod. French *deutéro-*.

15.6.2. Latin and Romance

Tremis. OEngl. *trimes trimesse -rimes* 'drachm', 'coin'.
Spanish *tres*. LG *dris* 'three' (at cards) and *drist* with added *t*; hence also *twist* 'two' (at cards).[537] These words have been borrowed into Scandinavian: Mod. Icel. *tvistur, þristur*; Færoese *tvistur*; Mod. Norw. *tvist, trest*; Mod. Swed. *tress, träss*; Mod. Danish *trest*.

Bilix, trillix. These are correctly adapted as OHG *zwilîh, drilîh*; MHG *zwilich, zwilch, drilich, drilch*; Mod. HG *zwilch, drillich*. The High German forms are borrowed into Dutch and Low German. Hence Mod. Dutch *zwilk* 'ticking' and **drilk*; this latter was apparently reformed to *dril* 'drill' (by analogy Mod. Engl. *drill*) under the influence *drillen* 'to bore'. In Low German the unsyncopated High German form must have appeared as **twilik, *drilik*; because of the system of *zerdehnte* forms, these will in part have become **twēlik*, **drēlik*. Hence MLG *drell, drelle* [538a] from this latter + **drillen* 'to bore';[538b] further MLG *dwelk* 'ticking' (early Mod. Swed. *dwälk* 'kind of linen') from **twēlik* + *drell(e)*. In English, Latin *trilix* correctly appears as OEngl. *þrilig* (spelt *þrielig*)[539] > *þrilī*;[540] *þrilīn* (> *þrylen*)[541] from this + *līn*, loan-word form, Latin *līnum*. Similarly *bilix* appears as OEngl. *twilic *twilig* > *twili*. In Middle English there are two developments; first, the normal one to *þrili*, **twili*; secondly, an abnormal one in which the *i* of the second syllable is treated as unstressed – hence MEngl. *þrile, twile*; this latter form will, in the North, give *twę̄l* (Luick 1921–1940: § 393). Hence, then, on the one hand Mod. Engl. *twilly* and on the other Mod. Scots *tweel*; further the derivatives *twilling, tweeling*. Mod. Engl. *tweed* is taken by OED (s. v.) as a trade-name due to a misreading to *tweel* (reinforced by the river-name *Tweed*) – the word is first recorded there in 1847. This explanation is not entirely satisfactory, for cf. Mod. Scots *tweddling*, a variant of *tweeling*, in which the *dd* is of obscure origin – OED: *tweddling* first records the word in 1541.[542] Finally, we make note that OED: *drilling* 'a coarse twilled linen or cotton fabric used for summer clothing', etc., regards this word as a corruption of Mod. HG *drillich*; more probably it is from *drill* + *twilling*.
'Five'. *Quintinus*. In MHG *quintîn, quentîn* 'one quarter of a drachm' (Mod. HG *quent* 'drachm') 'fifth' has been misunderstood as 'fourth'.

Notes

1. This chapter naturally owes very much to van Helten's celebrated article "Zum germanischen Zahlwort" (van Helten 1905–1906).
2. The late Professor Ross wished to express his gratitude to the following people for advice on various points: Dr. A. J. Aitken, Dictionary of the older Scottish tongue; Dr. J. B. Berns, Department of Dialectology of the P. J. Meertens-Instituut of the Royal Netherlands Academy of Arts and Sciences, Amsterdam; Professor J. A. Boyle (Manchester); the late Professor A. Campbell (Oxford); Sir Gerard Clauson; Professor Dowsett (Oxford); Professor D. M. Dunlop (Columbia); Mr. S. Ellis (Leeds); Professor S. Fries

(Umeå); Professor Tibor Halasi-Kun (Columbia); Dr. Ingeborg Hof (Oslo); Landsmål- och Folkminnesarkivet, Uppsala; Professor Angus McIntosh (Edinburgh); Professor J.-M. Michelena (Salamanca); Dr. David D. Murison, Scottish National Dictionary; Dr. Bent Jul Nielsen, Institut for Dansk dialekforskning; Dr. U. Scheuermann, Niedersächsisches Wörterbuch, Göttingen; Professor K. H. Schmidt (Bochum); Schweizerdeutsches Wörterbuch; Professor Denis Sinor (Indiana); Professor R. E. F. Smith (Birmingham); Dr. Jan Stroop, University of Amsterdam; Professor C.-E. Thors (Helsinki); Professor E. M. Uhlenbeck (Leiden); Professor Kjell Venås (Oslo) — and especially to Professor Nils Århammar (Flensburg), Professor W. B. Lockwood (Reading) and Professor E. G. Stanley (Oxford).

3. As in Cleasby — Vigfusson (1957).

4a. The author of the Ormulum (Holt — White 1878) has an extremely useful habit: he consistently writes the consonant double after a short vowel; the writing vowel + single consonant thus in general means that the vowel is long.

4b. For the first two sets of forms see, respectively, Holt and White (1878) and Wallenberg (1923); for the *Language AB*, see d'Ardenne (1936: ix). I have taken the numeral forms from the *Accidence* (§§ 99—101) and *Glossary* of this work.

5. But in later Germanic, adjectival endings are sometimes added.

6. Cf. the anomalous OHG dat. *drinzenin* 'thirteen', Notker (Piper 1895: i, 619, line 2), with both parts declined.

7. With one remarkable exception: ONorw. dat. *seawn* (= *sjám*), dated March 2, 1392.

8. Braune — Mitzka (1967: § 271b).

9. Franck (1910: 232.4).

10. In the reflexes of PIE *septm̥* 'seven' and *deḱm̥*, 'ten', final **-m* gives **-n*; then, in these forms, as also in PIE **newn̥* 'nine', final *-n* should regulary vanish (Streitberg 1896: § 129.7b); thus PGmc. **seƀu*, **newu*, **texu*, **texa*. But, in fact, it has been restored by analogy with the *i*-inflected forms **siƀuni-*, **niwuni-*, **tixuni-*, **texani-*; hence **seƀun*, **newun*, **texun*, **texan*. By a similar process, OEngl. *mægden* loses its final *-n* (> Mod. Engl. *maid*), but this is restored by analogy with the inflected forms (e. g., OEngl. gen. sing. *mægdnes* — Jordan 1925: § 170); hence Mod. Engl. *maiden*.

11. Paul — Mitzka (1966: § 6.1 and n. 1, where further literature).

12. We may note here a minor form of inflection: in Modern Islandic, cardinals are denominated as *fimma*, 'five', *sexa* 'six', *sjöa* 'seven'; these are substantivized feminine weak adjectives (hence by analogy and similarity *átta* = cardinal *átta* 'eight', *nía*, from *níu*, 'nine', *tía*, from *tíu* 'ten'). Cf. also Mod. Swed. *etta* 'ace', *tvåa* 'two', *trea* 'three', and, further, Mod. Norw. *tvåe* 'two-skilling-piece', North Gudbrandsdal — the corresponding masculine.

13. Crimean Gothic *ita* < Gothic acc. sing. neut. *ainata*? Von Grienberger (1896: 123—136).

14. Murray (1873: 105).
15. Ormulum (Holt – White 1878) *a*, Iuliene (d'Ardenne 1936) *a*, Ayenbite of Inwyt (Morris 1866) *a*.
16. Cf. Ross (1972: 94 ff.).
17. Wangeroog: *än* < Rüstingen: *enne*, with analogical *e* (instead of *anne*).
18. Cf. also *æn-iege* 'one-eyed'; shaped *on eage* to *an-eage*.
19. We leave out of account the nature and frequency of occurrence of the *æn-* and *an*-forms, which may well point to a similar conclusion. The *æn*-forms hardly survive in later English (except, of course, indirectly in 'one' – see 15.1.0.); see *OED*: *only* a. and *onlepy* – but cf. Lambeth Homilies *enlepi* (Morris 1867–1873: 75/29).
20. Except on Wangeroog, where there is gender-agreement between the two parts: *ainoget* 'one-eyed' but *änmastig* 'with one mast'.
21. Saterland *aenter* 'one-year-old horse' (Kramer 1965: ii, 76) = OEngl. *enetere* < **ain-wintri-* (Löfstedt 1968: 23 n. 8). Föhr and Amrum *enter* and, probably, West Frisian *inter* is a borrowing of Mod. Dutch *enter*.
22. See Franck (1910: § 225 n.) – where there is also some discussion of the difficult Mod. Dutch nom. sing. masc.; nom.-acc. sing. neuter *ene* (strong).
23. See Lasch (1914: § 101.2), MLG acc. sing. masc. *enne* is from *erre emme* + acc. sing. masc. *enen* (so Lasch 1914: § 396 n. 1).
24. Cf. *þe* immediately above.

    In Old East Norse, inflectional *R* is lost to a considerable, but variable, extent: nom. pl. OSwed. *fiska*, ODanish *fiskæ* = Icel. *fiskar*, 'fish'; see Noreen (1904: § 30.1); Brøndum Nielsen (1950–1957: § 399.2). A similar loss is evidenced in Norwegian; see Noreen (1923: § 301.2); Hægstad (1914–1915: 1; 67 n. 133; 2, 156 n. 360); Indrebø (1951: 239).
25. Cf. the discussion in Walde (1900; Chapter II).
26. But for another explanation of the Old East Norse forms, see Noreen (1904: § 509.11) and Brøndum Nielsen (1950–1957: § 574.B.II.5).
27. Cf. the fate of the parallel PIE **dwōw* 'two', below.
28. But the former has been taken as equivalent to **þøsi* (Noreen 1904: § 509.6) and the latter as due to a sound change (Brøndum Nielsen 1950–1957: § 17b).
29. So Kock (1891: 251); see also Jansson (1952: 180 ff.).
30. For these three endings cf. Ross (1954: 118).
31. Also used for the accusative. In Færoese nouns the accusative is not distinct from the nominative in the plural, nor is it in the definite article (*teir*), but it is in the masculine of adjectives; nom. *tungir*, acc. *tungar* to *tungur* 'heavy'. It is curious that the numeral form and the definite article should have been influenced by the substantive rather than the adjective. But, in the earlier language, acc. masc. *tvá* (= OIcel *tuá*), hence *tóa, tógva* (*tögva*) are also found (analogical cf. *tögvar*).
32. Instead of **tuair* like *þair*; see Pipping (1901: 95).

33. On MSwed. *tūgh* see Noreen (1904: § 73).
34. Norse development as described in 15.1.2.0.4.
35. North Northumbrian *tuu* is *twū*, by analogy with *tw*-forms – so van Helten (1906: 88) and see Ross (1937: 108, 160–161).
36. *Two* is actually recorded: The Rushworth Gospel 2 (Skeat 1871–1887: 12,52 bis); van Helten (1906: 88) takes this as genuine, but it is certainly due to Latin 'duo', which it glosses.
37. On Mod. Norw. *tuaug* see 15.1.7.5.
38. Cf. 15.1.2.0.4.
39. But OSwed. *twā*; ODanish *twā* (> *twō* > *tō*) are more probably analogical; see below.
40. Dialectal *zweu* from this + *dreu* 'three'. For 'two' in the dialects, see *Deutscher Sprachatlas*, Map 103.
41. *Ey*: Lasch (1914: § 99). *Twê* could represent the protoform directly, or it could be from *twey* + nom. acc. masc. *twêne* (so Lasch 1914: § 396 n. 4).
42. In "*.þ.þusundjos*" δισχίλιοι, Nehemiah 7, 19, the *.þ.* was formerly read as *twa*, and this supposed feminine form naturally gave rise to much discussion. See: Streitberg (1914: 226–227).
43. *Twaddje* (Skeireins 3, 21) has been taken as feminine (cf. Jellinek 1926: § 168 n.).
44. *Twiggia* from this + gen. *þriggia* 'three'.
45. *Zuano haupito* 'duorum capitum' (Kögel 1879: 177), [? read *zuaiio*] – PGmc. *ai* remains to a considerable extent in this text (Braune – Mitzka 1967: § 44 n. 3).
46. *Tweyer, twêner* from this + nom.-acc. masc. *twey*, nom.-acc. masc. *twêne*, respectively.
47. But *tweer* is formed directly on nom.-acc. *twee* (Franck 1910: § 232.2).
48. *Tueim, tuem* from this + respectively nom. masc. *tueir* (15.1.2.2.) and dat. *þrem* 'three' (= OSwed. *þræm*, 15.1.3.8.2.).
49. *Zwêm, zwên* by analogy with adjectival *-êm, -ên*, or from nom.-acc. masc. *zwene, zwim* by analogy with dative *drim* 'three'.
50. *Zweien* (> Mod. HG *zweien*) by analogy with the adjectives.
51. The forms are well discussed by Seebold (1968: 417–436: "ae. *twegen* und ahd. *zwēne* 'zwei'" (with references to earlier literature); we are however not able to agree with the explanation given.
52. Only dat. sing. fem. *geonre* Cura Pastoralis (Sweet 1871–1872: 443/25).
53. *twoegen* (Napier 1901).
54. Lindisfarne Gospels *tuoege* with loss of final *-n* – see Campbell (1959: § 472 [Rit.]), *twoego* 192/25 with adj. *-o*, Lindisfarne *twoge* from this + nominative accusative neuter **twō* (15.1.2.5.). Rit. *tuoegi* § 113/22 is used by van Helten (1906: 92) as evidence for the stage "*-ii-*" in his postulated development of the second element (see above) – but it merely has the frequent spelling *gi* for *ge* (see Ross 1972: 55).

55. But Kentish *twægen* could as well have the spelling *æ* for *oe* (Campbell 1959: § 289).
56. *Tweyer, twêner* from this + nom.-acc. neuter *twey*, nom.-acc. masc. *twêne*, respectively. Hammerich (1937: 356) takes this form to be a borrowing from Old Norse – he compares OIcel. *tueir* – a very improbable suggestion.
57a. Brøndum Nielsen (1950–1957: § 146.3) – but the form, like Swed. *twiggia* (15.1.2.6.), could be explained as due to analogy with 'three' (ODanish gen. *thriggia*).
57b. Note also *tuyggae* < *twiggia* (Brøndum Nielsen 1950–1957: § 133).
57c. The numeral forms afford examples of the following, perhaps rather rare, kind of analogy: OEngl. pret. sing. *bæd*, pl. *bædon* > early MEngl. *bad, beden*; the *ă* in the singular is then lengthened to *ā* because the vowel in the plural is long; hence MEngl. *băd* > Mod. Engl. *bāde*. So essentially Bülbring (1889: 61).
58. Zachrisson (1927: 198).
59. *Tween* occurs as an accusative – possibly also as a nominative – but this is merely the dative (Franck 1910: § 232.2).
60. *Zwo* has been artifically resurrected for use on the telephone, so as to be distinct from *drei*.
61. These spreads in German – High and Low – would of course be readily explained if we could assume that nominative masculine PGmc. **twae* existed there; this form would give MLG **twê* and OHG **zwê* (15.1.2.0.5. and 15.1.2.5.), which we could suppose to have become remodelled to **zwei* under the influence of the neuter, and these forms would account for the dominance. But the absence of the relevant forms in Old Saxon and early Old High German discredits such a view.
62. OEng. nominative-accusative feminine, nominative-accusative neuter *bā* > MEngl. *bā, bō,* (Ormulum, Holt – White 1878) *ba*, Iuliene (d'Ardenne 1936) *ba*.
63. Forms with weakened ending (cf. 15.1.2.9.1.): *bæggiæ, bæggæ, bæggi, beggi*; cf. also *bieggia, bieggie* (Brøndum Nielsen 1950–1957: § 187 n. 2).
64. The alteration does not imply that *boegra* is erroneous; cf. Ross (1968: 68 n. 1).
65. Lindisfarne *boege*, and *boego* Luke 1,6; cf. *twoege, twoego*, 15.1.2.8.
66. Noreen (1923: § 54.3a, 1904: § 80.I.4a); Brøndum Nielsen (1950–1957: § 104.2).
67. Noreen (1923: § 139, 1904: § 91.2); Brøndum Nielsen (1950–1957: § 120.1).
68. Note 24 should be kept in mind throughout this section.
69. Also as accusative masculine (cf. 15.1.2.2.).
70. Mod. Swed. *båda* < accusative masculine/nominative-accusative feminine *baþa*.
71. Cf. 15.1.2.5.
72. This is a better derivation of the first element than from a **bā*, parallel to OIcel. nominative-accusative neuter *tuá* (15.1.2.5.), for our genesis of this

latter implies a syncope, so that, no doubt, the form would be too late to be affected by *i*-umlaut.

73. < PGmc. **ƀae.*
74. On the appearance of this form as nominative plural masculine, see Siljestrand (1890: ii. 40).
75. For three forms in the modern languages, see below.
76. From a form with adj. *-ra*: *bæggers* < **bæggras* (Noreen 1904: § 339.2).
77. Cf. gen. *twiggi* (15.1.2.9.1.).
78. Falk — Torp (1900: XVn.).
79. So Shetlandic conjunction *bo* (Hægstad 1900: § 27.1).
80. > Mod. Swed. *både.*
81. MSwed. nominative-accusative neuter *badhan*, numeral, is from the parent of this form + nominative-accusative neuter OSwed. *båþen.*
82. There is some generalization of one form for all cases — of the nominative-accusative *bêde, beide* and also of dat. *bêden, beiden*; see Franck (1910: § 232.2). Singular forms are also found, e. g. gen. *beids* (rare).
83. There is also the curious derivate *biisinge* East Moringen, *biiring* (*biiðing*) Sylt. It seems to be due to analogy with certain pronominal, adjectival and adverbial forms; cf., from Wiedingharde, *jaring* 'your', *mening* 'many', *aliining* 'alone' — or, less probably, with the plural of nouns, cf. Föhr and Amrum *hüsing*, Sylt *hüüsing* to *hüs* 'house'.
84. Cf. *vnker bother*, Elfgar's Will (mid tenth century, preserved in fourteenth century copies) (Whitelock 1930).
85. Ormulum (Holt — White 1878) *baþe*, gen. *baþre*; AB (d'Ardenne 1936) *baðe*, dative *baðen*; Ayenbite of Inwyt (Morris 1866) *buoþe.*
86. Cf. Mossé (1950—1959: § 74). The forms in *-s* are merely *s*-genitives.
87. The corresponding Old Norwegian form, *báðen*, is not relevant, for, since it is borrowed from Old Swedish (15.1.2.11.2.), it is presumably too late to be a possible etymon.
88. Also used for the accusative masculine in West Germanic.
89. Færoese nominative-accusative masculine *tríggir* from nominative-accusative feminine *tríggjar*, because of the adjectival declension (nominative-accusative masculine *tungir*, nominative-accusative feminine *tungar* to *tungur* 'heavy').
90. Also as genitive and dative (15.0.2.).
91. See further Gradon (1962: 63—76).
92. Mod. Norw. *préa* (Hægstad 1900, 1: 37) is rare and obscure.
93. Færoese *tríggjar* < **tríiar* < **þríar* < **þriar* + nominative masculine **þrír*; see 15.1.10.0.
94. Tryå Halingdal, Valdres by analogy with neuter *try.*
95. Notker (Piper 1895) has *dri*, the masculine form, as in the adjective (cf. Braune — Mitzka 1967: § 248 n. 9).
96. And *drî*, because this was used beside *drîe* in the nominative-accusative masculine.

97. For **thria*; to be explained as was nominative-accusative masculine *threa* (15.11.3.3.).
98. Van Helten (1906: 93–94) takes OFr. *thrê* as due to analogy with the adjectival declension; from it descend Mod. Fr. East *träi*, Saterland *thrê* Wangeroog; North *tra, träi, trai* (all masculine) Coast.
99. See Århammar (1969: 61–62).
100. For Rit. *ðria* (102/27), see Ross (1960: 219).
101. ODanish *thræ, threa* have been otherwise explained. Brøndum Nielsen (1950–1957: § 160.1) postulates accusative masculine **þria*, nominative-accusative feminine **þriar*, both formed adjectivally.
102. Not explained: OIcel. *þrió*.
103. In Old East Norse, *iu* < *y* after *r* (Noreen 1904: § 122.2a; Brøndum Nielsen 1950–1957: § 179.3). The form survives in the Danish dialects, see Bennike – Kristensen (1898–1912: 165); Lech (1925: § 44). It is also borrowed into Færoese – unless Norwegian (*try*) is the source (nominative-accusative neuter *try*, early Færoese *tryggj* (Svabo *trujgj*, s. v. *Trujggjir*) from this + nominative masculine *tríggir*, nominative-accusative feminine *tríggjar*). Cf. further nominative Sjællandsk *troej* (Brøndum Nielsen 1927: 116).
104. All these forms can be derived from OSax. *thrio*; Cf. OSax. *liaf* > MLG *lêf, lif, lief* (Lasch 1914: §§ 111, 113); for *ŭ̂*, see Lasch (1914: § 187.III). Since the last three numeral forms mentioned are masculine (15.1.3.) as well as neuter, they come to be used for the feminine also.
105. But Lindisfarne *ðreo* is of a slightly different genesis, being due to a special sound change (Ross 1960: VIII, 219). In later English, the feminine and neuter form, OEngl. *þrēo*, becomes dominant: MEngl. *thrẹ̄* (Orm. *þreo þre*, AB [d'Ardenne 1936] *þreo*) > Mod. Engl. *three*.
106. Masculine, with *-e* as in genitive *twaddje* 'two' (15.1.2.6.).
107. Weak: Lindisfarne *ðreana* L 10,36: Hence North Northumbrian *ðrea* from this + the correct **ðria*. Then, because **ðria* could be used in both nominative-accusative and genitive, *ðrea* came to be used for the former also (Ross 1960: 219).
108. Færoese *trimum* from **trim* and adj. *-um*.
109. If this form exists (Lasch 1914: § 396 n. 6). MLG *drên* from this + nominative-accusative neuter *drê* (no doubt influenced by dative *twên* 'two'). MDutch *drien* – reformed on the rest of the paradigm.
110. *drîen* (> Mod. HG *dreien*) because of nominative-accusative masculine *drîe* beside *drî*.
111. For another explanation see Noreen (1904: § 103).
112. In Old Swedish there is a further development: since *þrī* occurs beside *þrē* in the nominative masculine, it came to be used beside *þrē* in the nominative-accusative neuter too; and, since *þrȳ* occurs beside *þrī, þrē* in this latter case, this came also to be used beside *þrī, þrē* in the nominative masculine (*þrī, þrȳ* are apparently not recorded in the nominative-accusative feminine, where they would have been equally explicable).

113. Middle Swedish genitive *þrȳ*, ODanish dative *thrȳ* – that is, nominative-accusative neuter, are further consequences of the variant.
114. For a view of 'four' different from that set out here, see Jansson (1936: 272–287).
115. Noreen (1913: § 61c; 1904: § 228); Brøndum Nielsen (1950–1957: § 248.2b).
116. Noreen (1904: § 244.3, 1913: § 85.9a); Brøndum Nielsen (1950–1957: § 270.2).
117. Noreen (1904: § 228, 1913; § 61c, 1923: § 123); Brøndum Nielsen (1950–1957: § 111.5, § 248.2b).
118. And cf. Shetlandic *feur-fetign* (15.3.2.3.).
119. This form survives in Mod. Swed. dialectal (Älvsdal) *fjūärer, fjūärär, fȳörer*.
120. OGut. *fiaurum* is a relic, since *fiaur-* = West Germanic **feur* (15.1.4.2.3.2.); see Noreen (1913: § 218.5), and cf. Noreen (1904: §§ 82, 122.1).
121. The diphthong is short in *fiŭrutighi*, from which nominative-accusative masculine **fiŭru* > *fyŭru* (Noreen 1904: § 270 n. 3) because of nominative-accusative masculine *fĭri* beside *fĭritighi*. But, here, *iŭ* may again have been lengthened by analogy with nominative masculine *fiūri*.
122. Brøndum Nielsen (1950–1957: § 140 n. 1) provides a detailed account of 'four' in the Old Danish dialects.
123. The form must have existed in Old Swedish too, for it is borrowed as Mod. Norw. *fyghura*.
124. Adapted as Færoese *fýra*; *í* and *ý* fell together in the sixteenth century, so that the *y* may well be only orthographic (see Hamre 1944: 24–25). On the other hand it could be due to the influence, orthographic or real, of nominative-accusative neuter *trý*. For final *-a* corresponding to Mod. Danish *-e*, cf. Færoese *kanska* 'perhaps', a loanword from Mod. Danish *kanske*. We may conclude this section by referring to Runic Swedish (Rök) accusative masculine *fiakura*, dat. *fiakurum*, which have caused difficulties. The development of the first form (cf. 15.1.4.1.1.) seems to be PN **feδuranR* > **fiuδuranR* (δ3) > **fiuδra* (γ); from this + the ordinal (15.2.4.), **fioδra* > **fiaδra* with delabialization before a following *a*; then *fiaʒura* from this + nominative-accusative neuter *fiughur*; dat. *fiaʒurum* formed on *fiaʒura*. So essentially Noreen (1904: § 118 n. 1).
125. See the discussion in 15.1.7.3. However, there is no direct evidence for this form.
126. It might be suggested that accusative masculine-femine **fewurunz* would also give this **fewuru* **fiwuru*. Streitberg (1896: 247) suggests that OHG acc. pl. *situ* has the ending *-unz*, and cf. Walde (1900: 29). But this view has not been accepted (Braune – Mitzka 1967: § 230 n. 3), and the phonology is against the suggestion.
127. *veir* in the Münster MS of the Freckenhorster Heberegister (Wadstein 1899: 24/10 and n. 4) is an error for **vier* (so van Helten 1906: 95 n. I), and was allowed to stand after some scribal alteration (Gallée 1894: 172, col. 2/14).

128. Cf. Krogmann (1952: 108, 1954: 222).
129. The orthography renders very diverse the forms actually recorded (Ross 1972: 58).
130. Rit. *fō̆ver* is quoted by Bülbring (1889: § 331); it derives from Lindelöf (1901: 105–220): *feover*; this work is based on the inaccurate edition (Stevenson 1839): Rituale Ecclesiae Dunelmensis (SSP X). Rituale Ecclesiae Dunelmensis (Lindelöf 1927: 197/15) gives the reading *f..ver* – that is, the form is partially illegible. Mrs. Squires (Durham), who has made a new collection of the Ritual (Notes and Queries ccxvi, 362–366) confirms this (letter to Ross of December 8th, 1970).
131. In some south-eastern dialects there are nasalized forms under High German influence (Weijnen 1966: 296).
132. Mod. Engl. [*faif*] is an artifically altered form made up for use on the telephone to avoid confusion with *nine*.
133. Mod. Norw. *femm* from OWN **fimm* + a borrowing of OSwed. *fem* – which last Mod. Norw. *fem* certainly is.
134. Runic Swed. (Rök) *fim* could be interpreted as *fem, fem, fimm*, or *fim*.
135. *Sex* because of Latin *sex* (Noreen 1904: § 24 n.).
136. *Seiss* (modern dialects *sæjs*): see Brøndum Nielsen (1950–1957: § 312.2).
137. MHG *sehs* from OHG nom. masc. *sechs* < MHG *sëhs* and/or *sehs*.
138. Lasch (1914: § 41). MLG *sös* (> LG *sös*, van Helten 1906: 98) from *söven* 'seven' – see Lasch (1914: § 175).
139. All the modern forms are developed from this (for West *seis* see Spenter 1968: 185) except Helgoland *sös* loan-word form, Low German.
140. Late WSaxon *seox* arises from the inflected forms with a back vowel in the second syllable, genitive **seoxa*, dative **seoxum*, in which palatal umlaut would not take place (Campbell 1959: § 305).
141. If the *ie* of early WSaxon *siex* is regarded as "genuine" (cf. 15.11.3.3.), the form could of course be derived from **sixsi-*. But this **siex* must give **six* in late West Saxon (Campbell 1959: § 301), which is indistinguishable from late WSaxon *six* above. There is thus no evidence for **sixsi-*.
142. Cf. Noreen (1904: § 78.3). The broken form survives in the Modern Swedish dialects: Vendell (1904–1907): [*sæx*] has *sı̯ı̯̄äks* and *sı̯ı̯̄öks*; Gustavson (1918–1945): *sex* has *siäx*.
143a. On the distribution of the various forms in the Old Danish dialects, see Brøndum Nielsen (1950–1957, § 545.2).
143b. See note 10.
144. Noreen (1923: § 223.3, 1904: § 243); Brøndum Nielsen (1950–1957: § 248.2a).
145. Noreen (1923: § 235.2, 1904: § 243); Brøndum Nielsen (1950–1957: §§ 264.1, 269).
146. *syū* (Noreen 1904: § 270 n. 3).
147. *Siban* from this + *zëhan* 'ten'.

148a. Assimilation to the labial according to Mausser (1932: 867).

148b. Kyes (1983: 85) gives s. v. *sivon-faldun* 'sevenfold', *sinuolualdun* 'septuplum' from Gl. 614 (11.7) and *siuuoluatdun* 'septuplum' from Ep. 597. (For the abbreviations see Kyes 1983, VI ff.)

149. The protoform may be evidenced as early as OSax. *sebun* Hêliand, Cottonianus v. 3245 (cf. Gallée 1910: § 65 n. 1), if this is not an error. For MLG *suwen*, cf. Lasch (1914: § 185).

150. Cf. Danneil (1859): *säöw'n* and Schütze (1800–1806) s. v. These Low German forms could as well derive from **sibun*.

151. Also *sueven*; cf. his remarks (van Helten 1895: 114).

152. Dat. *seven* < *sevene*.

153. Cf. Hofmann (1961: 327).

154. For a detailed discussion of the North Northumbrian forms, see Ross (1972: 58).

155. *Sefo* Matthew 18,21 has the spelling *e* for *eo*.

156. Quoted in the OED: *Seven*, without reference.

157. Late WSax. *syfon, sufon* do not survive.

158. AB (d'Ardenne 1936) *seove*, Ayenbite of Inwyt (Morris 1866) *zeue, zeuen*. Ormulum (Holt – White 1878) *seofenn, sefenn* – single *f* denotes preceding long vowel, infl. *seoffne, seffne* – double *ff* denotes preceding short vowel (from the ordinal, 15.2.7.).

159. This suggestion is essentially to be found in Noreen (1913: § 224) – "*siau*, das von *tuau* und *þau* beeinflusst worden ist". As stated, the analogy seems improbable because of the distance between 'seven' and 'two'. It can be improved by making the analogy: **siqu* (> OIcel. *siau*): **sīo* (> OIcel. *sió*) :: **twōu* (> OIcel. *tuau*): **twō* (> OIcel. *tú*); cf. 15.1.2.5.

160. Cf. Hægstad (1906–1942: II.1.76; II.2.i.170 nn. 365, 190).

161. It is of course possible to assume that the sound change started in one form (definite article?), and that the forms are due to analogy with this. For an enumeration of the Old Danish forms, a full discussion of them, and also for several modern dialect form, see Brøndum Nielsen (1950–1957: §§ 179 n. 5, 545.3).

162. > *āta* (see Noreen 1904: § 304 n. 3). But, in the Old Danish occurrences of *atæ*, the single *t* for the most part merely indicates that the preceding vowel is long.

163. *Oage deege* Saterland; *age digge* Wangeroog; *aage deege* North Coast; *aagi daar* Föhr and Amrum, Sylt 'eight days a week' < **age* < **agde* < **achte*.

164. [*æit*] [*ait*] Durham (SED i, 752), [*ait*] Shropshire (SED ii, 736), [*æit*] [*ɔit*] Herfordshire (SED ii, 736).

165. Umlaut from the next syllable but one (Paul – Mitzka 1966: § 40 n. 2.2). On *ehte, ähte* see 15.1.0.1., above.

166. See note 10.

167. This suggestion is essentially due to Pipping (1922: 159).

168. > **nīјo* – hence *niio nighio* (Noreen 1904: § 328.1b) and *nyio* (cf. Noreen 1904: § 108 n. 5).
170. For the Danish dialect forms see Brøndum Nielsen (1950–1957: § 545.5).
171. Inflected, see von Grienberger (1897: 131), and cf. *sevene*, 15.1.7.3.
172. Dative *neghen* < *neghenen*.
173. In some south-eastern dialects there are *g*-less forms under High German influence (Weijnen 1966: 296).
174. OKentish **niogon* (*niogen* Anglia xi, 4/no. 3/4, from this + *nigen*) > **neogon* (cf. *neogontyne* 'nineteen', 15.1.19., *neogonteoba* 'nineteenth', 15.2.19.) > Ayenbite of Inwyt (Morris 1866) *neȝen*.
175. OEngl. *nigan nygan* with *-an*, beside *-on, -en* because of the late Old English variation in 'seven'. But the variation in the ending may be due to weakening and confusion (Campbell 1959: §§ 381–389).
176a. Luick (1921–1940: § 401.2). There is no reason to suppose that this northern *nen* represents, even in part, Ru[2] *nione* (> **neone*).
176b. See note 10.
177. For the Færoese development see Matras (1952: 178).
178. *tiio*, MSwed. *tījo, tīghio, tīgio* (Noreen 1904: § 328.1b).
179. For the Danish dialect forms see Brøndum Nielsen (1950–1957: § 545.6).
180. Cf. MDutch *sien* = OHG *sëhan* 'to see' (Franck 1910: § 40; Schönfeld – Van Loey 1964: § 33).
181. Ed. in Smith (1933: 38–41).
182. On Lindisfarne *glóedi* 'prunas' John 21,9, see Elliot – Ross (1972: 69–70.
183. Contracted forms from **texan*, **texani-*: OHG *zên* (Braune – Mitzka 1967: § 154 n. 7a); MHG *zên, -zên, zîn* (see Mausser 1932: 15 ff.). Cf. also Mod. HG *zehn, -zehn*.
184. *teyen, teng* (Lasch 1914: § 118) *-tign, ting*. For this last form see Kahle (1908: § 42); he also notes *tyen*. On *-teyng, -tygn*, see Lasch (1914: § 398 n. 1).
185. The modern Frisian forms are borrowed from Low German (MLG *-tein*): West *-t(s)jin* (Schier *-tien*); East *-tien* Saterland, *-tîn* Wangeroog; North *-täin* (> *-tin*) *-tain* Coast; *-taanj* Föhr and Amrum (WFöhr *-tanj*); *-tain* Sylt, Helgoland.
186. Cf. Ru[2] *gifeo* = Lind *gefea* = OHG *gi-fëho*.
187. The shortening is unexplained; see Luick (1921–1940: § 388 n. 2).
188. Ormulum (Holt – White 1878) *tenn* (thus short *e*; cf. 15.1.7.3.), *-tene*; the language AB (d'Ardenne 1936) *ten, -tene*; Ayenbite of Inwyt (Morris 1866) *ten* (see Wallenberg 1923: 240 n. 1), *uyftene, uiftene*.
189. In 'fourteen' it is only indirectly attested by ordinal ONorw. *fiórtoánde* (*fiórtiánde*) (15.2.14.). Færoese *-tan* 'thirteen' to 'sixteen', *-tjan* 'seventeen' to 'nineteen'; Mod. Norw. *tan* 'thirteen' to 'sixteen' and 'eighteen', descendants of OWN **-tiān* in 'seventeen' and 'nineteen' (15.1.17., 15.1.19.).
190. See Rosenfeld (1956: 115–140).
191. For another – very poor – suggestion see Noreen (1923: § 172.1).

192. Crimean Gothic *thiinita*, that is 'ten' – one', is calqued on Turkic. This statement, however, requires clarification. In Old Turkic, the numerals of one set were originally formed by means of the next following ten; thus *üč älig* 'forty-three' (*üč* 'three', *älig* 'fifty'). But in later Old Turkic texts the type required to explain the Crimean Gothic formation is already present; cf. *säkiz on bis* 'eighty-five' for earlier *biš toquz on* (*biš* 'five', *säkiz on* 'eighty', *toquz on* 'ninety'). For this former type in the modern languages, cf. Nogai *ombir* (*on bir*) 'eleven', *on eki* 'twelve' (*on* 'ten', *bir* 'one', *eki* 'two'), Turkish *on bir* 'eleven', *on iki* 'twelve', *on üč* 'thirteen' (*on* 'ten', *bir* 'one', *iki* 'two', *üč* 'three').
193. Syncope and loss of *n* (cf. Mausser 1932: § 129). Mod HG (Bavarian) *ąuanlaf* from a form with MHG *-lîf*; see Mausser (1939: 53, 167).
194. This is a better explanation of the final *-u* than Noreen's suggestion (1923: § 406, n. 5) that the form has a weak plural ending – for there is no reason why only 'eleven' should have taken on this ending.
195. Pretonic *ai* > *a* (15.1.2.11.2.).
196. > OGut. *allivu* (γ) – cf. Noreen (1913: § 155a).
197. Brøndum Nielsen (1950–1957: § 215, n. 3) gives a number of Old Danish forms, and (§ 546.1) some modern dialect ones.
198. *i* > *e* by "vokalbalanz" (Brøndum Nielsen 1950–1957: § 204).
199. Unprinted forms (from the *Institut for dansk dialektforskning*) essentially congruent to *elleve: ölu, ălu* south-east Jutland, *æjlu* south and west Fyn; cf. further *æľua, æləua* Brøndum Nielsen (1950–1957).
200. The status of this final *-u* (also in *ellivu*) is not certain; there is variation between *-i* and *-u* in Færoese (cf. Lockwood 1950: 90 ff.).
201a. Dat. *elleven* < *ellevenen*; also *elven*.
201b. Many Old Frisian forms are given by van Helten (1890: § 22).
202. The regular form is found in the word for 'die', *alas*, probably originally 'dice'; see Århammar (1968: 69).
203. **ānli-* > **ǣnl-* > **ǣ̆nl* > **ĕnl-* (Campbell 1959: § 193d).
204. Campbell (1959: § 478.3).
205. This is a better explanation of the *-on* than that by van Helten (1906: 107): "ws. *endlufon* ... neben *endlufan* ... nach dem Muster von *nigon, -an, siofon, -an, seofon, -an*".
206. Crimean Gothic *thunetua* [? read *thiinetua*]; cf. 15.1.11.1.
207. But cf. *tuolf* (Þorkelsson 1925: IV, 153).
208. Noreen (1923: § 124.3). For MIcel. *tolb* see Noreen (1923: § 237.3).
209. For the long vowel cf. Færoese *gólv* 'floor' = OIcel. *golf*; Færoese *hálvur* = OIcel. *halfr* (15.4.6.); and Færoese *úlvur* 'wolf' = OIcel. *ulfr*. But in all these examples the vowel has become short again – thus (*tolv*].
210. Runic Swed. (Rök) *tualf* = *twolf* (so Noreen 1923: §§ 77, 10).
211. *Twalfe* influenced by the Low German of East Frisian, cf. *twalf* at Groningen.
212. Löfstedt (1932: 12).

213. But Hattstedt *twelf* from Low German (so Löfstedt 1933: 129).
214. Loss of *i* between *l* and *f* (Luick 1921–1940: § 341).
215. Ormulum (Holt – White 1878) *twellf*, Ayenbite of Inwyt (Morris 1866) *tuelf*. MEngl. *twellif, twellyf* are given in the *Oxford English Dictionary: twelve* without reference – presumably with svarabhakti. MEngl. *twel* by analogy with the ordinal *twelthe* (< *twelfþe*). Jordan (1925: § 216, n. 1) explains *twel* as from *twelmonth* 'year', with loss of *f* in the cluster (as in *twelthe*), and this word may certainly have played a part in the analogy. But the loss may have taken place in the inflected form; cf. Mod. Engl. dialectal *del* for *delve* (EDD s. v.); see also Luick (1921:1940: § 766).
216. The same explanation accounts for MLG *twalf*.
217. Kentish *twælf* is not of interest, for it may well have the spelling *æ* for *e*.
218. Infl. *zwilffe*, dat. *zwilffen*, Rechte von Meiningen a. 1450 (Grimm: 1840–1878: iii. 597/36, 39).
219. MHG *zweilf* from *zwelf* + *eilf* 'eleven'.
220. Mod. Fr. *tolf tolve* West – the latter derives from an inflected form, as does also Schiermonnikoog *tyəlvə* (see Spenter 1968: 224).
221. Crimean Gothic *thunetria* [? read *thiinetria*]; cf. 15.1.19.
222. *i* > *e* before *nt*, then lengthening, and *nt* > *tt* (Noreen 1923: §§ 110.1, 123, 266.2).
223. *ĭ* > *ē* (Noreen 1904: § 83.2b) > *æ* (Noreen 1904: § 114.1).
224. *ǣt* > *ăett* (Noreen: 1904: § 297 n. 2).
225. Mod. Danish dialectal (Skåne) *trætan* (Brøndum Nielsen 1950–1957).
226a. OSwed. *þrættam* has the well-known, but unexplained *-m* for *-n*, cf. Noreen (1904: § 277, n. 3).
226b. See note 57c.
227a. Formally, the first element could also be nominative-accusative feminine *þrēo*, but, in view of the other West Germanic forms, there is no reason to suppose that it is.
227b. See note 10.
228a. Noted as occurring sporadically in late West Saxon by van Helten (1906: 111), without references.
228b. See note 57c.
229. From this + *fiōr-* (n. 57c), OSwed. *fioghirtān, fioghartān*, and – cf. Noreen (1904: § 270 n. 3) – *fyoghętān*.
230. The language AB (d'Ardenne 1936) *fiftene*, Ayenbite of Inwyt (Morris 1866) *uyftene, uiftene*.
231. *Syæxten*: see Brøndum Nielsen (1950–1957: § 176, n. 3).
232. The modern dialects nearly all have pronunciations with *æj, aj* – for literature referring to the forms see Brøndum Nielsen (1950–1957: § 546.6). Cf. the pronunciations of the standard from as [*saisdn*]. Cf., however, South Jutland *sexstən* and *sækstan* in Skåne and Halland.
233. Also Low German *söstein* (Danneil 1859 *sösstein*, s. v. *söss*), *sosstein* (van Helten 1906: 114).

234. *Tj* and *kj* fall together in Norwegian (Indrebø 1951: 232); for the loss of *n*, cf. Indrebø (1951: 237).
235. PN *ǫu* appears as *ey* in Færoese whether umlauted or not, so this form could as well be regarded as being umlauted – but there is no reason to suppose it is.
236. *Sytten*, Danish (*syttan*, adaptation); *sykjan* from *syttan* + forms in *-kja(n)*.
237. Sywtten < **siūghtan* (Brøndum Nielsen 1950–1957: § 197.2). The various forms survive in the modern dialects, in general *sydən, sødən, ʃutan, ʃøtan, søtan* in Skåne, the last also on Bornholm.
238. The *Oxford English Dictionary* gives sets of forms for all the teens except 'seventeen', for which s. v. *seventeen* the reader receives the directive: "Forms: see *'seven'* and -'teen'" – but the forms of the numeral actually occurring cannot of course be reconstituted in this way. Ross therefore put a query (NQ 217: 29–30), asking for Middle English forms of 'seventeen', but received no replies. It may be, then, that the reason for the peculiar entry in the *OED* was that, by chance, forms of this numeral are very rare in Middle English. *Seuentene* occurs in The Holy Bible ... in the earliest English version made by J. Wycliffe and his followers (III Kings 14, 21; IV Kings 13, 1).
239. In some of the later languages, e. g. Middle English, the loss can, of course, be "regular".
240. Noreen (1904: § 266, n. 2) without references (and therefore suspect).
241. Wessén (1965: § 160).
242. *atertan* (Brandt 1865: 121/14) is surely a Swedicism.
243. Cf. *aagi daar* 'eight days', 15.1.9.
244. *eahtetēone* (Earle – Plummer 1892–1899: a. 1083) shows the influence of ordinal *eahtatēoþa* (15.2.18.).
245. Cf. *sjaukja* 'seventeen' (15.1.17.); *nitten*, Danish (*nittan*, adaptation).
246. *Nyttan, nytten* with *y* written for *i* (cf. Brøndum Nielsen 1950–1957: § 36, n. 1).
247. The modern dialects have *nidən* nitan notan *nedən* (Brøndum Nielsen 1950–1957: § 546.9).
248. For the immediately ensuing forms, reference should occasionally be made to the discussion of 'two' (15.1.2.0.).
249. The daggered numbers in square brackets are for reference – some of them to the discussion of the endings in Ross, others to the forms printed here.
250. Cf. OIcel. *sonr* 'son' (Noreen 1923: § 395, n. 2).
251. In Modern Icelandic, *tveir, tigir, tveir, tugir* is also used for 'twenty'.
252. Jóhannesson (1923: no. 60).
253. As *tiughi* > *tyghi* above; but, in both cases *y* may be a mere orthography for *i*.
254. It is convenient to consider this a separate, monir decad formation, which we shall here designate as A'. This formation carries with it, first – naturally

– the use of fully inflected forms (such as dative *fiurum tiughum* 'forty'), and, secondly – sometimes – a first element in the compositional case.

255. Brøndum Nielsen (1950–1957: § 547B, C) gives full references back to earlier sections of the work for the sound changes relevant to the forms of 'twenty' and '-ty' quoted.
256. The normal noun **teʒu-* survives both in Danish and Norwegian: ODanish *tiugh* > *tiw*, Skånsk *tjug, tju, tjyv*; Mod. Norw. *tjug*. But its meaning has changed from 'ten' to 'score' under the influence of 'twenty' (so Torp 1919: *Tjug*).
257. For the immediately ensuing forms, reference should occasionally be made to the discussion of 'three' (15.1.3.) and 'four' (15.1.4.3.).
258. Gallée (1910: § 256, n. 1b). Note also the spellings *c* and *hc* for *g* (Gallée 1910: §§ 169 n. 1, 169b; van Loey 1969: § 112; van Helten 1890: 140).
259. Except for those of Standard West Frisian and Saterland, the Modern Frisian decads above 'twenty' are Low German loans. So too are the Danish dialect forms around Flensburg: *fertig, føftig, søstig, søventig, tagentig, nægentig* (Bennike – Kristensen 1898–1912: 165).
260. Lindisfarne has some special forms: *-tig* > *-teig* by analogy with the ordinal, and *h* can be written for *g* in this position (Ross 1961: 145); hence *-tih, -teih*. See Britton – Ross (1960: 146, n. 4), where the relevant forms are enumerated.
261. Modern West Frisian forms with initial *t-* may be due to Dutch influence (though East and North *tachentich* is more probably from Low German); they occur in Japicx in the ordinals – we quote from Brouwer et al. (1966): *tsegstigste* i, 186; *tsestigste* i, 233; *tsantigste* i, 172; *tachtigste* i, 123; i, 221; *tachtighste* i, 169; *tnjueggentigste* i, 233; *tnjueggentighste*, i, 126; *tnjueggentichste* i, 149.
262. Since Osthoff – Brugmann (1878–1910) do not mark the *o* long, they presumably take it as identical with *o* of genitive plural *tago* to *tag* 'day'.
263. Rosenfeld is followed by Frings (1960: 7–39). Frings (1962: 4–5) gives a list of Rosenfeld's articles.
264. And see Schlüter (1892: i. 8 ff.).
265. See Battisti (1912: 166).
266. So Þórólfsson (1925: 40–41), he gives a valuable discussion of the history of the decads in later Icelandic.
267. Type F appears occasionally in Old Danish ordinals (15.2.21.).
268. Sometimes spelt with *y* (cf. Brøndum Nielsen 1950–1957: § 36 n. 1).
269. Crimean Gothic *stega* is a suppletive = Mod HG *stiege*, MLG *stîge*, MDutch *stîge*, Mod, Dutch *stijg*, OFr. *stîge* 'score'. For another suppletive, cf. OEngl. *scoru*, Mod. Engl. *score*, loan-word form, Scandinavian (: OIcel. *skor* 'notch, crevice in a precipice, four hundred'; Mod. Icel. *skor* 'notch, ledge, twenty'; Færoese *skor* mountain-ledge'; Mod. Norw. *skor* 'mountain-ledge, notch'; Mod. Swed. dialectal *skărr* 'mountain-ledge') – see Björkman (1900–1901: 129).

270. From this + nominative-accusative masculine *zwêne* 'two', we have *zwênzëc, zwênzic*.
271. On the *a*, see Kluge – Götze (1976: s. v.).
272. *twi-* in Middle Low German, Dutch, and Frisian is due to the influence of *twi-* (so van Helten 1906: 118).
273. With the same development as in acc. sing. masc. *enne* 'one' (15.1.1.).
274. The Rushworth Gospel 2 (Skeat 1871–1887): *twoegentig* J 6,19, by analogy with *twoegen* 'two'.
275. Mod. Scots *twantie, twontie*, with sound change due to *w* – for the latter cf. Gabrielson (1912: 206) – also *twinti*, with *en* > *in* (some dialects).
276. Hægstad (1900: 42) (*tretti*, loan-word form, Norwegian).
277. Spelling-pronunciation, for intervocalic *d* does not occur in native Færoese; the *t* is an orthographic naturalization.
278. But cf. 15.1.11.3.
279. Long vowel – despite van Helten (1890: § 235, Nachträge).
280. Holthausen (1886): *dẹЛRic*; Schambach (1858: s. v.).
281. Schütze (1800–1806): *Dörde*; Berghaus (1880–1884: s. v.); Danneil (1859): *Dörtein*.
282. OGut. *fiauratighi*, from this type + dative *flaurum*.
283. > MSwed. *fȳretighi* (> *fyrtyghi, fyrteghi*, cf. Noreen 1904: § 154C.1a).
284. Early Færoese *fjøriti* (Svabo, Matras 1943), by vowel-harmony?
285. Saterland *fithertich* has a compositional first element (15.3.3.).
286. Mod. Norw. *femti*, adapted as early Færoese *fimti*.
287. Cf. *vîftein, veftein, vöftein* 'fifteen'.
288. Danneil (1859): *föfftig* (s. v. *fîw*); Schambach (1858: s. v.).
289. Both given Schütze (1800–1806): *Fief* and Berghaus (1880–1884): *Foftig*; Dähnert (1781) gives the former (s. v.) and the Bremer Wörterbuch the latter (s. v. *Fofte*).
290. MLG *vechtych, vichteg*, LG *föchtig* however shows the change *ft* > *cht* (Lasch 1914: § 296).
291. Adapted as Færoese *hălvtrýsinstjúgu* (abbreviated *hálvtrýss*).
292. Early Færoese *sexti* (Svabo, Matras 1943).
293. Dähnert (1781: s. v.); Danneil (1859): *söss*; Schütze (1800–1806): *söss*.
294. Dative *siextegum* (Sweet 1883: 172/4).
295. Ormulum (Holt – White 1878) *sextiȝ*, The language AB (d'Ardenne 1936) *sixti*, Ayenbite of Inwyt (Morris 1866) *zixti*.
296. MLG *tsestich* (Lasch 1914: § 398 n. 2).
297. Weijnen (1962: 15).
298. *u* = *y*? (Cf. Brøndum Nielsen 1950–1957: § 52 n. 1.)
299. Adapted as Færoese *trysinstjúgu*, abbreviated *trýss*.
300. Some Low German forms have *s* from German: *sīwn̥tsich* Assinghausen, *siebmsich* Ostbevern.
301. Ormulum (Holt – White 1878) *seofenntiȝ*, Ayenbite of Inwyt (Morris 1866) *zeventy*.

302. For Lindisfarne forms in *un-* and *und-*, see Ross (1962a: 282).
303. Færoese *hálvfjerosinstjúgu*, abbreviated *hálvfjeros* (*o* etymological orthography).
304. *Achtsich* Assinghausen, Ostbevern, Stavenhagen, with *-s-* from German.
305. But on these two forms see Brøndum Nielsen (1950–1957: § 547C.7a).
306. Adapted as Færoese *fýrsynstjúgu* (*y* = *í*), abbreviated *fýrs*.
307. LG *niȝntsich* Assinghausen, *nieȝntsich* Ostbevern, with *-s-* from German. (MDutch *negenstich*, *-s-* from 'sixty'.)
308. See Weijnen (1962), where a map of *tnegentig/negentig* is given.
309. Adapted as Færoese *hálvfemsinstjúgu*, abbreviated *hálvfems*. Færoese *níti* is a literary creation (*níggjuti* from this + *níggju* 'nine').
310. "Extra" forms: (A4) OSwed. *siaxtantighi* 'one hundred and sixty'. I may mention here the higher vigesimal forms of Old Danish, which are not uncommon: *halffsiettesindzthiuffue* 'one hundred and ten'; *sexsinnetiuæ, sexsynnetywe, sexsintiwge, sexsindstiwe, sexsyndstiuffe* 'one hundred and twenty'; *sywsynnetywe, siuffsindstyffue* 'one hundred and forty'; *halfottendesynnetiwghw* 'one hundred and fifty'; *otthesindstiuge, ottesindstiuffue, ottesindstywe, ottesindztiuge* 'one hundred and sixty'; *nisintywæ, nysynetyffuenisindztiwe, nysyndtztiuge, nysinnestywe* 'one hundred and eighty'; *eloffsynnetywe* 'two hundred and twenty'; *søtthendindstywe* 'three hundred and forty'.
311. The *e* is a svarabhakti (Gallée 1910: § 133.1).
312. *ð* silent in pronunciation, etymological spelling.
313. With a loss comparable to that in the neuter suffixed definite article: *huset* 'the house' > **huseð* > *huse*, in the spoken language.
314. *hunderth* may be a Low German loan, but see Brøndum Nielsen (1950–1957: § 346.2,3).
315. Forms with a final vowel appear in East Norse: OSwed. *hundraþa* > *hundradhe* (Noreen 1904: § 149.1), *hundrattæ* (from *hundrat* + *hundraþa* – so Noreen 1904: § 487 n.), *hunderdha* (Noreen 1904: § 399.2), *hundradho* (from *hundraþa* (*a* + *-tio* of the decads [type F] – so Noreen 1904: § 487 n.); ODanish *hundratha, hundrathe, hundræþæ, hundredæ, hundride* (*hondride* – Brøndum Nielsen 1950–1957: § 167.1); Mod. Danish *hundrede*. The form has been taken as originally that of the genitive plural, but Brøndum Nielsen (1950–1957: § 548 n. 1) suggests that it may be adjectival. For ODanish *hunderthæ*, cf. *hunderth* above.
316. Also *hondertich*, from the decads.
317. On Helgoland *groothondert*, see Krogmann (1957–1967: 272). The remaining forms are borrowed from Low German: West *hûndert* (Schiermonnikoog *hyndəd*); East *hunnert* Saterland, Wangeroog, *hundert* Harlingen (see Spenter 1968: 238); North *hunert, honert* Coast, *hunert* Föhr and Amrum.
318. OEngl. North Northumberland *hundrað* (*hundræð* Lindisfarne, Matthew 13,23), The Rushworth Gospel 2 (Skeat 1871–1887): *hundreð*; MEngl.

hundreth (Jordan 1925: § 200 n. 4) is a Scandinavian borrowing (Björkman 1900–1902: 163).

319. But cf. Hungarian *száz*.
320. Crimean Gothic *hazer*, Iranian; cf. *ärzä, ärjä* in the Ossete epic (< OIr. **hazahra-*). There has been much discussion about Hungarian *ezer*; see Gombocz – Melich (1914 s. v.) (where the equivalents in Zyryene, Votyak, Vogul and Ostyak are also to be found).
321. *þúshund* from this + **hund* 'hundred', *þúsundraþ* from this + *hundraþ* 'hundred'.
322. Runic Swed. *þūshuntraþ* from this + *hundraþ* 'hundred'.
323. In East Norse there is a form with final vowel similar to that found in 'hundred', one for which there are the same explanations (15.1.30.): OSwed. *þusanda*; Mod. Swed. *tusende* neuter; ODanish *thusanda, thusande, thusandæ, thusændæthusende*, and with admixture of type 5, *thusindæ*, Mod. Danish *tusinde*. MEngl. *þousand* (Mod. Engl. *thousand*) is a Scandinavian borrowing (Jordan 1925: § 136.3; cf. Björkman 1900–1902: 17 n. 1). Færoese *túsund* is normally pronounced [*tuusin*] and is thus doubtless from Danish; the alternative pronunciation [*tuusun*] may represent type 2.
324. Further *tûsinc, tûseng, tûsig* with alteration of suffix (cf. Kluge 1926: §§ 159, 205).
325. So, essentially, Ritter (1922: 170–171).
326. The language AB (d'Ardenne 1936) *þusent*, Ayenbite of Inwyt (Morris 1866) *þousend, þouzend; þousond, þouzond* appear to show vowel-harmony, as do also Laȝamon (Brook – Leslie 1963–1978) *þusund* v. 234, *þusunde* v. 274, *þousunt* v. 43. Wallenberg (1923: note ad loc.) has a different explanation of the Ayenbite form. In Ormulum (Holt – White 1878) *þusennde*, the final vowel was apparently added metri causa: *Bitwenenn an þusennde shep* v. 1316.
327. But the majority of Modern Frisian forms have initial *d*, which reveals Low German influence: Schiermonnikoog diuzənd; East *duusend* Saterland, Harlingen, Wangeroog; North *duusend* Coast, *düüsen* Föhr and Amrum, *düüsent* Sylt, *duusent* Helgoland.
328. But there is of course also indirect borrowing; thus Mod. Icel. *milljón* no doubt derives proximately from Danish, Mod. Fr. *miljoen* from Dutch.
329. Hereafter gender as for 'million'.
330. Cf. Mod. Engl. *centillionth* (15.3.1.).
331. For the ordinals of Low German see Rosenfeld (1959: 16).
332. See Mausser (1932: 880). Bavarian still has *-gast* (MHG *-ost*) in the decads: *twantsgast* 'twentieth', etc.; see Mausser (1932: 881).
333. The descendant is prevalent in some Modern Dutch dialects (Weijnen 1966: 297).
334. For Middle Low German loanwords in Old West Norse, see de Vries (1962: XXIX–XXXI).

335. So Lockwood (1955: 66).
336. Luick (1921–1940: § 441); van Langenhove (1925: 49–54).
337. Oakden (1930: 34–35); van Langenhove (1925: 49–54).
338. Keller (1925: 87).
339. Jordan (1925: § 200) and cf. Dobson (1957: § 367).
340. So Wallenberg (1923: 81 n. 6) in his note to Ayenbite of Inwyt (Morris 1866) *eʒtende* 'eight'.
341. Rit. *fru'mes* 'prime' (35/13), *fru'mu'* 'primis'.
342. For variant forms see Noreen (1904: § 468.2).
343. For variant forms see Brøndum Nielsen (1950–1957: § 553).
344. For variant forms see Noreen (1904: § 490.2,3).
345. Mod. Frisian *twôd*, Wangeroog *twäide*, Saterland *tweede*, Helgoland *twiidi*, Sylt (obsolete) – or from Low German?
346. For the suggestion that this is present in Crimean Gothic *treithyen*, 'thirty' see 15.1.21.4.
347a. *þryþi* from this + gen. *þryggia*, dative *þrym*.
347b. Nom. sing. fem. *þriþa* (and cf. oblique, *þryba*) because of the juxtaposition of *j*- and *j*-less forms in the nominative singular masculine.
348. The distinction *e*/*i* survives in the modern dialects: Zealand *treδə træδə*; Jutland *trioi triδə*.
349. Mausser (1932: 535–537) (*derde* because of *vierde* beside *vierte* 'fourth').
350. Woeste (ed. Nörrenberg, 1930: s. v.); Danneil (1859): *drüdd*; also Assinghausen, Heide (Dithmarschen).
351. Wangeroog masculine *thrêst* (and feminine neuter *thrîûst* – cf. 15.0.2.1.), Sylt (recent) *trerst*.
352. Ormulum (Holt – White 1878) *þridde*, The language AB (d'Ardenne 1936) *þridde*, Ayenbite of Inwyt (Morris 1866) *þridde*.
353. Similar development to that in West Norse.
354. *fiærdhia* from this + *þriþie* 'third'.
355. MSwed. *fǣrdhe*, ODanish *færthæe*, Mod. Danish *dialectal fær* South Jutland, MLG *vêrde, verde*.
356. Lindisfarne *fearδa*. If this had occurred only once or twice, the *ea* could have been explained as due to the sporadic representation of normal *eo* as this (Britton 1961: 18). In fact, the form occurs frequently. Its explanation is the following. The diphthong usually written PGmc. *eu* is in reality a multipartite phoneme, which can materialize as *eu, eo* or *iu*. The first two materializations are distinct only in the North Northumbrian dialect of Anglo-Saxon – as *ēo, ēa* respectively (so Luick (1921–1940: § 127, and see Ross 1951: 8). In **feurþān*/*ōn*- the materialization before the back vowels of the inflectional endings *istoeo*, hence *fearδa*.
357. Ormulum (Holt – White 1878) *feorþe, ferþe*, The language AB (d'Ardenne 1936) *feoroe*, Ayenbite of Inwyt (Morris 1866) *uerbe*.
358. He also mentions early Modern English pronunciations influenced by that of the cardinal.

359. WSax. *fēowerþa* and MEngl. *fourthe* would thus seem to constitute independent carry-over from the cardinal.
360. Schambach (1858: s. v.); Dähnert (1781: s. v.); Danneil (1859): *föfft* (s. v. *fīw*).
361. Low German developments as in 'fifteen'. Both given by Berghaus (1880–1884): *Fofte*, the latter also by the Bremer Wörterbuch (s. v.).
362. The single consonant may do no more than indicate the preceding long vowel (Brøndum Nielsen 1950–1957: § 555.4). Both unbroken und broken forms survive in the Danish dialects; for the former, cf. *sæ.t, sæ't* Jutland, for the latter *sjətə* Sejerø, and *ʃæt* Bornholm (Bennike – Kristensen 1898–1912: 165).
363. Brøndum Nielsen (1950–1957: § 177) has some remarks on the modern forms.
364. Despite Braune (1961: § 278 n. 1) and Mausser (1932: 877).
365. The reanalogy may in part have taken place within the individual languages.
366. For the Rushworth Gospel 1 (Skeat 1871–1887): *syxta* 27,45; cf. Brown (1891–1892: i, 38).
367. Britton – Ross (1960: 148 n. 1); Elliot – Ross (1972: 69).
368. Mod. Norw. *sjaunde; sjuande* from *sju* + *attande* 'eighth'. ONorw. *siauði* is a curious form; may it be by analogy with *fiorþi* 'fourth'?
369. *syunde* (cf. Brøndum Nielsen 1950–1957: § 180.3); further analogy with the cardinal: *siuende, siwende, sywende* (*syffwinde* – cf. Brøndum Nielsen 1950–1957: § 446 n. 2), Mod. Danish *syvende*.
370. In the Rushworth Gospel 1 (Skeat 1871–1887): *siofund* 22, 26, the final vowel is erroneously omitted.
371. Ormulum (Holt – White 1878) *sefnnde* (on his *seoffnde, seffnde*, see Luick 1921–1940: § 458).
372. With "akzentumsprung" (c): OEngl. accusative singular *sufoþan* Anglo-Saxon Gospels (ed. Sweet 1871–1887): Mt 22, 26 (v. r.); MEngl. *sovethe*.
373. Mod. Swed. *åttonde* by analogy with *nionde* 'ninth', *tionde* 'tenth'.
374. On the shortening see Brøndum Nielsen (1919: 83). And for the single *t* (*atende, atændæ, atinde*), cf. 15.2.6.
375. Ormulum (Holt – White 1878) *ehhtennde*; Ayenbite of Inwyt (Morris 1866) *eȝtende* (*eȝtinde* 2/6 col. 2 has presumably been affected by pres. part. *-inde* – cf. Jensen 1908: 12, 32).
376. Because of MEngl. *tiȝethe* beside *teȝethe* (The language AB, d'Ardenne 1936, *teoheðe*) 'tenth', so **ihteþe* beside **ehteþe* 'eighth'. Some of the Modern English dialect forms descend from the former: [*æitθ*], [*aitθt*] Durham (SED i, 767), [*aiʔθ*] Shropshire (SED ii, 751), [*æitθ*] [*ɔ.tθ*] Herefordshire (SED ii, 751); these have influenced the cardinal (15.1.7.5.).
377. Mod. Norw. *niande* by analogy with *attande* 'eighth'.
378. Early Færoese *níggindi* (Svabo – ed. Matras 1943: *nujggjindi*), by vowel-harmony.

379. MEngl. *neoȝethe* (Black 1845: v. 617) ultimately by analogy with OEngl. *teogeþa* 'tenth' (15.2.10.).
380. Ormulum (Holt – White 1878) *niȝhennde*; Ayenbite of Inwyt (Morris 1866) *neȝende* < OKentish **neogunda* < **niogun* **nigunda* (back-mutation, Campbell 1959: § 216).
381. Mod. Norw. *tiande* by analogy with *niande* 'ninth' and *åttande* 'eighth'.
382. Early Færoese *tíggindi* (Svabo – ed. Matras 1943: *tujggjindi*).
383. Kristensen (1928 – 1933: 108/27).
384. Also *tynde, tyændhe* (Brøndum Nielsen 1950 – 1957: § 36.1).
385. See note 57c.
386. LG *-tende* Assinghausen, *tainte* Assinghausen, *tainte* Ostbevern, *tainte* Heide in Dithmarschen, *tait* Stavenhagen.
387. *-teingeste*: cf. LG *-tainste* Ostbevern, *-tainste* Heide in Dithmarschen, *-taist* Stavenhagen.
388. *zëhendiste, zëhendste, zëhenste, -zëhentest, -zëhentist, -zëhendest, -zëhendist.*
389. *-tunde, -tundi* apparently by analogy with *āttunde* 'eighth' (so Noreen 1904: § 493 n. 1). A similar form with original *-u-* is preserved in Skåne and on Bornholm (*trætənə* 'thirteenth', etc.); see Brøndum Nielsen (1950 – 1957: § 556 n. 1).
390. Weakened to *-tende* and *-tinde*, Brøndum Nielsen 1950 – 1957: § 146 n. 1), *-tennæ*; see Brøndum Nielsen (1950 – 1957: § 341.2).
391. Cf. furhter OSax. *tegetho*; MDutch *tiende*; Mod. Dutch *tiend*; OFr. *tegotha*; Mod. Fr. *teeged* Saterland; OFr. *tíanda*, Mod. Fr. *tinj* 'multure' Sylt – but this might be a borrowing from Jutland dialect, cf. *tiende* [*tiən*] with its normal Danish meaning 'tithe'; cf. further the verb *tinjigi* 'to deduct multure' Sylt with Jutland *tiende* 'to pay tithe'.
392. In Scandinavian, 'tithe' is by origin a *-ti*-abstract, but it has been influenced by the ordinal; see further 15.3.4.
393. The Rushworth Gospel 1 (Skeat 1871 – 1887): *tægþigeþ* 'decimatis' 23, 23; The Rushworth Gospel 2 (Skeat 1871 – 1887): *tegδigas*, Lindisfarne *gie teigδas* Luke 11, 42; *gitei/gδeges* Matthew 23, 23.
394. This coincides in form with another English word for 'tithe', the *-ungo*-abstract to the ordinal (15.4.6.).
395. Syncopated (Brøndum Nielsen 1950 – 1957: § 219.2): *elffthe, olffthe.*
396. Bavarian *ǫanlaft* with MHG **-lîft*.
397. *elftende* from this + *teinde* 'tenth'; *elvenich* – 15.2.0.
398. *aleveth* (MED: *elleventhe* without quotation) from this + **allef* < OEngl. *ællef*.
399. *elevend* from this type + *tend* 'tenth' and *-tend* 'teenth'; further *ellevent*. The final consonant is sometimes omitted before a following one; hence *elleven* 'eleventh'.
400. Also *twelftende, twelvich*, like *elftende, elvenich* 'eleventh'.
401. On the language AB *tweofte*, see d'Ardenne (1936: 232 n. 3).

402. See von Friesen (1934: *Exkurs III: Räkneorden pa fvn. -tán x*) *-tiá*, OSwed. *trittande*, with development parallel to that in *þrætan* > = *þrættan*.
403. ONorw. *þrentánde* OSax. *þræntāndi* by analogy with *þrenner, þrænne* (15.3.3.1.). Noreen (1923: § 258.2) takes the Old Norwegian form as with dat. *þrem* (*mt* > *nt*), but this suggestion has to be rejected.
404. *thredtînda, thredténdesta, dt* due to *dd* of *thredda* 'third'.
405. Noreen (1904: § 493, n. 2), unless this is a mere orthography for *fiūrtānde*.
406. For the explanation of *syøttonde*, see Noreen (1904: § 493 n. 3).
407a. For the curious Mod. Danish dialectal *syttens* South Jutland, see Brøndum Nielsen (1950–1957: § 556.7).
407b. See note 57c.
408. Noreen (1904: § 494) takes the sporadic *-tiiande* as meaning *-tīonde*, and *-tighiande* as meaning *-tījonde* (cf. MSwed. *tījo* 'ten', 15.1.10.1.).
409. Dat. sing. *twentugoðan* Anglo-Saxon Gospels Matthew 8, 14 (margin) Skeat: 1871–1887) and Gospel of Nicodemus MS A (Hulme 1898: 471/10).
410. The Kentish development follows a different route: **tiȝuþa* > **-tiuȝuþa* (*u*-umlaut before the guttural, Campbell 1959: § 210) > **-tiogoþa* > **tiogþa* > **-tiagþa* > Ayenbite of Inwyt (Morris 1866) *tiaȝte, -taȝte* (cf. Wallenberg 1923: 256 n. 3).
411. *Twinthechgista*, mixed spelling (*-tech* and *-teg*).
412. Ayenbite of Inwyt (Morris 1866) *uourtaȝte* — cf. *furteohte* Old English Homilies (Morris 1868–1873: 229/34).
413. Cf. also *in dem zwey und vouffzigstem iare*, Codex diplomaticus mœnofrancofurtanus in a document of March 10, 1352, Böhmer (1836).
414. Abbreviated form, see Britton — Ross (1960: 131–132).
415. Brøndum Nielsen (1950–1957: § 557.3), with references to the literature on 'hundredth' and 'thousandth' in the Modern Danish dialects.
416. Ayenbite of Inwyt (Morris 1866) *hondredaȝte*; also *hondraȝte* (234/8). Wallenberg (1923: 125 n. 1) does not wish to emend this latter, but gives no reason for his view; cf. however, MEngl. *hundreth* (admixture of *hund*?).
417. For dialect forms with *-s* as in *syttens* 'seventeenth', see the reference to Brøndum Nielsen (1950–1957) in section 15.2.17.
418. A phenomenon which indirectly confirms the lateness of the formation.
419. A nonce-form *centillionth* [10 600] is recorded in *Tait's Edinburgh Magazine* (xix: 473 col. 1/31).
420. Noreen (1923: § 111.1, 1904: § 83.3a), Brøndum Nielsen (1950–1957: § 101).
421. Noreen (1923: § 230.1, 1904: § 246), Brøndum Nielsen (1950–1957: § 273.1).
422. And related meanings, also in the plural, used as a cardinal.
523. See note 57c.
424. Also used as a cardinal in the plural.
425. *þrani* from this + *þranni* (15.3.3.1.); cf. n. 57c.
426. For 'one' in composition see 15.1.1.1.
427. But, occasionally, a cardinal form appears in compounds which is different from that normally used. Thus OIcel. *ní-røþr* 'in the tenth decade' as against

nío té-øþr 'in the eleventh decade' as against *tío – tí-røþr* by analogy with *ní-røþr*. (With OIcel. *átt-røþr* 'in the ninth decade' beside *átta*, cf. *áttián* 'eighteen').

428. Cf. Noreen (1923: § 122, 1904: § 87), Brøndum Nielsen (1950–1957: § 113).
429. But even in Old High German, the form tends to be replaced by the cardinal; cf. Notker (Piper 1895) *zwei-elnîg* (nominative-accusative neuter), *zweio-elnîg* (gen.) 'measuring two ells'; hence Mod. HG *zwei-*.
430. OEngl. *twi-wintre* 'having two winters' > Mod. Engl. *twinter* 'two years old' and, as noun, 'two year-old').
431. In Old West Norse, by well-known sound changes, (α) *é* > *æ* after *v* and before *tt* (< *xt*) as in Icel. *vættr* 'being' = Gothic *(ni) waíht* 'nothing' and (β) in Old Norwegian *e* > *æ* after *v* as in *væl* = Icel. *vel*, 'well' (Noreen 1923: § 108). In his discussion of (α), Noreen (1923: § 109) suggests that in part (γ) *é* > *æ* after *v* and before *a* lost (α) in positions other than before *t* as in Icel. *sværa* 'mother-in-law' = Gothic *swaíhro*. In this discussion he derives OIcel. *tuæ-* in *tuæ – uetr* 'two years old' from **twīh* (i. e. **twīxa-*); that would be then to equate it to OEngl. *(be-)twīh* (15.4.8.). But it is hard to see why this derivative should be used in composition. If we had an OIcel. **tuænn* beside *tuénn* < **twixna/ō-* (immediately above), we could explain the *æ* by (β) and suppose that *tuæ-* was due to analogy with **tuænn*. But in fact, this latter form seems not to exist. Perhaps the most probable explanation of *tuæ-* is that it is from *tué-* by a hitherto unpostulated sound change (δ) *é* > *æ* after *v*, parallel to (α).
432. Notker (Piper 1895) sometimes has *drî* – Braune (1961: 132) – (MHG *drî-*, Mod. HG *drei-*). Cf. also his *drîo-elnîg* (nominative-accusative feminine) 'measuring three ells' and *driunissa* 'Trinity' (Sievers 1874) beside *drînissa*.
433. Mod. Engl. *threeness* is a late formation.
434. But Campbell (1959: 287 n. 1) seems to suggest that the *m*-form arose in dative plural *þrimfealdum* (Liebermann: II Æthelstan 4, 6.1, i: 152, 154) with the *m* due to the following part; cf. Rushworth Gospel 1 *'twæ fældu'* 'duplo' 23,15 – if the *m* is not due to analogy with *þrimfald*, produced as we have suggested above.
435. Also *fjór-*, cf. Shet. *feurfetign* 'having four feet' with the cardinal (Hægstad 1900: § 20.3), which also appears in Mod. Norw. *fjøfit* (influence of ON *fit* 'webbed foot' – so Torp 1919: *Fjore*) beside the old compositional form in *firfôt* (both Østfold).
436. Also late WSax. *fiþer-, fyþer-* (with change *e* > *i* before a following *u-* (NQ 219: 123), MEngl. *fiðer*.
437. This survives as the Gothic prefix *twis-*. It has been suggested that the Gothic prefix *dis-* derives from a PIE **dis* (beside **du̯is*). On this point – and also on a possible connection between Gothic *dis-* and OSax. *te-*; OFr. *te-*; OEngl. *te-, ti-*; MEngl. *te-*; OHG *zi-, ze-* (OHG *zir-*, MHG *zer-*, Mod. HG *zer-* from this + OHG *ir-*, MHG *er*, Mod HG *er-* see.

438. *er-* will not be discussed here.
439. Of the same meanings as OIcel. *tuénn* (above).
440. Færoese neuter *tvint* 'set of two'; Mod. Norw. *tvinne* 'two'.
441. So by origin, but the word is normally indeclinable; cf. however dative *twinnum*.
442. Mod. Fr. *twane* 'two' North (so Dr. Århammar, letter to Ross of June 23, 1970).
443. OSwed. *twanni* from cardinal *twa* (note 57c).
444. *i* > *e* before *r* (Lasch 1914: § 61).
445. *i* > *e* before *r* (Franck 1910: § 67).
446. Cf. OEngl. *hād-* 'hair' = Icel. *haddr* 'hair of a womans head' < **xazda-* (Campbell 1959: § 404).
447. Cf. OEngl. *ærn* 'house' < **rænn* = Gothic *razn*; see Stanley (1952–1953: 107).
448. EDD: *twains* Cornwall 'twins' by analogy with Mod. Engl. *twain*.
449. Also *zwirnên*, but this is probably secondary.
450. Early Mod. Engl. *twind*, from this + *wind*, verb.
451. But Mod. HG *zwilling* etc. is of a different origin (15.4.17).
452. Mod. Norw. *tvinlast burt* 'to vanish away', etc., is not connected with 'two' (see Torp 1919: *tvinla*), but *tvintlast burt*, of the same meaning, shows confusion with *tvinta*. Mod. Norw. *tvingla* 'to reel' is from *tvinna* (above) + *svingla* 'to tremble'. But EDD: *twingle* v. Scots, Cornwall, Northamptonshire 'to twist closely round', 'to turn', 'to wriggle' is no doubt a word of the kind that Ross has called "autochthonous" (Proceedings of the Leeds Philosophical and Literary Society, Literary and Historical Section 1932, iii: 351–352); cf. EDD: *twangle* v. Yorkshire, Warwickshire Suffolk 'to twist', 'entangle', 'ruffle', 'to writhe from pain'.
453. *þranni* from *þrinni* + *twanni* (above).
454. Mod. Fr. *trane* 'three' North (so Prof. Århammar, personal communication; cf. 15.3.3.1.).
455. But Mod. Engl. dialectal *thrins* 'triplets' is no doubt formed on *twins*.
456. In addition to Icel. *tvenning, þrenning*, we have also Icel. *eining* 'a unity'; Færoese *á einingi* 'entirely'; Mod. Norw. *i eining, i einingo* Nordland *i einung*, Hardanger 'alone'; OSwed. *ivir enunga* 'in agreement'; Mod. Swed. *enings-band* 'bond of union'; Mod. Danish *ening*.
457. But Mod. HG *drilling* etc., is of a different origin (15.4.17.).
458. Cf. Mod. Dutch *zuster* = Gothic *swistar* 'sister' (Schönfeld, van Loey 1964: § 53).
459. Similarly – unmetathesized – Mod. Engl. dialectal *tweesht* (also *tweest*), Mod. Scots *betwisht*. Mirk *betwysse* (Festial, Erbe 1905: 292/33) may be from **twisk* with change *sc* > *s* before a following consonant; cf. also *flesse* (Erbe 1905: 290/26 and cf also Jordan 1925: § 183 n.). Pearl (Morris 1869: v. 464) *bytwyste* (rhymes with *gryste* 'anger' < OEngl. *grist-* 'gnashing of

teeth') may be from this with added *-t* (Jordan 1925: § 199). Derivative verb: PGmc. **twiskoþ* > OFr. *twiskia* 'to separate'.

460. OHG dative *feoriskeem* (Benediktinerregel: 197/15) is a nonce-formation on the basis of the cardinal.

461. The first accented form occurs once, the second several times.

462. Persson (1912: i, 552–553), followed by Pokorny (1959: 1140), who compares Armenian *gelum* 'to turn'.

463. For the ending, cf. Ross (1954: 119).

464. Cf. genitive singular Gothic *sunaus* < PGmc. **sunaus* or **sunauz; -z* of the latter form might, but need not necessarily, be preserved immediately before a voiced sound; the relevant examples are *sunaus* Skeirins Nehemiah 6, 18; *sunaus gudis* Mark 1, 1; Ephesians 4, 13; Galatians 2, 20; *sunaus mans* Luke 6, 22; Luke 17, 26; John 6, 53.

465. Icel. *eins* adverb 'in agreement', 'alone' (*fyrir eins* 'come what may'); Færoese *eins* adverb 'in the same way'; Mod. Norw. *eins* adverb 'like' (also 'alone'); OSwed. *ēns* adjective and adverb 'of the same kind', 'in agreement'; MSwed. *ens* adjective and adverb 'even', 'in agreement'; ODanish *ens*, Mod. Danish *ens* adjective and adverb 'identical, identically'. Numeral adverb 'once': OHG *eines*; MHG *eines*; Mod. HG *eins*; OSax. *ênes*; MLG *ênes*; LG *es* Ostbevern; MDutch *êns*; Mod. Dutch *eens*; OFr. *ênes* (*ênse* from this + instr. sing. **aini* – so van Helten 1890: § 240); Mod. Fr. *iens, iensen* West, *ins, insen* Saterland, Wangeroog, *iinjsen* East Moringen, *ens* Föhr and Amrum 'times' (unstressed) – and *iansis* 'once' stressed extended by OFr. *sîth* 'times', *jens* Sylt, *ens* Helgoland; OEngl. *ænes* (by analogy with instr. sing. *æne*); MEngl. *enes* and from this + *an, ǫn* 'one', we have *anes, ǫnes* (> Mod. Engl. *once*). Further (with added *-t* – see Loewe 1916: 141–146): OHG *einêst*; MHG *einest*; Mod. HG (Swiss) *einist* (and from this + *zwei*, we have *zweinist* 'twice'); with change of meaning, Mod. HG *einst*; cf. OHG *anderêst* 'for the second time' Notker (Piper 1895); MHG *anderst*; Mod. HG *anderst*. In Scandinavian the form has a life of its own; cf. Mod. Swed. *ense* 'in agreement with' (formed from the adjectives in *-se*), such as *gramse* 'bearing a grudge' beside early Mod. Swed. *gram* 'angry' – see Hellquist (Arkiv 7: 158) and the derivatives, ICel. *einsligr* 'alone'; Færose *einsligur*; Mod. Norw. *enslig*; OSwed. *enseliker*; Mod. Swed. *enslig*; Mod. Danish *enslig* 'single'; Mod. Norw. *ensling* 'recluse'; Mod. Swed. *ensling*.

466a. In *tuswar* the vowel is due to nominative-accusative neuter *tu* (see note 57c). *Twøsser, tuøsser* in the *Nøye testamenth paa danske* (Wittenberg 1524, fascimile: *Danske Bibelarbejder fra Reformationstiden* vol. I) show an orthography apparently due to *two*, a spelling for *to* 'two'.

466b. See note 57c.

467. Derivatives: Mod. HG (Swiss) *zwirisch* 'ambiguous', *zwurig* 'double', and, as adverb, 'twice'.

468. Also *tweisi(s)* extended by OFr. *sîth* 'times'. Hence further *thriisi(s)* 'thrice', etc., with the cardinal.

469. Orm *twiȝȝess* (representing OEngl. **twio*) and *twiȝess* (representing OEngl. **twīo*); cf. 15.1.7.5.
470. Early Mod. Engl. also *twist* (cf. Dobson 1957: § 437); Mod. Engl. dialectal [*twaist*] (EDG 295). *Twaisuer* Halligen, *tweisuar* Amrum (has added the Old Frisian adverb *over*) (= Mod. Engl. *over*).
471. *W*-umlaut here only in West Norse (Brøndum Nielsen 1950–1957: § 92).
472a. *Traiauer* Halligen; see 15.3.3.
472b. See note 57c.
473. Doubling of *u* before *w*.
474. Notker (Piper 1895) often marks long vowels, so the fact that the *o* is not marked affords some indication that it is short.
475. Cf. Gothic 3rd pers. pret. ind. *berun* < PIE **bhērn̥t* (Streitberg 1896: § 129. 7a).
476. Two *n*-forms occur in East Norse, namely ODanish *thys(s)wen* four times in Den ældste danske Bibeloversættelse (Molbech 1828: 178/15, 20; 199/24; 200/21) and OSwed. *thryswæn*, which occurs as a variant reading in the Konungx balker of Konung Magnus Erikssons Stadslag (Collin – Schlyter 1827–1877: xi. 42 n. 73). But both have been "explained away"; Brøndum Nielsen (1950–1957: § 542 n. 2) suggests that the *-n* of the Old Danish form is "analogical" (and refers to his § 345 n. 2), and Noreen (1904: § 500.2) tentatively suggests that the Old Swedish form is erroneous. The former explanation is certainly unsatisfactory. It may be, then, that one or both forms are genuine and do derive ultimately from **dwis-went*, **tris-went*.
477. OSwed. *sæxt, siæxt* 'twelve o'clock', Latin *sexta*.
478. See Bugge (1905–1917: 33–34).
479. *Annar* can be inflected weak in Middle Swedish (Noreen 1904: § 490), so can *annar* in later Old Danish (Brøndum Nielsen 1950–1957: § 554); and *anden* is weak in some Danish dialects (Bennike – Kristensen 1898–1912: 165).
480. Qvigstad (1893): *divad.*
481. The final Finnish *-i* is not to be brought into connection with the *-i-* of PGmc. **texundi-*, **tixundi-* as suggested by. Karsten (1943–1944). Many Finnish borrowing add *-i* to an etymon ending in a consonant (OSwed. *tiund*); cf. recent Finnish examples such as *bentsiini* 'petrol'.
482. By analogy. LG (Schleswig) *tult, tült*, Mod. Fr. *talt, telt* 'twelve planks' North (by analogy Mod. Dutch *tult*).
483. This abstract is also recorded, with fair certainty, in Salic Law plural *tualepti*; see van Helten (1906: § 11).
484. I give here the Icelandic form as OIcel. *-tøgr*, Mod. Icel. *-tugur*; *-togr* too is found in Old Icelandic and *tugr* in this and Old Norwegian.
485. Only a few other, specialized, meanings are therefore given here.
486. OSwed. *þrætiugh* = *thrætiught*, above, with loss of the final *-t* (Noreen 1904: § 454. 1c).

487. The *u* of *brætulfter* would seem to indicate that this is a Gutnish form (Noreen 1904: § 111.1), but the *þræ-* is Swedish; OGut. *þri-*.
488. Kluge (1926: §§ 3, 17).
489. See Hotzenköcherle (1961: 211 – 212).
490. "*n* +" means that the word has passed into the Germanic *n* – declension; this happens very frequently; see Brugmann – Delbrück (1897 – 1916: II.i. 303).
491. But *briggja*, Sonatorrek Stanza 2, is an error for *Friggjar* (Nordal 1955: 247, following Jónsson 1931: 34), and so does not represent a comparable PGmc. **brijjan-*.
492. Neckel – Kuhn (1962 – 1968: i, 240 – 247).
493. Cf. Gothic dative singular, gender not determined *wagggarja* *προσκεφάλαιον* Mark 4, 38, to OEngl. *wange* 'cheek' (Kluge 1926: 77).
494. Kluge (1926: § 144 ff.).
495. For the ending cf. Gothic *unweniggo* 'unexpectedly"; cf. Streitberg (1896: § 189. 1b).
496. Cf. also the Middle English noun *oninge*, Early English Psalter (Stevenson 1839: xxi. 21).
497. No umlaut in *-inga-* forms because of the influence of the unumlauted forms in *-unga-*.
498. The principal fraction "half" (Pokorny 1959: 926), however, does not belong here: Gothic *halbs*; OIcel. *halfr*; Mod. Icel. *hálfur* (Noreen 1923: § 124.3); Færoese *hálvur* (see 15.1.12.1.); Mod. Norw. *halv*; OSwed. *halver* (*haver*, Noreen 1904: § 315. 2b); Mod. Swed. *halv*; ODanish *halvær*, Mod. Danish *halv*; OHG *halb*; MHG *halp*; Mod. HG *halb*; OSax. *half*; MLG *half*; MDutch *half*; Mod Dutch *half*; OFr. *half*; Mod. Fr. *heal* West (*hail* Schiermonnikoog; cf. Spenter 1968: 177), *hoolf* Saterland, *halv* Wangeroog, *huulew* East Moringen, *hualev* Sylt, *hualew* Föhr and Amrum, *huálow* Helgoland; OEngl. *healf*; MEngl. *half* (Ormulum, Holt – White 1878) *halff*, AB *half* (Ayenbite of Inwyt, Morris 1866: *half*); Mod. Engl. *half*. The word is used "idiomatically" in numerals, as in Mod. HG *anderthalb* 'one-and-a-half'; cf. Icel. *halfr, fjórði* 'three-and-a-half'; Færose *hálvur fjórði* 'three-and-a-half'; OSwed. *halffiærþe* 'three-and-a-half'; Mod. Swed. *halvtredje* 'two-and-a-half'; ODanish *halffierde* 'two-and-a-half'; Mod. Danish *halvtredie* 'two-and-a-half'; OHG *anderhalb*; MHG *anderhalp*; OSax. *ôtherhalf*; MLG *anderhalf*; MDutch *anderhalf*; Mod. Dutch *anderhalf*; OFr. *ôtherhalf*; Mod. Fr. *oardeheal* West; Oengl. *eathoþe* healf 'seven-and-a-half'; MEngl. *other half*; "half" has derivatives: (1) *-iðō* abstract (Kluge 1926: § 121): OIcel. *helfþ*; MHG *helfte*; Mod. HG *hälfte*; MLG *helfte*; MDutch *helfde, helft*; Mod. Dutch *helft*; OFr. *helft*; Mod. Fr. *helt(e)* West (Spenter 1968: 177) and loanword from (Low) German *hälft* Wangeroog, *haleft* East Moringen, Helgoland, Amrum, *heleft* Föhr; there are also *t*-forms in Scandinavian: OIcel. *helft*; Færoese *helvt*; Mod. Norw. *helvt*; OSwed. *hælft*; these may be due to

the influence of the *-ti*-abstracts or to West Germanic influence or to both (so Noreen 1923: § 238. 7). (2) Masculine *-linga* derivative (Kluge 1926: § 55): OHG *helbelinc*, MHG *helbelinc* 'half-pfennig', OSax. *helfling* (MEngl. *halfling* 'half a silver penny', reformed on *half*); in Scandinavian the fraction **xelolingR *helöningR* by dissimilation > **helmingR* (Noreen 1923: § 237. 2) > **helmingR* (see Noreen 1923: § 254) and mixed forms: OIcel. *helfningr, helmingr*; ICel. *helmingr*; Færoese *helmingur*; Orkney *helmin* (measure of land) and *hemlin* 'a sheep-mark', 'a slice, cut diagonally from the ear' (Marwick 1929: s. vv.; cf. also his *hemliband* 'a tether which bifurcates after stretching out from stake [sic] for some length as a single line'); Mod. Norw. *helming*; OSwed. *hælfninger, hælfminger*. A derivative verb: OHG *bi-halbôn*; Mod. HG *halben*; MDutch *halven*; Mod. Dutch *halven*; MEngl. *halfen, halven*; Mod. Engl. *halve* — for the most part the verb is recent.

499. Only these derived meanings are given here, preceded by "specifying".
500. In the sense of 'territorial division' the word is borrowed into English: OEngl. *þriðing* (cf. acc. sing. *trydinge*, Liebermann 1903—1916: iii. 341; see further Ross, NQ 213: 444; Mod. Engl. *Riding* by false division of *norþ þriþing* etc.), see Smith (1956: ii. 213).
501. MSwed. *fǣrdhunger, fiǣrdhinger, fiǣrunger, fiǣring* adapted as MLG.
502. Kluge (1926: § 100a) puts OEngl. *teōþung* here, but this is wrong, for the word is feminine; it is an *-ingō- -ungō*-formation to the ordinal: OEngl. *tēoþung tēoþing* 'tithe, association of ten men'; The Rushworth Gospel 2 (Skeat 1871—1887): *tegðunge*, Lindisfarne *teigðuncgas* 'decimas' Luke 18, 12; MEngl. *teothinge, tueþyng, teþing, tiþing*, Mod. Engl. *tithing* 'tithe, tenth part, a company (originally) of ten householders, now only as a rural division, originally regarded as one tenth of a hundred'; Mod. Engl. dialectal also 'shock of ten sheaves'.
503. See Falkman (1884: 1,161 ff.).
504. Ormulum (Holt — White 1878) *aniȝ*, Iul *eanni*, Ayenbite of Inwyt (Morris 1866) *eni, eny* (see Wallenberg 1923: 84 n. 3).
505. OEngl. *ancummum* 'per singula' Lindisfarne, John 21, 25 is probably a Norse borrowing; see Ross (1932—1933: 344—345).
506. De Vries (1962): *ekkja*, suggests that Lappish (Norwegian) *akka* 'woman', 'wife' is a borrowing of this word from West Norse. But this is certainly not the case; the words like Finnish *akka* 'old woman', 'grandmother', etc., are no doubt autochthonous (15.3.3.1.); see Toivonen (1955): *akka*.
507. By analogy, Mod. Fr. (Sylt) *inki-* in *inki-man* 'widower', *inki-wiif* 'widow'.
508. Mod. Fr. *inkeld* West, *aonkeld, ankeld, aenkeld, onkeld* East, *énkelt* Wangeroog, *ainkelt, enkelt* East Moringen, plural *enkelten* Föhr and Amrum, Sylt, Helgoland (OFöhr also *eenkelt*). The North Frisian and Wangeroog forms are borrowings from Low German, the Saterland forms an adaptation; the West Frisian form may be from Dutch.

509. Kluge (1926: § 150). EDD: *twitch* sb. Yorkshire, Lancashire 'a narrow way', 'a passage', 'a short, steep twist or bend in a road' may represent the unextended form.
510. Esk. < **esken* is also from Low German; cf. LG *esch, esk* (*eschen, esken* along the Coast; further MLG *esken*. (In two Frisian dialects 'ace' is a diminutive to 'one' by means of the Low German suffix *-ken*: *áinken* Wangeroog and *înken*, Jensen 1927: 103).
511. MLG *tôch*, LG *touX* assimilated to feminine OSax. *twô*, MLG *twô* (Schönhoff 1908: § 551).
512. *i* > *e* in open syllable, cf. Torp – Falk (1898: 149).
513. But MHG *einzel*, Mod. HG *einzeln* is by origin a compound, OHG *einluzzi*.
514. But *twitter-light* 'twilight' is to Mod. Engl. *twitter* in the sense 'to move tremulously'; cf. *twatter-light'*.
515. 'Branch' and 'twine' survive in the dialects.
516. Mod. Danish *tvist* 'cotton-waste', 'kind of yarn'; Mod. HG *twist* (Germanized, *zwist*); Mod. Dutch *twist* 'kind of yarn'.
517. Note especially the sense 'a twig', 'a branch' (OED: *Twist* sb. 2), and early Middle English Modern. In respect of the Middle Scots occurrences, Flom (1900: 69), considers it to be a Scandinavian borrowing (Icel. *kvistr*), but this is not possible.
518. It is generally recognized – though the subject has been little discussed – that, for whatever reason, initial PGmc. *tw* can appear as if it had been PGmc. *kw*. De Vries (1962: sv. *kvísl*) notes a few probable examples. The phenomenon is found in Frisian; thus in the Moringer dialect we have *twaage* ~ Sylt *kweeken* 'yeast' (to Mod. Engl. *quick*); *twarn* ~ Föhr and Amrum *twarn* (Gothic *qaírnus*), and cf. Helgoland *kweebak* 'Zwieback'.
519. Torp (1919): *Kvist* and *Tvist* takes Mod. Norw. *tvist* 'porch', *kvist* 'attic'; Mod. Swed. dialectal *kvist, tvist* 'porch'; Mod. Danish *tvist* 'attic' as this same word (i.e. < PGmc. **twista-* masculine), the semantic development being via 'a branching-out'.
520. Cf. Olson (1916: § 52).
521a. It might well be suggested that Mod. HG *zwitter* (MHG *zwitar*) belongs here. But the word is in fact not a derivative, but a compound, although the nature of the second element is unclear. Cf., in the first place, OHG singular *zwitaran*; further MHG *zwidorn*; Mod. Swed. dialectal *tvetorna, tvetona* 'hermaphrodite'. (In Scandinavian there are several different compounds for this concept; see Hellquist 1922: *tve-* 1.) Cf. also Mod. HG dialectal *zwister* 'hermaphrodite'.
521b. We may note here that OEngl. *þrimen*, OFr. *thrimine* is not a suffixed form; it is a compound **þri-minnizi-* 'consisting of a quantity three times smaller'; see van Helten (1894: 330) Buma (1949: 280). OFr. *thrim(e)nath* 'one-third' is formed from it, by means of the suffix PGmc. *-oþu-*. Hence also *wêdnath* 'two-thirds', to *twêde* (15.4.13.). See Ahlsson (1960: 143–144).

522. Mod. HG *drilling* 'triplet' formed on *zwilling*. Mod. Dutch *drieling* – this and many other meaning, see Woordenboek der Nederlandsche Taal s. v. – is a recent *-ling-* formation on the cardinal. Cf. further Mod. Fr. *trijeling, trjilling* West (*tranling* East Moringen, Föhr and Amrum, *trenling* Sylt, reformed on *trane*, 15.3.3.1.).
523. Kluge (1926: § 138 ff.).
524. Cf. Rooth (1929: 33).
525a. Cf. Kluge (1926: §§ 89, 91).
525b. See note 518.
526a. See note 518.
526b. See note 518.
527. See Ståhl (1950).
528. See Sonderegger (1958: 81).
529. Witt (1912: 88).
530. This sense is due to the influence of Mod. Norw. *tulla* of the same meaning.
531. It is uncertain whether the word is masculine or neuter, for it only occurs as accusative singular *tweifl* (*Skeireins* 1834: 2, 14).
532. Old Saxon: derived adjective PGmc. **twifljа/ō-* > *twîfli* 'doubtful' and derived verb (see below).
533. Most of the corresponding Scandinavian words are borrowings from Low German: OSwed. *tvifl, tvifla*; Mod. Swed. *tvivel, tvivla*; ODanish *twivæl, twiflæ*; Mod. Danish *tvivl, tvivle* > *tvil, tvile*, with loss of *v* (Torp – Falk 1898: 225); Mod. Icel. *tvíla*; Færoese *tvílur* and *tvíl* neuter, *tvíla*, loan-word from Danish. Cf. also Mod. Norw. *tvil* 'doubt' and *tvila, tvela* 'to doubt, presuppose or be apprehensive about something'. Torp (1919: *tvil*) takes the Norwegian words as essentially from Danish, but suggests that the verb – and particularly its *-e*-form – may be in part from a PGmc. **twilōþ*; there seems, however no support for this form. (For other *l*-derivatives see 15.4.11.).
534. Kluge (1926: §§ 237–238).
535. Kluge (1926: § 239).
536. But Mod. Engl. '-some', as in *foursome*, noun – cf. *neynesom* 'group of nine' Morte Arthure (Brock 1865: v. 523) – is not of suffixal origin; it is merely the endproduct of constructions such as OEngl. *syxa-sum* 'one of six', i. e. 'with five others', in which OEngl. *sum* 'some' is the adjective. See OED: *-some*, suffix. Similar forms are found in Frisian; Mod. Fr. (West) *twaresom* 'with another person', *trijeresom* 'with two other persons', *fjouweresom* 'with three other persons', etc., are rather obscure; the *r* may derive from *fjouwer* 'four' and be extended to the other *two*; see Sipma (1948–1949: iii, 21 ff.) and, recently, Buma (1974: 93-4.2). There is a number of words, certainly derived from numerals, of which the precise morphology is uncertain; these are to be found, in the main, in the modern dialects. Cf., for instance the 'two'-forms, EDD: *tweag* Shropshire 'doubt', 'perplexity'; EDD:

tweagle Staffordshire 'doubt', 'preplexity', 'indecision'; EDD: *twiddick* Dorset 'a little twig'; EDD: *twifer* Norfolk 'a parting in two of the fibres of a root'; EDD: *twikle* Northumberland 'to walk awkwardly, as if with a twist in the legs'.

537. In Low German these two terms are used to denote the worthless cards "two" – "five" *twisten an dristen* Föhr and Amrum (borrowed from Low German); LG *de twischens un de drischens* (Mensing 1927–1935: i, 865); *twieschens und drieschens* (Teut 1959: i, 444); *twîsken un drîsken* Wangeroog (from Low German). These last are reformed on LG *esken, eschen* 'ace' (15.4.9.).

538a. Mod. Swed. *dräll* 'damask', early Mod. Danish *drell* 'figured linen'. (Mod. Danish *dreijl* by confusion with ODanish *dreil* < *dræghel* = Icel. *dregill* 'ribbon'.)

538b. See note 57c.

539. "Triligium, *þ*rielig hrægil" (Wright – Wülcker 1884: i, col. 279/3).

540. *ðrili* Corpus Glossary 29, *drili* Leiden Glossary (ed. Sweet 1885: 111–221; 158).

541. "Trilicis, þrylen hrægel" (Wright – Wülcker 1884: i, col. 151/34).

542. So, essentially, SND: *Tweed.*

Abbreviations

Language abbreviations

E	East	M	Middle
Engl.	English	Mod.	Modern
Fi.	Finnish	N	Norse
Fr.	Frisian	Nl.	Netherlands
Franc.	Franconian	Norw.	Norwegian
G	German	O	Old
Gmc.	Germanic	OCS	Old Church Slavonic
Gut.	Gutnish	OE	Old English
H	High	P	Proto
Icel.	Icelandic	R	Runic
IE	Indo-European	Sax.	Saxon
Ind.	Indic = Indian	Shet.	Shetlandic
It.	Italic	Swed.	Swedish
L	Low	W	West

Works cited

AB	The Language AB (d'Ardenne 1936)
Althochdeutsches Wörterbuch	Karg-Gasterstädt, E. – Th. Frings
ÆB	Molbech (1828)
Æthelstan	Liebermann (1903–1916)
Anglo-Saxon Gospels	See Sweet (1887)
Ayen.	Morris (1866)
Benediktinerregel	Steinmeyer (1916: 190–289)
Bremer Wörterbuch	Tiling (1767–1771)
Corpus Glossary	Sweet (1885: 35–107)
CP	Cura pastoralis (Sweet 1871–1872)
Cura Pastoralis	Sweet (1871–1872)
EDD	The English dialect dictionary (Wright 1898–1905)
EDG	The English dialect grammar (Wright 1905)
Festial	Erbe (1905)
Franck – van Wijk	Van Wijk (1912)
F. – v. W.	Franck's Etymologisch woordenboek der Nederlandsche taal (van Wijk 1912)
Hunsinger Codex	Hoekstra (1950)
Layamon	Brook – Leslie (1963–1978)
Language AB	d'Ardenne (1936)
Leiden Glossary	Hessels (1906)
Lind.	The Anglo-Saxon gloss to the Lindisfarne Gospels (see Ross 1937)
MED	Middle English dictionary (Kurath – Kuhn 1952)
Middelnederlandsch Woordenboek	Verwijs – Verdam (1885–1941)
Mittelhochdeutsches Handwörterbuch	Lexer (1872–1878)
Mittelhochdeutsches Wörterbuch	Benecke – Müller – Zarncke (1854–1866)
Mittelniederdeutsches Wörterbuch	Schiller – Lübben (1875–1881)
Morte Arthure	Brock (1865)
Notker	Piper (1895)
OEBede	Schipper (1898)
OED	The Oxford English dictionary
OEH	Old English homilies of the 12th ct. (Morris 1867–1873)
OEMart.	An Old English martyrology (Herzfeld 1900)
Ormulum	Holt – White (1878)
Pearl	Morris (1869)

Rit.	Rituale Ecclesiae Dunelmensis (Lindelöf 1927)
Ru[1], Ru[2]	Skeat (1871 – 1887)
Schönfeld – van Loey	Van Loey (1964)
SED	Survey of English dialects
SND	Scottish National dictionary
Svabo (ed. Matras)	Svabo (1966)
VP	Vespasian Psalter (Sweet 1885)

References

Periodicals

IF	Indogermanische Forschungen
KZ	Zeitschrift für vergleichende Sprachforschung auf dem Gebiete der indogermanischen Sprachen
LSE	Leeds Studies in English and kindred languages
NJb	Niederdeutsches Jahrbuch: Jahrbuch des Vereins für niederdeutsche Sprachforschung
NphM	Neuphilologische Mitteilungen
NQ	Notes and Queries (for Readers and Writers, Collectors and Librarians). London 1 – (1849 –)
NTS	Norsk tidsskrift for sprogvidenskap
PBB	(Paul und Braune's) Beiträge zur Geschichte der deutschen Sprache und Literatur
PMLA	Publications of the Modern Language Association
PPhS	Publications of the Philological Society
TsNTL	Tijdschrift voor Nederlandse Taal- en Letterkunde
TPhS	Transactions of the Philological Society
ZDA	Zeitschrift für deutsches Altertum
ZMaF	Zeitschrift für Mundartforschung
ZDPh	Zeitschrift für deutsche Philologie
ZRPh	Zeitschrift für romanische Philologie

References

Ahlson, Lars Erik
1960 *Die altfriesische Abstraktbildungen* (Uppsala: Almqvist & Wiksell).

d'Ardenne, Simone Rosalie Therèse Odile
1936 *An Edition of Þe liflade ant te passium of Seinte Iulienne* (*Bibliothèque de la Faculté de philosophie et lettres de l'Université de Liège, 64e fasc.*) (Paris: E. Droz) [²London: Oxford University Press, 1961 (*Early English Text Society 248*)].

Århammar, Nils
1968 "Die Herkunft des Inselnordfriesischen im Lichte der Wortgeographie", *Philologia Frisica Anno 1966* (Groningen: Wolters-Nordhoff).
1969 "Die friesische Wörter für 'Rad'", *Kopenhagener germanistische Studien* 1: 35–84.

Bartholomae, Christian
1890–1891 *Studien zur indogermanischen Sprachgeschichte* (Halle: Niemeyer).

Battisti, Carlo
1912 "Le dentali esplosive intervocaliche nei dialetti" (Beiheft *ZRPh*) (Halle: Niemeyer).

Benecke, Georg Friedrich — Wilhelm Müller — Friedrich Zarncke
1854–1866 *Mittelhochdeutsches Wörterbuch* 1–3 (Leipzig: S. Hirzel).
[1963] [Reprinted Hildesheim: Olms].

Bennike, Valdemar — Marius Kristensen
1898–1912 *Kort over de danske folkemål med forklaringer* (København: Gyldendal).

Berghaus, H.B.
1880–1884 *Der Sprachschatz der Sassen* 1 (Brandenburg: Müller), 2 and 3 (Berlin: Eisenschmidt).

Best, Richard Irvine et al. (eds.)
1954–1957 *The book of Leinster, formerly LEBAR na Núachongbála* 1–5 (Dublin: Institute for Advanced Studies).

Birch, Walter de Gray
1885–1899 *Cartularium Saxonicum: A collection of charters relating to the Anglo-Saxon history* 1–3 (London: Whiting and Co.).

Björkman, Erik
1900–1902 "Scandinavian loanwords in Middle English", *Studien zur englischen Philologie* 7: 1–193; 11: 194–360 (Halle: Niemeyer).

Black, W. H.
1845 *Robert of Gloucester, 1260–1300. The life and martyrdom of Thomas Becket Archbishop of Canterbury* (London: Percy Society).

Böhmer, J. D.
1836 *Codex diplomaticus mænofrancofurtanus. Urkundenbuch der Reichsstadt Frankfurt* 1 (Frankfurt/M: Varrentrap)

Bosworth, Joseph
1882–1892 *An Anglo-Saxon dictionary* (Oxford: Clarendon Press).
[1929, 1954] reprinted: Oxford: Oxford University Press.

Brandt, Carl Joakim
1865 *Kirkeårets Söndags-Evangelier* (*Dansk Klosterlæsning fra Middelalderen*) (København).

Braune, Wilhelm
1875 "Über die Quantität der althochdeutschen Endsilben", *PBB* 2: 125–167.

Braune, Wilhelm – Walter Mitzka
1967 *Alhochdeutsche Grammatik*[12] (Tübingen: Niemeyer).

Britton, G. C.
1961 "Alrediana IV: The *e*- and *u*- Diphthongs", *English and Germanic Studies* 7: 1–19.
1970 "Aldrediana XII: The *Æ – E*", *English Philological Studies* 12: 1–34.

Britton, G. C. – Alan S. C. Ross
1960 "Aldrediana X: Manifesta", *Anglia* 78: 129–168.

Brock, Edmond
1865 *Morte Arthure* (*Early English Text Society, Original Series* 8) (London: Trübner).

Brøndum Nielsen, Johannes
1927 *Dialekter og Dialektforskning* (*Acta philologica scandinavica 25*) (København: Schultz).
1950–1957 *Gammelsdansk grammatik i sproghistorisk fremstilling*[2] (København: Schultz).

Brook, George Leslie – Robert Frank Leslie
1963–1978 *Layamon, Brut* 1–2 (*Early English Text Society* 250, 277) (London: Oxford University Press).

Brouwer, Jelle Hindriks
1966 *Gysbert Japikcz wurken* 2 (Bolsward: Osinga).

Brown, Edward Miles
1891 *Die Sprache der Rushworth Gospels zum Evangelium Matthäus und der mercische Dialekt* (Göttingen: Dieterich).

Brugmann, Karl
1902 *Kurze vergleichende Grammatik der indogermanischen Sprachen* (Berlin: de Gruyter).
1907 *Die distributiven und die kollektiven Numeralia der indogermanischen Sprachen* (*Abhandlungen der königl. sächs. Gesellschaft der Wissenschaften zu Leipzig, Philologisch-historische Klasse*, 25: 3) (Leipzig: Teubner).

Brugmann, Karl – Berthold Delbrück
1897–1916 *Grundriss der vergleichenden Grammatik der indogermanischen Sprachen*[2] (Strassburg: Trübner).

Bülbring, Karl D.
1889 *Geschichte des Ablauts der starken Zeitwörter innerhalb des Südenglischen* (*Quellen und Forschungen zur Sprach- und Kulturgeschichte der germanischen Völker* 63) (Strassburg: Trübner).

Bugge, Sophus
1888 "Zur altgermanischen Sprachgeschichte: Germanisch *ug* aus *uw*", *PBB* 13: 504–515.
1905–1917 *Norges indskrifter med de ældre runer* (*Norges indskrifter indtil Reformationen* I) 1–3 (Christiania: A. W. Brøggers).
Buma, Wybren Jan
1949 *Die Brokmer Rechtshandschriften* (*Oudfriese Taal- en Rechtsbronnen* 4) (s' Gravenhage: Nijhoff).
1961 *De eerste Rüstringer Codex (Oudfriese Taal- en Rechtsbronnen 11)* (s' Gravenhage: Nijhoff).
1974 "Wurdsneuperijen, 50: Nijfrysk *trijeresom*", *Us Wurk* 23: 93–94.
Campbell, Allistair
1959 *Old English Grammar* (Oxford: Clarendon Press).
Carr, Charles T.
1939 *Nominal compounds in Germanic* (*St. Andrew's University Publications* 41) (London: Oxford University Press).
Cleasby, Richard – Gudbrand Vigfusson
1957 *An Icelandic-English Dictionary*[3] (edited by William A. Craigie) (Oxford: Clarendon Press).
Collin, H. S. – C. J. Schlyter
1827–1877 *Corpus iuris sueo-gotorum antiqui* 1–7 (Lund: Gleerup).
Collinder, Björn
1932–1941 *Die urgermanischen Lehnwörter im Finnischen* 1–2 (*Skrifter utg. av Humanist. Vatensk. Samf. i Uppsala*, 28.1, 34,3.) (Uppsala: Almqvist & Wiksell).
Cosijn, Pieter Jakob
1872 "De Oudnederlandsche Psalmen", *Taal- en Letterbode* 3: 25–48, 110–124, 257–270.
1873 "De Oudnederlandsche Psalmen", *Taal- en Letterbode* 4: 149–176.
1883–1886 *Altwestsächsische Grammatik* 1–2 ('s Gravenhage: Nijhoff).
Craigie, William A.
1931–1937 *Dictionary of the Older Scottish Tongue* 1– (Oxford: Oxford University Press) [1974] [Second impression: Chicago and London: The University of Chicago Press].
Dähnert, Johann Carl
1781 *Platt-deutsches Wörterbuch nach der alten und neuen pommerschen und rügischen Mundart* (Strahlsund: Struck).
Danneil, Johann Friedrich
1859 *Wörterbuch der altmärkisch-plattdeutschen Mundart* (Salzwedel: Schmidt).
Deutscher Sprachatlas
1927–1956 (Edited by F. Wrede – W. Mitzka – B. Martin) (Marburg: N. G. Elwert Verlag).

Dietrich, Ernst
1903 *Die Bruchstücke der Skeireins*, in: Friedrich Kaufmann (ed.), *Texte und Untersuchungen zur altgermanischen Religionsgeschichte* (Strassburg: Trübner) 2: 22.

Dobson, Eric John
1957 *English pronunciation 1500–1700* 1–2 (Oxford: Clarendon Press).

Earle, Johann – C. Plummer
1892–1899 *Two of the Saxon Chronicles parallel with supplementary extracts from the others* 1–2 (Oxford: Clarendon Press).

Ehrentreut, H. C.
1849 *Friesisches Archiv, eine Zeitschrift für friesische Geschichte und Sprache* 1 (Oldenburg: Schulzesche Buchhandlung).

Elliot, Constance O. – Alan S. C. Ross
1972 "Aldrediana XXIV: The linguistic pecularities of the gloss to St. John's Gospel", *English Philological Studies* 12: 49–72.

Endzelins, Janis
1944 *Altpreussische Grammatik* (Riga: Latvju Gramata).
1971 *Comparative phonology and morphology of the Baltic languages* (*Slavistic Printings and Reprintings* 85) (The Hague: Mouton).

Erbe, T.
1905 *Mirk's Festial: a Collection of Homilies by Johannes Mirkus*. (*Early English Text Society, Extra Series* 96) (London: Trübner).

Espersen, Johan Christian Subcleff
1908 *Bornholmsk ordbog. Med inledning og tillæag* (*Det Kgl. Danske Videnskabernes Selskab*) (København: Bianco Luno).

Falk, Hjalmar – Alf Torp
1900 *Dansk-norskens syntax i historisk fremstilling* (Kristiania: Aschehoug).

Falkman, Ludvig B.
1884 *Om mått ocht vigt i Sverige: historisk framstälning* (Stockholm: Förf).

Feist, Sigmund
1939 *Vergleichendes Wörterbuch der gotischen Sprache mit Einschluss des Krimgotischen und sonstiger verstreuter Überreste des Gotischen*[3] (Leiden: Brill).

Flom, George T.
1966 *Scandinavian influence on Southern Lowland Scotch* (Dissertation New York, 1900) (New York: AM Press).

Franck, Johannes
1910 *Mittelniederländische Grammatik mit Lesestücken und Glossar*[2] (Leipzig: Tauchnitz).
[1967] [Reprinted: Arnhem: Gysbers en Van Loon].

Friesen, Otto von
1934 *Rökstenen* (*Kungliga Vitterhets- Historie och Antikvitets-Akademien*) (Stockholm: Wahlström och Widstrand).

Frings, Theodor
1960 "Ingwäonisches in den Bezeichnungen der Zehnerzahlen", in: Klaas Dykstra et al. (eds.), *Fryske Stúdzjes oanbean oan Prof. Dr. J. H. Brouwer op syn sechstichste jierdei 23 augustus 1960* (*Fryske Akademy Publications* 180; *Studia Germanica* 2) (Assen: Van Gorcum), 7–39.
1984 "Ingwäonisches in den Bezeichnungen der Zehnerzahlen", *PBB* 8: 41–66.
Gabrielson, Arvid
1912 *The influence of w- in Old English as seen in the Middle English dialects* (Gothenburg – Leipzig: Eranos).
Gallée, Johann Hendrik
1903 *Vorstudien zu einem altniederdeutschen Wörterbuch* (Leiden: Brill).
1910 *Altsächsische Grammatik*[2] (edited by Johannes Lochner) (Halle: Niemeyer).
Gombocz, Zoltán – J. Melich
1914 ff. *A magyar nyelv etymologiai szótára* (Budapest: Magyar tudományos akad.).
Gradon, Pamela Olive Elisabeth
1962 "Studies in Late West Saxon labialization and delabialization", in: Norman Davis – C. L. Wrenn (eds.), *English and medieval studies presented to J. R. R. Tolkien on the occasion of his seventieth birthday.* (London: Allan and Unwin).
Grienberger, Theodor von
1897 Review of: Richard Loewe, *Die Reste der Germanen am Schwarzen Meere* (Halle: Niemeyer, 1896), *ZDPh* 30: 123–136.
Grimm, Jacob
1840–1878 *Weisthümer* 1–7. (Göttingen: Dieterich).
[1957] [Second edition: Berlin: Akademie Verlag].
Grimme, Hubert
1922 *Plattdeutsche Mundarten* (*Sammlung Göschen* 461)[2] (Berlin – Leipzig: de Gruyter).
Gustavson, Herbert
1918–1945 *Gotländsk ordbok på grundval av. C. och P. A. Säves samlingar* (*Skrifter utgivna genom Landsmålsarkivet i Uppsala* A. 2). (Uppsala: Almqvist & Wiksell).
Haan Hettema, Montanus de
1841 *Fivelgoër en Oldampster Landrecht. Een oudfriesch handschrift uit de 14de eeuw* (Workum: H. Brandenburgh en Zonen).
Hægstad, Marius
1900 *Hildinakvadet, med utgreiding um det norske maal paa Shetland i eldre tid* (*Vid. selsk. Skrifter* 2) (Kristiania: Dybwad).
1906–1942 *Vestnorske maalføre fyre 1350. (Innleiding; I Nordvestlandsk; II Sudvestlandsk. 1. Rygjamaal; 2. Indre sudvestlandsk, faerøymaal, islandsk, 1–4.). (Vid. Selsk. Skr. 2.* 1905. 7, 1907. 1, 1914. 5, 1915. 3, 1916. 4, 1935. 1, 1941. 1) (Oslo: Dybwad).

Hammerich, Louis L.
1937 "Über das Friesische", in: *Mélanges linguistiques offerts à M. Holger Pedersen à l'occasion de son soixante-dixième anniversaire* (*Acta Jutlandica* 9.1) (Aarhus: Universitetsforlaget, København: Levin & Munksgaard), 351–359.

Hamre, Håkon
1944 *Færoymålet i tiden 1584–1750* (*Skrifter utg. av Det Norske Videnskapsakademi* 2) (Oslo: Dybwad).

Heeroma, Klaas Hanzen
1939 "Ingwaeoons", *TsNTL* 58: 198–239.

Heinertz, Nils Otto
1912–1915 "Friesisches", *IF* 30: 303–388; 35: 304–336.

Hellquist, Elof
1948 *Svensk etymologisk ordbok*³ 1–2 (Lund: Gleerup).

Helten, Willem Lodewijk van
1890 *Altostfriesische Grammatik* (Leeuwarden: Kuipers en Wester).
1896 *Zur lexikologie des altostfriesischen* (*Verhandelingen der Koninklijke Akademie van Wetenschappen, Afdeling Letterkunde* 1.5.) (Amsterdam: Muller).
1900 "Zu den malbergischen Glossen und den salfränkischen Formeln und Lehnwörtern in der Lex Salica", *PBB* 25: 225–542.
1902 *Die altostniederfränkische Psalmfragmente, die Lipsius'schen Glossen und die altsüdmittelfränkischen Psalmenfragmente, mit Einleitung, Noten, Indices and Grammatiken.* 1: *Texte, Glossen und Indices* 2: *Die Grammatiken* (Groningen: Wolters) [Reprinted: New York: Johnson, 1969; Wiesbaden: Sändig, 1971].
1905–1906 "Zum germanischen Zahlwort", *IF* 18: 84–126.
1907 *Zur lexikologie des altostfriesischen* (*Verhandelingen der Koninklijke Akademie van Wetenschappen, Afdeling Letterkunde* n.s. IX) (Amsterdam: Muller).

Hench, Georg A.
1890 *The Monsee fragments. Newly collated text, with introduction, notes, grammatical treatise and exhaustive glossary* (Strassburg: Trübner).
1893 *Der althochdeutsche Isidor: Facsimile-Ausgabe des Pariser Codex* (*Quellen und Forschungen zur Sprach- und Kulturgeschichte der germanischen Völker* 72) (Strassburg: Trübner).

Henzen, Walter
1940 "Das Fortleben der alten schwachen konjugationsklassen im Lötschental", *PBB* 64, 283.

Hertzfeld, George
1900 *An Old English martyrology* (*Early English Text Society, Extra Series* 116) (London: Trübner).

Hessels, Jan Hendrik
1906 *A late eight-century Latin – Anglo-Saxon Glossary preserved in the Library of the Leiden University* (Cambridge: University Press).
Hoekstra, Jelle
1950 *De eerste en de tweede Hunsinger Codex* (*Oudfriese Taal- en Rechtbronnen* 6) (The Hague: Nijhoff).
Hofmann, Dietrich
1961 "Akzentverschiebung und Stammsilbenreduktion im Wurster Friesisch", *ZDA* 90: 303–322.
Holt, Robert – R. M. White
1878 *The Ormulum with Notes and Glossary of Dr. R. M. White* (Oxford: Macmillan).
Holthausen, Ferdinand
1886 *Die Soester Mundart. Laut- und Formenlehre, nebst Texten* (*Forschungen herausgegeben vom Verein für niederdeutsche Sprachforschung*, Band 1) (Norden – Leipzig: Soltau).
Hotzenköcherle, Rudolf
1971 "Historische und geographische Zahlwortprobleme im Schweizerdeutschen", in: Wolfgang Meid – H. M. Ölberg – Hans Schmeja (eds.), *Studien zur Namenkunde und Sprachgeographie, Festschrift für Karl Finsterwalder zum 70. Geburtstag* (*Innsbrucker Beiträge zur Kulturwissenschaft* 16) (Innsbruck: Kowatsch).
1961 "Zur Raumstruktur des Schweizerdeutschen", *ZMaF* 28: 207–227.
Hulme, Will Henry
1898 "The Old English Version of the Gospel of Nicodemus", *PMLA* 13: 457–542.
Indrebø, Gustav
1951 *Norsk målsoga. Edited by Per Hovda and Per Thorson* (Bergen: Grieg).
Jackson, Kenneth Hurlstone
1953 *Language and history in early Britain* (*Edinburgh University Publications, Language and Literature* 1) (Edinburgh: University Press).
Jansson, Valter
1936 "Räkneordet 'fyra'", in: *Bidrag till nordisk filologi tillägnade Emil Olson den 9. Juni 1936* (Lund: Gleerup).
Jellinek, Max Hermann
1926 *Geschichte der gotischen Sprache* (*Grundriss der germanischen Philologie*, 1.1.) (Berlin: de Gruyter).
Jensen, Peter J.
1927 *Wörterbuch der nordfriesischen Sprache der Wiedingharde* (Neumünster: Wachholtz).
[1967] [Reprinted: Wiesbaden: Sändig].
Jóhannesson, Alexander
1923 *Grammatik der urnordischen Runeninschriften* (Heidelberg: Winter).

Jónsson, Finnur

1925 *Det norsk-islandske skjaldesprog omtr. 800–1300* (*Udg. for Samfund til udgivelse af gammel nordisk literatur*) (København: J. Jørgensen & Co.).

Jordan, Richard

1906 *Eigentümlichkeiten des anglischen Wortschatzes* (*Anglistische Forschungen* 17) (Heidelberg: Winter).

1925 *Handbuch der mittelenglischen Grammatik* (Heidelberg: Winter).

Kahle, Bernhard

1908 *Die mittelniederdeutsche Urkunden- und Kanzleisprache Anhalts im XIV. Jahrhundert hinsichtlich ihrer lautlichen Verhältnisse untersucht* (Borna – Leipzig: Noske).

Karg-Gasterstädt, Elisabeth – Theodor Frings

1952–1968 *Althochdeutsches Wörterbuch: auf Grund der von Elias von Steinmeyer hinterlassenen Sammlungen im Auftrag der sächsischen Akademie der Wissenschaften zu Leipzig bearbeitet und herausgegeben.* (Berlin: Akademie Verlag).

1971 *Althochdeutsches Wörterbuch: auf Grund der von Elias von Steinmeyer hinterlassenen Sammlungen im Auftrag der sächsischen Akademie der Wissenschaften zu Leipzig bearbeitet und herausgegeben.*[2] Bearbeiter: Siegfried Blum, Sybille Blum, Heinrich Götz (Berlin: Akademie Verlag).

Karsten, Torsten E.

1943–1944 *Finnar og germaner* (Folkmålsstudier 9, 10) (Helsingfors: Akademiska bokhandeln).

Keller, Wolfgang

1925 "Skandinavischer Einfluss in der englischen Flektion", in: *Probleme der englischen Sprache und Kultur. Festschrift Johannes Hoops zum 60. Geburtstag überreicht von Freunden und Kollegen 80–87* (Heidelberg: Winter), 80–81.

Kluge, Friedrich

1926 *Nominale Stammbildungslehre der altgermanischen Dialekte*[3] (edited by L. Sütterlin and E. Ochs) (Halle: Niemeyer).

Kluge, Friedrich – Alfred Götze

1976 *Etymologisches Wörterbuch der deutschen Sprache*[2a] (edited by W. Mitzka, Berlin – New York: de Gruyter).

Kock, Axel

1891 "Zur Laut- und Formenlehre der altnordischen Sprache", *PBB* 15: 244–267.

Kögel, Rudolf

1879 *Über das Keronische Glossar. Studien zur althochdeutschen Grammatik* (Halle: Niemeyer).

Korenchy, É.
1972 *Iranische Lehnwörter in den obugrischen Sprachen*. Budapest. (Diss. in Hungarian: Budapest, 1971).
Kramer, Piet (ed.)
1965 *Minssen, Johann Friedrich: Mitteilungen aus dem Saterlande*[2], *fersuurged fon P. Kramer ätter de Aarhuser hondschrift* (*Fryske Akademy 270*) (Leeuwarden: Fryske Akademy).
Krapp, Georg Philip – Elliot van Kirk Dobbie
1936 *The Exeter Book* (*Anglo-Saxon Poetic Records* III) (London: Routledge, New York: Columbia University Press).
Kristensen, Marius
1928–1933 *En klosterbog fra Middelalderens slutning. (AM 76 8°)* (Udg. for Samfund til udgivelse af gammel nordisk literatur) (København: J. Jørgensen & Co.).
Krogmann, Willy
1952 "Friesische Relikte und Sonderentwicklungen", *ZMaF* 21: 106–116.
1954 "Amringisch *fi* > *si* in 'vier, feurig, föhren", *ZMaF* 22: 222–223.
1957–1967 *Helgoländer Wörterbuch* (*Akademie der Wissenschaften und der Literatur: Veröffentlichungen der Kommission für germanische Sprach- und Literaturwissenschaft* 1–5) (Wiesbaden: Steiner).
Kurath, Hans – Sherman M. Kuhn
1952 ff. *Middle English dictionary* (Ann Arbor: The University of Michigan Press).
Kyes, Robert L.
1983 *Dictionary of the Old Low and Central Franconian psalms and glosses* (Tübingen: Niemeyer).
Lange, Christian – Christoph Andreas – C. R. Unter
1904–1927 *Diplomatarium Islandicum* (Christiania: P. T. Malling).
Langenhove, George C. van
1925 *On the origin of the gerund in English* (Université de Grand: Recueil de travaux publiés par la Faculté de Philosophie et Lettres 56e fasc.) (Gand: Van Ryssenberghe & Rombaut/Paris: Eduard Champion).
Lasch, Agathe
1914 *Mittelniederdeutsche Grammatik* (Halle: Niemeyer).
[1974] [Reprinted: Tübingen: Niemeyer].
Lech, Gillis
1925 *Skånemålens böjningslära* (Lund: Blom).
Lexer, Matthias
1872–1878 *Mittelhochdeutsches Handwörterbuch* 1–3 (Leipzig: Hirzel).
Liebermann, Felix (ed.)
1903–1916 *Die Gesetze der Angelsachsen* 1–3 (Halle: Niemeyer).
Lindelöf, Uno
1901 *Wörterbuch zur Interlinearglosse des Rituale Ecclesiae Dunelmensis.* (*Bonner Beiträge zur Anglistik* 9, 105–220) (Bonn: Hanstein).

1927 *Rituale Ecclesiae Dunelmensis. The Durham Collectar. A new and revised edition of the Latin text with the interlinear Anglo-Saxon version.* (*Surtees Society* 140) (Durham: Andrews/London: Quatrich).

Lockwood, William Burley

1950 "Notes on the Faroese Language to-day", *TPhS* 1950: 88–111.

1955 *An introduction to modern Faroese.* (Copenhagen: Munksgaard).

Löfstedt, Ernst

1932 *Zwei Beiträge zur friesischen Sprachgeschichte* (*Lund Universitets Årsskrift* n.s. 1.2.) (Lund: Ohlsson).

1933 *Beiträge zur nordfriesischen Mundartforschung* (*Lund Universitets Årsskrift* n.f. avd. 1.29.2.) (Lund: Ohlsson).

1968 *Beiträge zu einer nordfriesischen Grammatik 1: Das Substantivum und das Adjektiv, das Zahlwort und der bestimmte Artikel* (*Acta Universitatis Upsaliensis: Studia germanistica Upsaliensia* 6) (Uppsala: Almqvist & Wiksell).

Loey, Adolphe van

1964–1965 *Middelnederlandse Spraakkunst* 1: *Vormleer*; 2: *Klankleer*[4] (Groningen: Wolters – Noordhoff/Antwerpen: De Sikkel).

Loewe, Richard

1916 "Die Anfügung von *-t* im Deutschen und das *e* von ahd. *einest*", *KZ* 47: 98–100.

Luick, Karl

1921–1940 *Historische Grammatik der englischen Sprache* 1.1–2 (Leipzig: Tauchnitz).

Mahlow, Georg Heinrich

1879 *Die langen Vocale A, E. O in den europäischen Sprachen. Ein Beitrag zur vergleichenden Lautlehre der indogermanischen Sprachen* (Berlin: Hermann).

Marwick, Hugh

1929 *The Orkney Norn* (Oxford: Oxford University Press).

Massmann, Hans Ferdinand

1841 "Gotthica minora", *ZDA* 1: 294–393).

Matras, Christian

1952 "Ljóđskrift i føroyskom av sama slag sum 'skerpingin' i frum norrønum og gotiskom. Frágreiđing fyri fyrst", *Fróđskaparrit* I, 177–180.

Mausser, Otto

1932 *Mittelhochdeutsche Grammatik auf vergleichender Grundlage* (München: Hueber).

1939 *Die Mundarten Bayerns: Registerband zu Schmellers Werk: Als Beitrag zu einer historischen Geographie der Mundarten Bayerns* (München: Hueber).

[1969] [Reprinted: Wiesbaden: Sändig].

Mensing, Otto
1927–1935 *Schleswig-Holsteinisches Wörterbuch* (Volksausgabe) (Neumünster: Wachholtz).
Möllencamp, Rudolf
1968 *Die friesischen Sprachdenkmäler des Landes Wursten* (*Sonderveröffentlichungen der Männer vom Morgenstern*) (Bremerhaven: Heimatverband an Elb- und Wesermündung).
Molbech, Christian
1828 *Den aeldste danske Bibeloversaettelse, eller det gamle Testamentes otte førske Bøger fordanskede efter Vulgata* (Kjøbnhavn: Andreas Seidelin).
Morris, Richard
1885 *Specimens of English literature, I: From 1150–1300* (Oxford: Oxford University Press).
1866 *The Ayenbite of Inwyt: or Remorse of Conscience* (*Early English Text Society, Original Series* 23) (London: Trübner).
1869 *Early English alliterative poems in the West-Midland dialect of the fourteenth century*[2] (*Early English Text Society* 1)[2] (London: Trübner).
Morris, Richard (ed.)
1867–1873 *Old English homilies of the 12th ct.* (edited by R. Morris/London: Trübner).
Morris, Richard – Walter William Skeat
1873 *Specimens of English literature, II: From 1298–1393* (Oxford: Clarendon Press).
Mossé, Fernand
1950–1959 *Manuel de l'anglais du moyen age des origines au XIVe siècle*[2] (Paris: Aubier).
Murray, James A. H.
1873 *The dialect of the southern counties of Scotland: Its pronunciation, grammar and historical relations, TPhS 1873* (London).
Napier, Arthur S.
1901 "The Franks Casket", in: *An English miscellany presented to Dr. Furnivall* (Oxford: Gay & B.), 362–381.
Neckel, Gustav – Hans Kuhn
1962–1968 *Edda. Die Lieder des Codex Regius nebst verwandten Denkmälern* 1. *Text*[4] 2. *Kurzes Wörterbuch*[3] (Heidelberg: Winter).
Nielsen, Niels Åge
1968 *Runestudier* (*Odense Studies in Scandinavian, Languages* 1) (Odense: Odense University Press).
Nordal, Sigurdur
1933 *Egils Saga Skalla-Grímssonar* (*Islenzk Fornrit 20*) (Reykjavík: Islenzka fornitafélag).

Noreen, Adolf
1892–1894 *Altschwedisches Lesebuch mit Anmerkungen und Glossar* (Halle: Niemeyer).
1904 *Altschwedische Grammatik. Mit Einschluß des Altgutnischen* (Halle: Niemeyer).
1913 *Geschichte der nordischen Sprachen*[3] (*Grundriss der germanischen Philologie* 4) (Strassburg: Trübner).
1923 *Altnordische Grammatik 1: Altisländische und altnorwegische Grammatik (Laut- und Flexionslehre) unter Berücksichtigung des Urnordischen* (Halle: Niemeyer).
[1970] [Reprinted Tübingen: Niemeyer].

Oakden, J. P.
1930 *Alliterative poetry in Middle English* 1–2 (Manchester: Manchester University Press).

Olson, Emil
1916 *De appellativa substantivens bildning i fornsvenskan. Bidrag till den fornsvenska ordbildningslärna* (Lund: Gleerup).

Osthoff, Hermann – Karl Brugmann
1878–1910 *Morphologische Untersuchungen auf dem Gebiete der indogermanischen Sprachen* 1–6 (Leipzig:S. Hirzel).
[1974–1975] [Reprinted Hildesheim/New York: Georg Olms].

Otfrid von Weissenburg
1831 (Handschriften kritisch herausgegeben von E. G. Graff) (Königsberg: Gebrüder Bornträger).

Ottmann, R. E.
1886 *Grammatische Darstellung der Sprache des althochdeutschen Glossars Rb* (Berlin: Weidmann).

Paul, Hermann
1901 *Grundriss der germanischen Philologie*[2] (Strassburg: Trübner).

Paul, Hermann – Walther Mitzka
1966 *Mittelhochdeutsche Grammatik*[19] (Tübingen: Niemeyer).

Persson, Pär
1912 *Beiträge zur indogermanischen Wortforschung* 1–2 (Uppsala: Akademiska Bokhandeln).

Piper, Paul
1895 *Die Schriften Notkers und seiner Schule* 1: *Schriften philosophischen Inhalts*, 2: *Psalmen und katechetische Denkmäler nach der St. Galler Handschriftengruppe* (*Germanischer Bücherschatz* 8–10) (Freiburg i. Br. – Leipzig: Mohr).

Pipping, Hugo
1922 *Gotländska studier. Inledning till studiet av de nordiska språkens ljudlära* (Helsinki: Söderström).

Pokorny, Julius
1959 *Indogermanisches etymologisches Wörterbuch* 1 (Bern – München: Francke).
Qvigstad, Just Knud
1893 *Nordische Lehnwörter im Lappischen* (*Christiania Videnskabs-Selskabs Forhandlinger* 1) (Christiania: Dybwad).
Ritter, Otto
1922 *Vermischte Beiträge zur englischen Sprachgeschichte* (Halle: Niemeyer).
Rooth, Erik
1929 *Nordfriesische Streifzüge,. Laut- und wortgeographische Studien mit einem Exkurs über den i-Umlaut der Velarvokale im Germanischen* (*Lund Universitets Årsskrift* 1.25.6) (Lund: Gleerup).
Rosenfeld, Hans-Friedrich
1956 "Die Elferzählung, ein niederdeutsches Zahlenproblem, zugleich ein Beitrag zur Volkskunde der Zahlen", *NJb* 79: 115–140.
1958 "Niederdeutsche Zahlwortstudien, 3", *NJb* 81: 59–103.
Ross, Alan S. C.
1932–1933 "Notes on some OE Words", *Englische Studien*, 67: 344–349.
1937 *Studies in the accidence of the Lindisfarne Gospels* (*Leeds School of English Language, Texts and Monographs* 2) (Leeds: Leeds University Press).
1951 *The essentials of Anglo-Saxon grammar with tables for Old English sound-changes* (Cambridge: Heffer).
1954 "Contributions to the study of U-flexion", *TPhS* 1954: 85–128.
1959 "Aldrediana I: Three suffixes", *Moderna Språk, Language Monographs* 3: 1–28.
1960 "Aldrediana VIII: A hitherto unnoticed Anglo-Saxon sound-change", in: Wolfgang Iser – Hans Schabram (eds.), *Brittanica, Festschrift für Hermann M. Flassdieck* (Heidelberg: Winter), 215–220.
1961a "Aldrediana XII: Observations upon certain words of the Lindisfarne Gloss", *Zeitschrift für vergleichende Sprachforschung* 77: 259–295.
1961b "Aldrediana XIV: Felle-Read", *NphM* 62: 1–22.
1967 "This in the Lindisfarne Gospels and the Durham Ritual: Aldrediana XVI", *NO* 212: 248–288.
1968a "Aldrediana XV: On the vowel of nominal composition", *NphM* 69: 361–374.
1968b "Aldrediana XX: Notes on the preterite-present verbs", *English Philological Studies* 11: 44–50.
1969 "Aldrediana XIX: On some forms of the anomalous and contracted verbs in the Anglo-Saxon glosses to the Lindisfarne Gospels and the Durham Ritual", *TPhS* 1968: 67–105.
1971 "Aldrediana XXIII: Notes on the accidence of the Durham Ritual", *LSE* 5: 53–68.
1973 "*I*- and *U*-adjectives in Germanic", *TPhS* 1972: 94–100.

Schambach, Georg
1858 *Wörterbuch der niederdeutschen Mundart der Fürstenthümer Göttingen und Grubenhagen oder Göttingisch-Grubenhagensches Idiotikon* (Hannover: Ruempler).
Schatz, Josef
1927 *Althochdeutsche Grammatik* (Göttingen: Vandenhoeck und Ruprecht).
Schiller, Karl – August Lübben
1875–1881 *Mittelniederdeutsches Wörterbuch* 1–6 (Bremen: Küthmann).
[1969] [Reprinted: Wiesbaden: Sändig].
Schipper, Jakob
1898 *Geschichte und Stand der gegenwärtigen Forschung über König Alfreds Übersetzung von Bedas Kirchengeschichte* (*Sitzungsberichte der kaiserlichen Akademie der Wissenschaften Wien*, 138.7) (Wien: Böhlau).
Schirmunski, Viktor M.
1962 *Deutsche Mundartkunde. Vergleichende Laut- und Formenlehre der deutschen Mundarten* [Aus dem Russischen übersetzt und wissenschaftlich bearbeitet von Wolfgang Fleischer] (*Deutsche Akademie der Wissenschaften zu Berlin: Veröffentlichungen des Instituts für deutsche Sprache und Literatur*, 25) (Berlin: Akademie Verlag).
Schirokauer, Arno
1923 "Studien zur mhd. Reimgrammatik", *PBB* 47: 1–126.
Schlüter, Wolfgang
1892 *Untersuchungen zur Geschichte der altsächsischen Sprache* 1. *Die schwache Deklination in der Sprache des Heliand und der kleineren altsächsischen Denkmäler* (Göttingen: Peppermüller).
Schmidt, Gernot
1970 "Zum Problem der germanischen Dekadenbildungen", *KZ* 84: 98–136.
Schmidt, Johannes
1889 *Die Pluralbildungen der indogermanischen Neutra* (Weimar: Böhlau).
Schönfeld, Moritz
1911 *Wörterbuch der altgermanischen Personen- und Völkernamen nach der Überlieferung des klassischen Altertums bearbeitet* (Heidelberg: Winter).
Schönhoff, Hermann
1908 *Emsländische Grammatik. Laut- und Formenlehre* (Heidelberg: Winter).
Schütze, Johann Friedrich
1800–1806 *Holsteinisches Idiotikon. Ein Beitrag zur Volkssittengeschichte* 1–4 (1–3: Hamburg: Villaume; 4: Altona: Hammerich).
Scottish National Dictionary
1946 (Edited by Will Grant) (Edinburgh: The Scottish National Dictionary association).

Seebold, Elmar
1968 "Ae. *twegen* und ahd. *zwene* 'zwei' ", *Anglia* 136: 417–436.
Sehrt, Edward Henry
1925 *Vollständiges Wörterbuch zum Heliand und zur altsächsischen Genesis* (Hesperia 14) (Göttingen: Vandenhoeck und Ruprecht [[2]1966, Göttingen: Vandenhoeck und Ruprecht]).
Sievers, Eduard (ed.)
1874 *Die Murbacher Hymnen* (Halle: Waisenhaus).
1875 "Kleine Beiträge zur deutschen Grammatik III: die starke Adjectivdeclination", *PBB* 2: 98–124.
1885 "Zur Rhythmik des germanischen Alliterationsverses. Erster Abschnitt", *PBB* 10: 220–314.
Siljestrand, K. K.
1890 *Ordböjningen i Västmanna lagen* (Liunköping).
Sipma, Pieter
1948–1949 *Ta it Frysk*. 1–3 (Utjeften fan de Fryske Akademy) (Leeuwarden: R. van der Velden).
Skeat, Walter William
1879 *Specimens of English literature III; from the 'Ploughman's Crede' to the 'Shepheardes Calender', 1394–1579* (Oxford: Clarendon Press).
1871–1887 *The Gospels according to Saint Matthew (Saint Mark, etc.) in Anglo-Saxon, Northumbrian, and Old Mercian versions* 1–4 (Cambridge: Cambridge University Press).
Skeireins Aivaggeljons thairh Johannen
1834 Auslegung des Evangelii Johannis in Gothischer Sprache (edited by F. Massmann) (München: George Jaquet).
Smith, Albert Hugh
1933 *Three Northumbrian poems: Cædmon's Hymn, Bede's Death-Song and the Leiden Riddle* (London: Methuen).
1956 *English place-name elements* (*English Place-Name Society Publications* 25.1, 26.2) (Cambridge: Cambridge University Press).
Sommer, Ferdinand
1951 *Zum Zahlwort* (*Sitzungsberichte der Bayerischen Akademie der Wissenschaften, philosophisch-historische Klasse*) (München: Akademie).
Sonderegger, Stefan
1958 *Die Orts- und Flurnamen des Landes Appenzell* (*Beiträge zur schweizerdeutschen Mundartforschung*, viii (Frauenfeld: Huber).
Spenter, Arne
1963 "Das Lautsystem der Schiermonnikooger Mundart", *Philologia Frisica Anno 1962* (Groningen: Wolters – Noordhoff), 69–75.
1968 *Der Vokalismus der akzentuierten Silben in der Schiermonikooger Mundart* (København: Munksgaard).

Ståhl, Harry
1950 *Kvill och tyll: En studie över några i svenska ortnamn ingående ord med betydelse 'åmote, ågren', o dyl* (*Skrifter utgivna av Kungl. Gustav Adolfs Akademien* 20) (Uppsala: Almqvist och Wiksell).
Stanley, E. G.
1952–1953 "The Chronology of *r*-Metathesis in Old English", *English and Germanic Studies* 5: 103–115.
Steinmeyer, Elias von
1916 *Die kleineren althochdeutschen Sprachdenkmäler* (Berlin: Weidmann).
Steinmeyer, Elias von – Eduard Sievers
1879–1922 *Die althochdeutsche Glossen* (Berlin: Weidmann).
Steller, Walther
1928 *Abriss der altfriesischen Grammatik mit Berücksichtigung der westgermanischen Dialekte des Altenglischen, Altsächsischen und Althochdeutschen mit Lesestücken und Wörterverzeichnis* (Halle: Niemeyer).
Stevenson, Joseph
1839 *Anglo-Saxon and Early English Psalter.* (Surtees Society Publications 16) (Durham and London: Andrews).
Streitberg, Wilhelm
1896 *Urgermanische Grammatik. Einführung in das vergleichende Studium der altgermanischen Dialekte* (Heidelberg: Winter) ([3]1963, Heidelberg: Winter].
1914 "Zur gotischen Grammatik", in: *Festschrift Ernst Windisch zum siebzigsten Geburtstag* (Leipzig: Harrassowitz), 217–227.
1920 *Gotisches Elementarbuch* [5/6] (Heidelberg: Winter).
1965 *Die Gotische Bibel* 1: *Der gotische Text und seine griechische Vorlage mit Einleitung, Lesearten und Quellennachweisen sowie den kleineren Denkmälern als Anhang* [5] [[1]1908, Heidelberg: Winter]. 2: *Gotisch-griechisch-deutsches Wörterbuch* [4] (Heidelberg: Winter) [[1]1910, Heidelberg: Winter].
Svabo, J. C.
1943 *Glossar til færøske Visehaandskrifter*, ed: Christian Matras (*Samfund til Udgivelse af gammel nordisk Litteratur*, 60] (København: Gyldendal).
1966 *Dictionarium f,earoense. Færøsk-dansk ordbog* (ed.: Christian Matras) 1. *Ordbogen* (Københvn: Munksgaard).
Sweet, Henry
1871–1872 *King Alfred's West-Saxon version of Gregory's Pastoral Care.* (*Early English Text Society, Original Series* 45, 50) (London: Trübner).
1883 *King Alfred's Orosius* (*Early English Text Society, Original Series* 79) (London: Trübner).
1885 *The oldest English texts* (*Early English Text Society Original Series* 83) (London: Trübner).

1887 A Second Anglo-Saxon Reader, Archaic and Dialectal (Oxford: Clarendon Press).

Teut, Heinrich
1959 *Hadeler Wörterbuch. Der plattdeutsche Wortschatz des Landes Hadeln (Niederelbe)* 1 – 4 (Neumünster: Wachholtz).

Þorkelssón, Jón
1876 – 1899 *Supplement til islandske ordbøger* 1 – 4 (Reykjavík: E. Þórdarson).

Þórólfsson, Björn K.
1925 *Um íslenskar orðmyndir á 14 og 15 öld og breytingar þierna úr formálinu* (Reykjavík: Fjelagsprentsmidjan).

Tiling, Eberhard
1767 – 1771 *Versuch eines bremisch-niedersächsischen Wörterbuches. Herausgegeben von dem Bremischen Deutschen Gesellschaft* 1 – 5 (Bremen: Karl Tannen) (²1869, Bremen: Karl Tannen).

Toivonen, Y. H.
1955 – *Suomen kielen etymologinen sanakirja* (*Lexica Societatis Fenno-ugricae* 12.3) 1 – 7 (Helsinki: Suomalais-Ugrilainen seura).

Toller, T. Northcote
1921 *An Anglo-Saxon dictionary: Supplement* (Oxford: Clarendon Press).

Torp, Alf
1919 *Nynorsk etymologisk ordbok* (Kristiania: Aschehoug).

Torp, Alf — Hjalmar Falk
1898 *Dansk-norskens lydhistorie* (Kristiania: Aschehoug).

Torvik, Ingvald
1966 *Nynorsk grammatik*² (Oslo: Universitetsforlag).

Vendell, Hermann
1904 – 1907 *Ordbok över de östsvenska, dialekterna* 1 – 4 (*Skrifter utgifna af Svenska Litteratursällskapet i Finland* 71) (Helsinki: Mercator).

Verwijs, Eelco — Jacob Verdam
1885 – 1941 *Middelnederlandsch Woordenboek* 1 – 11 ('s Gravenhage: Nijhoff).

Vries, Jan de
1962 *Altnordisches etymologisches Wörterbuch* (Leiden: Brill).

Wadstein, Elis
1899 *Kleine altsächsische Sprachdenkmäler mit Anmerkungen und Glossar* (Norden — Leipzig: Soltau).

Walde, Alois
1900 *Die germanischen Auslautgesetze. Eine sprachwissenschaftliche Untersuchung mit vornehmlicher Berücksichtigung der Zeitfolge der Auslautveränderungen* (Halle: Niemeyer).

Walde, Alois — Julius Pokorny
1927 – 1932 *Vergleichendes Wörterbuch der indogermanischen Sprachen* 1 – 3 (Berlin — Leipzig: de Gruyter).

Wallenberg, J. K.
1923 *The vocabulary of Dan Michel's Ayenbite of Inwyt* (Uppsala: Appelberg).

Weijnen, Antonius Angelus
1962 "De t van tnegentig", *Mededelingen van de Nijmeegse Centrale voor Dialect- en Naamkunde* 2: 14–16.
1966 *Nederlandse dialectkunde*[2] (*Taalkundige Bijdragen van Noord en Zuid* 10) (Assen: Van Gorcum).

Weinhold, Karl W.
1883 *Mittelhochdeutsche Grammatik*[2] (Paderborn: Schöningh).

Wessén, Elias
1965 *Svensk språkhistoria. 1 Ljudlära og ordböjningslära*[1] (Lund: Blom).

Whitelock, Dorothy (ed.)
1930 *Anglo-Saxon wills* (Cambridge: Cambridge University Press).

Wijk, Nicolaas van
1912 *Franck's Etymologisch woordenboek der Nederlandsche Taal*[2] (Supplement by C. B. van Haeringen 1936] ('s Gravenhage: Nijhoff).

Wiklund, Karl Bernhard
1903 *Virittäjä* (Koebenhavn:).

Witt, Fritz
1912 *Beiträge zur Kenntnis der Flussnamen Nordwestdeutschlands* (Kiel: Schmidt & Klaunig).

Woeste, Friedrich
1930 *Wörterbuch der westfälischen Mundart* (ed.: E. Nörrenberg) (Wiesbaden: Steiner).

Wright, Joseph
1898–1905 *The English dialect dictionary* 1–6 (London: Oxford University Press).
1905 *The English dialect grammar* (Oxford: Henry Frowdy).

Wright, Thomas – R. P. Wülcker
1884 *Anglo-Saxon and Old English vocabularies* 1–2 (London: Trübner).

Wright, William Aldis
1887 The metrical chronicle of Robert of Gloucester[2] (Rolls Series 86) (London: Eyre and Spottiswoode).

Wüllner, Ludwig
1882 *Das Hrabanische Glossar und die ältesten baierischen Sprachdenkmäler* (Berlin: Weidmann).

Zachrisson, Rob. Eugen
1927 *The English pronunciation at Shakespeare's time as taught by William Bullokar. With word-list from all his works* (Uppsala: Almqvist & Wiksell).

Chapter 16
Balto-Slavonic

Bernard Comrie

16.0. Introduction

The present chapter is an account of the historical development of numeral forms in the various Balto-Slavonic languages; whether or not there was ever a period of Balto-Slavonic unity, there are some common developments in the Balto-Slavonic numeral system that justify discussing numerals in Baltic and Slavonic in one chapter, although it should not be forgotten that there are also striking divergences (e. g. the formation of the cardinals 'five' to 'nine'; see 16.1.5.). The chapter is concerned primarily with morphology, though syntactic questions sometimes arise in the discussion of the morphology, especially in view of the complex system of numerals in many of the Slavonic languages.[1] In most of the Balto-Slavonic languages numerals have also a reasonably complex morphology, with declension, apart from languages like Bulgarian, Macedonian and Serbo-Croatian that have lost declension (in this last only of some numerals) completely or almost completely.

The languages treated are all the modern literary languages in their historical development, together with the following extinct languages: Old Prussian (clearly a distinct language), Old Church Slavonic (a literary language from an earlier period), Polabian (clearly a distinct language) and Slovincian (usually considered a dialect of Polish, but with some very aberrant numeral forms), the last usually only where its numerals diverge significantly from Polish. In addition, dialect material has been included where it illuminates the historical material, or shows sharply divergent developments.

To avoid unnecessary repetition, (masculine) (human) animate accusatives that are the same as genitives have not been taken into account in giving morphological forms; thus Ru. nom.-acc. *odín*, gen. *odnogó*, is taken to include masculine animate accusative (= gen.) *odnogó*. For further discussion of these forms, see 16.2.

16.0.1. General notes and sources

This section gives some general notes on the languages and sources used, to avoid unnecessary repetition in the discussion of the individual numerals. Forms which are taken from these standard sources and are noncontroversial are quoted without reference in the text; for all other forms, the source is given. Wherever possible, forms are cited in standard orthography (or transcription, see Table 1, for languages using the Cyrillic alphabet), with comments on relevant details of pronunciation not noted in the orthography.

Table 1. Transcription of Cyrillic orthographies

а	a	й	j	ў	ŭ
б	b	j	j	ф	f
в	v	к	k	х	ch
г	g (Uk., Br. h)	л	l	ц	c
д	d	љ	ĺ	ч	č
ѓ	ǵ	м	m	џ	ǯ
е	e	н	n	ш	š
ё	ë	њ	ń	щ	šč (Bg. št)
є	je	о	o	ъ	" (Bg. ъ)
ж	ž	п	p	ы	y
з	z	р	r	ь	′ (Bg., Uk. ьо jo)
ѕ	ʒ	с	s	э	ė
и	i (Uk y)	т	t	ю	ju
і	i	ќ	ḱ	я	ja
ї	ji	у	u		

Nonpredictable stress is marked with an acute accent.

Baltic (Old Prussian, Lithuanian, Latvian): Endzelīns (1971), Stang (1966).

Old Prusian: Endzelin (1944). The only attested Old Prussian numerals are: cardinals 'half', 'one', 'two', 'both', 'three', 'ten', 'thousand'; ordinals: 'first' to 'tenth'; collective: 'both'; 'two' in compounds.

Lithuanian: *Lietuvių kalbos žodynas; Dabartinės lietuvių kalbos žodyans; Lietuvių kalbos gramatika*; Zinkevičius (1966) and Fraenkel (1962–1965). Tone and length are indicated according to the usual system: ` (short falling), ´ (long falling), ˜ (long rising), the last two replacing the macron on *ū*.

Latvian: Mühlenbachs (1923–1932), *Latviešu literārās valodas vārdnīca*, and Endzelin (1922). Tone is indicated according to the usual system, the diacritics replacing the macron: ` (falling), ˜ (level/rising), ˆ (glottalised). Current orthography has been followed in writing *o* rather than *uo*; open *e* is indicated by *ę*.

Slavonic. South Slavonic: Old Church Slavonic, Bulgarian, Macedonian, Serbo-Croatian, Slovenian; East Slavonic: Russian, Ukrainian, Belorussian; West Slavonic: Czech, Slovak, Polish, Upper Sorbian, Lower Sorbian, Polabian; Suprun (1969) has unfortunately not been available to me.

Old Church Slavonic: Vaillant (1964), Suprun (1961). Old Church Slavonic has been taken in the traditional sense of non-East-Slavonic manuscripts written before 1100, though other Church Slavonic forms have been cited as such.

Bulgarian: *Rečnik na sŭvremenija bŭlgarski knižoven ezik* (the orthography of this dictionary has been followed), Beaulieux – Mladenov (1950), Mladenov (1929) and Mirčev (1963).

Macedonian: *Rečnik na makedonskiot jazik*, Koneski (1966), Koneski (1965). In the Macedonian ordinals, the widespread use of the (late) Indo-European ordinal suffix *-t* should be noted, leading to many ordinals in *-tt* (cardinal *-t*) for *-t* (cardinal and ordinal) in other Slavonic languages.

Serbo-Croatian: *Rečnik srpskohrvatskoga književnog jezika*, A. Leskien (1914), *Pravopis hrvatskosrpskoga književnog jezika*, M. Stevanović (1954), P. Skok (1971–1974). Forms are quoted in the standard Latin orthography, with the usual indications of tone and length: ˵ (short falling), ` (short rising), ˆ (long falling), ´ (long rising); also ˉ (posttonic long vowel), ˈ (stressed vowel irrespective of tone). Standard (Štokavian) Serbo-Croatian has usually shifted the stress one syllable back, so Čakavian forms (without stress-shift) are often cited in discussing stress. Both Ekavski and Jekavski variants are given, the latter preceded by "Je" in brackets.

Slovenian: *Slovar slovenskega knjižnega jezika*, Pleteršnik (1894–1895), Svane (1858), Ramovš (1952). Tone and length are marked according to the following system: ` (short falling), ˆ (long falling), ´ (long rising); also ˈ for a stressed vowel irrespective of tone. For close *e o*, the symbols *ẹ ọ* are used, while *ə* is used for schwa. In accordance with the Slavonic tradition, the symbols *ь* and *ъ* are used equivalently to *ĭ* and *ŭ*, respectively, in other traditions.

In the East Slavonic area, isoglosses between numeral forms often fail to coincide with the linguistic boundaries. Particularly for the numerals 'five' to 'eighty' ('ninety'), Standard Russian has an archaic system close to Common Slavonic, while Standard Ukrainian has both this system and an innovating system with endings from the plural of the pronominal declension. This innovating system is common to East Slavonic (Russian, Ukrainian, Belorussian) dialects. The current Belorussian norm favours a system like that of Standard Russian, although forms of the innovating system are frequent in literature; these forms are cited in smaller type in *Hramatyka belaruskaj movy*.

Russian: *Slovar' sovremennogo russkogo literaturnogo jazyka, Russkaja dialektologija*, Vasmer (1950–1958), Borkovskij – Kuznecov (1965), Kiparsky (1963–1967).

Ukrainian: *Slovnyk ukrajins'koji movy; Ukrajin'sko-rosijs'kyj slovnyk*; Ivčenko, *Sučasna ukrajin'ska literaturna mova* (1962).

Belorussian: *Belorussko-russkij slovar', Hramatyka belarusskaj movy*, Karskij (1955–1956), which dates from before the development of a literary language, gives a comprehensive list of dialect forms.

Czech: *Slovník spisovného jazyka českého*, Vážný (1964), Havránek – Jedlička (1960). Some eastern Czech dialects have a numeral system closer to that of Standard Slovak, while some western Slovak dialects have a system closer to that of Standard Czech. The numeral systems of the standard languages differ considerably. A monograph study of the historical development of Czech numerals is now available in Basaj (1974).

Slovak: *Slovník slovenského jazyka*, Stanislav (1958), Pauliny et al. (1955).

Polish: *Słownik języka polskiego, Słownik poprawnej polszczyzny PWN*, Klemensiewicz et al. (1965). The Polish numeral system has departed considerably from that of Common Slavonic, though using basically Slavonic material; the forms recommended in *Słownik poprawnej polszczyzny PWN* have been taken as normative. Irregular stress is marked by a preceding stroke ('); the acute accent is used in older and regional forms to mark a close (originally long) vowel.

Slovincian, although usually considered a dialect of Polish, has some particularly aberrant numeral forms, especially for the tens, with a vigesimal system (see 16.1.12.2.1.), which merit special attention. Some of these forms are also found in other Kashubian dialects of Polish. Sources: Lorentz (1903, 1925), Hinze (1972).

Upper Sorbian: Völkel (1970), Šewc (1968).

Lower Sorbian: Muka (1911–1915, 1926–1928), Šwela (1952), Schwela (1906). Forms are quoted primarily from Šwela, which is in the current orthography; but forms which are absent from Schwela, and therefore probably neologisms, are indicated as such.

Polabian: Polański – Sehnert (1967), Suprun (1962). Forms are normalized according to Polański – Sehnert, except for discussion of individual variants.

16.0.2. Decimal and non-decimal systems

Over almost the whole of the Balto-Slavonic area, the numeral system is rigorously decimal. There are separate words for the units 'one' to 'nine', for 'ten', 'hundred' and 'thousand' (if the last two, or any of the other forms, were originally complex formations, this is no longer apparent in the historical periods). Other numerals are formed by multiplication (i. e. 'twenty' is 'two tens', 'three hundred', 'three hundreds') and addition (i. e. 'thirty-four' is 'three tens and four', with variations in word order and conjunction); within addition, the teens are formed differently from the higher numerals (and within the teens, Lithuanian has a different formation from Latvian and Slavonic). With the teens and tens (in some languages also the lower hundreds), the transparency of this system has been somewhat reduced by subsequent modifications. Thus we may say that Balto-Slavonic is characterized by a decimal system using multiplication and addition for the formation of numerals other than those provided for by the simple morphemes.

Within individual languages, however, there are deviations from this regular system, deviations that can be classified as follows: subtraction (e. g. 'nineteen' as 'twenty minus one' rather than 'nine over ten'); division (e. g. 'fifty' as 'half of a hundred' rather than 'five tens'); intermediate forms (e. g. 'twenty-five' as 'five between twenty and thirty' rather than 'five and twenty'); overcounting (by addition, e. g. 'twenty' as 'ten over ten' rather than 'two tens', or by multiplication, e. g. 'hundred' as 'ten tens' rather than the simple morpheme); numeral systems with non-decimal bases (e. g. 'nine', 'twenty', 'ninety'); and portmanteau forms (e. g. a completely separate word for 'forty'). These forms are illustrated below. In discussing deviations from the decimal system, it is important to ensure that the forms under discussion are strictly numerals (this is particularly true with non-decimal bases and portmanteau forms), rather than the names of units, often commercial units, restricted to counting certain kinds of goods. In Russian, for instance, there is a term *gross* 'one hundred and forty-four', but it is not part of a duodecimal system (attested nowhere in Balto-Slavonic), because it exists solely as a mercantile term, as a unit of measurement for certain goods. The same is true of Ru. *djúžina* 'dozen', which is much less used than its English counterpart, and does not enter into the formation of other complex numeral expressions. Non-decimal bases and portmanteau forms in Balto-Slavonic often have their origin in commercial usage, but they enter into our field of concern only when they assume general numerical use.

16.0.3. Nonal system[2]

There is some evidence from Latvian and East Slavonic (especially North Russian) of a nonary system, in the following expressions, found especially in folk-tales: Le *trejdeviņi* 'three times nine', also less dommonly *trîsdeviņi* 'three nines', both used in the sense of 'many'; Ru. *za trídevjat' zemél'* 'beyond three-nine lands', i.e. 'a long way away', and with the same meaning *v tridevjátom cárstve* 'in the three-ninth kingdom' (in Russian folk-tales these are sometimes replaced by *tridesjátyj*, i.e. 'three-tenth', apparently an innovation). Some further evidence for a nonal system in East Slavonic is provided by the special form *devjanósto* 'ninety' (see section 16.1.12.2.). The origin of this system, which is at best marginal in Latvian and East Slavonic, is unclear: it is not found in the other Balto-Slavonic languages, and there is no concrete evidence of a Finno-Ugric origin.

16.0.4. Vigesimal system

Indirect evidence for a vigesimal system is sometimes sought in the difference in formation of complex numerals between the teens and formations over 'twenty' in Balto-Slavonic, but this is more likely to reflect a difference in the productive morphological patterns at the times when the two formations were created: the higher numerals would be required primarily as a function of increasing numeracy, and it is not therefore surprising that lower, more essential formations should have rather different structures. Evidence for this is also provided by the Old Czech formation '*x* between the tens' for '*x* and twenty' (section 16.0.8.): this does not reflect a system of counting by thirties, but a gradual process of construction of the higher numerals.

In Slavonic the only direct evidence of a vigesimal system comes from the far west of the Slavonic area, and involves a loan from German: Sc.

štǟgă (for **štyga*), Pb. *stig* (see section 16.1.12.2.1.). In the Slovenian dialect of Rezija vigesimal forms are used in *trikrat dveisti* 'three-times twenty', *trikatdveisti anu deset* 'three-times-twenty and ten', *štirkat dveisti* 'four-times twenty', *štirkat dveisti anu deset* 'four-times twenty and ten'.[3]

16.0.5. Quadragesimal system

Portmanteau forms for 'forty' exist in East Slavonic (e. g. Ru. *sórok*), and in Serbo-Croatian and Slovak dialects (SCr. *mérōv*, Sk. *meru*),[4] see section 16.1.20.2. In East Slavonic, at least, the form *sórok* functions as a regular cardinal numeral, and occurs in coordinate numerals, for instance; however, it is isolated within the system, and there is no general quadragesimal system as such. (The expression *sórok sorokóv* 'forty forties' is not a general numeral expression, but refers specifically to the (alleged) number of churches in Moscow.)

16.0.6. Sexagesimal system

The rudiments of a sexagesimal system, using *kopa* 'batch of sixty', are found in some forms for the decads in Slovincian and Polabian (see section 16.1.12.2.1.).

16.0.7. Overcounting

Overcounting by addition is found in Pb. *disǫtnocti* 'twenty', literally 'ten-teen, ten over ten'.

Overcounting by multiplication is rather commoner. For 'hundred' Polabian has both *disǫ(t)dišǫt* 'ten-ty, ten tens' and *pǫtstid'ĕ* 'five scores'. Slovincian also has *pjĩnc štĩǵ* 'five scores'. For 'thousand', Polabian has *disǫt pǫtstid'ĕ* 'ten hundreds', or rather 'ten five-scores', since *pǫtstid'ĕ* is itself an instance of overcounting. Lower Sorbian has, for 'thousand', *źaseś stow* and *źaseś hundertow*, both 'ten hundreds', and continues this system with *jadnasćo stow* 'eleven hundred', *pěśnasćo stow* 'fifteen hundred', *jaden a dwaźasća stow* 'twenty-one hundred', etc.[5]

16.0.8. Intermediate forms

In Old Czech, and occasionally in Church Slavonic without any specific Moravian connections,[6] one finds the numbers between 'twenty' and 'thirty' expressed as 'x between the tens', for 'x and twenty', e. g. Old Czech 'twenty-two' as: *dva-mezi(d)cietma, dva-mezi-cítma, dva-mezcítma, dvamecítma*. In this last form it survives in the dialect of the Třeboň fishermen, also in a few other archaic expressions.[7] This is at best a rare construction type in Slavonic, and cannot be continued indefinitely up into the higher numerals, since it depends on the convention that 'between the tens' means 'between twenty and thirty'. It may provide evidence of a gradual elaboration of the numeral system into the higher numerals: first the teens, then the twenties by a different process, until finally a general procedure is adopted whereby higher numerals can be created indefinitely. In Old Czech one occasionally finds a generalisation of this pattern in numerals of the type *šestdesát mezi dvěma* 'sixty between two hundreds', i. e. 'two hundred and sixty'.[7a]

16.0.9. Division

Simple division is rare in the strictly numeral system of Slavonic, though it is found in USo. *połsta*, LSo. *poł sta, poł hunderta* 'half of a hundred', Sc. *pòu̯lkŭ̀o̤pä* 'half of sixty' and *pòu̯lstã* 'half of a hundred', Pb. *pöl-t'üpě* 'half of sixty'.

A formation that is characteristic of Balto-Slavonic, however, especially in the earlier period, is the formation of vulgar fractions of the type $x\frac{1}{2}$ by division, i. e. $x\frac{1}{2}$ is expressed as 'half of the $(x + 1)$th'; see section 16.5.2. Complex numerals can also be formed on the same pattern, e. g. 'twenty-five' as 'half of the third ten', 'one hundred and fifty' as 'half of the second hundred', and such formations were the only possibilities in Slovincian for some of the tens (see section 16.1.12.2.1.).

16.0.10. Subtraction

Subtractive numerals are not found in any of the modern standard languages, although subtractive formations are attested, sporadically, in earlier periods and in nonstandard usage. Thus in Old Czech one finds instead of 'nine plus x tens' the formation '(x plus one) tens minus one',

e. g. for 'nineteen': *bez jednoho dvadcěti* 'without one twenty', *dvadcěti bez jednoho* 'twenty without one', *dvadcěti méně jednoho* 'twenty less (of) one'. Similar forms are found in nonstandard Lower Sorbian: *poł hunderta měńej jadnogo* 'half of a hundred less (of) one', i. e. 'forty-nine', *hundert měńej šesćich* 'a hundred less (of) six', i. e. 'ninety-four'.

16.1. Cardinal and ordinal numerals

The appearance of numerals for 'zero' is a recent phenomenon in the Balto-Slavonic languages, as elsewhere in Europe, and is intimately tied up with the increasing use of the Arabic system for writing numerals. Most of the Balto-Slavonic languages use derivatives of Latin *nullus* 'none', via French *nul*, German *Null*, even Swedish *noll* (in Russian); as the word is an internationalism, the precise developments are difficult to trace. Except where specified, declension is as for a noun; note that the gender varies from language to language:

Li. *nùlis* (masc.); Le. *nul̃le* (fem.); Bg. *núla*; Ma. *nula*; Scr. *nȕla*; Sn. *nìč* (indeclinable) or *níčla*, cp. the negative adjective-pronoun *nìč* 'nothing', nonstandard also *núla*;[8] Ru. *nol′*, gen. *noljá* (from Swedish *noll*), and *nul′*, gen. *nuljá* (from German *Null*);[9] Uk. *nul′*, gen. *nuljá*; Br. *nul′*, gen. *nuljá*; Cz. *nula*; Sk. *nula*; Po. *zero*, another internationalism (French *zéro*, Italian *zero*), deriving ultimately from Arabic *ṣifr* 'zero'; USo. *nula*.

Ordinal forms for 'zero' as such are rare, though some languages use adjectival derivatives in such expressions as 'zero hour' ('the zero-th hour'), 'zero-th degree' (cf. 'first degree'): Li. *nùlinis*; Le. *nul̃les* (the sg. gen. of *nul̃le*, therefore not declinable further); Bg. *núlev*; Ma. *nulev*; SCr. *nȕltī* (with the ordinal-forming suffix *-t*); Ru. *nolevój* and *nulevój*; Uk. *nuljovýj*; Br. *nuljavý*; Cz. *nultý* (ordinal *-t*); Sk. *nultý*; Po. *zerowy*; USo. *nulowy*.

16.1.1.1. 'One'

All the Balto-Slavonic forms derive from variants of IE **oi̯nos*, declined pronominally in Old Prussian and Slovenian (cf. 'two', 'three', 'four') and adjectivally in Lithuanian and Latvian (cf. the reformed declension of the numerals from 'four' on). The simplest form to explain is OPr. *ains*, with B-Sl. **a* for IE **o*. Sporadic spellings with *ei-* are probably scribal errors.[10]

Li. *víenas* and Le. *viêns* show parallel development, though the precise development is unclear. The vowel *ie* probably derives, in Lithuanian-Latvian, from both **ai* and **ei*, under conditions that are not clear,[11] but Li. *vičveĩnelis* 'a single' points to **ei*, in agreement with Slavonic rather than Old Prussian, and representing an Indo-European ablaut variant **e̯inos*. No satisfactory explanation has been offered for the prothetic *v*-. Phonetic prothetic *v*- is found sporadically in some Lithuanian dialects, but this would hardly explain the spread of prothetic *v*- here throughout Lithuanian-Latvian. Various suggestions concerning a possible prefix (**u*-, **u̯ē̆*-, **u̯i*-) are discussed by Endzelin.[12] The acute tone of the root vowel agrees with Slavonic, in particular Serbo-Croatian *ȉn, ȉno* 'other'.

In Slavonic, the simple form **ein*- survives only with shifted meaning, as 'other', e. g. SCr. *ȉn*, and in some compound words with the meaning 'one', e. g. OCS *inorogъ* 'unicorn'. Elsewhere, a prefix *ed-, jed-, od-* is added. The stem vowel *i* derives naturally from IE **ei̯*; whether Sl. **i* can derive from IE **oi̯* under acute intonation is dubious.[13] The prefix CSl. **ed*- is not fully clear in origin, though its probable meaning was 'only', cf. **(j)edъva* 'scarcely'. In Slavonic, initial **e* and **je* are not distinguished, most languages having *je*, although *e* is usual in much of Bulgarian and most of Macedonian, sporadically also in the rest of South Slavonic and even in Slovak; Old Church Slavonic spelling is not clear with the letter *e* (which can represent *e* or *je*), but there are also unambiguous spellings with the letter *je*, possibly both forms being possible, as in modern South Slavonic. In East Slavonic, initial **(j)e* sometimes shifts to *o*, the conditions perhaps being when stressed or immediately pretonic and before a front vowel;[14] at any rate, these conditions are satisfied in **(j)edín*-, giving ORu. *odín*-. Initial *o* (for general Sl. *(j)e*) is found in some words even outside East Slavonic; cf. perhaps Bg. dial. *adín*. Russian has numerous loans from Church Slavonic with initial *ed*-.

The vowel *i* is usual in all forms of this numeral in Old Church Slavonic, though in the Codex Suprasliensis forms other than the nominative-accusative singular masculine usually have *(j)edn-, (j)ed'n*-, and of the modern languages only East Slavonic and Bulgarian (some dialects and the standard language) retain the *i*, and then only in the nominative-accusative singular masculine, while Macedonian retains *i* in *edinaeset* 'eleven' (and in *edin* in some dialects). Derivatives of **edin*- are common in all Slavonic languages, e. g. Cz. *jediný*, Po. *jedyny* 'single' (the latter with *dy* for expected **dzi*, perhaps analogous to hard *d* in forms of *jedn*-). The usual assumption is that there was a Common Slavonic variant **edьn*-, probably as an allegro form, in those forms with stress on the flection in particular. This accounts without difficulty for Bulgarian dial. *edén* (for **edьnъ*, not **edъnъ*) and Ma. *eden*; in Serbo-Croatian, Slovenian and Czech the jers are not distinguished, so the forms give no evidence as to the jer. In West Slavonic, however, the evidence of the nominative-accusative singular masculine is rather for original *ъ: Po. *jeden* (not **jedzien*), Sk. *jaden* (with hard *d*), LSo. *jaden* (not **jeźen*), Pb. *jadån* (not **jad'ån*). Conceivably all of these represent analogical hardening, cf. the other flectional forms where the *d* would regularly be hardened before the *n* after the loss of the weak jer, also Po. *jedyny* noted above and *żaden* 'none', for older *żadzien*. Bulgarian and Macedonian, the only languages to have clear reflexes of *ь, do not retain palatalization (or never developed it) before front vowels, so there is no palatalization alternation to level out. Another possibility would be that the development of these forms postdates the Common Slavonic period, with different languages selecting different fill-vowels in the nominative-accusative singular masculine. This might account for USo. *jedyn* (if not a reflex of **jedinъ*, with analogical hardening), where *y* is common as a nonetymological fill-vowel (cp. *sym* 'I am' for **(je)smь)*. In this respect, it is worth noting that in Old Church Slavonic, especially the Codex Suprasliensis, where *i*-less forms are found, the spelling is almost never with ь, but rather with the apostrophe or nothing. In some languages, and more frequently in nonstandard dialects, the resulting consonant cluster *dn* has been simplified to *n*, in Slovenian also in the prenominal forms of the nominative-accusative singular masculine *èn*.

For accentuation, the evidence is overwhelmingly for desinence-stress throughout in Slavonic. The declension is that of the hard pronominal declension; deviations in the individual languages are noted below, though not deviations that are common to the pronominal declension as a whole, largely as a result of the influence of the soft pronominal and compound adjectival declensions.

OCS *(j)edinъ*, stem *(j)edin-*, rarely *(j)ed(ь)n-*. Bg. *edín* (stem *edn-́*), in western dialects *edén*, dial. also *adín*. Ma. *eden*, dial. also *edin*, stem *edn-*. SCr. *jèdan*, stem *jèdn-*; the short rising initial stress has been generalized to trisyllabic forms, e. g. gen. sg. masc.-neut. *jèdnoga*, though the older oxytonic stress survives in dialects (*jednòga*, Čak *jednegȁ*). Sn. *édən*, before nouns contracted to *èn*, stem *én-*, declined as an adjective; the lack of prothetic *j-* before initial *e* is rare in standard Slovenian, but found sporadically in dialects; the long rising tone on an open vowel represents recent retraction from final stress.

Ru. *odín*, stem *odn-́*. Where there were etymological alternations between hard pronominal endings with the vowel *ě* and soft pronominal endings with *i*, the two sets are redistributed lexically in Russian, and *odín* takes the soft set, e. g. instr. sg. masc.-neut. *odním*; other distributions are found in dialects. In counting, the numeral is replaced by *raz*, literally '(a, one) time'. Uk. *odýn*, with regular coalescence of **i* and **y* to **y*, stem *odn-́*. The declension is that of the hard pronouns, now largely the same as the adjectival declension, but the genitive singular feminine has the alternatives *odnóji* and *odnijéji*, and the instr. sg. fem. *odnóju* and *odnijéju*, for pronominal (and adjectival) *-oji, -oju* only. In the nominative-accusative singular neuter, both the original pronominal *odnó* and adjectival *odné* are normative. In western Ukrainian dialects forms more similar to those of West Slavonic are found, e. g. *jeden, oden, jedyn, jiden* (with *i* for *ē*, originally in the oblique forms by compensatory lengthening).[15] Br. *adzín*, stem *adn-́*; in literature, alongside *adnój* (*adnóju*) the gen.-dat.-loc. sg. fem. *adnḗj* (instr. also *adnḗju*), cf. the soft pronominal declension, is also found.

Cz. *jeden*, stem *jedn-*. Sk. *jeden* (the *d* is hard), stem *jedn-*; the development of the strong jers is complex in Slovak, perhaps as a result of dialect mixing, though *e* is the usual reflex of both jers in the standard language, while in dialects *jedon* is also found. Po. *jeden*, stem *jedn-*. In standard Polish, the oblique endings are the same in pronominal and adjectival declensions, though some dialects distinguish them by reflexes of vowel length (short in pronominal, long in adjectival; some dialects have long vowels, i. e. adjectival in origin, throughout). Of the nominative-accusative forms, masc. *jeden* and neut. *jedno* are unambigously pronominal, nom. fem. *jedna* is ambiguous, while acc. fem. *jedną* is in origin adjectival, like the accusative singular feminine of all pronouns except *ten* 'this'; the pl. *jedne* is adjectival, as in other pronouns. USo. *jedyn*, stem *jedn-* (nonstandard *jen-*); the *y*-vowel has already been discussed. The hard pronominal and adjectival declensions differ only in the nominative-accusative, genitive and dative singular masculine and neuter; *jedyn* has here the pronominal endings except in the nom.-acc. sg. neut. *jedne*. LSo. *jaden*, stem *jadn-*, with characteristic development of **je* to *ja* before a hard consonant; the declension is that of the hard pronouns, which differs from the adjectival declension in the singular masculine and neuter. Pb. *jadån*, with *ja* for **je* as in Lower Sorbian, stem *jan-*, attested in nom.-acc. sg. neut. *janü* and loc. sg. fem. *jană*; the vocalism of the last form suggests, unusually, stem stress; the ending cannot reflect the Common Slavonic pronominal ending **oi* (or reduced **oj*), and is probably from the ending **ě* of the substantival declension. While initial *ja-* is expected in Lower Sorbian and Polabian, it also occurs, irregularly, in Sc. *jȁděn* and in some Kashubian dialects of Polish. This *a* could either be a sporadic incursion of the **je* to *ja* change found in Lower Sorbian and Polabian (i. e. the extreme north-west of Slavonic territory), or derive from the (equally irregular) *ji*-forms found in some other Kashubian dialects.[16]

16.1.1.2. 'First'

Both Baltic and Slavonic have formations based on the root **pr-*, cf. Germanic forms like Gothic *fruma* and, rather less close in formation, Latin *prīmus*. The Baltic forms are particularly close to those of Germanic, having the suffix **-mo*; the Slavonic languages have a different suffix here (**-v*).

The Baltic forms derive from **pr̥̄mo-*,[17] giving Balt. **pirma-*. OPr. *pirmas* is accompanied by several other morphological forms of the same word of rather unclear formation: nom. sg. fem. *pirmoi*, perhaps a definite adjective, cf. Li. *pirmóji*; nom. sg. masc. *pirmois*, perhaps analogous to the feminine definite form; accusative singular (all genders) definite *pirmonnien, pirmannien, pirmannin*; nominative singular masculine definite *pirmonnis*, perhaps analogous to the accusative definite form. The tone of Li. *pìrmas* reveals the original length of the syllabic sonant, cf. also those Slavonic languages (Serbo-Croatian, Slovenian) that retain the original length distinctions, or rather the length correlates of the original tone distinctions (acute = long, circumflex = short) on syllabic sonants. Standard Latvian has *pìrmais*, but as dialects show both *pir̃mais* and *pir̂mais*, no solid conclusions as to original tone can be drawn from the Latvian evidence.

The Common Slavonic form for 'first' is **pr̥̄v-*; apart from the **v*, this accords exactly with Li. *pìrmas*, including the front vowel realization of the syllabic *r*. For the *v* formative, the closest parallels are forms like Sanskrit *pū́rvaḥ, pūrvyáḥ* 'first, front'. In Old Church Slavonic, there is in general (at least orthographically, probably also in pronunciation, judging by the modern Bulgarian dialects) confusion of **r̥*, **ŕ̥*, **rъ* and **rь*, all of which are usually written *rъ*, giving OCS *prъvъ*. In modern Bulgarian both *rъ* and *ъr* occur as reflexes of all of these, though the eastern dialects and the standard language tend towards a distribution with *rъ* in closed syllables and *ъr* in open syllables, thus Bg. *pъ́rvi* (dial. also [rare] *prъ̀vńi*), short form *prъv* (dial. *pъrv*). The other South Slavonic languages retain syllabic *r* (though the usual Slovenian pronunciation is with prothetic schwa): Ma. *prv(i)*; SCr. *pȓvī*; Sn. *pȓvi*.

In East Slavonic **ŕ̥* gives *er*; in some Russian dialects, the development is rather to *ere* (Second Polnoglasie), and some such forms have been accepted into the standard language (sporadically), either in that form, or in the form *er′*.[18] The older Russian form was *pér′vyj*, and though the soft *r* is no longer retained in pronunciation, it prevented the development of *e* to *o*, giving modern Ru. *pérvyj*. Ukrainian and Belorussian differ from Russian in having an additional suffix *-š*, cf. the comparative adjective (and Polish), before which the *v* is lost: Uk. *péršyj*; Br. *peršy*.

Czech and Slovak both retain syllabic *r*. Cz. *první* (less commonly: *prvý*) has added the adjective-forming suffix **-ьn*, giving, as often in Czech, a soft stem adjective. Slovak retains simply *prvý*. In Polish **ŕ̥* gives *iř*, later *eř* (*erz*), with later hardening before the hard consonant to give *pierw-*, as in the adverb *najpierw* 'firstly'; the ordinal has an additional suffix *-š*, the suffix of the comparative adjective, to give modern *pierwszy* (often pronounced *pierszy*). The Sorbian languages do not have this formation, but rather adjectival derivatives of CSl. **perd-* 'before, earlier', with the adjective-forming suffix **-ьn*. Lower Sorbian has *prědny*, with regular metathesis of CSl. **er* between consonants. USo. *prěni* shows simplification of **dn* to *n* intervocalically, and also the common confusion of the hard and soft stem adjectives, as in Czech. The attested Polabian forms are *pară* (for **pŕ̥(v)-*) and possibly *vå parėjsă* 'formerly' (for **vъ pŕ̥vějьšě*); the reason for the loss of the **v* is unclear. The German loan *erstě* (Middle Low German *êrste*) occurs in the expression for 'first quarter (of the moon)'. The word for autumn, *preńă zajmă*, i.e. 'pre-winter' or 'first winter', may include an ordinal on the same pattern as Sorbian. Pfeffinger[19] says that the Polabians used the cardinals for the ordinals.

16.1.2.1. 'Two'

For IE **d(u)u̯ō* 'two', Balto-Slavonic presents reflexes both with and without the vowel of the first syllable: forms with *u* are found in Slavonic and Latvian, while forms without are found in Old Prussian and Lithuanian. The original inflection was that of the dual pronominal declension, but various modifications have taken place in the individual languages, as noted below.

The only attested Old Prussian form is *dwai*, which appears to have the nominative plural masculine ending *-ai*, suggesting a shift to plural declension in Old Prussian (cf. the discussion of 'both', section 16.1.2.3.); the only other possibility would be a fossilized nominative-accusative dual neuter (IE **du̯oi̯*).

The current Lithuanian forms are *dù*, fem. *dvì*, the latter for **du̯ai̯*; the former seems to continue **du̯ō*, and dialectally *duò* is still found: *dù* is a contraction of the latter, perhaps influenced by the *-u* ending of the accompanying dual noun. The declension is that of the dual pronominal declension, though as with all Lithuanian genitive and locative duals, the original dual endings are replaced by those of the plural: gen. *dviejũ*, dat. *dvíem*, instr. *dviẽm*; loc. masc. *dviejuosè*, fem. *dviejosè*. For the locative, various contracted forms, as for other plural locatives, are found in dialects; as elsewhere, the locative plural endings are originally those of the substantive declension (using *dviej-*, from the genitive, as stem), whence the gender distinction. An older locative form survives in *dvíejau(s)* 'by twos'.

The current Latvian form *divi*, declined as a plural indefinite adjective, or indeclinable, derives from forms with the vowel *u* in the first syllable. *Divi* in feminine use derives directly from **duvai*, with the feminine dual ending **-ai* developing regularly to Latin *i*, and the shift of *u* to *i* before a labial (probably originally only in forms with a following *i* too) found in several Latvian forms.[20] As a masculine, *divi* is either the feminine form generalized, or a form with the plural ending following the loss of the dual category; the latter is clearly how the form is analyzed in the modern language, cf. the declension and the separate feminine (plural) form *divas*. Whether traces of a masc. du. **divu* (for **duvō*) survive in dialectal *diu̯, divudesmit* 'twelve', remains doubtful. Traces of the *u* vowel of the first syllable are found in the Curonian forms *duj* and *du* (the latter a result of contraction). Forms without the vowel of the first syllable, as in Lithuanian, seem to underlie the forms *dū, do* (i. e. *duo*), cf. Li. **d(v)uo*.

The Slavonic forms derive regularly from IE **du̯ō*, giving CSl. **dъva*, fem. **du̯ai̯* and neut. **du̯oi̯*, giving CSl. **dъvě*. The declension is that of the dual of the hard pronominal declension, i. e. gen.-loc. **dъvoju*, dat.-instr. **dъvěma*. Final stress in the instrumental form (by Fortunatov's Law) is suggested by all the languages that retain reflexes of mobile stress, except for the aberrant Pb. *dvemă* (alongside expected *dvemo*). The tone of the nominative-accusative is more complex, as the number of possible shifts obscures the original stress and tone. Most languages shorten all final vowels of monosyllables, and the circumflex tone of SCr. *dvâ, dvê* (Je. *dvȉje*), Sn. *dvâ, dvệ̂* could be secondary (cf. Sn. *stộ̂* for **sъto*, and *tộ̂* for **to*, both with original short vowels). The claim that IE **oi* gives different reflexes according to tone (acute **i*, circumflex **ě*) is also dubious. Moreover, the evidence from other Indo-European languages (Sanskrit, Greek) is conflicting.[21]

The declension has been reformed to some extent in all Slavonic languages, except Czech, largely as a result of the loss of the distinct dual declension and the ensuing arbitrariness of the endings of **dъva* synchronically. The gender distinction masculine versus feminine-neuter is replaced by masculine-neuter versus feminine in Serbo-Croatian, East Slavonic and Polish; this gives the position in the standard languages, though other distributions exist in dialects, e. g. in Polish, where Silesian dialects have the old distinction masculine versus feminine-neuter, while some northern dialects have generalized the masculine form throughout. An important factor in this re-alignment is undoubtedly the use of neuter nouns in *-a* (genitive singular or nominative plural) with this numeral. Gender distinction is sometimes introduced into the oblique cases by generalizing the vowel distinction of the nominative-accusative throughout the paradigm, in Belorussian by generalizing the hard versus soft consonant distinction. Generalization of one vowel, at least in the oblique cases, is more widespread. Other influences have been the plural endings (gen.-loc. *-ch*, dat. *-m*, instr. *-mi*), the substantival (especially *o*-stem) declension, and the numeral 'three'.

OCS *dъva*, fem.-neut. *dъvě*, gen.-loc. *dъvoju*, dat.-instr. *dъvěma*; the isolated instr. masc. *dъvama* (Codex Zographensis, Luke 16: 13) has generalized the vowel *a* from the nominative, as in some of the modern languages. Bg. *dva*, fem.-neut. *dve*, masc. hum. *dváma, dvamína*, dial. *dvóica*. Ma. *dva*, fem.-neut. *dve*, masc. hum. *dvajca*. SCr. *dvâ*, fem. *dvê* (Je. *dvȉje*), indeclinable or gen. *dvájū*, fem. *dvéjū* (Je. *dvíjū*), dat.-instr.-loc. *dvàma*/*dváma*, fem.[22] *dvèma*/*dvéma* (Je. *dvjèma*/*dvjéma*). The vowel of the nominative-accusative is generalized to the other cases; the long vowel in the dative-instrumental-locative is late and analogical, cf. the unusual correspondence Ekavski *ē*: Jekavski *jē* (not *ije*). As elsewhere, there is one form for dative-instrumental-locative in the dual/plural, historically the dative-instrumental dual. In dialects one also finds *dvíju* (i. e. even in Ekavski dialects), *dvíma*, with the stem vowel of 'three'. Sn. *dvâ*, fem.-neut. *dvệ*, gen.-loc. *dvẹ́h*, dat.-instr. *dvẹ́ma*. All Slovenian dual genitive-locatives are replaced by plural forms, as here; the oblique endings are those of the pronominal declension.

Ru. *dva*, fem. *dve*, gen.-loc. *dvuch*, dat. *dvum*, instr. *dvumjá*. The *u* vowel of the genitive-locative has been generalized throughout the oblique cases, replacing the ORu. dat.-instr. *dvěma*; the *u* is not a regular contraction of **oju* in Russian, and probably derives from the substantival declension. The oblique endings are those of the plural, except for the (uniquely Russian) instrumental in *-mja*, apparently a contamination of du. *-ma* and pl. *-mi* (the vowel of the former, the soft consonant of the latter); dialects have other instrumental plural endings, here as elsewhere. Some dialects have generalized *o* rather than *u* in the oblique cases (cf. 'three', or the *o*-stem noun declension). Some dialects have generalized the hard versus soft consonant distinction of the nominative-accusative into the oblique cases, as in Belorussian. Br. masc.-neut. *dva*, gen.-loc. *dvuch*, dat. *dvum*, instr. *dvumá*, fem. *dzve*, gen.-loc. *dzvjuch*, dat. *dzvjum*, instr. *dzvjumá*. The forms differ from those of Russian by the retention of the dual instrumental ending, and the generalization of the hard versus soft distinction of the masculine-neuter versus feminine nominative accusative into the oblique cases. In literature forms more like those of Ukrainian are found: obl. *dvoch, dvom, dvomá*, fem. *dzvëch, dzvëm, dzvjamá* (with jakanie). In the period 1933–1957, the masculine oblique forms were normative for all genders. Uk. *dva*, fem. *dvi* (for **dъvě*), gen.-loc. *dvoch*, dat. *dvom*, instr. *dvomá*, with the vowel *o*, possibly from the substantival declension, throughout the oblique cases.[23]

Cz. *dva*, fem.-neut. *dvě*, gen.-loc. *dvou*, dat.-instr. *dvěma*. The forms continue Common Slavonic exactly, with contraction of **oju* to OCz. *ú*, modern *ou*, in the genitive-locative. In some older texts and in dialects a generalized vowel *ou* (Old Czech and dial. also *ú*) is found throughout the oblique forms, e. g. instr. *dvouma*, and plural endings: gen.-loc. *dvouch*, dat. *dvoum*, instr. *dvoumi*. A special masculine animate form *dvá*, with a long vowel as in the corresponding form for 'three', is found in some texts from the sixteenth century.[23a] Sk. *dva*, fem.-neut. *dve*, masc. hum. *dvaja*, gen.-loc. *dvoch*, dat. *dvom*, instr. *dvoma*. The oblique endings are those of the *o*-stem substantival declension. Old Slovak has gen.-loc. *dvú*, dat.-instr. *dvema*. Some dialects have generalized *ú* (*dvúch, dvúm, dvúma*), while some have separate feminine forms with reflexes of **ě* in the oblique cases: *dvjech, dvjem, dvjema*. Po. *dwa*, fem. *dwie*, masc. hum. *dwaj*, gen.-loc. *dwóch* (also *dwu*), dat. *dwom, dwu* (also *dwóm*), instr. *dwoma, dwu*, fem. also *dwiema*. The gen.-loc. *dwu* arises by regular contraction of **dъvoju*. Forms with the vowel *o*, also lengthened to *ó*, are from the *o*-stem substantival declension. The instr. *dwiema*, originally for all genders, is now restricted to feminine use (where *dwoma* is also possible), cf. the strictly fem. nom.-acc. *dwie*. The spread of *dwu* to dative and instrumental use is part of the general Polish tendency to syncretize the oblique forms of numerals. Over the history of the language, and in current nonstandard usage, other permutations are found, e. g. gen.-loc. *dwuch, dwoch*, instr. *dwóma, dwuma*. Within Sorbian, the Lower Sorbian forms are closer to the original system: LSo. *dwa*, fem.-neut. *dwě*, gen. *dweju*, dat.-loc.-instr. *dwěma*. The realignment of the cases (locative with dative-instrumental rather than with genitive) is common to all Lower Sorbian duals. The gen. *-eju* (not *-ěju*) is from the (originally soft) pronominal declension. USo. *dwaj*, fem.-neut. *dwě*, gen. *dweju*, dat.-instr.-loc. *dwěmaj*. The nom.-acc. masc. *dwaj* (not specifically masculine human, unlike similar forms in Polish and Slovak) has the ending *-aj* of other duals; the etymology of this ending is not clear (but see section 16.2.), but in Upper Sorbian it is not restricted to the numerals; the same final *-j* is found in the dat.-instr.-loc. *dwěmaj*. In nonstandard Upper Sorbian, a declension closer to that of 'three' is found: *dwejo, dwejoch, dwejom*, with the *e* vowel of the (originally soft) pronominal declension. Pb. *dåvo*, fem. *dåve*, continue regularly CSl. **dъvá*, **dъvě́*, with retention of jer in immediately pretonic initial syllables. Also recorded are the gen. *dåvüx* (for **dъvóch*), with the plural ending and the vowel of the *o*-stem substantival declension; and dat.-instr. *dvemă, dvemo*. The latter form derives regularly from **dъvěmá*, with loss of the jer because it is not immediately pretonic. The alternative *dvemă* is probably a specifically Polabian development: the reduced vowel of the final syllable suggests **dъvě́ma*, which both goes against the evidence of the other languages, and fails to account for the loss of the jer in the first syllable, i. e. is a late development.

16.1.2.2. 'Second'

Despite the apparent similarity of the Baltic and Slavonic forms for 'second' (compare Li. *añt(a)ras* and OCS *vъtorъ*), it is in fact dubious whether both can be traced to the same etymon, and they will be treated separately here.

The Baltic forms find close parallels in Sanskrit *ántaraḥ* 'other' and Germanic forms like Gothic *anþar* 'second'. Li. *añtras* is paralleled by the dialect form *añtaras*, retaining the older disyllabic stem as in Sanskrit and Germanic. It is not clear whether the shorter form represents an ablaut variant, or rather a sporadic contraction. Standard Latvian has the shorter form *òtrs* (dialectally also *õtrs*), though older texts give evidence of a longer form (*otar-*, etc.), especially in the nominative singular masculine (i. e. where the shorter form leads to an uncomfortable consonant cluster); *o* (i. e. *uo*) is the regular Latvian development of **an* before a plosive. Of the Old Prussian forms, nom. sg. fem. *antrā* and acc.

sg. masc. *āntran* speak for a contracted form, and it is possible that nom. sg. masc. *antars, anters* (also dat. sg. masc. *antersmu*) reflects a pronunciation of the type *antr̥s*, for **antras* rather than **antaras* or **anteras*.

The oldest Slavonic form for 'second' is OCS *vъtorъ*, which survives in Bulgarian and Macedonian and, under Church Slavonic influence, in Russian, and survived also in Polabian. The other Slavonic languages have lost this word in the meaning 'second', though other derivatives of the root are sometimes retained. While it is tempting to try and link this to Baltic forms like Li. *añtras*, the evidence is against such an etymology: the hypothesis that Sl. **ъ* (with automatic prothetic **v-* in initial position) can derive from **n̥* is itself dubious,[24] and there is no solid evidence for an Indo-European zero-grade **n̥teros*, with the required syllabic nasal.[25] The closest forms to CSl. **vъtor-*, or perhaps rather **vъtor-*, with subsequent backing of the jer after **v* and/or before the following syllable with a back vowel, are Sanskrit *vítaraḥ* 'next, following', *vitarám* 'further'. Apart from the languages mentioned above, the ordinal for 'second' has been replaced by CSl. **drug-*, which in the languages that retain reflexes of **vъtor-* (and sometimes in those that do not) means 'other', and derives from the same root as **drugъ* 'companion, friend'.

The Old Church Slavonic form is *vъtorъ*, usually (if not always) kept distinct from *drugъ* 'other'. Bulgarian has *vtóri* (short form *vtor*), dial. also *dveḱi* for **dveti*, i. e. ordinal *-t* on cardinal *dve*;[26] Ma. *vtor(i)*. Both Serbo-Croatian and Slovenian have reflexes of **drug-*: SCr. *drȕgī*, Sn. *drúgi*. SCr. *ùtorak* 'Tuesday' contains the **vъtor-* stem. Ru. *vtorój* as a Church Slavonic form; in Old Russian we find *drugój*, which also survives in the formula *sam-drúg* 'with one other person'. The other East Slavonic languages do not have the Church Slavonic forms: Uk. *drúhy*, Br. *druhí*. The Russian and Belorussian forms suggest retention of original final stress, suggesting that the Ukrainian stress is a later development; this is confirmed by Cz. *druhý* with a short vowel, and is consistent with SCr. *drȕgī*, Sn. *drúgi*. The pattern is essentially the same as for the ordinals 'sixth', 'seventh', 'eighth' (see section 16.1.5.0.6.); final stress is also retained in Sc. *drä̂ʒí*. The West Slavonic forms are: Cz. *druhý*, Sk. *druhý*; Po. *drugi*; USo. *druhi*; LSo. *drugi*. In Polabian, *törě* occurs in the gloss to 'am anderen Tage', i. e. in the sense 'next' rather than strictly 'second', though it is a regular development of **(vъ)tor-*, with loss of the initial unstressed syllable and regular development of **o* to *ö* before a hard dental; *draug* (**drugъ*) occurs only in the meaning 'other'. Elsewhere in West Slavonic the **vъtor-* stem occurs for instance in archaic Po. *wtóry* 'second' and modern *wtórny* 'secondary', in Cz. *vteřina* 'second (of time)', with *er* as an ablaut variant, perhaps under the influence of the *or/er* alternation in collective numerals (see section 16.3.), and in LSo. *połtera* 'one and a half' (for **polъ (vъ)tera*).

16.1.2.3. 'Both'

Li. *abù*, Lavian dial. *obu* (short *o*), CSl. **oba*, correspond exactly, i. e. pre-Balto-Slavonic **abhō*. The second component, **bhō*, is widespread in Indo-European, usually with prefixal reinforcement (Gothic *baí*, Greek *ámphō*, Latin *ambō* (**ambh-bhō*), Tocharian B *ant-api*, Sanskrit *ubhā́u*). The Balto-Slavonic prefix (and preposition) (CSl. **ob*, which conflates IE **obhi* and **opi/epi*) corresponds to that in Greek and Latin.[27] For the original stress of this word in Balto-Slavonic there is conflicting evidence. Lithuanian has final stress (*abù*), whereas most of Slavonic has initial stress (Ru. *óba*, SCr. *ȍba*, Sn. *obâ* [for **òba*], Bg. dial. *óba*). However, final stress is also attested, though less widespread, in Slavonic: Ukrainian dial. *obá*, Belorussian dial. *abá*, Slovenian dial. *òba* (for **obà*). On the assumption that the nominative-accusative dual endings had acute tone, one would expect final stress, by Fortunatov's Law, since the stem vowel is short; thus the final stress is probably the older form, the initial stress a Slavonic innovation.[28]

Old Prussian nom. masc. *abbai*, acc. masc. *abbans*, both have plural inflections, cf., probably, *dwai*. Li. *abù*, fem. *abì*, declined like *dù*; there is also the form *abùdu*, fem. *abìdvi*, with declension of both parts, and in dialects forms with reduplication: *abùd(v)edu, abìd(v)edi*; in dialects also, with plural endings, *abìdveji, abìdvejos* (originally collectives), with invariable first component. Le. *abi*, fem. *abas*, is, like *divi*, now treated as a plural adjective; the old du. masc. *obu* (short *o*) survives in dialects, where one also finds compound forms like *abi divi* (both parts declined) and *aba-ivi*, with the bare stem as first component.

CSl. **oba*, declined like **dъva*; except where stated below, the declension is as for 'two'. OCS *oba*; Bulgarian dial. *óba*, though the standard language uses articled forms of 'two', i. e. *dváta, dvéte, dvámata*; Ma. (always articled) *obata*, fem.-neut. *obete*, masc. hum. *obajcata*. SCr. *ȍba*, fem. *ȍbe* (Je. *ȍbje*), gen. (rare) *obájū*, fem. *obéjū* (Je. *obíjū*), dat.-instr.-loc. masc.-neut. *ȍbama*, fem. (nonstandard also masc.-neut.) *ȍbema* (Je. *ȍ bjema*), and the compound form, with indeclinable first component, *ȍ badvā*, fem. *ȍbadvē* (Je. *ȍbadvije*), gen. *obadvájū*, fem. *obadvéjū* (Je. *obadvíjū*), dat.-instr.-loc. *obadváma/obadvàma*, fem. (nonstandard also masc.-neut.) *obadvéma/obadvèma* (Je. *obadvjéma/obadvjèma*). Sn. *obâ*, fem.-neut.

obę̑; there is also *obadvȃ* (*obȃdva*), fem.-neut. *obedvę̑* (*obę̑dve*), with both components or only the second component declined.

Ru. *óba*, fem. *óbe*, has completely refashioned the oblique cases: the current norm has masc.-neut. gen.-loc. *obóich*, dat. *obóim*, instr. *obóimi*, fem. gen.-loc. *obéich*, dat. *obéim*, instr. *obéimi*, but the gender distinction is an artificial introduction, and dialects have one or the other set for all genders; the forms are originally those of the collective numeral (with plural inflections) *óboi*, the vowel differences probably deriving from the difference between du. gen.-loc. **oboju* and dat.-instr. **oběma* (cf. also nom.-acc. fem. *obě*). The current Ukrainian forms are nom.-acc. masc. *obýdva* (first component invariable, and *-y-* as in Polish), fem. *obýdvi*, neut. *obóje* (originally a collective), and for the oblique cases forms of *obá*, which as nominative-accusative survives in dialects: gen.-loc. *obóch*, dat. *obóm*, instr. *obomá*, with *o* as in 'two'. In Belorussian, simple *abá* survives only in dialects, while the standard language has masc.-neut. *abódva* (with *-o-* either from the oblique cases, originally in dialects that have *o*-stem noun endings here, or as the usual connecting vowel in compounds), with invariable first component and the second component declined like *dva*, fem. *abédzve*, first component invariable, second component declined like *dzve*; variants as for 'two'.

Cz. *oba*; Sk. *oba*; Po. *oba*, also *obydwa* (invariable first component) and earlier *obadwa*; USo. *wobaj*; LSo. *wobej* (declined like a du. pronoun); Pb. *vibě/vübě*, also unclear *věbe*.[29]

16.1.3.1. 'Three'

IE **tre̯ies* has morphological forms with the full-grade of the stem suffix **ei̯* and with the zero-grade **i*, i. e. **tri-*. In Balto-Slavonic the full-grade is used in the nominative and genitive, the zero-grade in the other forms. The derivatives of the zero-grade **tri-* present few problems, but those of **trei̯-* are more complex: in Slavonic, all instances of heterosyllabic **ei̯* in fact give **ьj*, but there are few examples, and in all cases alternative morphological explanations are possible.[30] In Baltic, it is even more dubious whether IE **ei̯* can give **ij* rather than **ej*, and forms like Lithuanian-Latvian collectives in *trej-* (see section 16.3.) suggest that **ej* is the regular reflex. Forms like Li. *trijũ* are therefore problematic, and it must be assumed that the *i*-vowel here is the result of morphological analogy to the forms in *tri-*, the same being true, perhaps, of Slavonic. The declension of IE **trei̯es* is the same as the plural of an *i*-stem noun.

In Old Prussian, only the gen. *treon* is reasonably clearly attested in the place-name *Treonkaymynweysigis* 'trium villarum pratum'; the nominative may survive in the place-name *Triskaym*, if this is not a contraction of *Tristekaym*.

The current Lithuanian forms are: nom. *trỹs*, gen. *trijũ*, dat. *trìms*, acc. *trìs*, instr. *trimìs*, loc. masc. *trijuosè*, fem. *trijosè*. The nominative seems to represent a regular development, with contraction, of **trijes*. Gen. *trijũ* uses the same stem. The acc. *trìs* is an innovation, cf. the accusative plural of *i*-stem nouns, for older *trins, trįs* (IE **trins*); these older forms were also used as nominative, and it is possible that *trỹs* may, at least in part, continue such forms. The older locative is attested in the form *trisu*, the current form attaches the endings of the noun declension (whence the gender distinction) to the stem *trij-*. In dialects other forms from this stem are found (e. g. dat. *trijìms*, fem. *trijóms*). Dialects also show the influence of the declension of 'two', e. g. gen. *triẽj*.

The current Latvian forms are: nom.-acc. *trîs*, gen. *triju*, dat.-instr. *trim* (also masc. *trijiem*, fem. *trijām*), loc. *trîs* (also masc. *trijos*, fem. *trijās*). Nom. *trîs* parallels Li. *trỹs*, and has replaced the original accusative form. An older form for the dative-instrumental is *trims*, without loss of the final consonant; the alternative forms for the dative-instrumental and locative are formed from the stem *trij-*. Loc. *trîs*, as with similar forms in nouns, is an unclear Latvian innovation. In dialects dat.-instr. *trim* is also used as stem, giving: dat.-instr. *trimi(e)m*, fem. *trimām*, gen. *trimu*, loc. *trimos*, fem. *trimās*. *Trîs* also occurs as an indeclinable, and in nonstandard usage as *trîsi* with adjectival declension, cf. *divi, četri*, etc.

The Common Slavonic forms for 'three' are: nom. masc. **trьje*, fem.-neut. **tri*, acc. **tri*, gen. **trьjь*, dat. **trьmъ*, instr. **trьmi*, loc. **trьchъ*, with the same endings as pl. *i*-stem nouns. Nom. masc. **trьje* continues IE **treįes* (or **triįes*), the same full-grade stem gives gen. **trьjь*. Acc. **tri* continues IE **trins*, with the usual realization of *-*ins* in flections; nom. fem. **tri* is in origin the accusative (the original nominative was like the nominative masculine), as with all nominatives plural feminine; nom.-acc. neut. **tri* parallels Vedic *trī́*. The gender distinction is lost in all the modern languages except Slovenian; for the possibility of deriving current masculine human forms in the other languages from this form, see section 16.2.

Old Church Slavonic masc. *trije* (once only *tri*), fem.-neut. *tri*, acc. *tri*, gen. *trii* (*tri, trei*), dat. *trьmъ*, *tremъ*, instr. *trьmi*, loc. *trьchъ, trechь*. The vowel *i* in the nominative masculine and genitive represents the regular Old Church Slavonic development of the front jer before **j* (though spellings with *ь* also occur); in the dative and locative *e*, with vocalized strong jer, is in fact commoner than *ь*, and gen. *trei* also occurs. Bg. *tri*, masc. hum. *tríma* (analogical to *dvama*, i. e. *dva* + *ma* : *tri* + *ma*), dial. *tróica*. Ma. *tri*, masc. hum. *trojca*. SCr. *trî*, gen. *tríju*, dat.-loc.-instr. *tríma*, also indeclinable; the vowel *i* of the nominative-accusative is generalized throughout, and the oblique endings are those of the dual declension (cf. 'two'); in the older language dat. *trim*, with the original plural ending, is found. Slovenian masc. *trijẹ̑*, with neo-circumflex for older **trìje*, has the regular development of *ь to *i* before *j*; the oblique forms have the endings of the (originally soft) pronominal declension: gen.-loc. *trẹ́h*, dat. *trẹ́m*, instr. *trẹ́mi.*

In East Slavonic, the separate masc. nom. *trie* survives into the sixteenth century, as does the gen. *trej*, subsequently replaced by the locative, cf. the identity of genitive and locative plural in the pronominal declension. The current Russian forms are: nom.-acc. *tri*, gen.-loc. *trëch*, dat. *trëm*, instr. *tremjá*. In the instrumental the weak jer is irregularly developed to *e*, perhaps to avoid the consonant cluster, while the ending is as for 'two'; *trema*, with the dual ending, is the usual dative-instrumental form in Old Russian. Some dialects have the vowel *u* throughout the oblique cases (cf. 'two'), e. g. gen.-loc. *trjuch*; others have *i* from the (soft) pronominal declension, e. g. gen.-loc. *trich*. Uk. *try*, gen.-loc. *trjoch*, dat. *trjom*, instr. *trjomá*, with the vowel *o* in the oblique cases as in 'two' (Ukrainian does not have a general shift of *e* to *o* before hard consonants); the instrumental has the dual ending, cf. 'two'. Belorussian has, of course, hard *r* throughout: *try*, gen.-loc. *troch*, dat. *trom*, instr. *trymá*; in the instrumental, *ry* is the regular Belorussian reflex of **rь* between consonants.

The current Czech forms are nom.-acc. *tři*, gen. *tří*, dat. *třem*, instr. *třemi*, loc. *třech*. The retention of the old genitive, *tří* (by contraction from **trьjь*) is unique among the modern languages, though dialects also have *třech* (cf. the locative, as in the other languages). Old Czech has the distinct masculine form *třie*, and also instr. *třmi*, the current form having the consonant cluster broken by nonetymological *e*, which develops regularly in the other oblique forms from strong *ь. Dialects also have forms with the stem vowel *í* (of the compound adjective declension), e. g. dat. *třím*, and *o* (cf. the *o*-stem substantival declension), e. g. *třom*. Slovak has: nom.-acc. *tri*, masc. hum. *traja*, gen.-loc. *troch*, dat. *trom*, instr. *troma, tromi*, the oblique cases having the vowel of the *o*-stem nouns. Old Slovak has the distinct nom. masc. *tré* (contracted from **trьje*) and gen. *trí* (also *trech*); reflexes of **trьmi* are found only under Czech influence. Other instrumental forms attested are *trimi, trima, trema*; both dual and plural endings are normative in the current standard. Po. *trzy*, masc. hum. *trzej*, gen.-loc. *trzech*, dat. *trzem*, instr. *trzema*. The separate nom. masc. *trze* (i. e. *trzē*, by contraction from **trьje*) occurs rarely in Old Polish, in masculine human meaning; the gen. *trzy* (i. e. *trzȳ*) occurs into the fifteenth century. Older forms for the instrumental include *trzmi*,[31] *trzemi* (with irregular strengthening of the jer), *trzymi* (with analogical *y*, cp. the pronominal declension); the current form *trzema* has the dual ending, cf. 'two'. In Upper Sorbian, *o* from the *o*-stem nouns has been generalized throughout the oblique cases; in the nominative, the masculine human form *třo* continues **trьje*, with regular shift of final **e* to *o* in nominal (non-verbal) categories: nom.-acc. *tři*, masc. hum. *třo*, gen.-loc. *třoch*, dat. *třom*, instr. *třomi*. The Lower Sorbian forms are similar, except that in the non-masculine human forms the vowel *i* of the nominative-accusative is generalized throughout (and **ř* gives *ś* after *t* in Lower Sorbian): nom.-acc. *tśi*, gen.-loc. *tśich*, dat. *tśim*, instr. *tśimi*, masc. hum. nom.-acc. *tśo*, gen.-loc. *tśoch*, dat. *tśom*, instr. *tśomi*. The attested Polabian forms are nom.-acc. *tåri*, instr. *tåraimĕ*. The vowel of the first syllable, apparently continuing *ъ, is in fact analogical to the first vowel of *dåvo*.[32] The nominative-accusative (or more strictly, citation) form *tåri* presupposes a development from **tъre*, i.e. nom. masc. **trьje* (with contraction) rather than fem.-neut. **tri*, which would give **t(å)roi*, **t(å)rai*, cf. sections 16.1.11.3.3. and 16.4. The instrumental presupposes earlier **t(ъ)rimi*, with an analogical ending from the soft pronominal declension.

16.1.3.2. 'Third'

Balto-Slavonic, like some other Indo-European languages (e. g. Sanskrit *tr̥tī́yaḥ*) uses a double suffix in the ordinal 'third', with ordinal-forming *-t* followed by another suffix *-*ĭi̯o*-. The Slavonic forms derive from **tretii̯o*-, while the Lithuanian-Latvian proto-form has lost the first **i*. The root **tre*- is unusual, and is perhaps taken from the nominative of the cardinal **trei̯es*, before this was reformed to **trii̯es*.

The Old Prussian forms are: nom. sg. masc. *tīrts, tirts, tirtis*, dat. sg. masc. *tīrtsmu*, acc. sg. masc. *tīrtin*, nom. sg. fem. *tirti*, acc. sg. fem. *tīrtan, tirtin, tīrtian, tirtien*. The older forms seem to be masc. *tirtis, tīrtin*, fem. *tirti*, with a masculine *jo*-stem and a feminine *ē*- or *ī/jā*-stem. The vocalism of the first syllable has probably been influenced by *kettwirts* 'fourth'.[33] The form *tīrts* has been completely remodelled on the pattern of the ordinals from *kettwirts* onwards (cf. Bulgarian and Macedonian for similar developments in Slavonic). The Lithuanian form is *trẽčias* (for **tretjo-*), and is paralleled by Le *trešais* (with regular *š* for **tj*).

In Slavonic, the Common Slavonic form is **tretьjь*; this is the indefinite form, and the regular definite form would be **tretьjьjь*: reflexes of this are indeed found in Old Church Slavonic (e. g. nom. sg. masc. *tretьii*, nom. sg. neut. *treti(j)e(j)e*), but most of the modern languages have contracted the complex ending to simple *-i(jь)*, which in Bulgarian and Macedonian has been reanalyzed as the ending, rather than a stem-formative, giving a new short form *tret*. OCS *tretii*, also contracted *treti*; other forms from the stem *tretij-* are attested, e. g. gen. sg. masc. *tretijaago*, nom. sg. neut. *tretiee*. In Bg. *tréti*, short form *tret* (hard stem, i. e. fem. *tréta*, but dial. also soft, *trét'a*), the final *-i* has been reinterpreted as the adjective ending, giving rise to the nonetymological short form *tret*; similarly with Ma. *trét(i)*. SCr. *trȅćī* presupposes **tretjьjь*, contracted from **tretьjьjь*, with the usual contraction of the long adjective ending **ъjь/ьjь* to *ī*. In Slovenian the group *tj* that arises by contraction, as in Serbo-Croatian, is not simplified, leaving *trẹ́tji*. Ru. *trétij*, stem *trét'j-*, is declined as a possessive adjective, i. e. fem. nom. *trét'ja*, acc. *trét'ju*, neut. nom.-acc. *tret'e*, pl. nom.-acc. *trét'ji*; thus the stem derives from the Common Slavonic stem **tretьj-*. In the other East Slavonic languages the suffix of the nominative-accusative singular masculine has been reinterpreted as an inflectional ending, and the other forms amended accordingly: Uk. *trétij*, nom. sg. fem. *trétja*; Br. *tréci*, nom. sg. fem. *trécjaja*. In the form *sam-tretéj* 'with two others, threefold', Russian preserves a trace of original final stress on the ordinal, cf. the same stress in the Slovincian ordinal *třecí*; assuming that the final stress is original, the stress retraction must be of fairly recent date, cf. the ordinals 'sixth', 'seventh', 'eighth', and Slovenian *trẹ́tji* with neo-acute must be analogical (see section 16.1.5.0.6.). In all the West Slavonic languages the forms for 'third' behave as if they were from a soft stem **tret'-*: Cz. *třetí*, Sk. *tretí*, Po. *trzeci*, USo. *třeći*, LSo. *tśeśi* (with regular shift of **ć* to *ś*), Pb. *tritě* (with regular shift of **e* to *i*).

16.1.4.1. 'Four'

The Indo-European form most relevant to the Balto-Slavonic forms for cardinal 'four' is **k^{u}etur-*, cf. the Sanskrit 'weak form' *catúr-*. CSl. **četyre* suggests, unusually, a long vowel in the second syllable, the long vowel perhaps by analogy with the long vowel of the Indo-European form

k^{u}etu̯ō r-, as in the Sanskrit 'strong form' *catvā́r-* (there is also an Indo-European variant *k^{u}etu̯or-*, with short *o*). The original declension in Indo-European is of a consonantal stem (*r*-stem); this declension is preserved in part in the oldest Slavonic, but in Baltic only slight traces remain, and most of the modern languages have reformed the declension (in Baltic as a *jo/jā*-stem adjective, in Slavonic at least as an *i*-stem).

Current Li. *keturì* is declined as a *jo/jā*-stem adjective, e. g. nom. fem. *kẽturios*, although there is one survival of the original *r*-stem declension: the acc. masc. *kẽturis* (for *k^{u}eturn̥s*, cf. Sanskrit *catúraḥ*), although some dialects have even here the adjectival ending, *kẽturius*. The old locative survives in *keturíese* 'by fours', as in all the numerals 'three' to 'nine'. Dialects also have stress-shifted *kèturi*, and contracted *kètur*. Some dialects show loss of the second syllable, e. g. *kẽtrios* for standard *kẽturios*, perhaps to make this numeral disyllabic like its neighbours in counting (cf. the loss of the initial syllable in some Slavonic, where the second syllable is usually stressed).

Le. *četri* is declined as an adjective. The initial *č*, for expected **c*, is usually attributed to the influence of Sl. **četyre*; forms with *c-* occur in older texts, cf. also the ordinal *cę̄tur̃tais*. The vowel of the second syllable is lost in the cardinal, as in Lithuanian dialects, though some dialects show traces of the vowel in instr. *četuris, četuriem*, and even in the quality of the first vowel in dial. *čętri* (open *e*, i. e. originally the following vowel was not *i*); cf. also compounds of *četur-* in older texts, and the ordinal *cętur̃tais*.

In Slavonic, two forms of the root for 'four' are attested, **četyr-* and **čtyr-* (the latter in West Slavonic, except Polabian, and in Slovenian, though in Slovenian only in the cardinal; it may be further simplified, in pronunciation or nonstandard usage if not in the written standard, to **štyr-*). The latter is probably an allegro form, contracted to two syllables (cf. Baltic) because its neighbours in counting are also disyllabic in Common Slavonic, there being no concrete evidence for a Common Slavonic ablaut variant **čьtyre*. The declension is that of the plural of an *r*-stem noun, though as with consonantal stems generally the dative-instrumental-locative plural takes the endings of the *i*-stems (the instrumental plural in *-y* is not found for **četyre*), and in the later development of Slavonic the *i*-stem endings spread even further; Common Slavonic nom. masc. **četyre* (*k^{u}etūres*), fem. **četyri* (originally the accusative form, as in all feminine nominatives plural), neut. **četyri*, acc. **četyri* (*k^{u}etūrn̥s*, giving *-ins*, *-īs*), gen. **četyrъ* (*k^{u}etūrom*), dat. **četyrьmъ*, instr. **četyrьmi*, loc. **četyrьchъ*. In the modern languages, the gender distinction in the nominative is retained only in Slovenian; the other languages generalized the feminine-neuter form, except for Russian which generalizes the masculine form. In the nominative-accusative, the expected stress on **y* (by Fortunatov's Law) is found in the vast majority of the modern languages with free stress, except Bg. *čétiri* [34] and Pb. *citěr*, both with initial stress. In the oblique cases, desinence stress in East Slavonic is of recent provenance,[35] while the Serbo-Croatian gen. *četiríju* has analogical stress (and ending), contrast dat.-loc.-instr. *čètirma*; the older stress was on the **y*.

The Old Church Slavonic forms are those of an *r*-stem: nom. masc. *četyre*, fem.-neut. *četyri*, acc. *četyri*, gen. *četyrъ*, dat. *četyremь*, instr. *četyrьmi*, loc. *četyrechъ*; the dative and locative are only found with vocalized strong jers. The spelling *četyrь* in the genitive could be the general orthographic confusion of the jers, or analogical to the front vowels of the other endings (cf. Cz. *čtyř*). Bg. *čétiri* (older *čétire* is purely orthographical), masc. hum. *četiríma, četírma* (the latter with the same stress as in, e. g., Serbo-Croatian, and presumably Common Slavonic), dial. *četvórica*. Ma. *četiri*, masc. hum. *četvorica*. SCr. *čètiri*, usually indeclinable, though the older declension is: gen. *četiríju* (cf. *tríju*), dat.-loc.-instr. *čètirma*; an older dative is *četirim*, with the original plural ending and the vowel of the nominative-accusative generalized, and an older instrumental is *četirima*, again with the vowel of the nominative-accusative: modern *čètirma* could be a contraction of this form, rather than a direct reflex of **četyrьma*. Sn. *štírje*, fem.-neut. *štíri*, gen.-loc. *štîrich*, dat. *štîrim*, instr. *štîrimi*, is unusual among all modern Slavonic languages in retaining the gender distinction in the nominative (though the form *štírje*, for expected **štíre*, has been influenced by *trijệ*), and among South Slavonic languages in showing contracted **čt-* (simplified to *št-*), though in general Slovenian is the most 'western' of the South Slavonic languages, and the ordinal and collective numerals are in *čet-*. The oblique endings, as in the higher Slovenian numerals, are those of the adjective declension.

The current Russian forms are nom.-acc. *četýre*, gen.-loc. *četyrëch*, dat. *četyrëm*, instr. *četyr'mjá*; older forms are: nom.-acc. fem.-neut. *četyri*, gen. *četyrь* (not **četyrъ*, though even *četyrъ* occurs rarely, and could be the result of orthographic confusion of the jers, or of the influence of the other front vowel endings/forms with palatalized *r*), later *četyrej* (cf. *trej* for **trьjь*), finally replaced by the locative, which in the pronominal and adjectival declensions is the same as the genitive in the plural; dat. *četrma* (cf. *dvěma*; it remains doubtful whether modern *četyrëm* is a direct reflex of **četyrьmъ*, not attested in the older period, or an analogical innovation that happens to have the same form as the expected regular development); instr. *četyr'ma* (cf. *dvěma*), *četyr'mi* (the jer does not vocalize, being in weak position), with modern *četyr'mjá* as for *dvumjá*. Some dialects have generalized the vowel *u* (cf. 'two') throughout the oblique cases, e. g. gen.-loc. *četyrjúch*. Uk. *čotýry*, gen.-loc. *čotyrjóch*, dat. *čotyrjóm*, instr. *čotyrmá* show the usual Ukrainian development of *e* to *o* after a hushing sibilant, and as in the other numerals the oblique cases have endings from the *o*-stem nouns (except instr. *čotyrmá*, for **četyrьmi*). The Belorussian forms are similar, though the initial *ča-* is the result of jakanie, and all Br. *r*'s are hard: nom.-acc. *čatýry*, gen.-loc. *čatyróch*, dat. *čatyróm*, instr. *čatyrmá*.

Cz. *čtyři*, gen. *čtyř*, dat. *čtyřem*, instr. *čtyřmi*, loc. *čtyřech*, with retention of the distinct genitive form (though with *-ř* rather than *-r*, like the other case forms in the paradigm; older Czech also has the paradigm with the generalized stem *čtyr-*);[35a] older forms include: nom. masc. *čtyřie* (with the ending of *třie*, as in Slovenian; *štyre* and *štyře* still occur in dialects), gen. *čtř* (apparently an allegro form, cf. *čtrnáct* 'fourteen') and *čtyří* (cf. *tří*), and instr. *čtřmi* (cf. *třmi* and gen. *čtř*); other vowels are found before the endings in dialects, as in the other numerals, e. g. dat. *čtyřóm*. Sk. *štyry*, masc. hum. *štyria*, gen.-loc. *štyroch*, dat. *štyrom*, instr. *štyrmi*; in the oblique cases, apart from the instrumental, the *o*-stem noun endings are used; in the oldest Slovak the gen. *čtyr, štyr* occurs. Po. *cztery*, masc. hum. *czterej*, gen.-loc. *czterech*, dat. *czterem*, instr. *czterema*. The stem in Old Polish is *cztyrz-* (for **čtyr-* before a front vowel), which develops regularly to *cztérz-, czterz-*; the final hard *-r* of the stem, influenced by forms where the *r* hardens regularly before another hard consonant (e. g. *czternaście* 'fourteen'), subsequently replaces *-rz*. Older forms attested include: nom. masc. *cztyrze*, though only with human nouns; gen. *cztyr* (rare, usually replaced by the locative); instr. *cztyrzmi, cztyrmi, cztermi* (still in dialects), *czterma* (cf. *dwiema*): the current instrumental form *czterema* takes over the whole of the ending of *trzema*. USo. *štyri*, masc. hum. *štyrjo*, gen.-loc. *štyrjoch*, dat. *štyrjom*, instr. *štyrjoma*; LSo. *styri*, masc. hum. *styŕo*, declined like *tśi, tśo*. Lower Sorbian, like Polabian below, collapses **č* and **c* to *c*, i. e. **čtyri* > **ctyri* > *styri*. Pb. *citěr* (for **čétyr*, with loss of the final vowel) has initial stress (cf. Bulgarian), and unusually for West Slavonic retains the *e* vowel of the first syllable (presumably because it is stressed); the loss of the final vowel (cf. the forms for 'fourteen' and 'forty' in most Slavonic languages) makes the form disyllabic, like *dåvo* and *tåri*.

16.1.4.2. 'Fourth'

The Balto-Slavonic forms for the ordinal 'fourth' derive from the (late) IE **kᵘetu̯or̥-to-*, i. e. the stem **kᵘetu̯r̥-* (cf. **kᵘetur-* in the cardinal, where the following segment is a vowel, and so **u* rather than **r* is vocalized) with the ordinal-forming suffix **-to-*. The syllabic sonant, as usually (though not invariably) in Balto-Slavic after a dental, gives front vowel reflexes in those languages that do not retain the syllabic sonant.

OPr. *kettwirts* and Li. *ketvir̃tas* directly continue the Indo-European form; the tone of the Lithuanian form points to an original short syllabic sonant, i. e., in the same formalism as was used for 'first', **kᵘetu̯ŕ̥t-*. *Latvian has lost this formation, replacing it by cȩtur̃tais*, adding ordinal-forming *-t* to the stem of the older form of the cardinal **cȩturi*; in dialects the form *cȩtrutais*, with metathesis, occurs, and the form *cȩtortais*, once current in the written language, derives from dialects that regularly shift *ur* to *or* (i. e. *uor*).

The Common Slavonic form of the ordinal is **č(e)tvŕ̥t-*; for the development of Common Slavonic **ŕ̥*, see the discussion of 'first'. The forms in the individual languages are: OCS *četvrъtъ*; Bg. *četvъ̀rti* (short form *četvъ̀rt*; as elsewhere in Bulgarian, there is confusion between *rъ* and *ъr*, the distribution here avoiding the consonant cluster *-tvr-*); Ma. *četvrt(i)*; SCr. *čètvr̄tī*, where the long syllabic sonant suggests neo-acute; Sn. *četŕti*, with simplification of the group **tv* (dialectally [Rezija] this, and the higher ordinals, also occur with the suffix *-tn′i*, e. g. *šter-tn′i*);[36] Ru. *četvërtyj* which, unlike *pérvyj*, shows the shift of *e* to *o*, before the (presumably) hard *r*; Uk. *četvértyj*; Br. *čacvërty*; Cz. *čtvrtý*; Sk. *štvrtý*. The Polish forms require a more detailed discussion: CSl. **ŕ̥* is backed before a hard dental as part of the Lechitic przegłos, and in most of the Polish area the palatalization of the preceding consonant is lost, though it is retained in Kashubian and Slovincian (e. g. Sc. *čvjǻṛti̇̈*); the oldest Polish form is *cztwarty*, subsequently the initial consonant group is simplified by dropping the *t*; dialects that preserve reflexes of Old Polish long vowels have *czwárty*, suggesting, like Serbo-Croatian, neo-acute, i. e. an early shift (no Slavonic language presents final stress, cf. the ordinals 'fifth', 'ninth', 'tenth') from a later syllable onto the (originally short, cf. Lithuanian) syllabic sonant. USo. *štwórty*; LSo. *stworty*; Pb. *cit'ortě*, with przegłos of **ŕ̥* to *or* before the hard dental, with retention of the preceding palatalization, and the regular Polabian loss of the labial component of the consonant cluster **tv*, **t'v*.

16.1.5. 'Five' to 'ten'

In Indo-European, the cardinals 'five' to 'ten', unlike 'one' to 'four', were indeclinable, and declension in the individual Indo-European languages that have declension here is a later development. Both Baltic and Slavonic do in fact decline these numerals, though the precise line of innovation is different in the two groups.

16.1.5.0.1. Baltic 'five' to 'nine'

In Lithuanian-Latvian (the Old Prussian cardinals 'five' to 'nine' are not attested) these cardinals are transformed into adjectives, or more strictly follow the declension of *keturì*, itself an original consonant-stem adjective transformed (except for relic forms like acc. masc. *kẽturis*) into a *jo*/*jā*-stem adjective. For 'six' (Balt. **šeš*), 'seven' (**septin*) and 'nine' (**devin*), the adjective endings are simply attached to the older indeclinable cardinal form; for 'five' (Balt. **penke*) the final vowel is lost before adding the adjectival endings (in IE **penk*^{u}- functions regularly as the stem of **penk*^{u}*e* in derivation), while 'eight' (**aštō*) adds *-n* to the stem (cf. 'seven' and 'nine') before adding the adjectival endings.

16.1.5.0.2. Balto-Slavonic 'ten'

The formations for 'ten' are similar throughout Balto-Slavonic: there is a noun (Balt. **dešimtis*, Sl. **desętь*), in the oldest attested stages primarily an *i*-stem, but with clear vestiges of having been originally a consonantal *t*-stem (see section 16.1.10.1./2. for details), i.e. for IE **deḱm̥t-*. The traditional view[37] is that the Indo-European cardinal was **deḱm̥*, and the *-t* found in Balto-Slavonic is a noun-forming suffix; the only close parallels for 'ten' are the collective nouns Sanskrit *daśát-* and Greek *dekád-*, for **deḱm̥t-*, with secondary *-d-* for **-t-* in Greek, though the Slavonic formations 'five' to 'nine' and the Sanskrit collective *paṅktiḥ* 'group of five' are usually also adduced (see section 16.1.5.0.3.). The traditional view has been criticized strongly by Szemerényi,[38] who argues that there is no real evidence for **-t* as a collective noun suffix, and that indeed the suffix **-t* (whether in cardinals or ordinals) derives originally from false morphemic analysis of Indo-European **deḱm̥t* into **deḱm̥-t* because of the parallel form **deḱm̥*, probably originally the preconsonantal sandhi variant of **deḱm̥t*.[39] Under this analysis, which I follow here, Balt. **dešimt-* and Sl. **desęt-* simply continue IE **deḱm̥t*, with the addition of inflections from the nominal declension, i. e. originally as a consonantal *t*-stem, later refashioned (like nearly all consonantal stems in Balto-Slavonic) as an *i*-stem noun.

16.1.5.0.3. Slavonic 'five' to 'nine'

In Slavonic, the transformation of Indo-European 'five' to 'nine' has gone even further than in Baltic. The stems of cardinal and ordinal are the same, the cardinal being a noun of the *i*-declension, the ordinal declined as an ordinary adjective, e. g. CSl. **pętь* 'five', **pętъ* 'fifth'. The stem of 'seven' (**sedm-*, **sem-*) is in essence a direct continuation of IE **septm̥*, while 'eight' (**osm-*) has adopted the final *-m* of 'seven', probably originally only in the ordinal, a formation that is also found in Baltic (see section 16.1.8.1./2.); the other numerals have *-t* added to the Indo-European cardinal in both cardinal and ordinals forms (**pęt-* for **penkᵘ(e)*, **šest-* for **(k)seḱs*, **devęt-* for **neu̯n̥*). The traditional analysis links the Slavonic forms in *-t* (as cardinals) with Sanskrit *paṅktiḥ* 'group of five',[40] which then leads to the cardinal and ordinal having the same stem (irrespective of whether there is any relation between the *-t* that forms ordinals and the *-t* that forms collective nouns), drawing 'seven' and 'eight' into the same pattern. The traditional analysis again comes in for criticism from Szemerényi,[41] who argues that there is minimal evidence for collective nouns in *-t* in Indo-European, even less for collective nouns in *-ti* (only Sanskrit and Slavonic); moreover it is not clear, on the traditional analysis, why a different formation should have been chosen for 'ten' and for the lower numerals (in Sanskrit, apparently only for 'five'). This suggests that some other source should be sought for the origin of the pattern whereby cardinal and ordinal have the same stem in Slavonic. Szemerényi suggests 'seven' as the starting point, with the original cardinal **setь* (for **septm̥*) and ordinal **sedm-* (or perhaps **sem-*, see section 16.1.7.1./2.) influencing one another to give a new cardinal form **sedmь*, which, ending in **ь*, was then treated as an *i*-stem. Another possible point of departure would be 'ten', which in Slavonic was effectively an *i*-stem rather than a *t*-stem (the consonantal stem forms are most common in the formation of the teens and tens, a process that was fossilized before the earliest attested texts, elsewhere consonantal declension forms are much less common than *i*-stem forms, and for several cases only *i*-stem forms are attested, see section 16.1.10.1./2.); here, the cardinal stem is **desęt-*, and the ordinal stem is also **desęt-*, the former synchronically an *i*-stem, the latter a regular (*o*/*ā*-stem) adjective. Thus the *-t* of 'five', 'six', 'nine' would originally be that of the ordinal, transferred to the cardinal on the pattern cardinal stem = ordinal stem; since the ordinals for 'seventh' and 'eighth' have no ordinal *-t*, neither do the corresponding cardinals, a difficulty for the "collective noun" theory.

16.1.5.0.4. Morphology and syntax of Slavonic 'five' to 'ten'

Quite generally in Old Church Slavonic and the oldest attested stages of the other Slavonic languages, the cardinals 'five' to 'ten' are declined as singular *i*-stem nouns (with vestiges of consonantal-stem endings in the case of 'ten'); for purposes of concord they are feminine singular (rarely masculine singular for 'ten'); they require following nouns in the genitive plural, irrespective of the case of the numeral. This system is not retained in its entirety in any of the modern languages, all of which show a tendency to move from the older system with a numeral-noun plus genitive complement to one with a numeral-attribute plus noun in the case required by the syntax of the sentence; the following brief breakdown gives the position in the modern standard languages (excepting Bulgarian and Macedonian, with general loss of declension). In many languages these numerals now take plural (adjectival, pronominal) inflections in the oblique cases (Slovenian, optionally Ukrainian, Slovak, partially Polish, optionally Sorbian [unless indeclinable]); the older declension is retained more or less intact only in Russian, optionally Ukrainian, Belorussian, Czech; in Serbo-Croatian these numerals are indeclinable, while in Polish they have been integrated into the aberrant Polish numeral system as a whole. Concord as with a feminine singular noun is not retained in any of the modern languages, which treat the group numeral plus noun either as a plural or as a neuter singular (as with other quantity expressions), often both possibilities being present in the one language. In the oblique cases, including the Slovak masculine human forms, in all the modern languages the noun stands in the case required by the syntax of the sentence, whether or not the numeral is declined; in the nominative-accusative, however, numeral plus genitive plural is still the rule, and in Russian, for instance, the originally nominal nature of the numeral can still be seen in its failure to take on the form of the genitive when accusative and animate. The use of the genitive plural after the nominative-accusative numeral has proved particularly tenacious in Slavonic, indeed it is effectively the unmarked syntactic norm for numerals, being used for instance after mathematical expressions used as numerals (e. g.

Ru. *x jablok* '*x* apples'), and in nonstandard usage often occurring even with the numerals 'two' to 'four'.[42] In this context, it is worth looking briefly at the syntax of the higher numerals ('hundred', 'thousand', also the relatively recent internationalisms 'million', 'milliard', etc.; the following does not apply where these numerals are indeclinable, as they may be in some languages), which have generally retained more of their nominal origin in Slavonic, on the principle: the higher the numeral, the more nominal it is. Thus **sъto* 'hundred' has been integrated into the system of the lower numerals (i. e. genitive plural noun only after the nominative-accusative, otherwise agreement in case) in Russian and Polish, whereas in Czech it usually always takes the genitive plural. For 'thousand', Russian and, less commonly Czech, have optional agreement between numeral and noun in the oblique cases, while optionally (obligatorily in standard Polish) the noun may remain in the genitive plural. For the higher numerals, most Slavonic languages usually require the genitive plural throughout. Similarly with concord, where the numerals for 'thousand' and 'million' often induce concord according to their gender as nouns, rather than the unmarked (quantity expression) neuter singular.

16.1.5.0.5. Prosody of Slavonic 'five' to 'ten'

The stress pattern of these numerals has undergone several analogical changes in the various Slavonic languages, but some attempt can be made at the reconstruction of the Common Slavonic pattern. The most convenient language to start with is Russian, which retains both mobile accent and the original declension, and with the numeral 'nine', which, not being monosyllabic in the modern language, makes clearer the possible developments of various accent shifts. In Russian all numerals of this class have desinence stress in the oblique cases, and initial stress (*dévjat′*, not **devját′*) in the nominative-accusative; however, Russian also has initial stress in the instrumental when this is used as part of the multiplication formula (e. g. *dévjat′ju odínnadcat′* 'nine times eleven'). The closest noun accent type among the *i*-stems is the mobile paradigm, reconstructed by Stang,[43] on whom much of this account is based, as follows: nom. **devę́tь* (for **devętь̍*, with loss of stressability of jers); acc. **dévętь* (cf. Russian sg. acc. *gólovu* of *golová* 'head' in *a*-stems); gen. **devętí*; dat. **déveti*; instr. *dévętьjǫ*; loc. **devętí*. The nominative was subsequently replaced by the accusative, as in *i*-stem nouns of this type, and the dative took the desinence-stress of the genitive and locative (the reverse analogy of that usual in nouns); this general desinence-stress also affected the instrumental, though the older stress survives in the multiplication formula. For 'ten', we can also reconstruct the (expected) pl. gen. **desę́tъ* for **desętь́*, cf. Ru. *pjat′desját* 'fifty', *šest′desját* 'sixty'; otherwise in the modern languages the declension is as for 'nine'. In these numerals, the current nominative-accusative with initial stress is clearly the result of circumflex tone, not of later stress-shift following the loss of the jer, which would have given **devját′*; cf. also circumflex tone on prepositions with numerals, e. g. Ru. *ná desjat′* 'onto ten', *ná pjat′* 'onto five', though *ná sem′* 'onto seven' and *ná vosem′* 'onto eight' are analogical.

The other point of interest in the prosody of 'nine' and 'ten' is the length of the second vowel, deriving from Common Slavonic (long) **ę*. In the oblique cases, where the vowel is internal and pretonic, it is not clear what the general rule is for retention of vowel length, at best one can say that length is sometimes retained (Sk. *deviat-*, *desiat-*, Cz. *devíti, desíti*, alongside short *devěti, deseti*), sometimes not (Po. *dziewięciu, dziesięciu*).[44] Where the internal syllable is posttonic, as in the nominative-accusative, retention is usual, but not invariable,[45] but in the numerals we find it only in SCr. *dȅvēt, dȅsēt* (alongside *dȅvet, dȅset*), not in Cz. *devět, deset*, Sk. *deväť, desäť*, Po. *dziewięć, dziesięć*.

Turning now to 'five', the South Slavonic evidence points to original circumflex tone rather than neo-acute: neo-acute in Slovenian would give **pẹ́t*, not *pȇt*, similarly Čakavian has *pȇt* rather than **pét*. The same is true of 'six', where the long falling tones of Slovenian and Čakavian indicate lengthening of Common Slavonic (short) **e* with loss of an unstressed jer; neo-acute would have given Sn. **šȅst* (or possibly **šẹ́st*, though lengthening of *e* under neo-acute is not usual in Slovenian).[46] Similarly, SCr. *šȇst* represents lengthening with loss of an unstressed jer, since Serbo-Croatian also does not usually lengthen short vowels under neo-acute. In the oblique cases, the length in Sk. *šiest-* is analogical to the alternation in 'nine', 'ten', cf. the retained short vowel in Cz. *šesti*. In 'five', given that the **ę* is under circumflex tone, retention of length in pretonic position in a disyllable would not be expected in Slovak, and is again analogical; modern Czech has regularly short vowels in the same position, i. e. *pěti*, though a number of exceptions are found in Old Czech, which may rather have had the South Slavonic system with retained length, one of these examples being *pieti*.[47]

'Seven' and 'eight' are rather more complex. The Russian forms for 'eight' have prothetic *v-*, which in Russian (or rather, certain Russian dialects, not other East Slavonic languages, which have different systems here, see section 16.1.8.1./2.) arises only before *o* under neo-acute, i. e. **osmь̀*) **vósmь*; the *v*- in other inflectional forms must be analogical, but the nominative-accusative is the only possible source for the analogy. Sn. *sẹ́dəm* and *ọ́səm* also suggest neo-acute, which is consistent with the Serbo-Croatian forms. Only Sk. *osem* remains as a possible counterexample, since Slovak usually shows reflexes of neo-acute on *o*; but the Slovak forms have been remodelled as a morphological opposition (short vowel in the nominative-accusative, long vowel in the oblique cases), so the lack of neo-acute reflexes here is not too surprising. Russian provides further evidence for a distinction between 'seven', 'eight' on the one hand and 'five', 'six' on the other in the stress of the decads: *sém′desjat*, 'seventy', *vósem′desjat* 'eighty', versus *pjat′desját* 'fifty', *šest′desját* 'sixty'.[48]

Thus the available evidence suggests consistent desinence stress for Common Slavonic 'seven' and 'eight', but mobile stress for 'five', 'six', 'nine', 'ten'. Interestingly, this corresponds to a distinction in Indo-European between final and initial stress in these numerals, cf. Sanskrit *saptá, aṣṭā́*, versus *páñca, náva, dáśa*; Greek *heptá, oktṓ*, versus *pénte, ennéa, déka*.[49]

16.1.5.0.6. Prosody of Slavonic 'fifth' to 'tenth'

In some Slavonic languages, these ordinals fall into two groups according to stress or vowel length, in particular Ru. *pjátyj, devjátyj, desjátyj* versus *šestój, sed′mój, vos′mój*, and Cz. *pátý, devátý, desátý* versus *šestý, sedmý, osmý*. The difference corresponds to that between compound adjective types (b) (original circumflex tone on the root vowel) and (d) (original desinential stress), using the classes set up by Shevelov.[50] Although the ordinal numerals do not behave exactly as the most typical adjectives in either group, the distinction between the two groups is still quite clear in Russian and Czech. The Russian stress difference and the Czech length difference correlate as follows: the long vowels in Czech represent neo-acute, i. e. an early shift from final stress; the short vowels represent a later loss of final stress, subsequent to the development of neo-acute, and in these cases the final stress is retained in Russian. Most of the other languages that show reflexes of neo-acute have generalized apparent neo-acute (early stress-shifted) forms to all of these ordinals, i. e. they now show no difference between the two groups. Thus Ukrainian and Belorussian have stem stress throughout (Uk. *p′játyj, šóstyj*); Serbo-Croatian has apparent neo-acute throughout (*pêtī, šêstī*, Čak. *péti, šésti*), as do Slovak (*piaty, šiesty*, with the diphthongs that develop from long vowels) and Polish (*piąty, szósty*, with the vowel qualities resulting from Old Polish long vowels). Standard Slovenian also shows neo-acute (*pẹ́ti, šẹ́sti*), but there exists an alternative vowel quality under stress *péti, šésti*,[51] suggesting the existence of forms with later (post-neo-acute) stress retraction; presumably Slovenian originally has the two types distributed as in Czech, but with analogy working both ways the original distribution has been lost.

This line of analysis can also be extended to the ordinals 'second' to 'fourth'. For 'second', the evidence for **vъtorъjь* is conflicting: Ru. *vtorój*, but OPo. *wtóry* (neo-acute!); for the other formation, we have retained final stress in Ru. *drugój* (albeit with different meaning), Br. *druhí* and Sc. *drä́ʒī*, with no neo-acute in those languages that can show it, i. e. no early stress shift. For 'third', final stress is suggested by Ru. *sam-tretéj* 'with two others, threefold', though the current standard has *trétij* as ordinal, and by Sc. *třecī́*; SCr. *trȅćī* fits into the same pattern (no neo-acute, as the vowel is originally short), while Sn. *trẹ́tji*, with apparent neo-acute, must be analogical. For 'fourth', the evidence of Li. *ketvir̃tas* suggests original short **ŕ̥*, so the long vowels of SCr. *čètvr̄tī* and Po. (dial.) *czwárty* are probably analogous to the higher ordinals.

16.1.5.1./2. 'Five', 'fifth'

The Balto-Slavonic forms for 'five' continue the Indo-European (indeclinable) **penkᵘe*, or at least **penkᵘ-*; the Slavonic forms (but not those in Baltic) are equally consistent with the alternative **pn̥kᵘe*, although they provide no specific evidence for such a form. In all the languages, the Indo-European indeclinable has been reformed as a declined form, adjectival in Baltic, nominal (*i*-stem) in Slavonic.

Li. *penkì* continues IE **penkᵘ-*, with the addition of the plural adjectival ending, declined like *keturì*, e. g. nom. fem. *peñkios*; some dialects have *peñki* (cf. *kèturi*). Similarly Le. *pìeci* (with *ie* for **en* before a stop, and palatalization of **k* to *c* before *i*), declined as an adjective (nom. fem. *pìecas*).

The Baltic forms for the ordinal simply add ordinal *-t* to the stem of the cardinal: OPr. *piēncts*;[52] Li. *peñktas*; Le. *pìektais* (without palatalization of the *k*, as there is no following *i* in the ordinal).

The Common Slavonic form for the cardinal is **pętь*, declined as a singular *i*-stem feminine noun. OCS *pętь*, gen.-dat.-loc. *pęti*, instr. *pętiją* (*pętьję*, with orthographic variation in the representation of the jer); Bg. *pet*, masc. hum. *petíma*; Ma. *pet*, masc. hum. *petina, petmina*; SCr. *pêt* (Čak. *pêt*), indeclinable; Sn. *pệt*, with the endings of the compound adjective declension, gen.-loc. *pétich*, dat. *pétim*, instr. *pétimi*,[53] the open vowels of the oblique cases reflecting a recent stress retraction.

Standard Russian has a very archaic system: nom.-acc. *pjat'*, gen.-dat.-loc. *pjatí*, instr. *pjat'jú*; in older texts instr. *pjatma, pjatmja* (cp. 'two') are found; some modern dialects have the endings of the pronominal declension, with the vowel *u* from 'two' (i. e. gen.-loc. *pjacjúch*, dat. *pjacjúm*), the vowel *o* from 'three' or the *o*-stem nouns (*pjacjóch, pjacjóm*), or retaining the vowel *i* of *pjati* (*pjatích, pjatím*). Ukrainian and Belorussian have both an old system like standard Russian, and an innovating system with the vowel *o* and pronominal endings; in current standard Belorussian, only the former is normative, though gen.-loc. *pjacḗch*, instr. *pjac'má* are found in literature: Uk. *p'jat'*, gen.-dat.-loc. *p'jatý* or gen.-loc. *p'jatjóch*, dat. *p'jatjóm*, instr. *p'jat'má* or *p'jatjomá* (Ukrainian has lost the old instrumental); Br. *pjac'*, gen.-dat.-loc. *pjací*, instr. *pjaccjú* (with regular *CCjV* for *C'jV*).

Old Czech continues the Common Slavonic system with *pět* (*ę gives *ě* before a soft consonant, contrast the ordinal; final soft consonants were subsequently hardened in Czech and in numerals (unlike most nouns) are not reinstated by analogy with the oblique forms), gen.-dat.-loc. *pěti*, instr. *pět'ú*, giving regularly *pětí*; in the modern language, *pěti* is used for all the oblique cases. Sk. *päť*, masc. hum. *piati*, gen.-loc. *piatich*, dat. *piatim*, instr. *piatimi*, i. e. with soft adjectival endings (with short vowels by rhythmic shortening); the change in vowel length between the nominative-accusative (non-masculine human) and the other forms is generalized to all numerals 'five' to 'ten' in Slovak, see 'nine' to 'ten' (Sk. *ia* is for older *ā̈* for *ę); dialects sometimes show a system closer to that of Czech, with general obl. *piati*. Old Polish has regularly *pięć*, gen.-dat.-loc. *pięci*, instr. *pięcią*; other forms in the older language include dat. *pięciom* (cf. *dwom*), *pięciam* (cf. the pl. of *a*-stems), and forms still current in dialects like gen.-loc. *pięcich, pięciuch*; the current standard has *pięć*, obl. *pięciu* (cf. *dwu*), instr. also *pięcioma* (cf. *dwoma*). USo. *pjeć* (with regular *je* for *ę before a soft consonant, contrast the ordinal), indeclinable or gen.-loc. *pjećich*, dat. *pjećim*, instr. *pjećimi*, masc. hum. *pjećo*, gen.-loc. *pjećoch*, dat. *pjećom*, instr. *pjećomi*, i. e. declined as 'three' to 'four' except that *i* is retained throughout the non-masculine human paradigm; there is also a (nonstandard) general oblique form *pjeći*, continuing the Common Slavonic form, as in Czech. LSo. *pěś* is indeclinable or declined in the other case forms like *tśi, tśo* (e. g. gen.-loc. *pěśich*, masc. hum. nom. *pěśo*, gen.-loc. *pěśoch*), except that for the masculine human instrumental both *pěśimi* and *pěśomi* exist. Pb. *pąt* has *ą* for **ę* before the originally soft consonant, contrast the ordinal.

Since the Slavonic ordinals are formed from the same stem as the cardinals, they present few problems, once one notes those West Slavonic languages where the effects of przegłos (Polish, Polabian) or přehláska (Czech, Upper Sorbian) give rise to different stem vowels: CSl. **pętъ*; OCS *pętъ*; Bg. *péti* (short form *pet*); Ma. *petti*, with the extra ordinal *-t* as in all Macedonian ordinals 'five' to 'hundred'; SCr. *pêtī*; Sn. *pẹ́ti* (also *péti*); Ru. *pjátyj*; Uk. *p'játyj*; Br. *pjáty*; Cz. *pátý*, with *a* because of the following hard consonant, and the vowel long under neo-acute; Sk. *piaty*, with a long stem vowel as in all ordinals 'five' to 'ten'; Po. *piąty*, again with the reflex of a long vowel, as in all ordinals 'five' to 'ten'; USo. *pjaty* (*a* by přehláska); LSo. *pěty*; Pb. *ṕǫtě*, with *ǫ* for **ę* by przegłos, whence the retention of the palatalization of *ṕ*.

16.1.6.1./2. 'Six, sixth'

The traditionally assumed reconstructed form for IE 'six' is **seḱs*. Some Indo-European languages suggest a by-form (older?) **su̯eḱs*, but whatever the relation between forms with and without **u̯*, there are no traces of the former in Balto-Slavonic apart from the aberrant Old Prussian ordinal. There is evidence in Indo-Iranian for initial **k*, i. e. **ks(u̯)eḱs*, and the assumption of an original initial **k* in Slavonic would account for the initial **š* of **šestь*, since **s* regularly shifts to **ch* after **k*, and **ch* is palatalized to **š* before **e* by the First Palatalization; this avoids the assumption of dissimilation of **sestь* to **šestь*. In Li. *šešì*, the second *š* derives regularly from *ḱ*; the first *š* cannot be explained as in Slavonic, since Baltic does not have **š* for **ks*,[54] and here assimilation from **seši* (for **seḱs*, without **k-*) seems the most likely explanation.

Li. *šešì*, declined like *keturì* (nom. fem. *šẽšios*), has already been discussed above; in dialects initial-stressed *šèši* also occurs, cf. *kèturi*. In Le. *seši* (declined as an adjective, e. g. nom. fem. *sešas*) the medial *š* is not parallel to Li. *š* (for which Latvian would have *s*), but derives rather from other forms where the stem is **sesj-*, with the regular shift of **sj* to *š*, cf. the stem-final *-n* of the cardinals 'seven' to 'nine'.

The ordinals in Lithuanian and Latvian are formed by adding ordinal *-t* to the stem of the cardinal: Li. *šẽštas*, Le. *sęstais* (open *e* and *s* rather than *š*, as there is no following *i* or *j*). Old Prussian, however, has a different formation here, unique within Balto-Slavonic (and unusual, at least, in Indo-European as a whole), namely *usts, uschts* (i. e. *ušts*); the *š* of the second form cannot continue **ḱ* (which gives OPr. *s*, as in Latvian), and probably derives from forms of the cardinal in **-sj*, as in Le. *seši*. The only possible close cognate in Baltic is Li. *ušės* 'lying-in lasting six weeks', and this may be a loan from Old Prussian. Old Prussian suggests a derivation from **uḱtos*, where **u* would be the zero-grade of the **u̯e* of **su̯eḱs*; the lack of initial **s-* is still problematic, and it seems defeatist to treat the initial zero-consonant as the result of dissimilation from **susts*. Although Armenian *v* does not usually continue IE **u̯* (which gives Armenian *g*), it is still tempting to see in Armenian *veç* a reflex of **u̯eḱs*,[55] perhaps an older Indo-European form than **su̯eḱs*.

CSl. **šestь*, declined as **pętь*. The forms of the individual languages are as follows; all are declined like 'five', except where specified otherwise. OCS *šestь*; Bg. *šest*, masc. hum. *šestíma*; Ma. *šest*, masc. hum. *šestina, šestmina*; SCr. *šȇst*; Sn. *šẹ̑st*, stem *šést-*. Ru. *šest′* has from the fourteenth to eighteenth centuries an alternative stem *št-* in the oblique cases (e. g. gen. *šti*), for **šsti*, as if the etymology were **šьst-* (with vocalization of the jer to *šest′* in the nominative-accusative); this alternative stem is analogical to items where the alternation *e/Ø* does result from alternation between weak and strong jers within the paradigm; the current declension uses *šest-* as the stem. Uk. *šist′*, from **šēst′*, with compensatory lengthening after the loss of the weak jer, follows the two declension possibilities for *p'jat′*: in the gen.-dat. loc. *šestý* the stem vowel is *e*, according to the etymology as there is no lost jer here; but gen.-loc. *šistjóch*, dat. *šistjóm*, and instr. *šist′má* or *šistjōmá* have generalized the vowel of the nominative-accusative. Br. *šėsc′* has the oblique stem *šasc′-*, with jakanie; the instr. *šascjú* has single *-cj-*, not *-ccj-*, because of the consonant cluster. Cz. *šest*; Sk. *šest'*, obl. stem *šiest-* (with *ie* for**ē*); Po. *sześć*; USo. *šěsć*, with compensatory lengthening for the loss of the final jer, oblique stem *šesć-*; LSo. *šesć*, with retention of *ć* after *s*; Pb. *sist*, with initial *s* by mazurzenie.

The Slavonic ordinals, for CSl. **šestъ*, are: OCS **šestъ*; Bg. *šésti* (short *šest*); Ma. *šesti* (with single *t*, as **-stt-* would in any case give *-st-*); SCr. *šȇstī*; Sn. *šẹ́sti* (also *šésti*); Ru. *šestój*, with retention of final stress; Uk. *šóstyj* (with shift of *e* to *o* between a hushing sibilant and a hard consonant); Cz. *šestý*; Sk. *šiesty*, with long vowel as in the other ordinals; Po. *szósty*, with *o* for **e* by przegłos, and a long vowel as in the other ordinals; USo. *šěsty*, with *ě* from the cardinal; LSo. *šesty*; Pb. *sestě*, with *e* for **e* before a hard dental, contrast the cardinal.

16.1.7.1./2. 'Seven', 'seventh'

The Baltic forms for 'seven' present few difficulties. IE **septm̥* would give Balt. **septin*, which appears in the modern languages with adjectival endings. Li. *septynì* (declined like *keturì*, e. g. nom. fem. *septýnios*) has an unexpected long *ī*, probably by analogy with the long vowel of *aštuonì* (*uo*, for **ō*); dialects also have initial stressed *sèptyni* and contracted *sèptyn*. Le. *septiņi* (declined as an adjective) retains the short vowel in the second syllable (though *septîņi* occurs in dialects, parallel to the Lithuanian form), but has *ņ* in the nominative masculine by analogy with other forms having *-*nj*, which develops regularly to *ņ*, e. g. nom. fem. *septiņas*.

The ordinals in Lithuanian and Latvian have been reformed on the basis of the cardinal stem: Li. *septiñtas* (where the *i* must be short, as part of a nasal diphthong), Le. *septîtais* (with *ī* for **in* before a stop). The Old Prussian form is *sep(t)mas*, and an older Lithuanian form *sẽkmas*, both continuing the Indo-European ordinal stem **septm-*; the precise development of the Lithuanian form is not clear, as there are no other instances of the cluster *-*ptm-* for comparison, but **septm-* must have been simplified to either **sepm-* or **setm-*, then further to **sẽkmas*.[56]

The Common Slavonic cardinal is usually given as **sedmь*, although East Slavonic suggests rather **semь*, and the latter form is more in keeping with general Common Slavonic phonotactics, where dental stops are not permitted before nasals. The Indo-European ordinal form from which the Slavonic cardinal and ordinal derive is **septmos*.[57] Apart from Slavonic, voicing of the prenasal consonant is found only in Greek of the older Indo-European languages (ordinal *hébdomos*), although it is doubtful whether the Greek and Slavonic voicing date back to the same Indo-European dialectal process;[58] voiceless forms (*sėtäm, sėtmə*) are found in Kashubian dialects of Polish, but only in the (indeclinable) cardinal, and probably result from final devoicing rather than being a survival of Indo-European **t*.[59] The traditional explanation for the retention of a dental in the reflex of **septmos* is that, while the cluster **pt* simplifies regularly to **t*, the **t* of **ptm* is protected by the preceding stop at the time of the simplification of consonant clusters; apart from lack of phonetic plausibility, this fails to account for ESl **semь*. If the **m* of **septmos* were syllabic, then the **t* would not be expected to be lost, though again the East Slavonic form would be anomalous. Another possibility is that the Common Slavonic form could have been regularly **semъ* for the ordinal, as in Old Russian, with **setь* as cardinal from IE

**septm̥*; coalescence of the two forms would give cardinal **setmь* and ordinal **setmъ*, with subsequent voicing of the dental. The earlier loss of the weak jers in South Slavonic and West Slavonic means that the cluster **dm* became phonotactic in these Slavonic languages earlier than in East Slavonic, which may account for the failure of East Slavonic to share in this development.[59a]

The modern Slavonic languages that have reflexes of **sedmь* rather than **semь* usually have a fill-vowel between the *d* and the *m* in the endingless nominative-accusative. There is no trace of this vowel in Old Church Slavonic, and many of the modern languages have patently nonetymological fill-vowels, corresponding to neither of the Common Slavonic jers (thus Ma. *sedum*, Cz. *sedum* [the usual pronunciation of *sedm*], LSo. *sedym*, Pb. *siděm* [not **sidăm*]); of the other languages, some have vowels that could continue either jer (Bg. dial. *sédъm*, SCr. *sȅdam*, Sn. *sẹ́dəm*, Sk. *sedem*; in this Slovak form, unlike *jeden*, the *d* is soft, though *d'* before *e* from *ъ is not unknown elsewhere), while Bg. *sédem* suggests *ь, and Po. *siedem* suggests *ъ (Old Polish has usually *siedm*, without fill-vowel), as does USo. *sydom* (although Upper Sorbian does occasionally have *o* for *ь); even more so than with 'one', we seem to be dealing with the insertion of a fill-vowel postdating the Common Slavonic period. An unusual development is found in Kashubian, including Slovincian, in forms like *sètmə* (cf. also *u̯osmə* 'eight'), where *-mə* represents a different solution to vocalizing the syllabic sonant of **sedm*, following the loss of the final jer.

OCS *sedmь*, declined like *pętь*; in all the other languages, except where stated otherwise, the declension is as for 'five'. Bu. *sédem* (dial. *sédъm* in dialects where both jers give ъ even in suffixes), masc. hum. dial. *sedmína*; Ma. *sedum*, masc. hum. *sedmina* or, analogically to the citation form, *sedummina*; SCr. *sȅdam*; Sn. *sẹ́dəm*, stem *sédm-* (for the stress, see section 16.1.5.0.5.). Ru. *sem'*; Uk. *sim* (for **sēm*, with compensatory lengthening following the loss of the jer), gen.-dat.-loc. *semý* or, with the vowel of the nominative-accusative, gen.-loc. *simóch*, dat. *simóm*, instr. *sjomá* (an aberrant form, for expected **simmá*, perhaps influenced by the ordinal *sjómyj*) or *simomá* (the *m* is hardened regularly in final position, i. e. regularly in the nominative-accusative, and this hardening has been transferred to the oblique forms); Br. *sem* (with hardening of final *m*), gen.-dat.-loc. *sjamí*, instr. *sjamjú*, the oblique forms with jakanie. Cz. *sedm* (pronounced *sedum*), stem *sedm-*; Sk. *sedem*, stem *siedm-*; Po. *siedem*, stem *siedm-* (Old Polish usually *siedm*); Upper Sorbian both *sydom* (stem *sydmj-*) and *sedm*, the former, which is preferred in the current standard, deriving from **sēd(o)m*, with lengthening of the **e* following the loss of the final jer (i. e. before the insertion of the fill-vowel); LSo. *sedym*, stem *sedyḿ-*, i. e. with generalization of the fill-vowel to all forms; Pb. *sidĕm*. It will be noted that Russian is the only Slavonic language to retain distinctive palatalization of labials in final position.

The Slavonic ordinals, for CSl. **sedmъ/semъ*, are: OCS *sedmъ*; Bg. *sédmi* (no short form); Ma. *sedmi* (without ordinal *-t*, thus avoiding the consonant cluster **sedmti*); SCr. *sêdmī*; Sn. *sẹ́dmi* (also *sédmi*); Ru. *sed′mój*, a loan from Church Slavonic, cf. dialect forms *semój, sё́moj*, and the phrase *sam-sё́m* 'with six others, sevenfold' (the soft *d* of *sed′-mój* cannot be directly from OCS *sedmъ*, but is probably influenced by the reading of the Old Church Slavonic/Church Slavonic cardinal *sedmь* with a soft *d*, or by *vos′mój* 'eighth', where the soft *s* has a similar origin); Uk. *sjómyj*, with shift of **e* to *o*, sporadic in Ukrainian after consonants other than hushing sibilants, here perhaps influenced by the vowels of *šóstyj* 'sixth' and *vós′myj* 'eight'; Br. *sё́my*; Cz. *sedmý*; Sk. *siedmy*; Po. *siódmy* (the last two with analogical neo-acute); USo. *sydmy, sedmy*; LSo. *sedymy*, with the fill-vowel of the cardinal. For Polabian, the only attested form glossed as an ordinal is *sídim*;[60] either this is the cardinal *sidĕm* used as an ordinal, or a misspelling of **sidmĕ*.[61]

16.1.8.1./2. 'Eight', 'eighth'

Li.-Le. **aštuo* derives regularly from IE **oḱtō*, and is then reformed as an adjective, taking stem-final *-n* from the cardinals 'seven' and/or 'nine' to give Li. *aštuonì* (declined like *keturì*, e. g. nom. fem. *aštúonios*; in dialects also *àštuoni, àštuon*), Le. *astôņi* (in dialects also *astuņi*, with short vowel as in *septiņi, deviņi*, and *ostiņi* (short *o*), with the vowel of the neighbouring numerals).[62]

The current Baltic ordinals are based on the cardinal stem: Li. *aštuñtas*, with regular shortening of **uo* to **u* as part of a nasal diphthong, though dialects have analogical *aštuõntas, aštúontas*; L. *astôtais*, an even more recent re-formation on the basis of the cardinal *astôņi*, cf. the older form *astūts* (parallelling Li. *aštuñtas*, with regular Le. *ū* for **un* before a plosive) in dialects, also *ostīts* (short *o*) where the cardinal is *ostiņi* (short *o*). An older formation is found in OPr. *asmus*, Li. (archaic) *ãšmas*, surviving in Latvian dial. *asmīte* as a measure of land. These parallel Sl. **osm-*, and continue forms with an ordinal-forming suffix *-m*, derived from the numeral for 'seven'.

The Common Slavonic form for the cardinal is **osmь*, with *m* from the ordinal, where it is analogical to the form for 'seventh', as in Baltic. In the nominative-accusative most of the modern languages have a nonetymological fill-vowel, as with 'seven' (q. v.). OCS *osmь*, declined like *pętь*, this being true of the other languages, except where stated otherwise; Bg. *ósem*, msc. hum. dial. *osmína*; Ma. *osum*, masc. *osmina, osummina*; SCr. *ȍsam*; Sn. *ọ́səm* (stem *ósm-*). In Ru. *vósem'*, gen.-dat.-loc. *vos'mí*, instr. *vosem'jú* (the regular development of the apparent etymon **(v)osьmьjǫ*, though the first jer is of course nonetymological) or, more usually, *vos'm'jú*, prothetic *v-* in the nominative-accusative is a reflex of neo-acute, the *v-* being transferred to the other forms by analogy; Old Russian has variants without the *v*, and in the sixteenth and seventeenth centuries the historically correct distribution of nom.-acc. *v-*, oblique without *v*, is found. Uk. *vísim*, gen.-dat.-loc. *vos'mý*, or gen.-loc. *vis'móch*, dat. *vis'móm*, instr. *vis'má* or *vis'momá*; the prothetic *v* and vowel *i* again arise regularly only in the nominative-accusative: **o* gives *i* in Ukrainian when lengthened after the fall of the following jer, i. e. the **o* of *osmь* is lengthened to give, ultimately, *i*, and such lengthened *o*'s take prothetic *v*; the *i* of the second syllable cannot continue the (nonetymological) **ь*, and seems to be taken from *sim*; prothetic *v* now occurs in all forms, though in the older oblique case *vos'mý* the historically correct vocalism with *o* is retained. Br. *vósem*, gen.-dat.-loc. *vas'mí*, instr. *vas'mjú*, has prothetic *v* regularly in the nominative-accusative, since in Belorussian all initial stressed *o*'s take *v-*; where the stress shifts in the oblique cases, there should historically be no *v-*, but *v* has been inserted analogically. Cz. *osm* (pronounced *osum*), stem *osm-*; Sk. *osem*, stem *ôsm-*; Po. *osiem*, stem *ośm-* (Old Polish has usually *ośm*, and Kashubian dialects also have *u̯osmə*). In Upper Sorbian, Völkel[63] gives only *wosom*, stem *wos(o)mj-* (i. e. with or without fill-vowel in the oblique cases), though Šewc[64] cites all forms as *wósom*, stem *wósmj-*, with *ó* paralleling the *y* of *sydom*. In practice, variants of the nominative-accusative without the fill-vowel are also found, e. g. *wosm* (cf. *sedm*).[65] Similar variation applies to other derivatives of this stem. Prothetic *w* before initial *o* is regular in Sorbian. LSo. *wosym*, stem *wosyḿ-*; Pb. *visĕm/vüsĕm*,[66] with regular development of initial **o* to *vi/vü* before a soft consonant. It will be noted that several Slavonic languages and dialects have prothetic *v-* or *w-* before initial *o*, although the conditions for the appearance of this prothetic consonant differ from language to language. For other details of the phonetic development of 'eight', see 'seven', with a similar termination.

The Slavonic ordinals, for CSl. **osmъ*, are: OCS *osmъ*; Bg. *ósmi* (no short form); Ma. *osmi* (not **osmti*); SCr. *ôsmī*; Sn. *ọ́smi* (also *ósmi*); Ru. *vos′mój* (with initial *v* and soft *s* from the cardinal); Uk. *vós′myj*; Br. *vós′my*; Cz. *osmý*; Sk. *ôsmy*; Po. *ósmy* (the last two with analogical neo-acute); USo. *wosmy* (also *wósmy*); LSo. *wosymy*; Pb. *våsmě*, with *vå* for initial **o* before a hard consonant (but see also footnote 60).

16.1.9.1./2. 'Nine', 'ninth'

An innovation of Balto-Slavonic, with the exception of Old Prussian, is the replacement of the initial **n* of IE **neu̯n̥* (or **neu̯m̥*) by initial *d-*, either by dissimilation from the final *n* or, more probably, under the influence of the following numeral in counting, with initial *d* (IE **dek̑m̥(t)*).

IE **neu̯n̥* (or **neu̯m̥*, since both would give the same reflexes in Balto-Slavonic) gives Li.-Le. **devin*, to which adjective endings are added, as with the other cardinals 'five' to 'nine' (cf. especially 'seven'), giving: Li. *devynì* (declined like *keturì*, e. g. nom. fem. *devýnios*), with long *ī* analogously to the long vowel of *aštuonì*, in dialects also *dèvyni, dèvyn*; Le *deviņi* (declined as an adjective), with *ņ* from the other forms of the paradigm (e. g. nom. fem. *deviņas*), dial. also *devîņi* with a long vowel as in Lithuanian.

The Baltic ordinals simply add ordinal *-t* to the stem of the cardinal: OPr. *newīnts*, with retention of initial *n*; Li. *deviñtas* (where the *i* must be short, as part of a nasal diphthong); Le. *devîtais* (with regular *ī* for **in* before a plosive).

The Common Slavonic form of the cardinal is **devętь*; IE **eu* normally gives Sl. **ev* heterosyllabically before a front vowel (as opposed to **ov* before a back vowel), so there is no need to assume that the Slavonic vowel is analogous to that of **desętь*. Except where noted, the declension is as for 'five'. OCS *devętь*; Bg. *dévet*, masc. hum. *devetíma*, dial. *devetína*; Ma. *devet*, masc. hum. *devetina, devetmina*; SCr. *dȅvēt* (also *dȅvet*); Sn. *devệt*, with neo-circumflex, for **dèvet*, stem *devét-*; Ru. *dévjat′*; Uk. *dév′jat′*; Br. *dzévjac′*; Cz. *devět*, stem *devít-* or *devět-*; Sk. *deväť*, stem *deviat-*; Po. *dziewięć*; USo. *dźewjeć*; LSo. *źeẃeś*, with regular loss of occlusion in both affricates; Pb. *divąt*. For the stress and vowel length, see sections 16.1.5.0.5. – 6.; for other aspects of the development of the vowel of the second syllable (e. g. the different influence of przegłos and přehláska as between cardinal and ordinal), see the discussion of 'five' and 'fifth', with the same vowel and following consonant.

The Slavonic ordinals, for CSl. **devętъ*, are: OCS *devętъ*; Bg. *devéti* (short form *devét*, differing in stress from the cardinal); Ma. *devetti*; SCr. *dèvētī*; Sn. *devę́ti* (also *devéti*); Ru. *devjátyj*; Uk. *dev'játyj*; Br. *dzevjáty*, with no orthographic representation of jakanie; Cz. *devátý*; Sk. *deviaty*; Po. *dziewiąty*; USo. *dźewjaty*; LSo. *źeẃety*; Pb. *diẃǫtě*.

16.1.10.1./2. 'Ten', 'tenth'

For the Balto-Slavonic forms for 'ten' and 'tenth', it is most convenient to start from IE **deḱm̥t*, for the final *t* of which see section 16.1.5.0.3. Evidence from both Baltic and Slavonic suggests that the cardinal was originally a consonant (*t*-) stem, although this declension has been by and large abandoned, as in the case of other consonant-stems, in favour of the *i*-declension. The original gender is less clear, though the oldest Slavonic points to masculine, later replaced by feminine on the analogy of the numerals 'five' to 'nine'; within Baltic, both masculine and (more widespread) feminine are found.

Current standard Lithuanian has *dešimtìs*, a fem. *i*-stem noun, and also indeclinable *dẽšimt*, a truncated form of the singular accusative (*dẽšimtį*); other indeclinable forms found in dialects are *dešimts, dešims, dešim*, with various contractions. Dialects show traces of the original consonant declension: gen. sg. *dešimtès*, nom. pl. *dẽšimtes*, and the very widespread gen. pl. *dešimtų̃*; other declension types found in dialects include fem. *ē*-, *jā*-stems, and masc. *jo*-stem. The nominal origin of this numeral is reflected in its syntax: it takes the genitive plural of the following noun. The current standard Latvian form is indeclinable *desmit*, by metathesis from *desimt* (found in dialects), originally from the singular accusative; it either takes a genitive plural, or leaves the noun in the case required by the syntax of the sentence. In strictly nominal use there is also the *i*-stem *desmits*,[67] and in dialects the fem. *ā*-stem *desmita* and the masc. *o*-stem *desmits*; in the oblique cases also with plural endings. The Old Prussian forms are *dessimpts* (*dessempts*, i. e. open *i*), cf. Li. *dešimtìs*, also *dessimton*, with the neuter ending, perhaps by similarity with 'hundred' (OPr. *simtan*); the other attested form, plural accusative *dessimtons*, suggests agreement with the noun.

The Baltic ordinals simply add the adjetival endings to the stem of the cardinal, which already ends in *t*: OPr. *dessīmts*; Li. *dešim̃tas*; Le. *desmitais* (dial. *desimtais*, without metathesis). Note the contrast between the *m* of *dešim̃tas*, deriving regularly from **deḱm̥tos*, and the *n* of *septiñtas* 'seventh', where *t* has been added to the cardinal **septin* for **septm̥*, with the usual Balto-Slavonic loss of the distinction between word-final **m* and **n*.

Common Slavonic **desęt-* was originally a consonant (*t*-) stem, probably of masculine gender, and traces of the original declension (and masc. gender) are found in Old Church Slavonic and the oldest stages of some of the other languages. The declension was subsequently modified to that of the fem. *i*-declension, like the numerals 'five' to 'nine', though traces of the consonantal case-forms survive in some of the forms for the teens and tens. OCS *desętь*, declined basically as an *i*-stem, but with the following *t*-stem forms: sg. gen. *desęte* (not in canonical Old Church Slavonic, which has *desęti*), loc. *desęte* (especially in the formation of the teens; alongside *desęti*), du. gen.-loc. *desętu* (not in canonical Old Church Slavonic; moreover it is not clear whether this is an original consonant-stem ending, or taken from the *o*-stems), pl. nom. *desęte*, gen. *desętъ*, instr. *desęty* (not the *i*-stem ending, but probably borrowed from the *o*-stems, rather than original). In the modern languages, except where otherwise stated, the declension is as for 'five'; for relics of consonantal forms in the teens and decads, see sections 16.1.11.3. and 16.1.12.2. Bg. *déset*; Ma. *deset*, masc. hum. *desetmina*; SCr. *dȅsēt* (also *dȅset*); Sn. *desȇt* (with neo-circumflex), stem *desét-*; Ru. *désjat′* (in Old Russian we find the consonantal gen. sg. *desjate*, and perhaps the instr. du. *desjama* – for **desętma*, with regular loss of *t* before a consonant, unless the form is an orthographic abbreviation – and the old acc. (?) sg. *desja* – for **desęt*, with regular Slavonic loss of final obstruent –, though the latter form is particularly dubious);[68] Uk. *désjat′*; Br. *dzésjac′*; Cz. *deset*, stem *desít-* and *deset-*; Sk. *desat'* (*ä* occurs only after labials), stem *desiat-*; Po. *dziesięć*; USo. *dźesać* (with regular *a* for *ę* after *s*; cf. *wzać* 'to take' for **vъzęt'i*); LSo. *źaseś*, with regular shift of **e* to *a* before a hard consonant; Pb. *disąt*. For the treatment of the last vowel of the stem, in cardinal and ordinal, cf. the discussion of 'five'.

The ordinal forms, for CSl. **desętъ*, are: OCS *desętъ*; Bg. *deséti* (short form *desét*); Ma. *desetti*; SCr. *dèsētī*; Sn. *desẹ́ti* (also *deséti*); Ru. *desjátyj*; Uk. *desjátyj*; Br. *dzesjáty*, with no orthographic representation of jakanie (cf. 'ninth'); Cz. *desátý*; Sk. *desiaty;* Po. *dziesiąty*; USo. *dźesaty*; LSo. *źasety*; Pb. *diśǫtě*.

16.1.11. Teens

In Balto-Slavonic there are two formations for the teens: the one occurs only in Lithuanian (though it is similar to the formation of 'eleven' and 'twelve' in Germanic) on the pattern 'one left over (sc. after ten)'; the other occurs in Latvian and Slavonic (the Old Prussian teens are not attested), and uses the pattern 'one on ten') (Latvian rather 'one after/beyond ten'), a pattern found outside Balto-Slavonic in Albanian, Romanian (not the rest of Romance), Hungarian, Ancient Greek (dialectally), Celtic, Old Armenian, and Tokharian.[69] In addition, some Latvian dialects simply construct the teens like higher coordinate numerals, e. g. *viêndesmit viêns* for 'eleven', literally 'one-ty one'.

16.1.11.1. Lithuanian

The modern Lithuanian cardinal teens are: *vienúolika, dvýlika, trýlika, keturiólika, penkiólika, šešiólika, septyniólika, aštuoniólika, devyniólika,* all declined like singular nouns (with the following noun in the genitive plural) except that the accusative is the same as the nominative. The current forms for the ordinals add ordinal-forming *-t* to the stem of the cardinals: *vienúoliktas, dvýliktas, trýliktas, keturióliktas, penkióliktas, šešióliktas, septynióliktas, aštuonióliktas, devynióliktas*; the older language had formations of the type *liekas* (*pirmas liekas, vienas liekas*) 'eleventh', *antras liekas* 'twelfth', etc., i. e. 'the first (second, etc.) left over'. Following Stang[70] we may take this ordinal formation as the starting-point of the Lithuanian teen formation. The second component is *liẽkas* 'odd (i. e. not even)', cf. Le. *lìeks* 'extra, left over'; thus the ordinal (*pìrmas*) *liẽkas* meant originally 'the (first one) left over (sc. after ten)', while the cardinal *trýlika* would mean 'three left over (sc. after ten)'. Unstressed, *-lieka* was reduced to *-lika* (dialects also have *-li˙ka* and *-leka*); since the form was originally plural, *-lika* presumably derives from a nom.-acc. pl. neut. adj. **-liekā*. The form *try-* corresponds to the Old Church Slavonic neut. *tri*, and the higher forms in *-o* are probably nom.-acc. neut. *jo*-stem adjectives. The remaining problems are *vienúolika* and *dvýlika*, with unexpected vowels in stressed position. The vowel of *dvýlika* probably derives analogically from that of *trýlika*, though the original form is more difficult to reconstruct: the traditional assumption is that it was **dvōlika*, which influenced the form for 'eleven' to give **vienōlika* (modern *vienúolika*) before being modified itself. But with nominative-accusative plural neuter one would expect as first component not **dvō-* (masculine) but **dvie-*, unless the forms were redistributed, as in some Slavonic (section 16.1.2.1.). Thus the real remaining problem is *vienúolika*, whose vowel cannot, under this analysis, be attributed to **dvōlika*. Conceivably *vienuo-*, which occurs in other compounds, is originally a (sociative) instrumental, i. e. the original form was **(dešimtìs) vienúo liekúo* '(ten) with one extra', changed subsequently to *vienúolika* under the influence of the higher teens with *-lika*.

In the standard language, the accusative of the cardinal teens being like the nominative is a relic of the original plural neuter nature of these formation; in dialects, the regular accusative in *-ą* occurs, as also does a nominative in *-s* (*vienúliks*), cf. dial *dešim̃(t)s* 'ten'. Ordinal forms found in Lithuanian dialects include *vienúolikis*, without ordinal-forming *-t*, and *vienuoliktiñtas*, by analogy with *deviñtas* 'ninth'.

16.1.11.2. Latvian

The Latvian teens end in *-padsmit* (pronounced *-pacmit*, in colloquial speech and dialects even further reduced to *-pa*, cf. Slavonic forms in *-na*) and are indeclinable, dialectally also declinable in *-padsmits*. Dialects also retain older forms in *-padesmit(s)* (and *-padesimt*, without metathesis), without loss of the *e*. The final vowel of the unit is lost in the teens: *viênpadsmit, divpadsmit, trîspadsmit, četrpadsmit* (dial.: *četrupadsmit*, possibly for **četurpadsmit*, and unclear *četrapadsmit*; possibly these vowels are epenthetic to break up the consonant cluster), *pìecpadsmit, sešpadsmit, septiņpadsmit, astôņpadsmit, deviņpadsmit*. For the ordinals the current forms simply attach the adjectival ending to the cardinal: *viênpadsmitais, divpadsmitais, trîspadsmitais, četrpadsmitais, pìecpadsmitais, sešpadsmitais, septiņpadsmitais, astôņpadsmitais, deviņpadsmitais*. In older texts both unit and second component decline, e. g. acc. *vienu padesmitu*, loc. *vienā padesmitā*; possibly the oldest form was with invariable second component, as in the oldest Slavonic.

16.1.11.3. Slavonic

The Slavonic teens are formed on the pattern **pętь na desęte*, literally 'five on ten', with the original consonantal stem locative of **desętь*. In the modern languages the second part of the complex has been shortened in all the languages, often more so in dialects or other nonstandard usage than in the written standard. The shortest forms are simply with *-na*, e. g. in some Bulgarian and Kashubian dialects *dvaná* 'twelve',[71] though here the shortening could be morphological (loss of the element **desęte*) rather than phonological.

The construction in the older languages reflects the compound nature of the formation: the second part (**na desęte*) is invariable, while it is the first part (the unit) that declines and determines the form of the noun in the numeral phrase. Even in Old Church Slavonic, however, deviations from this pattern are found, which characterize the development in the modern languages; where the declension of the first part (the unit) is usually lost, the whole complex starts assuming declension (i. e. in effect the **deseęte* element), and the whole complex determines the form of the noun as if it were a simple numeral other than 'one', 'two', 'three', 'four'. Thus the morphological divisibility of the complex gradually plays a smaller role in the morphology and syntax of these formations.

The reflexes of **na desęte* in the individual languages may now be discussed, before turning to the individual teens in the various languages. It should be noted that the various contractions of **na desęte* attested in the individual languages do not always represent a single line of development; this is illustrated particularly clearly by Czech (see Table 2). Many languages suggest a development from **na desętь* rather than from **na desęte*: this could have an internal morphological explanation (*na* with the accusative meaning 'onto' rather than 'on'), though there is also the possibility that such forms were developed, or at least favoured, because they could then be declined like numerals of the **pętь* type.

Table 2. Development of '-teen' in Czech

-nádcěte	> -nádcete >			
		-nácte >		
	> -nácěte >			
			-nácte >	
	> -nádste	>		-náct > -nást
	> -ná(d)cět >	-ná(d)cet >	-nádst >	

OCS *na desęte*, once only *na desęti* (Gospel according to Matthew 26: 47, in the Codex Assemanianus), with the ending of the *i*-stem locative. Declension of the first part only is usual, though deviations from this are found even in the canonical manuscripts.

Bg. *-nádeset*, still the usual form in the written language, though *-nájset* is also possible; colloquially usually *-nájse*.

Ma. *-naeset*, colloqu. *-najse*.

SCr. older *-nadeste, -naeste* (also *-najeste*), *-najste; -nadeset, -nadest*. From the last form comes the current standard *-naest* and colloquial *-najst*. These numerals are indeclinable in the modern language; the stress falls on the syllable immediately preceding the *na*, representing original stress on the preposition.

Sn. *-najst*, the whole complex being declined like *pệt*, but with fixed stress/tone. Apart from *enájst*, which has only this stress, there are two possible stresses: one as in the other Slavonic languages on the preposition, *-nájst*, the other, analogical, on the unit, as in the simple form of the unit.

Russian older *-nadesjate, -nadsjat'*, the latter effectively the same, except in spelling, as the current standard *-nádcat'* (for the stress of *odínnadcat'* and *četýrnadcat'*, see below), declined like *pjat'*, but with fixes stress. The pronunciation with long affricate is insisted on by orthoepic handbooks, though the pronunciation *-nácat'* is common.[72]

Uk. *-nádcjat'*, with retention of softness from CSl. **sę*; the normative pronunciation is with single affricate, i. e. *-nácjat'*. Declension is as for *p'jat'*: the older form for the genitive-dative-locative has fixed stress (e. g. *odynádcjaty)*; whereas the other forms have final stress, as for *p'jat'* (e. g. gen.-loc. *odynadcjatjóch*, dat. *odynadcjatjóm*, instr. *odynadcjat'má, odynadcjatjomá*).

Br. *-náccac'*, the whole complex being declined like *pjac'*, but with fixed stress; in literature, also forms like Ukrainian: gen.-loc. *-naccacḗch*, dat. *-naccacḗm*, instr. *-naccac'má*.

The Czech forms can usefully be set up in tabular form, to show the varying paths of development (see table 2); the current norm is *-náct*, declined like *pět*.

Slovak older *-nádsťe, -nádsť* (cf. dial. *-nátsť, -nácť*), *-nác*, and the current standard *-násť*, declined like *päť* (obl. stem *-násť-*).

Polish older *-nadzieście, -naćcie, -naście* (the current standard form), *-nacie*. Minimal declension of the first part of the complex is retained in 'twelve', see section 16.1.11.3.2. In current usage the oblique form is *-nastu*, instr. also *-nastoma*; the hard consonant before the ending is unexpected, and perhaps due to the influence of the hard consonant in obl. *dwu* 'two' or *dwudziestu* 'twenty'. Declension of the second part is found from the sixteenth century (often together with declension of the unit), sometimes according to the neuter *jo*-stem substantival declension (cf. the nominative-accusative in *-cie*), or with oblique forms similar to those of the older declension of *pięć* (*jedenaści, jedenaścią*).

USo. *-naće*, declined like *pjeć*, with stem *-nać-* in oblique forms (and nominative masculine human *-naćo*).

LSo. *-nasćo*, with regular development of final **-e* to *o*. The declension is like that of *pěś*, except that the form in *-nasćo* is used in the nominative-accusative for non-masculine human too (the masculine human forms in the oblique cases are distinct, e. g. gen. *-naséich* for non-masculine human, *-naséoch* for masculine human).

Polabian: numerous variants are attested, and it is not always possible to reconstruct the exact form from the spellings of the manuscripts. The forms given by Polański and Sehnert[73] are: *-nădistě, -nădist, -năcti, -năcte, -noctě, -nocte*. The first three forms suggest primary stress on the unit, with secondary stress on the 'teen' part, given the reduction of the preceding vowel; the same is true of *-năcte*, though the vowel *-e* (CSl. **ě*, not **e*) is surprising (influence of the singular locative of the *o*- and *a*-stem substantival declensions?). Similarly, *-nocte* suggests primary stress on the last vowel, again with the unexpected *-e*. Only *-noctě* seems to agree with the pattern of the other languages, with stress on the original preposition. On the other hand, forms like *dvenăcti*, with loss of the jer in the initial syllable, suggest that primary stress was not originally on the first part of the complex; but contrast the variants *trainăcti* and *tåroinăcti*.[74]

Apart from the internally conflicting evidence of Polabian, the other languages suggest overwhelmingly stress on the preposition. It is possible that originally stress was on the unit, then attracted onto the preposition by the general rule (Fortunatov's Law) advancing stress from (originally only a short or circumflex) vowel to a following acute. This is confirmed by Ru. *odínnadcat'* 'eleven', *četýrnadcat'* 'fourteen', where the unshifted stress has been retained because the vowels in question were long and acute;[75] the other languages have levelled out this distinction.

Details of declension, except for individual exceptions, are not given again in the detailed discussion below.

16.1.11.3.1. 'Eleven'

Most of the modern languages use the nominative-accusative singular masculine as the invariable first part of the complex; in Sorbian the oblique stem is used (and in Slovenian the oblique stem is also possible as nominative-accusative singular masculine, see section 16.1.1.1.). All the modern languages have simplified the expected double *n*. OCS *(j)edinъ na desętе*; Bg. *edinádeset*, colloqu. *edinájse(t)*; Ma. *edinaeset*, colloqu. *edinajse* (for initial *edin-* rather than *eden-*, see section 16.1.1.1.); SCr. *jedànaest*; Sn. *enájst*; Ru. *odínnadcat'* (the normative pronunciation is with one *n*,[76] as in the other languages where it is reflected orthographically); Uk. *odynádcjat'*; Br. *adzináccac'*; Cz. *jedenáct*; Sk. *jedenásť* (hard *d*); Po. *jedenaście*; USo. *jědnaće* (the vowel *ě*, rather than *e*, represents lengthening after the loss of the vowel of the following syllable); LSo. *jadnasćo*. Pb. *jadånădistě, janădist, janünăcti*: the first form contains the nominative-accusative singular masculine, the second the oblique stem of the unit; the third form is unusual in showing the neuter form of the unit (**jedno na desęte*), and from the available evidence it is not clear whether the first part of the numeral was still declinable, or whether *janünăcti* was a fossilized form for all genders and cases (cf. Ru. *dvenádcat′* 'twelve' and the Polabian forms for 'twelve').

16.1.11.3.2. 'Twelve'

All the modern languages have generalized the masculine nominative-accusative form of the unit, except Russian and Polabian with generalization of the feminine form, and Polish retaining minimal declension of the unit. OCS *dъva na desęte*; Bg. *dvanádeset*, colloqu. *dvanájse(t)*; Ma. *dvanaeset*, colloqu. *dvanajse*; SCr. *dvánaest*; Sn. *dvánajst* or *dvanájst*; Ru. *dvenádcat′*, with generalization of the feminine form *dvě*; Uk. *dvanádcjat′*; Br. *dvanáccac′*; Cz. *dvanáct*; Sk. *dvanást′*; Po. *dwanaście*, obl. *dwunastu*, instrumental also *dwunastoma* (though not **dwomanastoma*), with minimal retention of declinability of the first component, the only Polish teen to retain this possibility; USo. *dwanaće*; LSo. *dwanasćo*; Pb. *dvenădist, dvenăcte, dvenăcti*, with generalization of the feminine form **dъvě*.

16.1.11.3.3. 'Thirteen'

All the modern languages have generalized the nom.-acc. fem.-neut. **tri* as first part of the complex. OCS *trъje na desęte*; Bg. *trinádeset*, colloqu. *trinájse(t)*; Ma. *trinaeset*, colloqu. *trinajse*; SCr. *trínaest*; Sn. *trînajst* or *trinájst*; Ru. *trinádcat′*; Uk. *trynádcjat′*; Br. *trynáccac′*; Cz. *třináct*; Sk. *trinást′*; Po. *trzynaście*; USo. *třinaće*; LSo. *tśinasćo*. Pb. *trainădist, trainăcti, tåroinăcti, trainoctě*; in general, the (nonetymological) jer of the initial syllable is lost, while *tåroinăcti* could represent analogical reinsertion of the jer rather than retention with original stress on the first part of the complex.

16.1.11.3.4. 'Fourteen'

Most languages lose the final vowel of the unit, presumably originally as an allegro form; the languages that retain the vowel (Bulgarian, Macedonian, Slovenian) do not use the nominative masculine form of the unit.

The softness of the final *-r* is lost, except in Lower Sorbian, before the hard *n*. Serbo-Croatian, Czech and Slovak have undergone further contraction by the loss of the **y* vowel; for Czech and Slovak, cf. forms like gen. *čtř* 'four'. OCS *četyre na desęte*; Bg. *četirinádeset*, colloqu. *četirinájse(t)*; Ma. *četirinaeset*, colloqu. *četirinajse*; SCr. *četr̀naest*; Sn. *štȋrinajst* (with the tone of the obl. cases of *štíri*) or *štirinájst*; Ru. *četýrnadcat'*; Uk. *čotyrnádcjat'*; Br. *čatyrnáccac'*; Cz. *čtrnáct*; Sk. *štrnásť*; Po. *czternaście*; USo. *štyrnaće*; LSo. *styŕnaśćo*; Pb. *citĕrnădist, citĕrnocti, citĕrnoctĕ*.

16.1.11.3.5. 'Fifteen'

All the modern languages lose the palatalization of the final *t* of the unit before the following hard *n*, except Lower Sorbian which has *ś* for **ť* in any case. In Czech and Upper Sorbian this hardening must have preceded the přehláska, giving *pat-* (USo. *pjat-*) rather than **pět-* (USo. **pjet-*) as the reflex of **ę* before a hard consonant. The hardening probably followed the Lechitic przegłos, but cf. 'sixteen'. OCS *pętь na desęte*; Bg. *petnádeset*, colloqu. *petnájse(t)*; Ma. *petnaeset*, colloqu. *petnajse*; SCr. *pètnaest* (short vowel as in the other higher teens); Sn. *pệtnajst* or *petnájst*; Ru. *pjatnádcat'*; Uk. *p'jatnádcjat'*; Br. *pjatnáccac'*; Cz. *patnáct*; Sk. *pätnásť*; Po. *piętnaście* (simplified in pronunciation to *pietnaście*); USo. *pjatnaće*; LSo. *pěśnaśćo*; Pb. *pą(t)nădist, pątnocti*.

16.1.11.3.6. 'Sixteen'

As in the other teens, the final consonant(s) of the unit lose their palatalization before the hard *n*, except in Lower Sorbian; this hardening must have followed the Lechitic przegłos, cf. the retention of *e* in Polish, and *i* (for **e* before a soft consonant) in Polabian. Many languages also simplify the consonant group *-stn-* to *-sn-*, probably quite generally in pronunciation if not in spelling (thus in Russian, the orthoepic pronunciation is without the *t*, despite the spelling).[77] OCS *šestь na desęte*; Bg. *šestnádeset*, colloqu. *šesnájse(t)*; Ma. *šesnaeset*, colloqu. *šesnajse*; SCr. *šèsnaest* (the conditions for the lengthening of **e* that apply in the simple numeral *šêst* do not hold here); Sn. *šệstnajst* or *šestnájst*; Ru. *šestnádcat'*; Uk. *šistnádcjat'*; Br. *šasnáccac'*, reflecting jakanie; Cz. *šestnáct*; Sk. *šestnásť*; Po. *szesnaście*; USo. *šěsnaće*; LSo. *šes(ć)naśćo*; Pb. *sis(t)nădist, sis(t)nocti*.

16.1.11.3.7. 'Seventeen'

The final *m* of the unit is hard in all the modern languages, including Russian. OCS *sedmь na desętе*; Bg. *sedemnádeset*, colloqu. *sedemnájse(t)*; Ma. *sedumnaeset*, colloqu. *sedumnajse*; SCr. *sedàmnaest*; Sn. *sẹ́dəmnajst* or *sedəmnájst*; Ru. *semnádcat'*; Uk. *simnádcjat'*; Br. *semnáccac'*, with no orthographic representation of jakanie, see also 'eighteen', and contrast 'sixteen'; Cz. *sedmnáct* (pronounced *sedumnáct*); Sk. *sedemnásť*; Po. *siedemnaście*; USo. *sydomnaće, sedmnaće*; LSo. *sedymnasćo*; Pb. *sidĕmnădist, sidĕmnocti*.

16.1.11.3.8. 'Eighteen'

All the modern languages have hard *m* at the end of the unit, including Russian. OCS *osmь na desętе*; Bg. *osemnádeset*, colloqu. *osemnájse(t)*; Ma. *osumnaeset*, colloqu. *osumnajse*; SCr. *osàmnaest*; Sn. *ọ́səmnajst* or *osəmnájst*; Ru. *vosemnádcat'*; Uk. *visimnádcjat'*; Br. *vasemnáccac'*, with no orthographic representation of jakanie, but with akanie of the first vowel, showing that there is no secondary stress to account for the lack of vowel reduction; Cz. *osmnáct* (pronounced *osumnáct*); Sk. *osemnásť*; Po. *osiemnaście*; USo. *wosomnaće, wósomnaće* (and other variants as for *wosom*); LSo. *wosymnasćo*; Pb. *visĕmnădist, visĕmnocti*.

16.1.11.3.9. 'Nineteen'

For the development of the second syllable of the unit, see the discussion of 'fifteen', with the same phonological make-up at this point. OCS *devętь na desętе*; Bg. *devetnádeset*, colloqu. *devetnájse(t)*; Ma. *devetnaeset*, colloqu. *devetnajse*; SCr. *devètnaest*; Sn. *devệtnajst* or *devetnájst*; Ru. *devjatnádcat'*; Uk. *dev'jatnádcjat'*; Br. *dzevjatnáccac'*; Cz. *devatenáct*, with unexpected *-e-*, between unit and ten; older Czech also *devatynáct* alongside only one known occurrence of *devietnadste*, the *-e-*/*-y-* probably deriving from ordinal formations of the type *devatenáctý, devatýnáctý*;[77a] Sk. *devätnásť*; Po. *dziewiętnaście* (pronounced *dziewietnaście*); USo. *dźewjatnaće*; LSo. *źewěśnasćo*; Pb. *divą(t)nădist, divą(t)nocti*.

16.1.11.3.10. 'Tenteen'

This particular instance of overcounting is attested only in Polabian, where *disą(t)nocti* (**desętь na desętе*) is the only attested word for 'twenty'. Further overcounting in the teens was probably not possible in

Polabian, the attested forms for 'twenty-one' being *jadån disǫtnocti* and *disǫtnocti jadån*, i. e. in higher coordinate numerals *disǫtnocti* behaves like the Common Slavonic word for 'twenty', **dъva desęti.*

16.1.11.3.11. Ordinals

The ordinals of the teens occur very rarely in Old Church Slavonic, though from the sparse data here and in the other early Slavonic languages the following patterns can be detected. The commonest is for the unit to appear as an ordinal, agreeing with the noun, while the second part of the complex remains invariable as *na desęte*, e. g. *pęto(j)e na desęte* 'fifteenth (nominative-accusative singular neuter)'. Under Church Slavonic influence this formation survived in Russian into the nineteenth century in the high style. Another common formation was for the second part of the complex to be declined, in the form *-nadesęt-*, i. e. without any specifically ordinal suffix, while the unit was attached in the form used in compounds (see section 16.5.), with the connecting vowel *o*, e. g. *osmonadesęto(j)e* 'eighteenth (nominative-accusative singular neuter)'. The third type, attested in the Codex Suprasliensis 273, is for the first part of the complex to be invariable in the nominative, while the second part attaches the adjective-forming suffix **-ьn* to *-nadesęt-*, giving *devętъnadesętьněmь* 'nineteenth'. All three formations are found in the Codex Suprasliensis.

All of the modern languages have abandoned these systems. Instead, the stem of the cardinal is used as stem of the ordinal without any ordinal-forming suffix (except in Macedonian, where as elsewhere ordinal-forming *t* is used), the adjectival ending being attached directly to this stem. The formation in the individual languages are given below.

Bg. *-nádeseti*, colloqu. *-nájseti*; there are also short forms without the final *-i*, though these are hardly used in the modern language. *Edinádeseti* (*edinájseti*), *dvanádeseti* (*dvanájseti*), *trinádeseti* (*trinájseti*), *četirinádeseti* (*četirinájseti*), *petnádeseti* (*petnájseti*), *šestnádeseti* (*šesnájseti*), *sedemnádeseti* (*sedemnájseti*), *osemnádeseti* (*osemnájseti*), *devetnádeseti* (*devetnájseti*).

Ma. *-naesetti*, colloqu. *-najsetti: edinaesetti* (*edinajsetti*), *dvanaesetti* (*dvanajsetti*), *trinaesetti* (*trinajsetti*), *četirinaesetti* (*četirinajsetti*), *petnaesetti* (*petnajsetti*), *šesnaesetti* (*šesnajsetti*), *sedumnaesetti* (*sedumnajsetti*), *osumnaesetti* (*osumnajsetti*), *devetnaesetti* (*devetnajsetti*).

SCr. *-naestī: jedànaestī, dvánaestī, trínaestī, četȓnaestī, pètnaestī, šèsnaestī, sedàmnaestī, osàmnaestī, devètnaestī.*

Sn. *-nájsti: enájsti, dvȃnajsti* or *dvanájsti, trȋnajsti* or *trinájsti, štȋrinajsti* or *štirinájsti, pę̑tnajsti* or *petnájsti, šę̑stnajsti* or *šestnájsti, sę̑dəmnajsti* or *sedəmnájsti, ọ̑səmnajsti* or *osəmnájsti, devę̑tnajsti* or *devetnájsti.*[78]

Ru. *-nádcatyj: odínnadcatyj, dvenádcatyj, trinádcatyj, četýrnadcatyj, pjatnádcatyj, šestnádcatyj, semnádcatyj, vosemnádcatyj, devjatnádcatyj.*

Uk. *-nádcjatyj: odynádcjatyj, dvanádcjatyj, trynádcjatyj, čotyrnádcjatyj, p'jatnádcjatyj, šistnádcjatyj, simnádcjatyj, visimnádcjatyj, dev'jatnádcjatyj.*

Br. *-náccaty: adzináccaty, dvanáccaty, trynáccaty, čatyrnáccaty, pjatnáccaty, šasnáccaty, semnáccaty, vasemnáccaty, dzevjatnáccaty.*

Cz. *-náctý: jedenáctý, dvanáctý, třináctý, čtrnáctý, patnáctý, šestnáctý, sedmnáctý* (pronounced *sedumnáctý*), *osmnáctý* (pronounced *osumnáctý*), *devatenáctý.*

Sk. *-násty: jedenásty* (hard *d*), *dvanásty, trinásty, štrnásty, pätnásty, šestnásty, sedemnásty, osemnásty, devätnásty.*

Po. *-nasty: jedenasty, dwunasty, trzynasty, czternasty, piętnasty* (pro- *pietnasty*), *szesnasty, siedemnasty, osiemnasty, dziewiętnasty* (pronounced *dziewietnasty*). The stem is that of the oblique form of the cardinal, i. e. *-nast-*, cf. in particular *dwunasty*, from obl. *dwunastu* rather than nom.-acc. *dwanaście.*

USo. *-naty: jědnaty, dwanaty, třinaty, štyrnaty, pjatnaty, šěsnaty, sydomnaty* (*sedmnaty*), *wosomnaty* (and variants as for *wosom*), *dźewjatnaty.*

LSo. *-nasty: jadnasty, dwanasty, tśinasty, styŕnasty, pěśnasty, šesnasty, sedymnasty, wosymnasty, źeẃeśnasty.*

16.1.12. Decads

In Balto-Slavonic, the Indo-European formations for the decads are lost completely (with the possible exception of the East Slavonic for 'ninety', q. v.), and are replaced by new formations on the transparent pattern '*x* tens', using the regular numeral (and noun) for 'ten' (**dek̂imt-*). These forms are still clearly transparent in the oldest Slavonic, and in one of the two formations in Lithuanian. Elsewhere, various contractions have taken place masking somewhat the original formation.

16.1.12.1. Baltic

The transparent formation in Lithuanian uses the appropriate form of the feminine noun *dešimtìs*, e. g. nom.-acc. pl. *dẽšimtys*, also nom.-acc. du. *dẽšimti* in the form form 'twenty': *dvì dẽšimti, trỹs dẽšimtys, kẽturios dẽšimtys, peñkios dẽšimtys, šẽšios dẽšimtys, septýnios dẽšimtys, aštúonios* *dẽšimtys, devýnios dẽšimtys.* These decline as ordinary adjective plus noun constructions. Alternatively, an indeclinable formation may be used with *-dešimt* (originally the accusative singular) as second component and the fossilized accusative plural feminine of the unit (though in the case of *dvìdešimt* the initial *dvi-* could be the regular form used in compounds, for IE **du̯i-*, see section 16.6.): *dvìdešimt, trìsdešimt, kẽturiasdešimt, peñkiasdešimt, šẽšiasdešimt, septýniasdešimt, aštúondiasdešimt, devýniasdešimt.*

In Latvian only the compound formation exists, with indeclinable *-desmit* as second component (dial. also *-desmits*, which can then decline), and the cardinal (minus the final *-i*) as first component: *divdesmit, trîsdesmit, četrdesmit, pìecdesmit, sešdesmit, septiņdesmit, astôņdesmit, deviņdesmit.* Other forms found in dialects include: *dividesmit* (with the full form of fem. du. *divi*), *divudesmit* (of unclear origin, perhaps with the masculine dual, cf. OCS *dъva desęti* with the original masculine form of this numeral) for 'twenty', and *četrudesmit* (for **četurdesmit*, or by analogy with *divudesmit*) and *četradesmit* (of unclear oigin) for 'forty' (cf. 'fourteen', section 16.1.11.2.).

The current forms for the ordinals in both Lithunian and Latvian simply add the adjectival endings to the stem of the cardinal, i. e. Lithuanian: *dvìdešimtas, trìsdešimtas, keturiasdẽšimtas, penkiasdẽšimtas, šešiasdẽšimtas, septyniasdẽšimtas, aštuoniasdẽšimtas, devyniasdẽšimtas*; Latvian: *divdesmitais, trîsdesmitais, četrdesmitais, pìecdesmitais, sešdesmitais, septiņdesmitais, astôņdesmitais, deviņdesmitais.* In older documents another formation is found, with 'twentieth' expressed as 'second tenth', Li. *añtras dešim̃tas*, Le. (loc.) *otrā desmitā*; cf. similar formations in the older Slavonic languages.

16.1.12.2. Slavonic cardinals

The Indo-European forms for the decads are lost in Slavonic (except perhaps for 'ninety' in East Slavonic, q. v., on one explanation of this form), and replaced by transparently multiplicative forms using the noun **desętь* in the appropriate form, either as a masculine and consonant-stem or, as elsewhere, as feminine and/or *i*-stem. The Common Slavonic and Old Church Slavonic forms will be discussed first, with indications of the main changes in the modern languages, followed by the forms language by language. Particularly aberrant forms are found in East Slavonic ('forty', 'ninety'), Slovincian (see section 16.1.12.2.1.), and Polabian ('twenty', 'thirty').

The Common Slavonic form for 'twenty' is **dъva desęti*, with the dual of **desętь*. This is also the usual Old Church Slavonic form, alongside one occurrence of *dъva desętě*, where *-ě* (orthographic for both **ě* and **ja*) seems to be the *jo*-stem ending. Despite the tendency for **desętь* to become feminine, there are no traces of **dъvě desęti* or its reflexes. The form **dъva desęti* is that from which most of the modern forms derive, except in those languages that have generalized the original genitive plural from the higher decads into the lower decads.

For 'thirty', the expected form is **trьje desęte*, with the nominative masculine of the first component and the nominative plural consonant-declension form of **desętь*. The nominative is not attested in Old Church Slavonic, and all the modern forms derive from forms with **tri* (i.e. feminine) in the first component. Many modern forms suggest a second component **desęti*, with the *i*-stem ending, cf. 'forty'.

The Common Slavonic form for 'forty' is **četyre desęte*, i.e. masculine consonant-declension. Old Church Slavonic has both *četyre desęte* and *četyri desęti*, the latter with feminine *i*-stem declension, and this latter form stands at the origin of many of the current forms. Many languages (especially South Slavonic) have replaced the original forms for 'twenty' to 'forty' by new formations with the genitive plural of **desętь*, on the analogy of the higher decads. Sometimes traces of the older forms are still present in stress differences: CSl. **désęti, *désęte* in the nominative dual and plural versus **desę́tъ* (for **desętъ̍*) in the genitive plural. For the lower decads, most languages that retain mobile stress point to original stress on the first part of the complex in the cardinals (nonapplicability of Fortunatov's Law, because of circumflex accent on the second component).

The higher decads are relatively straightforward, with the pl. gen. **desętъ: *pętь desętъ*, **šestь desętъ*; **sedmь desętъ*; **osmь desętъ*; **devętь desętъ*. The Old Church Slavonic forms, to the extent that they are attested, are the same. For the stress, see section 16.1.5.0.5.; the differentiation that is apparent in Russian has been levelled out in the other languages.

The modern languages have usually lost declension of the first part of the complex (except: 'twenty' in Polish; the higher decads in East Slavonic), and the medial consonant cluster is often simplified in much the same way as for the teens.

All the Bulgarian decads have *-deset* as second component, in some forms simplified to *-jse(t)* (after vowels) in colloquial usage. In 'twenty' to 'forty' the stress is on the first component, in the higher decads on the second. The generalized second component *-deset* represents either spread of the second component of the higher decads, or phonetic reduction of *-deseti*. The forms are (colloquial variants in parentheses): *dvádeset* (*dvájse(t)*), *trídeset* (*tríjse(t)*), *četírideset* (*četiríjse(t)*), *petdesét* (*pedesé(t)*), *šestdesét* (*šéjse(t)*), *sedemdesét* (*sedemdesé(t)*), *osemdesét* (*osemdesé(t)*), *devetdesét* (*devedesé(t)*).

The Macedonian forms are very similar (colloquial variants in parentheses): *dvaeset* (*dvajse*), *trieset* (*trijse*), *četirieset* (*četirijse*), *pedeset* (*pedese*), *šeeset* (*šeese*, dial. also *šiese*, by analogy with *triese*), *sedumdeset* (*sedumdese*), *osumdeset* (*osumdese*), *devedeset* (*devedese*).

The oldest Serbo-Croatian forms for the lower decads are *dva deseti, tri deseti, četiri deseti*, also contracted forms *dvadesti, tridesti, četir(i)desti*. Alongside these are found the current forms with *-desēt*, as in the higher decads; but the development could also have been via phonetic contraction, cf. the stress of 'twenty' and 'thirty' (but not 'forty', which has been assimilated to the higher decads). The current forms are (colloquial variants in parentheses): *dvádesēt* (*dvàest*), *trídesēt* (*trìest*), *četrdèsēt* (*če-tȑsēt*), *pedèsēt, šezdèsēt* (*šésēt*), *sedamdèsēt, osamdèsēt, devedèsēt*.

The Slovenian forms have generalized stress on the first component, and *-deset* as second component, except in the form for 'twenty': *dvȃjset* (contracted from **dva deset*) (dial. also *dvájsti*, for **dъva desęti*), *trȋdeset, štírideset, pę̂tdeset, šę̂stdeset, sę́dəmdeset, ǫ́səmdeset, devę̂tdeset*. They are declined like *pę̂t*, without any change in stress or vowel quality. Some dialects use *rę̂d*, literally 'row', originally a commercial term, instead of *-deset*, e. g. *pętrę̂d* 'fifty', in Rezija *paterdou* (**pętь rędovъ*);[79] for vigesimal forms in the Rezija dialect, see section 16.0.4.

The Common Slavonic system is still retained reasonably faithfully in the oldest Russian, though there are instances of etymologically incorrect declension, usually by failure to decline the second component. In the current forms for 'twenty' and 'thirty', the second component has been reduced from *desjate, desjati* to *-dcat'* (for **-dsjat'*), with variants in older manuscripts, dialects and other East Slavonic languages: *-cat', -dcjat', -cjat'*. The retention of the softness of the final consonant was no doubt fostered by the declension, parallel to that of *pjat'*, with indeclinability in the modern language of the first component: *dvádcat'* (gen.-dat.-loc. *dvadcatí*, instr. *dvadcat'jú*), *trídcat'* (gen.-dat.-loc. *tridcatí*, instr. *tridcat'jú*); the stress is that common to many Russian numerals, with initial stress in the nominative-accusative and desinence stress in the oblique forms.

For 'forty', Russian, like the other East Slavonic languages, replaces the Slavonic formation *četyre desjate* with the word *sorok*. Earlier attempts to derive this from Greek *sarákonta* (classical *tessarákonta*, modern *saránta*) 'forty' or *sarakostḗ* (from *tessarakostḗ*) 'fast lasting forty days' have been largely rejected:[80] since Greek early loses the *ko* of the former to give *saránta*, there are chronological difficulties with this explanation in view of the later development of Russian-Byzantine trading links, while *sarakostḗ*, apart from its more restricted meaning, fails to account for the other meaning of *sorok* in older north Russian, namely 'a sack of forty sable furs'. The latter meaning suggests rather a link with Ru. *soróčka* 'shirt, blouse', cf. Li. *šar̃kas* 'fisherman's coat', *švar̃kas* 'night-dress'; these are probably not loans from Old Norse *serkr* which is quite isolated in Germanic, suggesting that if there were any loan traffic it was in the reverse direction. The accentuation of the Lithuanian forms is paralleled by the accent in older Russian, fixed on the initial syllable.[81] The older declension was as a masculine *o*-stem noun (cf. the archaic expression *sórok sorokóv* 'forty forties', the number of churches in Moscow); the current norm is nom.-acc. *sórok* versus obl. *soroká*, cf. 'ninety' and 'hundred'. The current stress is as for *pjat'*, i. e. desinence stress in the oblique cases.

In Russian for the higher decads ('fifty' to 'eighty'), the first component retains its declension as in the simple cardinal (Common Slavonic), while the second component follows exactly the same declension in the oblique cases; in the oblique cases stress is always on the first component (original acute). In nonstandard usage, the first component in the oblique cases is often generalized throughout to the form in *-í*, possibly by analogy with the form used in compounds (see section 16.5.).[82] The forms are: *pjat'desját* (gen.-dat.-loc. *pjatídesjati*, instr. *pjat'júdesjat'ju*, colloqu. also *pjatídesjat'ju*), *šest'desját, sém'desjat, vósem'desjat*. In the spoken language the second component is often pronounced *-s'át*, unstressed *-s'ət*.[83]

For 'ninety', Russian again has a form diverging from the regular Slavonic pattern, namely *devjanósto*; this form occurs in the other East Slavonic languages, though in Ukrainian and Belorussian dialects forms of *devjat'desjat* are widespread. Several attempts have been made to explain this form,[84] the main ones being as follows. One suggestion links *devjanósto* to the Indo-European decads formation (i. e. prior to the Slavonic re-formations, i. e. as an archaic survival), as **ne̯uenə-(d)ḱm̥tə* 'nine tens' or 'ninth ten'; a more detailed etymology of this type is advanced by Szemerényi,[85] on the basis of extrapolated pre-Slavonic forms of the decads before the Slavonic re-formation, in particular **ostāsъ(n)* 'eighty' and **nevīnsъ(n)* (or **devīnsъ(n)*) 'ninety', the latter being influenced by the former to give **devinasъ*, then being influenced by the following word for 'hundred' to give **devinās(ъ)to*, then by *devętь* to give **devenasto*, and finally by assimilation *devenosto* (the earliest attested form of modern *devjanosto*); the number of necessary nonattested forms makes it difficult to assess the validity of this line of argument. Another approach suggests an original form **devętь do sъta* (or **devętь na sъto*), but this makes it difficult to account for the meaning (hundred less ten, not nine); a possible patching operation would be **desętь do sъta*, **desętь na sъto*, with reinterpretation (or dissimilation) to initial *devę-*. The most profitable line of attack seems to be that of treating *devjanósto* as the result of the intersection of a nonal and decimal system of counting, especially as the incidence of *devjanósto* is geographically very similar to that of nonal forms like *trídevjat′* in folklore;[86] one specific suggestion is that of Stang,[87] namely **devjano sъto*, where the first word is an adjective, i. e. 'the nonal hundred' (cf. the Germanic *Grosshundert* 'one hundred and twenty'), **devęnъ* being the adjective formed from **devę* (rather than the later *devętь*, cf. section 16.1.5.0.3.), attested in plant names like *devjasíl* 'Inula helenium'. The older declension of this form is as a neuter *o*-stem, the current declension distinguishes only nom.-acc. *devjanósto* and obl. *devjanósta*, cf. 'hundred'. In older Russian *devjat′-desjat* is also found, and in the standard language survives, alongside *devjanósto*, into the nineteenth century.

The Ukrainian forms for the decads are very similar to those of Russian in the nominative-accusative, though in the higher decads stress on the second component has been generalized to all numerals. The declension of 'twenty' to 'thirty' is similar to that of *p'jat′*: *dvádcjat′* (gen.-dat.-loc. *dvadcjatý*, or gen.-loc. *dvadcjatjóch*, dat. *dvadcjatjóm*, instr. *dvadcjat′má* or *dvadcjatjomá*), *trýdcjat′*. The word for 'forty' is as in Russian: *sórok*, obl. *soroká*. For the higher decads, the first component is invariable, and has a final hard consonant by assimilation to the following *d* (hard in Ukrainian before *e*); the second component declines like *p'jat′*: *p'jatdesját* (gen.-dat.-loc. *p'jatdesjatý* or gen.-loc. *p'jatdesjatjóch*, dat. *p'jatdesjatjóm*, instr. *p'jatdesjat′má* or *p'jatdesjatjomá*), *šistdesját, simdesját, visimdesját*. In current normative usage 'ninety' is *dev'janósto*, obl. *dev'janósta*, though until recently in the standard language, and still in dialects, the form *dev'jatdesját* was found.

The Belorussian decads are very similar in form, stress and declension to those of Russian, at least in the current standard, though they also appear as indeclinables, and in literature with variants as for 'five', and one source specifically notes a stress *šésc'dzesjat*,[88] though I have not found support for this form from elsewhere: *dváccac'* (gen.-dat.-loc. *dvaccací*, instr. *dvaccaccjú*), *trýccac'*, *sórak* (obl. *saraká*; instr. also *sarakmá* in literature), *pjac'dzesját* (gen.-dat.-loc. *pjacídzesjaci*, instr. *pjaccjúdzesjaccju*), *šèsc'dzesját* (gen. *šascídzesjaci*), *sémdzesjat* (gen. *sjamídzesjaci*), *vósemdzesjat* (gen. *vas'mídzesjaci*), *dzevjanósta* (indeclinable, the difference between *devjanósto* and obl. *devjanósta* being lost by akanie).

The Old Czech forms for the lower decads all derive from **desęti*, in the form *-dcěti, -cěti, -čet, -cet*, the latter with the regular Czech loss of the difference between *e* and *ě* after *c*, giving modern *dvacet, třicet, čtyřicet*. The older pattern was for declension of both parts, e. g. gen. *tří(d)cát*, loc. *třech(d)cětech*, or only of the first part, as in instr. *třmicát*, where the second component is a fossilized genitive plural. The current declension is as for 'five', obl. *dvaceti, třiceti, čtyřiceti*, also *dvacíti, třicíti, čtyřicíti*. The higher decads have in Czech *-desát* (dial. contracted to *-cát*), for **desętъ*, with dispalatalization of **ę* before a nonpalatalized consonant (also in the first component of 'fifty' and 'ninety'), and retention of length before a stressed jer: *padesát, šedesát, sedmdesát* (pronounced *sedumdesát*), *osmdesát* (pronounced *osumdesát*), *devadesát*, with contraction in the case of 'fifty', 'ninety', and especially 'sixty'. The original declension was either just of the first part, as in Common Slavonic, or of both parts; the current declension is of the whole complex like *pět*, i. e. obl. *padesáti*. The loss of final palatalization in numerals like *pět* facilitated the shift of the higher tens, with original hard consonants, into this declension pattern.

The Slovak forms are very similar, also in historical development, to those of Czech, though contraction is rather less marked in the higher decads. The current declension is of the second component only, i. e. of the whole complex, like *päť*; the higher decads have a dialectal form in *-desiať*, analogically removing the contrast between the hard stem nominative-accusative and the soft stem of the oblique cases: *dvadsať, tridsať, štyridsať, päťdesiat, šesťdesiat, sedemdesiat, osemdesiat, deväťdesiat*. In the higher decads, *-desiat* continues **ďesa̋t* for **desętъ*, without the characteristically Czech dispalatalization. Stanislav[89] notes a dialect form *meru* for 'forty', but it is not clear whether this is used in strictly numeral use. It derives from Hungarian *mérő* 'measure', originally the present participle of the verb *mér* 'measure', itself originally a loan from the Slavonic root **měr* 'measure'.

The Old Polish forms present considerable variety. The modern forms are: *dwadzieścia* (obl. *dwudziestu*, instrumental also *dwudziestoma*, with retention of minimal declension of the first component, the only such decad in modern Polish), *trzydzieści* (obl. *trzydziestu*, instrumental also *trzydziestoma*), *czterdzieści* (obl. *czterdziestu*, instrumental also *czterdziestoma*), *pięćdziesiąt* (obl. *pięćdziesięciu*, instrumental also *pięćdziesięcioma*; the higher forms are declined in the same way), *sześćdziesiąt, siedemdziesiąt, osiemdziesiąt, dziewięćdziesiąt*; in pronunciation, *ć* is silent before the *dź* in these forms ('fifty', 'sixty', 'ninety').

The form *dwadzieścia*, with analogical *-a* probably from the form *dwa*, is the commonest form from earliest times, and there is only one occurrence of *dwadzieści* for **dъva desęti*. Another form is OPo. *dwadzieście*, with *-ie* probably by analogy with the teen formations in *-nadzieście, -naście*; current orthoepic handbooks still find it necessary to warn against forms in *-dzieście* for the lower decads. The obl. *dwudziestu* directly continues the old gen.-loc. du. **dъvoju desętu*. Other forms that occur in earlier periods are dat. *dwudziestom*, instr. *dwiemadziestoma, dwiemadziesty, dwadzieścią, dwudzieścią, dwudziestą*, with various dual, plural, and singular (cf. *pięć*) endings of the instrumental.

For 'thirty' and 'forty' the oldest forms are *trzydzieści* and *czterydzieści* or contracted *czterdzieści* (for variants of the first component, see the discussion of 'four'). The rare alternatives in *-dzieście* are apparently by analogy with the teens rather than direct reflexes of CSl. **tri desęte*, etc., though the data are sparse; cf. also analogical *trzydzieścia* (with a neuter plural ending), *trzydziesiąt* (by analogy with *pięćdziesiąt*), and similar forms for 'forty'. The original declension was of both parts, replaced subsequently by declension of the second part only, finally on the pattern of *dwadzieścia* and the other numerals with a general oblique in *-u*. In the intervening period there are also instances of declension of the first component only, followed by invariable *-dziesiąt*, as in *pięćdziesiąt* in the older language.

For the higher decads the nominative-accusative forms *pięcdziesiąt*, etc., regularly continue **pętь desętъ*, with the genitive plural of **desętь*, and in Polish lengthening of the nasal vowel in a closed syllable after the loss of the final jer, represented in the modern language by *ą* rather than *ę*. Originally, only the first component declined, as in other noun phrases with a numeral between 'five' and 'nine' and a noun in the genitive plural, but the declension was subsequently transferred to the second component only, finally as a general oblique case in *-u*, and a soft stem in the oblique cases as in the lower decads. Occasional examples of declension of both parts are found in the nineteenth century.

In Upper Sorbian, the lower tens have the suffix *-ceći* (**desęti*): *dwaceći, třiceći, štyrceći*; while the higher decads have *-dźesat* (**desętъ*): *pjećdźesat* (also *połsta* 'half of a hundred'), *šěsćdźesat, sydomdźesat, wosomdźesat* (and variants as for *sydom, wosom*), *dźewjećdźesat*. The current declension (if the numerals are not used indeclinably) is of the second component only, following the declension of *pjeć*, with the stem *dwaceć-*, etc., *pjećdźesać-*, etc., the latter with analogical softness of the *ć*; e. g. gen.-loc. *dwacećich*, masc. hum. *dwacećoch, pjećdźesaćich*, masc. hum. *pjećdźesaćoch*.

In Lower Sorbian the suffixes are *-źasća* (probably by analogy with *dwa*, or with the neut. *o*-stems in the plural) and *-źaset: dwaźasća, tśiźasća, styŕźasća, pěśźaset* (or the divisional formations *poł sta, poł hunderta*, both 'half of a hundred'), *šesćźaset, sedymźaset, wosymźaset, źewěśźaset*. The lower decads ('twenty' to 'forty') are either indeclinable or declined like *pěś*, stem *dwaźasć-*, e. g. gen.-loc. *dwaźasćich*, masc. hum. *dwaźasćoch*. The higher decads are not declined in Lower Sorbian.

Polabian has *disątnocti* for 'twenty' (see section 16.1.11.3.10.) and *pöl-t'üpě* for 'thirty', the latter for **pol kopy*, i. e. 'half of sixty', see section 16.1.12.2.1.; CSl. **o* gives Pb. *ö* before hard dentals, elsewhere *ü*, and **k* is fronted to *t'* before front vowels. The higher decads all have *-diśǫt*, for CSl. **desętъ*, with Lechitic przegłos: *citěrdiśǫt* (with *-diśot* by analogy with the higher tens),[90] *pą(t)diśǫt, sis(t)diśǫt, siděmdiśǫt, visěmdiśǫt, divą(t)diśǫt*, and even *disą(t)diśǫt* by overcounting for 'hundred', cf. older German *zehanzec* 'ten-ty', alongside *pątstid'ě*; in the only compound of 'hundred' attested, *disąt pątstid'ě* 'thousand', the form 'ten-ty' is not used, so there is circumstantial evidence that this formation may not have been used beyond 'one hundred'. Some of Pfeffinger's forms[91] deserve comment: *Tújan Ziternístich* 'forty' and *Tewangtnótzti* 'ninety' are teens rather than decads, despite Pfeffinger's glosses, the former being wildly deformed;[92] *Schistisjunčt* 'sixty' has *š* distinct from *s* as in a few other forms, e. g. the collective numeral 'four' (see section 16.4.); *sibitisjunčt* 'seventy', i. e. probably *sibědiśǫt*, seems to represent a development *siděm* > **sidmᵉ̆* > **sibmᵉ̆* > *sibᵉ̆*.

16.1.12.2.1. Slovincian cardinals

In Slovincian, this system of forming the decads is lost, except in the one form *dvaʒię́scä* 'twenty', bearing witness to the fact that formations of this type were once possible in these dialects. For the other decads, the

Common Slavonic forms have been replaced by and large by a vigesimal system, using *štã̄gă* 'score', a loanword from German, cf. German *Steige*; the Slovincian form suggests an original form with the vowel **i*, rather than the standard German diphthong *ei*, as would be expected from the Low German that surrounded Slovincian. Similar forms are found, at least as alternatives for some of the decads, in other Kashubian dialects, also in the Polabian word for 'hundred'. Hinze[93] suggests that the Slovincian system is based on an old Low German vigesimal system. In Slovincian, the simplex *štã̄gă* is not used strictly as a numeral, though the other twenties are formed on the pattern '*x* twenties'. The odd decads are formed on the pattern '$\frac{1}{2}$ of the *x*th twenty', using the Common Slavonic fractions '$\frac{1}{2}$ of the $(x + 1)$th' for '$x\frac{1}{2}$' (see section 16.5.2.). In addition to this vigesimal system, there is also a sexagesimal system, using Common Slavonic **kopa*, with the basic meaning 'heap', but widely used in Baltic and Polish as a commercial term for a batch of sixty; again, similar forms are found in Polabian. The numerals are listed below, including comparisons with Polabian, but including only those forms that are strictly numeral in use.

Twenty: *dvaʒi̯ȩscä*, the only possibility in Slovincian.

Thirty: *pȯu̯lkṷ̀o̯pä*, i.e. 'half of sixty', **polъ-kopy*, cf. Pb. *pöl-t'üpě*. Note that in this form *štã̄gă* may not be used.

Forty: *dvještã̄ză*, i.e. 'two scores', using the dual of *štã̄gă*, where the ending **ě* automatically induces the First Palatalization of **g* to *z*; the numeral is in the feminine form, agreeing with the 'noun'.

Fifty: *pȯu̯lstã*, i.e. 'half of a hundred', the only possibility here, for **polъ-sъta*; cf. similar forms in Sorbian.

Sixty: *třäštã̄ʒ́ĭ*, i.e. 'three scores'; the second part of the complex is in the plural, with the regular Slovincian shift of **gi* (CSl. **gy*) to *ʒ́i*. Alongside this form, *kṷ̀ o̯pă* was also used in strictly numerical use (unlike Polabian).

Seventy: *pö̋˙u̯čvjarṭ štã̄ʒ́ĭ*, i.e. 'half of the fourth score'.

Eighty: *št˙ĕ̋räštȧʒ́ĭ*, i.e. 'four scores'.

Ninety: *pö̋˙u̯pjątäštã̄ʒ́ĭ*, i.e. 'half of the fifth score'.

Hundred: *stṷ̀o̯*, the commoner form, and the only form found in the higher hundreds, for CSl. **sъto*, alongside *pjĩnc štī́g*, i.e. 'five scores'. In the latter form, the 'noun' is in the genitive plural, with zero-ending and regular lengthening of the preceding vowel before a voiced obstruent (*ï* functions as the lengthened grade of *ȧ* for original **y*), and (nonphonemic) palatalization of the final *g* after *ï*. Cf. Pb. *pątstid'ě* 'hundred'.

From the above it will be seen that the Slovincian decads do not present a strictly vigesimal (or sexagesimal) system, though there are clear vigesimal and sexagesimal features. The decimal system is retained for 'twenty'; the vigesimal system cannot be used here, nor for 'thirty' and 'fifty'. The sexagesimal system only gives the base 'sixty' and one other form, 'thirty', but no multiplicative formations. The word for 'score' is not used itself in strictly numeral use. Vigesimal and sexagesimal forms are even less systematic in other Kashubian dialects and in Polabian. Use of the vigesimal system to form numerals higher than 'hundred' (e. g. 'one hundred and twenty' as 'six twenties') is not attested; even Pb. *disǫt pǫtstid'ĕ* is not a counterexample, since it is 'ten times (five times twenty)', rather than '(ten times five) times twenty', cf. the impossibility of **disǫt pǫt* 'ten fives' in the meaning 'fifty'.

16.1.12.3. Slavonic ordinals

The ordinals of the decads are very rare in Old Church Slavonic, though the following formations are attested in Old Church Slavonic and Church Slavonic. Perhaps the oldest formation was to put both the digit and the decad into the ordinal form, e. g. *sedmo(j)e desęto(j)e* 'seventieth', literally 'seventh tenth'. In Old Church Slavonic these ordinals are usually contracted into one word, often with the adjective-forming suffix *-ьn* attached to the whole complex, e. g. *dъvadesętьno(j)e* 'twentieth'; very occasionally, the digit is replaced by the form used in compounds (see section 16.6.), thus emphasizing the unity of the complex, e. g. *dъvodesętьno(j)e*. Finally, the stem of the cardinal may be used as stem of the ordinal, e. g. *sedmьdesęto(j)e*. It is this last formation that predominates in the modern languages, the only exceptions being the higher decads in East Slavonic, where the first component may occur in the form used in compounds (identical with the genitive, see section 16.6.), and in the Polish form for 'twenty'. For Bulgarian, Macedonian, and Slovenian, colloquial variants are given in parentheses.

Bg. *dvádeseti* (*dvájseti*), *trídeseti* (*tríjseti*), *četírideseti* (*četiríjseti*), *petdeséti* (*pedeséti*), *šestdeséti* (*šejséti*), *sedemdeséti, osemdeséti, devetdeséti* (*devedeséti*). Short ordinal forms without the final *-i*, i. e. identical with the cardinals, have at least a theoretical existence in Bulgarian.

Ma. *dvaesetti* (*dvajsetti*), *triesetti* (*trijsetti*), *četiriesetti* (*četirijsetti*), *pedesetti, šeesetti, sedumdesetti, osumdesetti, devedesetti.*

SCr. *dvádesētī* (*dváestī*), *trídesētī* (*tríestī*), *četrdèsētī* (*četȑestī*), *pedèsētī, šezdèsētī* (*šésētī*), *sedamdèsētī, osamdèsētī, devedèsētī.*

Sn. *dvâjseti, trîdeseti, štírideseti, pę̂tdeseti, šę̂stdeseti, sę̂dəmdeseti, ọ́səmdeseti, devę̂tdeseti.*

In East Slavonic, for the higher decads ('fifty' to 'eighty'), Russian and Belorussian (but not Ukrainian) use as first component the same form as in compounds, i. e. the genitive. Ru. *dvadcátyj, tridcátyj, sorokovój, pjatidesjátyj, šestidesjátyj, semidesjátyj, vos'midesjátyj, devjanóstyj.* Uk. *dvadcjátyj, trydcjátyj, trydcjátyj, sorokóvyj, p'jatdesjátyj, šistdesjátyj, simdesjátyj, visimdesjátyj, dev'janóstyj* (non-standard *dev'jatdesjátyj*). Br. *dvaccáty, tryccáty, sarakavý, pjacidzesjáty, šascidzesjáty, sjamidzesjáty, vas'midzesjáty, dzevjanósty* (nonstandard *dzevjacidzesjáty*).

Cz. *dvacátý, třicátý, čtyřicátý, padesátý, šedesátý, sedmdesátý, osmdesátý, devadesátý.* Sk. *dvadsiaty, tridsiaty, štyridsiaty, päť desiaty, šesť desiaty, sedemdesiaty, osemdesiaty, deväť desiaty.*

The Polish form for 'twentieth' is *dwudziesty*, with initial *dwu-* as in compounds (see section 16.6.), although this could also be generalization of *dwu-* to all forms other than the nominative-accusative of the cardinal; the special compound forms are not used with the other decads: *trzydziesty, czterdziesty, pięćdziesiąty, sześćdziesiąty, siedemdziesiąty, osiemdziesiąty, dziewięćdziesiąty.*

USo. *dwacety, třicety, štyrcety, pjećdźesaty, šěsćdźesaty, sydomdźesaty, wosomdźesaty* (and variants as for *sydom* and *wosom*), *dźewjećdźesaty.* LSo. *dwaźasty, tśiźasty, styŕźasty, pěśźasety, šesćźasety, sedymźasety, wosymźasety, źeẃeśźasety.*

Further comment is needed only for those numerals not based on the strict decimal pattern. ESl. *devjanóstyj* follows the usual pattern of having the same stem for cardinal and ordinal. The East Slavonic forms *sorokovój, sorokóvyj, sarakavój* use the adjective-forming suffix *-ov*. In Slovincian, *pòu̯lkŭ̀ọpnĭ* 'thirtieth' uses the adjective-forming suffix *-n* (**-ьn*), and is the highest ordinal used in Slovincian; the Polabian higher ordinals are not attested.

16.1.13. Hundreds

16.1.13.1. 'Hundred'

The derivatives of IE **ḱm̥tom* are relatively straightforward in Baltic. **ḱ* regularly gives Li. *š*, Le. *s*; the syllabic sonants are resolved to *i* plus sonant in all cases after palatovelars, giving Li. *šim̃tas*, Le. *sìmts*, in the modern languages masculine nouns (in Latvian only in nominal use) following the loss of the neuter. The accent pattern in Lithuanian is of type IV (nom. pl. *šimtaĩ*), though in dialects type II is also found (nom. pl. *šim̃tai*), especially in the formation of the higher hundreds.

In Lithuanian dialects the contracted form *šim̃ts* occurs, and in coordinate numerals a first component *šim*, e. g. *šim devynì* 'one hundred and nine'. In Latvian, in addition to nominal *sìmts*, in attributive use we find fossilized (invariable) *sìmts*, also *sìmtu* (originally accusative singular) and contracted *sìmt*. In Lithuanian *šim̃tas* still requires the genitive plural of the following noun. In Latvian before nouns the indeclinable forms are used, with the noun in the appropriate case as determined by the syntax of the sentence, although occasionally in dialects declined forms are found, including separate feminine forms.

The Slavonic forms for 'hundred' are much less clear than their Baltic, counterparts: the Common Slavonic form is **sъto* (cf. the Romanian loan *sută* from Slavonic). The reflexes in the modern languages are all monosyllabic, following the loss of the jer, so that it is difficult to determine the original accent. SCr. *stô* and Sn. *stộ*, with long vowels, seem to indicate shifted stress, i. e. original **sъ́to*, unless they are analogical (to the ordinals?).[94]

IE **ḱm̥tom* would be expected to give CSl. **sęto*; the actual Common Slavonic form **sъto* has unexpectedly no nasal vowel in the first syllable, and a back vowel there, although Indo-European syllabic sonants always give front vowel reflexes after palatovelars. Reconstruction of an Indo-European by-form **ḱutom* does nothing to explain the Slavonic developments, and other alleged instances of IE **m̥* giving Sl. **ъ* are dubious.[95] One traditional explanation, that Sl. **sъto* is a loan from Iranian, still fails to account adequately for the vocalism, for Iranian **satam* would give Sl. **soto* rather than **sъto*. The nonnasal vowel can perhaps be explained as an allegro form at the time when there was still a vowel followed by a nasal (i. e. **simt-* reduced to **sit-*), which would give Sl. **sьto* rather than **sъto*. Shevelov[96] suggests that a by-form **sumtom* of **simtom* may have arisen to parallel the attested vowel alternation in the Slavonic forms for 'thousand' (q. v.). Another recent suggestion[97] is that earlier **sintiⁿ* was influenced by the earlier forms of the decads, which Szemerényi reconstructs as ending in **-sъ*, before the decads were reformed in Slavonic on the basis of the nominal form for 'ten'; the main problem with this solution is the number of hypothetical forms that have to be accepted in early Slavonic.

CSl. **sъto* is a neuter *o*-stem noun, behaving morphologically and syntactically as such, though in the later development of the Slavonic languages it tends to lose its nominal character and be drawn into the general numeral system. In strictly nominal use, most of the languages use nominal derivatives of **sъto*; in much of South Slavonic (except Slovenian), one of these nominal derivatives, *stotina*, has itself been drawn into the strictly numeral system.

OCS *sъto* is morphologically and syntactically an *o*-stem neuter noun. Bg. *sto*, Ma. *sto* are of course invariable. Serbo-Croatian has invariable *stô* and the originally nominal derivative *stȍtina*, which either declines as a feminine *a*-stem noun or appears invariable in the fossilized accusative singular form *stȍtinu* (for the stress on *stȍtina*, see section 16.1.13.3.). Slovenian has indeclinable *stọ̑*.

In Russian the original nominal declension of *sto* proved very tenacious: it was still recommended by Lomonosov in the late eighteenth century, and even today forms like dat. *stu* (especially in *pó stu* 'hundred each') and loc. *stach* (a plural form, though in the meaning 'hundred') are encountered, at least in speech.[98] The current declension, which has dominated in practice from the early nineteenth century, is for nom.-acc. *sto* and a general oblique form *sta*. The same forms are found in Ukrainian (nom.-acc. *sto*, obl. *sta*) and Belorussian (nom.-acc. *sto*, obl. *sta*). In the modern East Slavonic languages, the nominative-accusative takes a following genitive plural, otherwise the noun is in the same case as *sto*, as determined by the syntax of the sentence.

Cz. *sto* is a neuter *o*-stem in form (loc. sg. *stu*), but is often indeclinable with a following noun; with a noun, if *sto* is declined the noun is usually in the genitive plural, but when *sto* is invariable the following noun goes into the case determined by the syntax of the sentence in the oblique cases, though it may also be genitive plural. The Slovak forms are the same as for Czech (*sto, o*-stem neuter, loc. sg. *stu*), though always invariable with a following noun, which will be in the case determined by the syntax of the sentence in the oblique cases.

Po. *sto* originally declined as an *o*-stem neuter, the locative singular being either *ście* (in the oldest Polish) or *stu* (with the *u*-stem ending, reducing the degree of allomorphic variation), and this declension survives, at least in part, into the nineteenth century. The gen. *stu* (cf. *dwu*) is found from the seventeenth century, and the current declension is with *stu* as a general oblique case, the following noun going into the case determined by the syntax of the sentence in the oblique cases, and into the genitive plural after the nominative-accusative; there is also a separate instr. *stoma*; the declension and syntax thus parallel that of the lower numerals. Other attested by-forms are instr. *stą* (cf. *piecią*) and *stema* (confusion of instr. sg. *stem* and pl. *stoma*, or by analogy with *trzema*). Slovincian has, in addition to *stùo̯*, the variant *pjĩnc štĩǵ* 'five scores', see section 16.1.12.2.1.; only the former is used in forming the higher hundreds.

USo. *sto* is a neuter *o*-stem noun when used alone, but with a following noun it is indeclinable, the form of the noun being determined by the syntax of the sentence in the oblique cases (in the nominative-accusative, it is genitive plural). In Lower Sorbian, except as a neologism, the loanword *hundert* from German is commoner than the Slavonic form *sto*. Polabian has no attested reflex of **sъto*, but only the forms *disą(t)diśǫt* 'ten tens, ten-ty' and *pątstid'ě* 'five scores', for which see also section 16.1.12.2.1.; the latter form has the nominative-accusative plural of *stig* 'score', rather than the genitive plural (expected in Slavonic, and probably usual in Polabian, after 'five'),[99] possibly calquing German (strictly, *-stid'ě* is the atonic form of the original acc. *stid'ai* (Sl. *-*y*), rather than the nom. *stiʒai* (Sl. *-*i*, with the Second Palatalization), but in Polabian both these forms are attested with no apparent case distinction between them).[100]

16.1.13.2. 'Hundredth'

In Baltic, the ordinal for 'hundredth' simply uses the stem of the cardinal. In Lithuanian, the resulting form *šim̃tas* (indefinite) is the same as the cardinal, and is usually replaced by the definite form *šimtàsis*; Endzelīns mentions a form *šimtìnis*,[101] with the adjective-forming suffix *-in*. Since Latvian only has the definite forms of ordinals, there are no problems with *sìmtais*.

The Slavonic formations are more varied. The simplest is the use of the cardinal stem, which with the loss of the weak jer is simply *st-*, an unusually short stem (no vowel) for an adjective in Slavonic. The principal extensions are the adjective-forming suffix *-*ьn*, added to the stem (i.e. **sъtьn-*, with loss of the second [weak] jer and vocalization of the first [strong] jer), and ordinal-forming *-t*, added to the nominative-accusative form; in South Slavonic both forms are also found combined.

OCS *sъtьnъ*, attested in the gen. sg. masc.-neut. *sъtъnaago*, with confusion of the jers, in Codex Suprasliensis 302/19; Bg. *stótni* (short form *stóten*), with both ordinal *-t* and adjective-forming *-*ьn*; Ma. *stoti*, but also *stoten*, the latter being used in the current standard as second component of the ordinals of the higher hundreds; SCr. *stôtī*, with neo-acute (or at least, apparent neo-acute); Sn. *stọ́ti*,[102] with (apparent) neo-acute, *stóti*,[103] *stọ̑ti*,[104] the last form perhaps with the prosody of non-standard *stọ̑tni*.[105]

The East Slavonic languages have: Ru. *sótyj*, Uk. *sótyj*, Br. *sóty*, all without any suffix, but with irregular retention of the weak jer in the first syllable, avoiding the vowelless stem *st-*.

Cz. *stý*, without any suffix or avoidance of the short stem; Sk. *stý*, also *stotý* (not in the higher hundreds). Po. *setny* (for **sъtьn-*). USo. *stoty*. The traditional Lower Sorbian form is *hundertny*, with *-*ьn* added to the German loanword *hundert*, and as a neologism *stoty*,[106] as in Upper Sorbian.

16.1.13.3. Hundreds: cardinals

The higher hundreds present few problems in Baltic. In Lithuanian they are formed with the plural of *šim̃tas*, i. e. *šimtaĩ* (dial. also *šim̃tai*, alongside *šimtaĩ* in strictly nominal use): *dù šimtaĩ, trỹs šimtaĩ, keturì šimtaĩ, penkì šimtaĩ, šešì šimtaĩ, septynì šimtaĩ, aštuonì šimtaĩ, devynì šimtaĩ*. The ordinals simply use the stem of the cardinal, retaining the spelling as two words: *dù šim̃tas, trỹs šim̃tas, keturì šim̃tas, penkì šim̃tas, šešì šim̃tas, septynì šim̃tas, aštuonì šim̃tas, devynì šim̃tas*.

In Latvian this formation for the cardinals is also possible: *divi sìmti, trîs sìmti, četri sìmti, pìeci sìmti, seši sìmti, septiņi sìmti, astôņi sìmti, deviņi sìmti*. An alternative formation is to use indeclinable *-simt* (dial. also *-simts*) as second component, in which case the first component usually loses its final vowel: *divsimt, trîssimt, četrsimt, pìecsimt, sešsimt, septiņsimt, astôņsimt, deviņsimt*, also *divisimt, četrisimt*, etc. The ordinals use this contracted form as stem: *divsìmtais, trîssìmtais, četrsìmtais, pìecsìmtais, sešsìmtais, septiñsìmtais, astôņsìmtais, deviñsìmtais*, also *divisìmtais, četrisìmtais*, etc.

In the older Slavonic languages, the higher hundreds were simply numeral phrases using **sъto* as a noun, i. e. CSl. **dъvě sъtě* (dual), **tri sъta*, **četyri sъta* (plural), **pętь sъtъ*, **šestь sъtъ*, **sedmь sъtъ*, **osmь sъtъ*, **devętь sъtъ* (genitive plural); in 'two hundred' to 'four hundred' both parts decline, while in 'five hundred' to 'nine hundred' the second part remains in the genitive plural, the numerals 'five' to 'nine' being treated as nouns. The changes over the history of the Slavonic languages include both those that result from the loss of noun status by the numerals 'five' to 'nine', and more general ones that are often parallel to changes in other complex numerals.

Bg. *dvéste* and *dvésta* (analogical to *trísta*), *trísta, čétiristotin, pétstotin, šéststotin, sédemstotin, ósemstotin, dévetstotin*. In the higher hundreds, the nominal derivative *stótina* or *sto* is used as a numeral, i. e. not only has the original noun **sъto* been converted to a numeral, but the same has happened to a certain extent to its nominal derivative. *Stótin* is originally the genitive plural of *stotína/stótina* (for the stress, see the discussion of Serbo-Croatian), *čétiristotin* is analogical to the higher forms.

Ma. *dveste, trista, četiristotini, petstotini, šeststotini, sedumstotini, osumstotini, devetstotini*; the forms are essentially as in Bulgarian, except that in the higher hundreds nom. pl. *stotini* is used, rather than the old genitive.

SCr. *dvȅsta* (Je. *dvjȅsta*) or *dvȇ* (Je. *dvȉje*) *stȍtine, trȉsta* or *trȋ stȍtine, čètiri stȍtine, pȇt stȍtīnā, šȇst stȍtīnā, sȅdam stȍtīnā, ȍsam stȍtīnā, dȅvēt* (or *dȅvet*) *stȍtīnā*. The form for 'two hundred' has final *-a* by analogy with *trȉsta*. In the older language, **sъto* could be used in the genitive plural (zero-ending) in forming the higher hundreds, i. e. *pȇt sȃt*, etc. The current forms use the nominative plural or genitive plural of **stotína*; the stress on this word would be regularly retracted in the genitive plural,[107] giving *stȍtīnā*; the stress on *stȍtine* is this stress generalized. There are also forms from 'four hundred' on with enlitic *-stō: čètiristō, pȇtstō, šȇststō, sȅdamstō, ȍsamstō, dȅvetstō*.

Slovenian hundreds all use the indeclinable *stọ̑*, which is often pronounced as an enclitic: *dvẹ̑ stọ̑, trȋ stọ̑, štíri stọ̑, pẹ̑t stọ̑, šẹ̑st stọ̑, sẹ́dəm stọ̑, ọ́səm stọ̑, devẹ̑t stọ̑*.

Russian hundreds still retain much of the compound character of the numeral (and new combinations, like *néskol'ko sót* 'several hundred' are still found, attesting to the lesser cohesion of these compounds), and in declension both parts of the compound change in accordance with the usual rules for combining a numeral with a noun: the forms of *sto* that occur, in the plural, are nom.-acc. *sta*, gen. *sot*, dat. *stam*, instr. *stámi*, loc. *stach*, i. e. regular neuter *o*-stem forms. The first part of the compound is usually unstressed, though does not necessarily have its vowel reduced (cf. *trëchsót*), and secondary stress on the first component is retained in the instr. *dvumjàstámi, tremjàstámi, četyr'mjàstámi*.[108] The forms are: *dvésti* (from earlier *dvěstě*, by analogy with the common plural ending *-i*), gen. *dvuchsót*, dat. *dvumstám*, instr. *dvumjàstami*, loc. *dvuchstách*; *trísta*, gen. *trëchsót*, dat. *trëmstám*, instr. *tremjàstámi*, loc. *trëchstách*; *četýresta*, gen. *četyrëchsót*, dat. *četyrëmstám*, instr. *četyr'mjàstámi*, loc. *četyrëchstách*; *pjat'sót*, gen. *pjatisót*, dat. *pjatistám*, instr. *pjat'justámi* (nonstandard also *pjatistámi*, cf. the discussion of the decads), loc. *pja-*

tistách (without secondary stress on the first part of these forms, and with vowel reduction; for the higher hundreds the full declension will not be given); *šest′sót*; *sem′sót; vosem′sót; devjat′sót*. Despite the spelling, in the forms 'five hundred' to 'nine hundred' the final consonant of the first component is hard, like the first consonant of the second component.

Ukrainian hundreds follow essentially the same system as their Russian counterparts; note that the first component of the higher hundreds is spelled, as well as pronounced, with a hard final consonant, and that in the declension of the higher hundreds the first component does not take the alternative pronominal-adjectival endings: *dvísti* (for **dъvě sъtě*; dialectally also *dvísta*), gen. *dvochsót*, dat. *dvomstám*, instr. *dvomastámy*, loc. *dvochstách*; *trýsta; čotýrysta; p'jatsót*, gen. *p'jatysót*, dat. *p'jatystám*, instr. *p'jatystámy, p'jat′mastámy* or *p'jatjomastámy*, loc. *p'jatystách; šistsót; simsót; visimsót, dev'jatsót*. In western dialects, indeclinable *-sto* is also found (e. g. *trysto*).

The Belorussian hundreds follow the same system: *dzvésce*, gen. *dvuchsót*, dat. *dvumstám*, instr. *dvumastámi*, loc. *dvuchstách*; *trýsta; čatýrysta; pjac′sót*, gen. *pjacisót*, dat. *pjacistám*, instr. *pjaccjustámi*, loc. *pjacistách; šèsc′sót* (gen. *šascisót*); *semsót* (gen. *sjamisót*), *vosemsót* (gen. *vas′misót*); *dzevjac′sót* (gen. *dzevjacisót*).

Czech hundreds contain the relevant form of *sto* as if it were an ordinary noun, and orthographically it is written as a separate word: *dvě stě* (with unusual retention of the dual, though only in the nominative-accusative), gen. *dvou set*, dat. *dvěma stům*, instr. *dvěma sty*, loc. *dvou stech; tři sta; čtyři sta*; *pět set* (dat. *pěti stům*); *šest set; sedm set; osm set; devět set*.

Slovak hundreds contain indeclinable *-sto*, and are not declined: *dvesto, tristo, štyristo, päť sto, šesť sto, sedemsto, osemsto, deväť sto*.

Polish hundreds still divide strictly into two groups, 'two hundred' to 'four hundred' and 'five hundred' to 'nine hundred'. For the former, the nominative-accusative forms are *dwieście* (**dъvě stě*), *trzysta, czterysta* (quite generally: monosyllabic forms of *sto* are enclitic in all of the hundreds). The older declension of both parts has been replaced by declension of the second part only, except in 'two hundred' (cf. 'twenty'): obl. *dwustu, trzystu, czterystu*, with the usual oblique ending *-u* and a hard consonant in *dwustu* by analogy with the other numerals (including obl. *stu*); there is also a separate instr. *dwustoma, trzystoma, czterystoma* (*-stoma*, not being monosyllabic, is not enclitic). Oblique forms like *dwochset, dwuchset, dwóchset* are found from the sixteenth to the nineteenth centuries, the latter (also *trzechset, czterechset*) occasionally in current usage, mirroring the construction of the higher hundreds. In these, the second component is invariable *-set*: this continues the use of the genitive plural after all cases of the (originally nominal) numerals 'five' to 'nine', an unusual retention of the earlier system, but one that has held throughout the recorded history of Polish: *pięćset*, obl. *pięciuset* (a separate instr. **pię'ciomaset* is not used), *sześćset* (pronounced *sześset* or *szejset*), *siedemset, osiemset, dziewięćset.*

Upper Sorbian hundreds use the appropriate form of *sto*, in the nominative-accusative, and are either indeclinable, or decline as an ordinary noun phrase with a numeral and a neuter noun: *dwě sće* (the dual is a live category in Sorbian), *tři sta, štyri sta, pjeć stow, šěsć stow, sydom stow, wosom stow* (variants as for *sydom, wosom*), *dźewjeć stow.*

Lower Sorbian hundreds follow essentially the same pattern, except that both native *sto* and the German loanword *hundert* are available; in the numerals requiring the plural genitive of 'hundred', the Slavonic forms in *stow* seem particularly common, and it is not clear from the discussion by Šẃela (Schwela) whether the forms in *hundertow* are always possible.[109] In Lower Sorbian the hundreds also participate in overcounting, in that they can be used to form the numerals 'ten hundred' to 'nineteen hundred', apparently also some higher numerals too (e. g. *jaden a dwaźasća stow* 'twenty-one hundred'). Examples are: *dwě sćě* (*dwa hunderta*), *tśi sta* (*hunderty*), *styri sta* (*hunderty*), *pěś stow, šesć stow, sedym stow, wosym stow, źeẃeś stow, źaseś stow* (*hundertow*) 'thousand' (q. v.), *jadnasćo stow, dwanasćo stow, pěśnasćo stow* (*hundertow*).

The only higher hundred attested in Polabian is *disąt pątstid'ě* 'thousand', literally 'ten hundreds' (where 'hundred' is already a complex formation, 'five scores'); the form is only attested with this word for 'hundred', not with *disątdiśǫt.*

16.1.13.4. Hundreds: ordinals

In Old Church Slavonic the ordinals for the higher hundreds are not attested, and even in other forms of Church Slavonic and the older Slavonic languages they are rare, though Church Slavonic does give forms like *pętьsъtьno(j)e* 'five hundredth'. The modern languages use the ordinal form of 'hundredth' as second component, with the first component either in the form used in compounds (see section 16.6.; thus East Slavonic, Czech, 'two hundredth' to 'four hundredth' in Slovak, Polish; 'two hundredth' in Upper Sorbian), or in the nominative-accusative (citation) form (elsewhere).

Bg. *dvestótni, tristótni, četiristótni, petstótni, šeststótni, sedemstótni, osemstótni, devetstótni*; also short forms *dvestóten*, etc.

Ma. *dvestoten, tristoten, četiristoten, petstoten, šeststoten, sedumstoten, osumstoten, devetstoten.*

SCr. *dvèstōtī* (Je. *dvjèstōtī*), *trȋstōtī, čètiristōtī, pȇtstōtī, šȇststōtī, sȅdamstōtī, ȍsamstōtī, dȅvetstōtī*; also *dvȇstotinitī* (Je. *dvȉjestotinitī*), etc.

Sn. *dvệstộti* (and prosodic variants of the second component as for 'hundredth'), *trȋstộti, štíristộti, pę̂tstộti, šę̂ststộti, sẹ́dəmstộti, ọ́səmstộti, devę̂tstộti.*

Ru. *dvuchsótyj, trëchsótyj, četyrëchsótyj, pjatisótyj, šestisótyj, semisótyj, vos'misótyj, devjatisótyj.*

Uk. *dvochsótyj, trjochsótyj, čotyrjochsótyj, p'jatysótyj, šestysótyj, semysótyj, vos'mysótyj, dev'jatysótyj.*

Br. *dvuchsóty, trochsóty, čatyrochsóty, pjacisóty, šascisóty, sjamisóty, vas'misóty, dzevjacisóty.*

Cz. *dvoustý, třístý, čtyřstý, pětistý, šestistý, sedmistý, osmistý, devítistý.*

Sk. *dvojstý, trojstý, štvorstý, päťstý, šesťstý, sedemstý, osemstý, deväťstý.*

Po. *dwusetny* (also *dwóchsetny*), *trzechsetny* (nonstandard *trzysetny*), *czterechsetny, pięćsetny, sześćsetny, siedemsetny, osiemsetny, dziewięćsetny.* For 'two hundredth' to 'four hundredth' only (cf. Slovak), Polish uses the genitive of the numeral as first component: *dwu-* cf. gen. *dwu, dwóch*), *trzech-, czterech-*; in the case of 'three hundredth', this genitive differs from the form used in compounds, which is *trzy-* — see section 16.6, though there is a nonstandard form *trzysetny.*

USo. *dwustoty* (a neologism, like all forms in *dwu*, see section 16.6.; the older form is *dwě stoty*, cf. *dwě sće*),[110] *třistoty, štyristoty, pjećstoty, šěsćstoty, sydomstoty, wosomstoty* (variants as for *sydom, wosom*), *dźewjećstoty.*

For Lower Sorbian, Schwela[111] lists only *dwahundertny*, with the ordinal corresponding to the German loan *hundert* (it will be recalled that for 'hundredth' only *hundertny* is given in the earlier edition, while *stoty* is a neologism); presumably *tśihundertny* and *styrihundertny* are also possible, but the traditional forms for the higher hundreds cannot be deduced from Schwela's examples. As neologisms, we have *dwěstoty, tśistoty, styristoty, pěšstoty*, etc.

16.1.14. Higher numerals

16.1.14.1. 'Thousand'

The Balto-Slavonic forms for 'thousand' (e. g. Li. *túkstantis*, OCS *tysęšti, tysǫšti*) have proved particularly recalcitrant to etymologizing. The forms are paralleled closely in Indo-European only by Germanic forms like Gothic *þūsundi* (perhaps for **þūs-hundi*), but there is no direct reason to suppose a loan from Germanic, especially as the formation is no clearer in Germanic than in Balto-Slavonic. The starting-point seems to have been a form like **tū(s)-ḱm̥t-*, where the first component is related to Sanskrit *tuvi-* 'very', perhaps also to OCS *tyti*, Li. *túkti*, Le. *tûkt* (dialectally also *tûskt*) 'to get fat', and the second component is the stem of the word for 'hundred', i. e. 'thousand' is the 'big hundred'. In Slavonic, this will give regularly **tysęt-*; in formation, this looks like a present participle, and was apparently reinterpreted as such, giving the variant **tysǫt-* (cf. the hesitation between *goręšt-* and *gorǫšt-* 'burning' in Old Church Slavonic), perhaps also the gender and declension-type fluctuations; the different vowels could also represent ablaut variants. The Baltic forms are more complex.[112] OPr. *tūsimtons* is close to the Slavonic forms (but see the detailed discussion below), but Li. *túkstantis* (older *túkštantis*) and Le. *tũkstôtis* are problematic in the appearance of *k*, of *s* rather than *š* in the modern Lithuanian form (Latvian and Old Prussian do not distinguish original **s* and **š*; a form with *š* is also suggested by the Finnish borrowing *tuhat*, stem *tuhante-*, 'thousand', with *h* regularly for **š*), of *t* in the second syllable, and *-an-* (Le. *o*) in the second syllable. The *k*, which is absent from an older Latvian form *tuustosch-*, may be from the root **tuk* (cf. Le. *tûkstu* 'I get fat'), synonymous with the first formative of the numeral, i. e. a recent analogical insertion. The *s*, again probably a recent development, may derive from other verbs with present stem in *-sta* not shifted to *šta* (the shift would occur regularly only after *k* and *r*). The *t* was apparently inserted into an earlier form **tūšant-*, reinterpreted as a present participle, by confusion of the present stem **tūša* (cf. Le. *tûskt*) and the newer present stem form **tū-sta*. The ending *-ant* is that expected in a present participle, but it is more difficult to see how Balt. **tūšimt-* could have been reinterpreted as a participle (**tūšamt-*), since the alternation of front and back vowel endings of Slavonic is not matched in Baltic. This is the major difficulty with the etymology **tū(s)-ḱm̥t-*; one solution would be to assume that the participial forms are in fact older, and that OPr. *tūsimtons*, with *-im-*, is a popular etymology based on the word for 'hundred'. Under this analysis, the original meaning of the form in Balto-Slavonic would be something like 'that which is fat (big)', not entirely satisfactory from the semantic viewpoint. One way round the problem of the vowel variants would be to assume reinterpretation of **-m̥t* (Sl. **-ęt*, Balt. **-imt*) as a suffix subject to ablaut variants (subsequently reinterpreted as the suffix of the present participle), in particular with the variant Balt. **-amt*, Sl. **-ǫt*, as if for IE **-omt*.[113]

The only Old Prussian form attested is acc. pl. *tūsimtons*. Li. *túkstantis* was originally a feminine *i*-stem (gen. *túkstanties*), but in the current standard is a masculine *jo*-stem (gen. *túkstančio*), perhaps under the influence of the masculine *o*-stem *šim̃tas* 'hundred'. In dialects it also appears as a feminine *jā*-stem (*túkstančia*), and a feminine *ē*-stem (*túkstantė*). Contracted *túkstan(t)*, probably for acc. sg. *túkstanti*, also occurs as first component of coordinate numerals, e. g. *túkstan(t) devynì* 'one thousand and nine'. Lithuanian dialects in a Belorussian environment also show loans from East Slavonic: *tỹsiačias, tỹsiačis, tìsėčia, tìsėčis*. Le. *tũkstôtis* is a masculine *jo*-stem, though *tũkstôts* also occurs, but in the standard language it usually appears as invariable *tũkstoš* before a noun; this form, for expected **tũkstot* (cf. Li. *túkstant*), is apparently taken from the contracted forms of the higher thousands, e. g. *divi tũkstoš* 'two thousand', see section 16.1.14.5.

The Slavonic languages, apart from those that have replaced reflexes of **tysǫtj-* or **tysętj-* by loans from other languages (Greek, German, Hungarian, Romance) or paraphrases, present variation in the vowel of the second syllable (**ę* in East Slavonic, Polish and older Slovak; **ǫ* in Serbo-Croatian and Slovenian; both in Old Church Slavonic, and confusion of the two forms in Czech) and in the gender and stem-class of the numeral-noun (*ja*-stem feminine in OCS [nom. sg. usually in *-i*, and traces of analogical *i*-stem forms], Serbo-Croatian, Slovenian dialects, and East Slavonic; *jo*-stem masculine in Slovenian and West Slavonic).

Old Church Slavonic has both *tysǫšti* and *tysęšti* (CSl. **tj* gives OCS *št*), with final *-i* in the nominative singular as with participles; the distribution of the two forms suggests that the *ǫ*-form was that of the Old Macedonian and Serbo-Croatian Church Slavonic (more western) tradition, the *ę*-form that of Bulgarian Old Church Slavonic and Russian Church Slavonic (i. e. the east). The gen. pl. *tysǫšti*, common in Croatian Church Slavonic, suggests a shift in these dialects to the *i*-declension.

Both Bulgarian and Macedonian have replaced this form with a loan from Greek *chiliáda* 'thousand' (a nominal derivative from the numeral), giving Bg. *chiljáda* (nonstandard also *chiljádo*, with *-o* from *sto* 'hundred'), Ma. *iljada* (initial *ch-* is unstable generally in Macedonian); in the plural

Bulgarian has *chíljadi*, originally the stress of the genitive plural, with neo-circumflex. In Serbo-Croatian, the eastern variety of the language prefers the Greek loan *hìljada* (gen. pl. *hȉljādā*, with neo-circumflex), while the western variety continues the original Slavonic form with *tȉsuća* (with regular *ć* for **tj*); the *u* is short, as usual in an internal posttonic syllable.[114] The Serbo-Croatian forms are either declined as feminine singular nouns or, if preceding a noun or as part of a coordinate numeral, appear in the fossilized accusative singular (*hìljadu, tȉsuću*). Serbo-Croatian dialects have loans from other languages too: *tâjzunt, tâvžan* and *tâȉnžic*, unexplained derivative of German *Tausend; jȅzero*, with regular prothetic *j-*, from Hungarian *ezer*; and *miljâr, mȉljār, mijõr*, from Romance *millearium*. Standard Slovenian has *tȋsoč*, as masculine noun or indeclinable, also *tísoč* (where the rising tone agrees with Serbo-Croatian and Baltic),[115] dialectally there is also the feminine noun *tisọ́ča*;[116] *č* is the regular Slovenian reflex of **tj*. In Slovenian dialects, loans from German and Hungarian are found, much as in Serbo-Croatian: *tavžent, jezer(o)*.[117].

The East Slavonic languages have consistently reflexes of **tysętj-* (**tj* gives ESl. **č*): Ru. *týsjača* (in strictly numerical use, the singular instrumental is *týsjač'ju*, with the ending *-'ju* from numerals like *pjat'*); Uk. *týsjača* (older Ukrainian also masc. *týsjač*, and instr. *týsjaččju*); Br. *týsjača* (instr. *týsjačeju* or *týsjačču*). Apart from the alternative instrumental singular forms, all are declined like feminine nouns.

The Czech form *tisíc*, declined as a masculine noun (gen. pl. *tisíců* in nominal use, but *tisíc* in numeral use), or indeclinable before a noun, is unusual in its initial *ť* (orthographically *t* before *i* rather than *y*), cf. OCz. *tis'úc*, the palatal *ť* apparently arising by assimilation to the palatalized *s'* in the earlier form. The Old Czech group *s'ú* is itself problematic: **sǫ* would give regularly **sú*, and **sę* would give **s'ā̈*, the actual form *s'ú* (giving regularly modern *sí*) being apparently a contamination of the two.[118] Sk. *tisíc*, declined as a noun or, more usually, indeclinable, is a loan from Czech; Old Slovak has *tysā̈c*, the regular development of **tysętj-*. This same form gives Po. *tysiąc* (in West Slavonic generally, **tj* gives *c*): the two modern Polish nasals reflect older differences in quantity, not quality, of the Common Slavonic nasals, but the palatalization of **s* points to original **ę*, not **ǫ*. Po. *ą* represents original length (cf. Czech), which is usually retained in a posttonic syllable before a jer,[119] though other flectional forms would have been expected to show **ę*, and variant forms found in the earlier language suggest that levelling must have taken place both ways. Po. *tysiąc* declines as a masculine noun, with the ending *-y* in the genitive plural, as in most nouns of the (historically) soft masculine declension; the actual form *tysięcy* has *ę*, but the front vowel here does not reflect historical quantitative alternation, but is analogous to the *o e* alternation (with *e* before "historically" soft dental plus *i*) resulting from the Lechitic przegłos.

Although current grammars of both Sorbian languages give the word *tysac* (declined as a masculine noun, gen. pl. *tysac(ow)* in Upper Sorbian, *tysac* in Lower Sorbian), these forms are neologisms, not direct continuations of CSl. **tysętj-*. USo. *tysac* first appears in the nineteenth century, replacing the earlier loan *tawzynt* (German *Tausend*);[120] LSo. *tysac* is even more recent, since it is not given by Schwela,[121] but does appear in the revised edition.[122] In Lower Sorbian the German loan *towzynt* is still current, as are instances of overcounting, namely *źaseś hundertow* and *źaseś stow* 'ten hundreds', see section 16.1.13.3. In Polabian, the form attested for 'thousand' is *disęt pętstid'ĕ*, literally 'ten hundreds' ('ten fivescores'), see section 16.1.22.1.

16.1.14.2. 'Thousandth'

The current Lithuanian and Latvian forms simply use the stem of the cardinal: Li. *túkstants*, Le. *tũkstôšais* (*š* for **tj*). However, a number of variant Lithuanian forms are given by Endzelīns:[123] *túkstantysis, túkstantinis* (with adjective-forming *-in*), and, with a trucated stem *túkst-, túkstinis* (adjective-forming *-in*) and *tūkstàsis* (a definite form using the simple stem *túkst-*, cf. *šimtàsis* 'hundredth').

The ordinals in Slavonic present much the same range of variation in formation as for 'hundredth'. In Old Church Slavonic, Codex Suprasliensis (272/30) has the form *tysęštьnu* (dative singular), though in the meaning 'thousand-year', suggesting formations **tysęštьnъ* and **tysǫštьnъ*. Bulgarian and Macedonian both have the adjective-forming suffix **ьn-*, in Bg. *chíljadni* (short form *chíljaden*), Ma. *iljaden*. In Serbo-Croatian the eastern variety has *hìljaditī*, with ordinal-forming *-t* and epenthetic *i*, while the western variety has both *tȉsućī* (stem as in the cardinal) and *tȉsućnī* (with **-ьn*), though the latter is not used in the ordinals for the higher thousands. Slovenian simply uses the stem of the cardinal: *tȋsoči*.[124]

The East Slavonic languages all use the suffix **-ьn*: Ru. *týsjačnyj*, Uk. *týsjačnyj*, Br. *týsjačny*.

Cz. *tisící*, Sk. *tisíci* (with rhythmic shortening) use the stem of the cardinal. Po. *tysiączny* has the suffix **-ьn*; since the *c* of *tysiąc* derives from **tj*, not **k*, the expected ending would be **-cny*, and the *c/cz* alternation is analogical to this alternation where both *c* and *cz* derive from **k* (contrast SCr. *tȉsućnī*; in ESl. **tj* gives *č* in any case). Polish has a by-form *tysięczny*, reflecting variation in the length of the nasal vowel at an earlier period, but this is nonstandard for the simple ordinal, though preferred to *-tysiączny* for the ordinals of the higher thousands. USo. *tysacty* has ordinal-forming *-t*; while LSo. *towzyntny*, and the neologism *tysacny*, both have adjective-forming **-ьn*. Some older sources give an Upper Sorbian form *tysači*,[125] analogous to the use of **-jь* as an adjective-forming suffix with reflexes of the First Palatalization (i. e. as if the *-c* of *tysac* were from **k* rather than **tj*), cf. Po. *tysiączny*; SCr. *tȉsućī*, Sn. *tîsoči*, Cz. *tisící*, Sk. *tisíci* are, strictly speaking, ambiguous as to whether they have the bare stem, or the suffix **-jь*, as the stem ends in **i* in any case in Common Slavonic.

16.1.14.3. 'Million', etc.

The Balto-Slavonic forms for 'million' all trace back ultimately to the Italian augmentative *millione* 'big thousand', though as the word is an internationalism, and is a fairly recent introduction to many of the languages, it is not always possible to trace the exact path of borrowing into each of the Balto-Slavonic languages. The same is true of the forms for 'milliard', a French coinage on the same root. Words of the form 'billion', etc. (i. e. other forms in *-illion*) do exist in the Balto-Slavonic languages, but tend to be less used than in English, perhaps because of uncertainty as to the exact value intended ('ten to the power of twelve' as in British and French usage, or 'ten to the power of nine' as in American and German usage).

The forms for 'million' in the individual languages are as follows; except where otherwise stated, they are morphologically and syntactically nouns, though they may also occur in coordinate numerals, and in some languages (Slovenian, Czech, Slovak, Sorbian) may be indeclinable when preceding a noun: Li. *milijõnas* (dial. also *milijònas, milijónas*; in all these forms, the *o* is usually pronounced open), Le. *miljons* (short *o*); Bg. *milión*, Ma. *milión*, SCr. *milìōn* (gen. *milióna*) or, especially in the western variety of the standard language,[126] *milìjūn* (gen. *milijúna*), Sn. *milijộn*; Ru. *millión* (pronounced *mil'jón* or *milión*; note that the less common *billión*, however, is more often pronounced as spelt, since divergence between spelling and pronunciation in foreign words is, rather, a characteristic of commoner words),[127] Uk. *mil'jón*,[128] Br. *mil'ё́n*; Cz. *milion, milión* (the *o* is pronounced long in either case), Sk. *milión*, Po. *milion* (pronounced *miljon*), USo. *milion*, LSo. *milion*.

The forms for 'milliard' are as follows; whereas 'million' is masculine in all Balto-Slavonic languages, 'milliard' appears as both masculine and feminine: Li. *milijárdas*, Le. *miljards*; Bg. *miliárd*, Ma. *milijárda*, SCr. *milìjārda*, Sn. *milijârda* (note the similarity among the three Yugoslavian languages); Ru. *milliárd* (pronounced *mil'járd* or *miliárd*),[129] Uk. *mil'-járd*, Br. *mil'járd*; Cz. *miliarda*, Sk. *miliarda*, Po. *miliard* (pronounced *miljard*), USo. *miliarda*.

16.1.14.4. 'Millionth'

The corresponding ordinals present considerable variety in Balto-Slavonic; the use of the adjective-forming suffix *-ski* in Macedonian, Serbo-Croatian and Slovenian (i. e. the languages of Yugoslavia) is found only for these higher ordinals in Slavonic, while Polish has adjective-forming *-owy* only for these forms; Lithuanian has a denominal adjective in *-in*. Li. *milijõninis* (open *o*), *milijárdinis*; Bg. *miliónni* (short form *miliónen*), *miliárdni* (short form *miliárden*), Ma. *miliónski*,[130] *milijárdski*, SCr. *mil-iònitī, milìōntī, milìōnskī, milìjūnskī, milìjūntī, milijùnitī, milìjardskī*, Sn. *milijọ̑nski, milijârden*; Ru. *milliónnyj, milliárdnyj* (for the pronunciation, see the cardinals), Uk. *mil'jónnyj* (archaic *miliónnyj*), *mil'járdnyj*, Br. *mil'ënny, mil'járdny*; Cz. *miliontý, milióntý* (the *o* is always pronounced long), *miliardtý*, Sk. *milióntу, miliardtý*, Po. *milionowy, miliardowy*, USo. *milionty, miliardny*.

16.1.14.5. 'Thousands', 'millions', etc.

Compounds of 'thousand', 'million', etc., are still transparent combinations in Balto-Slavonic, with the appropriate form of the power of ten determined by the usual syntactic requirements of the preceding numeral; only Slovenian departs from this pattern, with the power of ten usually indeclinable. Some sample numerals are given from the various languages below; except where otherwise stated, they are 'two thousand' and 'five thousand', with the nominative plural of 'thousand', in the former, the genitive plural (Baltic nominative plural) in the latter. Declension of the complex is as for any numeral plus noun complex, except in those languages where the higher numerals are normally indeclinable in numeral use: Li. *dù túkstančiai, penkì túkstančiai, dẽšimt túkstančių* 'ten thousand', the latter with the genitive plural of 'thousand'; Le. *divi tũkstoši, pìeci tũkstôši*, or contracted and indeclinable *divi tũkstoš, pìeci tũkstoš*; Bg. *dve chíljadi, pet chíljadi* (nominative plural); Ma. *dve iljadi, pet iljadi* (nominative plural); SCr. *dvȇ* (Je. *dvȉje*) *hìljade/tȉsuće, pȇt hȉljādā/tȉsūćā*; Sn. *dvȃ tȋsoč, pę̑t tȋsoč* (indeclinable *tȋsoč*); Ru. *dve týsjači, pjat' týsjač*; Uk. *dvi týsjači, p'jat' týsjač(iv)*; Br. *dzve týsjačy, pjac' týsjač*; Cz. *dva tisíce, pět tisíc*; Sk. *dva tisíce, päť tisíc*; Po. *dwa tysiące, pięć tysięcy*; USo. *dwaj tysacaj* (nominative dual), *tři tysacy* 'three thousand', *pjeć tysac(ow)*; LSo. *dwa towzynta* (nominative dual), *tśi towzynty* 'three thousand', *pěś towzynt(ow)*, also the neologisms *dwa tysaca, tśi tysace, pěś tysac*.

For the ordinals or compounds of 'thousand', 'million', etc., no difficulty arises in those languages that simply prefix the cardinal number (in the appropriate gender, where gender is distinguished) to the ordinal of the power of ten, e. g. SCr. *dvȃmiliōntī* (variants as for 'millionth') 'two millionth'; the languages in this group are Lithuanian, Latvian, Bulgarian, Serbo-Croatian, Slovenian, presumably also Lower Sorbian, though Šẃela does not list any ordinals as high as these. Upper Sorbian belongs essentially to the same group, except that it uses *dwu-* for 'two' (see section 16.6.; this form is a neologism); Slovak and Polish belong to this group except for compounds of 'two', 'three', 'four', where Slovak has special compound forms *dvoj-, troj-, štvor-*, and Polish has *dwu-* (*dwóch-* is nonstandard with these higher numerals), *trzech-* (and *trzy-*, which is standard here, unlike 'three hundredth'), *czterech-*; see section 16.6. As noted in section 16.1.14.2., in compounds the form *-tysięczny* is preferred in Polish to *-tysiączny*. Only East Slavonic and Czech rigorously use the compound form of the numeral which is the same as the genitive (see section 16.6.); the use of compound forms has certain practical disadvantages, since some complex numerals do not readily, or at all, form compounds: as pointed out to me by E. W. Browne (Cornell) there is apparently no way in Russian of saying 'twenty-one thousandth'.

As illustrative material, the forms for 'two thousandth' and 'five thousandth' in the individual languages are given below: Li. *dù túkstantas, penkì túkstantas*; Le. *divi tũkstôšais, pìeci tũkstôšais*; Bg. *dvechíljadni* (short *dvechíljaden*), *petchíljadni* (short *petchíljaden*); Ma. *dve iljaden, pet iljaden*; SCr. *dvȇhiljaditī/dvȇtisućī* (Je. *dvȉjehiljaditī/dvȉjetisućī*), *pȇthiljaditī/pȇttisućī*; Sn. *dvȃtȋsoči, pę̑ttȋsoči*; Ru. *dvuchtýsjačnyj, pjatitýsjačnyj*; Uk. *dvochtýsjačnyj, p'jatytýsjačnyj*; Br. *dvuchtýsjačny, pjacitýsjačny*; Cz. *dvoutisící, pětitisící*; Sk. *dvojtisíci, päťtisíci*; Po. *dwutysięczny, trzechtysięczny* or *trzytysięczny* 'three thousandth', *czterechtysięczny* 'four thousandth', *pięćtysięczny* (also variants in *-tysiączny*); USo. *dwutysacty* (traditional form: *dwaj tysacty*),[131] *třitysacty* 'three thousandth', *pjećtysacty*.

16.1.14.6. Other systems for counting beyond 'thousand'

Before the adoption of the international system with 'million', 'millard', etc., there was in Slavonic an older system; most of the data concerning this older system come from Old Church Slavonic and Old Russian.[132] These very high numerals were not always used with accurate numerical meaning, often signifying simply 'a very large number', but the terms *tьma, legion* and *legiodr*, in particular, did also have exact numerical values as noted below.

Old Church Slavonic and ORu. *tъma, tьma*, also *tma* with loss of the weak jer, 'ten thousand', used to translate Greek *mýrioi*. The etymology is unclear, as is the possible relation to *tьma* 'mist'; Vasmer suggests Turkic *tuman* 'crowd; mist' as the most likely etymon.[133]

OCS *leģeonъ*, ORu. *legion* 'one hundred thousand', from Greek *legeṓn, legiṓn*.

ORu. *leodor* (variants *legiodr, leodr*) 'million', of uncertain etymology, though non-Slavonic and probably connected with *legion*.

ORu. *vóron*, literally 'raven', 'ten to the power of seven'; ORu. *kolóda*, literally 'block', for an indefinitely large number, approaching the concept of 'infinity'.

Another counting system, known from the seventeenth century,[134] has *tьma* 'ten to the power of six', *legion* 'ten to the power of twelve', *leodr* 'ten to the power of twenty-four', *voron* 'ten to the power of twenty-five' or 'ten to the power of forty-eight', *koloda* 'ten to the power of fifty', the last two also as an indefinitely high number.

For a concept like our infinity, Old Church Slavonic has *nesъvěda*,[135] literally 'incomprehensibility'.

16.1.15. Coordinate numerals

In the Balto-Slavonic languages, numerals between the round decads (over 'twenty'), hundreds, thousands, etc., are expressed primarily by addition, i. e. 'twenty-two' is expressed as 'twenty and two'. The principal variants in this formula are the conjunction and the order: some languages have no conjunction (as in English), while others require one ('and'); the majority of Balto-Slavonic languages order the numbers as in English and most European languages, from the highest to the lowest, but in some languages (Slovenian, Czech, Slovak, Sorbian, Polabian), there is at least the possibility of the reverse order for the decads and digits, i. e. digits (usually in the fossilized nominative singular masculine form) plus decads: it can hardly be coincidence that these are precisely those languages that are contiguous with German and have otherwise been strongly influenced by German, with its order *zweiundzwanzig* 'two and twenty'. Below, examples of coordinate numerals are given for the individual languages, except where otherwise stated, it is assumed that the order is from highest to lowest numeral, and that each component of the cardinal declines (unless it is otherwise indeclinable), the syntax of the following noun being determined by the last component of the coordinate. A common pattern in the ordinals is for only the last component to be ordinal, the others in the citation form of the cardinal. The citation example is 'two hundred and twenty-two/twenty-second'.

Li. *dù šimtaĩ dvìdešimt dù*, ordinal: *dù šimtaĩ dvìdešimt añtras*, with only the last component as an ordinal. Le. *divsimt divdesmit divi*, ordinal: *divisimt divdesmit òtrs* (last component only cardinal).

In Old Church Slavonic the order is from highest to lowest, and each component is separated from its neighbour by the conjunction *i* (Codex Suprasliensis *ti*) 'and', e. g. *pętь sъtъ i tri* 'five hundred and three', *pęti desętъ ti pęti* 'fifty-five (genitive)'; for the ordinals, there are few examples, though both patterns with all ordinals and with only the last component as ordinal are found.

Bg. *dvéste dvádeset i dva*, with the last two constituents separated by *i*, ordinal: *dvéste dvádeset i vtóri*. Ma. *dveste dvaeset í dva*, with the conjunction *i* separating the last two components:[136] when this *i* occurs between a ten and a unit (but not in, e. g., *sto i éden* 'one hundred and one'), the conjunction plus unit function as one word for purposes of stress placement;[137] ordinal: *dveste (i) dvaeset i vtor*.

SCr. *dvȅsta* (Je. *dvjȅsta*) *dvádeset dvā* (with optional *i* before the unit and optional attraction of stress onto this conjunction from a unit with falling tone on the first syllable); ordinal: *dvȅsta* (Je. *dvjȅsta*) *dvádeset* (*i*) *drȕgī*, with only the last component as ordinal; in both cardinal and ordinal, the fossilized acc. sg. *stȍtinu, hìljadu* or *tȉsuću* are used for 'one hundred', 'one thousand'.

In Slovenian, for the decads and digits there are two possibilities: the commoner is for the digit to precede the decad separated from it by the conjunction *in* 'and', in which case the unit appears in the fossilized nominative singular masculine, except for *éna-* 'one', a fossilized feminine singular, e. g. *énaindvȃjset* 'twenty-one', *dvȃindvȃjset* 'twenty-two'; alternatively, the decad may precede as a separate word, e. g. *dvȃjset édən*, this being archaic in the current standard. With the ordinals, one has either *énaindvȃjseti* or *dvȃjseti pȓvi*, both components being ordinal in the latter. No conjunction is used between higher numerals: *stộ édən* 'one hundred and one', *dvệ stộ dvâindvâjset* 'two hundred and twenty-two'.

Ru. *dvésti dvádcat′ dva*, with all components declined in the standard language, though with long numerals in the spoken language there is a tendency to leave forms in the middle in their citation form; ordinal: *dvésti dvádcat′ vtorój*; in nonstandard usage, the higher ordinals are also found with acc. *týsjaču*, rather than nom. *týsjača*, e. g. in dates.[138] The other East Slavonic forms are similar: Uk. *dvísti dvádcjat′ dva*, ordinal *dvísti dvádcjat′ drúhy*; Br. *dzvésce dváccac′ dva*, ordinal *dzvésce dváccac′ druhí*.

In Czech, the digit may either precede the decad with the conjunction *a*, in which case the digit is indeclinable, e. g. *dvaadvacet* 'twenty-two', or follow it as a separate word, e. g. *dvacet dva*. For the numbers 'twenty-one' to 'ninety-nine' the former is more colloquial, while for higher numbers the latter is preferred: *dvě stě dvacet dva*. For numbers between 'one hundred' and 'two hundred' Old Czech also has the formation *padesát ke stu* 'fifty to a hundred, i. e. one hundred and fifty'.[138a] In ordinals up to 'ninety-nine', the forms are *dvaadvacátý* and *dvacátý druhý* (the latter with ordinals throughout), while for the higher ordinals, in principle at least, all components should be ordinal: *dvoustý dvacátý druhý*.

The Slovak system is similar to that of Czech, except that in Slovak the alternative with preposed unit is literary and rare. Thus for 'twenty-two' one has both *dvadsat'dva* (either indeclinable, or with both parts declined and written separately in the oblique cases, e. g. gen. *dvadsatich dvoch*) and *dvaadvadsat'* (usually indeclinable). If the digit is 'one', e. g. *dvadsat'jeden*, then the number, in this form, can only be indeclinable (cf. a similar phenomenon in Polish). Ordinal *dvesto dvadsiaty druhý*, with decads and digit as ordinals, but not the higher components, except for the last component (e. g. *tisíc dvojstý* 'one thousand two hundredth'), as in Polish.

Po. *dwieście dwadzieścia dwa*, with all components declined; but if one of the components is *jeden*, this component remains in the fossilized nominative singular masculine, and the case of the following noun is determined by the numeral preceding *jeden*. In the ordinal, the decads and digits must be in the ordinal form, otherwise (i. e. if there are no decads or digits) only the last component: *dwieście dwudziesty drugi*, but *tysiąc dwusetny* 'one thousand two hundredth'.

In Sorbian, the usual order is for the digits to precede the decads, and in either order the conjunction *a* 'and' must occur: USo. *dwě sće dwajad-*

waceći (ordinal *dwě sće dwajadwacety*); LSo. *dwě sćě* (*dwa hunderta*) *dwa a dwaźasća* (ordinal *dwě sćě* [*dwa hunderta*] *dwa a dwaźasty*). Note also the forms for 'one hundred and one': USo. *sto a jedyn*, LSo. *sto a jaden*, and LSo. *sto a pěšźasety* 'one hundred and fiftieth', where the last two components must be separated by the conjunction *a*. In both Sorbian languages, only the last component is declined.

In Polabian, both *janü disǫtnocti* and *disǫtnocti janü* are attested for 'twenty-one'; whether the digit, in the former order, was declinable or a fossilized neuter form is not clear.

The above gives the situation in the modern standard languages, though certain variations are found in the use of conjunctions and order of decads and digits in earlier periods and in nonstandard usage. Thus Old Czech had both orders of decads and digits with conjunctions: *jeden a dvadcěti, dvadcěti a jeden*, with declension of either or both parts; current *dvacet jeden* is apparently a later development. Another variant in Old Czech was the use of subtractive formations for coordinate numerals ending in 'nine': *bez jednoho dvadcěti, dvadcěti bez jednoho* ('twenty without one'), *dvadcěti méně* ('less') *jednoho*, for 'nineteen'. Similar formations, both additive and subtractive, are used in popular Lower Sorbian: *poł hunderta měńej jadnogo* 'forty-nine (half of a hundred less one)', *hundert měńej šesćich* 'ninety-four (hundred less six)', *jaden wušej połtera hunderta* 'one hundred and fifty one (one more than one-and-a-half hundred'.

In some dialects (though not, generally, in the standard languages) there is some seepage between the formation of coordinate numerals per se and the formation of the teens. Thus some Latvian dialects use the coordinate formation for the teens: *viêndesmit viêns* 'eleven'; cf. also the Czech subtractive formation for 'nineteen' above. Conversely, Old Russian has the occasional formation *pjata na dvadcat′* 'twenty-fifth', using the preposition *na* as in the teens.[139] See also section 16.0.8. for the special forms for numerals between 'twenty' and 'thirty' in Church Slavonic and Old Czech.

16.2. Masculine human forms

The existence of separate numeral forms for male humans is a characteristic feature of many Slavonic languages. In some of the languages there are general syntactic-morphological criteria that set off male human, or generally human, or generally animate nouns, in particular the use of the morphological genitive in place of the accusative. All Slavonic languages have accusative = genitive for singular masculine animate nouns (other than those declined as *a*-stems) and their attributes, including therefore the numeral 'one'. In the plural, this usage is more restricted, and the individual language situation (at least for the standard languages) is as follows: Serbo-Croatian, Slovenian and Czech do not have accusative-genitive in the plural; Polish, Slovak, Upper Sorbian and Lower Sorbian have accusative = genitive only for masculine human nouns (though in Sorbian there is some seepage into other human and animate nouns), for all numerals from 'two' to 'ninety-nine' inclusive (Polish 'two' to 'nine hundred and ninety-nine' inclusive); Ukrainian and Belorussian have accusative = genitive for all human plural nouns, but only for the numerals 'two' to 'four'; Russian has accusative = genitive for all animate plural nouns, but with numerals only with 'two' to 'four', and in coordinate numerals with 'two' to 'four' as last constituent there is a tendency to use the accusative = nominative, especially with animals.

Less commonly, with numerals (apparently not with other nonquantified phrases) the nominative plural is replaced by the genitive plural. This shows consistently in Polish, where for all numerals from 'two' to 'nine hundred and ninety-nine' inclusive the nominative plural when referring to male humans (or a mixed group including male humans) is replaced by the genitive plural, a phenomenon first noted in seventeenth-century texts (for the hundreds, only from the nineteenth century). In other languages, sporadic traces of similar constructions are found, e. g. Macedonian dial. *obev* 'both', apparently for older **oběchъ*, **oběichъ*, i. e. a genitive plural.[140]

Apart from these syntactic means of distinguishing male humans, the following languages have distinct morphological forms as indicated below; the distinct forms usually indicate a group of men, or a group of men and women.

Bulgarian has three types of formation here. The first derives from the original dative-instrumental dual, with the ending *-ma*; the Common Slavonic form for the dative-instrumental of 'two' is **dъvěma*, but even in Old Church Slavonic the form *dъvama* occurs once, with the vowel *a* from nom.-acc. masc. *dъva*, and this is the origin of Bulgarian masc. hum. *dváma* (colloquially also as a diminutive *dvámka* or *dvámca*); then follows *tríma* (with attachment of the 'suffix' *-ma* to the nom.-acc. *tri*), *četiríma* (with attachment of *-ma* to *čétiri*, alongside an etymologically more correct instrumental form *četírma*), *petíma, šestíma* (no forms for 'seven', 'eight'), *devetíma*. A second formation originally attached the noun-forming suffix *-ina* to the numeral, giving still current *petína,*[142] *šestína,*[142] *sedmína,*[141] *osmína,*[141] *devetína;*[141] from the forms for 'seven' and 'eight' a new suffix *-mina* was abstracted, giving the current forms: *dvamína, trimína,*[142] *četirmína,*[142] *petmína,*[142] *šestmína,*[142] *sedmína,*[141] *osmína,*[141] *devetmína.*[142] There are no distinct masculine human forms for the higher numerals, though the masculine human forms can be used as last component of a coordinate numeral. The use of these numerals is not obligatory in Bulgarian, so that for 'two sons', for instance, there are two possible constructions: the ordinary cardinal in *dvá sína*, with the numerical form (deriving from the old dual) of the noun, or *dváma* (*dvamína*) *sinové*, with the ordinary plural. On the basis of the *-mina* forms, colloquial Bulgarian has also *edín mín* 'one man'.[143] For 'two' to 'four' there are also dialectal masculine human forms deriving from the old collective noun in *-ica: dvóica, tróica, četvórica.*

In Macedonian there are fewer variants of the individual numerals, and the system goes up to 'thousand': *dvajca* (with the vowel of *dva*; dial. *dvojca*), *trojca, četvorica, pet(m)ina* (articled: *pettemina*), *šest(m)ina, sedmina* or *sedummina, osmina* or *osummina, devetmina,*[144] *desetmina, stomina, iljadamina.*[145]

Serbo-Croatian has optional masculine human forms for the numerals 'one' to 'ten', in origin collective nouns with the suffix *-ica* attached to the stem of the collective numeral: *dvòjica, tròjica, četvòrica, petòrica, šestòrica, sedmòrica, osmòrica, devetòrica, desetòrica.*

The East Slavonic languages have no specifically masculine human forms, though in Russian one of the uses of the collective numerals *dvóe*, etc., is in referring to a group of male humans. Slovenian and Czech also lack separate masculine human forms of numerals (Slovenian does have separate masculine forms for 'two' to 'four', e. g. masc. *štírje* vs. fem. neut. *štíri*, but they are not used exclusively for denoting humans).

In Slovak the numerals 'five' to 'ninety-nine' indicate the nominative masculine human by adopting the nominative plural adjectival ending *-i* (and the noun agrees in case, rather than being genitive plural); in the accusative, the form of the genitive is used for male humans, otherwise there are no separate forms. Distinct nominative forms exist, however, for the numerals 'two' to 'four': *dvaja* (cf. also *obaja*), *traja, štyria.* The origin of these forms is probably the ending, frequent in Slovak, *-ia* (earlier *-ā̈*) in masculine nouns, giving older Sk. *dvā̈* (*dvia*), *trā̈* (*tria*), and still current *štyria* (older *štyrā̈*). *Traja* has an alternative, still found in dialects, *trajā̈*, apparently the ending *-ā̈* attached to a stem form which has been influenced in its vocalism by *dva*; this would give regularly

**trajia*, whence modern *traja*. For 'two', *dvajā̃*, still found in dialects, seems to be by analogy with *trajā̃*. The forms for 'two' could also involve contamination with gen. **dvojú* (or **dvajú*, with the vowel of *dva*) or collective *dvoj-*.

Apart from the use of the genitive for the nominative-accusative, Polish has distinct nominative masculine human forms *dwaj* (cf. *obaj, obydwaj*), *trzej, czterej*. In Old Polish the etymologically masculine forms *trze* (i. e. *trzē*, for **trьje*) and (rare) *cztyrze* (**č(e)tyre*) are found, though only in masculine human use. It is possible that current *trzej* developed from *trzē* by diphthongization of the long vowel, the final *-j* then being tranferred analogically to give *dwaj,* and the final *-ej* to give *czterej*. Alternatively, the final *-j* may derive from contamination of the cardinals with the collectives *dwoj-, troj-*.[146] One advantage of explanations involving the collective numerals for West Slavonic is that they would permit a uniform explanation to be given of the appearance of apparently irregular *-j* in the Slovak and Polish forms, perhaps also of the Upper Sorbian (not specifically masculine human) form *dwaj* (whence the ending has spread to all dual forms originally in *-a*), and of the Polabian collectives *dåvoj, tåroj* (with *o* for **a*, see section 16.4.); in addition, such explanations provide a link to the masculine human forms in South Slavonic.

In Sorbian there are masculine human forms only for the numerals 'three' to 'ninety-nine' (though from 'five' upwards all numerals may be indeclinable). For 'three' Upper Sorbian has *třo*, probably from the original nom. masc. **trьje* by contraction, and the typical Sorbian shift of final *-*e* to *-o* (in Upper Sorbian, only in nonverbal forms); similarly *štyŕo*, and by analogy the higher forms *pěšo*, etc.; in the masculine human forms, the vowel *o* is generalized throughout the oblique cases too. LSo. has similarly *tśo, styŕo*, both with the vowel *o* throughout the oblique cases, and *pěšo*, etc., with the vowel *o* throughout the oblique cases, except for the instrumental. In Lower Sorbian and some Upper Sorbian dialects, these forms tend to be used also with feminine human nouns and other animate nouns, especially in the oblique cases.

16.3. Articled forms

16.3.1. Cardinals

In Old Church Slavonic, the cardinals 'one' to 'four' are adjectives, and therefore like other adjectives should be expected to take the compound adjective declension endings, i. e. the suffix *-*jь* in the appropriate form.

In practice, these forms are rare, though they do occur for 'one' to 'three': *(j)edinii* 'the one, unique', *dъvaja* 'the two', *trii* (i. e. *tri* [for masc. *trije*] + *i*) 'the three'; also for the teens: dat. sg. masc. *jedinujemu na desęte* 'eleven'. In place of the articled forms of *dъva, oba* 'both' is often found. The higher numerals, being strictly nouns, should not take this adjectival suffix, but a few examples do occur, presumably representing the general tendency in Slavonic to lose the strictly nominal character of these numerals: acc. pl. masc. *sedmiję* 'seven'; nom. pl. masc. *desętii* 'ten'; nom. pl. masc. *sedmь desętii* 'seventy'; acc. pl. fem. *devętь desętъje i devętь* 'ninety-nine'.

In Bulgarian and Macedonian, the only modern Slavonic languages to have an article as such, the article occurs with most numerals (except 'one' in Macedonian; Bulgarian has *edínijat, ednáta, ednóto*), as with most attributive adjectives in general. In Bulgarian the form of the article is determined by the final segment of the cardinal: if it is *-a* the article is *-ta* (*dváta, dvámata*, i. e. irrespective of gender), otherwise it is *-te* in the plural (*tríte, petté*). In some dialects rather than *-te* the old gen. *-tech* is used (cf. section 16.2.). The stress remains on the cardinal in 'two' to 'four', but in the higher numerals shifts onto the article, cf. the shift in feminine nouns in a consonant, e. g. *mládost* 'youth' but *mladosttá*. Macedonian has essentially the same system: *dvata, dvajcata, trite* ... *pette, šeste* (for **šest-te*), etc., also *iljadata* and *miliónot* (*milión* being a masculine noun). With internally complex numerals, the positioning of the article in Macedonian gives an insight into what is currently felt to be the divisibility of the complex into its components: *petmina* has *pettemina* (i. e. *pet-te* + *mina*), the teens and tens are indivisible (*edinaesette, dvadesette*), as are the lower hundreds (*dvestete, tristata*), but not the higher hundreds (*četiritestotini, pettestotini*, etc.). In coordinate numerals, only the last component takes the article, e. g. Bg. *osemdesét i petté*, Ma. *osumdeset i pette* 'eighty-five'.

16.3.2. Ordinals

The ordinals in Balto-Slavonic are *o/jā*-stem adjectives, and as such have both short (i. e. article-less) and long (articled) forms, though given the meaning of the ordinals, they in fact occur more frequently in the long form.

In Lithuanian, both long and short forms exist (though for 'hundredth' long form *šimtàsis* is preferred, as the short form is the same as the cardinal *šim̃tas*). Latvian in general has only the long forms, except for *ȍtrs* 'second', with both; but High Latvian has more general use of short forms.

In Old Church Slavonic, the long forms are commoner. Those Slavonic languages that have lost short forms of adjectives in general lose them here too, while some languages that in general retain both forms, e. g. Serbo-Croatian and Russian, have only long forms for the ordinals. In Russian, the short forms survive in the expressions *sam-drúg* 'with one other (literally oneself second), twofold', *sam-tretéj, sam-četvërt, sam-pját, sam-šëst, sam-sëm, sam-devját, sam-desját* (there is no equivalent form for 'with seven others', for which *sam-vos'mój* is used).[147] More generally, the fractions for '*x* and a half' (see section 16.5.2.) retain the short form of the ordinal '*x* plus one', e. g. Ru. *poltorá* for **pol vtora* 'half of the second', i. e. 'one and a half', as do various adverbial expressions.

A rather different situation obtains in Bulgarian and Macedonian, where generally it is the short form rather than the long form of the adjectives that survives into the modern languages (no ending in the masculine singular). Yet here the ordinals typically have the final *-i* in the long form in the masculine singular, in Bulgarian for all ordinals, in Macedonian for all those up to 'hundredth' (*stoti*, but *dvestoten* 'two hundredth'; 'first' to 'fourth' are commoner in Macedonian in the short form). Within the modern languages these forms are not felt as articled, and may take the regular article to give, e. g., Bg. *pъ́rvijat*, Ma. *prviot* 'the first'. The use of the 'long' forms here probably derives from the greater frequency of the long form over the short form in earlier periods when the two forms were distinguished semantically. For the lower numerals, Macedonian has 'short' forms for the ordinals 'first' to 'fourth' (*prv, vtor, tret, četvrt*); in Bulgarian these forms, together with 'fifth' (*pet*), 'sixth' (*šest*) and the higher ordinals (*stóten, chíljāden, miliónen, miliárden*), are the only ones used in practice, though grammars may list such forms for other ordinals, with the exception of *sédmi* 'seventh', *ósmi* 'eighth'. For the form *tret* 'third', see section 16.1.3.2.

16.4. Collective numerals

The Balto-Slavonic collective numerals derive from Indo-European formations with thematization of the full-grade of the corresponding cardinal, i. e. with thematization used twice over; this would give, for **d(u)u̯i-* (cf. the form used in compounds, section 16.6.) the collective **d(u)u̯ei̯-/d(u)u̯oi̯-* (with *e/o* ablaut variants), for **tri-* (cf. the form used in compounds) collective **trei̯-/troi̯-* (the latter variant, cf. Sl. **troj-*, need not necessarily have its *o* from **dъvoj-*, as is often assumed, since the ablaut variant found in the latter may equally well be operative in the former), and for **kᵘetur-* the collective **kᵘetu̯er-/kᵘetu̯or-*. The other forms in Balto-Slavonic are analogical formations based on one of these. In Lithuanian-Latvian the *e*-grade is used; the only attested Old Prussian collective *abbaien* 'both' has *o*-grade, as do Sl. **dъvoj-*, **troj-*, while for the higher collectives Slavonic has both *o* and *e*. The principal uses of the collectives are: in the sense '*n*-fold' or '*n* kinds of'; in place of the ordinary cardinals when referring to groups of people (especially if of mixed sex); and with *pluralia tantum*; for further details, see below, and discussions of the syntax of the individual languages. Close parallels to the Slavonic forms are found in Sanskrit *dvayá-* 'double', *trayá-* 'treble', *catváram* 'quadrangle', Greek *doioí* 'two, both'.

The only attested Old Prussian form is *abbaien* 'both', which in formation agrees with Slavonic rather than Lithuanian-Latvian.

In Lithuanian, the reflexes of the collective formation noted above are used only in the plural, and only with *pluralia tantum*. For 'one', in addition to *vienì*, the plural of the cardinal *víenas*, there is also the form *vienerì* (fem. *víenerios*), with a suffix abstracted from the higher collectives, in particular 'four'. For 'two', 'both', 'three', the forms are *dvejì* (fem. *dvẽjos*), *abejì* (fem. *ãbejos*) and *trejì* (fem. *trẽjos*) (in some dialects, this stem has replaced the ordinary cardinal 'three'); some dialects have *dvejerì* and *trejerì*, with the same suffix as in the higher collectives. For 'four' we have *ketverì* (fem. *kẽtverios*); originally, the *-er* was part of the stem but, as in all Balto-Slavonic languages that have retained these formations, the **or/er* is reinterpreted as a suffix, and appears as such with the higher collectives: *penkerì* (fem. *peñkerios*), *šešerì* (fem. *šẽšerios*), *septynerì* (fem. *septýnerios*), *aštuonerì* (fem. *aštúonerios*), *devynerì* (fem. *devýnerios*); *dešimterì* occurs only dialectally. Some dialects have *-elì* rather than *-erì*, perhaps under the influence of *kelì* 'some, several',[148] and even *ketverelì* 'four'. The singular of these formations occurs only in dialect usage, where the neuter singular has the meaning 'twice', etc., e. g. *dvẽja tíek* 'twice as much'. This formation in Lithuanian (the so-called *dauginiai skaitvardžiai* 'plural numerals') is not used as a strict collective, for which there are *kuopiniai skaitvardžiai* 'collective numerals' with the ending *-(e)tas* (probably for **-atas*, with *a* giving *e* originally only after *j*): *víenetas, dvẽjetas, ãbejetas, trẽjetas, kẽtvertas, peñketas, šẽšetas, septýnetas, aštúonetas, devýnetas*. This formation seems to parallel that of Sanskrit *pañcát-* 'group of five'.[149]

In Latvian, the forms used with *pluralia tantum* have generalized the ending *-ej*, from *divej-* (**duvej-*), *trej-*, to the higher numerals, i.e. the inverse of the Lithuanian and Slavonic pattern: *viênẽji, divẽji, abẽji, treji* (dialectally analogical *trejẽji*), *četrẽji, pìecẽji, sešẽji*. The long *ẽ* in these is unexpected, though short *e* is retained in *treji*, and dialectally in the other forms; they have probably been influenced by other nominal derivatives in **-ējo-*.[150] These Latvian forms also occur, in dialects, with collective meaning, and in the same meaning we find the neuter singular of the collective, followed by the noun in the genitive plural (cf. some Slavonic forms); Old Lithuanian had a similar use of *abeju* 'both'. Another Latvian collective formation is in *-at* (cf. Li. *-et* above), and is used in the locative singular, e.g. *divatā, trejatā, četratā, pìecatā, sešatā* 'in a group of two, three, etc.'.

Slavonic agrees with Lithuanian in generalizing the suffix *-er/-or* to the collectives higher than 'four' (though not to 'one'; with *pluralia tantum*, the plural of the cardinal 'one' is used), including such forms as **sъtor-* 'hundred'. The distribution of *-er* versus *-or* depends on the language (and dialect), though many languages have both forms, at least historically. In Slavonic, there are two syntactic uses of the collectives: one as an agreeing adjective (pronominal declension for 'two', 'both', 'three'; *o/a*-stem for the higher collectives), usually in the dual or plural; the other as a singular neuter, with the following noun in the genitive plural. The modern languages differ considerably in the extent to which collectives are used, though a discussion of this problem belongs in a treatment of the syntax of the individual languages.

CSl. **dъvoj-, *oboj-, *troj-, *četvor-/četver-, *pętor-/pęter-, *šestor-/šester-, *sedmor-/sedmer-, *osmor-/osmer-, *devętor-/devęter-, *desętor-/desęter-*, and possibly **sъtor-*, though the last is attested only in certain languages, and may be a later analogical form, as are the teens and tens, where they occur. The Old Church Slavonic forms are essentially the same, from 'one' to 'ten' (including 'both'), but in Old Church Slavonic proper only the *-or* variants are found, although the derivative *sedmerica* exists; the *-er* forms are found in Church Slavonic. Modern Bulgarian and Macedonian do not have these collectives, though there are derivatives from them, e.g. Bg. *dvójka, trójka, četvórka, petórka*, as collective nouns.

Serbo-Croatian has both the neuter singular and plural formations; for the higher collectives, both *-er* and *-or* forms are normative; the forms quoted are in the neuter singular: *dvȍje, ȍboje* (also *ȍbadvoje*, with invariable first component), *trȍje, čȅtvero* (and *čȅtvoro*, thus also for the higher collectives), *pètero, šèstero, sèdmero, òsmero, dèvetero, dèsetero*; and more recent creations for the teens and tens, following their reinterpretation as single complexes: *devétnaestero* 'nineteen', *trídesetero* 'thirty'. Serbo-Croatian also has collective coordinate numerals, with the last component only collective in form. The plural collectives, which are rare in the modern language, are declined as indefinite adjectives. The declension of the neuter singular collectives has been largely reformed: the original pronominal declension gen. *dvòjega* (still normative) contracted to *dvójga*, while dat. *dvòjemu* (still normative) contracted to *dvójmu*; these forms were subsequently replaced by adjectival endings, giving gen. *dvóga* (normative) and dat.-loc. *dvómu, dvóme* (both normative); finally, these dative forms were in turn optionally replaced by *dvóma*, with the plural (originally dual) ending, cf. *dvèma* (Je. *dvjèma*), and are now used as dative-instrumental-locative. The declension of *čètvero* is essentially the same: gen. *četvérga*, dat.-instr.-loc. *četvérma* (dat.-loc. also *četveróma, četveróme*), with endings from the lower collectives. In practice, these forms are often left indeclinable.

Slovenian, like Serbo-Croatian, has retained both singular and plural usage of the collectives, declined as adjectives: *dvộj, trộj, četvệr, petệr, šestệr*, etc., *stotệr*.

Old Russian had both singular and plural forms, but in the modern language only the originally neuter singular form survives for 'two' to 'ten', followed by the genitive plural in the nominative-accusative, although in the oblique cases forms of the original plural collectives are used, according to the pronominal declension. In modern Russian, the higher collectives (from 'five' onwards) tend to be avoided, and in the oblique cases cardinals are often used instead of the collectives. The forms are: *dvóe* (gen. *dvoích*, etc.), (for **óboe*, see section 16.1.2.3.), *tróe, čétvero* (gen. *četverých*), *pjátero, šéstero, sémero, vós'mero, dévjatero, désjatero.* Ukrainian has similar forms, except that in the oblique cases only the cardinals may be used: *dvóje* (for *obóje*, which is not now a collective, see section 16.1.2.3.), *tróje, čétvero, p'játero, šéstero, sémero, vós'mero, dév'jatero, désjatero.* Belorussian has *dvóe* (gen. *dvaích* or *dvajhá*, the latter for the original singular form **dvojego* with the genitive singular ending *-a* from the *o*-stem noun declension (cf. Polish), dat. *dvaím*, instr. *dvajmá* [cf. *dvumá*], loc. *dvaích*), *abóe, tróe, čac'vëra* (gen.-loc. *čac'vjaróch*, dat. *čac'vjaróm*, instr. *čac'vjarmá*, i. e. declined like the cardinal), *pjacëra, šascëra, sjamëra, vas'mëra, dzevjácera, dzesjácera.*

The current Czech forms are neuter singular (nominative-accusative only) and plural (plural forms given here): *dvojí, obojí, trojí, čtverý, paterý, šesterý, sedmerý, osmerý, devaterý, desaterý, sterý*. Some of these forms also exist with short final vowels (cf. the pronominal declension; the current adjectival declension is an innovation). Old Czech had *dvój*, etc., declined as a pronoun, *čtver*, etc., declined as short adjectives, and also contracted *dvé*, gen. *dvého, tré*, gen. *trého*; and the regular pronominal or adjectival declension of *dvój, dvojí*, etc., and pronominal (adjectival, in the oblique plural) of *čtver*, etc. Slovak has: *dvoje, oboje* (*obidvoje*), *troje, štvoro, pätero*, etc.; in the modern language they are indeclinable.

In Old Polish the full range of forms of collectives is found, but in the modern language only the neuter singular survives, with the following noun in the genitive plural: *dwoje, oboje, troje, czworo, pięcioro, sześcioro, siedmioro, ośmioro, dziewięcioro, dziesięcioro*, etc., to *dziewięćdziesięcioro*; from 'five' onwards, the ending *-oro* is added to the nominative-accusative of the cardinal (which in the modern language is the same as the stem), giving the forms in soft consonant plus *-oro*. The declension has been reformed: the old gen. *dwojego* was contracted to *dwojgo*, subsequently *dwojga*, with the *o*-stem ending *-a*, and the *-g-* reinterpreted as an increment forming the oblique stem, whence dat.-loc. *dwojgu* (earlier also *dwojgom*, with the plural ending), instr. *dwojgiem*. The higher collectives have adopted the same declension: *czworo, czworga, czworgu, czworgiem*.

The collectives in Sorbian are used primarily as adjectives ('*n*-fold'). USo. *dwoji, troji, štwory, pjećory, šěsćory, wosmory* (*wósmory*), *dźewjećory, dźesaćory, story* (also *stotory*), *tysacory*. LSo. *dwoji, tšoji* (with regular *tš* for *tr* before a back vowel), *stwory, pěšory* or *pěšery* (and similarly for the higher collectives), *šěsćory, sedymory, wosymory, źewéśory, źaseśory, dwaźasćory, hundertory* or (archaic) *story*.

The singular collectives were presumably very much alive in Polabian, as in the numeral lists they are often given in place of the cardinals: *dåvoj, våboj, tåroj* (to the extent that this is distinguishable from *tåroi*, the expected reflex of **tri*), *citvărü*,[151] *pątărü, sistărü, sidmărü, smărü* (also *vismărü/vüsmărü*), *divątărü, disątărü*. The collectives for 'two', 'both', 'three' presuppose **dъvaj-*, **obaj-*, **t(ъ)raj-*, with *a* probably from the cardinal **dъva*.[152] In the higher collectives, the final nonreduced vowel *-ü* (cf. also the apocopated form *smărü* 'eight') suggests final stress synchronically in Polabian, though this appears to be an innovation: the preceding vowel is reduced (normally, immediately pretonic vowels are not reduced), while the vowel on which the stress would have been expected from the evidence of the other Slavonic languages is not reduced (compare *citvărü* with Ru. *čétvero*). Possibly reflexes of both *-oro* and *-ero* were possible.[153]

16.5. Fractions

16.5.1. Simple fractions

Most of the Balto-Slavonic languages have a separate word for 'half', and numeral derivatives for the other fractions; for the higher denominators, many languages use ordinals, in the gender appropriate to the word for 'part'.

The distinctive words for 'half' may be treated first. Baltic and Slavonic diverge here. The Baltic forms are: Li. *pùsė*, Le. *puse*, OPr. *pausan, pauson.*[154] These forms also occur in the meaning 'side', and seem most closely related to Tocharian AB *poṣi* 'side, wall, rib', A *posac, posaṃ* 'beside'; the Old Prussian form has a different ablaut grade from its congeners. The Common Slavonic root is **pol*, possibly related to Albanian *pálë* 'side',[155] perhaps also IE **phel/phol*, cf. Sanskrit *phálati* 'splits', CSl. **polti* 'split in two', cf. Ru. *poléno* 'log'. In Slavonic, **pol-* is an *u*-stem, though in most of the modern languages, and occasionally in Old Church Slavonic, it is treated as an indeclinable, while in nominal use a nominal derivative (with the *o*-grade of the stem-formative) **polov-* is used: OCS *polъ* (*u*-stem noun or indeclinable); Bg. *polovína* (before a noun truncated to *polovín*), dialectally also *pol* (indeclinable); Ma. *polovina*, in some expressions also indeclinable *pol*; SCr. *pȏ, pòla* (indeclinable), *polòvina* (or *polovìna*), *polòvica*; Sn. *pộl* (indeclinable), *polovíca*; Ru. *pol-* (written as part of the following noun; the oblique cases have *polu-*, i. e. the (originally genitive-locative) *u*-stem ending), *polovína*; Uk. *piv* (indeclinable), *polovýna*; Br. *paŭ-* (written as part of following noun), *palavína*; Cz. *půl* (indeclinable), *polovina*; Sk. *pol* (indeclinable), *polovica, polovina*; Po. *pół* (indeclinable), *połowa*; USo. *poł* (indeclinable), *połojca*; LSo. *poł* (indeclinable); Pb. *pöl* (for **polъ*), as in *pöl-t'üpě* 'half of sixty, thirty'.

The higher denominators may now be given language by language. Lithuanian has two basic formations, one a compound with the ordinal of the denominator as first component and *-dalis* as second, i. e. *dalìs* (dial. *dalià*) 'part, piece', cf. Sl. *dolja*, e. g. *trẽčdalis, ketvirtãdalis, penktãdalis*, etc.; the other simply uses the definite ordinal for the denominator, feminine in agreement with *dalìs: vienà penktóji* 'one fifth', and even *vienà antróji* 'one half'. For 'quarter' there is also the noun *ketvir̃tis*. Latvian has the formations in *-daļa* (dial. *-dalis*), e. g. *trešdaļa, cętur̃tdaļa* (also *cętur̃knis*, as strict noun), and also formations with *daļa* as a separate word: *viêna trešā daļa*.

The Slavonic languages have typically an *i*-stem feminine noun based on the ordinal, or a nominal derivative of the ordinal in *-ina*. The attested

Old Church Slavonic forms are *četvrъtь* 'quarter', *desętina* 'tenth, tithe', and in Church Slavonic *tretina* 'third'. Bulgarian has forms in *-ina* (preferred for numerals up to 'ten') and *-inka* (originally diminutives, preferred in mathematical usage and for the higher denominators): *tretín(k)a, četvъrtín(k)a* (in nonmathematical usage also *čétvъrt* [feminine]), *petín(k)a*, etc., *edinadesetínka*, etc.; for coordinate numerals, and for 'hundred' and above, the ordinals are used, in the feminine: *dvádeset i pь̂rva, stótna, chíljadna, miliónna.* Macedonian has *-ina* derivatives up to 'ten': *tretina, četvrtina* (cf. *četvrt* 'quarter kilogramme'), *petina, šestina, sedmina, osmina, devetina, desetina*, but for higher denominators usually uses the ordinal, in the masculine form (cf. *del* 'part').[156] Serbo-Croatian (note the accent variants) *trèćina, četvr̀tina* (also *čȅtvr̄t*, feminine), *pètina, šèstina, sèdmina*, etc., *desètina, stòtīnka* (etymologically a diminutive), *tȉsućina.* Sn. *tretjína* (or *tretjȋnka*, similarly for higher denominators), *četrtína* (also *četȓt*), *petína*, etc., *desetína, stotína, tisočína.*

Russian has the *i*-stems *tret′* and *čétvert′* (Old Russian also contracted *čet′*), while for the higher denominators the feminine ordinal is used (cf. *čast′* (feminine) 'part'). Old Russian also had *-ina* derivatives (*tretina, pjatina, desjatina*), and also 'fractions of fractions', e. g. *polъ treti* 'one-sixth' (i. e. half of a third)', *polъ polъ treti* 'one-twelfth (i. e. half of half of a third)', *polъ polъ polъ četi* 'one thirty-second (i. e. half of half of half of a quarter)'.[157] Ukrainian has either the ordinal (*odná trétja*, etc.) or the *-yna* derivative throughout (*tretýna, četvertýna, p'jatýna*); for 'quarter', especially in clock-time, there is also the form *čvert′*, with contraction of **četv-* perhaps under Polish influence. Belorussian has much the same system as Russian: *trèc′, čvèrc′* (cf. the discussion of Ukrainian *čvert′*), for higher denominators the feminine ordinal.

Czech has consistently *-ina* derivatives: *třetina, čtvrtina* (also the feminine *i*-stem *čtvrt*, especially in clock-time), *pětina, šestina, sedmina, osmina, devítina, desetina* (with different reflexes of the originally long nasal in these two), *setina* (with irregular analogical strengthening of the weak jer, though *stotina* is also found), *tisícina, miliontina* (long *o*) or *milióntina.* The Slovak forms are similar: *tretina, štvrtina* (also *štvrt'*, indeclinable in the singular, pl. *štvrte*, indeclinable), *pätina*, etc., *stotina, tisícina, milióntina.* Polish agrees with East Slavonic, rather than the rest of West Slavonic, in preferring ordinals to the *-ina* derivatives: *jedna trzecia, ćwierć* (for **cztwierć*, with initial *ć* apparently by assimilation to the final consonant), *jedna piąta*, etc. Upper Sorbian has *-ina* derivatives, though many of the forms are recent neologisms: *třećina, štwórćina* (also indeclinable *štwórć*, pl. *štwórće*; these forms are used in clock-time, alongside the German loan *běrtl* [also diminutive *běrtlk*, and nonstandard *bětl*] 'Viertel'), *pjećina, šesćina, sedmina, wosmina* (*wósmina*), *dźewjećina, dźesaćina*, etc. *stoćina, tysaćina, milionćina*. In Lower Sorbian, the forms *stẃerś* and the German loan *běrtyl* are traditional forms for 'quarter', especially in clock-time; otherwise Lower Sorbian formed fractions of the type $(x - 1)/x$ on the pattern 'x parts', using *źěł* 'part', e.g. *dwa źěła* 'two-thirds', *tśi źěły* 'three-quarters', *pěś źěłow* 'five-sixths'; the forms in *-ina* (*tśeśina, stworśina, ṕeśina*, etc.) are blatant neologisms.[158] In Polabian, we find for 'quarter' the ordinal *cit'ortě*, and also the German loan *fardål* (Middle Low German *vêr-dêl*) and *fartin* (Middle Low German *vêrdink*).[158a]

16.5.2. '*x* and a half'

An interesting fraction formation, shared by Balto-Slavonic with some of the languages of Scandinavia (Swedish, Danish, Finnish), is the formation of fractions 'x and a half' on the pattern 'half of the $(x + 1)$th, i. e. 'one and a half' becomes 'half of the second', and so on. The productivity of this pattern is different in the various languages, and has tended to decline in use in the historical period. Few of the modern languages form compound numerals on this pattern, though Russian still has *poltorásta* (obl. *polútorasta*) 'one hundred and fifty', Sn. *poldrúgi stǫ̂* 'one hundred and fifty', *poldrúgi tȋsoč* 'one thousand five hundred', USo. *połdrasta* 'one hundred fifty', *połdra tysaca* 'one thousand five hundred', while Lower Sorbian has an even more productive system with the hundreds: *połtera sta* 'one hundred and fifty', *połtśeśa sta* 'two hundred and fifty', etc. Older Polish has *połtorasta* (obl. *połtorastu*), while in Old Russian, for instance, one finds forms like *poldevjatnadcata* 'eighteen and a half', *poltret'jadcat'* 'twenty-five' (i. e. 'half of the third ten'), *polšestadesjat* 'fifty-five', even *poldevjanosto* 'eighty-five', suggesting that *devjanosto* 'ninety' was at least at this period felt synchronically to have *devjat'*- as first component, cf. the impossibility of *polsorok(a)* for 'thirty-five' (for which Old Russian has *polčetvertadcat'*).[159] See also the formation of the odd decads in Slovincian, section 16.1.12.2.1.

Representative forms from the modern languages are as follows. Li. *pusañtro, pustrẽčio, pusketvir̃to*; *añtro*, etc., are genitive, cf. the meaning 'half of the xth', with the following noun equally in the genitive singular, and the ordinal part agreeing in gender; in the oblique cases, however, the whole complex *pusañtr-*, etc., is treated as one, going into the case determined by the syntax of the sentence, and agreeing with the noun. In Latvian, only *pusòtra* is in common use.

In Slavonic, the ordinal remains in the short adjectival form (apart from later changes, e. g. Polish fem. *połtorej* for older *połtory*). For 'one and a half', many languages have **(vъ)tor-* as second component, even when the simple ordinal is usually replaced by **drug-*. Current forms are: Sn. *poldrúgi, poltrẹ́tji, polčetŕti, polpẹ́ti, poldesẹ́ti* (all declined as adjectives); Ru. *poltorá* (fem. *poltorý*, obl. *polútora*; in the oblique cases, the following noun is in the plural, in the case determined by the syntax of the sentence), with *poltret'já* (for the stress, see section 16.1.3.2.) found into the nineteenth century; Uk. *pivtorá* (fem. *pivtorý*); Br. *paŭtará* (fem. *paŭtarý*), in dialects also *paŭtracja, paŭčvarta*, etc.; Czech (archaic) *půl druha*, current *půl čtvrta, půl páta*, etc., usually indeclinable; Sk. *pol druha, pol tret'a*, etc.; Po. *połtora* (fem. *połtorej*, older *połtory*), indeclinable; USo. *połdra* (for **pol druha*), *połtřeća, połštwórta*, etc.; LSo. *połtera, połtśeśa*, etc.

16.6. Numerals as first part of compound words

Ordinals as first part of a compound word present no problems, because the ordinals, being ordinary adjectives, combine with the second component as would any other adjective, i. e. with the vowel *-o-* in Slavonic (e. g. Ru. *pervo-*), *-e-* after a soft consonant, *-a-* in Lithuanian (e. g. *pirma-*), and in the stem form in Latvian (e. g. *pìrm-*).

The cardinals are more problematic, since they present various formations, either inherited from Indo-European, or a result of group or language-particular innovations.

The only attested Old Prussian compound is *dwi-gubbus* 'double', where *dwi-* corresponds to Sanskrit *dvi-*, Greek *di-*, i. e. IE **d(u)u̯i-*.

The Lithuanian forms are: *vien(a)-, dvi-, tri-, ketur-, penk(ia)-*, etc., *dešimt(a)-, šimt(a)-, tūkstant-*, and for 'half-' *pus-* (also sometimes the old loc. *pusiau-*). *Dvi-* and *tri-* continue Indo-European formations (cf. Sanskrit *dvi-, tri-*); for 'half-', 'four-' and 'thousand-' the stem is used as first component, while for 'one-', 'five-' to 'ten-', 'hundred-' the formative *-a-* is optionally present.

Latvian has more consistently generalized the stem: *viên-, div-* (the current stem of *divi*), *trij-* (based on the oblique stem form *trij-*) or *trîs-* (i. e. the citation form of the cardinal), *četr-, pìec-*, etc., *desmit-, sìmt-*, *tũkstôš-* (the last three forms being the usual prenominal forms of the cardinal too), and *pus-* 'half-'.

In Slavonic, traces of the older Indo-European formations are rare, and the more usual formations use one of the following: the stem with the connecting vowel *-o-* (*-e-* after palatalized consonants); the bare stem; the citation form (often the same as the stem in the modern languages); the genitive of the cardinal; the collective numeral (stem with or without connection vowel). Isolated formations are the ordinal (OCS *četvrъto-*) and the accusative (SCr. *hiljadu-, tisuću-* cf. the general use of this in numeral expressions).

OCS *(j)edino-* or *(j)edьno-*, also *ino-* (see section 16.1.1.1.); *dъvo-* (connecting vowel *-o-*) and *dъva-* (citation form); *tri-* and *trь-* (the latter, in *trьgub-* 'treble' being a survival of the Indo-European formation **tri-*); *četvrъto-* (an unusual ordinal formation) or *četvrě-* (the preconsonantal forms of **četver-*, i. e. the stem of the collective, with regular metathesis); *pęto-* or *pętь-* or (genitive) *pęti-*, etc. The evidence of the modern languages points to CSl. **sъto-* (where the final *o* may be interpreted, in accordance with the general productive formation of the language in question, as the connecting vowel or the final vowel of the citation form). For 'half-', we have gen. *polu-*, and also *pla-*, by metathesis from **pol-* before a consonant, i. e. the bare stem.

This system, barring those forms that are archaisms within Old Church Slavonic, is retained reasonably faithfully in Serbo-Croatian, though other collective formations are found less commonly: *jedno-, dvo-* (*dvoje-*), *tri-* (*troje-*), *četvoro-* (i. e. the collective with connecting *o*), *peto-* (*petero-, petoro-*), etc. *deseto-* (*desetero-, desetoro-*), *sto-*, and for 'half-' *polu-*; for 'thousand' the accusative is used: *hiljadu-* or *tisuću-*. Slovenian has *eno-, dvo-, tro-* (the usual form, alongside nonproductive *tri-*), *četvero-, pet-* and *petero-, deset-* and *desetero-, sto-, tisoč-, pol-*. Bg. *edno-, dvu-* (i. e. old gen.) and *dvoe-* (collective), *tri-, četiri-, pet-*, etc., *deset-, sto-, chiljado-, polu-*. Ma. *edno-, dvo-, tri-* and *tro-, četiri-* and *četvoro-, pet(o)-, deset-, sto-, iljado-, polu-*. Bulgarian has departed most from the Old Church Slavonic pattern, while Macedonian occupies an intermediate position.

In Russian, productive formations use the genitive consistently for numerals from 'two' to 'eighty', though traces of other formations (including earlier forms of the genitive) are found in individual words: *odno-* (alongside many Church Slavonic loans in *edino-*), *dvuch-* (also *dvu-* from the older form of the genitive; *dvoju-* in *dvojúrodnyj brát* 'cousin' has an even earlier genitive; occasionally *dvoe-* as in *dvoežё́nstvo* 'bigamy'), *trёch-* (occasionally *troe-*; also *tre-* in *treugól'nik* 'triangle', the same stem as is abstracted in the formation of *trétij* 'third'; *troju-* in *trojúrodnyj brát* 'second cousin', analogous to *dvoju-*), *četyrëch-* (alongside occasional *četvero-*, from the collective, e. g. *četveronógij* 'quadrupedal'), *pjati-*, etc. (note older *os'mi-* in *os'minóg* 'octopus', alongside the usual *vos'mi-*), *desjati-, dvadcati-, pjatidesjati-, dvuchsot-*; for the higher simplex numbers, we find the genitive in *soroka-*, cf. the other decads, but the *-o-* form in *devjanosto-* and *sto-*, also *tysjače-* (*e* for *o* after a palatalized consonant); for 'half-' we have *polu-* (for the 'prefix' *pol-*, see section 16.5.1.). Apart from 'two' to 'four', where the genitive forms have not been fully generalized, Ukrainian has much the same system as Russian here: *odno-, dvo-* (*dvoch-*, rarer *dvoje-*), *try-* (rarer *trjoch-, troje-*), *čotyry-* (rare *čotyrjoch-*), *p'jaty-*, etc., *desjaty-, soroka-, dev'janosto-, sto-, tysjačo-*. Br. *adna-, dvuch* (occasionally *dvu-, dvoe-/dvaja-*), *troch* (occasionally *troe-*), *čatyroch-, pjaci-, šasci-, dzesjaci-, saraka-, dzevjanosta-, sto-, tysjača-*.

Czech, like Russian, has generalized the genitive to the lower numerals too: *jedno-, dvou-* (also *dvoj-,* though usually in the sense of 'double-'), *tří-, čtyř-, pěti-*, etc., *devíti* (also *děvěti-*), *desíti* (also *deseti-*), *sto-, tisíci-* (e. g. *tisíciletí* 'millenium', with *-i* as in *pěti-*); for 'half-' there are *polo-* and *půl-*. Slovak differs markedly from Czech here: for 'two-' to 'four-' the collectives are used as bare stems, while for the higher numerals the citation forms are used: *jedno-, dvoj-, troj-, štvor-, päť-*, etc., *desäť-, sto-, tisíc-*; for 'half-' there is *polo-*, rarely *pol-*.

Polish uses basically the connecting vowel *-o-*, after the current form of the stem: *jedno-, dwu-* (i. e. genitive; the form *dwóch-* is used in some of the higher ordinals, see section 16.1.14.5.), *trzy-* (citation form; occasionally *trój-* as in *trójkąt* 'triangle', and gen. *trzech-* as in *trzechlecie* 'three-year period'), *cztero-, pięcio-*, etc., *dziesięcio-, stu-* (genitive, unlike all the other Slavonic languages), *tysiąc-*; also *pół-* 'half'.

The Upper Sorbian forms, which are basically the citation forms, are: *jedno-, dwojo-* (the traditional form, based on the collective) and *dwu-* (a neologism based on other Slavonic languages), *trojo-* and *tři-, štyri-, pjeć-*, etc., *dźesać-, sto-, tysac-*; in place of the forms in *-ć-* one also finds forms in *-ći-*, e. g. *pjećiletka* 'five-year plan', but these are artificial neologisms, and only in a few cases have they been accepted into the standard language (*pjećiletka* on the analogy of Ru. *pjatilétka*); for 'half-' the stem *poł-* is used. Lower Sorbian[160] *jadno-, dwa-* or *dwě-* (according to the gender of the noun component) (also *dwu-* in archaic *dwulětny* 'two-year'), *tśi-, styri-* (also *styŕ-, styro-*), *pěś-*. The attested Polabian forms are: *pül-ni* 'midday' (for **polъdьne*), *citěr-nordě* 'square' ('viereckig').

In some of the languages that do not use the citation form as first component with numerals from 'five' upwards, there is a tendency in nonstandard usage to have the citation form here; similarly, in Russian in a neologism like *čètvert'-finál'* 'quarter-final' (there are no traditional formations in 'quarter-') the citation form of the fraction is used.

16.7. Symbols for numerals

The modern Balto-Slavonic numerals, like the other European languages, currently use the Arabic numerals for most purposes, with the usual Continental conventions (e. g. decimal comma rather than decimal point), and Roman numerals for more restricted purposes. However, within Slavonic there was also an older tradition going back to the older Greek system of writing numbers, and found in Slavonic in two differing versions, the Glagolitic and Cyrillic, corresponding at least originally to the difference between the Glagolitic and Cyrillic alphabets (though some later Cyrillic manuscripts use the letters in their Glagolitic numerical values).

The Greek system[161] had separate symbols for each of the numerals 'one' to 'nine', for each of the decads 'ten' to 'ninety', and for each of the hundreds 'one hundred' to 'nine hundred'; the thousands were indicated by a diacritic before the corresponding unit; the order of the letters of the alphabet was used as the order of the numerals, with the addition of the three non-letters *stigma* ('six'), *koppa* ('ninety') and *sampi* ('nine hundred') to bring the total up to twenty-seven. This Greek system is followed most slavishly in the Cyrillic numeral system: the order of the letters follows exactly that of the Greek number system (the letters being pronounced according to their Byzantine sounds, e. g. *víta* for classical *bēta*), including those Greek letters that were not used in native Slavonic words, and excluding Cyrillic letters that did not have direct counterparts in the Greek alphabet (except for 'nine hundred' and, in later manuscripts, 'ninety'; cf. also 'six') (see Table 3).

Table 3. Numerical values of the Glagolitic letters

	Units		Tens		Hundreds		Thousands	
1	Ⰰ	a	Ⰹ, Ⰺ	i_1	Ⱃ	r	Ⱍ	č
2	Ⰱ	b	Ⰻ	i_2	Ⱄ	s	Ⱎ	š
3	Ⰲ	v	Ⰼ	ǵ	Ⱅ	t	Ⱏ	b
4	Ⰳ	g	Ⰽ	k	Ⱆ	ü	Ⱐ	ъ
5	Ⰴ	d	Ⰾ	l	Ⱇ	f	Ⱑ	ě/ja
6	Ⰵ	e	Ⰿ	m	Ⱒ	x_2	Ⱈ	x_1
7	Ⰶ	ž	Ⱀ	n	Ⱉ	o_2	Ⱖ	jo
8	Ⰷ	ʒ	Ⱁ	o_1	Ⱋ	št	Ⱓ	ju
9	Ⰸ	z	Ⱂ	p	Ⱌ	c	Ⱔ	ę

10 Corresponds to Cyrillic dotted *i*.
20 Corresponds to Cyrillic undotted *i*.
30 As a letter used primarily to indicate Greek *gamma* before a front vowel.
400 As a letter ususally primarily in Greek loans, for *ypsilon*; also in native words as second part of the ligature for *u*.
500 As a letter used in Greek loans.
600, 6000 The numerical differentiation of x_1 and x_2 is not absolutely clear; as a letter x_2 is used only in Greek loans, for *chi*.
500 The distinct symbol is due to Greek influence (*omega*), though it is also used as a letter in native words, phonetically indistinct from o_1.
500 The Glagolitic alphabet has one symbol for **ě* and **ja*.
7000 In practice, as a letter occurs only as first part of the ligature for *ję*; pre-CSl. **jo* gives CSl **je*.
7000 Although this is used as a separate letter (*ę*), it usually occurs as second part of the ligature for the nasal vowels.

In the Glagolitic system, the ascending order of numbers seems to have followed the order of the letters in the Glagolitic alphabet, as this is preserved in the surviving abecedaria,[162] including those Glagolitic letters that do not correspond directly to Greek letters, and with only a few specifically Greek letters. Although the thousands are not attested in the canonical Glagolitic manuscripts, later manuscripts suggest that the letters towards the end of the alphabet were used for this purpose, rather than diacritics with the units as in Greek and Cyrillic; only 'one thousand' and 'two thousand' are attested, the other values given in Table 4 are reconstructed from the abecedaria.[163]

Table 4. Numerical values of the Cyrilllic letters

	Units		Tens		Hundreds	
1	а	a	і	i (dotted)	р	r
2	в	v	к	k	с	s
3	г	g	л	l	т	t
4	д	d	м	m	υ	ü
5	е	e	н	n	ф	f
6	ѕ	ʒ	ξ	ks	х	ch
7	з	z	о	o	ψ	ps
8	и	i (undotted)	п	p	ω	o (omega)
9	θ	th	ч	č	Ѧ, ц	ę, c

6 Used as a number symbol even in manuscripts where it is not used as a letter. The Greek number system has the non-letter *stigma* here, also used as an abbreviation for *st*; originally this was the position of *vau* (*digamma*, i.e. *v*, *w*).

8, 10 These two symbols as letters, and the Glagolitic equivalents, are not distinguished phonetically in the manuscripts.

9 As a letter, only in Greek loans.

60 As a letter, only in Greek loans.

90 Originally the Greek (non-letter) numeral symbol *koppa* (*q*, borrowed from Semitic) was used here; later (from the fourteenth century) it was replaced by the graphically similar Cyrillic letter for *č*.

400 As a letter only in Greek loans, though it also forms the second part of the ligature for *u* in native words.

500 As a letter, only in Greek loans.

700 As a letter, only in Greek loans.

800 This letter, phonetically indistinct from *o*, is distinguished graphically from *o* under Greek influence, though also in native words.

900 Greek uses the non-letter *sampi* here; for *c*, cf. Table 3.

In writing coordinate numerals, the usual order in Greek, Cyrillic and Glagolitic is to start with the highest and work down to the units; in Cyrillic and Glagolitic the teens, however, are usually in the order 'unit followed by ten', corresponding to the order in reading the number (*x na desęte*).

In the manuscripts, the numerals are usually distinguished from letters as parts of words by being overlined, or by having a preposed and postposed point enclosing the whole number.

For the older terms for numerals above 'thousand', the symbols used were as in Table 5.[164]

Table 5. Symbols for numerals over 'thousand'

tьma	A
legion	A
legiodr (leodor)	A

Notes

1. For discussion of the syntax, see Basaj (1971), Šerech (1952), references cited there, and grammars of the individual languages.
2. Šerech (1952: 92–97).
3. Ramovš (1952: 112–113), who suggests Venetian commercial influence; variants *-krat, -kat* in original.
4. Machek (1957: 293).
5. For examples of counting above 'thousand' in hundreds elsewhere in Slavonic, see Suprun (1962: 25).
6. Vaillant (1964: 159, 162).
7. Vážný (1964: 152).

7a. Basaj (1974: 172–173).

8. Slovenski pravopis (1950: 422).
9. For differences between the usage of the two forms, see Tarabasova (1955).
10. Endzelin (1944: 107).
11. Under ictus? See Stang (1966: 52–68).
12. Endzelin (1922: 356).
13. Shevelov (1964: 285–288).
14. Kiparsky (1963–1967,1: 89–90).

15. Bulaxovs'kyj (1951: 64).
16. Hinze (1972: 347).
17. The palatalization mark over the *ṛ* is a convenient way of representing the subsequent development to **ir* in Baltic, and also those Slavonic languages that do not retain syllabic *r*; the reasons for the split of **r̥* (and likewise other Indo-European syllabic sonants) into Balto-Slavonic **ir* versus **ur* is not clear; see Shevelov (1964: 86–90).
18. For **ьrъ*, without vocalization of the second jer; see Kiparsky (1963–1967: 86–87).
19. Quoted in Olesch (1967: 45–46).
20. Endzelin (1922: 33–34).
21. Shevelov (1964: 287–288, 544).
22. Nonstandard also masculine-neuter, especially in the western variety of Serbo-Croatian; see Gudkov (1969: 41).
23. Šerech (1952: 99–102) suggests that this development originated in the dative, where the ending *-om* is common for nouns around the fifteenth century; cf. the similar development in Slovak.

23a. Basaj (1974: 60).

24. Shevelov (1964: 90–91).
25. Vasmer (1950–1958: 237).
26. Mladenov (1929: 247).
27. Ernout – Meillet (1959: 27); Vasmer (1950–1958: 236–237).
28. Shevelov (1964: 56).
29. Suprun (1962: 14).
30. Shevelov (1964: 359–360).
31. Hinze (1972: 355).
32. For possible similar developments elsewhere in Slavonic, see Suprun (1962: 11).
33. For discussion, see Szemerényi (1960: 82); Endzelin (1944: 109) suggests a direct parallel between OPr. *tirtis* and Sanskrit *tr̥tī́yaḥ*, but there are other possibilities.
34. Though some dialects have *četíri*; Mladenov (1929: 247).
35. Kiparsky (1962: 781).

35a. Basaj (1974: 90).

36. Ramovš (1952: 114).
37. Meillet (1925).
38. Szemerényi (1960: 85–87).
39. Szemerényi (1960: 68).
40. Meillet (1925: 177).
41. Szemerényi (1960: 108–114).
42. Šerech (1952: 83–91); Basaj (1971: 159–162).
43. Stang (1957: 86–88).
44. Shevelov (1964: 517).
45. Shevelov (1964: 519).

46. Shevelov (1964: 535).
47. Shevelov (1964: 511); for Old Czech examples, see J. Gebauer (1960: 351). Occasionally in Old Czech the long vowel is found, by paradigmatic levelling, in the nominative-accusative too, i.e. *pít*, less commonly *devít*, and by analogy even *šíst*; see Basaj (1974: 101–102).
48. Stang (1957: 183).
49. Stang (1957: 183).
50. Shevelov (1964: 545–550).
51. Jaksche (1965: 94).
52. For the vowel, see Stang (1966: 87).
53. Svane (1958: 68), gives an alternative instr. *petę̇mi*, with a pronominal ending.
54. The actual reflex of **ks* is unclear: perhaps **sk*, see Stang (1966: 95–96).
55. See Meillet (1936: 49–50).
56. The changes *tm* to *km*, and *bm* to *gm*, are attested sporadically in Lithuanian; see Stang (1966: 107).
57. Or perhaps **septm̥os*, by Sievers' Law; see Szemerényi (1960: 6–7).
58. Szemerényi (1960: 8–9).
59. Lorentz (1925: 88).

59a. Comrie (1975).

60. Hennig von Jessen (1959: 315); Hennig also cites 'ordinal' *wissem* 'eighth' (1959: 70).
61. Suprun (1962: 43–44).
62. For other analogical formations in Latvian, see Endzelin (1922: 368–369).
63. Völkel (1970: 776).
64. Šewc (1968: 140).
65. Wowčerk (1951: 64).
66. Suprun (1962: 12).
67. Masculine, according to *Latviešu literārās valodas vārdnīca*, 314; nonstandard also feminine.
68. Kiparsky (1963–1967,2: 78).
69. Reichenkron (1958).
70. Stang (1966: 280–281).
71. Hinze (1972: 348–349).
72. *Russkoe literaturnoe proiznošenie i udarenie* (1959: 694).
73. Polański – Sehnert (1967) (see relevant articles for individual teens).
74. For further details, see Suprun (1962: 15–17).
75. Kiparsky (1962: 280).
76. *Russkoe literaturnoe proiznošenie i udarenie* (1959: 335).
77. *Russkoe literaturnoe proiznošenie i udarenie* (1959: 648).

77a. Basaj (1974: 128); for the ordinal forms, compare the Old Church Slavonic ordinals in section 16.1.11.3.11.

78. The former variants are not given by all sources, but *dvânajsti* and *devêtnajsti* are given in *Slovar slovenskega knjižnega jezika* (1970: 532, 390).
79. Ramovš (1952: 112).

80. Vasmer (1950–1958,2: 698–699).
81. Kiparsky (1963–1967,2: 179–180).
82. *Russkij jaazyk i sovetskoe obščestvo* (1968: 95).
83. *Russkaja razgovornaja reč'* (1973: 117).
84. See Vasmer (1950–1958,1: 334); Šerech (1952: 92–97); Kiparsky (1963–1967,2: 180–181); Szemerényi (1960: 63–65); Stang (1964), for discussion and references.
85. Szemerényi (1960: 64).
86. Šerech (1952: 93–94).
87. Stang (1964: 129).
88. Jaŭnevič – Andrėenka (1971: 126).
89. Stanislav (1958: 362).
90. Though the syntax of Pb. *citěr* is not clear from the available material; possibly both nominative plural and genitive plural were current, see Suprun (1962: 57–59).
91. Quoted in Olesch (1967: 45).
92. Suprun (1962: 45, 55).
93. Hinze (1972: 351).
94. Shevelov (1964: 543–544).
95. Shevelov (1964: 90–91).
96. Shevelov (1964: 91).
97. Szemerényi (1960: 65).
98. *Russkij jazyk i sovetskoe obščestvo* (1968: 93–94).
99. Suprun (1962: 59).
100. Polański – Sehnert (1967: 137).
101. Endzelīns (1971: 185).
102. Jaksche (1965: 94).
103. Svane (1958: 70); I have not found this form listed elsewhere.
104. Pleteršnik (1894–1895,2: 581).
105. Pleteršnik (1894–1895,2: 582). *Slovenski pravopis* (1950: 769) has *stôto*, i. e. in the system used here *stȍto*, without indication of tone.
106. Not given in Schwela (1906: 34).
107. Shevelov (1964: 536).
108. See the relevant articles in *Russkoe literaturnoe proiznošenie i udarenie* (1959).
109. Schwela (1906: 31); Šẃela (1952: 31).
110. Mohelský (1948: 33).
111. Schwela (1906: 34); no additional forms are given in Šẃela (1952: 34).
112. The explanation below follows Endzelin (1922: 365–367).
113. Shevelov (1964: 91).
114. Shevelov (1964: 518).
115. Pleteršnik (1894–1895,2: 670) has only *tisȍč*.
116. Pleteršnik (1894–1895,2: 670).
117. Ramovš (1952: 113).
118. Machek (1957: 528–529).

119. Shevelov (1964: 519); contrast SCr. *tìsuća*, where the *u* is not before a jer; retention of long vowel reflexes in the oblique cases in Czech, Slovak and Polish is analogical.
120. Stone (1971: 89).
121. Schwela (1906: 31).
122. Śẃela (1952: 31). Muka (1926–1928,2: 827) cites it as a loan from Upper Sorbian, whence the *a*, and notes a (nonstandard, but more "etymological") by-form *tysec*.
123. Endzelīns (1971: 185).
124. Pleteršnik (1894–1895,2: 670) gives only *tisǒčni*.
125. Wjela (1949: 108), for instance.
126. Gudkov (1969: 40).
127. *Russkoe literaturnoe proiznošenie i udarenie* (1959: 48, 271).
128. *Slovnyk ukrajins'koji movy* (1970–).
129. *Russkoe literaturnoe proiznošenie i udarenie* (1959: 271).
130. Lunt (1952: 50) gives *milionit*, but this is not listed by *Rečnik na makedonskiot jazik* (1961–1966).
131. Wjela (1949: 108).
132. For references, see Borkovskij – Kuznecov (1965: 254) and Kiparsky (1963–1967,2: 183). For similar forms in Czech, see Basaj (1974: 282–283).
133. Vasmer (1950–1958,3: 162).
134. Borkovskij – Kuznecov (1965: 254).
135. Suprun (1961: 14).
136. Thus Koneski (1966: 207); but Lunt (1952: 49) gives *sto i pedeset í dva* 'one hundred and fifty two'.
137. Lunt (1952: 49).
138. Isačenko (1968: 534–535).
138a. Basaj (1974: 172).
139. Suprun (1961: 17).
140. Koneski (1965: 126).
141. Not given in *Rečnik na sŭvremenija bŭlgarski knižoven ezik* (1955–1959); see Beaulieux – Mladenov (1950: 100–101).
142. Dialectal according to *Rečnik na sŭvremenija bŭlgarski knižoven ezik* (1955–1959).
143. Beaulieux – Mladenov (1950: 101).
144. Omitted, apparently by oversight, from *Rečnik na makedonskiot jazik* (1961–1966).
145. Lunt (1952: 50), but not given by *Rečnik na makedonskiot jazik* (1961–1966); the forms given by Lunt differ occasionally in spelling from those of *Rečnik na makedonskiot jazik* (*šesmina, sedumina, osumina*).
146. For a comprehensive survey of explanations advanced for these numeral forms, see Suprun (1962: 32–39).
147. *Orfografičeskij slovar' russkogo jazyka* (1957: 938) also gives *sam-vósem'*.
148. Endzelīns (1971: 185).

149. Endzelīns (1971: 185).
150. Endzelin (1922: 204, 371).
151. Pfeffinger (quoted in Olesch 1967: 45) has *Tschütwarǜ*, i. e. *čitvărü*, with distinction of **č* from **c*; see also Pb. 'sixty', section 16.1.12.2.
152. For further discussion, see Suprun (1962: 32–39); *düjocě* 'zweierlei' apparently continues **dъvoj-*, contracted to *düj-* for **d(å)vüj-*.
153. Suprun (1962: 30–32).
154. Fraenkel (1962–1965,2: 676).
155. Vasmer (1950–1958,2: 390).
156. Lunt (1952: 50) notes that as a fraction *iljadit* is more usual than *iljaden*, though the former is not cited by *Rečnik na makedonskiot jazik* (1961–1966).
157. Borkovskij – Kuznecov (1965: 256).
158. Śẃela (1952: 37); they are not given in Schwela (1906).
158a. I am grateful to A. S. C. Ross for drawing this Middle Low German form to my attention.
159. Kiparsky (1963–1967,2: 184–185).
160. From items in Muka (1911–1915, 1926–1928).
161. Goodwin (1894: 78–81).
162. For the reconstruction, see Trubetzkoy (1968: 18–23).
163. Trubetzkoy (1968: 22).
164. Kiparsky (1963–1967,2: 183).

Abbreviations

Language and dialect names

Balt. Baltic
Bg. Bulgarian
Br. Belorussian
Čak. Čakavian (dialect area of SCr)
ChSl. Church Slavonic (other than OCS)
CSl. Common Slavonic
Cz. Czech
ESl. East Slavonic
IE Indo-European
Je. Jekavski (dialect area of SCr)
Le. Latvian (Lettish)
Li. Lithuanian
LSo. Lower Sorbian
Ma. Macedonian
O Old (prefixed to one of the other language abbreviations)
OCS Old Church Slavonic
OPr. Old Prussian
Pb. Polabian
Po. Polish
Ru. Russian
Sc. Slovincian (usually considered a dialect of Po.)
SCr. Serbo-Croatian
Sk. Slovak
Sl. Slavonic
Sn. Slovenian
So. Sorbian (Lusatian, Wendish) (i. e. LSo. and USo.)
SSl. South Slavonic
Uk. Ukrainian
USo. Upper Sorbian
WSl. West Slavonic

Grammatical terms

acc.	accusative	instr.	instrumental
colloqu.	colloquial	loc.	locative
dat.	dative	masc.	masculine
dial.	dialectal(ly)	neut.	neuter
du.	dual	nom.	nominative
fem.	feminine	obl.	oblique (i. e. not nom.-acc.)
gen.	genitive	pl.	plural
hum.	human	sg.	singular

References

Basaj, Mieczysław

1971 "Syntactyczne tendencje rozwojowe liczebników słowiańskich", *Studia z filologii polskiej i słowiańskiej* 10 (Warsaw: PWN), 155–162.

1974 *Morfologia i składnia liczebnika w języku czeskim do końca XVI wieku* (Polska Akademia Nauk, Komitet Słowianoznawstwa, Monografie Slawistyczne 26) (Wrocław, Warsaw, Kraków & Gdańsk: Zakład Narodowy imienia Ossolińskich, Wydawnictwo Polskiej Akademii Nauk).

Beaulieux, Léon – Stefan Mladenov

1950 *Grammaire de la langue bulgare* (Collections de grammaires de l'Institut d'Études Slaves 4) (2nd ed.) (Paris: Institut d'Études Slaves).

Belorussko-russkij slovar'

1963 (eds.: Kandrat K. Krapiva et al.) (Moscow: GIINS).

Borkovskij, Viktor I. – Petr S. Kuznecov

1965 *Istoričeskaja grammatika russkogo jazyka* (2nd ed.) (Moscow: Nauka).

Bulaxovs'kyj, Leonid A.

1951 "Z istoryčnyx komentarijiv do ukrajins'koji movy", *Movoznavstvo: Naukovi zapysky* 9 (Kiev: AN USSR), 61–70.

Comrie, Bernard

1975 "Common (?) Slavonic **sedmъ*", *Slavonic and East European Review* 53: 323–329.

Dabartinės lietuvių kalbos žodynas

1972 (eds.: Juozas Balčikonis, J. Kruopas et al.) (2nd ed.) (Vilnius: Mintis).

Endzelin, Jan (= Endzelīns, Jānis)

1922 *Lettische Grammatik* (Indogermanische Bibliothek, I. Reihe) (Heidelberg: Winter).

1944 *Altpreussische Grammatik* (Riga: Latvju Grāmata).

Endzelīns, Jānis
1971 *Comparative phonology and morphology of the Baltic languages* (Slavistic Printings and Reprintings 85) (The Hague & Paris: Mouton).
Ernout, Alfred – Antoine Meillet
1959 *Dictionnaire étymologique de la langue latine* (4th. ed.) (Paris: Klincksieck).
Fraenkel, Ernst
1962–1965 *Litauisches etymologisches Wörterbuch* (*Indogermanische Bibliothek*, II. Reihe) (2 vols.) (Heidelberg: Winter, Göttingen: Vandenhoek & Ruprecht).
Gebauer, Jan
1960 *Historická mluvnice jazyka českého*, díl III: *Tvarosloví*, 1: *Skloňování* (2nd. ed.) (Prague: ČSAV).
Goodwin, William W.
1894 *A Greek grammar* (new ed.) (London: Macmillan).
Grammatika russkogo jazyka
1960 (eds.: Viktor V. Vinogradov et al.) vol. 1 (revised ed.) (Moscow: AN SSSR).
Gudkov, Vladimir P.
1969 *Serboxorvatskij jazyk* (Jazyki mira 7) (Moscow: Moscow University).
Havránek, Bohuslav – Alois Jedlička
1960 *Česká mluvnice* (Prague: SPN).
Hennig von Jessen, Christian
1959 *Vocabularium Venedicum* (reprinted in: Olesch 1967) (Cologne & Graz: Böhlau).
Hinze, Friedhelm
1972 "Die Besonderheiten des pomoranischen Kardinalzahlworts gegenüber dem des Polnischen", *Zeitschrift für Slawistik* 17: 346–359.
Hramatyka belaruskaj movy
1962 (eds.: by Kandrat K. Krapiva – M. H. Bulaxaŭ) vol. 1 (Minsk: AN BSSR).
Isačenko, Alexander V.
1968 *Die russische Sprache der Gegenwart*, 1: *Formenlehre* (2nd. ed.) (Halle/Saale: Niemeyer).
Ivčenko, Makar P.
1962 *Sučasna ukrajins'ka literaturna mova* (Kiev: University Press).
Jaksche, H.
1965 *Slavische Akzentuation* 2: *Slovenisch* (Biblioteca Slavica) (Wiesbaden: Harrassowitz).
Jaŭnevič, M. S. – U. K. Andrėenka
1971 *Belaruskaja mova* (Minsk: Narodnaja Asveta).
Karskij, Evfimij F.
1955–1956 *Belorusy: jazyk belorusskogo naroda* (3 parts reprinted in 2 vols.) (Moscow: AN SSSR).

Kiparsky, Valentin
1962 *Der Wortakzent der russischen Schriftsprache* (Slavica, Sammlung slavischer Lehr- und Handbücher, Neue Folge) (Heidelberg: Winter).
1963–1967 *Russische historische Grammatik* (2 vols.) (Slavica, Sammlung slavischer Lehr- und Handbücher, Neue Folge) (Heidelberg: Winter).
Klemensiewicz, Zenon – Tadeusz Lehr-Spławiński – Stanisław Urbańczyk
1965 *Gramatyka historyczna języka polskiego* (3rd ed.) (Warsaw: PWN).
Koneski, Blaže
1965 *Istorija na makedonskiot jazik* (Skopje: Kočo Racin, Belgrade: Prosveta).
1966 *Grammatika na makedonskiot literaturen jazik* (2nd. ed.) (Skopje: Prosvetno Delo).
Latviešu literārās valodas vārdnīca
1972– (eds.: H. Bendiks, R. Grabis et al.) (Riga: Zinātne).
Leskien, August
1914 *Grammatik der serbokroatischen Sprache* 1 (Sammlung slavischer Lehr- und Handbücher, I. Reihe 4) (Heidelberg: Winter).
Lietuvių kalbos gramatika
1965 (eds.: A. Laigonaitė, K. Ulvydas et al.) vol. 1 (Vilnius: Mintis).
Lietuvių kalbos žodynas
1968– (2nd ed.) (Vilnius: Mintis).
Lorentz, Friedrich
1903 *Slovinzische Grammatik* (St. Petersburg: Vtoroe Otdelenie Imperatorskoj Akademii Nauk).
1925 *Geschichte der pomoranischen (kaschubischen) Sprache* (Grundriß der Slavischen Philologie und Kulturgeschichte) (Berlin & Leipzig: de Gruyter).
Lunt, Horace G.
1952 *Grammar of the Macedonian Literary Language* (Skopje: Državno Knigoizdatelstvo).
Machek, Václav
1957 *Etymologický slovník jazyka českého a slovenského* (Prague: ČSAV).
Meillet, Antoine
1925 "Les origines du vocabulaire slave, II: De quelques noms de nombre", *Revue des Études Slaves* 5: 177–182.
1936 *Esquisse d'une grammaire comparée de l'arménien classique* (2nd. ed.) (Vienna: Imprimerie des PP. Mekhitharistes).
Mirčev, Kiril
1963 *Istoričeska gramatika na bŭlgarskija ezik* (2nd. ed.) (Sofia: Nauka i Izkustvo).
Mladenov, Stefan
1929 *Geschichte der bulgarischen Sprache* (Grundriß der Slavischen Philologie und Kulturgeschichte) (Berlin & Leipzig: de Gruyter).

Mohelský, Vladimír
1948 *Mluvnice hornolužické srbštiny a slovník hornosrbskočeský* (Olomouc: Kroužek Přátel Lužických Srbů).
Mühlenbachs, K.
1923–1932 *Lettisch-deutsches Wörterbuch* (ed.: Jānis Endzelīns) (4 vols.) (Riga: Bildungsministerium, later Kulturfonds).
Muka, Ernst
1911–1915 *Słownik dolnoserbskeje rěcy a jeje narěcow* 1 (St. Petersburg: Russian Academy of Sciences).
1926–1928 *Słownik dolnoserbskeje rěcy a jeje narěcow* 2–3 (Prague: Czech Academy of Sciences).
Olesch, Reinhold
1967 *Fontes linguae Dravaeno-Polabicae minores* (Slavistische Forschungen 7) (Cologne & Graz: Böhlau).
Orfografičeskij slovar' russkogo jazyka
1956 (eds.: Sergej I. Ožegov – Abram B. Šapiro) (Moscow: GIINS).
Pauliny, Eugen – Jozef Ružička – Jozef Štolc
1955 *Slovenská gramatika* (2nd. ed.) (Martin: Osveta).
Pleteršnik, M.
1894–1895 *Slovensko-nemški slovar* (2 vols.) (Ljubljana: Knezoškofijstvo).
Polański, Kazimierz – James A. Sehnert
1967 *Polabian-English Dictionary* (Slavistic Printings and Reprintings 61) (The Hague & Paris: Mouton).
Pravopis hrvatskosrpskoga književnog jezika
1960 (eds.: Mate Hraste et al.) (Zagreb: Matica Hrvatska & Novi Sad: Matica Srpska).
Ramovš, Fran
1952 *Morfologija slovenskega jezika* (Ljubljana: Univerzitetna Studijska Komisija).
Rečnik na makedonskiot jazik
1961–1966 (eds.: Todor Dimitrovski et al.) (3 vols.) (Skopje: Institut za Makedonski Jazik).
Rečnik na sŭvremenija bŭlgarski knižoven ezik
1955–1959 (eds.: Stojan Romanski et al.) (3 vols.) (Sofia: Bŭlgarska Akademija na Naukite).
Rečnik srpskohrvatskoga književnog jezika/Rječnik hrvatskosrpskoga književnog jezika
1967– (eds.: Mihailo Stevanović, Ljudevit Jonke et al.) (Novi Sad: Matica Srpska & Zagreb: Matica Hrvatska).
Reichenkron, Günter
1958 "Der lokativische Zähltypus für die Reihe 11 bis 19: 'eins auf zehn'", *Südostforschungen* 17: 152–174.

Russkaja dialektologija
1965 (eds.: Ruben I. Avanesov – Varvara G. Orlova) (2nd. ed.) (Moscow: Nauka).
Russkaja razgovornaja reč'
1973 (ed.: Elena A. Zemskaja) (Moscow: Nauka).
Russkij jazyk i sovetskoe obščestvo: Morfologija i sintaksis sovremennogo russkogo literaturnogo jazyka
1968 (ed.: Mixail V. Panov) (Moscow: Nauka).
Russkoe literaturnoe proiznošenie i udarenie
1959 (eds.: Ruben I. Avanesov – Sergej I. Ožegov) (Moscow: GIINS).
Schwela, Gotthold (= Šẃela, Bogumił)
1906 *Lehrbuch der niederwendischen Sprache*, 1 (Heidelberg: Ficker).
Šerech, Jurij (= Shevelov, George Y.)
1952 *Probleme der Bildung des Zahlwortes als Redeteil in den slavischen Sprachen* (Lunds Universitets Årsskrift, N. F. Avd. 1, Bd. 48, Nr. 2) (Lund: C. W. Gleerup).
Šewc, Hinc
1968 *Gramatika hornjoserbskeje rěče*, 1 (Budyšin (Bautzen): Domowina).
Shevelov, G. Y.
1964 *A prehistory of Slavic: The historical phonology of Common Slavic* (Heidelberg: Winter).
Skok, Petar
1971–1974 *Etimologijski rječnik hrvatskoga ili srpskoga jezika* (4 vols.) (Zagreb: Jugoslovenska Akademija Znanosti i Umjetnosti).
Slovar slovenskega knjižnega jezika
1970– (Ljubljana: Slovenska Akademija Znanosti in Umetnosti).
Slovar' sovremennogo russkogo literaturnogo jazyka
1950–1965 (eds.: Vasilij I. Černyšev et al.) (17 vols.) (Moscow & Leningrad: AN SSSR, later Nauka).
Slovenski pravopis
1950 (eds.: Anton Bajec et al.) (Ljubljana: Slovenska Akademija Znanosti in Umetnosti).
Slovník slovenského jazyka
1959–1968 (eds.: Stefan Peciar et al.) (6 vols.) (Bratislava: SAV).
Slovnyk ukrajins'koji movy
1970– (eds.: Ivan K. Bilodid et al.) (Kiev: Naukova Dumka).
Slovník spisovného jazyka českého
1960–1971 (eds.: Bohuslav Havránek, Lubomír Doležel et al.) (4 vols.) (Prague: ČSAV).
Słownik języka polskiego
1958–1969 (eds.: Witold Doroszewski et al.) (11 vols.) (Warsaw: Wiedza Powszechna).
Słownik poprawnej polszczyzny PWN
1973 (eds.: Witold Doroszewski et al.) (Warsaw: PWN).

Stang, Christian S.
1957 *Slavonic accentuation* (Norske Videnskaps-Akademi i Oslo, Historisk-Filosofisk Klasse, Skrifter 3).
1964 "Russisch *devjanosto*", *Lingua viget: Commentationes Slavicae in honorem V. Kiparsky* (eds.: Igor Vahros & Martti Kahla) (Helsinki: Suomalaisen Kirjallisuuden Kirjapaino), 124–129.
1966 *Vergleichende Grammatik der baltischen Sprachen* (Oslo, Bergen & Tromsö: Universitetsforlaget).

Stanislav, Ján
1958 *Dejiny slovenského jazyka* 2: *Tvaroslovie* (Bratislava: SAV).

Stevanović, Mihailo
1954 *Gramatika srpskohrvatskog jezika za više razrede gimnazije* (2nd. ed.) (Novi Sad: Bratstvo – Jedinstvo).

Stone, Gerald
1971 "Lexical changes in the Upper Sorbian literary language during and following the national awakening", *Lětopis Instituta za Serbski Ludospyt w Budyšinje Němskeje Akademie Wědomosćow w Berlinje*, rjad A: *Rěč a Literatura*, c. 18/1: 1–127.

Suprun, Adam E.
1961 *Staroslavjanskie čislitel'nye* (Frunze: University Press).
1962 *Polabskie čislitel'nye* (Frunze).
1969 *Slavjanskie čislitel'nye* (Minsk).

Svane, Gunnar O.
1958 *Grammatik der slowenischen Schriftsprache* (Copenhagen: Rosenkilde & Bagger).

Šẃela, Bohumił
1952 *Grammatik der niedersorbischen Sprache* (2nd. ed.) (= revision of Schwela 1906) (Bautzen: Domowina).

Szemerényi, Oswald
1960 *Studies in the Indo-European system of numerals* (Indogermanische Bibliothek, 3. Reihe) (Heidelberg: Winter).

Tarabasova, N. I.
1955 "Nol' i nul'", *Voprosy kul'tury reči* 1 (Moscow: AN SSSR), 227–234.

Trubetzkoy, Nikolaus S.
1968 *Altkirchenslavische Grammatik* (2nd. ed.) (Cologne, Graz & Vienna: Böhlaus Nachf.).

Ukrajins'ko-rosijs'kyj slovnyk
1953–1963 6 vols. (Kiev: AN USSR).

Vaillant, André
1964 *Manuel du vieux-slave* 1 (Collection de manuels publiée par l'Institut d'Études Slaves 6), (2nd. ed.) (Paris: Institut d'Études Slaves).

Vasmer, Max
1950–1958 *Russisches etymologisches Wörterbuch* (Indogermanische Bibliothek, II. Reihe) (3 vols.) (Heidelberg: Winter).

Vážný, Václav
1964 *Historická mluvnice česká* 2: *Tvarosloví*, part 1: *Skloňování* (Prague: SPN).
Völkel, P.
1970 *Prawopisny słownik: Hornjoserbsko-němski słownik* (Budyšin [Bautzen]: Domowina).
Wjela, Jurij
1949 *Lehrgang der sorbischen Sprache* (Bautzen: Domowina).
Wowčerk, Pawoł
1951 *Kurzgefaßte obersorbische Grammatik* (Bautzen).
Zinkevičius, Zigmas
1966 *Lietuvių dialektologia* (Vilnius: Mintis).

Chapter 17
Albanian*

Eric P. Hamp

Dhet muej lopa viqin,	10 months the cow (bears) the calf,
Nand muej vasha djalin,	9 months the girl the son,
Tet cica na i ka dosa,	8 teats has the sow,
Shtat sy na i ka naleti,	7 eyes has the devil,
Gjasht muej bajn gjys vjeti,	6 months make half a year,
Pes gishta na i ka dora,	5 fingers has the hand,
Kater kamb' na i ka dhija,	4 legs has the goat,
Tri kamb' terezija,	3 legs the scales,
Dy lula na i ka vasha ...[1]	2 flowers has the girl ...
Dymbdhet muj na i ka motmoti,[2]	12 months has the year,
Njimbdhet muj pela mazin,[2]	11 months the mare (bears) the foal,
Te dheten e merr spahija,[2]	The 10th the army takes,
Non muej gruej djalin,[2]	9 months a woman (bears) the son,
Tet cica na i ka dosa,[2]	8 teats has the sow,
Shtat syna i ka 'shejtani,	7 eyes has Satan,
Gjasht muej na i ka gjys vjeti,	6 months has a half-year,
Pes gishta na i ka dora,	5 fingers has the hand,
Kater kom na i ka dhija,	4 legs has the goat,
Tri kam terezija,	3 legs the scales,
E dy molla na i ka vajza[2] *...*[3]	And 2 apples has the girl[4] ...

1. From Rogovë, sung in Prizren. This and the following are printed in full in Max Lambertz, *Lehrgang des Albanischen*, Teil III, Halle (Saale): Niemeyer 1959, 219–225.
2. Variants from Kamenicë:

Dymbdhet muj na i ka vjeti,	12 months has the year,
Njimbdhet vet na i ka shpija,	11 people the house has,
Dhet muj lopa viqin,	10 months the cow (bears) the calt,
Non muej grueja djalin,	9 months the woman the lad,
Tet muj pela mazin,	8 months the mare the foal,
...	...
Dy lule na i ka vasha ...	2 flowers has the girl ...

* In this chapter the notes follow the section to which they refer; references for the literature cited are included within the text.

3. From Deçan.
4. In the first song the two flowers could refer ambiguously to the girl's breasts, but here the apples are artfully ambiguous; for 'apple' is regularly a kenning for a rosy cheek. This must be an ancient Balkan metaphor; cf. Classical Greek μῆλον.

17.1. Numeral categories

The numerals of Albanian form a class apart. They are more like nouns, certainly, than verbs, or even than adjectives. They can be readily derived to form nouns. Yet morphologically they can be made to vary in a limited way to show gender. This might suggest that they are really a deviant class of adjective. However, such would be the case only in a rather perverse view: As a class they do not carry typical adjective morphology. They are not subject to comparison. They do not occupy the postposed adjunct position in the noun phrase, as all adjectives do. The principles for the use of the proclitic particle of concord with the numeral do not match those which apply with the adjective. When a noun phrase containing a numeral is definite the definite marking does not follow Wackernagel's Law, which governs both adjectives and nouns in that situation. In short, the numeral occupies a special place and syntax in an Albanian noun phrase.

Such syntaxes include interrogatives, indefinites, deictics, and pronominals such as *sā* 'how much/many', *disa* ~ *ca* 'some', *aq* ~ *kaq* 'so much/many, that much/many'; *shumë* 'much, many', *pak* 'little, few'. The last two behave also as adjectives, and are ancient borrowings from Latin *summum* or *summē* (or some such form, even *summā*, in a bleached sense common in colloquial exaggeration) and *paucus*. All the former forms are descended from the Indo-European interrogative-indefinite *$k^{w}ei/k^{w}e$-/$k^{w}o$-, *sā* < *k^{w}i̯a < *k^{w}iə = *$k^{w}i$-H_{a} (*Studia Celtica* 10–11, 1975–1976; 60), the old neuter plural, and *aqë* Blanchus *achie* 'tot' (from which *kaqë* Blanchus *ka(a)chie* 'tanti') < deictic *a-* + *ḱë* < *ke < *k^{w}ō or better *k^{w}ă̄-ai; cf. Old Prussian *qu-ai* (Chr. S. Stang, *Vergleichende Grammatik der baltischen Sprachen*, Oslo 1966, 240, 242, 286).

Albanian forms numerals of the following semantic classes:

CARDINAL: a lexeme specifying an amount expressed as an integer; a symbol corresponding to an aggregate of elements in a set; or to one of an ordered series of integers.

The cardinals form the basis on which the Albanian numerals are semantically and morphologically founded.

A cardinal may be accompanied by an adverb, e. g. 'exactly', *plot* 'fully' (: *i plotë* 'full'). An APPROXIMATIVE can be formed by joining two adjacent cardinals with *a* 'or', i. e. '2 or 3'; unlike English, Albanian may delete this *a*. Another approximative pre-poses *nja* 'circa', i. e. *nja* x 'about, ca. x', as an adverb. This expression presumably arose as an extension of the allegro contracted form of *një a dy* '1 or 2'.

A NOMINALIZED CARDINAL denotes a set comprising a cardinal number of members. Such a form may be pluralized to form a COLLECTIVE, e. g. *qinda, qindra* 'hundreds'. The category of definite applies to these formations through the medium of inflexion: *njër-i* 'the one', *të tre* (masc.) *të tria* (fem.) 'the 3'.

ORDINAL: denotes an element closing an ordered series which is indexed with cardinals. Except for 'first', which is suppletive, the ordinals are formed from the cardinals by addition of the suffix *-të*; however, if the cardinal ends in *-të* it is said that the suffix *-të* is suppressed (but there are dialects for which this contextual exception does not hold). The latter rule has the appearance of a euphonic haplology, but it seems probable that it is grounded in a fact of original Proto-Indo-European word formation: Since, as I claim, '6' to '8' (at least), have *-të* traceable to an original feminine **-ti-* suffix, we would not expect a source formation in †*-ti-to-*, with ordinal **-to-* suffix. Therefore, in these ordinals the *-të* must be, strictly, **-to-*. In the case of '10th', the observed *-të* would be **-to-* < **-t-o-* (see later discussion) with ordinal thema, while the cardinal *-të* of '10' reflects a resolution of the Proto-Indo-European final **-t* here.

Ordinals (*numërorët rrjeshtorë*) are adjectives, and can be nominalized or derived to yield adverbs in the elative by normal rules that apply to adjectives.

FRACTIONAL: An expression of the form 'one xth' denotes one out of a number x of equal parts which constitute the whole. Formally a fractional xth is a nominal in the feminine definite taken directly, from the ordinal.

It should be noted that 'half' is a feminine noun and is a prime in the numeral system.

MULTIPLICATIVE: a construction specifying a cardinal multiplier of a quantity. To express this Albanian adds the element *-fish*, which descends from *-fij-sh* (in the dialects where *ʎ has become *j*), the old ablative plural of *fill* (masc.) 'thread'.

From such a complex an adjective may be formed with *-të*, e. g. *e trefishtë* 'threefold (fem.)'.

ABSTRACTION of the cardinal: The quality or property of x; a unit x. This forms a noun with the suffix *-sh* (masc.), e. g. *tre-sh* 'a 3', def. *tresh-i*; or with the suffix *-(j)a* (fem.), *tri-a* 'a 3'. The formation with *-sh* makes plurals both with *-a* and with *-e*.

Because the *-sh* suffixation applies only through '3', i. e., through the gendered and productively declined cardinals, this ending must be traced to an origin in declension. We therefore assume that it originates in, or reflects conflation with, the ablative plural, i. e., the Proto-Indo-European locative plural * + *su*.

The cardinal elements (*numërorët themelorë* 'the basic numerals') are: the integers '1' to '10', *-zet* '20', (-)*qind* '100', *mijë* (dialectally *miʎë*) '1000', plus the modern neologisms for '$10^{3 \cdot 2 \ldots}$'.

Fine semantic and syntactic observations, mostly for the literary language, are to be found in Oda Buchholz and Wilfried Fiedler, *Albanische Grammatik*, Leipzig 1987, 349–360. Martin Camaj, *Albanian Grammar*, Wiesbaden 1984, 82–90, is more compact and less detailed, but highlights well the main features, giving fuller coverage of the total modern language, including Geg (important for earlier literature) and Arbëresh (strongly divergent, linguistically and culturally important).

Camaj's earlier, briefer *Lehrbuch der albanischen Sprache*, Wiesbaden 1969, 36–39, includes some variants which may here be noted: Camaj makes the clear statement that, except for the 'teens, *e* serves as link for the numerals. He includes also the formations *të dyja, të katra*, and *-qindë*, and gives the alternate *i mijtë*. His form *katërtë* conflicts only with the spelling rule of the current orthography. He includes *nji herë* and *dy herë* in the vocabulary list.

The category of NUMERAL is defined lexically within Albanian by the lexeme (verb) *njeh* 'count'.

17.2. The data

I present now the full inventory, abbreviated at times with the conventional "etc." where repetitious or easily generated mention would not add to our grasp of the material, an inventory of the observed forms of the language on which this study is based. The above-mentioned grammatical works list and cite forms of the numerals in ample number. However, these forms are given in the standard orthography of the literary language or in analogous normalizations. Such representations not only mask interesting phonetics and dialect diversity; they also deprive us *ab initio* of the features of vowel length and nasality.

I therefore draw my material from older texts, which of course require philological control, and from dialect sources which so far as possible have been observed at first hand. In all cases where the published source or collector is not acknowledged dialect material has been collected by me, normally *in situ*. I have tried to indicate the circumstances and date of my own collecting.

For a compact inventory of the dialect varieties and enclaves of Albanian see my survey of dialect studies in Thomas Sebeok, *Current Trends in Linguistics* 9 (2nd part) 1972, pp. 1640–1650. The following pages do not exhaust all the dialects for which I have collected material; there are some varieties for which I have extensive material but happen not to have a full set of numerals. I believe, however, that the following samples exemplify nearly all features of surviving Albanian numeral sequences. I feel confident that no distinctive phonological feature remains undocumented for extant Albanian in the numeral system.

It is to be hoped that scholars will fill in any gaps in documentation that they may notice.

Material is presented for the following varieties:

Geg:
Blanchus (1635)
Buzuku (1555)
Da Lecce (1716)
Bogdan (1685)[1]
Shala (Dukagjin)
Gusî/Gusinje (Crna Gora)
Tuzi (Crna Gora)
Bajgorska Šalja (Kosovë), from Mulaku
Drenica (Kosovë), from Kelmendi and Çetta
Upper Morava (Kosovë), from Halimi
Dushmani (Dukagjin), from Cimochowski
Arbanasi (Zadar, Croatia)
von Harff (1496–1499)
South Geg (1900), from Weigand
Tetovo/Tetovë (Makedonija).

Tosk:
Ohrid (Makedonija)
Elbasan (1882), from Kristoforidhi (Χριστοφορίδης)
Villa Badessa (Pescara, Italy)
Mandrìtsa (Ivajlovgrad, Bulgaria) and Mándres (Kilkís, Greece)
3 villages near Melitópol, Ukraine; from Kotova
Salamís (Arvanítika, Greece), from Haebler
Argolid (Arvanítika), from Reinhold (1855)
Sophikò (Arvanítika, Korinthía)
Kaskavélji/Λεοντάρι (Arvanítika, Boeotia)
Greci (Arbëresh, Avellino), from Camaj
Portocannone (Arbëresh, Campobasso)
Barile (Arbëresh, Potenza)
San Costantino Albanese (Arbëresh, Potenza), from Camaj and EPH
Plàtaci (Arbëresh, Cosenza)
Vaccarizzo Albanese (Arbëresh, Cosenza)
San Giorgio Albanese/Mbuzàt (Arbëresh, Cosenza)
Macchia (Arbëresh, Cosenza), from Giuseppe de Rada (1871) and Girolamo de Rada (1894)
Falconara Albanese (Arbëresh, Cosenza), EPH and Camaj
San Nicola dell'Alto (Arbëresh, Catanzaro)
Àndali (Arbëresh, Catanzaro), EPH and Gangale
Marcedusa (Arbëresh, Catanzaro), from Gangale
Vena di Màida (Arbëresh, Catanzaro)
San Marzano di San Giuseppe (Arbëresh, Tàranto)
Piana degli Albanesi (Arbëresh, Palermo), from Guzzetta and Luca Matrënga (ca. 1600)
Contessa Entellina (Arbëresh, Palermo)

The tabulations which follow are presented in the above order.

For remarks on the value of dialectology for history see in connexion with our subject A. V. Desnickaja, "Dialektologija – osnova istoričeskogo izučenija albanskogo jazyka", in *Sravitel'noe jazykoznanie i istorija jazykov*, Leningrad: Nauka 1984, 260–276.

1. My collections for the older Geg authors come from my own reading and are surely not exhaustive.

	Blanchus[1] Cardinals	Ordinals
1	*gna* (& 69, 186) *asgna* 'nullus' (68, 69) *gne-*[2] *gnæ mije* (69) '1000'[2]	*i pari*
2m.	*dȣ*	*i dȣȣti* (& 146) *i dȣte* indef. (75)
2f.	*dȣȣ* (21)	
3m.	*tre* (& 176), 'trinus' (176) *tre ȥambes* 'tridens' (176) *ntremueis* 'trimestris' (176) *terfoiene* 'trifolium' (176)[3]	*i treti* (& 173)
3f.	*per trij dit* 'triduum' (176) *trij viet* 'triennis, trieteris' (176) *Ntrij vietſ* 'trietericus' (176) *Ntrij giuhes* 'trilinguis' (176) *Ntrij cambes* 'tripes' (176)	
4	*cattere* *catere* (119) (*n*)*cater* (118)[4]	*i caterti*
5	*pesse* (& 69, 120) *mpesse mueiss* (120)	*i pesti* (& 120)
6	*giascte* *giaste* (151; 190 for '16' and '26') *giaste ghind* '600' (151) *ngiaste mueiss* 'semestris' (147)	*i giasti* (& 151)
7	*state* (& 149)	*i stati* (& 149)
8	*tete* (& 75)	*i teti, e teta* f. (75)
9	*nande* (& 68) *nandeghind* '900) (67)	*i nandi, enanda* f. (67)

(Table continued)

	Blanchus[1] Cardinals	Ordinals
10	*ȥiete* (& 17, 69)	*i ȥieti*
	ȥiete mije '10 000' (69)	*teȥietate* 'decimæ' (17)
11	*gnambeȥiete*	*igna mbeȥieti* (& 186)
12	*dȣmbeȥiete*	
	dȣȣmbeȥiete (21)	
13	*trembeȥiete*	
14	*catere mbeȥiete* (& 119)	unit ordinal -DEF + *mbe-* 10
15	*pessembeȥiete*	
	pesse mbeȥiete (120)	
16	*giaste embeȥiete*	*ipaʃti mbe* ... [sic]
17	*state mbeȥiete*	
18	*tete mbeȥiete*	unit ordinal -DEF + *mbe-* 10
19	*nande mbeȥiete*	
20	*gnaεet*	
	gna εet (183)	*igne*[2] *εeti*
21	*gnaεet egna*	
22	*gnaεet edȣȣ*[5]	
23	*gnaεet etrij*[5]	
30	*trijȥiete*	For the ordinal decades, the formation = '10th'
	trij ȥiete (176)	
40	*caterȥiete* (& 117)	
50	*pesseȥiete* (§ 120)	
	pesseȥȥiete (69)	
60	*giaʃte ȥiete*	
70	*state ȥiete*	
	stateȥiete (149)	
80	*tete ȥiete* (& 75)[7]	
90	*nande ȥiete* (& 67)[7]	

(Table continued)

	Blanchus[1] Cardinals	Ordinals
100[6]	*gneghind*[2] *gne*[2] *ghind* (69)	1 000 *gne*[2] *mije*
200	*dǒghind* *dǒgind* (& 21)	2 000 *dǒǒ mije*
300	*treghind*	
400	*catterghind*	4 000 *cater mije*
500	*pesseghind* *pesse ghind* (69) *pesse chind* (120)	
600	*giaſte ghind*	
700	*state ghind*	
800	*tette ghind*	
		10 000 *ʑiete mije* 400 000 *cater ghind mije* 2 000 000 *gne*[2] *εet ghind mije*
½	*g(i)ǒms(s)e* *g(i)ǒms(s)a* def. (148, 151)	

Multiples

pesse here 'quinquies' (120)
pesse ʑiete here 'quindecies' (120)
state here 'septies' (149)
nga εet here 'vicies' (183)

E cheſtu paa teſoſſune 'Et sic Ininfinitum' (193)

1. Mario Roques (ed.), *Le dictionnaire albanais de 1635*, Paris 1932. The numerals are to be found expecially on pp. 189–193; other paginations are indicated in parentheses.

2. This may be taken as vowel raising under secondary (combining) stress next to [ɲ]; it could be fronted [e] in some variety, or centralized *ë*.
3. I take the form with *ter-*/tër-/ as continuing the older state of affairs, with reduced unstressed vocalism; and forms with *tre-* as being rebuilt with the underlying full vocalism.
4. I take this as dropping the final *-ë* in combination. It could have even then been hard to hear *ë* next to a syllabified *r*.
5. These appear to be feminine.
6. The ordinal hundreds are formed with the concord particle (*i* + etc.) and the inflexional -DEF suffix (*-i* etc.).
7. Blanchus treats these as if '18th' and '19th'; cf. *vndeceni Nandeʒiete enande* (186), and '60' for '16' (151), and 50 · 10 · 100 *mije* for 50 000 (69). Perhaps his spoken forms syllabified like those of Shala.

   Blanchus gets muddled on high numbers: 500 000 'quinquies centena millia' becomes *Peſſe ʒiete here peſſegine mye* (69) '50 times 500 thousand'; and 1 000 000 '10 · 100 – 1000' becomes 10 *here* 10 · 100 *mije* (69).

These may be phonologized as follows; the same order is observed.

1	*ɲâ*	*i pari*
2m.	*dy*	*i dȳti, i dytë* (indef.)
2f.	*dȳ*	
3m.	*tre*	
	tër-	*i treti*
3f.	*trī*	
4	*katërë*	
	katër-	
5	*pesë*	*i pest-i*
6	*ǵaštë*	*i ǵašt-i*
7	*štatë*	*i štat-i*
8	*tetë*	*i tet-i*
9	*nândë*	*i nând-i*
10	*ðietë*	*i ðiet-i*
11	*ɲâ-mbë-ðietë*	*i ɲâ-mbë-ðiet-i*
12	*dy-, dȳ-* (is this fem.?)	
13	*tre-*	
14	*katërë* + 8	
15	*pesë* +	
16	*ǵaštë* +	
17	*štatë* +	
18	*tetë* +	

(Table continued)

19	*nândë* $^{+}$	
20	*ɲâ zet*	
30	*trī ðietë*	
40	*katër-ðietë*	
50	*pesë-ðietë*	
60	*ǵaštë* $^{+}$[9]	
70	*štatë* $^{+}$	
80	*tetë* $^{+}$	
90	*nândë* †	
100	*ɲë-ḱind*	1 000 *ɲë mijë*
200	*dy-ḱind*	2 000 *dȳ mijë*
300	*tre-ḱind*	
400	*katër-ḱind*	4 000 *katër mijë*
500	*pesë-ḱind*	
600	*ǵaštë* $^{+}$[9]	
700	*štatë* $^{+}$	
800	*tetë* $^{+}$	
		10 000 *ðietë mijë*
½	*ǵymsë* f.	

pesë herë '5 times'
štatë herë '7 times'
ɲâ zet herë '20 times'

e kështù pā të-sòsunë 'and thus without stopping; infinity'

8. It appears that the open juncture in '14–19' reflects the assignment of *-ë* in position before **(ë)mbë*.
9. The open juncture in '60–90' appears to reflect the fact that the old forms in suffixal *-të* < **-tā* ← **-ti-* (f.) formed phrasal structures. Apparently the same applies to '600' and up.

	Buzuku[1] Cardinals	Ordinals
1	*gneh* 'one single (God)' (XXI$_1$) *gneh* (XXI$_1$) *gne* (XXI$_2$, XXII$_1$) *gnani* def. (XX$_2$), *gnanah* f. (LV$_1$)[2] *e gnaih* gen. (XXII$_1$)	*hi pari* (XXII$_1$) *e para* (XXIII$_1$) *te paret* (XXI$_3$) *ende te paret* m. [3]abl. sg. (XXII$_1$)
2m.	*du* (LII$_1$)	*hi duti* (XXII$_2$), *dutet* *teh dutene* f. acc. sg. (LIV)[3] *ende te dutet* m. abl. sg. (XXII$_1$)
2f.	*duu* (XXI$_1$), *duu graa* '2 women' (LV$_1$) *nah teh duu* 'we 2', *teh dua* 'the two' (LV$_1$)	
3m.	*tre* (LII$_1$)	*hi treti* (XXII$_1$) *teh tretene* f. acc. sg. (LV$_1$) *ende teh tretet* m. abl. sg. (XXII$_2$)
3f.	*trij dit* 'triduum' (XLIV$_1$) *trii vieteh*[4] '3 years' (LI$_1$)	
4	*catere* (LIII$_3$)	*hi caterti* (XXI$_3$), *e c(h)aterta* f. (LXIX$_1$) *ende teh catert* m. abl. sg. (XXII$_2$)
5	*pesse* (B LV$_3$ Ç 171 R 55 V)	*hi pesti* (XXII$_2$) *ende e pesët* (XXII$_2$)
6	*ʎaste* (LIII$_2$) *gaste* (LVI$_1$) *ʎasteh muoih* (LI$_1$)	 *hi ʎasti* (XXI$_1$, XXII$_2$)
7	*state* (XXII$_1$)	*hi stati* (XXII$_1$) *e statet* (XXII$_1$) *endeh teh state* f. abl. sg. (B LXXI$_3$ Ç 303 R 89v)

(Table continued)

	Buzuku[1] Cardinals	Ordinals
8	*teteh* (XLV$_1$)	*i tehte* *teh tehtene* f. acc. sg.
9	*nande* (XXXII$_3$)	*hi nandi* (XXI$_4$)
10	*ʒiete* (XX$_1$) *ʒiete miieh* '10 000' (LXXII$_1$)	*ʒieti* (XXII$_1$); *teh ʒiete* pl. (XXII$_3$) *teh ʒieteteh* gen. (LX$_1$)
11	*gneh enbeh*[5] *ʒiete* (B LXIX$_1$ Ç 261 R 79)	*egneh enbeh ʒietah* f. (LXIX$_1$) *teh gnenbeʒietete* 'the 13th (pl.)' (B LXIV$_3$ Ç 243 R 74v)
12	*duu enbeh ʒiete(h)* (XXIII$_1$) *duu enbeʒiete* (XXIII$_1$) *meh teh duu enbeh ʒietet* (LXIV$_1$) 'with the 12'	17 *teh statene enbeh ʒiete* acc. (LX$_1$)
14	*catere enbeh ʒiete* (XL$_2$) *gneh en*[5] *seh duu enbeh*[5] *ʒietes* 'one of 12' (LXIV$_1$)	
15	*pese enbeh ʒiete* (LX$_1$)	
		15 *teh pestene enbeh ʒieteh* f. acc. sg. (B LXXIX$_1$ Ç 301 R 89)
20	*gneɛett* (LX$_1$) *gne ɛett* (LXI$_1$)	
30	*triʒiete* (XL$_1$)	70 *stateh ʒieteh* (LXII$_2$, B LX$_3$ Ç 231 R 70v)
40	*caterʒiete* (XLII$_1$, B LX$_3$ Ç 231 R 70v)	
46	*caterʒieteh eƙasteh* (LVI$_1$)	
49	*caterʒiete e nande* (XXXII$_3$)	
50	*pesse ʒiete* (LX$_1$, LXXII$_1$)	
100	*gne(h) ƙind* (XXII$_1$, LX, LXXII) *gneh ƙind* (B LX$_1$ Ç 229 R 70)	

(Table continued)

	Buzuku[1] Cardinals	Ordinals
120	*gneh ƛind e gneh εet* (LXX_1)	
200	*dȣ ƛind* (LV_2)	
300	*treƛind* (B LX_2 Ç 229 R 70)	
500	*en pese ƛintss vieteh* (B LX_1 Ç 229 R 70)	
600	*gaste ƛind* (B LX_3 Ç 231 R 70v)	*teh ƛasteneh ƛind* (B LX_3 Ç 231 R 70v)
5 000	*pesseh miieh* (LV_2)	
6 000	*ƛaste miieh* (LI_1)	
7 000	*stateh miieh* (B LXIV_2 Ç 241 R 74)	
10 000	*ʒiete miieh* (LXXII)	
½	*ƛimseh* (XVII_1)	
Multiples		
dupio 'doppio' (XXI_3)		*teh duteneh herre* acc. sg. 'per la seconda volta' (LX_1)
trii herre 'three times' (LXIV_2)		
stateh herreh '7 times' (LII_1)		
stateh herreh stateh ʒiete '7 × 70' (LII_1)		
Distributives		
chaa duu e chaa duu '2 by 2' (LX_2)		

1. Eqrem Çabej (ed.), *"Meshari" i Gjon Buzukut (1555)*, Tiranë 1968 (2 vols.); and N. Ressuli, *Il "Messale" di Giovanni Buzuku,* Studi e Testi 99, Città del Vaticano: Biblioteca Apostolica Vaticanos 1958. Numbers in parentheses refer to folios, but for Ç(abej) Arabic numbers are pages; subscripts are columns of B(uzuku). I am grateful to my dear friend Martin Camaj for help with the troublesome pagination and for spotting some valuable additional examples. So far as practicable I follow the ordering of the Blanchus citations.
2. Regardless of how the *e(h)* vocalism of '1' is to be interpreted, this *â* vocalism gives us the full underlying and original value.
3. The length of [y] here is subject to the allophonics of open syllables.
4. This old neuter is important in illustrating the feminine outcome in the ambigènes.
5. The exact status of the syllabic nasal is uncertain.

We may phonologize these forms as:

1	*ɲë*, gen.*ɲâi*	i pari, e para, të parët
	*ɲ*âni, *ɲ*âna	
2m.	*dy*	*i dyti, dytët, të dytënë*
2f.	*dȳ, të dya*	
3m.	*tre*	*i treti, të tretënë, të tretët*
3f.	*trī*	
4	*katërë*	*i katërti, e katërta. të ka-tërt*
5	*pesë*	*i pesti, e pesët*
6	*ǵaštë*	*i ǵašti*
7	*štatë*	*i štati, e štatët, të štate*
8	*tetë*	*i tetë, të tetënë*
9	*nândë*	*i nândi*
10	*ðietë*	*ðieti, të ðietëtë*, pl. *të ðietë*
11	*ɲë ëmbë ðietë*	*e ɲë ëmbë ðieta, të ɲëmbëðietëtë*
12	*dȳ ëmbë(-)ðietë*	17 *të štatënë ëmbë ðietë*
	me të dȳ ëmbë ðietët	15 *pestënë*
	ɲë ën së dȳ ëmbë ðietëš	
14	*katërë ëmbë ðietë*	
15	*pesë ëmbë ðietë*	
20	*ɲë(-)zet*	
30	*triðietë*	
40	*katërðietë*	70 *štatë ðietë*
50	*pesë ðietë*	
100	*ɲë ḱind*	
200	*dy ḱind*	
300	*treḱind*	
500	*ën pesë ḱindš*	
600	*ǵaštë ḱind*	*të ǵaštënë ḱind*
5 000	*pesë mijë*	
6 000	*ǵaštë mijë*	
7 000	*štatë míjë*	
10 000	*ðietë mijë*	
½	*ǵimsë*	

trī herë '3 times'
štatë-herë '7 times'

kā dȳ e kā dȳ '2 by 2'

Da Lecce (1716)			
1	*gnì* ~ *gnia*[1]	*i pari*	
	gnani def. m., gn(i)ana f.		
2	*dȣ* m. f.[2]	*i ddȣti* m., *e ddȣte* f., *e dȣta*	
	dȣue, dȣȣsc[3]		
3m.	*trè*	*i treti*	*e treta*
3f.	*trì*		
4	*kattre*	*i kattriti*[4]	*e katreta*
5	*pèss*	*i pesti*	*e pesta*
6	*giasct*	*i giàsti*	*e giàseta*[5]
7	*scttatt*	*i sctatti*	*e sctatta*
8	*tette*[6]	*i tetti*	*e tetta*
9	*nand*	*i nandi*	*e nanda*
10	*ʓiett*		
11	*gni mbeʓiet*		
12	*dȣ mbeʓiet*		
13m.	*tre mbeʓiet*		
f.	*tri mbeʓiet*		
15	*pes mbeʓiet*		
17	*sctat mbeʓiet*		
20	*gni εett*		
30	*tri ʓiett*		
40	*kattre ʓiett*		
50	*pes ʓiett*		
60	*giasct ʓiett*		
70	*sctatt ʓiett*		
80	*tett ʓiett*		
90	*nand ʓiett*		
100	*gni cint*[7]		
1 000	*gni mije* ~ *mii; gni mij viet* 'mille anni'		
2 000	*dȣ mije*		

Distributives

kaa gni kaa gni	'uno à uno'
kaa gni cint	'cento à cento'
kaa gni mije	'by the thousand'
kaʓiet ~ *kaa ʓiett*	'dieci a dieci'

(Table continued)

Da Lecce (1716)

Partials

'in due'	*Ndȣȣsc*
'in 3'	*Ntriisc* [8]
'in 4'	*Nkattresc*
'in 5'	*Npesctesc* [9]
'in 6'	*Ngiasctesc*
'in 7'	*Nsctattesc*
'in 8'	*Ntettesc*
'in 9'	*Nnandesc*

Except for loss of final *-ë*, these forms of Da Lecce[10] agree well with those of Blanchus and Buzuku.

1. It seems probable that this was a nasal *â*. The vowel *i* of *gnì* results from raising and fronting when unstressed next to [*ɲ*]; this result is widespread and probably independent also in Tosk.
2. This appears to be morphological levelling and not phonological merger.
3. Perhaps preserved length in a closed syllable.
4. Raising and fronting of *ë* before *i*.
5. Apparently *e* misprinted for *c*. Perhaps the masculine was meant to have *sc*.
6. Final *-e* is unexpected; cf. '80'.
7. Note the spelling *c*, presumably for an affricate.
8. Note the long vowel by comparison with *trì* above.
9. The first *sc* seems to be an error for *s*; cf. *i pesti* above.
10. P. Francesco M. Da Lecce, *Osservazioni grammaticali nella lingua albanese*, Roma 1716.

Bogdan (1685)[1]

1	*gni*	*i pari*	
	gniani def. m., *gn(i)ana* f.		
2m.	*dȣ*	*i dȣjti* [2] m., *e dȣita* [2] f.	
2f.	*dȣȣ* [3]		
	(*gniεet e dȣ vjetsc* 'from 22 years')[3]		
3m.	*tre*	*i tretti*	*e treta*
3f.	*trij* [3]	*i catèrti*	
4	*catter vjet, catter vjetsc* '4 years'	*catèrtit* (locative)	
			e caterta
	Eeretè janè cattèra 'Li Venti sono quattro'		

(Table continued)

Bogdan (1685)[1]			
5	*pens(s)e* [4]	*i pensti*	*e pensta*
6	*giascte*	*i giascti*	*e giascta*
7		*i statti*	
8		*i tetti*	
9		*i nandi*	
10		*i ʒjeti*	
12 000	*dŏmbeʒjetè mije*		
14	*catter mbè ʒjetè vjetsc* 'from 14 years'		
20	*gniεet* [5]		
30	*trijʒjetè* [5]		
40	*catter* [6] *ʒjetè e gni vjetti* 'from 41 years'[7]		
50	*pensse ʒjetè e giasctè vjetsc* 'from 56 years'[7]		
60	*giasctè ʒjetè e tettesc* 'from 68'[7]		
70	*sctatteʒjetè*[5]		
100	*gni chind*		
300	*tre chind*		
400	*catter chind*		
2 000	*dŏŏ mijè* [5]		
3 000	*trijmije* [5]		

1. Pjetër Bogdani, bishop of Shkodër, educated in Italy and a superb and sensitive connoisseur of his native language in the context of a sophisticated and erudite polyglot mastery of ancient and modern languages, tells us in his introduction that "being from Guri ndë Hast [in Hasi country], in the Sanjak of Dukagjin, in the Diocese of Prizren, I desired with great sweat to adjust many words to the territory of Shkodër", i. e., to the literary center and norm of the time. There is disagreement on the degree of this adjustment and the distance in dialect then between Kosovo/Kosovë and Shkodër; but there can be no doubt that Bogdan used frequently such Scutarene forms as *ghiuha* 'the language' and not **gunha*, and *ndeghiuem* 'hearing' instead of *n(d)gue* vel sim., while retaining alongside the last the Kosovar *zgheʒune* 'reading'.
2. It appears that in Bogdan's record long [ȳ] dissimilated into a diphthong [yi], unless this is a remarkable archaism.
3. Bogdan's conservation of vowel length is valuable. It may be that this length could be reduced by phrasal stress ranking, but perhaps *ata vjettè* 'quell'età' simply indicates masculine gender throughout.

4. This important form must be [pêsë].
5. It is difficult to say whether the junctural phenomenon of these complex numerals is phrasal, compounding, or phonological. Note such an example as *gni εet edδ̈mije* '22 000', lit. 'one twenty and-two-thousand'.
6. The frequent doubled *t* seems to point to a short *a*, while the ordinal may indicate a lengthened [*a·*]; but *cater* is also found.
7. These complex numerals are regularly printed with comma before *e*.

Shala (Dukagjin)
(Gusî/Gusinje)[1] M = Martìnaj, Gusî

1	*ni,*[2] *i* (unstressed) *ni̯â* (stressed), *ni̯ânɪ* def.		
2m.	*dy*	*i dȳti*	
f.	*dȳ*		
3m.	*tre,* M *trε*	*i trεti*	
f.	*trī*		
4	*katër, katra,* M *katè̈r*	*i katè̈rti*	*ε katè̈rta*
5	*pε̂s* [3]	*i pε̂sti*	*ε pε̂sta*
6	*ʒ́ašt* [4] ~ *ź-*		*ε źašt˙a*
7	*štat*[4]		*ε štat˙a*
8	*te˙t,*[4] M *tet*		*ε tet˙a*
9	*nân*		
10	*ϑ̌ε˙t* [5]		
11	*ňɪmϑ̌ε˙t,*[6] *ni̯âmϑ̌ε˙t*		
12	*dymϑ̌ε˙t, dȳ-*		
13	*trεmϑ̌ε˙t* [6]		
14	*katërmϑ̌ε˙t, ka…*		
15	*pε̂së mϑ̌ε˙t*		
16	*ʒ́aš tëmϑ̌ε˙t* [6] ~ *ź-*		
17	*štatëmϑ̌ε˙t* [6]		
18	*tεtëmϑ̌ε˙t* [6]		
19	*nânëmϑ̌ε˙t*		
20	*iz'εt,*[7] M *niz'εt*		
21	*iz'εt ε ní*		
30	*triϑ̌'ε˙t*		
40	*katè̈rϑ̌ε˙t*		
50	*pε̂sϑ̌ε˙t* M *pε̂s θεt*		
60	*ʒ́aštϑ̌ε˙t* [6] M *ʒ́aštθεt*		
70	*štatϑ̌ε˙t* [6] M *štatθεt*		

Table continued)

Shala (Dukagjin) (Gusî/Gusinje)[1] M = Martìnaj, Gusî	
80	*tɛtϑɛˑt*[6] M *tɛtθɛt*
90	*nânϑɛˑt*
100	*ićɪn*[7] ~ *iśɪn*, M *nićin*
200	*dyćɪn* ~ *-ś-*
300	*trɛćɪn* ~ *-ś-*
1 000	*imī*,[7] M *nimī*
2 000	*dȳ mī*
3 000	*trī mī*
½	*iʒ́ȳs*[7] ~ *-ź-*

	Qosaj, Gusî[1]	Tuzi[9]	Bajgorska Šalja[11]	Drenica[12]	Ordinals[13]	Upper Morava[14]	
1	*ni* '1, a(n)'	*i*	*ni*	*ni*	*i par*	*ni*	*i pari*
	ňâ (stressed)	*ňâ*	*njâ, njâni*	*njâ*		*njâni*	*e para*
2m.	*dy*	*dy*	*dy*	*dy*	*i dyt*	*dy*[16]	*i dȳt*
f.	*dy*	*dȳ*		*dȳ*		*dȳ*[15]	
3m.	*tre*	*tre*		*tre*	*i tret*		*i trēt*
f.	*trī*	*trī*		*trī*		*tri vjete*[15]	
4	*katër*	*katër*		*katër*[13]	*i katërt*		
5	*pɛ̂s*	*pɛ̂s*	*pês*		*i pêst*	*pēs*	
6	*ʒ́aš t*	*ʒ́aš t*	*ʒ́ā št*		*i ʒ́aš t*		
7	*štat*	*štat*			*i štat*		
8	*te˙t*	*te˙t*		*tet*[13]	*i tet*		
9	*nân*	*nât*[10]		*non*[13]	*i non*		
10	*ẟe˙t*[8]	*ẟe˙t*[8]				*ðēt*	
11	*ňimẟɛt*	*nimëẟɛt*					
12	*dymẟɛt*	*dymëẟɛt*					
13	*trɛmẟɛt*	*trɛmëẟɛt*					
14	*katërmẟɛt*						
15	*pɛ̂sm ẟɛt*						
16	*ʒ́aš tmẟɛt*						
17	*štatmẟɛt*						
18	*tɛtmẟɛt*						
19	*nânmẟɛt*						
20	*ňizɛt*	*izɛt*		*nizet e pes*[13]	'25'[15]	*nizet*	
30		*triẟɛt*				*triðet*	
40		*katërẟɛt*				*katerðet*	
50		*pɛ̂sẟɛt*					
100		*ićît*[10]				*ʒ̆ašθet*	
1 000		*imī*					

My speaker from Shala was born in Dukagjin, moved to Thethi at the age of 20, and came to Yugoslavia aged 55. She was the widow of a man from Martìnaj, and lived outside the center of Gusî near the huge spring called Ali Pašin Izvor. Her speech was noticeably and consistently different from that of Gusî. She was Roman Catholic; the Qosaj specimen is Moslem, and I also have Moslem material from Vûthaj. For brief remarks on Shala, Thethi, and their relation see A. V. Desnickaja, *Gjuha shqipe dhe dialektet e saj* (*Albanskij jazyk i ego dialekty*), Prishtinë 1972, p. 81.

1. This far North Geg variety of the region near the national Albanian border was studied by me in Gusî, Crna Gora, over a half dozen years in the 1970's. I have confidence therefore in the phonological transcription, which tries also to suggest some of the phonetics. Martìnaj is north of the center of Gusî, towards Plav; Qosaj and Vûthaj are slightly to the southeast of the center. Plav is Slavic.
2. Note the depalatalization compared with Da Lecce, Bogdan, and Buzuku. This is found independently in some other dialects.
3. The nasality is important; nasal was lost before original (Proto-Indo-European) **s*.
4. The vowel quality points to old lost *-ë*.
5. This [ɛ·] is very retracted.
6. The vowel quality and quantity is truncated in closed syllables by contrast with the simplexes.
7. Note the unstressed form of '1'.
8. The quality of this vowel seems significant. The role of vowel length in Qosaj is not entirely clear to me.
9. Tuzi is in Crna Gora at the Albanian border on the road from Titograd.
10. This treatment is regular for old nasal clusters in Tuzi.
11. From L. Mulaku, *Govor Albanaca Bajgorske Šalje*, Priština 1968.
12. From H. Kelmendi, *Disa veçori morfologjike të së folmes së lokalitetit të Turiçevcit*, in *Studime gjuhësore I (Dialektologji)* Prishtinë 1978, 453–479. A region in northwest Kosovo/Kosovë.
13. Anton Çetta, *Tregime popullore I Drenicë*, Prishtinë 1963.
14. M. Halimi, Disa tipare të së folmes së Moravës së Epërme, in *Studime gjuhësore I (Dialektologji)*, Prishtinë 1978, 353–402. A region in southeast Kosovo/Kosovë.
15. All numerals have short vowel before noun.
16. Bujanovac, at the eastern edge of Kosovo, north of the Lower Morava region and in contact with the unbroken Serbian speech area, has *di* '2' with unrounding corresponding to the Serbian vowel system.

	Dushmani[1]	Arbanasi[3]
1	*ńi*	*ńí; ní* 'a'
	ńâni m., *ńâna* f.	*ńáni; ńáj* 'a'
2m.	*dy, ńâni dyš* 'one of 2', *t dy(-t)*	*dỳ*
f.	*dȳ, ńâna dȳš* 'one of 2', *tdyja(-t)*	*dý*
3m.	*tre, t tre(-t)*	*trè*
f.	*trī, t trija(-t); dȳš, trīš* 'in 2, 3'	*trí*
4	*kátər, t kátər(-t)m., t kátra(-t)* f.	*kátər*
5	*pês*	*pés*
6	*ʒ́āšt*	*ʒ́ášt*
7	*štāt*	*štát*
8	*tēt*	*tét*
9	*nân*	*nánt*
10	*ðēt*	*ðiet*
11	*ńimðèt*[2]	*nimèt*
12	*dymðèt*	*dymèt*
13	*trémðèt*	*tremèt*
14	*kátərmðèt*	
15	*pêsmðèt*	
16	*ʒ́ā́štmðèt*	
17	*štātmðèt*	
18	*tḗtmðèt*	
19	*nânmðèt*	
20	*ńizet*	*ńizèt*
30	*trī́ðèt*	*triðèt*
40	*kátərðèt*	*katərðèt*
50	*pêsðèt*	
60	*ʒ́ā́štðèt*	
100	*ńi ćin*, pl. *ćina*	*ńi ćìnd*
200	*dy ćin*	
300	*tre ćin*	
1 000	*ńi mīj*	*ńi mí*
2 000	*dȳ mīj*	
3 000	*trī mīj*	

Ordinals

1	*i, e pār*	def. m. *i pari*, f. *e para*
2	*dȳt*	*i, e dyt-i, -a*
3	*trēt*	*tret-i, -a*

(Table continued)

	Dushmani[1]	Arbanasi[3]
5	*pêst*	*pêst-i, -a*
6	*ʒ́ăšt(t)*	*ʒ́ašt(t)-i, -a*
8	*tēt(t)*	*tett-i, -a*
9	*nânt(t)*	*nânt(t)-i, -a*
20	*ńizet(t)*	*ńizett-i, -a*
100	*ćint(t)*	*ćintt-i, -a*

Multiples

ńi, dȳ, trī hēr	'1, 2, 3 time(s)'
dy, tre fiš	'doubly, triply'

1. These data are taken from the cardinal description of Wacław Cimochowski, *Le dialecte de Dushmani*, Poznań 1951; reviewed by E. P. Hamp, *Language* 29, 1953, 500–512.

   Dushmani is located in the heart of Dukagjin, on the right bank of the river Drin.
2. For Cimochowski *ė* represents half-length; see my review. In these numerals this reduced length seems not to be independent, since it occurs pretty regularly with reduced stress indicated.
3. Arbanasi, formerly known as Borgo Erizzo, was an outlying village of, and is now englobed by, Zadar on the Dalmatian coast; it is surrounded by ikavski Croatian. It was settled in the 18th century by emigrants from near Lake Scutari, and is the only Geg enclave existing apart from the main mass of Albanian. My material was gathered personally in situ in July 1961, and a subsequent visit was made in 1978. My observation of the vowels (and details of the consonants) differs from that of earlier observers, I believe, unquestionably. Older descriptions will simply not give consistent results.

   The acute accent marks a tense (< *long) vowel; the grave a lax (< *short) vowel.

Arnold von Harff's numerals of 1496–1499 (Roques 1932: 49–50) provide very little information that we do not otherwise possess:

1	*nea*	presumably =	*ňâ* :	Blanchus *gna*, Da Lecce *gnia*
2	*dua*		*(të) dya* :	Buzuku *teh dua*
3	*trij*		*trī* :	Blanchus, Buzuku *trij*
4	*quater*		*kátër(ë)* :	Blanchus *(n)cater*
5	*pessa*		*(të) pésa* :	Kristoforidhi τε̱ πέσα[1]

(Table continued)

	Dushmani[1]		Arbanasi[3]
6	*jast*	? *ǵáštë* :	Blanchus *giascte*, Buzuku *ʄaste*
7	*statte*	*štátë* :	Blanchus, Buzuku *state*
8	*tette*	*tétë* :	Blanchus *tete*, Buzuku *te-teh*
9	*nante*	*nântë* :	Arbanasi *nánt*, Kristofori-dhi νέ̰ντε̰
10	*dieta*	*(të)ðíeta*[1] :	Kristoforidhi δίετε̰ in fem.
100	*nijtgint*	*ňi-ćint* :	Da Lecce *gni cint*
1 000	*nemijgo*	*ńë-mijë* (?) :[2]	Blanchus *gne mije*

It appears that von Harff's informant, from somewhere in the Geg region between Dulcina (Ulcinj) and Durazzo (Durrës), was largely counting feminines. The exact form of '10' is uncertain, as will be understood from our later difficulties in reaching a definitive reconstruction.

The shape of *nante* is valuable. The writing of *tg* in '100' appears to assure us at this early date of the affricate value (seen in Da Lecce) of the Geg reflex of *q*. In view of this last piece of evidence we may also see an affricate [ʒ́] behind the *j* in *jast* '6'.

1. Unless, unlike *dua*, these are abstracts (names of the number).
2. Perhaps a spirant [j] was heard.

	South Geg[1] Cardinals	Ordinals
1	*nji* *me-j thes* 'with -a bag' *do-j tshīk* 'I want a bit'[2] *def, njiu*[3] ~ *njani* m., *njana* f.	*i, e par-i, -a*
2m.	*dy*, gen. dat. *dyve*, abl. *dysh* *të dy burrat*[4] 'the 2 men'	*i dyti*
f.	*dy, def, të dyja*[4] *daj-e-dȳsh* 'divide it in 2'	
3m.	*tre*, def. *të tre*	*i, e tret-i, -a*
f.	*trī*, def. *të trija*[4] *daj-e trīsh* 'divide it in 3'	

(Table continued)

	South Geg[1] Cardinals	Ordinals
4	*katër*	*i, e katr-i, -a*
5	*pēs*	*i, e pest-i, -a*
6	*gjāsht*	*i, e gjasht-i, -a*
7	*shtāt*	*i, e shtat-i, -a*
8	*tēt*	*i, e tet-i, -a*
9	*nând*	*i, e nânt-i, -a*
10	*dhīt*	*i, e dhit-i, -a* [7]
11	*njimëdhīt*	
12	*dymëdhīt*	
13	*tremëdhīt*	
14	*katërmëdhīt*	
15	*pesmëdhīt* [5]	
16	*gjashmëdhīt*	
17	*shtatmëdhīt*	
18	*tetmëdhīt*	
19	*nânmëdhīt*	
20	*njizét*	
30	*tridhīt* [5]	
40	*dyzét*	
50	*pesdhīt* [5]	
60	*gjashdhīt*	
70	*shtatdhīt*	
80	*tetdhīt*	
90	*nândhīt*	
100	*nji kjînd* [6]	
200	*dy kjînd*	
300	*tre kjînd*	
1 000	*nji mî* [6]	

(Table continued)

	South Geg[1] Cardinals	Ordinals
3 000	*tri mî*	
1 000 000	*nji miliû* [8]	
3 000 000	*tre miliûj*	
½	*nji gjymës*	
¼	*nji tsherék*	

Multiples

nji hēr 'once'
Camaj (1984: 87–88):
dyfish -i, trefish -i 'double, triple'

Distributives

nji nga nji '1 by 1'
dy nga dy '2 by 2'
tre nga tre '3 by 3'

1. Based on the area of Durrës, Elbasan, and Tirana at the beginning of the 20th century; from G. Weigand, *Albanesische Grammatik im südgegischen Dialekt*, Leipzig 1913.
2. This enclitic form applies after a vowel within close phrasal units in the sentence. The form must be a non-syllabic variant of what appears elsewhere as *i*.
3. This is simply an analogical form fashioned with the rule for definitizing masculine stressed vowel finals; therefore the *i* of this form is restressed, or taken from the marginal seen in Tosk.
4. In a noun phrase the quantifier does not count as first element for purposes of affixing the enclitic definite marker by Wackernagel's Law. Thus, *të dy burravet* 'to the 2 men', *të dyja grāt* 'the 2 women', *të trija të bukèrat* 'the 3 beautiful females', but *këjó të dyja motra* 'these 2 sisters'.
5. The vowel quantity is truncated in closed syllables by contrast with the simplexes. Or is this reduction of length in other than rightmost elements of phrases? Some heavy consonantisms are also reduced.
6. Nasalization in South Geg is strongly tied to surface nasal consonants.

7. A new rule has evolved for the ordinals which requires simply that the base vowel be shortened. This rule was extracted from the ordinals '6th'–'8th', where the *-ë* which imparted length to the cardinals was missing.
8. M. Camaj, *Albanian Grammar*, Wiesbaden 1984, who presents a "unified language" taking account of the language reform and embracing Geg, Tosk, and Arbëresh, has the neologism *milión*, and also *miliárd* 'billion'.

	Tetovo/Tetovë[1]	Ohrid[4]
1	Indef. *ni*	*ňi*
	ňâ	
2m.	*di*[2]	*dy*
f.	*di*[2]	
3m.	*trɛ*	*trɛ*
f.	*trɛ*	
4	*katër*	*katër*
5	*pɛ̂s*	*pēs*
6	*ʒ́āšt*	*ǵašt(ë)*[5]
7	*štāt*	*štat(ë)*[5]
8	*tɛ̄t*	*tet(ë)*[5]
9	*nând*	*nëntë*
10	*ð'ɛjet*[3]	*ðetë*
11	*n'imðɛjit*[3]	*ňimbëðēt*
12	*dimðɛjit*	
20	*niz'ɛt*	*ňiz'ɛt*
30	*trài̯ðài̯t*[3] (Skopje, from Mladenov)	*trɛðēt*
40		*dyz'ɛt*
50		*pesðēt*[5]
60		*ǵaštᵊðēt*[5]
70		*štatᵊðēt*[5]
80		*tɛtᵊðēt*[5]
90		*nëntᵊðēt*
100		*ňiḱint*

1. A major city in the Albanian continuum of northwestern Makedonija, which is separated from Kosovo by the high mountainous mass of Šar Planina. Much of my materials were collected from the Moslem speakers (all men, of course) in conversations around the mosque. My fieldwork dates from the second half of the summer, 1961, when I was living in Skopje and spending the workday daily in Tetovo.

2. Unrounding of *y* is regular.
3. Diphthongization of long vowels is marked in the whole of northwestern Makedonija.
4. This specimen is from a polyglot (in five or six languages) native of the city of Ohrid in westernmost Makedonija, on the eastern shore of the lake of the same name. The north end of Lake Ohrid is at the northern limit of the Tosk speaking area, while just east of this lake we encounter along the eastern shore of Lake Prespa the easternmost limit of Albanian habitation and local speech. Prespa Albanian shows stronger acculturation to Makedonski structure. This Tosk variety is not very informative for our purposes, but is included to show the eastern extent and integrity of the language. I studied this speaker mainly in 1976.
5. Note the shortening and change in vowel quality in complex forms which we have seen in Geg dialects.

Kristoforidhi's Elbasan Tosk[1]
Ordinals

masc.				fem.			
indef.		def.		indef.		def.	
ι πάρε̮	πρῶτος	ι πάρι	ὁ πρῶτος	ε πάρε̮	πρώτη	ε πάρα	ἡ πρώτη
ι dύτε̮	δεύτερος	ι dύτι	ὁ δεύτερος	ε dύτε̮	δευτέρα	ε dύτα	ἡ δευτέρα
ι τρέτε̮	τρίτος	ι τρέτι	ὁ τρίτος	ε τρέτε̮	τρίτη	ε τρέτα	ἡ τρίτη
ι κάτρε̮τε̮	τέταρτος	ι κάτρε̮τι	ὁ τέταρτος	ε κάτρε̮τε̮	τετάρτη	ε κάτρε̮τα	ἡ τετάρτη
ι πέσε̮τε̮	πέμπτος	ι πέσε̮τι	ὁ πέμπτος	ε πέσε̮τε̮	πέμπτη	ε πέσε̮τα	ἡ πέμπτη
ι γ̇άστε̮	ἕκτος	ι γ̇άστι	ὁ ἕκτος	ε γ̇άστε̮	ἕκτη	ε γ̇άστα	ἡ ἕκτη
ι ὅτάτε̮	ἕβδομος	ι ὅτάτι	ὁ ἕβδομος	ε ὅτάτε̮	ἑβδόμη	ε ὅτάτα	ἡ ἑβδόμη
ι τέτε̮	ὄγδοος	ι τέτι	ὁ ὄγδοος	ε τέτε̮	ὀγδόη	ε τέτα	ἡ ὀγδόη
ι νέ̮ντε̮	ἔννατος	ι νέ̮ντι	ὁ ἔννατος	ε νέ̮ντε̮	ἐννάτη	ε νέ̮ντα	ἡ ἐννάτη
ι διέτε̮	δέκατος	ι διέτι	ὁ δέκατος	ε διέτε̮	δεκάτη	ε διέτα	ἡ δεκάτη etc.
ι ν̇ε̮-μbε̮-διέτε̮		ιν̇ε̮-μbε̮-διέτι		ε ν̇ε̮-μbε̮-διέτε̮		ε ν̇ε̮-μbε̮-διέτα	
ι dυ-μbε̮-διέτε̮		ι dυ-μbε̮-διέτι		ε dυ-μbε̮-διέτε̮		ε dυ-μbε̮-διέτα	
ι τρε-μbε̮-διέτε̮	etc.	ι τρε-μbε̮-διέτι	etc.	ε τρε-μbε̮-διέτε̮	etc.	ε τρε-μbε̮-διέτα	etc.
ι ν̇ε̮ζέτε̮		ι ν̇ε̮ζέτι		ε ν̇ε̮ζέτε̮	"	ε ν̇ε̮ζέτα	
ι ν̇ε̮ζέτ' ε ν̇έ̮jτε̮		ι ν̇ε̮ζέτ'ε ν̇έ̮jτι		ε ν̇ε̮ζέτ' ε ν̇έ̮jτε̮	"	ε ν̇ε̮ζέτ' ε ν̇έ̮jτα	
ι ν̇ε̮ζέτ' ε dύτε̮		ι ν̇ε̮ζέτ' ε dύτι		ε ν̇ε̮ζέτ' ε dύτε̮	"	ε ν̇ε̮ζέτ' ε dύτα	
ι ν̇εζέτ' ε τρέτε̮		ι ν̇ε̮ζέτ' ε τρέτι		ε ν̇ε̮ζέτ' ε τρέτε̮	"	ε ν̇ε̮ζέτ'ε τρέτα	
ι ν̇ε̮ζέτ' ε κάτρε̮τε̮	etc.	ι ν̇ε̮ζέτ'ε κάτρε̮τι	etc.	ε ν̇ε̮ζέτ' ε κάτρε̮τε̮	"	ε ν̇ε̮ζέτ' ε κάτρε̮τα	etc.
ι τρι-διέτε̮		ι τρι-διέτι		ε τρι-διέτε̮	"	ε τρι-διέτα	
ι τρι-διέτ'ε ν̇έ̮jτε̮	etc.	ι τρι-διέτ'ε ν̇έ̮jτι	etc.	ε τρι-διέτ'ε ν̇έ̮jτε̮	"	ε τρι-διέτ'ε ν̇έ̮jτα	"
ι dυζέτε̮		ι dυζέτι		ε dυζέτε̮	"	ε dυζέτα	
ι dυζέτ'ε ν̇έ̮jτε̮	etc.	ι dυζέτ'ε ν̇έ̮jτι	etc.	ε dυζέτ'ε ν̇έ̮jτε̮	"	ε dυζέτ'ε ν̇έ̮jτα	etc.

ι πεσε̰-διέτε̰	”	ι πεσε̰-διέτι	”	ε πεσε̰-διέτε̰	”	ε πεσε̰-διέτα	”
ι γ̇άσ̌τε̰-διέτε̰	”	ι γ̇ασ̌τε̰-διέτι	”	ε γ̇ασ̌τε̰-διέτε̰	”	ε γ̇ασ̌τε̰-διέτα	”
ι σ̌τάτε̰-διέτε̰	”	ι σ̌τατε̰-διέτι	”	ε σ̌τατε̰-διέτε̰	”	ε σ̌τατε̰-διέτα	”
ι τετε̰-διέτε̰	”	ι τετε̰-διέτι	”	ε τετε̰-διέτε̰	”	ε τετε̰-διέτα	”
ι νε̰ντε̰-διέτε̰	”	ι νε̰ντε̰-διέτι	”	ε νε̰ντε̰-διέτε̰	”	ε νε̰ντε̰-διέτα	”
ι ṅε̰-κ̇ίνττε̰	”	ι ṅε̰-κ̇ίνττι	”	ε ṅε̰-κ̇ίνττε̰	”	ε ṅε̰-κ̇ίνττα	”
ι ṅε̰-κ̇ίνττ᾽ε ṅέj̰τε̰	”	ι ṅε̰-κ̇ίνττ᾽ε ṅέj̰τι	”	ε ṅε̰-κ̇ίνττ᾽ε ṅέj̰τε̰	”	ε ṅε̰ κ̇ίνττ᾽ε ṅέj̰τα	”
ι dυ-κ̇ίνττε̰	”	ι dυ-κ̇ίνττι	”	ε dυ-κ̇ίνττε̰	”	ε dυ-κ̇ίνττα	”
ι τρε-κ̇ίνττε̰	”	ι τρε-κ̇ίνττι	”	ε τρε-κ̇ίνττε̰	”	ε τρε-κ̇ίνττα	”
ι κατρε̰-κ̇ίνττε̰	”	ι κατρε̰-κ̇ίνττι	”	ε κατρε̰κ̇ίνττε̰	”	ε κατρε̰-κ̇ίνττα	”
ι πεσε̰-κ̇ίνττε̰	”	ι πεσε̰-κ̇ίνττι	”	ε πεσε̰-κ̇ίνττε̰	”	ε πεσε̰-κ̇ίνττα	”
ι γ̇ασ̌τε̰-κ̇ίνττε̰	”	ι γ̇ασ̌τε̰-κ̇ίνττι	”	ε γ̇ασ̌τε̰-κ̇ίνττε̰	”	ε γ̇ασ̌τε̰-κ̇ίνττα	”
ι σ̌τατε̰-κ̇ίνττε̰	”	ι σ̌τατε̰-κ̇ίνττι	”	ε σ̌τατε̰-κ̇ίνττε̰	”	ε σ̌τατε̰-κ̇ίνττα	”
ι τετε̰-κ̇ίνττε̰	”	ι τετε̰-κ̇ίνττι	”	ε τετε̰-κ̇ίνττε̰	”	ε τετε̰-κ̇ίνττα	”
ι νε̰ντε̰-κ̇ίνττε̰	”	ι νε̰ντε̰-κ̇ίνττι	”	ε νε̰ντε̰-κ̇ίνττε̰	”	ε νε̰ντε̰-κ̇ίνττα	”
ι ṅε̰-μίλ̂ε̰τε̰	”	ι ṅε̰ μίλ̂ε̰τι	”	ε ṅε̰ μίλ̂ε̰τε̰	”	ε ṅε̰-μίλ̂ε̰τα	”
ι ṅε̰-μίλ̂ε̰τ᾽ε ṅέj̰τε̰	etc.	ι ṅε̰-μιλ̂ε̰τ᾽ε ṅέj̰τι	etc.	ε ṅε̰-μίλ̂ε̰τ᾽ε νέj̰ε̰τε̰		ε ṅε̰-μίj̰ε̰τ᾽ε ṅέj̰τα (sic!)	etc.
ι dυ-μίλ̂ε̰τε̰	”	ι dυ-μίλ̂ε̰τι	”	ε dυ-μίλ̂ε̰τε̰		ε dυ-μίλ̂ε̰τα	”
ι τρε-μίλ̂ε̰τε̰	”	ι τρι-μίλ̂ε̰τι	”	ε τρι-μίλ̂ε̰τε̰	”	ε τρι-μίλ̂ε̰τα	”
ι ṅε̰-μιλ̂ιбντε̰		ι ṅε̰-μιλ̂ιбντι	”	ε ṅέ̰-μιλ̂ιбντε̰	”	ε ṅέ̰-μιλ̂ιбντα	”
ι ṅε̰-μιλ̂ιбντ᾽ε ṅέj̰τε̰	”	ι ṅε̰-μιλ̂ιбντ᾽ε ṅέj̰τι	”	ε ṅε̰-μιλ̂ιбντ᾽ε ṅέj̰τε̰	”	ε ṅε̰-μιλ̂ιбντ᾽ε ṅέj̰τα	
ι dυ-μιλ̂ιбντε̰	”	ι dυ-μιλ̂ιбντι	”	ε dυ-μιλ̂ιбντε̰	”	ε dυ-μιλ̂ιбντα	etc.
ι τρε-μιλ̂ιбντε̰	”	ι τρε-μιλ̂ιбντι	”	ε τρε-μιλ̂ιбντε̰	”	ε τρε-μιλ̂ιбντα	”
ι ṅε̰-dυλ̂ιбντε̰	”	ι ṅε̰-dυλ̂ιбντι	”	ε ṅε̰-dυλ̂ιбντε̰	”	ε ṅε̰-dυλ̂ιбντα	”
ι ṅε̰-τρελ̂ιбντε̰		ι ṅε̰-τρελ̂ιбντι		ε ṅε̰-τρελ̂ιбντε̰		ε ṅε̰-τρελ̂ιбντα	etc.
ι ṅε̰-κατρε̰λ̂ιбντε̰		ι ṅε̰-κατρε̰λ̂ιбντι		ε ṅε̰-κατρε̰λ̂ιбντε̰		ε ṅε̰-κατρε̰λ̂ιбντα	”
ι ṅε̰-πεσε̰λ̂ιбντε̰		ι ṅε̰-πεσε̰λ̂ιбντι		ε ṅε̰-πεσε̰λ̂ιбντε̰		ε ṅε̰-πεσε̰λ̂ιбντα	”

Kristoforidhi's Elbasan Tosk[1]
Cardinals

1[2] m.	ν̇έ̰, def. ν̇έ̰ρι which I transcribe	*ňë, ňë́ri*
f.	ν̇ε̰̃, ν̇ε̰̃ρα	*ňë̄, ňë̄́ra*
2[2] m.	dύ, def. τε̰ dύ	*dy, të dy*
f.	dῦ, τε̰ dῦjα	*dȳ, të dȳ́ja*
3[2] m.	τρέ, τε̰ τρέ	*tre, të tre*
f.	τρῖ, τε̰ τρία	*trī, të tría*
4[2]	κάτρε̰, τε̰ κάτρε̰, τε̰ κάτρα	*kátrë, të kátr-ë, -a*
5	πέσε̰, τε̰ πέσε̰, τε̰ πέσα	*pésë, të pés-ë, -a*
6	ε̰άσ̈τε̰	*ǵáštë*
7	σ̈τάτε̰	*štátë*
8	τέτε̰	*tétë*
9	νέ̰ντε̰	*në́ntë*
10	δίετε̰ ~ διέτε̰	*ðietë ~ ðjétë*
11	ν̇ε̰ μbε̰-διέτε̰	*ňë-mbë-ðjétë*
12	dυ-μbε̰-διέτε̰	*dy-mbë-ðjétë*
13	τρε-μbε̰-διέτε̰	*tre-mbë-ðjétë*
20	ν̇ε̰ζέτ	*ňëzét*
21	ν̇ε̰ζέτ ε ν̇έ̰ m., ε ν̇ε̰̃ f.	*ňëzét e ňë, e ňë̄*
22	ν̇ε̰ζέτ ε dύ, ε dῦ	*ňëzét e dy, e dȳ*
23	ν̇ε̰ζέτ ε τρέ, ε τρῖ	*ňëzét e tre, e trī*
30	τρι-διέτε̰	*tri-ðjétë*
40	dυζέτ ~ (Σ̈κοdρα) κάτρε̰-διέτε̰	*dyzét ~ kátrë-ðjétë*
50	πεσε̰-διέτε̰	*pesë-ðjétë*
60	γ̇ασ̈τε̰-diétε̰ ~ (Ὕδρα) τρεζέτ	*ǵaštë-ðjétë ~ trezét*
70	σ̈τατε̰-διέτε̰	*štatë-ðjétë*
80	τέτε̰-διέτε̰ ~ (Ὕδρα) κατρε̰ζέτ	*tétë-ðjété ~ katrëzét*
90	νε̰ντε̰-διέτε	*nëntë-ðjétë*
99	ν̇έ̰ κ̇ίντ πα ν̇ε̰̃ '100 minus 1 fem.' etc. often used … *pa ňë̄*	
100	ν̇έ̰ κ̇ιντ	*ňë́ ḱint*
200	dύ κ̇ιντ	*dý ḱint*
300	τρέ κ̇ιντ	*tré ḱint*
1 000	ν̇ε̰̃ μίλ̇ε̰ ~ μίjε̰	*ňë̄ míljë ~ míjë*
2 000	dῦ μίλ̇ε̰ ~ μίjε̰	*dȳ míljë ~ míjë*
3 000	τρῖ μίλ̇ε̰ ~ μίjε̰	*trī míljë ~ míjë*

(Table continued)

Kristoforidhi's Elbasan Tosk[1] Cardinals		
1 000 000	ν̇έ̰ μιλ̇ιδ́ν	*ňë miljiún*
2 000 000	dύ μιλ̇ιδ́νε̰	*dy miljiúnë*
	ν̇έ̰ dυδ́ιλ̇ν ἓν δισεκατομμύριον 'billion'	*ňë dyljiún*
	ν̇έ̰ τρελ̇ιδ́ν 'trillion'	*treljiún*
	ν̇έ̰ κατρε̰λ̇ιδ́ν 'quadrillion'	*katrëljiún*
	ν̇έ̰ πεσε̰λ̇ιδ́ν 'quintillion'	*pesëljiún*
Distributives		
ν̇έ̰ νγα ν̇έ̰ ~ νγα ν̇έ̰, dύ..., τρέ... m. ἀνὰ ἕνα, etc.		
ν̇ε̰͂ νγα ν̇ε̰͂ ~ νγα ν̇ε̰͂, dῦ..., τρῖ... f. ἀνὰ μίαν, etc.		

1. I digest here the characteristically ample and meticulous inventory of forms to be found in the grammar of the great 19th century Elbasan scholar Konstantin Kristoforidhi: K. Χριστοφορίδης, Γραμματικὴ τῆς Ἀλβανικῆς γλώσσης κατὰ τὴν Τοσκικὴν διάλεκτον (τοῦ ἐξ Ἐλβασανίου), ἐν Κωνσταντινουπόλει 1882.
2. Kristoforidhi gives lengthy declensional paradigms for these forms which need not be repeated here since they are given by the rule formulated in note 4 to the tabulation of Weigand's South Geg.

	Villa Badessa[1]	Mandrìtsa[6]	Bulgarian	Ukraine[15]
1	Indef. *ňɨ* *ňë*	*ni* :	*edín*	*n'i*
2m.f.	*di*[2]	*ǵu*[7]	*dva*	*dy*
3m.f.	*tri*[3]	*tri*[8]	*tri*	*tr'i*
4	*katrë*	*kátrë*	*čétiri*	*kátre*
5	*pes*[3]	*pésë*	*pet*	*p'esë*
6	*ǵašt*	*ǵáštë*	*šes(t)*	*g'aštë*
7	*štat*	*štátë*	*sédem*	
8	*tet*	*tétë*	*ósem*	
9	*nënd*	*nḗntë*	*dévet*	
10	*diét*[4]	*zjétë*[9]	*déset*	
11	*ňëmbëdiét* ~ -*ð*-[4]	*nimbëzjetë*	*idinájsъ(t)*	
12	*dimbëdiét* ~ -*ð*-	*ǵumbëzjetë*	*dvanajsъ(t)*	
13	*trimbëdiét* ~ -*ð*-	*trimbëzjetë*		

(Table continued)

	Villa Badessa[1]	Mandrìtsa[6]	Bulgarian	Ukraine[15]
14		*katërmet* [10]	*čet-(i)rinájsъ(t)* [10]	
15		*pesëmet* [10]		
20	*ňëzét* [ɲɨzˈɛt]	*nizét*	*dvájsъ(t)*	
21		*nisteni* [11]	*dv-ájs(ъ)tiednó* [11]	
22		*nisteǵú* [11]...	*dvázdvá* [11]	
30	*triðiét* [4]	*trizjét* [9]	*tríjsъ(t)*	
31		*tristení* [11]		
40	*dizét*	*ǵuzét*	*č(e)tírisъ(t)* [10]	
50	*pesëðiét* [4]	*pezjét* [12]	*pedesé(t)* [12]	
60	*ǵaštëðiét*	*ǵažjét* [12]	*šejse(t)* [13]	
70	*štatëðiét*	*štatëzjét* [14]	*sedъmdesé(t)*	
80	*tetëðiét*	*tetëzjét* [14]	*osъmdesé(t)*	
90	*nëndëðiét*	*nëntëzjét* [14]	*devedesé(t)*	
100	*ňëḱínt*			
200	*diḱínt*			
300	*triḱínt*			
1 000	*ňë míjë* [5]			

1. This small village near Pescara, in the Abruzzi, was settled by refugee Albanians from Pikernion on the Epiros coast in 1745; the language is therefore not Arbëresh. M. Lambertz published exiguous text samples, *KZ* 53, 1925, 76–79; glossary notes 304–307. The dialect has been said to be extinct, even by natives I have questioned in the village; but on 7 October 1988 I located and interviewed the last surviving speaker Artemìsia Vlàsi (Vlaš) in Pescara, who displayed excellent command of forms and everyday vocabulary.
2. *y* and *i* have merged throughout.
3. I found no stable traces of distinctive length; but there may be [C:] after *V̌.
4. The structure of vocalisms resembles that of Italian. The voiced dentals *d* and *ð* behave largely, as in Italian, as còntextual variants.
5. *j* had slight friction.
6. The dialect of this village in southeasternmost Bulgaria, in contact with Bulgarian, Turkish, and Greek, and the most divergent variety of Albanian I know, is nearly identical with that of its offshoot Màndres, near Kilkís, which I have sketched, *Die Sprache* 11, 1965, 137–154, and revisited in 1982. In April 1969 I was able to visit Mandrìtsa and collect a serviceable sample; see also my article "The diphthongs of Mandrica", *Linguistique Balkanique*

14, 1970, 21–25. I have presented some aspects of the Mandrìtsa numerals at the Linguistic Society of America meeting, December 1969; see "A borrowed morphophonemic particularity", LSA *Meeting Handbook* 1969, 117–118.

7. We must see here: *dy* > **di̯u* (Bulgarian structure) > **d'u* > *ǵu*.
8. The Bulgarian homophony has favored the choice. I had the impression that at Villa Badessa **tre* had been rejected as seeming Italian. This would reflect the difference in emphasizing cultural identity.
9. *z*- is clearly Bulgarian or Turkish bilingual interference. The accidental result is that '10' and '20' nearly merge.
10. Metrical syncope occurs with numerals containing one extra syllable.
11. The vowel of the decade suffers anomalous syncope in these complex numerals.
12. Adjacent homorganic obstruents merge to voiced output.
13. Mandrìtsa follows Bulgarian in syncopating the interior syllable.
14. These follow Bulgarian metrically in conserving one additional syllable.
15. These materials from Russian sources, representing the three villages near Melitópol, are totally at second hand, since they and Greci (Avellino) are the only enclaves I have never visited. Note the consonant palatalization, reflecting bilingual interference. Selim Islami, *Buletin për shkencat shoqërore* 1955, 2, 163–180, suppresses dialect detail through normalizing.

	Salamís (Arvanítika)[1] Cardinals		Ordinals	
1	*ɲə*		*i párə*	
	def. *ɲə́ri* m., *ɲə́ra* f., *ñierene*[4] acc.			
2m.	*di*, nominalized[3]	*tə-dí te di*[4]	*i dítə*	
f.	*di*[2]	*tə-día te dia*[4]		
3m.	*tre*	*tə-tré te tre*[4]	*i trétə*	
f.	*tri*[2]	*tə-tría te tria*[4]		
4	*kátrə katter*[4]	*tə-kátr-ə* m., -*a*, f.	*i kátrətə*	
5	*pésə*		*i pésətə* ~	*i péstə*
6	*ɟáʃtə*		*i ɟáʃtətə*	*i ɟáʃtə*
7	*ʃtátə*		*i ʃtátətə*	*i ʃtátə*
8	*tétə*		*i tétətə*	*i tétə*
9	*nə́ndə*		*i nə́ndətə*	
10	*ðjétə*		*i ðjétətə*	*i ðjétə*
11	*ɲə́mbetə*	+ *mbe δiette*[4]	*i ɲə́mbetətə*	*i ɲə́mbetə*
12	*dímbetə*		*i dímbetətə*	*i dímbetə*
13	*trémbetə*			
14	*kátrəmbetə*			

(Table continued)

	Salamís (Arvanítika)[1] Cardinals			Ordinals	
15	*pésəmbetə*				
16	*ɟáʃtəmbetə*				
17	*ʃtátəmbetə*				
18	*téṭəmbetə*				
19	*nə́ndəmbetə*				
20	*ɲəzét*	*ñie ζet*[4]		*i ɲəzétətə* ~	*i ɲəzétə,* *i ñieζétim*[4]
30	*triðjétə*	*tri δiette*[4]		*i triðjétətə* ~	*i triðjétə*
40	*dizét*	*di ζett'*[4]			*i tri δiettete*[4]
48	*dizét (e) tétə*		45	*i dizétepéstə*	
50	*pesəðjétə*	*pesse δiette*[4]			
60	*ɟaʃtəðjétə*	*tre ζett'*[4]			
70	*ʃtatəðjétə*	*štatte δiette*[4]			
80	*tetəðjétə*	*katter ζett'*[4]			
90	*nəndəðjétə*	*nönde δiette*[4]			
100	*ɲəcínt* ~ *cint*	*kint*[4]		*i cíndətə*	*i kindete*[4]
200	*dicínt*	*di kint*[4]		*i dicíndətə*	
300	*trecínt*	*tre kint*[4]	362	*i trecíndeɟaštəðjétedítə*	
400	*katrəcínt*				
500	*pesəcínt*				
600	*ɟaʃtəcínt*				
700	*ʃtatəcínt*				
800	*tetəcínt*				
900	*nəndəcínt*				
1 000	*ɲəmíʎə*	*ñie mil̄l̄e*[4]		*i míʎətə*	*i mil̄l̄ete*[4]
2 000	*dimíʎə*	*di mil̄l̄e*[4]			
3 000	*trimiʎə*	*tri mil̄l̄e*[4]			
4 000	*katrəmíʎə*	*katter mil̄l̄e*[4]			
4 321	*katrəmiʎə e trecínt e ɲəzét e ɲə́*				
1 000 000	*ɲəmiʎún*	*ñie mil̄l̄iun,* *di mil̄l̄iune,* *tre mil̄l̄iune*			

Multiples: *trihérə* '3 times', etc.

Distributives: *didí* ~ *ŋgadí* '2 by 2', etc.

1. From Claus Haebler, *Grammatik der albanischen Mundart von Salamis*, Wiesbaden 1965.
2. In almost all of Arvanítika dialects surviving in 1950 there was no trace of inherited vowel length; nor is it recorded by Reinhold (1855).
3. The declension and phrasal expansion of these forms are governed by the rule formulated in note 4 to the tabulation of Weigand's South Geg.
4. From C. H. Th. Reinhold, *Noctes Pelasgicae* (Πελασγικά Α′), Athenis: Sophoclis Garbola, 1855, which was based on the speech of the Saronic islands of Póros, Ídhra (Hydra), and Spétsai.

	Sophikò, Korinthía[1] Cardinals		Ordinals	
1	*ňë*		*i pári* m., *e pára* f.	
	def. *ňë́ë ri* m., *ňë́ë ra* f., *ňë́ë së* f. marginal, *ňë́ë në* acc., Reinhold *n̄ie′ne* m. acc.			
2m.	*di*	def.[8] *të-dí*		
f.	*dii* [3]	*të-díia*		
3m.	*tre*	*të-tré*	*i tréti* m., *e tréta*	
f.	*trii*	*të-tríia*		
4	*kátrë*		*i kátrëti*	
5	*pésë*		*i pésëti*, etc.	
6	*ǵáštë*			
7	*štátë*			
8	*tétë*			
9	*në́ndë*		Kaskavélji (> Λεον-τάρι), Boeotia[2]	
10	*ðjétë*			
11	*ňë́mbjetë* [4]		*ňë́mbet*	
12	*dímbjetë*		*díbet*	
13	*trémbjetë*		*tríbet* [6]	
14			*kátërbet*	
15			*pésëmbet*	
16			*ǵáštëmbet*	
17			*štátëmbet*	
18			*tétëmbet*	
19	*në́ndë mjet* [5]		*në́ndë bet*	
20	*ňëzét*		*i ňëzétëti*	*ňëzét*
21	*ňëzeteňë́*			
30	*triétë*			*triðjét*

(Table continued)

	Sophikò, Korinthía[1] Cardinals	Ordinals
40	*dizét*	*dizét*
50	*pesiétë*	*pesëðjét*
60	*trezét*	*trizét*[6]
70	*štatëðjétë*[9]	*štatëðjét*
80	*katrëzét*	*katërzét*
90	*nëndëðjétë*[9]	*nëndëðjét*
100	*ňëḱindë*	*ňё́ḱind*[7]
200	*diḱindë*	*díḱind*[7]
300		*tréḱind*[7]
1 000	*ňëmiʎë*	*ňëmiʎ*
		dimiʎ
		trímiʎ ~ tré

1. This large village and an adjacent one are the only points of Arvanítika, and indeed of the entirety of Albanian, which retain proto-Tosk vowel length in all positions, while also conserving all instances of *ë* as a syllabic. My materials from Sophikò date from 1955 and later.
2. These divergent forms from Boeotia (fairly far north in the Arvanítika area) were collected for contrast in September 1988.
3. One often actually hears two pulses in Sophikò length.
4. Note the retraction of accent.
5. Cf. the reduction to *m* in Mandrìtsa.
6. Probably Greek interference produces the *tri-*.
7. Note the separate word stresses.
8. See note 3 to Salamís.
9. Preservation of -ð- here may point to old word juncture.

	Greci (Avellino)[1] Cardinals	Ordinals
1	*ɲ* ~ *ɲi*[2] marginal case *ɲéja*[3] (also *ɲẽ́ja*) def. *ɲéri*[3] m., *ɲéra*[3] f.	*i pári*
2m.f.	*di*	*i díti*
3m.	*tre*	*i tréti* m., *a tréta*[7] f.
f.	*tri*	
4	*katr*	*i kátrʃi* (probably = de Radas' "abl.")
5	*pes*	*i pési*
6	*ɟaʃt*	
7	*ʃtat*	
8	*tet*	
9	*nend*[3]	
10	*ðié(t)*	*i ðiéti*
11	*ɲimbðié(t)*	*i ɲimbðéu*[8] m., *a ɲimbðéa* f.
12	*dimbié(t)*[4] ~ *ɲ-ðet-e-di*	
13	*trembðié(t)*	
19	*nendmbðié(t)*	*i nendmbðéu*
20	*ɲizé(t)*	*i ɲizéu*[8] m., *a ɲizéa* f.
21	*ɲizét-e-ɲ*	*i ɲizét-e-pári*
22	*ɲizét-e-di*	*i ɲizét-e-díti*
29	*ɲizét-e-nend*	
30	*treðié(t)*[5]	*i treðéu*[8]
40	*dizé(t)*[5]	*i dizéu*
50	*pesðié* ~ *dizét-e-ðié(t)*[6]	*i pesðéu*
60	*ɟaʃtðié(t)* ~ *trezé(t)*[6]	*i trezéu*
70	*ʃtatðié(t)* ~ *dizét-e-ðié(t)*[6] [sic!]	
80	*katrzé(t)*	*i katrzéu*
90	*nendðié(t)*	*i nendðéu*
100	*ɲicínd* ~ *ɲ-cínd*	*i ɲicíndi*
101	*ɲicínd-e-ɲ*	
102	*ɲicínd-e-di*	
103	*ɲicínd-e-tre*	
200	*dicínd*	

(Table continued)

	Greci (Avellino)[1] Cardinals	Ordinals
300	*trecínd*	
1 000	*ɲi míʎ*	*i ɲimíʎi*
2 000	*di míʎ*	
3 000	*tre míʎ*	
4 000	*katr míʎ*	

Multiples: *tre her* '3 times'

Distributives: *ɲeɲ* '1 by 1'
di-e-di '2 by 2'
tre-e-tre '3 by 3'

1. From Martin Camaj, *La parlata albanese di Greci in Provincia di Avellino*, Firenze: Olschki 1971. I have never visited Greci, and did not learn about it during my first work on Arbëresh in the 1950s. This dialect has been neglected, and we are greatly indebted to Camaj for his work on this as on so many other things; cf. also M. Camaj, *Racconti popolari* (*di Greci* [*Katúndi*] *in Provincia di Avellino e di Barile* [*Baríli*] *in Provincia di Potenza*), Roma 1972, for a rich set of texts.
2. On the vocalism *i* cf. note 1 to Da Lecce.
3. Stressed **ë* apparently gives *e*.
4. Cf. Sophikò. Also *dimbðié*.
5. The units follow as with the 20s.
6. The units follow as with the 20s, formed on *pesðié, trezé(t)*, and *ʃtatðié(t)*.
7. Proclitic *e* becomes *a* in Greci.
8. These definite forms are treated productively as if terminating in stressed *-é* by suffixing *-u*, just as '5th' and '10th' suffix *-i*.

	Portocannone (Campobasso) Molise[1]
1	*ňë*
	marginal case { *ňëria* / *ňëja* / *ňëve* (analogy on higher numerals) }
2m.f.	*di*
3m.f.	*tre*
4	*katër*
5	*pes*
6	*ǵašt*
7	*štat*
8	*tet*
9	*nënd*
10	*ðíet*
11	*ňëmb(ë)ðíet* etc.
20	*ňëzét*
30	(= 13)[2]
40	(= 14),[2] *dizét*
50	
60	*trezét*
70	(= 17)[2]
80	*katërzet*
90	(= 19)[2]
100	*pez:ét* ~ *ðíetmb(ë)ðjet*[2] etc. by 20s

1. The Molise villages were the first Arbëresh dialects to be reported on a basis of modern linguistic, i. e., Neogrammarian, standards: Max Lambertz, "Italo-albanische Dialektstudien" I, *KZ* 51, 1923, 259–290 (Lautlehre); II, *KZ* 52, 1924, 43–90 (Formenlehre, Syntax); III, *KZ* 53, 1925, 66–79 (Volkstümliche Texte, including Villa Badessa); IV, *KZ* 53, 1925, 282–306 (Glossar). For this reason the Molise group was the last Arbëresh enclave I visited, in October 1988. I now realize that there are many corrections and improvements to Lambertz's record to be made, and of course a full and ample description by

today's standards for at least Ururi, Portocannone, and Montecilfone is urgently needed. I report elsewhere my 1988 findings in Portocannone.

2. It is clear that the speaker conflated the decades based on *ðíet* and the teens; the difference between these should be the presence and absence of *mb(ë)*. The form given for '100' suggests that the final element in the decades properly has the shape *-ðjet*. The series in *-zét* has been productively extended.

	Barile (Potenza)[1]	San Costantino Albanese (Potenza), Lucania[6]	Plàtaci (Cosenza)[8]
1	*ňɪ*	*një*	*ňë*
2m.	*di, dɪ-*	*di*[7]	*di*
f.	*di, dɪ-*	*dī*[7]	*di*[9]
3m.	*tri*	*tre*	*tre*
f.	*tri*	*tri*	*trī*
4	*katër*	*kater*	*katër*
5	*pɛs*		*pes*
6	*ǵašt*		*ǵašt*
7	*štat*		*štat*
8	*tɛt*		*tet*
9	*nënd*	*nə̃nd*	*nënd*
10	*ðit*	*ðiét*	*ðjet*
11	*ňɪmbðít*	*-ðjet*	*ňëmbëðjét*
12	*dɪmbðít*	⋮	*dímbëðjet*
13	*trɛmbðít*[2]		*trembëðjet*
14	*katrmbðít*		*katrmbëðjet*
15	*pɛsëmbðít*		*pesmbëðjet*
16	*ǵaštëmbðít*		*ǵaštmbëðjet*
17	*štatëmbðít*		*štatmbëðjet*
18	*tɛtëmbðít*		*tetmbëðjet*
19	*nëndëmbðít*		*nëndmbëðjet*
20	*ňɪzét*		*ň(ë)zét* *ňzeteňë́* *ňzetedī́*[10] *ňzetetré*, etc.
30	*tr̄ðít*[3]	*triðjet*	*triðjét*
40	*di zét*		*dizét*
50	*pɛzëðít*	*pesðjet*	*pes$^{(ë)}$ðjét*
60	*ǵažëðít*[4]	*trezet*	*trezet*
70	*štadðít*	*štatðjet*	*štatðjet*

(Table continued)

	Barile (Potenza)[1]	San Costantino Albanese (Potenza), Lucania[6]	Plàtaci (Cosenza)[8]
80	*katrzέt*		*katrzet*
90	*nëndðít*		*nënd^(ë)ðjet*
100	*ňıḱën* [5]	*ḱind*	*ňḱind*
200	*di ḱën*	*diḱind*	*diḱind*
300	*tri ḱën*		*treḱind*
400	*kátr ḱën*		
1 000	*ňı miĺ*	*miʎ*	*ň^(ë)miʎ*
2 000	*dı miĺ*	*di miʎ*	*di miʎ*
3 000	*tri miĺ*	*tre miʎ*	*tre miʎ*
1 000 000		*miʎun*	
½		*ǵims*[7]	*ǵims-a* (def.)

1. I studied the dialect during a stay of several days in July 1952, and these numerals were collected and checked during a stop in the village in October 1988. I published a diagram of the Barile vowel system in *Language* 34, 1958, 361. My system of ten vowels differs considerably from that of six presented by Martin Camaj in "Zur albanischen Mundart von Barile in der Provinz Potenza", *Dissertationes Albanicae*, München: Trofenik 1971, 127–140, esp. 129–131.
2. The conservation of *trε* in this complex form is important.
3. The attestation of the obviously archaic reduced unstressed syllable with *r*, now questionably syllabic, is highly important.
4. Note the absence, i. e., loss, of the vigesimal here.
5. The form of '100' seems to betray an old reduction in these complexes.
6. I am obliged to my dear friend Martin Camaj for making available to me these materials from the data he will present in his forthcoming work on this important and conservative village. Forms are cited only where they differ from those of Barile. For texts and traditional materials see Enza Scutari, *Plaka rrëfien ...: Vita e storia di una comunità albanese della Lucania attraverso la "voce" della sua gente*, San Costantino Albanese 1987.
7. These and some other forms are from material I collected in 1954 from an elderly emigrant from San Costantino in New York. I have examples for all vowels, including *ë*, showing the opposition of length.
8. This isolated village in northernmost Calabria on the slopes of Monte Pollino bequeaths us a highly conservative distinctive dialect. Leading facts have

been sketched for us by Francesco Solano, *Le parlate albanesi di S. Basile e Plataci*, Quaderni di "Zjarri", San Demetrio Corone 1979. I have collected material on two visits, in June 1956 and October 1988.

9. The vocalism here appears to result from morphological levelling.
10. The clearly audible length here is not functionally clear to me. I simply do not know the Plataci dialect well enough.

	Vaccarizzo Albanese (Cosenza)[1]	Giuseppe de Rada (1871) Macchia (Cosenza)[6]	Ordinals
1	*ňæ*, Mbuzát *ňã* [2]	*njē̱* m.f. marginal *(të)njiij, njē̱je*	*i paar*
2m.	*di*	*di*, gen. *diish*, dat. *dive*	*i diit*
f.	*di*	*dii* *diash* *diave*	
3m.	*tre* [3]	*tre*	*i tret*
f.	*tre* [3]	*trii* (Gir)[7]	
4	*káter*	*catër, kàtēr* (Gir)	
5	*pes*	*pes*, gen. *pessësh*, dat. *pessëve* m.[8] *p'ssash* *pessave* f.	
6	*ǵašt*	*gjasht, gjàšt* (Gir), def. *të gjashta(t)*	
7	*štat*	*shëtat*,[9] *štàt* (Gir)	
8	*tet*	*tet, tèt* (Gir)	
9	*næ*^{n}*d*, Mbuzàt *nãnt* [2]	*nē̱ē̱nt*	
10	*ðjet*	*δièt, të δiettësh*	
11	*ňæ*^{m}*bðjét* ~ *ň*^{m}*bðjét*, Mbuzàt *ňmbëðjét* [2]	*-mbë-δiètë*	
12	*di*^{m}*bðjét*	*-mbë-δièt* (Gir)	*-δiètë*
13	*tre*^{m}*bðjét*		
14	*kater*^{m}*bðjét*		
15	*pes*^{m}*bðjét*		
16	*ǵašt*^{m}*bðjét*		
17	*štat*^{m}*bðjét*		
18	*tet*^{m}*bðjét*		
19	*næ*^{n}*d*^{m}*bðjét*, Mbuzàt *nãndmbë ðjét* [2]		
20	*ňzet*	*një ζét, nē̱ζet* (Gir)	
21	*ňzeteňǽ*, Mbuzàt *ňzeteňã́*		
22	*ňzetedí*		
23	*ňzetetré*		

(Table continued)

	Vaccarizzo Albanese (Cosenza)[1]	Giuseppe de Rada (1871) Macchia (Cosenza)[6]	Ordinals
30	Mbuzàt *treðjet* [4] *tre*^{m}*bðjét* [5]	*triiδiet*	
31	*tre*^{m}*bðjéteňǽ* [5]		
40	*dizet*	*diζét, di ζèt* (Gir)	
50	*dizeteðjét*	*pesëδiét, pesδièt* (Gir)	
60	*trezet*	*treζét, trèζét* (Gir)	
70	*trezeteðjét*		
80	*katerzét*		
90	*katerzéteðjét*		
100	*peszet* ~ *ňḱí*^{n}*d*, Mbuzàt *ňḱint*	*ñë kjint* (Gir)	
200	*diḱí*^{n}*d*	*dì kjint* (Gir)	
300	*treḱí*^{n}*d*, Mbuzàt *tri-* ~ *tre-*		
400	*katerḱí*^{n}*d*		
500	*pesḱí*^{n}*d*		
1 000	*ňmíʎ*	*ñë miilj* (Gir)	
2 000	*dimíʎ*		
3 000	*tremíʎ*, Mbuzàt *tri-*		
1 000 000	*ňmiljún*		
2 000 000	*dimiljún*		
3 000 000	Mbuzàt *trimiljún*		
½	*ǵíms-a* (def.)		

1. This village, of falling population but increasing prosperity over the past 40 years, belongs to the chain of six villages on the right of the river Crati and on the slope of the Sila overlooking the plain of ancient Sybaris. Here the most important Albanian literature of the 19th century took root; the Crati basin is an important focus for Arbëresh culture. Vaccarizziote is the dialect of Albanian I know best; I began studying it in February 1950. I have described the phonology in *Vaccarizzo Albanese phonology: the sound-system of a Calabro-Albanian dialect*, Harvard University PhD dissertation, 1954. I have checked and completed the numerals in June 1989.
2. Mbuzàt = San Giorgio Albanese, the adjacent village to the east. The forms of Mbuzàt are phonetically the same as those of Vaccarizzo except for those indicated. My forms come from a 90-year old in 1989.

3. *tri* was given on a repetition, with the remark that *tre* is Italian.
4. *ňzeteðjét* offered by another Mbuzàt speaker.
5. 13 repeatedly given mistakenly for 30; cf. Portocannone. Perhaps the generalization of *tre* for '3' led to this confusion.
6. Guiseppe de Rada, *Grammatica della lingua albanese*, Firenze 1871 (reprinted Cosenza 1965), the work of an erudite scholar from Macchia, the second village west of Vaccarizzo.
7. Girolamo de Rada, *Caratteri e grammatica della lingua albanese*, Corigliano Càlabro 1894, by the great poet and patriot of the 19th century.
8. Gir (1894): m. gen. *pèssëš*, dat. *péssëve*, abl. *pésseši*
   f. *pessaš* *pessave* *pessaši.*
9. If taken at face value this form is highly important.

	Falconara Albanese (Cosenza)[1]
1	*ňë*
	ň(i) indef.
2m.	*di*
f.	*dī*
3m.f.	tre ~ *tri*
4	*kat·r*
5	*pes*
6	*ǵašt*
7	*štat*
8	*tet*
9	*nënd*
10	*ðiét*
11	*ňḗmbë ðjét* (~ *-ðét* Camaj)
12	*dimbëðjét*
13	*trembëðjét*
14	*kátrbëðjét* [2]
15	*pesmbëðjet*
16	*ǵaštmbëðjet*
17	*štatmbëðjet*
18	*tetmbëðjet*
19	*nëndmbëðjet*
20	*ň(i)zét*
21	*ň(i)zét eňḗ*
30	*ň(i)zét eðjét* [3] ~ *-ðét* (Camaj) ~ *tri-ðjét* (Camaj)
31	*ň(i)zét ðjet eňḗ*, etc.

(Table continued)

	Falconara Albanese (Cosenza)[1]
40	*dizét* ~ *kátrë-ðjét* (Camaj)
50	*dizét eðjét*[4] ~ *pes-ðjét* (Camaj)
60	*trezét* ~ *ǵašt-ðjét* (Camaj)
70	*trezét eðjét*[4] ~ *štat-ðjét* (Camaj)
80	*kátrzét*
90	*kátrzét eðjét*[4] ~ *nënd-ðjét*
100	*peszét*[4] ~ *ňḱind*
200	*duečénd* ~ *diḱínd*
300	*treḱind*
1 000	*ňë-míj* (Camaj)
2 000	*di-míj*
½	*ň(i)ǵíms*

1. I visited this village in October 1988 and June 1989, and I have collated my findings with Martin Camaj, *Die albanische Mundart von Falconara Albanese in der Provinz Cosenza*, München 1977. I discuss my results elsewhere in several articles.
2. Note the cluster reduction in the presence of two sonants.
3. Cf. Mbuzàt (Vaccarizzo, note 4).
4. Cf. Vaccarizzo Albanese.

	San Nicola dell'Alto (Catanzaro)[1]	Àndali (Catanzaro)[3]	Ordinals[5]	Vena di Màida (Catanzaro)[3]
1	*ńo*[2]	*ňë* M.[4] *njeera* m.f. *njare* adj.	*e paarë*	*ňë*
2	*di*	*di*	*e ddiitë*	*di*
3	*tre*	*tre*, M. *tre*[4]	*e trehtë*[6]	*tre*
4	*katr*	*katr*[5], M. *katrh*[4]	*e katrhëttë*[7]	*kátrë*
5	*pes*	*pésë*	*e pesëtë*	*pes*
6	*ǵašt*		*e gjashtëtë*	
7	*štat*		*e shtatëtë*	
8	*tet*			

(Table continued)

	San Nicola dell'Alto (Catanzaro)[1]	Àndali (Catanzaro)[3]	Ordinals[5]	Vena di Màida (Catanzaro)[3]
9	*nond*[2]		*e nandëttë*	
10	*ðiét*	*dhiétë*[5]		
		15 *pesëmbidhiétë*[5]		
20	*ńzet*			
Pallagorio/Puharí (L. Lorecchio) *gjimsa* def.		M.[4] *gjímis* '½'		
		katr heerë[5] '4 times'		

1. I visited San Nicola dell'Alto in March 1961 and again in 1974. I have published a brief phonological sketch in the *Bollettino dell'Atlante Linguistico Mediterraneo* N. 8, 1966, 61–64.
2. In this dialect **ë* regularly merges with *o* under stress.
3. My material for Àndali comes from a brief visit in March 1961. That journey also included Vena. The forms marked M are from Marcedusa in the Catanzaro area.
4. From G. Gangale, *Glossarium Arberiscum Marcidusiae*, Arberisca III, København 1977; and Arberisca IV, 1979.
5. From G. Gangale, *Fialja e Andalit*, Gluha 3, Hafniae (København): Munksgaard, 1964 [short texts in an idiosyncratic orthography, with brief notes on forms].
6. The spelling with *h* is unclear to me; perhaps cf. Piana.
7. *rh* represents the strong *rr*.

	San Marzano (Tàranto)[1]	Pre-form[3]
1	*ňë*	**ňə*
2	*di*	*di*
3	*tre*	*tre*
4	*káttrə*	*kátrə*
5	*péssə*	*pésə*
6	*ǵáštə*	*ǵáštə*
7	*štáttə*	*štátə*
8	*téttə*	*tétə*
9	*nḗndə*	*nə́ndə*

(Table continued)

	San Marzano (Tàranto)[1]	Pre-form[3]
10	*tiéttə*	*ðiétə*
20	*ditiéttə*	*diðiétə*
30	*trediét(ə)*[2]	*treðiét(ə)*
100	*ňë ḱində*	*ňə ḱind*

1. This is the last surviving Albanian-speaking village in the Apulian region; the dialect is, if taken together with Mandrìtsa and Mándres, one of the two most strikingly divergent varieties of Albanian in existence. I visited San Marzano and collected material in June 1956; I described the most remarkable aspects of the phonology in *Papers from the Fourth Annual Regional Meeting of the Chicago Linguistic Society*, 1968, 103–110. I discussed a sizeable sample of San Marzano data in relation to earlier work in "On Bonaparte and the Neogrammarians as field workers", chapter 16 in *Studies in the history of linguistics: Traditions and paradigms,* ed. Dell Hymes, Bloomington: Indiana 1974, 390–433. Since that time there has appeared Leonardo M. Savoia, "La parlata albanese di S. Marzano di S. Giuseppe: appunti fonologici e morfologici", *Zjarri* (San Demetrio Corone) 12, No. 27, 1981, 8–26.
2. This form is from Hanusz (1889) and Meyer (1890). They provide also other decad numerals but they are not of interest to us in furnishing additional testimony other than reflections of contact with the adjacent Italian.
3. These reconstructions observe the rules which I have formulated for gemination of intersonant consonants and the addition of *-ə* in word-final.

	Piana degli Albanesi (Palermo)[1]			Ordinals	Matrënga[7]
1	*një,*[2] marginal	*nji*		*i, e par*	*të parënë*
2	*di*	*dive*		*dit*	*të dijtënë*
3m.[3]	*tre*	*treve*, def.	*të tre*	*tret*	*të tretënë*
f.[3]	*tri*	*trive*	*të tria*		
4	*katr* Matrënga:[7]	*katër*		*kart*[4]	*i katërti*
5	*pes*	*pesë*		etc.[5]	*i pesti*
6	*gjasht* CE *jašt*				
7	*shtat*	*shtatë*			
8	*tet*	*tetë*			
9	*nönd* CE *nënd*				
10	*dhjet*	*dhjetë*			

(Table continued)

	Piana degli Albanesi (Palermo)[1]	Ordinals	Matrënga[7]
11	*njm(b)ëdhjet* CE *njëmbë-*		
12	*di-* *dimbëdhjetë*		
13m.	*tre-*		*i trem-bëdhjeti*
f.	*tri-*		
14	*katrë-* CE *katr̂mbë-*		
15	*pesë-* CE *pes-* def. *të pesë mbëdhjetë* 'the 15'		
16	*gjashtë-* CE *jašt-*		
17	*shtatë-*		
18	*tetë-*		
19	*nöndë-*		
20	*njëzet*		
21	*njëzet e një*, etc.		
30	*tridhjet* CE *treðjet*		
40	*dizet*		
50	*pesdhjet* ~ *dizet e dhjet*[6] CE *ǵims-ḱindje*		
60	*gjashtdhjet* ~ *trizet*[6] CE *trezet*		
61	*trizet e një*		
70	*shtatdhjet* ~ *trizet e dhjet*[6] CE *set-tanta*		
71	*shtatdhjet e një*		
80	*katrëzet* CE *katr-zet*		*katër zet*
90	*nön(d)dhjet* ~ *katrëzet e dhjet*[6]		
91	*nön(d)dhjet e një*		
100	*një qint* CE *një ḱind ḱind*		*një kjin(d) (chijn)*
101	*një qint e një*		
200	*di qint*		
300	*tri qint*		
1 000	*njëmijë*		
2 000	*dimijë*		
3 000	*trimijë*		
1 000 000	*njëmiliun*		

Distributives: *një e një* '1 by 1', etc.

1. This large and well-known Arbëresh village, certainly the predominant and most vigorously surviving settlement in Sicily, has produced notable scholars and literary figures. Settled by an emigration from the Pelopónnesos, it dates from slightly later than many other Arbëresh villages. Though I have on occasion observed Piana speech since 1950, I have not worked seriously on the dialect, and visited Piana only in 1988, because many others have studied it, and continue to do so, while I considered my efforts more needed in neglected areas.
   The forms presented here are from the manuscript *Grammatica* by Antonino Guzzetta in the possession of Martin Camaj and commented on by Camaj, both of whom I thank heartily for these valuable data. One should consult also A. Guzzetta, *La parlata di Piana degli Albanesi* I: *Fonologia*, Palermo 1978.
   I have also had the opportunity to collect the numerals up to 100, as well as some other diagnostic forms, from Contessa Entellina (CE), Prov. Palermo, diocese of Monreale, on the occasion of a visit to New Orleans (2 December 1990), where a considerable colony of Contessioti established itself a century ago. I am indebted to the kindness of Mr Bret Clesi for this valuable opportunity. For an account of CE see Alessandro Schirò, *Guida illustrata delle colonie albanesi di Sicilia: Contessa Entellina,* Palermo: Di Carlo [1924 †], in which the New Orleans emigration finds mention (p. 9). CE forms are listed below in instances where they diverge from Piana forms.
2. *ë* in Piana is a relatively low vowel.
3. Distinguished among old and cultivated speakers.
4. Showing dissimilation and interference from the Italian form.
5. With absorption of *-t* in forms terminating in *t*.
6. We have here the productive development of two systems, as Camaj and Guzzetta have observed. From CE I record *katrzet e ðjet*.
7. These forms from L. Matrënga (1560–1619), of Piana, are taken from the compilation of Matteo Sciambra, *La Dottrina cristiana' albanese di Luca Matranga*, Città del Vaticano 1964.

17.3. The reconstruction of Common Albanian

When we believe a group of dialects or languages to be genetically related we may, by employing well known (or much discussed and invoked) criteria and methods, formulate a reconstruction. When in a genetic family a number of such groups are believed to be traceable each to a separate node in the stemma, an equivalent number of independent reconstructions is possible. For well segregated speech communities such a Stammbaum model is feasible and yields productive and consistent results. For intercommunicating dialects or for descendants of unclear past association dialectology has taught us that such a Stammbaum model requires serious modification, or at least supplementation. Besides, Albanian dialectology is now only in its beginnings; it is still in the first phases of basic inventorizing, and that task of salvage is not yet reasonably completed.

We cannot therefore construct a proper stemma for the varieties of Albanian. For our present task I therefore employ two methods. For those varieties which I can reasonably trace to an independent node I offer a reconstruction. For those for which I have no such clear discreteness I assemble manageable and partly intuitive groups and offer an inference.

By working back (and forwards) through these two we reach a reconstruction for all of Albanian.

As a means of reducing the multiplicity of form and of bringing our problem into a range which we may intelligibly grasp, I now offer a number of inferences based on a large part of the data presented above:

Inference I: Blanchus, Buzuku, and Da Lecce.
Inference II: Bogdan, Shala, Dushmani, Gusî, Tuzi, and Arbanasi, to which the material from Kosovë and also Tetovë may also be joined.
Inference III: The Arbëresh dialects of Greci, Portocannone, Barile, San Costantino Albanese, Plàtaci, Vaccarizzo Albanese, Mbuzàt (San Giorgio Albanese), Macchia (i. e. the two de Radas), Falconara Albanese, San Nicola dell'Alto, Pallagarío, Àndali, Marcedusa, Vena di Màida.
Inference IV: The Arbëresh dialects of San Marzano di San Guiseppe and Piana degli Albanesi with Contessa Entellina.

I further reckon with additional inferences:

V: The Arvanítika dialects of Greece;
VI: the remainder of the Tosk data given;

but these will not require elaborate and explicit separate tabulation as in the case of the first four.

I. We may infer from Blanchus, Buzuku, and Da Lecce the following elements and complexes.

	Cardinals	Ordinals
1	**ňâ, ňân-i -a*	*i, e pár-i -a*
	ňë (unstressed)	
2m.	*dy*	*dý̄t-i -a*
f.	*dȳ, të dya*	
3m.	*tre*	*trét-i -a*
f.	*trī*	
cpd.	*tër-* (unstressed)	
4	*kátërë*	*kátërt-i -a*
cpd.	*katër-*	
5	*pésë*	*pést-i -a*
6	*ǵáštë*	*ǵášt-i*
7	*štátë*	*štát-i*
8	*tétë*	*tét-i*
9	*nândë*	*nând-i*
10	*ðietë*	*ðiet-i*
11	*ňë (ë)mbë-ðietë*	*i, e ňë(ë)mbë-ðiet-i -a*
12	*dȳ̆ ëmbë-ðietë*	
13	*tre (ë)mbë-ðietë*	
15	*pesë ëmbë(-)ðietë*	*i pest-i ëmbë-ðietë*
17		*i štat-i ëmbë-ðietë*
20	*ňë-zet*	
30	*trī(-)ðietë*	
40	*katër-ðietë*	
50	*pesë(-)ðietë*	
60	*ǵaštë ðietë*	
70	*štatë ðietë*	
80	*tetë ðietë*	
90	*nândë ðietë*	
100	*ňë-ḱind*	
200	*dy(-)ḱind*	
300	*tre(-)ḱind*	
400	*katër(-)ḱind*	
500	*pesë(-)ḱind*	
600	*ǵaštë ḱind*	*të ǵaštënë ḱind* (acc. sg.)
700	*štatë ḱind*	
800	*tetë ḱind*	

(Table continued)

	Cardinals	Ordinals
1 000	*ňë mijë*	
2 000	*dȳ mijë*	
4 000	*katër mijë*	
5 000	*pesë mijë*	
6 000	*ǵaštë mijë*	
7 000	*štatë mijë*	
10 000	*ðietë mijë*	
½	*ǵýmsë* f.	
	trī, pésë, štátë hérë '3, 5, 7 times'	
	kaa + Numeral 'Distributive x by x, by x – s'	

II. We infer from Bogdan, Shala, Dushmani, Gusî, Tuzi, and Arbanasi the following elements and complexes. The data from Kosovë and from Tetovë appear to fit within this inferential set.

	Cardinals	Ordinals
1	**ňâ, ňân-i -a* [1]	*i, e pár-i -a*
	ňi, i (unstressed)	
2m.	*dy, të dy(-të)*	*dȳ́t-i* [2] *-a*
f.	*dȳ, të dýja(-të), dȳš*	
3m.	*tre, të tre(-të)*	*trét-i -a*
f.	*trī, të tríja(-të), trīš*	
4	*kátër, kátëra,* m. *të kátër(-të)*	*kā́tërt-i -a*
	f. *të kát(ë)ra(-të)*	
5	*pêsë*	*pêsët-i -a*
6.	*ʒ́áštë*	*ʒ́áštët-i* [3] *-a*
7	*štátë*	*štátët-i -a*
8	*tétë*	*tétët-i -a*
9	*nântë ∼ nândë* [4]	*nândët-i -a*
10	*ðietë* [5]	? *ðíetët-i* [6] *-a*
11	*ňim(b)ëð(j)ét* [7]	
12	*dym(b)ëð(j)ét*	
13	*trem(b)ëð(j)ét*	
14	*kátërm(b)ëð(j)ét*	
15	*pêsëm(b)ëð(j)ét*	

(Table continued)

	Cardinals	Ordinals
16	*ǯá štëm(b)ëð(j)ét*	
17	*štátëm(b)ëð(j)ét*	
18	*tétëm(b)ëð(j)ét*	
19	*nân(d)ëm(b)ëð(j)ét*	
20	*ňizét* ~ *izét*	*ňizét(ë)t-i -a*
21	*izét e ňi*	
30	*trīðí etë* ?, *trið(j)ét* ?	
40	*kátër* +	
50	*pêsë* +	
60	*ǯáštë* +	
70	*štátë* (–)	
80	*tétë* +	
90	*nân(d)ë* +	
100	*ňi ćind* ~ *ićínd*	
200	*dy(-)ćind*	
300	*tre(-)ćind*	
1 000	*ňi mijë* ~ *imíjë*	
2 000	*dȳ mijë*	
3 000	*trī mijë*	
½	*i-ǯý së*	
	ňi, dȳ, trī, hérë '1, 2, 3 time(s)'	

1. This leaves Arbanasi *ńáj* unaccounted for in detail. Modern Kosovë shows *ňi* depalatalized, as does Tetovë also.
2. Note Shala and Bogdan for length. Presumably Dushmani has absorbed the length by the open-syllable rule.
3. Presumably in Dushmani after loss of internal *ë* the vowel was shortened before the heavy consonant cluster.
4. The form with *d* is inferred from Bogdan's ordinal and from Tetovë. It is not clear whether the pre-form in all cases had *t* or *d*.
5. Arbanasi and Shala are important here; Arbanasi very much so for the nature of the diphthong (cf. Arbanasi *díeli* 'the sun'). Shala shows a diagnostic contrast with '8'. The final *-ë* will account for the lengthening in Gusî and Tuzi.
6. Bogdan is ambiguous here. The form is reconstructed by inferred rule.
7. For the final syllable note especially Qosaj, Tuzi, and Arbanasi.

III. We infer the following for Arbëresh on the basis of the data presented, apart from San Marzano and 16th century Piana.

	Cardinals	Ordinals
1	**ňë*, def. *ňë̄́r-i* [1] m. *-a* f.	*i pār* [2]
	ňi (indef. & unstressed)	
	marginal *(të)ňīj*, *ňë́je*, *ňë́ja*	
2m.	*di*, gen. *dīš*, dat. *dive*	*i dīt* [2]
f.	*dī* *diaš* *diave*	
3m.	*tre*	*i tret*
f.	*trī*	
4	*kátër*, *kátr(ë)* [3]	*e kátrëtë* [4]
5	*pes* [6], gen. *pésëš*, dat. *pésëve*, abl. *pésëši* m.	
	pésaš *pésave* *pésaši* f. [5]	*e pésëtë* [4]
6	*ǵašt*	*e ǵáštëtë* [4]
7	*š(ë)tát*	*e štátëtë* [4]
8	*tet*	
9	*në̄nd*	*e në́ndë të* [4]
10	*ðjet*, gen. *ðjétëš*; *ðíet* [7]	
11	*ňë-mbë-ðjét(ë)*	*-ðjétë*
12	*di-mbë-ðjét(ë)*	
13	*tre-mbë-ðjét(ë)*	
20	*ňëzét*	
21	*ňëzéteňë* ~ *eňë́*	
	etc.	
30	*tër-ðjét* [8] ~ *trī ðjet* [9]	
40	*dizét*	
50	*pes(ë)ðjét* [10]	
60	*trezét* [10]	
70	*štat(ë)ðjét* [10]	
80	*kátrëzét* [10]	
90	*nënd(ë)ðjét* [10]	
100	*ňëḱind* ~ *-ḱënd* [8] (?)	
200	*di(-)ḱind*	
300	*tre(-)ḱind* [11]	
1 000	*ňë mīʎ*	
½	*ǵímës* [12]	

1. The length is from Marcedusa.
2. The length is from de Rada and Àndali.
3. On the basis of the Catanzaro dialects and Falconara.
4. On the Àndali evidence.
5. Such gendered stems seem to have been possible in the nominalized syntax of an indefinite range of numerals.
6. Gangale reports *peesu* from Àndali, with a long *ē*.
7. On the basis of Portocannone; see also note 2 there.
8. On the basis of Barile.
9. See especially de Rada.
10. Guaranteed by Plataci, Portocannone, and the units and ordinals of Greci.
11. Guaranteed by Plataci.
12. On the basis of Marcedusa.

IV. Now if we pool our data from San Marzano and Piana degli Albanesi with Contessa Entellina we arrive at the following elements and complexes.

	Cardinals			Ordinals
1	**ňë*, marginal case	*ňi*		*të párënë* (acc. sg.)
2	*di* [1]	*díve*		*të dī́tënë*
3m.	*tre*	*tréve*; def.	*të tre*	*të trétënë*
f.	*tri* [1]	*tríve;*	*tëtría* [1]	
4	*kátër, kátrë*			*i kátërt-i*
5	*pése* [1]			*i pést-i*
6	*ǵáštë*			
7	*štátë*			
8	*tétë*			
9	*nḗndë*			
10	*ðjétë*			
11	*ňëmbëðjétë* [2]			
12	*dimbëðjétë*			
13m.	*tre-*			*i trembëðjéti* [4]
f.	*tri-*			
14	*kátrë mbëðjétë* [4]			
15	def. *të pésë mbëðjétë* [4]			
20	*ňëzét*			
21	*ňëzét e ňë* [3]			
30	*triðjét(ë)* [1,5]			

(Table continued)

	Cardinals	Ordinals
40	*dizét*	
50	*pes(ë)ðjet(ë)* [6] ~ *ǵimës ḱindje*[6]	
60	*tre-zet* [6, 7]	
70	*štat(ë)ðjet(ë)* [6]	
80	*kátër zét* [4]	
90	*nënd(ë)ðjet(ë)* [6] ~ *kátër zét e ðjétë*	
100	*ňë ḱind* [8]	

The above tabulation suffers from the known difficulties of a two-member comparison.

1. Remember that San Marzano and modern Piana give us no information on vowel length.
2. The status and reality of the *-ë* is not at all as certain as we should like.
3. This is only an approximate inference.
4. The junctural phenomena are interesting to note.
5. Outside knowledge has been used here to choose *tri-*.
6. Here we use the evidence of the unit complexes, as well as invoking Meillet's rule of "irregularity", which is really a special case of the *lectio difficilior*.
7. The combining form *tri-*, found also in '300', has probably been propagated in Piana from the lower, and hence more salient, numeral '30'.
8. The higher numerals of Piana furnish us no additional information.

Because I have long been convinced of the close genetic relation of Arbëresh and Arvanítika, and on grounds other than the numerals, I will now provide a reconstruction for these based on inferences III and IV and on inference V, which can easily be extracted from the tabulations for Salamís with Reinhold and for Sophikò with Kaskavélji (Λεοντάρι). We may call that reconstruction SOUTHERNMOST TOSK:

	Cardinals	Ordinals
1	*ňë; indef. unstressed *ňi* marginal *(të)ňīj, ňë́je, ňë́ja* def. m. *ňë́r-i*, acc. *ňë́në* f. *ňë́r-a,* *ňë́r-ënë*, marg. *ňë́së*	*i párë*, def. *i, e pár-i -a*

(Table continued)

	Cardinals	Ordinals
2m.	*di*; nominal. *të-dí*, gen. *dīš*, dat. *dive*	*i, e dī́t-i -a*
f.	*dī; të-dī́a, dī́aš,*[1] *dī́ave*	
3m.	*tre; të-tré, tréve*	*i, e trét-i -a*
f.	*trī; të-trī́a, trī́ve*[2]	
4	*kátrë, kátër*; m. *të-kátr-ë*, f. *-a*	*i kátrëtë, i, e kátrët-i -a*
5	*pésë*	*i pés(ë)të*[3], *i pésët-i*
6	*ǵáštë*	*i ǵášt(ët)ë*[3]
7	*š(ë)tátë*[4]	*i štát(ët)ë*[3]
8	*tétë*	*i tét(ët)ë*[3], etc.
9	*nḗndë*	*i nḗndëtë*
10	*ðjétë, ðíet*	
11	*ňë(-)mbë-ðjet(ë) ~ ňë-m(b)jet(ë)*[5]	
12	*di(-)*	
13	*tre(-)*	
14	4 (–)	
20	*ňëzét*	
30	*trīðjét(ë) ~ tërðjét(ë)*	
40	*dizét*	
50	*pesë(-)ðjét(ë)* (~ ½ of 100?)	
60	*tre(-)zét*	
70	*štátë ðjétë*	
80	*kátrë(-)zét, kátër* +	
90	*nḗndë ðjétë* (80 *e* 10?)	
100	*ňë(-)ḱind*	
200	*di(-)ḱind*	
300	*tre(-)ḱind*	
1 000	*ňë(-)miʎë*	
2 000	*di(-)miʎë*	
3 000	*tri(-)miʎë*	
½	*ǵimësë* f.	

Multiples: x(-)*hérë*
Distributives: x(*e*)x ~ ^{n}*ga* x

1. Perhaps the *-a* was generalized in the feminine to disambiguate the gender in such an oblique case as this.
2. On the basis of Piana, thus motivating note 1.
3. We will ignore henceforth these haplologies or syncopes between voiceless obstruents in the ordinals, which especially affected the decads and which must have given rise to duplicate formation rules for the ordinals. No doubt the situation arose because of ambiguity in function between dental terminals and suffixes with reduced (neutralized) vocalisms. The outcome with '5th' resulted from the creation of an especially acceptable cluster.
4. It is quite possible that the form with *šët-* lived on in a marginal way with conservative speakers, while the allegro form reflecting the devoicing from the obstruents bestowed a productivity on *št-* which conformed to the phonotactics of initial clusters. I have from Lakonía and Triphylía Arvanítika the invaluable form *e šëtúnë* 'Saturday', which is normally *e shtunë.*
5. The teens give the appearance of having been rebuilt at some time.

We will now consider the material united under inference VI (Ohrid, Villa Badessa, Mandrìtsa, Ukraine, and Kristoforidhi's Elbasan) in relation to Southernmost Tosk, whereby we reach a reconstruction of the elements and complexes of PROTO-TOSK at a time depth approximating the end of the first millennium AD.

	Cardinals		Ordinals	
1	**ňë*;[1] unstressed *ňi* marginal *(të) ňīj, ňë́j-* def. m. *ňë̄́r-i*,[1] acc. *ňë̄́-në* f. *ňë̄́r-a,*	 *ňë̄́r-ënë*, marg. *ňë̄́së*	*i párë*, def.	*i, e pár-i -a*
2m.	*dy*; nominal.	*të-dý*, gen. *dȳš*		*i, e dȳ́t-i -a*
f.	*dȳ*	*të-dȳ́ja*		
3m.	*tre;*	*të-tré*		
f.	*trī*	*të-trī́a*		*i, e trét-i -a*
4	*kátrë, kátër;*	m. *të-kátr-ë*, f. *-a*	*i kátrëtë*	*i, e kátrët-i -a*
5	*pésë* [2]	m *të-pés-ë*, f. *-a*	*i pésëtë*	*i, e pésët-i -a*
6	*ǵáštë*		*i ǵášt(ët)ë*	*i, e ǵášt(ët)-i -a*
7	*š(ë)tátë*		*i štát(ët)ë*	
8	*tétë*		*i tét(ët)ë*	
9	*nḗndë*,[3] *nḗntë*		*i nën(dë)të*	
10	*ðjétë, ðíet(ë)* [4]		*i ðjétë* [6]	
11	*ňë(-)mbë-ðjet(ë)* [5]		*i -ðjétë*	

(Table continued)

	Cardinals	Ordinals
12	*dy(-)*	
13	*tre(-)*	
20	*ňëzét*	*i ňëzétë*
21		*i ňëzét e ňḗjtë*
30	*trī ðjétë* ~ *tërðjét*	*i triðjétë*
40	*dyzét*	*i dyzétë*
50	*pesë(-)ðjétë*	*i pesëðjétë*
60	*tre(-)zét*	
70	*štátë ðjétë*	
80	*kátrë(-)zét*	
90	*nḗndë ðjétë, nḗntë* +	
100	*ňë(-)ḱind*	
200	*dy(-)ḱind*	
300	*tre(-)ḱind*	
1 000	*ňë(-)miʎë*	
2 000	*dȳ(-)miʎë*	
3 000	*trī(-)miʎë*	
½	*ǵýmësë* f.	

Distributives: (x) *nga* x

1. The correlation of length with gender in this numeral in Elbasan must be an innovation.
2. Note the short *e*. It seems to be a regularity that an original nasal vowel of early date in position before a spirant gives a common Tosk short vowel. Cf. Sophikò *gʎúxë* 'tongue', with simple short *u*, < Southernmost Tosk **gluhë* = Tetovë *gûh* < **dlunhë* < **dl̥ńǵhu̯ā*; for detail on this etymon see my article in *Studia Linguistica et Orientalia Memoriae Haim Blanc Dedicata*, edd. P. Wexler, A. Borg, and S. Somekh, Wiesbaden 1989, 121–124.
3. Note that *nḗndë* is assured by Southernmost Tosk and by Villa Badessa. It is possible that this could be derived from an earlier **nḗntë* by contact interference from neighbouring Greek.
4. The forms of '10' are extremely difficult. There are clearly two treatments of the diphthong. Then *je* seems to have been reduced to *e*. But *íe* appears to have yielded divergent reductions, and to this I credit Ohrid *ē*.

5. It seems likely that the teens did not originally have *-ë*. The form would then have been **-ðjet*.
6. From here on the ordinals are based on Kristoforidhi.

Next, we reconstruct the elements and complexes of PROTO-GEG by comparing our South Geg specimen with the results of inferences I and II.

	Cardinals		Ordinals
1	**ňâ*; unstressed *ňë, ňi* [1]		*i, e pár-i -a*
	proclitic *i*		
	def. m. *ňân-i,* f. *ňân-a*		
2m.	*dy*; nominal	*te-dý(-të)*	
		gen. dat. *dýve*, abl. *dyš*	*i, e dȳ́t-i -a*
f.	*dȳ;*	*të-dýja(-të),* *dȳš*	
3m.	*tre;*	*të-tré(-të)*	*i, e trét-i -a*
f.	*trī*	*të-tríja(-të)*, abl. *trīš*	
cpd.	*tër-* (unstressed)		
4	*kátër(ë), kátëra*; m. *të-kátër*, f. *-a*		*i, e kắtërt-i -a*
cpd.	*katër-*		*kátr-i* [2] *-a*
5	*pêsë*		*i, e pêsët-i* [4] *-a*
6	*ǵáštë*		*i, e ǵášt(ët)-i* [4] *-a*
7	*štátë*		*i, e štát(ët)-i* [4] *-a*
8	*tétë*		*i, e tét(ët)-i* [4] *-a*
9	*nândë,* [3] *nântë*		*i, e nând(ët)-i* [4] *-a*
10	*ðietë*		? *i, e ðiet(ët)-i -a*
11	*ňë (ë)m(b)ë- ð(j)ét* [5]		*i, e -ð(j)ét-i -a*
12	*dȳ̆* +		
13	*tre* +		
15	*pêsë* +		
17	*štátë* + [5]		*i štát(ët)-i*
			ëm(b)ë-ð(j)ét
19	*nân(d)ë* + [6]		
20	*ňëzét* ~ *izét*		*i ňëzétët-i*
21	*izét e ňâ*		
30	*trī ðietë, trið(j)ét?*		
40	*katër-ðiete, dyzét* [7]		

(Table continued)

	Cardinals	Ordinals
50	*pêsë(-)ðietë*	
60	*ǵáštë ðietë*	
70	*štátë ðietë*[8]	
80	*tétë ðietë*	
90	*nân(d)ë ðietë*	
100	*ňë(-)ḱínd ~ iḱínd*	
200	*dy(-)ḱínd*	
300	*tre(-)ḱínd*	
600	*ǵáštë ḱínd*	*të ǵášt(ët)ënë ḱínd* (acc. sg.)
1 000	*ňë míjë*	
2 000	*dȳ míjë*	
3 000	*trī míjë*	
½	*ǵýmësë* f.	
(¼)	*čerék*)[9]	

Multiples: *ňë, dȳ, trī, pêsë, štátë hérë* '1, 2, 3, 5, 7 time(s)'
dy-fijš -i, tre-fijš -i 'double, triple'.

Distributives: x *nga* x, *kā* x

1. This vocalism, provoked by the lack of stress and the presence of the palatal consonant, may then have been restressed.
2. This appears to be an analogical short stem formed on the model of the numerals in *-t* as seen in South Geg.
3. South Geg is particularly instructive here.
4. In South Geg because of the shortened vowels in '6th', '7th', and '8th', as well as in the consonantism of *nânti*, we must see the former presence of the suffix found in **ǵáštëti* etc.
5. Note the probable accentuation in these complexes.
6. With probable cluster reduction.
7. The South Geg evidence may reflect diffusion from Tosk.
8. It is difficult to say how rapidly the unification of these phrases proceeded.
9. It is not clear what, if anything, this lexeme borrowed from Turkish *çeyrek* replaced.

We are now in a position to reconstruct the recoverable elements and complexes of Common Albanian by comparing our results for Proto-Tosk and Proto-Geg.

	Cardinals	Ordinals
1	**ňâ*, unstressed *ňë* → *ňi*	*i párë*, def. *i, e pár-i -a*
	marginal *(të) ňīj, ňâj-*[1]	
	proclitic *i*	
	def. m. *ňân-i*, acc. *ňân-në*	
	f. *ňân-a* *ňân-ëňë*, marg. *ňâ-së*	
2m.	*dy*; nominal. *të-dý(-të)*, gen. abl. *dȳš*	*i, e dȳ́t-i -a*
f.	*dȳ* *të-dȳ́ja(-të),* *dȳš*	
3m.	*tre;* *të-tré(-të)*	*i, e trét-i -a*
f.	*trī* *të-trī-a(-të)*, abl. *trīš*	
cpd.	*tër-́*	
4	*kátër(ë), kátëra*; m. *të-kátr-ë*, f. *-a*	*i, e kắtërt-i -a*
		kátrët-i -a
cpd.	*katër-*	
5	*pêsë*[2] *të-pêsë*	*i, e pêsët-i -a*
6	*ǵáštë*	*i, e ǵášt(ët)-i -a*
7	*š(ë)tátë*	*i, e štát(ët)-i -a*
8	*tétë*	*i, e tét(ët)-i -a*
9	*nândë, nântë*	*i, e nând(ët)-i -a*
10	*ðietë*	*i, e ðjét(ët)-i -a*
11	*ňë (ë)m(b)ë-ðjét*	*i, e -ðjét-i -a*
12	*dy*	
13	*tre*	
15	*pêsë*	
17	*štátë*	*i štát(ët)-i ëm(b)ë-ðjét*
19	*nândë*	
20	*ňëzét ~ izét*	*i ňëzét(ët)-i*
21	*izét e ňâ*	*i ňëzét e ňâjtë*
30	*trī ðietë, tërðjét*	*i triðjétë*
40	*dyzét*	*i dyzét(ët)-i*
50	*pêsë(-)ðietë*	*i pêsëðjétë*
60	*tre(-)zét*	

(Table continued)

	Cardinals	Ordinals
70	*štátë ðietë*	
80	*kátrë(-)zét*	
90	*nândë ðietë, nântë +*	
100	*ñë(-)ḱind ~ iḱind*	
200	*dy(-)ḱind*	
300	*tre(-)ḱind*	
600	*ǵáštë ḱind*	*të ǵášt(ët)ëñë ḱind* (acc. sg.)
1 000	*ñë miʎë*	
2 000	*dȳ miʎë*	
3 000	*trī miʎë*	
½	*ǵýmësë* f.	

Multiples: *ñë, dȳ, trī, pêsë, štátë hérë* '1, 2, 3, 5, 7 time(s)'
dy-fiλ(ë)š -i, tre-fiλ(ë)š -i 'double, triple'

Distributives: (x) *ngā* x, *kā* x

1. This will explain the troublesome Arbanasi form.
2. We have already remarked that the Tosk outcome is a short vowel. Note also that Tosk does not here show *ë* in correspondence with Geg *ê*, and that only North Geg shows *ê* in such words as this. In short, the nasality in this category of forms disappeared early enough through South Geg and Tosk to leave the modern forms of these areas unaffected by this nasalization.

17.4. Meyer's study

Gustav Meyer's *Albanesische Studien* II: *Die albanesischen Zahlwörter*, Sitzungsberichte der phil.-historischen Classe der Kaiserlichen Akademie der Wissenschaften (Wien) 107, 1884, 259–338, esp. 264 ff., was really a preliminary pioneering study in the comparative-historical accounting for Albanian phonology on Neogrammarian principles. It is therefore convenient as well as instructive to discuss the main features of Meyer's analysis in one place, rather than scattered among the other commentary. We take up matters in the order of his argument:

'20': *$\acute{k}$ is stated to yield *s*, and then is voiced (somehow) to *z* (279). Pedersen later clarified and corrected these general Lautgesetze. An initial *$v\bar{\imath}$ is discussed (280) inconclusively. The outcome of *$\mathring{n}$ is thought to be *e* (281); this erroneous formulation persists as recently as M. Huld, *KZ* 98, 1985, 101.

'2' is discussed 282–299, and at 283 attested forms (NB de Rada's) are presented. 284–297 is occupied with the problem of a reflex *d* vs. *ð*; here we find many examples, and a prelude to *Albanesische Studien* III. Finally (297), Meyer could not find a rule; we will see that this problem waited until Cimochowski for the principles of a solution. The question of *u* vs. *ü* is discussed 297–299. In the end Meyer has no result. He debates whether the form is of Proto-Indo-European or of Latin origin; in my view, entertaining a Latin origin here violates the principle in comparison of continuity as the first assumption.

'3': Meyer gives forms (299–300), of which only Kristoforidhi's are clear. He rightly observes (300) that the feminine cannot be descended from Proto-Indo-European and that we must have an old neuter, but his formulation **tria* > *trię* is incorrect. Meyer refers to *Albanesische Studien* I 99; one may now consult my analysis, *Romance Philology* 12, 1958, 147–155. Again he violates the principle of the assumption of continuity when he vacillates between a Proto-Indo-European and a Latin source.

'4': The matter is left inconclusive whether we have *-ër* or *-rë* (301). It is then decided (301–302) that the form cannot be inherited because of the lack of **e*, and that it must be Latin in origin. Von Harff's *quater* is taken naïvely as proof.

'5': Good forms are offered (303), but it is believed that *s* cannot reflect *k^w; this was of course later refuted by Pedersen. As a consequence *-sę* is taken (303–306) as *-*ti̯*-, and the numeral is reconstructed as **penkti-*. The discussion (307) on Slavic anticipates Szemerényi, but also assumes the existence of *-ti-* forms. Thus the Albanian is held (308) to be as in Slavic. The *-sę* is explained as in *besę*, but on the latter see now Hamp, *KZ* 77, 1961, 252–253, and *Živa Antika* 35, 1985, 85–86. There then follows an inconclusive discussion (308–312) of nasal vowels.

'6': 312–313 opens with an exposition of the difficulty in establishing the Proto-Indo-European form. Meyer then settles (313) on **seks* for Balto-Slavic, Germanic, Latin, and Albanian. He then (313–314) removes *-te̥*, leaving *ǵas-*, with loss of k_1, before *s*. A long section (314–320) follows on the sources of *ǵ*; this analysis is later superseded by Pedersen.

'7': Meyer registers the attested forms (320), including Arbëresh with *-e̥-* (cf. our own data and commentary). Then he discusses (320–321) the assumed Indo-European accentuation, for which Albanian would support Vedic and Greek on Osthoff's formulation. However, after this commendable approach Meyer (321) concludes that Arbëresh *e̥* is not original to the first part of the word, since then an initial *ǵ-* (*gj-*) would be expected; but of course Pedersen's later formulation depending on the Indo-European accent successfully explains the observed phenomena and rescues what might have been Meyer's reconstruction. Meyer is needlessly puzzled (322) by the vocalism *a*, since he expects *e* from syllabic nasal. But most others (except V. I. Georgiev) have been similarly misled or else inattentive. Meyer suggests an *a* from the influence of '6'. This is unnecessary, but there is also no guarantee that the diphthong *i̯a* of '6' was of the correct chronology to affect the simple syllabic *a* of '7'.

'8': Meyer's account is nearly correct. He assumes (322) a loss of the first syllable from Tonlosigkeit; that may well be, but the reduction and then complete loss is regular for first syllables (unaccented at a particular, post-Roman time) only when the vowel, which is not *u-*, was initial. Meyer looked for **as-*; but that is unnecessary since **ḱt* reduced regularly to *-t-*, cf. *dritë* 'light' < **driḱtā* < **driḱti-* (f.) < **dr̥ḱ-ti-* (f.), or < **driti-* (f.) < **driḱti-* (f.) < **dr̥ḱ-ti-* (f.).

'9': After presenting the known forms (322–323), Meyer doubts Kristoforidhi's *ne̥nte̥* and invokes the Lautgesetz giving a voiced obstruent in nasal clusters (323–324). Meyer did not realize that we have here a more complex situation. He thought that Piana *ne̥ne̥te̥* '9th' must be a dissimilative result (!), but his entire discussion (324–325) is based on outmoded views of Proto-Indo-European '9'. Meyer also thought needlessly that Geg *â* is not a normal development.

'10': This is the most difficult numeral in Albanian, from the point of view of multiplicity of forms and situations in the system, of dialect variants, and of possible Indo-European sources. It is not surprising, then, that Meyer did not get very far with its solution. He presents the forms he had (325–326), and rehearses older sources, *ðjetë, ðietë, ðiét* (de Rada), *ðet(ë)* (Geg), but he did not possess enough dialect material to see the distribution accurately. He considered the reconstructed Proto-

Indo-European forms (326), but was puzzled by the seeming truncation in Albanian. A merit of his discussion is his consideration (326–327) of the accent movement on the Albanian diphthong; cf. *mbíel : mbiél*, etc. This question was not placed in its relevant phonotactic contexts until my proposals of *BSL* 66, 1971, 221–223, and *KZ* 84, 1970, 140–141. Note further that Meyer failed to consider the important variations and contexts for '10' in the simplex vs. the 'teens and the decads; the alternation or opposition of *-ë* with zero; the varying gender; and the sandhi conditions for *-ð-*.

'1': Meyer cites (328–329) useful forms, but his analysis is superseded by mine, *IJSLP* 16, 1973, 1–6.

The ordinal form *parę* is equated with Skt. *pára-* 'highest'! Apart from the semantics, such a comparandum does not assure an accounting of the *-ë*. Besides, it is vastly preferable to be able to equate our form with other Indo-European exemples of 'first'.

Ordinals: Meyer detects traces of **-mo-* (330). In this connection see my analysis of the related participles, *Baltistica* 9, 1973, 45–50.

His discussion (331–336) of *-tę* suffixes in Albanian is implicitly criticized in detail by my analysis elsewhere in the present paper.

17.5. The prehistory of Common Albanian

Regardless of the critical remarks just made, Meyer's study was a major original contribution to the basic elaboration of comparative Indo-European scholarship. It also laid the foundation of the comparative and historical study of the Albanian numerals. Corrections and refinements have since been offered, especially by Pedersen but have largely remained unnoticed by later Indo-European scholarship; no adequate revised account of the Albanian numerals has been presented since Meyer: Pedersen came too soon after Meyer apparently to think a total revision worthwhile, and besides he was visibly busy at other things; Jokl tragically was not allowed to live to complete his life's work, but he was also not a synthesizer; Tagliavini did not reach the numerals in his start at stratifying the Indo-European lexicon of Albanian, yet he did bequeath us a valuable etymological glossary, which is conveniently referred to below for most of the cardinals; Çabej's work in the last half-century has often enriched our documentation, but his theoretical outlook for the prehistory of

Albanian and for Indo-European remains that of Jokl. For the rest I draw mainly on my own work.

A compressed account of the primes follows first.

'1' M. Huld (*Basic Albanian etymologies*, Columbus: Slavica 1984, 101) summarizes several earlier attempts, and then offers an implausible proposal deriving the Albanian by back-formation from a Proto-Indo-European feminine *$smieH_a$*. No motivation is offered for the successful emergence of a feminine in a language that conserves three Indo-European genders, and two of these in the lower numerals; the case of Armenian *mi* is of course not comparable since Armenian has lost gender and has had such choices forced by the resulting system. It is also not clear that **mi̯* would give *nj* in Albanian; note such an isolated form as *qime* 'single strand of hair' < **-miā*, def. *qimja*, pl. *qime*. Furthermore Huld unaccountably chooses for Common Albanian only *ňi* and *ňë*, seemingly restricting himself to unstressed and uninflected instances; perhaps this is what permitted him to consider only a single gendered pre-form. He seems also not to have taken account of the syntactic possibilities of Albanian. But more immediately, Huld does not notice my article on this numeral, *IJSLP* 16, 1973, 1–6.

First of all, it is easy to derive **ňë* as an unstressed form from **ňâ* vel sim. One can in turn derive unstressed **ňi* from **ňë* by vowel colouring in the presence of palatal *ň*, as has been earlier suggested in the presentation of the data. However, it will be seen that one may also explain **ňi* (perhaps via **ňë*) as having another origin. The marginal case form **ňâj-* is readily derived from an earlier refashioning as **ňâ-i*. Likewise it is possible to derive *ňīj-* from **ňë-i* or **ňi-i*.

We are then in a position to trace **ňâ* and all the inflections of the definite to a single stem **ňân-*, which can be internally reconstructed as **ni̯ēn-*. Associating this stem with the Balto-Slavic evidence, I have proposed (*IJSLP* 16,3–5; cf. also on Crimean Gothic, *Kwartalnik Neofilologiczny* 24, 1977, 275–276) **ni̯ēn-* < **(V)ni-ain-* < **Vni-oino-* (perhaps **eni-oino-*): Slavic *onŭ* etc., Armenian *-n*; cf. Baltic **uV-oino-*: Slavic *ovŭ*; and Slavic **ed-oino-*, apparently < **edh-*: OPruss. anaphora *-din* (acc.). In parallel fashion we have (*ibid.* 6) Alb. Geg *tânë*, Tosk *tërë* 'all' < **tod-oino-* with the same pattern and syntax *deictic + numeral. Thus we recover an extended formation, matching Balto-Slavic, of PIE **oino-*.

The reduction leading to unstressed **ňë* and an indefinite article is paralleled in Romanian *unu/a* → *un/o* + Noun. The Romanian result may well reflect a carry-over of the autochthonous (Albanoid) noun-phrase accent pattern, just as Romanian word accent mirrors the Albanian.

It is difficult to be sure of the exact background of the proclitic *_i_, but it is reasonable that this reflects the Proto-Indo-European anaphora *_ei_, neuter *_i-d_; cf. for example the paradigm I assume, _AJP_ 107, 1986, 398–400. In view of this and of the structure of *_ňân-_ above, it seems plausible that a suppletive pair of proclitics for individuation was furnished by *_ei_ and *_eni-_ (: Gk. ἔνιοι 'some', ἔνη and ἐκεῖνος κεῖνος κῆνος 'that').

In that case, *_eni-_ could be the source of unstressed *_ňi_. We would then have a succession somewhat as follows:

Proclitic	Head
*_ei_, *_eni-_	*_oino-_
> *_ei_, *_eni-_	*_enioino-_
> *_i_, *_ňi_	*_ňân-_
> *_i_, *_ňi_	*_ňân-_, *_ňâ_
> *_i_, *_ňi_, *_ňë_	*_ňân-_, *_ňâ_
> dialect/contextual choice	*_ňâ(n-)_

In consequence of this it seems possible that whatever form(s) of *_ei_ we find continued in Geg Albanian may be cognate at bottom with Epic ἴα (fem.), on which so much has been written. Certainly we cannot derive ἴα in a principled way from μία and PIE *_sem-_. This leads us to consider once again in the context of the above tabulation the possibility that *_oino-_ (along with *_oiuo-_ and *_oiko-_) was an ancient derivative in Proto-Indo-European of *_ei_, which we know as the anaphora.

In this fashion we would reduce the amount of unmotivated suppletion in the ancestral paradigm.

'1st'. *_párë_ has been correctly seen by virtually all modern scholars as reflecting, in agreement with Slavic, Indo-Iranian, and Armenian, what we now would write as PIE *_prH_$_o$_-uo-_; see, e.g., _Glossologia_ 2–3, 1983–1984, 64. If we recall the meaning of _(për)para_ 'before' we see that the Romanian ordinal _întîi_ < *_antaneus_ (← Latin _ante_) is simply a native calque in Dacian Latin on the indigenous Albanoid morpheme structure of the ordinal; it is a borrowing, or native carry-over, in Latin dress of the autochthonous morphology.

Though the etymology and Proto-Indo-European origin of *_párë_ are not in question, so great a master as Meillet was able to overlook the

Albanian agreement with Indo-Iranian and Slavic on this point; cf. E. P. Hamp in H. Birnbaum — J. Puhvel (eds.), *Ancient Indo-European dialects*, Berkeley and Los Angeles 1966, 116—117.

'2'. Tagliavini (*L'albanese di Dalmazia* 109) is properly dubious on both Pedersen's **duo* and Skok's **dui*; since **u̯* is lost after **d* before vowel (cf. *degë* 'branch' ≅ Eng. *twig*) these vocalisms will not suffice to explain *y*. Çabej offers no improvement. Huld (57) has a circular argument by deriving the masculine from the feminine of Proto-Indo-European.

Since *dy* stands rather isolated it will be best for us to approach the problem via *sȳ* 'eyes'. We may assume that *sȳ* has developed its singular Geg *sŷ*, def. *sŷni*, Tosk *sy, syri* on the model of such monosyllables as *drū* (collective) 'wood', sg. *drû, drûni*. Thus the fundamental form for us is the plural *sȳ*, and we do best to follow the brilliant insight of Pedersen who recognized here the Proto-Indo-European base of Slavic *oči* etc. We must therefore reconstruct *s-* < **okʷi̯-*, which is appropriate to a dual equivalent to Gk. ὄσσε. On this reasoning *sȳ* is an old neuter dual, which would have fallen in formally with a feminine in Albanian and hence matches *dȳ*. This morphological argument assures us that *-y* is the correct dual reflex in Albanian, and that we must find a plausible Proto-Indo-European pre-form for *-y* as an inflectional nominative-accusative.

We cannot have PIE **-ū* (**-uH*) since in a monosyllable this yields *-i*; cf. *mi* 'mouse'. Nor can we have **-ō* pure and simple, since that yields *e*. The only possibility seems to be **-ōu*, which must have yielded a later **-ū*. Now we know that the ultimate development of both **ō* and **-ū-* are post-Roman, so that it is plausible to assume that PIE **du̯ōu* > **dōu* > Roman period **dū* > *dy*, just as non-final **ū* > *y*. Alongside Indo-Iranian this is a significant finding.

The feminine would then reflect (as in Sardinian) **dū* + *ās* > **dū(u̯)ā* > **dyë* > *dȳ*; cf. E. P. Hamp, *RPh* 12, 1958, 147—155. An old (yet modern) length that could have been appropriate for the neuter would then have been indiscriminable from the feminine, thus fitting in with the categorial development of gender in Albanian.

We must now explain the "ablative" **dȳš*. With its length this cannot be derived from **du̯ōu*. Alternatively, it would be an artifice to derive this inflected form like the feminine from a derivation. Therefore it seems we must look to an original polysyllable with the potentiality of both lengthening and fronting the vowel. Such conditions point to a form related to **du(u̯)oi* or **du(u̯)(e)i*. Moreover, in view of the apparent 'thematic" **du̯ōu* (cf. Mycen. *du-wo-u-pi* instrum.), an original Proto-Indo-European locative plural in *-*oi* + *su* (cf. OCS *vlcěxŭ*, Lith. adverbial numeral _keturíese_, Rietavas dialect _ḱaturẹisu_ 'in(to) 4') makes a perfect morphological fit. Thus I reconstruct _*du(u̯)oi + su_ > _*du̯eisu_ > _*du̯īsu_ > _*dü(u̯)īsu_ > _*dyëš_ > _dȳš_.

'2nd'. On the other hand, we must explain the length in the ordinal _*dȳt-_ differently. The earliest Proto-Indo-European form should have been _*dui-o-_; this was then revised to _*du(u̯)i-to-_. From here on the way is clear: _*du̯ito-_ > _*dü(u̯)ito-_ > _*dyët-_ > _*dȳt-_, perhaps Bogdan's _dyit-_ (cf. _dēt_, Vaccarizzo _dejt_ 'sea'). The Albanian ordinal is thus seen to be reasonably ancient.

Basically we have reflexes of: _*du̯ōu_, _*dui-_, and _*du̯oi-_ in _degë_ 'branch'.

For the numeral '2' E. Çabej, _Studime gjuhësore_ I, Prishtinë 1976, 149–150, reviews in some detail the earlier rejected scholarship, summarizing (149) "po me formë historikisht të pasqaruar" (= but in form historically unspecified/unaccounted for). But, Çabej fails to address the various problems presented by the Albanian and Proto-Indo-European for mations and to assemble the pertinent Albanian forms. We have tried to improve on all these aspects in the present essay.

'3'. Tagliavini (_AD_ 270) had essentially the two ancestral forms that must underlie the two primary cardinal forms _tre_ (masc.) and _trī_ (fem.), which he cited from Meyer as _*trejes_ and _*tria_. Huld (117) essentially repeats this. The principal shortcoming with these reconstructions is their lack of precision in phonology and morphology. It is necessary to explain the length of the vowel in _trī_ and to justify the morphological status of the feminine.

The masc. _tre_ has been nearly completely explained. The intervocalic _*i̯_ of _*tréi̯es_ (nom.) (> Skt. _tráyas_, Cretan τρέες) was lost early, and the loss of a final syllable is of course normal. The diphthongization of _*e_ which we might look for fails to occur, or else survive, after consonant plus _r_; cf. _bredh_ 'jump(s)': Lith. _brẽda_ 'wades'; _dredh_ 'twist(s)', from a problematic base _*d(h)reǵh-_, on which see most recently E. Çabej, _Studime gjuhësore_ I, Prishtinë 1976, 137–138.

The fem. _trī_ must essentially depart from the Proto-Indo-European neuter _*triH_$_a$. Since this would give _*tri_ we may suppose that the neuter ending was extended as _*tri-ā_. This ending would have become indiscriminable from a rebuilt feminine plural _*tri-ā(s)_. Thus we arrive at _*trië_ > _trī_. We see now that the neuter-feminine of '3' must be regarded as the model for the new feminine of '2'.

An explanation is now needed for the length in the "ablative" _trīš_. The original locative (Lith. dialect _trisù_) should have given _*tri + su_ >

**triš*. We may therefore assume a levelling of the neuter-feminine stem **tri-ā-su* > **triēš* > *trīs*, or else a formation patterned on what we have seen for '2': **tri-ī-su* > **triēš* > *trīš*.

There are two possible explanations for the unstressed compounding form **tër-*. One simple source may be sought in the reduction of the Proto-Indo-European compounding state **tri*.

However, the remarkable Barile form for '30', which should originate syntactically in '3 tens', and which, we see, calls in Albanian for a feminine concord', leads us to consider the Indo-European feminine numeral, which we know from Indo-Iranian and Celtic: **tisres*, dissimilated from **tri-sr-es*. In Albanian, if this were to have survived, we should find **tisres* > **tīres* > **tir* > **tir-́* > **tër-́*. The medial cluster **sr* would have lengthened the preceding vowel while losing the **s*, as I have shown for *dorë* 'hand' < PIE **ǵhesr*.

'3rd'. The ordinal **tret-* could be derived from the same preform as the Balto-Slavic **tret(i)os*. But it is also possible to see a feminine **tritā* > **tretā* contributing to this. It is further possible to derive **trit-* from PIE **trt(i)o-*, on which see my remarks, *Foundations of Language* 11, 1974, 463.

'4'. As recently as Tagliavini (*AD* 144) and A. V. Desnickaja ("K izučeniju latinskix ėlementov v leksike balkanskix jazykov", in *Romano-Balcanica*, Leningrad: Nauka 1987, p. 18; but not listed *Albanskaja literatura i albanskij jazyk*, Leningrad: Nauka 1987, p. 223) *katër* was thought to be a borrowing from Latin. However, Huld (79) is surely right in insisting, as I have (*IF* 74, 1969, 153; *IJSLP* 16, 1973, 1–2; etc.), that this numeral must be an Indo-European inheritance, and not a lone unmotivated borrowing in the entire series below '100'. There is, moreover, no reason to be troubled, as some scholars have been, that the vocalism of *katër* fails to match that of Skt. *catvāras*, Attic τέτταρες, Lesbian πέσσυρες, OCS *četyre*, Lith. *keturì*, and Welsh *pedwar*. As I have pointed out (*IF* 74, 1969, 153), an explanation of *katër* involves no extra formulation beyond what is required for Lat. *quattuor*, Homeric πίσυρες, and Czech *čtyři*; see also my remarks and references, *Nestor* 9: 1 (January 1982), 1586–1587. Additionally, in view of this consideration I have tried to give an integrated explanation of the Latin facts to embrace *quattuor, quadru-*, and *quadrāgintā; Studii Clasice* 17, 1977, 149–151.

In the last-mentioned study I have offered, as also in *Ériu* 24, 1973, 17, a paradigm of crucial case forms for the Proto-Indo-European numeral '4':

nom.	*k^{w}etuóres	= [k^{w}etu̯óres]
acc.	*k^{w}túrms	= [k^w(ə)túrm̥s]
dat.-instr.	*k^{w}tur + bh...	= [k^w(ə)tuu̯r̥]
loc.	*k^{w}tur + su	

Note that [(ə)] is not one of the PIE "schwas prima".

Nine different phenomena could result from the above phonological sequences in a single dialect:

a) The sequence *k^{w}t could be preserved (Avestan *āxtūirīm*);
b) initial *k^w could be lost (Av. *tūirya-* '4th', Armenian *kʻar̄asun* '40', Gk. τράπεζα);
c) a relieving conditioned vocalism could be inserted (Latin *quattuor*, Homeric πίσυρες, Slovene *štirje* < *čĭtyr-);
d) a sequence syllabic *u + non-syllabic *r could result (Skt. *catúras* = Lith. *kẽturis* [acc.] = πίσυρες, generalized in Toch. B *śtarte*, Latv. *ceturtais* '4th'; Skt. *cátur-* = Lith. *ketur-*, Umbr. *petur-*, Mercian *feoðor-*);
e) a sequence with non-syllabic *u̯ could appear in Sievers post-light position (Skt. *catvā́ras*, Av. *čaθwārō*, Welsh *pedwar*, OIr. *cethair*, Toch. B *śtwer*, Goth. *fidwor* < *k^{w}etu̯ór-es; Boeotian πέτταρες, Gaulish *petuar(io-)* '4th', Lith. *ketvir̃tas* < *-tu̯r̥-);
f) and with *uu̯ in Sievers post-heavy position (Slavic *čĭtyr-* < *kitūr- < *ktuur- < *k^{w}tuu̯r̥-; *IF* 85, 1980, 41);
g) the last variant apparently also underwent metathesis to *k^{w}tr̥ru- (ultimately to Lat. *quadru-*, *Studii Clasice* 17, 1977, 151); this could have happened in compounding with *-roto- 'wheeled';
h) and this in Sievers post-light position gave *(k^{w}e)tru- (Av. *čaθru-*, Gaulish *petru-*, OIr. *cethor-cho* '40' < *k^{w}etru-k̑ont-s; τρυ-φάλεια 'a helmet with 4 φάλοι' < *tru- < *k^{w}tru-);
i) finally, *k^{w}tu̯r̥- and, less likely, *k^{w}tru- were perceived as containing but one instance of lip-rounding and this was attributed to the *k^w; thus *k^{w}tr̥- was extracted, and with initial simplification this gave *(k^{w}e)tr̥- (τρά-πεζα = Mycenaean *to(r)-peza* 'table' < *(k^w)tr̥-pedi̯H$_a$ '4-footed', ταρτη-μόριον '¼'; τετρά-φαλος 'with 4 helmet φάλοι', Mycenaean *qe-to-ro-we qet(o)rōwes* '4-eared, -handled', Attic τέταρτος, Boeotian πέτρατος, Arcadian τέτορτος '4th' < *k^{w}etr̥-; Czech *čtr-náct* '14' presumably *k$^{w(ə)}$tr̥- and not *k$^{w(ə)}$tur-); the re-

vocalization of this variant in the paradigm then gave Doric τέτορες = Armenian *č‘ork‘*, *č‘orek‘-* '4', Oscan *petora* (neut.).

We must now attempt to place the observed Albanian forms plausibly among these possibilities. It is not enough merely to find a possible antecedent; in such problems one must search for a motivated ancestor consistent with other observed forms.

The reason why the vocalism of the first syllable of '4' was treated differently – and to a degree unpredictably – in the Indo-European dialects was twofold: First, the intrinsically phonetic aspect of the heavy cluster *k^wt-* permitted different optional resolutions or reductions, either loss of the first element or intercalation of a helping syllabic; cf. the references mentioned above, and *Studia Celtica* 12–13, 1977–1978, 14, and *Annual of Armenian Linguistics* 6, 1985, 51–52. Secondly, the ambiguity as to whether *k^wtur-* was to be treated as a polysyllabic base (like Greek κτείς = Latin *pecten*, or Lith. *žẽmė* = Greek χθών = Hittite *DeGan*) or a monosyllabic base, which required vowel insertion in zero-grade (as with **pod-* 'foot', **pd-* → *ped-*); cf. *FLH* 4, 1983, 137–138, and *Chicago Linguistic Society* 23/1, 1987, 116–117, and *Ériu* 24, 1973, 17. Interpretation under the last provision permitted speakers to generate as regular forms the feminine *k^wéte-sr-es* (Skt. *cátasras* = Av. *čataŋrō* = Welsh *pedair*) as well as the types with *k^we-* given under (d), (h), and (i) above.

It is clear that Albanian preserved no forms of this numeral in *k^we-*; if it had, we should find a modern reflex in *s-*. Therefore, we find that the initial *ka-* must reflect a generalization, or levelling, of (c) above, with *k^wət-*.

The next important fact to be noted is the clear open-syllable lengthening to be seen in the North Geg ordinal. This means that we must regard the instances of short first syllable as pointing to an ancient ancestry of closed-syllable configuration, i. e., of an old consonantal cluster following the vowel. It is easy to see that the forms with Common Albanian *kátr-* go back to a shape *k^watrV-*. The difficulty in this framework arises with the cardinal *kátër(ë)*.

Here we may first note that Albanian '2' and '3' have been seen to be still today declined and gendered, as they were in Proto-Indo-European. We are therefore justified in supposing that this remained true for '4' also for a considerable time. For this reason I regard *kátërë* as the earlier feminized form *k^watVr-ā* (perhaps also lineally neuter), from still earlier *-ās*, of a masc. *k^watVr*. It is even possible to imagine that *k^watVrā(s)* was descended from *k^watēr-ās* < *k^watesr-es*.

We must now account for the lack of open-syllable lengthening in masc. **kátër* < **k^{w}atVr*. Notice that **párë* < **pr̥Hu̯o-* shows no signs of lengthening, and, more significant, that *bir* 'son' shows a relatively late truncation of a diphthong in **bir(ë)* < **bi(e̯)ru̯V* < **b(h)eru̯-*, as I think I have shown, *BSL* 66, 1971, 220–225, esp. 223–225[1].

Therefore we may assume that post-consonantal **u̯* or its successor retained a capacity for creating closed syllables relatively late in Albanian. This gives us the possibility of suggesting that masc. **kátër* is to be derived from **k^{w}atu̯or-es* or **k^{w}atu̯r̥-*, as in (e) above.

To give the open syllable environment the ordinal must now be derived from **k^{w}atur-to-*, which would have developed naturally from an earlier **k^{w}tur-to-*, the expected shape for the ordinal and more conservative than the Baltic **k^{w}etur-to-* (*FL* 11, 1974, 463). This development follows variant (d) or perhaps even (f).

The other ordinal shape **kátrët-* must be traced to **k^{w}atru-to-* (i. e., variant h) or **k^{w}atri-to-*, which would reflect **k^{w}tr̥-* (variant i). The latter variant would not only match Greek τέταρτος closely, but it would correspond in formation to **tr̥-to-* '3rd' earlier referred to.

The compounding **katër-* could match either of the ordinal stem variants under secondary stress, i. e. either (d) or (h).

It is hard to suggest a precise and uniquely conclusive ancestor for the definite nominalization **kátrë*. A reasonable possibility is that this was an old neuter collective **k^{w}atro-m*. Such a form would be fashioned on the variant stem (i) and related to Skt. *catváram* = Old Slovene *četvero,* 16th cent. *zhetuero, (→ Lith. ketverì*, gen. *kẽtverios*) 'a group of 4' < **k^{w}etuéro-m*. I have explained the vocalism of the last in *Studia Celtica* 18–19, 1983–4, 128–132.

The Albanian vocalism would of course be carried over from the primary stem forms of '4'.

'5'. The primary form **pêsë* for Common Albanian is assured. Huld's account (102–103) is far too lax, though it usefully reviews earlier expositions. The crucial discovery was Pedersen's: the *s* is adequately explained as **k^w* before front vowel, and therefore **ti̯* (equally possible for *s*) is unnecessary. In any case, as we shall see, a suffix *-*ti*- should not lead to *-*ti-ā*, which such a **ti̯* really implies, since in our numerals we have to do with a feminine suffix *-*ti*- which leads us to an Albanian feminine *-*tā*.

---

[1] In footnote 13, p. 224, correct "*i* syllabique bref" to "*a* syllabique bref".

Moreover, any **-t-* suffix implies at a sufficiently early date a zero-grade state of the base: OHG *funfto*, Av. *puxδa-*, RV (x61,1[d]) *pakthás*; cf. Chr. S. Stang, *Vergleichende Grammatik der baltischen Sprachen*, Oslo 1966, 283. Therefore **pn̥k*^{w}*-tó-* would have given Albanian **pakta-* > **pata-*; cf. my discussion of Meyer's analysis of '20' and my analysis of '7' below for the outcome of Proto-Indo-European syllabic nasal. There is a further morphological argument against **ti̯* for **pêsë*: I have argued in the opening section on "categories" that the suppression of ordinal *-të* in '6th'–'8th' is to be traced to the Indo-European exclusion of such a suffix sequence as **-tí-* plus **-tó-*. If we take that seriously we might then expect some trace in the descendant dialects of a corresponding variant of '5th' with only *-së* or *-të*; but we find no such form.

We therefore credit **pêsë* with Pedersen to **pénk*^{w}*e*. I have already remarked that **ê* in this position seems not to yield *ë* in Tosk; this phonetic development matches the outcome observed for **ê* in Tosk in the situation calling for *i*-umlaut. We may assume, then, that **ć* (> *s*) had a fronting effect.

Huld (102) is troubled by the vocalism, declaring that he expects †*pîs* since "**en* before sibilants becomes *i* elsewhere, e.g. *mish* 'meat' < **memsos*". But Huld seems to forget that the sibilant of 'meat' has always been a sibilant, whereas the *s* of **pêsë* was an affricate as late as the coming of the Slavs, and earlier was a palatalized labialized stop.

There remains the question of the unexpected *-ë*. In the definite form, as with '4', we may see an old neuter collective **penk*^{w}*e-om* > **penk*^{w}*e̯an* > **penć*^{w}*an* > *pêsë*. In the cardinal, however, which was uninflected in Proto-Indo-European, we expect only †*pês*; note that Da Lecce's *pèss* is not significant with its lack of *-ë*. But recall now that '5' can be gendered (and inflected) in the nominalization. We may therefore derive **pêsë* from a marked plural **pénk*^{w}*e-ā(s)*.

The vocalism of the ordinal **pêsët-* can be adequately explained from **penk*^{w}*e-to-*, which is the exact equivalent of Gaulish *pinpetos* < **k*^{w}*enk*^{w}*e-to-*. These must have replaced, doubtless independently, the original **pnk*^{w}*-tó-*. Cf. *Studia Celtica Japonica* 2, 1989, 41–43.

'6'–'9'. The Albanian cardinals in *-të* exactly match the Indo-Iranian decads in *-tí-* (feminine):

'6'	**ǵáš-të*	= Vedic	*ṣaṣ-ṭí-*	'60'
'7'	**š(ë)tá-të*		*sapta-tí-*	'70'
'8'	**té-të*		*aśī-tí-*	'80'
'9'	**nân-dë*, **nân-të*		*nava-tí-*	'90'

Notice that the span covered ('6' to '9') by this formation exactly coincides, and excludes:

'5'	**pêsë* < **pénkʷe-ā(s)*	: Vedic	*pañcā-śát-*	=	πεντήκοντα '50'
'10'	**ðietë* (see below)		*śatá-m*	=	ἑ-κατόν

This morphological formation is clearly of Indo-European ancestry, and its scope is defined precisely. We therefore recover a suffix **-ti-* (feminine) which formed numeral abstracts and which was replaced by **-tā* > *-të* in Albanian; see my formulation, *Word* 17, 1961, 102. This mechanism for forming abstracts or an entity specified by the numeral was the same as that which formed action nouns from verb bases, as seen in Vedic *iṣṭí-* 'desire', *rā-tí-* 'gift', *gá-ti* 'motion'; cf. *dritë* 'light' < **dr̥ḱ-ti-* = Skt. *dŕ̥ṣ-ṭi-* 'vision, a glance'. These examples, of course, constitute but one situation of the more general Albanian feminizing inflection seen in *natë* 'night', *derë* 'door'; cf. *Sprachwissenschaftliche Forschungen: Festschrift für Johann Knobloch*, Innsbruck 1985, 145.

I have pointed out, *Kwartalnik Neofilologiczny* 24, 1977, 277, that Crimean Gothic showed a suffix *-e* exactly in the numeral series '7'–'10', i.e. beginning with the numeral which terminated in an inherited nasal. We appear here to have an areal feature. However in that discussion my statement for Slavic is imprecise in the same way that others' have been from the beginning of serious Albanian studies; we cannot equate the Albanian series with the Slavic. For Slavic we must juxtapose the ordinals and the cardinals: a solution which will not explain the Albanian in the way Huld's vague allusion (166) mistakenly states.

Ordinals	Cardinals
pętŭ (Lith. *peñktas*) < **p(e)nkʷto-*	*pętĭ*
šestŭ (Lith. *šẽštas*, Lat. *sextus*)	*šestĭ*
sedmŭ (Olith. *sekmas*, OPruss. *septmas*)	*sedmĭ*
osmŭ (OLith. *ãšmas*, Skt. *aṣṭamás*)	*osmĭ*
devętŭ (Lith. *deviñtas*)	*devętĭ*
desętŭ (Lith. *dešim̃tas*)	*desętĭ* (Lith. *dẽšimt*, *acc. with loss of *-i̯* → *dešimtìs*)

Apart from the fact that we have to do here with '5'–'10' it is seen that we cannot explain the cardinals completely by invoking an integral cardinal suffix; even Vaillant (*Grammaire comparée des langues slaves* II

2, 1958, 632 § 305) errs by speaking of a derivative "en *-tĭ*" and by entertaining a chronologically piecemeal derivation. In fact, aside from the question of '7' and '8', '5' cannot be explained at all in this way since **p(e)nk*^{w}*-ti-* (with front vowel following) would yield †*pęštь* etc. (cf. *noštь* etc. 'night'). On the other hand, once we recognize that **oš(t)mo-* was formed by analogy on **sebdmo-* and that *pętŭ* is a correct outcome for **p(e)nk*^{w}*-to-* (with back vowel; cf. *potŭ* 'sweat' < **pok*^{w}*-to-*) all the ordinals have perfectly normal explanations: **p(e)nk*^{w}*-to-*, **kseḱs-to-*, **sebdmo-* < **septm-o-*, **deu̯n-to-* < **ʔneun-o-*, **dešm-to-* < **deḱmt-o-*.

Furthermore, since *desęt-* < **dešmt-* was earlier an obstruent stem (cf. the decads and 'teens), by the Balto-Slavic rule we expect an *i*-stem to result. Hence **dešmt-o-* came to oppose a new cardinal **dešmt-i-* and the relation ordinal **-o-* : cardinal **-i-* was established. From this a new set of cardinals in *-ĭ* took root for the old indeclinables; Vaillant *op. cit.* 637–638 fails to see this source.

The Slavic *-tĭ* therefore has no common origin with the Albanian cardinal *-të*, and no direct source in a Proto-Indo-European suffix.

'6'. Huld's account (68) is so brief as to be barely adequate to indicate the simple fact of Indo-European descent; it certainly does not deal with the inherent complexities of this numeral. Huld mentions Jucquois (1965) for the equation with Vedic *ṣaṣ-ṭí-*, but he adduces this as an isolated fact and does not notice my analysis of the systematic behavior of this suffix in these numerals, *Word* 17, 1961, 102. The fullest segmental comparandum, which I cite there, is Avestan *xšvašti-*. The full Albanian form is therefore an abstract nominalization, and, as I have remarked earlier, not appropriate for a further suffixation as an ordinal; the ordinal was therefore formed on the base.

Huld also missed my article "Indo-European '6'", in *Linguistic and literary studies in honor of Archibald A. Hill*, edd. M. A. Jazayery, E. C. Polomé, and W. Winter, The Hague 1978, vol. 3, 81–90,[1] which presents a detailed reconstruction of this numeral and a specific account (86–87) of the Albanian development: **ksu̯eḱs* > **kseḱs* → **seḱs-ti-* (fem.) → **séśt-ā* > **ǵiǽstā* > **ǵáštë*. Every development here is regular and nothing is obscure. Since I pair Albanian with Balto-Slavic the stage with **ks-* is assured.

---

[1] It is convenient to add here to the documentation Mycenaean *we-pe-za* ϝε( )-πεζα. Note also *Indo-Iranian Journal* 25, 1983, 102.

'7'. The termination *-të* of **š(ë)tá-të* is explained as in **ǵáštë*. The first *-t-* can result from the simplification of a medial **-pt-*; phonological parallels are morphologically complex, and would be too distracting to review here. The initial *š* is the expected reflex for a PIE **s-* in an unaccented syllable, as opposed to the *ǵ-* seen in '6'. This fact, and not just the simple presence of the word accent on the next syllabic in the historically attested form, is a valuable piece of evidence for the Proto-Indo-European accent to be placed beside the Indic *saptá*, Greek ἑπτά; but not Germanic *sibun* (*Word* 8, 1952, 136–139, where I now reject fn. 1).

These observations allow us to reconstruct at least **septá-ti-* (fem.). Since the reflex *š-* points simply to an originally unaccented syllable it would be equally possible to reconstruct **septa-tí-* to agree with Vedic *sapta-tí-*. But this would lead us to assume for '6' a form **seḱs-tí-*, which would in turn destroy the argument for the initial *ǵ-*. We must therefore recover **sé(ḱ)s-tā* and **se(p)tá-tā* < **septá-ti-* (fem.), with the reflexes of the **s-* based on the Proto-Indo-European accent of the simplex. Whether, of course, **pt* and **á* and **-ti-* all precisely coexisted chronologically cannot be said on this evidence; but an interim reconstruction **septá-ti-* is undeniable.

The syncope of the first syllable with unstressed *ë* is quite normal in Albanian when an acceptable cluster is produced; cf. *flas* 'speak': *fjalë* 'word'.

The remaining point to be settled is the reflex of PIE [m̥]. Huld (154) dismisses *a* as "superficial", but has only weak arguments of analogy or assimilation to offer in order to set aside the couple of cases he mentions. In fact, the instances of *a* are not inconsequential, and the occurrences of apparent *e* are always susceptible of explanation as umlaut of **a*. I have argued this in a paper "The IE syllabic nasals in Albanian" presented to the Linguistic Society of America in December 1967, and V. I. Georgiev has maintained this on less evidence in *Akten des internationalen albanologischen Kolloquiums Innsbruck 1972 zum Gedächtnis an Norbert Jokl*, 1977, 232–233.

The precise reconstruction of the cardinal then becomes **septḿ̥ + ti-*.

'8'. In light of the foregoing discussion the reconstruction of *tétë*, while not immediately obvious from the surface shape of the Albanian, does not give rise to any serious doubts. Again we have **-ti-* (fem.). The stressed *e* is best credited to **ŏ́*. The first *t* can be derived from an old medial cluster **-ḱt-*, contrary to *AD* 267. And an unstressed initial vowel other than *u- could have been lost, as in *mik* 'friend' < Latin *amīcus*. Thus we arrive at *a(ḱ)tṓ-ti- and *oḱtṓ + ti-.

The superficial comparamdum for this last form is Avestan *aštāiti-*, which is shown to be analogical by Vedic *aśītí-* '80'; cf. *Word* 17, 1961, 102 fn. 3, and *Indo-Iranian Journal* 24, 1982, 37–38.

'9'. Although previous accounts of '9' (Huld 155, Tagliavini *AD* 201) are unsatisfactory, I think that the shape of PIE '9' is now clear to us as *ˀnéun (i. e. *$H_e$néun) = [ˀnéu̯n̥], [ˀneun-]; for detail see my discussions *Istituto Universitario Orientale Annali* (Sez. Linguistica) II 2, 1960, 186; *Foundations of Language* 11, 1974, 463–464; *Russian Linguistics* 2, 1975, 221–222; *Michigan Germanic Studies* 2, 1976, 1–2 (where one should read *H_e throughout); *Münchener Studien zur Sprachwissenschaft* 37, 1978, 61 (to which add the Mycenaean compounding form *e-ne-wo* < *ˀneu̯n̥-); *Zbornik za filologiju i lingvistiku* 19, 1976, 13–14; *CLS Book of Squibs* (1977) 46–48; *Glotta* 59, 1981, 228 f.

Once again the dental termination of Albanian '9' can be equated with *-tí-* of Vedic *navatí-*, Avestan *navaiti-* '90' (: Vedic *náva* '9'); *Word* 17, 1961, 102.

The distinctively Albanian problem with our Common Albanian result lies in finding an exact explanation for the double reflex seen in the cardinal *nândë, nântë. The regular outcome in Albanian of a stop immediately after a nasal is the voiced stop following the nasal, which is homorganic with the stop. Therefore *nândë can be adequately explained with a pre-form in *-nt-. It is possible that the cardinal *ˀnéun [ˀnéu̯n̥] first gave *néu̯in; cf. *emër* 'name' < *émëno- < *émin- < *ámin < *n̥mn̥ < PIE *ˀnmn. But *néu̯in should have yielded in turn *ni̯eu̯in > *ń-, of which we find no trace. It seems, then, that we must look to a pre-form *ˀneun- + -tí- (fem.), or other appropriate dental suffix.

On the other hand, an early nominalization *ˀnéun-ti- would have given *ˀnéu̯n̥ti- > *ni̯eu̯atā > *ni̯eëtë. While an ordinal matching OLith. *dewintas* would also produce *ˀneu̯n̥to- > *ni̯eu̯at- > *ni̯eët-, or *neu̯át- > *nëát-, we find in Common Albanian no trace of the early-layer *-t- in the ordinal. I therefore attribute the ordinal to an original conservative *ˀneun-o-.

In sum, we start from *ˀneun-t- > *nēnt- and *ˀnéu̯n̥ti- (fem.) > *ni̯eu̯atā. The first of these gave directly *nândë, while the second conflated with the first yielded *nân(ë)të. The ordinal produced immediately *nândë.

I have discussed these matters in detail in connection with the autochthonous name *Neunt(i)us* attested at Ig near Ljubljana in *IF* 81, 1976, 43–44.

'10'. I have already reviewed the inadequacies of Meyer's analysis of '10'. All discussions of this Albanian numeral up to the present have been multiply unsatisfactory because of deficiencies in the evidential data used as a basis and of the insufficiency of prevailing views (including my own until two decads ago) regarding the original Proto-Indo-European form of '10' and the sources of the Slavic higher units. These various shortcomings have led all earlier accounts astray. Huld (60) makes a good attempt, but his data are deficient, he did not look far enough, he did not seriously consider (143) the initial *ð-* and errs in his view (154) of the outcome of the Proto-Indo-European syllabic nasals; but his critique of earlier proposals is good so far as it goes.

There are several particulatirities of the forms of '10' that must be satisfied: Two different resolutions of the diphthong coexist; the apparent absence of PIE **ḱ* must be explained; the initial spirant must be exactly accounted for; the finals of the two shapes and the gender of the word must find plausible histories; the syntax of these forms must be taken into account.

The fundamental answer for the initial spirant *ð-* has surely been given by W. Cimochowski, *Lingua Posnaniensis* 2, 1950, 220–255, who attributes the dual representation (*d* and *ð*, i. e. orthographic *dh*) of both PIE **d/dh* and **ǵ/ǵh* to old *sandhi*, a source for the differenciation which had already been invoked by Pedersen. Cimochowski's main contribution was a general discussion of sandhi in Albanian, which I have reviewed critically in *Hanǰamana*, ed. S. K. Sen (Calcutta: Calcutta University 1989) 6–9. However the conditions for the sandhi manifested in Albanian '10' must be stated specifically: it is clear that we have here the generalization of a contextual feature. Unlike other units, such as *dy* '2', '10' occurred in two crucially categorial contexts: immediately after **(ë)m(b)ë* in the 'teens, and after **trī* or **tri-* and **pesë* in the decads; a form of '3' ending in PIE **-s* would also combine with **d-* to yield **ð-* in Albanian. Therefore because of the presence of these preceding elements in close-knit phrases the conditions were provided to produce a spirantization of the initial by lenition; this lenited form was then generalized.

We might have expected PIE **déḱmt* (*Foundations of Language* 11, 1974, 463, and rejecting *Word* 8, 1952, 136, footnote 1) to yield **djeθat(V)* > **ðjéθët(ë)*, or **ðëθát(ë)*. On the other hand PIE **-(d)ḱmt-* '-ty' would presumably give *-*θat*. However, from my argument in *Studi Linguistici e Filologici per Carlo Alberto Mastrelli* (Pisa: Pacini, 1985) 217–218 and *Slavistična Revija* 28, 1980, 97–101, these forms at an early time would have been rather **djetθat(V)* > **ðjétθët(ë)*, or **ðëtθát(ë)*, with an affricate descendant of PIE *ḱ. The presence of this affricate implies for some stage the possibility of a complex dissimilation in this remarkable series of dentals: **ðjétθët(ë)* > **ðjétët(ë)*, with dissimilation of the spirant segments, or **ðjétθët(ë)* > **ðjéθët(ë)* with either dissimilation of the stops or else ultimate resolution of **tθ* > *θ*. In any case **ðjétët(ë)* could give *ðjét(ë)* just as **só-dit-* gave *sot* ~ *sod* 'today'; see *Acta Linguistica Hafniensia* 12, 1969, 154. On the other hand **ðjéθët(ë)* by a further dissimilation would yield **ðjéët(ë)*, with a syllabic configuration like that of **dheubeto-* > **dheubeta-* > **déubeta-* > **déƀët-* > **déët-* > *dēt* 'sea'. We might then expect **ðjéët(ë)* to resolve itself as a long syllable, giving **ðīēt(ë)*, i. e., *ðiet(ë)*. The status of *jé* and *íe* throughout all of this is still subject to consideration and further exploration. For the basic developments of PIE **e* see my formulation *BSL* 66, 1972, 221–224.

Now that we have seen an avenue of explanation for the dual vocalism and the fate of *ḱ, which must both be linked, we do best to proceed at the same time to the analysis of the 'teens and the decads.

**déḱmt* was an obstruent athematic stem. It is clear that in Albanian this indeclinable became, as in Slavic, a noun. However, unlike Slavic where it was masculine (see Vaillant *op. cit.* 636 § 306; but not with a derivation in *-t-* as Vaillant 637 has it), in Albanian our noun was feminine; note significantly **trī ðietë* '30'. This fact is important in correcting a universal misapprehension of the history of the Romanian numerals and decads. These last are continually said to be patterned on Slavic, an impossible explanation. In Romanian, *zece* < Latin *decem* has become a noun, with a plural *zeci*; this is shown by the syntax from '20' on with *de: trei zeci de lei* '30 lei', *două mii de oameni* '2000 men', *cinzeci de mii de oameni* '50 000 men'. Now in Daco-Romanian, as opposed to Aromân, Latin *uīginti* '20' has been replaced by '2 × 10', *douăzeci*. Note that we have here *două* feminine, and not *doi* masculine. It is therefore not possible that *zece* (fem.), pl. *zeci* was calqued on Slavic, which had a masculine (not, however, so identified in even the greatest Old Slavic lexica). We must therefore add *zece* (fem.) to the inventory of "autochthonous" elements of Romanian, and derive it as a borrowed grammatical feature from an early Albanian dialect of Dacia or Moesia.

Thus we are assured that Alb. **déḱm̥t-* was feminine like *ditë* (pl. *dit*) 'day' < **di-t-*. In stem form the Albanian agreed with Lith. *dẽšimt* < acc. *dẽšimtį* (see B. J. Darden, in H. Aronson (ed.), *The Non-Slavic languages of the USSR: Linguistic studies*, Chicago: Chicago Linguistic Society 1989, 56–79, esp. 77), to *dešimtìs*, gen. pl. *dešimtų̃* (= OCS *desętŭ*), OPruss. *dessimpts*, gen. pl. *dessimton* (Vaillant *op. cit.* 637). The forms *ditë* and **ðietë* have been feminized from old obstruent feminine stems just as we have with both the strong and weak stems in *darkë* 'supper' < **dorkʷ-* and *drekë* 'lunch' < **dr̥kʷ-* (cf. French *dîner* and *déjeuner*). We have now explained **ðietë* as far as I know how for the present; but note too that the Vedic decads are feminine.

The 'teens are formed with a transparent close-knit phrase linked by *mbë* < *mbi* 'on'. It is universally recognized that Romanian *ùn-spre-zece, dòi-spre-zece, dòuă-spre-zece* etc. (~ *-șpe*) agrees with this. But now in light of what has been determined above for *zece* we do best to credit this Romanian calque not to Slavic but to Albanian, i. e., to the autochthonous pre-Roman speech. This is valuable in dating the Albanian locution.

Nevertheless the Slavic construction *na desęte*, differing from the Baltic and hence an areal diffusion of very early date, is useful in suggesting to us the locative case government of **(ë)m(b)ë* 'on' (< **ambhi* or **embhi*; see *Ériu* 24, 1973, 164–166; 28, 1977, 145–146; 33, 1982, 180–181). Thus **ëmbi* + *ðjét* 'on 10' must be an old inflected locative, and phonologically as well as morphologically it matches *sot* 'today' < **só-dit-* (or rather **ćā́-dit-* < **tįā-dit-*) 'on this day', with an Albanian "ablative-locative". I therefore reconstruct **diétθat-i* > **ðjétët*.

In similar phonological circumstances **tërðjét* '30' derives from **tri-diétθat-es* just as we have the old consonant-stem plurals *net* and *dit* to *natë* 'night' and *ditë* 'day'. I have pointed out a corresponding relation in the Crimean Gothic pair *-thien* '-ty' : *thiine* '10'; *Kwartalnik Neofilologiczny* 24, 1977, 276–277.

The original coexistence of **déḱmt* '10' and **deḱmt-o-* '10th' (*FL* 11, 1974, 463), later resegmented to **deḱm-to-*, accounts for the ordinal **-ðjét-i -a* of the 'teens as well as being at the root of the seeming haplology of **-ët-* in the decade ordinals.

The archaic **tri-diétθat-es* < **tri-deḱmt-es* '30' may be compared directly with Vedic *triṃśát-am* (acc.). It seems possible that the duplicate **nândë* and **nântë* in '90' matches the appearance of the ordinal in Latin *nōnāgintā*, though not in Russian *devjanosto*.

'20'. Though I had formulated the regular change of PIE **uiḱ-* to Albanian *z-* by ca. 1961 (see the reference in Huld 133), I had not by that time seen that Proto-Indo-European syllabic nasal must give only Albanian **a*. Ever since my paper on the Proto-Indo-European syllabic nasals in Albanian before the Linguistic Society of America in 1967 I have reconstructed *-zet* < **ʒ́*^{ü}*äti* < **ʒ́*^{ü}*atī* < **u̯(i)ǵatī* < **u̯iḱm̥̍tī*, i.e. **uī̆ḱmtī* or **ui-dḱmt-iH* < **dui-dḱmt-iH*.

No other treatments of *-zet* up to the present have satisfied me. Çabej (*Studime gjuhësore* II 1976, 318–319, based on a 1956 article) concentrates on the vigesimal system, mentioning the form *trezét* from Shalë e Shosh; but his reconstruction **ieuk-t-* from the base of Eng. *yoke* is quite impossible and unnecessary.

From our discussion of '2' and *sȳ* 'eyes' we have seen that an Albanian dual may emerge naturally as a neuter > masculine singular. Because the formal dual **uī̆ḱmtī*, in an opaque shape that appeared to be a simplex, was used in the vigesimal system as the basic form and was taken as a singular, it is natural that it has become a masculine. It is interesting that '60' and '80' have not developed as solidly and universally in close compound as has '40' and, of course, '20'.

The ordinal is surely a fresh formation.

'100'. Everyone agrees (cf. Tagliavini *AD* 95) that **ḱind* (masc.) is borrowed from Latin *centum*; it is a classic example for Latin *c-* before front vowel.

Although one could entertain the possibility (*IJSLP* 16, 1973, 1) that the *ḱ-* stemmed from the regular Albanian depalatalization of Proto-Indo-European palatals before sonants, the result of a cognate to Vedic *śatám* (neut.) = Lith. *šim̃tas* should be Alb. **kat*.

The syntax of **ḱind* is important. It will be seen that with an ordinal it behaved early as a simple noun. The noun **ḱind* (*qind* in the orthography) does not appear alone, as do its cognates; we find it united with **ňë-* and **i-*. This syntax is replicated with Romanian *o sută* '100' and *o mie* '1000'.

'1' in complex phrases. However, we seem to have in Albanian a remnant of the Proto-Indo-European rule deleting '1' in complex phrases; on this rule see my observations *Glotta* 46, 1968, 278; *Baltistica* 8, 1972, 55–56; *Kwartalnik Neofilologiczny* 24, 1977, 275–276. It is notable that in the 'teens ('11') and the decads ('21' etc.) and higher the ancient ordinal *i.e. parë* 'first' is not used. This is reminiscent of OLith. *liekas* '11th'.

Perhaps there once was **i, e ňë-zét-i -a* 'the 20th', but **i, e zét-i -a e x* 'the 21st x' (lit. 'the 20th and x').

It may also be that *i-zét, i-ḱind* are remnants of the syntactic situation where a full form of '1' was not allowed.

'1000'. Albanian does not show the North European form **tuH-sḱ-ont-*; see E. P. Hamp, *Papers from the Ninth Regional Meeting of the Chicago Linguistic Society*, edd. C. Corum, T. Cedric Smith-Stark, A. Weiser, 1973, 172–178.

**míʎë* is a clear borrowing from Latin *mīlia*, the plural which has given a feminine in Albanian. On Latin *mīlle* see my analysis *Glotta* 46, 1968, 274–278. Our form **míʎë* cannot be derived from *mīlle* itself, as A. V. Desnickaja would have (*Romano-Balcanica*, Leningrad 1987, 18), for that would result in **mil'*; nor from a surprising *mīli*, as A. Ju. Rusakov has it (*ibid.* 143), for such a form would give **miʎ*.

'half'. **ǵýmësë* (fem.), despite the ambiguity, in principle, of the sources for initial *ǵ-*, indubitably goes back to **i̯umi-ti̯ā*, with an old suffix or suffixal conglomerate with "abstract" value. As I have shown (*Studii şi cercetări lingvistice* 27, 1976, 34–35), this structure finds an exact match in the autochthonous element of Romanian *jumătate* < *jumetate*, with the same meaning, Aromân *ǧumitate*. We have here a borrowing (or continuation) of the substratum base **i̯umi-*, with substitution of Latin *-tate* for the native *-*ti̯ā*. This abstract is derived from **iumi-to-* 'twinned', with cognates for its base in Latvian and Sanskrit *yam-*, as I have proposed in *Ériu* 24, 1973, 160 ff.

Syntax of the cardinals. It is to be noted that the definite form of the cardinals, which also covers the sense 'both', treats unity as a noun **ňâ(n-)* to which the definite and case forms are simply added, but all higher numbers as members of an old phrase *të* + Numeral, forming a sort of collective. Therefore we analyze this as **tod* or **tā* + Numeral suffixed with *-*om* or *-*ā* 'that dyad, etc.', to which the (head) noun stood in apposition. This source construction will serve to explain why the enclitic passed directly to the (head) noun, rather than affixing in the customary position of the Albanian NP which follows the dictates of Wackernagel's Law. Thus, in fact, Wackernagel's Law is not violated in this construction.

The syntax of the cardinals in the NP otherwise has been dealt with in the introductory presentation of numeral categories.

Ordinals. The morphology and syntax of the ordinals has been summarized in the introductory matter on categories. It seems clear that the original formation of ordinals in Proto-Indo-European was simple thematization of the cardinal (e. g. Gaulish *suex-os*, Latin *septim-us*, Greek ὄγδοϝ-ος i. e. [ὀγ]δόϝα, SC de Bacch, *noun-dinum*, Gaulish fem. acc. δεκαντ-εμ) at an early time in zero-grade (e. g., Avestan *tūir-ya-*, Greek ταρ-τη-). It is likely that **(d)k̑mt-ó-m* '100' is a residue of the last condition.

Then the ancestor of δέκατ-ος, Arc. Lesb. δέκοτ-ος was resegmented δέκα-τος. This gave rise to a freshly productive suffix **-to-* (e. g., ϝέκ-τος, OPruss. *uschts* '6th', OLith. *sekmas* → Lith. *septiñ-tas* '7th', OLith. *asch-mas* : Alb. *i té-ti* '8th', Att. ἔνα-τος Ion. εἴνα-τος Lesb. ἔνο-τος < *ἐνϝŋ̥-τος). That formation, seen in πέμπ-τος, Lith. *peñk-tas*, Lat. *quīntus*, was then extended more mechanically to produce Gaulish *pinpe-tos*, and then *sextam-etos* '7th', *oxtu-m-etos*, etc. See my analyses of these series, *FL* 11, 1974, 463–464, and *Studia Celtica Japonica* 2, 1989, 41–43.

The generalization of **-to-* is seen clearly in Albanian. The source of this has already been discussed in detail under the rubric '10'. The exact source of the final **-ë* is however not clear; it could, of course, reflect **-om* or **-ā*, but that would be an arbitrary and indecisive proposal. We certainly cannot have **-t̯io-* here.

The suppletive *parë* 'first' has been discussed above. I have taken up allied IE formations in *ZCP* 33, 1974, 15–18.

Multiples. The only matter requiring attention in these phrases is the noun *hérë*. In this, see my analysis, *Glotta* 67, 1989, 41.

Distributives. The source of **kā* (→ **n-kā* > *ngā*) is ambiguous.

Note of Acknowledgement

For help and support in my work over the past forty years leading to the results reported in this paper, I am obligated for financial assistance and stipends to a Sheldon Travelling Fellowship from Harvard University, to two Fulbright-Hays stays in Greece and Yugoslavia, to the Social Sciences Research Council and American Council of Learned Societies for research grants to Italy, Greece and Yugoslavia, to the Bulgarian Academy of Sciences, to the hospitality of the Region of Kosovë and the Republic of Makedonija (each many times), to the Division of Humanities (over all these years) and the Center for Balkan and Slavic Studies (over many years since 1966) of the University of Chicago, to the John Simon Guggenheim Foundation (who now receive the first installment of a debt after fifteen years); for scholarly help and friendship to Professors Carlo Tagliavini and Vladimir I. Georgiev (both sadly now departed), Božo Vidoeski, Blaže Koneski, Pavle Ivić, Vida Marković, Ranko Bugarski, the late Liljana (and Rade) Mihailović, Idriz Ajeti, Rexhep Ismajli, Xrisoúla Kardará, Martin Camaj, Francesco Altimari, Geraint Gruffydd, Gabriel and Angelikí Drachman; to Eileen Petrohelos, Mr. John Jones (who never fails to keep my car running and travel costs therefore feasible); to Jean and Madeleine Soulas, to Tom and Pat Markey; to countless speakers of their language who will be listed as fully as possible at a later time; to the ever patient Julijana and Alexander Hamp, to cheerful and loving Gwen; to the incomparable Margot who has suffered uncomplainingly through it all.

Appendix I
List of lesser-known languages

Alan S. C. Ross

For a linguistic placement of the languages mentioned in the various chapters, the reader is referred to the following surveys:

Carruba, Onofrio
1970 *Das Palische* (Text, Grammatik, Lexikon) (Studien zu den Boğazköy-Texten, Heft 10) (Wiesbaden: Harrassowitz).

Dirr, Adolf
1928 *Einführung in das Studium der kaukasischen Sprachen* (mit einer Sprachenkarte) (Leipzig: Verlag der Asia Major).

Elcock, W. D.
1960 *The Romance Languages* (London: Faber & Faber).

Fussman, Gérard
1972 *Atlas linguistique des parlers dardes et kafirs*. I: *Cartes*, II: *Commentaire* (Paris: École Française d'Extrême Orient).

Grierson, G.A.
1927 *Linguistic survey of India* Vol I. (Delhi/Varanasi/Patna: Motilal Banarsidass).

Lorimer, D. L. R.
1938 *The Burushaski language* (Oslo: H. Ahenoug & Co.).

Meillet, Antoine – Marcel Cohen
1952 *Les langues du monde* (par un groupe de linguistes, sous la direction de A. Meillet et M. Cohen) (Paris: Centre National de la recherche scientifique).

Sinor, Denis
1969 *Inner Asia* (History – Civilization – Languages) (Bloomington: Indiana University).

Zinkevičius, Z.
1966 *Lietuvių dialektologija* (Vilnius: Mink).

The list of lesser-known languages gives references to places where the languages concerned are mentioned. Pure numbers, such as "456", are page references to Meillet – Cohen (1952). *LSI* here means *Linguistic survey of India*, especially "Index of language names", I.i.425–517. If a language reference occurs frequently in a publication, the author only is listed.

Agul	234
Akhwakh	Dirr p. 210
Andi	233
Archi	Dirr p. 253
Areti	Fussmann p. XI
Ashkun	21
Aukštaitic	Zinkevičius
Aunus	Szinnyei, *Unkarin kieloppi,* Helsinki (1950: 8)
Awadhī	23
Awar	238
Bashgalī	21
Bashghārik	*LSI*
Bhadrawāhī (LSI)	*LSI*
Bhalēsī	*LSI*
Bhaṭeālī	*LSI*
Bhojpurī	23
Birhor	630
Bodo	556
Botlikh	Dirr p. 196
Budukh	234
Burushaski	507
Čakavian	66
Chamalal	233
Chechen	234
Cheremyss	283
Chilīs	*LSI*
Chorasmian	30
Chumash	995
Curonian	64
Dameli	21
Darrai-i-Nuri	Fussmann p. XI
Dido	233
Digor	34
Ḍōgrī	*LSI*
Ḍumāki	D. L. R. Lorimer, *The Dumāki language* (*Publications de la Commission d'enquête linguistique* IV)
Erzä	283
Gabrī	*New Encyclopaedia britannica, Macropaedia* ix,452
Gauro	*LSI*
Gawar-Bati	21
Gayo	*ATN*
Geg	45
Godoberi	233

Gurēzī	*LSI*
Hova	564
Ingush	235
Iron	34
Iškāšmī	34
Jek	234
Jijelut	Fussmann p. X
Juang	623
Kalasha	21
Kandia	Fussmann p. VIII
Kanyawālī (Maiyā̃)	Fussmann p. IX
Karaim	Sinor p. 52
Karata	Dirr p. 202
Kati	21
Kayapo	1151
Khētrānī	*LSI*
Khinalug	Dirr p. 300
Khiurkila	Dirr p. 219
Khowār	22
Khvarshi	Dirr p. 215
Kipchak	*New Encyclopaedia britannica, Micropaedia* x, 195
Kiuri	234
Kohistānī	22
Kōṅkaṇī	*LSI*
Kubachi	Dirr p. 235
Kumaunī	*LSI*
Kuanada	Dirr p. 204
Lahndā	22
Lak	233
Lauṛowānī	Fussmann p. XI
Lo-lo	554
Luvian	17
Māgahī	23
Maithilī	23
Maiyā̃	*LSI*
Māṛwāṛī	22
Mech	*LSI*
Mēwāṛī	*LSI*
Minangkabau	*Atlas van tropisch Nederland*, map 96
Miskito	1077
Moksha	283
Mordvin	283
Munjī	*see* Yidghā-Munjī

Ngadju-Dyak	*Atlas van tropisch Nederland*, map 96
Nogai	Sinor p. 65
Occitan	49
Oguz	*New Encyclopaedia britannica, Micropaedia* x, 195
Oṛiyā	23
Ormuṛī	34
Ostyak	284
Otati	*Anthropological Linguistics* VIII p. 67
Pahāṛī	22
Palaean	O. Carruba
Palesī	Fussmann p. X
Parāčī	34
Pashai	21
Pāzand	29
Phalūṛa	21
Prasun	21
Rutul	234
Salinan	995
Sanglēčī	34
Sarīkolī	34
Savara	491
Savi	Fussmann p. X
Semang	652
Shina	22
Shoshon	1050
Shumashti	Fussmann p. X
Sindhī	22
Šughnī	34
Surselvan	Elcock p. 479
Tabasaran	234
Tagalog	650
Tangut	E. D. Grinstead, *Tangut studies*
Tashlayt	162
Tati	32
Tindi	233
Tirāhī	21
Toba-Batak	651
Tōrwālī	*LSI*
Tosk	45
Tsakhur	234
Tukano	1142
Udi	234
Vannetais	55

Appendix II
List of lesser-known place-names

Alan S. C. Ross

In the case of large features (rivers, areas, etc.), the reference is to an abitrary point on or in them. A few now vanished place-names are perforce omitted.

Achin	4°00′ N × 97°00′ E
Adour	43°15′ N × 0°15′ E
Aegina	37°43′ N × 23°26′ E
Älvdal	61°14′ N × 14°05′ E
Alghero	40°34′ N × 8°19′ E
Allgau	47°40′ N × 10°00′ E
Als	56°46′ N × 10°18′ E
Amaseno	41°28′ N × 13°20′ E
Amorgus	36°50′ N × 26°00′ E
Amrum	54°20′ N × 8°23′ E
Anzasca	45°55′ N × 8°10′ E
Aphrodisias	37°40′ N × 28°22′ E
Apollonia	40°53′ N × 19°34′ E
Ardea	41°36′ N × 12°33′ E
Arezzo	43°28′ N × 11°54′ E
Assinghausen	51°18′ N × 8°30′ E
Axum	14°10′ N × 38°45′ E
Bagnes	46°00′ N × 7°20′ E
Batz	47°15′ N × 3°32′ W
Baunei	40°02′ N × 9°41′ E
Behistan	34°23′ N × 47°26′ E
Bigeste	43°12′ N × 17°32′ E
Bitti	40°29′ N × 9°23′ E
Boğazköy	40°02′ N × 34°37′ E
Bregu i Bunës	41°57′ N × 19°25′ E
Bregu i Detit	41°52′ N × 20°11′ E
Bulgarec	40°39′ N × 20°43′ E
Calydon	38°22′ N × 21°30′ E
Çamëria	39°43′ N × 20°09′ E
Campidano	39°30′ N × 8°45′ E
Citium	34°53′ N × 33°40′ E

Cnidus	36°40′ N × 27°24′ E
Corcyra	39°25′ N × 20°05′ E
Cosenza	39°17′ N × 16°16′ E
Cyrene	32°30′ N × 21°52′ E
Dalecarlia	61°00′ N × 15°00′ E
Dibra	41°55′ N × 19°50′ E
Didyma	38°32′ N × 14°49′ E
Diecimo	43°58′ N × 10°30′ E
Drisht	42°08′ N × 19°36′ E
Einang	61°05′ N × 9°00′ E
Elis	37°50′ N × 21°30′ E
Emilia	44°30′ N × 10°30′ E
Fretria	38°26′ N × 23°49′ E
Failaka	29°26′ N × 48°20′ E
Falster	54°45′ N × 12°00′ E
Föhr	54°44′ N × 8°24′ E
Forez	45°30′ N × 3°45′ E
Futuna	19°32′ S × 170°12′ E
Fyn	55°15′ N × 10°30′ E
Ghadames	30°10′ N × 9°30′ E
Gilgit	35°54′ N × 74°20′ E
Girnār	21°32′ N × 70°32′ E
Gjirokastra	40°05′ N × 20°10′ E
Goeree	51°50′ N × 4°00′ E
Gortyn	35°04′ N × 24°59′ E
Gudbrandsdal	61°30′ N × 9°17′ E
Hädel	47°50′ N × 8°43′ E
Halland	56°40′ N × 12°45′ E
Halligen	54°35′ N × 8°42′ E
Hallingdal	60°35′ N × 8°00′ E
Hardanger	60°15′ N × 7°30′ E
Harlingen	53°10′ N × 5°25′ E
Hattstedt	54°32′ N × 9°02′ E
Heide in Dithmarschen	54°12′ N × 9°05′ E
Heraclea	40°15′ N × 16°43′ E
Himera	38°00′ N × 13°41′ E
Hindeloopen	52°57′ N × 5°24′ E
Iguvium	43°21′ N × 12°35′ E
Ile de Groix	47°39′ N × 3°27′ W
Inari	68°54′ N × 27°05′ E
Innherad	63°40′ N × 12°30′ E
Issa	43°00′ N × 16°34′ E
Istaby	56°01′ N × 14°39′ E

Iulis	37°40′ N × 24°45′ E
Jemdet Nasr	32°45′ N × 44°43′ E
Karashahr	42°04′ N × 86°34′ E
Keos	37°38′ N × 24°20′ E
Kermān	30°18′ N × 57°05′ E
Kjølevig	59°06′ N × 5°57′ E
Krujë	41°31′ N × 19°35′ E
Kucha	41°43′ N × 82°58′ E
Kululu	38°59′ N × 36°09′ E
Kurvelesh	40°12′ N × 19°53′ E
Labëria	40°29′ N × 19°36′ E
La Gleize	50°24′ N × 5°51′ E
La Graufesenque	44°05′ N × 3°05′ E
Lakhimpur	27°52′ N × 80°47′ E
Lanuvium	41°41′ N × 12°45′ E
Larvik	59°04′ N × 10°02′ E
Logudoro	40°40′ N × 8°45′ E
Lolland	54°50′ N × 11°30′ E
Lucania	40°16′ N × 15°07′ E
Lule	65°40′ N × 21°45′ E
Lyttos	35°12′ N × 25°24′ E
Macugnaga	45°58′ N × 7°59′ E
Maine	47°30′ N × 0°30′ W
Makrān	26°30′ N × 62°00′ E
Malcija	42°23′ N × 19°27′ E
Mandalen	58°02′ N × 7°30′ E
Manigod	45°52′ N × 6°22′ E
Mantinea	37°36′ N × 22°26′ E
Mat	41°40′ N × 19°35′ E
Megara	38°00′ N × 23°21′ E
Metapontium	40°21′ N × 16°48′ E
Mezzoiuso	37°52′ N × 13°28′ E
Miletus	37°29′ N × 27°18′ E
Møn	54°54′ N × 12°20′ E
Moringen	51°42′ N × 9°52′ E
Mylasa	37°19′ N × 27°48′ E
Mzab	32°24′ N × 4°36′ E
Naqš-i-Rustam	30°00′ N × 52°53′ E
Nikaj-Mërkuri	42°17′ N × 19°52′ E
Niya	37°02′ N × 82°47′ E
Nordfjord	61°55′ N × 5°30′ E
Nordhordland	60°40′ N × 5°30′ E
Nordland	67°00′ N × 15°00′ E

Numedal	60°00′ N × 9°23′ E
Núoro	40°41′ N × 9°25′ E
Østfold	59°20′ N × 11°15′ E
Oetaea	38°49′ N × 22°17′ E
Ostbevern	52°03′ N × 7°51′ E
Oudenard	50°50′ N × 3°37′ E
Overflakkee	51°40′ N × 4°08′ E
Pas	43°10′ N × 3°46′ W
Perga	36°59′ N × 30°53′ E
Perinthus	40°58′ N × 27°58′ E
Phocis	38°25′ N × 22°30′ E
Piana degli Albanesi	37°59′ N × 13°17′ E
Rezija	46°08′ N × 13°36′ E
Rhegium	38°04′ N × 15°41′ E
Rök	58°18′ N × 14°46′ E
Sa'a	9°50′ S × 161°30′ E
Salento	40°25′ N × 18°00′ E
Sanabria	42°04′ N × 6°42′ W
San Giorgio Albanese	39°35′ N × 16°27′ E
Saterland	53°05′ N × 7°43′ E
Schiermonnikoog	53°28′ N × 6°10′ E
Sejerø	55°53′ N × 11°10′ E
Setesdal	59°08′ N × 7°30′ E
Shāhbāzgaṛhi	34°14′ N × 72°10′ E
Shkodra	42°03′ N × 19°01′ E
Shlaku	42°06′ N × 19°44′ E
Shpat	41°03′ N × 19°45′ E
Sogn	61°11′ N × 6°00′ E
Sophikon	37°48′ N × 23°03′ E
Stavenhagen	53°42′ N × 12°55′ E
Stentofta	56°06′ N × 14°37′ E
Sterdebüll	54°39′ N × 8°24′ E
Stienta	44°57′ N × 11°33′ E
Straum	63°40′ N × 8°45′ E
Strücklingen	53°07′ N × 7°40′ E
Sunnmøre	62°22′ N × 7°00′ E
Sylt	54°55′ N × 8°18′ E
Tauromenion	37°51′ N × 15°17′ E
Tegea	37°28′ N × 22°28′ E
Terina	38°57′ N × 16°09′ E
Terschelling	53°25′ N × 5°20′ E
Thasos	40°40′ N × 24°28′ E
Thera	36°20′ N × 25°35′ E

Toprā	30°07′ N × 77°10′ E
Tras os Montes	41°35′ N × 6°45′ W
Třeboň	49°01′ N × 14°50′ E
Treger	48°47′ N × 3°14′ W
Troizen	37°25′ N × 23°20′ E
Tune	55°36′ N × 12°12′ E
Tusculum	41°48′ N × 12°41′ E
Twisselbach	52°08′ N × 8°18′ E
Upgant	53°31′ N × 7°17′ E
Vaccarizzo Albanese	39°35′ N × 16°26′ E
Valdres	61°00′ N × 9°00′ E
Valtellina	46°11′ N × 10°00′ E′
Van	38°33′ N × 42°46′ E
Vaux-le-Vicomte	48°34′ N × 2°43′ E
Vefsn	65°51′ N × 13°10′ E
Venusia	41°00′ N × 15°40′ E
Vernole	40°17′ N × 18°19′ E
Veroli	41°41′ N × 13°26′ E
Voss	60°40′ N × 6°20′ E
Wangeroog	53°47′ N × 7°58′ E
Warka	31°09′ N × 46°47′ E
Wiedingharde	54°51′ N × 8°43′ E
Wursten	53°41′ N × 8°31′ E
Zadrima	41°58′ N × 19°37′ E
Zwieselberg	46°42′ N × 5°17′ E

Author Index